The Blue Guides

Please write in with your comments, suggestions, and corrections for the next edition of the Blue Guide. Writers of the most helpful letters will be awarded a free Blue Guide of their choice.

New York

Carol von Pressentin Wright
Stuart Miller and Sharon Seitz

BLUE GUIDE

A & C Black Limited • London
W. W. Norton & Company Inc. • New York

Third edition 2002

Published by A & C Black Publishers Limited
37 Soho Square, London W1D 3QZ

A CIP catalogue record of this book is available from the British Library.

ISBN 0-7136-6316-2

Published in the United States of America by
W. W. Norton & Company, Inc.
500 Fifth Avenue, New York, NY 10110

Printed in the United States of America

The text and display of this book are composed in Photina
Composition by Allentown Digital Services
Manufacturing by the Haddon Craftsmen, Inc.
Production manager: Julia Druskin

ISBN 0-393-31985-7 (pbk.)

W. W. Norton & Company, Inc., 500 Fifth Avenue, New York, N.Y. 10110
www.wwnorton.com

W. W. Norton & Company Ltd., Castle House, 75/76 Wells Street, London W1T 3QT

1 2 3 4 5 6 7 8 9 0

Authors' Note

The attack that ravaged the World Trade Center on Sept 11, 2001, came just as this book was going to press. As of early Oct, the World Trade Center site and much of the surrounding neighborhood remain in turmoil. Several buildings near the site have suffered major damage and their future is uncertain: these include the American Express headquarters and the Winter Garden (both in the World Financial Center), One Liberty Plaza, the Millenium Hilton Hotel, St. Nicholas Greek Orthodox Church, and 90 West St. Some downtown businesses, absorbing financial losses caused by the shrinking of the local and national economy, also face unclear prospects. Transportation, especially the subway system under and near the Trade Center site, has been disrupted, and here, too, the long view is uncertain. Except for the sections of this book discussing the World Trade Center itself, the descriptions of buildings near the site reflect the area before the tragedy, partly because information is only gradually becoming available and partly in the hope that the downtown area may once again look as it did on Sept 10, 2001.

Acknowledgments

We would like to thank Tabitha Griffin for her energy and enthusiasm getting the project underway and Drake Bennett for his willingness to confront and resolve the many problems involved in such a complex undertaking. Morgen Van Vorst brought the project to conclusion under difficult and trying circumstances with tact and commitment. Don Rifkin has carefully read every single word, uncovering errors and rooting out discrepancies; his patience and judgment have made the book far better than it would otherwise have been. We thank Patricia Chui for giving us access to her years of editorial experience and Diana Perron for her personal observations.

We are also grateful to Joy Holland at the Brooklyn Collection of the Brooklyn Public Library, Marianne Malec at the Landmarks Preservation Commission, Susan Tobin at Congregation Shearith Israel, and Gemma Davies and Samantha McLean in England, all of whom provided information otherwise difficult to find.

Carol Wright would also like to acknowledge Paul Langridge, editor of the first edition, who has watched the Blue Guide to New York for more than 25 years and kindly given a helping hand from abroad. She thanks her agent, Mildred Marmur, for her continued support and friendship and her many contributions in matters both literary and worldly. Finally, she would like to thank Fred and Catherine Wright, both of whom probably know more obscure bits of New York history than they might wish.

Contents

Borough of the Bronx/Bronx County   567

Borough of Brooklyn/Kings County   619

Borough of Queens/Queens County   725

Borough of Staten Island/Richmond County   789

Maps

Introduction by Carol von Pressentin Wright

Since I wrote the first edition of this book, a project that began when I was pregnant with my daughter, who is now a college graduate, the configuration of the city has so changed that a single person can no longer adequately do the job. Although the original Blue Guide to New York was cited for leaving "no pothole uncatalogued" and for giving the outer boroughs more than the cursory nod usually cast in their direction, in this edition the focus has been enlarged.

Manhattan, formerly synonymous with "New York City," may still be the center of interest for most visitors, but the other boroughs are exerting an increasingly strong centrifugal pull. When the first edition was written, the Brooklyn Academy of Music was just beginning to emerge from a long period of relative dormancy. On Staten Island, Sailors Snug Harbor had been rescued from development and the restoration of its beautiful 19C buildings had begun, but the museums, art spaces, and botanical gardens that are there today had yet to emerge. The work of Sharon Seitz and Stuart Miller, which documents the changes of the last ten years and adds much fascinating material to the coverage of the outer boroughs, has given me the pleasure of viewing much of the city with fresh eyes.

It has also been a pleasure over the years to watch history unfold, to see the city recover from fiscal disaster, and to observe the fruits of investment by private and public organizations. Grand Central Terminal, the reading room of the New York Public Library on Fifth Ave, and the Chrysler Building, to mention a few Midtown sites, have been restored to their former glory. Preservationists have succeeded in getting landmark designations for many buildings and historic districts, more than 90 in the few years since 1998, helping preserve the city's architectural heritage. The Central Park Conservancy and Prospect Park Alliance have made these parks the urban oases that their designers intended. Watching these and other improvements has been truly gratifying.

The walking tours of this book, with their emphasis on history, architecture, and culture in its most inclusive sense, will take you to every corner of the city, from the asphalt of midtown Manhattan to the sands of Coney Island. If you are a visitor, I hope the guide will show why New York is the world's preeminent city; if you already know and love New York, I hope the book will show you things you have not yet discovered or present familiar things in a new and exciting way.

Introduction by
Stuart Miller and Sharon Seitz

New York is a city made for walking. But most of the time we are consumed by rushing to work or running errands and don't take the time to really look around. So it was a genuine pleasure and quite rewarding to undertake all the walks in this book, to have a reason to stop and soak in the details of a building, a block, a neighborhood. We spent over a year exploring the city's world-famous tourist attractions and its more obscure nooks and crannies, toting Caleb, our then-newborn son, everywhere from a historic walking tour of Jackson Heights to the Ferragusto di Belmont, a festival in an old Bronx Italian enclave.

We were asked to update the New York edition of the Blue Guide because while much of New York's charm and character is wonderfully preserved, no city changes more rapidly, and no guide to it could possibly remain current. Imagine reading a book that describes Times Square in 1990, or Bryant Park, Red Hook, or even the South Bronx. Back then, this was also a city without a Hudson River Park, without a museum devoted to its skyscrapers or its immigrants. And, of course, no change was more startling or traumatic than the destruction of the World Trade Center, which came, oddly enough, on the day we were due to hand in our final revisions of this manuscript.

We were honored to be chosen to build upon the impressive, nearly monumental work compiled by Carol von Pressentin Wright in the first two editions of the Blue Guide to New York. For us the appeal of revising the Blue Guide was not just in updating it, but in expanding it. From the renowned W. 4th St basketball courts to the influential rock club CBGB, we've added a taste of the city's contemporary cultural life.

As native Brooklynites, we also are acutely aware that most guide books make short-shrift of the "outer" boroughs (as Manhattan-centric folks describe them). We have attempted to flesh out the character of the city's many neighborhoods and have added numerous attractions. Some are quintessentially New York—no comprehensive guide to the city can truly be complete without Junior's restaurant in downtown Brooklyn or Fort Greene's Lafayette Avenue Church, where an early draft of the Emancipation Proclamation was hammered out. And because this city has a closer connection to nature than many people realize, we've added attractions like Staten Island's Lemon Creek and Blue Heron Parks.

Our walking tours cover Manhattan's neighborhoods and the major sights in Brooklyn, Queens, the Bronx, and Staten Island. Points of interest inconvenient to reach on foot have been organized in gazetteer form: for these you will need either a car or a lot of time and a good map.

Restaurants, hotels, and a few notes on creature comforts and conveniences have been covered briefly for the sake of completeness, but there are more detailed sources on all of these (see the section on Practical Information).

The abbreviation *DL* indicates designated landmarks, that is, buildings or other sites chosen by the city's Landmarks Preservation Commission for their historic, architectural, or cultural value and protected by law from destruction or undue alteration. The symbol ⦿ used on the maps indicates subway stops. URL addresses of Web sites sometimes extend over two lines of text but should be read as a single unit.

Practical Information

Planning Your Trip

Sources of Information

NYC & Company, formerly the New York Convention and Visitors Bureau, is the mother lode of New York City information. The **Visitor Center** at 810 Seventh Ave (between W. 52nd and W. 53rd Sts) is open weekdays 8:30–6, weekends 9–5; ☎ (212) 484-1222; Web site: www.nycvisit.com. The center has brochures describing attractions, discounted theater tickets, subway and bus maps, lists of hotels and restaurants. NYC & Company publishes the quarterly *Official NYC Guide* (information about hotels, attractions, performing arts, restaurants, nightlife, sports, and calendar of events). Order by calling ☎ (212) 397-8222 or, outside New York, ☎ (800) NYC-VISIT.

The **Times Square Visitors Center** in the former Embassy Theatre, 1560 Broadway (between W. 46th and W. 47th Sts), is open daily 8–8 (no phone); Web site: www.timessquarebid.org/visitor. It has an ATM machine, MetroCard sales, currency exchange, theater tickets, sightseeing and airport transportation bookings.

The Virtual City

The following Web sites can help you plan your trip or find out what to do and where to go once you have arrived.

About.com: www.gonyc.about.com. Part of the About network, which features pages hosted by individual guides; info on hotels, museums, neighborhoods, bed-and-breakfasts, tours, shopping, and even weather.

CitySearch: www.newyork.citysearch.com. Part of a network that includes Ticketmaster and other media companies; has extensive listings of what to do and what to see, as well as "best of" lists and editors' "new and noteworthy" picks.

***Time Out* New York: www.timeoutny.com.** The Internet location of the hip entertainment magazine. Reviews of restaurants, events, movies, shops, etc. Also archived articles, so you can find out what used to be trendy.

New York Today: www.nytoday.com. The *New York Times* guide to cultural events, restaurants (includes reviews), sports; a great site, easy to use. To see the news, access: www.nytimes.com.

***New York* magazine: www.newyorkmetro.com.** Reviews, political articles, opinion, events. Archived articles and good shopping tips for sales and bargains.

The *Village Voice*: www.villagevoice.com. Opinionated (left-of-center) reviews of films, theater, music, books. Calendar of events. Even the personals and your horoscope.

For Visitors from the UK

The U.S. government no longer operates a national tourist office in the UK. However, **NYC & Company** has a walk-in facility at 33–34 Carnaby St, London; open Mon–Fri 10–4; ☎ [44] (0)20 7437 8300; fax: [44] (0)20 7437 8100. The organization supplies maps, lists of hotels and tour operators, and the *Official NYC Guide*, with useful addresses, a calendar of events, and contacts. Web site: www.nycvisit.com.

Visit USA, a private nonprofit group, offers information on U.S. travel; ☎ 09069 101020. This is a premium-rate number available only to callers from the UK; calls are charged at 1 pound per minute.

When to Go

You can enjoy New York at any time of the year, but the most predictably pleasant seasons are spring and fall. Winter can be invigorating, though it can also be bleak, gray, and bitterly cold. The maximum and minimum daily averages in Jan, the coldest month, are 38°–25°F (3°– –4°C). Summer can be warm and pleasant, but there are usually periods of a week or so in July and/or Aug when it is stiflingly hot and humid, with heat radiating off buildings and condensation dripping from air conditioners to the pavement. Average ranges in July, statistically the hottest month (though plenty of New Yorkers would argue empirically for Aug), are 85–68°F (29–20°C). Fortunately, most public facilities, including subway cars but not the platforms in the stations, are air-conditioned.

The cultural calendar is most crowded Sept–May, but there is plenty to do and see all year, with special outdoor events and festivals in summer. Attractions as

New York Weather				
	Temperature		**Rainfall**	
	F°	**C°**	**Inches**	**Cm**
Jan	32	0	3	8
Feb	33	1	3	8
March	41	5	4	11
April	52	11	4	10
May	63	17	4	10
June	71	22	4	10
July	77	25	4	10
Aug	75	24	4	10
Sept	70	21	4	9
Oct	58	14	3	9
Nov	47	8	4	10
Dec	37	3	4	10

well as restaurants and stores may be less crowded in summer, when New Yorkers vacation. Christmas, when the city is brilliantly decorated, draws thousands of visitors; expect crowds and high prices.

Hotel rates, not unexpectedly, vary inversely to the popularity of the season, so if money is the prime consideration, come in winter (after the Christmas season through March) or summer (July and Aug).

Passports and Visas

The United States has a Visa Waiver Program that allows citizens of the UK, Ireland, and most western European countries to enter for business or pleasure without a visa. To enter without a visa, you must have an unexpired national or EC passport, plan to stay fewer than 90 days, and have a return or onward ticket. The 90-day limit cannot be extended once you are in the United States, so if you wish to stay longer you must get a visa beforehand. The **State Department Web site,** with detailed information about visas and passports, is at: www.travel.state.gov.

If you do need a visa, you must submit an application in person or by mail, accompanied by two 1½-inch-square photos and a fee of $45. It may take longer than 24 hours during the summer rush period.

For further information about visas, UK citizens should contact the **U.S. Embassy Visa Information Line** (toll call): ☎ (01891) 200-290. For information **by mail** (enclose a stamped self-addressed envelope), **in England** write to: U.S. Embassy Visa Branch, 5 Upper Grosvenor Square, London W1A 1AE. In **Northern Ireland:** U.S. Consulate General, Queens House, Queen St, Belfast BT1 6EO. In **Ireland:** 42 Elgin Rd, Ballsbridge, Dublin 4, Ireland.

Take Care of Your Passport

It is a good idea to photocopy the page of your passport with your photo and passport number. Leave one copy at home and take another, keeping it in a safe place (but not with your passport). Some travelers carry an expired passport or official copy of their birth certificate for identification. If you lose your passport, call your consulate and notify the police.

Customs Regulations

Nonresidents who are at least 21 years old may bring in, free of duty, up to one liter of alcoholic beverages—beer, wine, and liquor—for personal use; 200 cigarettes (one carton) or 50 non-Cuban cigars, or two kilograms (4.4 pounds) of smoking tobacco; and $100 worth of merchandise for gifts. Various U.S. governmental agencies prohibit bringing in certain plant and animal products; the best source of information is the **U.S. Customs Service Web site**: www.customs.ustreas.gov; you can also phone the Customs Service at ☎ (202) 927-1770.

Obviously, narcotics and dangerous drugs are prohibited. If you take **medications** with ingredients that can be habit-forming (some cough medicines, tranquilizers, sleeping pills, antidepressants, stimulants), you should bring along a

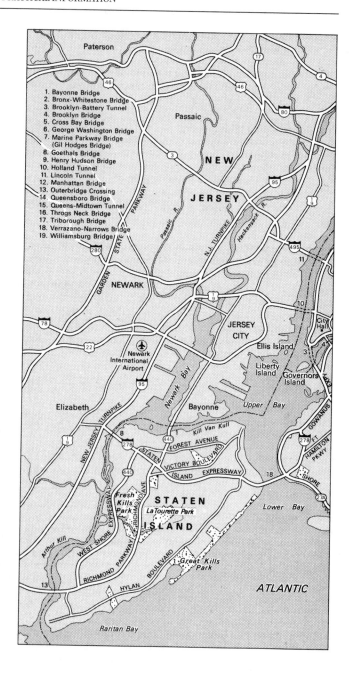

1. Bayonne Bridge
2. Bronx-Whitestone Bridge
3. Brooklyn-Battery Tunnel
4. Brooklyn Bridge
5. Cross Bay Bridge
6. George Washington Bridge
7. Marine Parkway Bridge
   (Gil Hodges Bridge)
8. Goethals Bridge
9. Henry Hudson Bridge
10. Holland Tunnel
11. Lincoln Tunnel
12. Manhattan Bridge
13. Outerbridge Crossing
14. Queensboro Bridge
15. Queens-Midtown Tunnel
16. Throgs Neck Bridge
17. Triborough Bridge
18. Verrazano-Narrows Bridge
19. Williamsburg Bridge

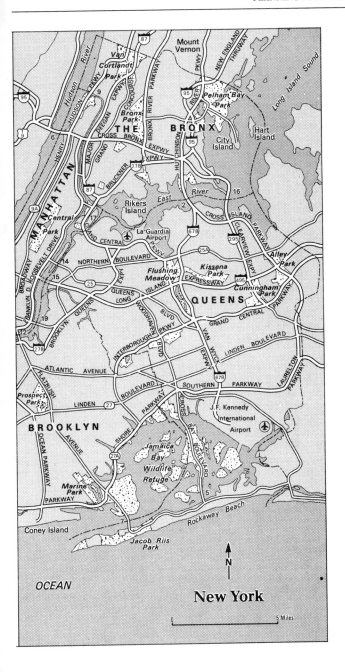

written prescription and carry enough of your medication only for your personal use. Bring prescriptions in their original containers.

Chances are you won't be stopped, but Congress grants customs inspectors the right to search every passenger who arrives in the United States. If you are searched, you should behave in a courteous manner (no matter how the customs inspector behaves).

Currency Regulations

Foreign tourists may bring any amount of money of any currency into the United States. However, if you bring in or take out more than $10,000 (U.S. or foreign equivalent, or a combination of the two), you are required by law to file a report on Form CM 4790 with the United States Customs Service.

Health Regulations and Insurance

The U.S. does not require inoculations or vaccinations for entry unless you are coming from a country with a known epidemic, especially yellow fever or cholera. For information contact the Centers for Disease Control and Prevention (CDC): toll-free ☎ (888) 232-3228; Web site: www.cdc.gov.

Check with your insurance company to see whether your **health insurance** is valid while traveling. Health care is expensive in the U.S. Doctors and hospitals usually require either proof of insurance coverage or payment in advance for nonemergency care, though emergency rooms will treat you first and bill you later. Avoid anxiety by making sure your policy covers you in the U.S. or by purchasing special health insurance.

Accessibility for Disabled Visitors

New York is not totally accessible to disabled visitors but is manageable. The **airports** have accessible restrooms, telephones, and restaurants, as well as handicap parking spaces close to the terminals. The Web site of the Port Authority of New York and New Jersey has detailed information about airport facilities: www. panynj.gov. **Upward Mobility Limousine** operates roll-in wheelchair vans for transportation from airport to city or within the city; ☎ (718) 645-7774. **Symphony Transportation Service** also operates wheelchair vans, which go anywhere within the city. Call ☎ (800) 253-1443 at least 24 hours in advance. **Public transit buses** have wheelchair lifts and kneelers, which lower the steps.

The **subways,** however, are not easily accessible, though some stations have been upgraded with elevators and other facilities. For information about a particular station or for help routing a journey, call New York City Transit at ☎ (718) 596-8585. The Mayor's Office for People with Disabilities (MOPD) also has information on accessible transportation: ☎ (212) 788-2830 or (212) 788-2838 (TTY); fax: (212) 788-2858; Web site: www.nyc.gov/html/mopd/home.html.

If you use a wheelchair and are unable to use public transportation, contact Paratransit Access-A-ride program; ☎ (877) 337-2017. While taxis are not equipped to accommodate wheelchairs, many drivers will help stow folding wheelchairs in the trunk. Many public buildings, especially newer ones, are accessible to wheelchairs, including most museums, theaters, and many major tourist attractions. Some Broadway theaters have induction loops for hearing-impaired people. **Hospital Audiences, Inc.**, a nonprofit organization dedicated to making **cultural events** accessible, maintains a hotline with accessibility information: ☎ (888) 424-4685; Web site: www.hospitalaudiences.org. They also publish ***Access for All,*** a book with detailed information about museums, theaters, and other cultural sites; to order it, ☎ (212) 575-7663.

Restaurants vary in accessibility; dining rooms may be accessible, restrooms may not. Hotels also vary widely. Call ahead. **Big Apple Greeters,** a nonprofit organization, offers free neighborhood visits guided by volunteers. Visitors with disabilities are especially welcome; guides are knowledgeable about facilities for the disabled; ☎ (212) 669-8159 or (212) 669-8273 (TTY); Web site: www.big applegreeter.org.

Maps
Good maps of New York are easy to come by. You can get free ones at NYC & Company, 810 Seventh Ave (at W. 53rd St) and the Times Square Visitors Center, 1560 Broadway (between W. 46th and W. 47th Sts). Hagstrom and Rand McNally publish both pocket and large folded maps of the city.

Money: Know before You Go
Major **credit cards** are accepted in most stores and restaurants and may be used for cash withdrawals at automatic teller machines (ATMs). The major cards are Visa (Barclaycard, Carte Bleue), American Express, Diners Club, and Mastercard (Access, EuroCard).

There are **automatic teller machines** (ATMs) throughout the city. If you use a major credit card for a cash advance from an ATM, the advance is treated as a loan for which interest is charged from the moment of withdrawal. You may also use a debit (money) card if your bank belongs to one of the money networks at the ATM you are using. The two major international networks are Cirrus, ☎ (800) 424-7787, and PLUS, ☎ (800) 843-7587.

For ATM transactions you will need a **Personal Identification Number (PIN),** supplied by your credit card company or bank at home. The exchange rates at ATMs are usually favorable. It is difficult to cash a **personal check** at a New York bank without having an account there.

Travelers' checks, to some extent superceded by ATMs nowadays, are accepted in most places, supported by photo identification (a passport or driver's license). Make sure you get your checks in **dollar amounts.** The most familiar are Thomas Cook/MasterCard, Visa, and American Express. Less familiar ones may not be recognized or honored. You can always cash travelers' checks at banks and may be able to do so at other businesses as long as the checks are in dollars.

Getting to New York

Tour Operators
Package-tour operators in the U.S. offer arrangements that include hotels, sightseeing, city tours by bus or Circle Line, and sometimes tickets to popular Broadway shows. Some advertise in the Sunday Travel section of the *New York Times.* American airline companies also offer vacation packages to New York. Two U.S. package-tour operators are:

Liberty Travel: ☎ (888) 271-1584; Web site: www.libertytravel.com.
New York City Vacations: ☎ (888) 692-8701; Web site: www.nycvp.com.

The following **UK tour operators** have packages to New York City:

Bon Voyage Travel and Tours Ltd, 16–18 Bellevue Rd, Southampton, SO15 2AY; ☎ 0800 316 3012; Web site: bon-voyage.co.uk.

City Cruiser Holidays, Lingley House, Commissioners Rd, Strood, Rochester, Kent ME2 4EE; ☎ 01634 291 101; Web site: www.citycruiser.co.uk.

Funway Holidays International Inc., 1 Elmfield Park, Bromley, Kent BR1 1LU; ☎ 0208 466 0222; Web site: www.funwayholidays.co.uk.

Major Travel plc, Fortess Grove, 28–34 Fortess Rd, Kentish Town, London NW5 2HB; ☎ 020 7393 1070; Web site: www.majortravel.co.uk.

North America Travel Service, 7 Albion St, Leeds LS1 5ER; ☎ 0113 246 1606; Web site: www.northamericatravelservice.co.uk.

Premier Holidays, Westbrook Centre, Milton Rd, Cambridge CB4 1YG; ☎ 0870 789 6688; Web site: www.premierholidays.co.uk.

Trailfinders, 215 Kensington High St, London W8 6BD; ☎ 020 7937 5400; Web site: www.trailfinder.com.

Travelbag plc, 3–5 High St, Alton, Hampshire GU34 1TL; ☎ 0870 900 1352; Web site: www.travelbag.co.uk.

Virgin Holidays, The Galleria, Station Rd, Crawley, West Sussex RH10 1WW; ☎ 01293 617 181; Web site: www.virginholidays.co.uk.

By air

Most major airlines fly to one of New York's three airports—John F. Kennedy International Airport, LaGuardia Airport, and Newark International Airport. Flight schedules and online booking are available on airline Web sites.

Airlines in North America

Air Canada, ☎ (800) 776-3000; Web site: www.aircanada.ca
American Airlines, ☎ (800) 433-7300; Web site: www.aa.com
Continental, ☎ (800) 525-0280; Web site: www.flycontinental.com
Delta, ☎ (800) 241-4141; Web site: www.delta.com
Midwest Express, ☎ (800) 452-2022; Web site: www.midwestexpress.com.
United Airlines, ☎ (800) 538-2929; Web site: www.ual.com
U.S. Airways: ☎ (800) 428-4322; Web site: www.usairways.com.

Airlines in Britain

British Airways, ☎ 0845 77 333 77; in the U.S., ☎ (800) 247-9297; Web site: www.british-airways.com.

Virgin Atlantic, ☎ 01293 747 747; in the U.S., ☎ (800) 862-8621; Web site: www.virgin-atlantic.com.

Airlines in Ireland

Aer Lingus, Dublin, ☎ 01 886 8888; in the U.S., ☎ (800) 474-7424. Web site: www.aerlingus.ie.

British Airways, Belfast, ☎ 0345 222111; Web site: www.british-airways.com.

Discounted Tickets

From the U.S. and abroad, the cheapest regularly available flights are **Apex tickets** (Advance Purchase Excursion), which must be booked at least 21 days before departure and have length-of-stay requirements. If you plan to come in summer, the heaviest time for international travel, book well in advance. Some airlines offer low-price tickets at the last minute or other special rates. Check with carriers by phone or at their Web sites.

Consolidators buy tickets for scheduled flights at reduced prices from the airlines and then resell them to passengers. Read the fine print carefully for information about penalties for changes in schedule and cancellations. Always call the airlines to confirm your consolidator reservation. Some consolidators are:

Cheap Tickets, Inc, ☎ (800) 377-1000; Web site: www.cheaptickets.com.
Ticket Planet, ☎ (800) 799-8888; Web site: www.ticketplanet.com.

STA Travel specializes in student travel but its resources are available to others; there are offices in the UK and throughout the U.S.; in the U.S., ☎ (800) 781-4040; Web site: www.statravel.com.

On Arrival

Arriving at the airport

Most international and many domestic flights arrive at **John F. Kennedy International Airport,** ☎ (718) 244-4444. Known as JFK, the airport faces Jamaica Bay in the southeastern section of the borough of Queens, about 15 miles from midtown Manhattan (60 minutes in moderate traffic). JFK has a complex of terminals serving more than 90 airlines, some with their own passport control and customs offices. Many international flights are channeled through Terminal 4, formerly the International Arrivals Building.

The **Travelers Aid Society,** located in Terminal 4, provides services to lost, stranded, or needy travelers. Services include emergency travel assistance and counseling; ☎ (718) 656-4870. You can reach them Mon–Thurs 10 A.M.–7 P.M.; Fri 10 A.M.–6 P.M.; Sat 11 A.M.–6 P.M.; Sun noon–6 P.M.

LaGuardia Airport—also in Queens, on the East River, about eight miles (30–45 minutes) from Midtown—primarily serves domestic flights; ☎ (718) 533-3400. Most flights arrive at and depart from the two-level Central Terminal Building; Delta Airlines has its own terminal; US Airways shuttle flights to Washington and Boston operate from the US Airways Shuttle Terminal; the Marine Terminal handles the Delta shuttle.

Newark International Airport, near Newark Bay in New Jersey, is about 16 miles (45–60 minutes) from Midtown; ☎ (973) 961-6000. Many international flights originate and terminate there, and its location makes it convenient for travelers headed for Manhattan's West Side. The airport has three terminals (A, B, and C); Terminal B includes the International Arrivals Facility.

Transportation to and from Airports

The Port Authority of New York and New Jersey, which operates the three major airports, maintains a Web site at www.panynj.gov. The site has detailed information about ground transportation to Manhattan and the suburbs. The Port Authority also has a telephone hotline with similar information; ☎ (800) AIR-RIDE (i.e., 247-7433). Live operator available Mon–Fri 9 A.M.–5 P.M.; recorded information all other times.

Taxis

Taxis to Midtown are available at all three airports. During peak hours uniformed dispatchers will direct you to a cab. Licensed taxis (the legal ones) are yellow and have a medallion shield on the hood. When uniformed taxi dispatchers are not on duty, you must hail your own cab; New Yorkers are assertive in this respect.

Ignore offers of transportation from people who approach you in the terminal; visitors unfamiliar with New York have been grossly overcharged and sometimes intimidated by these **taxi hustlers.** Go to information counters, bus stops, or taxi dispatchers for safe and legitimate transportation.

Taxi drivers are required legally to stay inside their cabs except to help with luggage, etc. Drivers will expect a 15–20 percent tip.

Taxis from Newark and LaGuardia are metered. From **LaGuardia** you pay the meter amount plus bridge and tunnel tolls. From **Newark,** you pay the meter amount, plus $10 and tolls. Estimate $16–26 from LaGuardia and $30–32 from Newark. Taxis from **JFK** are charged at a flat rate of $30, a blessing when you are stalled in traffic. One fare covers all passengers.

Rental cars

It is nonsensical to rent a car for use in New York City unless you're staying in remote parts of the outer boroughs. Just getting to Manhattan from the airport can be a hassle. Parking and driving around once you do get there can be even worse. Major rental companies do maintain fleets at all three airports, with counters or courtesy phones in the arrival areas of the terminals.

Ground Transportation from Kennedy Airport

Ground Transportation Information counters are located on the baggage-claim level of all terminals.

Express Bus Service

New York Airport Service buses run from JFK terminals to the Port Authority Bus Terminal (W. 42nd St and Eighth Ave), Grand Central Terminal (E. 42nd St and Park Ave) and Penn Station (W. 34th St and Eighth Ave). Transfers are available from Grand Central to Midtown hotels. Buses run every 15–30 minutes from 6 A.M. to midnight, less frequently late at night; ☎ (718) 875-8200 or (800) 872-4577. Fare is $13.

Shared Minibus Service

Express Shuttle USA (formerly Gray Line Air Shuttle) vans run on demand to Midtown hotels, 7 A.M.–11:30 P.M., at about 45–60 minute intervals, longer at peak hours. Make arrangements at the Ground Transportation Desk. Travel time depends on how many hotel stops the van makes. Call ☎ (212) 315-3006 in New York or toll-free (800) 451-0455; Web site: www.graylinenewyork.com. Fare is $14.

SuperShuttle runs door-to-door service 24 hours, 365 days; fare based on destination, about $16 to Midtown. Call ☎ (800) 258-3826 or (212) 258-3826; Web site: www.supershuttle.com.

Subway-Bus Combinations

You can get to Midtown inexpensively using public transportation, though it is neither convenient nor quick and is not recommended late at night or when you have heavy luggage. If you are stout-hearted, strong-armed, and patient, take the blue, white, and yellow **Long-Term Parking Lot Bus,** which departs about every 15 minutes from all JFK terminals. Buses connect at the **Howard Beach–JFK Airport subway station** with the **Eighth Ave Express (A train),** which wends its way to the West Side of Manhattan, stopping in Queens and Brooklyn. The trip takes approximately 60–90 minutes. The shuttle bus is free, but the subway costs $1.50 (cash, token, or MetroCard required).

A Future Rail Link to JFK

In 1998 the Port Authority began construction of **AirTrain,** a light rail link that will loop eight passenger terminals at JFK and connect to the Howard Beach subway station and the Jamaica railroad station. From these stations, passengers will be able to transfer to the Long Island Rail Road, subway, or bus lines. If all goes well, the first section of Airtrain (to the Howard Beach subway station) is scheduled to open in 2003.

Ground Transportation from LaGuardia Airport

Ground Transportation Information counters are located on the baggage-claim level of all terminals.

Express Bus Service

New York Airport Service runs between the airport and the Port Authority Bus Terminal in Manhattan (W. 42nd St and Eighth Ave), Grand Central Terminal (E. 42nd St and Park Ave), Penn Station (W. 34th St and Eighth Ave) and hotels between 27th and 63rd Sts. Buses run at least every half hour from early morning until late evening; ☎ (718) 875-8200. Fare is $10.

Shared Minibus Service

Express Shuttle USA (formerly Gray Line Air Shuttle) vans run on demand to Midtown hotels, 7 A.M.–11:30 P.M., at about 45–60 minute intervals, longer at peak hours. Make arrangements at the Ground Transportation Desk. Travel time depends on how many hotel stops the van makes. Call ☎ (212) 315-3006 in New York or toll-free (800) 451-0455; Web site: www.graylinenewyork.com. Fare is $13.

SuperShuttle Manhattan provides door-to-door service to all Manhattan locations, 24 hours, 365 days; ☎ (212) 209-7000 or (800) 258-3826; Web site: www.supershuttle.com. Fare is $13–15, depending on destination.

Ground Transportation from Newark Airport

Ground Transportation Information counters are located on the baggage-claim level of all terminals.

Express Bus Service

Olympia Airport Express provides express bus service between all terminals and the Port Authority Bus Terminal in Manhattan (W. 42nd St and Eighth Ave), Grand Central Terminal (E. 42nd St and Park Ave), and Penn Station (W. 34th St and Eighth Ave). Buses go to the Port Authority Terminal around the clock at intervals of 20–30 minutes (less frequently after midnight and during peak hours) and to Penn Station and Grand Central 6 A.M.–midnight. Call ☎ (212) 964-6233 in New York or (908) 354-3330 in New Jersey. The fare is $11; connecting service from Grand Central to many hotels is available for an extra fee.

Shared Minibus Service

Express Shuttle USA operates on demand (30–60 minute intervals, longer at peak hours), 7 A.M.–11:30 P.M. from terminals to midtown Manhattan hotels (23rd–63rd Sts). Make arrangements at the Ground Transportation Desk or dial 24 at the Gray Line courtesy phone in the baggage-claim area. Call ☎ (212) 315-3006 or (800) 451-0455; Web site: www.graylinenewyork.com. Fare is $14.

Super Shuttle Manhattan offers door-to-door service to locations in Manhattan between Battery Park and 227th St. Available 24 hours, at 30–60 minute intervals, longer at peak hours. Call ☎ (212) 209-7000 or (800) 258-3826. Fare is $17–22.50.

By train

The main railroad stations are Pennsylvania Station (W. 34th St and Eighth Ave) and Grand Central Terminal (W. 42nd St and Park Ave). Long-distance **Amtrak** trains from points east, north, and west arrive and depart from Penn Station; ☎ (800) USA-RAIL; Web site: www.amtrak.com. The northeast corridor, from Boston to Washington, D.C., is served by new high-speed Acela Express trains. Book well ahead (for example, six months) for best rates; ask about cheaper weekend rates.

Commuter lines from the New Jersey and Long Island suburbs also arrive and depart from Penn Station. For **New Jersey Transit:** outside N.J., ☎ (973) 762-5100; inside N.J., ☎ (800) 772-2222; Web site: www.njtransit.state.nj.us. For the **Long Island Rail Road (LIRR):** ☎ (718) 217-LIRR (217-5477); Web site: www.mta.nyc.ny.us/lirr.

The **PATH (Port Authority Trans-Hudson)** system runs between Newark or Hoboken in New Jersey and either the World Trade Center (Church St between Liberty and Vesey Sts) or Penn Station in New York. Call ☎ (800) 234-PATH (234-7284); Web site: www.panynj.gov/path.

The northern and eastern suburbs in Westchester County and Connecticut are served by the **Metro-North Railroad,** part of the city's Metropolitan Transit Authority. Its commuter lines (the Harlem, Hudson, and New Haven lines) operate from Grand Central Terminal. Call ☎ (212) 532-4900; outside of New York City, ☎ (800) METRO-INFO (638-7646); Web site: www.mta.nyc.ny.us/mnr.

By bus

Long-distance bus travel in the U.S. is much slower and less pleasant than train travel. Long-distance buses (as well as commuter lines) arrive at the mammoth **Port Authority Bus Terminal** (W. 42nd St and Eighth Ave), located west of Times Square. Recently modernized, the terminal provides information services, connections to local buses and subways, an updated security system, shops, restaurants, ATM machines, a post office, and hotel reservation phones (on the subway level). There is a taxi dispatch stand on Eighth Ave, 7 A.M.–11 P.M. While security at the Port Authority Terminal itself and in its immediate neighborhood has improved in recent years, you should still be cautious, particularly late at night.

For **bus information,** ☎ (212) 564-8484. Or call individual bus lines:
Adirondack Trailways, Pine Hill Trailways, New York Trailways, serving New York State; ☎ (800) 858-8555 or (800) 225-6815.
Bonanza Bus Lines, serving Connecticut, Rhode Island, Massachusetts, and Vermont; ☎ (800) 556-3815; Web site: www.bonanzabus.com.
Greyhound Lines, nationwide service; ☎ (800) 231-2222 or (212) 971-6300; Web site: www.greyhound.com.

By car

Manhattan island is joined to the mainland by tunnels and bridges. The **Holland Tunnel** connects New Jersey (from route I-95, the N.J. Turnpike) with downtown Manhattan (Canal St). The **Lincoln Tunnel** links Midtown (40th St) with New Jersey (I-95). The **George Washington Bridge** connects northern Manhattan (via the Henry Hudson Pkwy or the Harlem River Drive) with New Jersey (links to I-95, I-80, and the Palisades Pkwy). The **Triborough Bridge** links Connecticut and Westchester County with the FDR Drive on the East Side and also provides access to the airports in Queens.

Getting around New York

Finding Your Way

In Lower Manhattan the street plan, which reflects historical development, is irregular; you probably will need a map to get around. North of about 14th St, a grid system makes it easier to find your way.

Avenues run north and south and are named (Park, Lexington, West End), numbered (First Ave, Fifth Ave), or lettered (Ave A, B, C, and D on the Lower East Side). Sixth Ave, officially the Ave of the Americas, is still Sixth Ave to New Yorkers. Traffic on most avenues flows in one direction, with alternate avenues running north and south, though there are exceptions to this rule.

Streets run east and west and are numbered east or west of Fifth Ave with the smallest numbers closest to Fifth Ave; thus 12 E. 72nd St lies east of Fifth Ave but fairly close to it. Broadway, originally an Indian trail and the major exception to the grid, runs diagonally from northwest to southeast.

Traffic generally flows east on even-numbered streets and west on odd-numbered ones, though again there are exceptions. Major crosstown streets with two-way traffic are 14th St, 23rd St, 34th St, 42nd St, 57th St, and 72nd St. Transverses cross Central Park at 65th/66th St, 79th/80th St, and 96th/97th St. Uptown means north; downtown means south; crosstown means either east or west. Midtown is the part of Manhattan from about 34th to 59th Sts.

Using Public Transportation

Public transportation will take you most places you want to go. Subways are quick, fairly reliable, and reasonably easy to negotiate. Buses allow you to see the passing scene, though sometimes they get stalled in traffic or stuck in snow. During the rush hours at the beginning and ending of the business day, buses and subways are unpleasantly crowded.

Official **bus and subway maps,** including bus maps of the outer boroughs, are available at the Information Booth on the Main Concourse in Grand Central Terminal. Subway maps are available at the token booths of subway stations and are posted inside the stations and in the trains; bus maps are available on buses. Maps are also available online at www.mta.nyc.ny.us/nyct/maps.

You can also request a map from the **NYC Transit Customer Assistance;** ☏ (718) 330-3322. Do not expect a swift response.

MetroCards

MetroCards are prepaid fare cards with magnetic strips that can be read by the scanners installed in subway turnstiles and bus fare boxes. They offer discounts and convenience.

There are three types of cards: the **Unlimited Ride MetroCard** with a 7-day ($17) or 30-day ($63) expiration date; the **Fun Pass** ($4), which allow you unlimited local bus and subway rides for one day; and the **Pay-Per-Ride Metro-Card** ($15) which gives you 11 rides for the price of 10. If you plan to use public transportation frequently, buy a MetroCard.

Manhattan Address Finder

To find the nearest cross street on any avenue in Manhattan, take the address number, cancel the last digit, divide by two, and add or subtract the key number below. Example: Where is 500 Fifth Ave? Cancel the last 0 and divide 50 by 2. Add the appropriate key number (18) to 25 and get 43. Thus, 500 Fifth Ave is near 43rd St.

Ave A	Add 3
Ave B	Add 3
Ave C	Add 3
Ave D	Add 3
First Ave	Add 3
Second Ave	Add 3
Third Ave	Add 10
Fourth Ave	Add 8
Fifth Ave	
63 to 108	Add 11
109 to 200	Add 13
201 to 400	Add 16
401 to 600	Add 18
601 to 775	Add 20
776 to 1286	Cancel last figure of building number and subtract 18; do not divide building number by 2.
1286 to 1500	Add 45
above 2000	Add 24
Sixth Ave	Subtract 12
Seventh Ave	
1 to 1800	Add 12
above 1800	Add 20
Eighth Ave	Add 9
Ninth Ave	Add 13

Tenth Ave	Add 14
Amsterdam Ave	Add 59
Broadway	
Anything from 1 to 754 is south of 8th St; cross streets are named, not numbered.	
756 to 846	Subtract 29
847 to 953	Subtract 25
above 953	Subtract 31
Columbus Ave	Add 60
Lexington Ave	Add 22
Madison Ave	Add 27
Park Ave	Add 34
Park Ave South	Add 8
West End Ave	Add 59
York Ave	Add 4
Central Park West	Cancel last digit and add 60
Riverside Drive	Cancel last digit and
up to 567	Add 72
568 and up	Add 78

Reduced fare cards (half-price) are available for travelers with disabilities and the elderly (65 and older); ☎ (718) 243-4999 or (718) 596-8273 (TTY).

MetroCards allow you to **transfer** free from bus to subway or vice versa, and from one bus to another one crossing its route. When your card is swiped, the scanner automatically records a transfer, good for the next two hours. You can check your MetroCard balance when using the card on the bus or in the subway stations at a MetroCard reader near the token booth. If you swipe the card several times and the subway turnstile does not open, check with the station agent in the ticket booth.

You can buy a MetroCard at any subway station or at any of over 3,000 participating neighborhood merchants (news centers, pharmacies, delicatessens and grocery stores, check-cashing centers, etc.). Fun Passes are available at MetroCard vending machines in stations, at participating merchants, at the Times Square Visitors Center, NYC & Company, and the N.Y. Transit Museum Gallery and Store at Grand Central Terminal. For current sales locations, ☎ (212) METROCARD (i.e., 638-7622) from within the city or (800) METROCARD from elsewhere. Metrocards are also available online; Web site: www.metrocard.citysearch.com.

Buses

The Metropolitan Transit Authority (MTA) operates some 4,000 buses over 234 routes, a network of about 1,700 miles. Buses are relatively cheap and moderately reliable, though they have become increasingly crowded since 1997, when Metro-Cards enabled free transfers between buses and subways. They are the best way to travel short distances or east–west in Manhattan (subways run primarily north–south).

Pay with exact change (no bills), a token (available at toll booths in the subway stations), or a MetroCard. Many stores refuse to give change without a purchase, so stock up on tokens, hoard change, or buy a MetroCard. A single ride costs

$1.50 and a transfer (free, ask the driver when you board) enables you to change within two hours to a second bus on an intersecting route.

Buses stop on demand about every two blocks going uptown and downtown and every block crosstown. Most buses run on a 24-hour schedule with reduced service at night.

For late-night safety, **Request-A-Stop** bus service (every day from 10 P.M. to 5 A.M.) allows you to get off along the route between regular stops. Tell the bus driver where you want to get off and he or she will let you off there or at the closest corner where it is safe to stop the bus.

Subways

Subways are the fastest but not always the most pleasant way to get around. As ridership has risen, the subways have become increasingly crowded, and, according to recent surveys, less clean. Like other public facilities within the city, the subways attract people who loiter on the platforms and panhandle in the cars.

The trains run 24 hours a day across a 244-mile route (468 stations) in four boroughs (excluding Staten Island), serving about 4.3 million riders on an average weekday. The fare is $1.50, paid by tokens or MetroCard (both available in booths inside the stations). You can purchase packets of ten tokens, which can be used on buses as well.

Express trains make only certain stops; **local trains** stop at every station. Trains to widely different destinations often travel on the same track, so check the number on the front of the train before you board. Announcements are made over a public address system but they are often garbled and impossible to understand.

Routes to outlying areas can involve changing trains, but it is easy to travel up- and downtown along major avenues. Avoid rush hours (7:30–9:30 A.M., 5–6:30 P.M.) if you are claustrophobic.

Subway Service Changes

Until 2004, the **rehabilitation of the Manhattan Bridge** will cause major and fairly complex service changes on the Sixth Ave Express lines. The B and D trains between the Bronx and Manhattan will terminate at 34th St–Herald Square. South of 34th St–Herald Square and in Brooklyn, the former Sixth Ave Express trains (B, D, and Q) will have new names and new routes: the B will become the W; the D will become the Q Local; the Q will become the Q Express. For more information, pick up a pamphlet in Sixth Ave line subway stations, check the red-and-white posters in the subway stations, or call the Manhattan Bridge Hotline, ☎ (718) 521-3333. The MTA Web site also has information: www.mta.nyc.ny.us; click on "NYC Transit" and then on the "Service Alert" icon.

Following the destruction of the World Trade Center, there is no service on the Broadway–Seventh Ave Local (1) to the Cortlandt St, Rector St, and South Ferry stations. The Cortlandt St station on the Broadway Local (N, R) is temporarily closed. The World Trade Center station on the Eighth Ave Local (E) is closed. For updated information about these and other **service changes in downtown Manhattan,** check the MTA Web site or ask at the token booth in a subway station.

Taxis

The city fleet contains about 12,000 cabs, a statistic difficult to believe during a rainy rush hour. Yellow cabs are licensed and regulated by the New York City Taxi and Limousine Commission and may be identified by their color and the medallion displayed on the hood. Rates, which cover up to four passengers, are posted on the door; they are currently $2.00 for the first ⅕ mile, 30¢ for each additional ⅕ mile, and 20¢ for each minute of waiting time. A 50¢ surcharge from 8 P.M. to 6 A.M. is in effect on all cabs. Fares to destinations outside the city should be negotiated before you start.

Your driver may not speak fluent English and may drive imaginatively. (You are required by law to wear your seatbelt.) It is a good idea to know more or less how to get to your destination, since drivers have been known to take unsuspecting tourists via circuitous routes. Make sure the meter is turned on when the ride begins. Get a receipt in case you leave something in the cab or later want to register a complaint.

There are dispatcher-controlled taxi stands at major transportation terminals and more than 200 taxi stands within the city, but most cabs cruise looking for passengers. The lighted sign on top of the car indicates whether the cab is available; if the center panel is lit, the cab is empty.

To inquire about lost property or to register complaints, ☎ (212) NYC-TAXI (i.e., 692-8294). You must have either the taxi identification number from the lighted roof panel or the driver's identification number, which is posted inside the cab. Your receipt has the taxi ID number printed on it.

"Gypsy" cabs operate in the outer boroughs and in Manhattan outside the central and downtown districts; they are painted colors other than yellow and may have "livery" license plates. They are not authorized to pick up passengers who hail them on the street and are not recommended to visitors. In 1984 these cabs, an estimated 35,000 of them, came under city regulation, though the fares remain unregulated.

Walking

Walking is one of the best ways to enjoy New York. There are 20 north–south blocks to a mile (crosstown blocks, except between Lexington and Madison Aves, are about three times as long).

Driving

Unless you plan excursions to the outer boroughs, a car is no advantage in New York. Traffic can approach gridlock. Street parking is hard to find; parking garages are expensive; parking tickets are even more so. To the uninitiated, the city's alternate-side-of-the-street parking regulations (parking allowed on one side one day, on the other side the next day) may seem byzantine. If you do have a car and are staying at a hotel, check with the doorman about parking facilities.

Cars parked illegally may be towed and impounded. It is expensive in time, emotional energy, and money (cash, certified check, or credit card only, currently about $200, plus poundage and storage fees) to retrieve your vehicle. To find out if the Department of Transportation has your car, call ☎ (212) TOW-AWAY.

Other hazards to the uninitiated include New York drivers and roads. The former can be aggressive and impatient but are generally predictable. The latter, frequently under repair, are pocked with bone- and metal-jolting potholes, sometimes impressive in their dimensions.

Theft, either of your car or its contents, is another possibility. If you park on the street, do not leave valuables in your car. You may see parked cars bearing signs that announce "No radio in car," testimony to the frequency of radio theft. Consider using a "club" that locks the steering column.

Where to Stay

Hotels

Hotels in New York are expensive; the average room rate in June 2000 was $224.83, with prices headed up. In a city built vertically, space is money. Rooms, even in expensive hotels, tend to be small. It is possible to find comfortable, clean places to stay in safe neighborhoods, but they will not be inexpensive. If you are on a budget and are willing to sacrifice some privacy, you can find modest accommodations with shared bathrooms. You might also consider hostels, YMCAs, and hotels outside the center of Manhattan.

The rates given here are "rack rates," the hotels' published prices, but you may be able to negotiate a discount: ask about rates for seniors, special packages, weekend or out-of-season specials, and rates for extended stays. Try discounters on the Internet. If smoke bothers you, ask about nonsmoking rooms.

Reserving a Room

Tourism is currently booming in New York, so reserve before you arrive, well in advance for less-expensive hotels, which are in great demand. The easiest way to book a hotel room, either from the United States or abroad, is by fax or phone, using a major credit card to guarantee your room. Many hotels have Internet sites and e-mail addresses.

NYC & Company lists hotels in their publications and on their Web site: www.nycvisit.com. The **Hotel Guide** provides online access to more than 30,000 hotels worldwide: www.hotelguide.com. Published sources include *The New York Times Guide to Hotels in New York City* (2000) by Charles Suisman and *New York's 60 Best Wonderful Little Hotels* (1999) by Allen Sperry; both have detailed reviews.

Rates

In general, luxury hotels charge more than $350 per night for a standard double room (and some charge more than $400); expensive hotels charge more than $250; moderately expensive, more than $200; moderate, more than $150; and budget, less than $150. In addition, New York hotels must tack on a city tax of 13.25 percent and a per-room fee of $2.00.

Luxury Hotels

Carlyle, 35 E. 76th St (at Madison Ave), New York, NY 10021. ☎ (212) 744-1600 or (800) 227-5737; fax: (212) 717-4682; no Web site. Elegant, low-key, much-loved hotel (190 rooms). Bemelmans Bar, with murals by Ludwig Bemelmans, is a well-known watering spot.

Essex House/A Westin Hotel, 160 Central Park South (between Sixth and Seventh Aves), New York, NY 10019. ☎ (212) 247-0300 or (888) 625-5144; from abroad, ☎ (800) 937-8461; fax: (212) 315-1839; Web site: www.essex house.com. Grand, old 39-story hotel (597 rooms), famous Art Deco lobby spruced up in 1993. Some rooms have park views, some are small.

Four Seasons, 57 E. 57th St (between Park and Madison Aves), New York, NY 10022. ☎ (212) 758-5700 or (800) 332-3442; fax: (212) 758-5711; Web site: www.fourseasons.com. Designed by I. M. Pei; architecturally stunning lobby; 52-story building (370 rooms) with big rooms, beautiful appointments, stunning prices.

The Mark, 25 E. 77th St (at Madison Ave), New York, NY 10021. ☎ (212) 744-4300 or (800) 843-6275; fax: (212) 744-2749; Web site: www.mandarinoriental.com. Excellent traditional hotel (180 rooms), attentive service. Complimentary shuttle service to Wall St (Mon–Fri mornings); near Madison Ave boutiques and Central Park.

Mercer Hotel, 147 Mercer St (at Prince St), New York, NY 10012. ☎ (212) 966-6060 or (888) 918-6060; fax: (212) 965-3838; Web site: none. Small-scale hotel (75 rooms), in SoHo with "downtown" atmosphere, hip and high concept. High-tech bathrooms; Mercer Kitchen headed up by celebrity chef.

New York Palace Hotel, 455 Madison Ave (between E. 50th and E. 51st Sts), New York, NY 10022. ☎ (212) 888-7000 or (800) 697-2522; fax: (212) 303-6030; Web site: www.newyorkpalace.com. The ground floor occupies land-marked former Villard Houses. Three levels (900 rooms) of prices and amenities.

Peninsula-New York, 700 Fifth Ave (at W. 55th St), New York, NY 10019. ☎ (212) 956-2888 or (800) 262-9467; fax: (212) 903-3943; Web site: www. peninsula.com. Prime location in landmarked building. Elegantly refurbished (241 rooms), high-tech tools for business travelers. Rooftop health club, swimming pool.

Pierre, 2 E. 61st St (between Fifth and Madison Aves), New York, NY 10021. ☎ (212) 838-8000 or (800) 332-3442; fax: (212) 940-8109; Web site: www.fourseasons.com. Elegant Old World hotel (202 rooms), emphasis on service and comfort. Some rooms have views of Central Park.

Royalton, 44 W. 44th St (between Fifth and Sixth Aves), New York, NY 10036. ☎ (212) 869-4400 or (800) 635-9013; fax: (212) 869-8965; no Web site. High-style boutique hotel (168 rooms); sleek and modern. Round Bar in lobby is famous gathering place. Small rooms.

Sherry-Netherland, 781 Fifth Ave (at 59th St), New York, NY 10021. ☎ (212) 355-2800 or (800) 247-4377; fax: (212) 319-4306; Web site: www.sherry netherland.com. Worldly and elegant (168 rooms and suites); fine, unobtrusive service; large rooms, many with views of Central Park and Fifth Ave. Cipriani's restaurant for celebrity watching; a grande dame.

SoHo Grand Hotel, 310 West Broadway (between Grand and Canal Sts), New York, NY 10013. ☎ (212) 965-3000 or (800) 965-3000; fax: (212) 965-3244; Web site: www.sohogrand.com. New hotel (369 rooms), highly designed and quintessentially SoHo. Close to art galleries and shopping. Some rooms are small.

St. Regis, 2 E. 55th St (between Fifth and Madison Aves), New York, NY 10022. ☎ (212) 753-4500 or (800) 759-7550; fax: (212) 787-3447; Web site: www.starwood.com/stregis. Built in 1904 (313 rooms), Gilded Age ambience with modern amenities. High ceilings, chandeliers, marble bathrooms.

Expensive Hotels

Algonquin, 59 W. 44th St (between Fifth and Sixth Aves), New York, NY 10036. ☎ (212) 840-6800 or (800) 555-8000; fax: (212) 944-1419; Web site: www.camberleyhotels.com. Landmarked 165-room hotel with historic literary associations, well-known cabaret. Refurbished in 1998. Small rooms, pleasantly decorated.

The Benjamin, 125 E. 50th St (at Lexington Ave), New York, NY 10022. ☎ (212) 715-2500 or (888) 4-BENJAMIN; fax: (212) 465-3697; Web site: www.the benjamin.com. Formerly the Hotel Beverly, redone (209 rooms) and renamed in 1999; high-tech gear, well-designed rooms with large desks, large in-room safes, big beds, many thoughtful amenities.

Doubletree Guest Suites, 1568 Broadway (at W. 47th St), New York, NY 10036. ☎ (212) 719-1600 or (800) 222-TREE; fax: (212) 921-5212; Web site: www.hilton.com. Large hotel (460 suites) in the Theater District. Kid-friendly amenities (children 12-and-under are free). Suites with living room, dining area, bedroom, kitchenette.

Grand Hyatt New York, Park Ave at Grand Central (E. 42nd St between Park and Lexington Aves), New York, NY 10017. ☎ (212) 883-1234 or (800) 233-1234; fax: (212) 697-3772; Web site: www.newyork.hyatt.com. Very large hotel (1,337 rooms) next to Grand Central. Large-scale lobby with cascading water, greenery marble, and bronze. Refurbished 1980.

Hotel Wales, 1295 Madison Ave (at E. 92nd St), New York, NY 10128. ☎ (212) 876-6000 or (877) 847-4444; fax: (212) 894-5220; Web site: www.wales hotel.com. Small (87 rooms) stylish hotel in Carnegie Hill neighborhood. Guests can use the 92nd Street Y for a small fee. Complimentary breakfast buffet.

Inn at Irving Place, 56 Irving Place (between E. 17th and E. 18th Sts), New York, NY 10003. ☎ (212) 533-4600 or (800) 685-1447; fax: (212) 533-4611; Web site: www.innatirving.com. Twelve guest rooms in a landmarked three-story town house in the historic Gramercy Park district. Victorian ambience with modern conveniences.

Lombardy, 111 E. 56th St (between Park and Lexington Aves), New York, NY 10022. ☎ (212) 753-8600 or (800) 223-5254; fax: (212) 754-5683; Web site: www.lombardyhotel.com. Built in the 1920s by publisher William Randolph Hearst; public spaces express his opulent tastes. Has 125 rooms, none nonsmoking. Marble bathrooms, big closets.

Morgans, 237 Madison Ave (between E. 37th and E. 38th Sts), New York, NY 10016. ☎ (212) 686-0300 or (800) 334-3408; fax: (212) 779-8352; no Web site. Boutique hotel (113 rooms) in Murray Hill, run by the people who run the Royalton. Private, quiet, contemporary.

Plaza, Fifth Ave at Central Park South, New York, NY 10019. ☎ (212) 759-3000 or (800) 759-3000; fax: (212) 546-5234; Web site: www.fairmont.com. Big, famous hotel (805 rooms) overlooking Central Park; wide variety of rooms, many services; can be overcrowded.

Millennium Hotel United Nations Plaza, One United Nations Plaza (E. 44th St at First Ave), New York, NY 10017. ☎ (212) 758-1234 or (800) 222-8888; fax: (212) 702-5051; Web site: www.millennium-hotels.com. Built to house UN executives, then converted (427 rooms). Rooms start on the 28th floor, well above street noise; many have spectacular views. Indoor swimming pool, tennis court.

Waldorf-Astoria, 301 Park Ave (at E. 50th St), New York, NY 10022. ☎ (212)

355-3000 or (800) 925-3673; fax: (212) 872-7272; Web site: www.hilton.com. One of the grandest of New York's old hotels, this landmarked building (1,401 rooms) is famous for its Art Deco lobby and its history. Recently refurbished. Rooms in the Waldorf Towers have private entrance and special amenities.

Moderately Expensive Hotels

Crowne Plaza Hotel at the United Nations, 304 E. 42nd St (between First and Second Aves), New York, NY 10017. ☎ (212) 986-8800 or (800) 879-8836; fax: (212) 297-3440; Web site: www.crowneplaza-un.com. Formerly the Tudor Hotel (300 rooms). Walking distance to Grand Central Station and Midtown. Upscale branch of Holiday Inn.

Fitzpatrick Grand Central Hotel, 141 E. 44th St (between Lexington and Third Aves), New York, NY 10017. ☎ (212) 351-6800 or (800) 367-7701; fax: (212) 317-0572; Web site: www.fitzpatrickhotels.com. Part of family-owned chain (155 rooms). Complimentary newspapers, use of nearby sports club.

Kimberly Hotel, 145 E. 50th St (between Lexington and Third Aves), New York, NY 10022. ☎ (212) 755-0400 or (800) 683-0400; fax: (212) 750-0113; Web site: www.kimberlyhotel.com. Hotel (186 rooms) has spacious one- and two-bedroom suites, some with terraces. Faxes, kitchenettes. Use of nearby health club.

Millenium Hilton, 55 Church St (between Fulton and Dey Sts), New York, NY 10007. ☎ (212) 693-2001 or (800) 835-2220; fax: (212) 571-2316; Web site: www.hilton.com. Next to the World Trade Center, modern hotel (561 rooms), views of downtown and Hudson River. Geared to business travelers, health club, swimming pool. **Note:** Because of its proximity to the World Trade Center site, this hotel is currently (Oct 2001) closed and not accepting reservations.

New York Marriott East Side, 525 Lexington Ave (at E. 49th St), New York, NY 10017. ☎ (212) 755-4000 or (800) 242-8684; fax: (212) 751-3440; Web site: www.marriott.com. Built as Shelton Towers (1924), was once NY's largest hotel (646 rooms); attractive rooms, amenities for business travelers; gracious atmosphere.

New York Marriott Marquis, 1535 Broadway (between W. 45th and W. 46th Sts), New York, NY 10036. ☎ (212) 398-1900 or (800) 843-4898; fax: (212) 704-8930; Web site: www.marriott.com. Blockbuster (1,919 rooms) hotel in Times Square, guest rooms begin on ninth floor. Huge atrium lobby, business center; often used by convention goers and business groups.

Shelburne Murray Hill, 303 Lexington Ave (at E. 37th St), New York, NY 10016. ☎ (212) 689-5200 or (800) 637-8483; fax: (212) 779-7068; Web site: www.mesuite.com. All-suite hotel (263 suites). Built as Shelburne Hotel (1926), rooms fairly spacious, full kitchens or kitchenettes, grocery-shopping service, laundry, restaurant.

Wall Street Inn, 9 South William St (between Broad and Beaver Sts), New York, NY 10005. ☎ (212) 747-1500; fax: (212) 747-1900; Web site: www.thewallstreetinn.com. Opened July 1999 in renovated building. Quiet, small (46 rooms) hotel, good service, multiline phones, health club, laundry, business center.

Moderately Priced Hotels

Best Western Seaport Inn, 33 Peck Slip (at Front St), New York, NY 10038. ☎ (212) 766-6600 or (800) HOTELNY (i.e., 468-3569); fax: (212) 766-6615; Web site: www.bestwestern.com. In historic, quiet neighborhood (71 rooms) near

South Street Seaport, Financial District, and Chinatown. Some rooms have terraces with view. Restaurant next door.

Hotel Chelsea, 222 W. 22nd St (between Seventh and Eighth Aves), New York, NY 10011. ☎ (212) 243-3700; fax: (212) 675-5531; Web site: www.hotel chelsea.com. One of New York's most famous, not for the accommodations but for its clientele—from O. Henry to Sid Vicious. The *International Herald Tribune* called it a "Tower of Babel of creativity and bad behavior." Walls are famously thick, rooms are reasonably clean. Check its Web site for an idea of the ambience.

Holiday Inn Wall Street District, 15 Gold St (at Platt St), New York, NY 10038. ☎ (212) 232-7700 or (800) 465-4329; fax: (212) 425-0330; Web site: www.holidayinnwsd.com. Small (138 rooms), new (opened 1999), high-tech member of national chain; T-1 lines in every room, also Nintendo; automated check-in and checkout. Weekend packages.

Hospitality House, 145 E. 49th St (between Third and Lexington Aves), New York, NY 10017. ☎ (212) 965-1102 or (800) 987-1235; fax: (212) 965-1149; Web site: www.hospitalitycompany.com. Renovated apartment building in Midtown, simple (35 apartments) accommodations for short and longer stays, full kitchens. No smoking, no maid service. Basement laundry room.

Inn on 23rd Street, 131 W. 23rd St (between Sixth and Seventh Aves), New York, NY 10011. ☎ (212) 463-0330 or (877) 387-2323; fax: (212) 463-0302; Web site: www.bbonline.com/ny/innon23rd. Small family-run bed-and-breakfast (11 rooms) in Chelsea town house. Rooms on five floors, elevator. All rooms nonsmoking.

Marmara-Manhattan, 301 E. 94th St (at Second Ave), New York, NY 10128. ☎ (212) 427-3100 or (800) 621-9029; fax: (212) 427-3042; Web site: www.marmara-manhattan.com. An extended-stay hotel (107 suites) on the Upper East Side. Japanese courtyard garden. Kitchens, some suites with washers and dryers. Rates based on monthly stay.

Washington Square Hotel, 103 Waverly Place (at MacDougal St), New York, NY 10011. ☎ (212) 777-9515 or (800) 222-0418; fax: (212) 979-8373; Web site: www.wshotel.com. Family-run hotel in Greenwich Village; recently renovated (170 rooms in two connecting buildings). Front rooms overlook Washington Square; some back rooms very dark. No nonsmoking rooms. Popular for price and location.

Wellington Hotel, 871 Seventh Ave (at W. 55th St), New York, NY 10019. ☎ (212) 247-3900 or (800) 652-1212; fax: (212) 581-1719; Web site: www.wellingtonhotel.com. Large (617 rooms) hotel in good Midtown location, draws tour groups and many European travelers. Small but adequate rooms. Voice mail. Lobby and many rooms recently renovated.

Wyndham, 42 W. 58th St (between Fifth and Sixth Aves), New York, NY 10019. ☎ (212) 753-3500 or (800) 257-1111; fax: (212) 754-5638; no Web site. Independently owned older hotel (210 rooms), great Midtown location, repeat visitors and European tourists. Spacious by New York standards. No fancy amenities or room service; good value.

Budget Hotels

In a city where hotel rooms are high-priced, budget hotels offer few services and, often, little cheer. Some, however, are in very good locations.

Americana Inn, 69 W. 38th St (at Sixth Ave), New York, NY 10018. ☎ (212) 840-

6700 or (888) Hotel58; fax (212) 840-1830; Web site: www.newyorkhotel.com. Good location close to Macy's and within walking distance of the Theater District; very clean, air-conditioned, simply furnished rooms; shared bathrooms.

Carlton Arms Hotel, 160 E. 25th St (at Third Ave), New York, NY 10010. ☎ (212) 679-0680; fax: none; Web site: www.carltonarms.com. Small, old hotel (54 rooms); high-energy ambience. Check the Web site to get an idea of the ambience. No phones in rooms, no TV, no air-conditioning, some shared baths. Discounts for students and visitors from abroad. Pleasant, safe neighborhood.

Chelsea Savoy Hotel, 204 W. 23rd St (at Seventh Ave), New York, NY 10011. ☎ (212) 929-9353; fax: (212) 741-6309; Web site: www.chelseasavoynyc.com. Opened 1997 in a plain, new building in a burgeoning neighborhood; 90 rooms; rooms have big closets, clean bathrooms, fridges, and safes.

Comfort Inn Midtown, 129 W. 46th St (between Sixth Ave and Broadway), New York, NY 10036. ☎ (212) 221-2600 or (800) 567-7720; fax: (212) 764-7481. Web site: www.comfortinn.com. Pleasant member (79 rooms) of the familiar chain; renovated in 1998. There are also Comfort Inns on 35th St (near Fifth Ave), ☎ (212) 947-0200; and near Central Park on W. 71st St, ☎ (212) 721-4770.

Gershwin Hotel, 7 E. 27th St (at Fifth Ave), New York, NY 10016. ☎ (212) 545-8000; fax: (212) 684-5546; Web site: www.gershwinhotel.com. An older hotel (134 rooms), favorite with European students. All rooms have TV and telephones, some have air-conditioning. Many activities: jazz, video programs, art gallery.

Herald Square Hotel, 19 W. 31st St (between Fifth Ave and Broadway), New York, NY 10001. ☎ (212) 279-4017 and (800) 727-1888; fax: (212) 643-9208; Web site: www.heraldsquarehotel.com. Under the same management as the Portland Square Hotel; good location, low prices, attractive facade. Rooms are basic though clean; some shared bathrooms. Ask about discounts.

Hotel Edison, 228 W. 47th St (between Broadway and Eighth Ave), New York, NY 10036. ☎ (212) 840-5000 or (800) 637-7070; fax (212) 596-6850; Web site: www.edisonhotelnyc.com. Big (941 rooms) hotel in Theater District; recently renovated, clean, basic, and very popular.

Hotel Newton, 2528 Broadway (between W. 94th and W. 95th Sts), New York, NY 10025. ☎ (212) 678-6500; (800) 643-5553; (888) HOTEL58; fax: (212) 678-6758; Web site: www.newyorkhotel.com. An excellent uptown value (115 rooms, 6 suites); clean, well-kept, and comfortable; popular with European visitors; near W. 96th St subway stop; good neighborhood; some rooms have shared bathrooms.

Larchmont Hotel, 27 W. 11th St (between Fifth and Sixth Aves), New York, NY 10011. ☎ (212) 989-9333; fax: (212) 989-9496; Web site: www.larchmont hotel.citysearch.com. Quiet hotel (55 rooms) in Greenwich Village. Clean, small rooms (smoking in all rooms). Wash basin in each room, shared bathrooms. Continental breakfast.

Malibu Studios, 2688 Broadway (between W. 102nd and W. 103rd Sts), New York, NY 10025. ☎ (212) 222-2954 or (800) 647-2227; fax: (212) 678-6842; Web site: www.malibuhotelnyc.com. Clean, recently refurbished uptown hotel (150 rooms), popular with students and travelers from abroad. Some shared bathrooms. Deluxe rooms (private bath) have TV and air-conditioning. No elevator. No phones in rooms. No credit cards. Close to subway.

Portland Square Hotel, 132 W. 47th St (between Sixth and Seventh Aves), New York, NY 10036. ☎ (212) 382-0600 or (800) 388-8988; fax: (212) 382-0684; Web site: www.portlandsquarehotel.com. Older hotel (formerly the Rio) in Theater District. Rooms (145 rooms in two sections) are small and clean; some are dark; some shared baths. Laundry facilities, TV, in-room safes, voice mail.

Washington Jefferson Hotel, 318 W. 51st St (between Eighth and Ninth Aves), New York, NY 10019. ☎ (212) 246-7550 or (888) 567-7550; fax: (212) 246-7622; Web site: www.wjhotel.com. Basic accommodations (260 rooms), close to the Theater District. Clean, spartan; many shared bathrooms; modem lines. Many long-term residents.

Alternative Housing

Bed-and-Breakfasts (B&Bs)

Bed-and-breakfasts offer fewer conveniences and sometimes less privacy than commercial hotels. Most are in apartments, all or part of which are rented to visitors. "Hosted" B&Bs are in owner-occupied apartments; "unhosted" ones are in apartments with absentee owners. Most require a three-night stay. Reserve early; cancel early, as refunds, minus a service fee, are usually given up to ten days before scheduled arrival. Rates, which vary according to neighborhood and quality of accommodation, can be as low as $100 per night but range upward to $150–200.

Abode Ltd, P.O. Box 20022, New York, NY 10021. ☎ (212) 472-2000 or (800) 835-8880; no fax; Web site: www.abodenyc.com.

New York Habitat, 307 Seventh Ave, Suite 306, New York, NY 10001. ☎ (212) 255-8018; fax: (212) 627-1416; Web site: www.nyhabitat.com.

Urban Ventures, 38 W. 32nd St, Suite 1412, New York, NY 10001. ☎ (212) 594-5650; fax: (212) 947-9320; Web site: www.nyurbanventures.com.

Hostels

If price is a primary consideration, consider hosteling. Although many hostel patrons are students, guests of all ages are welcome. Room types include dormitories, single rooms for couples, or family accommodations. Some hostels require you to bring or rent sheets.

If you are planning to use hostels elsewhere as well, you might join **Hostelling International–American Youth Hostels,** which has more than 300 hostels in this country. They can be contacted at 733 15th St N.W., Suite 840, Washington, D.C. 20005; ☎ (202) 783-6161; fax: (202) 783-6171; Web site: www.hiayh.org.

Aladdin Hotel, 317 W. 45th St (between Eight and Ninth Aves), New York, NY 10036. ☎ (212) 977-5700; fax (212) 246-6036; Web site: www.alladin hotel.com. Low-budget hotel/hostel near Times Square; dormitory-style and private rooms; shared bathrooms. Well-worn and spartan but popular with students and backpackers. Requires out-of-state ID or international passport.

New York International HI–AYH Hostel, 891 Amsterdam Ave (at W. 103rd St), New York, NY 10025. ☎ (212) 932-2300 or (800) 909-4776; fax: (212) 932-2574; Web site: www.HInewyork.org. A landmarked building on the Upper West Side with 624 beds in 90 rooms. Reserve by phone or fax with credit card deposit; book early for summer and Christmas season.

YMCA/YMHA

The Young Men's Christian Association (YMCA) and the Young Men's Hebrew Association (YMHA) offer private rooms (communal bathrooms) and are less expensive than hotels but more expensive than hostels. Most offer access to athletic facilities. Popular with foreign travelers, reserve well in advance. Check out the individual branches at the Web site: www.ymcanyc.org.

De Hirsch Residence at the 92nd Street Y, 1395 Lexington Ave (at E. 92nd St), New York, NY 10128. ☎ (212) 415-5650 or (800) 858-4692; fax: (212) 415-5578; Web site: www.92ndsty.org. Long and short stays, three-day minimum; basic, clean, secure accommodations; cultural programs; fitness center.

McBurney YMCA, 206 W. 24th St (between Seventh and Eighth Aves), New York, NY 10011. ☎ (212) 741-9226; fax: (212) 741-8724. Athletic facilities, good security; basic no-frills rooms, some air-conditioned.

Vanderbilt YMCA, 224 E. 47th St (between Second and Third Aves), New York, NY 10017. ☎ (212) 756-9600; fax: (212) 755-7579. Convenient Midtown location. Many athletic facilities. Shuttles to airport; luggage storage.

West Side YMCA, 5 W. 63rd St (at Central Park West), New York, NY 10023. ☎ (212) 875-4100 or (212) 875-4273 for room reservations; fax: (212) 875-1334. The largest of New York's YMCAs, close to Lincoln Center. Clean, secure; single and double rooms, air-conditioning, luggage storage, safe-deposit boxes, housekeeping, access to athletic facilities.

Additional Information

Alcoholic Beverages

Liquor stores are open daily except Sun, holidays, and election days while the polls are open. Beer is sold in grocery stores and delicatessens, as well as liquor stores, except on Sun mornings. The legal drinking age is 21; many bars will request photo ID. Bars can remain open until 4 A.M.

Banking and Business Hours

Most New York banks are open Mon–Fri 9–5, and some are open Sat morning as well. Banks are closed on legal holidays. Business hours for most offices are Mon–Fri 9–5. Department stores and many shops open Mon–Sat at 10 A.M. and stay open until 6 or 7; some are open later on Thurs evening; many are open Sun from noon until 5. Groceries, pharmacies, and other service shops may open earlier.

Clothing

Raincoats are useful in spring and fall. Bring clothing you can layer since air-conditioning can be chilly in summer and heating can be overpowering in winter. Bring comfortable walking shoes; the pavements are hard.

Consulates and Government Information Services

Australian Consulate General, 150 E. 42nd St (34th floor), New York, NY 10017-5612; ☎ (212) 351-6500.

Canadian Consulate General, 1251 Sixth Ave, New York, NY 10020-1175; ☎ (212) 596-1628.

Consulate General of Ireland, Ireland House, 345 Park Ave (17th floor), New York, NY 10154-0037; ☎ (212) 319-2555.

New Zealand Consulate General, 780 Third Ave, Suite 1904, New York, NY 10017-2024; ☎ (212) 832-4038.
South Africa, 333 E. 38th St, New York, NY 10016; ☎ (212) 213-4880.
United Kingdom, 845 Third Ave, New York, NY 10022; ☎ (212) 745-0200.

Crime and Personal Security

The crime rate has been falling in New York for the past decade. FBI statistics for the first six months of 2000 place New York 160th of 205 major cities, and among the ten cities whose population exceeds one million, New York has the lowest crime rate. Nevertheless it is wise to be cautious about personal security, as in any large city. Traditional, common-sense advice includes being alert to your surroundings and looking confident about where you are going. (No statistics exist, however, as to the effectiveness of this posture.) If your instincts tell you the neighborhood is unsafe, leave. Don't flash cash or jewelry on the street.

Safety on Foot

Walking is generally safe in New York. During the day you can go almost any-where, especially in company, and at night you can certainly walk on busy streets. Avoid deserted streets. Do not wander in the parks after dark unless attending a concert or other activity and even then stay with the crowds; do not walk alone in the isolated, remote parts of parks. Hang on to your handbag. Shoulder bags are safer than backpacks. Put your wallet in a front pants pocket.

Tourists are targets because they often carry a lot of cash. Use travelers' checks or ATMs for smaller amounts. Be alert when using an ATM; if you are uncomfortable about the people around you, go elsewhere.

Panhandlers may assail you with requests for money. In general, it is wise to resist intimidation. Don't play three-card monte; you won't win. A very real pedestrian hazard is the corps of **bicycle messengers,** most of them deeply committed to speed. Since these cyclists often ride against the flow of traffic and not infrequently run traffic lights, look both ways, carefully, before stepping into the street.

Subway Safety

The New York subway system has a reputation for crime and dirt that is exaggerated but not entirely undeserved. Use common sense; be alert to your surroundings; stay with other people; avoid going down empty stairwells or riding in empty cars; don't lean over the edge of the platform. Panhandlers, pickpockets, and purse snatchers work the subways as well as the street.

If possible, take a taxi or ride the bus instead of the subway late at night, especially when you are alone. If you do take the subway during off-hours, ride in the car with the transit policeman, if there is one, or the conductor, who has a telephone. Avoid waiting on an empty platform; use the Off-Hours Waiting area.

Electrical Current

Electricity in the U.S. is 110–120V, 60-cycle AC current. Unless you have a dual-voltage appliance (for example, a hair dryer or shaver) with flat pins, you will need an adapter. You can buy one at hardware stores, some pharmacies, and airports.

Emergency Information

For fire, police, or medical emergency, dial 911. For the location of the nearest police precinct, ☎ (212) 374-5000.

Poison Control: ☎ (212) 340-4494.
Rape Hotline: ☎ (212) 267-7273
Suicide Prevention Hotline: ☎ (212) 673-3000.
Victims' Services: ☎ (212) 577-7777.

Hospital Emergency Rooms

Hospital emergency rooms, open at all times, are often crowded, and waits can be very long. You will be billed for emergency treatment. If you have health insurance, call your company's emergency number to find which hospitals accept your insurance.

Bellevue Hospital Center, 462 First Ave (at E. 27th St); ☎ (212) 562-4141. Adult emergency room, ☎ (212) 562-3015; pediatric emergency room, ☎ (212) 562-3025.
Beth Israel Medical Center, First Ave at E. 16th St; ☎ (212) 420-2000. Emergency room, ☎ (212) 420-2840.
Cabrini Medical Center, 227 E. 19th St (between Second and Third Aves); ☎ (212) 995-6120.
Columbia Presbyterian Medical Center, 21 Audubon Ave (at W. 166th St); ☎ (212) 305-2500. Adult emergency room, ☎ (212) 305-2255; pediatric emergency room, ☎ (212) 305-6628.
New York Weill Cornell Medical Center, 528 E. 68th St (at York Ave). Adult emergency room, ☎ (212) 746-5050; pediatric emergency room, ☎ (212) 746-3300.
Roosevelt Hospital, W. 59th St (between Ninth and Tenth Aves); ☎ (212) 523-6800.
St. Vincent's Hospital, Seventh Ave at W. 12th St. Emergency room, ☎ (212) 604-8000.

Internet Access

There are computer terminals at the Times Square Visitors Center, 1560 Broadway (between W. 46th and W. 47th Sts) for e-mail. Kinko's copy centers offer high-speed Internet access; for locations, check the Yellow Pages or their Web site at www.kinkos.com. Among the branches are those at 21 Astor Place (between Lafayette St and Broadway), ☎ (212) 228-9511; 245 Seventh Ave (at W. 24th St), ☎ (212) 929-2679; 191 Madison Ave (at E. 34th St), ☎ (212) 685-3449; 100 Wall St (at Water St), ☎ (212) 269-0024; and 16 E. 52nd St (at Madison Ave), ☎ (212) 308-2679. There are branches of Cybercafé—where you can snack, play games, or surf the Net—in SoHo at 273 Lafayette St (at Prince St), ☎ (212) 334-5140; and north of Times Square at 250 W. 49th St (between Eighth Ave and Broadway), ☎ (212) 333-4109. Public libraries have computer terminals, but you may have to wait in line and access time may be limited.

Legal Holidays

Legal holidays are New Year's Day (Jan 1), Martin Luther King Day (third Mon in Jan), President's Day (third Mon in Feb), Memorial Day (fourth Mon in May), Independence Day (July 4), Labor Day (first Mon in Sept), Columbus Day (Oct 12, celebrated the Mon on or near this date), Veterans Day (Nov 11), Thanksgiving (fourth Thurs in Nov), and Christmas (Dec 25). Christmas Eve (Dec 24) is an unofficial holiday for many businesses, but not, of course, for stores.

Schools and some businesses in New York are closed on major Jewish holidays: Passover (March or April), Rosh Hashanah (Sept or Oct), and Yom Kippur (Sept or Oct).

Newspapers and Magazines

New Yorkers can choose from more than 100 newspapers, both dailies and weeklies, in English and other languages, some international in scope, many reflecting neighborhood and ethnic interests. The *New York Times* is the doyenne of daily papers, in print since 1851, offering, as its front page states, "All the News That's Fit to Print." Other major dailies are the *New York Post* and the *Daily News,* both tabloids, and the *Wall Street Journal,* with a focus on business and the financial markets. The *Amsterdam News,* published uptown in Harlem, carries news and features of particular interest to the black community. The leading Spanish-language dailies are *Noticias del Mundo* and *El Diario.*

The *Village Voice,* an alternative weekly, free in New York, has political articles, good movie reviews and listings of nightlife, and occasional investigative reports. The *New York Press,* politically more conservative than the *Voice* and also free, has a large following. The *New York Observer,* published weekly on the Upper East Side and printed on pinkish paper, carries articles on the media and society, arts and entertainment, city politics, and real estate.

Among the city's weekly **magazines** are *New York,* which carries news about city life and politics as well as extensive listings. *The New Yorker* has long been known for fine writing (both fiction and nonfiction), reviews of cultural events, and urbane humor (including cartoons). *Time Out New York,* which arrived here from London in 1995, is the best single source for listings of what's going on—in art galleries, restaurants, clubs, concert halls, and movie theaters.

Pharmacies

Most pharmacies are open Mon–Sat 9 A.M.–5 P.M. (or later). The **Duane Reade** at W. 57th St and Broadway has a pharmacist on duty 24 hours a day; ☎ (212) 541-9708. Other branches open late are at Broadway and W. 91st St, ☎ (212) 799-3172; and Third Ave and W. 74th St, ☎ (212) 744-2668.

Physician Referrals

Mount Sinai Hospital, Doctor Referral Call Center: ☎ 1-800-MD-YOURS (1-800-639-6877).
New York–Presbyterian Hospital, ☎ (toll-free) 1-877-NYP-WELL (1-877-697-9355).

Post Offices

Most post offices are open weekdays 9 A.M.–5 P.M. and Sat until noon or 1 P.M. The **main post office,** the James A. Farley Building on Eighth Ave at W. 33rd St, is open daily 24 hours, though all services are not available outside regular business hours. The branch at 90 Church St (between Barclay and Vesey Sts), near the World Trade Center, also has extended hours (weekdays 7 A.M.–midnight; Sat 9–5). Branch post offices are located throughout the city; to find the nearest one, look in the blue section in the Yellow Pages of the telephone book under "United States Government, Postal Service" or ☎ (800) 275-8777. Most branches are open Mon–Fri 8–5 (or sometimes 6 P.M.) and Sat 9–3. Mailboxes are located on street corners in all boroughs; many hotels will perform postal services.

Telephones

General Information
The U.S. phone system is run by private corporations; rates for long-distance calls vary from carrier to carrier. The local service provider is Verizon, formerly Bell Atlantic. Hotels add surcharges for both local and long-distance calls, so it is cheaper to use a calling card or a public pay phone.

Pay phones can be found on the streets and in building lobbies. Most belong to Verizon. Some phones, especially in train stations and airports, will accept credit cards instead of coins. You can buy a **prepaid calling card** in denominations up to $50 at chain pharmacies (Duane Reade and Rite Aid), convenience stores, or newsstands. Private pay phones may charge exorbitant rates.

All telephone numbers in the United States consist of a three-digit area code, a three-digit exchange, and a four-digit number. To make a local call, you need only dial the three-digit exchange plus the four-digit number (seven digits).

Information and Directory Assistance
To reach an operator, dial 0. To reach local directory information, dial 411. For information in Manhattan or the Bronx, dial 411 or 555-1212 with no area code from Manhattan telephones. For information in Queens, Brooklyn, or Staten Island from Manhattan, dial 1-718-555-1212. To reach directory assistance for other parts of the United States, dial the area code, then 555-1212. These calls are free at pay telephones.

The **area codes** for Manhattan are 212 and 646; for Brooklyn, Queens, the Bronx, and Staten Island, 718 and 347. The 917 code is used for cell phones and pagers in all five boroughs.

To make a **local call** on a public pay telephone, deposit 25¢ in change (no pennies) for the first three minutes, listen for the dial tone, and dial the seven-digit number. The operator (either a live person or a recording) will cut in and tell you to deposit more money when the time has elapsed.

To make a **direct long-distance** call to any place in the United States or Canada, you must dial 1 plus the area code plus the seven-digit number. To make a **direct international call** dial 011 plus the country code, city code, and telephone number of the person you wish to reach.

To dial an **operator-assisted long-distance call** (collect calls, person-to-person calls, etc.), dial 0 plus the area code plus the local number; the operator will come on the line and assist you.

Although the numbering system in the United States is uniform, there are several long-distance providers. To reach the long distance carrier of your choice, dial their 800 number to be connected to their operator as a local call: **AT&T,** ☎ (800) 225-5288; **MCI,** ☎ (800) 888-8000; **Sprint,** ☎ (800) 366-2255. This method can be used to avoid hotel surcharges.

The "area" codes 800, 888, 877, and 866 designate **toll-free numbers.** The code 900 indicates a toll call for some kind of "service" (e.g., to speak with a psychic); these calls are often expensive.

Time

Depending on the season, New York is either on Eastern Standard Time (EST) or Eastern Daylight Saving Time (EDT). Eastern Standard Time is five hours behind Greenwich Mean Time (GMT). Daylight saving time begins at 1 A.M. on the first Sun in April and continues until 1 A.M. the last Sun in Oct. During this period, New York time is four hours behind GMT. To find the correct local time, ☎ (212) 976-1616.

Tipping

In restaurants the usual tip is 15–20 percent; many people double the 8.25 percent sales tax. Coat-check attendants will expect $1 per coat. Room service waiters and taxi drivers should also receive at least 15 percent (no less than 25¢ for cab drivers); bellhops expect about $1 per suitcase, $2 in luxury hotels. Porters in airports expect $1 per bag. Others to tip include doormen who help with packages or summon a taxi (about $1), hotel chambermaids ($1 or $2 per day), and delivery people ($1 or more, depending on the size of the object delivered). Do not reward rude service.

Toilets

Public toilets are not easy to find in New York. Restaurants are usually unwilling to let noncustomers use their facilities, though you may succeed if you walk boldly and look like a customer. Try department stores, free museums, libraries, hotel lobbies (ask at the desk if necessary), church parish houses, buildings with public atriums (Trump Tower, Citicorp Building), megastores with cafés (Barnes & Noble), stores that cater to children (FAO Schwarz, Disney stores), and the Times Square Visitors Center (1560 Broadway between W. 46th and W. 47th Sts).

Best Toilets of New York is a regularly updated Web site, organized by neighborhood, at www.besttoilets.com. There is also a legendary book by Ken Eichenbaum, *The Toilets of New York: A Handy Guide to the Best (And the Worst) Public and Semipublic Relief Stations for Those with a Need-To-Know* (Milwaukee, Wis.: 1990). Contact Litterati Books, 9470 N. Broadmoor Rd, Milwaukee, WI 53217; ☎ (414) 352-4755.

Weather Information

For the current temperature or the forecast, ☎ (212) 976-1212. The *New York Times* and other dailies print the daily forecast. Online you can check **www.weather.com** or **www.cnn.com/weather** for detailed forecasts and maps. Television's Weather Channel (36 in New York) will tell you more than you want to know.

Food and Drink

Restaurants

New York is the nation's dining capital. There are restaurants of every price range featuring all of the world's great cuisines and many of the lesser ones. The following list has been compiled from personal experience, advice from friends, and reviews to include choices for every pocketbook and taste. Because restaurants open and close in the twinkling of an eye, as fashion shifts, those on the list have shown some staying power.

Restaurant Guides and Reviews

To keep up with the rapidly changing restaurant scene, look at *Zagat's Restaurant Guide,* published yearly, which surveys diners' experiences. On the Internet, check out *New York Today* (www.nytoday.com/restaurants) and *Time Out New York* (www.timeout.com/newyork). CuisineNet offers restaurant reviews submitted by patrons; Web site: www.cuisinenet.com. Many restaurants post their own Web sites, where you can survey the ambience, read the menu, check the prices, and make reservations—do everything, that is, except taste the food.

Price Guidelines and Reservations

For a Three-Course Meal Excluding Beverages	
Very expensive	$55 or more (and it can be considerably more)
Expensive	$40–55
Moderate	$25–40
Inexpensive	less than $25

The tax on restaurant meals is currently 8.25 percent. In some restaurants the same dishes at lunch are less expensive than at dinner. Most establishments accept major credit cards. Make reservations on weekends for all restaurants and at all times for expensive restaurants, though it may be easier for a camel to pass through the eye of a needle than to get a weekend reservation at a currently "hot" restaurant. **Reservation books** usually open a month ahead of time, at 9 A.M. Call early and often. It is usually better to get a table early or late at popular restaurants.

If in doubt, ask about credit card policy when you reserve. Some restaurants are closed for lunch on weekends, all day Sun, and for vacations during the summer.

Lower Manhattan and TriBeCa

Lower Manhattan was formerly a gustatory wasteland. No longer. The lunch crowd in the Financial District can be overwhelming, so eat early or late there if possible.

American Park at the Battery, in Battery Park (near State St); ☎ (212) 809-5508. New American cuisine, especially seafood, beautifully sited restaurant. Outdoor tables in season. Expensive.

Arqua, 281 Church St (at White St); ☎ (212) 334-1888. Stylish Italian restaurant, named after Italian hill town. Northern Italian food; sometimes noisy. Expensive.

Bouley Bakery, 120 West Broadway (at Duane St); ☎ (212) 964-2525. Stellar French restaurant with celebrity chef; exquisite food. Very expensive.

Bridge Cafe, 279 Water St (at Dover St); ☎ (212) 227-3344. Small pub-tavern with pressed-tin ceiling in shadow of Brooklyn Bridge; new American food; often crowded. Expensive.

Chanterelle, 2 Harrison St (at Hudson St); ☎ (212) 966-6960. Founded in SoHo in 1979. One of New York's finest; graceful decor, fine service, superb food. Very expensive.

Fraunces Tavern, 54 Pearl St (at Broad St); ☎ (212) 968-1776. Reconstructed 18C house; famous for history, not food. Stick to simple fare. Moderate.

Montrachet, 239 West Broadway (between White and Walker Sts); ☎ (212) 219-2777. TriBeCa's first French restaurant, in recycled industrial building. Softly lit, elegant dining room; lunch Friday, otherwise dinner only. Very expensive.

Odeon, 145 West Broadway (at Thomas St); ☎ (212) 233-0507. An early TriBeCa outpost and celebrity hotspot, still going strong. New American food in former Art Deco cafeteria. Closely spaced tables; high-decibel level. Open late. Moderate.

Salaam Bombay, 319 Greenwich St (at Duane St); ☎ (212) 226-9400. Pleasant Indian restaurant; lunch buffet. Moderate.

Wall Street Kitchen and Bar, 70 Broad St (at Beaver St); ☎ (212) 797-7070. Noisy and crowded at lunch, informal; sandwiches, hearty fare. Moderate.

Chinatown

Compared to their uptown analogues, most Chinatown restaurants lack refinements of decor; think Formica tabletops, fluorescent lights, and paper napkins. In some restaurants, you may be asked to share your table. Toilet facilities are inelegant. Many restaurants do not take reservations and some do not take credit cards. Their reputations can be as volatile as dry tinder, with "hot" restaurants attracting long lines of customers for a while only to relapse into relative obscurity. However, the food is often excellent and inexpensive. You can bring your own beer and wine to those restaurants lacking a liquor license.

Bo Ky, 80 Bayard St (between Mott and Mulberry Sts); ☎ (212) 406-2292. No-frills noodle shop with Vietnamese specialties, soups. Cash only. Inexpensive.

Grand Sichuan, 125 Canal St (at Bowery); ☎ (212) 625-9212. Authentic regional cooking. Menu in English and Chinese. Does take reservations. No credit cards. Moderate.

Jing Fong, 20 Elizabeth St (between Bayard and Canal Sts); ☎ (212) 964-5256. Huge restaurant, serves dim sum from 10 A.M. Also Cantonese food. Red lanterns and lion statues. Does take credit cards. Inexpensive.

Joe's Shanghai, 9 Pell St (between Bowery and Mott St); ☎ (212) 233-8888. Hong Kong– and Shanghai-style cooking. First branch in Queens. Inexpensive.

New York Noodle Town, 28½ Bowery (at Bayard St); ☎ (212) 349-0923. Despite its name and modest storefront appearance, offers good, authentic Hong Kong food. Noodle dishes, but also large menu. No credit cards. Inexpensive.

Nom Wah Tea Parlor, 13 Doyers St (between Pell St and Chatham Square); ☎ (212) 962-6047. One of Chinatown's oldest dim sum parlors. No atmosphere but lots of dim sum. No credit cards. Inexpensive.

Sweet 'n' Tart Café, 76 Mott St (at Canal St); ☎ (212) 334-8088. Features "tong shui," sweet and tart "soups" with medicinal properties. Also noodle and dumpling dishes. Plain decor. No credit cards. Local clientele. Inexpensive.

Little Italy and NoLIta

Most of the Italians are gone from Little Italy, but some old-time restaurants remain, family-run places with plentiful southern Italian food (red sauce and garlic) served in a convivial atmosphere. Newer restaurants are likely to be more sophisticated and more expensive, and to reflect the changing character of the neighborhood.

Benito's (I and II); 174 Mulberry St (between Broome and Grand Sts), ☎ (212) 226-9171; and 163 Mulberry St (between Broome/Grand Sts), ☎ (212) 226-9012. Two old-timers. Sicilian and southern Italian food. Moderate.

Caffè Palermo, 148 Mulberry St (between Grand and Hester Sts); ☎ (212) 431-4205. Recently renovated pastry-and-coffee shop. Closed Mon.

Il Cortile, 125 Mulberry St (between Hester and Canal Sts); ☎ (212) 226-6060. Northern and southern Italian dishes, handsome restaurant with tile floors, pressed-tin ceiling. Expensive.

Lombardi's, 32 Spring St (between Mulberry and Mott Sts); ☎ (212) 941-7994. Historic pizzeria with noteworthy thin-crust pizza, good atmosphere. Inexpensive.

Puglia, 189 Hester St (at Mulberry St); ☎ (212) 966-6006. Another old-timer; informal; hearty fare in large portions; long communal tables, lots of noise. Closed Mon. Inexpensive.

Rialto, 265 Elizabeth St (between E. Houston and Prince Sts); ☎ (212) 334-7900. Nouveau American cuisine; pleasant garden; casual. Moderate.

Rice, 227 Mott St (between Prince and Spring Sts); ☎ (212) 226-5775. As Chinatown has spilled over into Little Italy, so have Asian restaurants. Rice dishes from Vietnam and Thailand, as well as China. No credit cards. Inexpensive.

Lower East Side and East Village

Acme Bar & Grill, 9 Great Jones St (between Lafayette St and Broadway); ☎ (212) 420-1934. Home-style southern cooking in funky truck-stop setting. Rock club downstairs. Inexpensive.

Circa, 103 Second Ave (at E. 6th St); ☎ (212) 777-4120. Stylish crowd, attractive surroundings, lots of noise and energy. New American food. Moderate.

Cyclo, 203 First Ave (at E. 12th St); ☎ (212) 673-3975. Fine Vietnamese food; dinner only. Understandably crowded. Inexpensive.

Dok Suni's Restaurant, 119 First Ave (between E. 7th St and St. Mark's Place); ☎ (212) 477-9506. Hip attitude, superior Korean cooking. Inexpensive.

Flor's Kitchen, 149 First Ave (at E. 9th St); ☎ (212) 387-8949. Small, colorful, Venezuelan restaurant. Inexpensive.

Frank, 88 Second Ave (at E. 5th St); ☎ (212) 420-0202. Popular Italian restaurant; crowded because the food is good and the prices are low. Inexpensive.

Great Jones Cafe, 54 Great Jones St (between Lafayette St and Bowery); ☎ (212) 674-9304. Small, informal café with downtown crowd and Cajun cooking. Cash only. Moderate.

Holy Basil, 149 Second Ave (between E. 9th and E. 10th Sts); ☎ (212) 460-5557. Excellent Thai restaurant; pretty dining room; occasional jazz. Dinner only. Inexpensive.

Katz's Delicatessen, 205 E. Houston St (at Ludlow St); ☎ (212) 254-2246. A century-old deli with attitude; among the city's best. Serves meat dishes, including corned beef and pastrami. Inexpensive.

Kiev, 117 Second Ave (at E. 7th St); ☎ (212) 674-4040. Eastern European in ethnic neighborhood. Good breakfasts; short on atmosphere. Inexpensive.

Mama's Food Shop, 200 E. 3rd St (between Aves A and B); ☎ (212) 777-4425. Good homey food to eat in or take out. Closed Sun. No credit cards. Inexpensive.

Sammy's Roumanian Restaurant, 157 Chrystie St (between Delancey and E. Houston Sts); ☎ (212) 673-0330. Jewish restaurant with Roumanian meat dishes, boiled beef, sausages, and other rich fare. Expensive.

Second Avenue Delicatessen, 156 Second Ave (at E. 10th St); ☎ (212) 677-0606. Kosher deli with long tradition, perhaps fallen from former glory. Chopped liver, stuffed veal breast, other meat dishes, and sandwiches. Inexpensive.

Veselka, 144 Second Ave (at E. 9th St); ☎ (212) 228-9682. Informal eastern European restaurant has served blintzes and borscht for decades. Good place for breakfast. Inexpensive.

SoHo

Alison on Dominick, 38 Dominick St (between Varick and Hudson Sts); ☎ (212) 727-1188. Romantic French restaurant, excellent food and wine. Very expensive.

Aquagrill, 210 Spring St (at Sixth Ave); ☎ (212) 274-0505. Fine seafood in friendly, understated restaurant. Expensive.

Blue Ribbon, 97 Sullivan St (between Prince and Spring Sts); ☎ (212) 274-0404. Open practically all night; crowded, and noisy; good new American food. Expensive.

Blue Ribbon Sushi, 119 Sullivan St (between Prince and Spring Sts); ☎ (212) 343-0404. Small and busy sushi shop with large menu. Dinner only. Expensive.

Cendrillon, 45 Mercer St (between Broome and Grand Sts); ☎ (212) 343-9012. Good Filipino food, in modest storefront setting. Moderate.

Cupping Room, 359 West Broadway (between Broome and Grand Sts); ☎ (212) 925-2898. A SoHo pioneer; burgers and straightforward American food. Moderate.

Fanelli's, 94 Prince St (at Mercer St); ☎ (212) 226-9412. Popular bar, everyday food; a SoHo institution. Inexpensive.

Honmura An, 170 Mercer St (between Houston and Prince Sts); ☎ (212) 334-5253. Upscale Japanese restaurant, offshoot of Tokyo original, features soba (traditional buckwheat noodles). Expensive.

Jean Claude, 137 Sullivan St (between Prince and Houston Sts); ☎ (212) 475-9232. Good, satisfying bistro food, understandably busy restaurant. Dinner only; no credit cards. Inexpensive.

Jerry's, 101 Prince St (between Mercer and Greene Sts); ☎ (212) 966-9464. Good place for lunch or a modest dinner. Sandwiches and burgers. Moderate.

Mercer Kitchen, 99 Prince St (at Mercer St); ☎ (212) 966-5454. Stylish food from celebrity chef; restaurant in high-style Mercer House Hotel. Expensive.

Omen, 113 Thompson St (between Prince and Spring Sts); ☎ (212) 925-8923. SoHo branch of family-run Kyoto restaurant; wood-and-brick decor suggestive of a Japanese country inn. Specialty is Omen soup, a spicy broth for plunging vegetables and noodles. Dinner only. Expensive.

Palacinka, 28 Grand St (at Sixth Ave); ☎ (212) 625-0362. Small restaurant featuring sweet and savory crepes. No credit cards. Inexpensive.

Pão, 322 Spring St (at Greenwich St); ☎ (212) 334-5464. Small, modest Portuguese restaurant, very good food. Inexpensive.

SoHo Steak, 90 Thompson St (between Spring and Prince Sts); ☎ (212) 226-0602. Affordable French bistro with small dining room, young crowd. No credit cards. Inexpensive.

Spring Street Natural, 62 Spring St (at Lafayette St); ☎ (212) 966-0290. For the vegetarians in your crowd. Inexpensive.

Zoë, 90 Prince St (between Mercer St and Broadway); ☎ (212) 966-6722. Pleasant American food in large dining room with viewable kitchen. Moderate.

Greenwich Village

Babbo, 110 Waverly Place (between Sixth Ave and Washington Square West); ☎ (212) 777-0303. Robust Italian restaurant in former Coach House; unusual specialties; reserve well in advance. Very expensive.

Bar Pitti, 268 Sixth Ave (between Bleecker and Houston Sts); ☎ (212) 982-3300. Italian café setting, outdoor tables, Tuscan favorites. Inexpensive.

Blue Ribbon Bakery, 33 Downing St (at Bedford St); ☎ (212) 337-0404. Downstairs bistro and upstairs café in old building with old-fashioned oven; eclectic menu including baked goods. Moderate.

Clementine, 1 Fifth Ave (at 8th St); ☎ (212) 253-0003. Young crowd, very good new American cuisine; casual and noisy. Moderate.

Corner Bistro, 331 W. 4th St (at Jane St and Eighth Ave); ☎ (212) 242-9502. Bar food, including one of the best burgers in the city. Inexpensive.

Florent, 69 Gansevoort St (between Greenwich and Washington Sts); ☎ (212) 989-5779. In an old meat market, now a bistro. Informal French food, good value. Popular and busy; open 24 hours on Sat and Sun. No credit cards. Moderate.

Gotham Bar and Grill, 12 E. 12th St (between Fifth Ave and University Place); ☎ (212) 620-4020. High-ceilinged, multilevel dining room; very superior food by celebrity chef, beautifully presented. Expensive.

Home, 20 Cornelia St (between W. 4th and Bleecker Sts); ☎ (212) 243-9579. Small storefront with homey American food. Inexpensive.

John's Pizzeria, 278 Bleecker St (between Seventh Ave and Morton St); ☎ (212) 243-1680. Small and mildly run-down. Famous among pizza aficionados, who rate it among the best in the city; busy. Cash only. Inexpensive.

La Metairie, 189 W. 10th St (between W. 4th and Bleecker Sts); ☎ (212) 989-0343. Small neighborhood bistro; good traditional Provençal food. Romantic. Moderate.

Le Gans, 46 Gansevoort St (at Greenwich St); ☎ (212) 675-5224. Bistro food, brick wall; also light menu. Inexpensive.

Malatesta Trattoria, 649 Washington St (at Christopher St); ☎ (212) 741-1207. Small trattoria, generous portions, convivial. No credit cards. Moderate.

One If by Land, Two If by Sea, 17 Barrow St (between Bleecker and W. 4th Sts); ☎ (212) 228-0822. Ultraromantic and ultrapricey. Located in Aaron Burr's former carriage house. Very expensive.

The Pink Tea Cup, 42 Grove St (between Bleecker and Bedford Sts); ☎ (212) 807-6755. Cheap eats, in the soulful style of the American South. Tasty (and huge) breakfast dishes.

Po, 31 Cornelia St (between Bleecker and W. 4th Sts); ☎ (212) 645-2189. Topflight Italian food in a narrow, intimate space at reasonable prices. Moderate.

White Horse Tavern, 567 Hudson St (at W. 11th St); ☎ (212) 989-3956. Historic bar where Dylan Thomas drank too much; bar food. Inexpensive.

Gramercy Park, Flatiron District, and Murray Hill: East Side, 14th–42nd Streets

Blue Water Grill, 31 Union Square West (at E. 16th St); ☎ (212) 675-9500. Fresh seafood in many guises; in former bank. Moderate.

Caffé Adulis, 39 E. 19th St (between Broadway and Park Ave South); ☎ (212) 358-7775. The city's only Eritrean restaurant, specializes in northeast African and Mediterranean cuisine. Traditional spicing with modern touches. Good wine list. Moderate.

Campagna, 24 E. 21st St (between Broadway and Park Ave); ☎ (212) 460-0900. Italian food attractively presented to a chic clientele; bustling and entertaining. Expensive.

Chat 'n' Chew, 10 E. 16th St (between Fifth Ave and Union Square West); ☎ (212) 243-1616. Friendly, homely restaurant with hearty American food. Good for children. Inexpensive.

Cinque Terre, 22 E. 38th St (between Park and Madison Aves); ☎ (212) 213-0910. Small Italian restaurant features the cooking of Liguria. Moderate.

Coach House, 16 E. 32nd St (at Fifth Ave); ☎ (212) 696-1800. Reincarnation of legendary New York restaurant retains some old favorite dishes; new American cuisine; urbane surroundings. Very expensive.

Da Ciro, 229 Lexington Ave (at E. 33rd St); ☎ (212) 532-1636. Pizza baked in wood-burning oven; other good Italian specialties. Inexpensive.

Gramercy Tavern, 42 E. 20th St (between Broadway and Park Ave South); ☎ (212) 477-0777. Famous for the food; celebrity chef, new American cuisine. Large and bustling dining room; less expensive bar room in front. Very expensive.

Mavalli Palace, 46 E. 29th St (between Madison and Park Aves); ☎ (212) 679-5535. Indian vegetarian restaurant, attractive ambience, pleasant service. Inexpensive.

Nadaman Hakubai, 66 Park Ave (at E. 38th St in Hotel Kitano); ☎ (212) 885-7111. Elegantly prepared and served traditional Japanese food; tatami rooms, kimono-clad servers; a cultural and gustatory experience. Very expensive.

Park Bistro, 414 Park Ave South (between E. 28th and E. 29th Sts); ☎ (212) 689-1360. Authentic French bistro food in simple Parisian setting. Moderately expensive.

Patria, 250 Park Ave South (at E. 20th St); ☎ (212) 777-6211. Lively Latino restaurant with imaginative, eclectic cooking. Stylish and fun. Prix fixe. Expensive.

Pete's Tavern, 129 E. 18th St (at Irving Place); ☎ (212) 473-7676. Great neighborhood bar, good Italian and American food. Moderate.

Sal Anthony's, 55 Irving Place (at E. 17th St); ☎ (212) 982-9030. Large, handsome, enduring Italian restaurant; all the old standard Italian dishes served up in generous portions. Moderate.

Tabla, 11 Madison Ave (at E. 25th St); ☎ (212) 889-0667. Destination restaurant with new American–Indian fusion food. Gorgeous decor. Downstairs bar with tandoori oven. Reserve far in advance. Very expensive.

Union Square Cafe, 21 E. 16th St (between Fifth Ave and Union Square West); ☎ (212) 243-4020. Much-loved restaurant with locals and visitors alike. Excellent new American cuisine, excellent wine list, excellent service. Expensive.

Water Club, 500 E. 30th St (East River at FDR Drive); ☎ (212) 683-3333. American-style seafood, lovely views from restaurant afloat in the East River. Very expensive.

Zen Palate, 34 Union Square East (at E. 16th St); ☎ (212) 614-9291. Modest Asian vegetarian restaurant; good food. Other branches at Ninth Ave and W. 46th St and on Broadway between W. 76th and W. 77th Sts. Inexpensive.

Chelsea and Garment District: West Side, 14th–40th Streets

Bottino, 246 Tenth Ave (between W. 24th and W. 25th Sts); ☎ (212) 206-6766. Handy to Chelsea galleries, Italian food, good wine bar. Dinner only. Moderate.

Chelsea Bistro & Bar, 358 W. 23rd St (between Eighth and Ninth Aves); ☎ (212) 727-2026. Classic neighborhood bistro; fireplace, mirrors, brass fittings; good wine list. Moderate.

Empire Diner, 210 Tenth Ave (at W. 22nd St); ☎ (212) 243-2736. Art Deco interior; simple food; touristic. Open late. Moderate.

Follonico, 6 W. 24th St (between Fifth and Sixth Aves); ☎ (212) 691-6359. Enjoyable Tuscan food, appealing pasta dishes, in relaxed restaurant with wood-burning oven. Expensive.

Frank's, 85 Tenth Ave (at W. 15th St); ☎ (212) 243-1349. Italian steakhouse, large portions, friendly service. Expensive.

Kang Suh, 1250 Broadway (at W. 32nd St); ☎ (212) 564-6845. Fine Korean restaurant in Korean neighborhood. Sushi, charcoal-grilled dishes. Moderate.

Le Madri, 168 W. 18th St (between Sixth and Seventh Aves); ☎ (212) 727-8022. Italian cooking in a handsome, elegant room with a festive atmosphere. Very expensive.

Lola, 30 W. 22nd St (between Fifth and Sixth Aves); ☎ (212) 675-6700. Caribbean and American cooking. Pretty setting though noisy. Expensive.

Los Dos Rancheros, 507 Ninth Ave (at W. 38th St); ☎ (212) 868-7780. Modest restaurant with bona fide Mexican food. No credit cards. Inexpensive.

Periyali, 35 W. 20th St (between Fifth and Sixth Aves); ☎ (212) 463-7890. Superior Greek food in attractive Mediterranean setting. Popular. Expensive.

The Red Cat, 227 Tenth Ave (at W. 23rd St); ☎ (212) 242-1122. Good American cooking with some Mediterranean touches; young crowd; casual. Moderate.

Rocking Horse Café, 182 Eighth Ave (at W. 19th St); ☎ (212) 463-9511. Fine Mexican food with imaginative flair. Convivial and crowded. Inexpensive.

Siena, 200 Ninth Ave (at W. 22nd St); ☎ (212) 633-8033. Pastas and other simple Italian food. Busy restaurant, can be noisy. Inexpensive.

Supreme Macaroni Company, 511 Ninth Ave (between W. 38th and W. 39th Sts); ☎ (212) 564-8074. Good old-fashioned, no-frills Italian eatery, left over from the days when this neighborhood was Hell's Kitchen; hearty, simple food. Inexpensive.

Theater District: West Side, 42nd–59th Streets

Bali Nusa Indah, 651 Ninth Ave (between W. 45th and W. 46th Sts); ☎ (212) 265-2200. Attractive Indonesian restaurant; spicy food in serene setting. Inexpensive.

Bryant Park Grill, 25 W. 40th St (between Fifth and Sixth Aves); ☎ (212) 840-6500. Behind the library in Bryant Park; new American cuisine, beautiful setting. Moderate.

Cabana Carioca, 123 W. 45th St (between Sixth and Seventh Aves); ☎ (212) 581-8088. Long-lived Brazilian restaurant; feijoada, black bean dishes; good food served up in large portions. Moderate.

Carmines, 200 W. 44th St (between Seventh Ave and Broadway); ☎ (212) 221-3800. Pleasant Italian restaurant. Draws crowds. Moderate.

Carnegie Deli, 854 Seventh Ave (at W. 56th St); ☎ 757-2245. Famous deli, huge corned beef and pastrami sandwiches. Crowded; assertive waiters. Good for kids. Open late. No credit cards. Moderate.

Chez Josephine, 414 W. 42nd St (between Ninth and Tenth Aves); ☎ (212) 594-1925. Theatre Row bistro-cabaret whose decor celebrates Josephine Baker, the sultry 1920s Parisian nightclub singer; clientele includes musicians, singers, dancers; good bistro food. Expensive.

Jezebel, 630 Ninth Ave (at W. 45th St); ☎ (212) 582-1045. Southern cooking and soul food (corn bread, sweet potato pie, ribs, shrimp, fried chicken); lots of decor. Expensive.

Joe Allen, 326 W. 46th St (between Eighth and Ninth Aves); ☎ (212) 581-6464. Casual restaurant on Restaurant Row; theater clientele; hamburgers and simple food. Popular at show time. Moderate.

John's Pizzeria, 260 W. 44th St (between Seventh and Eighth Aves); ☎ (212) 391-7560. Uptown branch of Village original. In a converted church. Inexpensive.

Le Bernardin, 155 W. 51st St (at Sixth Ave); ☎ (212) 489-1515. Superb food, fine service, luxurious dining room; menu focuses on seafood. Reserve well ahead. Very expensive.

Orso, 322 W. 46th St (between Eighth and Ninth Aves); ☎ (212) 489-7212. Casual, new-style Sardi's with theatrical and journalistic clientele but better food. Individual pizzas, pasta, grilled dishes, Italian desserts. After-theater supper. Expensive.

Palio, in the Equitable Building, 151 W. 51st St (between Sixth and Seventh Aves); ☎ (212) 245-4850. Stunning, colorful decor, evoking traditional Sienese horse race; opulent appointments; regional Italian menu. Very expensive.

Patsy's, 236 W. 56th St (between Broadway and Eighth Ave); ☎ (212) 247-3491. Veteran Italian restaurant with good food in generous portions. Moderate.

Petrossian, 182 W. 58th St (at Seventh Ave); ☎ (212) 245-2214. Parisian caviar firm presents exquisite foods—caviar, foie gras—in elegant, civilized surroundings. Pretheater and lunch prix fixe moderate, otherwise expensive.

Russian Tea Room, 150 W. 57th St (between Sixth and Seventh Aves); ☎ (212) 974-2111. Historic restaurant, reopened Oct 1999 with buffed-up decor (some leftovers from previous incarnation). Russian food. Tourist destination, very popular, sometimes boisterous. Very expensive.

Sardi's, 234 W. 44th St (between Seventh and Eighth Aves); ☎ (212) 221-8440. Formerly famous for its theatrical clientele and conviviality. Still a tourist spot. Expensive.

"21," 21 W. 52nd St (between Fifth and Sixth Aves); ☎ (212) 582-7200. Haunt of businessmen (lunch), celebrities, and celebrity watchers. Steak, Continental cuisine. Expensive.

Wu Liang Ye, 36 W. 48th St (between Fifth and Sixth Aves); ☎ (212) 398-2308. Szechuan food, well-prepared. Other branches at E. 86th St and 3rd Ave and on Lexington Ave between E. 39th and E. 40th Sts. Inexpensive.

Midtown East: 42nd–59th Streets

Many good restaurants, but few inexpensive and moderately priced ones.

Chola, 232 E. 58th St (between Second and Third Aves); ☎ (212) 688-4619. Busy Indian restaurant with unpretentious decor, very good pan-Indian food. Moderate.

Cosi Sandwich Bar, 38 E. 45th St (between Madison and Vanderbilt Aves); ☎ (212) 949-7400; 165 E. 52nd St (between Lexington and Third Aves); ☎ (212) 758-7800; 60 E. 56th St (between Fifth and Madison Aves); ☎ (212) 588-0888; other locations. Chain of sandwich restaurants serving fresh flatbreads with custom toppings; espresso. Inexpensive.

Dawat, 210 E. 58th St (between Second and Third Aves); ☎ (212) 355-7555. Popular and comfortable Indian restaurant. Expensive.

Deniz à la Turk, 400 E. 57th St (between First Ave and Sutton Place); ☎ (212) 486-2255. Turkish-Mediterranean restaurant specializing in seafood. Moderate.

Felidia, 243 E. 58th St (between Second and Third Aves); ☎ (212) 758-1479. Brick-walled, two-level restaurant with regional Italian menu (Veneto, Friuli, Istria). Superior food, sometimes crowded and cramped in evenings. Very expensive.

Four Seasons, 99 E. 52nd St (between Park and Lexington Aves); ☎ (212) 754-9494. Elegant, modern American food. Handsome decor; gracious, unhurried service; upper-echelon executives dominate Grill Room at lunch; Pool Room offers more romantic atmosphere. Very expensive.

Hatsuhana, 17 E. 48th St (between Fifth and Madison Aves); ☎ (212) 355-3345. Also 237 Park Ave (entrance on E. 46th St); ☎ (212) 661-3400. Comfortable but authentic Japanese restaurant; seafood, superb sushi. Expensive.

Jubilee, 347 E. 54th St (between First and Second Aves); ☎ (212) 888-3569. Small French restaurant, bistro food, busy. Moderate.

La Côte Basque, 60 W. 55th St (between Fifth and Sixth Aves); ☎ (212) 688-6525. Classic French restaurant, pretty dining room, handsomely presented food, ample portions. Prix fixe. Expensive.

La Grenouille, 3 E. 52nd St (at Fifth Ave); ☎ (212) 752-1495. Another of the city's classic French restaurants. Mirrored dining room, celebrated flower arrangements, haute cuisine. Courteous professional service, highly praised food. Like others of its ilk, has an air of exclusivity. Expensive.

Le Cirque 2000, in the Villard Houses, 455 Madison Ave (between E. 50th and E. 51st Sts); ☎ (212) 303-7788. One of the city's stars. A place to see and be seen. New American cooking; charming service. Very expensive.

Lespinasse, 2 E. 55th St (at Fifth Ave, in the St. Regis Hotel); ☎ (212) 339-6719. Elegant restaurant, with exquisite food, luxurious surroundings, fine service. Very expensive.

Lutèce, 249 E. 50th St (between Second and Third Aves); ☎ (212) 752-2225. Long the domain of the legendary André Soltner and still known for fine French cuisine. In former town house; unpretentious but elegant, gracious service. Expensive.

March, 405 E. 58th St (between First Ave and Sutton Place); ☎ (212) 754-6272. Romantic restaurant in town house, with garden for outdoor seasonal dining; excellent, updated American food with Japanese overtones. Very expensive.

Meltemi, 905 First Ave (at E. 51st St); ☎ (212) 355-4040. Greek restaurant specializing in seafood; grilled dishes, other straightforward dishes prepared in open kitchen; cheerful ambience. Moderate.

Michael Jordan's, in Grand Central Terminal, 23 Vanderbilt Ave; ☎ (212) 655-2300. Celebrity steakhouse in one of New York's great interiors. Good food. Expensive.

Oceana, 55 E. 54th St (between Madison and Park Aves); ☎ (212) 759-5941. Elegant seafood in town house setting. American-style with Asian and European influences. Prix fixe. Very expensive.

Oyster Bar & Restaurant, in Grand Central Terminal, lower level (E. 42nd St near Vanderbilt Ave); ☎ (212) 490-6650. Tiled and vaulted rooms deep in the station; counter for quick service; long recognized for seafood; many varieties of oysters in season. Crowded at noon. Expensive.

Palm, 837 Second Ave (at E. 45th St); ☎ (212) 687-2953. Grand old steakhouse with sawdust on the floors, cartoons of celebrities on the walls, brusque service. Crowded. Expensive.

Rosa Mexicano, 1063 First Ave (at E. 58th St); ☎ (212) 753-7407. Longstanding restaurant with classic Mexican food; friendly, welcoming atmosphere. Expensive.

Shun Lee Palace, 155 E. 55th St (between Lexington and Third Aves); ☎ (212) 371-8844. Glossy Chinese restaurant, Szechuan dishes, Peking duck, pleasant decor, good service. Expensive.

Zarela, 953 Second Ave (between E. 50th and E. 51st Sts); ☎ (212) 644-6740. Home-style, authentic Mexican cooking; fine appetizers, imaginative entrées ranging in heat from mild to murderous. Good desserts. Moderate.

Upper East Side, Yorkville: 59th Street and North

Arizona 206, 206 E. 60th St (between Second and Third Aves); ☎ (212) 838-0440. Latin American restaurant with very good food. Noisy. Moderate.

Aureole, 34 E. 61st St (between Madison and Park Aves); ☎ (212) 319-1660. Stellar restaurant with stellar new American food, fine service. Longstanding favorite. Very expensive.

Barking Dog Luncheonette, 1678 Third Ave (at E. 94th St); ☎ (212) 831-1800. Modest restaurant, with homey, familiar diner food. Good for kids. No credit cards. Inexpensive.

Bistro Le Steak, 1309 Third Ave (at E. 75th St); ☎ (212) 517-3800. Friendly neighborhood restaurant, with good steak, fries, simple bistro dishes. Inexpensive.

Café Boulud, 20 E. 70th St (at Madison Ave); ☎ (212) 772-2600. Celebrity chef serves adventurous and globally influenced French food. Casual, sometimes noisy. Reserve well in advance. Very expensive.

Cello, 53 E. 77th St (between Madison and Park Aves); ☎ (212) 517-1200. Elegant French seafood in turn-of-the-20C town house; serene and quiet; small dining room with garden view. Expensive.

Elaine's, 1703 Second Ave (at E. 88th St); ☎ (212) 534-8103. Famous for the clientele—writers, journalists, assorted celebrities—not for the food (mostly Italian) or the service. Expensive.

Etats-Unis, 242 E. 81st St (between Second and Third Aves); ☎ (212) 517-8826. New American cooking in small, family-run restaurant. Dinner only. Expensive.

Guastavino's, 409 E. 59th St (at First Ave); ☎ (212) 980-2455. Large brasserie restaurant in the vaulted landmarked space under the bridge. French-American-English food. Moderate.

J & J Neopolitano, 1606 First Ave (at E. 84th St); ☎ (212) 396-9401. Classic pizzeria with coal oven. Thin, crisp crusts; good toppings. Inexpensive.

Jo Jo, 160 E. 64th St (between Lexington and Third Aves); ☎ (212) 223-5656. Outstanding, imaginative French food; small, sometimes crowded dining rooms. Very expensive.

L'Ardoise, 1207 First Ave (between E. 65th and E. 66th Sts); ☎ (212) 744-4752. Neighborhood French restaurant, with bistro dishes, traditional food. Low on decor but high on value. Moderate.

Luca, 1712 First Ave (between E. 88th and E. 89th Sts); ☎ (212) 987-9260. Modest but attractive restaurant with good Italian food. Inexpensive.

Maya, 1191 First Ave (between E. 64th and E. 65th Sts); ☎ (212) 585-1818. Engaging Tex-Mex food in busy (and noisy) restaurant. Old favorites and more imaginative specialties. Expensive.

Parioli Romanissimo, 24 E. 81st St (between Fifth and Madison Aves); ☎ (212) 288-2391. Long a topflight northern Italian restaurant with highly reputed food; town house setting. Dinner only. Very expensive.

Park View, Loeb Boathouse in Central Park (latitude of 72nd St); ☎ (212) 514-2233. In historic building with idyllic setting. Eclectic new American food. Expensive.

Pig Heaven, 1540 Second Ave (between E. 80th and E. 81st Sts); ☎ (212) 744-4333. Good Chinese food, porcine decor; kids like the piggy decorations and some of the food. American desserts. Moderate.

Primavera, 1578 First Ave (at E. 82nd St); ☎ (212) 861-8608. Mahogany walls, low lights, potted palms. Well-heeled, conservative clientele, who rate it highly. A longtime favorite for classic Italian food; closely spaced tables. Dinner only. Very expensive.

Rafina, 1481 York Ave (at E. 78th St); ☎ (212) 327-0950. Greek food, especially seafood. Straightforward cooking, pleasant room. Inexpensive.

Sultan, 1435 Second Ave (at E. 74th St); ☎ (212) 861-2828. Good Turkish food in storefront restaurant; good value. Inexpensive.

Sushihatsu, 1143 First Ave (at E. 62nd St); ☎ (212) 371-0238. One of the city's best sushi bars. Other Japanese dishes served in restaurant dining room. Very expensive.

Usküdar, 1405 Second Ave (between E. 73rd and E. 74th Sts); ☎ (212) 988-2641. Good Turkish restaurant, small and pleasant. Moderate.

Vinegar Factory, 431 E. 91st St (between York and First Aves); ☎ (212) 987-0885. Owned by Eli Zabar of delicatessen fame, open weekends only. Moderate.

Wu Liang Ye, 215 E. 86th St (between Second and Third Aves); ☎ (212) 534-8899. Uptown branch of small Chinese restaurant chain. Szechuan food, well-prepared. Inexpensive.

Lincoln Center: West Side, 59th–72nd Streets

The Lincoln Center area, one of the most popular with visitors, does not offer a plethora of wonderful dining choices. The restaurants closest to Lincoln Center are very crowded around concert time, so try to arrive early enough to have a relaxed meal.

All State Café, 250 W. 72nd St (between Broadway and West End Ave); ☎ (212) 874-1833. Small neighborhood café with beer, wine, and simple food. Hamburgers, bar food. Good for kids. Inexpensive.

Atlas, 40 Central Park South (between Fifth and Sixth Aves); ☎ (212) 759-9191. Small, stylish restaurant with cutting-edge cuisine, celebrity chef; dinner only. Very expensive.

Café des Artistes, 1 W. 67th St (between Central Park West and Columbus Ave); ☎ (212) 877-3500. Howard Chandler Christy murals; romantic 1930s decor; French and Continental food. Expensive.

Cafe Luxembourg, 200 W. 70th St (between Amsterdam and West End Aves); ☎ (212) 873-7411. Art Deco café attracts arty, late-night crowd but more conservative folks for dinner. New American, Italian, and bistro food. Pleasant, casual service. Pretheater prix fixe dinner. Expensive.

China Fun, 246 Columbus Ave (between W. 71st and W. 72nd Sts); ☎ (212) 580-1516. Chinese food within striking distance of Lincoln Center. Good for children. Noisy sometimes. Inexpensive.

Gabriel, 11 W. 60th St (between Broadway and Columbus Ave); ☎ (212) 956-4600. Pleasant Italian restaurant with imaginative, hearty food, friendly service. Expensive.

Fiorello's, 1900 Broadway (between W. 63rd and W. 64th Sts); ☎ (212) 595-5330. Bustling, noisy Italian restaurant across Broadway from Lincoln Center. Large antipasto bar; pizza in the evening. Moderate.

Jean-Georges, 1 Central Park West (at W. 60th St); ☎ (212) 299-3900. Elegant dining in quiet, luxurious restaurant, celebrity chef; eclectic, imaginative American cuisine. Very expensive.

John's Pizzeria, 48 W. 65th St (between Columbus Ave and Central Park West); ☎ (212) 721-7001. Uptown branch of favorite pizzeria. Inexpensive.

Merlot Bar and Grill, 48 W. 63rd St (between Broadway and Columbus Ave); ☎ (212) 363-7568. New American food in former jazz club. Dinner only. Expensive.

Penang, 240 Columbus Ave (at W. 71st St); ☎ (212) 769-3988. Belongs to a chain of Malaysian restaurants, authentic food. Moderate.

Picholine, 35 W. 64th St (between Broadway and Central Park West); ☎ (212) 724-8585. Elegant French restaurant emphasizes Mediterranean cuisine. Excellent cheese tray. Pretty dining room; good service. Very expensive.

The Saloon, 1920 Broadway (at W. 64th St); ☎ (212) 874-1500. Across the street from Lincoln Center, American food; large restaurant, good for children, noisy. Moderate.

Shun Lee West, 43 W. 65th St (between Broadway and Central Park West); ☎ (212) 595-8895. Perhaps the city's finest Chinese restaurant. Large dining room with striking decor; Chinese specialties from several regions. Expensive.

Sugar Bar, 254 W. 72nd St (between Broadway and West End Ave); ☎ (212) 579-0222. Small restaurant with good food from the American South. Expensive.

Tavern on the Green, in Central Park (Central Park West and W. 67th St); ☎ (212) 873-3200. Large restaurant glitters with chandeliers and floral displays; pretty views of the park. New American food. Can be crowded and slow. Very expensive.

Vince & Eddie's, 70 W. 68th St (between Columbus Ave and Central Park West); ☎ (212) 721-0068. American food in simple setting. Outdoor tables. Moderate.

West 63rd Street Steakhouse, 44 W. 63rd St (between Columbus Ave and Broadway); ☎ (212) 246-6363. Upstairs dining room with view of Lincoln Center; quiet and relaxing; steak, roast chicken, veal chops, and other hearty American food. Expensive.

Upper West Side: 72nd Street and North, Harlem, Upper Manhattan

The Upper West Side is not known for its restaurants, though the choices have been broadening recently.

Afghan Kebab House, 2680 Broadway (at W. 102nd St); ☎ (212) 280-3500. Kebabs and rice; grilled meats; hearty portions. Other branches within city. Inexpensive.

Alouette, 2588 Broadway (at W. 97th St); ☎ (212) 222-6808. Small French bistro, good food; dining rooms upstairs and down; spotty service, popular with neighborhood folk. Inexpensive.

Barney Greengrass, 541 Amsterdam Ave (between W. 86th and W. 87th Sts); ☎ (212) 724-4707. Great smoked fish and other deli foods; low on decor, but no one cares. Moderate.

Café con Leche, 726 Amsterdam Ave (between W. 95th and W. 96th Sts); ☎ (212) 678-7000. Dominican and Cuban food in ample portions; colorful café. Other branch at 424 Amsterdam Ave, between W. 80th and W. 81st Sts. Friendly. Inexpensive.

Calle Ocho, 446 Columbus Ave (between W. 81st and W. 82nd Sts); ☎ (212) 873-5025. Large, noisy Latin American restaurant with flashy decor, high energy ambience, stylish Nuevo Latino cooking; busy bar scene. Expensive.

Charles' Southern Style Chicken, 2839 Eighth Ave (between W. 151st and W. 152nd Sts); ☎ (212) 926-4313. The whole menu may be great, but most folks never stray from the city's best fried chicken. Inexpensive.

Emily's, 1325 Fifth Ave (at W. 111th St); ☎ (212) 996-1212. Like Sylvia's, it has great soul food; unlike Sylvia's, it's not packed with tourists. Inexpensive.

Gennaro, 665 Amsterdam Ave (between W. 92nd and W. 93rd Sts); ☎ (212) 665-5348. Fabulous and original Italian food in a tiny storefront. Moderate.

La Casa de los Tacos, 2277 First Ave (at E. 117th St); ☎ (212) 860-6858. East Harlem neighborhood taquería; some sandwiches, some English spoken. Inexpensive.

Les Routiers, 568 Amsterdam Ave (between W. 87th and W. 88th Sts); ☎ (212) 874-2742. Charming and delicious French fare. Expensive.

Métisse, 239 W. 105th St (between Amsterdam Ave and Broadway); ☎ (212) 666-8825. French bistro with well-prepared food; neighborhood favorite. Good desserts. Moderate.

Niko's Mediterranean Grill and Bistro, 2161 Broadway (at W. 76th St); ☎ (212) 873-7000. Down the block from the beloved Big Nick's Burger Joint, its sibling serves massive portions from an unending menu. Moderate.

Pampa, 768 Amsterdam Ave (between W. 97th and W. 98th Sts); ☎ (212) 865-2929. Meat, Argentine style, and lots of it. Moderate.

Patsy's Pizzeria, 2287 First Ave (between E. 117th and E. 118th Sts); ☎ (212) 534-9783. Classic pizzeria left over from the days when East Harlem was an Italian neighborhood. New York thin-crust pizza baked in coal-fired oven. No credit cards. Inexpensive.

Rain, 100 W. 82nd St (between Amsterdam and Columbus Aves); ☎ (212) 501-0776. Superb Asian food. Expensive.

Ruby Foo's, 2182 Broadway (at W. 77th St); ☎ (212) 724-6700. Fancy Asian restaurant, plenty of decor, plenty of choices (Chinese, Thai, Southeast Asian); good for children and adults alike. Moderate.

Sylvia's, 328 Lenox Ave (between W. 126th and W. 127th Sts); ☎ (212) 996-0660. Informal, friendly restaurant in Harlem, noted for soul food. European and other tourists as well as locals. Inexpensive.

Terrace in the Sky, 400 W. 119th St (at Morningside Drive); ☎ (212) 666-9490. The Terrace offers a beautiful view of the city and fine French and New American cuisine. Expensive.

Restaurants in the Outer Boroughs

Many restaurants in the outer boroughs reflect the ethnicity of their neighborhoods. Some do not take credit cards; a few do not have a liquor license. Call ahead to make sure.

The Bronx

In Belmont (Near the Zoo)

Casual, homey southern Italian restaurants, some in the same family for generations.

Amici's, 566 E. 187th St (at Hoffman St); ☎ (718) 584-6167. Dinner only. Moderate.

Ann & Tony's, 2407 Arthur Ave (at E. 187th St); ☎ (718) 364-8250. Moderate.

Dominick's, 2335 Arthur Ave (at E. 187th St); ☎ (718) 733-2807. A bar with a few tables in front, no menu; small, homey, and famous enough to have lines in front. No credit cards. Moderate.

Mario's, 2342 Arthur Ave (between E. 184th and E. 186th Sts); ☎ (718) 584-1188. Family-run since 1919. Large pasta menu. Moderate.

In City Island

Expect crowds of tourists and visitors on spring and summer weekends.

Le Refuge, 620 City Island Ave (at Sutherland St); ☎ (718) 885-2478. French restaurant in an inn. Expensive.

In Highbridge, (Near Yankee Stadium)

Feeding Tree, 892 Gerard Ave (at E. 161st St); ☎ (718) 293-5025. Caribbean restaurant with jerk chicken, seafood, spicy dishes. Moderate.

Brooklyn

On Atlantic Ave

Brawta Caribbean Cafe, 347 Atlantic Ave (at Hoyt St); ☎ (718) 855-5515. Well-prepared, spicy Jamaican food and beverages. Inexpensive.

La Bouillabaisse, 145 Atlantic Ave (between Clinton and Henry Sts); ☎ (718) 522-8275. French bistro specializing in seafood. Popular and very busy. Moderate.

Tripoli, 156 Atlantic Ave (at Clinton St); ☎ (718) 596-5800. Veteran Lebanese café-restaurant, down-to-earth ethnic food, many appetizers, also full meals. Moderate.

In Bay Ridge

Lento's, 7003 Third Ave (at Ovington Ave); ☎ (718) 745-9197. Old-fashioned neighborhood restaurant, good pizza. No credit cards. Inexpensive.

In Bensonhurst

Tommaso, 1464 86th St (between Fourteenth and Fifteenth Aves); ☎ (718) 236-9883. Southern Italian cooking with opera on the weekends. Moderate.

In Brooklyn Heights

Caffé Buon Gusto, 151 Montague St (between Clinton and Henry Sts); ☎ (718) 624-3838. Simple Italian restaurant, many pasta dishes. Outdoor tables. Inexpensive.

Grimaldi's, 19 Old Fulton St (between Front and Water Sts); ☎ (718) 858-4300. Excellent coal-oven pizza. A New York classic. No credit cards. Inexpensive.

Henry's End, 44 Henry St (at Cranberry St); ☎ (718) 834-1776. A Brooklyn Heights institution that has held up through the years. Moderate.

Monty Q's, 158 Montague St (between Clinton and Henry Sts); ☎ (718) 246-2000. Good neighborhood brick-oven pizza restaurant, also serves pasta, salads. Inexpensive.

River Café, 1 Water St (under the Brooklyn Bridge); ☎ (718) 522-5200. One of the borough's most elegant. Very good American food; beautiful view of Manhattan skyline; music. Very expensive.

In Carroll Gardens and Boerum Hill

Banania Café, 241 Smith St (between Butler and Douglass Sts); ☎ (718) 237-9100. French bistro food with cosmopolitan touches. No credit cards. Inexpensive.

Boerum Hill Food Company, 134 Smith St (between Dean and Bergen Sts); ☎ (718) 222-0140. Small café; sandwiches, salads, also take-out food. Inexpensive.

Patois, 255 Smith St (between DeGraw and Douglass Sts), ☎ (718) 855-1535. The first, and still one of the finest, Smith St restaurants. Moderate.

Saul, 140 Smith St (at Bergen St); ☎ (718) 935-9844. Top-notch New American cuisine. Moderate.

In Coney Island

Gargiulo's, 2911 W. 15th St (between Surf and Mermaid Aves); ☎ (718) 266-4891. Once-famous, still popular restaurant; old-fashioned red-sauce Italian food and seafood.

Totonno's, 1524 Neptune Ave (between 15th and 16th Sts); ☎ (718) 372-8606. Modest surroundings in Italian enclave; historic pizzeria; irregular hours. No credit cards. Moderate.

In Downtown Brooklyn

BAMcafé, in the Brooklyn Academy of Music, 30 Lafayette St (at Ashland Place); ☎ (718) 636-4111. Features live music, spoken-word performance; open evenings during week, Sun afternoons. Moderate.

Gage & Tollner, 372 Fulton St (at Jay St); ☎ (718) 875-5181. American cooking, emphasis on seafood. Beautifully restored 19C restaurant illuminated by gaslight. Moderate.

Junior's, 386 Flatbush Ave Extension (at DeKalb Ave); ☎ (718) 852-5257. Deli with famous cheesecake; open late; near Brooklyn Academy of Music. Moderate.

In Fort Greene

A Table, 171 Lafayette Ave (at Adelphi St); ☎ (718) 935-9121. Long tables, rustic ambience, good French food. Moderate.

In Greenpoint

Thai Café, 923 Manhattan Ave (at Kent St); ☎ (718) 383-3562. Simple but good Thai restaurant. No credit cards. Inexpensive.

In Park Slope

Al di La, 248 Fifth Ave (at Carroll St); ☎ (718) 636-8888. Northern Italian food in attractive trattoria. Moderate.

Coco Roco, 392 Fifth Ave (between 6th and 7th Sts); ☎ (718) 965-3376. Pleasant Peruvian; includes seafood, chicken dishes, tamales. Inexpensive.

Cucina, 256 Fifth Ave (between Carroll St and Garfield Place); ☎ (718) 230-0711. This Italian restaurant is among Brooklyn's finest. Expensive.

Lento's, 833 Union St (at Seventh Ave); ☎ (718) 399-8782. Newer branch of Bay Ridge pizzeria; in old firehouse. Inexpensive.

Max and Moritz, 426A Seventh Ave (between 14th and 15th Sts); ☎ (718) 499-5557. Very good French cooking, popular restaurant; outdoor dining. Moderate.

In Sunset Park

Jade Plaza Restaurant, 6022 Eighth Ave (at 60th St); ☎ (718) 492-6888. Large dining room, good food, especially seafood, popular neighborhood restaurant. Inexpensive.

Ocean Palace, 5423 Eighth Ave (at 55th St); ☎ (718) 871-8080. The biggest and best restaurant in Brooklyn's Chinatown. Inexpensive.

Tequilita's, 5213 Fourth Ave (between 52nd and 53rd Sts); ☎ (718) 492-4303. Neighborhood taquería with excellent tacos, enchiladas, etc. Inexpensive.

In Williamsburg

Bamonte's, 32 Withers St (between Lorimer St and Union Ave); ☎ (718) 384-8831. Old-style neighborhood southern Italian. Often crowded. Moderate.

Peter Luger Steak House, 178 Broadway (at Driggs Ave); ☎ (718) 387-7400. Famous old steakhouse retains old tavern atmosphere with wood beams, scrubbed tables. Superb steak, lamb chops. No credit cards (they have their own). Very expensive.

Plan Eat Thailand, 141 N. 7th St (between Bedford Ave and Berry St); ☎ (718) 599-5758. Large Thai restaurant with sushi, hibachi tables. Inexpensive.

Vera Cruz, 195 Bedford Ave (between 6th and 7th Sts); ☎ (718) 599-7914. Mexican, with classic food, margaritas, homemade salsas. Inexpensive.

In Sheepshead Bay
Café Istanbul, 1715 Emmons Ave (at Sheepshead Bay Rd); ☎ (718) 368-3587. Small Turkish restaurant, with brick oven; specializes in lamejuns (meat or vegetable toppings on pizzalike crusts). No credit cards. Inexpensive.
Lundy Brothers, 1901 Emmons Ave (at Ocean Ave); ☎ (718) 743-0022. Gargantuan seafood restaurant overlooking Sheepshead Bay; once-glorious past, more mundane present. Moderate.

Queens

In Astoria
Christos Hasapo-Taverna, 41-08 23d Ave (at 41st St); ☎ (718) 726-5195. Attractive family-owned butcher shop plus restaurant. Steaks, Greek appetizers, rotisserie-grilled meats; Greek wines. Inexpensive.
Elias Corner, 24-02 31st St (at 24th Ave); ☎ (718) 932-1510. Very fresh grilled fish in established restaurant; outdoor tables in season. Sometimes harried service. No credit cards. Moderate.
Karyatis, 35-03 Broadway (between 35th and 36th Sts); ☎ (718) 204-0666. Traditional food, live music; attractive surroundings. Moderate.
Piccola Venezia, 42-01 28th Ave (at 42nd St); ☎ (718) 721-8470. Pleasant northern Italian restaurant; good cooking, agreeable service. Expensive.

In Corona
Green Field Churrascaria, 108-01 Northern Blvd (between 108th and 109th Sts); ☎ (718) 672-5202. All-you-can-eat Brazilian barbecue; huge restaurant, huge salad bar. Inexpensive.
Parkside Restaurant, 107-01 Corona Ave (between 108th St and 51st Ave); ☎ (718) 271-9276. Relaxed restaurant in old-time Italian neighborhood; a Queens institution. Moderate.

In Flushing
East Lake, 42-33 Main St (at Franklin Ave); ☎ (718) 539-8532. Small, simple Chinese restaurant, known for fresh seafood and dim sum. Local clientele. Inexpensive.
Golden Monkey, 133-47 Roosevelt Ave (at Prince St); ☎ (718) 762-2664. Basement restaurant, Szechuan dishes. No credit cards. Inexpensive.
Joe's Shanghai, 136-21 37th Ave (between Main and Union Sts); ☎ (718) 539-3838. The first of a small, family-owned chain; specializes in soup dumplings; busy. No credit cards. Inexpensive.
Kum Gang San, 138-28 Northern Blvd (between Main and Union Sts); ☎ (718) 461-0909. Fine Korean barbecue and other specialties in pleasant restaurant with outdoor waterfall, piano music. Moderate.

In Jackson Heights
Delhi Palace, 37-33 74th St (between 37th and Roosevelt Aves); ☎ (718) 507-0666. Very good northern Indian food; pleasant service, attractive restaurant. Inexpensive.

Pearson's Texas Barbecue, in Legend's Sports Bar, 71-04 35th Ave (between 71st and 72nd Sts); ☎ (718) 779-7715. A real pit barbecue, with beef, chicken, sausages. Very casual (plastic utensils and paper napkins); friendly. Inexpensive.
Tierras Colombianas, 82-18 Roosevelt Ave (between 82nd and 83d Sts); ☎ (718) 426-8868. Colombian food served in large portions; friendly, menu in both Spanish and English. No credit cards. Inexpensive.

In Long Island City
Water's Edge, 44th Drive (at the East River); ☎ (718) 482-0033. Good new American cuisine at Midtown prices. Spectacular view from barge-based restaurant. Free ferry from Manhattan. Very expensive.

In Rego Park
Goody's, 94-03 63rd Drive (between Booth and Saunders Sts); ☎ (718) 896-7159. Shanghai specialties (i.e., soup dumplings). Storefront with pleasant service. No credit cards. Moderate.
London Lennie's, 63-88 Woodhaven Blvd (between 63rd Drive and Fleet Court); ☎ (718) 894-8084. Busy, homey fish house; expect to wait during peak hours. Moderate.

In Steinway
Ubol's Kitchen. 24-42 Steinway St (at 25th Ave); ☎ (718) 545-2874. Small, simple restaurant with authentic (fiery), well-regarded Thai food. Pleasant service. Inexpensive.

Staten Island

In Charleston (Near Clay Pits Pond Park)
Killmeyer's, 4254 Arthur Kill Rd (at Sharrotts Rd); ☎ (718) 984-1202. A Bavarian restaurant, complete with beer garden. Moderate.

In Eltingville
Angelina's, 26 Jefferson Blvd (at Annadale Rd); ☎ (718) 227-7100. Italian food, casual restaurant in small mall. Expensive.

In New Dorp
Goodfella's Brick Oven Pizza, 1718 Hylan Blvd (at Seaview Ave); ☎ (718) 987-2422. Traditional and revisionist pizza, pasta, and casual Italian food in family-style restaurant. Inexpensive.
Mauro's Restaurant, 121 Roma Ave (at New Dorp Lane); ☎ (718) 351-8441. Simple Italian. Inexpensive.
Taste of India, 287 New Dorp Lane (between Clawson and Edison Sts;) ☎ (718) 987-4700. Small casual restaurant with northern Indian cuisine. Tandoori dishes, many breads. Inexpensive.

In Rosebank (Near Alice Austen Cottage, Not Too Far from Garibaldi-Meucci Museum)
Aesop's Tables, 1233 Bay St (between Maryland Ave and Hylan Blvd); ☎ (718) 720-2005. Charming French restaurant, open for lunch and dinner, with outdoor dining in season. Moderate.

In Rossville

Historic Old Bermuda Inn, 2515 Arthur Kill Rd (between Bloomingdale Rd and Rossville Ave); ☎ (718) 948-7600. Popular spot for weddings, receptions, celebratory dining; in old house. Continental cuisine. Moderate.

In St. George (Near the Ferry and Staten Island Museum)

Side Street Saloon, 11 Schuyler St (at Richmond Terrace); ☎ (718) 448-6868. Quiet restaurant with Italian American food; popular with courthouse workers during the week, couples and singles on weekends. Inexpensive.

In Stapleton

Patricio Ristorante, 695 Bay St (between Vanderbilt Ave and Broad St); ☎ (718) 720-1861. Comfortable restaurant with windows looking out on the Verrazano Bridge; Italian regional food. Moderate.

Bars

New York offers a wealth of places to imbibe, from historic taverns where famous writers overindulged to chic wine bars in trendy neighborhoods. Bars stay open until 4 A.M. The legal drinking age is 21.

Downtown, SoHo, and TriBeCa

Bridge Café, 279 Water St (at Dover St); ☎ (212) 227-3344.

Fanelli's, 94 Prince St (at Mercer St); ☎ (212) 226-9412.

Screening Room, 54 Varick St (at Canal St); ☎ (212) 334-2100.

SoHo Kitchen and Bar, 103 Green St (between Prince and Spring Sts); ☎ (212) 925-1866.

Spy, 101 Greene St (between Prince and Spring Sts); ☎ (212) 343-9000.

Lower East Side, East Village, Gramercy Park

Barmacy, 538 E. 14th St (between Aves A and B); ☎ (212) 228-2240.

Beauty Bar, 231 E. 14th St (between Second and Third Aves); ☎ (212) 539-1389.

Fez, 380 Lafayette St (at Great Jones St); ☎ (212) 533-2680.

Idlewild, 145 E. Houston St (between Eldrige and Forsythe Sts); ☎ (212) 477-5005.

Jules, 65 St. Mark's Place; ☎ (212) 477-5560.

McSorley's Old Ale House, 15 E. 7th St (between Second and Third Aves); ☎ (212) 473-9148.

Greenwich Village

Automatic Slim's, 733 Washington St (at Bank St); ☎ (212) 645-8660.

The Village Idiot, 355 W. 14th St (between Eighth and Ninth Aves); ☎ (212) 989-7334.

The White Horse Tavern, 567 Hudson St (at W. 11th St); ☎ (212) 989-3956. Dylan Thomas is said to have drunk himself to death here.

Union Square, Gramercy Park

Heartland Brewery, 35 Union Square West; ☎ (212) 645-3400.

Pete's Tavern, 129 E. 18th St (at Irving Place); ☎ (212) 473-7676.

Midtown, Theater District

Algonquin Hotel Lounge, 59 W. 44th St (between Fifth and Sixth Aves); ☎ (212) 840-6800.

Barrymore's, 267 W. 45th St (between Broadway and Eighth Ave); ☎ (212) 391-8400.

Café Un Deux Trois, 123 W. 44th St (between Broadway and Sixth Ave); ☎ (212) 354-4148.

Landmark Tavern, 626 Eleventh Ave (at W. 46th St); ☎ (212) 757-8595.

Morgans Bar, 237 Madison Ave (at E. 37th St); ☎ (212) 686-0300.

Oak Bar, Plaza Hotel, Fifth Ave at 59th St; ☎ (212) 759-3000.

Royalton Hotel Bar, 44 W. 44th St (between Fifth and Sixth Aves); ☎ (212) 869-4400.

"21 Club," 21 W. 52nd St (between Fifth and Sixth Aves); ☎ (212) 582-7200.

Upper West Side, Harlem

Café des Artistes, 1 W. 67th St (at Central Park West); ☎ (212) 877-3500.

Hi-Life, 477 Amsterdam Ave (at W. 83rd St); ☎ (212) 787-7199.

Leonx Lounge, 288 Lenox Ave (between W. 124th and W. 125th Sts); ☎ (212) 427-0253.

O'Neals', 49 W. 64th St (between Central Park West and Broadway); ☎ (212) 787-4663.

Yogi's, 2156 Broadway (at W. 76th St); ☎ (212) 873-9852.

Midtown East

Bateau Ivre, 230 E. 51st St (between Second and Third Aves); ☎ (212) 583-0579.

Beer Bar, 200 Park Ave (at E. 45th St); ☎ (212) 818-1333.

Divine Bar, 244 E. 51st St (between Second and Third Aves); ☎ (212) 319-9463

King Cole Bar, St. Regis Hotel, 2 E. 55th St (at Fifth Ave); ☎ (212) 753-4500.

Top of the Tower, Beekman Hotel, 26th floor, 3 Mitchell Place (between E. 49th St and First Ave); ☎ (212) 355-7300

Upper East Side

Bemelman's Bar, Carlyle Hotel, 981 Madison Ave (between E. 76th and E. 77th Sts); ☎ (212) 744-1600.

Elaine's, 1703 Second Ave (at E. 88th St); ☎ (212) 534-8103.

États-Unis Wine Bar, 396 E. 81st St (at First Ave); ☎ (212) 517-8826.

P.J. Clarke's, 915 Third Ave (at E. 55th St); ☎ (212) 759-1650.

What to See

The Classic Sights

These are the places that mean "New York City" to the world. They're famous because they deserve to be, so don't expect to be alone when you visit. Check the index for more information about hours, locations, and what to expect.

The Staten Island Ferry, at the foot of South and Whitehall Sts. A free ride with glorious views of the Lower Manhattan skyline, the Statue of Liberty, and the action in the harbor. About 30 minutes one way.

The Statue of Liberty and **Ellis Island Immigration Museum,** in New York Harbor, accessible from Battery Park at the foot of Broadway. Visiting the statue and the historic buildings of Ellis Island is an emotionally moving experience; more than 5.5 million visitors come yearly to the statue, so plan accordingly.

The South Street Seaport, along the East River, between John St and Peck Slip. New York's maritime past is enshrined in renovated buildings and historic ships; shopping galore.

The Brooklyn Bridge, from Park Row at Centre St in Manhattan to Adams St in Brooklyn. New York's most beautiful bridge. Whether you look down, up, left, or right, the views are stunning. Walk across to Brooklyn and back, or take the subway to High St in Brooklyn and make the one-way jaunt to Manhattan.

Chinatown, centered around Mott St south of Canal St. New York's original Chinese immigrant community. Crowded, colorful, and vital.

The Empire State Building, Fifth Ave at 34th St. Not the tallest but the most historic skyscraper. In addition to the (real) breathtaking views from the observation deck, New York Skyride "tours" city sights via big-screen motion simulators.

Times Square and the **Broadway Theater District,** focused on W. 42nd St and Broadway. Cleaned up (some say sanitized) during the 1990s, Times Square is still a crossroads of the entertainment world. Theaters, tourist hotspots (e.g., Madame Tussaud's), media glitz, and all the rest, illuminated after dark by miles of neon.

Rockefeller Center, between Fifth and Sixth Aves from 48th to 51st Sts. The city's best-ever urban renewal project, still elegant after all these years. Includes Radio City Music Hall, the Channel Gardens, and the famous ice skating rink overlooked by a gilded statue of Prometheus.

Central Park, 59th St to 110th St, Fifth Ave to Central Park West. Landscaped by Frederick Law Olmsted and accessorized with architectural enhancements by Calvert Vaux, Central Park is an inestimable green space in Manhattan's asphalt grid. Zoos, gardens, places for sports and strolling, performance spaces.

Lincoln Center for the Performing Arts, between Amsterdam and Columbus Ave from W. 62nd to W. 66th Sts. The nexus of classical music in New York, including the Metropolitan Opera, Avery Fisher Hall, the Juilliard School, the New York Public Library for the Performing Arts, among others.

American Museum of Natural History, Central Park West from W. 77th to W. 81st Sts. Celebrated for the scientifically up-to-date installations of dinosaurs and the Rose Center for Earth and Space, the museum has wonderful Native American artifacts, gems and minerals, historic animal dioramas, and myriad specimens of birds and bugs, as well as bones.

The Metropolitan Museum of Art, Fifth Ave from 80th to 84th Sts. Hands down the best art museum in the Western Hemisphere; world-famous collections of paintings, sculpture, decorative objects, musical instruments, weapons, and other artifacts—more than 2 million altogether—drawn from 5,000 years of human history.

The Bronx Zoo, Fordham Rd at Bronx River Pkwy in the Bronx (of course). World-famous, but perhaps overshadowed nowadays by more spacious and less urban wildlife parks elsewhere, the Bronx Zoo remains the largest metropolitan zoo in the U.S. with more than 6,000 animals, many in habitat exhibitions.

The Brooklyn Botanic Garden, 1000 Washington Ave near Prospect Park in Brooklyn. Intensely planted, this beautiful space has a famous Japanese garden, outstanding collections of roses and cherry trees, and greenhouses with a famous bonsai collection. Nearby are the **Brooklyn Museum of Art,** known for its fine permanent collection and adventurous changing exhibitions, and **Prospect Park,** considered by some to be the masterpiece of Frederick Law Olmsted and Calvert Vaux.

Less Famous but Equally Interesting

Skyscrapers
The Woolworth Building, Broadway between Barclay St and Park Place. Cass Gilbert's opulent Gothic skyscraper built with the proceeds of F. W. Woolworth's dime-store empire.
The Flatiron Building, between Fifth Ave and Broadway, 22nd and 23rd Sts. A turn-of-the-20C steel-skeleton skyscraper whose triangular form follows Broadway's diagonal course.
The Chrysler Building, Lexington Ave at E. 42nd St. An Art Deco masterpiece with a richly detailed lobby (including the elevator cabs) and a famous skyline crown.
The Seagram Building, Park Ave between E. 53rd and E. 54th Sts. An influential international style work by Mies van der Rohe and Philip Johnson.
The Citicorp Building, Lexington Ave between E. 53rd and E. 54th Sts. Known for its slashing diagonal skyline silhouette and its inclusion of St. Peter's Church.
The Sony Building (formerly the AT&T Headquarters), Madison Ave between E. 55th and E. 56th Sts. One of New York's first postmodern skyscrapers; its "Chippendale top" stirred up controversy.

Other Historic and Grand Buildings
City Hall, City Hall Park between Broadway and Park Row. A neoclassical Franco-American triumph, now unfortunately fenced off.
The "Tweed Courthouse," Chambers St at City Hall Park. Soon to be the home of the Museum of the City of New York (projected opening 2003), this building is infamous for graft and admirable for Victorian opulence.
The General Post Office (now the James A. Farley Building), Eighth Ave between W. 31st and 33rd Sts. A McKim Mead & White masterpiece that is going to be recycled as the next Penn Station.
New York Public Library, Center for the Humanities, Fifth Ave between 40th and 42nd Sts. A famous Beaux Arts monument; check out the beautifully restored Main Reading Room and enjoy the exhibits in cool, marbled Gottesman Hall.
Grand Central Terminal, E. 42nd St between Vanderbilt and Lexington Aves. One of the city's great interior spaces, recently restored to its former splendor and fitted out with a marketplace that will siphon cash from your wallet.
The Solomon R. Guggenheim Museum, Fifth Ave between 88th and 89th Sts. Features Frank Lloyd Wright's great interior design. Look up from the ground floor and down from the top circle; enjoy the art as you pass by.

Green Spaces
Central and Prospect Parks are the city's most famous parks (don't forget the **Conservatory Gardens** in Central Park opposite 105th St), but if you're looking for a respite from asphalt, there are other refuges.

New York Botanical Garden, in Bronx Park, north of Fordham Rd (and near the Bronx Zoo). Acres of gardens, seasonal plantings, a beautiful conservatory recently restored, and a stand of virgin forest. Combine it with a trip to the Bronx Zoo if you have time.

Wave Hill, W. 252nd St and Sycamore Ave in the Riverdale section of the Bronx. Rolling lawns, wonderful views across the Hudson River to the Palisades, fine gardens.

Snug Harbor Cultural Center, on Richmond Terrace, facing the Kill van Kull in Staten Island. Once a home for retired sailors, Snug Harbor includes the Staten Island Botanical Garden, lovely Greek revival architecture overlooking rolling lawns, several art exhibition spaces, and the Staten Island Children's Museum.

Peaceful Indoor Oases

The Frick Collection, Fifth Ave at 70th St. Quiet and civilized, a stunning collection of Old Masters, French furniture, and bibelots in an opulent town house. The Garden Court with its murmuring fountain encourages contemplation.

The Morgan Library, Madison Ave and 36th St. J. P. Morgan's private library and anterooms, plus newer galleries and a courtyard café. Morgan's treasures include Gutenberg Bibles, medieval manuscripts, rare books, drawings, and other beautiful objets d'art.

The Cloisters, in Fort Tryon Park, Fort Washington Ave and Margaret Corbin Plaza, Upper Manhattan. Artifacts from a spiritual age displayed in a reconstructed medieval setting; the museum overlooks the Hudson River and the Palisades to the west (thank John D. Rockefeller Jr. for preserving the view). Home of the Unicorn Tapestries.

Tours and Sightseeing Services

The quarterly *Calendar of Events* published by NYC & Company contains a list of commercial sightseeing services. Pick up a copy at the Visitors Center at 810 Seventh Ave (between W. 52nd and W. 53rd Sts).

General Tours

General tours can help first-time visitors or sightseers with limited time who want an overview.

Boat Tours

Circle Line Cruises, Pier 83 at the foot of W. 42nd St; ☎ (212) 563-3200. Three-hour cruises around Manhattan with lively commentary. Year-round.

South Street Seaport, Pier 16, at the seaport; ☎ (212) 748-8786. Two-hour voyages in the harbor on the schooner *Pioneer,* views of Statue of Liberty, skyline, sunset tours, charters.

Spirit Cruises, Pier 62 at Chelsea Piers (W. 23rd St at Twelfth Ave); ☎ (212) 727-2789. Harbor cruises, dancing, live entertainment.

World Yacht Enterprises, Pier 81 (W. 41st St at the Hudson River); ☎ (212) 630-8100. Luxury restaurant-yacht tours for lunch, dinner, and brunch.

Bus Tours

Gray Line New York Tours, Port Authority Bus Terminal (Eighth Ave and W. 42nd St); ☎ (212) 397-2600; Web site: www.graylinenewyork.com. Double-decker and regular coach tours, lasting 2–12 hours to all areas of the city. Also coach trips to Atlantic City casinos, shopping in nearby malls.

Helicopter Tours
Liberty Helicopters, heliports at W. 30th St and Twelfth Ave and Pier 6 at the East River; ☎ (212) 967-6464; for same-day reservations from the W. 30th St location, ☎ (212) 967-4550. Web site: libertyhelicopters.com.

Specialized Tours
These tours include guided visits by bus, bike, van, or car, as well as walking tours. Some tours are organized for groups only, but individuals may join if all places are not taken. Call for description of tour, prices, and meeting place. In addition to tours that are offered all year or during the warm months, many thematic tours are offered on a onetime or occasional basis. Check *Time Out New York, New York* magazine, and the listings in the Fri edition of the *New York Times.*

Adventure on a Shoestring, ☎ (212) 265-2663. Inexpensive weekend tours, year-round, of New York neighborhoods. Reservations required.

Apollo Theater, ☎ (212) 222-0992. Backstage tours, jazz history.

Big Onion Walking Tours, ☎ (212) 439-1090; Web site: www.bigonion.com. Organized thematically. University-trained historians lead ethnic, literary, architectural tours. Weekends all year; some weekdays.

Central Park Bicycle Tours, ☎ (212) 541-8759; Web site: www.centralpark biketour.com. Guided two-hour bike tours through the park, bicycle rental included.

Central Park Conservancy, ☎ (212) 360-2726; Web site: centralparknyc.org. Free guided walks through the park focused on nature and history.

Gracie Mansion Conservancy Tour, ☎ (212) 570-4751. See the inside of the historic residence of New York's mayor. By reservation only. Wed, Nov–March.

Grand Central Station, ☎ (212) 935-3960. Tour of the public and private spaces in this historic building by the Municipal Art Society; meets every Wed at 12:30 P.M. at the Information Booth, Main Concourse.

Harlem Spirituals, Inc., ☎ (212) 391-0900; Web site: www.harlemspirituals. com. Gospel, jazz, and soul food tours of Harlem, also other ethnic neighborhoods.

Joyce Gold History Tours of New York City, ☎ (212) 242-5762; Web site: www.nyctours.com. Joyce Gold has been leading tours since 1976; themes include Diplomatic New York, Macabre Greenwich Village, and The New Meat Market—Butchers, Makers, and Art Scene Makers.

Lincoln Center for the Performing Arts, ☎ (212) 875-5350. Daily tours meet on concourse level, downstairs from the Met. Include Metropolitan Opera, Avery Fisher Hall, New York State Theater.

Lower East Side Conservancy. ☎ (212) 598-1200; Web site: www.nycjewish tours.com. Visits on foot or by minibus to historic synagogues, kosher food shops, and Judaica stores; special events. Advance ticket purchase required.

Lower East Side Tenement Museum, ☎ (212) 431-0233. Tours of ethnic neighborhoods on Lower East Side; Web site: www.tenement.org.

Madison Square Garden, ☎ (212) 465-5800. Behind-the-scenes tours of this sports-entertainment facility. Tickets also available from Ticketmaster; ☎ (212) 307-7171.

Metropolitan Opera House, ☎ (212) 769-7020. Tour the nonpublic spaces of the opera, including costume and scenery areas, stage, rehearsal spaces.

Municipal Art Society, ☎ (212) 935-3960; Web site: www.mas.org. Walking tours focus on history and architecture; tours have included Midtown Manhattan in the Age of Morgan the Magnificent and The Best of the West Side.

Museum of the City of New York, ☎ (212) 534-1672; Web site: www.mcny. org. Historical and architectural tours, April–Oct.

New York City Cultural Walking Tours, ☎ (212) 979-2388; Web site: nyc walk.com. Both public and private tours offered, focusing on landmarks, architectural and historic sites.

New York Like a Native, ☎ (212) 334-0492; Web site: www.nylikea native.com. Tours of Brooklyn (from Park Slope to Brooklyn Heights and Williamsburg) and the Lower East Side.

92nd Street Y, ☎ (212) 415-5500; Web site: www.92ndsty.org. Cultural and ethnic tours, including places normally not open to the public (artists' studios, homes), neighborhood tours, bus trips to outlying areas.

Radio City Music Hall Productions, ☎ (212) 632-4041. Backstage at Radio City.

Savory Sojourns, ☎ (212) 691-7314 or (888) 9-SAVORY; Web site: www. savorysojourns.com. Tours to ethnic neighborhoods and other places of culinary interest, also meals at top restaurants, cooking instruction.

Urban Park Rangers, ☎ (212) 427-4040. Explore history and ecology of the city's parks; workshops and programs for children. For Prospect Park in Brooklyn, ☎ (718) 438-0100.

Historical societies in the outer boroughs sometimes offer neighborhood walking tours.

Brooklyn Historical Society, ☎ (718) 254-9830; Web site: www.brooklyn history.org. Ongoing series of walking tours and lectures about Brooklyn neighborhoods, cemeteries, history.

Bronx County Historical Society, ☎ (718) 881-8900; Web site: www.bronx historicalsociety.org.

Queens Historical Society, ☎ (718) 939-0647.

Staten Island Historical Society, ☎ (718) 351-9414.

Shopping

Shopping is a major tourist attraction and, for some New Yorkers, a hobby.

Shopping Hours

Most department stores open at 10 A.M. and remain open until 6 P.M. or later; some are open in the evening one day a week; some are open Sun 11–5 or 12–6. Specialty shops and boutiques may open and close later.

Where to Shop

In former days, Midtown was the focus of fashionable shopping, with outlying neighborhoods known for special products, sold in specialty stores clustered together for the convenience of buyers. Thus there were districts for lighting, kitchen supplies, flowers, notions, millinery supplies (including feathers), and musical instruments. While traces of this older economy remain, shopping areas all over the city reflect the general economic level of the neighborhood rather than a specific trade or product.

Manhattan's Old Shopping Neighborhoods

Dealers in musical instruments can still be found on W. 45th St between Sixth and Seventh Aves and also on W. 48th St in the same crosstown block. There are antique (and junk) shops in the E. 30s on Second and Third Aves as well as on Columbus Ave in the low W. 80s. Camera stores used to be clustered in the low W. 30s west of Seventh Ave. Shops with notions (haberdashery), trimmings, millinery supplies, and similar paraphernalia can be found in the Garment District (mid- to high W. 30s around Seventh Ave). West 47th St, just off Fifth Ave, is "Diamond Street," with upscale jewelers located nearby on the avenue itself.

Although New York, like other towns and cities in the U.S., has seen an influx of chain stores whose presence homogenizes the experience of shopping, there are still some neighborhoods with their own special ambience. The following summary begins downtown and works north.

The **South Street Seaport** has a large shopping mall, the Fulton Market Building, which is currently under redevelopment.

The **Lower East Side,** once home to a large Jewish immigrant population from eastern Europe, has traditionally been the center of bargain shopping. Orchard St is known for discounted clothing and lingerie stores. Grand St, intersecting Orchard St, has linens, towels, and other household goods. The Bowery, between Grand and Delancey Sts, still has lighting fixtures. Stores on the Lower East Side are closed on Sat.

In the **East Village** are shops with books, used records and CDs, vintage clothing, and other paraphernalia.

SoHo, now too expensive to be home turf for any but the most successful artists, has become a focal point of style—fashions for men and women, furniture (especially on Lafayette St), cosmetics, even stylish food. Major designers like Louis Vuitton and Prada Sport have set up shop here. Dean & DeLuca is one of the city's best-known gourmet food emporiums; Enchanted Forest is an upscale toy store. Zona and Moss are well known for home furnishings.

Chelsea and the Flatiron District have large chain stores—including Barnes & Noble, Filene's Basement, and Loehmann's—and stylish clothing stores (Emporio Armani) as well as discounters. Art galleries have moved to the western fringes of the district near Tenth Ave.

Fifth Ave from Central Park South down to about 50th St has a mix of very expensive shops, department stores, and the kind of chain stores familiar from malls across the country. In addition to the classic American department stores—Bergdorf Goodman, Henri Bendel, and Saks Fifth Avenue—the Japanese department store chain Takashimaya has a branch on Fifth Ave. The jewelers Cartier, Tiffany, Harry Winston, and Bulgari are also located here. Trump Tower and Rockerfeller Center have boutiques and shops.

57th St, like Fifth Ave, is a center for luxury shopping, with Chanel, Burbery, Escada, and Hermès among the boutiques offering expensive wares. New, and more affordable, arrivals are NikeTown and a Warner Bros. Studio Store. West of Fifth Ave are more modest stores, including occasional bookshops and a few fabric shops, which will probably be replaced by fancier establishments in the near future.

Madison Ave north of 57th St is a center of couture boutiques and art galleries. Giorgio Armani, Valentino, Prada, Donna Karan—all have shops here. There is a branch of Cartier and menswear stores such as Alfred Dunhill.

The Grand Old Department Stores

Department stores are known for their wide range of goods and services, and many of the country's most famous have their flagship locations in New York. They offer convenience, service (usually), and ambience but not bargain prices. The most notable are Bergdorf Goodman (Fifth Ave at 58th St), Bloomingdale's (E. 59th St and Lexington Ave), Henri Bendel (Fifth Ave between 55th and 56th Sts), Lord & Taylor (Fifth Ave at 39th St), Macy's (Herald Square, Sixth Ave and W. 34th St), and Saks Fifth Avenue (Fifth Ave at 50th St).

Museums and Galleries

New York has more than 150 museums and hundreds of art galleries. Most museums are open six days a week, with Mon the preferred closing day. However, the Museum of Modern Art is closed Wed, the Brooklyn Museum of Art is closed both Mon and Tues, and the Guggenheim is closed Thurs. If in doubt, call ahead.

Some museums are free, but most have **admission charges.** Most have reduced rates for children, students, and seniors; some have hours when the entrance fee is reduced or canceled altogether. Many museums now have Web sites, with information about current and upcoming exhibitions; these are also listed in *Time Out New York,* the Fri edition of the *New York Times, New York* magazine, and *The New Yorker.* A quarterly magazine, *Museums: New York,* offers comprehensive listings, a calendar of events, and tips on what is new and newsworthy.

The Museum of Modern Art is open on Mon and closed on Wed. Most other museums are closed on Mon but open on Wed.

Museums with Special Collections: Where to Find . . .

African Art
Brooklyn Museum of Art, 200 Eastern Pkwy, Brooklyn.
Metropolitan Museum of Art, 1000 Fifth Ave (at 82nd St).
Museum for African Art, 593 Broadway (between Houston and Prince Sts).
Studio Museum in Harlem, 144 W. 125th St (between Adam Clayton Powell Jr. Blvd [Seventh Ave] and Lenox Ave [Sixth Ave]).

African American Art and Culture
Bronx Museum of the Arts, 1040 Grand Concourse (at E. 165th St).
Brooklyn Historical Society, 128 Pierrepont St (at Clinton St), Brooklyn.

Louis Armstrong Archives, Rosenthal Library, Queens College, Kissena Blvd, Flushing, Queens.
Museum for African Art, 593 Broadway (between Houston and Prince Sts).
Schomburg Center for Research in Black Culture, New York Public Library, 515 Malcolm X Blvd (W. 135th St and Lenox Ave).
Studio Museum in Harlem, 144 W. 125th St (between Adam Clayton Powell Jr. Blvd [Seventh Ave] and Lenox Ave [Sixth Ave]).

American Painting
Brooklyn Museum of Art, 200 Eastern Pkwy, Brooklyn.
City Hall, Governors' Room, City Hall Park (Broadway, south of Chambers St).
Metropolitan Museum of Art, 1000 Fifth Ave (at 82nd St).
Museum of Modern Art, 11 W. 53rd St (between Fifth and Sixth Aves).
Museum of the City of New York, 1220 Fifth Ave (at 103rd St).
New-York Historical Society, 2 W. 77th St (at Central Park West).
Queens Museum of Art, New York City Building, Flushing Meadows–Corona Park, Queens.
Whitney Museum of American Art, 945 Madison Ave (at E. 75th St).

Architecture and Urban Planning
Municipal Art Society, 457 Madison Ave (between E. 50th and E. 51th Sts).
Museum of Modern Art, 11 W. 53rd St (between Fifth and Sixth Aves).

Bibles
American Bible Society, 1865 Broadway (at W. 61st St).
Morgan Library, 29 E. 36th St (at Madison Ave).

Books and Manuscripts
Grolier Club, 47 E. 60th St (between Madison and Park Aves).
Morgan Library, 29 E. 36th St (at Madison Ave).
New York Public Library: Humanities and Social Sciences Library (Fifth Ave and 42nd St).
New York Public Library: Science, Industry and Business Library, 188 Madison Ave (at E. 34th St).
New York Public Library for the Performing Arts, Lincoln Center, 40 Lincoln Center Plaza (Broadway and W. 65th St).

Children's Museums, Collections Interesting to Children
American Museum of Natural History, Central Park West at W. 79th St.
Aquarium for Wildlife Conservation, W. 8th St at Surf Ave, Brooklyn.
Bronx Zoo, Fordham Rd at Bronx River Pkwy, Bronx.
Brooklyn Children's Museum, 145 Brooklyn Ave (at St. Marks Ave), Brooklyn.
Brooklyn Historical Society, 128 Pierrepont St (at Clinton St), Brooklyn.
Brooklyn Museum of Art (Egyptian collection, special exhibitions), 200 Eastern Pkwy, Brooklyn.
Central Park Wildlife Center, in Central Park, 64th St and Fifth Ave.
Children's Museum of Manhattan, 212 W. 83rd St (between Broadway and Amsterdam Ave).

Children's Museum of the Arts, 182 Lafayette St (between Broome and Grand Sts).

The Cloisters, Metropolitan Museum of Art, Fort Tryon Park.

Coney Island Museum, 1208 Surf Ave (at W. 12th St), Brooklyn.

Cooper-Hewitt National Design Museum, Smithsonian Institution, 2 E. 91st St (at Fifth Ave).

Ellis Island Immigration Museum, Statue of Liberty National Monument.

Forbes Magazine Galleries, 62 Fifth Ave (at 12th St).

General Grant National Memorial, in Riverside Park (Riverside Drive and W. 122nd St).

Historic Richmond Town, in La Tourette Park, 441 Clarke Ave (at St. Patrick's Place), Staten Island.

Intrepid Sea Air Space Museum, Pier 86 (W. 46th St and Twelfth Ave).

Lefferts Homestead Children's Historic House Museum, in Prospect Park, Flatbush Ave and Empire Blvd, Brooklyn.

Lower East Side Tenement Museum, 90 Orchard St (at Broome St).

Metropolitan Museum of Art, 1000 Fifth Ave (at 82nd St).

Museum of Television and Radio, 25 W. 52nd St (between Fifth and Sixth Aves).

Museum of the City of New York, 1220 Fifth Ave (at 103rd St). Scheduled to move to 52 Chambers St in 2003.

National Museum of the American Indian, 1 Bowling Green (between State and Whitehall Sts).

New York City Fire Museum, 278 Spring St (between Hudson and Varick Sts).

New York City Police Museum, 100 Old Slip (near Front St).

New York Hall of Science, in Flushing Meadows–Corona Park, 47-01 111th St (at Forty-ninth Ave), Queens.

New York Transit Museum, in former subway station, Boerum Place and Schermerhorn St, Brooklyn. Also branch museum in Grand Central Terminal.

New York Unearthed, 17 State St (across from Battery Park); enter from Pearl St.

Prospect Park Wildlife Center, in Prospect Park, entrance on Flatbush Ave, Brooklyn.

Queens County Farm Museum, 73-50 Little Neck Pkwy, Floral Park, Queens.

Queens Wildlife Center, in Flushing Meadows–Corona Park, 53-51 111th St, Queens.

Sony Wonder Technology Lab, 550 Madison Ave (at E. 50th St).

Staten Island Children's Museum, at Snug Harbor Cultural Center, 1000 Richmond Terrace, Staten Island.

Staten Island Zoo, 614 Broadway (between Forest Ave and Clove Rd), Staten Island.

Statue of Liberty National Monument, Liberty Island.

Coins, Medals

American Numismatic Society, Audubon Terrace (Broadway and W. 155th St). Scheduled to move to 140 William St in 2002.

Jewish Museum, 1109 Fifth Ave (at 92nd St).

Metropolitan Museum of Art, 1000 Fifth Ave (at 82nd St).

Costume and Fashion
Brooklyn Museum of Art, 200 Eastern Pkwy, Brooklyn.
Metropolitan Museum of Art, 1000 Fifth Ave (at 82nd St).
Museum at FIT, Seventh Ave at W. 27th St.

Craft
American Craft Museum, 40 W. 53rd St (between Fifth and Sixth Aves).
American Folk Art Museum, 45 W. 53rd St (between Fifth and Sixth Aves) and 2 Lincoln Square (Columbus Ave, between W. 65th and W. 66th Sts).
American Museum of Natural History, Central Park West at W. 79th St.
Historic Richmond Town, in La Tourette Park, 441 Clarke Ave (at St. Patrick's Place), Staten Island.
National Museum of the American Indian, Smithsonian Institution, 1 Bowling Green (between State and Whitehall Sts).

Decorative Arts
American Craft Museum, 40 W. 53rd St (between Fifth and Sixth Aves).
American Folk Art Museum, 45 W. 53rd St (between Fifth and Sixth Aves) and 2 Lincoln Square (Columbus Ave, between W. 65th and W. 66th Sts).
Brooklyn Museum of Art, 200 Eastern Pkwy, Brooklyn.
Cooper-Hewitt National Design Museum, Smithsonian Institution, 2 E. 91st St (at Fifth Ave).
Frick Collection, 1 E. 70th St (at Fifth Ave).
Historic Richmond Town, in La Tourette Park, 441 Clarke Ave (at St. Patrick's Place), Staten Island.
Jewish Museum, 1109 Fifth Ave (at 92nd St).
Metropolitan Museum of Art, 1000 Fifth Ave (at 82nd St).
Museum of Modern Art, 11 W. 53rd St (between Fifth and Sixth Aves).
Museum of the City of New York, 1220 Fifth Ave (at 103rd St). Scheduled to move to 52 Chambers St in 2003.

Dinosaurs
American Museum of Natural History, Central Park West at W. 79th St.

Fire-Fighting Equipment
New York City Fire Museum, 278 Spring St (between Hudson and Varick Sts).
New-York Historical Society, 2 W. 77th St (at Central Park West).

Folk Art
American Folk Art Museum, 45 W. 53rd St (between Fifth and Sixth Aves) and 2 Lincoln Square (Columbus Ave, between W. 65th and W. 66th Sts).
American Museum of Natural History, Central Park West at W. 79th St.
El Museo del Barrio, 1230 Fifth Ave (at 104th St).
Museum for African Art, 593 Broadway (between Houston and Prince Sts).
Ukrainian Museum, 203 Second Ave (between E. 12th and E. 13th Sts).

Gardens
Alice Austen House Museum, 2 Hylan Blvd (at Bay St), Staten Island.
Bartow-Pell Mansion Museum, Pelham Bay Park, 895 Shore Rd, Bronx.
Brooklyn Botanic Garden, 1000 Washington Ave (at Eastern Pkwy), Brooklyn.
Central Park, Conservatory Garden (Fifth Ave and 103rd St).

The Cloisters, Metropolitan Museum of Art, Fort Tryon Park.
Mount Vernon Hotel Museum and Garden, 421 E. 61st St (between First and York Aves).
New York Botanical Garden, E. 200th St and Southern Blvd, Bronx.
Queens Botanical Garden, 43-50 Main St (at Dahlia Ave), Flushing, Queens.
Snug Harbor Cultural Center, 1000 Richmond Terrace, Staten Island.
Staten Island Botanical Garden, Snug Harbor Cultural Center, 1000 Richmond Terrace, Staten Island.
Wave Hill, W. 249th St and Independence Ave, Bronx.

Historic Buildings, Local History

Alice Austen House Museum, 2 Hylan Blvd (at Bay St), Staten Island.
Bartow-Pell Mansion Museum, Pelham Bay Park, 895 Shore Rd, Bronx.
Bowne House, 37-01 Bowne St (at 37th Ave), Flushing, Queens.
Brooklyn Museum of Art, 200 Eastern Pkwy, Brooklyn.
Brooklyn's History Museum, 128 Pierrepont St (at Clinton St), Brooklyn.
Castle Clinton National Monument, Battery Park.
Conference House, Conference House Park, 7455 Hylan Blvd, Staten Island.
Cooper-Hewitt National Design Museum, Smithsonian Institution, former Andrew Carnegie Mansion, 2 E. 91st St (at Fifth Ave).
Dyckman Farmhouse Museum, 4881 Broadway (at W. 204th St).
Edgar Allan Poe Cottage, in Poe Park, 2460 Grand Concourse (at E. Kingsbridge Rd), Bronx.
Ellis Island Immigration Museum, Statue of Liberty National Monument.
Federal Hall National Memorial, 26 Wall St (at Broad St).
Fraunces Tavern Museum, 54 Pearl St (at Broad St).
The Frick Collection, 1 E. 70th St (at Fifth Ave).
The Friends Meeting House, 137-16 Northern Blvd (at Main St), Flushing, Queens.
Garibaldi-Meucci Museum, 420 Tompkins Ave (at Chestnut Ave), Staten Island.
General Grant National Memorial, in Riverside Park (at Riverside Drive and W. 122nd St).
Gracie Mansion, in Carl Schurz Park, (at E. 89th St and East End Ave).
Hall of Fame for Great Americans, Bronx Community College of the City University of New York (at University Ave and W. 181st St), Bronx.
Hamilton Grange National Memorial, 287 Convent Ave (between W. 141st and W. 142nd Sts).
Harbor Defense Museum of New York City, Fort Hamilton (at 101st St and Fort Hamilton Pkwy), Brooklyn.
Historic Richmond Town, in La Tourette Park, 441 Clarke Ave (at St. Patrick's Place), Staten Island.
Jewish Museum, former Felix Warburg Mansion, 1109 Fifth Ave (at 92nd St).
King Manor Museum, 150th St and Jamaica Ave, Jamaica, Queens.
Kingsland Homestead, in Weeping Beech Park, 143-35 37th Ave, Flushing, Queens.
Lefferts Homestead Children's Historic House Museum, in Prospect Park, at Flatbush Ave and Empire Blvd, Brooklyn.

Lower East Side Tenement Museum, 90 Orchard St (at Broome St).
Merchant's House Museum, 29 E. 4th St (between Lafayette St and Bowery).
Morgan Library, 29 E. 36th St (at Madison Ave).
Morris-Jumel Mansion, in Roger Morris Park, 65 Jumel Terrace (at W. 160th St, east of St. Nicholas Ave).
Mount Vernon Hotel Museum and Garden, 421 E. 61st St (between First and York Aves).
Museum of Bronx History, Valentine-Varian House, 3266 Bainbridge Ave (at E. 208th St), Bronx.
Museum of the City of New York, 1220 Fifth Ave (at 103rd St). Scheduled to move to 52 Chambers St in 2003.
National Museum of the American Indian, 1 Bowling Green (between State and Whitehall Sts).
New-York Historical Society, 2 W. 77th St (at Central Park West).
New York Public Library: Humanities and Social Sciences Library (at Fifth Ave and 42nd St).
Queens County Farm Museum, 73-50 Little Neck Pkwy, Floral Park, Queens.
Seguine Mansion, in Lemon Creek Park, 440 Seguine Ave, Staten Island.
Snug Harbor Cultural Center, 1000 Richmond Terrace, Staten Island.
South Street Seaport Museum, 12 Fulton St (near the East River).
Theodore Roosevelt Birthplace, 28 E. 20th St (between Broadway and Park Ave South).
Van Cortlandt House Museum, in Van Cortlandt Park (Broadway at W. 246th St), Bronx.

Judaica and Jewish History
Center for Jewish History, 15 W. 16th St (between Fifth and Sixth Aves).
Ellis Island Immigration Museum, Statue of Liberty National Monument.
Hebrew Union College–Jewish Institute of Religion, 1 W. 4th St (at Mercer St).
Judaica Museum, Hebrew Home for the Aged at Riverdale, 5961 Palisade Ave (at W. 261st St), Bronx.
Jewish Museum, 1109 Fifth Ave (at 92nd St).
Lower East Side Tenement Museum, 90 Orchard St (at Broome St).
Museum of Jewish Heritage: A Living Memorial to the Holocaust, 18 First Place (in Battery Park City).

Maritime History
Harbor Defense Museum of New York City, Fort Hamilton (at 101st St and Fort Hamilton Pkwy), Brooklyn.
Intrepid Sea Air Space Museum, Pier 86 (at W. 46th St and Twelfth Ave).
Museum of the City of New York, 1220 Fifth Ave (at 103rd St). Scheduled to move to 52 Chambers St in 2003.
South Street Seaport Museum, 12 Fulton St (near the East River).

Medieval Art
The Cloisters, Metropolitan Museum of Art, Fort Tryon Park.
Metropolitan Museum of Art, 1000 Fifth Ave (at 82nd St).
Morgan Library, 29 E. 36th St (at Madison Ave).

Modern Art

Brooklyn Museum of Art, 200 Eastern Pkwy, Brooklyn.
Metropolitan Museum of Art, 1000 Fifth Ave (at 82nd St).
Museum of Modern Art, 11 W. 53rd St (between Fifth and Sixth Aves).
New Museum of Contemporary Art, 583 Broadway (between Prince and Houston Sts).
P.S. 1 Museum, 22-25 Jackson Ave (at 46th Ave), Queens.
Solomon R. Guggenheim Museum, 1071 Fifth Ave (at 89th St).
Whitney Museum of American Art, 945 Madison Ave (at E. 75th St).

Planetarium

Rose Center for Earth and Space, American Museum of Natural History, Central Park West at 81st St.

Science and Technology

American Museum of Natural History, Central Park West at W. 79th St.
Brooklyn Children's Museum, 145 Brooklyn Ave (at St. Marks Ave), Brooklyn.
Children's Museum of Manhattan, 212 W. 83rd St (between Broadway and Amsterdam Ave).
Intrepid Sea Air Space Museum, Pier 86 (at W. 46th St and Twelfth Ave).
New York Academy of Sciences, 2 E. 63rd St (at Fifth Ave).
New York Hall of Science, in Flushing Meadows–Corona Park, 47-01 111th St (at Forty-ninth Ave), Corona Park, Queens.
Sony Wonder Technology Lab, 550 Madison Ave (at E. 50th St).
Staten Island Children's Museum, in Snug Harbor Cultural Center, Staten Island.

Zoos, Aquarium

Aquarium for Wildlife Conservation, W. 8th St at Surf Ave, Brooklyn.
Bronx Zoo, Fordham Rd at Bronx River Pkwy, Bronx.
Central Park Wildlife Center, in Central Park, at 64th St and Fifth Ave.
Prospect Park Wildlife Center, in Prospect Park, Brooklyn.
Queens Wildlife Center, in Flushing Meadows–Corona Park, Queens.
Staten Island Zoo, 614 Broadway (between Forest Ave and Clove Rd), Staten Island.

Art Exhibitions

Most **art museums** are open Tues–Sat 10–5 and Sun 12–5, and many are open at least one evening per week. **Galleries,** like museums, are usually open Tues–Sat from around 10 or 11 in the morning until 5 or 6 in the afternoon. Many close for part of the summer. There are extensive gallery listings in *Time Out New York, New York* magazine, *The New Yorker,* and the Weekend section in the Fri edition of the *New York Times.*

Commercial Art Galleries

New York has hundreds of commercial art galleries, where you can search out emerging talent or view the work of established artists. Some have historical or thematic exhibitions of museum quality that explore in depth a particular artist or some aspect of art.

Before the 1970s, the center of gallery activity was around E. 57th St and Madison Ave. SoHo burgeoned in the 1970s; for a while in the early 1980s the East Village was a hotbed of artistic activity. As SoHo became too expensive, the art scene expanded south into TriBeCa and then north to western Chelsea, around W. 22nd St on the far West Side. Other galleries and art spaces are scattered throughout the city including the boroughs. The best sources of information about current exhibitions are the *New York Times* (Fri and Sun editions), *New York* magazine, *The New Yorker*, and *Time Out New York*.

Auction Houses

New York is a major world auction center, where everything from van Gogh masterpieces to last year's memorabilia goes on the block. *The New Yorker, New York* magazine, and the Sunday *New York Times* have schedules of sales, as do the Web sites of the individual houses. The auction season runs Sept–June.

Christie's, 20 Rockefeller Plaza (at Fifth Ave), ☎ (212) 636-2000; **Christie's East,** 219 E. 67th St (at Third Ave), ☎ (212) 606-0400; Web site for both galleries: www.christies.com. The gallery at Rockefeller Plaza auctions major paintings, jewelry, antique furniture, and rare wines; the East Side branch sells less expensive works.
Sotheby's, 1334 York Ave (at E. 72nd St); ☎ (212) 606-7000; Web site: www.sothebys.com. Offers a wide range: baseball cards, Rembrandts, Tiffany lamps.
Swann Galleries, 1025 E. 25th St (at Lexington Ave); ☎ (212) 254-4710. Auctions of rare and antiquarian books, maps, autographs and manuscripts, photographs, prints and drawings, and vintage posters.
William Doyle Galleries, 175 E. 87th St (at Third Ave); ☎ (212) 427-2730; Web site: www.doylenewyork.com. The house is especially known for its sales of porcelain and silver, jewelry, furniture and decorative arts, and its auctions of the estates of celebrities, including Gloria Swanson and cookbook author James Beard.

Calendar of Events, Festivals, and Parades

This is just a sampling of the parades, festivals, street fairs, and other events that take place, often on weekends, in the city. For dates, times, locations: call NYC & Company, ☎ (212) 484-1200; Web site: www.nycvisit.com. Two other informative Web sites are: www.carnaval.com/cityguides/newyork/parades.htm and www.metrobase.com/newyork/metro.exe?homepage.exe.

January

Jan 1, New Year's Day, public holiday.
Three Kings Day Parade, Spanish Harlem, begins at Fifth Ave and 104th St.
National Boat Show, at Javits Center.
Martin Luther King Jr. Birthday (Mon closest to Jan 19), public holiday.
Chinese New Year, end of Jan or early Feb, Chinatown.

February

President's Day, third Mon in Feb, public holiday.
Black History Month, citywide programs.

Westminster Kennel Club Dog Show, Madison Square Garden.

Empire State Building Run-Up. Invitational race up 86 stories.

March

St. Patrick's Day Parade, March 17, Fifth Ave from 44th to 86th Sts. Bands and marchers from Ireland and elsewhere, bagpipes, and beer (much of it green, served at pubs and bars). Reviewing stand at 65th St.

Ringling Bros. and Barnum & Bailey Circus, Madison Square Garden. Late March or early April.

Greek Independence Day Parade, March 25 or a Sun near that date (date shifted during Orthodox Lent), Fifth Ave from 61st to 79th Sts. School bands, floats, Greek music.

April

April Fool's Day Parade, April 1, Fifth Ave from 59th St to Washington Square Park. Since 1986. Floats, bands, spectator participation. Produced by prankster Jerry Scaggs.

New York International Auto Show, Javits Center. Hot cars of today plus hundreds of concept cars for the future.

Easter floral displays: Rockefeller Center, Brooklyn Botanic Garden, New York Botanical Garden in the Bronx.

Easter Parade on Fifth Ave, Easter Sun 10–4. Informal parade (no bands), but extravagant costumes, spring finery, creative hats. Fifth Ave from 49th to 57th Sts. Open to all.

Macy's Flower Show. Thousands of plants from around the world.

Cherry Blossom Festival, Brooklyn Botanic Garden.

May

Memorial Day, last Mon, public holiday.

Bike New York. Five-borough bike tour; 42 miles of traffic-free roads.

Ninth Avenue International Food Festival, weekend event, 11 A.M.–7 P.M.; Ninth Ave between W. 37th and W. 57th Sts. Ethnic food in abundance.

Cuban Day Parade, early May, Sun, on Sixth Ave from W. 44th to W. 58th Sts.

Norwegian American Parade, Sun closest to May 17, 90th St and Fifth Ave, Brooklyn.

Fleet Week, *Intrepid* Sea-Air-Space Museum, W. 46th St and Twelfth Ave (at Hudson River). Military and naval celebration, parade of ships, events, thousands of sailors in uniform.

Turkish American Day Parade, 1 P.M.; from Madison Ave between E. 56th St and E. 57th Sts to Dag Hammarskjöld Plaza at Second Ave and E. 47th St.

Memorial Day Parades, all boroughs.

Washington Square Outdoor Art Show, Greenwich Village, weekends, noon–sundown, late May or early June.

June

Metropolitan Opera in parks, all five boroughs.

Museum Mile Celebration, Fifth Ave between 82nd and 105th Sts. Museums stay open late, special exhibitions, weekday, early June.

Welcome Back to Brooklyn Festival at Grand Army Plaza, Brooklyn. An international exposition of food, music, and entertainment. Early June.

Feast of St. Anthony of Padua, Sullivan St south of Houston St in SoHo, early to mid-June. Italian street fair, procession with saint's image.

Church of Our Lady of Carmel, St. Anthony's Feast, E. 187th St near Arthur Ave, Bronx.

Belmont Stakes at Belmont Racetrack, Elmont, Long Island. The third jewel of the Triple Crown.

Puerto Rican Day Parade, Fifth Ave between 44th and 86th Sts, usually first or second Sun in June.

JVC Jazz Festival, mid-June. Famous jazz festival, originated at Newport, Rhode Island; performances in various venues.

St. Paulinus Festival, Williamsburg, Brooklyn. Italian street festival, late June–mid-July. Procession with towering monument to Our Lady of Mt. Carmel Church.

Mermaid Parade, Sat in late June, boardwalk at Coney Island. Marchers dressed as mermaids and King Neptune.

Gay and Lesbian Gay Pride March, Sun in late June, from Columbus Circle to Christopher St. Commemorates Stonewall Riots of 1968. Other events citywide.

Shakespeare in the Park, through Aug. Delacorte Theater, Central Park at 81st St.

Restaurant Week, lunch for $20 at top restaurants. Check the *New York Times* or www.restaurantweek.com.

July

Independence Day, July 4, public holiday. Events at Battery Park and in the rivers around Lower Manhattan. Great fireworks displays from barges in rivers around the city, sponsored by Macy's.

Nathan's Fourth of July Hot Dog Eating Contest, at Nathan's Famous in Coney Island, Brooklyn.

Mostly Mozart Festival at Lincoln Center, Avery Fisher Hall.

Feast of Our Lady of Mt. Carmel, E. 116th St and 1st Ave, in former Little Italy; evening celebrations, mid-July. Also festivals in Our Lady of Mt. Carmel Churches in Brooklyn and Bronx.

New York Philharmonic concerts in major parks, free, late July–early Aug.

Lincoln Center Festival, with drama, dance, opera, and other events.

August

Harlem Week, mid-Aug. Parades, art exhibitions, jazz, dance contests, sports clinics taught by prominent athletes, tours of Harlem landmarks.

India Day Parade, third Sun, Madison Ave between E. 41st and E. 23rd Sts.

Pakistani Independence Parade, fourth Sun, Madison Ave between E. 41st and E. 23rd Sts. Celebrates Pakistani independence. Also smaller street festival.

Tap-O-Mania, mid- or late Aug; W. 34th St between Seventh Ave and Broadway. Another of Macy's contributions to city life; thousands of dancers tap out a routine in front of the store.

Tugboat Challenge, *Intrepid* Sea-Air-Space Museum. Crews from New York tugboats, pushing competition, races, line-throwing contest.

Lincoln Center Out-of-Doors. Free music and dance.

New York International Fringe Festival (Fringe NYC), mid- to late Aug. Two weeks of theater, dance, puppetry, multimedia, and other events, held in 20 different venues throughout the Lower East Side. Close to 200 different theater companies and performing artists from all over the world participate.

U.S. Open Tennis Championships at the National Tennis Center in Flushing Meadows–Corona Park, Queens, late Aug–early Sept. America's Grand Slam tennis event.

September

Labor Day, first Mon in Sept, public holiday.

Labor Day Parade, Fifth Ave from 44th to 72nd Sts, first Mon, morning.

West Indian American Day Carnevale in Brooklyn. Labor Day weekend with parade on Mon, all day, along Eastern Pkwy from Utica Ave to the Brooklyn Museum. Floats, extravagant costumes, West Indian music, dancing in the streets, food. Huge event.

BAM Next Wave Festival, Brooklyn Academy of Music. Showcase of avant-garde music, dance, drama, of famous and lesser-known artists.

Broadway on Broadway. Free outdoor show in Times Square features music from current Broadway shows.

Fall Flower Exhibition, New York Botanical Garden, Bronx.

Brazilian Day, W. 46th St, first Sun. Street festival commemorating Brazil's independence from Portugal. Food, music, crafts, samba performances, dancing in the street.

Feast of San Gennaro in Little Italy on Mulberry St between E. Houston St and Worth St, morning–night, about ten days in mid-Sept. Street fair, food and games, procession with saint's image carried through the streets.

New York Film Festival, Lincoln Center, late Sept to early Oct.

New York Is Book Country, Fifth Ave between 48th and 57th Sts, and Madison Ave between E. 52nd and E. 53rd Sts, Sat in mid-Sept, 11–5. Stalls, carts, booths with publishers, authors, books, clowns, balloons.

German American Steuben Day Parade, third Sat, on Fifth Ave from 63rd to 86th Sts, noon. Bands, floats, costumed folk dancers march to honor Baron von Steuben, who assisted Washington during the Revolutionary War.

October

Columbus Day, second Mon in Oct, public holiday.

Feast of St. Francis, blessing of the animals, Cathedral of St. John the Divine (Amsterdam Ave at W. 112th St). Booths with environmental themes.

Pulaski Day Parade, Fifth Ave from 26th to 52nd Sts, first Sun, noon. Celebrates Polish hero of the American Revolution.

Hispanic Day Parade, Fifth Ave from 44th to 72nd Sts and east to Third Ave, second Sun mid-month, 11 A.M.

Columbus Day Parade, Fifth Ave between 44th and 79th Sts, 11 A.M., with Italian American groups, bands, floats, beauty queens. Street festival on Lower Broadway.

Halloween events: Parade in Greenwich Village, Sixth Ave from Spring St to W. 23rd St (Oct 31, early evening). Halloween on Haunted Walk, at New York Botanical Garden, Bronx. Halloween Carnival, Chelsea Piers. Boo at the Zoo, Halloween events at Bronx Zoo. Other events.

November

Election Day, first Tues, public holiday.

Thanksgiving, fourth Thurs, public holiday.

Big Apple Circus, tent in Damrosch Park, Lincoln Center.

New York City Marathon, 26.2-mile race through the five boroughs, Sun late in Oct or early in Nov. Begins at Verrazano Bridge 10:30 A.M. and finishes at Tavern-on-the-Green in Central Park.

Veterans Day Parade, Fifth Ave from 39th to 24th Sts, Nov 11 (morning).

Thanksgiving Parade, Thanksgiving Day, Central Park West from W. 77th to W. 59th Sts, then down Broadway to Macy's at W. 34th St. Floats, bands, giant helium-filled balloons pulled by more than 1,000 attendants. When the parade reaches Macy's, Santa Claus arrives, opening the Christmas season.

Christmas windows along Fifth Ave. Especially: Lord & Taylor (39th St), Saks Fifth Ave (50th St), F.A.O. Schwarz (58th St). The tree and illuminated angels in the Channel Gardens at Rockefeller Center attract large crowds. Office buildings on Park Ave below 50th St have lavish displays.

Singing Christmas Tree, South Street Seaport, through Jan.

Radio City Music Hall Christmas spectacular begins. Christmas pageant, Rockettes, mid-Nov to early Jan.

Planetarium Christmas show begins, late Nov or early Dec, Hayden Planetarium, Rose Center, American Museum of Natural History.

New York City Ballet, fall season, New York State Theater, Lincoln Center, including the ever-popular *Nutcracker.*

December

Christmas, Dec 25, public holiday.

Christmas and Hanukkah holiday celebrations citywide. Christmas tree lightings at Rockefeller Center, City Hall, other borough halls. Hanukkah candle lighting at City Hall. Hanukkah Menorah, Grand Army Plaza, 5th Ave at 59th St. Tuba Christmas, Rockefeller Center, brass choirs.

Christmas decorations and programs in museums. Large Christmas tree with 18C Neapolitan carved angels and crèche figures in Medieval Sculpture Hall, Metropolitan Museum of Art. Special holiday displays at The Cloisters, Museum of the City of New York, Jewish Museum.

New Year's Eve in Times Square, recommended only for those undaunted by celebratory crowds. Midnight ball drop. Midnight fireworks and a midnight run in Central Park sponsored by the New York Road Runners Club. New Year's Eve Concert for Peace at Cathedral of St. John the Divine.

Sports

Spectator Sports

New York has professional baseball, football, basketball, and ice hockey teams and hosts important tennis tournaments and track and field meets. New York fans are intensely loyal to their teams, and tickets are often difficult to get.

Many events (basketball, boxing, figure skating, indoor track, and others) take place at **Madison Square Garden** (Seventh Ave and W. 33rd St); box office ☎ (212) 465-6741, or Ticketmaster, ☎ (212) 307-7171.

Baseball

The season runs from early April to Oct with New York's two teams, the Yankees and the Mets, each playing 81 home games, many at night. The **Yankees** occupy **Yankee Stadium** (E. 161st St and River Ave in the Bronx). For tickets, call Ticketmaster, ☎ (212) 307-1212. For stadium tours, ☎ (718) 579-4531. Web site: www.yankees.com. Tickets are also available at the stadium and at Yankee Clubhouse Stores.

Getting to Yankee Stadium

Subway: Lexington Ave Express (4) uptown to 161st St–Yankee Stadium or Sixth Ave Express (D) to the same stop.

Car: Take Major Deegan Expwy to Grand Concourse; go north on Grand Concourse to E. 161st St; turn left to the stadium. Car parking available; traffic is usually heavy just before game time.

Boat: New York Waterway's *Yankee Clipper* travels upriver to the stadium from the East Side; ☎ (800) 533-3779 or (800) 755-4000 (outside New York, New Jersey, Connecticut); Web site: www.nywaterway.com.

The **Mets'** home turf is **Shea Stadium** at Flushing Meadows–Corona Park in Queens; for tickets, ☎ (718) 507-8499, or access their Web site: www.nymets.com. Tickets are also available at the stadium and at New York Mets Clubhouse Shops.

Getting to Shea Stadium

Subway: Flushing Local (7) to Willets Point–Shea Stadium.

Car: Take Grand Central Pkwy or Northern Blvd to Flushing Meadows Park; follow signs to Shea Stadium.

Boat: New York Waterway's *Mets Express* travels to the stadium from the East Side; ☎ (800) 533-3779 or (800) 755-4000 (outside New York, New Jersey, Connecticut); Web site: www.nywaterway.com.

The **Brooklyn Cyclones** occupy **KeySpan Park**, 1904 Surf Ave (between W. 17th and W. 19th Sts in Coney Island). Their 76-game season runs from June through Sept, with 38 home dates. Game times: Mon–Fri 7 P.M.; Sat 6 P.M.; Sun 5 P.M. Tickets range from $5 to $10; ☎ (718) 449-8497. Web site: www.cyclones.net.

Getting to KeySpan Park

Subway: Sixth Ave Express or Local (B, D, F) or Broadway Local (N) to Coney Island–Stillwell Ave. Walk toward Surf Ave. The ballpark is two blocks away.

Bus: B36, B64, or B74 to Stillwell and Surf Aves.

Car: Take the Belt Pkwy to Ocean Pkwy South. Drive on Ocean Pkwy to Surf Ave. Continue for half a mile on Surf Ave.

The **Staten Island Yankees** play at **Richmond County Bank Ballpark at St. George,** 2025 Richmond Terrace, from June through Sept. Game times: Mon–Sat 7:35 P.M.; Sun 5:05 P.M. Tickets for their 38 home games range from $8 to $10; ☎ (718) 698-9265. Web site: www.siyanks.com.

Getting to Richmond County Bank Ballpark

Subway and ferry: Take the Lexington Ave Express (4, 5) to Bowling Green, then catch the free Staten Island Ferry. Depart the ferry from the bottom deck; the park is on your right.

Car: Cross Verrazano-Narrows Bridge to the Hylan Blvd exit. Take a right on Hylan Blvd and drive to Bay St. Turn left on Bay St and drive for about 2.3 miles, just past the ferry terminal.

Basketball

The **New York Knicks** (officially the Knickerbockers) play home games (Oct–April) at Madison Square Garden; for ticket information, call the New York Knicks Fanline, ☎ (212) 465-5867, or Ticketmaster, ☎ (212) 307-7171. Web site: www.nba.com/knicks.

The **New Jersey Nets,** formerly of New York, now play in East Rutherford, New Jersey, at the Meadowlands in the Continental Airlines Arena (on Rte 3); for ticket information, call the box office, ☎ (201) 935-3900, or Ticketmaster, ☎ (201) 507-8900 or (212) 307-7171. Web site: www.nba.com/nets.

The **New York Liberty,** in the Women's National Basketball Association, play home games in the summer (June–Aug) at Madison Square Garden; for ticket information, ☎ (212) 564-9622 or Ticketmaster, ☎ (877) WNBA-TIX. Web site: www.wnba.com/liberty.

Boxing

Once the top venue for boxing, Madison Square Garden still hosts professional matches; ☎ (212) 465-6741.

Football

The two professional teams, the **New York Jets** and the **New York Giants,** now play at Giants Stadium in the New Jersey Meadowlands. The season runs Sept–Jan. Tickets are extremely difficult to get.

For **Jets** ticket information, ☎ (201) 935-3900; or access their Web site: www.newyorkjets.com. For **Giants** ticket information, ☎ (201) 935-8222; or check out their Web site: www.nfl.com/giants.

Getting to the Meadowlands

Bus: Buses leave from the Port Authority Bus Terminal (W. 42nd St and Eighth Ave) two hours before game time and return up to one hour after the game (20-minute travel time); ☎ (212) 564-8484.

Car: Take the Lincoln Tunnel from Manhattan; follow Rte 3 west to exit 16W.

Ice Hockey

The season runs Oct–April. The **New York Rangers** play at Madison Square Garden. For ticket information, ☎ (212) 465-6741, or Ticketmaster, ☎ (212) 307-7171; Web site: www.newyorkrangers.com.

The **New York Islanders** skate at Nassau Veterans Memorial Coliseum in Uniondale, Long Island. Call the box office at ☎ (516) 888-9000 or (516) 794-

9300, or Ticketmaster at ☎ (212) 307-7171; Web site: www.newyork islanders.com.

Getting to the Nassau Coliseum

Train and Bus: Take the Long Island Rail Road to the Hempstead train station; walk one block to the Hempstead Bus Terminal. Take bus N70, N71, or N72, which will drop you off on Hempstead Turnpike opposite the coliseum. For information for all buses to and from the Nassau Coliseum, ☎ (516) 766-6722.

Car: From Manhattan, take Midtown Tunnel to Long Island Expwy (I-495); follow expressway east to exit 38 (Northern State Pkwy); continue to exit 31A (Meadowbrook Pkwy South); continue to exit M4; follow signs to the Nassau Coliseum. Or take Triborough Bridge to Grand Central Pkwy, which turns into the Northern State Pkwy; follow it to exit 31A (Meadowbrook Pkwy South); continue to exit M4; follow signs to the Nassau Coliseum.

The home ice of the **New Jersey Devils** is the Continental Airlines Arena at the Meadowlands in New Jersey. For tickets, ☎ (201) 935-3900, or Ticketmaster, ☎ (201) 507-8900 or (212) 307-7171; Web site: www.newjerseydevils.com. For directions, see above section on Football.

Horse Racing

Aqueduct Racetrack, at Rockaway Blvd and 110th St in Ozone Park, Queens; ☎ (718) 641-4700; Web site: www.nyra.com/aqueduct. Thoroughbred racing Oct–May; closed Mon and Tues.

Getting to Aqueduct

Subway: Eighth Ave Express (A) to Aqueduct–N. Conduit Ave station. Courtesy Bus service is available to the Admission Gate.

Car: From Manhattan, take Midtown Tunnel to Long Island Expwy East; continue to Van Wyck Expwy South; take exit 3 (Linden Blvd). Turn right on Linden and follow signs to track.

Belmont Park, at 2150 Hempstead Turnpike in Elmont, Long Island, just beyond the Queens border; ☎ (718) 641-4700; Web site: www.nyra.com/belmont. Season runs May–July, late Aug–mid-Oct. The Belmont Stakes in June is the final leg of the Triple Crown for three-year-olds after the Kentucky Derby and the Preakness Stakes.

Getting to Belmont

Subway: Sixth Ave Local (F) to 169th St or 179th St; then take the N6 or the Q2 bus to Belmont. Or Eighth Ave Local (E) to Jamaica Center–Parsons/Archer and Q10 bus to Belmont.

Car: From Manhattan, take Queens Midtown Tunnel to Long Island Expwy; continue east to Cross Island Pkwy; then go south to exit 26D.

Meadowlands Racetrack, at the Meadowlands Sports Complex, ☎ (201) 935-8500; Web site: www.thebigm.com. Harness racing, Jan–Aug; thoroughbred racing, Sept–Nov. For directions, see above under Football.

Running

The biggest event of the year is the New York City Marathon, an early-Nov institution since 1970, organized by the New York Road Runners Club; ☎ (212) 860-4455; Web site: nyrrc.org. The course covers all five boroughs and finishes in Central Park.

Soccer

The **MetroStars** play at Giants Stadium in the Meadowlands. The season runs Apr–Sept; ☎ (201) 395-3900 or (888) 4METROTIX; Web site: www.metro stars.com.

Tennis

The **U.S. Open Tennis Championships,** are played (late Aug–early Sept) at the National Tennis Center in Flushing Meadows–Corona Park, Queens. Tickets go on sale in May; ☎ (888) OPENTIX. Tickets for the second week of the tournament are usually sold out well in advance, but it is possible to get tickets to the earlier rounds when more matches are played on a single day.

Participant Sports

Most public parks have **playing fields.** In Central Park the athletic fields are south of 66th St on the West Side and south of the reservoir in the center of the park. A circular drive, called Park Drive in its entirety, girds the park. Its name changes according to its location (i.e., East Drive on the East Side); several side roads cross from east and west.

Cycling

Central Park is closed to vehicular traffic weekdays 10 A.M.–3 P.M. and 7 P.M.–10 P.M.; weekends from 7 P.M. Fri until 6 A.M. Mon. On holidays the automobile ban begins at 7 P.M. the night before the holiday and lasts until 6 A.M. the day after. The circular drive offers a 6.1-mile route with several hills as well as several shorter options.

In **Central Park,** you can rent bicycles at Loeb Boathouse (East Side between 74th and 75th Sts); ☎ (212) 861-4137. Expect to leave a hefty deposit or a credit card. There is a shorter (3.3 mile) circular road in **Prospect Park** in Brooklyn, with equally pretty views. **Riverside Park,** between W. 72nd and W. 110th Sts, offers views of the Hudson River.

Ice Skating

The most memorable place to skate, especially during the Christmas season, is the **Rink at Rockefeller Plaza,** open from about Nov to March; ☎ (212) 332-7654. Telephone ahead for schedule; there are several skating sessions daily and the admission price applies only to one session. The rink is often very crowded; it's better for ambience than it is for serious skating.

Central Park rinks (generally open Nov–March for ice skating): **Wollman Memorial Rink** in Central Park (East Side between 62nd and 63rd Sts), ☎ (212) 396-1010; **Lasker Memorial Rink** in the northern part (midpark between 108th and 109th Sts); ☎ (212) 396-1010. Lasker is usually less crowded than Wollman.

Riverbank State Park Skating Rink, 679 Riverside Drive (at W. 145th St), ☎ 694-3642, is a covered outdoor rink with good ice conditions.

Also in Manhattan, at **Chelsea Piers** (Pier 61, W. 23rd St at the Hudson River) is the **Sky Rink,** ☎ (212) 336-6100. The two indoor rinks at this facility have recreational skating, ice hockey, lessons, and special events.

In **Brooklyn's Prospect Park,** the **Kate Wollman Memorial Rink** is open in season; ☎ (718) 287-6431. In **Queens,** there's the **World's Fair Ice Skating Rink,** (Flushing Meadows–Corona Park, in the former New York City Building); ☎ (718) 271-1996.

Horseback Riding

For Central Park, call the **Claremont Riding Academy,** 175 W. 89th St (between Columbus and Amsterdam Aves); ☎ (212) 724-5100. For experienced riders.

Rollerblading and Skating

Central Park draws skaters of all levels. The circular road (East Drive, North Drive, etc.) makes a 6.1-mile circuit of the park. The New York Roller Skating Association sets up weekend slalom courses on West Drive near W. 67th St. The **Central Park Skate Patrol** gives free stopping clinics on weekends, April–Oct; ☎ (212) 439-1234. Center Drive, east of the Sheep Meadow, is also known as Skaters Rd; the part just south of 72nd St draws roller dancers on weekends.

Time's Up!, an environmental group, organizes bike rides and skating tours; ☎ (212) 802-8222; Web site: www.times-up.org. The **Empire Skate Club** organizes group events; ☎ (212) 774-1774; Web site: www.empireskate.org.

Other venues: **Hudson River Park Esplanade** (W. 14th St to Battery Park); **Chelsea Piers** (W. 23rd St at the Hudson River) has two outdoor rinks and a skatepark, ☎ (212) 336-6200; the **Roxy,** 515 W. 18th St (between Tenth and Eleventh Aves), ☎ (212) 645-5156.

Running

In **Central Park** the favorite spot is the track circling the **Jacqueline Kennedy Onassis Reservoir,** but other park roads are also well used. **Riverside Park** has beautiful views for runners and cyclists. Downtown sites include the **Battery Park City Esplanade** and the **East River Esplanade** (E. 59th St and north).

Views of the Manhattan skyline add to the appeal of the **Brooklyn Heights Promenade** (only about ⅓ mile long). There is a loop in **Prospect Park** (3.3 miles).

The New York Road Runners Club, 9 E. 89th St, ☎ (212) 860-4455, Web site: www.nyrrc.org, sponsors the New York Marathon and organizes group runs in Central Park all year. Groups meet at the Safety Kiosk in the park at 90th St and Fifth Ave: weekdays at 6:30 A.M., and 6:30 P.M.

Swimming

The Parks Department operates 33 outdoor and 10 indoor pools, and while free, they are often very crowded and sometimes rowdy. Two pools near Midtown are the **John Jay Pool,** east of York Ave and E. 77th St, ☎ (212) 794-6566; and the **Asser Levy Pool,** at Asser Levy Place and E. 23rd St, ☎ (212) 447-2020.

The **Westside Y,** 5 W. 63rd St (between Central Park West and Broadway), ☎

(212) 787-4400 has pools, sauna, running track, exercise rooms, handball, squash, and racquetball courts. The **Vanderbilt YMCA,** 224 E. 47th St (between Second and Third Aves), ☎ (212) 756-9600 has a pool, gym, and sauna.

Chelsea Piers Sports Center, Pier 60 (W. 23rd St at the Hudson River), ☎ (212) 336-6000, features a pool (25 yds) overlooking the Hudson River. Day passes available.

Tennis

The Parks Department maintains public courts for city residents, open mid-April–Oct; seasonal passes available at the Arsenal (in Central Park, at Fifth Ave and 64th St); ☎ (212) 360-8131 for permit information. You can buy a daily pass at the Central Park Courts (midpark between W. 94th and W. 95th Sts) for one hour of singles on any city-owned court (list of courts obtainable from the Parks Department in the Arsenal or at their Web site: www.ci.nyc.ny.us/html/dpr). There are 26 fast-dry and 4 hard courts in Central Park. ☎ (212) 280-0201 for the Central Park Tennis Center.

USTA National Tennis Center, at the Flushing Meadows–Corona Park in Queens, ☎ (718) 760-5100 has 36 courts outdoors and 9 indoors. It's open to the public except when the national championships are being played (late Aug–early Sept).

Performing Arts

Theater

Theater in New York can be divided into three categories: Broadway, Off-Broadway, and Off-Off-Broadway. Proximity to or distance from Broadway in these terms, however, is not merely geographical but also economic and artistic. The **Broadway** theater represents the Establishment, the center of commercial theater in America. Its houses are located mainly north of Times Square between about W. 42rd and W. 53rd Sts; most are large, seating more than a thousand spectators. They have given rise to a special genre, the Broadway Production, gargantuan in scale, expensive in details of production, star-studded in personnel, and popular in appeal.

While the **Off-Broadway** movement may have originated in the years around World War I, when such groups as the Provincetown Players and the Washington Square Players burst upon the scene in Greenwich Village, it truly began to flourish in the early 1950s, notably with Jose Quintero's production in 1952 of Tennessee Williams's *Summer and Smoke,* which had failed four years earlier on Broadway but which became the first major theatrical success south of 42nd St in thirty years. According to Actors' Equity, Off-Broadway is defined by an exclusion clause that relegates its theaters (necessarily holding fewer than 300 spectators) to areas outside the Times Square Theater District, but which permits smaller work crews and lower wages, allowing for less-expensive productions and hence experimentation.

However, as Off-Broadway became more successful and less innocent commercially, the **Off-Off-Broadway** movement began to flourish, filling the spot that Off-Broadway occupied in its early days. Historians trace its beginnings to Alfred Jarry's *King Ubu,* which opened in the Take 3 coffeehouse in Greenwich Village in 1960, or to Ellen Stewart's Café La MaMa, which opened in a cellar on E. 12th St the same year. Off-Off-Broadway productions frequently occupy nontheatrical buildings—lofts, churches, coffeehouses—all over the city. Plays tend to be headily experimental or to deal with themes too radical for Broadway.

How to Get Tickets
Top prices for Broadway shows are currently around $80 (with the exception of the megahit, *The Producers*, where the best seats cost $100); Off-Broadway shows may run as high as $60; Off-Off-Broadway tickets usually cost less than $20.

By Phone
Tele-charge, ☎ (212) 239-6200; Web site: www.telecharge.com.
Ticketmaster, ☎ (212) 307-4100; Web site: www.ticketmaster.com.
   Both services allow you to reserve tickets for Broadway and Off-Broadway shows by using a major credit card; both add a surcharge and handling fee to the ticket price. Newspaper ads usually say which service handles tickets for a particular event. Ask about seat locations. The tickets can be mailed to you or held at the box office. Some Off- and Off-Off-Broadway productions accept Theater Development Fund (TDF) vouchers; a book of four costs $28; ☎ (212) 768-1818.
Ticket Central, ☎ (212) 279-4200, Web site: www.ticketcentral.org, acts as a box office for some Off-Broadway and Off-Off-Broadway shows; call 1–8 P.M. daily.

Ticket brokers sell tickets to popular, even sold-out, events. Expect to pay top dollar, sometimes more than triple the ticket price. NYC & Company has lists of brokers. Among them are: **Applause Entertainment NY,** ☎ (212) 307-7050 or (800) 451-9930; **Global Tickets from Edwards & Edwards,** ☎ (800) 223-6108; and **Keith Prowse & Co.,** ☎ (212) 398-1430 or (800) 669-8687; Web site: www.keithprowse.com.

In Person
Full-price tickets to Broadway shows are available at the **Broadway Ticket Center** in the Times Square Visitor Center at 1560 Broadway (between W. 46th and W. 47th Sts), open Mon–Sat 10 A.M.–7 P.M.; Sun 11 A.M.–6 P.M. You can also stop by a theater's box office for advance or same-day tickets.

Discounted tickets, available the day of performance, may be purchased at **tkts,** a service of the nonprofit Theater Development Fund (Web site: www.tdf.org). Their booth is located at the north end of Times Square (W. 47th St and Broadway). Prices depend on the show's popularity, but discounts can reach 50 percent of the box office price plus a handling fee. No phone purchases; no credit cards (cash, travelers' checks only). Many, but not all, shows are available, so have several choices in mind when you go. Hours: Mon–Sat 3–8 P.M.; Wed, Sat 10 A.M.–2 P.M.; Sun 11 A.M.–7 P.M.
   Same-day standing room tickets for sold-out shows and less desirable locations (front row, side orchestra, rear mezzanine) are sometimes available at the box office at reduced prices.

By Mail

Send a stamped self-addressed envelope, a list of several alternate dates, and a certified check or money order to the box office well in advance.

Broadway Theaters

Tickets for Broadway productions are handled by Ticketmaster, ☎ (212) 307-4100; or Tele-charge, ☎ (212) 239-6200.

Broadway theaters have devices for the hearing-impaired; for information, call Sound Associates, ☎ (212) 582-7678. For information about wheelchair accessibility, call Tele-charge, ☎ (212) 239-6200, or the box office of the individual theater. Most theaters are accessible to wheelchairs, but some restrooms are not.

Ambassador, 215 W. 49th St (between Broadway and Eighth Ave).
American Airlines Theatre, 227 W. 42nd St (between Seventh and Eighth Aves).
Belasco, 111 W. 44th St (between Sixth and Seventh Aves).
Booth, 222 W. 45th St (between Broadway and Eighth Ave).
Broadhurst, 235 W. 44th St (between Broadway and Eighth Ave).
Broadway, 1681 Broadway (at W. 53rd St).
Brooks Atkinson, 256 W. 47th St (between Broadway and Eighth Ave).
Cort, 138 W. 48th St (between Sixth and Seventh Aves).
Circle in the Square, 1633 Broadway (at W. 50th St).
Ethel Barrymore, 243 W. 47th St (between Broadway and Eighth Ave).
Eugene O'Neill, 230 W. 49th St (between Broadway and Eighth Ave).
Ford Center for the Performing Arts, 213 W. 42nd St (between Seventh and Eighth Aves).
Gershwin, 222 W. 51st St (between Broadway and Eighth Ave).
Golden, 252 W. 45th St (between Broadway and Eighth Ave).
Helen Hayes, 240 W. 44th St (between Broadway and Eighth Ave).
Imperial, 249 W. 45th St (between Broadway and Eighth Ave).
Longacre, 220 W. 48th St (between Broadway and Eighth Ave).
Lunt-Fontanne, 205 W. 46th St (between Broadway and Eighth Ave).
Lyceum, 149 W. 45th St (between Sixth and Seventh Aves).
Majestic, 245 W. 44th St (between Broadway and Eighth Ave).
Marquis, 1535 Broadway (between W. 45th and W. 46th Sts).
Martin Beck, 302 W. 45th St (between Eighth and Ninth Aves).
Minskoff, 1515 Broadway (at W. 45th St).
Music Box, 239 W. 45th St (between Broadway and Eighth Ave).
Nederlander, 208 W. 41st St (between Seventh and Eighth Aves).
Neil Simon, 250 W. 52nd St (between Broadway and Eighth Ave).
New Amsterdam, 214 W. 42nd St (between Seventh and Eighth Aves).
New Victory, 209 W. 42nd St (between Seventh and Eighth Aves).
Palace, 1564 Broadway (at W. 47th St).
Plymouth, 236 W. 45th St (between Broadway and Eighth Ave).

Richard Rodgers, 226 W. 46th St (between Broadway and Eighth Ave).
Royale, 242 W. 45th St (between Broadway and Eighth Ave).
Shubert, 225 W. 44th St (between Broadway and Eighth Ave).
St. James, 246 W. 44th St (between Broadway and Eighth Ave).
Virginia, 245 W. 52nd St (between Broadway and Eighth Ave).
Winter Garden, 1634 Broadway (between W. 50th and W. 51st Sts).

Major Off-Broadway Theaters

Actors Playhouse, 100 Seventh Ave South (between Grove and Bleecker Sts), ☎ (212) 239-6200.

American Place Theater, 111 W. 46th St (between Sixth and Seventh Aves), ☎ (212) 840-3074.

Astor Place Theatre, 434 Lafayette St (between Astor Place and E. 4th St), ☎ (212) 254-4370.

Cherry Lane Theatre, 38 Commerce St (between Bedford and Hudson Sts), ☎ (212) 239-6200.

Classic Stage Company, 136 E. 13th St (between Third and Fourth Aves), ☎ (212) 677-4210.

Daryl Roth Theatre, 20 Union Square East (at E. 15th St); ☎ (212) 375-1110.

Dixon Place, 258 Bowery (between Houston and Prince Sts); ☎ (212) 219-3088.

Douglas Fairbanks Theatre, 432 W. 42nd St (between Ninth and Tenth Aves); ☎ (212) 239-6200.

Ensemble Studio Theatre, 549 W. 52nd St (between Tenth and Eleventh Aves); ☎ (212) 247-3405.

47th Street Theatre, 307 W. 47th St (at Eighth Ave); ☎ (212) 239-6200.

Gramercy Theatre, 127 E. 23rd St (between Park Ave South and Lexington Aves); ☎ (212) 777-4900.

Irish Repertory Theatre, 132 W. 22nd St (between Sixth and Seventh Aves); ☎ (212) 727-2737.

Jane Street Theatre, Hotel Riverview, 113 Jane St (at West St); ☎ (212) 239-6200.

Jewish Repertory Theatre, Playhouse 91, 316 E. 91st St (between First and Second Aves); ☎ (212) 831-2000.

John Houseman Theatre, 450 W. 42nd St (at Tenth Ave); ☎ (212) 239-6200.

Joseph Papp Public Theater, 425 Lafayette St (between Astor Place and E. 4th St); ☎ (212) 260-2400.

The Kitchen, 512 W. 19th St (between Tenth and Eleventh Aves); ☎ (212) 255-5793.

La MaMa E.T.C., 74A E. 4th St (between Second Ave and Bowery); ☎ (212) 475-7710.

Lamb's Theatre, 130 W. 44th St (between Sixth and Seventh Aves); ☎ (212) 997-1780.

Lucille Lortel, 121 Christopher St (between Hudson and Bleecker Sts); ☎ (212) 239-6200.

Manhattan Theater Club, City Center, 131 W. 55th St (between Sixth and Seventh Aves); ☎ (212) 581-1212.

Martin R. Kaufman Theater, 534 W. 42nd St (between Tenth and Eleventh Aves); ☎ (212) 244-7529.

Minetta Lane Theatre, 18 Minetta Lane (between Sixth Ave and MacDougal St); ☎ (212) 420-8000.

Mitzi Newhouse Theater, Lincoln Center, 150 W. 65th St (at Broadway); ☎ (212) 239-6200.

Ontological Theater, St. Mark's-in-the-Bowery Church, 131 E. 10th St (at Second Ave); ☎ (212) 420-1916.

Orpheum Theatre, 126 Second Ave (between St. Mark's Place and E. 7th St); ☎ (212) 477-2477.

Pearl Theatre Company, 80 St. Mark's Place (between First and Second Aves); ☎ (212) 598-9802.

Players Theatre, 115 MacDougal St (at Minetta Lane); ☎ (212) 254-5076.

Playwrights Horizons, 416 W. 42nd St (between Ninth and Tenth Aves); ☎ (212) 279-4200.

Primary Stages, 354 W. 45th St (between Eighth and Ninth Aves); ☎ (212) 333-4052.

Promenade Theatre, 2162 Broadway (at W. 76th St); ☎ (212) 580-1313.

Second Stage, 307 W. 43 St (at Eighth Ave); ☎ (212) 246-4422.

Signature Theatre Company, 555 W. 42nd St (between Tenth and Eleventh Aves); ☎ (212) 244-7529.

SoHo Playhouse, 15 Vandam St (between Sixth Ave and Varick St); ☎ (212) 239-6200.

Sullivan Street Playhouse, 181 Sullivan St (between Bleecker and Houston Sts); ☎ (212) 674-3838.

Triad Theatre, 158 W. 72nd St (between Columbus and Amsterdam Aves); ☎ (212) 799-4599.

Vineyard Theatre, 108 E. 15th St (between Union Square East and Irving Place); ☎ (212) 353-3366.

Vivian Beaumont Theater, Lincoln Center, 150 W. 65th St (at Broadway); ☎ (212) 787-6868.

Westside Theatre, 406 W. 43rd St (between Ninth and Tenth Aves); ☎ (212) 307-4100.

York Theatre Company, Theatre at St. Peter's Church, 619 Lexington Ave (at E. 54th St); ☎ (212) 935-5820.

Music

Major Performing Arts Centers

Brooklyn Academy of Music (BAM), 30 Lafayette Ave (at Ashland Place), Brooklyn; ☎ (718) 636-4100; Web site: www.bam.org. Has a full schedule of music, dance, and drama, including the Brooklyn Philharmonic. The **Next Wave Festival** is a premier showcase for contemporary performing arts. Summer events include DanceAfrica and outdoor concert series at the MetroTech Center in downtown Brooklyn and in city parks. Facilities include the Opera House (2,000 seats) and the Majestic Theatre (900 seats), a restored vaudeville palace, and the four-screen BAM Rose Theatre.

Brooklyn Center for the Performing Arts, Brooklyn College of the City University of New York, 2900 Campus Rd and Hillel Place, Brooklyn; for box office information, ☎ (718) 951-4500; Web site: www.brooklyncenter.com. In its 2,450-seat Walt Whitman Theater and other smaller performance spaces, the center offers classical music and Broadway musicals; ethnic theater, music, and dance; classic and experimental films; and family programs.

Carnegie Hall, 154 W. 57th St (at Seventh Ave); ☎ (212) 247-7800; Web site: www.carnegiehall.org. The city's best-loved concert hall, relished both for its acoustics and its tradition. Major orchestras perform here as well as world-class instrumental soloists and recitalists; emphasis on classical music, but also jazz and pop concerts. Less prominent artists appear at Weill Recital Hall at Carnegie Hall (formerly Carnegie Recital Hall; same telephone number).

City Center, 131 W. 55th St (between Sixth and Seventh Aves); ☎ (212) 247-0430. For tickets, call CityTix, ☎ (212) 581-1212; Web site: www.citycenter.org. A venue for dance, theater, and concert versions of great American musicals. The **Manhattan Theatre Club** produces a full season of plays and the Writers in Performance series.

Lincoln Center for the Performing Arts, Broadway at W. 65th St; ☎ (212) 875-5000; Web site: www.lincolncenter.org. Occupying three city blocks, Lincoln Center is the home of the Metropolitan Opera, the New York City Opera, the New York Philharmonic, the Chamber Music Society of Lincoln Center, Jazz at Lincoln Center, the New York City Ballet, the American Ballet Theater, the Film Society of Lincoln Center, the Lincoln Center Theater, and the Juilliard School. In addition, it houses the New York Public Library and Museum of the Performing Arts.

For tickets to events at Avery Fisher and Alice Tully Halls, call CenterCharge, ☎ (212) 721-6500. Tickets for Lincoln Center events are also available by mail (order at least a month ahead) and at the box offices.

For Lincoln Center Programming and Ticket Information

The Lincoln Center Web site has links to all theaters and events: www.lincoln center.org.

Alice Tully Hall, ☎ (212) 875-5050.
Avery Fisher Hall, ☎ (212) 875-5030.
The Chamber Music Society of Lincoln Center, ☎ (212) 875-5788.
Jazz at Lincoln Center Hotline, ☎ (212) 875-5299.
The Juilliard School, ☎ (212) 769-7406.
Lincoln Center Theater, ☎ (212) 362-7600.
The Metropolitan Opera House, ☎ (212) 362-6000.
New York State Theater, ☎ (212) 870-5570.
Walter Reade Theater, ☎ (212) 875-5601.

Tickets are also available through booking agencies. For Walter Reade Theater films, call Moviefone, ☎ 777-FILM (theater code 954). For Lincoln Center Theater productions, call Tele-charge, ☎ (212) 239-6200. For New York State Theater performances, call Ticketmaster, ☎ (212) 307-4100.

Classical Music

New York is certainly the classical music center of this country, possibly even the world. Classical music is performed in concert halls, churches, and museums throughout the city. Churches offer special concerts around significant religious holidays. Check the newspapers and other listings for current events.

Aaron Davis Hall, at City College, W. 133rd St and Convent Ave; ☎ (212) 650-6900. Classical concerts, dance, world music.

Alice Tully Hall, at Lincoln Center, 1941 Broadway (at W. 65th St); ☎ (212) 875-5050. Home of the Chamber Music Society of Lincoln Center, also hosts recitals and other events requiring a moderately intimate theater.

Avery Fisher Hall, at Lincoln Center, 10 Lincoln Center Plaza (at Broadway and W. 65th St); ☎ (212) 875-5030. The home of the New York Philharmonic and the Mostly Mozart Festival; hosts visiting orchestras and famous soloists including big-name pop and jazz musicians.

Bargemusic, Fulton Ferry Landing (at Old Fulton and Furman Sts), Brooklyn; ☎ (718) 624-4061. Chamber music and small ensembles on a barge in the East River; great views.

Brooklyn Academy of Music (BAM), 30 Lafayette Ave (between Flatbush Ave and Fulton St), Brooklyn; ☎ (718) 636-4100. Home of the Brooklyn Philharmonic and many adventurous, avant-garde programs.

Brooklyn Museum of Art, 200 Eastern Pkwy (at Washington Ave), Brooklyn; ☎ (718) 638-5000. Programs of world music, dance, held on the first Sat of each month, when the museum remains open until 11 P.M.

Carnegie Hall, 154 W. 57th St (at Seventh Ave); ☎ (212) 247-7800. One of the world's greatest concert halls; famous soloists and orchestras perform in the large main auditorium and smaller Weill Recital Hall.

Cathedral of St. John the Divine, 1047 Amsterdam Ave (at W. 112th St); ☎ (212) 749-6600. Concerts of medieval and Renaissance music, ethnic music, organ recitals.

Church of St. Ignatius Loyola, 980 Park Ave (at E. 84th St); ☎ (212) 288-2520. Choral and organ concerts.

Church of the Ascension, Fifth Ave at 10th St; ☎ (212) 254-8553. Known for its choir, the Voices of Ascension.

The Cloisters, Fort Tryon Park; ☎ (212) 650-2290. Medieval music and drama amidst medieval masterpieces of art.

The Frick Collection, 1 E. 70th St (at Fifth Ave); ☎ (212) 288-0700. Free Sun afternoon concerts or soloists and chamber groups during fall and winter. Contact the museum for information about tickets.

Kaye Playhouse, at Hunter College, E. 68th St (between Park and Lexington Aves), ☎ (212) 772-4448. The performing arts series, soloists, chamber music.

Manhattan School of Music, 120 Claremont Ave (between Broadway and W. 122nd St), ☎ (212) 749-2802, ext. 428.

Mannes College of Music, 150 W. 85th St (between Columbus and Amsterdam Aves); ☎ (212) 580-0210.

Merkin Concert Hall, Abraham Goodman House, 129 W. 67th St (between Broadway and Amsterdam Aves); ☎ (212) 501-3303. Chamber music, recitals. Adventurous programming choices including the work of lesser-known composers, ethnic music, and unusual ensembles.

Metropolitan Museum of Art, 1000 Fifth Ave (at 82nd St); ☎ (212) 570-

3949. Chamber music, recitals, jazz. Christmas concerts in the Medieval Sculpture Hall.

Miller Theatre, at Columbia University, Broadway at W. 116th St; ☎ (212) 854-7799. Jazz, new music; also dance and film.

The New York State Theater, at Lincoln Center, 20 Lincoln Plaza (at Broadway and W. 65th St, ☎ (212) 870-5570. The home of the New York City Opera Company and the New York City Ballet, which rose to fame under George Balanchine. The opera season runs from about late Feb to early May and from early Sept to mid-Nov. The ballet season runs from mid-Nov to the end of Feb, with numerous performances of the *Nutcracker* (get tickets well in advance) in Dec. The spring seasons runs from late April through mid-June.

92nd Street Y, 1395 Lexington Ave (at E. 92nd St); ☎ (212) 996-1100.

St. Peter's Lutheran Church, Citicorp Building, Lexington Ave at E. 54th St; ☎ (212) 935-2200. Has an extensive jazz program, which includes a regular Jazz Vespers, Sun at 5 P.M.; also classical music, including a Bach Festival.

Town Hall, 123 W. 43rd St (between Sixth and Seventh Aves); ☎ (212) 840-2824. Another venerable city institution; offers a wide range of concerts, lectures, and other cultural events.

Trinity Church. Presents noonday concerts; Mon at St. Paul's Chapel (Broadway at Fulton St) at noon; on Thurs at Trinity Church (Broadway and Wall St) at 1 P.M.; ☎ (212) 602-0747. Suggested donation.

Opera

Amato Opera Theater, 319 Bowery (at E. 2nd St); ☎ (212) 228-8200. Small theater, focuses on aspiring singers, full and abbreviated operas.

Brooklyn Academy of Music, 30 Lafayette Ave (at Ashland Place), Brooklyn; ☎ (718) 636-4100. Known for its artistically adventurous productions, especially baroque operas.

The Metropolitan Opera, at Lincoln Center, 30 Lincoln Center Plaza (at Broadway and W. 65th St); ☎ (212) 362-6000. The nation's premier opera company, with a glorious orchestra, star singers, and lavish productions. The opera season runs from late Sept through mid-April; the ballet season, divided into two sections, runs from Oct through Nov and again from mid-April through June.

The New York City Opera, New York State Theater, at Lincoln Center, 20 Lincoln Center Plaza (at Broadway and W. 65th St); ☎ (212) 870-5570. The New York City Opera Company, a "starless" company whose casts feature up-and-coming singers, offers more adventuresome productions than the Met. The opera season runs from about late Feb to early May and from early Sept to mid-Nov.

New York Grand Opera, headquarters at 154 W. 57th St, Suite 125 (at Seventh Ave); ☎ (212) 245-8837. Presents free summer performances of Italian operas in Central Park. Since 1994, its Viva Verdi! festival has been performing all of Verdi's 28 operas in chronological order.

Opera Orchestra of New York, P.O. Box 1226, New York, NY 10023-1226, ☎ (212) 799-1982. Much-admired organization, performs lesser-known operas in concert form, often with famous soloists. Performances usually at Carnegie Hall.

Jazz

You can hear jazz in clubs and at major concert halls. **Jazz at Lincoln Center,** headed by Wynton Marsalis, offers a series of concerts, films, and lectures; ☎ (212) 875-5299. The **Carnegie Hall Jazz Band series** (offered in the fall) focuses on jazz history, especially big band music; for tickets, ☎ (212) 247-7800; or access the Carnegie Hall Web site (www.carnegiehall.org) up to ten days prior to the concert.

The **JVC Jazz Festival** takes place in mid-June, with events throughout the city; some are outdoors and some are free. For information, ☎ (212) 501-1390; Web site: www.festivalproductions.net. **Central Park Summerstage,** a free summer arts festival, has American and world music, dance, spoken-word performances, and opera, as well as jazz; ☎ (212) 360-2777.

Check out the listings in *Time Out New York,* the *New York Times, New York* magazine, and other publications.

BAMcafé, 30 Lafayette Ave (at Ashland Place), Brooklyn; ☎ (718) 636-4139.
Birdland, 315 W. 44th St (between Eighth and Ninth Aves); ☎ (212) 581-3080.
Blue Note, 131 W. 3rd St (between Sixth Ave and MacDougal St); ☎ (212) 475-8592.
Café Carlyle, Carlyle Hotel, 95 E. 76th St (at Madison Ave); ☎ (212) 570-7189.
Fez, 380 Lafayette St (at Great Jones St); ☎ (212) 533-2680.
Granite Room at City Hall, 131 Duane St (between Church St and West Broadway); ☎ (212) 227-7777.
Iridium, 444 W. 63rd St (at Columbus Ave); ☎ (212) 582-2121.
Jazz Standard, 116 E. 27th St (between Park and Lexington Aves); ☎ (212) 576-2232.
Knitting Factory, 74 Leonard St (between Broadway and Church St); ☎ (212) 249-3055.
Merkin Concert Hall, 129 W. 67th St (between Broadway and Columbus Ave); ☎ (212) 501-3330.
Nuyorican Poets Café, 236 E. 3rd St (between Aves B and C); ☎ (212) 505-8183.
Smalls, 183 W. 10th St (between Seventh Ave South and W. 4th St); ☎ (212) 929-7565.
Smoke, 2751 Broadway (between W. 105th and W. 106th Sts); ☎ (212) 864-6662.
Swing 46, 349 W. 46th St (between Eighth and Ninth Aves); ☎ (212) 262-9554.
Tonic, 107 Norfolk St (between Delancey and Rivington Sts); ☎ (212) 358-7503.
Up Over Jazz Café, 351 Flatbush Ave (at Seventh Ave), Park Slope, Brooklyn; ☎ (718) 398-5413.
Village Vanguard, 178 Seventh Ave South (between W. 11th and Perry Sts); ☎ (212) 255-4037.
Zinc Bar, 90 Houston St (between La Guardia Place and Thompson St); ☎ (212) 477-8337.

Pop and Rock

Big-name stars appear at big venues, including Madison Square Garden, ☎ (212) 465-6741; the Continental Air Arena at the Meadowlands in New Jersey, ☎ (201) 935-3900; and Radio City Music Hall, ☎ (212) 632-4000.

Beacon Theatre, 2124 Broadway (between W. 74th and W. 75th Sts); ☎ (212) 496-7070.

Bitter End, 147 Bleecker St (between Thompson St and La Guardia Place); ☎ (212) 673-7030.

Bottom Line, 15 W. 4th St (at Mercer St); ☎ (212) 228-7880.

Bowery Ballroom, 6 Delancey St (at Bowery); ☎ (212) 533-2111.

Brownie's, 169 Ave A (between E. 10th and E. 11th Sts); ☎ (212) 420-8392.

CBGB, 315 Bowery (at Bleecker St); ☎ (212) 982-4052.

The Cooler, 416 W. 14th St (between Ninth and Tenth Aves); ☎ (212) 229-0785.

Irving Plaza, 17 Irving Place (at E. 15th St); ☎ (212) 777-6800.

Knitting Factory, 74 Leonard St (between Broadway and Church St); ☎ (212) 249-3055.

Mercury Lounge, 217 E. Houston St (at Essex St); ☎ (212) 260-4700.

Roseland, 239 W. 52nd St (between Eighth Ave and Broadway); ☎ (212) 249-8870.

Dance

Dance performances take place all over the city, in theaters and other performing arts spaces, churches, and, occasionally, museums. Ballet companies regularly appear at City Center, the New York State Theater, and the Metropolitan Opera.

American Ballet Theater; spring season: Metropolitan Opera House, Lincoln Center, 30 Lincoln Center Plaza (at Broadway and W. 65th St); ☎ (212) 362-6000; autumn season: City Center, 131 W. 55th St (between Sixth and Seventh Aves), ☎ (212) 247-0430. Founded in 1940, performs classic ballet and contemporary repertoire.

Brooklyn Academy of Music, 30 Lafayette Ave (at Ashland Place), Brooklyn; ☎ (718) 623-2770. Modern dance groups in Next Wave Festival in the autumn. Also the Mark Morris Dance Group.

City Center, 131 W. 55th St (between Sixth and Seventh Aves); ☎ (212) 581-1212. The Alvin Ailey American Dance Theater, the Paul Taylor Dance Company, Dance Theater of Harlem, and ballet companies from aboard all appear here.

Dance Theater Workshop, Bessie Schonberg Theater, 219 W. 19th St (between Seventh and Eighth Aves); ☎ (212) 924-0077.

Danspace Project, in St.-Mark's-in-the-Bowery Church, 131 E. 10th St (at Second Ave); ☎ (212) 674-8194. Avant-garde series, from fall through spring.

Joyce SoHo, 155 Mercer St (between Prince and Houston Sts); ☎ (212) 334-7949. Owned and operated by the Joyce Theater, this three-story former firehouse was purchased by them in 1996.

The Joyce Theater, 175 Eighth Ave (at W. 19th St); ☎ (212) 242-0800. An old movie theater gutted and remodeled in 1982, this is an important center for modern dance.

New York City Ballet, New York State Theater, Lincoln Center, 20 Lincoln Plaza (at Broadway and W. 65th St); ☎ (212) 870-5570. Founded by George Balanchine and Lincoln Kirstein, has winter (Nov–Feb) and spring seasons (April–June), also *Nutcracker* performances at Christmas.

Film

New York is for film lovers. In addition to first-run movies, theaters offer revivals, art films, and festivals. Museums and other cultural organizations (for example, Goethe House and the Japan Society) also organize film series. The most important film event in the city is the **New York Film Festival** at Lincoln Center (usually late Sept to mid-Oct), where foreign and American films deserving of special attention get their first American showing. For information, ☎ (212) 875-5610.

In March the Museum of Modern Art, in collaboration with the Film Society of Lincoln Center, produces **New Directors/New Films,** which focuses on emerging or overlooked talent. For ticket information, ☎ (212) 708-9500.

First-Run Movies

You can book seats by phone or over the Internet at some theaters. To find times, call Moviefone, ☎ (212) 777-3456 (777-FILM), or access their Web site: www.moviefone.com. You can also check listings in the newspapers and periodicals such as *Time Out New York, New York* magazine, *The New Yorker,* and the Fri edition of the *New York Times.*

If you arrive without a ticket and find a line outside the theater, be sure to inquire whether the line is for ticket buyers or ticket holders before you settle in; be prepared to arrive at least a half hour to 45 minutes before a popular show if you wish to get a good seat.

Revival Houses, Art Houses, Film Societies, and Museums

American Museum of the Moving Image, 35th Ave at 36th St, Astoria, Queens; ☎ (718) 784-0077.

Angelika Film Center, 18 W. Houston (at Mercer St); ☎ (212) 995-2000, or 777-FILM 531.

Anthology Film Archives, 32 Second Ave (at E. 2nd St); ☎ (212) 505-5181.

BAM Rose Cinemas, Brooklyn Academy of Music, 30 Lafayette Ave (at Ashland Place), Brooklyn; ☎ (718) 623-2770.

Cinema Classics, 332 E. 11th St (between First and Second Aves); ☎ (212) 971-1015.

Cinema Village, 22 E. 12th St (between University Place and Fifth Ave); ☎ (212) 924-3363.

Eastside Playhouse, 919 Third Ave (between E. 55th and E. 56th Sts); ☎ (212) 755-3020 or 777-FILM.

Film Forum, 209 W. Houston St (between Varick St and Sixth Ave); ☎ (212) 727-8110.

Film Society of Lincoln Center. Walter Reade Theater, 70 Lincoln Center Plaza (at Broadway and W. 65th St); ☎ (212) 875-5600.

Lincoln Plaza Cinemas, 1886 Broadway (between W. 62nd and W. 63rd Sts); ☎ (212) 757-2280.

Makor, 35 W. 67th St (between Columbus Ave and Central Park West); ☎ (212) 601-1000.
Museum of Modern Art, 11 W. 53rd St (between Fifth and Sixth Aves); ☎ (212) 708-9490.
Paris, 4 W. 58th St (at Fifth Ave); ☎ (212) 688-3800.
Pioneer Theater, 155 E. 3rd St (at Ave A); ☎ (212) 254-3300.
Quad Cinema, 34 W. 13th St (between Fifth and Sixth Aves); ☎ (212) 255-8800.
Screening Room, 54 Varick St (at Canal St); ☎ (212) 334-2100.
Symphony Space, 2537 Broadway (at W. 95th St); ☎ (212) 864-5400.

The New York League for the Hard of Hearing, 71 W. 23rd St, ☎ (917) 305-7700 (voice) or (917) 305-7999 (TTY), compiles schedules of captioned films for the hearing-impaired in commercial theaters. Check their Web site at www.lhh.org.

Background Information

Chronology

1524   Giovanni da Verrazano, working for Francis I of France, explores New York Bay and the North American coastline.

1525   Esteban Gómez explores what was probably the Hudson River for Charles V of Spain.

1609   Henry Hudson, seeking a water route to the Orient for the Dutch East India Company, explores the harbor and sails upriver to the site of Albany.

1613   Adriaen Block and crew winter in Lower Manhattan, building a new ship after their first, the *Tyger*, burns.

1614   Block explores Long Island Sound, discovers Block Island, and makes the first map of Manhattan.

1624   Thirty Dutch and Walloon families sent by the Dutch West India Company settle in New Netherland, a territory reaching from the Delaware to Connecticut Rivers.

1625   First permanent settlement is made in Lower Manhattan and named New Amsterdam.

1626   Governor General Peter Minuit "purchases" Manhattan Island from the Native Americans for 60 guilders (estimated at $24).

1628   First church (Dutch Reformed) founded with arrival of its first minister.

1633   First church building, constructed at site of 39 Pearl St.

1636   Settlers Jacques Bentyn and Adrianse Bennett buy land from Native Americans in Brooklyn near Gowanus Creek. Jacobus Van Corlaer buys Corlaer's Hook.

1638   First ferry line established from Fulton Ferry in Brooklyn to about present-day Dover St in Manhattan. Earliest Manhattan land grant given to Andries Hudd in what is now Harlem.

1639   Jonas Bronck, a Dane, buys part of the Bronx from Native Americans. David de Vries and others settle Staten Island but are driven out by Native Americans.

1642   Religious tolerance of New Amsterdam attracts dissidents from New England, including John Throgmorton (Throg's Neck) and Anne Hutchinson (Hutchinson River).

1643   Native American uprisings in New Amsterdam, New Jersey, and Staten Island; they continue intermittently until 1655.

1645   First permanent settlement in Queens at Vlisingen (Flushing).

1647   Peter Stuyvesant becomes governor.

1653   New Amsterdam receives charter establishing the municipal government. Peter Stuyvesant builds a fortified wall, river to river, at the present latitude of Wall St, to keep out the British, trading rivals of the Dutch.

1654   First permanent Jewish settlement; Asser Levy and 22 others arrive, fleeing persecution in Brazil.

1655   Flatbush Dutch Reformed Church founded, Long Island's first church.

1661   First permanent settlement on Staten Island at Oude Dorp. Bowne House built in Flushing.

1664   The British capture New Amsterdam without a fight and rename it after James, Duke of York, brother of King Charles II.

1665   Thomas Willett becomes first mayor of New York.

1673   The Dutch capture New York, again without a fight, and rename it New Orange.

1674   Treaty of Westminster brings Anglo-Dutch War to a close; makes New York British once again.

1676   Canal on Broad St filled.

1682   Jews establish cemetery (still extant) at Chatham Square.

1686   The Dongan Charter gives the city a form of municipal government that remains in force until modern times.

1689   In England King James II, facing rebellion, abdicates and flees to France. Jacob Leisler leads uprising against the British in New York.

1693   Frederick Philipse builds Kingsbridge across Harlem River, joining Manhattan Island to the mainland.

1713   First Staten Island ferry.

1725   *New-York Gazette* founded by William Bradford.

1729   First synagogue of Congregation Shearith Israel built on Beaver St.

1732   First theater opens near present Maiden Lane.

1733   John Peter Zenger publishes the *New-York Weekly Journal*, an antigovernment paper.

1734   Zenger jailed for slander; issues of his paper are publicly burned.

1735   Zenger acquittal establishes precedent for freedom of the press.

1754   King's College, now Columbia University, founded near Trinity Church as city's first college.

1762   Samuel Fraunces buys DeLancey house, opens tavern.

1763   French and Indian War closes with Treaty of Paris, confirming English control of North America.

1765   British Parliament passes Stamp Act, raising revenues to support British troops in America. Stamp Act Congress meets with delegates from nine colonies in New York and denounces British policies of taxation.

1766   Stamp Act repealed in England. St. Paul's Chapel, oldest remaining church in New York, dedicated. Roger Morris House built, now the Morris-Jumel Mansion in Harlem.

1767   Townshend Acts, named after the British chancellor of Exchequer, increase taxes and restrict colonial self-government. Although repealed three years later, they fuel anti-British sentiment.

1776   Declaration of Independence marks beginning of Revolutionary War. British occupy Brooklyn after Battle of Long Island and take control of all of Manhattan by Nov 17.

1783   Treaty of Paris concludes Revolutionary War as Britain recognizes independence of the 13 colonies. British Army leaves New York.

1784   New York City becomes the capital of the state and nation.

1787   Erasmus Hall Academy opens in Flatbush, Brooklyn.

1789   U.S. Constitution ratified. George Washington takes oath as nation's first president in Federal Hall on Wall St.

1790   Federal capital moves to Philadelphia. First census puts city population at 33,000.

1791   Yellow fever epidemic stimulates development of Greenwich Village.

1792   Buttonwood Agreement leads to formation of New York Stock Exchange.

1794   City buys Bellevue, an East River estate, and opens contagious disease hospital.

1796   Robert Fitch tests experimental steamboat on Collect Pond.

1797   Albany becomes state capital. Washington Square purchased as a potter's field.

1798   Yellow fever epidemic claims 2,086 lives.

1799   Aaron Burr founds Manhattan Company to provide drinking water, but clause in charter allows him also to found bank.

1800   Alexander Hamilton builds the Grange.

1801   Brooklyn Navy Yard founded.

1803   Cornerstone laid for present City Hall. Another yellow fever epidemic.

1806   First New York free school opens.

1807   Robert Fulton demonstrates his steamboat *Clermont* on the Hudson River.

1810   Fulton opens steam ferry service to New Jersey.

1811   John Randel Jr. heads group of commissioners who plan New York's rectilinear street grid, known as the Commissioner's Plan, or Randel Survey.

1812   City Hall opens. U.S. declares war on Britain; port suffers in trade war and is fortified against possible British attack.

1814   Treaty of Ghent ends War of 1812.

1816   Village of Brooklyn incorporated on site of present downtown Brooklyn.

1820   New York becomes nation's largest city, with population of 123,706.

1823   City buys site of Bryant Park for another potter's field.

1825   Erie Canal opens, greatly enhancing the importance of New York as a port and making it the gateway to the Midwest.

1827   State legislature ends all slavery in New York State.

1828   Washington Square Park laid out in old potter's field.

1829   Large reservoir built on 14th St at the Bowery, one of numerous stopgap measures aimed at solving the city's water problems.

1831   New York University founded as University of the City of New York. Gramercy Park laid out.

1832   New York and Harlem Railroad, a horsecar line, opens along the Bowery and Fourth Ave from Prince St to 14th St as city's first railroad.

1834   Village of Brooklyn incorporated as City of Brooklyn.

1835   "Great Fire" destroys 674 buildings near Hanover and Pearl Sts.

1837   Business panic; city losses total some $60 million. New York and Harlem Railroad reaches Harlem. First steam locomotives added in 1839.

1840   City's population reaches 312,710.

1841   St. John's College, now Fordham University, founded in the Bronx.

1842   Croton Aqueduct brings water to city; stored in reservoir on site of Bryant Park. John Jacob Astor founds Astor Library. Charles Dickens visits the city.

1843   Potter's field established on Randall's Island.

1846   Potato famine in Ireland swells immigration. Tensions between Catholics and Protestants arise over such issues as aid to parochial schools.

1847   Madison Square Park laid out, replacing potter's field.

1848   Political uprisings increase immigration from Germany.

1849   Free Academy (chartered 1847), the precursor of City College, opens on Lexington Ave at 23rd St. Astor Place Riot demonstrates incompetence of police force.

1850   P. T. Barnum organizes concert with Jenny Lind at Castle Garden. Giuseppe Garibaldi arrives in Staten Island during period of exile.

1851   *New York Daily Times*, now the *New York Times*, begins publication. Hudson River Railroad links New York City and Albany.

1852   William M. "Boss" Tweed begins political career as alderman of Seventh Ward.

1853   State legislature authorizes Central Park. World's Fair held at Crystal Palace in Bryant Park.

1855   Castle Garden becomes immigrant station. Construction of many inhumane tenements leads to tenement-reform movement; first model tenement built at Elizabeth and Mott Sts.

1856   City buys land for Central Park.

1857   Another financial panic.

1858   Calvert Vaux and Frederick Law Olmsted chosen to design Central Park; work is begun. Fire destroys Crystal Palace. Macy's founded.

1859   Cooper Union opens. State legislature authorizes Prospect Park. Otis passenger elevator installed in Fifth Avenue Hotel.

1860   City's population reaches 813,669, including large numbers of immigrants.

1861   Civil War begins.

1862   *Monitor*, an ironclad ship designed by John Ericsson, launched in the Greenpoint section of Brooklyn.

1863   Draft Riots against conscription into the Union Army (those who could pay a $300 fee were exempted) paralyze the city for three days.

1865   Civil War ends. Municipal fire-fighting system replaces volunteer companies.

1867   Prospect Park opens in Brooklyn. First tenement house law attempts to set standards for ventilation, sanitation, and room size.

1868   Andrew H. Green proposes consolidation of boroughs. First elevated railroad opens on Greenwich St from the Battery to Cortlandt St, a cable system with both moving and stationary engines.

1869   Rutherford Stuyvesant builds city's first known apartment house on E. 18th St. Potter's field moved to Harts Island, where it remains today. Jay Gould and Jim Fisk corner the gold market.

1870   Work begins on Brooklyn Bridge. First building with passenger elevators (Equitable Life Assurance Building at 120 Broadway; burned down

1912). Joseph Warren Beach opens pneumatic subway under Broadway from Warren to Murray Sts. Ninth Avenue El reaches 30th St.

1871 Grand Central Depot opens. Boss Tweed arrested, closing a period during which city government reached a low point of inefficiency and corruption.

1873 Another financial panic.

1874 P. T. Barnum opens Hippodrome at Madison Square. Part of the Bronx annexed to New York City.

1877 Alfred Tredway White opens model tenement houses in Brooklyn. Museum of Natural History opens at its present site.

1878 Sixth Avenue El opens from Rector St to Central Park.

1879 "Dumbbell" tenement plan by James F. Ware wins competition for model tenement sponsored by magazine. Plan condemned by tenement reformers but widely adopted.

1880 Sixth Avenue El reaches 155th St. Metropolitan Museum of Art opens. Broadway illuminated by Brush electric arc lamps.

1882 Thomas Edison opens generating plant at 257 Pearl St, making electricity commercially available.

1883 Brooklyn Bridge opens. Metropolitan Opera opens on Broadway between 39th and 40th Sts (demolished 1967). New York Giants baseball team founded.

1885 Elevated railway opens in Brooklyn.

1886 Statue of Liberty inaugurated on Bedloe's (now Liberty) Island. Elevated railway joins Manhattan and Bronx.

1888 Great Blizzard. First building with steel skeleton erected (Tower Building at 50 Broadway).

1890 Madison Square Garden, designed by Stanford White, opens at the northeast corner of Madison Square.

1891 Carnegie Hall opens. New York Botanical Garden opens in the Bronx.

1892 Immigration station opens on Ellis Island.

1895 Harlem Ship Canal opens along Harlem River with channel dug south of Spuyten Duyvil Creek. Rest of Bronx annexed to New York City.

1898 Greater New York created by joining the five boroughs under a single municipal government. Population of 3.4 million makes it the world's second largest city behind London (4 million).

1899 Bronx Zoo opens. Brooklyn Children's Museum established. Croton Reservoir in Bryant Park razed.

1900 Subway construction begins. Blacks begin moving to Harlem. Census shows tenements house 70 percent of city's population.

1901 Tenement House Law institutes "New Law" tenements, superseding dumbbell plan. Macy's opens on Broadway.

1903 Williamsburg Bridge opens, making northern Brooklyn accessible to the poor of the Lower East Side.

1904 IRT subway opens from City Hall to W. 145th St.

1905 Municipal Staten Island ferry opens, with 5¢ fare.

1906 Harry K. Thaw, deranged Pittsburgh millionaire, shoots and kills architect Stanford White on the roof of Madison Square Garden.

1908 East River subway tunnel between Bowling Green and Joralemon St links Manhattan and Brooklyn. First Hudson Tube, the McAdoo Tunnel, links Manhattan and Hoboken, New Jersey. IRT Broadway line reaches Kingsbridge section of the Bronx.

1909 Queensboro and Manhattan Bridges open.

1910 Pennsylvania Station opens.

1911 Triangle Shirtwaist Company fire kills 145. Brooklyn Botanic Garden opens.

1913 The present Grand Central Terminal opens. The Armory Show at the 69th Regiment Armory introduces New York to "modern art."

1916 Nation's first zoning resolution, divides city into residential and commercial areas and restricts height and bulk of buildings.

1923 "Setback" law restricts configuration of tall buildings. New York Yankees move into Yankee Stadium; Babe Ruth hits home run in first game at the stadium.

1925 Columbia University and Presbyterian Hospital join to form Columbia-Presbyterian Medical Center at W. 168th St and Broadway. Stanford White's Madison Square Garden at Madison Square demolished.

1927 Holland Tunnel (for vehicular traffic) opens between New York and New Jersey.

1928 Cornell University and New York Hospital join forces as New York Medical Center, York Ave and E. 70th St. Goethals Bridge and Outerbridge Crossing open, linking Staten Island and New Jersey.

1929 Stock market crashes; Great Depression begins.

1931 Empire State Building and George Washington Bridge open. Floyd Bennett Field opens as city's first municipal airport. Bayonne Bridge opens, linking Staten Island and New Jersey.

1932 Mayor James J. ("Beau James") Walker resigns after Seabury Investigations reveal rampant corruption.

1933 Fiorello La Guardia elected mayor. IND subway opens to Queens.

1934 New York City Housing Authority formed to clear slums and build low-rent housing.

1935 Work begins on East River Drive (now FDR Drive).

1936 Triborough Bridge opens. First Houses (Ave A at E. 3rd St) open.

1938 La Guardia's City Charter of 1936 goes into effect, centralizing municipal power and giving full legislative authority to City Council.

1939 North Beach Airport opens; soon renamed for La Guardia. New York World's Fair of 1939–40 opens in Flushing Meadows Park, Queens.

1940 Queens-Midtown Tunnel opens, linking mid-Manhattan and Queens. Brooklyn Battery Tunnel begun.

1941 U.S. enters World War II. New York becomes major Atlantic port. Brooklyn Navy Yard operates at full capacity.

1945 World War II ends. Army bomber crashes into Empire State Building. United Nations charter passed.

1946 U.N. selects New York as permanent headquarters. Army plane crashes into Bank of Manhattan Co. building's 58th floor.

1947 Rockefellers donate $5.8 million site of U.N. headquarters. Stuyvesant Town, middle-income housing for returning war veterans and their families, is built by Metropolitan Life Insurance Co. along East River Drive, E. 14th–E. 20th Sts.

1948 Subway and bus fares rise to 10¢. New York International Airport, known as Idlewild, officially opened, greatly expanded from original plans; now called John F. Kennedy International Airport.

1950 Brooklyn Battery Tunnel opens after construction delay caused by war. City population at all-time high: 7,891,957. Mayor William O'Dwyer, on the verge of exposure for corruption and links with organized crime, is appointed ambassador to Mexico by fellow Democrat, President Harry Truman.

1952 Lever House opens, first of glass-box skyscrapers. Transit Authority established.

1954 Robert F. Wagner elected mayor. Decline of older American cities begins in mid- to late 1950s. Puerto Rican immigration increases, as does influx of poor blacks.

1955 Brooklyn Dodgers win the World Series, at last.

1956 Yankee pitcher Don Larsen pitches perfect game, the only in World Series history.

1957 Fair Housing Law outlaws racial discrimination. Manhattantown scandal reveals housing project sponsors have failed to develop site while pocketing tenants' rents.

1958 Brooklyn Dodgers move to Los Angeles. Baseball Giants move to San Francisco.

1959 Ground broken for Lincoln Center.

1960 World Trade Center proposed at estimated cost of $250 million. Completion of Chase Manhattan Bank marks beginning of construction boom in Lower Manhattan. Ebbets Field razed for housing project.

1961 New zoning law offers incentives for public amenities, plazas, arcades.

1962 Philharmonic Hall, now Avery Fisher Hall, opens as first building of Lincoln Center for the Performing Arts.

1963 Pennsylvania Station demolished, despite protests.

1964 Race riots in Harlem and Bedford-Stuyvesant. World's Fair of 1964–65 opens in Flushing Meadows, Queens. Fair plagued by financial difficulties and controversy but attracts 51 million visitors. Verrazano-Narrows Bridge opens, ending relative isolation of Staten Island.

1965 Landmarks Preservation Commission established to save city's architectural heritage. New laws allow increased Asian, Greek, Haitian, Dominican, etc. immigration. First power blackout.

1966 Ground broken for World Trade Center.

1968 City teachers strike in battle over school decentralization, an issue with racial overtones.

1970 First New York City Marathon is run, completely in Central Park, with 126 males and 1 female participating. McSorley's Old Ale House is forced by the courts to admit women.

1971 Football Giants move to New Jersey. Construction begins on 63rd St subway tunnel. *All in the Family,* a TV sitcom with Archie Bunker (Carroll O'Connor) as the main character, brings Queens to the small screen.

1973 Construction of Twin Towers at World Trade Center completed. Welfare Island renamed Roosevelt Island as redevelopment begins. Dump truck plummets through deteriorated section of West Side Highway.

1974 Project to replace West Side Highway and to redevelop West Side corridor officially named Westway. Opponents file first lawsuit to stop project. City's financial position worsens, as loss of middle class and departure of businesses erode tax base while costs of social services increase.

1975 Cash-flow problems and inability to sell more municipal bonds bring city to verge of insolvency. Federal government staves off default on city notes by offering loans. South Bronx becomes symbol of urban despair as 13,000 fires break out in 12-square-mile area.

1977 Power blackout, lasting 25 hours, results in widespread looting and vandalism. David Berkowitz, self-styled "Son of Sam," arrested for murder. Studio 54 opens and becomes the quintessential disco. *A Chorus Line* opens.

1978 Radio City Music Hall saved from demolition. Supreme Court decision preserves Grand Central Terminal in its present form. *Herald Tribune* ceases publication. Federal government gives city $1.65 billion in long-term loan guarantees. "Pooper scooper" law requires pet owners to clean up after their dogs, gives pedestrians safer footing and cleaner shoes.

1980 Census assesses population at 7,086,096, with sharp decline in city's white population, moderate increase in black population, and substantial increase in Hispanic population. Blacks and Hispanics account for 48 percent of city's population. Mark David Chapman assassinates John Lennon in front of the Dakota Apartments.

1981 City reenters long-term municipal bond market. Construction begins at Battery Park City. Mysterious virus afflicting gay men is identified as AIDS; Gay Men's Health Crisis formed to deal with new epidemic.

1982 Morosco and Helen Hayes Theatres demolished despite protest as hotel project begins in Times Square. IBM Building opens on Madison Ave. *Cats* opens, ushering in era of Broadway blockbuster.

1983 City celebrates Brooklyn Bridge Centennial. Statue of Liberty restoration begun. Trump Tower opens. *A Chorus Line* sets Broadway record with 3,389th performance. Midtown suffers blackout after fire erupts in electrical substation; 12 blocks of Garment District darkened during crucial marketing week. City enacts "antisliver" law, which limits height of buildings that are less than 45 ft wide.

1985 Columbia University sells land under Rockefeller Center to Rockefeller Group for $400 million. After 12 years of struggle, Westway project ($2.3-billion, 4.2-mile highway) abandoned because of lack of federal financial support, potential harm to striped bass, hostility of environmentalists and public.

1986 Two British parachutists jump from 86th floor observation deck of Empire State Building, landing two blocks away. Carnegie Hall reopens after complete refurbishing. Statue of Liberty celebrates 100th anniversary amid fireworks, speeches, and parade of tall ships. Corruption probe uncovers kickback schemes involving parking ticket collection contracts; scandal spreads to other city agencies.

1987 Stock market crashes as Dow Jones average plunges 508 points in one day. World Financial Center opens in Battery Park City.

1988 City signs first comprehensive antismoking bill, limiting smoking in public places. Williamsburg Bridge closes for repairs after bridge approaches, long neglected, are deemed unsafe to carry traffic.

1989 David Dinkins is elected first black mayor of the city. B. Altman & Company department store closes after 124 years in business.

1990 Ellis Island reopens to public as museum of immigration. The U.S. Census pegs city population at 7,322,564; for the first time whites, though still the largest racial group, are in the minority.

1991 The last automat (on W. 42nd St) closes. The African Burial Ground, an 18C cemetery for blacks, is discovered near City Hall during construction. Riots take place in Brooklyn's Crown Heights after a Hasidic driver accidentally kills a black child.

1992 Police corruption leads to formation of Mollen Commission to investigate reports of theft and police brutality.

1993 World Trade Center is bombed. Six die, thousands are injured. Rudolph W. Giuliani becomes mayor, the first Republican since 1969. Staten Island's Republican vote tips the scales Giuliani's way. Staten Island votes to secede from Greater New York.

1994 High-tech industries reach New York with development of "Silicon Alley" around Broadway in the W. 20s. State legislature and courts quash Staten Island's bid to secede from New York City.

1997 Times Square rehabilitation in full swing. New Amsterdam Theatre reopens. Crime rate falls. *Cats* establishes new record for Broadway longevity, with 6,138 performances.

1999 Brooklyn Museum draws protest over *Sensation,* an exhibit of British artists; mayor threatens to end city subsidies of museum. Police slay Amadou Diallo, unarmed immigrant from West Africa, triggering protests across country. Yankee pitcher David Cone pitches perfect game, 16th in history of baseball.

2000 City's population tops 8 million for first time (rising to 8,008,278, an increase of 9.4 percent in the last decade), confirming it as nation's largest. Census tallies 3.6 million whites, 2.2 million Hispanics (the group with largest increase), 2.1 million blacks, and fewer than 800,000 Asians. Rose Center Planetarium opens at American Museum of Natural History. *Cats* finally closes after 7,485 performances. Guggenheim Museum announces plans for building by architect Frank Gehry that will change downtown skyline.

2001 On the morning of Sept 11, eighteen minutes apart, two commercial airliners hijacked by terrorists slam into the Twin Towers of the World Trade Center, exploding into catastrophic fires. Both buildings collapse within an hour and a half of impact, killing more than 3,500 people and shattering the life of the city and the nation. On Sept 17, when the stock market reopens after the tragedy, the Dow Jones Industrial average falls 685 points, reflecting concerns about the economy and the country's future. Billionaire Republican Michael Bloomberg, in his first run for a political office, is elected mayor.

Glossary of Architectural Terms

ANTHEMION: Stylized honeysuckle form, used in classical and Greek revival architecture.

ARCHITRAVE: The lowest part of an entablature; in classical architecture it rested directly on a column and usually supported a frieze and cornice.

BARREL-VAULT: A vault in the form of a very deep arch.

CHAMFER: Cuts the edge off a corner or rectangular shape, usually at 45 degrees.

CLERESTORY: Part of an interior raised above adjacent rooftops, usually windowed to allow light into the central part of the building. Typically used in Gothic churches, where the nave is built higher than the aisles, allowing windowed clerestory walls above the aisles.

COFFER: Recessed ceiling ornamentation, usually square or polygonal.

COLONNETTE: Small column, used for decorative purposes.

CONSOLE: Ornamental bracket, sometimes of stone, to support cornices, balconies, or other elements.

CORBEL: Block or bracket projecting from a wall to support timbers, girders, or masonry.

CORNICE: A prominent, continuous, horizontal projection surmounting a wall.

CRENELATIONS: Battlements, the toothed ramparts of a medieval fortification designed to protect a shooter or archer.

CRESTING: Decorative coping or ornamental ridge to give a building an interesting skyline.

ENTABLATURE: The upper section of a classical order, resting on the capitals and including the architrave, frieze, and cornice.

GAMBREL ROOF: A gabled roof with two pitches, the upper-half gentler, the lower-half steeper.

IMPOST: A bracketed piece of masonry projecting from a wall to support an arch or part of a roofing structure.

LINTEL: A beam supporting weight over a window or door opening.

LUNETTE: Area of wall enframed by a vault or arch, often penetrated by a window.

MACHICOLATION: A projecting gallery on top of a castle wall, supported by corbeled arches with an opening through which boiling liquids or missiles can be dropped on attackers.

MANSARD ROOF: Steep attic urban roof that allows an added story on a building.

MODILLION: A carved scroll of a bracket, placed horizontally.

MULLION: The major support between adjacent panels of glass or doors, or window sash; the vertical strip dividing panes of glass in a window.

NARTHEX: Originally the open porch of a church; now any kind of vestibule to the nave.

OCULUS: Eye or eyelike. A round window.

ORIEL: A high, projecting bay window, supported by corbels or brackets.

PEDIMENT: The triangular gabled end of a temple roof-front; in classical architecture supported by the colonnade and often decorated with sculpture.

PENDENTIVE: Triangular piece of a sphere that fills the space between a round dome and the supporting structure.

PERISTYLE: The series of columns surrounding a building or courtyard.

PIER: A vertical supporting structure, the portion of a wall between windows.

PILASTER: Attached, rectangular column used decoratively.

QUOIN: Corner stone of a building.

REREDOS: A background for an altar, often carved.

SPANDREL: The flat space between two arches and the surrounding rectangular framework. Also, the material between the head of one floor's windows and the sill of the next.

TIE-ROD: A tensile member to hold together parts of a building that tend to separate.

TYMPANUM: The sculptured pediment, or triangular end crest, of a Greek or Roman temple. Later, the arched space over Romanesque or Gothic doors, often filled with sculpture.

ZIGGURAT: Terraced pyramids used as holy places by the ancient Assyrians and Babylonians; hence, a stepped pyramid.

Further Reading

This list barely scratches the surface. Many of the older, now classic, books on the list are out of print; try your library.

History, Architecture, and Memoirs

Abbott, Berenice. *Changing New York* (1997). A thorough collection of photos depicting the city through the eyes of one of the top photographers of the 1930s.

Berger, Meyer. *Meyer Berger's New York* (1960). Berger's classic columns reprinted from the *New York Times* of the 1950s.

Brown, Claude. *Manchild in the Promised Land* (1965). An autobiographic novel about growing up on Harlem's mean streets, by a child of the first generation of urban pioneers who left the rural South for the "promised land" of the urban North.

Burns, Ric, and James Sanders, with Lisa Ades. *New York: An Illustrated History* (1999). A profusely illustrated companion to a television documentary that contains hundreds of rare photographs, paintings, lithographs, prints, and period maps.

Burrows, Edward, and Mike Wallace. *Gotham: A History of New York City to 1898* (1999). This authoritative chronicle includes a wealth of information and an abundance of lively anecdotes from the city's rich past.

Caro, Robert A. *The Power Broker: Robert Moses and the Fall of New York* (1974). Caro's classic indictment of Robert Moses is an extensively researched book offering a detailed view of Moses's impact on the physical environment of the city.

Cudahy, Brian J. *Under the Sidewalks of New York: The Story of the Greatest Subway System in the World* (1995). An illustrated history of the city's subways from 1904 to the present.

Diamonstein, Barbaralee. *The Landmarks of New York III* (1998). A black-and-white photo of every landmark building in the city with accompanying text.

Dolkart, Andrew S. *Guide to New York City Landmarks* (2nd edition, 1998). Short descriptions of all designated landmarks and historic districts.

Federal Writers' Project. *New York City Guide* (1939; reprint, 1982). Published the year of New York's great World's Fair, this classic account of the city was written during the Depression by a group of federally supported writers, including John Cheever.

Fischler, Stan. *Uptown, Downtown* (1976). A lively history of the subways, by a man who rode all of its 722 miles.

Galusha, Diane. *Liquid Assets: A History of New York City's Water System* (1999). A native of the Catskills, where New York City gets its water, the author chronicles the supply system as well as its impact on upstate New York communities.

Gayle, Margot, and Michele Cohen. *The Art Commission and the Municipal Art Society Guide to Manhattan's Outdoor Sculpture* (1988). The definitive work on this subject, for the casual onlooker and the scholar as well.

Gillespie, Angus Kress. *Twin Towers: The Life of New York City's World Trade Center* (1999). A detailed account of the World Trade Center as American icon and neighborhood to the people who worked there.

Homberger, Eric. *The Historical Atlas of New York City* (1994). Charts, maps, pictures, and texts depict the evolution of the city's populace, commerce, and culture.

Jackson, Kenneth T., editor. *The Encyclopedia of New York City* (1995). This massive tome, with more than 4,000 entries written by 650 contributors, is the standard reference to the city and its history.

Koeppel, Gerard T. *Water for Gotham: A History* (2000). A well-researched treatise on the complexity of New York City's water supply system and the historically difficult job of delivering this resource.

Kouwenhoven, John A. *The Columbia Historical Portrait of New York* (1953; reprint, 1972). A classic, originally published to honor the city's tricentennial and later reprinted. Lots of good historical pictures.

Lockwood, Charles. *Bricks and Brownstone: The New York Row House* (1972) and *Manhattan Moves Uptown* (1976). Illustrated histories of the city and its domestic architecture; pioneering studies.

Metzker, Isaac. *The Bintel Brief: Sixty Years of Letters from the Lower East Side to the Jewish Daily Forward* (1990). The life of the Jewish immigrants as told by their personal letters.

Mitchell, Joseph. *Up in the Old Hotel* (1992). A collection originally published between 1938 and 1964 by the legendary *New Yorker* writer. The people who interested Mitchell were, as he said, "visionaries, obsessives, imposters, fanatics, lost souls, the end-is-near street preachers, old Gypsy kings and old Gypsy queens, and out-and-out freak-show freaks."

Rogers, Elizabeth Barlow. *The Forests and Wetlands of New York City* (1971) and *Frederick Law Olmsted's New York* (1972). These books, by the founder of the Central Park Conservancy, focus on the natural environment of the city and the changes wrought upon it by Olmsted.

Seitz, Sharon, and Stuart Miller. *The Other Islands of New York City: A Guide and History* (2001, 2nd edition). A comprehensive exploration of the city's vast archipelago.

Stern, Robert A. M., et al. *New York 1880: Architecture and Urbanism in the Gilded Age* (1999); *New York 1900: Metropolitan Architecture and Urbanism, 1890–1915* (1995); *New York 1930: Architecture and Urbanism between the Two World Wars* (1987); *New York 1960: Architecture and Urbanism between the Second World War and the Bicentennial* (2nd edition, 1998). A series of hefty architectural histories, with many period photos, architectural drawings, and well-researched, exhaustive discussions.

Stokes, Isaac Newton Phelps. *The Iconography of Manhattan Island, 1498–1909* (1915–1928; reprint, 1967). Stokes, an architect and member of a prominent

New York family, labored on this masterpiece for most of his adult life. The six large, heavy volumes contain reproductions of historic maps and documents as well as a chronology of events, great and small, culled from public and private sources.

White, E. B. *Here Is New York* (1949; republished, 1999). An elegant homage to the city by a famous writer and editor.

White, Norval, and Elliott Willensky. *The AIA Guide to New York City* (4th edition, 2000). Each edition of this guide, which first appeared in 1967, has gotten bigger and better. It is the single best source of information on the city's architecture, enlivened by a witty commentary and thousands of photos.

Environment and Nature

Fowle, Marcia T., et al. *The New York City Audubon Society Guide to Finding Birds in the Metropolitan Area* (2001). An instructive manual for novice and expert birders alike.

Kershner, Bruce. *Secret Places of Staten Island: A Visitor's Guide to Scenic and Historic Treasures of Staten Island* (1998). A must-have for anyone interested in going beyond Staten Island's suburban subdivisions.

Matthews, Anne. *Wild Nights: Nature Returns to the City* (2001). Engaging and well-written proof that wildlife in the city goes beyond squirrels and pigeons.

Miller, Benjamin. *Fat of the Land: The Garbage of New York—The Last Two Hundred Years* (2000). A history of New York City's garbage.

Mittelbach, Margaret, and Michael Crewdson. *Wild New York: A Guide to Wildlife, Wild Places, and Natural Phenomena of New York City* (1997). A comprehensive look at nature in the city, complete with walking tours.

Waldman, John R. *Heartbeats in the Muck: A Dramatic Look at the History, Sea Life, and Environment of New York Harbor* (2000). An intimate natural and human history of the harbor from the 17C through the present day.

Literature and Ficton

Baldwin, James. *Go Tell It on the Mountain* (1953). A classic novel of moral and spiritual awakening, set in Harlem.

Capote, Truman. *Breakfast at Tiffany's* (1958). Adventures of the stylish Holly Golightly, made even more famous by the 1961 movie with Audrey Hepburn.

Carr, Caleb. *The Alienist* (1994). Yes, it's fiction, but the author vividly re-creates New York City in the 1890s.

Crane, Stephen. *Maggie: A Girl of the Streets* (1893). Realistic 19C fiction.

Doctorow, E. L. *Ragtime* (1975); *World's Fair* (1986); *Billy Bathgate* (1989); *The Waterworks* (1994); *City of God* (2001). Novels with New York settings at various times in its history.

Finney, Jack. *Time and Again* (1970). A favorite of New York buffs, the story of a man who shuttles back and forth in time between 1880 and the 20C; a detailed picture of the city in the 19C.

Fitzgerald, F. Scott. *The Great Gatsby* (1925). An American classic; New York in the Jazz Age.

James, Henry. *Washington Square* (1881). A Jamesian morality tale set in Greenwich Village, where the author's aunt lived.

Lopate, Philip, editor. *Writing New York: A Literary Anthology* (1998). Excerpts from more than 100 authors, including Washington Irving, Jane Jacobs, Louis Auchincloss, Zora Neale Hurston, and Oscar Hijuelos.

Roth, Henry. *Call It Sleep* (1964). Jewish immigrants on the Lower East Side.

Smith, Betty. *A Tree Grows in Brooklyn* (1943). A poor Irish Catholic girl grows up in Brooklyn around the turn of the 20C.

Wharton, Edith. *The Age of Innocence* (1920). Wharton won the Pulitzer Prize for this understated indictment of the manners and morals of the privileged classes to which she was born.

Winn, Marie. *Red-Tails in Love: A Wildlife Drama in Central Park* (1999). You don't have to be a birdwatcher to enjoy this romantic, wonderfully entwined story of big-city birders and the resilient hawks they observe.

Wolfe, Thomas. *Of Time and the River: A Legend of Man's Hunger in His Youth* (1935). Epic sequel to *Look Homeward, Angel.*

Wolfe, Tom. *The Bonfire of the Vanities* (1987). Wolfe's satire on the nastiness of 1980s New York society.

THE GUIDE

Borough of Manhattan / New York County

To many people New York is synonymous with Manhattan, a slender island 12.5 miles long, 2.5 miles wide, with a total area of 22.6 square miles. It is the third largest borough in population (1.6 million) behind Brooklyn and Queens, and the smallest in size. Manhattan also ranks third in attracting immigrants, with 152,000 settling in the borough from 1990 to 1996. Nearly 60,000 of those newcomers were from the Dominican Republic, and another 31,000 were Chinese, most heading for Chinatown. While half of the Dominicans are clustered in Washington Heights, they have become a strong presence throughout Manhattan and indeed throughout the city, particularly as the Puerto Rican population has diminished. (Puerto Ricans are not immigrants, since the island belongs to America; many longtime Puerto Ricans have begun moving to the suburbs, while poorer ones have returned home.)

City Hall, the center of the borough politically if not geographically, lies at a latitude of 40° 42′ 26″ and a longitude of 74° 0′ 23″. Manhattan's highest altitude is about 268 ft and its lowest is at sea level. Topographically there remain only a few vestiges of Manhattan's appearance before the Dutch came. Southern Manhattan is flat, a coastal plain lying over a fairly shallow stratum of Manhattan schist, the bedrock on which its skyscrapers stand. Again in Midtown, bedrock lies close to the surface, supporting a second great concentration of towering buildings. A large pond near City Hall and swamps in the West Village and near Turtle Bay have been filled; streams and rivers have been drained, filled, or channeled underground as sewers so that Manhattan's topography from the Battery to Central Park is uniform and undistinguished, with the exception of a few unimpressive rises like Murray Hill.

In its more northerly reaches, however, the island's natural terrain is more evident: in Central Park's outcroppings of Manhattan schist, laced with granite intrusions and striated by glacial scratches; in Fort Tryon Park and Inwood Hill Park, two schist ridges bisected by the fault valley that underlies Dyckman St; in the ridges of Morningside Heights, once used by rock climbers to hone their skills; and in the valley of W. 125th St, slashing diagonally across the regular north–south street grid.

Manhattan is encircled by rivers: the Hudson (once called the North River) on the west; the East River, actually a tidal inlet from Long Island Sound, on the east; and the Harlem River on the northeast, part of which, the Harlem Ship Canal on the north, is an artificial channel dug at the end of the 19C to facilitate navigation.

The island was settled from south to north, with its oldest neighborhoods in what is today called Lower Manhattan. The first Dutch settlement was near Battery Park, an area of marshy flatness similar to the Dutch lowlands. The Financial District, a residential area for the Dutch, had already begun to assume some public functions when the British took over in 1664. North of it are the Civic Center, and then the Lower East Side, Chinatown, and Little Italy, which became home to the city's large immigrant population toward the end of the 19C. To the north and west are TriBeCa and SoHo, former industrial areas that have now become chic residential and shopping districts. Above Houston St are Greenwich Village and the East Village, long home to the city's counterculture. (The East Village formerly was part of the Lower East Side and still houses many immigrants, especially in Alphabet City to the far East.) Also south of Midtown are the increasingly trendy Chelsea and tony Gramercy Park.

The western half of Midtown, which stretches from 34th to 59th Sts, includes Herald Square, Penn Station, Madison Square Garden, Bryant Park, and the newly rejuvenated Times Square. The eastern section features Grand Central Terminal and the office towers of Madison and Park Aves, and to the far east, the United Nations and the affluent residential neighborhoods of Murray Hill, Kips Bay, and Turtle Bay. Dividing east from west is Fifth Ave, along which are ranged the Empire State Building, the New York Public Library, Rockefeller Center, St. Patrick's Cathedral, and the city's monuments to shopping, department stores Saks Fifth Avenue, Lord & Taylor, and Bergdorf Goodman.

Central Park divides the East Side from the West Side above 59th St. The Upper East Side includes the most expensive homes in the city—particularly along Fifth Ave and in elite neighborhoods like Sutton Place and Beekman Place—and Yorkville, an increasingly pricey area that was formerly an uptown immigrant neighborhood for Germans, Czechs, and Hungarians. Fifth Ave between 82nd and 104th Sts is home to Museum Mile, a stretch of world-famous institutions, including the Metropolitan Museum of Art, the Solomon R. Guggenheim Museum, and the Jewish Museum. Above 96th St lies East Harlem, formerly an Italian enclave, now known as El Barrio or Spanish Harlem.

On the West Side, Central Park West and Riverside Drive are the finest residential areas, with their views of greenery and the Hudson River respectively, while the commercial streets—Broadway, Amsterdam and Columbus Aves—house countless restaurants, bars, and shops, as well as Lincoln Center for the Performing Arts and the Promenade and Beacon Theaters. North of 96th St is Morningside Heights, dominated by Columbia University, the Cathedral of St. John the Divine, and other major educational and religious institutions. To the east and below Morningside Heights lies the Harlem plain, embracing the nation's most famous black community. Upper Manhattan consists of the residential neighborhoods of Washington Heights and Inwood, with their own impressive parks, including the relatively untamed Inwood Hill Park. The Cloisters in Fort Tryon Park is the major cultural institution in Upper Manhattan. Across the Harlem River is Marble Hill, physically attached to the Bronx but politically a part of Manhattan, to which it was joined before the digging of the Harlem Ship Canal.

While the city as a whole has flourished in the last decade, the spotlight, particularly for visitors, has naturally been on Manhattan. Neighborhoods like TriBeCa, Chelsea, and Times Square have undergone dramatic rebirths as have public spaces like Bryant Park. City, state, and government agencies have undertaken impressive restorations (for example, Grand Central Terminal) as well as ambitious new projects like Hudson River Park and the new Penn Station. Much of this was due to a vibrant national economy and what seemed to be an endless Wall Street boom, but much of the credit also goes to the tough-on-crime, business-friendly mayoralty of Rudolph Giuliani (1994 to 2001), who made the city seem like a welcoming place to investors, developers, tourists, college students, and young professionals. At the same time, the mayor's policy and demeanor badly strained relations with minorities while many middle-class residents and mom-and-pop businesses have been forced out by soaring real estate prices and rules designed to encourage suburban-style superstores. Additionally, new condos and co-ops for the very affluent in neighborhoods such as Chelsea and TriBeCa and high-density developments such as Donald Trump's new East Side tower and Riverside South can send costs skyrocketing for the surrounding community, again forcing out the working and middle class. (The proposed sale of air rights from Broadway theaters to Clinton-area developers would also compound this problem.) These additions also place major new burdens on the city's infrastructure, especially its streets and subways, while the government (particularly the state) has been unwilling to push for ambitious but desperately needed solutions, like a full-fledged Second Ave subway line that would ease East Side crowding.

Another major factor in restoring the city's image has been the growth and increased influence of Business Improvement Districts (BIDs), the most prominent of which—the Grand Central, 34th St, and Bryant Park BIDs—have done an astonishing job of polishing up large swaths of Midtown. First authorized by the City Council in the 1980s, these quasi-governmental agencies impose mandatory taxes on neighborhood property owners and, in turn, provide security, clean-up crews, and social services where the city has fallen short. In recent years, however, it has become apparent that BIDs also can be a morass of conflicts of interest and just as inefficient as government in delivering services for a good price. Equally problematic is the realization that BIDs can undermine democracy: the executives running them aren't held accountable to voters, and BIDs are subject to minimal public oversight. Like highly successful public-private partnerships such as the Central Park Conservancy, BIDs may ultimately harm the city's residents more than they help, since government uses them as an excuse to cut services, further widening the division between haves and have-nots.

Note: Until 2004, the rehabilitation of the Manhattan Bridge will cause major service changes on the Sixth Ave Express lines (B, D, and Q). Because of the destruction of the World Trade Center, service to some stations on several downtown lines has been lost indefinitely or disrupted temporarily. For further information, see Subways in Practical Information.

1 · Statue of Liberty, Ellis Island, and Governors Island

Subway: Broadway–Seventh Ave Local (1, 9) to South Ferry. Lexington Ave Express (4, 5) to Bowling Green. Broadway Local (R) to Whitehall St.
Bus: M1, M6, M15.

Statue of Liberty National Monument

Liberty Island, New York, NY 10004. ☎ (212) 363-3200 for recorded information. Web site: www.nps.gov/stli. Open every day at least 9:30–4; extended hours in summer and holiday periods. Closed Dec 25. Free; charge for ferry; credit cards or personal checks not accepted for ferry tickets.

Ferries bound for the Statue of Liberty and Ellis Island leave from Battery Park in New York and Liberty State Park in Jersey City, N.J.; for information about departures from Liberty State Park, ☎ (201) 435-9499. The **ticket kiosk** in Battery Park is located in Castle Clinton, the low red sandstone structure on the west side of the park. Boats leave at least once each half hour all year at least 9–3:30 with additional sailings and extended hours during peak season. For schedule information call the Circle Line–Statue of Liberty and Ellis Island Ferry, Inc, ☎ (212) 269-5755. The round trip takes about 1 hour and 15 minutes, with stops at Ellis Island and the statue. During peak season the waiting time for a boat can stretch to two hours.

Crowds are often very heavy and the time required to ascend the statue lengthens proportionally. To make the ascent with the shortest waiting time, take the first boat (telephone for the time of first sailing), stay downstairs on the boat near the gangway, and hurry from the dock to the statue.

Museum in statue interior. Restaurant; gift shop. Complete access for handicapped visitors to museum, restrooms, and restaurant; no wheelchair access above museum level. No facilities for checking parcels.

Climbing the Statue

The crown is a 22-story climb from ground level. An elevator reaches the top of the pedestal, but from this level ascent to the crown is only by a narrow spiral stairway, the equivalent of 12 stories. Although the statue interior is air-cooled (not air-conditioned), temperatures rise in summer. Visitors with physical disabilities, asthma, heart ailments, fear of heights, or claustrophobia are urged not to make the climb. From the tenth-floor pedestal there are breathtaking panoramic views of the city's skyline, the harbor, Staten Island, and New Jersey. From the crown, the view is a limited southern one of the harbor, and the endless crowds allow for only a brief glimpse. At peak times, the ascent may take more than two hours.

The Statue of Liberty (dedicated 1886; sculptor, Frédéric Auguste Bartholdi; DL), surely the most famous piece of sculpture in America, rises in towering majesty on Liberty Island in direct view of ships entering the Upper Bay. A gift of the people of France, the figure stands on a granite pedestal, donated by the American public. Her head is surrounded by a radiant crown, while her feet step forth from broken shackles; in her uplifted right hand is a torch; her left holds a tablet representing the Declaration of Independence.

History: The Island
The Mohegan Indians called the island *Minnissais* (Lesser Island); early colonists called it Great Oyster Island, but it was more familiarly known as Bedloe's Island after Isaac Bedloe acquired it in 1667 from the English colonial governor. (It was renamed Liberty Island in 1956.) In 1738, fearful of a smallpox outbreak, New York took over the island, establishing the city's first formal quarantine station. On the eve of the American Revolution, British troops seized the island, establishing a refuge for Tory sympathizers. The U.S. government acquired it in 1800 to build Fort Wood (1808–11). Named after a now-obscure hero of the War of 1812, Fort Wood later served as a Civil War recruitment camp and an ordnance depot; in 1877 the government donated it to the Liberty project.

History: The Statue
The inspiration for the Statue of Liberty, originally called "Liberty Enlightening the World," came primarily from Édouard de Laboulaye (1811–1883), a noted ju-

Enlarging Liberty's hand (1876–81). Bartholdi's clay model of the statue was enlarged in three stages to full scale. The sculptor, bareheaded in the foreground, modified the form each time as increased size created unexpected visual effects. (New York Public Library)

rist, professor, and authority on U.S. Constitutional history, and Frédéric-Auguste Bartholdi (1834–1904), a sculptor of monumental ambitions. Laboulaye, wanted to identify the destiny of France, then ruled by a monarch, with that of a democracy, but knew anything too close to home would be inflammatory. He proposed a joint Franco-American monument in 1865 and introduced Bartholdi to the project. The statue's iron skeleton was devised by Alexandre-Gustave Eiffel (1832–1923), whose reputation at the time rested with his iron trusswork railway bridges.

Statue Statistics	
Height of statue alone	151 ft
Height of pedestal	89 ft
Height of torch above sea	305 ft
Weight	225 tons
Waist measurement	35 ft
Width of mouth	3 ft
Length of index finger	8 ft

The size of the statue imposed technical difficulties, which Eiffel solved with great ingenuity. He devised an interior framework consisting of a heavy central iron pylon supporting a lightweight system of trusswork that reaches out toward the interior surface of the statue. The hammered copper "skin" of the figure, only $\frac{3}{32}$ of an inch thick, is bound together in sections by steel straps and joined to the trusswork in such a way that it "floats" at the ends of hundreds of flexible attachments and can accommodate both thermal changes and wind.

The French people raised about $400,000 for the statue, which was constructed in Paris by the firm of Gaget, Gauthier, et Cie and assembled outside Bartholdi's workshops. On July 4, 1884, the figure was formally presented to the United States. Then it was dismantled and shipped to New York in 214 crates. The crates were royally welcomed but sat unopened for more than a year as a Franco-American committee struggled to raise money to build the pedestal (designed by French-trained architect Richard Morris Hunt). In 1885, the committee was considering returning the statue or letting another city have a go at it when *New York World* publisher Joseph Pulitzer, an immigrant from Hungary, promised to print the name of every donor in his paper, even if the gift were only a penny. Within three months the final $102,000 had been raised—from 80,000 donations.

On Oct 28, 1886, President Grover Cleveland dedicated it during spectacular ceremonies climaxed by fireworks and the unveiling of the face. The statue soon became a tourist attraction, later a promise of hope offered to immigrants, and eventually a powerful symbol for the U.S. itself. As such it has been the target of extremist groups: in 1965 four terrorists attempted to blow off its head and the arm holding its torch; in 1971 a group of Vietnam veterans occupied it for several days as a war protest; in 1980 two men protesting "injustice" climbed the exterior and spent a night enveloped in the folds of the robe.

The Statue of Liberty under construction in Paris (1881–84). The statue was completely assembled outside Bartholdi's studio and presented ceremoniously to the U.S. ambassador before being dismantled and shipped. (New York Public Library)

After nearly a century of wear and tear, a restoration campaign refurbished Lady Liberty in time for her centennial celebration. The only visible exterior change is the replacement of the former glass torch by a gilded one, as Bartholdi had envisioned. Inside, the wire mesh that long enclosed the spiral staircase has been cleared away so that the great volumes of the body and the billowing folds of the robe soar above the visitor in their full glory. The architectural firm of Swanke Hayden Connell, working with Ammann & Whitney, engineers, undertook the restoration.

The unveiling of the statue was climaxed by a July 4 celebration truly American in its exuberant excess. Naval warships fired 21-gun salvos and military planes performed aerobatics over the harbor; a fleet of 150 tall ships sailed from the Narrows up the Hudson River; a 40,000-shell fireworks display illuminated the harbor at night. Some 25,000 vessels clogged the harbor; helicopters, jet fighters, and six blimps buzzed, soared, and hovered overhead. An estimated 1.5–2 million people jammed the streets, parks, and buildings with a view of the statue. It may have been the city's largest party ever.

Exterior
The statue is supported by Hunt's pedestal of concrete and Stony Creek granite. The stepped terrace between the pedestal and Fort Wood at the base was added in 1965, belatedly fulfilling Hunt's original vision. The massive bronze doors at the entrance, installed in the 1980s, detail the labor that went into the restoration.

Interior
On view in the lobby is the copper-and-amber glass torch designed by Mt. Rushmore–creator Gutzon Borglum, which Lady Liberty held from 1916 to 1984. Upstairs is the **Statue of Liberty Museum,** devoted to the conception and construction of the statue, its impact on new arrivals, and its exploitation as a commercial image or vehicle for propaganda.

Ellis Island National Monument
Ellis Island, New York, NY 10004. ☎ (212) 363-3200 for recorded information. Web site: www.nps.gov/stli. Open every day at least 9:30–4; with extended hours in summer and holiday periods. Closed Dec 25. Free; charge for ferry; credit cards or personal checks not accepted for ferry tickets.

Permanent exhibitions, guided and audio tours, films. Cafeteria, gift shop. Accessible to wheelchairs: elevators to all levels; services for sight- and hearing-impaired.

Ferry: See Statue of Liberty ferry.

Originally a low-lying sandbar, Ellis Island lies about a mile southwest of Battery Park in Upper New York Bay, not far from the Statue of Liberty. It is the site of the former U.S. Immigration Station through which an estimated 12 million immigrants passed on their way to a new life in America. The U.S. Census Bureau estimates that perhaps two Americans in five can trace their ancestry to Ellis Island. The island now consists of two land masses—the original island (about 3 acres), where the museum stands; and a southern portion (about 24.5 acres), mostly landfill, home primarily to ruins from the days of the immigration service.

History

The Indians called Ellis Island *Kioshk* (Gull Island); the Dutch bought it in 1630, named it Little Oyster Island, and then ceded it to a patroon—a sort of feudal landowner—who also held title to what is now Hoboken, Staten Island, and Jersey City, but never left Amsterdam to enjoy his territories. During much of the 18C the British called it Gibbet Island, after several pirates who were hanged there in the 1760s. At the time of the Revolution it was owned by Samuel Ellis (died 1794), who had a farm in New Jersey, sold general merchandise in Manhattan, and leased out part of the island to a fisherman's tavern. After his death, the federal government acquired it (1808) for a then-exorbitant $10,000 to build a fort. Like the three other fortifications built at about this time (see Castle Clinton National Monument in Walk 2), it was intended to protect the city from a British naval invasion in the War of 1812, but saw no action. Named Fort Gibson in 1814, it is the only one of the four harbor fortifications of which no trace remains. From 1835 to 1890 it served as an ammunition dump, threatening nearby New Jersey residents with the possibility of accidental explosions.

In 1890, when the federal government took over the immigration service, Ellis Island was designated as the site of the main receiving station almost by default: the army did not want immigrants on Governors Island, New Yorkers did not want them on Manhattan, and the public considered the use of Bedloe's Island, already the site of the Statue of Liberty, an outrage. An immigrant station, therefore, was built on Ellis Island and opened in 1892.

Primarily constructed of Georgia pine, it burned to the ground five years later, fortunately without loss of life, but with the destruction of most of the immigration records for 1855–90. In 1898 the firm of Boring & Tilton began to construct the present station, while the immigration service was moved to Battery Park. The new fireproof buildings opened on Dec 17, 1900, and that day received 2,251 immigrants.

Inside the station, federal inspectors processed the immigrants, detaining those who would be incapacitated from earning a living and weeding out paupers, criminals, prostitutes, the insane, and those suffering from contagious diseases or professing beliefs such as anarchy or polygamy. Persons not admitted were either detained (20 percent) until their cases could be resolved or held for deportation (2 percent); they were housed and fed in the dormitories, hospitals, and dining halls.

Until 1902, when President Theodore Roosevelt appointed William Williams as commissioner of immigration, immigrants were often abused or robbed. After Williams's reforms, problems arose primarily from overcrowding. In 1907, the peak year of immigration, 1,004,756 people entered the U.S. through Ellis Island, approximately twice the number the station was designed to handle.

The heavy influx continued until 1915, when World War I closed transatlantic shipping. In the period of isolationism and racism that followed the war, a series of laws passed in the 1920s imposed an overall annual ceiling as well as quotas for particular nationalities, discriminating against Latins, Slavs, and Jews. Under the National Origins Act (1924) immigrants were processed in their own countries, and thereafter Ellis Island became underused and increasingly expensive to maintain. In 1954 the last detainee, a Norwegian sailor who had jumped ship, was released; the station closed and the island was vacated. All of the island's buildings, including the majestic Main Building, began to deteriorate rapidly, ravaged by weather and damp sea air and stripped by vandals. Gradually, the government became mindful of the island's historical importance, and in 1965 it became part of the Statue of Liberty National Monument. In 1976 the island opened to visitors on a small scale, allowing tours of the ruins. Four years later, the rehabilitation of Ellis Island was included in the Statue of Liberty restoration project, with its primary focus restoring the Main Building as a museum (reopened 1990). The rest of the island was left mostly untouched, its old buildings—formerly home to insane wards and hospitals—rotting away and still closed to the public. Work is currently under way to stabilize these ruins; numerous plans for future redevelopment include centers devoted to immigrant contributions and public health, along with conference facilities.

In 1993, New Jersey brought suit in the U.S. Supreme Court laying claim to the southern portion, stating that an 1834 compact between New York and New Jersey gave the Empire State jurisdiction only over the original three-acre island, not the 24.5 acres of landfill. New York maintained that the compact gave it jurisdiction over the entire island. In 1998, the Court ruled that most of the island is in New Jersey, with the original island and its museum in New York.

Exterior
The **Main Building** (1897–1900; Boring & Tilton), formerly the Immigrant Receiving Station, is built of red brick and limestone, with intricate stonework and four towers capped with cupolas and spires. To the right of the Main Building is the 652 ft American Immigrant Wall of Honor, with the names of thousands of immigrants whose descendants donated $100 to have their names inscribed.

Interior
Inside the main entrance is the **Baggage Room,** with displays of the original luggage—from wicker baskets to heavy trunks—toted by immigrants. Baggage handlers could often identify an immigrant's country of origin from these humble suitcases and parcels.

On the second floor is the historic **Registry Room** (200 × 100 × 56 ft), left empty to heighten its emotional impact; until 1911 it was divided by barriers of iron pipe into smaller areas reminiscent of cattle pens and handled 5,000 immigrants daily. The majestic vaulted ceiling was installed (1918) after a 1916 explosion detonated by German saboteurs on Black Tom Wharf in New Jersey brought down the earlier plaster ceiling. Engineered by Rafael Guastavino, an immigrant from Spain, the self-supporting tile proved so resilient that during the recent renovation only 17 of the 28,880 tiles had to be replaced. The former processing rooms now house exhibits that re-create the process by which immigrants were screened and chronicle the history of immigration from 1880 to 1924.

On the third floor, exhibits display artifacts and photographs brought by immigrants, recount the island's history, and depict the deterioration and restoration of the island.

Governors Island
East of Liberty and Ellis Islands is Governors Island, the nation's oldest continuously active military base until 1997, when its Coast Guard base closed. Situated in New York Harbor between Lower Manhattan and Brooklyn, this piece of history, and prime piece of real estate, is poised for redevelopment and faces an uncertain future. Currently it is not open to the public.

History

When the Dutch arrived in 1625, they noted the island's strategic importance and built a fort on what they called *Nooten Eylandt* (Nut Island) even before settling New Amsterdam. (The island then had vast groves of nut trees.) When the British took New Amsterdam in 1664, renaming it New York, they later proclaimed the island "the Denizen of His Majestie's Governors," giving it its current name. The flamboyant Lord Cornbury, Sir Edward Hyde, built himself a manor on the island but was yanked from office after it was discovered that he misused money intended for fortifications. In the early 18C, the island quarantined thousands of Palatine refugees—German Protestants expelled from the lower Palatinate of the Rhine by Louis XIV—after they had wandered into England. One of them, John Peter Zenger, later became the controversial publisher of the *New York Weekly Journal* (see Federal Hall National Monument in Walk 3). In 1755, during the French and Indian War, the 51st Regiment of the British Colonial Militia became the first troops stationed on Governors Island.

Threatened with involvement in the ongoing military tension between Britain and France, the new federal government took over the island, erecting Fort Jay (1798; rebuilt 1803), named for John Jay, who had helped negotiate peace with Great Britain after the Revolution, and served as the first secretary of foreign affairs. Castle Williams, named for its designer, Col. Jonathan Williams of the U.S. Army Corps of Engineers, was completed in 1811.

A year later, the South Battery was built to guard Buttermilk Channel. With all these fortifications, the British made no attempt to enter New York Harbor, and the fortresses never fired a shot. By 1900, the 160-acre island had been eroded to 70 acres; the Army Corps of Engineers used fill to increase the island by 103 acres. During World War I, and again in World War II, the island functioned as an embarkation point for troops.

In 1966, the army base was one of 95 closed around the country, and the baton was passed to the Coast Guard, establishing Governors Island as the largest Coast Guard base in the world. The Coast Guard base closed in 1997, and the island became federal surplus property. President Bill Clinton promoted the idea of selling the 173-acre island to the state and city for one dollar if they could agree on a plan that would serve the public good while providing the private funding necessary to maintain the island and its historic structures. Congress, however, presumed a $500 million price tag and included the revenue from its sale in the Balanced Budget Act.

The city and state's long-delayed plan was finally presented in 2000, calling for 50 acres of public parkland, cultural destinations, and commercial facilities to generate the necessary income. Republicans in Congress, however, show little inclination to return the island to New York (the state gave the island to the federal government in 1800 for coastal defense). Despite recent deadlines, it is likely that the fight over Governors Island will continue for some time. In 2001, as one of his final acts in office, President Bill Clinton designated the two forts as national monuments.

2 · Lower Manhattan: Battery Park to South Street Seaport

Subway: Broadway–Seventh Ave Local (1, 9) to South Ferry. Lexington Ave Express (4, 5) to Bowling Green. Broadway Local (R) to Whitehall St.
Bus: M1, M6, M15.

New York City owes its historic supremacy among American cities to its closeness to the sea, and nowhere are these ties more obvious than at the southernmost tip of Manhattan, where the East and Hudson Rivers converge and empty into New York Bay.

In 1624 the Dutch ship *Nieu Nederlandt* deposited eight men on what is now Governors Island and continued upstream to settle others at the present site of Albany. These men, sponsored by the Dutch West India Company, and the families who followed them, moved to the southern shore of Manhattan, where they built rude shelters and a fort to protect themselves from Native Americans.

The original fort (1626), Fort Amsterdam, consisted of a crude blockhouse protected by a cedar palisade. As the town grew and alternately fell under the jurisdiction of the Dutch, the British, the Dutch again, and the British once more, the fort was strengthened and appropriately renamed. The last such structure, called Fort George after the reigning British monarch, remained until after the Revolution, when it was torn down in 1789 to make way for Government House, intended as the residence for the new nation's President.

Alexander Hamilton Custom House
The former **United States Custom House** (1907; Cass Gilbert; DL), 1 Bowling Green, on the site of Government House is now the Alexander Hamilton Custom House, and is home to the U.S. Bankruptcy Court and the National Museum of the American Indian.

History
In 1892 the U.S. Treasury announced an architectural competition for a custom house—a building of great importance as customs revenue was integral to the nation's budget in the years before the income tax. Cass Gilbert, who had earlier apprenticed with the firm of McKim, Mead & White and established his reputation working in the Midwest, won the competition with a design that symbolized the commercial greatness of the nation and of the city. The building also made Gilbert one of the city's leading architects. After the U.S. Customs Service moved to the World Trade Center in 1973, the building stood empty for long periods. In 1994, the George Gustav Heye Center of the National Museum of the American Indian moved here from Washington Heights.

Exterior
Adorned with emblems of commerce and the sea, the Custom House facade is a triumph of Beaux-Arts exuberance. In the window arches are heads of the eight "races" of mankind. Above the cornice, statues representing 12 great commercial nations of history stare down on the vicissitudes of Broadway, while the head of

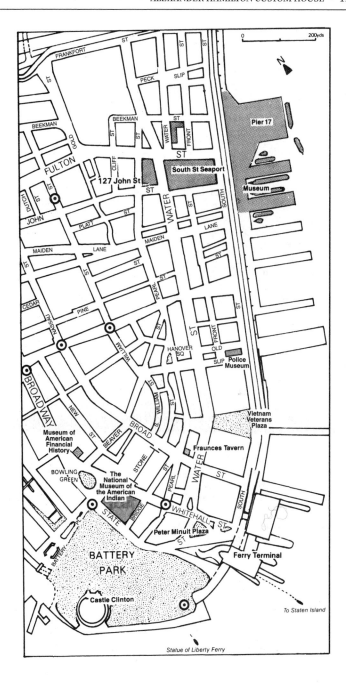

Mercury, Roman god of commerce, crowns the capital of each of the 44 Corinthian columns encircling the building.

Gilbert commissioned Daniel Chester French, best known for his statue of Abraham Lincoln in the Lincoln Memorial (Washington, D.C.), to design the heroic limestone statues of *The Four Continents* (left to right): Asia, America, Europe, and Africa. The groups reflect early-20C cultural attitudes: Asia and Africa, meditative and somnolent, sit at the periphery; Europe, robed in a Grecian gown, sits enthroned among the achievements of the past; America looks dynamically forward. On her right, Labor turns the wheel of progress; on her left a Native American kneels, eyes downcast.

Interior

In the center of the main floor is the great **rotunda** ($135 \times 85 \times 48$ ft high). The ceiling, constructed of 140 tons of tile and plaster (no steel), was engineered by Rafael Guastavino, whose tilework also appears in the Cathedral of St. John the Divine, Ellis Island's Registry Room, and Grand Central Station. Just below the dome are frescoes (1937) by Reginald Marsh. The panels depict early explorers and an ocean liner entering New York harbor. One famous panel shows the movie star Greta Garbo, surrounded by the press.

National Museum of the American Indian, Smithsonian Institution

George Gustav Heye Center, 1 Bowling Green (Broadway at Battery Park), New York, NY 10004. ☎ (212) 668-6624 for recorded information; to reach a live person, ☎ (212) 514-3700. Web site: www.si.edu/nmai. Open daily 10–5; Thurs until 8. Closed Dec 25. Free. Changing exhibitions, demonstrations, and performances. Gift shop. Accessible to wheelchairs.

The New York branch of the National Museum of the American Indian, Smithsonian Institution (chartered by Congress 1989) opened here in 1994. It merges the collections of the Smithsonian with those of the former Museum of the American Indian/Heye Foundation (founded 1916).

Highlights

The museum's astonishing collections range geographically from the Arctic to Tierra del Fuego and chronologically from prehistoric times to the present. Highlights include 18C clothing, farm implements and tools for gathering wild rice from the Great Lakes tribes; feathered headdresses and buffalo hide robes from the Plains Indians; masks and ceremonial wood carvings from the Northwest Coast tribes; featherwork from the Amazon; and Peruvian and Navajo fabrics. The photographic collection, with antique daguerreotypes as well as modern color prints, is world famous.

History

The Museum of the American Indian was born from the obsession of George Gustav Heye (1874–1957), who gathered most of its collection. The son of a wealthy German oil baron, Heye took a job in Arizona as an electrical engineer and soon began collecting Native American artifacts. At first he acquired things a few at a time. Later (he eventually became an investment banker), Heye collected wholesale, crisscrossing the West and financing expeditions to Central and South America. The collection opened (1922) to the public in a building at Audubon Terrace (Broadway at W. 155th St) in Washington Heights.

Though successful for decades, financial difficulties, a location far from the cultural center of the city, and crowded facilities eventually led the museum to consider moving. After several years of failed negotiations with city institutions, the museum merged (1989) with the Smithsonian Institution. The Custom House—federal property vacant since 1973—became the new Heye Center, which will continue as a satellite space of the Smithsonian's larger National Museum of the American Indian in Washington, D.C.

The museum's goals reflect attitudes toward Native American cultures and art that have evolved since Heye died. Heye's own insatiable methods of collecting are no longer condoned, and the museum is required by law to return to the tribes sacred objects and human remains.

The small fenced plot just north of the main facade of the Custom House is **Bowling Green Park,** the city's first park. During the Dutch colonial period, this area was an open place at the southern end of *de Heere Wegh* ("the Main Street," now Broadway) and was used as a cattle market; hence the name of Marketfield Street, a block east. Later the area became a parade ground and still later a bowling green, leased in 1733 for the annual fee of one peppercorn per year. The Bowling Green Fence (1771; DL) was built to keep the park from collecting "all the filth and dirt in the neighborhood" and to protect an equestrian statue of George III (erected 1766), but it was torn down on July 9, 1776, by a crowd of patriots, stirred to action by a public reading of the Declaration of Independence. Pieces of the lead statue were melted down and cast into bullets. The original fence survives, although the mob made off with the ornaments which capped the posts. A fountain is now the park's centerpiece.

Just beyond the park is a **flag pole** that honors the evacuation of the British troops. On Nov 25, 1783, a man named John Van Arsdale climbed a nearby flag pole—greased by the departing Tories—and replaced the last Union Jack with the Stars and Stripes.

While Lower Broadway no longer harbors the offices of the great transatlantic steamship lines, it still maintains fragile ties to its maritime past. The building at **1 Broadway** (1884; Edward H. Kendall) on the west side of Bowling Green, occupies the site of the Archibald Kennedy House (1771–1882), which was used by George Washington and General Howe during their respective periods of residence in New York during the Revolutionary War. Its tenure as the United States Lines Building is marked by decorative tridents, shells, and fish on the facade and doorways labeled for first- and cabin-class passengers. Inside is a large floor mosaic of a compass and a huge painting of the world highlighting steamship routes.

The U.S. Post Office at 25 Broadway is the former **Cunard Building** (1921; Benjamin Wistar Morris; DL). Behind the Renaissance facade lies one of the city's great interiors. The vaulted vestibule has a tall wrought-iron gate by Samuel Yellin and an ornate ceiling by Ezra Winter featuring cherubic figures riding dolphins and pelicans. The room beyond, now housing the drab apparatus of the postal service, once proclaimed the romance of steamship travel in a manner suitable to the company that launched the *Queen Mary* and the *Queen Elizabeth*. A dome, 68 ft high, rises loftily above the octagonal room (185 × 74 ft). The ceiling designs, again by Ezra Winter, were executed by Italian craftsmen brought in for the work;

the pendentives supporting the dome are covered with frescoes depicting the ships of Columbus (southeast), Sir Francis Drake (northeast), John Cabot (northwest), and Leif Eriksson (southwest). The maps of world steamship routes on the north and south walls were designed by Barry Faulkner.

On an island in front of 25 Broadway is **Charging Bull** (1989; Arturo Di-Modica), a bronze sculpture symbolizing the city's financial district.

A Bull on Broadway

At midnight on Christmas Eve in 1989, DiModica, a Sicilian-born artist who had spent three years creating the 3-ton, 16-ft bull in his SoHo studio, left it under a Christmas tree outside the New York Stock Exchange. His gift was immediately impounded by the police. Parks Commissioner Henry Stern rescued the bull and found it a permanent home at its present location.

Across the street at 26 Broadway is the former **Standard Oil Building** (1922; Carrère & Hastings). The facade of this elegant office building curves to follow Broadway, but the tower, best seen from Battery Park, is aligned with the north–south grid of the streets, an architectural concession to the uptown skyline. On top is a structure resembling an oil lamp, which conceals a chimney. Oil lamps also flank the main entrance, and the names of company executives, including John D. Rockefeller, adorn the marble walls.

Museum of American Financial History

28 Broadway, New York, NY 10004. ☎ (212) 908-4110. Web site: www.financial history.org. Open Tues–Sat 10–4. Closed Sun, Mon, public holidays, stock market holidays. Free. Walking tours, Fri at 10 A.M. Gift shop. Not accessible to wheelchairs.

Next door at 28 Broadway is the tiny Museum of American Financial History. Founded in 1988 by John Herzog, a businessman and collector of financial documents, the museum is, fittingly, on the site of Alexander Hamilton's law office. The collection includes an impressive array of financial arcana, including a 13 ft section of ticker tape from the first minutes of trading at the New York Stock Exchange on "Black Tuesday," Oct 29, 1929.

Battery Park

Return south along Broadway to Battery Park, whose name recalls a row of cannons that defended the original fort and stood near the present sidewalk west of the Custom House. Situated on filled land, the park offers spectacular views of the harbor and a group of monuments recalling New York's maritime and commercial history.

Near the intersection of State St, Bowling Green, and Battery Place just outside the fence is the **Battery Park Control House** (1904–5; Heins & La Farge; DL), the original entrance to the Bowling Green station of the city's first subway and a fine example of the influence of the École des Beaux-Arts. Designed by an architectural firm better known for its work on the Cathedral of St. John the Divine, its monumental quality suggests the city's pride in its new subway system.

The flagpole near the park entrance is the **Netherlands Memorial Monument,** given to the city in 1926 by the Dutch as a token of affection for the city's founders. The flagpole base bears a map (now barely visible) of Manhattan in Dutch times and a representation of the legendary event of Native Americans receiving $24 for the island. Between the flagpole and Castle Clinton stretches the **Eisenhower Mall** (1970). When the Dutch arrived, New York's shoreline only extended to about the midpoint of the present mall.

Just beyond the mall's halfway point is the **Hope Garden,** which honors victims of HIV and AIDS. Off to the right is a bronze **statue of John Ericsson** (1902; Jonathan Scott Hartley), the designer of the ironclad *Monitor,* whose clash with the Confederate frigate *Merrimac* in 1862 marked the beginning of the end for wooden warships.

In front of Castle Clinton stands *The Immigrants* (1973, dedicated 1983; Luis Sanguino), a bronze statue paying homage to the 8 million immigrants who passed through Castle Clinton's gates during its 35 years as the Immigrant Depot Station. The monument depicts new arrivals in highly dramatic poses of hope and despair.

Castle Clinton National Monument

Battery Park, New York, NY 10004 (c/o 26 Wall St, New York, NY 10005). ☎ (212) 344-7220. Web site: www.nps.gov/cacl. Open seven days 9–5; earlier in peak season. Closed Dec 25. Free. Tours, special events. Book shop. Accessible to wheelchairs.

The park's centerpiece is Castle Clinton National Monument (1807; John McComb Jr.; DL), whose squat red sandstone walls were raised before the War of 1812 to protect the harbor from a naval invasion.

History

The original fort, the Southwest Battery, was situated on an island about 200 ft from the mainland and connected to it by a wooden causeway with a drawbridge. It was built between 1807 and 1811, when British attacks on American ships suggested war might be imminent. Virtually defenseless at the time, New York began the construction of four forts: Fort Wood on Bedloe's (now Liberty) Island, Fort Gibson on Ellis Island, Castle Williams on Governors Island, and the Southwest Battery here.

Built from plans by John McComb Jr., one of New York's earliest native architects, the walls facing the harbor were pierced by a row of 28 black 32-pounders which could sweep the harbor shore to shore; those facing the land housed powder magazines and officers' quarters. The fort was untested during the war.

After the war the Southwest Battery was renamed Castle Clinton to honor De Witt Clinton, who served during a distinguished career both as mayor of the city and governor of the state. In 1824, it opened as an entertainment center called Castle Garden. Audiences enjoyed balloon ascensions, fireworks, scientific demonstrations (Samuel F. B. Morse's "wireless telegraph"), band concerts, political speeches (Daniel Webster, Henry Clay), and receptions for heroes (the Marquis de Lafayette, Andrew Jackson). In 1845 the old fort was roofed over, and Castle Garden became a venue for more serious cultural fare, reaching its apogee on Sept 11, 1850, when P. T. Barnum staged the American debut of Jenny Lind, the "Swedish Nightingale," before a sellout crowd of more than 6,000 people.

After more than a quarter of a century as a theater, Castle Garden closed its doors to the public and reopened them (1855) to immigrants streaming in from abroad. By this time the island had been joined to Manhattan by landfill, forcing immigration officials to fence off the depot from the city and the swindlers who preyed on bewildered new arrivals. The station welcomed more than 8 million people from 1855 until 1890, when the Immigration Service became a function of the federal government. Two years later Ellis Island opened.

In 1896 Castle Garden became the New York Aquarium and was remodeled once again. In 1941, despite the aquarium's immense popularity, Robert Moses, then commissioner of Parks and head of the Triborough Bridge Authority, closed the aquarium, determined to raze the fort as an act of revenge for the defeat of his proposed Brooklyn-Battery Bridge Crossing. Concerned citizens successfully lobbied to preserve the fort, and in 1946 Congress declared it a national monument.

Beyond the main gate, the passageway opens into a circular parade field surrounded by the fort's massive walls. To the right of the entrance is a small exhibit with dioramas and photographs illustrating the fort's history. In the center of the fort is the ticket kiosk for the Circle Line **ferry to the Statue of Liberty and Ellis Island** (for ferry information, see Walk 1).

To the right of Castle Clinton, is the **Korean War Memorial** (1991; Mac Adams), *The Universal Soldier,* a 20 ft sculpture of polished black granite with the stainless-steel outline of a soldier cut out of the center. Along the shoreline runs the **Admiral George Dewey Promenade,** with a spectacular panorama of New York Harbor.

At the north end of the promenade on **Pier A** (1884–86; DL) is the former Fireboat Station. The pier is one of the oldest piers remaining in the Hudson River. The tower, originally used as a lookout, now holds a clock donated (1919) by Daniel Reid, a founder of U.S. Steel, to honor servicemen who died in World War I. Until 1959 the pier served as headquarters for the Harbor Police and thereafter was used by the Fire Department's marine division. It is now being transformed into a visitors' center with restaurants and a marina for excursion boats.

South of the pier, 30 ft out in the water, is perhaps the most haunting and powerful piece of public sculpture in the city. The **American Merchant Marine Memorial** (1991; Marisol Escobar) was inspired by a photograph of merchant marines whose ship, the SS *Muskogee,* was destroyed during World War II by a German submarine. The seamen were left to die by the enemy (one of whom took the photo). The bronze and stainless steel sculpture, 7½ ft high, depicts one man kneeling on a raft and another shouting for help as a third man stretches down into the water to grasp the hand of a drowning comrade. The water provides a real background for the sculpture, and the figure of the drowning man emerges and recedes with the ebb and flow of the tide. Former merchant marines spent 15 years raising money and lobbying the government for the recognition afforded other veterans.

The promenade leads south along the shoreline. Beyond Castle Clinton and a few yards inland from the walkway is the **monument to Giovanni da Verrazano** (1909; Ettore Ximenes), the Florentine explorer employed by the king of France, who, in 1524, became the first known European to sail into New York harbor. Claiming the land for France, he wrote an enthusiastic description of his surroundings and of the Native Americans who welcomed him. The bronze statue was donated by a group of Italian American citizens who made their presentation during the Hudson-Fulton Festival to point out that Verrazano got here 85 years before Henry Hudson. The female figure in front of the granite base represents Discovery.

To the right of Verrazano, a small stone honors Peter Caesar Alberti, the first Italian settler in New York (June 2, 1635).

A few steps further along is the **Norwegian Maritime Memorial** (c. 1982), a tribute to the people of the U. S. by the veterans of the Norwegian Navy and Merchant Marine who fought in World War II. Many of the sailors looked upon New York, their principal port of call, as their home port. The memorial is constructed from two boulders from the coast of Norway. A little further inland is the **Wireless Operators' Memorial,** dedicated to radio operators who perished at sea, the most famous of whom was Jack Phillips, radioman of the *Titanic,* which struck an iceberg and sank on the night of April 14, 1912.

Further south is the **East Coast War Memorial** (1961; Albino Manca), with its great bronze eagle facing out to sea. The eight marble pylons bear the names of 4,596 Americans who perished in Atlantic coastal waters during World War II. Between the war memorial and the ferry terminal at the southern tip of the park is the **U.S. Coast Guard Memorial,** an eight-ft bronze statue of two guardsmen supporting an injured comrade. The statue (1947; Norman M. Thomas) was financed by individual $1 contributions from Coast Guard personnel. (The concrete structure nearby is a ventilator for the Brooklyn-Battery Tunnel.)

The path leads east out of the park, past the Marine Flagpole. Just inside the park fence is the unintimidating **Oyster Pasty Cannon,** discovered (1892) during excavations at 55 Broadway and Exchange Alley. It may date back all the way to 1695.

Leave the park and cross State St. Herman Melville (1819–1891), author of *Moby-Dick,* was born at 6 Pearl St, now the site of **17 State St** (1988; Emery Roth & Sons), one of the downtown skyline's more noticeable structures. Flanked by two dark boxy buildings, the wedge-shaped tower with its curved wall of mirrored glass has been likened to a modern beacon or lighthouse. The 43-story office tower was built by developer Melvyn Kaufman, whose earlier buildings at 77 Water St and 127 John St included whimsical details.

New York Unearthed

17 State St (in courtyard facing Pearl St), New York, NY 10004. ☎ (212) 748-8628. Open Mon–Fri 12–6. Free. Gift shop. Accessible to wheelchairs.

New York Unearthed, a satellite of the South Street Seaport Museum, provides a look not only at the artifacts found underneath modern New York, but also at the history they represent.

History

Construction began on 17 State St before approval was received from the Landmarks Preservation Commission, which had the right to study the site for potential archaeological significance. (The lot had been largely undisturbed since the 18C and possibly contained artifacts dating back to its 18C Jewish owner.) As a penalty the developer helped fund a museum on the site.

Exhibits

The museum contains a simulation of an archaeological site demonstrating how the layers containing artifacts were deposited. You can see clay pipes, ceramics, and other objects recovered in New York digs and watch workers in a glass-enclosed lab restoring and stabilizing archaeological finds.

At 7–8 State St is the **Rectory of the Shrine of the Blessed Elizabeth Bayley Seton** (originally the James Watson House), the only survivor of a time when State St was an upper-crust residential street. Designed in two sections (east wing 1793, west wing 1806; DL), it has been attributed to John McComb Jr. The details of the facade reflect its Georgian and Federal heritage: the marble plaques in the brickwork, the oval windows on the west wall, the splayed lintels above the rectangular windows. Its most distinctive feature, however, is the curved wooden portico that follows the street line, its tapered Ionic columns said to be made from ships' masts. During the Civil War the Union Army commandeered the house, which overlooked its encampment in the park. After the war an Irish immigrant, Charlotte Grace O'Brien, inspired the Roman Catholic Church to buy the house and establish the Mission of Our Lady of the Rosary, a haven for immigrant Irish girls. The mission now operates the building as a shrine to the Blessed Elizabeth Seton (1774–1821), the first American-born saint, canonized in 1975.

South of State St is **Peter Minuit Plaza,** a small triangular park named for the Dutch governor, who in 1626, according to legend, made the most famous real estate deal in the city's history, "purchasing" Manhattan from Native Americans for 60 guilders, a sum worth $24 according to traditional rates of exchange. (The Native Americans had a very different conception of the deal.) The park also contains a **monument to New York's first Jewish immigrants,** a group of Sephardic refugees fleeing persecution in Brazil. Their ship, bound for Holland, was seized by pirates; a few days later the pirates were overtaken by a French frigate whose captain charged the refugees for a voyage to Amsterdam but brought them to New Amsterdam instead. The Jews arrived in Sept 1654, and despite Peter Stuyvesant's opposition they were allowed to remain and engage in commerce.

At or near the present intersection of State and Whitehall Sts stood Peter Stuyvesant's town house, built in about 1657 and renamed Whitehall by the first English governor of New York.

Visible to the south along the water are two ferry stations. One is the **Whitehall Terminal** for the **Staten Island Ferry,** the only direct commuting link between the boroughs of Richmond and Manhattan and one of New York's great sightseeing bargains. After a damaging 1991 fire, plans for a new terminal began, but years of design delays imperiled funding. A modern terminal is now being built.

To the left of the ferry terminal is the **Battery Maritime Building** (1909; DL), 11 South St, a fine old relic of the days when many ferries plied the East River. Constructed of sheet steel and painted green to imitate verdigris, it is elaborately decorated with rivets, latticework, rosettes, and marine designs. The terminal is most dramatic seen from the water, its openmouthed arches gaping against the severe geometry of the skyscrapers behind it. Public ferries docked here until 1938, and more recently it was used by the Coast Guard and the Department of Ports and Terminals. The Governors Island ferry, which runs infrequently nowadays, leaves from this terminal.

New York Plaza

Walk north along Water St for a view of some of the skyscrapers that have radically altered the historic downtown skyline: **One New York Plaza** (1969; William Lescaze & Assocs.), facing Water St between Whitehall and Broad Sts, and **33 Whitehall St,** (1986; Fox & Fowle Architects) with its silver-blue mirrored glass facade.

History

The New York Plaza buildings are the products of a construction boom that began in Lower Manhattan in the late 1950s and continued into the 1970s, culminating in the building of the World Trade Center. During this period the brick and granite warehouses and small homes that graced Front and Water Sts were destroyed and the contours of the streets altered in the interests of efficiency and profit. Front St, south of Wall St, has been absorbed into "superblocks" created by developers building ever larger buildings.

To compensate for the forbidding scale of the new buildings, the city passed the Zoning Resolution of 1961, which states that for every square ft of "plaza" space, the builder was allowed an additional ten square ft of floor space. Unfortunately, the law lacked significant design requirements, and many of the plazas suggested that building owners wished to discourage public use. The city then amended the Zoning Resolution, requiring such amenities as trees, seating, and shops.

At the north side of New York Plaza, Water St (the eastward extension of State St) intersects with Broad St. During the Dutch colonial period, Broad St *(de Heere Gracht)* was a canal for drainage and shipping. The British filled it about 100 years before the Revolution, by which time it was polluted, but the extra width of Broad St remains as a reminder of the former canal.

Walk one block inland along Broad St to the corner of Pearl St. Pearl St, once on the shore of the East River, was named for the opalescent shells that dotted its beaches. At Bridge St, which joins Pearl St at this intersection, once stood the first bridge across the Broad St canal.

Fraunces Tavern and Fraunces Tavern Museum

54 Pearl Street, New York, NY 10004. ☎ (212) 425-1778. Fraunces Tavern Museum open Mon–Fri, Washington's Birthday, and July 4 10–4:45. Closed weekends. Admission charge. Changing exhibitions, children's programs, special events. Gift shop. Not accessible to wheelchairs.

On the southeast corner of Broad and Pearl Sts is Fraunces Tavern, the centerpiece of the Fraunces Tavern Block Historic District, one of the few full blocks of 18C and 19C buildings to have escaped both the Great Fire of 1835 and successive downtown building booms. There are 11 buildings here (for example, 62 Pearl St) built between 1827 and 1833. Fraunces Tavern itself is a reconstruction (1907; William Mersereau; DL) of a mansion built (c. 1719) for Stephen (or Etienne) De Lancey. Since no graphic records survived, Mersereau's reconstruction was based on an analysis of the structure of the building and studies of similar buildings. A 1781 advertisement describes the house as having "9 spacious rooms plus 5 bedchambers, 13 fireplaces . . . and an exceeding good kitchen, and a spring of remarkable fine water therein."

The ground floor contains a restaurant; the two upper stories house the Fraunces Tavern Museum.

History

In 1762, Samuel Fraunces, a West Indian, possibly of French ancestry, bought the De Lancey house and opened it as the Queen Charlotte Tavern; he renamed the tavern after himself, rather than British royalty, after the start of the American Revolution. Fraunces was well known as a cook, especially for his desserts, which may have influenced George Washington in his selection of Fraunces Tavern for his farewell (1783) to his officers when he temporarily retired to private life. Fraunces's abilities later earned him the position of chief steward to Washington during most of Washington's presidency.

In 1785 Fraunces leased the building to the government for office space; later he sold it to a Brooklyn butcher. During the 19C the building deteriorated along with the rest of the neighborhood, at its nadir becoming a hotel for transients. After being badly burned several times (1832, 1837, 1852), it remained derelict until its purchase (1904) by the Sons of the Revolution of the State of New York, who restored it.

Fraunces Tavern Museum

On the second floor are two period rooms: the **Long Room,** where the farewell actually took place, now refurbished as a late-18C tavern room, and the **Clinton Room,** furnished as a dining room, notable for its historic wallpaper. Galleries on the third floor offer changing exhibits on early American history and culture.

Occupying the block between Pearl and South William Sts and Coenties Alley is **85 Broad St** (1983; Skidmore, Owings & Merrill), housing the offices of Goldman Sachs. The huge 30-story building is permitted in the area because it bought the air rights from the small-scale Fraunces Tavern Block Historic District buildings across the street. In front of the building on Pearl St is an exhibit of early artifacts (displayed below sidewalk level), unearthed 1979–80, during the city's first archaeological dig, which was required by the Landmarks Preservation Commission when 85 Broad St was constructed.

Urban Archaeology

The dig proved that urban areas could contain significant finds, encouraging future excavations. The display contains remains from three structures, including the Dutch colonial Stadt Huys, or City Hall, which began as a waterside tavern in about 1641. It was converted to the Town Hall when New Amsterdam was granted its municipal charter in 1653, and served not only as a meeting place but as a jail, debtors' prison, courthouse, and public warehouse. The British demolished the building in 1699. The dig found tiles, clay pipes, liquor bottles, and jugs, along with pieces of the structures. Nearby is a cistern from the early 18C.

At 75 Broad St is the former **International Telephone & Telegraph headquarters** (1929). This 33-story Art Deco building has a corner entrance on South William St with an intricate mosaic. Used as a communications center for submarines in the Atlantic Ocean during World War II, the building became an office tower after ITT moved out. Across the street at 70 Broad St (corner of Beaver St) is the former **American Bank Note Company** (1908; Kirby, Petit & Green; DL), with two classical columns framing a large window on the second floor.

Return to Pearl St and turn left; turn right at Coenties Alley, following it toward the river. The brick plaza across Water St, formerly Jeannette Park, is now **Vietnam Veterans Plaza.** Dominating it is a greenish glass-brick wall (1985; William Britt Fellows and Peter Wormser), 70 ft long and 14 ft high, etched with words written home by American soldiers in Vietnam. Once the park was a favorite haunt of idle seamen, a tree-shaded trapezoidal plot of land created when Coenties Slip was filled in during the late 19C. Named after the ship *Jeannette,* which took part in the tragic polar expedition of 1879–81, the park originally followed the shape of Coenties Slip.

Return up Coenties Alley and walk halfway through the 85 Broad St Plaza. On the right is **Stone St,** so named because it was city's first paved street (1658). The name was later extended to include High St on the other side of what is now Broad St (in those days it was a canal). In 1980, the middle section of Stone St was obliterated by the construction of 85 Broad St, but paving stones from that section run through the building lobby, whose walls make two slight bends following the former path of Stone St.

Continue through the plaza to South William St, part of the **Stone St Historic District,** created to preserve the counting houses and other Greek revival commercial structures built on Stone, Pearl, and South William Sts after the Great Fire of 1835 (see Hanover Square), as well as several redesigned in the early 20C. The most unusual is **21 South William St** (1928; William Neil Smith), a massive brick building with neo-Tudor decor and a steep mansard roof. Named Block Hall and built as a private clubhouse, it became the Italian Alps restaurant in the 1960s but has sat vacant for nearly a decade.

Next are three 19C buildings with facades added in the early 20C. The one at **17 South William St** (1906; Edward Tilton) has a Renaissance-style facade, while **15 South William St** (1908; C. P. H. Gilbert) and **13 South William St** (1903; C. P. H. Gilbert) look Dutch, with large second-story windows and crow-stepped gables. The neo-Gothic building at **9 South William St** (1929; William Neil Smith), at the corner of Mill Lane, formerly an annex to the nearby Lehman Brothers offices, was converted to a hotel in 1999.

Mill Lane is named after a large windmill built by the Dutch in 1626, which once stood approximately at the intersection of Mill Lane and Mill St (now called South William St). Used primarily for grinding grain, the mill had a meeting room on the second story that was rented (1680s) to the city's first Jewish congregation, Shearith Israel. Two millstones can be seen at Shearith Israel's current synagogue on Central Park West (see Congregation Shearith Israel in Walk 26). In 1729 the congregation, many of whose members were descendants of those refugees from Brazil who had arrived in 1654 (see Peter Minuit Plaza), purchased land south of the mill for 100 pounds sterling plus a loaf of sugar and a pound of tea and built their first synagogue there (site of 26 South William St).

Delmonico's Restaurant

Continue along South William St to its intersection with William and Beaver Sts. On the left, at 56 Beaver St, is Delmonico's Restaurant (1891; James Brown Lord;

DL). This eight-story masterpiece with a cast-iron and steel-framed structure has a brownstone base and orange brick and terra-cotta trim.

History

The original Delmonico's opened at 21–25 William St in 1827 and fast became America's most famous restaurant, at one point offering 47 different veal dishes and 50 fish dishes. Chef Charles Ranhofer invented baked Alaska and lobster Newburg. After the restaurant was destroyed in the Great Fire of 1835, a new lavish building, marked by four entryway columns believed to have been excavated from Pompeii, was built at 56 Beaver St. Two of the "Pompeii" columns remain in front of the present building.

The building was converted to condominiums in 1996. The restaurant closed in 1917 and operated under different names or remained vacant until the 1990s, when it was restored to its 19C splendor with mahogany panels, etched glass windows, and a portrait of Chef Ranhofer above the fireplace.

Across the street at 1 William St is the former headquarters of the Lehman Brothers investment banking firm, originally the **Seligman Building** (1907; Francis H. Kimball and Julian Levi). This Beaux-Arts skyscraper is now the headquarters of the Banca Commerciale Italiana.

Walk past the bank down William St toward Hanover Square. Named after the English royal family of the Georges, **Hanover Square** was once a public common in a fine residential district. The most notorious resident was William Kidd, a sea captain. Though a respected New York citizen and a contributor to Trinity Church, he was hanged in England in 1701 for piracy. At the end of the 17C the area was the city's first Printing House Square, home of New York's first newspaper (1725), the *New-York Gazette*, published weekly by William Bradford.

The Great Fire

Hanover Square was the center of the **Great Fire of 1835.** On the night of Dec 17, a gas explosion ignited stockpiles of dry goods and chemicals, and, whipped by winter winds, the blaze raged out of control. Subzero temperatures froze the fire hoses and by noon the fire had incinerated Hanover Square. When the blaze finally burned itself out, it had destroyed over 20 acres and more than 650 buildings, including all the Dutch colonial structures in downtown New York.

India House, 1 Hanover Square, is one of the city's finest surviving Italianate brownstones (architect unknown; 1854; DL). Built for the Hanover Bank and later home to New York Cotton Exchange (1870–86), India House is also a prototype for the New York brownstone row house. India House is now owned by a private men's club.

The bronze **statue of Abraham De Peyster** (1896; George Edwin Bissell), commissioned by his great-great-great-grandson, honors a tireless public servant whose offices included alderman, mayor, chief justice of the colony, colonel of the militia, and acting governor.

Walk toward the East River. The **East River slips** (Old Slip, Burling Slip, Coenties Slip, and others) were originally docking areas for ships. As the coastline was pushed out by landfill, breakwaters were built and the slips were dredged to provide adequate draft. Eventually they were filled in to create new land, but their rectangular outlines remain in the shape of these streets.

New York City Police Museum

100 Old Slip, New York, NY 10005. ☎ (212) 301-4440. Web site: www.nyc policemuseum.org. Open Tues–Sat 10–6. Closed Sun, Mon, Thanksgiving, and Dec 25. Free. Gift shop. Accessible to wheelchairs.

In the middle of Old Slip sits the former **First Precinct Station House** (1909–11; Hunt & Hunt; DL) designed like a fortified Italian Renaissance palazzo. In 2001, the New York City Police Museum (founded 1929) moved into the building, bringing with it one of the nation's finest collections of police memorabilia. Visitors can see weapons, uniforms, police shields, and even vehicles, notably a green-and-white squad car from 1972 and a vintage red NYPD Highway Patrol Indian motorcycle. The ground floor entrance hall, dominated by a large desk that served the 64th Precinct in the Bronx until 1999, has been restored to look like a station house at the turn of the 20C. There are exhibits on forensics and notorious criminals, a simulated crime scene, and a Wall of Heroes honoring police officers who have died performing their jobs.

From 1909 until 1973, the building served as the First Precinct Station House, watching over the commercial and financial interests of Wall St and Lower Manhattan. It was closed amidst allegations of police corruption, and the First Precinct headquarters was transferred to Ericsson Place. Although the return of the building to police business seems appropriate, the move has displaced the Landmarks Preservation Commission, located here since 1993.

The museum has stirred controversy over several issues, including staffing by on-duty police officers and allegations of preferential funding by the city.

Along the waterfront are four piers, **Piers 9, 11, 13, and 14,** stretching about to Pine St, which the city hopes to redevelop. Among the proposals is one by the Solomon R. Guggenheim Museum, which would like to erect on a platform above the piers an irregularly shaped, 45-story building, with a branch museum. Frank O. Gehry, who created the Guggenheim Museum Bilbao in Spain, conceived the unique design.

Return to **77 Water St,** an office tower with a whimsical plaza (1970; Emery Roth & Sons) and sculptures (1969) on each corner. To the southwest is *Rejected Skin* (William Tarr), inspired by aluminum rejected as sheeting for the building and compacted in a scrap yard; to the southeast is George Adamy's work *Month of June;* to the northeast is *City Fountains* by Victor Scallo; and to the northwest is Rudolph de Harak's *Helix,* made of 120 one-inch-thick stainless steel squares, arranged to create the illusion of a continuous spiral. A pool with rockpiles and water jets runs the length of the plaza, while the sculpture *Herring-Like Fishes Swimming Upstream* (1985; Pamela Waters) commands the north end. The building was developed by Melvyn and Robert Kaufman, who became known for their adventurous approach to design. The roof's Astroturf runway (visible from other skyscrapers) features *Sopwith 19* (1970; William Tarr), a sculptural Sopwith Camel (the World War I fighter plane).

Walk north on Water St to the intersection of Pine St. In front of the aluminum-and glass-clad **Wall Street Plaza** (1973; I. M. Pei & Assocs.) at 88 Pine St stands *Moon Gate* (1973; YuYu Yang), a vertical slab with a circular opening facing a polished disk (diameter 12 ft, weight 4,000 pounds). A nearby tablet recalls the history of the *Queen Elizabeth I*, the Cunard liner that burned in Hong Kong harbor in 1972; Morley Cho, owner of the building, was the last owner of the fabled liner.

Continue north to Maiden Lane, so named by the Dutch, after a footpath used by neighborhood girls on their way to the brook where they washed laundry. Visible to the east at 180 Maiden Lane is the **Continental Center** (1983; Swanke Hayden Connell), a 41-story tower sheathed in greenish glass.

Continue north on Water St. In Jan 1982, during construction of the National Westminster Bank USA (1983; Fox & Fowle), 175 Water St, an archaeological team uncovered thousands of small items—mostly dishes and bottles—in the hull of an 85 × 26 ft 18C merchant ship with a rounded bow. The archaeologists fixed its arrival sometime after 1746, the date on a ceramic lid found below its decks. Since building construction was already delayed a month by the dig, only one side of the ship was excavated.

Filling the block between John and Fulton Sts, **127 John St** (1969; Emery Roth & Sons), another building developed by the Kaufman Organization, beguiles pedestrians with amusing sidewalk artifacts: an immense digital clock, a sculptural phone booth (1972; Albert Wilson) with cutout figures, and a neon tunnel (1972; Rudolph de Harak).

Moving Downtown

In 2002 the **American Numismatic Society** plans to move its headquarters and museum to the former Fidelity and Deposit Company Building, 140 William St (at Fulton St). For information about the Society, the museum, and its collections, see Walk 29.

Walk north to Fulton St, turn east, continue to Water St, and turn left. At the southeast corner of Water and Fulton Sts, a 35-story office building, One Seaport Plaza Plaza (1984; Swanke Hayden Connell), towers over the restored South Street Seaport. The south and west facades, which face the Financial District, look like those of many modern office buildings. But the windows on the north and east sides, which face the historic seaport and other 19C buildings, echo an older design—its old-fashioned individual windows are framed by stone lintels and sills. The building's lobby features three works from the *Protractor* series painted in the late 1960s by Frank Stella.

South Street Seaport

Walk north to Fulton St, turn east, continue to Water St, and turn left. The historic South Street Seaport begins at the intersection of Water, Pearl, and Fulton Sts, where the **Titanic Memorial** commemorates those who perished aboard the sinking ocean liner in 1912. Originally built (1913) atop the former Seamen's Church Building on South St near Jeannette Park, the statue was relocated after the building was demolished in 1968.

The South Street Seaport is a collection of historic buildings clustered around Fulton St and the East River piers. They include the former counting houses, saloons, hotels, and warehouses that were once at the center of the city's maritime industry. The South Street Seaport Museum features restored ships, exhibitions, galleries, and shops scattered throughout the site. The museum is undertaking a massive project to centralize its holdings.

History

Until the years after the Civil War, the city's maritime activity focused on the East River, less affected than the Hudson River by ice floes, flooding, and westerly winds. During the early 19C Fulton St became a major thoroughfare leading to the waterfront and Fulton Ferry (1814) to Brooklyn. The Fulton Market opened, initially as a produce market for Brooklyn and Long Island farmers; it eventually became a fish market. With the opening of the Erie Canal, New York was flooded with midwestern industrial and farm products; 500 new shipping firms sprouted up to handle the new business. By the 1840s, trade to California and to China burgeoned, spearheaded by the firm of A. A. Low on Burling Slip (now John St). After 1880, when steamships superseded the clippers and trade moved to the Hudson's deep-water docks, the area fell into decline.

After nearly a century of neglect, preservationists began working to save the old port, chartering the museum (1967) and acquiring historic buildings and ships. However, by the mid-1970s, financial and political forces thrust the historic-minded museum into an uncomfortable partnership with the city and the Rouse Company, a commercial developer. In 1983 a large part of the present restoration opened, including a rehabilitated Schermerhorn Row and a new Fulton Market, housing a mall in addition to fishmongers. In 1985 another shopping mall opened on Pier 17. The bottom-line commercialism of the Rouse Company put it constantly at odds with the South Street Seaport Museum and by the mid-1990s, the seaport was struggling as national chain stores filled the mall. The museum, while fighting with Rouse over direction and money, lost members before rebounding in the late 1990s.

The old seaport is alive in the flourishing Fulton Fish Market, founded in 1822 (see Fulton Fish Market), and at Pier 17 with the museum's seafaring ships and the ferries now transporting people upriver to Shea and Yankee Stadiums. However, part or all of the fish market is expected to move to Hunt's Point in the Bronx within the next five years, in order to comply with federal health regulations.

South Street Seaport Museum

Visitors' Center, 209 Water St (at Fulton St), New York, NY 10038. ☎ (212) 748-8600. Web site: www.southstseaport.org. Open Apr–Sept weekdays 10–6, weekends 11–5; Dec–March weekdays 11–4, weekends until 5. Closed Jan 1, Thanksgiving, Dec 25. Admission charge. Admission tickets sold until one hour before closing at Visitors' Center, at the ticket booth on Pier 16, or at any of the galleries.

Tours, children's programs, craft workshops, special events. Harbor excursions

South St in 1898, when sailing vessels still docked in the East River. In the background is the Brooklyn Bridge rising above the Fulton Ferry Terminal. (Courtesy of The New-York Historical Society, New York City)

in season: ☎ (212) 964-9082. Sailing cruises, ☎ (212) 669-9416. Restaurants. Shops. Wheelchair access limited.

Subway: Seventh Ave Express (2, 3) to Fulton St. Lexington Ave Express (4, 5) to Fulton St. Nassau St Express or Local (J, M, Z) to Fulton St. Eighth Ave Express or Local (A, C) to Broadway-Nassau. Bus: M15.

Note: Schermerhorn Row is currently (2001) undergoing restoration and the installation of the core exhibit, World Port New York. When the project is completed, the main entrance to the museum will be at 12 Fulton St. The **Visitors' Center** is temporarily located at 209 Water St. While construction is underway, visitors can still tour the historic ships and the satellite galleries.

Highlights

Onboard the four-masted barque ***Peking,*** you can view the crew's quarters, an exhibit of historic photos of the ship during her working years, and a film of the ***Peking*** rounding Cape Horn in heavy weather.

The **Wavertree,** undergoing a long-term restoration to its original appearance as a sailing ship, has been refitted with new masts and yards. Guided tours of the restoration are available.

The permanent **ocean liner exhibit** in the Whitman Gallery features impressive ship models of liners from Cunard, Holland-American, and other steamship companies as well as artifacts relating to the *Titanic,* posters, and other memorabilia.

World Port New York (opening 2003) in Schermerhorn Row, the core exhibit of the revitalized museum, will document New York's history as a port and will offer visitors a chance to see the restored buildings of this important architectural treasure.

To the left of the *Titanic* Memorial are three **Greek revival storefronts** (207–211 Water St) with granite steps, lintels, piers, and cornices. The museum's administrative offices are in 207 Water St. **Whitman Gallery,** featuring model ships, is at 209 Water St (1835–36). At 211 Water St is the city's sole remaining on-site letterpress shop. Here the museum has re-created the 19C printing shop of **Bowne & Co. Stationers,** whose working presses are used for demonstrations. The next building, 213 Water St (1868; Stephen D. Hatch; restored 1983) features a ground-floor cast-iron facade and upper stories faced in limestone. Originally a warehouse for a tin company, this Italianate structure now houses both the museum's **Melville Gallery,** with photo exhibits, and its library. Plans call for turning it into a children's center.

Return to Fulton St and turn left (east). At 19 Fulton St is the **Bogardus Building** (1983; Beyer Blinder Belle), whose facade was to have incorporated ironwork from the city's first cast-iron building erected by James Bogardus. The pieces, unfortunately, were stolen from storage, so the building uses similar materials and proportions to suggest the appearance of a Bogardus facade.

Schermerhorn Row

Schermerhorn Row (1812; DL), the seaport's architectural centerpiece, dominates the south side of Fulton St, with its buildings stretching around Fulton St to Front, John, and South Sts.

History

Peter Schermerhorn, a ship chandler, got the land in 1793 as water lots and filled them in. He then built 12 Georgian-Federal–style red brick commercial buildings with warehouse space downstairs and accounting offices above. The corner building was later converted into the Fulton Ferry Hotel; its mansard roof was added in 1868 for extra space. (This conglomeration of buildings will house a central museum. A new building on the corner of John and South Sts will have space for large exhibits like a steam engine or an America's Cup yacht.)

The Piers

Cross South St to the pier area. On the left is **Pier 17 Pavilion** (1984; Benjamin Thompson & Assoc), a massive mall with shops, restaurants, and a gorgeous view of the Brooklyn waterfront and Brooklyn Bridge. To the right is **Pier 16,** home to the museum's ships, which are open to the public. On the south side of the pier are three vessels. The massive *Peking,* a four-masted ship (1911) from Hamburg, is one of the last sailing vessels built for commercial purposes. The *Wavertree* (1885), a square-rigged iron-hulled ship from England, used to carry freight from India. The *Pioneer* is used for harbor trips and sail-training programs.

On the north side of Pier 16 is the *Ambrose Lightship*, built in 1908 to mark the entrance to the deepwater Ambrose Channel, which leads to New York Harbor. The lightship was replaced in 1932 by a tower and beacon. Next to the *Ambrose* is the *Lettie G. Howard*, an 1893 Gloucester fishing schooner, typical of many that brought their catches to the market. (Seaport Liberty Lines, affiliated with the Circle Line, takes visitors into Upper New York Bay. Tickets are sold on the pier.)

Between Piers 16 and 15 to the south is the ship preservation barge, the seaport's floating workshop. Moored there also is the tugboat *W.O. Decker*, used for waterfront trips. On the wooden apron at the edge of **Pier 15** is the Maritime Crafts Center, which features woodcarvers working on museum projects and commercial carvings.

Fulton Fish Market

On the north side of Fulton St is the **Fulton Market Building** (1983; Benjamin Thompson & Assoc.), which, with its impressive suspended iron canopy, suggests the original Fulton Market Building (1883), razed in 1948.

On the South St end of the market is the **Tin Building** (1909), which houses part of the Fulton Fish Market. (Market operators are also in city-owned buildings to the north at Beekman St and Peck Slip and in individually owned buildings in the square block of South, Front, Beekman Sts, and Peck Slip.)

History

The Fulton Market dates back to 1822 when vendors were allowed to set up stalls in a wooden building here. By 1831, the butchers downstairs were complaining that the runoff from the upstairs fish-gutting operations was seeping down to their stands. The fish dealers were exiled to their own wooden shed on the water, behind which floated fish cars with live fish. This lasted until the turn of the century, when polluted waters poisoned the fish. Today the market bustles in the predawn hours, although the catch arrives by truck, not by boat.

Return to South St and walk south to John St. This block of John St was known as **Burling Slip** until 1835 when it was filled in. At 167–171 John St stands the former **A. A. Low Building** (1850; DL), which was built by Abiel Abbot Low, pioneer of the China trade. Low founded his firm in 1840 after learning the trade in Canton; the speed of Low's clipper ships enabled him to provide fresher (and thus more expensive) tea than his competitors. In 1850 he demolished the brick buildings here and erected this elegant Greek revival brownstone-faced counting house. The cast-iron storefront was made by one of the city's most famous firms, Badger's Architectural Iron Works. Today teas, silks, and porcelains have been replaced by the museum's Norway Galleries with long-term exhibitions.

Next door is the **Children's Center,** 165 John St, housed in a building (1811; DL) leased by flour merchants and grocers during the 19C. The former **Baker, Carver & Morrell Building** (1840; DL) across the street, 170–176 John St, is one of the few surviving Greek revival warehouses with an all-granite front. The top story was added in 1981 to provide space for apartments.

Walk west to Front St and turn right. Walk past Fulton St to the corner of Beekman St. The building at **142 Beekman St** (1885; George B. Post), built for a Schermerhorn family member in the fish business, is replete with architecturally appropriate details: starfish on the tie-rod ends, cockleshells on the cornice, and fish wriggling on the terra-cotta keystones.

Walk one block west to Water St and turn right. The lobby of 241 Water St, the new home for the **Seamen's Church Institute** (1991; James Stewart Polshek & Partners), features a Sir Galahad figurehead, a bell from the liner *Normandie,* and models of the institute's original floating chapel and Henry Hudson's *Half Moon.* Walk north to **Peck Slip,** named for Benjamin Peck, who had a house and wharf here before the Revolution and in 1763 erected a brick building to house the Peck Slip Market. Turn right and walk one block east. On the walls of the power station is a trompe l'oeil mural (1979; Richard Haas) depicting Federal and Greek revival buildings with a fanciful arcade through which the Brooklyn Bridge is visible.

Next door is the former **Jasper Ward Store** (1807; restored 1983), 45 Peck Slip, built for the politician and real estate speculator for whom Ward's Island is also named. Initially it faced the water on two sides since Peck Slip was not filled in until 1817. The former **Meyer's Hotel** (1873; John B. Snook), 119 South St, sits on the opposite corner from the Jasper Ward Store. According to legend everyone from Diamond Jim Brady to Annie Oakley stopped by the hotel for a sip or two.

Joseph Rose House

At 273 Water St is the Joseph Rose House, commonly credited with being the oldest building in the neighborhood and the third oldest in Manhattan (after St. Paul's Chapel and the Morris-Jumel Mansion). That legacy depends on the definition of "building"—while the house had been constructed by 1781, fires and alterations left little of the original, and, in fact, until recently it was merely a brick facade and a pile of rubble.

History

Joseph Rose, who imported mahogany from Honduras, kept his boat moored outside his back door until 1800, when Front St was extended. The house served as an apothecary, rooming house, and a brothel, before reaching a new low at midcentury as Kit Burns's "Sportsmen's Hall," which featured dog and rat fights. Burns later underwent an unexpected religious conversion and offered the house to a missionary who opened the Water Street Home for Women, a rehab center for repentant prostitutes.

By 1976, after decades as a loft and storehouse, the building had been abandoned. Squatters set a fire that caused tremendous damage. The roof was destroyed and eventually parts of the interior collapsed. Then in 1998 the old house was renovated as a luxury apartment building.

Just to the north, at 279 Water St, is the **Bridge Café.** In recent years it was embroiled in a dispute with McSorley's Old Ale House (see Walk 10), each advertising itself as the oldest drinking establishment in the city. McSorley's laid claim to 1854, but Richard McDermott, history buff and publisher of the tiny *New York Chronicle,* proved that McSorley's didn't open until 1862. This building, he discovered, dates to 1794, when it served as a grocery store and residence, and has been selling food and drink continuously since 1826. Others, however, say both are trumped by the Ear Inn on Spring St, which dates to 1817 (see Walk 8).

3 · The Financial District

Subway: Seventh Ave Express (2, 3) to Wall St. Lexington Ave Express (4, 5) to Wall St. Broadway Local (R) to Rector St.

Bus: M1 (marked South Ferry), M6.

When to visit: Weekdays during business hours are frenzied and fascinating, while weekends can be quiet to the point of desolation. If you go during the week, try to eat lunch early or late, since restaurants in the area are hectic from about noon to 2:00.

Wall Street

Wall St, symbol of money and power, is a small street only about a third of a mile long, running between Broadway and the East River.

History

The street gets its name from a wall, erected in 1653 during Peter Stuyvesant's tenure, which stretched river to river to protect the Dutch town from its British neighbors to the north. Fortunately for the townspeople the wall was never needed for defense, since it suffered the indignities frequently attendant upon municipal projects. Though the original plan called for a palisade to be made of whole tree trunks sharpened and driven into the ground, the wall was actually constructed of planks instead. These proved overpoweringly attractive to homeowners as sources of firewood or lumber for household repairs, and so in 1699 the British had the wall torn down as useless. The imposing buildings give the street a monumental quality, and indeed they are monuments to the titans of finance and industry who built the institutions they represent.

Trinity Church

Broadway at Wall St, New York, NY 10006. ☎ (212) 602-0800. Web site: www.trinity wallstreet.org. Open weekdays and Sun about 7:30 A.M.–8 P.M.; earlier closing Sat. Concerts (Thurs 1 P.M.), tours, small museum. For recorded concert information, ☎ (212) 602-0747. Gift shop. Limited wheelchair accessibility: a few, small steps up from street level.

At the head of Wall St on Broadway stands **Trinity Church** (1846; Richard Upjohn; DL), once the loftiest building in the neighborhood, now overshadowed by gigantic office buildings. Despite its modesty in size and conception by today's standards, Trinity Church is probably New York's most famous house of worship because of its dramatic setting. It is also one of the wealthiest, as befits a parish situated in a district so unabashedly devoted to Mammon.

History

The wealth of the parish stems from the original 215-acre land grant made in 1705 by Queen Anne, which included the land west of Broadway between Fulton and Christopher Sts, an impressive chunk of Lower Manhattan. Although the parish no longer owns the entire parcel, it still has extensive real estate holdings, including 27 buildings with 6 million square ft of commercial space; the income supports philanthropic projects. (The queen also extended to the church the rights to all unclaimed shipwrecks and beached whales.)

Financial District as of Sept 10, 2001

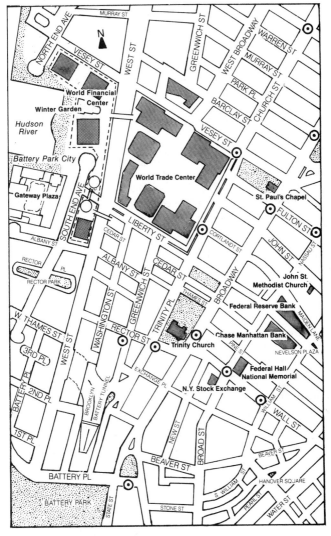

The present church is the third on the site. The first, finished in 1698, was a stone building facing the river, paid for by all citizens of the colony; everyone was taxed for the construction regardless of religious preference. The pirate William Kidd also lent his tackle for hoisting the stones. The church burned in 1776 and remained in ruins until long after the Revolution. A second church (completed 1790) had to be demolished in 1839 after a heavy snowfall damaged the roof.

Exterior

The current building is 79 ft wide and 166 ft long; the tower, including the spire, stands 281 ft above the ground. The building was the first Gothic revival church in the city. Its flying buttresses, stained glass windows, Gothic tracery, and medievally inspired sculpture impressed and pleased 19C New Yorkers, but the use of brownstone on the facade drew criticism. Until the construction of Trinity Church, brownstone was generally used as a cheap substitute for marble, granite, or limestone. Since Trinity parish could well have afforded marble, the choice was probably made for aesthetic reasons. The romantic movement, making itself felt in architecture as well as the other arts, favored the use of dark building materials, which were considered "picturesque" and "natural"—that is, close to the colors of the landscape.

The doors of the church, modeled after the famous Ghiberti doors on the baptistery of the cathedral in Florence, were designed by Richard Morris Hunt and donated by William Waldorf Astor. Karl Bitter, who won the competition for the construction, executed the main doors, whose panels illustrate biblical scenes. J. Massey Rhind and Charles H. Niehaus designed those on the north and south.

Interior

The chancel window designed by architect Richard Upjohn is among the earliest American examples of stained glass, though the glass itself came from Germany. The altar screen behind the main altar was given by John Jacob and William Astor in memory of their father. Made of Caen stone and marble, it was designed by Frederick C. Withers. The addition on the south side of the church contains a small museum, ☎ (212) 602-0872.

The Churchyard

The church sits in a beautiful churchyard (DL), its two acres among the few unpaved spots in the Financial District. Some of the gravestones are quite old and striking, their incised frizzle-haired angels and grinning death's heads reminding onlookers of mortality and what lies beyond. The oldest stone belongs to Richard Churcher (north of the church), who died at the age of five in 1681. Others are more elaborate and mark the burial places of renowned figures: Robert Fulton, whose *Clermont* proved that steamboat travel was economically viable; Alexander Hamilton; William Bradford, the publisher of the *New-York Gazette*; and Captain James Lawrence, whose nautical tombstone brings to mind his famous remark about not giving up the ship. Near the Broadway sidewalk on the north side of the church is the burial place of Charlotte Temple, a young lady of genteel background who was seduced and abandoned by a British officer and immortalized in a long but popular novel by Sarah Haswell Rowson. *Charlotte, A Tale of Truth* was published in 1791 in London, reprinted in Philadelphia in 1794, and quickly went through 160 editions. The largest monument is a statue of John Watts, a congressman, judge, and philanthropist.

The impressive graveyard cross in the center of the northern portion of the cemetery is a monument to the memory of Caroline Webster Astor, queen of New York society at the turn of the 20C (see The First Waldorf Astoria in Walk 16 and Mrs. Astor's Mansion in Walk 22). At the northeast corner of the plot is a large tribute to the Martyrs of the American Revolution, who died while imprisoned by the British in a sugarhouse (see Police Plaza in Walk 5).

The **American Stock Exchange,** 86 Trinity Place, is visible to the west of the graveyard. This handsome Art Deco building (1930; Starrett & Van Vleck) holds the city's second major stock exchange. It was known as the New York Curb Exchange, because before 1929 its brokers stood on the curb at the north end of Broad St and signaled with hand and arm movements to their colleagues in the windows of the New York Stock Exchange.

Return to Broadway. Just south is the **Empire Building** (1898; Kimball & Thompson; DL) at 71 Broadway. The headquarters of J. P. Morgan's U.S. Steel from 1907 to 1976, this classically decorated skyscraper became a rental apartment as part of a boom in residential development downtown. Between 1995 and 2002 an estimated 7,000 new units were converted or built from scratch. While there are few basic services in the area, the Alliance for Downtown New York brought residential landlords together and convinced them to partially subsidize the Amish Market gourmet food shop on Cedar St (heavily damaged in the catastrophe of Sept 11, 2001) and a more standard supermarket that later opened on John St.

Down the block at 65 Broadway is the former **American Express Building** (1917; James Aspinwall; DL), with a handsome white brick and terra-cotta facade. American Express was headquartered here from 1917 until 1975.

Across Broadway from Trinity Church is the Bank of Tokyo, originally the **American Surety Company** (1895; Bruce Price), at 100 Broadway. Above the ground floor is a row of allegorical stone figures by J. Massey Rhind, who sculpted the north doors of Trinity Church. In 1975 Isamu Noguchi, commissioned to design a sculpture for the lobby, designed a 17 ft long aluminum rhomboid that was hung, point down, from the ceiling. In 1980, the bank removed it because customers felt unsafe.

One block north, at 120 Broadway, is the **Equitable Building** (1915; Ernest R. Graham; DL), which was controversial in its day. In order to maximize available rental space and hence profits, the Equitable Building was built 40 stories straight up without setback, filling almost the entire site. This goliath darkened side streets and the windows of adjacent buildings; although the setback of the new Marine Midland Bank to the north has alleviated the problem somewhat, Pine St is still dark and gloomy. The following year the city passed the Zoning Resolution of 1916, which determined the "wedding cake" silhouette of so many early skyscrapers.

"Wedding Cake" Skyscrapers

The amount of setback required was determined by running an imaginary plane up from the center of the street at a predetermined angle and requiring the profile of the building to remain within this boundary. After setbacks had reduced the building size to 25 percent of the site, the tower could rise straight up. (In 1961 amendments allowed buildings to rise straight up without stepping back while covering 40 percent of the site; it also established absolute limits on building size and offered incentives for including public amenities.)

Across the street are the **Trinity** and **U.S. Realty Buildings** (1905 and 1906; Francis H. Kimball; DL), 111 and 115 Broadway, two fine early-20C Gothic skyscrapers, designed to complement Trinity Church. The Gothic decoration continues inside the lobbies, which have polychromed ceilings, sculptured corbels, and elaborate tracery around the elevators.

Return to Broadway and Wall St. The former **Irving Trust Company** (1932; Voorhees, Gmelin & Walker, with an addition in 1965), 1 Wall St, is a fine 1930s skyscraper, whose exterior detail emphasizes its verticality and whose setbacks illustrate the provisions of the Zoning Resolution of 1916. The curtain wall is designed to suggest fabric folds and is incised with a fabric pattern. The large windows that appear at the top of the faceted tower open into a lounge (not open to the public) with a high-faceted ceiling. The reception room facing Wall St contains glass mosaics (Hildreth Meiere) in oxblood, red, and orange with a web of gold and bronze lines. (Irving Trust was taken over by the Bank of New York in 1988.)

The **Bankers Trust Building** (1912; Trowbridge & Livingston; DL; addition, 1933; Shreve, Lamb, and Harmon), 14 Wall St, has a stepped pyramid atop a limestone tower. This handsome peak ultimately became the symbol of Bankers Trust. (Bankers Trust sold the building in 1987.)

New York Stock Exchange

20 Broad St (visitors' entrance), New York, NY 10005. ☎ (212) 656-5168. Web site: www.nyse.com. Open weekdays 9:30–4. Closed weekends, holidays. Free. Exhibits, tours, Visitors' Gallery overlooking the trading floor. Accessible to wheelchairs.

On Wall St between New and Broad Sts is the New York Stock Exchange (1903; George B. Post; DL), one reason why New York is the preeminent city of the capitalist world. Like Federal Hall up the street, the Stock Exchange is a "temple," dating from the period when classical architecture was de rigueur for all important public buildings. The sculpture on the pediment, *Integrity Protecting the Works of Man,* is by John Quincy Adams Ward and Paul W. Bartlett. To Integrity's left are figures symbolizing the mechanical arts, electricity, surveyors, and builders; on the other side are mining and agriculture.

History

Shortly after the end of the American Revolution, the Congress sitting in Federal Hall issued about $80 million in bonds to pay for the war debt. A central marketplace became necessary for these securities, and after a few years of informal trading outdoors and in coffeehouses, a group of 24 brokers got together and drew up the "Buttonwood Agreement" (May 17, 1792), which marks the formal beginnings of the New York Stock Exchange. The name of the document commemorated a buttonwood or sycamore tree on the north side of Wall St between William and Pearl Sts, near which the brokers used to meet.

The **Morgan Guaranty Trust Company** (1913; Trowbridge & Livingston; DL), 23 Wall St, was the bank of J. Pierpont Morgan, who more than any other man epitomized Wall St, power, and the stupendous acquisition of wealth. The Wall St facade still bears traces of a tragic explosion caused by a carriage loaded with TNT that killed 33 passersby and injured 400 others in 1920. The explosion was believed to be part of a Bolshevik plot, but the case was never solved.

Federal Hall National Memorial

26 Wall St (Nassau St), New York, NY 10005. ☎ (212) 825-6888. Open Mon–Fri 9–5. Closed weekends, except in July and Aug, and most federal holidays. Free. Exhibits, tours. Gift shop. Wheelchair access from 15 Pine St; restrooms accessible to wheelchairs.

Subway: Nassau St Express or Local (J, M, Z) to Broad St. Lexington Ave Express (4, 5) or Seventh Ave Express (2, 3) to Wall St. Broadway–Seventh Ave Local (1, 9) to Rector St. Bus: M1 (marked South Ferry), M6, M15.

Across the street is Federal Hall National Memorial (1842; Town & Davis with John Frazee; DL), one of the finest Greek revival buildings in the city and one of New York's most important historic sites, although the great events that took place here predate the present building.

History

In the early 18C the British City Hall (begun 1699; demolished 1812), stood on this site. There John Peter Zenger, the argumentative publisher of the *New York Weekly Journal*, was tried in 1735 for libeling the Royal Governor; Zenger's acquittal established a precedent for freedom of the press that would later be reaffirmed in the Bill of Rights.

After the Revolution, the Congress met here. George Washington took the oath of office in 1789 on the second floor balcony, wearing what was for the period a simple suit. The hall was renamed Federal Hall in honor of New York's prestigious position as the nation's capital (the federal government was moved to Philadelphia in 1790). Later the building functioned as the U.S. Custom House and as one of the six government subtreasuries.

Exterior

A wide flight of steps leads to eight 32 ft fluted Doric columns of Westchester marble that support an architrave and unadorned pediment. On the steps is a renowned **statue of George Washington** (1883) by John Quincy Adams Ward.

Interior

Inside, the handsome rotunda has one of the vaults from the subtreasury open for display. Beyond the rotunda is a historical museum with exhibits on New York as the nation's capital, Washington's inauguration, and the history of the site. On the ground floor are coin vaults (1878) dating from the building's period as a U.S. subtreasury, which at the end of the 19C contained as much as 1,700 tons of gold and silver coins.

The building at **30 Wall St** was once the site of a Greek revival bank (1826; Martin E. Thompson), which later became the U.S. Assay Office. In 1915 the building was torn down and its marble facade eventually incorporated in the American Wing of the Metropolitan Museum of Art (see Walk 24). The present Renaissance-style building (1919; York & Sawyer) served as the new home of the Assay Office; in 1955 it was bought by the Seamen's Bank for Savings, which built an eight-story addition but preserved the limestone facade. (The bank used the Assay Office's five underground floors of bullion vaults for archive storage.) The marble cornerstones of the 1826 and 1919 buildings are in the lobby.

At 40 Wall St is the former **Bank of Manhattan** (1929; H. Craig Severance & Yasuo Matsui; DL), now the **Trump Building,** its owner's name proclaimed in big gold letters on the facade. Planned as the world's tallest building during a period when architects were exercising secrecy and cunning to top their competitors, 40 Wall St lost out to the Chrysler Building. The uptown architects surreptitiously added a stainless steel spire to their canyon, previously two ft shorter than 40 Wall St, making it the tallest skyscraper in the world—until the completion of the Empire State Building two years later. The pyramidal tower and spire atop this bank make it a familiar part of the downtown skyline. (For the history of the Bank of Manhattan, see Chase Manhattan Bank).

At 48 Wall St is the **Bank of New York** (1927; Benjamin Wistar Morris), distinguished in the downtown skyline by its Georgian-style cupola. Founded by Alexander Hamilton in 1784, it is the oldest commercial bank in the country; plaques on the west corner describe its beginnings and the original Wall St wall.

Across the street at 55 Wall St is the venerable **National City Bank Building,** remarkable for having been constructed in two stages. The first section (1842; Isaiah Rogers; DL), a three-story Ionic temple with an imposing domed central hall, belongs to the same period and architectural tradition as Federal Hall. The 16 granite columns, quarried in Quincy, Massachusetts, and hauled up Wall St by 40 teams of oxen, make an impressive facade for the building, which first served as the new Merchants Exchange, replacing the one destroyed in the Great Fire of 1835. Later used as the custom house, the building was remodeled by the firm of McKim, Mead & White in 1907 when the Custom House at Bowling Green opened. The architects doubled the volume of the building by adding the upper stories, which are surrounded by a tier of Corinthian columns. In 1999 the building was converted into the Regent Wall Street Hotel.

Continue along Wall St and turn right on Hanover St. Go one block to 20 Exchange Place, the **City Bank–Farmers Trust Company Building** (1931; Cross & Cross; DL). Its spectacular ornamentation includes giant coins above the limestone base and stylized figures known as the "giants of finance" at the first setback.

Continue down Hanover St to Beaver St, named for that furry rodent whose pelts played such a large part in the early economy of the city that it appears on New York's coat of arms. One block to the left is the flatiron-shaped 82–92 Beaver St, known as the **Beaver Building** or the **New York Cocoa Exchange Building** (1904; Clinton & Russell; DL). It was one of the city's first "skyscrapers" (it has only 15 stories) to feature polychromatic glazed terra-cotta.

Return up Hanover St to Wall St and turn right. At the corner of Wall and Pearl Sts is 74 Wall St, originally headquarters of **Seaman's Bank for Savings** (1926; Benjamin Wistar Morris). The building features a high arched doorway framed by stone reliefs of nautical scenes and creatures. The original charter of the Seamen's Bank restricted its clients to sailors, encouraging them to invest their pay instead of squandering it on the transient pleasures of the port of New York.

Walk back to William St and go a block north to Pine St. Turn right. The Romanesque revival masterpiece at **56–58 Pine St** (1894; Oswald Wirz; DL) is a 12-story brick and stone structure with spiky terra-cotta swirls, bearded faces, and sea creatures among the arches, and deep-set windows offset by truncated marble columns. The **Down Town Association Building** at 60 Pine St (1887; Charles Haight; DL; addition 1911; Warren & Wetmore) has terra-cotta ornamentation and, above its large arched entrance, even larger arched windows than its neighbor.

The block is dominated by **70 Pine St** (1932; Clinton & Russell), recognizable on the skyline by its Gothic crown and steel spire. Near the Pine and Cedar St entrances are large models of the building. During the 1920s and 30s designers made considerable use of sculptural models, and it is possible that the architect, having gone to so much trouble to construct the models, had them installed here. Formerly the Cities Service Building, 70 Pine St has a lavish Art Deco lobby, with brown and beige tones of marble and polished aluminum decoration.

Chase Manhattan Bank

Return to Pine and William Sts. The Chase Manhattan Bank (1960; Skidmore, Owings & Merrill), which occupies the enlarged block bounded by Pine, William, Liberty, and Nassau Sts, is now an ordinary-looking skyscraper, but in 1960 it was considered remarkable. First, its presence here was testimony to the bank's decision in the late 1950s to remain downtown when the financial community seemed on the brink of flight uptown, a decision that stimulated the rapid growth of the area in the late 1960s. Second, with its severe, unembellished forms and surfaces of glass and steel, the building became the first example in Lower Manhattan of the international style. The outdoor plaza was also the first in the area, a gratuitous act at the time, since the building predates the Zoning Resolution of 1961.

History

The Chase Manhattan Bank is the successor to the Chase Bank (named after Salmon P. Chase, secretary of the Treasury under Abraham Lincoln and originator of the national banking system) and the bank of the Manhattan Company, formed by Aaron Burr and others. In 1799 Burr and a group of investors organized the Manhattan Water Company, with the apparent intent to provide the city with an adequate, safe water supply. An unobtrusive clause included in the charter gave the investors the right to form a bank and engage in financial activities. Although the Manhattan Water Company did lay several miles of wooden pipe to carry water, its primary interest quickly became banking—and maybe always had been. Alexander Hamilton claimed that Burr used his banking privileges to enhance his political career, and this vociferous and sustained criticism of the bank was yet another source of hostility between the two men.

The Plaza

The plaza, a large expanse of pavement inaccessible from Liberty St, is adorned by Isamu Noguchi's sunken Japanese garden, whose black basalt rocks were brought from Japan by the sculptor. Originally the fountain contained fish, but they had to be rescued from the effects of air pollution and from people's irrepressible desire to throw coins into fountains.

In 1972 the owners installed the sculpture *Group of Four Trees* by Jean Dubuffet, a 43 ft, 25-ton fabrication supported by a steel skeleton and constructed of fiberglass, aluminum, and plastic resin, materials the artist hoped would withstand air pollution; the polyurethane paint used on the surface is essentially the same kind used to paint lines on streets. The sculpture has been called handsome, humane, amusing, and ominous; critics were quick to point out the ironic juxtaposition of an institution that epitomizes the moneyed establishment and a work by an artist who called himself antibourgeois and claimed to be influenced by children, criminals, and psychotics.

Continue uptown on William St. Between Cedar and Liberty Sts is an empty lot. Above the lot on the wall belonging to 27 Cedar St and 80 Maiden Lane, a massive mural re-creates Georges Seurat's masterpiece *Sunday Afternoon on the Island of La Grande Jatte*; the mural was painted for the 1995 film *Die Hard with a Vengeance.*

The triangular park at the intersection of Maiden Lane and Liberty St, **Louise Nevelson Plaza,** contains *Shadows and Flags,* a four-piece black sculptural group by Nevelson, donated anonymously in 1978.

Turn right into Maiden Lane. The building at **90–94 Maiden Lane** (1871; attrib. Charles Wright; DL) is the city's sole remaining commercial structure from the post–Civil War era built in the French Second Empire style. The former **Roosevelt & Son Store** was given a cast-iron facade in the early 1870s by James Alfred Roosevelt, Teddy's uncle; it is the southernmost cast-iron facade in the borough.

Federal Reserve Bank of New York
Return to the triangle and go west on Liberty St. The Federal Reserve Bank of New York (1924; York & Sawyer; DL), 33 Liberty St, fills the entire block bounded by Maiden Lane, Liberty, William, and Nassau Sts with its massive institutional stolidity. Philip Sawyer, the architect, studied in Italy, and his design reflects the fortified palaces of the great Renaissance families whose wealth and power made them institutions in their own right. The Strozzi Palace in Florence is the bank's principal model, and the superbly crafted wrought-iron lanterns flanking the doorway on Maiden Lane are almost exact replicas of their Florentine predecessors. They were executed by Samuel Yellin, whose work also adorns the Cunard Building on Lower Broadway.

Beneath the imposing bank are five levels containing offices and bullion vaults, where gold from foreign countries is stored. International transactions are consummated by simply moving the gold from one vault to another without its ever seeing the light of day. For tours (reservations required), ☎ (212) 720-6130.

Drachmas, Doubloons, and Dollars
Until the end of 2006, *Drachmas, Doubloons and Dollars: The History of Money,* an exhibition mounted by the American Numismatic Society, is on view on the first floor of the bank. Among its treasures are a Brasher doubloon, a Confederate States half-dollar, and a 20-dollar gold piece, often considered America's most beautiful coin, designed by Augustus Saint-Gaudens. Open Mon–Fri 10–4, free.

Continue west on Liberty St. **Liberty Tower** (1909; Henry Ives Cobb; DL), 55 Liberty St on the corner of Nassau St, is an early skyscraper, now converted to housing; birds and alligators ornament the white terra-cotta facade. It was once the Sinclair Oil Building.

At 65 Liberty St, the International Commercial Bank of China occupies the former **Chamber of Commerce of the State of New York** (1901; James B. Baker; DL), a fine remnant of the Beaux-Arts tradition, with a copper mansard roof and dormer windows. The asymmetrical placement of the entrance is unusual.

Return to Nassau St and turn left. The columned cast-iron facade of **63 Nassau St** (c. 1860) may be the work of cast-iron founding father James Bogardus (see Cast-Iron Architecture in Walk 8). Adorning the building are busts of Benjamin Franklin and George Washington.

John Street Methodist Church

At John St, turn right. At 44 John St stands the **John Street Methodist Church,** which has steadfastly occupied this property since 1768. It is the oldest Methodist society in the country. The present building (1841; DL) is the third on the site and an early example of the Italianate style. The wide-board flooring, entrance stairway, pews, and light brackets along the balcony were preserved from an earlier building of 1817, demolished when John St was widened.

History

The first congregation, consisting mainly of Irish Methodist immigrants who had come to this country in the early 1760s, was led by Philip Embury and Barbara Heck. Mrs. Heck, Embury's cousin, came home one day to find her husband, brother, and friends gambling at cards in the kitchen; she broke up the game (an early illustration shows her tossing the cards into the fire) and entreated her cousin, a former preacher, to reassume his duties. Embury began preaching at his home in 1766, but when his living room became too crowded, the group rented the upper story of a rigging loft to hold their services. In 1768 the society purchased this property on John St, and Embury drew up plans for the original chapel, a stone building faced with plaster, which he literally helped build.

Peter Williams

One of the early sextons of the church was Peter Williams, a black man whose parents were slaves of a family living on Beekman St. Williams converted to Christianity and became sexton of the church. When his owner returned to England after the Revolution, the church trustees, thinking it embarrassing for a well-known Christian to be sold publicly at auction, bought Williams privately for 40 pounds. He repaid his purchase price over a period of years and was formally emancipated in 1785. Williams went into the tobacco business, prospered, and eventually founded the Mother Zion Church, the first black Methodist church in New York.

Wesley Chapel Museum

In the basement of the church is the Wesley Chapel Museum, with the church's first altar rail, a clock sent by John Wesley, and Embury's Bible and lectern.

Walk west across Nassau St. This section of John St was called **Insurance Alley** in the 1930s, because many insurance companies maintained offices here. Since city tax breaks started inspiring downtown residential conversions in the 1990s, John St has become home to nearly a third of the neighborhood's new housing. The former **Tyler Building** (1926), 17 John St, a 15-story Art Deco office building with a limestone facade and cast-iron details, underwent a $20-million conversion to apartments and is now **The Metro.**

Continue west to Broadway. The former **American Telephone and Telegraph Building** (1915–22; William Welles Bosworth), 195 Broadway (between Fulton and Dey Sts), was once topped off by a gilded statue, *Genius of the Telegraph* (Evelyn Beatrice Longman), nicknamed "Golden Boy." The exterior has eight tiers of Ionic columns resting on a tier of Doric columns. The record-setting parade of columns continues in the lobby, which also has a plaque memorializing the inventor of the telephone, Alexander Graham Bell, and a bronze and marble work by Chester Beach entitled *Service to the Nation.* Its central figure, wearing headphones, his hair frizzled by lightning bolts, poses before a map of the U.S., its major cities linked by long-distance telephone wires.

Walk south down Broadway. At the northwest corner of Liberty St and Broadway is **One Liberty Plaza** (1972; Skidmore, Owings & Merrill). It replaces the much-admired Singer Tower (1908; Ernest Flagg), which at 41 stories was the tallest building in the world for 18 months and is still the tallest building ever demolished.

Across the street at 160 Broadway is an unusual McDonald's, geared toward tourists in this moneyed neighborhood: it features a doorman, hostess, table service, grand piano, and gift shop.

On the southeast corner of the same intersection, 140 Broadway, is the **Marine Midland Bank Building** (1967; Skidmore, Owings & Merrill), a smooth, dark building that soars straight up without setbacks (it occupies 40 percent of its site; the rest is plaza). On the Broadway side stands Isamu Noguchi's red steel-and-aluminum *Cube* (1973), a 28 ft outdoor sculpture that required a building permit because it is an enclosed mass.

On a bench in the small park bounded by Liberty and Cedar Sts to the west sits *Double Check* (1982; J. Seward Johnson Jr.), a bronze businessman, reviewing his correspondence.

One block north, at 26 Cortlandt St (northwest corner of Cortlandt and Church Sts), is the former **East River Savings Bank** (1934; Walker & Gillette), an Art Deco building with a panoramic mural (Dale Stetson) of the East River and its environs as they appeared in 1935. Today the building is the **Century 21 Department Store.**

4 · World Trade Center, World Financial Center, and Battery Park City

Subway: Broadway–Seventh Ave Local (1, 9) to Cortlandt St. Eighth Ave Express or Local (A, C) to Chambers St. Eighth Ave Local (E) to World Trade Center. Broadway Local (N, R) to Cortlandt St.
Bus: M1, M6, M9, M20, M22.

Note: These directions reflect the subway system as it existed before Sept 11, 2001. The Broadway–Seventh Ave Local (1, 9) service from Chambers St to South Ferry may not be restored for several years. The World Trade Center station on the Eighth Ave Local (E) is currently closed, and stops on other lines are being bypassed until the cleanup has been completed.

September 11, 2001

At 8:48 on the morning of Sept 11, 2001, a hijacked commercial jet laden with fuel for a transcontinental flight slammed into One World Trade Center, the north tower, setting off a fire whose temperature may have significantly exceeded 1,000 degrees Fahrenheit. Eighteen minutes later a second hijacked jet rammed into Two World Trade Center, the south tower, igniting a second firestorm. At 9:59, the south tower collapsed, some of its steel columns blown away by the explosion, others melted by the heat of the blaze. When the supporting columns gave way, the upper floors, above the blast, came down like a pile driver on the floors below and drove the building to the ground. At 10:28, the north tower, too, sank to street level in a cloud of smoke, ash, and tangled steel.

The two towers, architectural symbols of American corporate and financial power, housed major banks, brokerages, insurance companies, and law firms, as well as the Port Authority of New York and New Jersey, which had developed the trade center in the 1970s. The 22-story Marriott World Trade Center Hotel, between the towers, was irreparably damaged; nearby buildings, both in the World Financial Center to the west and across Church St to the east, suffered grave structural injury. By the end of the day, Seven World Trade Center, a 46-story office building, had fallen. Telephone landlines and electrical lines were severed; subway tunnels were clogged with debris; residents of Lower Manhattan were evacuated.

The human toll was far greater. Approximately 50,000 people worked in the buildings. While most escaped unharmed, 3,682 persons died, including 157 on the hijacked planes (these figures reflect the tabulation of late Nov 2001). A high percentage of the bodies will never be recovered. Among the dead were police, rescue workers, and more than 300 firefighters, many of whom had rushed up the tower stairs, trying to put out the fires and help fleeing office workers. Relatives and friends of people missing in the tragedy walked the streets carrying photos of loved ones and searching hospital lists for information. Rescue workers dug through the rubble for days and nights, first hoping to find survivors, later trying to recover human remains, and finally simply clearing the streets.

The collapse of the towers and nearby buildings left some 16 acres of rubble—estimated as high as 1.2 million tons—which was taken from the site one truckload at a time and then barged to the Fresh Kills Landfill on Staten Island, which reopened to receive this mournful cargo.

Note: The attack that ravaged the World Trade Center on Sept 11, 2001, came just as this book was about to go to press. A month has passed: the World Trade

Center site and much of the surrounding neighborhood remain in turmoil. Buildings near the site have suffered varying degrees of damage. Many face uncertain futures. Some downtown businesses, absorbing financial losses caused by the shrinking local and national economy, also confront unclear prospects. Transportation, especially the subway system, has been disrupted, and here, too, the long view is uncertain. Because this book aims to provide a detailed look at the city's landscape and how it changes over time, the sections discussing the World Trade Center and the surrounding buildings are being included as they would have been written on Sept 10, 2001—a reminder of downtown as New Yorkers have known it for the past quarter century. However, we are also including a note indicating the status of each building at press time, and present tense, when no longer appropriate, has been changed to past tense.

World Trade Center

Bounded by Church, Vesey, Liberty, and West Sts, and dominating the neighborhood with its huge twin towers stood the World Trade Center (1972–77; Minoru Yamasaki and Assocs; Emery Roth & Sons).

The World Trade Center complex was made up of seven buildings centered around a five-acre plaza opening on Church St. Developed by the Port Authority of New York and New Jersey, the Trade Center housed government agencies, trade organizations, importers, freight handlers, the U.S. Custom House, steamship lines, brokerages, and international banks.

History

The World Trade Center was seriously proposed in 1960 and opened for business some ten years later, although the towers weren't completed until 1973. Virtually a city within a city, the complex had its own medical facility and police station, shops, banks, restaurants, and even a pistol range for Port Authority policemen. Like Battery Park, much of the Trade Center stood on man-made land, once the bed of the Hudson River.

In 1916, subway excavations at Greenwich and Dey Sts uncovered the charred timbers of the Tyger, the ship on which Dutch explorer Adraien Block had sailed across the Atlantic in 1612. The Tyger burned in the harbor in 1613, and Block and his followers spent the winter in New Amsterdam, building another vessel, the Onrust (Restless), in which they explored Long Island Sound before returning to Holland. In 1967, during excavations for the World Trade Center, workmen unearthed a bronze breech-loading swivel deck gun also probably from the Tyger, since Block was sued by the Dutch Admiralty for loss of the ship's cannons. The exhumed relics are now at the Museum of the City of New York, while the rest of the Tyger lies buried some 20 ft below the World Trade Center site.

The excavated dirt and rubble was dumped into the Hudson behind a retaining wall, forming 23.5 acres of filled land between Rector and Cortlandt Sts, now part of Battery Park City.

Like the Brooklyn Bridge and the Empire State Building, the Twin Towers drew their share of publicity seekers. In 1974, Philippe Petit, a French aerialist, shot a rope across the gap between the two towers with a crossbow and then walked across. In 1975, Owen J. Quinn, an unemployed construction worker from

Queens, parachuted from the top of the Trade Center to dramatize the plight of the world's poor. In 1977, George Willig, a mountaineer and toy factory employee, scaled the South Tower using equipment he had designed to fit the tracks of the window-washing apparatus. And in 1999, Thor Alex Kappfjell, a Norwegian, parachuted off the observation deck of the South Tower, completing an unusual troika—months before he had jumped off the Chrysler and Empire State Buildings. He died shortly after while jumping off a mountain in Norway.

Until recently, it seemed that nothing could be more horrific than the events of Feb 26, 1993, when terrorists exploded a car bomb in a parking garage beneath the World Trade Center, killing six people, injuring thousands, and badly damaging the buildings. The blast left a crater 150 ft in diameter in the steel-reinforced concrete floor; it also knocked out the power plant, leaving 50,000 people in darkness without elevator service as the towers filled with smoke. There was remarkably little panic. Afterward, Muslim terrorists were quickly arrested and ultimately convicted. (Authorities were tipped off when the group tried to get back the deposit for the truck they had rented and blown up.) The $250-million cleanup reportedly involved removing 2,500 tons of rubble and required 160,000 gallons of cleaning fluid and 200,000 gallons of detergent.

Twin Towers

The 110-story Twin Towers, One and Two World Trade Center, were the tallest buildings in New York City; when built they were the tallest skyscrapers in the world.

Beneath the buildings was a **concourse level** with shops, banks, and restaurants. The Port Authority Trans Hudson (PATH) rail line linking lower Manhattan with New Jersey had its terminal here, and the Broadway, Eighth Ave, and Broadway–Seventh Ave subways all had stops on the concourse level.

Twin Tower Statistics

Each had 104 elevators, 21,800 windows, and an acre of rentable space per floor. Since the windows could not be opened, and since buildings so large obviously posed certain dangers to their inhabitants, the interior environment was controlled by a central computer with 6,500 sensors that fed it information about the temperature, humidity, and water and power needs. An estimated 50,000 people worked here, while 100,000 business and tourist visitors passed through daily.

One World Trade Center

In the mezzanine of One World Trade Center facing the plaza hung a textured wall sculpture *Sky-Gate New York* (1977–87) by Louise Nevelson. At the top of this tower was one of the city's most famous restaurants, Windows on the World, which received a $25-million makeover after the 1993 bombing.

Two World Trade Center

In Two World Trade Center, the south tower, a monumental tapestry (35×20 ft) by Joan Miró hung in the mezzanine.

Two World Trade Center also boasted the **Observation Deck** on the 110th floor, open when wind and weather permited, and an enclosed **Gallery** on the 107th floor, both offering stunning views of the city, the harbor, New Jersey, and Long Island.

Four and Five World Trade Center

Other buildings in the World Trade Center complex included Four and Five World Trade Center (1977 and 1972, respectively), located along Church St on either side of the plaza. Three commodity exchanges—the New York Cotton Exchange, the New York Coffee, Sugar and Cocoa Exchange, and the Commodity Exchange—were housed in Four World Trade Center, on the south side of the plaza.

The Plaza

At the Church St entrance to the plaza stood the largest free-standing stone carving of modern times, a highly polished, asymmetrical work (untitled; 1967–72) of black granite by Masayuki Nagare.

In the plaza's center, surrounded by a fountain, stood the bronze, broken-surfaced *Globe* (1975) by Fritz Koenig. Between the twin towers was James Rosati's polished stainless steel sculpture, *Ideogram* (1973).

Other Buildings

Also facing the plaza, between the north tower and Vesey St, was the **United States Custom House,** Six World Trade Center (1974), which handled the customs and collections activities for the New York–New Jersey port, replacing the old Custom House at Bowling Green. The 22-story **Marriott World Trade Center Hotel** (1981; Skidmore, Owings & Merrill), Three World Trade Center, was the first major hotel built in Lower Manhattan since 1836.

Seven World Trade Center (1987; Emery Roth & Sons), bounded by Vesey, Barclay, and Greenwich Sts and West Broadway, was the complex's last addition. On the Vesey St overpass was Alexander Calder's 25-ton *World Trade Center Stabile* (1971), enlarged from a work entitled *Three Wings.*

Adjacent to the World Trade Center but not part of it is the **New York Telephone Company Building,** 140 West St (between Barclay and Vesey Sts), also known as the **Barclay-Vesey Building** (1926; McKenzie, Voorhees & Gmelin; DL), an office tower and switching center. The first major building by architect Ralph Walker, the Barclay-Vesey Building has long been admired for the arcaded sidewalk along Vesey St and for the lavish Art Deco ornament on the exterior—plant forms, baby flutists, elephants whose ears spiral into nautilus shells, and bells. From the entrance you may admire the lobby ceiling paintings (Mack, Jenney & Tyler) illustrating the history of human communications—from the glazed brick reliefs of Babylon to the age of radio. (**Note:** This building suffered structural damage caused by debris falling from the World Trade Center, but within a month of the attack it was being used again as an office tower.)

The block bounded by Washington, West, Liberty, and Cedar Sts was occupied almost entirely by a parking lot, between whose parked cars rose the solitary **St. Nicholas Greek Orthodox Church** (1832), 155 Cedar St. It was built in the 19C, when a Middle Eastern colony of Turks, Armenians, Greeks, and especially Syrians lived along Washington St from the Battery to Rector St. As late as the 1930s the congregation observed the ceremony of the Rescue of the Cross each Jan 6, throwing into the harbor at the Battery a small wooden cross, which would be rescued by a stalwart swimmer. Construction for the Brooklyn-Battery Tunnel displaced these ethnic colonies; the Greeks crossed the East River to Astoria and the Arabs settled around Atlantic Ave and elsewhere in Brooklyn. (**Note:** The church was destroyed during the World Trade Center collapse, but the congregation plans to rebuild it on this site. The town of Bari, Italy, which considers St. Nicholas its patron saint, has pledged $500,000 for the reconstruction.)

At **90 West St** (1907; Cass Gilbert) is one of Gilbert's lesser-known masterpieces, a handsome limestone building featuring clustered piers, upper-floor colonnettes, and on top, a three-story arcade and a row of dormer windows amidst Gothic trefoils beneath a copper mansard roof. The upper floors are trimmed with yellow, pink, green, blue, and black glazed terra-cotta. Although it no longer stands at river's edge (because of landfill for Battery Park City), the building is dramatically illuminated at night, making it a visual feast for drivers on West St. (**Note:** Although badly damaged by fires caused by the attack on the World Trade Center, the building has been pronounced structurally sound. There is speculation that the high cost of repairs might deal a fatal blow to this elegant structure.)

Battery Park City and the World Financial Center

Follow Liberty St across West St to Battery Park City, Manhattan's newest neighborhood, rising on 92 acres of man-made land in the Hudson River. The hub of Battery Park City is the World Financial Center, whose office towers are occupied by major members of the financial community, employing 40,000 people. A marina, parks, shops, and restaurants enrich the area for its residents.

Important buildings in the World Financial Center were also damaged on Sept 11, 2001, when the World Trade Center was destroyed. This description shows the buildings as they were before the tragedy.

History

In the mid-1960s, as commerce fled uptown and the unused Hudson River piers rotted in the water, Governor Nelson Rockefeller conceived of Battery Park City as a way to revitalize the downtown area and the decaying waterfront, simultaneously providing housing and saving millions of dollars by finding a place to dump the rock and earth excavated from the World Trade Center site. In 1968 the state, which owned all landfill in the river, created the Battery Park City Authority to develop the area west of the World Trade Center.

In 1979 architects Alexander Cooper and Stanton Eckstut created the master plan that determined the present outlines of the area and is largely responsible for its aesthetic success. The plan extended the Manhattan street grid into the land-fill area, linking it to the larger city, and called for a north–south esplanade join-ing the commercial central area with residential neighborhoods proposed for both ends. It laid down design guidelines and emphasized the human scale and variety found in New York's successful older neighborhoods. The Cooper-Eckstut pro-posal called for 14,000 residential units and 6 million square ft of commercial space and required that least 30 percent of the total land be set aside for parks, plazas, and esplanades (one-quarter of the authority's budget now goes to park-land maintenance). The development, which now has about 8,000 residents, has been praised as a model of urban planning.

A recent construction boom is pushing Battery Park City toward completion but threatens to undermine its success. By 1999, about 4,500 residential units had been built, but the tenants were less diverse and more affluent than had been originally conceived. To change that situation, the Battery Park City Authority has built some housing for senior citizens and offered some rent-subsidized apart-ments.

Recent development includes a Ritz-Carlton hotel at the southern end and an Embassy Suites hotel with a 16-screen multiplex north of the World Financial Center. Many observers are concerned that the development is going too far, too fast, carving up the open space that makes Battery Park City attractive. Com-mercial space has already surpassed the originally stipulated 6 million square ft mark and the authority is considering another 1.4 million square ft.

World Financial Center

All four commercial towers of the World Financial Center are clad in granite and reflective glass, but have different heights and different roof forms. Just south of Liberty St is **One World Financial Center** (1985; Cesar Pelli, design architect; Adamson Assocs, architects), the corporate home of Dow Jones & Co. and Op-penheimer & Co., 40 stories high and topped with a sloping rectangular roof.

Walk through the South Gatehouse, which adjoins One World Financial Cen-ter to the north, and continue through its mirror image, the North Gatehouse. North of that gatehouse is **Two World Financial Center** (1987; Cesar Pelli, de-sign architect; Haines Lundberg Waehler, architects), one of two towers occu-pied by Merrill Lynch & Co. Recognizable by its domed roof, it is, with 51 stories, the tallest building in the project.

The Winter Garden

Just to the north is the Winter Garden (1988; Cesar Pelli, design architect; Adam-son Assocs., architects), the centerpiece of the financial sector, a glassed-in, barrel-vaulted plaza as large as Grand Central Terminal. Its 50 ft palm trees were imported from California's Mojave desert. After four years spent beneath a canopy acclimatizing to the limited light they would receive in New York, the trees were hauled in on flatbed trucks and planted while the building was still under con-struction.

Within the Winter Garden are shops, a café, and a performance space for the center's Arts & Events Program—☎ (212) 945-0505 for information; events also held in other locations within the World Financial Center.

(**Note:** The Winter Garden suffered severe structural damage from debris falling during the World Trade Center collapse. While it is very likely that this area will eventually reopen, its repair will necessitate almost a complete overhaul and re-building.)

Continue on to the pyramidally roofed **Three World Financial Center** (1985; Cesar Pelli, design architect; Adamson Assocs, architects), headquarters of the American Express Company. Between Three and Four World Financial Center is the glass-roofed, canopied **courtyard,** inspired by European open-air piazzas, with restaurants and cafés. **Four World Financial Center** (1986; Cesar Pelli, design architect; Haines Lundberg Waehler, architects), also occupied by Merrill Lynch & Co., is the last and smallest of the original towers, ending in a truncated stepped pyramid. West of this is the **New York Mercantile Exchange,** which moved to 1 North End Ave in 1997.

North of the Mercantile Exchange, at the foot of Vesey St, is the **Irish Hunger Memorial** (2002). Its centerpiece is an abandoned stone farmhouse (c. 1838) that was brought piece by piece from County Mayo in Ireland, where it had remained uninhabited for 40 years. Stone walls, potato furrows, and Irish grasses and wildflowers surround the reconstructed cottage. The site commemorates the Irish potato famine, which sent hundreds of thousands of immigrants to the New World beginning in the 1840s, and also calls attention to world hunger today. The memorial was designed by Brian Tolle, an artist; Juergen Riehm and David Piscuskas, architects; and Gail Eileen Wittwer, a landscape architect.

Battery Park City

At the north end of Battery Park City is **Stuyvesant High School,** 346 Chambers St, one of the nation's premier high schools, which moved here from E. 15th St and Second Ave in 1992. Founded as a manual trade school for boys, it later became a specialized high school emphasizing mathematics, science, and technology. Notable alumni include Robert William Fogel, 1993 Nobel Prize winner for economics; Roald Hoffmann, who shared the 1981 Nobel Prize in chemistry; Roy Innis, chairman of the Congress of Racial Equality; Walter Becker, cofounder of the band Steely Dan; civil rights activist Robert Moses; screenwriter-director Joseph Mankiewicz *(All About Eve);* and actors Robert Alda, Jimmy Cagney, Gorge Raft, John Garfield, Paul Reiser, and Tim Robbins.

Walk west toward the water and then south along the esplanade. The plaza, west of the buildings, borders **North Cove.** The marina is used by ferries coming from and going to New Jersey, private yachts, sightseeing charters, and sailing schools. A new $24-million Port Authority ferry terminal will open in 2003.

Continue south, walking around the plaza and back to the Hudson River beyond Liberty St. At the south end of the cove, overlooking a small fountain and pool is the **New York City Police Memorial** (1997; Stuart Crawford), a black wall inscribed with the names of policemen who have died in the line of duty. Between the esplanade and South End Ave rise the unattractive towers and lowrises of Gateway Plaza (1982; Brown & Gershon), designed before the Cooper-Eckstut master plan.

The Esplanade

Continue south. The esplanade (1983–90; Cooper & Eckstut) is one of the glories of Battery Park City. A wide, thoughtfully designed walkway, it once more gave pedestrians, after long exile, access to the river. At the intersection of Albany St is Ned Smyth's *The Upper Room* (1987), an elevated bluestone plaza surrounded by terra-cotta columns, which suggests a ruined temple or courtyard. Between the columns is a long table inlaid with six chess boards. It is part of Battery Park City's public art project, in which artists have created works intrinsic to several sites in the neighborhood.

Continue south one block. On the left is **Rector Park,** a residential square surrounded by apartment buildings, designed to recall the quiet elegance of Gramercy Park. At the mouth of the park, facing the esplanade, is *Rector Gate* (1989; R. M. Fischer), a Calderesque 43 ft skeletal gateway of stainless steel and decorative metal. A block south, at West Thames St, is Richard Artschwager's *Sitting/Stance* (1988), with outsized, outdoor furniture in granite, aluminum, and wood.

Next comes **South Cove** (1988; Mary Miss, artist; Stanton Eckstut, architect; Susan Child, landscape architect), landscaped with rock outcroppings and wild plantings.

Museum of Jewish Heritage: A Living Memorial to the Holocaust

18 First Place, New York, NY 10004. ☎ (212) 509-6130 for recorded information. Web site: www.mjhnyc.org. Open Sun–Wed 9–5; Thurs 9–8; Fri 9–3 (extended Fri hours in summer). Closed Sat, Jewish holidays, and Thanksgiving. Admission charge. Group tours, gallery talks, films, events: ☎ (212) 968-1800. Café, gift shop. Accessible to wheelchairs.

Subway: Broadway–Seventh Ave Local (1, 9) to South Ferry. Lexington Ave Express (4, 5) to Bowling Green. Broadway Local (N, R) to Whitehall St. Bus: M1 (marked South Ferry), M6, M9, M15.

South of the cove is the Museum of Jewish Heritage: A Living Memorial to the Holocaust. Installed in a six-sided, six-tiered building (1997; Kevin Roche, architect; Patrick Gallagher, exhibit designer), the museum explores Jewish life and culture from the late 19C to the present. Although the museum was originally conceived decades ago as a Holocaust Memorial, plans changed several times and ultimately were shaped by the opening of the United States Holocaust Museum in Washington, D.C.

The core exhibit moves chronologically from the first floor to the third. On the **first floor,** a colorful multimedia display introduces Jewish traditions, rituals, and holidays, but most exhibits emphasize the years 1880–1930, when Jewish culture flourished and Jews emigrated from eastern Europe to Palestine, the U.S., and even China. The **second floor** explores Nazism and the Holocaust. Exhibits on the **third floor,** the only rooms with natural light, remind visitors that while the world's Jewish population was decimated by Hitler, it was not destroyed. The focus here is postwar Jewish life: the settlement of Israel, contributions to American popular culture, the Jewish response to intolerance since World War II, and the struggle to ensure that the Holocaust is never forgotten. Artifacts—a hand-painted Succoth tapestry from the 1920s, a German board game called *Juden Raus* (whoever "deports" the most Jews wins)—are supplemented by moving videotaped interviews with survivors and their families, photos, film footage, and computer displays.

In May 2000, the museum approved plans for a 45,000-square-ft expansion. The museum has been chosen as one of the initial five repositories for the archives of Steven Spielberg's Survivors of the Shoah Visual History Foundation.

Robert Wagner Jr. Park

At the south end of Battery Park City is the 3.5 acre Robert Wagner Jr. Park (1996; architects, Rodolfo Machado and Jorge Silvetti; landscape architects, Hannah/Olin; garden designer, Lynden Miller). Named for the former deputy mayor, Board of Education president, and City Council member, who died suddenly at 49 in 1993, the park is lush and tranquil. The centerpiece is a green lawn enclosed by low granite walls and backless teak benches. Rising above the lawn is a brick structure with a café at the base and platforms above for contemplating the harbor views. There are also wonderful gardens.

Skyscraper Museum

39 Battery Place (at First Place), New York, NY 10280. ☎ (212) 968-1961. Web site: www.skyscraper.org. Call the museum or check the Web site for hours and exhibition schedule. Changing exhibitions, walking tours, lectures, publications. Bookstore. Accessible to wheelchairs.

Across Battery Place from the park is the new **Ritz-Carlton Hotel and Condominiums** (2001; Gary Edward Handel and Polshek Partnership). On the ground floor is the Skyscraper Museum, which was founded in 1996 and offers changing exhibitions on the history, technology, and design of skyscrapers, as well as their importance as real estate. After wandering from one temporary exhibition space to another for the first six years of its existence, the museum moved here in 2002. The core exhibition, **Skyscraper\City,** details the evolution of New York's commercial skyline. Other exhibitions have chronicled the astonishingly swift construction of the Empire State Building and looked at the world's biggest (by volume) and tallest skyscrapers of the 20C, most of them in New York. The museum is beginning to acquire a permanent collection of architectural photos, drawings, construction records, and other high-rise artifacts.

Across from Battery Park City, at 21 West St, is the **Downtown Athletic Club** (1926; Starrett & Van Vleck), whose Art Deco exterior features salt-glazed tile and patterned brick work with corbeled arches. A private club, it is best known as presenter of the Heisman Trophy, college football's highest individual honor. Public access is limited to the lobby, where the original trophy (with all the winners' names etched on it) is on view.

5 · Park Row, City Hall, and the Civic Center

Subway: Broadway–Seventh Ave Local (1, 9) to Cortlandt St. Seventh Ave Express (2, 3) to Fulton St. Lexington Ave Express (4, 5) to Fulton St. Eighth Ave Express (A) to Broadway-Nassau. Broadway Local (R) to Cortlandt St. Nassau St Local or Express (J, M, Z) to Fulton St.
Bus: M1, M6, M9, M15, M22.

St. Paul's Chapel and Churchyard

Facing Broadway between Fulton, Church, and Vesey Sts is St. Paul's Chapel and Churchyard (1766; Thomas McBean; tower and steeple added 1794, James C. Lawrence; DL), built as a subsidiary chapel of Trinity Church for worshipers who lived too far uptown to make it down to Wall St. It is the city's oldest church and the site of the service following George Washington's inauguration as president. (Mon noon concerts; for program information, ☎ (212) 602-0747, or ☎ (212) 602-0768 for a live person.)

Exterior

Commonly attributed to Thomas McBean, of whom little is known, St. Paul's shows the influence of St. Martin's-in-the Fields, London, though executed in homely native building materials, including rough, reddish gray Manhattan schist and smooth brownstone. When built, the Georgian-style church faced west to the river, but as Broadway became an important thoroughfare, a portico and entrance were added facing east. On the east porch is the tomb and monument of Brig. Gen. Richard Montgomery, mortally wounded in the Battle of Quebec, Dec 25, 1775. The monument by sculptor Jean Jacques Caffieri pays tribute to the cause of freedom: on the right of the obelisk are a Phrygian cap (given to freed Roman slaves), broken swords, and a club of Hercules with a ribbon inscribed "Libertas Restituta" (Liberty Restored).

Interior

The interior is beautiful, painted in pale colors, graced by slender Corinthian columns supporting a barrel-vaulted ceiling. The chancel wall has a Palladian window glazed with clear glass. The 14 Waterford crystal chandeliers, the organ case, and the elaborately carved pulpit and communion rail all date from before the Revolution. Over the pulpit are three feathers, the emblem of the Prince of Wales. Pierre L'Enfant, best known as city planner of Washington, D.C., may have designed the gilded wooden sunburst behind the altar. At the rear of the church is a memorial to John Wells (died 1823), a prominent lawyer, the earliest known marble portrait bust by an American sculptor (1824; John Frazee).

History

Spared by the Fire of 1776, as old Trinity Church was not, St. Paul's Chapel became the most important Anglican church in the city and was used by George Washington following his inauguration at Federal Hall. The pew where he worshipped, originally canopied, is in the north aisle; in the south aisle is the Governor's Pew, reserved first for royal governors, now for the state governor. During the British occupation, while other churches became stables, prisons, and hospitals, St. Paul's Chapel served British officers as their own house of worship.

The Graveyard

At the rear of the church is a burial ground with gravestones of moderately prominent early New Yorkers (the most famous were buried in Trinity churchyard). Among them are: George Frederick Cooke (died 1812), a famous English actor whose monument was financed by Edmund Kean, an even more famous

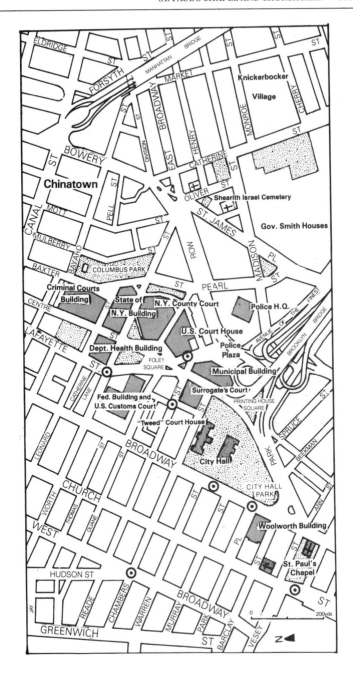

English actor; and Thomas Addis Emmet (died 1827), an Irish patriot and lawyer exiled from British territory after serving a prison term for treason.

Just north of the graveyard, at 14 Vesey St, is the **New York County Lawyers' Association** (1930; Cass Gilbert; DL), a white marble and limestone neo-Georgian building. Just to the west, at 20 Vesey St, is the former **New York Post Building** (1906; Robert D. Kohn; DL), home of the *New York Evening Post* from 1907 to 1930. Trademarks of famous early printers decorate the spandrels between windows, and statues high up on the facade represent the Four Periods of Publicity. Gutzon Borglum, best known for his gigantic portrait heads at Mt. Rushmore in North Dakota, and Estelle R. Kohn, wife of the architect, designed the statues.

Continue to Church St. Turn right and walk a block north to Barclay St. **St. Peter's Roman Catholic Church** (1838; John Haggerty and Thomas Thomas; DL), 22 Barclay St, is Manhattan's oldest Roman Catholic church, standing on the site of its predecessor, the first Catholic church in the city. Since the regulations outlawing Roman Catholicism in Britain applied to the U.S. during the colonial period, it was not until 1785 that the congregation was able to purchase this land from Trinity Parish and lay the cornerstone for the original building. The present granite church has an Ionic portico with six massive columns and a wood-framed pediment. In the central niche is a statue of St. Peter holding the keys to the eternal kingdom.

The Woolworth Building

Walk east, back to Broadway. The **Woolworth Building** (1913; Cass Gilbert; DL), 233 Broadway, was the world's tallest when completed, and though it was eclipsed in 1930 by the Chrysler Building, it remains one of the city's most luxuriantly detailed skyscrapers.

History

F. W. Woolworth enjoyed a classic 19C American rags-to-riches career, starting out as a farm boy and beginning his life's work clerking in a general store. During this apprenticeship Woolworth became convinced that customers would patronize a store where they could see and even finger the merchandise and buy without having to haggle over prices with intimidating clerks. After a few false starts he proved himself right in a grand way, opening his first successful five-and-ten-cent store in 1879 and expanding it eventually into a chain of stores. By 1913 he was able to pay $13.5 million in cash for this building.

The care and attention that Woolworth devoted to the smallest detail (he personally picked out the bathroom fixtures and the mail chutes), the extravagant expenditures for beautiful materials and fine craftsmanship, and the grandiose conception of the whole make the building a monument to its owner's career and a visual delight in a less opulent age.

The Woolworth Building was officially opened at 7:30 in the evening of April 24, 1913, by President Woodrow Wilson in Washington, who at a signal from a telegrapher pressed a button that illuminated 80,000 light bulbs in the tower in New York. The Reverend S. Parkes Cadman, known for the intensity of his sentiments, noted that the building inspired "feelings too deep even for tears," words that echo the final line of Wordsworth's "Ode: Intimations of Immortality." Cadman dubbed it "The Cathedral of Commerce," a nickname that stuck. In 2001, developers began converting the top 27 floors into ultraluxury condominiums.

Exterior

Predating the 1916 zoning restrictions, the building covers its entire site. It rises about 300 ft straight up from the street, its verticality emphasized by the light-colored piers that ascend in an unbroken line straight to the top of the main section. The tower then soars another 400 ft, ending in a delicate crown surrounded by four smaller towers (total height, 792 ft). At street level around the elaborate doorway arch are carved figures of young men and women at work, earning the money, according to some early observers, they will use to shop at Woolworth's. Masks above the second floor represent four centers of civilization—Europe, Africa, Asia, and America—a motif Cass Gilbert used earlier on the Custom House at Bowling Green.

Interior

The walls are covered with golden-toned marble quarried on the Isle of Skyros; the vaulted mosaic ceilings in blue, green, and gold have bird and flower patterns intended to recall the mosaics of Ravenna. In the side hallways at the mezzanine level are murals by C. Paul Jennewein representing Commerce and Labor (south and north respectively).

The only relief in all this magnificence (neither Gilbert nor Woolworth was known for a sense of humor) comes from a set of sculpted figures beneath the arches leading to the lateral hallways near Broadway, which depict Woolworth and some of his builders: Woolworth clutches a big nickel; Cass Gilbert peers through his pince-nez at a large model of the building; Lewis E. Pierson, president of the Irving Bank, first tenant of the building, gazes at a stock ticker tape; Edward Hogan, the renting agent, negotiates a rental; Gunvald Aus, the structural engineer, measures a girder.

North of the Woolworth Building, at 257 Broadway, is the former **Home Life Insurance Company Building** (1894; Napoleon Le Brun & Sons and Harding & Gooch; Pierre Le Brun, architect in charge; DL), a classic three-part skyscraper (elaborate base, simple tower, ornate crown) with a pioneering steel-skeleton frame beneath its marble Renaissance-style facade.

South of the Woolworth Building is the **Transportation Building** (1927; York & Sawyer), 225 Broadway, which occupies the site of the Astor House Hotel. Built in 1834 by John Jacob Astor, it was the city's first famous hotel, in its day a palace of luxury. Among its conveniences were bathing facilities and gaslights on every floor, indulgences then unknown even in the finest mansions. By 1870, however, fashion had deserted Lower Broadway and the Astor House began taking in mercantile visitors and a few older people who remembered its finer days. It was demolished in 1915.

Continue south on Broadway. From 1842 to 1865, the southeast corner of Broadway and Ann St was the site of **P. T. Barnum's American Museum,** which delighted and deceived the public with a "Feejee Mermaid," a bearded lady (possibly not a lady at all), and Gen. Tom Thumb, a midget from Bridgeport, Connecticut. The museum burned in 1865, and Barnum went on to organize the "Greatest Show on Earth," a circus that opened in Brooklyn in 1871.

Park Row

Cross to the east side of Broadway and walk uptown along Park Row, an early center of theatrical activity. The Park Theatre, New York's most famous early playhouse, which faced a small street parallel to Park Row still known as Theater Alley, saw the comings and goings of such notable performers as Edmund Kean, Edwin Booth, and Fanny and Charles Kemble. The Park Theatre opened in 1798 and lasted until 1848, when a fire and the changing character of the neighborhood closed it forever.

Park Row eventually became the center of the city's newspaper industry, close to City Hall (political news) and to the slums of the Lower East Side (sensational human interest stories). In its prime "Newspaper Row," as the street was known, ran from Ann St (where James Gordon Bennett's marble New York Herald Building was built on the site of P. T. Barnum's American Museum in 1866) to Chatham Square and was divided by the approaches to the Brooklyn Bridge into a northern section for the foreign language press and a southern section that belonged to the great New York dailies.

History

In one grand row facing City Hall Park stood buildings housing four of the city's greatest papers: Joseph Pulitzer's *New York World;* Charles Anderson Dana's *New York Sun;* the *New York Tribune,* founded by Horace Greeley; and the *New York Times,* revitalized by Adolph Ochs. When Joseph Pulitzer died in 1911, New York had 14 daily newspapers, 12 of them published on Park Row.

The 33-story, 386 ft **Park Row Building** (1899; R.H. Robertson) also called the Ivins Syndicate Building, 15 Park Row, was an early titleholder in the world's-tallest-building contest, holding the record from 1899 until 1908. On top are twin towers, and on the way up, four caryatids at the fourth floor.

The **Potter Building** (1886; Norris G. Starkweather), 38 Park Row, converted to apartments in 1979, is named after its politician-developer, Orlando B. Potter. Potter wanted state-of-the-art fireproofing because his earlier building here had burned in 1882. He pioneered the use of terra-cotta to fireproof structural steel, and went on to found the New York Architectural Terra Cotta Company in Queens. The deep window bays are framed by corbels, pediments and heavily ornamented brick pilasters.

At 41 Park Row, between Beekman and Spruce Sts, is the former **New York Times Building** (original building, 1857; considerably enlarged and altered, 1889, George B. Post; altered again, 1905, Robert Maynicke). The first home (1858–1904) of the *Times* was both imposing (its height of more than 80 ft gave it a grand panoramic view) and elegant, with plate glass windows on the ground level, frescoed walls, and marble floors. This luxury started a trend in newspaper buildings, which until then had humbly reflected the status of the industry. It was also fireproof, surviving the 1882 blaze that destroyed its neighbor.

Continue north on Park Row. The area around Nassau and Spruce Sts and Park Row was known as **Printing House Square** when the **statue of Benjamin Franklin** (c. 1872; Ernst Plassmann), publisher of the *Pennsylvania Gazette,* was erected. Today the ramps to the Brooklyn Bridge fill much of the former open space.

The **New Building** (1970; Eggers & Higgins; enlarged 1984) **of Pace University** is just to the east, bounded by Nassau, Frankfort, Gold, and Spruce Sts. Founded in 1906 as an accounting school, Pace University offers courses in the arts and sciences, education, nursing, and business. On the facade is *Brotherhood of Man*, a welded-copper relief by Henri Azaz.

City Hall Park and City Hall

Once known as the Commons, 8.8-acre City Hall Park still functions as a place for communal experience.

History

The park was a shared cow pasture during Dutch times, a parade ground during colonial times, and the site where, on July 9, 1776, the Declaration of Independence was publicly read for the first time to Gen. George Washington, the Continental Army, and a supportive crowd. Thereafter, the Commons housed an almshouse, debtor's prison, burial ground, and soldiers' barracks.

In 1691, Jacob Leisler, lieutenant governor of the colony and a militant anti-Catholic antagonist of the British royal governors (appointed by King James II, a Catholic) was hanged on the Commons for treason. In 1695, his sentence was reversed by the British Parliament, restoring his reputation and enabling his body to be exhumed and buried in hallowed ground. Throughout the years, the park has continued as ground zero for public protests, riots, and strikes, including the 1837 Bread Riot protesting the price of flour, a clash between rival city and state police forces in 1857, and an 1889 newsboy strike.

Traditionally, public heroes have been driven up Broadway from Battery Park to City Hall Park and showered with miles of ticker tape (paper strips on which news and stock market quotes are electronically printed), tossed from buildings in the Financial District.

Top Ticker-Tape Parades

The first "ticker-tape parade" was spontaneously initiated by enthusiastic office workers during the 1886 parade celebrating the dedication of the Statue of Liberty. The first person marched beneath the festive paper rain was Theodore Roosevelt upon his 1910 return from an African safari. Gertrude Ederle was the first woman so honored (1926), after becoming the first woman to swim the English Channel. Two weeks later, Mrs. Clemington Corson, the second woman to swim the channel was also honored. From 1919 until 1965, nearly every visiting foreign leader received a parade, and in 1928 alone there were six of them. The sky-bound were next most honored, with 14 parades for aviators, including Amelia Earhart, Charles Lindbergh and Howard Hughes, and six parades for astronauts, including John Glenn (1962) and Neil Armstrong, Buzz Aldrin, and Michael Collins (1969). Today, modern office buildings have sealed windows and ticker tape has been replaced by computers, so the tonnage of celebratory paper has declined. The New York Mets' 1986 championship parade produced 648 tons of paper, while in the late 1990s, the Yankees' three championship parades combined totaled only 160 tons. (No downtown parade, however, can match Times Square during V-J Day celebrations in 1945 when 5,438 tons of paper fell.)

City Hall Park

In 1999, City Hall Park underwent a ten-month, $14-million restoration, during which old coins and bones, including 15 skeletons, were discovered. The grave site remains in the park's northeast corner, now covered by a flower bed. The **new fountain** incorporates the basin of an original fountain (1871) by Jacob Wrey Mould, shunted off in the 1920s to Crotona Park in the Bronx. Four two-tiered bronze lampposts surround the four-spouted fountain. The new iron fence is cast from the original, discovered in a Bloomingburg, New York, cemetery.

As part of the redesign, a bronze **statue of Nathan Hale** (1890; Frederick W. MacMonnies) returned from a site near Broadway to center stage. Hale, the Revolutionary spy hanged by the British, who allegedly regretted having but one life to give for his country, is depicted as a handsome youth (he was 21) in an impassioned attitude of defiance. The portrayal represents MacMonnies's romantic conception of Hale, since a contemporary described him as having "shoulders of moderate breadth, his limbs straight and very plump."

On the west lawn is a **monument to the Liberty Poles,** erected by the Sons of Liberty in the years preceding the Revolution. Symbols of resistance to the British crown and rallying points for demonstrations, Liberty Poles were raised throughout the city, five successive ones in City Hall Park. Topped off with an emblem saying "Liberty," the poles were deliberately provocative, erected in sight of British barracks. The Liberty Boys, as the Sons of Liberty were also called, were disgruntled tradesmen, workers, and army veterans who propagandized against taxation policies and harassed British troops.

While the park's upgrade has been welcomed, the new guard posts and chains that close off the park plaza from City Hall have been criticized. Before the park reopened, the New York Civil Liberties Union sued Mayor Rudolph Giuliani for restricting public access to City Hall's steps, citing that forbidding their use as a public forum was a First Amendment violation. In April 2000 a federal judge struck down the city regulation governing the number of protesters allowed on the steps of City Hall.

History

Beneath the park (not open to the public) is **the city's first subway station.** Mayor George McClellan was at the throttle when the line running from City Hall to 137th St in the Bronx opened as part of the Interborough Rapid Transit system in 1904. The line was shut down Dec 31, 1945, since the station had become too short for modern subway cars. The station was sealed until the 1990s, when the Metropolitan Transit Authority began fund-raising to restore the site. The station has a grand entry hall with a domed ceiling, leaded stained-glass panels, terra-cotta tile work, chandeliers, and the original brass plaque marking "The First Municipal Rapid Transit Railroad of the City of New York." The Transit Museum sponsors several tours of the station each year; ☎ (718) 243-3060.

City Hall

City Hall, New York, NY 10007. ☎ (212) 788-6865. Tours (45 minutes) offered Mon–Fri at 10, 11, and 2; must have groups of at least 13 people. Reservations required. On days of public hearings the Council Chamber is open to the public. Accessible to wheelchairs.

Subway: Eighth Ave Express or Local (A, C, E) to Chambers St–World Trade Center. Broadway Local (N, R) to City Hall. Nassau St Express or Local (J, M, Z) to Chambers St. Seventh Ave Express (2,3) to Park Place. Lexington Ave Express or Local (4, 5, 6) to Brooklyn Bridge–City Hall. Bus: M1, M6, M9, M15, M22, M103.

The centerpiece of the park is City Hall (1802–11; Joseph Mangin and John Mc-Comb Jr; DL), one of New York's architectural jewels: elegant, gracefully proportioned, and attractively situated. Oddly enough, the building has not always been treasured.

History

The present City Hall is the third building to house the municipal government, following the Stadt Huys on Pearl St and the 18C City Hall on Wall St that later became Federal Hall. John McComb Jr. and Joseph François Mangin, two established New York architects, won the design competition, taking home a prize of $350, for which (plus construction costs estimated at a half-million dollars) the city got one of its outstanding public buildings.

The cornerstone for City Hall was laid in 1803, but a yellow fever epidemic, labor disputes, and financial difficulties delayed the official opening until July 4, 1811. The 35,000 cubic ft of marble to face the front and sides of the building were quarried in West Stockbridge, Massachusetts, while the north facade was originally faced in brownstone because the city fathers wished to save money and felt that the north side was safely out of sight. During a 1950s restoration the base was covered with red granite and the walls with Alabama limestone; the only original exterior marble is on the porch roof.

Exterior

City Hall is an elegant Federal-style building elaborated with French details, perhaps the contribution of Mangin, a French émigré, believed to have been the exterior's principal designer. The French influence appears particularly in the long rows of windows ornamented with pilasters and swags instead of the usual more severe classical orders. The tower, however, belongs to the native tradition, as does the interior. The dome is crowned by a copper, mass-produced statue of Justice, manufactured in Ohio and restored in 1998. It replaced the original Justice carved in wood in 1812 by John Dixey, which was destroyed by fire in 1858.

Interior

Ground floor. The lobby walls are covered with the original white Massachusetts marble. To the right of the entrance is a bronze copy (1857) of a sculpture of George Washington made from a marble original by Jean-Antoine Houdon in

City Hall (built 1802–11), an elegant example of the Federal style. The uptown facade was not clad in decorative marble, as hardly anyone, at the time of building, lived north of Chambers St to admire it. (Landmarks Preservation Commission, New York City. Photographer: John B. Bayley)

1787; the original, in the state capitol at Richmond, Virginia, is based on life casts Houdon made in 1785. The mayor's office is at the end of the left corridor.

Beyond the lobby is the **rotunda,** with a beautiful circular staircase. In the center of the rotunda, supported by ten marble Corinthian columns, is a dome with a clear glass oculus. The design for this space is probably McComb's.

Second floor. To the east of the rotunda on the second floor is the **City Council Chamber,** designed in about 1898 when the five boroughs were joined to make Greater New York, a union commemorated by the low-relief sculpture in the corners of the ceiling. The plaster statue of Thomas Jefferson is the original model for a bronze (1833) by Pierre Jean David d'Angers, a student of Houdon's. The ceiling painting, *New York Receiving the Tributes of the Nation* (1903), is by Taber Sears, George W. Breck, and Frederick C. Martin. The painting of the Marquis de Lafayette (1824) is by Samuel F. B. Morse, who had ambitions as a history painter but had to settle for portraiture, which he eventually abandoned in favor of inventing.

The Governor's Room

At the head of the stairs is the Governor's Room, originally set aside as an office for the state governor when he visited the city. The portraits inside on permanent display include 9 of the 13 paintings the city commissioned from John Trumbull. On the west wall is *George Washington on Evacuation Day* (Nov 24, 1783), which depicts Washington standing by his horse, with a background view of Bowling Green and the Upper Bay. Over the opposite mantel is his portrait of *George Clinton, Brigadier General in the American Army*, with the Hudson River highlands in the background.

Other Trumbull portraits, mainly of mayors and governors, include Governors John Jay and Daniel D. Tompkins, Mayors Richard Varick and Marinus Willett, and Secretary of the Treasury Alexander Hamilton. The portrait of Peter Stuyvesant is a copy by Trumbull of an earlier painting. Among the furniture is a writing table used by George Washington at Federal Hall on Wall St when New York was the nation's capital.

The Grounds

North of City Hall on the east side of the park is a bronze **statue of Horace Greeley** (1890; John Quincy Adams Ward) showing the famous newspaperman relaxing in a bronze upholstered chair with delightful bronze fringes, a newspaper draped over his right knee. Greeley founded the *New York Tribune* and guided it to eminence. Famous also for his advice to an unknown fortune seeker—"Go West, young man"—Greeley is known to have been careless about his dress and personal appearance, a quality Ward has caught in the statue.

Former New York County Courthouse

At the north end of City Hall Park, behind City Hall and facing Chambers St, is the former New York County Courthouse (1872; John Kellum; DL; rear addition, 1880, Leopold Eidlitz), a three-story, flat-roofed structure of Massachusetts marble, formerly white but now weathered to a dark gray. In the mid-1970s the courthouse was slated for demolition but the high cost plus resistance by preservationists saved it. It is now being renovated, and will become the home of the Museum of the City of New York (see Walk 23); the projected opening date is 2003. The building is known as the "Tweed Courthouse" because William M. "Boss" Tweed and his "ring" embezzled impressive sums of money from the city during its construction.

History

In 1858 the city Board of Supervisors agreed to a preliminary expenditure of $250,000 for a new criminal courthouse, the cornerstone of which was laid in Dec 1861. By the time the building was finished ten years later, the cost had risen to somewhere between $12 million and $13 million—the exact figures were concealed during the ensuing scandal—of which an estimated $8.5 million ended up in the pockets of Tweed and his cronies. They hired contractors who padded their accounts and then kicked back to the politicians most of the difference between what the work actually cost and what the city paid for it. Thus a plasterer named Andrew J. Garvey appeared in the records as receiving $45,966.89 for a single day's work, a sum which earned him the title "Prince of Plasterers." Although the Tweed Ring fleeced the city in other ways, it was the disclosure of these cost overruns that precipitated Tweed's exposure, downfall, and ultimate imprisonment.

Tweed, who rose from humble beginnings to wealth, power, and fame through the machinery of Tammany Hall, the most powerful organization in Democratic

Party politics, never held a high city office himself, but was a kingmaker who profited from friends in high places. His fall was swift and spectacular, and he died in prison (1876), poor and friendless.

The Civic Center

Beyond City Hall, the focal points of the municipal government are centered around the Municipal Building and Police Plaza to the east and Foley Square, which is north of City Hall. The location was chosen almost by default, the boggy ground making the neighborhood unsuitable for high-rise commercial construction and the nearby slums making it unattractive for anything else.

Municipal Building

Just east of City Hall is the magnificent Municipal Building (1907–14; McKim, Mead & White; DL) at 1 Centre Street. Applauded as a great civic skyscraper and an example of the eclectic style at its grandest, it replaced the Staats-Zeitung Building, home of the city's most important German language newspaper.

Exterior

Like other early skyscrapers, the Municipal Building is divided horizontally into an elaborate base (impressive to the pedestrian), a simple central tower, and a monumental top planned to take a conspicuous place in the skyline. The central arch in the ground-level colonnade formerly straddled Chambers St, forming a monumental gateway to the slums of the Lower East Side, but now acts as a grand entrance to Police Plaza. Above the colonnade are shields with the insignia of Amsterdam, Great Britain, New York City, and New York State. The winged figures flanking the arch represent Guidance (left) and Executive Power (right). The panels over the smaller arches are (left) Civic Duty, which shows the city conferring the law upon its citizens, and (right) Civic Pride, depicting the citizens returning the fruits of their labors to the city. Above, relief medallions depict Progress (left) and Prudence (right). Crowning the building is Adolph A. Weinman's 25 ft statue, *Civic Fame* (1913–14), holding a laurel branch and a crown with five turrets symbolizing the five boroughs. Made of copper hammered over a steel frame (like the Statue of Liberty) the gilded statue stands 582 ft above the street.

Interior

Walk through the central arch to see the coffered ceiling and the bronze ornamental work inside the lobby. On the south side of the building is an arcade with a vaulted ceiling, making the subway entrance there one of the most imposing in the city. Among the city offices is the Marriage Chapel, where couples getting married "at City Hall" take their vows.

Police Plaza

Walk through the central arch to Police Plaza. Bounded by the remnants of a former warehouse district on the east, by the Brooklyn Bridge approaches on the south, and by existing municipal buildings and irregular streets in other directions, the site recommended itself to planners only because the city could conveniently purchase its many small land parcels at a reasonable price.

Turn right. On the south side of the plaza is the **Rhinelander Sugar House Prison Window Monument.** During the 18C one of the city's prime industries was distilling rum, for which raw sugar was a principal ingredient; the rum, made of sugar or molasses from the West Indies, was exported to Africa in exchange for slaves, a series of transactions known as the "Triangular Trade." The Rhinelander Sugar Warehouse built (1763) on the corner of Rose (formerly the name of the southern extension of Madison St) and Duane Sts became a prison for American soldiers when the British occupied New York during the Revolutionary War. The sugar house was razed in 1892, but a window was incorporated in the Rhinelander Building (1895), which stood here until it was demolished (1968) for Police Plaza.

In the center of the three-acre brick plaza stands a sculpture of five interlocking oxidized steel disks by Bernard (Tony) Rosenthal (1971–74), entitled *Five in One* and said to symbolize the five city boroughs. Each disk weighs 15,000 pounds, is 20 ft in diameter, and 10 inches thick. Its installation aroused adverse comment, perhaps because it appeared merely rusty at the time. One correspondent to the *New York Times* likened it to the "rusty propeller of a supertanker," but since then its weathering steel has taken on a dark reddish brown color.

Police Headquarters (1973; Gruzen & Partners), dominating the plaza and bounded by Park Row, Pearl, Henry, and New Sts, is a 15-story, $58-million building of brick and reinforced concrete, its ground level containing an auditorium, meeting rooms, and holding and interrogation rooms for prisoners.

Walk back toward Centre St. On the right before you reach the Municipal Building is **St. Andrew's Church** (1939; Maginnis & Walsh, Robert J. Reiley), which bears the coats of arms of Pope Pius XI (central door) and Cardinal Hayes (side doors), who were in office when the church was consecrated. The present building replaces an earlier one known as Carroll Hall, which became the first Church of St. Andrew, ministering to the Catholic immigrants pouring into this neighborhood in the mid-19C. In 1900, when the printing industry dominated the area, the church began offering a Printer's Mass at 2:30 A.M. for newsmen and other late-night workers, making St. Andrew's the first work-centered parish in the city.

Surrogate's Court

Cross Centre St and walk west along Chambers St. At 31 Chambers St (northwest corner of Centre St) is the Surrogate's Court, also known as the **Hall of Records** (1899–1907; John R. Thomas and Horgan & Slattery; DL). Like the Woolworth Building, with which it is roughly contemporary, the Surrogate's Court was built as a monument, and the impulse of civic pride that inspired the design is expressed in the elegance and costliness of both the facade and the interior. Originally it was intended as a repository for municipal records and as a surrogate's court administering trusts and guardianships, but since the building has been used more and more by the court, the name was officially changed from Hall of Records to Surrogate's Court in 1963.

Exterior

The facade is lavishly ornamented with sculpture appropriate to the building's first function as a guardian of historical records. Flanking the Chambers St entrance are two sculptural groups by Philip Martiny: *New York in Revolutionary Times,* represented by a proud female figure wearing a helmet, and (right) *New*

York in Its Infancy, a woman wearing a feathered headdress. The frieze above the portico bears eight figures representing prominent early New Yorkers, including Peter Stuyvesant (third from left) and De Witt Clinton (third from right). The cornice figures facing Reade and Centre Sts represent the arts, professions, and industries.

Interior

The walls of the foyer are faced with yellow-toned Siena marble. Above the doorways at each end of the rooms are sculptural groups by Albert Weinert: *The Consolidation of Greater New York* (east door) and *Recording the Purchase of Manhattan Island* (west door). On the ceiling a mosaic by William de Leftwich Dodge, a Paris-trained muralist, is organized into panels depicting Greek and Egyptian deities. The Greek gods in the corners are Themis (Justice), Erinys (Retribution), Penthos (Sorrow), and Ponos (Labor). On the end walls are mosaics also by Dodge with the unimaginative but descriptive titles *Searching the Records* and *Widows and Orphans Pleading Before the Judge of the Surrogate's Court*. Above the central landing of the grand staircase in the lobby is a stucco relief of the seal of New York City, upon whose shield are the sails of a windmill; between the sails are beavers and flour barrels, both important elements of the early economy. A sailor and Native American support the shield, which rests on a horizontal laurel branch bearing the date 1664, the year the British captured New Amsterdam and named it New York.

The former **Emigrant Industrial Savings Bank Building** (1909–12; Raymond Almirall; DL) at 51 Chambers St (between Broadway and Elk St) is a familiar though unwelcome place for drivers who come here to ante up their parking fines. Founded in 1850 by the trustees of the Irish Emigrant Society to protect the financial resources of Irish immigrants and to teach those without such resources the virtues of thrift and industry, the bank succeeded from the outset, gradually widening its dealings to include people of many nationalities. The large oval stained glass skylights, whose themes represent aspects of economy, are perhaps as appropriate for the injudicious parker as they were for the arriving immigrant.

Sun Building

On the northeast corner of Broadway and Chambers St is the former Sun Building, 280 Broadway, originally the **A. T. Stewart Marble Palace** (1846; Trench & Snook; restored 1999, Beyer Blinder Belle; DL), the nation's first department store. City-owned since 1970, the building has large stores downstairs and the City Buildings Department upstairs. The $37-million restoration was complicated because the African Burial Ground (see African Burial Memorial) extends beneath the building.

History

Alexander Turney Stewart did for merchandising at the upper end of the economic scale what F. W. Woolworth did at the lower end. He brought together many different types of merchandise under a single roof, selling clothing in fixed sizes at fixed prices and freeing shoppers from the psychological demands of bargaining. Furthermore, Stewart shrewdly saw the need to turn shopping into entertainment, and to that end built the Marble Palace, which initially drew shoppers in droves. By 1862, however, fashionable society had begun shopping further uptown, so Stewart moved up Broadway to a new palace, the Cast Iron Palace, between 9th and 10th Sts, retaining the Chambers St store as a warehouse. Stewart also built himself a mansion on Fifth Ave at 34th St, a $3-million extravagance that set the standard for younger generations of millionaires.

From 1917 to 1950, this building was home to the *New York Sun*. The four-faced bronze clock on the Chambers St corner bears the motto, "The Sun, it shines for all."

Exterior

The building is an early example of the Italianate style, which replaced the Greek revival style as the city's dominant architectural fashion. Contemporaries admired the store for its palatial dimensions, beautiful white marble facade, and elegant details (for example, the classical masks in the keystones over the second-story windows). When the building opened, the slender Corinthian columns on the ground floor framed display windows so large that Stewart had to order the plate glass from France.

Look across Broadway to the northwest corner of Broadway and Chambers St and the **Broadway Chambers Building** (1899–1900; Cass Gilbert), 277 Broadway, Gilbert's first New York office building, with the oldest architectural polychrome terra-cotta in New York. At the time of completion, this 18-story tower, with its pink granite base, beige and red brickwork, and green copper cornice, was considered the city's finest skyscraper.

Walk north on Broadway. At **287 Broadway** (1872; John B. Snook; DL) is a handsome cast-iron commercial building erected on speculation. To enhance its market value, the developer added a fancy mansard roof with delicate iron cresting and an Otis passenger elevator.

Museum of the American Piano

291 Broadway, New York, NY 10007. ☎ (212) 406-6060. Web site: www.piano museum.com. Call for hours and wheelchair accessibility. Admission charge. Lecture-recitals; exhibitions.

At 291 Broadway (between Reade and Duane Sts) is the new home of the Museum of the American Piano. The museum, which opened (1984) uptown near Carnegie Hall in founder Kalman Detrich's piano workshop and showroom, documents the craft of American piano making, which flourished in the 19C. On view are representative examples of major American 19C instruments, including pianos by Chickering, Osborne, Steinway, Weber, and Boardman & Gray.

African Burial Memorial

Turn right on Duane St and walk to Elk St to reach the African Burial Memorial. The African Burial Ground Historic District extends down through City Hall Park and east to Centre St.

History

The burial ground, discovered during excavations for the Federal Building (290 Broadway) in 1991, is the one surviving trace of a large African community that existed in New York during the colonial period. Written records have shown that blacks, both free and slaves, buried their dead here as early as 1712 (most likely because they were no longer allowed burial in Trinity churchyard after 1697), and the area was also probably a focal point of community life for blacks in the 17C and 18C. Approximately 400 skeletons were unearthed, about 40 percent of them children; many others lie undisturbed. The remains were reinterred at the site, and a permanent memorial will be constructed here. (The federal government has allocated space for an interpretative center inside the building at 290 Broadway.)

Foley Square

North of Centre Street lies Foley Square, named after Tammany politician Thomas F. Foley (1852–1925), a kingmaker but never an officeholder. Foley helped Al Smith become governor and kept William Randolph Hearst, who had attacked him in his newspapers, from becoming either governor or U.S. senator.

History

Until the beginning of the 19C much of the present square lay beneath the waters of the Collect Pond (from the Dutch *kolch*, a small body of water), also known as the Freshwater Pond. Known for its depth (60 ft) and purity, the spring-fed pond drained west into the Hudson. Much of the land on that side was marshland called the Lispenard Meadows. In the 18C tanners settled here because the water supply was essential to their business, but in 1730 Anthony Rutgers, a landowner, petitioned the city for the swamp and pond, which he then began to drain, much to the distress of the tanners. The city gained title to the pond in 1791. In 1796 John Fitch tested a prototypical steamboat on its waters. Though successful technologically, the boat never achieved the fame of Robert Fulton's *Clermont*, which steamed up the Hudson in 1807. Fitch eventually abandoned his craft in the pond and left town.

Around 1800 the city began filling the pond and draining the Lispenard Meadows. By 1807, cartloads of dirt and garbage were being dumped into the pond; they eventually formed a foul-smelling island some 12–15 ft above the water. In 1809 Canal St was laid out and a sewer built beneath it to drain the springs that formerly fed the pond. By 1811 the pond had disappeared altogether.

The stench, the sinking of land still undermined by springs, and the encroachment of the dry goods trade into nearby streets drove out people who could afford to live elsewhere. By the early 19C the neighborhood was a slum, inhabited by freed slaves, immigrants, and the undifferentiated poor. By 1840 it had become notorious for crime, its worst section called Five Points at the intersection of Park, Baxter, and Worth Sts. Houses were rotten and overcrowded, with people packed into windowless basements or relegated to "back buildings" hastily erected in dark rear yards by eager landlords.

A central feature of Five Points was the Old Brewery, on part of the site of the present New York County Court House, once used for making beer but by the mid-19C the dwelling of some 1,200 people. In 1852 the Ladies' Home Missionary Society bought it and eventually replaced it with the Five Points Mission and House of Industry, a nursery school with about 400 students and boarders. Before demolishing the building, however, the missionary ladies, with remarkable public relations skills, opened the brewery for tours, allowing middle-class visitors to see just how the poor lived.

At 1 Foley Square (southeast corner) is the **United States Courthouse** (1933–36; Cass Gilbert; completed by Cass Gilbert Jr.; DL). Gilbert, who also designed the Supreme Court in Washington, intended this to be a counterpart. It has a gilded top like the Municipal Building and a heroic portico (50 ft Corinthian columns) facing Foley Square like the County Courthouse to its north. The building houses the U.S. District Court and the Federal Court of Appeals.

The square was recently refurbished, with a new sculpture, *Triumph of the Human Spirit* (2000; Lorenzo Pace), installed as its centerpiece. The work honors the slaves in the nearby African Burial Ground.

New York County Courthouse

On the northeast corner of Pearl St at Foley Square is the New York County Courthouse (1913–27; Guy Lowell; DL), home of the New York State Supreme Court.

Exterior

The grand portico in the Roman Corinthian style is three columns deep and about 100 ft wide. The carving in the tympanum above the portico (sculptor, Frederick W. Allen) shows *Justice with Courage and Wisdom*. Atop the pediment are statues representing Law (center) flanked by Truth and Equity. The niches of the porch shelter two female figures (by Philip Martiny) removed from the Surrogate's Court on Chambers St in 1961 when the city widened traffic lanes there. The figure with the shield and city coat of arms (left) is Authority, while her companion Justice (right) rests her foot upon a bundle of records.

Interior

The central saucer dome is supported by Corinthian columns of Tennessee marble. Ceiling frescoes by Attilio Pusterla depict scenes from the history of jurisprudence. The oculus, originally open to the sky, is now shielded by glass against the elements and, presumably, pigeons. On the floor beneath the dome is a colored marble design with bronze figures representing the signs of the zodiac.

Just behind the New York Supreme Court is a new 27-story **United States Courthouse** (1995; Kohn Pedersen Fox Associates), 500 Pearl St, used for naturalization ceremonies, judicial inductions, trials, and certain sessions of the Court of Appeals.

On the north edge of Foley Square stand two Art Deco buildings. The **State of New York Building** (1930; Sullivan W. Jones & William E. Haugaard) on the northeast corner of Worth and Centre Sts has a classic frieze and sculptured cornice. The former Department of Health Building, now the **Health, Hospitals, and Sanitation Departments Building** (1935; Charles B. Meyers), on the northwest corner of the same intersection, bears a molding inscribed with the names of great men of medicine.

Turn left on Worth St and walk west to Lafayette St; turn right. Walk a half-block north to Catherine Lane. Between Catherine Lane and Leonard St on Lafayette is the former **New York Life Insurance Co. Building** (1870; Stephen D. Hatch and McKim, Mead & White; 1984–99; DL), whose main entrance is at 346 Broadway. After decades of disrepair, the four-faced clock—the city's largest weight-driven clock—now ticks off the hours, revived in 1980 by two city workers, Martin Schneider and Eric Reiner. The city got New York Life Insurance to donate an insurance policy, and Schneider and Reiner devoted their lunch hours to the task on a volunteer basis. Schneider has since restored other city clocks, including seven at City Hall, and in 1992 he was officially named New York City Clock Master, caring for and winding 13 clocks a week, with Reiner serving as backup.

Clocktower Gallery

108 Leonard St (at Broadway), 13th floor, New York, NY 10013. ☎ (212) 233-1096. Open Wed–Sat noon–6. Closed mid-June–Aug and major holidays. Requested donation. Changing exhibitions, studio program. No restaurant. No wheelchair access.

Subway: Eighth Ave Express or Local (A, C, E) to Canal St. Broadway–Seventh Ave Local (1, 9) to Franklin St. Bus: M1, M6.

The building's first 12 floors are used for municipal offices while the 13th floor houses the Clocktower Gallery: Institute for Contemporary Art, formerly the Institute for Art and Urban Resources.

Founded in 1971, the institute devoted itself to salvaging abandoned buildings (or parts thereof) and using them as studio and exhibition space for new and experimental artists. The Clocktower is one such rehabilitated space; P.S. 1 Contemporary Art Center in Long Island City is another. The Clocktower mounts four or five shows annually, focusing on contemporary painting, sculpture, installations, and other media by artists from the United States and abroad.

Continue north on Lafayette St, named for the Marquis de Lafayette, who aided the colonies in the Revolutionary War. At 60 Lafayette St (between Leonard and Franklin Sts) is the **Family Court of New York City** (1975; Haines Lundberg Waehler), shaped like a cube partially sheered off on one surface. A statue (1972–76) entitled *Three Forms* by Roy Gussow stands before the entrance.

New York City Criminal Courts Building

Across the street and parking lot looms the bulk of the New York City Criminal Courts Building (1939; Harvey Wiley Corbett; redesigned 1986, The Gruzen Partnership) at 100 Centre St (between Leonard and White Sts), formerly the Manhattan Detention Center for Men and better known as "the Tombs."

History

The name originated with an earlier prison on the site, built in a gloomy hollow so deep that the massive prison walls hardly rose above the level of Broadway some hundred yards to the west. Officially known as "The Halls of Justice," it was built (1836–38) in the Egyptian revival style, with trapezoidal windows, lotus columns, and emblems of the sun god. This prison was called the Tombs partly because of the funereal associations of the architectural style and partly because of its dismal function and appearance. The building served as the city jail until 1893, when a second prison, Romanesque revival in style but still called the Tombs, replaced it.

Exterior

The present building is the third penal institution on the site. Built in the Art Moderne or Art Deco style of the 1930s, with ziggurat-shaped towers and cast-aluminum detail, it is laid out in four main blocks. The northernmost block contains the prison cells, while the others have offices and courtrooms.

In the foreground is the **Municipal and Civil Court Building** (1960; William Lescaze & Matthew Del Gaudio), 111 Centre St (southwest corner of White St), a plain white marble cube with a vertical stripe of windows down the south facade. On the east side are granite reliefs (c. 1959) representing Law by William Zorach; on the west facade is Joseph Kiselewski's relief (1960) depicting Justice flanked by an infant and a serpent.

Walk north on Lafayette St to the former site of **Engine Company Number 31** (1895; Napoleon Le Brun; DL) at 87 Lafayette St (northeast corner of White St). Built like a French Renaissance château with a steep slate roof and a corner turret, this firehouse was in its day a showcase of technology, with automatic stall latches that released the horses at the sound of the alarm. Today it houses the **Downtown Community Television Center.**

6 · Chinatown, Little Italy, and NoLIta

Subway: Lexington Ave Local (6) to Canal St. Nassau St Express or Local (J, M, Z). Walk four blocks east on Canal St and two blocks south on Mott St to Chatham Square. Broadway Local (N, R) to Canal St. Walk five blocks east to Mott St and two blocks south to Chatham Square.
Bus: M1, M6 to Worth St; walk east to Chatham Square (five blocks, counting on the north side). M15, M103 to Chatham Square

Chinatown
Chinatown, originally a tiny area bounded by Pell and Doyer Sts, has expanded uptown through Little Italy to the fringes of SoHo, into the Lower East Side, and downtown as far as Worth St.

History
Chinese sailors and merchants began arriving in New York in 1784 but generally did not remain. A handful of immigrants settled here in the early 19C, but in 1859 there were only about 150 Chinese men living in Lower Manhattan. However, in the second half of the 19C, political battles, floods, starvation, and limited economic opportunity in China, along with its soaring population, prompted massive emigration. Most Chinese originally landed in San Francisco, but many, driven away by violence and racial hostilities, began coming to New York. They settled in what is now Chinatown, known then as the Plow and Harrow District after a tavern of that name founded in the 17C.

Congress banned new Chinese arrivals with the Exclusion Acts of 1882, but New York's Chinese population tripled within a decade as "paper" families proliferated—men sold illegal papers to get entry for their "son," a "shareholder" in a fake Chinatown business.

The Chinese, most of whom came from the area around Canton, were restricted by language barriers, racism, and lack of skills to menial jobs, laboring as cigar makers, sign carriers, laundry and restaurant workers. (Most restaurants were

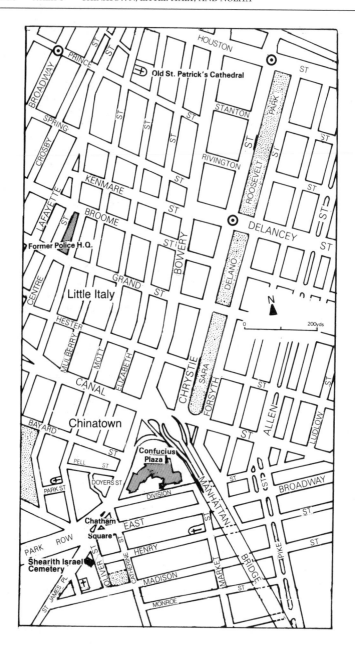

Cantonese in style, until after World War II when refugees from all over China emigrated to America and Szechuan and Hunan cooking became popular.)

Family or clan associations, or tongs, were originally formed of people with the same surname. The tongs were especially important during the early days, when male immigrants without families found themselves isolated and unfamiliar with English and local customs. Later they became social agencies for families as well, acting as employment brokerages and organizing social functions, while enabling businessmen to band together to enhance their commercial strength.

Some tongs, like Mafia families, became involved in vice. Through the 1920s tong wars, fought mainly by hired assassins wielding either guns or cleavers (hence the term *hatchetman*), were luridly exploited by the American press, and for years Chinatown bore the image of a place of sinister crimes and exotic sins.

Meanwhile, in 1883, the local Cantonese formed the Chinese Consolidation Benevolent Association (CCBA), eventually bringing together 60 regional, business, and family associations. It was long the area's most important umbrella organization and representative to the city's politicians.

In 1960 there were fewer than 20,000 Chinese (still mostly male) in New York, but in 1965 the restrictive immigration quotas were lifted. Today that number has increased tenfold. In recent years, however, Chinese immigration patterns have changed dramatically. For starters, only a third of the new Chinese (including people from the mainland, Taiwan, Hong Kong, or ethnic Chinese from Vietnam) have been settling in Manhattan's Chinatown. Most others moved to blossoming Chinatowns in Flushing, Queens, and Sunset Park in Brooklyn. The Taiwanese, more likely to be middle class and educated, have mostly settled in Queens, while Manhattan's Chinatown has increasingly attracted mainland immigrants, particularly the poor and uneducated from the rural province of Fujian. Many of the Fujianese arrived illegally and most live in extreme poverty—beyond typical immigration challenges, many bear debts from being smuggled in and they face prejudice from the Cantonese oldtimers, who are less supportive of mainland China. Fujianese gangs further exacerbated tensions, and many older Cantonese began moving to Queens and the suburbs. Unlike the insular CCBA, which has lost influence in recent decades, new Fujianese groups like the United Chinese Associations of New York worked hard on public image, became involved in New York politics, and cooperated with police in battling crime. Mandarin, which the Fujianese speak, has replaced Cantonese at many public events, and even Cantonese officials are learning the language.

No matter what group dominates, for the hundreds of thousands of Chinese living legally and illegally in ever-expanding Chinatown, the neighborhood remains plagued by poverty, overcrowding, and physical deterioration. Although most housing and business space is substandard, rents are rising, propelled by the population explosion. Meanwhile, there has been a resurgence in sweatshops both here and in Sunset Park, forcing thousands of immigrants to work long hours for low pay in unsafe conditions. Union experts say the problem is so deeply entrenched that change will have to come from crackdowns on retailers and manufacturers. Restaurant workers in the area also have a difficult time organizing and challenging the traditional power structure, largely because of high turnover and other immigrants willing to take their jobs.

Chatham Square

Begin at Chatham Square, the intersection of Park Row, St. James Place, Oliver St, East Broadway, Catherine St, Division St, the Bowery, Doyers St, Mott St, and Worth St. Before Chinatown overflowed its traditional boundaries, Chatham Square marked the border between Chinatown to the west and the Lower East Side to the east. The city is upgrading this congested, poorly designed intersection.

On one of the traffic islands is the **Kimlau War Memorial** (1962; Poy G. Lee), an arch with a pagoda-style top, dedicated to Chinese Americans who died in the U.S. armed services. On another traffic island east of the arch is a branch of the **Republic Savings Bank** (1977; George W. Clark Assocs.), brightly painted and topped with a traditional Chinese curved roof, one of the first buildings in Chinatown that was architecturally "Chinese."

On the east side of Chatham Square is a neighborhood once considered part of the Lower East Side, now part of an expanded Chinatown. During the early 19C it was prosperous, the home of successful merchants and ships' captains, a few of whose homes and churches still remain.

Cross the square and walk south along St. James Place. Between Oliver and James Sts is the small, forlorn **First Shearith Israel Graveyard** (1682–1831; DL), the earliest surviving burial ground of the city's first Jewish congregation. An earlier cemetery, then outside the city, was consecrated c. 1656 on land granted by Peter Stuyvesant, but its location is unknown. The earliest stone in the present graveyard dates from 1683. During the Revolutionary War, Gen. Charles Lee placed several guns in "the Jew Burying Ground" as part of the city's fortifications; 18 Revolutionary soldiers and patriots are buried here, among them Gershom Mendes Seixas, who removed the Torah scrolls to Stratford, Connecticut, during the British occupation. As the congregation moved uptown following the general development of the city, it established two other cemeteries, one at W. 11th St and another at W. 21st St.

At the south corner of James St is the Hall of St. James School, with a plaque on the doors announcing that Alfred E. Smith, who became one of New York's most beloved politicians, received his entire formal education here. At 32 James St, between St. James Place and Madison St, is the **St. James Roman Catholic Church** (1835–37; DL), a severe brownstone Greek revival building, its facade ornamented only by rosettes on the door lintels and a carved scroll and anthemion above the central doorway. Originally the church served Irish immigrants—Smith was baptized here and a street sign honors the block as the founding site of the Ancient Order of the Hibernians. Today the congregation is largely Spanish speaking.

Continue along St. James St. to Madison St. Turn left and left again on Oliver St. At **25 Oliver St** is the shabby walk-up where Al Smith spent his childhood. Smith rose from these lowly beginnings to become a social reformer, four-time governor of the state, and Democratic candidate for President in 1928.

Continue to 12 Oliver St (northwest corner of Henry St). The **Mariners' Temple** (1844–45; attrib. Isaac Lucas; DL), originally built as the Oliver Street Baptist Church, was bought by the Mariners' Temple in 1863, serving as a social mission for seamen, immigrants, and later for Bowery derelicts. Today its congregation is largely Chinese. The building, roughly contemporary with the St. James Church, is constructed of stone laid in random courses, plastered over (where visible to the street), and grooved with false joints to give it the smooth appearance characteristic of the Greek revival style.

Walk north along Henry St to 48 Henry St, the **Chinatown Mission** (1830), originally built as a subsidiary chapel of Trinity Church and later the Church of Our Savior. Now part of the social ministry of the Episcopal Church, the mission is housed in three Federal houses, of which the central one is the best preserved.

Continue north to the **First Chinese Presbyterian Church** (1817–19; DL), 61 Henry St, originally the Northern Reformed Church. Constructed of local materials, the church has brownstone quoins and trim, rubble masonry, steep gabled ends, and a square tower. The tall side windows with pointed arches are unusual in a church predating the Gothic revival period by about two decades. As the Sea and Land Church, after 1866, it served seamen.

Turn left on Market St just before the bridge and walk past the jam-packed commercial strip on East Broadway to **Division St,** so named because it marked the division between the farms of James De Lancey and Henry Rutgers in pre-Revolutionary New York.

Turn left on Division St. On the north side of the street is **Confucius Plaza** (1976; Horowitz & Chun), the only new housing built in Chinatown between the 1960s and early 1980s. The project includes an elementary school and 764 apartments, 20 percent of which are reserved as low-income housing.

Facing Chatham Square at Division St and the Bowery is Taiwanese sculptor Liu Shih's bronze **statue of Confucius,** standing on a base of green marble mined in Taiwan. It aroused a flurry of controversy when the Chinese Consolidated Benevolent Association presented it (1976) to the city as a gift from the Taiwanese government because it was a symbol of opposition to China's Cultural Revolution. At the time the People's Republic of China had denounced Confucius's teachings, and Chinatown residents who followed the party line found the traditional authoritarian philosopher an unsuitable representative of China's cultural heritage. In 1997, Fujianese residents put up their own statue, which honors **Lin Ze Xu** (1785–1850), a Fujianese official who in 1839 retaliated against British imperialists by confiscating and destroying 2.6 million pounds of opium, igniting the Opium War. Lin Ze Xu was selected because many Fujianese were concerned that they were being stereotyped, like Sicilians or Colombians, as gangsters and drug dealers. The statue's base, made of red granite from Xiamen in Fujian, is inscribed with the words "Say No to Drugs" in both English and Chinese. The figure, which is also intended to proclaim the ascendancy of Fujianese immigrants, faces East Broadway, nicknamed Fouzhou Street because so many Fujianese live here.

Continue past the plaza and across the Bowery. Head north to 18 Bowery, at the southwest corner of Pell St. The **Edward Mooney House** (c. 1785; DL) is the city's oldest row house. Mooney, a meat wholesaler and amateur racehorse breeder, built the house on land forfeited after the Revolution by the Tory James De Lancey. The house is Georgian in its proportions and in its details: the door hood, the lintels with splayed keystones, the quarter-round and round-headed windows facing Pell St. The generous number of windows reveals Mooney's wealth, since glass, manufactured in the middle colonies only after about 1740, was an expensive commodity. By 1840, however, the neighborhood had deteriorated and the house had become a brothel.

Turn onto Pell St. At 10 Pell St is the Chin Family Association and at 13 Pell St the headquarters of the Hip Sing Association, two influential family groups—the latter once a leading organized crime family.

Turn left into Doyers St, a crooked, narrow street that was originally a cart lane leading to Anthony Doyer's distillery at the south end. The bend in Doyers St was once known as "Bloody Angle," recalling a turn-of-the-20C tong war, during which the two most powerful families, the Hip Sings and On Leongs, battled ruthlessly.

On the site of the present post office at 6 Doyers St once stood the Chatham Club, where Irving Berlin—born Israel Baline—waited tables. Across the street at 5–7 Doyers St is the site of the original Chinese Opera House, which stood here until 1910, when it was acquired for a mission run by Tom Noonan, an ex-convict who dispensed charity to Bowery bums until his death in 1935. Follow Doyers St to the Bowery.

On the southwest corner of the intersection is a small Federal house remaining from 1809, when Anthony Doyer built it as one of four. Today it is recognizable only by the spacing of the windows and its diminutive size.

Mott Street

Turn right and walk to **Mott St,** Chinatown's main street, named after Joseph Mott, a prosperous pre-Revolutionary butcher, who also ran a tavern at what is now W. 143rd St and Eighth Ave. The tavern served as Washington's headquarters before he moved into the Morris-Jumel Mansion (see Walk 29).

Turn right onto Mott St. In 1896, Sun Yat-sen, the future founder of the Chinese Republic, hid out on the third floor of 7 Mott St, organizing a local branch of his secret Revolutionary party and recruiting people to support his plan to overthrow the Qing Dynasty.

The **Chinese Consolidated Benevolent Association,** an umbrella organization of Chinese family and regional associations, was formed at 16 Mott St in 1883. The association provided translation services and employment referrals and even raised money to ship bodies back to China for burial. The CCBA could not only mediate disputes between local groups but also tax businesses and regulate commerce for the greater good, resembling today's popular Business Improvement Districts. In the late 19C–early 20C, this building had a house of worship on the first floor and a gambling hall in the basement. In 1933, the **Chinese Hand Laundry Alliance** was formed here to combat a proposed city ordinance designed to drive Chinese laundries out of business. Less influential than formerly, it is now based on Canal St.

Continue along Mott St. Just beyond Mosco St is the **Church of the Transfiguration** (1801; DL), 25 Mott St, built as the Zion Episcopal Church. This modest rubblestone building has a triangular pediment, simple tower, and unusual pointed arch windows. The copper-clad spire was added in 1868.

Just to the north is **Quong Yuen Shing,** 41 Mott St, the neighborhood's oldest grocery, started by the Lee Family Association, the largest and most influential of the family groups. The first grocery in Chinatown was reportedly Wo Kee, established in 1872 at 34 Mott Street.

Return to Mosco St and walk west to Mulberry St. Columbus Park (opened 1897), facing Mulberry St between Bayard and Worth Sts, represents a triumph for early social reformers who spurred passage of the Small Parks Act in 1887.

This park, formerly known as Mulberry Bend Park, replaced Mulberry Bend, a violent slum that reformer Jacob Riis called "the worst pigsty of all."

The Museum of Chinese in the Americas

70 Mulberry St, New York, NY 10013. ☎ (212) 619-4785. Open Tues–Sat 12–5 P.M. Closed major holidays. Admission charge. Not accessible to wheelchairs.

Turn right and head north along Mulberry St. At 70 Mulberry, on the northeast corner of Bayard St, is the Museum of Chinese in the Americas, on the second floor of the former P.S. 23. The building also houses other arts groups, including H. T. Chen & Dancers (founded in 1979) and the Mulberry Street Theatre.

The museum, formerly the Chinatown History Museum (opened 1980), uses photos, documents, and artifacts to explore the history of Chinatown's laundry workers, cooks, cigar makers, merchants, and garment workers. Changing exhibits explore such themes as Chinatowns across the U.S. and Chinese immigration to Latin America.

Turn right and walk east along Bayard St to the **Chinatown Ice Cream Factory,** 65 Bayard St, whose homemade ice cream comes in flavors running from prosaic vanilla to exotic lichee, red bean, green tea, and ginger.

Return to Mott St and continue north. The telephone booths with pagoda tops were inspired by similar ones in San Francisco. Some of Chinatown's larger vegetable and fish stores line Mott St, which still remains the East Coast supply center of Chinese foodstuffs.

At 62 Mott St is the present headquarters of the Chinese Consolidated Benevolent Association and the Chinese School (opened 1915), which works to preserve Chinese language and culture. At 83–85 Mott St (southwest corner of Canal St), is an architectural melange of East and West, housing the **Chinese Merchants' Association,** which evolved from the On Leong tong.

Canal St, once the northern border of Chinatown, takes the pedestrian and auto traffic chaos of the rest of Chinatown and multiplies it exponentially. In addition to the apparel factories and sweatshops, the street has become the Chinese equivalent of W. 47th St in the Diamond District and is lined with jewelry stores, where non-Chinese come to haggle and buy.

Walk two blocks east along Canal St to the southwest corner of the Bowery and the monumentally domed **Republic Savings Bank** (1924; Clarence Brazer) at 58 Bowery. Here stood the Black Horse Inn and Bull's Head Tavern, from which, on Nov 25, 1783, George Washington began his triumphant march into the city to mark the Revolution's end.

Manhattan Bridge

Across the street is the Manhattan Bridge, the third East River crossing, notable for its ceremonial approach, arch, and colonnade (1912; Carrère & Hastings; Gustav Lindenthal, bridge engineer).

History

Feelings ran high over the design of the Manhattan Bridge, for though the Brooklyn Bridge, which opened in 1883, had evoked enthusiasm both as a feat of engineering and as an object of beauty, the Williamsburg Bridge, which followed in 1903, was considered ugly. The disputing parties were engineers, whose interests were primarily technological, and architects, whose goals were aesthetic. Because of these opposing interests and the political factions expressing them, plans for the Manhattan Bridge went through numerous modifications as architects and bridge commissioners came and went.

An early plan was scrapped in about 1901 and the bridge was redesigned by Henry Hornbostel, an architect whose belief in "artistic" engineering resulted in a proposal that included the use of eye-bars instead of the usual cables to support the roadway. City officials, however, preferred the older suspension cable system, and Carrère & Hastings (designers of the New York Public Library and the Frick Museum) were hired to replace Hornbostel. The bridge, with its 1,470 ft span, opened in 1909.

Meanwhile, the World's Columbian Exposition in Chicago (1893) had awakened public interest in neoclassic architecture, prompting the birth of the City Beautiful movement. From these enthusiasms sprang plans for improving the approaches to the bridge. Carrère & Hastings, who had studied at the École des Beaux-Arts in Paris, the cradle of the neoclassical movement, were well qualified for such an undertaking.

The Manhattan approach originally featured an elliptical landscaped plaza, which surrounded the actual roadway. Eight rail lines carried subways and surface railroads while the paved roadways accommodated both vehicular and foot traffic. Nowadays the subways are carried on the lower deck of the bridge, and a small parking area has replaced the landscaping.

The approach ends in a monumental arch and colonnade, the arch modeled after the 17C Porte St. Denis in Paris, the colonnade after Bernini's colonnade at St. Peter's Square in Rome. The frieze over the arch opening by Charles Cary Rumsey (1879–1922) is said to have been inspired by the Panathenaic procession on the Parthenon frieze, suitably Americanized. It depicts a group of four Native Americans on horseback hunting buffalo. The choice of this subject matter may seem peculiar on a classical arch signaling the approach to a modern steel suspension bridge linking two boroughs of a large city, but such frontier themes were then extremely popular.

Flanking the arch opening are two large granite sculptural groups by Carl Augustus Heber: the *Spirit of Commerce* on the north side and the *Spirit of Industries* on the south. Above the arch opening (36 × 40 ft) is a cornice and a low attic story decorated with lions' heads. The interior of the arch is barrel vaulted and coffered. The arch is set in the middle of a colonnade of Tuscan columns (31 ft high), above which are cornices with balustrades that connect the columns to one another and to the arch.

Return west along Canal St to its intersection with Centre St and the headquarters of the former Golden Pacific National Bank (1983; George Rycar), now the **Hongkong and Shanghai Bank.** This is one of Chinatown's newer architectural attractions, vividly decorated in blue, red, gold, and green, and styled with sweeping tile roofs and galleries. The Golden Pacific National Bank, once the pride of Chinatown, collapsed in 1985, causing economic hardship among the families who had deposited their savings in uninsured certificates.

Little Italy

Return to Mulberry St and turn left into the spine of Little Italy, an ethnic enclave dating from the 1880s, whose population dramatically increased between 1890 and 1924 before restrictive laws stanched immigration. As you turn the corner, the change in ambience—from the bustle of Chinatown to the quiet of Little Italy—is palpable. The neighborhood is barely surviving: while tens of thousands of Chinese arrived in the 1990s, fewer than 100 Italians settled in Little Italy. What was a 24-square-block neighborhood only 30 years ago is now a two-block strip: Mulberry St from Canal to Grand St, and Grand St from Mulberry to Mott St. (There are some Italian stores and restaurants scattered further north on Mulberry and on side streets.)

There have been tensions between the Chinese and the Italians in the past, but nowadays the fate of the neighborhood is accepted as inevitable. The northeast section of Little Italy has become a gentrified extension of SoHo, filled with trendy bars, restaurants, and stores. Few Italians live here anymore, and even the merchants commute from Brooklyn, Queens, or the suburbs. Consequently Little Italy can feel like a made-for-tourism theme park, though the food and products in the stores are authentic.

Many Italians, mingling with tourists, return to the neighborhood for two annual festivals: the Feast of St. Anthony of Padua, held evenings during the first two weeks of June and centered on Sullivan St, and the Feast of San Gennaro, held around the week of Sept 19 and occupying several blocks of Mulberry St. Images of the saints are carried through the streets, and at night arcades of lights turn the neighborhood into a carnival. (Another, more intimate festival is the Ferragosto di Belmont in the Bronx; see Belmont in Walk 32.)

Walk north on Mulberry St, where there are many Italian restaurants, some with the maître d' outside trying to coax passersby inside. Paolucci's (149 Mulberry St near Grand St) occupies the original **Stephen van Rensselaer House** (1816; DL), which dates from the Federal period and still retains its original dormers.

Authentic Italian

Old-style Italian shops near the corner of Grand and Mulberry Sts include **Alleva Dairy,** 88 Mulberry St, founded in 1892; the **Italian Food Center,** 186 Grand St, a relative newcomer dating back only to 1969; **Piemonte Home Made Ravioli,** 190 Grand St, founded 1920; **Ferrara** pastry shop, 195–201 Grand St, founded 1892; and **DiPalo Fine Foods,** 206 Grand St, founded 1925.

Turn left at Grand St to the former **Odd Fellows Hall** (1847–48; Trench & Snook; DL), one of the city's earliest Italianate buildings, 165 Grand St (southeast corner of Centre St). This immense brownstone pile was built as the home of a fraternal and mutual aid society. The two top stories were added in 1881–82.

Look west to the southwest corner of Centre and Grand Sts, where one of the city's few antique bishop's crook lamp posts remains (see 515 Broadway in Walk 8).

Former Police Headquarters Building

At 240 Centre St is the former Police Headquarters (1905–9; Hoppin & Koen; DL), set apart from the surrounding tenements and loft buildings by its grand scale and baroque flamboyance. Its grandeur was intended to enhance the image of the relatively new and rapidly expanding police force. The main entrance on Centre St is flanked by lions and embellished by a large New York coat of arms and five statues representing the five boroughs. The police moved out in 1973, and in 1987 the building was converted into luxury condominiums. The still-majestic lobby features two sets of marble columns, a double stairwell, and gorgeous chandeliers. Celebrity residents have included tennis star Steffi Graf and models Christy Turlington, Cindy Crawford, and Linda Evangelista. Residents have opposed a city plan to build a senior center for Chinese immigrants in the basement (the city took over the lower level after the developer defaulted on property taxes).

Bowery Savings Bank

Return to Grand St and walk east to the Bowery. The Bowery Savings Bank (1894; McKim, Mead & White; DL), 130 Bowery, embodies the classical revival that swept the country after the World's Columbian Exposition in 1893 and set the fashion for many banks that followed it. Because it fronts on both Grand St and the Bowery, Stanford White designed two grand limestone entrances, each with a Roman Corinthian portico, and hired Frederick W. MacMonnies to sculpt a pediment for each. The main banking room—with its coffered ceiling, ornate metal and glass skylight, yellow Siena marble teller's counter, and massive columns painted to resemble marble—must have dazzled the humble depositors of this poor neighborhood.

NoLIta

Walk one block west to Elizabeth St, then north into a neighborhood now known as NoLIta (North of Little Italy). It was once a hub of iron and steel manufacturing and part of Little Italy, with Sicilians living on Elizabeth St, Neapolitans on Mulberry St, and immigrants from Abruzzi on Mott St, but its Italian flavor faded in the 1970s as the population aged or moved away. Today these long-overlooked streets are increasingly lined with galleries and small chic shops selling home furnishings, vintage clothing, and crafts. The once-empty lot at 207 Elizabeth St is now the **Elizabeth Street Company,** an outdoor sculpture garden and gallery filled with statuary and fountains.

Turn left at Prince St and walk west one block to Mott St. On the southwest corner is the former **Roman Catholic Orphan Asylum** (1825–26; DL), 32 Prince St, an unusually large Federal-style building with brownstone trim, its handsome doorway framed with slender Corinthian columns and topped with a fanlight (now filled with stained glass). It is currently St. Patrick's Convent and Girls' School.

On Mott St between Prince and Houston Sts is **Old St. Patrick's Cathedral** (1809–15; Joseph François Mangin; DL), 233 Mott St, started in 1809 and finished six years later (the War of 1812 intervened). Until the present St. Patrick's Cathedral on Fifth Ave was completed in 1879, this was the cathedral church of the see of New York. It is also America's second Gothic revival church (the first was the Chapel of St. Mary's Seminary in Baltimore, which dates from 1807). It was altered after a fire in 1866 and its present appearance only hints at its former self. In the rear of St. Patrick's is a churchyard (usually locked) that includes the grave of Pierre Toussaint (1766–1853), born a slave in Haiti and revered for his ministrations to the poor and plague stricken.

Continue to 256–258 Mott St, the former **Fourteenth Ward Industrial School of the Children's Aid Society** (1888–89; Vaux & Radford; DL), later the Astor Memorial School, a Gothic revival reminder of Little Italy's past as an immigrant slum, now converted to cooperative apartments. Industrial schools were established by charitable organizations to fill the gap between the tenement and the public school, taking in street children and teaching them the rudiments of citizenship as well as reading and writing.

Puck Building

Continue north to Houston St and walk west. At 295–309 Lafayette St (filling the block between Mulberry, Houston, Lafayette, and Jersey Sts) is the imposing brick Romanesque revival Puck Building (1885–86; addition 1892–93; Albert Wagner, Herman Wagner; DL), which long served the printing industry, first as the home of the humor magazine *Puck*. In 1983 it reopened as a condominium with offices, studios, galleries, and showrooms for graphic designers, filmmakers, photographers, and architects, as well as rental space for art shows and other events. At the corner of Houston St and above the main entrance on Lafayette St are figures of Puck, top-hatted and cherubic, by Caspar Buberl, an immigrant from Bohemia.

Pratt Manhattan Gallery

295 Lafayette St, New York, NY 10012. ☎ (212) 925-8481. Web site: www.pratt.edu. Open Mon–Thurs 10 A.M.–9 P.M.; Fri–Sun 10–4. Free. Accessible to wheelchairs: ask on ground-floor level to have elevator opened.

Subway: Lexington Ave Local (6) to Bleecker St. Sixth Ave Express or Local (B, D, Q, F) to Broadway–Lafayette St. Bus: M1, M6, M103.

The second floor of the Puck Building contains the Manhattan gallery space of Brooklyn's Pratt Institute. Shows feature the work of students, faculty, and alumni.

7 · Lower East Side

Subway: Sixth Ave Local (F) to East Broadway.
Bus: M9, M15.
When to visit: Sun is a good day to visit the Lower East Side, since shops and markets are open and lively. Many are closed on Sat, the Jewish Sabbath. If you are interested in serious shopping, however, go during the week, when the crowds are thinner.

The Lower East Side has always defied tidy summary. Historically, it was a sprawling neighborhood encompassing areas that today have distinct identities—the East Village, Alphabet City, Chinatown, and Little Italy. Today, however, the name

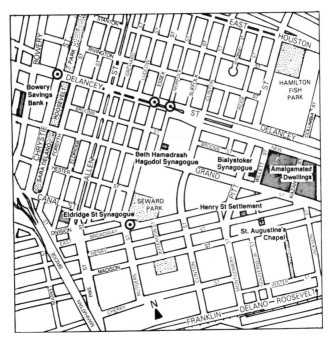

usually apples to the area south of Houston St and east of the Bowery. Chinatown is encroaching from the south and young East Villagers are moving into the northern part.

The Lower East Side has long been a poor neighborhood, the home of immigrants struggling for a foothold in the new world. It is short on famous landmarks, fine buildings, museums, and luxury shops (although it is a good place for bargain hunters). In many places you must use your historical imagination to look through layers of peeling paint and beyond shattered windows to see the once-proud synagogue, or visualize from tenements what life was like within their walls for the immigrants who lived and labored there.

History

In the 18C much of what is now the Lower East Side belonged to the city's great landowning families, the Rutgers and the De Lanceys, early settlers of French Huguenot origin. The De Lanceys, Tory sympathizers during the Revolution, owned much of the land north of Division St until after the war, when it was confiscated and sold off. Merchants and lawyers bought these block-size parcels and began developing this once-rural area after about 1800.

Soon the area became the city's manufacturing center, with shipyards and slaughterhouses lining the waterfront. Since transportation was limited, most people, especially the working poor, lived near where they worked, many of them in Five Points (where Foley Square is today). In 1833, the first tenement was erected on Water St near Corlear's Hook.

While the Irish settled all through the city, German immigrants—some Jews and Protestants, but mostly Bavarian Catholics—stuck together in an enclave north of Division St, which became known as *Kleindeutschland* (Little Germany). By 1871, Kleindeutschland's population made it the fifth-largest German "city" in the world. Many of these immigrants were skilled workers and craftsmen who pursued their trades, forming trade unions and workingmen's associations. They became assimilated with relative ease and took their places in society as merchants, jewelers, clothing manufacturers, furriers, bankers, and professionals.

In 1881, however, revolutionary terrorists assassinated Czar Alexander II of Russia, and in the pogroms and repressive political climate that followed, a wave of Russian and east European Jewish immigration began that entirely changed the Lower East Side and still affects the ethnic makeup of New York. (Italians and other immigrant groups also arrived, but the Jewish population was largest and had the greatest impact.) Of the almost 2 million Jews who came to the U.S. between 1881 and 1914, many settled at least temporarily on the Lower East Side, 60,000 between 1880 and 1890. Between 1918 (the end of World War I) and 1924 (when immigration quotas were imposed), another large group arrived.

Hungarian Jews settled above Houston St (in today's East Village) but the Jewish Quarter, the heart of the Lower East Side, ran from Rivington to Division Sts and from the Bowery to Norfolk Sts; it was filled with Jews from Russia, Poland, Romania, and even Turkey. At the century's end it was the most densely populated place on earth.

The life in store for most immigrants was not the American Dream. They had to accept the constant crowding and lack of privacy of tenement life, the pitiful wages their jobs offered, the loss of identity, the inability to communicate in English, and the family struggles as children assimilated and rejected the traditions of their parents. Many immigrants fell prey to physical and mental illness, especially tuberculosis (the worst tenement areas were called "lung blocks" and claimed mortality rates twice as high as the rest of the city) and depression; suicide was not uncommon.

Most of the Jewish immigrants found work peddling or in the needle trades, whose skills could be learned quickly. They toiled 12–14 hours a day for little money and under miserable conditions—lighting, ventilation, and toilet facilities were pitifully inadequate. Women and children contributed by sewing, making paper flowers, and shelling nuts at home.

Immigrant suffering awoke the compassion of reformers, some of them coreligionists like Lillian Wald, others nonsectarian humanitarians like Jacob Riis. American social work began on the Lower East Side and some social agencies founded then—the Henry Street Settlement and the Educational Alliance—remain active today.

Following a long cultural tradition, the Jews also helped each other. Various ethnic or local groups formed *landsmanshaftn* to offer financial and social support. They formed labor unions in the various trades and a central organization called the United Hebrew Trades (1888). Often risking personal injury, immigrant workers went out on strike, facing down threats from thugs hired to intimidate them. Women at home "organized" in other ways: the members of the Ladies Anti-Beef Trust, for example, instituted a meat boycott and poured kerosene over extortionately priced kosher beef.

Another bright spot in the general grayness of the slums was the intellectual life that the immigrants, despite the rigors of their working hours, carried on with undiminished passion. Lower East Side cafés became informal institutions where socialism, industrialism, Zionism, literature, and drama were discussed.

The Lower East Side was also a hotbed of political activity, with clubs and organizations (mostly left-wing) meeting in the cafés and meeting halls. Some organizations put out their own propaganda; the most successful of these left-wing publications was the *Jewish Daily Forward,* but there was also the Yiddish Communist daily, *Freiheit,* and Emma Goldman's anarchist *Mother Earth.* Lower East Side socialists even had victories at the polls, electing Meyer London (1871–1922) to Congress in 1914, 1916, and 1920 and putting three Socialist assemblymen in office in 1918. Morris Hillquit (1869–1933), a leader of the American Socialist Party, ran for mayor of New York in 1917 and got five times the number of votes garnered by the previous Socialist candidate.

The high-water mark of immigration came in the early years of the 20C, but while new arrivals were pressing at the barricades of Ellis Island, established residents were beginning to move on. Thanks to new bridges and subways they moved to Harlem and the Bronx and out to Brooklyn. The immigration laws of 1924 virtually stopped all new arrivals from eastern Europe and as the existing population drained away through the newly opened portals, the area became less crowded and also less vital. The 1930s saw tenements razed and huge housing projects constructed in an effort to improve the quality of life. At Catherine, Market, Monroe, and Cherry Sts, for example, is Knickerbocker Village (1934; Van Wart & Ackerman), where an apartment rented for $12.50 per room per month, a price out of reach for the former slumdwellers who then had to move on.

After immigration laws were eased in 1965, the neighborhood began attracting a new wave of immigrants, mostly Asian and Latino. Unfortunately the problems facing the new immigrants—poverty, poor housing, cultural alienation, and discrimination—are essentially those encountered by the Jews, Italians, and Irish before them.

The immigrants' plight will probably be aggravated as the Lower East Side's northwest section—closest to the East Village and SoHo—becomes gentrified. Since the mid-1990s, young people have spilled over from the East Village and SoHo. Theaters, bars, and rock clubs opened, to be replaced by trendy clothing boutiques and chic houseware shops, especially along Ludlow and Orchard Sts, as gentrification continues.

Off-Off-Broadway on the Fringe

Each summer, during the last two weeks of Aug, the **New York International Fringe Festival** occupies theaters and other neighborhood sites, attracting tens of thousands of visitors. For information, ☎ (212) 420-8877; Web site: www.fringenyc.org.

Begin at Grand and Kazan Sts (sometimes called Columbia St), site of the **Amalgamated Dwellings** (1930; Springsteen & Goldhammer), built as cooperative apartments and sponsored by the Amalgamated Clothing Workers of America. Though commended architecturally for their "complete elimination of meaningless ornament," the apartments, with an average rent of $12.33 per room per month, were too expensive for most clothing workers. A larger project, the **Hill-**

man Houses (1951; Springsteen & Goldhammer), was subsequently built just to the west on Grand St. It is named in honor of Sidney Hillman (1887–1946), a Lithuanian immigrant, union organizer, and prominent labor leader.

Because the area reflects its Jewish heritage, it has in recent years attracted a younger generation of Orthodox Jews back to the Lower East Side their grand-parents struggled to escape. (Cheap rents also are part of the appeal.) The build-ing at the southeast intersection of East Broadway and Grand St (311–313 East Broadway), once the Young Men's Benevolent Association, is today the **East Side Mikvah,** the last remaining public ritual bath in the area. Although individual synagogues often have their own mikvahs, public ones were necessary in a neigh-borhood where synagogues were often converted from churches or from store-fronts.

Walk north, just beyond the intersection of Grand St and Bialystoker Place to the **Bialystoker Synagogue** (1826; DL), 7–13 Bialystoker Place (formerly Wil-let St), originally the Willett Street Methodist Episcopal Church, a plain late-Federal building with masonry walls of random fieldstone. The congregation, founded in 1878 by Russian Jews from Bialystock (now in Poland), bought the building in 1905.

Abrons Arts Center

466 Grand St, New York, NY 10002. ☎ (212) 598-0400. Web site: www.henry streetarts.org. Open Tues–Sat 12–6 and before evening performances. Free. Ac-cessible to wheelchairs.

Subway: Sixth Ave Local (F) to East Broadway or Delancey St. Sixth Ave Ex-press (B, D, Q) to Grand St. Nassau St Express or Local (J, M, Z) to Essex St. Bus: M9, M14, M15 to Grand St. M22 to Montgomery St.

Return to Grand St, turn right and walk west to 466 Grand St and the Abrons Arts Center of the **Henry Street Settlement** (1975; Prentice & Chan, Ohlhausen), a red brick building that has won awards for architectural excel-lence. The center, along with the adjoining **Harry De Jur Henry Street Settle-ment Playhouse,** is the focal point of the settlement's arts programs.

Art exhibitions and cultural programs at the center reflect the neighborhood's diversity and include work by artists-in-residence, faculty, and local artists. Shows have included photographs of the Lower East Side from the 1940s and '50s, works by homeless women, and photographic portraits of people helped by the organi-zation over the past 75 years. For many years the playhouse was the permanent home of the **New Federal Theatre,** showcasing the work of black playwrights; since 1996 New Federal has shared the space with other ethnic theater groups.

Walk south on Pitt past East Broadway to Henry St, then turn left to **Saint Au-gustine's Episcopal Church** (1827–29; enlarged, 1849; DL), 290 Henry Street, originally the All Saints' Free Church ("free" because there was no charge for the pews). Formerly a chapel of Trinity parish, it is now independent.

Henry Street Settlement

Continue along Henry St. The buildings of the **Henry Street Settlement** (1827, later additions; DL) at 263–267 Henry St (between Montgomery and Grand Sts) attract attention architecturally as late-Federal residences, built in what was once a semirural setting at the edge of town.

History

Lillian Wald (1867–1940), who founded the Henry Street Settlement, remains one of New York's great figures, a compassionate, gentle, yet shrewd and worldly woman who devoted herself tirelessly to the poor. Awakened to a sense of vocation by a visit to a poor home, she moved to a fifth-floor walk-up at 27 Jefferson St and began her rounds, fighting ignorance, disease, malnutrition, rats, and bigotry. She raised money, largely through the assistance of Jacob Schiff, the philanthropist who gave two of the Henry St buildings to the settlement. Coming from a bourgeois German Jewish family, Wald gradually grew to accept these strange eastern European immigrants as her own people and became an important liaison between the "uptown" and "downtown" Jews, who often found themselves at odds with one another.

After Wald retired in 1933, her work was carried on by Helen Hall, whose career was as distinguished as the founder's. The organization's programs, adapted to reflect changing social conditions, include a credit union (founded in 1937 to offer the needy an alternative to street-based loan sharks), a day care center, and a companions' program for the elderly.

Exterior

Only the center building has survived with original details intact: the wrought-iron stoop railing with open box newel posts; the areaway fence with knobby finials (sometimes said to be acorns symbolizing hospitality, an attribute also attached to the pineapple, one of which appears as a finial on the newel post of 263 Henry St), the louvered shutters on the first-story windows; and the paneled doorway flanked by slender columns. The cornice above the doorway and the lintels above the windows came later.

Return to **East Broadway** and turn left. The street still bears traces of its former importance as the center of Orthodox Judaism in New York. At 225 East Broadway is the **Young Israel Synagogue,** home to a group founded in the early 20C to counteract what its young Orthodox members considered the triple threat of Reform Judaism, rising crime among second-generation Jews, and socialism. Although the founders were deeply committed to Orthodoxy, they also considered themselves Americanized, and so shaved their beards, accepted mixed social dancing, dressed in modern style, and listened to sermons in English, all of which would be anathema to the Hasidic and other ultra-Orthodox Jews. Today they continue their social programs, promoting Orthodox styles of living and worship. The building formerly belonged to the Hebrew Immigrant Aid and Sheltering Society (see Joseph Papp Public Theater in Walk 10).

The Educational Alliance

The Educational Alliance at 197 East Broadway near Jefferson St, organized in 1889, was one of the most important early agencies formed to help the massive influx of eastern European Jews adapt to the bewildering, alien culture of America.

History

The alliance was founded by a group of German Jewish philanthropists, many of them immigrants who had arrived a generation earlier, prospered, and moved out of the ghetto. These "uptown" Jews, as the German philanthropists were known, saw Americanization as the key to self-reliance and freedom from want. The alliance brought together the Aguilar Free Library Society, the Young Men's Hebrew Association, and the Hebrew Free School Association. It provided education for the ignorant, recreation for the weary, and, most important, knowledge of American institutions and language for the foreigner.

The Educational Alliance held classes for immigrant children to prepare them for the public school system and gave courses in English and civics to adults to ready them for naturalization. It showed movies about American history and held Legal Holiday parties (on July 4th, Lincoln's Birthday, and so on). It opened a library before the free public system existed and offered adult education in everything from Greek and Roman history to physics and stenography. It presented lectures that probed moral, philosophical, and literary topics. It provided a gymnasium and facilities for taking showers, an important service in a tenement-ridden slum where bathtubs were rare.

Relations between the "uptown" Jews who founded the alliance and "downtown" Jews who used it remained prickly for a long time. The assimilated uptowners found the new immigrants backward, "Oriental," and slovenly—people who needed lessons in hygiene as well as English. The "greenhorns," or new immigrants, found the German Jews condescending and insensitive to their natural desire to perpetuate their eastern European culture. Yet despite such strains, the Educational Alliance survived to make life better for many. Today it carries on its work, although those who use its facilities are Puerto Rican, Asian, and black, as well as Jewish.

Opposite Jefferson St in Seward Park is the **Seward Park Branch of the New York Public Library** (1909; Babb, Cook & Welch), 192 East Broadway, founded as an early branch of the public system. It offered a large collection of books in Yiddish, and long lines sometimes formed at the door as people waited to get in. Today it attracts Asian and Latino immigrants and older Jewish residents.

Seward Park, created from land acquired in 1897 and opened officially in 1903, is named after William H. Seward (1801–1872), governor of the state of New York, U.S. senator, and secretary of state under Abraham Lincoln.

Forward Building
Across from the park is the **Forward Building** (1912; George A. Boehm; DL), built for the *Jewish Daily Forward,* the most influential Yiddish daily newspaper. The first floor frieze includes portraits of Karl Marx and Friedrich Engels. In recent decades the building was home to a Chinese church; in 1998 it was converted into condominiums.

History
The *Jewish Daily Forward* (founded 1897) rose to prominence under Abraham Cahan (1860–1951), an immigrant from Lithuania. Cahan dictated the editorial policy of the paper, which had close ties to the Socialist Party, but reported the whole spectrum of immigrant Jewish experience. Intimate in tone and straightforward in diction, the *Forward* told of the everyday events of the Lower East Side. Cahan wrote about the prostitution of Allen St and the iniquities of bosses who imposed unbearable working conditions; his paper explained baseball to the

greenhorn and offered advice on the use of the pocket handkerchief. The paper's most famous feature was the "Bintel Brief" (Bundle of Letters), a column in which readers unburdened themselves of their personal problems. A mother wrote that her adult daughter ridiculed the old-country modes of dress, speech, and even cooking. A working father worried because his daughters hung around with street boys, no better than gangsters. Cahan's detractors criticized the paper as vulgarly anti-intellectual and degradingly commercial; according to the intellectual component of the community, it had the mind of a child and the lusts of a grown scoundrel. Cahan also leased some of the building to labor organizations like the Workman's Circle, which offered everything from affordable medical care to summer camps.

Since 1974 the newspaper has been located at 49 E. 33rd St in generic midtown Manhattan. Now a weekly with a readership of about 45,000 (its 1917 circulation was 238,000), it publishes editions in English, Russian, and Yiddish.

Continue along East Broadway to **Rutgers St;** the original landowner, Hendrick Rutgers, had a farm stretching from Division St to the East River. The Rutgers Mansion (1754) in the block bordered by Cherry, Jefferson, Monroe, and Clinton Sts remained until 1875, when it was razed in favor of tenements and sweatshop loft buildings.

Nathan Straus Square, at the intersection of East Broadway and Canal St, honors the Jewish philanthropist and businessman perhaps best remembered for his campaign to provide pasteurized milk to city children. Straus was Parks commissioner from 1889 to 1892 and president of the Board of Health in 1898. With his brother Isidor, Nathan (1848–1931) owned two of the city's largest department stores, acquiring R.H. Macy & Co. and entering into a partnership with Abraham Abraham to form Abraham & Straus.

Walk west on Canal St and turn right onto Ludlow St. The building at 5 Ludlow St formerly belonged to the **Independent Kletzker Brotherly Aid Society** and served both as a synagogue and a mutual-aid organization. The Kletzker Society (founded 1892), composed of immigrants from the Polish village of Kletsk, was one of many *landsmanshaftn* on the Lower East Side around 1900. These groups made burial and funeral arrangements, cared for the sick, and served as social centers. The building reflects the neighborhood's evolution: its facade retains a Jewish star, but the building serves as an Italian funeral home, and has information written in Chinese.

Jarmulowsky's Bank

Continue west on Canal St. The former Jarmulowsky's Bank, 15–16 Canal St, founded in 1873, was one of several small private Jewish banks established when financial conditions eased enough for local residents to save a few dollars. Unfortunately, several of these institutions failed, taking with them savings painfully culled from sweatshops, factories, and small businesses.

History

The bank survived until Aug 1914, when the state banking superintendent closed it with assets of $654,000 and liabilities of $1,703,000. A month later an angry crowd swarmed around the entrance of Jarmulowsky's apartment, while he and his family scurried to safety over the rooftops. Jarmulowsky was given a suspended sentence for mismanaging the bank's assets. The depositors eventually recovered some of their losses.

Eldridge Street Synagogue

Continue west on Canal St to Eldridge St. Turn left (south). At 12–16 Eldridge St is Congregation Khal Adath Jeshurun with Anshe Lubz (Community of the People of Israel with the People of Lubz), better known as the Eldridge Street Synagogue (1886–87; Herter Bros.; DL), crammed into a side street but towering above the neighboring tenements. Other Lower East Side synagogues had been built by western European Jews, but his was the first established by eastern European Ashkenazi Jews, a congregation sufficiently wealthy to hire the prestigious architectural firm of Herter Bros. Built in a mixture of Gothic, Romanesque, and Moorish revival styles, it shows the mid-19C trend in synagogue architecture toward Oriental motifs.

The barrel-vaulted upstairs sanctuary was once an outstanding example of synagogue decoration, with great brass chandeliers (gaslit in early days) and Victorian glass shades, a large rose window in the west wall, a towering ark carved in walnut, elaborately designed pews, galleries, and a vaulted ceiling.

History

By the 1930s, immigration had dwindled and many prosperous Jews had moved away from the Lower East Side. By the 1940s, the sanctuary was used only on special occasions, with regular services held in the basement study area. The sanctuary was closed in the 1950s. The nonprofit Eldridge Street Project, incorporated in 1986, has been restoring the synagogue and raising the nearly $9 million necessary for a full restoration. (Through it all, a small Orthodox congregation of 30–50 people has continued holding services in the basement, without missing a Sabbath or holiday in over a century.) By 1999 the slate roof had been restored and the sanctuary skylights, boarded up since World War II, had been reopened. For tour information, ☎ (212) 978-8800.

Walk north on Eldridge St to **Hester St,** named for Hester Rynders, daughter of Jacob Leisler, who was hanged for treason in 1691 (see City Hall Park and City Hall in Walk 5). During the late 19C, Hester St had the area's busiest street market, as well as sweatshops and tenement houses. Writers of the period found it the quintessential ghetto street, ringing with the shouts of vendors, the haggling and chattering of women, the cries of children who darted through the crowds playing games and making swift raids on the pushcarts. A sympathetic reporter from the *Times* in 1898 found the street scene touching and attractive. Another reporter for the same journal described it as a filthy place whose inhabitants were slatternly, lawless (they had failed to empty their garbage cans at a specified hour), and indecent.

One block to the left is **Sara Delano Roosevelt Park,** named after the mother of Franklin D. Roosevelt. The park was created in 1934 by widening Chrystie and Forsyth Sts and tearing down seven blocks of tenements between them.

Turn around and walk east on Hester St to **Allen St.** During the closing years of the 19C, Allen St, darkened and dirtied by the Second Avenue El, became a haven for prostitution. A local minister complained that the women openly solicited from the stoops of tenements adjoining his church. Michael Gold, in his novel *Jews Without Money*, recalled the time when prostitutes sat out on the sidewalks in chairs sunning themselves, their legs sprawled indolently in the way of anyone who wanted to pass by. After the street was widened in 1930 and the El torn down in 1942, the south part of Allen St near the Manhattan Bridge became a center for antiques, especially copper and brass ware.

Continue east along Hester St and turn left onto **Orchard St,** named for the apple orchards on the 18C farm of James De Lancey. The district's main shopping street, Orchard St is jammed with bargain hunters on Sundays. Like Hester St, it had a pushcart market that stretched a few blocks north and south from Delancey St. Some of the present businesses grew out of the pushcart trade and are still owned by descendants of peddlers. For unskilled immigrants with little English, the pushcarts represented one of the few ways to eke out a living. The carts, obstructive and unsanitary, were outlawed by the city in the 1930s.

Orchard St, between Delancey and Houston Sts, retains the boisterous atmosphere of the old days. Racks of clothing and leather coats and displays of jewelry and luggage pack the sidewalks and streets (closed to traffic during business hours), with barkers constantly urging potential customers to haggle with them for a good price. In recent years the old businesses have been joined by boutiques, some of which are owned by young people attracted by the relatively low rents.

> ### Lower East Side Tours
> The **Lower East Side Business Improvement District,** 261 Broome St, offers free tours of the Orchard Street Shopping District on Sundays Apr–Dec. Tours leave Katz's Deli (corner of Ludlow and E. Houston Sts) at 11 A.M. ☎ (212) 226-9010

Lower East Side Tenement Museum

Visitors' Center: 90 Orchard St, New York, NY 10002. ☎ (212) 431-0233. Web site: www.tenement.org. Open Mon, Tues, Wed, and Fri 11–5:30; Thurs 11–7; Sat–Sun 11–6. Free admission to Visitors' Center exhibits and films. The tenement can only be viewed by guided tour (admission charge). Reservations suggested weekends. Call for times.

Art exhibits, lectures, special events, and neighborhood walking tours. Gift shop. Tenement building not accessible to wheelchairs; Visitors' Center is accessible.

Subway: Sixth Ave Local (F) to Delancey St. Sixth Ave Express (B, D, Q) to Grand St. Nassau St Express or Local (J, M, Z) to Essex St. Bus: M15.

Continue north on Orchard St to 90 Orchard St (corner of Broome St), the Visitors' Center of the Lower East Side Tenement Museum, whose prime exhibition is **97 Orchard St,** a six-story Italianate brownstone tenement built in 1863. Seven thousand immigrants from more than 20 nations lived in the building between 1863 and 1935. The museum was founded in 1988 by Ruth J. Abram and Anita Jacobson, first operating out of the ground-floor storefront, offering walking tours and organizing traveling exhibits. Slowly, the building was restored and eventually purchased, opening to the public in 1994.

Tenement History

Tenements, built to exploit all available space and maximize profit, were one of the horrors of immigrant life. They can be classified as pre–Old Law (before 1879), Old Law (1879–1901), or New Law (after 1901) tenements; in general, the earlier buildings were worse than later ones, since each successive law laid new restrictions on landlords and builders. The Tenement Museum building is a pre–Old Law tenement, built when no laws whatsoever applied.

In 1850 one Silas Wood built a "model" tenement on Cherry St "with the design of supplying the laboring people with cheap lodging." His tenement, Gotham Court, was five stories tall and had about 144 two-room apartments. Six years after its completion, it housed over 1,000 tenants and had become a scandal.

In 1867 the city passed an act that promised improvement but lacked teeth. Technically, landlords were required to provide fire escapes and to connect toilets with sewers instead of with cesspools, but for every requirement the law provided a loophole. The next attempt at amelioration came in 1878 with a contest for a design that fit the standard New York 25 × 100 ft lot and would afford safety and convenience for the tenant along with profit for the landlord. The prize winner, the "dumbbell" tenement, soon became synonymous for all that was miserable in tenement design: two tenements were constructed side by side with an airshaft, often only a ft or so wide, between them, which gave the buildings their characteristic dumbbell shape, but provided virtually no air or light to the lower rooms on the airshaft. The population of a five-story building based on this plan could and often did reach 100–150 people, since poor families sublet space. The Tenement House Act of 1879 provided some improvements: there had to be running water either in the house or yard; buildings had to contain one toilet for each two apartments.

In 1901 the reformer Lawrence Veiller helped enact a law forbidding further construction of dumbbell tenements. Instead of the narrow airshaft, the law required a light court at least 4½ ft wide. Toilets were required in each apartment and windows in each room. Unfortunately the 1901 law came too late, since by 1893 some 1,196 dumbbell tenements already blighted the Lower East Side. In the mid-1990s, according to the Department of City Planning, 5,561 Old Law tenements were still occupied, while New Law tenements housed 624,958 tenants.

97 Orchard Street

The tenement at 97 Orchard St (1863) was built by Lucas Glockner, a tailor from Germany. At that time virtually no building codes existed, so Glockner had a free hand in its construction. His tenement was better than most of its contemporaries—Glockner even lived there himself. Each floor had four three-room apartments (a total of 325 square ft), with daylight reaching only one room of each apartment; the first floor was reserved for businesses. There were no bathrooms, running water, or electricity. The privies were in the backyard. Often seven or more people, and sometimes 12–15, were crammed into each apartment.

As housing laws changed, so did 97 Orchard St, although existing buildings were exempt from some requirements of new laws. To comply with the Tenement Act of 1901, the landlord installed two bathrooms per floor (one toilet per two families). No law required the installation of electricity, and the building wasn't wired until after 1918—the last time it was upgraded. In 1929 further stringent laws were passed, but the owners of 97 Orchard St, like many others, decided to close the building rather than comply. In 1935 the upper floors were sealed.

The guided tour takes visitors to the restored apartments of former residents Natalie Gumpertz, a German Jew who supported her family as a seamstress (apartment restored to the 1870s); the Rogarshevskys, the family of a Lithuanian Jewish garment worker who died at 47 of tuberculosis (apartment restored to 1918); and the Baldizzis, a Sicilian Catholic family who eked out their living during the Depression (apartment restored to the 1930s).

Continue north several blocks to Rivington St, named after James Rivington (1724–1803), publisher of *Rivington's New York Gazetteer,* a Tory newspaper that attacked the American Revolutionary movement. Rivington's sentiments and abrasive personality earned him the hostility of American patriots, who destroyed his presses and stole his type fonts, a serious theft since no American foundries produced type of the same high quality as Rivington's imported English fonts. Undaunted, he returned to England and got new equipment, came back to New York, and started another loyalist newspaper. In 1781 he had a change of heart and became a spy for General Washington.

Turn right on Rivington St. Organized as early as 1860, the **First Roumanian-American Congregation,** Shaarai Shamoyim (Gates of Heaven) bought the former Allen Street Methodist Church, 89 Rivington St, around 1890 and remodeled it into a synagogue (many Christian congregations moved away as Jewish immigrants poured in). One of the few Romanesque revival buildings in the area, the synagogue has a simple brick facade and round arched windows. In the days when cantors were lionized as opera stars are today, Shaarai Shamoyim was a springboard to vocal success; two famous operatic singers, Jan Peerce (then Jacob Pincus Perelmuth) and Richard Tucker (then Reuben Ticker), started here as cantors.

Turn left onto **Ludlow St,** the center of the Lower East Side's downtown scene. Among the pioneers of the area's revival are **Collective Unconscious** (145 Ludlow St), a theater; **Luna Lounge** (171 Ludlow St), known for its alternative-style comedians; **Max Fish** (178 Ludlow St), a bar that opened in 1989 when the street was still dominated by drug dealers; the **Pink Pony Café** (176 Ludlow St), its alcohol-free counterpart; and **Nada** (167 Ludlow St), the first and most influential theater in the area.

Walk north on Ludlow to the corner of Houston St, where **Katz's Delicatessen,** 205 Houston St, still stands. This old-timer is a no-frills, cafeteria-style deli that opened in 1888; during World War II its slogan was "Send a Salami to Your Boy in the Army." It still sells some of the city's finest and thickest pastrami sandwiches.

Turn left on Houston and walk west to **Russ & Daughters,** 179 Houston St. Polish immigrant Joel Russ started selling Polish mushrooms from a wagon in 1911, opened a store on Orchard St in 1914, and moved to this location in the 1940s. Russ wasn't great with the customers, so his three daughters—Ida, Anne, and Hattie—cheerfully became the front people. The family-owned store sells caviar, smoked and salted fish, and, of course, Polish mushrooms.

Return east along Houston St to **Red Square** (1989), 250 Houston St, a red, square apartment building. (It was constructed by developers with a sense of humor, at a time when the Soviet Communist regime was under intense pressure.) On its roof is an 18 ft **statue of Lenin** (Yuri Gerasimov) with his right arm raised. A Soviet commission, the statue was abandoned during the political turmoil in Russia and later salvaged by the developers from the backyard of a dacha outside Moscow. The developers have noted that Lenin faces both Wall St (symbol of capitalism) and the Lower East Side (destination of the socialist-minded Jews fleeing Russia). Behind Lenin, covering the water towers, is a clocktower with two huge clock faces whose numbers are out of sequence.

Turn right on Norfolk St. **Congregation Anshe Chesed** (1850; Alexander Saeltzer; DL), 172 Norfolk St, is the oldest surviving structure in the city built as a synagogue and the original home of New York's third Jewish congregation (after Shearith Israel and B'nai Jeshurun). Designed by the architect of the Astor Library (see Joseph Papp Public Theater in Walk 10), it was once resplendent with Gothic revival pointed arch windows and delicate tracery. Like other downtown houses of worship, its various owners reflect the successive waves of Jewish immigration in the neighborhood: built by a German congregation, Anshe Chesed (People of Kindness), it later housed a Hungarian immigrant group, Ohab Zedek, and, eventually became Congregation Anshe Slonim (People of Slonim), named for a fondly remembered village in Poland. Anshe Slonim, dwindling in size and resources, abandoned the building in 1974. In the early 1980s it was sealed against vandalism and threatened with demolition. Spanish sculptor Angel Orensanz bought the building (1986) and restored it. Sabbath services resumed in 1997. The building houses the Angel Orensanz Foundation and Center for the Arts, and is used for performances and exhibits.

Return to Houston St and walk two blocks east to Clinton St. Turn right. **Chasam Sopher Synagogue** (1853), 8 Clinton St, is the second-oldest surviving synagogue in the city, built for a German Jewish congregation that moved uptown in 1886. A group from Poland purchased the property and renamed it Chasam Sopher (Seal of the Scribe) to honor Moshe Sofer (or Schreiber, in the Germanicized form), a scholar and rabbi who was born in Frankfurt in 1762. This red brick building is constructed in the round-arch Romanesque revival style, although its appearance has been altered by the loss of the original parapets topping off the towers.

Across the street at 5–7 Clinton St is a quintessentially modern addition to the Lower East Side, the **Freakatorium,** a novelty gift shop with a free Freak Museum that includes shrunken heads, Siamese piglets, and banners from sideshows.

Walk south along Clinton to Stanton St, then walk west one block to Suffolk where there are new low- and middle-income row houses built by Asian Americans for Equality (AAFE), a community development organization.

Walk south to Rivington St. **Streit's Matzoth Company** (150 Rivington St) is the sole remaining bakery in Manhattan producing matzoth, an unleavened bread used especially during Passover. Walk west to **Schapiro's Wine Company,** 126 Rivington St (between Essex and Norfolk Sts), the only remaining kosher wine firm in Manhattan, founded in 1899 by the present owner's grandfather, who performed his own charitable work, giving new immigrants a free meal, 50 cents, and a bottle of honey wine. The kosher wine, billed as "The Wine You Can Almost Cut with a Knife," is made from grapes grown in upstate New York and pressed there under rabbinical supervision.

Turn left on Essex St. and walk south. Occupying most of the blocks from Stanton to Broome Sts, the **Essex Street Market** (1940) was built to house pushcart peddlers after Mayor Fiorello La Guardia cleared them off Orchard St. Today, the building between Rivington and Delancey Sts still houses ethnic food merchants; another building has become a hospital annex.

Turn left at **Delancey St,** a chaotic shopping strip leading to the Williamsburg Bridge; it is named after the landholding De Lancey family. When the street was widened, it was renamed Schiff Pkwy to honor Jacob Schiff, financier and philanthropist, but the new name never took hold.

A half-block east, at 138 Delancey, is **Ratner's Delicatessen** (founded 1905), a family-owned restaurant famous for its soups. In 1997, as its old-time Jewish clientele dwindled, a member of the younger generation opened **Lansky's**—named for gangster Meyer Lansky, a one-time Ratner's regular—as a pseudo-speakeasy in the back room. By 2000, Lansky's had taken over the whole place, serving steakhouse fare. The traditional Ratner's menu is now available only on Sun, and the food is no longer kosher.

Return to Essex St and walk south to **75 Essex St** (at the corner of Broome St), which long ago housed the Eastern Dispensary, one of several privately endowed clinics serving the poor. The clinic was founded in 1832; in 1891, as the Good Samaritan Dispensary, it treated about 160,000 patients annually.

Diagonally opposite is **Seward Park High School** (between Ludlow, Essex, Broome, and Grand Sts), which occupies the site of the old Essex Market Court House and Ludlow Street Jail. The jail held prisoners whose offenses came under the jurisdiction of the sheriff of the county of New York, as well as violators of federal laws. Sheriff's prisoners with enough money could buy fancier accommodations in the jail, a system that naturally led to abuse. William M. Tweed (see New York County Courthouse in Walk 5), jailed here while he served time for defrauding the city, availed himself of these privileges: he occupied a two-room cell with flower pots on the windowsills and even had a piano to ease the tedium of prison life. Tweed died in the jail in 1878.

Continue south to Grand St and turn left. **Kossar's Bialys,** 367 Grand St, sells bagels, bulkas, garlic knots, pletzels, salt sticks, and, of course, bialys, reputedly invented by the bakers of the Russian (now Polish) town of Bialystok. The bakery, founded in 1933, stays open until around midnight.

Return to Essex St and walk south. The Lower East Side's last remaining pickle place, **Guss' Pickles** (officially renamed Essex Street Pickles, but still called Guss'), is at 35 Essex St. Since 1910 it has sold pickles straight from the barrels, along with pickled tomatoes, peppers, and sauerkraut.

Continue south and make a right on Hester St. **Gertel's,** 53 Hester St, an old-fashioned kosher bakery, has served rugelach and potato kugel since 1904.

8 · SoHo

Subway: Lexington Ave Local (6) to Spring St. Broadway Local (N, R) to Prince St. Eighth Ave Express or Local (A, C, E) to Spring St. Sixth Ave Express or Local (B, D, Q, F) to Broadway–Lafayette St.
Bus: M1, M5, M6, M21.

SoHo, an acronym for *So*uth of *Ho*uston, has been integral to New York's art scene for more than three decades, but it came upon this identity by accident.

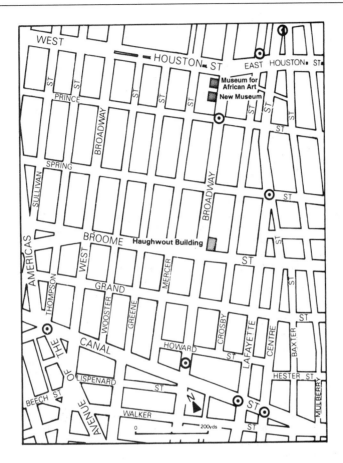

History

Before the Revolution, what is now SoHo was mostly farmland. At the end of the 18C the area became a quiet residential suburb (the oldest remaining house dates only from around 1806). By 1825 the area was the most densely populated part of the city, built up with Federal and Greek revival townhouses, and by 1840 it was highly fashionable. During the 1850s, while expensive hotels and retail stores of sterling reputation lined Broadway, the side streets began sporting brothels, dance halls, and casinos, some of them elegant in their own way.

Commerce pushed out the carriage trade, and industry came in to fill the vacuum. During the decades between 1860 and 1890, most of the cast-iron architecture so admired today was constructed, the buildings serving as factories or warehouses, often with shop fronts on the ground floor. Appealing as they may seem now, with their Corinthian columns or French Second Empire dormers, many functioned as sweatshops where immigrants from southern and eastern Europe endured 12 or more hours a day of tedious labor in degrading surroundings for the sake of their offspring. SoHo and Little Italy still rub elbows, and much of the remaining Italian population, visible in warm weather on Sullivan St and the other streets west of West Broadway, is descended from those overworked immigrants.

Although the sweatshops were legislated out of existence and immigration quotas cut off the flow of cheap, uneducated, and hence acquiescent labor, SoHo remained industrial until about 1960. Gradually, the cast-iron buildings became outmoded and inconvenient, and light industry—paper-box companies, tool and die factories, wool remnant companies—moved elsewhere. In 1959 the City Club of New York published an influential report labeling the area, then known as Hell's Hundred Acres (because of its frequent fires), or as the Valley (a lowland between the architectural highs of the Financial District and Midtown), an industrial slum with no architecture of note.

In the early 1960s, artists attracted by the empty commercial buildings began moving in, illegally converting spaces to apartments and installing plumbing, household wiring, and adequate heating. To protect themselves from profiteering landlords, artists' cooperatives began buying entire buildings and tenants' associations began lobbying for legalization of the status quo. In the late 1960s, SoHo was an artist's Eden. Rents were cheap, space was plentiful, and society was made up mostly of other artists. By 1970 SoHo had become a boomtown for real estate dealers, art dealers (some had headed downtown from the pricey reaches of the Upper East Side), and artists who, if not becoming rich, were at least forming a coherent artistic community with its own aesthetics and codes of living. Film, video, and performance art—the avant-garde media of the 1960s—became staple commodities of SoHo artistic life. Experimental dance and drama flourished. Cooperative galleries opened.

Today SoHo is cleaner, slicker, and more expensive. In recent years, high-end home furnishings stores and other retailers have arrived, joining the trendy restaurants that come and go with stunning rapidity. In 1996 the luxurious SoHo Grand Hotel opened at West Broadway and Grand St, the first major hotel built in the area since the 1800s.

Some complain that SoHo is simply returning to its 19C roots as an expensive shopping district, once defined by Lord & Taylor, Brooks Brothers, and E.V. Haughwout & Co. Many galleries have relocated to Chelsea, where space is cheaper, and many artists, unable to pay the steep rents, have moved to the Lower East Side and Brooklyn neighborhoods such as Williamsburg. While SoHo still does have working artists and others in arts-related fields, newcomers are more likely to be lawyers, investment bankers, and people working in the entertainment and fashion industries. Still, despite all the changes, SoHo remains close to the center of the art world, with about 200 commercial art galleries and many of the city's premier alternative art spaces.

Cast-Iron Architecture

SoHo's cast-iron architecture, a major architectural innovation hailed for its strength and versatility during the later half of the 19C, arouses passionate emotions in the hearts of admirers. Once a source of personal and civic pride, these buildings later suffered the ravages of neglect—disfigured by ugly ground-floor modernizations or dimmed by layers of dull paint. In

1973 the SoHo–Cast Iron Historic District was created to protect a 26-block tract—bounded by West Broadway, Houston, Crosby, and Canal Sts—with the largest concentration of cast-iron architecture in the world. Today many of these structures have been handsomely restored.

Early cast-iron architecture, adorned with the familiar quoins, columns, and consoles of the classical tradition and painted tan, buff, or cream, was designed to imitate marble or limestone. Sometimes cast-iron plates were even grooved to resemble blocks of stone mortared together. Eventually iron founders, many of whom had previously dealt in stoves, safes, and lawn furniture, began offering catalogs of ornaments from which the client could select, combining the elements in simple or lavish compositions. The ease of creating details in any architectural style was a major attraction of cast iron. As long as patterns could be carved and molds made, elaborate ornaments could be cheaply reproduced, allowing businessmen who could not afford the extravagance of stonecutting the prestige of fluted Corinthian columns, floral swags, anything they wanted, all bolted onto their buildings and painted to look like stone. While the earliest cast-iron buildings hark back stylistically to Italy (Sansovino's Library in Venice and the Roman Colosseum were much admired), later examples were based on French Renaissance, Second Empire, or neo-Grec styles.

James Bogardus is generally considered to be the father of cast-iron architecture, though his importance arises primarily from his patents for constructing buildings with mass-produced cast-iron sections and as a building contractor. He left little documentable work (see 254–260 Canal St in this walk and 85 Leonard St in Walk 9) and does not appear to have operated a large foundry of his own.

Begin at Houston St and Broadway and walk south. On the east side of the street are clothing boutiques for the young and adventurous as well as branches of national chain stores (for example, Pottery Barn). The west side of Broadway (between Houston and Prince Sts) is SoHo's "Museum Row," its lineup diminished by the closing of the Guggenheim SoHo in 2001.

Museum for African Art

593 Broadway, New York, NY 10012. ☎ (212) 966-1313. Web site: www.african art.org. Open Tues–Fri 10:30–5:30; Sat and Sun 12–6. Closed Mon, holidays. Admission charge, but free Sun. Gift shop. Accessible to wheelchairs. Publications, workshops, films, lectures, music, dance.

The Museum for African Art is one of only two museums in the country devoted exclusively to African art. (The other is the Smithsonian's National Museum of African Art.) Formerly the Center for African Art, founded in 1984 and located on the Upper East Side, it changed its name in 1992 and moved to SoHo a year later. The museum interior was designed by Maya Lin, architect of the National Vietnam Veteran's Memorial in Washington, D.C.

Its exhibitions, which explore Africa's rich artistic, traditional, and cultural heritage or showcase contemporary African art, have traveled to more than 50 national and international museums. Shows have included photographs of Africa by Africans, beaded objects (from thrones to necklaces) made by Yoruba-speaking people, and hair in African art and culture.

New Museum of Contemporary Art

583 Broadway, New York, NY 10012. ☎ (212) 219-1222. Web site: www.new museum.org. Open Tues–Sun 12–6; Thurs 12–8. Closed Mon. Admission charge, but free Thurs 6–8. Limited wheelchair access. Lectures, tours, performance events, poetry readings, films, videos. Bookshop.

The oldest museum on the block is the relatively young New Museum of Contemporary Art, dedicated to works of emerging and established contemporary artists. The museum was founded in 1977 by Marcia Tucker, formerly a curator of the Whitney Museum of American Art, to collect and show truly contemporary art. The three galleries on the ground floor and mezzanine level showcase installations, video, painting, and sculpture from around the world. Many exhibitions have a political bent. **"Downstairs"** is a large reading room and exhibition space for interactive projects, installations, and performances.

The museum building (1896; Cleverdon & Putzel), originally a store and manufacturing loft, was constructed as an investment by John Jacob Astor well after elegance had departed from this part of Broadway.

Walk south on Broadway and cross Prince St. During the 1850s and 1860s, this neighborhood glittered with the bright lights of theaters and music halls, including Niblo's Garden (1827) at the intersection of Broadway and Prince St, a theater known for its extravagant productions, 75 ft stage, and illuminated marquee with red gas jets.

Continue south on the east side of Broadway. Many art galleries are concentrated in **560 Broadway**—essentially a vertical art mall. On the ground level of 560 Broadway is **Dean & DeLuca,** one of the city's great gourmet food stores, whose extravagant displays of produce, cheeses, cakes, fish, and prepared foods are rightfully housed in a building committed to art. The store first opened in SoHo in 1977 and moved to this location in 1988.

Near the southwest corner of Prince St and Broadway is the former **"Little Singer Building"** (1904; Ernest Flagg), 561–563 Broadway, so called because there once existed a bigger Singer Building, demolished in 1967 (see One Liberty Plaza in Walk 3). Despite ugly ground-floor modifications, this steel-framed skyscraper (a building type less than ten years old when it was built) is extremely handsome. Most notable are the terra-cotta panels, delicate curls of dark green wrought iron, large expanses of plate glass admitting plenty of light and air, and a great arch beneath the cornice. The 12-story loft structure was built as a product showroom with rental space filled mostly by clothing manufacturers. The building is L-shaped and wraps around the corner of Prince St, enveloping 565 Broadway (1859; John Kellum) next door, whose carved marble Corinthian columns evoke the days when Ball, Black & Co. purveyed jewelry to society. Today the building has both residential and commercial units.

The handsomely maintained **Rouss Building** (1889; Alfred Zucker), 555 Broadway, still proclaims the aplomb of merchant Charles "Broadway" Rouss, who came debt-ridden to New York from Maryland and so flourished that he took the street's name as his own and had it emblazoned on his storefront.

The Haughwout Building. One of the earliest (1856–57) of SoHo's cast-iron masterpieces, the building reflects the economy and beauty of the architectural detail achieved by casting repeated forms from one mold. (Landmarks Preservation Commission, New York City. Photographer: John B. Bayley)

On the east side of Broadway is **550 Broadway** (1854), one of the last masonry buildings to be modernized with a cast-iron facade (1901), though the use of cast-iron to spruce up old-fashioned masonry or to convert a residence into a commercial building was common earlier. The building housed Tiffany & Co. until 1870.

Cross Spring St and continue south on Broadway. The **bishop's crook lamppost** in front of **515 Broadway** dates from around 1900, when it and others of its kind replaced older gaslights that had been introduced in the 1860s. In 1896 this classic lamppost—with its tendrils, scrollwork, and acanthus leaves—designed by Richard Rodgers Bowker began to appear on city streets. About 50, documented for preservation, still remain among the city's 350,000 streetlights.

Continue south along Broadway to the northeast corner of Broome St and the once supremely elegant **Haughwout Building** (1856–57; John P. Gaynor; DL) at 488–492 Broadway. Eder V. Haughwout sold china, glassware, chandeliers, and silver (to the White House and lesser establishments) from the ground-floor showroom (now an office supply store). After he retired in 1869, the building became a loft, including among its occupants M. H. Pulaski & Co., manufacturers of embroidery. Designed in the Italianate palazzo style common to many early cast-iron buildings and perhaps even modeled on the Sansovino Library in Venice, the Haughwout Building (sometimes inappropriately called the Parthenon of Cast-Iron Architecture) was nonetheless a pioneering structure. It was one of the first New York buildings whose floor loads were carried by a cast-iron skeleton instead of masonry walls and the very first to feature a passenger elevator with a safety device, a steam-driven, cable-and-drum contraption invented by Elisha Otis. The economy of casting many forms from the same mold fostered the repetition of detail on cast-iron buildings such as this one, whose basic motif—a round-arch window between slender Corinthian colonnettes flanked by larger Corinthian columns—is repeated 92 times in four tiers on two facades. The building, whose ironwork was cast by Daniel D. Badger & Co., is painted its original bright cream.

Less than a half-block south of the Haughwout Building is the **Roosevelt Building** (1874; Richard Morris Hunt), 478–482 Broadway, one of two cast-iron buildings by an architect better remembered for the base of the Statue of Liberty and the facade of the Metropolitan Museum of Art. The decoration (tracery arches at the fourth floor, an outleaning fifth-floor cornice, neo-Grec motifs on the ground-floor pilasters) is quite original, in no way imitating stonework. Roosevelt Hospital inherited the site from James H. Roosevelt, who lived and practiced law here (1843–61), and constructed the building as an investment. It extends through the block to Crosby St, where its narrow rear facade echoes the side facing Broadway.

Broome Street

Return to Broome St and turn left. Broome St was named in 1806 after John Broome, a prominent businessman involved early in the China trade.

History

Previously called Bayard Lane, the street led across the Bayard family farm to the Bowery Rd past Bayard's Mount, once the highest point in the developed part of Manhattan. When the hill was leveled between 1807 and 1811, and its earth dumped as landfill into the Collect Pond (see Foley Square in Walk 5), Broome St became a major east–west access route, a function it still maintains, linking the Holland Tunnel with the Williamsburg Bridge. Its function as a crosstown artery made it the target of Robert Moses's missionary zeal; his projected Lower Manhattan Expwy, an elevated highway above Broome St, would have carried heavy traffic from tunnel to bridge across the midsection of what is now SoHo. Moses's plan, conceived as early as World War II, was rejected by the Board of Estimate in 1968.

One building in from the corner on the north side of the street is **448 Broome St** (1875; Frederick Clarke Withers), a warehouse with unusual floral and filigree decorations. It is the only known cast-iron building by the architect responsible for the Church of the Good Shepherd on Roosevelt Island and the Jefferson Market Court House.

Continue west. On the south side of the street is a fine stretch of cast-iron architecture, including **453–455 Broome St** (1873; Griffith Thomas), a six-story structure originally home to the Welcome G. Hitchcock silk and veilings firm. Hitchcock came to New York as a poor boy from Montrose, Pennsylvania, and, according to a contemporary, achieved success by "industry, economy, ability, fidelity to each and every obligation, knowledge of his business, and proper consideration of his customers." Among his partners were Aaron Arnold and James Constable, founders of the Arnold Constable Department Store. From 1969 to 1994, the building housed A. Millner Company, a specialty food importing business; today the trendy **Gourmet Garage** occupies the ground floor.

Continue west on Broome St across Greene St. At **464–466 Broome St,** on the northeast corner of the intersection, is a building (1861) constructed for Aaron Arnold of the Arnold Constable Dry Goods Co., who left it to his son and daughter.

The Drawing Center

35 Wooster St, New York, NY 10013. ☎ (212) 219-2166. Open Tues–Fri 10–6; Sat 11–6. Suggested donation. Accessible to wheelchairs (lift available). Exhibitions, lectures, symposia, workshops.

Subway: Broadway–Seventh Ave Local (1, 9), Lexington Ave Local (6), Eighth Ave Express or Local (A, C, E), Broadway Local (N, R), or Nassau St Express or Local (J, M, Z) to Canal St. Bus: M1, M6, M21.

Continue west on Broome St; turn left (south) on Wooster St to the Drawing Center, a nonprofit exhibition space devoted to fostering appreciation of drawing as a major art form. The Drawing Center, founded in 1976, mounts six to seven exhibitions yearly both in its main space at 35 Wooster St and across the street in the **Drawing Room** at 40 Wooster St. Exhibitions have included work by Victor Hugo and Willem de Kooning, computer-generated art, and wall drawings.

Return to Broome St. On the northwest corner of Wooster St, **484–490 Broome St** (1890; Alfred Zucker) is a fine Romanesque revival brick-and-rockface brownstone building. It was once the warehouse and salesrooms of a company dealing in dry goods and tailors' trimmings.

Walk west on Broome St and turn right on Sullivan St, temporarily stepping outside the historic district to explore what locals still call the "South Village." The Italian population is dwindling, but some neighborhood institutions survive among the new arrivals. Just past the **Sullivan Street Bakery** (73 Sullivan St), known for its breads, is a charming pair of Federal-style town houses at **83–85 Sullivan St** (1819; DL), the only two remaining on a block once filled with them. Originally one-family, 2½-story homes, third floors were added when they became multiple dwellings.

Continue north on Sullivan St to the northwest corner of Spring St; **Frank's Hairstylists** retains the ambience of the old neighborhood. Walk north on Sullivan St to another pristine Federal-style row house at **116 Sullivan St** (1832; DL), notable for its doorway, which is topped with a fanlight and flanked by Ionic colonnettes and intricate sidelights whose design simulates a cloth curtain drawn through a series of rings.

Continue north to Prince St and turn left. The beautifully restored Federal house at **203 Prince St** (1834; third-floor addition, 1888; DL) stands on part of the former Aaron Burr estate.

Turn around and walk east on Prince St. Since 1920 the **Vesuvio Bakery,** 160 Prince St, has been a neighborhood institution and a family business, turning out handmade Italian bread.

Return to Sullivan St and walk north to the northwest corner of Houston St, widened when the IND subway tunnels were carved out in 1936. **Joe's Dairy,** 156 Sullivan St, a neighborhood fixture for 75 years, is known for its mozzarella cheese. It is a gathering spot for local men, who roost on folding chairs and watch the world go by.

West Broadway

Walk two blocks east to West Broadway. Turn right. Long SoHo's main drag, West Broadway is known for shopping, restaurants, and galleries. Like its mirror, East Broadway, the street got its name from its intended function, relieving the congested traffic on Broadway, which is four blocks east. It is also SoHo's widest street and the western boundary of the SoHo–Cast Iron Historic District. Since only the east side of the street lies within the protected district, the building fronts on the west side have been altered extensively.

At **472–478 West Broadway** is a one-time brick warehouse whose first-floor pilasters have been decorated with floral designs including cast-iron sunflowers. Next door, **468 West Broadway** is a brick Romanesque revival building (c. 1885) with round arches relieved by cast-iron floral swags in the spandrels.

The block between Spring and Prince Sts was once the center of SoHo's gallery scene, with **420 West Broadway** standing at ground zero. It was long the home of the legendary **Leo Castelli Gallery,** which moved downtown from 57th St in 1971 and relocated to 59 E. 79th St after Castelli's death in 1999.

Leo Castelli

Leo Castelli (1907–1999) has long been acknowledged as a major force in contemporary art and the dean of the pop art movement. He made his name representing Jasper Johns, Robert Rauschenberg, Roy Lichtenstein, and Andy Warhol and thereafter showed minimalists, conceptualists, and neo-expressionists. Castelli was famous for discovering unknown artists and nurturing them through long careers and for convincing Europeans of the importance of American art.

Continue south past Spring St to **393 West Broadway.** Installed upstairs here is an 18¾-ton exhibition sponsored by the Dia Center for the Arts (see Walk 12). *The Broken Kilometer* (1979), by Walter De Maria, consists of 500 highly polished, round solid-brass rods, each measuring two meters in length and five centimeters in diameter. The 500 rods are placed in five parallel rows of 100 rods each; if joined end to end they would measure 3,280 ft. The free exhibition is open Wed–Sat 12–6 (closed 3–3:30; closed summers).

Return to Houston St; walk east one block to Wooster St; turn right. Upstairs at **141 Wooster St** is *The New York Earth Room* (1977), a 280,000-pound interior earth sculpture by Walter De Maria, another exhibition installed by Dia. The work—250 cubic yds of dark, moist soil covering the floor of a stark white room to a depth of 22 inches—takes up 3,600 square ft of floor space. Raked and watered weekly, the exhibit tickles the nose with the moist reality of freshly tilled soil and summons up an urge to plant; it has been a welcome refuge in this rapidly changing neighborhood since it opened to the public in 1980. Open Sept–June Wed–Sat 12–6; closed 3–3:30; ring bell to left of door for entry. Free. ☎ (212) 473-8072.

Return to Houston St and walk one block east to Greene St, named after Revolutionary War general Nathanael Greene. The brick Federal house (c. 1824) at **139 Greene St** is still graced by its original dormers and lintels and is one of the few buildings remaining from SoHo's early period of residential development.

Across the street is **142 Greene St** (1871; Henry Fernbach). Behind most cast-iron fronts are buildings of conventional internal structure with brick-bearing walls, wooden beams, and joists supporting wooden floors. But occasional buildings, like this one, have a system of slender cast-iron columns supporting the floors, an arrangement that permits a very open interior. Such columns, usually painted white, were often fluted and embellished with elaborate Corinthian capitals.

Walk south on Greene St. The elaborate building (1883; Henry Fernbach) at **121–123 Greene St**—with its fluted pilasters, Corinthian columns, and ornate cornice, all painted a smooth cream color—is a fine example of this prolific architect's work. The sidewalks are granite, some with their original self-curbing.

Continue south to Prince St. On the northwest corner of the intersection is **109 Prince St** (1882; Jarvis Morgan Slade), a cast-iron building with a chamfered entrance, built as a warehouse. The foundry label for "Architectural Iron Works, Cheney & Hewlett" is visible on the base of the column at the corner of Greene St.

At the south corner of the same intersection is a famous trompe l'oeil **mural** (1973) by Richard Haas, sponsored by City Walls Inc., an organization dedicated to enlivening such blank outdoor surfaces. With wit and precision the mural imitates in paint on the brick east wall of the building (1889; Richard Berger) the cast-iron detail of the northern facade. The cast iron in turn imitates masonry construction—banded corner pilasters resembling masonry blocks, colonnettes standing on pedestals, protruding cornices ending in decorative blocks.

The buildings on the north side of the street, **113–115, 117–119,** and **121 Prince St** (1890; Cleverdon & Putzel), were built as warehouses; the facades are lavishly ornamented with geometric, floral, foliate, and heraldic motifs, egg and dart moldings, and scrollwork. Like many of SoHo's architectural gems, they now house high-end retailers.

Return to the intersection of Greene and Prince Sts and continue south on Greene St, taking note of the cobblestone streets. The building at **114–120**

Greene St (1882; Henry Fernbach) was built as a branch of the Frederick Loeser Department Store, whose flagship store was in Brooklyn; **113 Greene St** (1883; Henry Fernbach), across the street, was built as a shop and warehouse for a seller of caps and imported headgear. A cast-iron ground-floor facade was added to this masonry building. The unusual and restrained ornamentation includes an Art Nouveau molding with entwined leaves below the architrave and incised ornament on the vertical supports flanking the central door and at the edges of the building.

On the same side (west) of Greene St are three cast-iron buildings (93–95, 97, and 99), all designed in the neo-Grec style by Henry Fernbach in 1881.

Continue south to **Spring St,** named after a spring tapped by Aaron Burr's Manhattan Water Company, whose ostensible purpose was to supply drinking water but which quickly evolved into a banking company (see Chase Manhattan Bank in Walk 3). Local legend maintains that a well at Broadway and Spring St became the grave of one Juliana (or Gulielma) Elmore Sands, whose body minus shoes, hat, and shawl was found floating there on Jan 2, 1800. Her fiancé was acquitted of the crime, but her ghost has been seen occasionally in the area; in 1974 a resident of 535 Broadway (at Spring St) reported that a gray-haired apparition wearing mossy garments emerged from his waterbed. The same year the spring burst its underground channel and flooded a basement on West Broadway.

The building at **72–76 Greene St** (1872; J. F. Duckworth), is actually two structures designed as one. The monogram on the central pilaster between the doorways belongs to the Gardner Colby Co., which used the building as a warehouse. Most of the other buildings on the block, designed by Henry Fernbach and John B. Snook in the early 1870s, were used by firms dealing in rug clippings, wool rags, and fabric remnants but now have been converted into galleries and antique shops. The building at **66 Greene St** (1873; John B. Snook) was built as a store for P. Lorillard and Company, the tobacco firm.

Further down Greene St, at the southwest corner of Broome St (469–475 Broome St), is the **Gunther Building** (1871–72; Griffith Thomas), built as a warehouse for the furrier William H. Gunther. The elegant corner turning with curved panes of glass is a notable feature of this cast-iron building, which now consists of luxury condos.

Cross Broome St; **44** and **46–50 Greene St** are masonry structures with cast-iron ornaments. The ground-floor pilasters of 46–50 Greene St (1860) are decorated with scrollwork and ornate medallions bolted onto the long horizontal panels of the pilasters. Some of the acanthus leaves, cast separately and bolted to the capitals, have fallen off.

Artists Space

38 Greene St, 3rd floor, New York, NY 10013. ☎ (212) 226-3970. Web site: www.artistsspace.org. Open Tues–Sat 1–6. Closed major holidays, the month of Aug, and Dec 25–Jan 1. Free admission to gallery; admission charge for events. Exhibitions, music, films, lectures, publications. Accessible to wheelchairs; ramp and elevator available.

Subway: Lexington Ave Local (6) to Spring or Canal St. Eighth Ave Local (C, E) to Spring or Canal St. Broadway Local (N, R) to Prince St or Canal St. Broadway–Seventh Ave Express or Local (1, 2, 3, 9) to Canal St. Nassau St Express or Local (J, M, Z) to Canal St. Bus: M1, M6.

Between Broome and Grand Sts is Artists Space, a nonprofit organization founded in 1972 in TriBeCa to help emerging and unaffiliated artists find a place to show their work. It works to encourage experimentation in the arts by mounting exhibitions that are not influenced by what is currently successful. Artists Space maintains a digitized image database and slide registry of works by more than 3,500 contemporary artists.

Continue south to Grand St and turn left (east). The buildings at **91** and **93 Grand St** (1869; John B. Snook) are iron-fronted, resolutely imitating stone. The iron plates, cast in large sections and bolted through the brick front wall of the house, are grooved to look like uniform blocks of stone mortared together. The houses, which originally cost $6,000 apiece, were built in 4½ months from a design offered in the catalog of ironworker J. L. Jackson & Bros.; attached to the west pier of 91 Grand St is the company's foundry label. The columns of **89 Grand St** (1885) are identical to those of 31 and 72 Grand St, no doubt cast from the same mold.

Return to Greene St and continue south. The vista along this block has hardly changed since the 19C; it reveals the city's longest continuous row of cast-iron architecture, from **8 to 34 Greene St**, as well as several other superlative examples of the form: 34 Greene St (1873) by Charles Wright; 28–30 Greene St (1872) and 32 Greene St (1873) by J. F. Duckworth; 16–18 Greene St (1880) and 20–26 Greene St (1880) by Samuel A. Warner; 8 Greene St (1883) and 10–14 Greene St (1896) by John B. Snook. As the dates indicate, SoHo became industrial very rapidly in the 1870s and 1880s. Many of these buildings were erected with retail space on the ground floor and lofts for warehouses or workshops above.

The "Queen of Greene Street"

On the block between Grand and Canal Sts proudly stands the "Queen of Greene Street" (1872; J. F. Duckworth), 28–30 Greene St, a grandly ornate Second Empire building crowned with a stupendous mansard roof and painted a pale gray-blue. The tall, broad windows flanked by half-round columns, the central two-window bay rising the full height of the building to a broken pediment, and the elaborate dormers offer a wealth of architectural ornament.

History

During the 1850s, when nearby Broadway sparkled with theaters, hotels, and casinos, Greene and Mercer Sts were notorious for their brothels. While the houses on the south end of the streets near Canal St catered to sailors from the ships docked in the Hudson, the houses further north appealed to a wealthier clientele. An 1859 Directory to the Seraglios in New York written by an anonymous "Free Loveyer" recommends a Miss Clara Gordon at 119 Mercer St, "beautiful, entertaining and supremely seductive," who is patronized by Southern merchants and planters, and a Mrs. Bailey of 76 Greene St, whose comfortable and quiet "resort" is within a few moments' walk of Broadway and the principal hotels.

Canal Street

Continue south to Canal St, a shock after the fashionable streets of inner SoHo. The street is both a gateway to Chinatown and a chaotic bazaar of nuts, bolts, spare machine parts, Plexiglas and Lucite, sheet metal, tools, surplus office furniture, assorted cheap goods, and novelties.

History

Canal St owes both its name and its exceptional width to a canal proposed by the city fathers in 1805 to serve as a storm drain, a household sewer, and a conduit siphoning off the waters of the Collect Pond (near present Foley Square). By the 1820s both street and canal had been paved over, a mixed blessing: while the covered sewer alleviated the mosquito problem, the stench it created depressed both property values and morale until adequate air traps were installed.

Turn left (east) and walk a block along Canal St to Mercer St. On the northeast corner of Canal and Mercer Sts stands the former **Marble House** (1856–65; Griffith Thomas), 307–311 Canal St, now covered with graffiti and in sad decline from its heyday as home of the Arnold Constable Dry Goods Store. Only the Canal St facade of Marble House actually involved marble; the sides and rear of the building made do with humble brickwork. During the 1850s and 1860s the neighborhood boasted several fine stores, including Lord & Taylor, ultimately the victor in its perennial rivalry with Arnold Constable's store, then located a block north at Broadway and Grand St.

Turn left on Mercer St, still paved with its 19C Belgian blocks and named after Hugh Mercer, a surgeon and brigadier general in the Revolutionary War. The building at **11 Mercer St** (1870; F. E. Graef) began as a warehouse for the India Rubber Company. It still retains its vault cover, also known as an illuminated sidewalk or light platform, with glass disks embedded in the iron stoop to admit sunlight to the storage vault below.

If you are a hard-core cast-iron enthusiast, go back down Mercer St and walk a block east along Canal St past Broadway to Lafayette St. On the southwest corner of the intersection is **254–260 Canal St** (1857), an early cast-iron building whose Italianate half-round window arches and Medusa-head keystones over the fourth-floor windows suggest that it may have been designed by James Bogardus.

Charlton-King-Vandam Historic District

Below Houston St to the west of SoHo is a neighborhood without a name. Included in this roughly half-mile-square tract is the Charlton-King-Vandam Historic District, whose Federal houses date from the 1820s and 1830s.

History

In the 18C the district belonged to Abraham Mortier, who built (c. 1767) a fine mansion overlooking the Hudson. Washington used it for his headquarters; John and Abigail Adams lived there while he was vice president in 1789; Aaron Burr bought it in 1793 to further his colossal social ambitions. Never one to overlook his business interests, Burr had the estate mapped for development in 1797 and laid out the present Vandam, King, and Charlton Sts. In 1817 he sold the property to John Jacob Astor, who cut down the hill and sold off the land as 25 × 100 ft building lots to the speculators who constructed the present houses. (The mansion was demolished in 1849.) The first homeowners were lawyers, builders, and merchants whose livelihood was tied to the Hudson River wharves nearby.

The best preserved street in the district is **Charlton St,** which has the longest unbroken row of Federal houses in the city. They have brick facades laid in Flemish bond; doorway and window trim of modest brownstone, granite, or more refined marble; high stoops guarded by wrought-iron railings, sometimes with hollow cage newel posts; paneled front doors surrounded by leaded top- and sidelights; and steep roofs pierced by dormers.

New York City Fire Museum

278 Spring St (between Hudson and Varick Sts), New York, NY 10013. ☎ (212) 691-1303. Web site: www.nycfiremuseum.org. Open Tues–Sun 10–4. Closed Mon, holidays.

Admission charge. Gift shop. Accessible to wheelchairs.

Subway: Broadway–Seventh Ave Local (1, 9) to Houston St; walk three blocks south on Varick to Spring St. Eighth Ave Local (C, E) to Spring St; walk west past Varick St. Bus: M21.

Outside the historic district, at 278 Spring St, is the New York City Fire Museum, housed in the Renaissance revival former Engine Company 30 (1904–5; Edward Pierce Casey). The museum, which opened in 1987, has one of the nation's most important collections of fire equipment and memorabilia, including horse-drawn vehicles and hand pumpers dating back to colonial times, and early motorized vehicles. There are exhibits on the city's most famous fires, as well as toy fire engines from the 19C–20C, and antique equipment from the days when firefighters were eager volunteers.

Ear Inn

Further west at 326 Spring St, between Greenwich and Washington Sts, is the wooden gambrel-roofed **James Brown House** (1817; DL), which has allegedly held a tavern since it was built, making it the winner in the contest for the city's oldest continuously operating watering hole (see Bridge Café in Walk 2). Brown, an African American, is believed to have been an aide to George Washington and to have worked as a tobacco trader after the Revolutionary War.

History

Before landfill moved the shoreline west, the house stood on the edge of the Hudson River. Once it was a dive called the Green Door, frequented by sailors and prostitutes; more recently it has attracted an artier crowd, including Salvador Dalí and John Lennon. Since the 1970s it has been owned by Richard Hayman, who named it the Ear Inn by painting over parts of the B in the 1940s neon BAR sign. Today's customers range from artists to "suits," attracted at least in part by the good food.

9 · TriBeCa

Subway: Broadway–Seventh Ave Local (1, 9) to Canal St or Franklin St. Seventh Ave Express (2, 3) to Chambers St. Eighth Ave Express or Local (A, C, E) to Canal St.
Bus: M1, M6.

TriBeCa didn't exist in name until the 1970s when a realtor created the acronym from *Tri*angle *Be*low *Ca*nal St as a marketing ploy; before that it was simply the Lower West Side. The neighborhood is actually trapezoidal, bounded by Canal St, Broadway, Vesey St, and the Hudson River. Like SoHo, it is rapidly gentrifying.

History

TriBeCa left its rural roots behind in the early 19C as the city proceeded northward, becoming a well-to-do residential area with 2½- and 3½-story brick and brick-and-frame Federal houses. St. John's Park, an elegant open space anchored by St. John's Chapel (an outpost of Trinity Church that resembled St. Paul's Chapel), occupied the area bounded by Hudson, Varick, and Laight Sts and Ericsson Place. Businesses started intruding into the neighborhood's residential quiet as early as the 1840s, but the neighborhood was doomed in 1866 when Commodore Cornelius Vanderbilt bought the park for $1 million, felled the trees, and constructed a freight warehouse for the Hudson River Railroad. Today the ramps for the Holland Tunnel occupy the site of the park.

The Holland Tunnel

The Holland Tunnel, the first Hudson River vehicular tunnel, was completed in 1927 and named after its chief engineer, Clifford M. Holland. Today, operated by the Port Authority of New York and New Jersey, it annually carries more than 17 million cars eastbound—the direction in which the tolls are collected.

After the Civil War, many of the earlier houses and shops were torn down in favor of larger industrial buildings. Thus, like SoHo to the north, TriBeCa has substantial offerings of cast-iron architecture. TriBeCa achieved economic importance with the opening of the **Washington Market** (1880s), a wholesale distribution center for meat and produce, cheese, butter, eggs, and candy. The market building occupied the square bounded by Fulton, Vesey, Washington, and West Sts (Washington St formerly ran one block west of Greenwich St). Inside were stalls that offered everything from codfish tongues to bear steaks. Warehouses and market-related businesses spread into the surrounding streets, reaching from Washington St to West St, and as far north as Canal St by the third decade of the 20C. By 1939, Washington Market had a greater volume of business than all other markets in the city combined.

In the early 1960s, fruit and produce distribution moved to Hunts Point in the Bronx and many of the old market buildings were demolished for urban renewal.

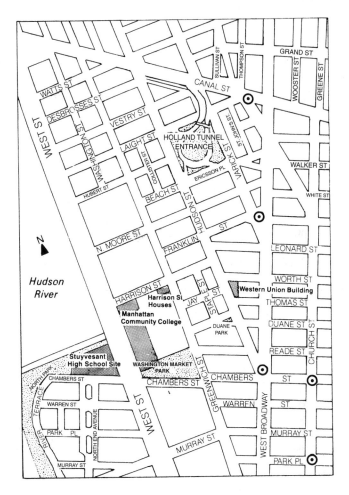

The last butter-and-egg dealer, Steve Wils, moved his family business, Harry Wils & Co., from Duane St to Secaucus, New Jersey, in 1998. Beginning in 1976, zoning changes permitted residential loft conversions, transforming the neighborhood from a market and industrial area to a middle-class residential and commercial neighborhood. As nearby SoHo became expensive, TriBeCa began attracting artists, galleries, museums, and avant-garde clubs. The most famous was the Mudd Club (1978). One of downtown's earliest nightclubs, it has been celebrated in song by the Talking Heads in "Life During Wartime" and by Frank Zappa in "Mudd Club."

In the 1980s and 1990s, the neighborhood saw the arrival of luxury condominiums and chic restaurants, attracting the wealthy, the hip, and the celebrated, including the late John F. Kennedy Jr. and movie star Robert De Niro. De Niro, in fact, was one of the driving forces behind the new chic TriBeCa, with a television and film production company and various restaurant partnerships (including Montrachet, the Tribeca Grill, Tribakery, Nobu, and Layla).

Gentrification in TriBeCa reached a fever pitch in the late 1990s, sending some pioneers packing for less expensive neighborhoods. Further signs of change include the presence of the four-story neon red umbrella, logo of the Travelers Group, on its building at 388 Greenwich St and the arrival of the **TriBeCa Grand Hotel** (2 Sixth Ave, between Walker and Church Sts). The 203-room hotel—with a screening room, open-air atrium, restaurant, and business center—was built by Hartz Mountain Industries, developer of the successful SoHo Grand Hotel. In addition, Franklin and Duane Sts have evolved from a gritty stretch into an "antiques row," with shops moving downtown from the Upper East Side and SoHo. Despite TriBeCa's new personality, many of the community's historic and architecturally significant buildings have been protected from indiscriminate change by the creation of four historic districts: TriBeCa North, TriBeCa East, TriBeCa West and TriBeCa South.

Begin at Canal St and Broadway. Walk south on Broadway past Lispenard St. The paterfamilias of the Lispenard family was Antoine L'Espinard, who fled religious persecution in France in the 17C. A later Anthony Lispenard became an important figure in local politics and married Alice Rutgers in 1741. During the early 18C, the low-lying rural was called Lispenard Meadows.

Continue past Walker St, named for Benjamin Walker, a captain of the Second New York Regiment during the Revolution and a representative to Congress. Continue two blocks south on Broadway to Franklin St and the **James S. White Building** (1881–82; W. Wheeler Smith; DL), 361 Broadway, a cast-iron palazzo with beautifully decorated columns. Between 1853 and 1859, photographer Mathew Brady's portrait studio occupied the three top floors of the Italianate stone building next door, **359 Broadway** (1852; DL). Brady photographed many of the celebrities of his day, including Abraham Lincoln, but his photos of the Civil War earned him a place in the annals of American photography.

Turn left on Franklin St, then left to the southwest corner of Franklin Place and White St. The building at **55 White St** (1861; John Kellum & Son; DL) was deemed so handsome by Daniel D. Badger, whose architectural ironworks cast the facade, that he featured it in his 1865 catalog. The building was commissioned by saddlers Samuel I. and John Elliot Condict; in later years drapers and textile firms tenanted the space.

The triangular pediment of 46–50 White St identifies the **Woods Mercantile Buildings** (1865; DL), two Italianate buildings designed as one. They are faced in Tuckahoe marble and have cast-iron shop fronts. Across the street at 49 White St (between Broadway and Church St) is the **Civic Center Synagogue** (1967; William N. Breger Assocs.), a modern building with an undulating marble facade, starkly out of place with its 19C neighbors. The **Synagogue for the Arts Gallery Space** opened in 1994. For information, ☎ (212) 966-7141.

Walk to the corner of Sixth Ave and White St, and turn right to 32 Sixth Ave, the former **Long Distance Building of the American Telephone & Telegraph Company** (1930–32; Voorhees, Gmelin & Walker; DL). When completed, this Art Deco building contained the largest long-distance communications center in the world, through which every overseas phone call to or from America was routed.

Inside the large bronze doors a tile wall map of the world proclaims: "Telephone Wires and Radio Unite to Make Neighbors of Nations." The floor is terrazzo and the ceiling features an earth-toned mosaic whose allegorical figures link the world. The building was AT&T's headquarters from 1992 to 1999, when it was sold to a developer.

Cross the triangle to 260 West Broadway, the former **American Thread Building** (1897), one of the first TriBeCa buildings converted to condominiums (1982; Stephen B. Jacobs).

Continue south on West Broadway to the northeast corner of West Broadway and White St. The small, brick-and-frame two-story Federal house with its original gambrel roof and dormers at **2 White St** (1809; DL) dates back to the time when the neighborhood was residential. This house was built for the plaster factory owner Gideon Tucker. The bottom floor, always a shop and long a liquor store, is now the **Liquor Store Bar.**

Continue south down West Broadway. One of the more colorful spots in this somber industrial neighborhood is **El Teddy's,** a Mexican restaurant, 219 West Broadway, whose funk decor features a wavy stained glass mosaic canopy and glitter-sprayed ceilings. On top is a 2,500-pound replica of the Statue of Liberty's crown (1985; Antonio Miralda).

Continue south on West Broadway. Turn left onto Leonard St, named for Leonard Lispenard, son of Anthony. At 74 Leonard St (between Broadway and Church St) is the **Knitting Factory,** founded (1987) in the East Village. The club, now an institution in New York night life, moved to TriBeCa in 1994. It has two bars, a video and recording studio, and its own music label, Shimmy Disc. Live concerts range from klezmer music to a popular annual jazz festival.

At **85 Leonard St** (1861; James Bogardus; DL) is the only structure in the city that can be positively attributed to James Bogardus. (Two other buildings in TriBeCa, 75 Murray St and 254–260 Canal St, are also thought to be his work.) Bogardus, the father of cast-iron architecture, foresaw the possibilities of bolting together sections of cast iron to make facades or even whole buildings. This building is practically a catalog of decorative possibilities, featuring fluted columns, lions' heads, rope moldings, dentiled moldings, bearded faces, faceted keystones, egg-and-dart trim, stylized leaves, and (best of all for cast-iron fanciers) Bogardus's own nameplate, embossed in the window ledge to the left of the door: JAMES BOGARDUS, ORIGINATOR AND PATENTEE OF IRON BUILDINGS. MAY 7, 1856.

Return to West Broadway and walk south. The **Western Union Building** (1928–30; Voorhees, Gmelin & Walker; DL), between Thomas and Worth Sts (main entrance at 60 Hudson St), is a massive Art Deco building by the architects of the Barclay-Vesey Building (see Walk 4) and the Long Distance Building. Nineteen tons of brick shade the facade from deep red brown at the bottom to bright salmon at the top. When it opened, the building housed telephone, telegraph, and ticker machinery, and classrooms where Western Union messenger boys could continue high school; today it is a modern telecommunications center. The lobby gloriously exemplifies Art Deco materials and techniques, finished in brown brick, with recessed lighting and geometrically patterned brickwork. Wall sconces cast mysterious shadows, elegant grillwork abounds, and large leaded glass windows in bronze casings let in sunlight at both ends.

Return to West Broadway and continue downtown. On the southeast corner of Thomas St, named for Thomas Lispenard, another son of Anthony Lispenard, is the **Odeon,** 145 West Broadway, converted in 1980 from an Art Deco 1930s cafeteria to a restaurant. It was the first of many stylish restaurants to follow the artists to TriBeCa.

At **147 West Broadway** (1869; John O'Neil), near the southeast corner of Thomas St, is a cast-iron building that closely imitates stone—look at the incised blocks on the facade and the quoins on the corners. Early cast-iron buildings, like this one, often simulated stone; later ones, exploiting the natural properties of cast iron, were often more elaborate.

Continue south past Reade St to Chambers St. At 125 Chambers St (corner of West Broadway) is possibly New York's oldest extant hotel. Formerly the Hotel Bond (c. 1850), it was renovated and reopened in 1995 as the **Cosmopolitan Hotel,** a budget hotel catering to tourists.

Continue south on West Broadway to the northwest corner of West Broadway and Warren St. An inscribed block embedded in the brick identifies West Broadway as College Place. Between 1760 and 1857, Kings College, now Columbia University, occupied the blocks bounded by West Broadway, Murray, Church, and Barclay Sts, the first of its locations in the city.

Continue south on West Broadway to Murray St, named after Joseph Murray, a pre–Revolutionary War lawyer. In 1728 Murray and John Chambers, another lawyer and contributor to Trinity Church, were commended by the Common Council and given the "freedom of the city" (presumably something like getting the key to the city today) for refunding the five-pound fees they had been paid for legal work. Walk west toward the river. At **75 Murray St** (1857; DL), originally the glassware business of Francis and John Hopkins, is one of the earliest extant cast-iron fronts in the city, possibly designed by James Bogardus. Italianate in style, it still retains Medusa-headed keystones over the arches on the third and fifth floors. Medusa-headed keystones also appear on 254–260 Canal St, which is usually attributed to Bogardus (see Walk 8).

Continue west to **Greenwich St** and turn right (north). Greenwich St was so named because when New York was centered south of Wall St, it was the high road out of town to Greenwich Village. Many of the industrial buildings along Greenwich St were formerly occupied by food wholesalers and processors serving the nearby Washington Market. When Washington Market closed in the 1960s, many buildings were razed as part of the Washington Market Urban Renewal project. They were replaced by a park and new buildings, including **P.S. 234** (1988; Richard Dattner) on the northwest corner of Warren and Greenwich Sts. Its imaginative design (for example, the iron gates decorated with sailing ships) suggests a childlike whimsy. Next to the school is **Washington Market Park** (1983), on the site of part of the former market.

Walk north to Duane St, turn right and walk inland a block. **Duane Park** (between Greenwich and Hudson Sts), a small triangle with benches and plantings, was the first park created by the city after the Revolution. In 1636 this land belonged to Annetje Jans, the widow of a Dutch farmer and a sharp businesswoman. The farm was later sold to the English governor and then given to the duke of York, who in turn gave it to Trinity Church. The city bought it in 1795 for a park, at a bargain-basement price of $5.

Duane St, between the park and Greenwich St, has a collection of small, late-19C Italianate and Romanesque revival buildings, including **173–175 Duane St**

(1879; Babb & Cook), one of the area's earliest Romanesque revival buildings. In the Aug 1884 edition of *Century,* the architectural critic Mariana van Rensselaer called it "a simple but successful solution to the problem of warehouse design." The Dutch Renaissance–inspired brick building with curving gable at **168 Duane St** (1886–87; Stephen Decatur Hatch) and the Romanesque revival brick warehouse (1880) on the northwest **corner of Duane and Hudson Sts,** designed for the spice merchant Leopold Schepp, are also notable.

Return to Greenwich St and continue north. The large apartment complexes, Independence Plaza North and Independence Plaza South (1975; Oppenheimer, Brady & Vogelstein), bounded by Greenwich, Duane, Washington, and North Moore Sts, part of the neighborhood's urban renewal, were probably the last middle-income housing to be built in now-trendy TriBeCa.

West of Independence Plaza, bounded by Duane, West, Greenwich, and North Moore Sts, is **Manhattan Community College** (1983; Caudill, Rowlett, Scott, and Assocs.), part of the City University of New York. In the plaza by the college entrance near West and Chambers Sts is Roy Shifrin's *Icarus* (1976), a bronze torso of the mythological flyer who, according to the sculptor, "represents the uncertainties of our age."

In the shadows of Independence Plaza on Harrison St—named for Harrison's Brewery, which stood near the river in pre-Revolutionary days—to the north is a row of nine 18C Federal-style brick town houses known as the **Harrison St houses** (1796–1828; DL), 25–41 Harrison St. During the years when Washington Market thrived, some of them were indiscriminately used as commercial spaces; three of them, formerly around the corner on Washington St, were moved to the L-shaped site when the college was built. The ones at 25 and 27 Harrison St were built by John McComb Jr., New York's first native-born architect (he designed City Hall), who lived in no. 27.

Continue east on Harrison St to the northwest corner of Hudson and Harrison Sts. The former **New York Mercantile Exchange** (1886; Thomas R. Jackson), 6 Harrison St, is a five-story, gabled brick Queen Anne building with a handsome tower looking toward the Hudson River. The tall second-story windows opened onto the trading floor, where on a good day at the turn of the 20C $15,000 worth of eggs changed hands in one hour. The exchange was organized in 1872 as the Butter and Cheese Exchange, for commercial objectives (fostering trade, reforming abuses) and social ones (promoting fellowship, providing for the widows and orphans of members). The building has been converted to condominiums; the present exchange stands on North End Ave, not far south.

On the southwest corner of Harrison and Hudson Sts is **Puffy's Tavern,** which dates back to Prohibition and still has its old-fashioned bar, tile floor, jukebox, and neighborhood atmosphere.

Walk north on Hudson St to Franklin St. The **Pierce Building,** later known as the **Powell Building** (1892; Carrère & Hastings), 105 Hudson St, is a Beaux-Arts building of white limestone, brick and terra-cotta, rich in sculptural detail. Built for Washington Market businesses, it was made taller and wider in 1905.

Turn right onto Franklin St. This block, between Varick and Hudson Sts, has the neighborhood's highest concentration of Romanesque revival brick warehouses. At the corner of Varick and Franklin Sts is the former **D. S. Walter & Company factory** (1887; Albert Wagner), 132 Franklin St, a monumental yellow brick building with two- and four-story arches trimmed in yellow terra-cotta. Its stately clock tower and other roof adornments have disappeared, and it is being renovated into yet another luxury condominium building.

10 · East Village

Subway: Lexington Ave Local (6) to Bleecker St. Sixth Ave Express or Local (B, D, Q, F) to Broadway–Lafayette St.
Bus: M1, M5, or M6 to Houston St.

Once considered part of the Lower East Side, the East Village today boasts an eclectic population of Bowery derelicts; working-class families of many races; students; aging Polish, Russian, and Ukrainian immigrant communities; middle-class, sometimes middle-aged "hippies"; artists; merchants; and punks. Culturally the East Village includes established institutions—Cooper Union, the *Village Voice*, and the New York Public Theater—as well as experimental theaters and ethnic shops and restaurants. Because of historical circumstance—sudden and rapid development as a fine residential area in the early 19C followed by an equally rapid decline when commerce invaded Broadway and immigrants crowded into the Tompkins Square neighborhood—the district preserves in strange juxtaposition architectural traces of its evolution.

History
Starting in the mid-19C, the East Village, like the Lower East Side of which it was the northward extension, has hosted waves of immigration. The immigrants established churches and social clubs and opened restaurants, some of which still remain. In the late 1950s writers and poets arrived, some of them members of the "Beat Generation": Jack Kerouac, Allen Ginsberg, William Burroughs, and Norman Mailer. The 1960s brought an influx of "hippies," who, viewed historically, were just one more wave of immigrants seeking cheap rents and a place to establish new lives. They, too, left their mark on the neighborhood—book and "head" shops (stores selling drug paraphernalia) and avant-garde theatrical establishments.

The lifestyles of these newcomers often ran counter to the values of the aging immigrant society. By the mid-1970s, the decaying neighborhood was beset by drug abuse and crime. But during the early 1980s, despite these problems, the East Village began attracting young professionals driven downtown by the shortage of rental housing elsewhere and attracted by relatively cheap rents. In their wake came upscale restaurants, gourmet food stores, cafés, nightclubs, performance spaces, and a profusion of art galleries. Gentification, as elsewhere, caused tensions between those who had little and those who had more.

In Aug 1988, when the city enforced a 1:00 A.M. curfew in Tompkins Square Park, designed to kick out squatters, anarchists, and drug addicts, a riot broke out, resulting in 40 civilian and 13 police injuries, and more than 100 complaints of police brutality.

In the 1990s, as the city began to recover economically, gentrification of the East Village continued, both for better and for worse. There are fewer drunks, drug addicts, skinheads, homeless men, and antiyuppie anarchists in the streets and park. Many new businesses have opened, mostly bars and restaurants geared

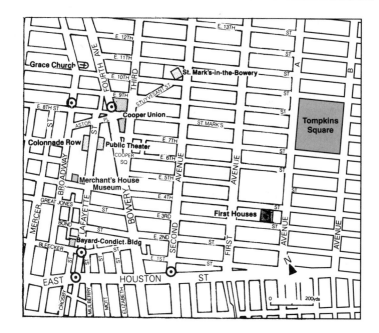

toward new arrivals in their twenties, but also bookstores and new shops located as far east as Alphabet City (Ave A to Ave D).

This former hinterland, long poor and crime-ridden, has begun to get services and conveniences—the first cash machine east of Ave A (Ave B and E. 3rd St), a drug store on Ave D and E. 7th St, and a health club (3rd St, east of Ave A). Tompkins Square Park, where moms with baby carriages are more common than anarchists, has been refurbished and closes at midnight, without protest.

Cable Building

Begin at Broadway and Houston St. In 1999 the city designated a sliver of the East Village (bounded more or less by Wanamaker Place, Lafayette St, Houston St, and Broadway) the **NoHo Historic District** (i.e., North of Houston) to preserve the 19C loft buildings, many of them cast iron. On the northwest corner of this intersection is the former Cable Building (1894; McKim, Mead & White), 611 Broadway, built as an office building and power station for the Metropolitan Traction Company, which operated cable cars along Broadway from 36th St to the Battery. Sculptor J. Massey Rhind (Trinity Church doors) designed the female figures flanking the door.

History

In the basement were huge winding wheels (26 ft in diameter) over which the 1½-inch steel cables were pulled at a steady 30 mph by steam power. The cables weighed 40 tons apiece and pulled 60 cars, which clamped onto lines installed just below the street level. The system operated until 1901, when electricity replaced steam.

Across the street is one of the city's earliest cast-iron buildings, 620 Broadway, named the **"Little Cary Building"** (1858; John B. Snook) because its facade was cast from the same molds as the larger Cary Building (now the Marketplace on the west side of Church St between Chambers and Reade Sts).

The original **New York Mercantile Exchange** (1882; Herman J. Schwarzmann), 628 Broadway, still retains its unusual cast-iron facade adorned with roses, lilies, slender colonnettes ridged to suggest bamboo, and Oriental filigree arches. The **Atrium** (1889; Stephen D. Hatch), 644 Broadway, is a brownstone, terra-cotta, and brick building with intricate cast-iron work and lions adorning the facade.

Continue north on Broadway to Bleecker St and turn right (east); walk a block to Crosby St, named after William Bedlow Crosby (1786–1865). Orphaned at the age of two, Crosby had the good luck to be adopted by his great-uncle Henry Rutgers, whose fortune he inherited and then devoted to good works.

Bayard-Condict Building

The Bayard-Condict Building (1897–99; Louis H. Sullivan; DL), 65–69 Bleecker St, tucked away at the north end of Crosby St, is one of Manhattan's little-known architectural treasures, the city's only building by Louis H. Sullivan. (The best view is from Crosby St near Houston St.)

History

First called the Bayard Building to honor one of the city's oldest families (though no Bayards were involved in the project), this 13-story office tower was undertaken by the United Loan and Investment Co., which hired Sullivan. Already known for his work in Chicago, Sullivan had attracted attention for his radical theories on skyscraper design, which stressed function as a determinant of form, the importance of new building materials, and their influence upon design.

His first plan incorporated a freestanding steel skeleton with 14-inch structural columns and exterior brick walls only 12 inches thick. Unfortunately, the conservative city building code ruled against this design and insisted upon thickening the lower walls and columns. With the loss of floor space and rental income, the United Loan and Investment Co. became unable to afford the building and sold it to Silas and Emmeline Condict.

Exterior

The building reflects Sullivan's dictum that a skyscraper should be a proud and soaring thing. Slender vertical piers over the interior structural columns alternate with even more slender vertical columns between the windows. The sumptuous terra-cotta surface decoration of leafy and geometric forms culminates in an ornate cornice, beneath which hover six angels with outspread wings. Beneath the angels are ten lions with bared teeth.

Return to Broadway; turn right and walk one block north. The ornate building at 670 Broadway at Bond St is a former **Brooks Brothers clothing store** (1874; George E. Harney). The ironwork (attrib. Michael Grosz and Sons) is noteworthy for the geometrically designed bases and graceful leaf forms on the capitals of the street-level columns. Originally located at Cherry and Catherine Sts, where it was looted during the Draft Riots of 1863, Brooks Brothers moved uptown, first to

Broadway and Grand St, then here, then to the 23rd St area, and finally (1915) to its present location at E. 44th St and Madison Ave.

Walk a short block east on Bond St. For a while in the 1830s and 1840s, **Bond St** was the cynosure of fashion, but the creep of commerce up Broadway put an end to its eminence; its fine homes became boarding houses and offices. By 1870 it was solidly commercial. Now converted to apartments, 1–5 Bond St, the former **Robbins & Appleton Building** (1879; Stephen D. Hatch; DL), was built for Henry Robbins and David Appleton, proprietors of the American Waltham Watch Co. The ground floor was also headquarters for publisher D. Appleton & Co., whose torches of learning are above the main doorway. The building, with its tall mansard roof, is a dramatic example of the French Second Empire style. The large expanses of plate glass were made possible by the strength of iron under compression so that a few widely spaced columns could support a sizable facade.

The Bowery

Continue two blocks east on Bond St to the Bowery, one of Manhattan's oldest streets. It runs about one mile, from Chatham Square to Cooper Square, and has long been associated with loneliness, poverty, and alcoholism.

History

Originally an Indian trail, the Bowery got its name from the Dutch word for farm *(bouwerie)* when the area was farmland on the northern fringes of the city. During the 18C the Bowery was part of the Boston Post Rd. In the early 19C, the street was a fine residential neighborhood, though the side streets further downtown (Chrystie, Elizabeth, and Forsyth Sts) had already become a center for slaughterhouses and factories for lard, soap fats, and candles. In the mid-19C, the Bowery glittered with the lights of theaters; it witnessed the first blackface minstrel show in the city, the first stage version of *Uncle Tom's Cabin,* and, in 1892 the first Yiddish theater production.

After about 1870, as the slums encroached on both sides, it began a long slide into poverty, with the arrival of beer halls, distilleries, and cheap lodgings. The worst were flophouses, where the lodger flopped on the floor, his space chalked out for him by the proprietor.

During the Depression the Bowery's cheap hotels, doorways, and all-night restaurants offered the army of the unemployed a place to spend the night, or wait until times got better. In the 1940s and 1950s there were still several bars per block, and until 1968 the Salvation Army operated a mission, doling out free food, coffee, and counseling.

The Bowery has not entirely recovered, but most of the flophouses are gone and certain stretches of the street have come to life. The blocks north of Grand St constitute the center of the city's lighting fixture trade, established here during the gaslight era.

At the corner of Bond St and the Bowery is the **Bouwerie Lane Theatre** (1874; Henry Engelbert; DL), 330 Bowery, built as the Bond Street Savings Bank. The architect, working with a modest 25 × 100 ft building lot, has managed to suggest the massive grandeur formerly associated with bank architecture, a difficult undertaking since the short side of the lot faces the Bowery, the more important thoroughfare. The Corinthian columns, the cornices at every floor, the quoins and rusticated piers all masquerade as stone, though they are cast iron. Since 1974 the building has housed the Jean Cocteau Repertory, one of the longest-running classical theaters in the nation (founded 1971).

Cross the street and turn right. Walk south on the Bowery. At 319 Bowery is the charming 107-seat **Amato Opera Theatre,** home to a company founded in 1948 and still run by Anthony Amato. The Amato Opera's first permanent home was the Bleecker Street Theatre; in 1964, it moved to this building, replacing the Holy Name Mission and a restaurant supply store. The Amato nurtures developing singers and brings opera to the masses at reasonable prices.

Just south of the Amato, opposite the dead end of Bleecker St, is **CBGB,** 315 Bowery, founded in 1974 as a home for country music. Its full name, CBGB & OMFUG, is an acronym for Country, Bluegrass, Blues and Other Music For Uplifting Gourmandizers. As a club for down-home music it failed, but punk and new wave flourished here as CBGB provided a launching pad for such legendary groups as the Talking Heads, the Police, Blondie, and the B-52s.

Return north on the Bowery to E. 2nd St and turn right. Cross Second Ave to the **New York City Marble Cemetery** (1831; DL), 52–74 E. 2nd St, whose handsome monuments and gravestones are visible through the fence. John Ericsson and James Monroe were interred here but later removed; still remaining are early mayor Marinus Willett, several Roosevelts, and Preserved Fish, member of a fine New York family, and seemingly the victim of his parents' fondness for punning. The cemetery name includes the word *city* to distinguish it from its nearby predecessor, the New York Marble Cemetery.

The **New York Marble Cemetery** (1830; DL), on the west side of the street, halfway up the block of Second Ave between E. 2nd and E. 3rd Sts, was the city's first nonsectarian graveyard, built as a commercial venture after burials were outlawed south of Canal St. The vaults are underground, but the names of the families who bought them are inscribed in plaques on the wall. (Not open to the public.)

First Houses

Continue east to First Ave and turn left (north); at E. 3rd St turn right (east) and continue a quarter-block to the **First Houses** (1935–36; N.Y.C. Housing Authority; Frederick L. Ackerman; DL). The first project of the New York City Housing Authority, created during the Depression, the First Houses were rebuilt from existing tenements using work-relief labor and bricks salvaged from demolished buildings. The Housing Authority purchased many of the tenements at a fraction of their value from Vincent Astor, who had inherited them from his grandfather John Jacob Astor, real estate entrepreneur and slumlord. Every third house was demolished to create light and air for the remaining tenements, which had to be reinforced with structural steel after the removal of adjoining structures made them unsound.

History

In two months of 1935, the Housing Authority was flooded with more than 3,000 applications for the 122 units. Social workers chose the tenants, giving preference to those from the worst slums and those with small families. The new apartments, renting for $6.05 per room, were luxurious, each equipped with a refrigerator, a stove, and a bathroom. Though attacked as a boondoggle, the First

Houses remain a source of pride to the city and a residential haven for an ethnically mixed, predominantly elderly group of tenants.

Turn around and walk west on E. 3rd St. At 77 E. 3rd St is the city's Hell's Angels headquarters. Continue past the Bowery, where the block briefly becomes Great Jones St. The land was ceded to the city by Samuel Jones, a prominent lawyer and the city's first comptroller (1796–99), with the stipulation that the street bear his name. New York already had a Jones St; for a while it had two, until Samuel Jones suggested calling his street "Great Jones St."

Continue west. At 44 Great Jones St is the **firehouse of Engine Company 33** (1898; Ernest Flagg and W.B. Chambers; DL), a satisfyingly flamboyant, impeccably maintained Beaux-Arts building dominated by a monumental three-story arch. Among its elegant details: a deep cornice with scroll brackets, tall French windows, and ornamental railings.

Continue west on Great Jones St to Lafayette St. On the northwest corner is **376 Lafayette St** (1888; Henry J. Hardenbergh; DL), also known as the **Schermerhorn Building,** originally a warehouse, designed by the architect better known for the Plaza Hotel and the Dakota Apartments.

De Vinne Press Building

On the northeast corner of the intersection at 399 Lafayette St is the former **De Vinne Press Building** (1885; Babb, Cook & Willard; DL), a stark Romanesque revival building of dark brick with terra-cotta trim. Massive and simple, the De Vinne Press Building is remarkable for its appearance of weight and strength: look at the deeply recessed window arches and the restrained trim on the rounded corner turning.

History

Theodore De Vinne (1828–1914) was a successful printer and distinguished scholar of the history of printing. The De Vinne Press published *Scribner's Monthly* and the *Century* magazine, but De Vinne's more enduring achievements were his edition of the *Book of Common Prayer* and the *Century Dictionary.*

Merchant's House Museum

29 E. 4th Street, New York, NY 10003. ☎ (212) 777-1089. Web site: www. merchantshouse.com. Open Thurs–Mon 1–4. Closed Tues, Wed, major holidays. Admission charge. Changing exhibitions, tours, lectures, special events. Gift shop. Not accessible to wheelchairs.

Subway: Lexington Ave Local (6) to Astor Place. Broadway Local (N, R) to 8th St. 6th Ave Express or Local (B, D, Q, F) or 8th Ave Express or Local (A, C, E) to 4th St. Bus: M1, M5, M6, M101, M102, M103.

Turn right (east) on E. 4th St and walk a half-block to the Merchant's House Museum, a remarkable survivor from the days when the Bond St neighborhood was the city's finest.

History

Known also as the Seabury Tredwell House, the Merchant's House Museum, formerly the Old Merchant's House (1832; attrib. Minard Lafever; DL), was built on speculation by a hat merchant dabbling in real estate. The three-story brick town house was then purchased in 1835 for $18,000 by Seabury Tredwell, a prosperous hardware merchant and importer. (The Tredwells' late Federal, American Empire, and Victorian furniture remains there today.) The house stayed in the family until Tredwell's daughter, Gertrude, died there in 1933. It has been a museum since 1936.

Exterior and Interior

The outside of the house has a steeply slanted dormer roof and a handsomely detailed doorway typical of the late Federal period. Inside are three floors of period rooms, with the Tredwells' original possessions (Gertrude did not throw things away). In the **front parlor** are the Tredwells' gondola chairs covered with black horsehair and a Federal sofa with handcarved eagles. On the third floor are **bedrooms** with Victorian and American Empire furniture.

Small theaters, long an East Village staple, also make their home along E. 4th St, including the **New York Theater Workshop,** 79 E. 4th St, which helped nurture *Rent,* perhaps the most successful new American musical of the 1990s.
    Return to Lafayette St; turn right (north) and walk uptown.

Lafayette Street

In 1804 John Jacob Astor paid $45,000 for the land where Lafayette St now runs. While waiting with his usual acumen for land values to rise, Astor leased it to a Frenchman, who created a pleasure ground called Vauxhall Gardens with summer pavilions where visitors could buy light refreshments and a remodeled greenhouse where those so inclined could indulge in heavier drinking. In 1825 Astor reclaimed the gardens, carved out the street, originally named Lafayette Place, and sold lots facing the new street for more than $45,000 apiece, the price of the entire parcel only 20 years earlier.

John Jacob Astor never lived on Lafayette St, but his son William B. Astor did—opposite Colonnade Row at 34 Lafayette Place, in a house described by a contemporary as a "plain but substantial looking brick mansion."

The **Durst Building** (1891; Alfred Zucker), 409–411 Lafayette St (between E. 4th St and Astor Place), is a cast-iron and brick building with terra-cotta trim, designed for Simon Goldenberg's haberdashery and workshops. On the ground floor are great iron-clad piers and freestanding iron columns ornamented with beaded rings.

Colonnade Row

On the west side of Lafayette St stand the remains of Colonnade Row (1833; attrib. Alexander Jackson Davis; DL), 428–434 Lafayette St, once a highly desirable building, now suffering the indignities of neglect.

History

First named La Grange Terrace, after the country home of the Marquis de Lafayette, Colonnade Row originally had nine houses joined by a monumental two-story colonnade of Corinthian columns. The houses, built on speculation, were faced with white Westchester marble cut by Sing Sing prisoners. They were purchased eagerly by such notables as Franklin Delano, grandfather of Franklin D. Roosevelt. Colonnade Row enjoyed only a brief moment of social splendor, as commerce continued moving up Broadway, depressing residential land values. By the 1860s the Astor Mansion had become a restaurant, a neighborhood church had been converted to a boxing ring, and the five southernmost houses of Colonnade Row opened as the Colonnade Hotel. When Lafayette St was extended south to the City Hall area in the 1880s, the remaining houses on the street became tenements and rooming houses or were torn down to make way for warehouses and factories. In 1901 the Wanamaker warehouse replaced the Colonnade Hotel.

The ground floor is home to the Astor Place Theater; the long-running show *Tubes* performed by Blue Man Group has played there since 1991. (A similar success story, *Stomp*, has played at the Orpheum Theater at 126 Second Ave since 1994.)

Joseph Papp Public Theater
Directly opposite Colonnade Row is the Joseph Papp Public Theater, 425 Lafayette St (between E. 4th St and Astor Place). Originally the Astor Library (south wing, 1849–53, Alexander Saeltzer; center wing, 1856–59, Griffith Thomas; north wing, 1879–81, Thomas Stent; remodeled, 1966, Giorgio Cavaglieri; DL), this complicated building has a complicated pedigree. Architecturally it is a Victorian version of a Renaissance Italian palace.

History
The building opened in 1854 as the Astor Library, the only public benefaction of tightfisted John Jacob Astor, who ostensibly dedicated it to working people but kept it open only during the day when workers couldn't use it. When the Astor Library merged with the Lenox and Tilden collections in 1912 to form the nucleus of the New York Public Library system, the Hebrew Immigrant Aid Society (HIAS) took over and used the building from 1921 to 1965 in its work of resettling eastern European immigrants. In 1966, after HIAS moved out, Joseph Papp convinced the city to buy the building and remodel the interior under the guidance of Giorgio Cavaglieri, renovator of the Jefferson Market Courthouse (see Walk 11).

Joe Papp
Born Yosl Papirofsky in 1921 to poor immigrant parents in Williamsburg, Joe Papp began as a telegraph messenger, laundry delivery man, and chicken plucker, but grew up to become the nation's most important theater impressario of the 20C. He first staged free Shakespeare in 1954 on the Lower East Side and in 1957 moved the New York Shakespeare Festival to Central Park, where it continues today. Brash and temperamental, Papp was a larger-than-life figure who took on and defeated powerful Parks Com-

missioner Robert Moses when Moses threatened the Shakespeare Festival's right to perform in the park in 1959.

Papp's first production in the Public Theater was the 1967 world premiere of *Hair.* Ultimately he produced more than 350 plays, including early works by David Mamet, John Guare, Sam Shepard, and Vaclav Havel. He was one of the first producers to cast blacks and other minority actors in Shakespeare, and he nurtured the careers of James Earl Jones, Meryl Streep, and Kevin Kline. His biggest hit, *A Chorus Line,* ran for a then-record 6,137 performances from 1975 until 1990, providing a financial cushion that allowed Papp to produce more adventurous works. Although he was noisily antiestablishment, when Papp died in 1991 Broadway dimmed its lights. As of this date, the Public has transferred 20 plays to Broadway and earned 32 Tony Awards and 120 Obies along the way.

The building now houses five performance spaces and a movie theater, offering jazz, films, and poetry readings. For the box office, ☎ (212) 260-2400.

Next to the Public Theater, on the south end of Astor Place, is the proposed site of the Astor Place Hotel. Hotelier Ian Schrager, who created the chic Royalton Hotel, working with Cooper Union, which owns the land, has promised a hotel with a visually extraordinary design. Schrager and the developer are paying virtually all of the $9.6 million in rent up front to enable Cooper Union to continue providing free education for its arts students.

Continue north on Lafayette St to Astor Place. On the traffic island on the right (east) side of the intersection is a 15 ft weathering steel cube (1966) by Bernard (Tony) Rosenthal. Balanced on one apex so that it will revolve when pushed, the work is entitled **Alamo,** a name derived from a remark by the sculptor's wife that the piece had the strength and feeling of a fortress.

The **Astor Place subway entrance** across the street (Fourth Ave and E. 8th St) is a cast-iron reproduction (1985) of an original subway kiosk. The station below (1904; Heins & La Farge; DL) is one of the best subway restorations in the city. Milton Glaser designed the new murals.

Across Lafayette St to the west at 13 Astor Place is the **District 65 Building**, originally the Mercantile Library Building (1890; George E. Harney), home of the district offices of the United Auto Workers.

The Astor Place Riot

The building stands on the site of the old Astor Place Opera House, now remembered chiefly for the Astor Place Riot (May 10, 1849). An already bitter theatrical rivalry between English actor William Macready and his American counterpart Edwin Forrest—fanned by working class anti-British and antiaristocratic sentiments—erupted into violence during a performance of *Macbeth.* The audience hurled garbage at Macready while a mob outside assaulted the building with bricks and paving stones. The militia summoned from the nearby Tompkins Market Armory was eventually ordered to fire into the crowd. Estimates of casualties differ, but the usual count is about 30 dead and 150 wounded.

Walk west on Astor Place to Broadway. Once a shopping area filled with funky stores, this stretch of Broadway is increasingly dominated by chain stores. One breath of fresh air, however, is **Audubon House,** 700 Broadway, the city's first environmentally responsible building. Formerly the Schermerhorn Building (1890; George Post), the structure was purchased in 1993 by the National Audubon Society, which spent $24 million proving that commercial spaces can be sound both environmentally and economically. Ordinary office buildings not only consume tremendous amounts of energy but pollute the air, producing 15 percent of the gases that cause acid rain in America. Audubon House has three times the legally required insulation and is "daylighted"—large windows and glass partitions maximize natural light, while occupancy and daylight sensors automatically switch off or dim lights. Food and other biodegradables are mulched in on-site composting machines and used in office planters and the rooftop garden. Floor tiles are partly made from waste glass while bathroom partitions contain plastic from recycled bottles. To avoid "sick building syndrome," the air in Audubon House circulates twice as often as in most buildings.

Walk north on Broadway. Along E. 8th St (north of the District 65 Building) is the one-time annex of the famous **Wanamaker Department Store** (1904, addition 1907; Daniel H. Burnham & Co.), today used by the Parking Violations Bureau.

The next stretch of Broadway was once part of **Ladies' Mile,** which extended from 8th to 23rd Sts and spilled over to Fifth and Sixth Aves. Ladies' Mile was a promenade for women of taste and means, with elegant stores where they could buy the clothing and furnishings essential to displaying their position in society. Much of this area is included in the Ladies' Mile Historic District, which continues in Walk 13.

Grace Church

Continue north along Broadway to E. 10th St, where Grace Church (Protestant Episcopal) lifts its delicate spire. Praised as New York's finest Gothic revival church (1843–47; James Renwick Jr.; DL), it was also once its most socially desirable, especially for weddings. In 1995, the church embarked on a $3-million restoration project, focusing on the marble exterior and the stained glass windows. Parishioners donated more than $1 million.

Exterior

The white marble facade, quarried by Sing Sing convicts as an economy measure, is known for its delicate stonework and fine proportions. The octagonal spire (1888) rising from the central tower replaced a wooden steeple—another economy measure instituted by the building committee. Unfortunately the marble spire cost two-thirds the original cost of the whole church.

Interior

The chancel window known either as the "Te Deum" window or the "Church Tri-umphant" window is by Clayton and Bell (1879), an English firm with a conservative, quasi-medieval style. Henry Holiday's Pre-Raphaelite windows in the north and south aisles represent a bolder attempt to fuse medieval and 19C sensibilities. In the north transept is a bust of architect Renwick.

The Rectory

Leave the church and walk around to its north side. The Rectory (DL), also designed by Renwick at the same time as the church, is one of the city's earliest Gothic revival dwellings, replete with pinnacles, gables, quatrefoil ornamentation, and traceried windows.

James McCreery Dry Goods Store

Across the street from the Rectory is a light gray apartment building, 67 E. 11th St, formerly the James McCreery Dry Goods Store (1868; John Kellum; converted, 1971; Stephen P. Jacobs). Known as the Cast Iron Building, it has a handsome colonnade with three-quarter round Corinthian columns on paneled pedestals along 11th St. The first floor, 20 ft high, has broad glass show windows whose light once flooded the sales counters. The fifth floor is an addition, replacing a mansard roof. James McCreery arrived as an Irish immigrant in 1845 and began trade as a lace merchant. Eventually, McCreery had his own store, which long adhered to its original line, dry goods, and at the end of the 19C was known for its fabrics, especially its silks and woolens, wedding and trousseau gowns. McCreery dedicated his fortune to the arts and became a patron of the Metropolitan Museum of Art. His store moved uptown as fashion dictated, closing finally in 1954.

Grace Memorial House

Walk along E. 10th St, passing the south side of Grace Church, to Fourth Ave and turn left. Grace Memorial House (1882–83; James Renwick Jr.; DL), 94–96 Fourth Ave, is now used by the Grace Church School. By the late 1870s the parish served by Grace Church was no longer exclusively wealthy, and the church needed facilities for its poorer members. Levi P. Morton, vice president of the United States under Benjamin Harrison, donated money in memory of his wife for Grace Memorial House, first a day nursery, then a home for young women of modest means, and still later a rehabilitation center for girls. The building, originally two Greek revival town houses, was altered to its present appearance by Renwick, who added the facade, the gable, and other features. The building at **96 Fourth Ave** was later duplicated by **Clergy House** at 92 Fourth Ave (1902; Heins & La Farge) to make a symmetrical group of buildings. Later **Neighborhood House** (1907; Renwick, Aspinwall, & Tucker), 98 Fourth Ave, was added in the same style.

The stretch of Fourth Ave between Cooper Square and Union Square on 14th St was once **Book Row,** lined with shops for used and antiquarian books. In the 1950s some 50 dealers in this neighborhood offered their wares, but since a used book store requires low rent and high traffic, irreconcilable conditions in New York today, such stores have all but disappeared. (The primary survivor in the area is **Strand Book Store** at Broadway and E. 12th St, which stocks some 2 million books.)

At Fourth Ave and E. 11th St, turn right and walk east. **Webster Hall** (1886; Charles Rentz), 119 E. 11th St, was built as a dance hall and later became a ballroom. During the 1980s, this surprisingly sedate red brick building was a rock club called the Ritz. It is still a place for concerts and dancing but has returned to its original name.

St. Mark's Historic District

Continue east to Third Ave and turn right to E. 10th St. The St. Mark's Historic District lies within the boundaries of Peter Stuyvesant's original farm, or *bouwerie*, purchased in 1651 from the Dutch West India Company, extending from the East River to Fourth Ave and from about present-day 5th to 17th Sts. (The Stuyvesant Mansion's probable foundations were uncovered in 1854 during excavations at 129 E. 10th St.)

History

The governor's great-grandson, Petrus Stuyvesant, developed part of the estate. In the late 1780s his property was mapped into lots along a grid of streets oriented to the points of the compass. Building began around 1800, but the city moved to impose its own scheme for development based on the Commissioners' Plan of 1811, which featured a street grid oriented to the long axis of Manhattan Island. Although the city generally closed existing streets or tore down buildings that did not conform to its plan, the Stuyvesant St neighborhood was allowed to remain, largely in deference to its wealthy families, including the Stuyvesants.

The houses at 112–128 E. 10th St and those directly behind them (23–35 Stuyvesant St) comprise **Renwick Triangle** (1861; attrib. James Renwick Jr.). This group of 16 residences was built on land belonging to Hamilton Fish, who sold it under the condition that no "noxious or offensive establishments"—breweries, slaughter houses, soap or glue factories, tanneries, cattle yards, or blacksmith shops—be built there. Before restrictive zoning laws, such covenants were the sole means of ensuring residential tranquility.

The houses, built in the Anglo-Italianate style with red Philadelphia pressed brick and brownstone trim, have rusticated ground floors, bold cornices, and fully enframed upper-story windows; many have fine cast-iron railings.

Continue along E. 10th St to Stuyvesant St and return west along the other long leg of Renwick Triangle. At 21 Stuyvesant St near Third Ave is the **Stuyvesant-Fish residence** (1803–4; DL), which dates from the earliest period of development of the Stuyvesant property. Built by Petrus Stuyvesant as a wedding present for his daughter Elizabeth and her husband, Nicholas Fish, the house is one of the city's grandest Federal residences, declaring the Stuyvesant wealth in its unusual height and width (28¾ ft). The east windows indicate that it was built as a freestanding (not a row) house. Hamilton Fish (1808–1893), born in this house to Elizabeth and Nicholas Fish, inherited from a childless relative $500,000 and went on to become governor of New York, U.S. senator, and secretary of state.

Cooper Union

Continue southwest along Stuyvesant St, crossing Third Ave to Cooper Square (intersection of E. 7th St, the Bowery, Astor Place, and Fourth Ave). The **Cooper Union Foundation Building** (1859; Frederick A. Peterson; DL; additions 1890s; Leopold Eidlitz; remodeling 1975; John Hejduk) embodies the innovative genius of its founder both in its physical plant and in the institution it houses.

History

Peter Cooper (1791–1883), a self-educated genius, designed the first American locomotive, promoted the Atlantic cable with Cyrus W. Field, and helped develop Morse's telegraph, but made his fortune largely through an ironworks in Trenton, New Jersey, and a glue factory in Baltimore. Unlike others of his breed, Cooper recognized that his wealth had come from the "cooperation of multitudes," and turned his millions to philanthropy. By establishing the Cooper Union as a free educational institution to give students the equivalent of a college degree while stressing also the practical arts and trades, Cooper provided for others the education he would have wished for himself. Requiring no other credentials than a good moral character, Cooper Union opened its doors to women as well as men, to adults as well as young people.

Exterior

Built of brownstone in the Italianate style, the building incorporates some of the first wrought-iron beams used anywhere, beams which Cooper developed from train rails and for which he built the necessary rolling machinery in his Trenton plant. Later Cooper's beams evolved into I-beams, which when translated into steel became the backbone of the modern skyscraper.

Interior

The upper stories, added in the 1890s, once housed the collection of decorative arts that later became the nucleus of the Cooper-Hewitt Museum. In 1973–74 the interior, except for the Great Hall, was gutted and the interior beams and columns encased in noncombustible materials; the new interior bears little relation to the old one except in its general proportions.

Toward the north end of the lobby an elaborately carved Victorian "birthday card" from the Cooper Union Foundation thanks its benefactor for a donation of $150,000 on the occasion of his 80th birthday. Cooper donated over $650,000 to the school, but didn't endow it, thinking that rentals from shops that once occupied the street-level arcade (east and west sides of the building) and offices would provide adequate operating income.

On the right side of the lobby a staircase leads down to the **Great Hall,** an auditorium with arcades of supporting granite arches. One of Cooper's aims in founding the Union was to establish a forum where great issues of the day could be freely discussed. Here Henry Ward Beecher, William Cullen Bryant, and William Lloyd Garrison spoke against slavery. Here Abraham Lincoln made his famous "right makes might" speech in 1860, winning the support of the N.Y. press and hence the presidential nomination. Later the auditorium housed the People's Institute, offering lectures to education-hungry Jews from the Lower East Side.

Just south of the main entrance to Cooper Union is a **statue of Peter Cooper**

(1894, installed 1897; Augustus Saint-Gaudens) by a sculptor who had received his early training as a night student at Cooper Union. The bronze statue sits beneath a marble canopy designed by the sculptor's friend Stanford White.

Across Third Ave to the east (between E. 6th and E. 7th Sts) is the **Abram S. Hewitt Memorial Hall** of Cooper Union (1905; Clinton & Russell). Active in founding and managing Cooper Union, Hewitt established the first American open-hearth furnace with Cooper's son Edward; later he became a U.S. congressman and mayor of New York (1887–88).

The Village Voice

The *Village Voice*, New York's most influential alternative publication, is based at 36 Cooper Square. Founded in 1955, by a group that included Norman Mailer, this weekly countercultural sounding board has played a major role in the city's life, investigating political stories ignored by the mainstream media and covering the arts. To boost circulation, largely in response to pressure from the conservative weekly *New York Press* (free) and *Time Out New York* (oriented to the arts and events), the *Voice* began free distribution in 1996. It was sold in 1999 to a chain of alternative weeklies.

Little Ukraine

Walk to Third Ave at E. 7th St, which is the heart of the city's Ukrainian enclave, stretching along Second Ave from about 4th St to 14th St. Little Ukraine reached a population of around 60,000 after World War II as Ukrainians fled Soviet control. The community dwindled steadily through the decades, but has seen a resurgence since the collapse of the Soviet Union. Although the current Ukrainian population is only about 20,000, the community is flourishing, its churches and ethnic associations full and active, its members prospering.

The grand marble edifice at the northeast corner (59 Third Ave), the former **Metropolitan Savings Bank** (1868; Carl Pfeiffer; DL) is now a Ukrainian church. This French Second Empire–style building is, in marble, what the cast-iron Bouwerie Lane Theatre (also formerly a bank) pretends to be—massive and imposing, with quoins at the corners and cornices articulating every floor.

On the south side of E. 7th St is the onion-domed, Byzantine-style **St. George's Ukrainian Catholic Church** (1977; Apollinare Osadca), the largest institution in the community. On the north side of the street is the **Surma Book and Record Company,** 11 E. 7th St, a family business since 1918. It sells traditional Ukrainian Easter eggs *(pysanky)*, embroidered Ukrainian clothing, and banduras, the harplike national instrument.

McSorley's Old Ale House

A beloved New York institution, McSorley's Old Ale House (formerly McSorley's Saloon), stands at 15 E. 7th St. McSorley's has long billed itself as the city's oldest saloon, with a sign in the window proclaiming a founding date of 1854. It has also claimed that Abraham Lincoln drank there in 1860. Amateur historian Richard McDermott discovered that John McSorley didn't arrive in America until

1855 and that the bar probably did not open until 1862. McDermott subsequently proved that the Bridge Café is the oldest drinking establishment (see Walk 2), although others argue in favor of the Ear Inn (see Walk 8).

McSorley's, which serves only ale, has been visited by Joseph Kennedy, Babe Ruth, and Will Rogers, among others. There is a wishbone collection at the bar—soldiers going off to war have left behind turkey wishbones to be picked up when they return. The wishbones on display (some supposedly dating back to the Civil War) belonged to soldiers who did not come back. McSorley's was also immortalized by John Sloan's painting *A Mug of Ale at McSorley's* (1913) and Joseph Mitchell's 1943 collection of *New Yorker* profiles, *McSorley's Wonderful Saloon.* Women were not permitted until 1970, when it became illegal to exclude them.

St. Mark's Place

Return to Third Ave and E. 7th St. Turn right (north) and walk one block along Third Ave to St. Mark's Place, actually the section of E. 8th St between Third Ave and Ave A. Turn right onto St. Mark's Place.

History

When first developed in the early 19C, St. Mark's Place was a fashionable street, its houses set back from the sidewalks to give a street of standard width (60 ft) the impression of spacious elegance. During the 1960s St. Mark's Place became the Main Street of the East Village, the focus of New York's counterculture. Today the streets overflow with street vendors and young shoppers. The block is home to record stores selling new, used, and bootlegged albums, as well as several tattoo and piercing parlors. (Tattoos were legalized in New York in 1997, after 36 years as an outlaw practice.) Chain stores have begun to encroach on the strip, which may threaten its countercultural identity.

The building at **12 St. Mark's Place** (1885; William C. Frohne) was once the social hall of a German shooting club, the Deutsch-Amerikanische Schuetzen Gesellschaft, its identity marked by the ornamental terra-cotta target and crossed rifles on the upper part of the facade.

The **Daniel LeRoy House** (1832; DL), 20 St. Mark's Place, has a Federal doorway ornamented with splayed triple keystones, reminiscent of the doorway of the Merchant's House Museum four blocks south.

In the 1920s the Polish National Home combined 19, 21, 23 and 25 St. Mark's Place into a home for Polish organizations, including the **Dom,** a Polish American social club. During the 1960s the Dom became a downstairs nightclub, while an alcohol-free but drug-soaked dance hall called the **Electric Circus** opened above it, with strobe lights, pulsating beats, and performance artists. Today the building is home to the nonprofit **All-Crafts Centre,** which provides social services ranging from shelter to job training to self-help programs. The organization operates an arts-and-crafts boutique, a home improvement school, a holistic health market, and the New Edge Cabaret (no liquor).

Continue east to Second Ave. One block south at 105 Second Ave was Bill Graham's **Fillmore East** (1968–71), one of rock's most vibrant clubs. The Who performed *Tommy* live for the first time here in 1969; Jimi Hendrix, the Doors, the Grateful Dead, and Otis Redding all performed there as well as newer groups like the J. Geils Band, Traffic, and the Allman Brothers. The theater was demolished in 1997 and the entrance is now part of a bank.

Around the same time Fillmore East was gearing up, the first Indian restaurants were opening around the block on E. 6th St between First and Second Aves. Today **Little India** is a block-long stretch of nearly two dozen small, inexpensive Indian restaurants.

On the west side of Second Ave is the **Ottendorfer Branch of the New York Public Library** (1884; William Schickel; DL), 135 Second Ave, originally the Freie Bibliothek und Lesehalle, a bright red brick building with terra-cotta ornament, donated by Oswald and Anna Ottendorfer to the local German immigrant community. Anna Ottendorfer immigrated to the U.S. in 1844 with her first husband, Jacob Uhl, who purchased the *New Yorker Staats Zeitung;* six years after Uhl's death in 1853, she married Oswald Ottendorfer, the paper's editor in chief, who personally selected the library's original collection of books.

Stuyvesant Polyclinic Hospital

Next door at 137 Second Ave is the more impressive Stuyvesant Polyclinic Hospital (1884; William Schickel; DL) founded and endowed by the Ottendorfers as the German Dispensary. Designed in an energetic neo-Italian Renaissance style, the clinic is architecturally noteworthy for its terra-cotta ornament, which includes portrait busts of physicians and scientists: Celsius, Hippocrates, Aesculapius, and Galen on the porch; Harvey, Linne (Linnaeus), Humboldt, Lavoisier, and Hufeland on the frieze beneath the cornice.

History

In 1866 the dispensary, which provided free outpatient care to the poor, became a branch of the German Hospital at Park Ave and E. 77th St (now Lenox Hill Hospital). In 1906 the German Polyklinik, another charitable organization, bought the building. During World War I, because of intense anti-German sentiment, the clinic's name was changed to the Stuyvesant Polyclinic. Between the wars it reverted to its original name, only to become the Stuyvesant Polyclinic again during World War II. It is now part of Cabrini Medical Center.

At 139 Second Ave is the Ukrainian-run **East Village Meat Market,** and across the street is the **Ukrainian National Home,** 140–142 Second Ave, a community center with an inexpensive, home-style Ukrainian restaurant whose specialties include kielbasa, stuffed cabbage, and pierogi.

The Jewish Rialto

Second Ave from Houston St to 14th St, once called the Jewish Rialto, was the home of a vital Yiddish theater, whose musical comedies and melodramas often outshone those produced by the rest of the New York theater community. Between the turn of the 20C and the 1930s it nurtured such stars as Jacob Adler, Boris Thomashefsky, David Kessler, and later Molly Picon, Menashe Skulnik, Muni Weisenfreund (Paul Muni), and Luther and Stella Adler. Along with the theaters were restaurants—Russian, Polish, Hungarian, and Romanian—serving the immigrant clientele.

> The most famous of the few remaining old-style restaurants is the **Second Avenue Delicatessen,** 156 Second Ave (at E. 10th St). Founded in 1954, it features pastrami and corned beef that rank among the best in the city; metal stars embedded in the sidewalk commemorate the greats of Yiddish theater. Owner Abe Lebewohl was mourned throughout the city when he was murdered in 1995.

St. Mark's Church-in-the-Bowery

On the west side of Second Ave at E. 10th St is St. Mark's Church-in-the-Bowery (1799; DL). This Protestant Episcopal church is the second oldest in the city after St. Paul's Chapel and is built on the probable site of Governor Stuyvesant's own chapel. St. Mark's Church-in-the-Bowery originally served an affluent, conservative congregation but is now one of the city's most socially active churches and has become an important cultural center. During the late 1950s and 1960s, as artists migrated to the area, theater began to flourish locally. The church is now home to Richard Foreman's avant-garde Ontological Hysteric Theater as well as other arts programs.

Exterior

The rubblestone walls and simple triangular pediment date from its late-Georgian, rural beginnings. The lovely Greek revival steeple was added in 1828 (Ithiel Town) and an Italianate cast-iron portico was built in 1854 keeping the church abreast of the architectural fashions. Flanking the main doorway are two Florentine marble lions and, outside the portico, two granite statues of Native Americans by Solon Borglum (1868–1922), brother of the more famous Gutzon Borglum. At the west end of the porch is a bust (1939; O. Grymes) of Daniel Tompkins (1774–1825), who as governor of New York was known for liberal reforms in education, the criminal code, and human rights.

Interior

The interior, steeple, and roof were severely damaged in 1978 when a worker's acetylene torch ignited the wooden gallery on the second floor. In 1980 a new bell was installed, dedicated to the workers, many of them youthful laborers from the neighborhood, who rebuilt the church. After the fire, the interior was restored, retaining much of the original detailing, including the 19C stained glass windows on the lower level. The upper windows (1982; Harold Edelman) are replacements.

The Graveyard

The graveyard (left side of church, sometimes locked) was the scene of a ghoulish kidnapping in 1878 when the body of department store millionaire A. T. Stewart (see Sun Building in Walk 5) was exhumed and carted off for $20,000 ransom. It was recovered two years later. Resting more peaceably here are Commodore Matthew Perry, Daniel Tompkins, and members of the prominent Fish, Goelet, Schermerhorn, Stuyvesant, and Livingston families.

The entrance to the churchyard is on the other (north) side of the church. Here stands the **old church bell,** cracked by the heat of the 1978 fire. Unlike the pre-

St. Mark's Church-in-the-Bowery (built 1799), the second oldest church in the city. In the graveyard are the remains of Governor Peter Stuyvesant, whose bouwerie, or farm, lent its name to the church and a nearby avenue. (Landmarks Preservation Commission, New York City)

sent electronically operated carillon, it was rung by a rope, and it tolled the deaths of John F. Kennedy, Robert F. Kennedy, and the Reverend Dr. Martin Luther King; after Dr. King's assassination it was rung only to celebrate the end of the Vietnam War. Here also are the remains of Peter Stuyvesant, entombed in the church wall, and a statue (to the right of the porch) of the governor sculpted in the Netherlands (1911) by Toon Dupuis. A plaque memorializes W. H. Auden, who lived in the neighborhood and was a parishioner of the church.

At 189 Second Ave the Village East City Cinemas occupy the home of the **Yiddish Art Theater** (1926; Harrison Wiseman; DL), later the Yiddish Folks Theater. In 1953 the renowned Phoenix Theater, a pioneer in the Off-Broadway movement, opened here. Its repertory company included Hume Cronyn, Jessica Tandy, Eli Wallach, and Lillian Gish.

Ukrainian Museum

203 Second Ave (between E. 12th and E. 13th Sts), New York, NY 10003. ☎ (212) 228-0110. Web site: www.ukrainianmuseum.org. Open Wed–Sun 1–5 P.M. Admission charge. Changing exhibitions, workshops, lectures, educational programs. Gift shop. Accessible to wheelchairs.

Walk north to the Ukrainian Museum, at 203 Second Ave. The museum, founded in 1976, has one of the largest collections of Ukrainian art in the West. Its folk art collection contains embroidered and woven textiles, *pysanky* (Easter eggs), ceramics, woodwork, and metalwork dating from the 19C to the mid-20C. Works by Alexander Archipenko and Alexis Gritchenko highlight the fine arts collection. The archives document more than 100 years of Ukrainian immigration to the U.S. and record the life of the community here.

In 2001, the museum announced plans for a new, 25,000-square-ft building at 222 E. 6th St. The larger space will allow more of the collections to be on view.

Turn around and walk south on Second Ave; turn left on E. 11th St to First Ave. Here on the southwest corner is a bit of Italian flavor mixed in with the continuing Polish and Ukrainian presence. **Veniero's Café,** 342 E. 11th St, is a tile-floored coffee shop and pasticceria founded in 1894 by immigrants from Sorrento. It bakes traditional Italian pastries, while **Russo's** next door has been producing fresh pastas, sauces, and cheeses since 1908.

Turn right (south) on First Ave. Also venerable is the **De Robertis Pasticceria,** 176 First Ave (between E. 11th and E. 10th Sts). Its tiled floors and walls and the old-fashioned showcases hark back to 1907.

Turn left on E. 10th St to the **Tenth Street Baths** (1892), 268 E. 10th St (between First Ave and Ave A), probably the only traditional Russian-Turkish steam bath remaining in Manhattan. Years ago many such establishments modeled after their Old World predecessors served people without bathtubs, but were consequently shunned as too old-fashioned by the children of immigrants. Many that remained acquired sexual connotations and have since closed.

Continue east along E. 10th St to Ave A. One sign of change in the East Village is the collection of new middle-income condos being built from Ave A to Ave C and from 13th to 10th Sts. On the southwest corner of E. 10th St and Ave A is **St. Nicholas Carpatho Russian Orthodox Greek Catholic Church** (1883; James Renwick Jr. and W. H. Russell), founded by the Rutherford-Stuyvesant family as St. Mark's Chapel. The interior is distinguished by tiled walls, stained glass, and carved wooden beams.

Tompkins Square Park

Across Ave A is Tompkins Square Park, named after Daniel Tompkins, whose remains lie at St. Mark's-in-the-Bowery. Along the north side of the park is a handsome row of houses built in 1846 when the Tompkins Square neighborhood was felt to have an auspicious future. The houses on the south side, built just a year later, were described at the time of completion as "new and desirable tenements," but their ground floors were designed as stores to be rented for $200 a year, an indication of the coming decline of the area. By the 1850s German immigrants had begun to displace the previous residents and the one- and two-family houses were sliced up into rooming houses or razed to make way for profitable tenements. By the 1860s the area was described as dirty, seedy, and dusty; 4th St between Aves A and B was called "Ragpickers' Row," while 11th St from First Ave to Ave B became "Mackerelville."

History

Originally part of a salt marsh called Stuyvesant Swamp, Tompkins Square Park was given to the city by the Stuyvesant family in 1833. It was a recruiting camp during the Civil War and witnessed riots in 1874 when 7,000 people hoping for "work relief" in the midst of a financial panic battled police. Three years later, it was the gathering spot for railway workers supporting the nation's first railroad strike.

In 1991, as an outgrowth of the 1988 riots, the park was closed for reconstruction. It has had a distinctly different feel since reopening in 1993, in large part because of the midnight curfew, but also because the neighborhood is more stable. It is relatively peaceful today with a population reflecting the ethnic and racial mix of the neighborhood: aging Russians, Ukrainians, and Poles along with younger people of every race.

The Park

Enter the 16-acre park along the north walkway near E. 10th St. Walk southeast. Visible through a gate about halfway through the park along the walkway is a nine-ft-high monument made of pink marble whose eroded features depict a boy and girl looking at a steamboat. It is a memorial to the victims of the *General Slocum*, an excursion steamer that burned in the East River on June 15, 1904, because of extraordinary criminal negligence on the part of the captain, crew, and steamboat company. Some 1,021 people, virtually all of them women and children from this then-predominantly-German neighborhood, burned or drowned in the tragedy. Many men, kept from the outing by their jobs, lost their entire families. For the bereaved, the Tompkins Square neighborhood became too full of painful memories, and an exodus to other German communities within the city followed the disaster. As the Germans moved out, Jews moved in, changing the ethnic character of the area within a few years.

Near the 9th St entrance is the **Temperance Fountain** (1888; Henry D. Cogswell), given to the city by the Moderation Society. It has a statue of Hebe (the water carrier) on its peak and a water fountain within to encourage the healthful consumption of water instead of alcohol.

Near the southwest entrance to the park is a **statue of Samuel Sullivan Cox,** "the letter carrier's friend," an Ohio congressman who earned this appellation by sponsoring legislation that raised wages and gave salaried vacations to postmen. The statue (1891; Louise Lawson) was commissioned by the mailmen of America and first erected in Cooper Square, where it occasioned criticism that the figure resembled a floor walker beckoning an approaching customer. When Saint-Gaudens's figure of Peter Cooper was installed there, Congressman Cox was moved here.

Christodora House

Across from the park, at 145 Ave B (on the northeast corner of E. 9th St), is **Christodora House** (1928; Henry C. Pelton), one of the area's few tall buildings and one whose history reflects that of the neighborhood.

History

In 1897 Sara Libby Carson and Christina MacColl founded a settlement house at 1637 Ave B, calling it Christodora House, a name suggested by a college professor to mean "gift of the Christ." In 1928, Christodora House moved to this 17-story brick building, financed by Arthur Curtiss James, a railroad magnate. George Gershwin, whose brother Ira headed the house Poets' Guild, is said to have given his first public concert on the third floor. Christodora House functioned successfully until after World War II when it was sold to the city, which turned it over (late 1960s) to community groups. After a group of political activists destroyed the electrical system, the building was sealed. In 1975 it sold at public auction for a mere $62,500. Rehabilitated in 1986–87, Christodora House, the one-time "skyscraper settlement house," now contains luxury condominiums.

At 151 Ave B (between E. 9th and E. 10th Sts) is the former **Charlie Parker House** (c. 1849; DL), where the great saxophone player lived with his companion, Chan Richardson, from 1950 to 1954. The couple had an apartment on the ground floor; two children were born during their stay. At the time Parker was world-famous, already recognized as a major innovator in jazz, but his life was spinning out of control. He died in 1955, his death hastened by drug use; she died in 1999 in France. The house itself, mildly remarkable as one of the city's few remaining Gothic revival town houses, retains its original pointed-arch entranceway and double wooden doors.

11 · Greenwich Village

Greenwich Village is remarkable for its variety—its people, architecture, institutions, and street life. There is so much to see in this ever-vital village-within-the-city that this section has been divided into three routes.

History

When Washington Square was still marshland traversed by Minetta Brook, a Native American settlement called Sapokanican stood in the general area of present-day Greenwich Village. The Dutch took over and divided the land into large farms. Under the British, the area became known as Greenwich (Green Village), a name that first appeared in city records in 1713. A few large landholders dominated the rural landscape—Trinity Church, which held considerable property in the West Village south of Christopher St; Capt. Peter Warren, who purchased 300 acres in 1744; and such established families as the De Lanceys, Lispenards, and Van Cortlandts. By the 1790s, however, as the city spread northward, some of its residents fleeing epidemics of yellow fever and other diseases, the large estates were breaking up.

Between 1825 and 1850 the population of the Village quadrupled. Since its inhabitants were predominantly native born, the area became known as the "American Ward," a title that lost its accuracy toward the end of the century. By 1870 the Village had become a backwater: fashionable commerce had swept north along Broadway, first enveloping the area and then passing it by, leaving a vacuum filled by immigrants. First came the Irish and a black population, who settled south of Washington Square; they were displaced by Italians in the 1890s and a second, poorer, wave of Irish who settled around Sheridan Square. Row houses gave way to tenements, while shops and hotels were converted to warehouses or manufacturing lofts suitable for exploiting immigrant labor.

Around the turn of the century, the Village entered its halcyon period. Because of its relative isolation, its historic charm, and the indifference of a foreign population who adhered to the spiritual precepts of the Roman Catholic church and the political dictates of the Democratic Party machine, the Village offered a haven for the radical, avant-garde element of American society. Here were cheap rents and freedom from the late-Victorian sexual and materialistic attitudes that dominated middle-class American culture.

Soon the place swarmed with radical social and artistic activity: Max Eastman founded *The Masses* (1910), a radical paper whose publication was suppressed in 1918 because it opposed the war; the *Seven Arts* (founded 1916), whose columns integrated political and artistic ideas, met a similar fate. Clubs like the "A" Club and the Liberal Club became forums for woman suffrage, birth control, anarchy, and free love.

Among the theater groups flourishing in the opening decades of the 20C were the Provincetown Players, whose productions displayed the talents of such playwrights and performers as Eugene O'Neill, Edna St. Vincent Millay, and Bette Davis. The Theater Guild, which started as the Washington Square Players, moved uptown in 1919 and became an innovative force in American theater. Resident Village writers included Sherwood Anderson, Theodore Dreiser, John Dos Passos, and Van Wyck Brooks, as well as poets E. E. Cummings, Hart Crane, and Marianne Moore.

The isolation of the Village, however, soon came to an end. Seventh Ave South was built south of Greenwich Ave and W. 11th St in 1919, Sixth Ave was extended south of Carmine St in the 1920s, and in the 1930s the IND subway joined the old IRT (opened 1904), linking the Village to the rest of the city. Real estate developers began tearing down the old row houses and replacing them with highrise, high-rent apartments, a process that accelerated after World War II.

Still, the Village remained the heart of the city's counterculture in the 1940s and 1950s. Beats like Jack Kerouac, Allen Ginsberg, Gregory Corso, and William Burroughs all either lived in the Village or spent a great deal of time drinking, thinking, and talking at places like the San Remo Café (Bleecker and MacDougal Sts), which was also popular with James Baldwin, James Agee, and socialist writer Michael Harrington. The Cedar Tavern on University Place was a favorite hangout of artists like Jackson Pollock, Willem de Kooning, and Larry Rivers. Woodie Guthrie and Pete Seeger were among those who helped make the neighborhood a mecca for folksingers and songwriters.

One of the centers for the Beat movement was Eighth St, which was filled with cabarets and quirky literary venues like Ted and Eli Wilentz's Eighth Street Book Shop. The Wilentz brothers not only sold books, they published poetry by Kerouac, Ginsberg, and others. In its own way, the street stayed hip even after the Beat movement died; Jimi Hendrix opened Electric Lady Sound Studio here in 1970, and although he died soon after, groups like Led Zeppelin and the Rolling Stones have recorded there.

For nearly two decades beginning in the mid-1970s, the Eighth Street Playhouse was home to the midnight screening of *The Rocky Horror Picture Show*, a campy film that became a cult classic with audience members dressing up, shouting responses to the dialogue, and even bringing props with which to participate. Record stores also flourished here, many selling underground copies of studio and live recordings by bands such as the Beatles and the Grateful Dead.

Because of its longstanding tolerance, the Village has a significant homosexual community and has been a base for feminist and gay activists, but it also attracts middle-class and professional people who, perhaps because of the traditional Village sense of community, have frequently and visibly exercised themselves in political and social causes.

Sheridan Square, Washington Square, New York University, and the South Village

Subway: Broadway–Seventh Ave Local (1, 9) to Christopher St–Sheridan Square. Sixth Ave Express or Local (B, D, Q, F) or Eighth Ave Express or Local (A, C, E) to W. 4th St. Walk west on W. 4th St to Seventh Ave and Sheridan Square.
Bus: M10 to Sheridan Square.

Begin at **Sheridan Square,** a triangle of asphalt bounded by Washington Place, Barrow, Grove, and W. 4th Sts (cross Seventh Ave to the east from the downtown Christopher St–Sheridan Square subway stop and walk a few yards along W. 4th St). **Christopher Park,** around the corner to the north, is often mistaken for Sheridan Square, understandably since it contains a statue (1936; Joseph Pollia) of Gen. Philip Sheridan (1831–1888). Sheridan, a successful Union general during the Civil War and exterminator of Native Americans thereafter, made the (usually misquoted) remark that "the only good Indians I saw were dead."

At 10 Sheridan Square is the **Shenandoah** (1929; Emery Roth), an apartment building with a jutting corner held up by the figures of two bearded men straining under the weight. The multicolored brick building is decorated with a sea horse, elephants, and a dragon.

Across the street, at 61 Christopher St, is the **Duplex,** a piano bar and cabaret theater for more than a half century. Once a proving ground for talents like Woody Allen and Joan Rivers, the Duplex draws tourists and a local gay crowd.

Next door at 59 Christopher St is the **Kettle of Fish,** a Village institution since 1950. The bar was originally on MacDougal St; it moved to W. 3rd Street in 1986 and then here in 1999. The walls feature a 1950s photo of Jack Kerouac in front of the neon BAR sign from the original tavern and wall sconces from the now-defunct Bleecker Street Cinema. Also notable is the name plaque remaining from the site's previous incarnation as the **Lion's Head,** a legendary writers' tavern, where Norman Mailer planned his 1969 mayoral run and where countless journalists and novelists drank and talked and drank some more. The bar also was popular with actors; Rod Steiger at one point had his mail delivered here. Other Lion's Head regulars included a small-time actor named Malachy McCourt and his schoolteacher brother, Frank, who often regaled their pals with childhood stories, many of which later found their way into Frank's memoir, *Angela's Ashes.* The Lion's Head closed in 1996, after 38 years in business.

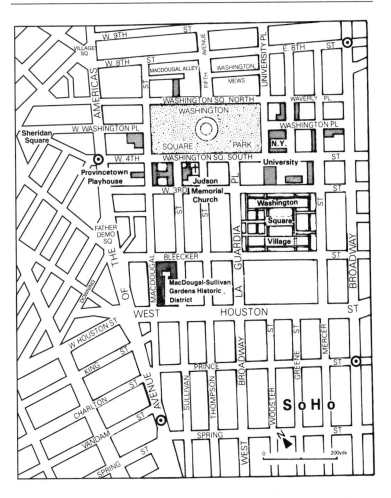

The Stonewall Bar (opened 1989) occupies the the site of the **Stonewall Inn,** 53 Christopher St, a landmark in the struggle for gay civil rights. On June 27, 1969, police raided the club. Previously, gay bar personnel and patrons had meekly accepted such raids, fearing arrests and publicity. This time, however, customers and passersby fought back, attacking with rocks and bottles. The rioting continued throughout the Village for two days and is considered the spark that ignited the battle for civil rights for homosexuals.

Follow Christopher St northeast to Waverly Place. Except for City Hall, the **Northern Dispensary** (1831; Henry Bayard, carpenter, and John C. Tucker, mason), a triangular building sited on a triangular plot, is the only public building from the Federal period still standing. Austerely constructed of red brick, the dispensary was originally two stories high; the addition of a third story (1854) can be detected by a line in the brickwork. It was chartered in 1827 to offer free medical care to the poor (Edgar Allan Poe was treated for a cold in 1837) and functioned as a public clinic until 1989.

The vagaries of Greenwich Village geography make it possible for the building to have two different sides facing a single street and one side facing two streets, since Waverly Place forks at its southeast corner and Christopher St joins Grove St along its north facade.

Follow Waverly Place along the south side of the dispensary to **Gay St,** still graced by several small, dormered Federal houses. During the mid-19C, Scottish weavers lived on this crooked, block-long street; off and on until about 1920 it was a residential enclave for the Village's black population. During Prohibition it harbored the Pirate's Den, a speakeasy where the waiters reputedly refused to give change. Novelist Ruth McKenney, who lived at no. 14, made Waverly Place famous in her play *My Sister Eileen,* later adapted as the musical comedy *Wonderful Town,* which recounted her adventures in the Village bohemia of the 1930s. The building at 13 Gay St was the longtime home of the radical law practice of William Kunstler and Ronald Kuby.

Continue east along Waverly Place. At no. 138 is a brick-and-brownstone Gothic revival town house (1895; George H. Streeton), formerly the rectory of St. Joseph's Church, which is around the corner.

At Sixth Ave, turn right. Down the block (corner of Washington Place) is **St. Joseph's Church** (1833; John Doran), the city's oldest Roman Catholic Church and one of its earliest Greek revival church buildings. The main facade belongs to the then-emerging Greek revival tradition, with its smooth surface, two large Doric columns, low pediment, and frieze. The rubblestone masonry on the side walls, corner quoins, and tall, round-headed windows hark back to the Federal period. John McCloskey (1810–1885), an early rector, became America's first cardinal. The interior preserves many of the original architectural features but suffers from the addition of stained glass windows.

Walk two blocks south on Sixth Ave to Bleecker St and turn right. At the intersection of Bleecker and Carmine Sts, a block west of Sixth Ave, is the **Church of Our Lady of Pompeii** (1926), which replaced a church of the same name where the first American citizen to be canonized, St. Frances Xavier Cabrini (1850–1917), once worshipped.

While chain stores have overrun much of the city, old-time shops, many of them holdovers from the neighborhood's Italian past, still occupy this stretch of Bleecker St (between Sixth and Seventh Aves).

Shopping, Italian Style

Some notable veterans are **Faicco's Pork Store** (founded 1900), at 260 Bleecker St for 54 years; **Zito's** bread bakery at 259 Bleecker St, owned by the Zito family for 76 years; **Murray's Cheese Shop,** which opened nearby on Cornelia St in 1940 and moved to 257 Bleecker St in the 1990s; and the original **Ottomanelli's,** an upscale butcher, which opened at 285 Bleecker St more than 50 years ago and now has other stores uptown. **John's Pizzeria** opened in 1929 on Sullivan St and moved to its present location at 278 Bleecker St in 1934.

At the corner of Bleecker and Barrow Sts, turn right on Barrow St, named after Thomas Barrow, a prominent early-19C artist. Originally named Reason St to honor *The Age of Reason* by Thomas Paine, who died nearby at 59 Grove St, the name was eventually corrupted to Raisin St, and was changed at the prompting of Trinity Church, a major landowner in the area.

Greenwich House, 27 Barrow St, was originally a settlement house founded (1902) by social worker Mary Kingsbury Simkhovitch in a nearby tenement. Greenwich House first directed its major efforts toward the children of the nearby immigrant and black population, which reached the shocking density of 975 people per acre around the turn of the 20C. Today, the building (1917; Delano & Aldrich) is a bit worse for wear, but the organization hopes to refurbish it for its 2002 centennial.

Continue along Barrow St to W. 4th St and turn right. Bob Dylan lived at 161 W. 4th St in the 1960s (also at 94 MacDougal St and later at the Chelsea Hotel). This block features some of the Village's individualistic entrepreneurs, including **Music Inn World Instruments** (169 W. 4th St), a store that has been selling and repairing instruments here since 1958, and the **Pink Pussycat Boutique** (167 W. 4th St), which has provided customers with erotica for 30 years.

Continue to Sixth Ave and cross the street. The fenced-in West 4th Street Playground (actually closer to W. 3rd St) known as **"The Cage,"** is one of the country's most famous outdoor basketball courts, where generations of future stars from all over the city—for example, Lew Alcindor (later Kareem Abdul-Jabbar) and Julius Erving—have come to prove themselves.

Washington Square

Walk east on W. 4th St to Washington Square West and turn left. Washington Square Park, now the heart of Greenwich Village, was once marshland through which Minetta Brook wandered on its way to the Hudson River.

History

The square's first inhabitants, after the Native Americans, were some black slaves freed by the Dutch beginning in 1644 and granted land for farming. Toward the end of the 18C the land became a potters' field and a hanging ground. In 1826 the field was converted to a parade ground and in 1827 the park was laid out, attracting the well-to-do, whose houses rose along its perimeter. In 1835 the park was the site of the first public demonstration of the telegraph by New York University professor Samuel F. B. Morse. In 1837 New York University constructed its first building on the east side of the park, a handsome Gothic revival building.

In the early 1950s Robert Moses, then the Parks commissioner and always a highway advocate, decided to push a highway over, under, or through the park to ease downtown traffic on Fifth Ave, a project that Villagers defeated after a decade-long struggle. In the 1960s, folksingers performed regularly by the fountain. Today the park swarms with activity during good weather: its denizens include parents and children, students, chess players, performers, and the inevitable drug dealers and their customers.

Washington Square North

Walk north to Washington Square North and turn right. Throughout the 19C, attractive row houses faced the square on three sides, but now only Washington

Square North suggests the former gentility of the neighborhood. The row here, on the western portion of the street, was developed (late 1820s–50s) by individual owners, and the houses reflect various styles—Federal, Greek revival, and Italianate. The buildings at **nos. 21–23** are Greek revival mansions (1835–36) with columned doorways, long parlor windows, and fine ironwork, considered in its day especially suited to park settings. The parlor window balcony on no. 21 with anthemion and Greek key motifs combined on a wheel is especially handsome.

The earliest house on the square **(no. 20)** is one of the city's few remaining Federal mansions, constructed 1828–29 as a country residence and converted into apartments in 1880 by Henry Hardenbergh, architect of the Plaza Hotel. The keystone and blocks in the arched doorway and the panels in the lintels are decorated with a vermiform design.

The original buildings from 18 Washington Square North to Fifth Ave have been demolished, including two matching Rhinelander family mansions and Henry James's grandmother's Greek revival house (no. 18), which provided the setting for his 1880 novel *Washington Square*. In 1951 the entire site with adjoining property on Fifth Ave was sold for an apartment house, dismaying the locals, who waged a battle against what they considered the wanton development of their neighborhood. The only concession the developers made was to scale down the wing facing the park, but the result is bland and unappealing.

Washington Mews

At Fifth Ave, turn left and walk north. A half-block north on the east side of the avenue is Washington Mews, a private alley. The buildings on its north side were stables built in the 19C, as the configuration of their doors suggests, while those on the south were built in the 1930s on land formerly part of the back gardens of the houses facing Washington Square.

Continue north on Fifth Ave to the corner of 8th St. The apartment tower on the southeast corner, **One Fifth Avenue** (1929; Helmle, Corbett & Harrison and Sugarman & Berger), is a handsome Art Deco building with "Gothic" details: stylized gargoyles, pointed window arches over the balconies, and simulated vertical piers achieved by using different colors of brick. During the 1920s the "A" Club met here; the club claimed among its members Rose O'Neill, inventor of the Kewpie doll, and Frances Perkins, secretary of labor during Franklin D. Roosevelt's presidency.

Washington Arch

Return to Washington Square North. Washington Arch (designed 1892, dedicated 1895; Stanford White), modeled on the Arc de Triomphe in Paris, dominates the northern entrance to Washington Square Park. The present marble arch replaced a temporary wood and plaster arch erected (1889) to commemorate the centennial of George Washington's inauguration. Fifth Ave ran through the arch until 1964, when the park was redesigned and closed to traffic at the urging of Village residents. Through the years the arch has been defaced by political, religious, feminist, and racial slogans spray-painted in several languages, a sign of the Village's political activism and linguistic competence. A fence currently surrounds it, as it is closed off to the public while being repaired.

Arch Statistics	
Height	77 ft high
Width between piers	30 ft
Height of arch opening	47 ft

The frieze is carved with a design of 13 large stars, 42 small stars, and the initial *W* repeated at intervals between emblems of war and peace; in the spandrels of the arch are figures of Victory. Sculpted against the north side of the east pier is *Washington in War* (1916; Hermon A. MacNeil), the commander in chief flanked by Fame (right) and Valor. On the west pier is *Washington in Peace* (1918; A. Stirling Calder), showing the statesman with Justice and Wisdom, holding a book inscribed (faintly nowadays) *"exitus acta probat"* (the end justifies the deed). The sculptor was the father of Alexander Calder.

The Row

Turn left on Washington Square North. One of the architectural jewels of this part of the Village is the group of houses extending from Fifth Ave east to University Place, nos. 1–13 Washington Square North, known simply as the Row. Built in 1831–33 on land belonging to Sailors' Snug Harbor (see Snug Harbor Cultural Center in Walk 55), they form one of the city's first examples of controlled urban design.

The fronts are red brick; the basement stories and trim are marble, as are the porches and massive balustrades. Along the street runs an iron fence with anthemia, lyres, and Greek key motifs. Yet even this fine row has not escaped alteration. The house at no. 3 is a Victorian replacement. Today the buildings are used by New York University, largely as offices. Among the famous residents of the row have been Edith Wharton, Edward Hopper, William Dean Howells, and John Dos Passos, who at no. 3 wrote *Manhattan Transfer,* and architect Richard Morris Hunt, who lived at no. 2 from 1887 to 1895.

New York University (NYU)

Turn right on Washington Square East. On this corner is the **Main Building** of New York University (NYU), which was founded in 1831 by a group of business and professional men including Albert Gallatin, secretary of the Treasury under Thomas Jefferson.

History

The university, nonsectarian and "modern" in its curriculum, offered practical as well as classical courses to a middle-class student body, providing an alternative to Episcopalian and conservative Columbia College. Among its early faculty members was Samuel F. B. Morse, painter, sculptor, and inventor of the telegraph and Morse code. The Main Building replaces a Gothic revival structure torn down in 1894, whose tower rooms were rented to students, including Winslow Homer, Walt Whitman, and the inventor Samuel Colt.

For years the school has been Greenwich Village's largest landowner, which has prompted squabbles with residents over expansion plans. During the early

1960s, architects Philip Johnson and Richard Foster produced a master plan to unify the campus that, though originally more ambitious, resulted only in three bulky buildings faced with bright red sandstone—the Tisch Building, the Meyer Physics Building, and Bobst Library—all at odds with the neighborhood's character. Despite its holdings, the school had fiscal woes and sold its University Heights campus (see Bronx Community College in Walk 32) in 1973 to meet its payroll. In the 1990s, thanks partially to a $1-billion fund-raising drive and the economic resurgence of the city, NYU has solved its fiscal problems and elevated itself to an upper-echelon university.

Grey Art Gallery and Study Center

33 Washington Place (100 Washington Square East), New York, NY 10003. ☎ (212) 998-6780. Website: www.nyu.edu/greyart. Open Tues, Thurs, Fri 11–6; Wed 11–8; Sat 11–5. Closed Sun, Mon, major holidays. Suggested admission. Lectures, special events. Accessible to wheelchairs.

Subway: Sixth Ave Express or Local (B, D, Q, F) or Eighth Ave Express or Local (A, C, E) to W. 4th St. Broadway Local (N, R) to 8th St. Lexington Ave Local (6) to Astor Place. Broadway–Seventh Ave Local (1, 9) to Christopher St–Sheridan Square. Bus: M1, M2, M3, M5, M6 to 8th St.

Continue along the front of the Main Building to Washington Place and turn left. In the southwest corner of the building (entrance at 33 Washington Place) is the Grey Art Gallery and Study Center (1975), the university's fine arts museum.

Exhibitions at the Grey Art Gallery have drawn praise from the city's art community for their quality and imagination. The permanent collection includes American paintings from 1940 onward, European prints, and contemporary Asian art. Recent shows have included *Ben Shahn's New York*—his photos from the 1930s—and *Shiseido and the Manufacture of Beauty, 1900–2000.*

The NYU building at 29 Washington Place, now called the **Brown Building**, was the site of a disastrous industrial fire.

The Triangle Shirtwaist Company Fire

Built in 1900 as a manufacturing loft called the Asch Building, the owners spent $400,000 to construct it but then declined to have a sprinkler system installed for another $5,000 because they considered the structure fireproof. On March 25, 1911, fire broke out at about 4:30 P.M. in the upper stories, where the Triangle Shirtwaist Company employed some 500 workers, mainly Jewish and Italian immigrant girls. Most of the stairwell doors had been locked to prevent employees from stealing, the stairways were narrow and winding, the fire escape tore free from the wall, and the fire department ladders reached up only six stories. Before the fire was brought under control, perhaps 20 minutes later, 146 workers had died, most jumping for their lives and perishing on the pavement of Washington Place ten floors below. The owners were acquitted of manslaughter and received some $65,000 more in insurance than they paid out in claims (making a profit of

$6,445 per victim). The fire, however, eventually brought about improved safety regulations for the workplace and still remains a landmark event in the history of labor reforms (although sweatshop conditions persist throughout the city).

Walk to Mercer St, turn right, and walk to W. 4th St. The **Bottom Line,** 15 W. 4th St, opened in 1974; its performers have ranged from Miles Davis to Philip Glass to Dolly Parton to Barenaked Ladies. Bruce Springsteen became a national star in the 1970s when his Born to Run concerts here landed him simultaneously on the covers of *Time* and *Newsweek.*

Hebrew Union College

Hebrew Union College–Jewish Institute of Religion: Joseph Exhibition Center, Brookdale Center. 1 West 4th St, New York, NY 10012. ☎ (212) 674-5300. Web site: www.huc.edu/outreach.html. Open Mon–Thurs 9–6, Fri 9–3. Closed Jewish and legal holidays. Free. Changing exhibitions, lectures. Accessible to wheelchairs.

Across the intersection is **Brookdale Center** (1979; Abramowitz, Harris, and Kingsland), Hebrew Union College. Within the building are the **Petrie Synagogue,** with windows, ark, and eternal light by Yaacov Agam, and the **Joseph Gallery,** whose changing exhibits focus on Jewish life and culture. Formerly located on W. 68th St, Hebrew Union College is an important center of Reform Judaism, whose programs reach both students and the public.

History

Founded in 1875 in Cincinnati by Rabbi Isaac Mayer Wise, Hebrew Union College was the first institution of Jewish higher education in the country, its function to train rabbis for the Reform movement. In 1922 Rabbi Stephen S. Wise founded the Jewish Institute of Religion in New York, and in 1950 the two institutions, similar in orientation, merged.

Walk west on 4th St toward the park. Across from the Bottom Line is **Warren Weaver Hall,** an unattractive NYU effort at contemporary architecture (1966; Warner, Burns, Toan & Lunde). Next to it is **Tisch Hall** (1972; Philip Johnson and Richard Foster), a product of the master plan.

Continue to the intersection of Washington Square East and W. 4th St. Follow W. 4th St west past the red sandstone **Elmer Holmes Bobst Library** (1973; Philip Johnson and Richard Foster). Fourth St, now Washington Square South, is occupied mainly by NYU buildings.

Judson Memorial Church

Continue west across Thompson St to the **Judson Memorial Church** (1892; McKim, Mead & White; DL), named by its founder, Edward Judson, after his father, Adinoram Judson (1788–1850), first Baptist missionary to Burma and compiler of an English-Burmese dictionary. Designed by Stanford White, the building and adjoining square bell tower, built of amber Roman brick with terra-cotta moldings and panels of colored marble, are generally Romanesque revival in style. The auditorium (usually open weekdays 9–5) has stained glass windows by John La Farge; the marble relief on the south wall was designed by Augustus Saint-Gaudens.

History

The younger Judson focused his missionary zeal close to home and set the church on the path of social and political activism it still follows today. At the turn of the 20C, Judson Church offered health care and philanthropic services for children. In the 1960s it opened the first drug treatment clinic in the Village, made referrals to women for abortions (then illegal), and offered experimental theater, music, and dance performances. In the 1970s, the church provided health care referrals to prostitutes and supported politically controversial art. In the 1990s, it was the starting point for an open-casket AIDS funeral designed to raise awareness. **Judson Hall,** next door, was once a hotel whose revenues supported church programs. Both the bell tower and hall are now NYU residences.

Continue west past the NYU Law School to MacDougal St and turn south (left). The **Provincetown Playhouse,** 133 MacDougal St, founded by a group of struggling actors and writers as a Cape Cod summer theater (1915), made American theatrical history when it introduced the plays of Eugene O'Neill. One of them, *Bound East for Cardiff,* achieved such success that the group opened a New York season in 1916 using the parlor floor of a house at 139 MacDougal St. In 1917 they remodeled a stable and bottling works at 133 MacDougal St into a 182-seat theater. Among the plays first produced here were *Aria da Capo* by Edna St. Vincent Millay and *The Emperor Jones* and *The Hairy Ape* by O'Neill, whose work changed the shape of American drama. The playhouse disbanded in 1929. The theater had other owners through the years, then sat empty before being taken over and revived by NYU in 1998.

The building next door, **137 MacDougal St,** once housed the Liberal Club, organized as a meeting place for those interested in new ideas. Downstairs in the same building was Polly Holliday's restaurant, a famous eating and meeting place for artists and intellectuals. Polly's lover, anarchist Hippolyte Havel, who served as cook and waiter, gave the place its own cachet by shouting "bourgeois pigs" and other insults at the patrons, who nonetheless remained loyal. Another popular watering place at the corner of W. 4th St and Sixth Ave was the Golden Swan, known by its intimates as the Hell Hole, whose clientele included thugs as well as bohemians, and which later provided the setting and some characters for O'Neill's *The Iceman Cometh.*

The small Federal houses at **127–131 MacDougal St,** next to the theater, their facades altered for commercial purposes, were built (1829) on speculation for Aaron Burr, who invested heavily but with little success in Greenwich Village real estate. At no. 129 the original pineapple newel posts, symbolic of hospitality, remain.

Walk down MacDougal St to Minetta Lane. **Minetta Lane** commemorates Minetta Brook, which flowed from former hills near Fifth Ave and 21st St to the Hudson River near Charlton St. Some sources say the name comes from a Native American name *Manetta* (devil water); others say the Dutch called it *Mintje Kill* (little stream). Minetta St, which intersects Minetta Lane a half-block West, follows the course of the brook.

Cafe Wha?, 115 MacDougal St, was once the launching pad for Bob Dylan, Janis Joplin, and, later, Bruce Springsteen. Jimi Hendrix got his big break here in 1966, when Chas Chandler, bass player of the Animals, a British rock group, heard him play with a band called Jimmy James and the Blue Flames. Impressed with the virtuosity and passion of the guitarist, whose real name was James Hendricks, Chandler invited him to England. A year later Jimi Hendrix was an international superstar.

On the southwest corner of MacDougal St and Minetta Lane is the **Minetta Tavern,** 113 MacDougal St, whose walls are covered with pictures of illustrious clients dating back to 1937. Perhaps the tavern's most unusual patron was Joe Gould. Member of an old New England family and a graduate of Harvard, Gould lived in the Village by his wits and on the charity of friends for three decades, gathering material for his magnum opus, "An Oral History of Our Time." The work, consisting of innumerable conversations, was reputed to have reached 11 million words when Gould died in a mental institution in 1957. The manuscript was never found. Joseph Mitchell, legendary writer for *The New Yorker,* chronicled Gould's saga; the Lions' Club of the Village paid for Gould's funeral.

Continue south to **Bleecker St,** named after Anthony Bleecker, an early-19C man of letters and owner of the land ceded to the city for the street. After World War II, Bleecker St was bohemia's Main Street, home to important jazz, folk, and avant-garde theater venues, like Café au Go Go, where comedian Lenny Bruce was arrested on indecency charges for uttering obscenities. **Le Figaro Café** (186 Bleecker St), which flourished during the "beatnik" era, is among the Village's classic coffeehouses and still offers espresso, food, and a setting for conversation. Other local examples include the **Caffe Reggio,** 119 MacDougal St, and the **Caffe Dante,** 81 MacDougal St.

Look right (west) on Bleecker St. At the corner of Sixth Ave is the **Little Red Schoolhouse,** an innovative school founded as part of the public school system in 1921, by Elisabeth Irwin, a pioneer in progressive education. In 1932, after feuding with school officials and losing funding, Irwin moved the school from its original location on E. 16th St to 196 Bleecker St, where it continues as a private school.

Cross Bleecker St and walk south on MacDougal St a half-block. The **MacDougal-Sullivan Gardens Historic District** is a group of 24 houses (1844–50) sharing a common back garden. In the mid-19C this land, bounded by MacDougal, Bleecker, Houston, and Sullivan Sts, belonged to Nicholas Low, a banker, land speculator, and legislator, who subdivided the property and built the houses as an investment. Although a large immigrant population altered the social makeup of the neighborhood in the late 19C, the Low family resisted the temptation to tear down the houses and replace them with more profitable tenements. Then in 1920 William Sloane Coffin, scion of the W. & J. Sloane furniture company, hit upon the idea of modernizing the old row houses to provide moderate-cost housing for professionals. He bought the block and converted the buildings to apartments, selling off the houses facing Bleecker and Houston Sts to finance the project. Although the facades have been significantly altered, the district remains interesting as an example of early urban renewal and for creating a common garden from small individual plots.

Return to Bleecker St and turn right (east). Walk one block to Sullivan St and turn right. At 181 Sullivan St is the **Sullivan Street Playhouse,** former home to what was the world's longest-running musical, *The Fantasticks,* which played here from May 3, 1960, till its close on Jan 13, 2002.

Two doors down, at 177 Sullivan St, was the birthplace of Fiorello La Guardia. The building collapsed in 1987 and the site is now a parking lot.

Fiorello La Guardia

Mayor from 1934 to 1945, La Guardia was renowned for his fighting spirit and ferocious temper, his boundless energy and ambition, and his facility in seven languages. He had a Jewish mother and an Italian father, and he was married first to a Catholic and then to a Lutheran, which made him a living example of his city's ethnic diversity. He was a liberal, a reformer, and an irate opponent of graft. He remains one of the city's iconic figures.

The Atrium

Return to Bleecker St. At 160 Bleecker St is the massive Atrium, originally Mills House No. 1 (1896; Ernest Flagg).

History

Flagg designed the Singer Tower (see One Liberty Plaza in Walk 3) and homes for the wealthy, including the Scribners, but he was also interested in high-density housing for the less affluent. Palatial in scale but cut up into tiny single rooms, this building was intended for men who could not afford boarding-house rates. It was named for Darius Ogden Mills, who philanthropically financed the building expecting only a modest 5 percent profit. With some justification, *Scribner's* magazine described Mills House as "A Palace at Twenty Cents a Night." Its 1,500 rooms faced either the streets or the open, grassy interior courts, and the hotel had modern bathrooms, lounges, restaurants, and smoking rooms. Eventually it deteriorated into the Greenwich Hotel with a down-and-out clientele. In 1976 the building was converted into apartments and its interior courts reconstructed.

The commercial space of the building was the longtime home of the beloved **Village Gate** cabaret-theater, which opened in 1958 and made its fame with a dazzling mix of performers, including musicians Miles Davis, Sonny Rollins, Dizzy Gillespie, John Coltrane, Thelonious Monk, Chuck Berry, Pete Seeger, and Blondie; poet Allen Ginsberg; and comedians Bill Cosby, Woody Allen, and Mort Sahl. The Village Gate closed in 1994, but in 2001, 158 Bleecker was revived as the Village Theater with the hit *Love, Janis,* a musical about Janis Joplin's life.

Chaim Gross Studio Museum

526 La Guardia Place (between W. 3rd and Bleecker Sts), New York, NY 10012. ☎ (212) 529-4906. Open Tues–Fri 12–6 by appointment. Free. Permanent exhibition, gallery talks, tours of collection. Accessible to wheelchairs except for studio floor, which is down a short flight of steps.

Continue east along Bleecker St to La Guardia Place and turn left. The Chaim Gross Studio Museum (1994) at 526 La Guardia Place occupies the house where sculptor Chaim Gross (1904–1991) lived and worked for more than 30 years. This small, very personal museum has examples of his work from the time he arrived in this country as a 17-year-old immigrant until his death in 1991.

In addition to a permanent collection of sculpture in bronze, wood, and stone, you can see Gross's skylit studio, with his workbench, tools, and the last sculpture on which he worked still clenched in its vise. The museum also mounts changing exhibitions featuring some aspect of Gross's work or career.

The massive apartment complexes across La Guardia Place are called **Washington Square Village** and **University Village;** the buildings, most of them owned by NYU, tower above the surrounding streets. The oldest group (1956–58; S. J. Kessler, Paul Lester Weiner) are institutional in feeling; the newer buildings (south of Bleecker St, 1966; I. M. Pei & Partners) have been admired for their design and for the technological achievement of their cast-in-place concrete. In the center of the Pei group is a monumental sculpture after a smaller work (1934) by Pablo Picasso, entitled ***Bust of Sylvette.*** The original, representing the profile of a girl with a ponytail, was only two ft high, painted on a piece of bent metal. The present adaptation (1968) by Carl Nesjar and Sigurd Frager is 36 ft high and is made of concrete with black basalt aggregate revealed by sandblasting.

Walk south to Houston St and turn right. The name "Houston" (its first syllable is pronounced *house*) is a corruption of "Houstoun," after William Houstoun, a Georgia delegate to the Continental Congress (1784–86), who got a New York street named for him by marrying the daughter of Nicholas Bayard III, owner of the land where the west side of the street now runs.

The patch of vegetation sprouting from the concrete at the intersection of La Guardia Place and Houston St is an environmental sculpture, ***Time Landscape*** (planted 1978; Alan Sonfist), composed of trees, shrubs, and plants that grew on Manhattan before Europeans arrived. Some of the trees were transplanted as saplings from Bronx Park, where the New York Botanical Garden now maintains the last virgin forest in the city.

Walk west to Sullivan St. On the south side of Houston St is the **Church of St. Anthony of Padua** (c. 1895). During the first two weeks of June this church sponsors the Feast of St. Anthony of Padua, beginning with a procession during which the saint's image is carried through the streets. The outdoor fair in the evenings offers rides, carnival games, and staggering quantities of Italian street food.

West Village from St. Luke's Place to Bank Street
Subway: Broadway–Seventh Ave Local (1, 9) to Christopher St–Sheridan Square or to Houston St.
Bus: M5, M6, or M10.

St. Luke's Place
The route begins at **St. Luke's Place,** the name of Leroy St between Hudson St and Seventh Ave South. Head west from Seventh Ave South. The north side of St. Luke's Place has a fine collection of Italianate houses whose aura of settled repose characterizes much of the West Village. Built in the early 1850s for prosperous merchants, many of whose livelihoods were tied to the Hudson River, the houses still have the red brick facades typical of the earlier Greek revival style. However,

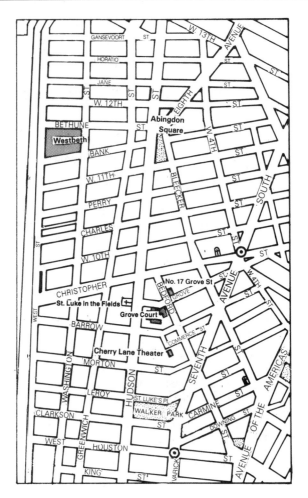

they also incorporate fashionable Italianate details such as brownstone trim, door hoods supported by carved consoles, bold cornices, tall stoops with rather elaborate cast-iron railings, high rusticated basements, and deeply recessed doorways with double doors.

History

Radicals from Max Eastman to Timothy Leary, writers Theodore Dreiser, Sherwood Anderson, and Marianne Moore, and painter Paul Cadmus lived here. The exterior of no. 10 was Bill Cosby's home in the 1980s hit television comedy *The Cosby Show*. But the block's most famous resident was James J. "Jimmy" Walker, the popular, high-living mayor of New York from 1926 until his resignation under a cloud of fiscal scandal in 1932. His home was at 6 St. Luke's Place.

James J. Walker Park

The playground across the gingko-lined street is James J. Walker Park, originally St. John's Burying Ground of Trinity Parish (which owned the West Village up to Christopher St under a 1705 land grant from Queen Anne). In 1898, under the guidance of architects Carrère & Hastings, the deteriorating cemetery was dug up and landscaped as Hudson Park. During excavations, workers uncovered a stone marked "Leroy" which rumor identified as the grave marker of Louis Charles, son of Louis XVI and Marie Antoinette. Although the dauphin may have been smuggled out of prison after his parents' death, he surely did not die in Greenwich Village. Leroy St is named after Jacob Leroy, alderman and successful merchant. Just inside the fence is a small coffinlike monument for Eugene Underhill and Frederick A. Ward, two firemen of Eagle Engine Company No. 13, who died in 1834 while performing their duties.

Continue west on St. Luke's Place to Hudson St, turn right, then turn right again onto **Morton St,** which features an eclectic mix of houses. Some of the houses on the west end of Morton St (for example, no. 68) remain from the early 19C, when tradespeople and craftsmen lived in the West Village, many of them sail makers and building suppliers involved with the city's maritime trades. At no. 59 is a fine Federal doorway. Toward the east end, smaller row houses give way to Old Law tenements—bigger, bulkier, built right up to the sidewalk—dating from the late 19C when the Village experienced the influx of a large Italian and Irish immigrant population.

Turn left at Bedford St, mapped before 1799 and named after its precursor in London. On the east side of the block stands a row of early-19C houses (nos. 64–70) in fine condition, though suffering various alterations. James Vandenburgh, master mason of Trinity Church, lived at no. 68 in 1821, another reminder of Trinity's influence in the West Village.

Edna St. Vincent Millay Residence

Across the street at 75½ Bedford St is a house only 9½ ft wide, distinguished both as the narrowest house in the Village and as a residence of Edna St. Vincent Millay. Built in 1873, it was wedged into a former carriage alley; the pink brick facing came later.

History

Edna St. Vincent Millay (1892–1950), poet, playwright, and actress, arrived in Greenwich Village in 1917, illuminating bohemian society with her beauty and intoxicating personality. Millay is probably one of very few people named after a hospital: her middle name honors the Greenwich Village hospital, where the staff had saved the life of a family member. In 1923, when she won the Pulitzer Prize, she married Eugen Boissevain and lived briefly in this house.

The **Isaacs-Hendricks House** next door, 77 Bedford St (southwest corner of Bedford and Commerce Sts), was built in 1799 by Joshua Isaacs, but was altered in 1836 and 1928 and retains little of its original appearance.

Turn left onto Commerce St. Formerly called Cherry Lane, the street took its present name from the rapid arrival of many downtown business firms during the smallpox epidemic of 1822. The **Cherry Lane Theatre** (38 Commerce St) was founded (1924) in this former brewery or malt house by Edna St. Vincent Millay and others as an experimental theater; it has evolved into an Off-Broadway house.

Around the sharp bend in the street are two remarkable houses, **39** and **41 Commerce St** (1831 and 1832), facing one another across a central courtyard. Although local legend says a sea captain built them for two feuding daughters, records attribute them to a local milk seller. The mansard roofs were added in the 1870s.

At the intersection of Commerce and Barrow Sts, turn right and walk back to Bedford St, then turn left. The inhospitable-looking building at 86 Bedford St is **Chumley's** restaurant, a remnant from Prohibition days, when it opened in 1927 disguised as a garage. It operated as a speakeasy, catering to Edna St. Vincent Millay, John Dos Passos, and others whose thirst was not quenched by the Volstead Act. Inside, wooden booths and photos of Eugene O'Neill and Fiorello La Guardia help recall an earlier era; book jackets of New York writers line the walls. During Prohibition, patrons entered through the alley door leading to Pamela Court (and exited the same way during police raids). In commemoration of those clandestine times, the restaurant does not advertise its presence with a sign, although the liquor license is visible through the barred window.

The attractive small apartment house diagonally opposite (**95 Bedford St**) was built in 1894 (Kurzer & Kohl) as a stable for J. Goebel & Co., dealers in wine, and converted to a residence in 1927.

Continue to the corner of Bedford and Grove Sts. The clapboard house at **17 Grove St** (northeast corner of the intersection) was built in 1822 by William Hyde, a window-sash maker. Although the house has been considerably altered—a Greek revival doorway added in the 1830s or 1840s, a third story with a gingerbread cornice in 1870, and an obtrusive fire escape later—it is still the best preserved of the Village's few wood frame houses. Behind it at **100 Bedford St** stands Hyde's workshop (1833). Designer Clifford Daily, whose greatest project stands next door, "renovated" it in the 1920s using moldings and other trim salvaged from demolished 19C houses.

The bizarre house known as **"Twin Peaks,"** 102 Bedford St, was built in 1830 as an ordinary frame house. Clifford Daily, who believed that Village artists needed inspirational surroundings to court the muse, persuaded financier Otto Kahn to undertake renovation of the house, which would be turned over to artists, writers, and actors who could then live free from financial pressures. The resulting house, said to be a replica of a house in Nuremberg, contains bricks from the old Madison Square Garden, a Second Ave tenement, and an Upper West Side apartment. The opening ceremonies of this stuccoed, gabled, and half-timbered extravagance were held in 1926. Princess Amelia Troubetzky sat on one peak making a burnt offering of acorns (to the god Pan) while actress Mabel Normand sat atop the other peak christening the building with the customary bottle of champagne.

Return to the corner of Grove and Bedford Sts; walk west on Grove toward the river. This block, between Bedford and Hudson Sts, is especially attractive. First is a row of vine-covered Greek revival houses, 14–16 Grove St, built in 1840 by Samuel Winant and John Degraw. Between 10 and 12 Grove St is the entrance to one of the Village's hidden architectural enclaves, **Grove Court,** a group of shuttered brick houses built (1853–54) as dwellings for workmen. Remarkable nowadays for its serenity, the court has a more boisterous past, earning at different times in its history the names Mixed Ale Alley and Pig's Alley. A group of Federal houses at nos. 4–10 Grove St (1834; James N. Wells) retain many original features: hand-wrought ironwork including boot scrapers in the stoop fences at nos. 6 and 8, small dormers, and paneled doorways.

Church of St. Luke in the Fields
Follow Grove St to Hudson St. Directly across Hudson is the Church of St. Luke in the Fields (1822; DL).

History
Trinity Church donated the land for this, the city's third oldest church behind St. Paul's Chapel and St. Mark's Church-in-the-Bowery. According to church records, congregation member Clement Clarke Moore (see Chelsea History in Walk 12) drew up plans for the building, which was constructed by John Heath. In the late 19C, when immigrants overwhelmed the neighborhood, the fashionable congregation built a new church uptown on Convent Ave at W. 141st St, and in 1891 Trinity Church bought this St. Luke's, making it a chapel of Trinity Parish. It became independent again in 1976.

Exterior
Built of brick rather than the more customary rubble stone, St. Luke's has a low, bulky, square tower unadorned with a steeple, reflecting the austerity of the Federal style, and a parklike setting, surviving from the builder's original plan. Fires in 1886 and 1981 badly damaged the church; it was reconstructed and expanded (1981–85) by Hardy Holzman Pfeiffer Assocs.

In its early years, the church was flanked by 14 town houses, built by James N. Wells (who also built houses on nearby Grove St) as part of the original plan. Six remain (nos. 473–477 and 487–491 Hudson St, all built in 1825), as does the handsome vicarage in the churchyard.

Walk north on Hudson St. Just east of the intersection with Christopher St is the **Lucille Lortel Theatre,** 121 Christopher St, named after its former owner, who was known as "the Queen of Off-Broadway." Lortel (1900–1999), who gave up acting at her husband's request when she married, founded the White Barn Theatre in Westport, Connecticut, in 1947 as a home for new or experimental writers. In 1955 her husband bought this theater, then called the Theatre de Lys, as an anniversary present. Her first production here was a revival of the *Threepenny Opera,* which opened with Lotte Lenya and ran for seven years. Lortel brought playwrights like Jean Genet, Eugene Ionesco, Samuel Beckett, and Athol Fugard to American audiences, and she also produced such contemporary American playwrights as Edward Albee, Adrienne Kennedy, and Terrence McNally.

Turn west (left) on Christopher St and walk toward the river. Because of its generally permissive attitudes, the Village has long had a sizable homosexual community focused around Christopher St in the West Village and particularly visible at night. Various bars, clubs, and clothing stores cater to this clientele, though the AIDS epidemic has closed a number of the clubs on West St.

The ten-story dark brick building filling the block bounded by Washington,

Greenwich, Christopher, and Barrow Sts was originally the **U.S. Appraiser's Stores** (1899; Willoughby J. Edbrooke and others; DL), a warehouse for goods passing through customs. Later it served as a federal archives building and a post office; it has been renamed **The Archives** and converted to condominiums. Imposing in scale, it typifies the Romanesque revival style at its best, with strong brick arches at ground level, rounded corner turnings, and successive bays of arched windows.

Turn right and walk north up Washington St. The large apartment building at 277 W. 10th St on the northeast corner of the intersection, with its bold Romanesque revival facade of brick and unfinished stone, was originally **Everhard's Storage Warehouse** (built c. 1894). It was renovated for condominiums in 1978.

The **West Village Houses** (1974; Perkins & Will), stretching along Washington St from W. 10th St to Bank St, represent the outcome of another territorial struggle between Village activists and the city bureaucracy. Led by Jane Jacobs, whose book *The Death and Life of Great American Cities* (1961) has become a classic, locals succeeded in having the scale of a proposed high-rise development reduced, but the walkups are institutional and bleak.

Continue north along Washington St. Turn right at Charles St. The Gendarme Arms, 135 Charles St, a half-block inland from Washington St, occupies the former **Ninth Precinct Station House** (1895; John Du Fais), another example of the conversion of older commercial or public buildings to residential uses. Next door, at **131 Charles St** (1834; DL), is a beautiful, restrained Federal-style house.

Continue east on Charles St to the next intersection at Greenwich St. The house at **121 Charles St** on the northeast corner is oddly rural, with wide clapboards, double-hung windows, and unexpected angles and proportions. Tucked away on a small triangular plot amidst larger commercial buildings, the house, which may date from the 18C, has been moved twice. It was brought to its present location in 1968 from York Ave and 71st St, where it was a back house with no street frontage. When the building was threatened with demolition, the owner purchased this small piece of land and had the house trucked here through five miles of city streets.

Turn left on Greenwich St and walk north to **Bank St,** once an important financial center. In 1798 the Bank of New York, on Wall St, established a branch bank on a nameless Greenwich Village lane to be used for emergencies (the downtown branch was threatened with quarantine for yellow fever); during the smallpox epidemic of 1822 other banks came for similar reasons. Today, attractive homes line the block and cobblestones line the street.

Turn left on Bank St and return to Washington St. The bulky industrial building with the address of 155 Bank St, but which fills the entire street between Bank and Bethune Sts is **Westbeth,** the former **Bell Telephone Laboratories** (c. 1861–98; Cyrus L. W. Eidlitz). Among the technological advances engineered here were the transistor and the transatlantic telephone, but its greatest artistic contribution in the old days was the production on its sound stage of parts of *The Jazz Singer,* the first commercially successful "talkie." In 1969, after the phone company had moved its laboratories to New Jersey, the building was renovated by Richard Meier, a pioneer in the reuse of old buildings, and converted to studios and artists' housing with federally subsidized rents. At one time or another Robert De Niro, Merce Cunningham, and Diane Arbus lived and/or worked within its walls. Within the complex are the **Westbeth Theatre Center,** an Off-Off-Broadway house with three theaters, an art gallery, a sculpture studio, and the Gay Synagogue.

Walk one block north on Washington to **Bethune St** and turn inland (east). The block between Washington and Greenwich Sts is lined with Greek revival houses. The ones at 19–29 Bethune St were built in 1837 by Henry S. Forman and Alexander Douglass. At no. 25 note the unusual ironwork anthemion motifs on the door. Those at nos. 24–34 date from 1845 (builder, Alexander R. Holden).

Abingdon Square

Continue east on Bethune St to Abingdon Square (intersection of Hudson and Bethune Sts and Eighth Ave), named after Charlotte Warren, who married the earl of Abingdon. Although many British place names were changed in 1794, after due consideration by the City Council Abingdon Square was allowed to remain Abgingdon Square because the earl and his wife had been sympathetic to the American Revolution.

History

Charlotte's father, Adm. Sir Peter Warren, was one of Greenwich Village's great 18C landholders. A true adventurer, Warren went to sea as a 12-year-old, rose to his own command at age 24, made a fortune as a privateer, and married Susannah De Lancey. He eventually owned some 300 acres and built a mansion on the block now bounded by Charles, Perry, Bleecker, and Washington Sts. He returned to England before the Revolution.

Abingdon Square contains the *Greenwich Village War Memorial* (1921; Philip Martiny), a bronze figure of an American soldier carrying a flag.

As Bethune St crosses the intersection just south of the square, it becomes Bleecker St. Follow Bleecker St for a half-block as it curves, then turn left on Bank St, where there is an attractive group of 19C houses including **76 Bank St** (1839–42; Andrew Lockwood), which has small top-story windows surrounded by cast-iron wreaths, a Greek revival ornament that survived only rarely. Other good row-house blocks in this vicinity are W. 4th St between Bank and W. 12th Sts, and W. 11th and Perry Sts both east and west of W. 4th St.

Return to Bleecker St. Turn left and walk south on **Bleecker St,** which along this stretch is one of the Village's most appealing shopping streets. It is lined with antique shops, clothing boutiques, small restaurants, and other attractive (generally expensive) places to spend money. The street also has "only-in-the-Village" shops like Condomania, 351 Bleecker St, which sells a dizzying array of condoms.

At the intersection of Bleecker and W. 11th Sts, walk a block west to the **White Horse Tavern,** 567 Hudson St (corner of W. 11th St). This old-fashioned bar (founded 1880) was a favorite haunt of Norman Mailer, William Styron, Jack Kerouac, and other writers. But it was made famous by Dylan Thomas, who slowly drank himself to death here, culminating with a final night of excess in 1953 when, according to lore, he downed 18 drinks.

Along the Hudson River

Until recently, there has been little reason to venture to the far western edge of the Village. West St runs north and south along the river and once serviced the Hudson River Piers, most of which are now abandoned. Some of the piers berthed ocean liners, for example the now-unused Cunard–White Star facility at the foot of W. 13th St; others accommodated freighters or served as loading piers for the Lehigh Valley Railroad. Later, when the piers were no longer a factor in the city's economy, the neighborhood was mostly known as a pick-up area for cruising gays and the site of the controversial and litigious Westway, a superhighway and luxury real estate development to be built on landfill in the Hudson River. (After years of litigation dedicated activists led by Marcy Benstock and the New York Clean Air Campaign triumphed in 1990.)

Now, however, all that has changed. After years of delay, the city and state are creating the $330-million **Hudson River Park,** which will reach from Battery Park to 59th St and include 13 reconstructed piers, an esplanade with gardens, playgrounds, and running and biking trails (targeted completion, 2005).

Northern Greenwich Village, 9th Street to 14th Street

Subway: Eighth Ave Express or Local (A, C, E) or Sixth Ave Express or Local (B, D, Q, F) to W. 4th St.
Bus: M5, M6 to W. 4th St.

Balducci's

At the intersection of Sixth Ave and W. 9th St is Balducci's, an upscale food market, long in the Balducci family.

History

Louis Balducci, an Italian immigrant, opened his first produce stand in Greenpoint, Brooklyn, in 1915. His business eventually outgrew the stand, and Balducci moved to Greenwich Village in 1946. The market, which eventually became a favorite with culinary gurus (for example, James Beard and Craig Claiborne) is stocked with dewy produce, exotic cheeses, and whatever is simultaneously chic and edible. Its Italian origins show up in the apparently infinite variety of pastas. In 1999 the store was sold by the Balducci family to a Washington gourmet food company.

Jefferson Market Courthouse

At the intersection of Sixth Ave and W. 10th St stands the remarkable Jefferson Market Courthouse (1877; Vaux & Withers; DL), now a branch of the New York Public Library system. Turreted, towered, gabled, carved, and further embellished with stained glass and ironwork, the building exemplifies Victorian Gothic architecture at its most flamboyant. Voted the nation's fifth most beautiful building in 1855, it stood empty from 1945 until 1967, when Giorgio Cavaglieri remodeled it for its present use.

History

The courthouse stands on the site of the Jefferson Market, one of the city's primary 19C produce markets. The old market (founded 1833) had a tall wooden fire tower with a bell to alert volunteer fire fighters, the precursor of the present main tower originally used for the same purpose. Assembly rooms above the market sheds doubled as courtrooms, so that when the present courthouse was built, it became part of a complex that included a brick jail and a reconstructed market building. In 1927 the jail was demolished and replaced by the infamous Women's House of Detention (1931; Sloan & Robertson), a massive, Art Deco building, long a Village landmark or eyesore, depending on the beholder's point of view. The women's prison, originally intended for the temporary detention of women awaiting trial, was more successful architecturally than socially, and as conditions within it deteriorated, its grim bulk bore unpleasant associations for Villagers, especially since the inmates could often be heard shouting out of the windows. In 1973–74 it was demolished. Its site has been converted to a garden maintained by volunteers with aid from the Vincent Astor Foundation.

Cross W. 10th St on the north side of the courthouse and turn left. In the middle of the block west of Sixth Ave is **Patchin Place,** a secluded mews with ten brick houses built in 1848 by Aaron D. Patchin. Theodore Dreiser lived here in 1895 while still an obscure journalist, and E. E. Cummings, the occupant of no. 4, presumably enjoyed its serenity for some 40 years.

Walk back around the corner of Sixth Ave and a half-block north to the entrance of **Milligan Place,** another enclave of 19C houses clustered around a tiny triangular courtyard. The street is named after Samuel Milligan, who purchased farmland here in 1799 and, according to legend, hired Aaron Patchin, later his son-in-law, to survey it. The houses (c. 1852) are said to have accommodated Basque waiters from the Brevoort Hotel on nearby Fifth Ave and French feather workers who dealt in ostrich and egret plumes for millinery.

Walk south to W. 9th St and turn left (east) toward Fifth Ave. Beginning in 1701, much of this area—stretching north and south from about 8th to 13th Sts and east and west between Fourth and Sixth Aves—belonged to the Brevoort family.

A Masked Ball

Henry Brevoort, one of New York's few millionaires in the 1840s, built a Greek revival mansion on the corner of Fifth Ave and 9th St, partly with the proceeds from real estate sales. The house became famous for a scandalous masked ball during which two of the guests took advantage of their disguises to elope. Afterward, masked balls were briefly forbidden and the sponsors of such dangerous entertainments were liable for fines of up to $1,000.

At 23 Fifth Ave, on the northeast corner of 9th St, stood a house where Mabel Dodge held her famous "evenings." In 1912 Mrs. Dodge and her wealthy husband rented the second floor of the house, which she had fitted up in white, including a white bearskin rug in front of a white marble fireplace. Inviting anarchists, poets, artists, sculptors, and journalists, she organized her evenings around a theme—psychoanalysis, birth control, or the labor movement. Featured speakers included A. A. Brill, "Big Bill" Haywood (leader of the Wobblies, or Industrial Workers of the World), and the anarchist Emma Goldman. The evenings, covered by the press, sometimes degenerated into quarrels, but were nonetheless considered symbolic of the Village's artistic and intellectual eminence.

Cross Fifth Ave and walk a block north to 10th St. Just east of the avenue, at 7 E. 10th St, is the former **Lockwood de Forest residence** (1887; Van Campen Taylor; DL) and an adjoining apartment building, **9 E. 10th St** (1888; Renwick, Aspinwall & Russell). The house has unusual East Indian decorative details, including an ornate bay window and carved door frame, both of teakwood. A celebrated designer, de Forest worked in India, where he developed an interest in traditional Indian woodcarving. He also designed the teakwood trim for the Carnegie Mansion family library (see Cooper-Hewitt National Design Museum in Walk 23), and with his brother gave a room from an Indian Jain temple to the Metropolitan Museum of Art. Today the house is NYU's Center for Jewish Life.

Return to Fifth Ave. On the northwest corner of Fifth Ave and 10th St is the **Church of the Ascension** (1840–41; Richard Upjohn), a fine brownstone Gothic revival church by the architect who later designed Trinity Church (Wall St and Broadway). In 1844 it witnessed the wedding of President John Tyler and Julia Gardiner, whom a contemporary diarist described as "one of those large fleshly Miss Gardiners of Gardiners Island." Julia, who lived on Colonnade Row (see Walk 10), apparently knew the value of publicity, since she had already allowed herself to appear in an advertisement for a nearby department store. The church has stained glass windows and an altar mural by John La Farge, and a marble altar relief by Augustus Saint-Gaudens.

Next to the church, at 7 W. 10th St, is the **Rectory** (1839–41), a 2½-story Gothic revival row house, daringly innovative for its day, with asymmetrical massing, drip moldings, a steep roof and large chimney, pointed dormers, and a rough brownstone facade.

The building at **12 W. 10th St** (1846, renovations 1895; Bruce Price) was once the home of the etiquette expert Emily Post (1873–1960); her architect father, Bruce Price, subdivided the house into apartments for his four daughters. Sugar refiner Moses Lazarus lived at **18 W. 10th St;** his daughter Emma lived here when she wrote "The New Colossus," chosen as the inscription for the pedestal of the Statue of Liberty.

The row of houses at 20–38 W. 10th St is known as **Renwick Terrace** (1856–58; attrib. James Renwick Jr.), or as the English Terrace since it was influenced by rows or "terraces" of town houses in London. Stylistically these Anglo-Italianate, or "English basement," houses depart from the usual Italianate brownstone in having low stoops (three or four steps instead of ten or twelve) and round-arched single windows and doorways on the ground floor. Like other mid-19C brownstones, Renwick Terrace was planned as part of a unified streetscape, with cornices, rooflines, and window levels aligned to create an impressive architectural vista.

The house at 50 W. 10th St, built shortly after the Civil War as a stable, has been converted to a residence. The small dormered house at 56 W. 10th St (1832) dates back to the Federal period and is one of the oldest houses in this part of Greenwich Village; its keyhole is two inches high. Next to it is another early house, 58 W. 10th St, built c. 1836 and remodeled by Stanford White. Behind it stood a back house (now joined to the main building) where the Tile Club once met. This nationally important society of artists claimed such members as Augustus Saint-Gaudens, Daniel Chester French, and John Singer Sargent.

Across the street stood Richard Morris Hunt's Studio Building at 51 W. 10th St. Clients included Winslow Homer, John La Farge, Albert Bierstadt, Frederick Mac-Monnies, Saint-Gaudens, and French.

Second Shearith Israel Graveyard

Continue west to Sixth Ave. Walk a block north and turn east onto W. 11th St. About a quarter-block along the south side of the street is the small triangular remnant of the Second Shearith Israel Graveyard (also called the cemetery of the Spanish and Portuguese Synagogue), once a larger, rectangular plot.

History

This graveyard opened in 1805 when the synagogue's first burial ground at Chatham Square (see First Shearith Israel Graveyard in Walk 6) was full. It was used until W. 11th St was cut through in 1830, obliterating most of it, though the congregation petitioned the city to retain the part of the cemetery that did not lie in the way of the street. Still buried here is Ephraim Hart, a founder of the New York Stock Exchange. (Most of the bodies were removed to W. 21st St west of

Sixth Ave, where the congregation established its third graveyard, used until 1851 when a new law prohibited burials south of 86th St.) The present Shearith Israel cemetery is on Long Island.

Continue east along W. 11th St. The new town house (1978; Hardy Holzman Pfeiffer Assocs.) at **18 W. 11th St** replaces one that belonged to the lyricist Howard Dietz, which was destroyed by an explosion in 1970. Members of the Weather Underground, a radical sect born in the politicized 1960s, were concocting explosives in the basement when one misfired, killing three of the bomb makers and sending the others into hiding.

Continue east to Fifth Ave and the **First Presbyterian Church** (1846; Joseph C. Wells; south transept, 1893; McKim, Mead & White; 1919; chancel), 48 Fifth Ave, one of three handsome Gothic revival churches built in the area in the mid-19C (the others are Grace Church and the Church of the Ascension). British architect Joseph C. Wells modeled the crenellated central tower on that of Magdalen College, Oxford. The Church House around the corner on W. 12th St was designed by Edgar Tafel (1960) in dark brown Roman brick to blend with the brownstone of the church itself.

Salmagundi Club

Across the avenue at 47 Fifth Ave is the Salmagundi Club (1852–53; DL), the only survivor of the great mansions that once ennobled lower Fifth Ave. Built for Irad Hawley, president of the Pennsylvania Coal Company, the building is now owned by the Salmagundi Club, the nation's oldest artists' club, founded in 1870. Among its members were John La Farge, Louis Tiffany, and Stanford White. The name Salmagundi (whose origins cannot reliably be traced back beyond the French *salmigondis*—a salad of minced veal, anchovies, onions, lemon juice, and oil) was adopted by Washington Irving and his collaborators as the title of a periodical whose pages satirized New York life.

Exterior

The building belongs to the Italianate tradition, with its boldly rusticated basement, high stoop and grand balustrade, ornate door hood supported on foliate consoles, and lavish cast-iron work on the parlor window balconies.

Interior

The inside (open during exhibitions) provides a glimpse into the pleasures of wealth in 19C New York. The ceilings are embellished with ornate plasterwork; the marble mantels are handsomely carved; Corinthian columns separate the two first-floor parlors, and elaborate chandeliers glitter overhead. For all its opulence, however, this house was nothing spectacular in its day; contemporary guidebooks wax eloquent on the nearby Lenox, Schiff, Belmont, and Haight mansions but do not mention this one.

Forbes Magazine Galleries

60 Fifth Ave (at 12th St), New York, NY 10011. ☎ (212) 206-5548. Open Tues–Wed and Fri–Sat 10–4. Closed Sun, Mon, legal holidays. Reserved Thurs for group tours. Free. Permanent collection, changing exhibits. Limited wheelchair accessibility; ramps available.

Subway: Broadway Local (N, R) to 14th St–Union Square. Lexington Ave Express or Local (4, 5, 6) to 14th St–Union Square. Broadway–Seventh Ave Express or Local (1, 2, 3) to 14th St. Sixth Ave Local (F) to 14th St. Bus: M1, M2, M3, M5 to 12th St.

Continue north to the Forbes Magazine Galleries (1985), located in the former Macmillan Company Building (1925; Carrere & Hastings), 60 Fifth Ave. The galleries showcase the eclectic collections of the eccentric magazine publisher, Malcolm S. Forbes (1919–1990).

On display are hundreds of toy boats, thousands of toy soldiers, and a gallery of trophies, including some rather odd testimonials to moments of triumph, along with the usual cups and urns. Also here are documents and memorabilia revealing the personalities and problems of various American presidents. The highlight of the museum, however, is the **Fabergé room,** a glittering collection that includes a dozen jewel-encrusted Easter eggs made for the last two Russian czars and many more delicate and extravagant trinkets.

Walk south to W. 12th St and turn west. At 31–33 W. 12th St are the **Ardea Apartments** (1895 and 1901; John B. Snook & Sons), built for the department store baron George A. Hearn. Next door at **35 W. 12th St** stands a narrow house (c. 1840), only 13 ft wide, with a basement and two stories plus an anachronistic mansard roof with a single dormer. In 1867 when the house, then 25 ft wide, was cut in half to widen its eastern neighbor, the mansard roof and dormer were added without altering the Federal lintels and doorway. During this period homeowners commonly topped off their Federal and Greek revival houses with mansard roofs, partly to follow fashion and partly to gain additional space in a city where housing was already cramped.

Next to this attractive little house is a highly lauded apartment building, **Butterfield House** (1962; Mayer, Whittlesey & Glass), which sits agreeably alongside the older buildings of the street. On 12th St it rises only seven stories to conform to the existing 19C scale; on 13th St it rises to thirteen stories in a more commercial block.

At **45 W. 12th St** is another curious small house (c. 1846) whose right-side wall slants to follow the course of Minetta Brook, which is now channeled underground.

The New School

At 66 W. 12th St is the main building of the New School University, formerly the New School for Social Research (1929–31; Joseph Urban; DL), an early New York example of European modernism. Known for his stage sets and theatrical designs, Urban made this large building as unobtrusive as possible on a street where most structures are small. His auditorium (restored 1992; Prentice and Chan Olhausen) was a model for Radio City Music Hall. The courtyard was redesigned (1997) by sculptor Martin Puryear and architect Michael van Valkenburgh.

History

The New School, founded in 1919 as a small, informal adult learning center, has evolved into a university whose major commitment is still innovative adult education. In the 1920s it brought psychoanalysis to the public and was the first college to offer courses on black culture (taught by W. E. B. DuBois). During the following decades it became a "university in exile" for intellectuals fleeing Nazi Germany. Lecturers have included Aaron Copland, Lewis Mumford, John Maynard Keynes, Bertrand Russell, Martha Graham, Frank Lloyd Wright, Hannah Arendt, Margaret Mead, John Cage, Berenice Abbott, W. H. Auden, and Stuart Davis. The Writers Workshop was attended by James Baldwin, Mario Puzo, William Styron, and others. The Dramatic Workshop program (1940–49) helped shape the talents of Marlon Brando, Tennesee Williams, Rod Steiger, Walter Matthau, Shelley Winters, Harry Belafonte, Elaine Stritch, Ben Gazzara, and Tony Curtis.

Today the New School's academic divisions include the Actors Studio, the Parsons School of Design, and the Mannes College of Music. A recent $200-million campaign has enabled the school to expand to a new building at 72 Fifth Ave.

The Art Collection

Works from the New School's collection are on rotating display in the hallways, classrooms, and lobbies of the W. 12th St building. Most of the collection is contemporary, much of it from the last decade; works reflect the school's diversity and commitment to freedom of expression. Recent artists include David Hammons, Glenn Ligon, and Joseph Beuys. The **murals by José Clemente Orozco** (1930–31, restored 1988), explore themes of exploitation, revolution, the brotherhood of man, and the dignity of labor. They are the only murals by this artist in New York City.

Continue west on W. 12th St. At the corner of Sixth Ave turn right (north) and walk a block to W. 13th St. Turn left (west) to the Portico Place Apartments (converted 1982), 143 W. 13th St, built as the **Thirteenth Street Presbyterian Church** (1846; attrib. Samuel Thompson). One of the finest Greek revival churches in the city, at one time it simultaneously housed Presbyterian and Jewish congregations. Its first rector was Dr. Samuel D. Burchard, best known for having undermined the presidential hopes of Republican James G. Blaine in 1884 by making an inflammatory speech in which he labeled the opposition, Grover Cleveland's Democratic Party, the party of "rum, Romanism, and rebellion." In part because of the Catholic backlash that followed, Blaine lost New York City, New York State, and the nation.

Continue west to Seventh Ave, then turn right and head north to **14th St,** which marks the northern boundary of Greenwich Village but seems miles from its quaint and historic insularity. It is a broad, busy, rundown, gritty commercial thoroughfare, though some of the richly ornamental facades of bygone days still hover above street level.

Between Seventh and Sixth Aves is the headquarters of the Salvation Army in **Centennial Memorial Temple** (1930; Voorhees, Gmelin & Walker), 120 W. 14th St, a grandiose Art Deco monument to a spiritual soldiery. Across the street at 125 W. 14th St is the **42nd Division Armory of the New York National Guard** (1971; N.Y. State General Services Administration, Charles S. Kawecki, architect), a piece of modern military architecture that makes one long for the castles and crenellations of old.

Turn around and walk west on 14th St. Facing each other across Eighth Ave are two former banks. On the southwest corner is the former **New York County National Bank** (1907; DeLemos & Cordes with Rudolph L. Daus; DL), 77–79 Eighth

Ave, a Beaux-Arts structure with four 100 ft tall bay windows on the sides. The companion piece on the northwest corner is the former **New York Savings Bank** (1897; R.H. Robertson; DL), 81 Eighth Ave, a classical revival "temple" with a marble facade, Corinthian columns, and a copper dome. It was restored and converted into a carpet store in 1994.

Gansevoort Market

The western extreme of 14th St is the northern boundary of the Gansevoort Market wholesale meat-packing district. Hectic and noisy in the predawn hours, the market is crowded into a clutter of 19C buildings facing narrow stone streets. On weekend nights, it vibrates with energy, with nearly a dozen restaurants and a half-dozen bars and clubs attracting wildly diverse crowds. As part of this revival, a few art galleries have trickled down from Chelsea to the north.

History

The district is named after Peter Gansevoort (1749–1812), a colonel during the Revolutionary War, who later attained the rank of brigadier general and died in active command during the War of 1812. The present Gansevoort Market is descended from two major 19C markets: the West Washington Market at the foot of W. 12th St, through whose buildings and piers passed cargoes of produce from southern and Caribbean ports as well as much of the city's oyster supply; and the old Gansevoort Market across from it, a large paved area where New Jersey and Long Island farmers drove their wagons to await the beginning of their predawn workday. Herman Melville, author of *Moby-Dick*, his literary career apparently in ruins, worked as a customs inspector on the former Gansevoort dock for 19 years beginning in 1866.

Later, in the late 1920s when the Ninth Avenue El was torn down, the city decided to restructure the Gansevoort area as a meat-packing and distribution center, a function it still maintains. Though the markets at the Hunts Point Terminal in the Bronx and the advent of meat prepacked at the slaughterhouses of the Midwest are cutting into its profits, the Gansevoort Market still supplies the meat for most Manhattan restaurants.

12 · Chelsea

Subway: Broadway–Seventh Ave Local (1, 9) to 18th St. Lexington Ave Express or Local (4, 5, 6) or Broadway Local (N, R) to 14th St–Union Square. Seventh Ave Express (2, 3) to 14th St. Sixth Ave Express or Local (B, D, Q, F) to 14th St.
Bus: M2, M3, M5, M6, M7.

Chelsea, centering in the West 20s, formerly a mixed bag of factories, urban renewal projects, and tenements, with a few elegant town houses thrown in, is rapidly gentrifying. It has become in the last decade one of the artistic hot spots of the city. Chelsea owes its name and approximate boundaries to Capt. Thomas Clarke, a retired British soldier who bought a tract of land in 1750 and named the estate after the Chelsea Hospital in London, a refuge for old and disabled soldiers. Clarke's descendents added to the lands that ultimately reached from present-day 14th St to 24th St, and from Eighth Ave to the Hudson River. Today, however,

Jacob K. Javits Convention Center

N

0   200yds

WEST   HIGHWAY

MILLER

TWELFTH

Former 30th St Terminal

W 40TH ST
W 41ST ST
W 39TH ST
W 38TH ST
W 37TH ST
W 36TH ST
W 35TH ST
W 33RD ST
W 32ND ST

THIRTY FOURTH

AVENUE

ST

W 31ST ST
W 30TH ST
W 29TH ST
W 28TH ST
W 27TH ST
W 26TH ST
W 25TH ST
W 24TH ST

ELEVENTH

General Post Office

Starrett-Lehigh Building

CHELSEA PARK

Church of the Holy Apostles

WEST

Chelsea Piers

London Terrace Apartments

W 22ND ST

TWENTY THIRD

Dia Center for the Arts

W 21ST ST

CLEMENT CLARKE MOORE PARK

W 20TH ST

TENTH

Penn Station South Apartments

The Kitchen

General Theological Seminary

NINTH

Chelsea Hotel

St. Peter's Church

W 19TH ST
W 18TH ST

EIGHTH

Joyce Theater

W 17TH ST

SEVENTH AVENUE

W 16TH ST
W 15TH ST

Chelsea Markets

W 14TH ST

SIXTH AVENUE

DISTANCES FROM FIFTH AVENUE TO EIGHTH AVENUE FORESHORTENED

Center for Jewish History

FIFTH AVENUE

Chelsea is considered to extend northward to about 30th St and east to Sixth Ave. The original Clarke family mansion stood between what is today Ninth and Tenth Aves and 22nd and 23rd Sts until it was demolished in 1854.

Chelsea owes its most attractive streets to Clarke's grandson, Clement Clarke Moore, who developed it as a residential neighborhood; it owes its ethnic diversity and slums to the New York Central Railroad.

History

Clement Clarke Moore (1779–1863) compiled the first Hebrew lexicon published in the U.S. but is best remembered for his poem *A Visit from St. Nicholas*, which begins " 'Twas the night before Christmas. . . ." (Recent scholarship indicates Moore may not have written the poem but instead stole credit from Henry Livingston of Poughkeepsie). Moore summered in Chelsea until it became clear that the pressures of the city's northward growth would engulf its rolling hills and meadows. He began selling building lots with controls attached: no alleys, no stables, no "manufactures," but a mandatory ten-ft setback for all houses.

Chelsea's residential tranquillity was disrupted when the Hudson River Railroad, later absorbed by the New York Central, laid tracks down Eleventh Ave (c. 1847), attracting breweries, slaughterhouses, and glue factories, which in turn attracted job-hungry immigrants, including Irish immigrants fleeing the potato famines. The Ninth Ave El (1871), an elevated railway whose overhead tracks plunged the avenue below into shadow, further depressed the area. Although the El was dismantled before World War II, the western part of Chelsea remained run-down.

The eastern part, however, fared better. During the 1870s and 1880s a theatrical district flourished on W. 23rd St, home of Edwin Booth's theater (1869–83), Proctor's (opened 1888), and Pike's Opera House (1868). Although the theater district moved uptown later in the century, Chelsea enjoyed a brief artistic revival around World War I as the center of early moviedom, before a better climate and more open space lured the industry to California. The Famous Players' Studio (221 W. 26th St) was based in an old armory and released some of Mary Pickford's early films. Other studios, like the Reliance and the Majestic (both at 520 W. 21st St) and the Kalem Company (235 W. 23rd St), attracted stars such as Alice Joyce and Wallace Reid.

Chelsea has long embraced many ethnic groups: one of the city's oldest Spanish communities; Scottish, German, and British immigrants; the once-predominant Irish; a French colony; a Greek enclave on Eighth Ave; and a Puerto Rican population that poured in after World War II. Tolerance has been extended also to union activists, to artists and their followers who spilled over from Greenwich Village, and to a gay population, which soared in the 1990s. (Chelsea's population reached 60,000 in the mid-1960s, dipped to 41,000 in 1990, and is again rising.)

Today there are many Chelseas, including the gay community, which now rivals that of Greenwich Village, and the arts community, which has attracted Off-Off-Broadway companies and art galleries. Western Chelsea, where most of the galleries are located, nevertheless still harbors thousands of the poor, who live in tenements and housing projects—for example, the Robert Fulton Houses and Elliott Houses. The far west also hosts the Chelsea Piers, a venue for recreational sports (and children's birthday parties). Ladies Mile, in the mid-19C a district of fashionable department stores along Sixth Ave in eastern Chelsea, has been revived as a shopping strip filled with the same chain stores that flourish in malls across the nation.

Central Chelsea is gentrifying rapidly. A 1995 rezoning has encouraged residential development along the avenues (excluding the side streets for now), allowing condos and co-ops in former office buildings and factories, and apartment towers are rising on former parking lots. As the boundary of bustling Midtown is pushed south to 23rd St, lower-middle-class residents and longstanding small businesses—furriers, flower dealers, and printers—are being pushed out. New construction recently displaced the much-loved outdoor antiques market that attracted hundreds of thousands of visitors to Chelsea each year.

Begin on W. 16th St, just off Fifth Ave, with its row of Greek revival houses. Between 1930 and 1973 Margaret Sanger ran her pioneering Birth Control Clinical Research Bureau at **17 W. 16th St** (1846; DL). The bow front is unusual in New York.

Center For Jewish History

15 W. 16th St, New York, NY 10011. ☎ (212) 294-8301 for the center; (212) 294-8330 for Yeshiva University Museum. Web site: www.centerforjewish history.org. Museum open Tues, Wed, Sun 11–5; Thus 11–8. Closed Mon, Sat, Jewish holidays. Admission charge. Exhibitions, lectures, children's discovery room, facilities for genealogical research. Library; gift shop; kosher cafeteria (to open). Accessible to wheelchairs.

At 15 W. 16th St is the Center for Jewish History (opened 2000), an umbrella organization that brings together the American Jewish Historical Society, the American Sephardi Federation, the Leo Baeck Institute, Yeshiva University Museum, and YIVO Institute for Jewish Research.

Each institution at the center emphasizes a different aspect of Jewish experience: the **Yeshiva University Museum** (founded 1973) looks at Jewish intellectual and cultural achievements over 3,000 years of history; the **Leo Baeck Institute** (founded 1955) documents the history of German-speaking Jews; the **American Jewish Historical Society** (founded 1892) works to illuminate American Jewish life from 1500 to the present; the **American Sephardi Federation** (founded 1984) focuses on Jews whose families originated in Syria, Turkey, Morocco, Yemen, and Egypt; **YIVO Institute for Jewish Research** (founded 1925 in Vilna) is the only pre-Holocaust scholarly institution that successfully transferred its holdings to the Western Hemisphere. The collections, shown in changing exhibitions, include 100 million archival documents, a half-million books, and more than a thousand family trees. The tens of thousands of artifacts range from Emma Lazarus's handwritten sonnet "The New Colossus," to a letter of Thomas Jefferson denouncing anti-Semitism, to Sandy Koufax's first baseball uniform (signed), to Yiddish sheet music commemorating the sinking of the *Titanic.* In addition to a regular schedule of exhibitions, the center offers a children's discovery center and an outdoor sculpture garden.

Ladies' Mile Historic District

Walk west to Sixth Ave; turn right. This section of the Ladies' Mile Historic District on the eastern edge of Chelsea is once again flourishing.

History

In its heyday, from about 1860 until the years just before World War I, Ladies' Mile, called Fashion Row by those who shopped there, was the city's prime shopping district. It ran from about 9th St, where A. T. Stewart entertained customers at his Cast Iron Palace with continuous organ music, to about 23rd St, where Stern Brothers' uniformed doormen stood waiting to help ladies from their carriages.

At 604–612 Sixth Ave (between W. 17th and W. 18th Sts) the **Price Building** (1912; Buchman & Fox), adorned with lions' heads and a metal cornice, is now home to **Old Navy,** a store for moderately priced clothing. At 616–632 Sixth Ave (between W. 18th and W. 19th Sts) is the former **Siegel-Cooper Dry Goods Store** (1896; DeLemos & Cordes). With almost 16 acres of floor space this was the world's largest store until Macy's Herald Square building opened in 1902. Siegel-Cooper's opulently ornamented building has a triple-arched entrance (mutilated by modernization) and terra-cotta shields bearing the firm's initials. Inside, the store, whose motto was "A City in Itself," offered a photo studio, a telegraph office, a barber shop, and a plant nursery. Its centerpiece was a fountain containing an 18 ft replica of Daniel Chester French's *The Republic,* a female figure with a marble head and arms clad in a gown of polished brass; the figure now resides in California's Forest Lawn Cemetery. Today the building holds branches of three national chains: **T. J. Maxx; Bed, Bath & Beyond;** and **Filene's Basement.**

Across the street at 621 Sixth Ave is the original **B. Altman Dry Goods Store** (1877; David & John Jardine; additions 1887; William Hume; 1910; Buchman & Fox), housed in a cast-iron building with neo-Grec detailing. Today another chain store, **Today's Man,** occupies the space where yesterday's ladies rode up and down in Altman's carpeted and upholstered elevator.

On the next block at 641 Sixth Ave was **Simpson Crawford & Simpson Dry Goods** (1900; William Hume & Son), one of the first stores with escalators. Under the dome of the conservative granite and limestone building are a **Radio Shack** and other tenants.

At the northeast corner of Sixth Ave and W. 20th St is the former **Church of the Holy Communion** (1846; rectory and parish house, 1850; Sisters' House, 1854; all by Richard Upjohn; DL). Influential in its day as the first asymmetrical Gothic revival church in the nation, the church houses the **Limelight,** a popular dance club since the early 1980s.

Another highlight of Ladies' Mile is the block-long former **Hugh O'Neill Dry Goods Store** (1875; Mortimer C. Merritt), 655–671 Sixth Ave (between W. 20th and W. 21st Sts), whose name is still visible on the pediment. When the store opened, the cast-iron facade with its parade of Corinthian columns was even more spectacular: great bulbous domes crowned the curved corner towers. O'Neill aggressively undercut his competition and lured shoppers into the store with heavily advertised sales and loss leaders. Today Elsevier Science Publishing tenants the space.

Just to the west on 21st St is the **Third Shearith Israel Graveyard,** a tiny cemetery that served the city's earliest Jewish congregation (see Congregation Shearith Israel in Walk 26) from 1829 to 1851.

The ornate light brick building on the next block at 675–691 Sixth Ave used to house the **Adams Dry Goods Store** (1900; DeLemos & Cordes). A helmeted female head (over the main entrance) and lions' heads (above the other entrances) overlook the scene. Passengers riding by on the El could enjoy the terra-cotta detail and massive limestone columns above the arched doorways. Today the building contains a **Barnes & Noble** and **Mattell/Tyco** toys. **Staples** office supply store and the **Burlington Coat Factory** have taken over the cast-iron **Ehrich Brothers Emporium** (1889; William Schickel) at 695–709 Sixth Ave.

Shakespeare on Sixth Avenue

Between 1869 and 1883 the French Second Empire **Edwin Booth Theatre** stood on the southeast corner of W. 23rd St and Sixth Ave, managed by the famous actor, who also took leading roles onstage. When the theater failed, James W. McCreery, already a successful merchant, took over the site, demolished the theater, and put up his second New York store. In his theater Booth had displayed a bust of Shakespeare (perhaps with himself posing as the Bard), which McCreery installed on the store's facade. In 1907 McCreery's moved uptown to 34th St, but the building on 23rd St survived until it was razed in 1975; the bust was subsequently donated to New York University.

The main attraction on W. 23rd St between Fifth and Sixth Aves is the former **Stern's Dry Goods Store** (32–36 W. 23rd St: 1878; Henry Fernbach; 38–46 W. 23rd St: 1892; William Schickel). This Italian Renaissance cast-iron extravaganza belonged to the four Stern brothers and three Stern sisters, who had previously run a small dry goods shop on 22nd St. The building now contains a toy company showroom and ad agencies.

Other cast-iron buildings that once housed esteemed retailers line the rest of the block. The building at **35–37 W. 23rd St** (1880; David & John Jardine), where Villeroy & Boch and F.A.O. Schwarz once offered their wares, has an iron cornice with leaves and sunflowers (F.A.O. Schwarz later moved to 39–41 W. 23rd St); **58 W. 23rd St** was home to Teller & Company, which became Bonwit Teller; and **61–65 W. 23rd St** (1886; John Snook), with its white tiered colonnade, was Horner's Furniture Store, which became Flint and Horner when it merged with Flint Furniture at 45–47 W. 23rd St.

Chelsea Hotel

Walk west past Sixth and Seventh Aves to the Chelsea Hotel (1884; Hubert, Pirsson & Co.; DL), 222 W. 23rd St, an architectural and literary landmark. Visually, it is most remarkable for its cast-iron balconies, with their interlaced sunflowers stretched row upon row across the long facade, but the building is also replete with gables, chimneys, dormers, lancet and semielliptical windows, terra-cotta reliefs, and bands of white stonework.

History

The Chelsea, one of the city's earliest cooperative apartment houses, was the first apartment building to reach 12 stories and to feature a penthouse. It was converted into a hotel in 1905. Writers Mark Twain and O. Henry (William Sydney

Porter) lived here in the early days, but its artistic heyday came after the 1930s, when Thomas Wolfe, James T. Farrell, Mary McCarthy, Arthur Miller, Brendan Behan, Vladimir Nabokov, Gregory Corso, John Sloan, Sarah Bernhardt, and Yevgeny Yevtushenko all enjoyed its hospitality. Dylan Thomas lapsed into a fatal coma in room 205 after allegedly remarking to his female companion, "I've had my eighteenth whiskey, and I think that's the record." The hotel was also at various points home to Eugene O'Neill, Tennessee Williams, and the composer Virgil Thompson, who lived here from 1940 until his death in 1989. Jackson Pollock, Willem de Kooning, and Larry Rivers stayed here, and Andy Warhol portrayed it as a wild and impetuous place in his movie *Chelsea Girls*. In the 1960s, rock musicians Janis Joplin, the Grateful Dead, and Bob Dylan joined the list of notables, and in 1978 Sid Vicious, bass player for the Sex Pistols, a punk rock group, was indicted for murdering his girlfriend with a hunting knife in the hotel. (He died of a heroin overdose before standing trial.) The hotel's most eccentric resident, perhaps, was George Kleinsinger, a composer who wrote a children's musical called *Tubby the Tuba* and is said to have been fond of composing at the piano with his pet boa constrictor encircling his body.

Today, the lobby features paintings and sculptures from residents past and present. The Chelsea continues as both a residential and guest hotel.

Opera on Eighth Avenue

On the northwest corner of Eighth Ave and W. 23rd St stood Pike's Opera House (1868), bought by financier Jay Gould and Erie Railroad partner Jim Fisk in 1869. Fisk and Gould renamed their building the Grand Opera House and produced opera and plays, while installing plush offices for the Erie Railroad upstairs. Attached to the building by tunnel was a brownstone mansion where high-living "Jubilee Jim" Fisk kept his mistress Josie Mansfield. Fisk was murdered in 1872 by Mansfield's subsequent lover, Edward S. Stokes, and his body lay in state in the opera house. The building, later a vaudeville house and movie theater, was demolished in 1960.

Turn left and walk south on Eighth Ave to 19th St. The **Joyce Theater** (1942; Simon Zelnick), 175 Eighth Ave, was once the Elgin Theater, a movie house, which by the 1970s was reduced to showing pornography. In 1982, it was gutted and dramatically returned to its original Art Moderne style (Hardy Holzman Pfeiffer Assocs.) and is now one of the principal venues of modern dance in the city.

Return to W. 20th St and turn right (west). At 346 W. 20th St is **St. Peter's Church** (Protestant Episcopal), a modest early–Gothic revival fieldstone church (1836–38; James W. Smith, builder, from designs by Clement Clarke Moore; DL). At the west end of the tract is the **Rectory** (1832), which first served as the church, and is built in the Greek revival style, though with engaged brick pilasters instead of the usual freestanding columns. According to legend, the foundations for the present church had already been laid when a vestryman returned from England, so enthralled with the Gothic parish churches there that he persuaded his colleagues to redesign the new church. The resulting structure, therefore, is Gothic more in its details than in its proportions and materials. The newest building, the brick **Parish Hall,** now used by the **Atlantic Theater,** was started in 1854 and completed in 1871, when the churchlike facade was added. Trinity Parish donated the wrought-iron fence (1790), formerly used in front of St. Paul's Chapel.

General Theological Seminary

Continue to Ninth Ave. Filling the block bounded by Ninth and Tenth Aves between 20th and 21st Sts, known as **Chelsea Square,** is the General Theological Seminary (Main Building, 1960; O'Connor and Kilham; West Building, 1836; other principal buildings, 1883–1900; Charles C. Haight). Clement Clarke Moore, who taught Hebrew and Greek here, donated the land on which the seminary (founded 1817) stands.

Enter through the modern building on Ninth Ave (between W. 20th and W. 21st Sts) and walk straight back to the courtyard. With the exception of the Gothic revival **West Building** (1836), most of the college was built from 1883–1900; Charles C. Haight designed the collegiate Gothic **quadrangle.** Especially attractive is the central **Chapel of the Good Shepherd,** with its 161 ft tower and bronze doors by J. Massey Rhind.

Return to Ninth Ave. Just north of the seminary on the northwest corner of 21st St is a small Federal house, **183 Ninth Ave** (1831), with fine Flemish bond brickwork. The three houses adjacent to it—185 Ninth Ave (1856) and 187 and 189 Ninth Ave (1868)—are among the few wooden houses remaining in Manhattan. They were built by James N. Wells, one of Chelsea's major 19C developers.

Return to W. 20th St and turn right (west). The block of W. 20th St between Ninth and Tenth Aves has gracious Greek revival and Italianate row houses. The building at **402 W. 20th St** (1897; C. P. H. Gilbert) is remarkable for the concave facade that curves back from the corner tenement to meet the ten-ft setback of the adjoining row of older houses. The letters *DONAC* above the door commemorate Don Alonzo Cushman, not a Spanish grandee but a dry goods merchant, friend of Clement Clarke Moore, parish leader, and land developer who made a fortune building in Chelsea. The brick-fronted frame house at 404 W. 20th St (1830) is the earliest house in the area.

From 406 to 418 W. 20th St is **Cushman Row,** named after the developer. Completed in 1840, these brick, brownstone-trimmed Greek revival houses still have many original details: fine cast-iron wreathes around small attic windows, paneled doors, iron stoop railings and areaway fences, and pilastered doorways with slender sidelights. The buildings at 416–418 still have their pineapple newel posts. This spot also offers a lovely view of the Chapel of the Good Shepherd in the seminary quadrangle.

Further down the block are some exceptional Italianate houses (**446–450 W. 20th St**) built in 1853 with round-headed ground-floor windows and doorways, as well as unusual trim beneath the cornices. Arched windows and doorways, exemplifying the Italianate style's attraction to circular forms, appeared only on expensive houses, since they were relatively difficult to execute. Jack Kerouac lived at 454 W. 20th St while writing his celebrated novel *On the Road.*

Turn right (north) at Tenth Ave and walk one block north to W. 21st St. At 193 Tenth Ave (northwest corner the intersection at W. 21st St) is the **Guardian Angel Roman Catholic Church** (1930; John Van Pelt), an elaborate red brick and limestone Romanesque-style church with a tile roof and frieze depicting biblical scenes. Before the Chelsea Piers closed (1968), the church served seamen and dockworkers, and in the 1930s its pastor was the port chaplain.

Another group of fine Italianate houses (465–473 W. 21st St) stretches along the north side of the 21st St just east of Tenth Ave.

Continue up Tenth Ave to the northeast corner of the intersection at 22nd St. The **Empire Diner** (1943, altered 1976; Carl Laanes) refurbished in black and chrome appropriate to its Art Deco origins, serves updated diner food. The large sign, whose blinking lights command passersby to E-A-T, makes it a popular visual landmark and meeting place.

The block of W. 22nd St, at Chelsea's far west, between Tenth and Eleventh Aves, is the newest frontier in the city's evolving art scene. Many SoHo galleries have relocated here, forced out of the old neighborhood by rising rents, and been joined by new galleries. In 1997 the warehouse at 525 W. 22nd St was converted to a condominium complex, complete with doorman, a sure sign of the revitalization of the neighborhood.

Dia Center for the Arts

Administrative offices, 542 W. 22nd St (at 11th Ave), New York, NY 10011. Galleries, 545 and 548 W. 22nd St. ☎ (212) 989-5566. Web site: www.diacenter. org. Open Wed–Sun noon–6. Closed Mon, Tues, Thanksgiving, Dec 24, 25, and 31, Jan 1, closed summer (mid-June–mid-Sept). Admission charge. Exhibitions, poetry readings, lectures, video programs. Café; bookstore. Accessible to wheelchairs.

Subway: Eighth Ave Local (C, E) to 23rd St. Bus: M11, M23.

The Dia Center for the Arts, which pioneered the transformation of western Chelsea, is its premier art institution.

History

Dia was established in 1974 by Philippa de Menil Friedrich, daughter of a Houston art patron, and Heiner Friedrich, a German-born art dealer, to support a selected group of artists outside the usual institutional system. Once based in SoHo, Dia opened here in 1987 in this four-story, 19C, renovated brick warehouse, expanding in 1998 to 545 W. 22nd St. The name, from the Greek *dia* meaning "through," suggests the center's role in making possible projects of a scale or character that might not find support elsewhere.

Dia became known in the 1970s for its monumental single-artist projects, including Walter De Maria's *The Broken Kilometer* (1979; see 393 West Broadway in Walk 8) and *The New York Earth Room* (1977; see 141 Wooster St in Walk 8). Between 1974 and 1984, the museum collected the works of Joseph Beuys, John Chamberlain, Walter De Maria, Dan Flavin, Donald Judd, Cy Twombly, Andy Warhol, and others. In addition, Dia has commissioned musical works, funded poetry translations, and commissioned projects from artists who are interested in exploring the potential of the Web. The gallery, with its raw unfinished exhibition space offers artists the opportunity to present large-scale work on a full floor of the building.

7000 Oaks

Along W. 22nd St between Tenth and Eleventh Aves is an installation of 23 basalt stone columns, each paired with a tree—part of a work by German artist Joseph

Beuys called *7000 Oaks.* In 1988 Dia put in the first five columns and planted gingko, linden, Bradford pear, sycamore, and oak trees. In 1996 Dia added 18 new trees and columns. The project carries on a work Beuys began in 1982 in Kassel, Germany, where 7,000 trees and columns have been planted, which the artist intended as the first stage in a scheme of worldwide tree planting.

Walk east on W. 22nd St, crossing Tenth Ave. Renowned 19C actor Edwin Forrest, now remembered primarily as one of the dramatic antagonists in the Astor Place Riot (see Walk 10), lived at **436 W. 22nd St** (1835) from 1839 to 1850. The building has been stripped of some of its ornamentation and converted to apartments.

Further east, beyond James Phelan Row (424–428 W. 22nd St, built 1843), is the only surviving five-bay Greek revival house in Manhattan at **414–416 W. 22nd St** (1835; James N. Wells). Wells, who also built 400–412 W. 22nd St in 1856, lived here briefly; in 1864–66 the building was remodeled with Italianate details.

Continue to Ninth Ave and walk north to W. 23rd St. Filling an entire block–23rd to 24th Sts and Ninth to Tenth Aves—are the **London Terrace Gardens,** an early modern apartment project (1930; Farrar & Watmaugh) named for a row (i.e., "terrace") of 19C colonnaded town houses torn down to make way for the present 14 buildings. When it first opened, amenities such as a central garden, swimming pool, solarium, gymnasium, and doormen dressed as London bobbies attracted tenants to its 1,665 apartments. On the top level was a clubhouse and the Marine Roof, fitted out like the deck of a transatlantic liner, complete with life buoys and folding deck chairs. Some of the buildings were converted to co-ops in the 1980s.

Walk north on Ninth Ave to 28th St. On the southeast corner of Ninth Ave and W. 28th St is the Protestant Episcopal **Church of the Holy Apostles** (1848; Minard Lafever; transepts 1858; Richard Upjohn & Sons; DL). This small brick church with its copper-covered, slate-roofed spire and bracketed eaves, is set in the midst of an overscaled modern housing project, but the surrounding open space gives it breathing room and allows it to stand out against the sky. Windows by William Jay Bolton, one of America's earliest stained glass artists, enhance the interior (open during Sunday services). Today the church serves the area's poor with a substantial soup kitchen.

Walk west to Eleventh Ave. The far west of Chelsea, once dominated by piers and railroads, still bears traces of that past. Between 27th and 28th Sts and Eleventh and Twelfth Aves, are the **Central Stores of the Terminal Warehouse Company** (1891), originally 25 storage buildings with 24 acres of warehousing space walled into one massive fortress surmounted by a Tuscan tower. The great arched doorway at one time admitted locomotives on a spur line of the New York Central Railroad, while the west facade opened onto the deepwater Hudson River piers. Cool cellars running beneath the entire structure were used to store wines, liquors, gums, and rubber. In the ultimate example of adaptive reuse, the lower reaches of the Terminal Warehouse were transformed in 1987 into one of the city's most popular dance clubs, the **Tunnel.** The club has drawn artists, celebrities, and onlookers into the cavernous cellars that are decorated with industrial hardware, red velvet couches, chandeliers, abstract paintings, and railroad tracks running off into nothingness. (In recent years, drug use and violence have created legal headaches for the club, and its future is in doubt.)

Across the street at 270 Eleventh Ave, **Dezerland** sports one of the city's most memorable storefronts with large classic cars sculpted into the facade. Inside is a drive-in theater where couples sit in classic cars under a fake sky and watch classic movies (available for private parties).

Starrett-Lehigh Building

A block to the south is the 19-story Starrett-Lehigh Building (1931; Russell G. and Walter M. Cory with Yasuo Matsui, assoc. architect; DL), an imposing Art Deco industrial building often overlooked because of its industrial surroundings. Admirers praise the building's dramatic exterior—horizontal bands of glass, concrete, and brown brick wrapped around curved corners—and its innovative concrete column-and-slab construction. It was one of the few American designs included in the Museum of Modern Art's 1932 international style exhibition.

History

Built over a spur line of the Lehigh Valley Railroad, the building was intended for freight handling, warehousing, and manufacturing, and was equipped with powerful elevators that could lift loaded boxcars from the tracks to the warehouse above. The railroad tracks inside the building were never built and those at street level were torn out, but the elevators still hoist 15-ton trucks into the vast interior.

Sold in 1998, the building was refurbished at a cost of $40 million and renamed the **Center for Creative Arts, Media and Technology.** Present tenants include media, Internet, and communications companies, as well as photography and art studios and galleries.

Chelsea Piers

Further south, stretching from W. 23rd St down to W. 17th St along the water is Chelsea's most significant recent addition, the Chelsea Piers, an entertainment and recreation complex.

History: 1902–1968

Piers 54–62 (1902–7; Warren & Wetmore) were designed specifically to receive the great transatlantic liners built around the turn of the 20C. In fact, the 800 ft finger piers were finished just in time to receive the *Mauretania* and the *Lusitania* (both 790 ft), then the pride of the Cunard Line. The *Titanic* was to dock here, but instead 675 of its passengers arrived on Cunard's *Carpathia,* which had rescued them from the frigid seas. In 1915 the *Lusitania* departed for England from these piers but was sunk by a German U-boat; 1,198 people died, including 124 Americans. Many immigrants landed here, only to be ferried directly to Ellis Island before they could truly enter the New World. The Depression debilitated the Atlantic trade and after World War II the Chelsea Piers never regained their importance for passenger shipping. With the decay of New York as a port in succeeding decades, this segment of Chelsea's economy atrophied and the piers closed in 1968. (In the early 1970s the city lost 20,000 waterfront jobs.) Many of the Irish American dockworkers who once lived here moved to New Jersey, where the piers are still active.

History: The 1990s

In the 1990s, the piers were converted into a production studio and a giant indoor playground for children and adults alike. The 30-acre site offers space-starved New Yorkers two roller rinks, two ice rinks, a tiered golf driving range, a health club, a "field house" (with a gymnastics center, a 50 ft high rock-climbing wall, a health club, basketball courts, soccer fields, and batting cages) and 40 bowling lanes. There are also two catering halls and the 200,000-square-ft Silver Screen Studios, which have attracted television and film production.

The Chelsea Piers were brought to life by Roland Betts and Tom Bernstein, entrepreneurs who had helped finance successful films and were part owners of the Texas Rangers baseball team. Their Chelsea Piers Management arrived in 1992 when New York State was looking for commercial development along the river to help pay for the future Hudson River Park (see Along the Hudson River in Walk 11). The management group leased the piers from the state. By the opening of the first phase in 1995, the project was way over budget. As problems mounted—lackluster response to the restaurants, pedestrians' complaints about crossing the West Side Highway, and continuing cost overruns—it appeared the whole project might sink. Ultimately, the owners poured $100 million into the project and were able to refinance their debt. As time went on, the piers grew rapidly in popularity: in 1998 they received 3.8 million visitors, third behind the Metropolitan Museum of Art and Madison Square Garden.

The Kitchen

512 W. 19th St (between Tenth and Eleventh Aves), New York, NY 10011. ☎ (212) 255-5793. Web site: www.thekitchen.org. Art gallery open Tues–Sat 2–6 and an hour before performances. Free; admission charge for performance events. Changing exhibitions, video, dance, children's programs, video archive. Accessible to wheelchairs.

Subway: Eighth Ave Express or Local (A, C, E) to 14th St; Eighth Ave Local (C, E) to 23rd St. Bus: M11, M14, M23.

Cross West St, walking east to Tenth Ave. Then walk south to W. 19th St and turn left. At 512 W. 19th St is The Kitchen, a center for interdisciplinary and experimental art: video, music, dance, performance, and film.

Founded in 1971 in the former kitchen of the now-defunct Broadway Central Hotel, The Kitchen began as a space for video art and soon expanded to include experimental music and other avant-garde performance arts. In 1974, it moved to SoHo, where it remained for about a dozen years, increasingly beset by such problems as skyrocketing SoHo rents and the relocation of the avant-garde artistic community to the East Village and elsewhere. In 1985, The Kitchen moved here, occupying a 19C ice house later used as a film studio. It has fostered the careers of Laurie Anderson, Eric Bogosian, David Byrne with the Talking Heads, Bill T. Jones and Arnie Zane, Nam June Paik, Meredith Monk, Robert Mapplethorpe, and Cindy Sherman.

Chelsea Market

Walk east to Ninth Ave, then south to W. 16th St. Between 15th and 16th Sts, and Ninth and Tenth Aves is the new Chelsea Market, 75 Ninth Ave, filling the ground level of a former Nabisco Cookie Factory.

History

A consolidation of 17 buildings built at various times between the 1890s and the mid-1930s, the factory was the birthplace of the Oreo, invented in 1912. Trains once delivered flour straight from the docks into the building on special tracks. (Nabisco departed in 1958.)

The market opened in 1997 for wholesalers willing to let the public see them at work—visitors can look into the kitchens—and to sell goods at less than retail. The **Lobster Place, Ruthy's Cheesecake, Amy's Breads,** and other firms that supply the city's restaurants are located here. The market has its own architectural ambience—sculptures by Mark Mennin decorate the long narrow hallway of exposed wood and brick; at odd intervals cast-iron ears and noses appear, a granite sleeping head, a massive coil of canvas industrial hose, knobby carved feet sticking out beneath a brick wall, and an iron heart on a stone ledge. Even the bathrooms are unusual, decorated with funky, colorful mosaics. Two ragged-edged brick arches—blasted through solid walls to create the walkway—suggest that you have stumbled upon some strange ruin. The hall's centerpiece is an urban waterfall—a large cast-iron pipe spilling water into a well, a welcome relief from the city's noise or the Muzak of conventional malls.

13 · Stuyvesant Square, Union Square, Madison Square, Gramercy Park, and the Flatiron District

Subway: Lexington Ave Express or Local (4, 5, 6) or Broadway Local (N, R) to 14th St–Union Square. From Union Square, walk east to Second Ave and then one block north to Stuyvesant Square.
Bus: M15 downtown via Second Ave to 14th St.

Stuyvesant Square

Begin at Stuyvesant Square, a four-acre park bisected by Second Ave and running from E. 15th to E. 17th Sts. Once part of Peter Stuyvesant's farm, the land was "sold" to the city by Stuyvesant's great grandson for $5 in 1836. The park was landscaped a century later with shade trees and small pools. The bronze **statue of Peter Stuyvesant** (1936, installed 1941) in the western half is by Gertrude Vanderbilt Whitney, founder of the Whitney Museum.

East of Stuyvesant Square

The area east of Stuyvesant Square is becoming home to an increasing number of Filipinos, many of whom who work as doctors and nurses at the nearby hospitals. There are several Filipino restaurants around E. 14th St and First Ave, a neighborhood sometimes known as Little Manila. Nearly half the congregation at **Immaculate Conception Church,** 406–412 E. 14th St between First Ave and Avenue A, is Filipino. The church and clergy

---

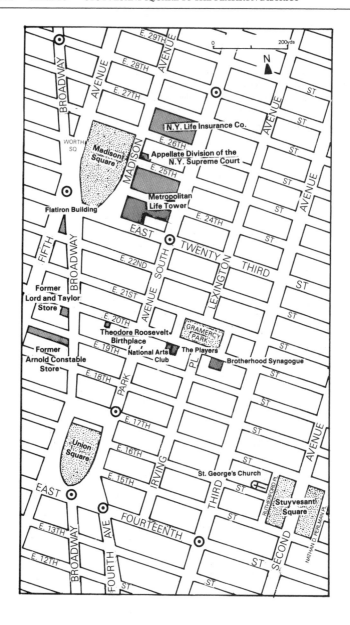

house (1894–96; Barney & Chapman; DL) were constructed in a French Gothic style as a chapel and hospital by Grace Church (Broadway at E. 10th St). The chapel, unlike its wealthy parent church, did not charge pew rents, allowing less affluent Episcopalians to attend. The Roman Catholic archdiocese bought the property in 1943 and converted the hospital to a residence for clergy.

Stuyvesant Town (1947; Irwin Clavan and Gilmore Clarke), fondly known as "Stuy Town," runs from First Ave to the FDR Drive and from E. 14th to E. 20th Sts. This immense and institutional-looking middle-income housing project was built by the Metropolitan Life Insurance Company, which got a sizable tax abatement for redeveloping 18 blocks of slums as affordable housing for returning World War II servicemen. In 1947 the waiting list numbered some 110,000; while the number nowadays is less than 10 percent of that figure, families still must wait several years to get into one of the 8,756 rent-stabilized apartments. From E. 20th to E. 23rd Sts is the slightly more upscale **Peter Cooper Village** (1947; Irwin Clavan and Gilmore Clarke).

Bellevue Hospital (1908–39, McKim, Mead & White; New Building between E. 27th and E. 28th Sts, 1974; Katz, Waisman, Weber, Strauss; Joseph Blumenkranz; Pomerance & Breines; Feld & Timoney) sits between First Ave and the FDR Drive and E. 25th and E. 30th Sts. It began as an infirmary in New York's first almshouse, erected 1736, on the site of City Hall Park. In 1794, following an epidemic of yellow fever, the almshouse was moved to Chambers St, but the facilities were inadequate to deal with the epidemic, so the city fathers bought an estate about three miles away, sufficiently remote to isolate the victims. The mansion house, Belle Vue, became a pesthouse. The hospital built on the site gradually became one of the city's principal municipal hospitals. Bellevue boasts a number of pioneering achievements: the colonies' first recorded instruction in anatomy dissection (1750), the city's first lying-in wards (1799), America's first appendectomy (1867), the world's first hospital-based ambulance service (1869), first hospital cesarean section (1887). The Bellevue Hospital emergency service is one of the most famous in the nation. Today the hospital treats about 400,000 patients annually.

From Stuyvesant Square, walk north on Second Avenue to 303–305 Second Ave (between E. 17th and E. 18th Sts), the former **Lying-In Hospital** (1902; R. H. Robertson) was built when most women gave birth at home. During its early years, 60 percent of all Manhattan hospital births took place here. The building, which is topped with a Palladian crown, now contains apartments and medical offices.

Return to E. 17th St and turn right (west). The **Stuyvesant Square Historic District** is filled with Greek revival and Italianate houses dating to the 1850s.

At Rutherford Place, turn left. The building at 4 Rutherford Place is the **chapel of St. George's Church** (1911; Matthew Lansing Emery and Henry George Emery), an elaborate Byzantine-Romanesque companion to the more somber church next door. **St. George's Church** (Protestant Episcopal), a formidable Romanesque revival brownstone (1856; Otto Blesch and Leopold Eidlitz; DL), is probably best remembered as J. P. Morgan's church; as an elder he ruled it with an iron hand. He also donated the land on which the present parish house stands. The first church (1847) burned in 1865 but was rebuilt according to the original plans, although at the time of the reconstruction the rector insisted on an evangelically simple interior without the customary altar and reredos. The original church had two tall spires, but they were weakened by the fire and removed (1888).

One block south is the **Friends' Meeting House and Seminary** (1860; Charles T. Bunting; DL), a red brick Greek revival building with brownstone quoins, austere like all Quaker houses of worship.

Walk west on E. 16th St past the original rectory at 209 E. 16th St, built in the early 1850s by Leopold Eidlitz. At 205–207 E. 16th St (1888; Cyrus Eidlitz) is the original parish house, a Gothic brownstone building replete with stained glass and turrets.

Union Square

Continue west on E. 16th St to Union Square, bounded by E. 18th and E. 14th Sts and Broadway and Park Ave South/Union Square East. It is the centerpiece of a neighborhood also known as Union Square (roughly 21st St to 14th St and Third Ave to Sixth Ave). The square was first named Union Place (1811) because it stood at the junction of the two main roads out of town, the Boston Post Rd and the Albany Post Rd (now Fourth Ave and Broadway).

History

The area was part of the Brevoort farm in the 18C. It was left open by decree when the 1811 grid (see Chronology in Background Information) was laid out, and in the 1830s it remained vacant land with a few shacks and a potter's field. In 1832 Samuel Ruggles (who had already developed Gramercy Park, see later in this walk) leased nearby land from the city and got the city to grade and enclose the square and lay out surrounding streets; Ruggles then sold his leases as building lots.

Before long, fashionable residences (including Ruggles's own) and theaters surrounded the square. In 1854 the Academy of Music, a grand opera house, opened at E. 14th St and Irving Place. Within a decade, Wallack's Theatre (E. 13th St and Broadway) and Irving Hall (later the Irving Place Theatre at E. 15th St and Irving Place) followed as did stylish restaurants—Delmonico's (which moved from downtown) and Luchow's, which lasted well into the 20C.

In the 1870s Frederick Law Olmsted and Calvert Vaux redesigned the park, removing its fence and placing a large fountain in the center. Toward century's end, Union Square was the heart of Ladies' Mile, a promenade of fashionable stores that stretched along Broadway from 9th St to 23rd St. By 1900 both commerce and art had moved uptown to Madison Square, and burlesque houses and shooting galleries moved into the area.

Many old homes became tenements housing laborers, including workers in the needle trades. In 1882 the park saw the nation's first Labor Day Parade. After the turn of the 20C and before World War I, the park became a center of political dissidence for anarchists, socialists, "Wobblies" (members of the Industrial Workers of the World), and communists. A decade later, mass meetings sometimes developed into confrontations with the police: most famous were a gathering protesting the execution of anarchists Nicola Sacco and Bartolomeo Vanzetti (Aug 22, 1927) and a Depression labor demonstration (March 6, 1930) attended by 35,000 workers and sympathizers. Public outcry after police injured 100 demonstrators at this meeting secured the park as a place of assembly, making it the heart of radical political activities in the city. During the 1930s various radical, progressive, and labor groups established headquarters in the area: the Socialist Party, the Communist Party, the American Civil Liberties Union, the Amalgamated Clothing Workers of America, and the International Ladies Garment Workers Union. In 1998 the park was named a National Historic Landmark because of its role in American labor history.

During the building of the BMT subway (1935–36) the park was raised four ft above street level and a perimeter wall added. By the 1970s, failing businesses and deteriorating buildings surrounded the park, which was dominated by drug dealers strolling its paths and hawking their wares.

Several factors have contributed to the neighborhood's recovery from hard times: the development of Zeckendorf Towers (completed 1987) east of the park; the presence of the city's first and most popular green market; the redesign and restoration of the park in the mid-1980s; and the doubling of the park's size in the late 1990s, with the conversion of adjacent pavement into parkland. Once again bustling shops, vital theaters, and busy restaurants surround the park, as residents and workers enjoy the green open space.

Flowers, Flags, and Candles

After the terrorist attack that brought down the World Trade Center on Sept 11, 2001, Union Square became a pilgrimage site for people mourning and honoring the victims of the attack. Homemade "missing" posters were taped to the lampposts, curbs, pavement, and the equestrian statue of George Washington. Incense, American flags, and bunches of flowers were strewn among banks of candles. Poems, thoughts, and prayers were written on the sidewalks, or taped to the low fencing on butcher paper, T-shirts, and drawings by schoolchildren. Local residents and visitors from the world over added their words and set down candles and flowers. Other city sites, including the black-draped, flower-strewn entryways to fire stations, were similarly decorated and used in this ceremonial way; but because 14th St was the southernmost point allowed for nonresident pedestrians and nonemergency vehicles in the days immediately following the disaster, and because of the square's proximity to Beth Israel and St. Vincent's Hospitals, it served as the logical choice for New Yorkers' largest spontaneous memorial to their loss.

Turn left and walk south to the **Union Square Savings Bank** (1907; Henry Bacon; DL), 20 Union Square East. The Corinthian colonnade recalls Bacon's most famous accomplishment, the Lincoln Memorial in Washington, D.C. Today the bank is home to the Daryl Roth Theatre, which along with the Vineyard Theatre (108 E. 15th St), Union Square Theatre (100 E. 17th St), and Century Center for the Performing Arts (1869; Gambrill & Richardson; DL) at 109–111 E. 15th St has brought theater back to Union Square after a century's absence.

At the southern edge of the park near E. 15th St (adjacent to Union Square East) stands a bronze **statue of the Marquis de Lafayette** (1876; Frédéric Auguste Bartholdi), a gift from France for American support during the Franco-Prussian War. Bartholdi, best known for that other monument of Franco-American friendship, the Statue of Liberty, depicts Lafayette offering his sword to the cause of American independence.

At 10 Union Square East (between E. 15th and E. 14th Sts) stands **Zeckendorf Towers** (1987; Davis, Brody and Assoc.), occupying the former turf of **S. Klein's-on-the-Square,** which between 1921 and 1975 offered discount clothing and the occasional fashion find to the determined shopper. The Zeckendorf development includes 670 residential units, offices, and the Vineyard Theatre.

Turn right (west) at 14th St. The massive **One Union Square South** (1999; Davis Brody Bond) epitomizes the resurgence of Union Square. Its ground-floor tenants include a Virgin Records Megastore and a multiplex theater (with New York's first stadium seating). Dominating the facade is *Metronome* (1999; Kristin Jones and Andrew Ginzel), a ten-story sculpture whose themes are place and time. The work emits light, steam, and sound, and even tracks the phases of the moon. Concentric circles of brickwork radiate from a central sunburst; a concrete "rock" plummets through space; a 67 ft long bronze pendulum swings. The bronze hand was enlarged from the park's equestrian statue of George Washington.

Facing E. 14th St at the south end of the park is the equestrian **statue of George Washington** (1856; Henry Kirke Brown with John Quincy Adams Ward), a 14 ft bronze work considered the sculptor's masterpiece. It commemorates Washington's entrance to the city on Evacuation Day (Nov 25, 1783), when British occupation of the city ended. In the southwest corner is Kantilal B. Patel's bronze **statue of Mohandas Gandhi** (1986), the Indian nationalist and advocate of nonviolent resistance, appropriately sited in a park long associated with political protest.

Turn right at Union Square West. The nine-story Romanesque revival **Lincoln Building** (1890; R. H. Robertson; DL), 1–3 Union Square West, was one of the neighborhood's earliest tall commercial structures; the facade sports terra-cotta griffins and heads of men and beasts.

At 5 Union Square West, the **Spingler Building** (1896) is named for the family whose farm once covered much of this area. Visible on the west side of Union Square West are two other turn-of-the-20C office buildings. At 31 Union Square West (northwest corner of E. 16th St) is the former **Bank of the Metropolis** (1893; Bruce Price; DL), a narrow graceful limestone tower with an Ionic portico of dark granite columns and a large cornice. Next door at 33 Union Square West is the Moorish-influenced **Union Building** (1893; Alfred Zucker; DL), originally the Decker Building, headquarters of the Decker Piano Company.

Union Square Park

Enter Union Square Park at Union Square West and E. 15th St. On the west side of the park is a **fountain** (1881; Adolph Dondorf) with a figure of a woman and children. Near the center of the park stands the base (36 ft diameter; 9½ ft high) of the **Independence Flagstaff** (1926; Anthony De Francisci), whose bronze reliefs symbolize the forces of Good and Evil during the American struggle for independence. Formerly called the Charles F. Murphy Memorial, after the Tammany Hall boss (1858–1924), the flagpole was financed by $80,000 of Tammany money collected on the 150th anniversary of the signing of the Declaration of Independence. The pedestal bears the text of the Declaration and a quotation from Thomas Jefferson.

At the north end of the park is a bronze **statue of Abraham Lincoln** (1868; Henry Kirke Brown). Erected three years after Lincoln's assassination, the figure, dressed in a baggy suit, was criticized for its uninspiring dowdiness. North of the statue is a colonnaded pavilion dating from the 1930s.

Visible beyond the park to the north of the pavilion, at 33 E. 17th St, is the ornate red brick **Century Building** (1881; William Schickel; DL), which features classical motifs and sunflowers in the Queen Anne style. At one time the *Century Illustrated* and *St. Nicholas* magazines were published here; the building now contains a Barnes & Noble bookstore.

Visible to the northeast, crowned by a tremendous mansard roof, is the W New York Hotel, formerly the **Guardian Life Insurance Co.** (1911; D'Oench & Yost; DL), 201 Park Ave South. The Guardian was originally called the Germania Life Insurance Co., but the name became a liability during World War I. Guardian moved out in 1999.

Diagonally across the street at 100 E. 17th St is the **Union Square Theatre** and **New York Film Academy** (1928; Thompson, Holmes & Converse), originally built for Tammany Hall, the city's notorious political machine.

Tammany Hall

Tammany Hall, founded in the late 18C as a fraternal society and political club, later grew into the Democratic Party machine, long the most potent factor in city politics. By the mid-19C, Tammany had become synonymous with corruption and crooked elections (notably with bought immigrant votes), and its leaders were known as "bosses" (e.g., "Boss" Tweed).

Leave the park on the west side. North of the park, Union Square West becomes Broadway. One-time palatial department stores and fine office buildings occupy the prominent intersections, reminders of the time this stretch of Broadway belonged to **Ladies' Mile,** a high-end shopping district. The **MacIntyre Building** (1892; R. H. Robertson) at 874 Broadway (northeast corner of the intersection at E. 18th St) is an office tower adorned with Romanesque arches, finials, and a spectacular heraldic device. Across from it, Paragon Sporting Goods, 867 Broadway, which opened in 1908, now stands as Manhattan's last large independent sporting goods store.

At 881–887 Broadway, stands the former **Arnold Constable Dry Goods Store** (1869, extended 1873 and 1877; Griffith Thomas), with its awesome block-long, two-story mansard roofs. Thomas, architect of Marble House, the Arnold Constable store on Canal St, faced the original Broadway wing with marble—the only suitable material according to Aaron Arnold. As the store grew, Thomas expanded it along E. 19th St and eventually duplicated the Broadway facade in cast iron along Fifth Ave, wrapping the mansard roof around the entire building.

On the southeast corner of the same intersection (880–888 Broadway) is the former **W. & J. Sloane Store** (1882; W. Wheeler Smith), a six-story brick building with cast-iron decoration, wide windows, and classical detailing. Originally dealers in carpets, Oriental rugs, lace curtains, and upholstery fabrics, W. & J. Sloane followed the carriage trade uptown in 1912. Fittingly, **ABC Carpets,** which has expanded into furnishings, occupies both the Sloane and Constable buildings.

On the northwest corner of the intersection is the former **Gorham Manufacturing Co.** (1883; Edward H. Kendall; DL), 889 Broadway, a Queen Anne brick structure with a chamfered corner turning that once rose to a tower. Built as an investment by the Goelet family, whose mansion stood across Broadway, it was an early multiuse building, with showrooms downstairs and apartments above.

Continue north on Broadway. Another family investment, the one time **Goelet Building** at 900 Broadway (1887; McKim, Mead & White), is conspicuous for its fine brickwork.

Cross to the east side of Broadway to see the former **Lord & Taylor Store,** 901 Broadway (southwest corner of the intersection at E. 20th St). The fourth and grandest Lord & Taylor emporium (1869; James H. Giles; DL) is a cast-iron French Second Empire extravaganza now sadly reduced in circumstance, though the restored Broadway section suggests the grandeur of the original. The two-story arched entranceway on Broadway and the corner turning with tall display windows and marble columns are gone, but the imposing corner tower and its high mansard roof remain. (Lord & Taylor is now at 424 Fifth Ave.)

Theodore Roosevelt Birthplace

28 E. 20th St, New York, NY 10003. ☎ (212) 260-1616. Web site: www.nps.gov/thrb. Open Mon–Fri 9–5. Tours on the hour; last tour at 4. Closed national holidays. Admission charge. Guided tours; occasional concerts. Gift shop. Not accessible to wheelchairs.

Subway: Lexington Ave Local (6) to 23rd St. Broadway Local (N, R) to 23rd St. Bus: M2, M3, M5, M23.

Turn right on E. 20th St and walk a half-block to the Theodore Roosevelt Birthplace (original building, 1848; replicated, 1923; Theodate Pope Riddle; DL). The house has five rooms of period furniture (about 40 percent of it originally in the family and another 20 percent contributed by other Roosevelts); a small museum displays memorabilia including TR's christening gown and Rough Rider uniform, diaries, photographs, and other documents relating to his life and achievements. The building, which replicates Roosevelt's birthplace, was reconstructed using architectural details from an identical house next door that had belonged to Roosevelt's uncle.

Walk west past Broadway to Fifth Ave. On the southwest corner is the former **Methodist Book Concern** (1889; Edward H. Kendall), 150 Fifth Ave, a Romanesque revival building whose rock face granite lower stories and brickwork arches survive above an unattractively modernized ground floor. Originally it was the headquarters of the *Christian Advocate,* a weekly Methodist journal that apprised its readers of the progress of humanity along religious and philanthropic lines.

On the northwest corner of the intersection, at 156 Fifth Ave, the Romanesque revival former **Presbyterian Building** (1895; James Baker) has housed architectural firms as well as Presbyterians: Baker himself, York and Sawyer, and the New York Chapter of the American Institute of Architects. McKim, Mead & White set up shop next door at 160 Fifth Ave.

Across the street at 153–157 Fifth Ave (between 21st and 22nd Sts) is the United Synagogue of America Building, originally the **Scribner Building** (1894; Ernest Flagg; DL). This small, classically elegant limestone building was the first commercial work by the Scribner family's architect, who also obliged them with a printing plant, the uptown Scribner's store, and two houses. Admired for its metal-and-glass storefront, which would have been at home on the Rue de la Paix, the Scribner Building once had a salesroom reminiscent of a library in a great private house and a metal-and-glass canopy over the entrance.

At 170 Fifth Ave is a skinny 13-story Beaux Arts building, the former **Sohmer Piano Company Building** (1898; Robert Maynicke), topped off with a gleaming gold-leafed octagonal dome. It is being converted to condiminiums.

Flatiron Building

For a good view of the Flatiron Building, continue north on Fifth Ave to W. 23rd St and look back. The Flatiron Building (1901–3; D. H. Burnham & Co.; DL), filling the elongated triangle where Broadway joins Fifth Ave at 23rd St, was the world's tallest building (300 ft) when completed and one of the first to be supported by a steel skeleton.

Exterior

Dramatically sited and radically constructed, it is nonetheless conservatively garbed in limestone and terra-cotta. The rounded corner turning (only six ft wide at the north end), and the eight-story undulating bays in the midsection of the side walls soften its severity. First called the Fuller Building after its developer, the Flatiron Building has evoked strong responses from such diverse observers as H. G. Wells (1906), who admired its "prow . . . ploughing up through the traffic of Broadway and Fifth Avenue in the afternoon light," and Edward Steichen, whose photos of it are famous. In 2001, reproductions of two cherubs that had broken off in the 1980s were installed on the building.

On the southwest corner of 23rd St just west of the Flatiron Building is the former **Western Union Telegraph Company Building** (1884; Henry J. Hardenbergh), 186 Fifth Ave. Small in scale, this red brick building with limestone trim, a gabled roof, dormers, and odd, octagonal chimney towers. It is an early work by the architect of the Dakota Apartments and the Plaza Hotel. Between 23rd and 24th Sts on the west side is a **sidewalk clock** (Hecla Iron Works; 1909; DL), one of four such landmarks in Manhattan.

Madison Square

Enter Madison Square Park—6.8 acres of green crisscrossed by walkways and studded with statuary—from the southwest.

History
The land was successively a marsh, a potter's field, and a parade ground before the Commissioners' Plan of 1811 designated as parkland the entire area bounded by 23rd and 34th Sts and Third and Seventh Aves. In 1844 the city fathers reduced the park to its present size and named it after President James Madison; it was designed by Ignatz Pilat, an assistant to Frederick Law Olmsted, and opened officially in 1847.

The Birthplace of Baseball
The park (or perhaps a lot at Madison Ave and E. 27th St) is generally considered the birthplace of baseball. It was here in 1842 that the game first took form; in 1846 the players, led by Alexander Cartwright, formalized the rules and created the Knickerbocker Club. The claims of Cooperstown, New York, and Abner Doubleday have long been discounted as myth. The claims of Hoboken, New Jersey, can also be dismissed because, although the Knickerbockers played their first officially recorded game there, both teams hailed from New York. Furthermore, the Knickerbockers codified the rules while playing in New York.

During the late 19C, Madison Square Park was the centerpiece of the city's most glamorous neighborhood. This happy time ended in 1902, when the skyscraping Flatiron Building arrived, signaling in a grand way the arrival of commerce. Madison Square Park, like Union Square and Bryant Park, is currently making a comeback from a period of decline, benefiting from a publicly and privately funded restoration project initiated in 1999.

Madison Square Park
At the south end of the park is a **statue of William Henry Seward** (erected 1876; Randolph Rogers), U.S. senator and secretary of state under Lincoln and Andrew Johnson, best known for purchasing Alaska from Russia. The bronze figure, admired when first installed, drew scorn when a rumor (never totally disproved) spread that Rogers had recast the body from a figure of Lincoln made earlier and simply attached Seward's head to Lincoln's neck.

To the east is the ***Star of Hope***—a five-pointed star atop a 35 ft pole, donated in 1916 by artist Minnie Dwight—moved here from the center of the park during the renovation. Further east is the only modern work in the park, ***Skagerrak*** (1972; Antoni Milkowski), three rectangles ($7 \times 7 \times 16$ ft) of weathering steel named for a waterway separating Norway, Sweden, and Denmark. Beyond that is a bronze **statue of Roscoe Conkling** (1893; John Quincy Adams Ward), a U.S. senator and presidential candidate who died of exposure after walking home from his downtown office in the Blizzard of 1888.

Return west and walk northwest through the park toward Broadway. The 120 ft flagpole near the sidewalk bears the **Eternal Light Memorial** (1924; Thomas Hastings and Paul Bartlett), which commemorates American soldiers fallen in France during World War I. The light has not burned unceasingly: it went dark briefly in 1933 when the Parks Department ran out of 250-watt bulbs, and at several other times it short-circuited. During its early years, crowds of up to 50,000 would gather for remembrances on Armistice Day. In 1973 the original wood pole and glass star were removed, and in 1976 a steel pole was installed.

Visible from here is a 51 ft granite obelisk outside the park on the traffic island between Fifth Ave and Broadway. It marks the **grave of Gen. William Jenkins Worth** (1857; James Goodwin Batterson), hero of the Mexican War, whose mortal remains lie below the roaring traffic. A 19C cast-iron fence of swords embedded in the ground surrounds the grave.

Continue clockwise through the park. Toward the center nearer the north end is the fine **Adm. David G. Farragut Monument** (1880; Augustus Saint-Gaudens; base by Stanford White). The bronze figure of the admiral, whipped by an imaginary wind, gazes off at the horizon from his pedestal (a replica of the original) on which two low-relief female figures, Courage and Loyalty, emerge from a swirl of ocean currents. The statue was unveiled (1881) by John H. Knowles, the sailor who lashed Farragut to the mast during the Civil War battle of Mobile Bay so that gunfire would not knock him overboard.

In the northeast corner of the park is **a statue of Chester A. Arthur** (1898; George E. Bissell), twenty-first president of the United States.

Leave the park. Occupying the east side of Madison Ave, between E. 26th and E. 27th Sts is the **New York Life Insurance Company** (1928; Cass Gilbert; DL), 51 Madison Ave. Its limestone Italian Renaissance base rises to a brightly gilded pyramidal tower, a feature Gilbert also used on the Woolworth Building and the Federal Courthouse at Foley Square. The grandiose lobby, with its imposing scale, coffered ceiling, bronze appointments, and great staircase, suggests the wealth of the institution that commissioned the building.

The First Two Madison Square Gardens

On this site stood an abandoned railroad depot of the New York and Harlem Railroad, which P. T. Barnum opened as an entertainment hall, the Hippodrome, in the 1870s. William Vanderbilt took over the building and converted it in 1879 to the first Madison Square Garden, which staged boxing matches and other sporting events. This money-loser was eventually razed, and the National Horse Association hired Stanford White to build a new Madison Square Garden on the site. From 1890 to 1925, this grand and elaborate Garden overlooked Madison Square. The walls were of yellow brick and white terra-cotta; the sidewalks were arcaded and the roof ornamented with six open cupolas, two small towers, and a large tower (249 ft to the base of the cupola) modeled after the Giralda in Seville. On top stood Augustus Saint-Gaudens's gilded statue *Diana*, whose nudity distressed the city's more proper citizens; her anatomical charms, however, could be glimpsed only remotely, since the goddess's head towered 332 ft up from the sidewalk.

Inside were a restaurant, theater, and roof garden as well as a sports arena. Ironically, architect White was murdered in Madison Square Garden, shot by Pittsburgh millionaire Harry K. Thaw, whose young wife, the former showgirl Evelyn Nesbit, had in earlier days enjoyed a well-publicized affair with White.

Just south of this building is perhaps the neighborhood's ugliest structure, the **Merchandise Mart** (1973; Emery Roth & Sons), a big, shiny, black box at 41 Madison Ave that replaced the Leonard Jerome Mansion.

The Leonard Jerome Mansion
Leonard Jerome's 1859 mansion had a 600-seat theater and stables paneled in black walnut. Daughter Jennie Jerome grew up to become Lady Randolph Churchill, mother of Winston Churchill. The Manhattan Club later leased the site, and this is reportedly where the Manhattan cocktail was invented.

Appellate Division of the New York State Supreme Court
Walk south along Madison Ave on the park side to the northeast corner of E. 25th St and the **Appellate Division of the New York State Supreme Court** (1900; James Brown Lord; DL), 27 Madison Ave. The building is remarkable for its sculpture and decoration.

Exterior
Built of white marble with a Corinthian portico facing E. 25th St and four columns along Madison Ave, the courthouse cost $633,768, of which more than one-third went for statuary and murals. Along Madison Ave on the roof balustrade, walking from north to south are: *Confucius* (Philip Martiny); *Peace,* flanked by *Wisdom* and *Strength* (Karl Bitter); and *Moses* (William Couper). The four caryatids below (Thomas Shields Clarke) represent the four seasons. Along the balustrade on E. 25th St, walking from west to east are: *Zoroaster* (Edward C. Potter); *Alfred the Great* (Jonathan Scott Hartley); *Lycurgus* (George Edwin Bissell); *Solon* (Herbert Adams); *Justice* flanked by *Power* and *Study* (Daniel Chester French); *Louis IX* (John Donoghue); *Manu* (Augustus Lukeman); and *Justinian* (Henry Kirke Bush-Brown). Formerly a statue of Mohammed stood next to Zoroaster, but it was removed and destroyed (1955) at the request of the city's Islamic community because religious law forbids images of the prophet. The pediment above the main doorway bears a sculptural group, the *Triumph of Law* (Charles H. Niehaus). Flanking the steps are *Wisdom* and *Force* (Frederick Wellington Ruckstuhl). The statuary and the stained glass dome in the courtroom were renovated in 1983 at a cost greater than the original cost of the building.

Interior
The interior of the building (open weekdays during working hours) is lavishly decorated with murals, beaded chandeliers, and paneling. In the courtroom is a stained glass skylight bearing the names of famous American lawyers.

Directly across E. 25th St is the **North Building of the Metropolitan Life Insurance Company** (1932; Harvey Wiley Corbett and D. Everett Waid), 11–25 Madison Ave, a massive limestone Art Deco building (best viewed from the park). Its high vaulted entrances and elaborate, angled setbacks have been praised for lightening the apparent mass of the building. Here stood Stanford White's Madison Avenue Presbyterian Church (1906), a white marble, domed, and colonnaded temple demolished in 1919.

In the block downtown from the North Building is the **Metropolitan Life Tower** (1909; Napoleon Le Brun & Sons; DL) at Madison Ave and E. 24th St, which surpassed the Flatiron Building as the world's tallest, only to be topped by the Woolworth Building four years later. The tower (700 ft high, 75 ft wide on Madison Ave, 85 ft wide on E. 24th St) was one of the first to use the steel columns and skeletal structure that allow skyscrapers to stand tall. Its design was inspired by the Campanile in St. Mark's Square in Venice. The four clock faces on the tower are 26 ft in diameter; each minute hand is 17 ft long and weighs a thousand pounds. The tower's light inspired the company slogan, "The Light That Never Fails," because ships maneuvering through New York Harbor used it as a beacon. Unfortunately, much of the building's ornamentation and detail were removed during an early-1960s renovation, including its white marble facing.

Walk east to Park Ave South and north to E. 25th St; turn right (east). The barrel-vaulted drill hall of the former **69th Regiment Armory** (1904–6; Hunt & Hunt; DL) fills the block of E. 25th St between Park Ave South and Lexington Ave. It is the only armory in the city not designed to look like a medieval fort. It is also the armory of the famous Armory Show (1913), where Marcel DuChamp's cubistic *Nude Descending the Stairs* stunned the New York art world. Today it hosts antiques shows, fashion award ceremonies, and other noncontroversial fare.

Across the street on the southwest corner of Lexington Ave and E. 25th St is the **Friends House in Rosehill,** built as the B. W. Mayer Building (1916; Herman Lee Meader). Like other of Meader's buildings, including the Cliff Dwellers' Apartments (see Walk 26), this one is dramatically ornamented: look for snakes, cattle skulls, and a Mayan head guarding the entrance. The International Ladies Garment Workers Union and later the first Labor College in the country (part of the State University of New York) held forth here. Today it is a Quaker-run AIDS hostel.

Turn right and walk south on Lexington Ave. On the southwest corner of the intersection at E. 22nd St is the former **Russell Sage Foundation** (c. 1914; tower added 1919; Grosvenor Atterbury), converted to apartments in 1975. The building, a lavishly handsome Renaissance revival palace (Florentine style), bears a frieze proclaiming its purpose: "For the Improvement of Social and Living Conditions." Sage—financier, railroad builder, stock market entrepreneur—left a fortune of some $60 million, much of which his wife gave to charity. Among the philanthropies of the foundation was the construction of Forest Hills Gardens in Queens, an attempt at model housing (see Walk 51).

Turn right and walk west to Park Avenue South—Fourth Ave prestigiously renamed. This area was once filled with charitable organizations. On the northeast corner the intersection at E. 22nd St is the former **United Charities Building** (1891; R. H. Robertson and Rowe & Baker), 287 Park Ave South. On the southeast corner is the Federation of Protestant Welfare Agencies, 281 Park Ave South, located in the **Church Missions' House Building** (1893; Robert W. Gibson and Edward J. N. Stent; DL) formerly headquarters of the Episcopal Church's missionary societies. Constructed of rock-face granite and Indiana limestone over a steel skeleton, the building has a tympanum above the entry that depicts St. Augustine preaching to the heathen in England and Bishop Seabury doing the same in America.

Look across the street at the former **New York Bank for Savings** (1894; Cyrus L. W. Eidlitz; apartment tower and bank alterations 1987), 280 Park Ave South, now an overly dignified supermarket.

Walk south along Park Ave South. **Calvary Church** (Protestant Episcopal), 273 Park Ave South (northeast corner of the intersection of E. 21st St) (1846; James Renwick Jr.), is a minor work by the architect of Grace Church and St. Patrick's Cathedral.

Gramercy Park

Turn left and walk one block east to Gramercy Park, New York's only private residential square.

History

The name *Gramercy* harks back to the Dutch colonial period when the area was called *Krom Moerasje* (crooked little swamp) after a marshy brook that wandered from Madison Square to the East River near 18th St. Later the neighborhood was called Crommashie Hill, and eventually Gramercy Park.

The park was created by Samuel Bulkley Ruggles, a small-scale urban planner and descendant of Peter Stuyvesant. Ruggles bought a 20-acre farm in 1831, drained the marshland, and laid out a park to increase the value of his land. Around the park he designated 66 building lots and sold them with the stipulation that only lot owners could have access to the park. His wishes are still in force: except for a brief period during the Draft Riots of 1863, when troops camped inside the eight-ft iron fence, the park trustees have resisted all intrusions, including a proposed cable car line (1890) and an extension of Lexington Ave (1912) through the park. Only residents facing the square who pay a yearly maintenance fee are granted keys. Famous residents of the neighborhood have included Stanford White and Eleanor Roosevelt.

Around Gramercy Park

Walk south along Gramercy Park West, with its fine Greek revival town houses (numbered counterclockwise). Dr. Valentine Mott (died 1865), prominent surgeon and a founder of Bellevue Hospital, lived at no. 1. The buildings at **nos. 3 and 4 Gramercy Park West** (c. 1840; attrib. Alexander Jackson Davis) are distinguished by their original cast-iron verandas with profuse Greek revival ornamentation—anthemions, meanders, and floral motifs. This lacy ironwork, more familiar in southern cities like Charleston and New Orleans, was considered a rustic touch especially appropriate to houses facing parks or enjoying deep front yards. A pair of Mayor's Lamps stand at no. 4, once the home of James Harper, mayor of the city (1844–45) and a founder of Harper & Bros. publishers.

At no. 15 on the south side of the park is the **National Arts Club** (1845, remodeled 1884; Vaux & Radford; DL). This brownstone was built as two houses during the Gothic revival period of the 1840s and remodeled for Samuel J. Tilden during the heyday of a more flamboyant Victorian Gothic style. Tilden, scourge of the Tweed Ring (see New York County Courthouse in Walk 5), governor of New York State, and the Democratic presidential candidate who lost by one electoral vote in 1876, was wary of assassination attempts, so he had rolling steel doors installed behind the lower windows and an escape tunnel built to 19th St. Tilden spent much of his money on his collection of rare books, which along with the Astor and Lenox endowments formed the core of the New York Public Library collection. Architecturally, the building's attractions include polychrome decoration, asymmetric bays, heavy lancet windows, and a set of medallions portraying Goethe, Dante, Franklin, Shakespeare, and Milton. The National Arts Club bought the property in 1906; occasionally it is open to the public for exhibitions.

Next door at no. 16 is **The Players** (1845; remodeled, 1888; Stanford White; DL), a simple Gothic revival brownstone (note the drip moldings on the upstairs windows) until actor Edwin Booth bought it and hired Stanford White to remodel it as an actors' club. At the end of his tragic and rootless life, Booth, one of the finest actors of his time, lived on the top floor of the club overlooking the park.

Cross Gramercy Park South and look into the park for a view of the **statue of Edwin Booth** in the character of Hamlet (1917, dedicated 1918; Edmond T. Quinn).

At 19 Gramercy Park South (southeast corner of Irving Place) stands **Evyan House,** the former Benjamin Sonnenberg Mansion, a five-story red brick house built in 1845 and updated with a mansard roof in 1860. Stuyvesant Fish, whose business interests included railroads, insurance, and banking, bought it in the 1880s. After Fish and his socially ambitious wife moved uptown near the turn of the century, the house declined, although John Barrymore lived here while acting on Broadway. Public relations counsel Benjamin Sonnenberg bought it in 1931 and restored it to its former glory, both architecturally and socially.

Continue east. On the southeast corner of Gramercy Park South and Gramercy Park East is the former **Friends' Meeting House** (1859; King & Kellum; DL), 144 E. 20th St, an austere Italianate building whose severity is broken only by the arched pediment above the doorway. Saved in 1965 from a developer, the meeting house was renovated as the Brotherhood Synagogue (1975; James Stewart Polshek). On its east side is a **Garden of Remembrance,** dedicated (1982) to Jews who perished in the Holocaust.

The **Gramercy** (1883; George da Cunha), 34 Gramercy Park East, an ornately detailed red brick building with an octagonal turret and a lavish mosaic lobby floor, is one of the city's earliest cooperative apartments. The building at **36 Gramercy Park East** (1908; James Riely Gordon) has elaborate terra-cotta Gothic ornament and two cast-stone armored knights guarding the entrance.

Return to Irving Place and walk south. Irving Place was named (1831) by Samuel Ruggles for Washington Irving, writer and diplomat. The block of E. 19th St between Irving Place and Third Ave is known as "The Block Beautiful" for its small but charming 19C houses and converted stables. During the 1930s a small artists' colony flourished here, its residents including muckraker Ida Tarbell *(The History of the Standard Oil Company)* and painter George Bellows.

Pete's Tavern

Pete's Tavern, formerly Healy's Café, on the northeast corner of Irving Place and E. 18th St, claims to be one of the city's oldest taverns, having opened in 1864; recently, however, amateur sleuth Richard McDermott (see McSorley's Old Ale House in Walk 10) uncovered tax records and city directories showing that the site was a grocery from 1851 to 1890 and did not become Healy's until 1899.

History

Its most illustrious client, writer O. Henry (William Sydney Porter), lived at 55 Irving Place and described the café in a story, *The Lost Blend.* According to legend he wrote *The Gift of the Magi* in either the first or second booth, although there is some evidence he wrote it in his apartment. Still, having survived Prohibition as a speakeasy with an entrance through a flower shop, the tavern is rich in ambiance and history.

Continue south to E. 17th St. The house at 40 Irving Place (southwest corner of the intersection) has been erroneously identified as Washington Irving's home. It wasn't. Built c. 1845, its most famous residents were Elsie de Wolfe (later, Lady Mendl) and Elisabeth Marbury, two ladies of taste and social ability who became famous respectively as an interior decorator and a literary agent. During their stay in this house at the turn of the 20C, the ladies ran a Sunday salon, which attracted so many foreign celebrities that it was known as the "Immigrants' Home."

14 · Herald Square and the Garment District

Subway: Broadway–Seventh Ave Express or Local (1, 2, 3, 9) to 34th St–Penn Station. Sixth Ave Express or Local (B, D, Q, F) or Eighth Ave Express or Local (A, C, E) to 34th St–Penn Station. Broadway Local (N, R) to 34th St.
Bus: M4, M6, M7, M10.

Herald Square took its name from the newspaper the *New York Herald,* which occupied a McKim, Mead & White palazzo just north of 35th Street from 1895 to 1921. Both the palazzo and the paper are long gone. The area, long dominated by Macy's and Gimbels, remains a major retail shopping district.

History

During the 1870s and 1880s Herald Square was the center of the notorious **Tenderloin District,** which stretched from about W. 24th to W. 40th Sts, between Fifth and Seventh Aves. When Police Inspector Alexander Williams was transferred to this precinct from quieter streets, he remarked: "I've had nothing but chuck steak for a long time, and now I'm going to get a little of the tenderloin." He promptly began supplementing his modest salary with protection money extorted from the local proprietors of saloons, gambling houses, and brothels, eventually owning a city home, a Connecticut estate, and a yacht. The area was so famous for its brothels, saloons, and dance halls that Brooklyn reformer T. DeWitt Talmadge called it "Satan's Circus." One of the most notorious spots was a variety theater, dance hall, and restaurant called the Haymarket at the southeast corner of Sixth Ave and W. 30th St. Through the efforts of reformers and the Lexow Committee (1894), the involvement of public officials in vice and crime became a source of general indignation; Williams was retired "for the good of the force."

Herald Square

Begin at Herald Square, not really a square at all but two triangles (W. 32nd to W. 35th Sts) created by the intersection of Broadway and Sixth Ave. Despite previous attempts at reconstruction, Herald Square remains hellishly congested for both pedestrians and drivers and continues to inspire pleas for redesign. Recently, however, Herald Square and Greeley Square, the southern triangle between W. 32nd and W. 33rd Sts, have been spruced up with plantings and movable chairs and tables provided by the local business improvement district.

Herald Square contains the **bell and clock** that once adorned the *New York Herald* building. When the Sixth Ave El was torn down (1939–40), they were installed as a memorial to *Herald* publishers James Gordon Bennett and his son James Gordon Bennett Jr. (pedestal and redesign of square, 1940; Aymar Embury II). Two muscular bronze figures nicknamed Stuff and Guff, or alternately Gog and Magog, seem to hammer out the hours on the Meneeley bell (actually the bell is struck from within), while a bronze Minerva and her owl observe the proceedings (statuary, 1894; Antonin Jean Paul Charles). **Greeley Square** contains a statue of *New York Tribune* founder Horace Greeley (1892; Alexander Doyle).

Macy's

Walk north to W. 34th St. **R. H. Macy & Co.** (original building facing Broadway, 1901; DeLemos & Cordes; Seventh Ave building, 1931; Robert D. Kohn) occupies a square block (W. 34th to W. 35th Sts and Broadway to Seventh Ave), contains 2.2 million square ft of selling space, and is a popular destination for tourists and New Yorkers alike. It is the largest department store in the world and sponsor of the huge annual Macy's Thanksgiving Parade.

History

Rowland Hussey Macy was a Nantucket Quaker who went to sea at the age of 15 and returned four years later with $500 and a red star, now Macy's logo, tattooed on his hand. After six failures in merchandising and additional disappointments in real estate and the stock market, Macy founded (1858) his New York store on Sixth Ave near 14th St, an enterprise he developed to the point where he could bill it as "the world's largest store."

A decade after its founder's death, the store passed in 1887 to Isidor and Nathan Straus, who had leased space in the basement (1874) to run a china-and-glassware department. Macy's moved to its current Herald Square flagship location in 1902. Isidor Straus and his wife, Ida, died aboard the *Titanic,* but the Straus Family maintained its association with Macy's for five generations. In 1994 the store merged with Federated Department Stores, Inc. to form the nation's largest department store company.

Macy's is known for the variety of its merchandise, stocking furs and diamonds, caviar and raspberries, as well as the more humble articles needed in this life. Among its more spectacular sales have been plumbing fixtures for Liberia's presidential palace and a length of silk to outfit a Saudi Arabian harem.

Across 34th St to the south is the **Herald Center,** a vertical mall replacing the former E. J. Korvette discount store, which in turn, replaced Saks–34th St (1902; Buchman & Fox), the original Saks department store in the city.

A block south, on Broadway between W. 32nd and W. 33rd Sts, is the **Manhattan Mall,** another blend of suburban-style chain stores under one neon roof. It opened in 1989 and has 100 stores on 9 floors. This site briefly hosted a branch of Brooklyn's Abraham & Straus and, before that, the legendary **Gimbel Brothers Department Store,** long famous as Macy's competitor. Adam Gimbel, a Bavarian immigrant who started his career in this country as a pack peddler, founded Gimbels in 1842 in the Midwest. The store arrived in New York in 1910 and rose to fame for its "feud" with Macy's, romanticized in the film *Miracle on 34th Street.* The rivalry was generally profitable to both stores, but Gimbels fell on hard times in the 1970s and was bought out and closed in 1986.

Across the triangle at Broadway and W. 32nd St is the Beaux-Arts **Hotel Martinique** (1897; Henry Hardenbergh; DL). A palace of luxury at the turn of the 20C, the hotel gradually declined until in 1970 the city began renting rooms as emergency housing for the homeless. Thereafter it became notorious as one of the city's most crime-ridden welfare hotels. It closed as a welfare hotel in 1989 and in the late 1990s was converted into a 500-room Holiday Inn. This move sparked the landmark designation as fears arose that the hotel chain would alter the fine exterior details—ornate dormers, rusticated stonework, balconies, and a mansard roof.

The Garment District

Walk west along W. 33rd St to Seventh Ave. The street signs for Seventh Ave as it passes through the Garment District are subtitled "Fashion Ave," a name imposed with some bravado on an area beset with problems. The American garment industry as a whole is shrinking in the face of cheaper imported goods, and the New York sector is further threatened with transportation difficulties and high labor costs. Nonetheless, the Garment District, bounded roughly by W. 30th and

W. 41st Sts and Fifth and Eighth Aves, houses one of the city's most important industries, which moved uptown from the sweatshops of the Lower East Side around the time of World War I, following the northward progress of the major department stores. Until recent years the entire industry—from designers to cutters, button makers, and seamstresses, to marketing professionals—crowded within the borders of the district. Nowadays, with gentrification encroaching on the area and an increasingly Asian labor force, many of the manufacturing operations (including illegal sweatshops) have moved to cheaper quarters in Chinatown and Sunset Park. Many have also gone to developing countries overseas.

For the most part, however, the showrooms remain here and, to a certain extent, the old lines of demarcation can still be discerned. What is left of the fur industry centers around the southern part of the district, W. 27th to W. 30th Sts and Sixth to Eighth Aves. Only a few buildings—for example, 150 W. 30th St—are still occupied entirely by furriers. Children's-wear firms cluster around W. 34th St; north of W. 36th St are businesses dealing in women's apparel. On the fringe of the Garment District are allied industries—firms dealing in millinery, hosiery, buttons, thread, trimmings, and fabrics.

Although the workforce has shrunk and the old-time restaurants for buyers and bosses are gone, the Garment District still has more than its share of congested traffic. Only the ignorant or sublimely patient driver will try to negotiate the crosstown streets during working hours, when double-parked trucks and occasionally wheeled clothing racks, called hand trucks, clog both the roadway and the sidewalk.

On the southeast corner of W. 33rd St and Seventh Ave is the **Hotel Pennsylvania** (1918; McKim, Mead & White), which has one of the city's most famous phone numbers: it was immortalized by big band legend Glenn Miller in his song "Pennsylvania 6-5000." During the 1930s the hotel was a center for big bands as well as a gathering place for buyers who arrived in town to stock their stores from the offerings of the Garment District.

Pennsylvania Station

Pennsylvania Station is still across the street, at W. 33rd St and Seventh Ave, but it is now stripped of its former glory and relegated to a hole in the ground.

History

Until wantonly destroyed in 1963, the former Pennsylvania Station (1906–10) was McKim, Mead & White's masterpiece, a symbol of the power of the Pennsylvania Railroad and a happy union of history and technology. The facade, with its imposing Doric colonnade, and the General Waiting Room, with its vaulted ceiling, were modeled on the Roman Baths of Caracalla, while the steel and glass arches, domes, and vaults covering the concourse belonged to the tradition of crystal palaces and glass exhibition galleries.

In 1962, the financially troubled Pennsylvania Railroad sold the air rights above the station for a new Madison Square Garden, which would rise above a smaller, underground station. The demolition of the old station was considered a monumental act of vandalism and led to the enactment of landmark preservation laws. Among the glories of the former station were a row of 22 granite eagles on the cornice and a great stone clock framed by two classical figures that were carted off and dumped in Secaucus, New Jersey.

The concourse of the former Pennsylvania Station in 1910. The demolition of this magnificent building and its replacement by the present nonentity mark one of the saddest episodes in the city's architectural history. (Courtesy of The New-York Historical Society, New York City)

Madison Square Garden

In its place rose the present graceless **Madison Square Garden Center** (1968; Charles Luckman Assocs.). The complex includes the fourth Madison Square Garden (see The First Two Madison Square Gardens in Walk 13 and The Third Madison Square Garden in Walk 15), a 20,000-seat arena enclosed in a precast concrete-clad drum, the Theater at Madison Square Garden (5,600 seats), and an office building (29 stories). The New York Rangers (ice hockey) and the New York Knicks (basketball) call the Garden home; other events include track meets; dog shows; ice shows; tennis tournaments; the Ringling Brothers, Barnum and Bailey circus; rock concerts; and boxing matches. The current owner, Cablevision, is considering destroying the building in favor of a new, more attractive and fan-friendly one.

The Fourth Madison Square Garden

While the architecture lacks style, the "World's Most Famous Arena" has been home to many memorable sporting events. Among the more notable have been the 1970 championship game between the Knicks and the Los Angeles Lakers and Muhammad Ali's first loss (1971), which he suffered at the hands of Joe Frazier in a brutal 15-round fight that ranks among the greatest bouts ever. In the 1990s the Knicks were the hottest ticket in town, with faithful fans like movie directors Spike Lee and Woody Allen and other celebrities in the expensive seats.

The Present Penn Station

Beneath the Garden is the present Penn Station, still giving access to the old tracks laid down when its predecessor was completed. Nearly 100 million train riders use the station annually, the vast majority of them commuters on the Long Island Railroad (LIRR), the nation's busiest commuter line. New Jersey Transit, Amtrak (the national intercity passenger system), and the PATH (Port Authority Trans-Hudson) system also contribute, though Amtrak's 7 million annual total is less than one-tenth that of the LIRR.

Walk west to Eighth Ave. On the west side of the avenue (between W. 31st and W. 33rd Sts) is the **General Post Office** (1913; McKim, Mead & White; DL), with a two-block colonnade of 53 ft Corinthian columns. Around the frieze marches the postal workers' motto, loosely adapted from Herodotus: "Neither snow nor rain nor heat nor gloom of night stays these couriers from the swift completion of their appointed rounds."

The Next Penn Station

The building, officially the **James A. Farley Building,** is being renovated as an Amtrak station, where passengers will once again (scheduled opening, 2004) enjoy the distinction of a Pennsylvania Station arrival. Plans for the monumental interior (architects Skidmore, Owings & Merrill) include tiers of skylit concourses to allow daylight to illuminate the tracks and let riders see the trains coming and going. The postal service will share space with the train station.

Continue walking west along W. 33rd St. In 1995 the *Daily News* moved from its landmark East Side building (see News Building in Walk 19) to **450 W. 33rd St** at Tenth Ave. Developers hoped the move would spur redevelopment, but progress has been slow because little public transportation reaches this far west.

Before the diesel truck supplanted the locomotive as America's prime freight hauler, this neighborhood was the hub of the city's freight distribution system. The **Thirtieth Street Yards** of the New York Central Railroad (W. 30th to W. 37th Sts between Eleventh and Twelfth Aves, with two additional blocks, W. 30th to W. 32nd Sts between Tenth and Eleventh Aves) received trains from a railroad that stretched far into the hinterlands. Additional yards at W. 60th St were connected to this facility by a freight line down Eleventh Ave, known as Death Ave until the 1930s, when the tracks were dropped beneath street level. South of the yards an elevated rail viaduct (parts still visible) led to the St. John's Park Freight Terminal (1934) between Charlton and Clarkson Sts, west of Washington St.

Jacob K. Javits Convention Center

After years of controversy in governmental and financial circles, the northern section of the abandoned yards, from W. 34th to W. 39th Sts, was transformed into the Jacob K. Javits Convention Center. The massive five-square-block complex (1986; I. M. Pei & Partners) was completed 17 years after being conceived, much-delayed by political squabbling.

History

Built as a 20C Crystal Palace of glass enframed by a metal grid, the center gleams like a many-faceted jewel when illuminated from within at night. It incorporates some 16,000 glass panels and 100,000 square ft of skylights. While the center generates more than $1 billion annually for the local economy, it has remained a magnet for controversy. It has been criticized for being too small (many of the largest trade shows cannot be accommodated; it is not among the nation's 15 largest convention facilities) and for lacking adequate parking space and public transportation. Studies have suggested nearly doubling its size. In the mid-1990s new work rules and a new hiring system were implemented to break the Mafia's hold on the center's labor force.

Other Points of Interest

Embedded in the sidewalk of Seventh Ave from W. 35th to W. 41st Sts are the granite-framed bronze plaques of the **Fashion Walk of Fame** (instituted 1999). The first eight honorees were Rudy Gernreich, Halston, Claire McCardell, Norman Norell, Geoffrey Beene, Bill Blass, Calvin Klein, and Ralph Lauren.

In front of 555 Seventh Ave (between W. 39th and W. 40th Sts) is a sculptural tribute to garment industry workers, a larger-than-life bronze figure of a Jewish man operating a sewing machine. Entitled *The Garment Worker* (Judith Weller; 1984), it was inspired by the sculptor's father, who for many years was a member of the International Ladies Garment Workers Union.

Fashion Institute of Technology

The Fashion Institute of Technology (FIT) (1958–77; DeYoung & Moscowitz), facing Seventh Ave from W. 26th to W. 28th Sts, is a professional school for those seeking careers in the clothing industry. FIT began (1944) as a technical institute for high school graduates and became, successively, a community college (1951) and a part of the state university system (1975). Students earn degrees in fields such as fashion design, advertising design, cosmetics and fragrance marketing, computer animation, toy design, and museum studies.

In the plaza facing Seventh Ave and W. 27th St is Robert M. Cronbach's hammered brass *Eye of Fashion* (1976).

The Museum at FIT

Shirley Goodman Resource Center, Seventh Ave at W. 27th St, New York, NY 10001. ☎ (212) 760-7760. Web site: www.fitnyc.suny.edu. Open during exhibitions Tues–Fri noon–8; Sat 10–5. Closed Sun, Mon, legal holidays. Free. Accessible to wheelchairs. Occasional lectures and seminars with major exhibitions. Library.

Subway: Broadway–Seventh Ave Local (1, 9) to 28th St. Broadway Local (N, R) to 28th St. Bus: M4, M5, M6, M7, M11.

The school has the world's largest collection of textiles, clothing, and costumes;

its exhibition space, the Museum at FIT, mounts several stylish exhibitions each year.

The elegant cast-iron **Gilsey House** (1871; Stephen Decatur Hatch; DL), 1200 Broadway (at W. 29th St) was one of the premiere hotels of the 19C. The building rises five stories to a three-story mansard embellished with dormers, oculi, and cresting. Two mermaids support the corner clock. The 300-room hotel was built by Peter Gilsey, a Danish immigrant and city alderman. The hotel closed in 1911, was used for manufacturing and gradually decayed until in 1979 it was converted into co-op housing. In 1992 it was restored and repainted its original cream color.

Keen's Steak House

Keen's Steak House, formerly Keen's Chophouse, one of New York's oldest eateries, opened in 1878 at 72 W. 36th St (just east of Sixth Ave). It served as the dining room for the adjacent Lamb's Club until 1885, when manager Albert Keen went independent. Until 1901, when actress Lillie Langtry sued on grounds of discrimination and won, women were excluded. Keen's dished up its millionth mutton chop in 1935, but eventually suffered a lean period, closing in the 1970s. It reopened in 1982 and changed its name from "chophouse" to "steak house" in 1995 when the owners decided "chophouse" was obsolete.

Interior

Inside are leaded casement windows, mahogany and brass bars, and theatrical memorabilia. On the ceiling are racks filled with 50,000 long-stemmed clay pipes, each numbered for its owner. Among the celebrities who dropped by for a smoke were Douglas MacArthur, Theodore Roosevelt, William Howard Taft, Herbert Hoover, Stanford White, Babe Ruth, Enrico Caruso, Albert Einstein, and theater luminaries John Barrymore, Florenz Ziegfeld, and Will Rogers.

15 · West 42nd Street and the Times Square Theater District

Subway: Broadway–Seventh Ave Express or Local (1, 2, 3, 9), Broadway Local (N, R), or Flushing Local (7) to Times Square–42nd St.
Bus: M6, M7, M10, M20, M27, M42, M104.

Times Square changed more dramatically and more rapidly than any other neighborhood in New York during the 1990s, undergoing a remarkable transformation from a tawdry run-down area seemingly beyond reform to the glittering symbol of the city's rebirth. This splashy tourist mecca capped its comeback by hosting the city's largest public event ever on New Year's Eve, 1999, when, according to some reports, 2 million people peacefully crammed into Times Square for the millennium celebration.

Depending on how the boundaries are drawn, Times Square extends from about Eighth Ave to Sixth Ave and from W. 40th St to as far north as W. 54th St. But the heart of Times Square, the "Crossroads of the World," is the area where Broadway and Seventh Ave intersect, bounded roughly by W. 42nd and W. 48th Sts.

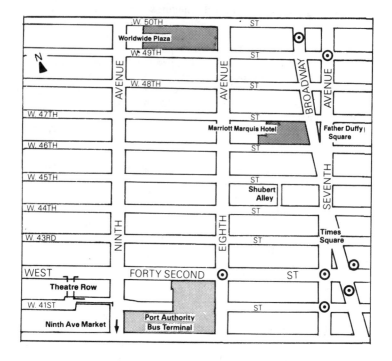

Times Square History

Before 1904 Times Square was called Longacre Square and was dominated by horse exchanges, carriage factories, stables, blacksmiths' shops, and upscale brothels. On its eastern side was the 12th Regiment Armory. The Astor family owned much of the western part of the district as part of a tract that ran from W. 42nd to W. 46th Sts, along Broadway and west to the Hudson River.

The area acquired its present name in 1904, when the *New York Times* moved in, persuading authorities to open a subway stop and rename the area Times Square. To celebrate the newspaper's Dec 31 arrival, publisher Adolph Ochs held a public New Year's Eve celebration, beginning the annual Times Square tradition.

In 1905, not long after theaters began moving uptown, the entertainment trade publication *Variety* was founded at 154 W. 46th St. Along with such nationally syndicated newspaper writers as Damon Runyon and Walter Winchell, *Variety* helped focus the spotlight on the new theater district. Although it was geared to those in the business, *Variety* coined or popularized numerous words and phrases that entered the lexicon, including *gams* (female legs), *hoofer* (a dancer), *soap opera*, and, much later, *sitcom*. In 1987 *Variety* moved from then-seedy Times Square to Park Ave South, before shifting its headquarters to Los Angeles in 1993.

By the time the *Times* and *Variety* arrived, the area had been electrically lighted for nearly a decade. O. J. Gude, an advertising man, is said to have coined "the Great White Way" in 1901, when he realized the commercial potential of electrically enhanced billboards. Through the years memorable Times Square billboards have included a gigantic smoker emitting real smoke rings, a shower of golden peanuts cascading from an illuminated bag, and a figure of Little Lulu and a giant electric Kleenex made of some 25,000 light bulbs. One of the all-time favorites was a 1930s sign for Wrigley's gum, with illuminated waves, glowing tropical fish each more than a story tall, and bubbles that floated up past a neon pack of gum (larger than a city bus) where a Wrigley boy fished calmly.

The city's Theater District developed around Times Square during the first three decades of the 20C. First came a few pioneers creeping up Broadway from Herald Square: Charles Frohman's Empire Theatre (1893) on Broadway at W. 40th St and the former Metropolitan Opera House (1883) between W. 39th and W. 40th Sts. However, Oscar Hammerstein—opera impresario, composer, and cigar maker—was the first to forge north of 42nd St, and while his Olympia Theatre (1895) on Broadway between W. 44th and W. 45th Sts lasted only two years, Hammerstein rebounded from bankruptcy and resiliently built three more theaters in Times Square—the Victoria, the Republic, and the Lew Fields—earning himself kudos as "the man who created Times Square."

As advances in transportation made the district widely accessible and investors realized the profits of theaters as real estate, Times Square flourished. Theaters were built either by speculators aware that a hit show could gross a million dollars in a single year—roughly the price of building a theater in the 1920s—or by financial backers working with independent producers such as Charles Frohman, David Belasco, and Harrison Grey Fiske. Times Square began attracting agents, producers, theatrical publications, restaurants, hotels, and theatrical clubs. New York's best season came in 1927–28 when 280 productions were mounted and 80 theaters were in operation. (Today there are 37 Broadway theaters, although several are often unoccupied.)

Talkies and then the Depression devastated Broadway: tickets went unsold; actors were unemployed; even the mighty Shubert family went into receivership. The Federal Theater Project kept some actors and writers in work during these years, but the Times Square Theater District began a process of attrition that lingered for decades, abetted by rising land values and the inroads made by movies and, later, television. More and more houses were converted for vaudeville, movies, and burlesque.

Even so, Times Square was a crossroads, a place for celebrations. Perhaps its greatest moment came at the end of World War II, when the city's jubilation was captured in Alfred Eisenstadt's famous V-J Day photo of a sailor kissing a nurse in Times Square.

Gradually, glamour dissipated and honky-tonk slid into sleaze. Crime increased, particularly drug dealing and prostitution. The area reached its nadir in the 1970s and 1980s when porno and kung fu movies seemed to be the highest forms of culture on 42nd St. Although revelers still thronged to Times Square for New Year's Eve, the area had sunk so low that even the most optimistic urban planners could not have envisioned such a remarkable reversal.

Times Square continued suffering until the 1992 formation of the Times Square Business Improvement District (BID) began to turn things around. The BID assessed $6 million annually from about 400 merchants to be spent on issues like antipornography cleanup, safety, and marketing.

Gretchen Dykstra, BID president from 1992 to 1998, is given the lion's share of credit for managing the egos, political issues, aesthetic considerations, and commercial decisions. Two other key players were Rebecca Robertson, then president of the 42nd Street Development Project, the state agency in charge of the transformation of 42d St between Seventh and Eighth Aves (the state took over much of the block and relocated some 280 occupants), and Cora Cahan, president of the New 42d Street, a nonprofit organization established by Robertson's group and responsible for restoring use to eight once-grand but outmoded theaters on that block.

The first small step, the success of a Gap clothing store, encouraged other retailers. But the most significant newcomer was the Walt Disney Company, which first looked into the area in 1993 and reopened the New Amsterdam Theatre in 1995 after a $36-million renovation (aided by a low-interest $26-million loan from the 42nd Street Development Project). Even before the theater reopened, Disney's presence encouraged retailers, speculators, and others to invest in the area. Disney's influence in Times Square (it also runs an ESPN theme restaurant, the ABC *Good Morning America* studio, and a Disney Store) has, however, inspired some backlash. Critics complain, justifiably that Times Square is not a place for New Yorkers—the Disney Store, Madame Tussaud's Wax Museum, the relentless blast of neon and exposed-to-the-street TV studios—have turned it into a multimedia theme park almost totally disconnected from the rest of the city. Still, there are few who would argue that the restored theaters or the decrease in the number of prostitutes and porno theaters are negatives. It is estimated that some 20 million tourists now spend $3.5 billion annually in Times Square.

Begin at the southeast corner of W. 42nd St and Broadway. The **former Knickerbocker Hotel** (1902; Marvin & Vavis, architects with Bruce Price, consultant; DL), is the only survivor of several elegant hotel buildings that were built in the area at the turn of the 20C. Commissioned by John Jacob Astor, this Beaux-Arts red brick building with terra-cotta and limestone pediments and a copper mansard roof had dining rooms that could serve 2,000 people and provide solid-gold cutlery for every guest. George M. Cohan stayed here, and the hotel was Enrico Caruso's home when he was performing in New York. In 1921 the hotel closed and 1466 Broadway became just another office building, home to *Newsweek* from 1940 to 1959, and later to sportswear manufacturers.

Across the street on the northwest side of W. 42nd St and Broadway is a quintessentially modern building, the **Condé Nast Building** (1999; Fox & Fowle), 4 Times Square. The 52-story tower is granite on the 42nd St side but glass facing Broadway, keeping with Times Square's shiny new image. On street level at the corner is **ESPN Zone,** a sports bar that also promotes the cable TV sports network. The bar has unusual artwork—a stained glass portrait of Jackie Robinson, a painting depicting basketball legend Walt Frazier as Thomas Gainsborough's *Blue Boy,* and a computer-generated image of Babe Ruth made from 2,000 Yankee baseball cards.

On the south strip of W. 42nd St. between Broadway and Seventh Ave is a newly renovated entrance to the **Times Square Subway Station** with glittering electric lights.

On the north side of the triangle where Broadway intersects Seventh Ave is 1 Times Square, originally the **Times Tower** (1904; Eidlitz & MacKenzie). When the *New York Times* moved in on Dec 31, 1904, the building had a granite base, a fine marble lobby, and 25 floors sheathed in ornamental terra-cotta. (The *Times* moved to W. 43rd St in 1913.) When the building was "improved" (1966; Smith, Smith, Haines, Lundberg & Waehler), a slick marble surface replaced the terra-cotta and granite.

Three floors up is the famous 369 ft "zipper," a wraparound moving sign that has announced the headlines since 1928 and been operated by Dow Jones (owner of the *Wall Street Journal*) since 1995. In 1997, 235,000 amber light-emitting diodes (LEDs) replaced the former 12,400 incandescent light bulbs, which were hard to read in bright sunlight.

New Amsterdam Theatre

Next door at 214 W. 42nd St is the New Amsterdam Theatre (1903; Herts & Tallant; restored 1995; Hardy Holzman Pfeiffer Assoc; DL), home of the *Ziegfeld Follies* from 1913 to 1927. For information on touring the theater, ☎ (212) 282-2900.

History

This lavish entertainment palace included a 1,800-seat main theater, the Aerial Theatre on the roof, and a ten-story office tower. Like other Times Square theaters, it became a movie house, and then closed in 1981. Pigeons and rats moved in and the building slowly collapsed. Disney's restoration replaced 10–15 percent of the exterior brick and terra-cotta, and 70 percent of the auditorium's wall surface, which required 13,000 square ft of new wood paneling to match the surviving white oak woodwork. When 800 pieces of ornamental wood detailing were found to be substandard, the architects had new ones cast of resin and painted to look like wood.

The theater has hosted two Disney blockbuster musicals since opening in 1994, *Beauty and The Beast* and, since 1997, *The Lion King.*

The white terra cotta-clad **Candler Building** (1914; Willauer, Shape & Bready, renovated 2000), 220 W. 42nd St, is named after its builder Asa Candler, then president of the Coca-Cola Company.

On the northwest corner of Seventh Ave and W. 42nd St, at 3 Times Square, is the **Reuters Building** (2001; Fox & Fowle), a 32-story office tower and corporate icon for the global news and financial data service. Along the Seventh Ave side is a glass-walled lobby with 30 ft-high video monitors that broadcast Reuters news. Above on the facade is a vertical LED that flashes news and financial data. On the roof are antennae and satellite dishes. The building occupies the site of the former Rialto Theatre, famous and infamous for its attractions, which in recent decades have included, simultaneously, pornography in the auditorium and television shows like *Romper Room* and *Bowling for Dollars* in the production studios upstairs.

Continue along the north side of W. 42nd St. The building at 207 W. 42nd Street was 42nd St's first theater, the Republic (1900; J. B. McElfatrick & Co.), now called the **New Victory Theater.** Oscar Hammerstein, the builder, was soon forced to sell the Republic to impressario David Belasco, who quickly renamed it after himself. In 1931 the 500-seat theater became a burlesque house, and after 1942, when it was renamed the Victory, it became a movie house; its 1995 reopening was a first step in reclaiming 42nd St. The $11-million restoration produced an impressive exterior staircase. The lamp posts with glass globes hark back to the Hammerstein days. The auditorium reflects Belasco's ornate additions—carved bees, golden domes, and other details in vibrant colors. Run by a nonprofit organization, the New Victory has been transformed into the city's first performing arts center for children.

Next door is the **Ford Center for the Performing Arts** (1997; Beyer Blinder Belle), 213 W. 42nd St, with its main entrance on 43rd St. It is one of Broadway's three largest theaters (1,839 seats) and combines architectural details from the two theaters—the Lyric and the Apollo—demolished to make way for it. The Ford Motor Company reportedly paid $8–10 million for the naming rights.

The Times Square and Selwyn Theatres once stood just beyond the Lyric and Apollo Theatres. Today, the site has been converted by the New 42nd Street Project into retail space (where the Times Square Theatre stood), a home for the Roundabout Theatre (in the Selwyn Theatre), and a ten-story tower with rehearsal studios.

The painstakingly restored 740-seat Selwyn Theatre (1918; George Keister) is the new **American Airlines Theatre**, 219 W. 42nd St, home of the Roundabout Theatre Company. The company was founded in a Chelsea basement in 1965, survived bankruptcy and several moves before settling on Broadway and transforming itself into the nation's second-largest nonprofit theater (after Lincoln Center). The $22-million restoration was financed largely by the sale of naming rights: $75,000 for a restroom, about $10 million for the theater itself. Although much of the Selwyn's outer shell had collapsed, many of the interior details, including the mezzanine cornices and boxes, have been restored. The rooftop lobby for preshow and intermission gathering is a new addition. The ticket lobby is inside the building that houses the **New 42nd Street Studios** and **The Duke,** a 200-seat experimental theater, owned by New 42nd Street, Inc.

Further west on the north side of W. 42nd St is **E-Walk** (1999; D'Agostino Izzo Quirk and Gensler Assocs), a retail and entertainment complex that includes **Broadway City,** a wholesome modern video arcade with a New York motif. Its decor includes a sculptural construction crew on an overhead beam and replicas of the Brooklyn Bridge's towers, the New York Public Library's lions, and Coney Island's Cyclone roller coaster. In a bit of unintended irony, a snack stand beneath a giant replica of the Statue of Liberty's face juxtaposes the line "Give Me Your Tired, Your Poor . . ." with pretzels that cost $1.60—another reminder of the distance between the new Times Square and the real world.

On the south side of W. 42nd St is another large retail and entertainment complex. The only remnant of the old 42nd St is the lobby of the multiplex theater, once the entryway to the **Empire Theatre** (1912; Thomas Lamb). The Empire, formerly called the Eltinge after Julian Eltinge, a popular turn-of-the-20C female impersonator, was further east, but the developer moved the 7.4-million-pound theater 170 ft west so it could be integrated into the multiplex.

Madame Tussaud's Wax Museum

234 W. 42nd St, New York, NY 10036. ☎ (212) 512-9600. Web site: www.madame-tussauds.com. Open Sun–Thurs 10–6; Fri and Sat 10–8. Admission

charge. Accessible to wheelchairs. Permanent exhibition; film. Snack bar. Gift shop.

This branch (opened 2000) of the famous waxworks is a popular and crowded tourist attraction, well-suited to its glitzy Times Square setting.

Exhibits

The exhibition begins with a top-floor **"Opening Night Party,"** attended by replicas of the mayor, state governor, and celebrities from stage and screen. A waxen-faced Woody Allen sits anxiously alone in a corner; flesh-and-blood female tourists cluster around wax movie star Brad Pitt, posing up close for snapshots. Exhibit areas include: a gallery celebrating Madame Tussaud's story, featuring grisly reddish and greenish recreations of heads and bodies, mostly unattached to one another; a behind-the-scenes look at how the lifelike figures are created; a gallery of historical celebrities (such unlikely roommates as Abraham Lincoln, the Dalai Lama, and Princess Diana); and a multimedia exhibit of popular culture, where you can hear Bob Dylan's nasal twang and Richard Nixon's uninflected protestations that he is not a crook. The approximately 200 wax figures stand on the exhibit floor (not in glass cases), where their relative heights evoke interest: Marilyn Monroe is shorter than her myth suggests; basketball star Kareem Abdul-Jabbar is not.

Who Was Madame Tussaud?

Madame Tussaud, née Marie Grosholtz (b. 1761), was apprenticed as a child to Philippe Curtius, a doctor and wax modeler. Hired as an art tutor for the sister of the ill-fated Louis XVI, she lived at Versailles for 11 years and when the French Revolution came, she was an obvious candidate to make death masks of guillotined aristocrats. When Curtius died in 1794, Marie inherited his collection of models. She took them as well as her souvenirs of the revolution to London and opened her first wax museum there in 1835.

Port Authority Terminal

Continue west, across Eighth Ave to the Port Authority Bus Terminal, now filling two city blocks from W. 40th to W. 42nd Sts between Eighth and Ninth Aves (1950; decks added 1963; expansion to W. 42nd St 1982; Port Authority Design Staff). Vast and efficient, this terminal is a weekday way station for 187,000 commuters transported here by 7,200 buses. While commuter buses make up 80 percent of the traffic, most long-distance buses entering New York use the terminal as well. Vehicular ramps feed directly into the Lincoln Tunnel without impeding traffic on the streets below, and subterranean pedestrian passageways connect with the 42nd St stations of the Eighth Ave, Seventh Ave, Broadway, and Flushing subways.

Interior

Near the 42nd St entrance is an audio-kinetic sculpture, *42nd Street Ballroom* (1983; George Rhoads), an entertaining contraption of rolling balls and dinging bells. In the waiting room in the South Wing is a life-size bronze group, *The Commuters* (1980) by George Segal, made from plaster casts of Segal's wife and friends.

Operation Alternative

The terminal was long considered one of the city's more unpleasant places because of the legions of homeless men and women living there. However, beginning in 1991, the Port Authority's Operation Alternative, a social services outreach program, helped clean up the terminal. The Port Authority also closed off many nooks and crannies and began redeveloping the retail areas.

Just west of the terminal, at 330 W. 42nd St, is the former **McGraw-Hill Building** (1931; Raymond Hood, Godley & Fouilhoux; DL), a revolutionary skyscraper in its day. Because the building originally contained printing presses, it was relegated to the fringes of Midtown by the Zoning Resolution of 1916, which prohibited light industry further inland, a law enacted in part to restrain the Garment District from encroaching on the theaters and restaurants of Times Square. McGraw-Hill's executives nonetheless hoped that the fortunes of the neighborhood would rise, a hope never fully realized. The building is much admired for its blue-green terra-cotta sheathing, which helps it blend with the sky, as well as its horizontal bands of strip windows, which were needed to illuminate the loft and factory floors. McGraw-Hill long ago departed for more genteel surroundings uptown.

Cross Ninth Ave to **Theatre Row.** A group of Off-Off-Broadway theaters opened here, officially in 1978, although three of the companies had started several years earlier. The goal of these theatrical pioneers was to reclaim the derelict west end of 42nd St for the Theater District. Today the row boasts commercial, nonprofit, and small studio theaters, including Playwrights Horizons, the John Houseman Theatre Center, and the Douglas Fairbanks Theatre (432 W. 42nd St), a commercial Off-Broadway house. In fact, it has fared so well that the 42nd Street Development Corporation, which owns the buildings, has torn down several of the theaters and is constructing, in conjunction with the Shubert Organization, a residential apartment tower, a 499-seat theater, and several smaller stages. Theatre Row's success has drawn restaurants and other attractions: Kramer's Reality Tour, which visits city spots related to the 1990s television show *Seinfeld* is based at the Pulse Ensemble Theatre (432 West 42nd St); the West Bank Café across the street (407 W. 42nd St) adds cabaret, comedy, and jazz to the mix. The Signature Theatre Company (555 W. 42nd St) has ventured even further west, opening a theater on 42nd St between Tenth and Eleventh Aves.

Dyer Ave, which breaks into W. 42nd St. between Ninth and Tenth Aves, exists primarily as part of the ramp system for the **Lincoln Tunnel.** The tunnel, owned and operated by the Port Authority of New York and New Jersey, links Midtown with Weehawken, New Jersey, and the interstate highway system. Its three tubes were opened in 1937 (center), 1945 (north), and 1957 (south) and now carry over 22 million vehicles annually.

Tunnel Statistics

Maximum depth from mean high water to roadway	97 ft
Longest tube (center) from portal to portal	8,216 ft
Typical weekday traffic (eastbound)	62,500 vehicles
Original cost	$75 million

Return to Ninth Ave, turn left, and walk north one block. Turn right on W. 43rd St and walk to Eighth Ave. In 1999 **Second Stage** moved into an Art Deco former bank (1927; Rene Chambellan and Dennison & Hirons; restoration, Rem Koolhaas and Richard Gluckman) at 307 W. 43rd St. The move gave new theatrical life to a spot beyond the 42nd Street reclamation project and the glitter of Times Square.

Continue east to 229 W. 43rd St, the **New York Times Building.** Founded in 1851, the *Times* rose to prominence under Adolph S. Ochs (publisher 1896–1935) who increased its daily circulation from 19,000 to 490,000 and established it as the nation's most respected newspaper. It remains the newspaper of record, distinguished for its reliability, coverage of foreign news, and editorial restraint. Today the "Gray Lady" has color photos and enough clever writing and quirky subject matter to occasionally infuriate critics. The newspaper moved its last printing presses from this building to College Point, Queens, in 1997. In 1999 the paper, a major player in the redevelopment of Times Square, began planning a move to a new 40-story office tower at Eighth Ave between W. 40th and W. 41st Sts at the southern edge of Times Square.

Walk east back toward the center of Times Square. Between Eighth and Seventh Aves on the south side of the street is the main entrance to the Ford Center. It incorporates parts of the facade of the former **Lyric Theatre** (1903; V. Hugo Koehler), including figures of Athena and Hermes, ram's-head masks, banded columns, oculi, wreaths, and the busts of three men, two of whom are thought to be Gilbert and Sullivan. Also from the Lyric is the plaster medallion depicting Zeus, installed above the first landing of the grand staircase. From the **Apollo Theatre** (1920; De Rosa & Pereira) comes the auditorium's 39 × 28 ft elliptical dome and the proscenium arch and side boxes. The lobby-floor mosaic of masks of Tragedy and Comedy, comprised of 172,800 green, gray, black, brown and ivory marble tiles, was made by 18 artisans in a Williamsburg studio.

Return on W. 43rd St to Times Square and the Broadway side of the **Condé Nast Building** (1999; Fox & Fowle), 4 Times Square, with the NASDAQ stock market's $37-million, 90 × 120 ft video screen and the world's largest outdoor video screen with 18 million LEDs. In the building is a visitors' center with exhibits on the stock market and a street-level studio used by network business reporters. The building to the north at 1500 Broadway (between W. 43rd and W. 44th Sts) contains the ABC studio for *Good Morning America.*

On the west side between W. 43rd and W. 44th Sts, at 1501 Broadway, is the **Paramount Building** (1927; Rapp & Rapp; DL), once the tallest skyscraper in Times Square with a clock tower and an illuminated glass globe on top. It was built as offices for Paramount Pictures but is best remembered as the site of the "bobby-soxer riots." In 1937, 21,000 fans showed up to see Benny Goodman's debut in the 3,900-seat Paramount Theatre. On Oct 12, 1944, when Frank Sinatra, whose rise to stardom had been sparked by his 1942 Paramount concerts, made his triumphant return, 30,000 youngsters rushed the doors. In the 1960s, the theater was dismantled, though the tower remains an important Times Square landmark. After decades of darkness, the clocks and globe were restored in 1997. The lobby is still theatrical, with its heavily ornate gilded ceiling, black marble-faced walls, opulent chandeliers, and paneled bronze elevator doors. In addition, the upper levels of the building now sport speakers that blare out a tape of a carillon playing George M. Cohan's "Give My Regards to Broadway" 15 minutes before curtain time for every show.

Performances of a different sort arrived in 1999. In a perfect blend of old Times Square (cheesy honky-tonk) and new Times Square (entertainment as big business), the World Wrestling Federation, opened a theme restaurant with a full stage, retail space, and a production studio in the Paramount.

Even the U.S. Army, whose recruiting station has long been located on an island between Seventh Ave and Broadway, has been smitten with Times Square fervor: a giant American flag with red-, white-, and blue-colored light bulbs now decorates the recruiting station.

Cross Broadway and Seventh Ave, walking east along 44th St, where land-marked buildings stand almost shoulder to shoulder. The **Manhattan Church of the Nazarene** at 130 W. 44th St was originally home to the Lambs Club (1904; McKim, Mead & White; DL), the city's oldest theatrical club, founded in 1875. The club, still active, is now at 3 W. 51st St, but the Lamb's Theatre continues in this building, a Georgian revival brick, marble, and terra-cotta structure with lambs' heads between the window spandrels. Members have included Mark Twain, Edwin Booth, and David Belasco. The building was sold to the church in 1974.

Across the street is the **Hudson Theatre** (1904; J. B. McElfatrick & Son and Israels & Harder; restored 1990; Stonehill & Taylor; DL), 139–141 W. 44th St, a Beaux-Arts building with a rich interior that includes a ceiling with domes of Tiffany glass, floral reliefs, Corinthian columns, and other lavish touches. Built for producer Henry Harris, who later died aboard the *Titanic*, it was restored in 1990 by the builders of the Millenium Hotel next door.

The **Gerard Apartments** (1894; George Keister; DL), 123 W. 44th St, originally the Hotel Gerard, is an ornately dormered brick and limestone residential hotel for middle-class residents.

The **Belasco Theatre** (1907; George Keister; DL), at 111 W. 44th St, was built by playwright and producer David Belasco as a showcase for his technical innovations; it included an elevator stage, a sophisticated lighting system, and a studio for developing special effects, as well as a grandly furnished apartment for Belasco himself.

Return to Broadway. Between W. 44th and W. 45th Sts is 1515 Broadway, originally named One Astor Plaza (1969; Kahn & Jacobs). The "Astor" part comes from the Astor Hotel (1904), which once but unfortunately no longer stands here. Architecturally the building is recognizable at some distance by the concrete fins adorning its upper stories, suggestive to one critic of an Edsel crashing into it from outer space. This was the first building in the specially designated Times Square Theater District to take advantage of zoning bonuses that allow extra floor space to a building that includes a new legitimate theater (the Minskoff). Today the building is the **Viacom Building,** home to MTV (Music Television) Networks. The mezzanine-level studio attracts hordes of screaming teens hoping for a glimpse of their favorite star or perhaps their own 15 minutes of fame on the network.

Continue west on W. 44th St. On the south side of the street is **Sardi's** restaurant, 234 W. 44th St, onetime haunt of actors, writers, and theater people, who traditionally held opening night celebrations here while awaiting the newspaper reviews. Today its clientele includes tourists and celebrity watchers.

Shubert Theatre

Across the street at 225 W. 44th St is the Shubert Theatre (1913; Henry B. Herts; DL), named after Sam S. Shubert, who with his brothers Lee and J. J. founded a theatrical empire.

The Shuberts

The Shubert brothers, offspring of a Syracuse peddler, came to New York around the turn of the 20C. Beginning with a single theater, they took on and bested the ruling monopoly of the day, the Klaw and Erlanger Syndicate, emerging as the most powerful force in the American theater. In their heyday the Shuberts controlled the production, booking, and presentation of shows, dominating the try-out circuits through their ownership of theaters outside New York and forcing producers to book exclusively through their organization. A decree issued in 1956 as the result of an antitrust action brought by the federal government required them to stop their restrictive booking practices and to sell 12 theaters in six cities. Yet the Shubert Organization remains the leading force on Broadway, controlling 16.5 Broadway theaters (Irving Berlin's estate owns a half-interest in the Music Box), nearly half of the 37 existing houses.

The Shubert Theatre, whose upper floors house the headquarters of the Shubert Organization, has had a resoundingly prosperous career, beginning with its opening production, *Hamlet*, and including *A Chorus Line*, which won the Pulitzer Prize in 1976 and ran until 1990. The building has an impressive curved corner entrance and a mansard roof with dormer windows.

There are several other landmark theaters on this block. The **Helen Hayes Theatre** (1912; Ingalls & Hoffman; DL), 240 W. 44th St, was originally the Little Theatre, so named because with 299 seats it was designed for small-scale plays. Even after 200 seats were later added it remains Broadway's smallest auditorium. In 1983 it was named after Hayes—star of *Mary of Scotland*, *Victoria Regina*, and *Happy Birthday*—when an earlier Helen Hayes Theatre was torn down for the Marriott Marquis Hotel.

The stucco facade of the **St. James Theatre** (1927; Warren & Wetmore; DL), 246–256 W. 44th St, is decorated with theatrical masks and a wrought-iron loggia. The St. James has seen its share of classics, including *Oklahoma!*, *The King and I*, and *Hello, Dolly*.

The **Broadhurst Theatre** (1918; Herbert J. Krapp; DL), 235–243 W. 44th St, was designed by the noted theater architect for the Shuberts as a companion to the Plymouth Theatre behind it on W. 45th St. The **Majestic Theatre** (1927; Herbert J. Krapp; DL), 245–257 W. 44th St, was part of a trio with the Royale Theatre and Theatre Masque (now the John Golden Theatre) on W. 45th St, created for developer Irving Chanin as part of a hotel complex. Krapp's efforts here were more ambitious than his earlier work; the three theaters share what he called a "modern Spanish" look that includes a terra-cotta base beneath a Roman brick wall and Spanish-style ornamentation. The Majestic's hits have included *Carousel, South Pacific, The Music Man, The Wiz,* and *The Phantom of the Opera.*

To the east of the Shubert Theatre is **Shubert Alley,** now a promenade for theatergoers, formerly a gathering place for singers, actors, and dancers who hoped to be cast in Shubert-produced plays.

Walk through Shubert Alley to the **Booth Theatre** (1913; Henry B. Herts; DL), 222 W. 45th St. Named after the legendary actor Edwin Booth, and built by Lee Shubert and the producer Winthrop Ames, the Booth is a small theater (783 seats; the Shubert has 1,483). The modesty came perhaps because its developers had just emerged from the spectacular failure of the New Theatre on Central Park West, a palatial marble-faced edifice that collapsed financially after two seasons. Like the Helen Hayes, the Booth showcased dramas and smaller-scale musicals, including *That Championship Season* and *Sunday in the Park with George.*

Friezes and elaborate plasterwork featuring urns, wreaths and figures holding musical instruments distinguish the **Plymouth Theatre** (1918; Herbert J. Krapp; DL), 234 W. 45th St, from the less elaborate Broadhurst. The **Royale Theatre** (1927; Herbert J. Krapp; DL), 242–250 W. 45th St, annother Irwin Chanin Spanish-inspired house, has a vaulted ceiling and a mural by Willy Pogany called *Lovers of Spain.* Julie Andrews's career got a jump start when she made her American debut in *The Boy Friend* here. The **John Golden Theatre** (1927; Herbert J. Krapp; DL), originally the Theatre Masque, 252–256 W. 45th St, another small theater, has been home to *The Gin Game, Crimes of the Heart,* and *'Night Mother.* The **Music Box Theatre** (1920; C. Howard Crane & E. George Kiehler; DL), 239–247 W. 45th St, its exterior balcony fronted by an Ionic limestone colonnade and its mansard roof with a wrought-iron balustrade, was built by Sam Harris for Irving Berlin's *Music Box Revues,* which ran for five years.

Inside the **Imperial** (1923; Herbert J. Krapp; interior DL), 249 W. 45th St, is impressive ornamental plasterwork. There are friezes, floral and geometric designs, and fairy figures with the masks of Comedy and Tragedy. One of the city's premier theaters, it has witnessed productions of *Annie Get Your Gun, Gypsy, Oliver, Fiddler on the Roof, Dreamgirls,* and *Les Miserables.*

Just west of Eighth Ave is the **Martin Beck Theatre** (1924; C. Albert Lansburgh; restored 1997; Francesca Russo Architects; DL), 302–314 W. 45th St, Broadway's only Moorish-style theater. Designed for Beck, a Czech immigrant turned producer, it is ornate both outside and in—the exterior has a line of three-story arches with detailed capitals, the inner lobby has three domes each with mural paintings, and the auditorium has a ceiling designed by painter Albert Herter along with boxes featuring Byzantine capitals.

Return to Broadway. Dominating the west Side of Broadway between W. 45th and W. 46th Sts is the **Marriott Marquis Hotel** (1985; John C. Portman), a 50-story tower. The luxury hotel features a dramatic atrium, a glass elevator, 1,877 rooms for visitors, the 1,600-seat Marquis Theatre, and a revolving lounge and restaurant on top. In Oct 1982, despite protests from actors, directors, producers, and preservationists, the historic Helen Hayes and Morosco Theatres were demolished in favor of the hotel, whose presence, it was hoped, would help revitalize this part of Times Square. Hayes declined to have the theater named for her, in part because she wanted her name on an intimate space, not one designed for commercial spectacles.

Continue east along W. 45th St to the **Lyceum Theatre** (1903; Herts & Tallant; DL), 149 W. 45th St, the oldest surviving legitimate New York theater and its grandest. Now a part of the Shubert Organization, whose archives occupy the onetime apartment of entrepreneur Daniel Frohman, the building stands out for its Beaux-Arts facade, its undulating marquee, its elaborate columns, and its high mansard roof pierced with oval windows.

Return to Seventh Ave, turn right, and walk past the Virgin Record Store/Loews Movie Theater that dominates this block. At the northeast corner of W. 46th St and Seventh Ave is the **I. Miller Building** (1929; Louis Friedland; DL). The shoe business, founded by Polish immigrant Israel Miller, long catered to the theater trade; niches on the facade hold life-size marble statues of ladies of the theater selected by the voting public; the winners: Ethel Barrymore (drama), Marilyn Miller (musical theater), Mary Pickford (film), and Rosa Ponselle (opera)—all sculpted by Alexander Stirling Calder, father of Alexander Calder.

The north end of Times Square is properly known as **Father Duffy Square**, named for Father Francis P. Duffy (1871–1932), the "Fighting Chaplain" of the 69th Regiment during World War I. A figure of Duffy (c. 1936, installed 1937; Charles Keck) stands near W. 47th St in the middle of the traffic island. As pastor of Holy Cross Church (at 333 W. 42nd St), Father Duffy served a parish that embraced the slums of Hell's Kitchen, the burlesque houses and dance halls of Times Square, and the legitimate theaters of Broadway. When the statue was unveiled, a crowd of 30,000 including prize fighters, political figures, and Broadway characters came to pay him tribute, joining the 69th Regiment and military bands, which struck up *Onward Christian Soldiers*. Father Duffy is shown in his World War I uniform holding the New Testament, his back to a granite Celtic cross.

Near the 46th St end of the square is a bronze **statue of George M. Cohan** (1958; George Lober), the song-and-dance man (1878–1942) best known for writing *Give My Regards to Broadway, Over There,* and *I'm a Yankee Doodle Dandy.* The statue was unveiled in a ceremony with Oscar Hammerstein II presiding, George Jessel acting as master of ceremonies, and a crowd of 45,000 attending. At the conclusion, everyone broke into *Give My Regards to Broadway.*

Just north of Father Duffy Square is **tkts** (short for Times Square Ticket Center), W. 47th St between Seventh Ave and Broadway, a kiosk run by the Theater Development Fund, selling day-of-performance discounted theater tickets. Lines form well in advance of curtain time and as many as 4,000 tickets may be sold in the two hours before showtime.

Times Square Visitors Center

On Seventh Ave (between W. 46th and W. 47th Sts) is New York's first full-fledged comprehensive visitors center, the Times Square Visitors Center at 1560 Broadway, housed in the former **Embassy Theatre** (1925; Thomas Lamb with Rambusch Studio; interior DL).

History

The Embassy, one of 300-plus theaters that Thomas Lamb designed around the world, was built by Metro-Goldwyn-Mayer to elevate the status of movies. Marble, blond wood paneling, Louis XV furniture, and mirrors visually enlarging the inner lobby gave the interior a French flavor. Inside the auditorium were tapestried chairs and elegant pastoral murals by Arthur Crisp. The Embassy sold reserved seats, like the legitimate theater, for $2.20, about ten times the price of an average ticket in 1925. The idea never caught on and in 1929 the Embassy became America's first newsreel theater, lasting until the 1950s, when it became a traditional movie house.

Interior

While the Louis XV furniture is long gone and the auditorium seats were donated to Brooklyn churches, the interior retains its original detailing. The two surviving murals were restored for the 1998 grand opening, and a new painting was added with faces of Broadway celebrities. Run by the Times Square Business Improvement District, the tourist center offers multilingual guides, an automated teller machine, foreign currency exchange, and free Internet surfing.

Next door at 1564–1566 Broadway is the **Palace Theatre** (1913; Kirchoff & Rose; interior DL), once the premier vaudeville theater. Built by Martin Beck but run by E. F. Albee, grandfather of the playwright Edward Albee, it became almost instantly successful with Sarah Bernhardt's appearance in May 1913. The stage was a proving ground for up-and-comers: among them the Marx Brothers, Mae West, Jack Benny, Harry Houdini, Bob Hope, Jimmy Durante, W. C. Fields, and Will Rogers. By 1932, vaudeville was losing ground and movies moved in; in 1966 it became a Broadway house.

Look across to the west side of Times Square between W. 47th and W. 48th Sts. The **Morgan Stanley Dean Witter Building**, 1585 Broadway, with another recent addition to Times Square's neon lineup, offers three tickers full of financial information.

Continue north on Seventh Ave to W. 48th St; turn right. Musical instrument dealers have long occupied 48th St between Seventh and Sixth Aves: among them are **Manny's Music,** 156 W. 48th St; **Rudy's Music Stop Inc,** 169 W. 48th St; and, largest of all, the **Sam Ash Music Store,** 163 W. 48th St. Halfway down the block, at 138–146 W. 48th St, is the **Cort Theatre** (1913; Thomas Lamb; DL), one of Lamb's oldest remaining New York theaters. Modeled on the Petit Trianon, Marie Antionette's favorite Versailles residence, the interior is decorated with a mural depicting Versailles's gardens.

Turn around, walk west, crossing Seventh Ave and Broadway to the **Longacre Theatre** at 220 W. 48th St (1913; Henry Herts; DL), distinguished by its French neoclassical facade. It was built for the Broadway producer Harry Frazee, who also owned the Boston Red Sox and later sold Babe Ruth to the New York Yankees for cash to finance a musical starring his girlfriend.

Return to Broadway and turn left, walking north one block to W. 49th St. The northwest corner of Broadway and W. 49th St has been renamed Jack Dempsey

Corner, after the prizefighter. Dempsey had a restaurant here when the third Madison Square Garden (W. 49th St at Eighth Ave) attracted gymnasiums and fight managers' offices to the neighborhood.

Brill Building

On this corner is also the Brill Building (1931; Victor Bark, Jr.), 1619 Broadway. Abraham Lefcourt, a clothing manufacturer who built up much of the Garment District and amassed a fortune of about $100 million, bought the site from clothiers Samuel, Max, and Maurice Brill. Lefcourt named the building for his son Alan, who had died in a car crash. (The bronze bust above the door and the larger stone one in the 11th floor recess are thought to be the two Lefcourts.) When Lefcourt lost his money in the Depression, Samuel Brill bought back the building and renamed it after himself. This building was the final stop for Tin Pan Alley, the district for music publishers and aspiring songwriters, that started downtown.

Tin Pan Alley

During the mid-19C, Tin Pan Alley was a strip of 14th St near Broadway. By the turn of the 20C, it had moved north to W. 28th St, before finally migrating uptown to the Brill Building. The Brill Building sound of the 1950s and 1960s became so famous that the term eventually referred also to hits written across the street at 1650 Broadway in an office headed by impresario Don Kirschner.

Among the leading producer-writers at the Brill Building were Jerry Leiber and Mike Stoller, who together had previously written hits such as "Hound Dog." Other songwriters included Neil Sedaka, Neil Diamond, and Carole King. Producer Phil Spector developed his "wall of sound" at the Brill Building. Among the hits churned out were "You've Lost That Loving Feeling," "On Broadway," "The LocoMotion," "One Fine Day," "Breaking Up Is Hard to Do," "I'm a Believer," "Up on the Roof," and "Leader of the Pack." The Beatles, who wrote their own songs and created an aural revolution, killed off the Brill Building sound and Tin Pan Alley.

Today there still are entertainment companies (many music-related) in both 1650 Broadway and the Brill Building. On the ground floor of the Brill Building is **Colony Record and Music Center,** which opened in 1948 and has the largest collection of sheet music available in the city.

Across the street, 1626 Broadway, Caroline's Comedy Club occupies the site of the **Rivoli Theatre,** a 2,100-seat movie palace where *Oklahoma!, The Grapes of Wrath, Around the World in 80 Days,* and *The Sound of Music* made their debuts. Above the ornate marquee rose a Greek temple facade with eight five-story Doric columns and an elaborately carved pediment. The theater, never landmarked, was demolished by 1988 to make way for the Morgan Stanley Building (1988–90; Kevin Roche John Dinkeloo & Assocs.).

Walk west along W. 49th St. The third Madison Square Garden (1925; Thomas Lamb) was built on the northwest corner of Eighth Ave and 49th St by John Ringling, a circus entrepreneur, and Tex Rickard, a sometime gambler, cattleman, and promoter of prizefights.

The Third Madison Square Garden

The first event in the third Garden was New York's introduction to professional hockey, with the New York Americans losing to the Montreal Canadians. Rickard later took over a team sportswriters nicknamed "Tex's Rangers." Although Tex and this building are gone, the Rangers remain a Madison Square Garden institution.

Presidential history was twice made here, first in 1932 when candidate Franklin Roosevelt accepted the nomination and then 30 years later when Marilyn Monroe sang her sultry "Happy Birthday" to President John Kennedy.

The Garden's staple offerings were boxing matches (Joe Louis defended his title eight times here), ice hockey and basketball games (the Knicks were born here in 1946), ice shows, the circus, rodeos, and expositions. Its social peak came with the annual horse show, for which a box cost $315 in 1939; its social nadir was probably the Six-Day Bicycle Race for which in the same year a one-week admission cost a dollar. Today, **Worldwide Plaza** (1989; Frank Williams, apartment towers; Skidmore, Owings & Merrill, office tower), a mixed-use project, occupies the site.

Hell's Kitchen

Continue west to Ninth Ave, leaving Times Square behind for the once-notorious neighborhood of Hell's Kitchen, today generally known as **Clinton.**

History

During the mid-19C, Hell's Kitchen, a slum stretching from about W. 30th St to W. 57th St west of Eighth Ave, held some of the city's worst tenements as well as some of its least desirable industries: slaughterhouses, gas plants, glue and soap factories. These industries were attracted by the Hudson River Railroad (later the New York Central Railroad) on Eleventh Ave. As elsewhere, immigrants (mostly Irish, with some Germans and blacks) were attracted to the jobs these industries promised.

Local gangs preyed on the railroad yards and so terrorized the neighborhood that policemen from the nearby 20th Precinct would venture out only in groups larger than three. Bearing such colorful names as the Hudson Dusters, the Gophers, the Gorillas, and Battle Row Annie's Ladies' Social and Athletic Club, the gangs gave Hell's Kitchen a reputation as one of the most dangerous spots on the American continent. Supposedly two policemen watching a street fight on a muggy summer night gave the district its name. Said one, "This neighborhood is hot as hell." "Hell is cool," corrected the other. "This here's Hell's Kitchen."

After 1910, when the New York Central Railroad hired a strong-arm squad who clubbed, shot, arrested, and otherwise incapacitated most of the old-style gangsters, life in the area mellowed for a while, only to resume its former vehemence with the arrival of bootleggers during the 1920s. After World War II, southern blacks and Puerto Ricans moved to the neighborhood, which became the setting for the 1957 musical *West Side Story.* The elimination of the Ninth Avenue El and the Eleventh Ave grade-level railroad tracks, as well as the demolition of many tenements that stood in the way of the ramps for the Lincoln Tunnel, paved the way for social changes now taking place.

The far West Side now is showing distinct signs of gentrification and residents prefer to call their neighborhood Clinton after DeWitt Clinton Park (west of Eleventh Ave, between W. 52nd and W. 54th Sts). Indeed, much of the neighborhood's character—mostly residential low-rises, mixed income and mixed ethnicity—is being threatened by the development of luxury high-rises. Ninth Ave is a hot spot for moderately priced ethnic restaurants. During the annual **Ninth Avenue International Food Festival** (a weekend in mid-May), the avenue is closed to traffic from W. 37th to W. 57th Sts as an estimated 1 million people stroll and eat.

Intrepid Sea-Air-Space Museum

Pier 86, 1 Intrepid Square (W. 46th St and Twelfth Ave), New York, NY 10036. ☎ (212) 245-2533; for recorded information, ☎ (212) 245-0072. Web site: www.intrepidmuseum.org. Open every day Memorial Day–Labor Day, Mon–Fri 10–5; Sat, Sun 10–6. Last tickets sold 1 hour before closing. Restricted hours in winter. Call for holiday closings.

Tours; films; special events often scheduled around military holidays. Snack bar, gift shop. Be prepared in winter for chilling winds on the flight deck. Complete wheelchair access to Hangar Deck; elevator, restrooms, and telephones accessible to handicapped visitors. Elevator to flight deck under construction; for updated access information, call the museum.

Subway: There is no subway stop near Twelfth Ave. Take any subway to 42nd St (Grand Central, 42nd St–Sixth Ave, Times Square, or 42nd St–Eighth Ave) and transfer to the 42nd St crosstown bus. Bus: M11, M42, M50.

Located at Pier 86 in the Hudson River at W. 46th St is the Intrepid Sea-Air-Space Museum. The aircraft carrier *Intrepid* (launched 1943, decommissioned 1974), whose planes destroyed 650 enemy planes and 289 enemy ships in World War II, was refurbished as a museum of technology and naval history in 1982.

In the forward theater of the *Intrepid,* a film offers thrilling shots of planes thundering onto the flight deck. Elsewhere are exhibits on the *Intrepid's* World War II history, undersea and space exploration, and the history of aviation including a collection of wood-and-canvas planes from the early days of flight. On the flight deck you can examine real aircraft, including helicopters and a Lockheed A-12 Blackbird, and climb up (sometimes a wait) to view the captain's bridge and the admiral's bridge. You can board the USS *Growler,* one of the first guided-missile submarines, the USS *Edson,* a destroyer whose guns once pounded the shores of Vietnam, and for an extra fee, take a turn in the *Intrepid's* flight simulator.

16 · Fifth Avenue and Vicinity: 34th Street to 59th Street

Subway: Lexington Ave Local (6) to 33rd St. Sixth Ave Express or Local (B, D, Q, F) to 34th St. Broadway Local (N, R) to 34th St.
Bus: M1, M2, M3, M4, M5

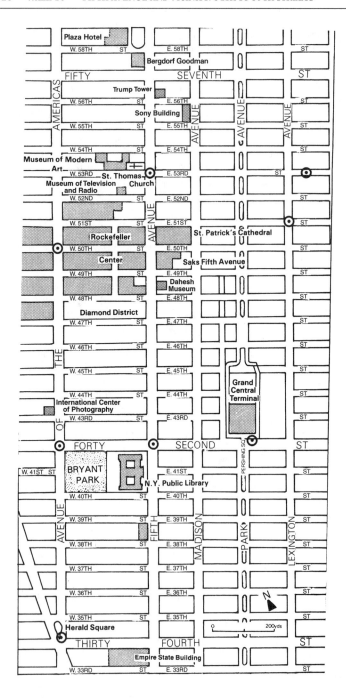

Among the streets of New York, **Fifth Ave** is preeminent. It is *the* avenue, the most famous, most glittering promenade in the city, the route of grand processions, and one of the best places to observe the chic and the famous on their daily rounds.

History

In the late 19C and early 20C, Fifth Ave was the city's most desirable residential address. Then commerce invaded, first with the old Waldorf-Astoria Hotel at 34th St, then with B. Altman and Co. a block north. The early Fifth Ave stores were uniformly upscale—Lord & Taylor, B. Altman, Gorham Silver—but now parts of the avenue have lost their former sheen. In the blocks of the 30s and 40s there are shops selling electronic gadgetry and garish bric-a-brac. Theme stores crammed with knickknacks based on corporate logos or cartoon characters clutter the area around 57th St. Much of Fifth Ave, however, still glitters, with jewelers, international boutiques, and expensive apartment houses.

Fifth Ave is also the prime route for annual ethnic parades, most notably the St. Patrick's Day Parade. On Easter Sunday, the fashion-minded informally parade in their finery. Between Thanksgiving and Christmas the stores—especially Lord & Taylor, F.A.O. Schwarz, and Saks Fifth Avenue—offer extravagant window displays with elaborately costumed dolls and mechanical figures. Hordes of people are drawn to this holiday ritual, resigned to inch along the pavement for a peek at the decorations while Salvation Army workers and Santas of all shapes, sizes, and colors ring bells soliciting money for charitable causes.

Fifth Avenue and Vicinity: 34th to 44th Streets

Empire State Building

The Empire State Building (1931; Shreve, Lamb & Harmon; DL), 350 Fifth Avenue (between W. 33rd and W. 34th Sts) is no longer the world's tallest building (surpassed in the 1970s by the World Trade Center and then by Chicago's Sears Roebuck Building). It regained its status as New York's tallest building in 2001, when the Twin Towers of the World Trade Center were destroyed, but it has always been for many people the quintessential skyscraper.

Empire State Building Statistics	
Height to 102nd floor observatory	1,250 ft
Height to top of TV tower	1,472 ft
Weight	365,000 tons
Volume	37,000,000 cubic ft
Area of site	2 acres
Number of bricks	10,000,000
Ft of electrical wire	2.5 million

And it has enough steel to build a double-track railroad from New York to Baltimore (187 miles). The site, however, was famous even before the building arrived.

The First Waldorf-Astoria

In 1859, John Jacob Astor III and William Backhouse Astor Jr. built adjoining mansions here. William married the socially ambitious Caroline Webster Schermerhorn. A feud developed between Caroline Astor and her nephew, William Waldorf Astor, who had inherited the southern house. William spited his aunt by tearing down his mansion and putting up a hotel, which he named the Waldorf after the ancestral Astor home in Germany. Caroline, offended by the towering hotel, moved uptown, leaving her house to her son, John Jacob IV, who tore it down and built the Astoria part of the Waldorf-Astoria. He named it after a city in Oregon that was originally a trading post in the first John Jacob Astor's fur empire.

The Waldorf-Astoria (opened 1893) flourished both financially and socially. Its dining room was ruled by the legendary Oscar Tschirky, known better as Oscar of the Waldorf, a maître d' who imperiously deployed his expertise in social discrimination. In 1929, the hotel moved uptown to its present location at Park Ave and E. 50th St.

Empire State Building History

The concept of the Empire State Building—the world's tallest skyscraper, budgeted at $60 million—was a product of the optimistic 1920s, but the building itself was a child of the Depression, demolition beginning in 1929 just two months before the stock market crash. Remarkably it was finished ahead of schedule and under budget, setting construction records still unrivaled, rising an average of 4½ stories a week and 14 stories during the ten peak working days. Steel was set in place as little as 80 hours after leaving the furnaces of Pittsburgh, and the supply and delivery of other materials were superbly coordinated with the building schedule. Lewis Hine's photographs of the "skyboys" at work on the high steel are a tribute to them and a landmark in American photography.

Because of the Depression, actual costs came only to $40,948,900. But despite the promotional efforts of former governor Al Smith (the figurehead president of the Empire State Corporation), the economic climate prevented full occupancy until almost the beginning of World War II, a period during which the building was nicknamed the "Empty State" building. Only tourists visiting the observation deck kept the company solvent. The building's most famous visitor in those years was King Kong; in the classic 1933 film, the mythical giant ape climbed atop the tower and attempted to fight off a squadron of army planes.

The building has also known its share of tragedy, beginning in 1933 when a woman named Irma Eberhardt became the first suicide to leap from the top. Then on a foggy July 28, 1945, after threading its way among the pinnacles of Midtown, an Army B-25 crashed into the 79th floor, killing 14 people. In 1997, just four years after a terrorist bombing at the World Trade Center, a Palestinian teacher killed one tourist and wounded six on the 86th floor observation deck before killing himself.

Exterior

The facade consists of a limestone curtain wall trimmed with vertical strips of stainless steel running the height of the building, a design chosen after 15 discarded attempts, in part because it would facilitate rapid construction. Everything possible—windows, spandrels, steel strips, even slabs of stone—was fabricated at the site of origin and shipped to be installed without further handfitting or stonecutting. Originally the building was to end at the 86th floor, but one of the backers determined that it needed a mast for mooring zeppelins, which added 150 ft to the projected height. Several attempts were made, but the mast never succeeded, though a navy blimp managed to dock long enough in 1931 to dump its ballast—water—on pedestrians several blocks away.

While the Empire State Building is a visual landmark 24 hours a day, it is particularly noticeable when illuminated at night. The colored lights change to celebrate various holidays. Some of the choices are easy to understand: red for Valentine's Day; red and green at Christmas; red, white, and blue for patriotic holidays. Through the years, however, the list of holidays has grown and some color choices have become less obvious: red and white for Pulaski Day (honoring the Polish war hero), purple and green for Alzheimer's Awareness Week.

Interior
The lobby, three stories high, is lined with marble imported from France, Italy, Belgium, and Germany. A marble panel with an aluminum relief of the skyscraper superimposed over New York State faces the main entrance. Next to it is a 1938 scale model ($\frac{1}{16}$ inch equals one ft) of the building. Along the north corridor are hypercolorful illuminated panels (1963) by Roy Sparkia and Renée Nemorov depicting the eight wonders of the world—the traditional seven plus the Empire State Building. On the mezzanine level is the **New York Skyride,** a tourist trap with a simulated thrill ride through the city.

Observatories
The ticket office for the observatories (86th and 102nd floors) is on the concourse level, one floor below the main lobby (open every day 9:30 A.M.–11:30 P.M., observatory open until midnight). Admission charge; ☎ (212) 736-3100.

On a clear day visibility reaches 80 miles. The view, spectacular day or night, peaks on July 4th when fireworks fill the sky with color (and the observation deck is elbow-to-elbow with onlookers).

Science, Industry, and Business Library
Walk north on Fifth Ave. Between 34th and 35th Sts on the east side is the New York Public Library's Science, Industry, and Business Library in the former building of **B. Altman & Company** (1906; Trowbridge & Livingston; DL). As the first department store to intrude on the previously residential area, Altman's was modeled like a great palazzo, perhaps to soften the blow to disgruntled neighbors.

History
Founder Benjamin Altman, son of a Lower East Side milliner, opened his first shop on Third Ave near E. 9th St and worked his way uptown via a stylish store in Ladies' Mile (Sixth Ave and W. 19th St). When Altman died unmarried in 1913, he left his art collection to the Metropolitan Museum of Art and $20 million in Altman's stock to a philanthropic foundation. Never trendy, the store was known through the years for its high-quality conservative clothing, home furnishings, dishes, and glassware; it went out of business in 1989.

In 1996, the building was restored as the Science, Industry, and Business Library (the entrance is on Madison Ave). The library has 250 personal computers and 500 reading-room seats wired for laptop use, in addition to circulating and research collections. The City University of New York has also moved into the building, consolidating its Graduate Center here.

Continue north to the former **Gorham Building** (1906; McKim, Mead & White), 390 Fifth Ave (southwest corner of the intersection at 36th St). The lower facade of this Italian Renaissance palace built for the jeweler and silver company has been unfortunately altered. At 409 Fifth Ave (southeast corner at 37th St) is the former home of **Tiffany's** (1906; McKim, Mead & White), modeled after the Venetian Palazzo Grimani.

Lord & Taylor
Between W. 38th and W. 39th Sts is Lord & Taylor (1914; Starrett & Van Vleck), the finest remaining store on this stretch of the avenue.

History
Samuel Lord, born in England, was the youngest of nine children. Orphaned before he was six, he worked in an iron foundry until he was 21, when he married the boss's daughter and emigrated to America. George Washington Taylor was his wife's cousin. Lord opened his first store in 1826 on Catherine St on the Lower East Side. In 1853 it moved to more fashionable surroundings at Grand and Chrystie Sts; after a stop on Broadway, where it anchored Ladies Mile, Lord & Taylor moved here. The store is known for traditional women's sportswear and American designer clothing. It is now part of the May Department Store Company.

Continue north on Fifth Ave. Arnold Constable & Co., the traditional rival of Lord & Taylor's, formerly stood on the northeast corner of 39th St. The building now houses the **Mid-Manhattan Branch of the New York Public Library.**
On the southwest corner of Fifth Ave and W. 40th St is the former **Knox Building** (1901–2; John H. Duncan; DL), a limestone and white brick Beaux-Arts showroom built for the hatter Edward M. Knox.

Humanities and Social Sciences Library of the New York Public Library
Fifth Ave at 42nd St, New York, NY 10036. ☎ (212) 661-7220 for recorded information. Web site: www.nypl.org. Open Mon, Thurs, Fri, Sat 10–6; Tues, Wed 11–7:30. Closed Sun, holidays. Hours vary for specific collections. Free. Tours Mon–Sat 11 and 2. Concerts, lectures. Exhibitions in several galleries. Recorded announcement of major exhibitions and events, ☎ (212) 869-8089. Gift shop; outdoor café in season.
Subway: Sixth Ave Express or Local (B, D, Q, F) to 42nd St. Lexington Ave Express or Local (4, 5, 6) to 42nd St–Grand Central. Flushing Local (7) to Fifth Ave. Bus: M1, M2, M3, M4, M5, M6, M7, M42, Q32.
Continue north. The Humanities and Social Sciences Library of the New York Public Library (1911; Carrère & Hastings; DL) occupies the west side of Fifth Ave between 40th and 42nd Sts. Formerly known as the Central Research Branch, it

is one of four research centers of the public library system, which are organized by subject matter. The others are the Science, Industry and Business Library (in the former B. Altman Building); the Schomburg Center for Research in Black Culture (see Walk 28); and the New York Public Library for the Performing Arts (see Lincoln Center in Walk 26).

History

The great collections of the New York Public Library developed from the consolidation of two privately endowed libraries, the Astor and Lenox Libraries, and the Tilden Trust, a bequest of $2 million and 15,000 books from Samuel J. Tilden, lawyer, governor, and unsuccessful presidential candidate. Immigrant **John Jacob Astor,** hardly a bookish man, was persuaded by Joseph Green Cogswell, bibliographer for the Astor Collection, to establish a public library as a testimonial to his adopted country. Astor, who had for a while favored a huge monument to George Washington, bequeathed $400,000 and a plot of land for its foundation (see Joseph Papp Public Theater in Walk 10). The books, largely chosen by Cogswell, were in the fields of greatest public interest, including books on the "mechanic arts and practical industry" and books on languages, since Cogswell saw the American nation coming "into near relation with countries formerly the most remote." **James Lenox,** on the other hand, was a scholar whose particular interests are reflected in his collection: American literature and history, the Bible, Milton, Shakespeare, Bunyan, and Renaissance literature of travel and discovery. Lenox built his own library (1875) on the site of the present Frick Collection but at his death (1880) left his 85,000 peerless books and an endowment of $505,000 to the New York Public Library. The gift of bachelor **Samuel J. Tilden,** a bequest reduced from $4 million to $2 million by relatives who contested the will, was sorely needed; by 1886 the Astor and Lenox libraries already lacked funds for new books and maintenance. In 1895 the three gifts were united as the New York Public Library, Astor, Lenox, and Tilden Foundations.

In 1901 **Andrew Carnegie,** realizing that the city had nothing comparable to the public circulating systems of other American cities, gave $52 million for the building of branch libraries. Today the library has 85 branches and four research libraries. The circulating collections are publicly supported, while the research libraries depend upon endowment and contributions.

Exterior

The building sits on a wide terrace running the length of the Fifth Ave facade. The steps, which have long attracted tourists, pigeons, footsore shoppers, and office workers at lunch, are flanked by two famous **marble lions** by Edward C. Potter (1911). Originally criticized as mealymouthed, complacent creatures, they are now well loved. At first they were called Leo Astor and Leo Lenox after the library's wealthy founders, but were renamed Patience (on the south side) and Fortitude (on the north) by Mayor Fiorello La Guardia, who wanted a visible symbol of the qualities he felt would enable New Yorkers to survive the Depression. The lions are now the official trademarked mascots of the New York Public Library.

In niches behind the fountains against the facade are statues (1913; Frederick W. MacMonnies) of Truth, a man leaning against a sphinx, and Beauty, a woman seated on the winged horse Pegasus. Above the entrance on the frieze are six allegorical figures (left to right) representing History, Romance, Religion, Poetry,

Drama, and Philosophy by Paul Wayland Bartlett. The pediment figures at the ends of the facade are Art (south) and History (north) by George Grey Barnard.

Interior

The **entrance hall** is finished in white Vermont marble, with an elaborate vaulted ceiling, heroic marble candelabra, and wide staircases. Behind it is **Gottesman Hall** (restored 1984), which features major exhibits of objects from the collection.

Take the elevator (end of the right corridor) to the third floor, or walk up the marble stairs that crisscross back and forth under marble barrel vaults. Visible from the stairway are the large interior courts that provide natural light for the catalog and reading rooms. A major new structure in the south courtyard for library orientation and Internet training will open in 2002.

The stairway rises to the **Rotunda** (third floor), decorated with murals (1940) by Edward Laning depicting the Story of the Recorded Word. The Public Catalog in room 315 formerly held more than 10 million cards; most have now been recorded electronically in the library's computerized catalog system, CATNYP.

Beyond is the monumental **Main Reading Room** (restored 1998) with a shelf collection of about 30,000 reference books—readers from Chester Carlson, inventor of the photocopier, to Norbert Pearlroth, researcher for *Ripley's Believe It or Not!,* have pored over books here. At 297 ft long, 78 ft wide, and 51 ft high, the reading room is reportedly one of the country's largest rooms without supporting columns. The 42 oak tables have chairs for 636 researchers. The beautifully decorated ceiling, tall, arched windows, and the furniture designed by Carrère & Hastings make it one of the city's great interiors.

Special Collections

Room 318 is an exhibition room with treasures from the **Berg Collection** (room 320), which contains some 127,000 items mostly in the fields of American and English literature: manuscripts from the 15C–20C, authors' corrected proofs, family correspondence, and rare books. The Prints Division (room 308) includes the **Phelps Stokes Collection of American Historical Prints,** one of whose treasures is an engraving by Paul Revere of the British landing in Boston in 1768. The **Spencer Collection** (room 308) has illuminated manuscripts from the 9C–16C and finely illustrated and bound books. The **Arents Collection** (room 328) has books published in serial form and documents (1507–present) concerned directly or tangentially with tobacco. The **Rare Book Division** (room 328) has more than 122,000 volumes and 21,500 broadsides including such treasures as a **Gutenberg Bible,** the only known copy of the original folio edition (in Spanish) of Christopher Columbus's letter describing his discoveries (dated 1493), the first full folio of Shakespeare (1623), and a Bay Psalm Book (1640) from Cambridge, Massachusetts, the first book printed in America in the English language.

Walk back to 40th St and turn right (west). A series of handsome buildings line the block (between Fifth and Sixth Aves), including two–32 W. 40th (1906; Whitfield & King) and 54–56 W. 40th St (1904; York & Sawyer) with large columns that echo the library's architecture. The **American Standard Building,** formerly the American Radiator Building (1924; Hood & Fouilhoux; DL), 40 W. 40th St, is a black brick and gold terra-cotta tower with a Gothic crown. The color of the facade elicited comment that the building suggested what the American Radiator Co. manufactured—the black evoking a pile of coal, the gold of its higher points the glow of flames.

Further west at 80 40th St is the **Bryant Park Studios** (1901); Charles Rich; DL), a pink brick and terra-cotta building with double-height windows: the building was designed to provide affordable housing as well as studio and exhibition space for artists. Fernand Léger and Edward Steichen both worked here.

Bryant Park
Directly behind the library is Bryant Park (DL), named after William Cullen Bryant (1794–1878), editor, writer, abolitionist, and proponent of such projects as Central Park and the Metropolitan Museum of Art.

History
During the 1820s, before these 9.6 acres became Bryant Park (1884), the land was used as the city's Potter's Field. Later, it was called Reservoir Park after the Croton Reservoir (1837–1900), which stood where the library is now, a walled and buttressed mass of gray granite with a wide promenade on top. In June 1842 the first water poured into the reservoir from man-made Lake Croton behind a dam in the Croton River, a tributary flowing into the Hudson north of Ossining, New York. Leaving Lake Croton, the water coursed along 33 miles of aqueduct, across the Harlem River on High Bridge, through pipes in the Manhattanville Valley, and into a tunnel that emptied into the reservoir. A jubilant crowd listened to speeches and a 38-gun salute as water filled the two basins within the aqueduct to a capacity of 150 million gallons. The opening of the reservoir ended a period of more than 200 years when the city, dependent on shallow wells and springs, was subject to frequent outbreaks of cholera and uncontrollable fires. The Croton system, enlarged, updated, and supplemented by the Catskill system, today provides about 10 percent of the city's water.

In 1853 a world's fair, complete with a Crystal Palace, opened in the park behind the reservoir, showing off the new technology: pumps, hardware, and sewing machines. The Crystal Palace burned down in 1858, and the reservoir was moved in the late 1890s.

By the 1970s and 1980s, Bryant Park had degenerated into a seedy, run-down park populated with drug dealers. In 1987, the year before the park closed while the library expanded its underground stacks, a reported 144 muggings took place there. Happily, the park has made an elegant comeback. Redesigned (Hanna/Olin and Lynden B. Miller, landscape design) with improved lighting, food kiosks and restaurants, a security force overseen by the Bryant Park Business Improvement District, and relandscaped without concealing hedges, it reopened in 1991. Even the restrooms are safe and clean. A stage added for performances has made Bryant Park a popular location in warm weather.

The Park
A **statue of William Cullen Bryant** (1911; Herbert Adams) as an elderly sage sits just behind the library (center of park) shaded by an elaborate pillared architectural setting by Thomas Hastings, one of the designers of the library. On the east side is a bronze **statue of Gertrude Stein** (1991; Jo Davidson). At the south end of the park near W. 40th St is a bronze **bust of Goethe** (1932; Karl Fischer);

New York, looking south from 42nd St in 1855. The Croton Distributing Reservoir and the Crystal Palace occupy the site of the Public Library and Bryant Park, while surrounding blocks remain sparsely developed. (Museum of the City of New York)

toward 42nd St is a bronze **statue of William Earl Dodge** (1885; John Quincy Adams Ward), wealthy industrialist and supporter of virtuous causes (founder of the American YMCA, president of the National Temperance Society). Just outside the park on the west side between W. 40th and W. 41st Sts is a bronze **statue of José Bonifacio de Andrada,** scholar, poet, and patriarch of Brazilian independence, by José Lima, cast from an original (1889) and presented to the U.S. in 1954 as a gift from Brazil. At the west end of the park, at W. 41st St, the **Josephine Shaw Lowell Fountain** (1912; Charles Platt), dedicated to a social reformer, was the city's first major monument dedicated to a woman.

Walk east along W. 42nd St. The **W. R. Grace Building** (1974; Skidmore, Owings & Merrill), 41 W. 42nd St, stands out for its swooping facade. At the northwest corner of 42nd St and Fifth Ave (500 Fifth Ave) is **Nat Sherman,** "Tobacconist to the World," a family business dating back to 1930 that moved to this site in 1990. A child of Hungarian immigrants, Sherman was a Lower East Side peddler who later owned a pool hall but rose to local stardom when he started importing Cuban cigars. A loquacious character who sang along with the piano players at New York nightclubs and smoked cigars until the age of 80, he died in 1990.

Continue north on Fifth Ave. The steel-and-glass box at the southwest corner of the intersection at W. 43rd St (510 Fifth Ave) is the former **Manufacturers Hanover Trust Co.** (1954; Skidmore, Owings & Merrill; DL), now merged into

Chase Manhattan Bank. It was considered architecturally innovative in 1954, when banks still resembled palazzos or ancient temples. While the building was designed expressly so that it could be turned to other uses, the 30-ton Mosler safe in the window identifies it as a bank.

At 7 W. 43rd St is the **Century Association** (1891; McKim, Mead & White; DL). Founded by William Cullen Bryant, the club has long been known for its intellectual and cultural orientation. In the late 1980s, there were both intramural and legal battles over admitting women as members. Members Charles Follen McKim and Stanford White designed here one of their first neo-Italian Renaissance clubhouses, notable for its mixture of materials (terra-cotta, granite and yellow brick) and its second floor ironwork beneath a Palladian window once part of an open loggia.

Continue west on W. 43rd St. to Sixth Ave. On the west side of Sixth Ave (between W. 42nd and W. 43rd Sts) is the **National Debt Clock,** which has publicly calculated this astonishing figure since 1986, adding about $10,000 a second to a number that has topped $5 trillion. The debt clock, installed by developer Seymour Durst, cost $150,000 to install and costs $3,000 a year to maintain. When the clock reached $5.5 trillion, a new, more powerful computer had to be installed to continue calculating the debt.

International Center of Photography (ICP)

1133 Avenue of the Americas, New York, NY 10036. ☎ (212) 860-1777. Web site: www.icp.org. Open Mon–Wed 10–5; Thurs–Fri 10–8; Sat–Sun 10–6. Closed holidays. Admission charge; Fri 5–8 pay-what-you-wish. Bookshop; café. Accessible to wheelchairs.

On the northwest corner of W. 43rd St and Sixth Ave is the International Center of Photography (formerly ICP Midtown), whose main gallery was previously located at 94th St and Fifth Ave.

History

ICP was founded (1974) by Cornell Capa to preserve the memory of four photographers who died pursuing their work, one of them his brother, Robert, a photojournalist killed in Vietnam. Today ICP is New York's foremost exhibitor of photography, as well as a school and center for photographers, editors, artists, and others interested in the medium. Exhibitions range from the historical to the contemporary, from photojournalism to the frankly experimental. ICP has shown fashion photography, holography, video art, and computer-based works as well as fine art photography of all kinds. The center's archives include some 55,000 prints, including the Robert and Cornell Capa Collections, and the Roman Vishniac and Weegee (Arthur Fellig) Archives and Collections.

Nearby, at 123 W. 43rd St (between Sixth Ave and Broadway), is **Town Hall** (1921; McKim, Mead & White; DL), commissioned by the League for Political Education to provide a forum on issues of the day. Speakers have included Theodore Roosevelt, Woodrow Wilson, Winston Churchill, Booker T. Washington, and Margaret Sanger. The hall, which has top-notch acoustics, is popular for concerts, and has featured jazz, folk, classical, and cabaret performers.

Walk north along Sixth Ave and turn right (east) onto W. 44th St. The Hippodrome Garage, 50 W. 44th St, marks the site of the **Hippodrome Theatre** (1905; Frederick Thompson and Elmer S. Dundy), which faced Sixth Ave and once was the largest legitimate theater in the world, seating 5,000. Because it was so large that the audience couldn't hear words or lyrics, the Hippodrome specialized in spectacles—elephants pulling automobiles, horses or girls plunging into giant tanks, and ballets featuring as many as 700 singers and dancers.

Algonquin Hotel

The 165-room Algonquin Hotel, originally the Puritan Hotel, (1902; Goldwin Starrett; DL), 59 W. 44th St, rose to fame as a literary hangout after H. L. Mencken made it his New York residence, beginning in about 1914.

History

Because the manager (and later owner) Frank Case was willing to extend credit to actors and writers, the hotel opened its doors to many authors, both budding and successful. William Faulkner drafted his 1950 Nobel Prize acceptance speech here. Gertrude Stein, James Thurber, Booth Tarkington, John Barrymore, Marian Anderson, Helen Hayes, Sinclair Lewis, F. Scott Fitzgerald, Tennessee Williams, and Graham Greene all partook of the Algonquin's hospitality. Beginning in 1919, Robert Benchley, Dorothy Parker, and Robert Sherwood, all of whom worked at nearby *Vanity Fair* magazine, held forth at the Round Table, amusing one another with clever conversation. Harold Ross, founder of *The New Yorker* magazine, belonged to the coterie and created his magazine partly to enshrine the sophisticated, incisive humor of his friends. (The hotel gives out complimentary copies of the magazine to guests.)

In 1997, the hotel's second makeover of the decade attempted to capitalize on its history. Tabletop bells once again summon waiters in gray-and-red waistcoats; reproduction Victorian planters, a new Round Table, an oil painting of the old one with its original guests, and old *New Yorker* covers and cartoons all recall the good old days. As a nod to its literary beginnings, authors on book tours get a free night in return for an autographed copy of the new book.

The **Royalton Hotel,** (1898: Ehrich Rossiter) across the street at 44 W. 44th St, was also a literary hotel, where *Smart Set* editor George Jean Nathan maintained an apartment and Robert Benchley, the writer and humorist, lived in a suite furnished with the Victorian red draperies and appointed with two portraits of the queen. More recently (1988) the Royalton was refurbished as a conspicuously high-style luxury hotel by Ian Schrager of Studio 54 fame (see Walk 17). Since its public space was redesigned in the 1990s, it has been one of the city's hippest lunch places, attracting fashion designers and magazine editors hungering for a lunch spot at which they can be spotted.

Across the street, built on land donated by J. P. Morgan (commodore of the club, 1897–99), is the **New York Yacht Club** (1901; Warren & Wetmore; DL), 37 W. 44th St. This wonderfully eccentric Beaux-Arts clubhouse is festooned with ropes and pulleys, anchors and hooks, adrip inside and out with seaweed. Truly astonishing, however, are the three windows fashioned like the sterns of ships ploughing through ossified seas whose stony waves curl over the sidewalk. The keystone above the main entrance represents Poseidon. Until the 1983 defeat of its entry, *Liberty*, by the Australian challenger *Australia II*, the club housed the America's Cup, given in 1851 by Queen Victoria and considered the ultimate prize in yachting.

Further east, at 27 W. 44th St, is the **Harvard Club** (1894; McKim, Mead & White, additions 1905 and 1915; DL), a handsome neo-Georgian clubhouse whose restrained brick-and-limestone facade recalls the early architecture of the college itself.

Mechanics' and Tradesmen's Institute

At 20 W. 44th St is a more humble institution, the Mechanics' and Tradesmen's Institute (1891; Lamb & Rich; DL), originally the Berkeley Preparatory School, which still offers courses to technical students. Inside, its three-story gymnasium and drill hall have been converted to a library and museum. The Mechanics' and Tradesmen's Institute Library on the ground floor is open by membership to the public and is stocked with novels, poetry, books on religion, and, oddly, a good collection on Gilbert and Sullivan.

The John M. Mossman Collection of Locks

20 W. 44th St, New York, NY 10036. ☎ (212) 840-1840. Open Mon–Fri 10–12 and 1–4. Closed weekends, July, and first Wed of every month, major holidays. Admission free. Limited wheelchair access; elevator to second floor.

The curious John M. Mossman Collection of Locks is installed on the balcony. The collection, displayed in old cases, consists of some 400 antique and modern locks, including such surprises as a Very Complicated lock, which more than justifies its name. Mossman (1850–1912) was a member of the Society of Mechanics and Tradesmen.

A 1996 renovation at the 128-room **Mansfield Hotel,** 12 W. 44th St (1904), revealed the original high lobby ceiling decorated with three rectangles outlined by plaster rosette light fixtures. In the lobby is a painting, *Seated Officer* (c. 1913; Paul Kotlarevsky).

Fifth Avenue and Vicinity: 45th to 59th Streets

On the northeast corner of Fifth Ave and 45th St is the 38-story **Fred F. French Building** (1927; John Sloan and H. Douglas Ives; DL), 551 Fifth Ave, which typifies the better skyscrapers of the 1920s. It has an ornate lobby and unusual faience polychromy delineating the upper-story setbacks and the top of the building. The panels concealing the water tower on the roof are decorated with symbolic motifs chosen by architect Ives: north and south, the rising sun (Progress) amid winged griffins (Integrity and Watchfulness) and golden beehives with bees (Thrift and Industry); east and west, heads of Mercury, god of commerce. The building is probably the first New York flattopped skyscraper.

Unimposing though it may be, the block of W. 47th St between Fifth and Sixth Aves is the city's **Diamond District.** In the 1920s and early 1930s the diamond business centered around the Bowery and Canal St, but the refugees who later fled the Amsterdam and Antwerp ghettos ahead of Hitler established themselves uptown. The glittering ground-floor shops are for the tourist trade, while the real business is transacted in trading clubs or upstairs in old buildings equipped with ultrasensitive cameras and sophisticated alarm systems. Until recently virtually all the brokers and diamond cutters were Jewish, using skills passed down the generations from as far back as the 16C, when stonecutting was one of the few trades open to Jews. The community still includes a large number of Hasidic Jews, drawn to the trade partly by tradition and partly because the flexible hours permit them to observe the strict schedule of their religion. Today, however, other ethnic groups—Indians, Russians, and Koreans—and women are gaining a foothold in the city's diamond industry, said to handle 90 percent of all the diamonds that come into this country.

The **Gotham Book Mart,** 41 W. 47th St, is a national literary landmark. Frances Steloff, friend and supporter of such American writers as William Carlos Williams, Henry Miller, and T. S. Eliot, established this new and used book emporium on New Year's Day, 1920. Thousands of books, especially a wide selection of 20C poetry and prose and literary magazines, cram the shelves. The James Joyce Society was organized here in 1947, with T. S. Eliot purchasing the first membership. The current owner, Andreas Brown, plans to sell the entire building (which he also owns) and reopen elsewhere in the area.

Return to Fifth Ave and continue north. In these blocks Fifth Ave still lives up to its reputation, though less-exclusive stores have begun to intrude even here. (For Rockefeller Center, which begins at Fifth Ave and W. 49th St, see Walk 17.) After more than seven decades in this location the former **Charles Scribner's Sons Bookstore,** 597 Fifth Ave (between E. 48th and E. 49th Sts), closed in 1989. It reopened as Brentano's, another well-known bookseller, which lasted less than a decade, and in 1996 Benetton, the clothing retailer, took over. The Charles Scribner's Sons Building (1913; Ernest Flagg; DL), however, endures. The black iron-and-glass storefront is reminiscent of fin de siècle Paris, and the dignified vaulted interior suggests a private library.

Dahesh Museum

601 Fifth Ave, New York, NY 10017. ☎ (212) 759-0606. Web site: www.dahesh museum.org. Open Tues–Sat 11–6. Free. Changing exhibitions, catalogs. Accessible to wheelchairs.

Subway: Lexington Ave Local (6) to 51st St. Sixth Ave Express or Local (B, D, Q, F) to 47th–50th Sts–Rockefeller Center. Broadway Local (N, R) to 49th St. Bus: M1, M2, M3, M4, M5, M27, M50.

Next door on the second floor is the small Dahesh Museum, which opened in 1995. It is the only museum in America devoted to 19C–early-20C European academic art, with a collection whose big-name stars include Jean-Léon Gérôme, Alexandre Cabanel, Rosa Bonheur, and Adolphe-William Bouguereau.

The nucleus of the collection was acquired by the Palestinian-born mystical writer Salim Moussa Achi (1909–1984), who later settled in Beirut, where he was known as Dr. Dahesh ("inspiring wonder" in Arabic). Dahesh became the leader of a movement known as Daheshism, whose beliefs include reincarnation and the redeeming power of art and literature. He began collecting academic art when it was neglected and ridiculed in Europe and the U.S., where it was accused of cloying sentimentality and empty technique, a reputation from which it is only beginning to recover. The collection of some 2,700 works—pastoral landscapes, historical events, exotic "Oriental" scenes, portraits—is shown in well-mounted, changing exhibitions.

Note: In 2000 the museum bid to acquire the building at 2 Columbus Circle, which originally housed the former Huntington Hartford Gallery of Modern Art.

On the west side of Fifth Ave is the Swiss Center Building, formerly the **Goelet Building** (1932; Victor Hafner and Edward Hall Faile; DL), 608 Fifth Ave. In 1880 the Goelets, one of New York's old landed families who had prospered in real estate, built a mansion here. When Rockefeller Center was announced, Robert Goelet demolished the house and erected this building, with retail space below and offices above. The first two floors of retail space (restored 1998) are sheathed in plate glass; the building is finished in green and cream marble, limestone, and stainless steel. The Goelet family crest, interlaced Gs beneath a swan, appears on the Fifth Ave facade. The beautiful Art Deco lobby has more marble, more swans, and elaborately ornamented elevator doors.

Saks Fifth Avenue

On the east side of Fifth Ave between 49th and 50th Sts is **Saks Fifth Avenue** (1924; Starrett & Van Vleck; DL), a department store known for its high-fashion boutiques, excellent service, and fine merchandise.

History

In 1902 Andrew Saks, who had begun his career as a peddler in Washington, D.C., established Saks Thirty-fourth on 34th St near Herald Square. In 1923 Saks's son Horace, who had attended Princeton, sold that less-exclusive store to the now-extinct Gimbels for $8 million in order to follow the carriage trade uptown. The next year he opened the present store with show windows offering a pigskin trunk ($3,000), raccoon coats ($1,000), and chauffeurs' livery.

St. Patrick's Cathedral

St. Patrick's Cathedral (1879; towers, 1888; James Renwick Jr.; DL), filling the block between E. 50th and E. 51st Sts on Fifth Ave, is the seat of the Roman Catholic Archdiocese of New York, a famous city landmark, and a symbol of the success in New York of its immigrant Irish Catholic population. Designed by James Renwick with William Rodrigue, whose contribution seems to have been minimal, it draws on the decorated Gothic style of the 13C. It is the largest Catholic cathedral in the U.S. and the eleventh largest in the world.

History

In 1828 the two major Catholic churches of New York, St. Peter's and St. Patrick's—then at the corner of Prince and Mott Sts—bought the plot where the cathedral now sits, intending it as a burial ground. Unfortunately the buyers neglected to examine the land, which turned out to be far too rocky for its intended purpose. In 1850 Archbishop John Hughes announced his intention to build a new cathedral on the site. Hughes had arrived in America from Ireland in 1817, an uneducated 20-year-old eager to become a priest. He arrived in New York 19 years later a bishop, a skillful administrator, and a flamboyant orator. By 1858, Hughes had raised the money to lay the cornerstone and begin construction (1858); in 1879 the cathedral was dedicated, having cost twice as much and taken four times as long to build (including an interruption during the Civil War) as estimated. It was consecrated, debt free, in 1910.

Cathedral Statistics	
Length	332 ft
Width	174 ft
Height from street to top of spire	330 ft
Height of central gable	156 ft
Length of nave and transept	144 ft
Width of nave	48 ft
Height of nave	108 ft

Exterior

The general plan is a Latin cross with traditional east-west orientation. The facade is marble. Because the interior vaulting is brick and plaster, not stone, flying buttresses were not needed, but the pinnacles of the buttresses exist, perhaps because Renwick originally called for stone interior vaulting supported by flying buttresses.

The bronze doors (added 1949) at the west entrance were designed by Charles Maginnis with figures by John Angel. The figures on the doors represent (top to bottom, left to right): St. Joseph, patron of this church; St. Isaac Jogues, first Catholic priest in New York; St. Frances X. Cabrini, founder of the Missionary Sisters of the Sacred Heart and "Mother of the Immigrant"; the Blessed Kateri Tekakwitha, an Indian maiden called the "Lily of the Mohawks"; and St. Elizabeth Ann Seton, first American-born saint.

Interior

Two rows of clustered columns divide the nave. Above the arches runs the triforium, divided into four sections by the arms of the cross. Above the triforia rise clerestory windows (14×26 ft in the nave, 28×58 ft in the transept). The ceiling is groined with (plaster) ribs.

Chapels and aisle windows in the south aisle include a modern shrine of St. Elizabeth Ann Seton (1975; sculptor Frederick Shrady), with the window above dedicated to St. Henry, 11C Holy Roman Emperor.

In the **south transept,** the stations of the cross were designed by Peter J. H. Cuypers in Holland. Over the entrance is a window devoted to St. Patrick, depicting 18 scenes from his life, given by Old St. Patrick's Cathedral. In the west wall of the transept is another St. Patrick's window, given by architect Renwick, who appears in the lower panels. Featured in the **south ambulatory,** beyond the sacristy, is a marble *Pietà* (1906; William O. Partridge) based on Michelangelo's famous work.

The **Lady Chapel** at the east end of the church, begun in 1901 and completed in 1906, was designed by Charles T. Matthews and is patterned after 13C French Gothic architecture. The stained glass windows (Paul Woodroffe) over this altar and the two flanking it depict the mysteries of the rosary. Directly opposite the Lady Chapel is the entrance to the crypt, in which are buried the earthly remains of Archbishop Hughes, the other cardinals of New York, and several rectors of this church, as well as Archbishop Fulton J. Sheen. (The crypt is not open to the public.)

North ambulatory: Adjacent to the Lady Chapel on the north side is the Altar of St. Michael and St. Louis, designed by Charles T. Matthews and executed by Tiffany & Co. Beyond the usher's office and bride's room are the altar of St. Joseph and the chancel organ (1928) with 2,520 pipes. **North transept:** In front of the altar of the Holy Family is the marble baptistry. The focal point of the **sanctuary** is the high altar with its baldachin or canopy designed by Charles D. Maginnis, made of bronze and rising to a height of 57 ft. Suspended from the ceiling of the sanctuary above the altar are the *galeros,* or ceremonial hats, of all the cardinals of New York.

From the crossing is a good view of the **West** (or **Rose**) **Window,** 26 ft in diameter and filled with stained glass in geometric patterns. In the loft beneath it is the Great Organ (1930), with 9,000 pipes, ranging from 3 inches to 32 ft in length.

North aisle: The shrine of St. John Neumann (the middle one in the south aisle) was erected in 1978 to honor this missionary in western New York State and bishop of Philadelphia, elevated to sainthood in 1977. The metal church depicted is Old St. Patrick's Cathedral, where he was ordained.

Fifth Avenue between 51st and 52nd Streets

Continue north on Fifth Ave. On the northeast corner of E. 51st St is **Olympic Towers** (1976; Skidmore, Owings & Merrill), an outscale luxury multiuse building (shops at ground level, offices above, and apartments on the highest floors) constructed by a consortium headed by Greek shipping colossus Aristotle Onassis.

The Vanderbilt Mansions

At the turn of the 20C, the block of Fifth Ave between 51st and 52nd Sts was Vanderbilt territory. Three brownstone mansions built by William Henry Vanderbilt for himself and his two daughters occupied the west side of the avenue. The socially competitive Alva Smith Vanderbilt, wife of his second son, William Kissam Vanderbilt, wanted something better than brownstone and had Richard Morris Hunt build a bigger, more luxurious limestone mansion at the northwest corner of 52nd St. (All are now gone.)

On the east side of the street, at **647 Fifth Ave,** is the last remaining Vanderbilt home (1905; Hunt & Hunt; DL) in the area, designed by Richard Morris Hunt's sons. It was built for George W. Vanderbilt, who then sold it to his brother William K. before the house was even finished. The only residents were Robert Goelet and his wife, Elsie. Since 1917 it has been a retail and office space; the current tenant, Versace, oversaw a restoration in 1996.

Meanwhile, William K. Vanderbilt, alarmed by the northward sweep of commerce, sold the southeast corner lot to the millionaire banker Morton F. Plant on the condition that the site remain residential for 25 years. Plant, commodore of the New York Yacht Club, obliged with a five-story neo-Italian palazzo of marble and granite (1905; Robert W. Gibson and C. P. H. Gilbert; remodeled as a store, 1917; DL), but by 1916 he found the area too commercial and built a new mansion at the northeast corner of Fifth Ave and 86th St. Vanderbilt bought Plant's mansion for $1 million and quickly rented it to Cartier's for $50,000 a year (despite a legend that Plant traded the house to Cartier for a perfect pearl necklace).

Cartier, jeweler to the French court in the 18C and to numerous later millionaires, movie stars, and members of royalty, still occupies the mansion, offering the general public its exquisite window displays and **Les Musts,** a boutique with more affordable items.

Continue north on Fifth Ave to **666 Fifth Ave** (1957; Carson, Lundin & Shaw), between W. 52nd and W. 53rd Sts. A gaudy National Basketball Association outlet occupies the street-level retail space. However, the office building lobby ceiling and the outdoor fountain, both designed by sculptor Isamu Noguchi were restored in 1998. The ceiling, *Landscape of the Clouds,* consists of rows of white-enameled metal louvers; the 40 ft wide waterfall has become the focal point of a new entrance.

St. Thomas Church

On the northwest corner of 53rd St and Fifth Ave (1 W. 53rd St) is Protestant Episcopal **St. Thomas Church** (1914; Cram, Goodhue & Ferguson; DL), picturesque, asymmetrical, and French Gothic in antecedents. It was originally built without steel, following the principles of Ralph Adams Cram (also architect of St. John the Divine), who believed that if a church were Gothic in style it should be Gothic in construction, its columns supporting its weight. However, 11 years after completion, with the unbuttressed north wall bulging dangerously, steel beams were placed across the columns above the ceiling. Later, during blasting for the subway tunnel under 53rd St, a steel beam was installed under the altar.

Exterior

Bertram G. Goodhue (architect of St. Bartholomew's on Park Ave) planned the limestone facade, which is notable for its single corner tower. Above the double entrance doors a gilded relief depicts the four different buildings in which the congregation has worshiped, two on Houston St and Broadway, and two here. The central figure on the facade is St. Thomas. Left of the main portal is the Bride's Entrance; above the doorway some observers have discerned a stylized dollar sign, whose presence recalls medieval times when carpenters and stoneworkers left tokens of social criticism in obscure parts of their cathedrals.

Interior

The remarkable 80 ft reredos of ivory-colored Dunville stone (Ohio) is pierced by three stained glass windows. Lee Lawrie, known for his work at Rockefeller Center, and architect Goodhue designed it, though the central portion depicting the cross and kneeling angels was copied from a smaller reredos by Augustus Saint-Gaudens in the previous church on this site (burned down 1905). In the **chancel**, the carved panels on the kneeling rail in front of the choir stalls have designs representing important historical events and fields of human endeavor (from the left): Christopher Columbus's ship, Theodore Roosevelt, Lee Lawrie (between the steamship and the telephone), a radio, finance (with the initials of J. P. Morgan), and medicine.

At 5 E. 53rd St is small, serene **Paley Park** (1967; Zion & Breen, landscape architects; Albert Preston Moore, consulting architect), measuring only 42 × 100 ft but graced with ivy, a dozen honey locust trees, and a "waterwall," whose white noise obliterates the whine of traffic. Before William S. Paley, chairman of the board of CBS, donated the park in memory of his father, Samuel, the site was occupied by the Stork Club, a nightclub beloved of café society and gossip columnists.

In the next block uptown, the Banco di Napoli occupies **4 E. 54th St,** a neo-Italian town house (1900; McKim, Mead & White; DL), remodeled for William H. Moore, a Chicago industrialist, whose résumé included United States Steel, the American Can Co., and the National Biscuit Co. The building is now dwarfed by its neighbors.

Return to Fifth Ave. On the northwest corner of 54th St is the **University Club** (1899; McKim, Mead & White; DL), 1 W. 54th St, a grand neo-Italian palazzo. It was built during a time when clubmen like Cornelius Vanderbilt belonged to as many as 16 clubs and spent in dues what average workers earned in a year. Above the main door is a head of Athena modeled after a statuette owned by Stanford White. The interior (not open to the public) is remarkable for its opulent decoration: hallways paved with marble, ceiling paintings by H. Siddons Mowbray (of Pierpont Morgan Library fame), pilasters of Italian walnut.

Turn left (west). When St. Luke's Hospital vacated W. 54th St in 1896, new dwellings began to rise on both sides of the street. Five adjoining houses from this period, designed by the city's most prestigious architects in styles ranging from Georgian revival to French Beaux-Arts, have been landmarked (most now occupied by businesses): **5 W. 54th St** (1899; R.H. Robertson; DL), **7 W. 54th St** (1900; John H. Duncan; DL), **nos. 9–11 W. 54th St** (1898; McKim, Mead & White; DL), **13 W. 54th St** (1897; Henry Hardenbergh; DL), and **15 W. 54th St**

(1897; Henry Hardenbergh; DL). The financier Robert Lehman lived at no. 7; his art collection is now exhibited in the Metropolitan Museum of Art in a wing that replicates the rooms of the townhouse. The Rockefellers owned townhouses at nos. 13 and 15; Governor Nelson Rockefeller installed the Museum of Primitive Art, now also part of the Metropolitan, at 15 W. 54th St. He died in 1979 at 13 W. 54th St.

Standing on the site of the senior John D. Rockefeller's town house at 17 W. 54th St are the **Rockefeller Apartments** (1936; Harrison & Fouilhoux; DL), an experiment in middle-class apartment design financed by John D. Rockefeller Jr. The project has two buildings running back-to-back (the other faces W. 55th St) with a central garden between to admit light but not noise to the rear bedrooms. Because the cylindrical bays were designed as "dinettes," their windows face away from one another, insuring privacy.

Return to Fifth Ave and walk north. Fifth Ave between 54th and 55th Sts is a great shopping block, catering to the carriage trade. **Bijan,** a men's clothier (by appointment only) whose blazing white facade is more suggestive of its earlier Beverly Hills incarnation than of staid Fifth Ave, **Gucci, Elizabeth Arden,** and **Christian Dior** give the block the élan of yesteryear.

On the southeast corner of 55th St (2 E. 55th St) is the **St. Regis Hotel** (1904; Trowbridge & Livingston, with an addition to the east, 1925; DL), a venture of John Jacob Astor IV, who realized from his experience with the Waldorf-Astoria that expensive hotels in fine residential neighborhoods attracted a clientele eager for proximity to social splendor. Astor named it after the French monk and patron saint of hospitality to travelers. The Beaux-Arts exterior has stone garlands, a mansard roof with bull's-eye windows and copper cresting, and on E. 55th St, a brass and glass kiosk for the top-hatted doormen. Inside, Astor provided automatic thermostats in every room, a system for heating, cooling, moistening, or drying the air (predating air-conditioning), 47 Steinway pianos, a service of gold-plated flatware, and other decorative touches that cost him $1.5 million. Once famous for its restaurants, including a palm room where members of both sexes could smoke publicly at all hours, the St. Regis is now known for the **King Cole Room,** with Maxfield Parrish's mural of the king holding court (originally commissioned for another Astor enterprise, the Knickerbocker Hotel in Times Square).

Across the street on the southwest corner (700 Fifth Ave) is the Italian Renaissance–style **Peninsula New York,** formerly the **Gotham Hotel** (1905; Hiss & Weekes; DL). Built by speculators, the Gotham ran into early financial difficulties: it was denied a liquor license because it stood within 200 ft of the Fifth Avenue Presbyterian Church and was saddled with unpaid bills by its socially elite but financially straitened clientele. It underwent an expensive facelift in 1998 that included luxury touches like televisions over the bathtubs and high-speed phone lines for bedside Internet access.

On the northwest corner is the **Fifth Avenue Presbyterian Church** (1875; Carl Pfeiffer). Next to it at 714 Fifth Ave is the **Henri Bendel Building,** which incorporates the former Rizzoli Building (1907–8; Albert S. Gottlieb; DL) and its neighbor the Coty Building (1907–8; Woodruff Leeming; DL). The building retains René Lalique's architectural glass storefront (for the Coty Building). Inside, the store has galleries of specialty boutiques surrounding a four-story central atrium. Developers used the air rights purchased from the adjacent church for

$15.75 million to construct **712 Fifth Ave** (1998; Kohn Pederson Fox Assocs.), the 44-story skyscraper that rises over the department store.

Continue uptown. **Harry Winston** at 718 Fifth Ave, southwest corner of the intersection at 56th St, is a jeweler of international reputation. Across the avenue, on the southeast corner of Fifth Ave and 56th St (717 Fifth Ave), is the **Corning Glass Building** (1959; Harrison, Abramovitz & Abbe), a 28-story tower with greenish glass facing. On the ground floor are the Steuben Glass Co. showrooms, whose windows, convex to prevent glare, seem invisible. Inside is an array of crystal figurines, sculptures, and accessories.

Continue north. Occupying most of Fifth Ave between 56th and 57th Sts is **Trump Tower** (1983; Der Scutt, design architect; Swanke Hayden Connell) at 725 Fifth Ave, the work of Donald J. Trump, the conspicuous real estate entrepreneur. The lavish six-story atrium surfaced with pink marble provides an opulent setting for shops that now include such improbabilities as Niketown. Trump Tower's residents have included Sophia Loren, Johnny Carson, Dick Clark, Steven Spielberg, Martina Navratilova, Fay Wray, and Andrew Lloyd Webber. The building replaced Bonwit Teller, a women's apparel store, which had moved here in 1930.

At the southeast corner of 57th St and Fifth Ave is **Tiffany & Co.,** 727 Fifth Ave, another of the avenue's renowned jewelers. It was founded by Charles L. Tiffany, father of Louis Comfort Tiffany, the famous designer of stained glass, jewelry, enamels, and interiors. The firm moved to this modest granite palazzo (1940; Cross & Cross) from a fancier palace on 37th St and Fifth Ave. Tiffany's sophisticated window displays have long been famous, especially since Audrey Hepburn stared longingly at them in *Breakfast at Tiffany's.*

Return to Fifth Ave. On the southwest corner of the intersection at 57th St (730 Fifth Ave) is the **Crown Building** (1921; Warren & Wetmore), originally the Heckscher Building. This 25-story limestone and buff brick structure was the first tall building to invade Upper Fifth Ave and the first office building built after the Zoning Resolution of 1916. The tower, adorned with stone and terra-cotta bands, parapets, and dormer windows, once had a weathercock on top. The Museum of Modern Art got its start here in 1929, renting space on the 12th floor.

The building at **9 W. 57th St** (1972; Skidmore, Owings & Merrill), with its glassy swooping facade, is a more expensive version of the W. R. Grace Building on W. 42nd St. The red 9 on the sidewalk was designed by sculptor Ivan Chermayeff.

Bergdorf Goodman

On the west side of Fifth Ave (between 57th and 58th Sts) once stood the Cornelius Vanderbilt Mansion, a 137-room castle, filling the whole block with peaks, gables, dormers, and other Victorian extravagances. Today the site is home to Bergdorf Goodman.

History

Like so many of the city's other luxury stores, Bergdorf Goodman (1928) had humble beginnings. Herman Bergdorf, a tailor known for adapting men's suits to the female figure, founded the firm, but Edwin Goodman, who bought out Bergdorf in 1901, raised the store to its present heights, moving it in 1928 to this white marble building, initially built as seven distinct storefronts. The store is known for its luxury European clothing and accessories, its fur collection, and its service.

17 · Rockefeller Center, Museum of Modern Art, and Carnegie Hall

Subway: Broadway–Seventh Ave Local (1, 9) to 50th St. Lexington Ave Local (6) to 51st St. Sixth Ave Express or Local (B, D, Q, or F) to 47th–50th Sts–Rockefeller Center. Broadway Local (N, R) to 49th St.
Bus: M1, M2, M3, M4, M5, M6, M7, M27.

Rockefeller Center

Rockefeller Center is the world's largest privately owned business and entertainment center, the first architecturally coordinated development in New York City, and a major tourist attraction that nonetheless maintains high aesthetic standards. This complex of 19 commercial buildings, theaters, plazas, streets, underground pedestrian passageways, and shops sits on some of the world's most valuable real estate in midtown Manhattan.

History

In 1927 the Metropolitan Opera, seeking to replace its outmoded house at Broadway and W. 40th St, became interested 12 acres of land—between Fifth and Sixth Aves and W. 48th and W. 51st Sts—owned by Columbia University. The land had blossomed briefly (1801–11) as the Elgin Botanic Garden but now held speakeasies, rooming houses, and brothels. The opera company approached John D. Rockefeller Jr. as a possible benefactor, hoping he might donate land for a plaza in front of the new opera house. Rockefeller in turn began exploring the possibilities of leasing the land himself, making the central portion available to the opera, and then subleasing the rest to commercial interests who would construct their own buildings. Since property experts led him to believe that he could realize as much as $5.5 million dollars annually on the property, he signed a contract with Columbia University in Oct 1928 to lease the property for a 24-year period with renewal options to 2019, later extended to 2069.

Then the stock market crashed (1929) and the Metropolitan Opera Co. abruptly dropped its plans for a new house, leaving Rockefeller with a lease under which he owed more than $3.8 million a year on property that brought in only about $300,000. Rockefeller's only real choice was to develop the property without the opera house. He directed his planners to design a commercial center "as beautiful as possible consistent with maximum income," and work began on the city's first integrated commercial center, where skyscrapers could be planned in relation to one another with due consideration of open space, light, and traffic control. Largely responsible for the early project were developers Todd, Robertson & Todd, and three principal architectural firms—Reinhard & Hofmeister; Corbett, Harrison, and MacMurray; and Hood & Fouilhoux, who worked under the name of The Associated Architects—making it impossible nowadays to assign specific credit for individual buildings in the original development.

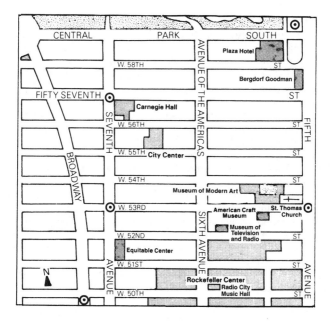

Between 1931 and 1940, 228 buildings were demolished and 4,000 tenants were relocated to make way for 14 new buildings—75,000 workers were employed on the job during the Depression. Architect Raymond Hood proposed that the Radio Corporation of America (RCA), still prospering during the Depression, become the center's major tenant. For years most radio programs of NBC, a subsidiary of RCA, were produced here, and Rockefeller Center was known popularly as Radio City.

Although Rockefeller drove the "last" rivet into the "last" building, the United States Rubber Co. Building (now the Simon & Schuster Building) in 1939, development continued after World War II, when the Esso Building (now the Warner Communications Building) pushed the center beyond its original boundaries. During the 1950s and 1960s, Rockefeller Center expanded west to Sixth Ave, replacing nondescript low buildings and small business tenants with stiff, ponderous office towers that mostly express the affluence of their corporate tenants.

In 1985 Columbia University sold its land under the center to the Rockefeller Group for $400 million, the largest price ever paid for a single parcel of real estate in the city. On the 11.7-acre plot sit Radio City Music Hall, the skating rink, the GE Building (formerly the RCA Building), and other buildings of the original development. These remain in the hands of Rockefeller's heirs, who control the stock of Rockefeller Center, Inc., the corporation that developed and still maintains the property.

The most dramatic approach to Rockefeller Center is from Fifth Ave between 49th and 50th Sts. Flanking a central promenade are two low buildings, the **British Building** (completed 1933; DL) on the north and **La Maison Française** (1933;

DL) on the south, buildings whose modest scale reflects an earlier Fifth Ave. By placing these low structures on the avenue, the developers gained rights to build the towering RCA Building in the center of the block, simultaneously preserving neighborhood property values by leaving the side streets unshadowed.

Over the main entrance of the British Building (formerly the British Empire Building) is a bronze panel (1933) by Carl Paul Jennewein with figures representing nine major industries of the British Commonwealth. At the bottom, a bronze sun symbolizes the empire on which the sun never set. Above the panel is a cartouche with the British coat of arms and the mottoes of British royalty and the Order of the Garter.

Across the promenade is La Maison Française. A bronze strip in the sidewalk near the building line at the entrance to the promenade marks the boundary of the property formerly owned by Columbia University. Over the main door of La Maison Française a bronze panel (1934) designed by Alfred Janniot depicts Paris and New York joining hands above figures representing Poetry, Beauty, and Elegance. Inscribed on a ribbon behind the figure of Paris is that city's motto: "*Fluctuat nec mergitur*" (It is tossed by waves but does not sink). Above the panel soars an Art Deco version of the traditional symbol of France, a woman holding the flaming torch of Liberty.

The promenade itself is popularly known as the **Channel Gardens** (1933; DL) because it separates the British and French buildings; the walkway (60 ft wide and 200 ft long) is embellished with granite pools, seasonal floral displays, and fountains. The bronze fountain heads (1935), designed by René Chambellan, represent Tritons and Nereids riding dolphins that symbolize (east to west) Leadership, Will, Thought, Imagination, Energy, and Alertness—qualities chosen as those contributing to human progress. Most of the themes of the center's artwork were chosen by Professor Hartley Burr Alexander of the University of Southern California, hired to impose unity on the whole development. He decided upon the general topic "New Frontiers and the March of Civilization." Professor Alexander's themes have resulted in artworks with a technological bent and clunky titles.

The Lower Plaza

The promenade opens into the **Lower Plaza** (DL). At the top of the stairway leading to the lower level is a commemorative plaque inscribed with John D. Rockefeller Jr.'s personal credo: "I believe in the supreme worth of the individual . . . every right implies a responsibility, every opportunity an obligation."

The Lower Plaza is dominated by an 18 ft **figure of Prometheus,** designed by Paul Manship (1934). The eight-ton gilded bronze statue resting on a gilded mountain peak is encircled by a ring containing the signs of the zodiac. On the red granite wall behind it is a quotation from Aeschylus: "Prometheus, teacher in every art, brought the fire that hath proved to mortals a means to mighty ends." Fifty jets of water surrounding the statue form a summer backdrop for an electronically controlled lighting display. During the Christmas season, a large tree is installed on the sidewalk behind the plaza and illuminated by thousands of lights, accounting in part for the spectacular crowds who pack the area during the holidays. During the summer, the sunken plaza becomes an outdoor café; during the winter it is flooded and becomes an ice rink.

NBC's *Today* show spent $15 million to build production studios on the 49th St side of Rockefeller Center; through the first-floor windows you can see yourself on TV and watch the broadcasts.

Rockefeller Plaza separates the Lower Plaza from the GE Building. The idea of breaking up the long east–west block with a private street was a happy inspiration. Rockefeller Plaza remains one of the few private streets in the city and is closed to all traffic, vehicular and pedestrian, once a year, usually a Sunday in July, to preserve its private status.

GE Building

The most famous and imposing building at Rockefeller Center is the GE Building, formerly the **RCA Building,** (1933; DL) at 30 Rockefeller Plaza, directly west of the plaza. It was the first building constructed for the center. The 70-story building is roughly rectangular, with its thin edge facing east–west and a broad, slab-like wall on the north and south. It owes its disproportionate length to Rockefeller's desire to include within its walls some potentially unprofitable lots he owned on Sixth Ave, which were still overhung by the elevated railway. Skillfully designed setbacks give the building the impression of soaring height. An 11-story wraparound structure houses NBC's studios, constructed free from the rest of the building to minimize vibrations. The RCA building and NBC were bought by General Electric in 1986.

Tours
NBC studio tours include visits to sets and control rooms; for information and schedule, ☎ (212) 664-4000.

Exterior

Over the east entrance is a stone relief by Lee Lawrie (1877–1963), whose subject is *Wisdom, Which Interprets to the Human Race the Laws and Cycles of the Cosmic Forces of the Universe, Making the Cycles of Light and Sound.* Wisdom, a giant with a remarkable Art Deco beard, spreads a compass above a glass screen made of 240 blocks of glass, cast in relief in 84 different molds. Only when the work was well under way did the art committee notice the embarrassing similarity between Lawrie's work and William Blake's frontispiece to *Europe: A Prophecy* (1794).

Flanking the 49th St entrance are two limestone pylons with sculptures by Leo Friedlander representing *Transmission Receiving an Image of Dancers and Flashing It Through the Ether by Means of Television to Reception, Symbolized by Mother Earth and Her Child, Man.* At the 50th St entrance two more pylons, also sculpted by Friedlander, represent *Transmission Receiving Music and Flashing It Through the Ether by Means of Radio to Reception.* Rockefeller found these works "gross and unbeautiful"; critics generally concur.

Interior

Directly in front of the main entrance is a large mural by José Maria Sert (1876–1945), originally entitled *Triumph of Man's Accomplishments Through Physical and Mental Labor,* now called *American Progress.* Sert's moralistic painting

(1937) is famous primarily for replacing the controversial Diego Rivera fresco destroyed by the Rockefellers.

The Diego Rivera Fresco

Commissioned to paint a mural illustrating the theme "man's new possibilities from his new understanding of material things," Rivera submitted a sketch acceptable to his patrons but then produced a fresco that included a portrait of Lenin, a crowd of workers near Lenin's tomb carrying red flags, and a scene of rich people playing cards while venereal disease germs hover over them. When asked to substitute another face for Lenin's, Rivera replied that he would prefer to destroy the painting, at least preserving its integrity. The fresco remained shrouded in canvas during opening ceremonies and eventually the Rockefellers had it destroyed. In the recriminations that followed, cowboy humorist and sage Will Rogers "advised" Rivera that he "should never try to fool a Rockefeller in oils."

The massive ceiling painting, again by Sert, is entitled *Time,* while the murals against the elevator banks in the north and south corridors by Sert and Frank Brangwyn illustrate themes of progress against such obstacles as disease, slavery, and crushing physical labor.

Walk down the north corridor to the elevator banks, which contain the first high-speed elevators in New York City. Take a car in the last row to the **Rainbow Room** on the 65th floor. The nightclub opened in 1934, the first dining spot on top of a skyscraper, and was through the years celebrated for its view and handsome trappings. Noel Coward and Cole Porter came on opening night; the great dance bands of the 1930s and 1940s played there—Duke Ellington, Glen Gray, and Ray Noble. Built as a two-story cylinder with no internal columns and called the Stratosphere Club, the place was renamed the Rainbow Room for its "color organ," which threw colored lights corresponding to musical pitches on the domed ceiling.

From the main floor, stairways behind the elevator banks lead down to the **concourse,** with more than two miles of underground passageways lined with shops, services, and restaurants.

The **Sixth Ave entrance,** less opulently decorated than the east facade, features a glass mosaic by Barry Faulkner made of about 1 million pieces of colored glass and entitled *Intelligence Awakening Mankind.* Four limestone panels by Gaston Lachaise on the west facade depict *Genius Seizing the Light of the Sun, Conquest of Space, Gifts of Earth to Mankind,* and *Understanding—Spirit of Progress.*

Across Sixth Ave from the GE Building loom four later additions to the center. Architectural critics have found them sadly wanting, charging that the buildings lack sympathetic human scale, that they drove small businesses from the area, that their plazas are cold and ill-planned, and that their use of modern technology has allowed them to contain maximum permissible space at the expense of light, air, and human values.

The southernmost of these towers, the **Celanese Building** (1973; Harrison,

Abramovitz & Harris) occupies the block between W. 47th and W. 48th Sts. Like its companions, it is a slab divided vertically into columns and vertical window strips. It now houses Rupert Murdoch's media empire—Fox Television, *TV Guide,* and the *New York Post.* Outside are a news ticker and several televisions blaring the Fox News channel. In the lobby is a white-on-crimson mosaic mural, *Reclining Figure,* developed from a design by Josef Albers. To the west of the building is a lackluster shopping plaza, which enabled developers to exceed building limits according to the Zoning Resolution of 1961.

Just north of the Celanese Building is the **McGraw-Hill Building** (1972; Harrison, Abramovitz & Harris). In the sunken plaza is a steel sculpture (1973) by Athelstan Spilhaus, a meteorologist, entitled *Sun Triangle.* The three sides of the triangle point to the sun's noon position at the equinoxes and solstices.

Cross W. 49th St to the former **Exxon Building** (1971; Harrison, Abramovitz & Harris), a 54-story rectangular slab clad in limestone, with a seven-story wraparound wing on the west. Like its neighbors, it has an austere facade of vertical columns alternating with vertical window strips. On the west was a small park with a waterfall, but in 1999 the Rockefeller Group bulldozed it to develop the lot.

Return to Sixth Ave and cross W. 50th St to the **Time & Life Building** (1959; Harrison & Abramovitz), the earliest of the new buildings across Sixth Ave. Along its east facade is a plaza with a central pool and basin surrounded by a low wall that serves as a bench. The undulating gray-and-white pattern on the pavement and extending into the building's lobby is similar to one that architect Wallace K. Harrison admired in Rio de Janeiro. *Cubed Curve,* the blue-painted steel sculpture on the southeast corner of the lot, is by William Crovello and was installed in 1971. Inside the lobby are (west end of elevator banks) a glass-and-metal mural (1961) by Josef Albers entitled *Portals* and (east end of elevator banks) an oil-on-canvas mural, *Relational Painting #88* (1960), by Fritz Glarner.

Radio City Music Hall
On the northeast corner of W. 50th St and Sixth Ave is Radio City Music Hall (1932; Edward Durell Stone, design architect; DL), the nation's largest indoor theater and a masterpiece of Art Deco decoration. You can see the interior only by attending a performance or joining a Music Hall tour; ☎ (212) 632-4041.

History
Samuel Lionel Rothafel (1882–1936), better known as Roxy, was a self-made man who began his career showing movies in the back room of a bar and rose to become a show business mogul, producing radio programs and stage shows and managing several New York theaters including the opulent Roxy. Because he enjoyed the reputation of knowing infallibly what the public wanted, he was given broad powers by the RKO Corporation, a subsidiary of RCA, who hired him as director of the Music Hall. He contributed to the design of the theater and shaped its general policies, intending to revive vaudeville and produce spectacular variety shows.

Unfortunately Roxy's variety shows lost $180,000 in the first two weeks, and the format was changed. Until television began competing strenuously, the Music Hall successfully presented a long list of wholesome movies paired with stage shows, drawing 5 million patrons yearly through 1967. But by 1977 attendance had fallen to less than 2 million and the theater lost $2.3 million. In 1978, the

Music Hall was threatened with demolition, but a wave of public support resulted in its interior being designated a landmark. In 1979, the parent company, Rockefeller Center Inc., reopened it with a new format of elaborate musical shows, rock concerts, and special events, preserving its ever-popular Christmas Spectacular. In 1999, a $70-million renovation (Hardy Holzman Pfeiffer Associates) returned much of the luster to the faded building. The artwork, the Wurlitzer pipe organ, the marquee (where the words MUSIC HALL glisten in their original golden hue), and even the upholstered furniture were restored to their original appearance.

Interior

The interior of the Music Hall, climaxed by the great auditorium, is one of the high points of American theater design and one of the city's grandest and most sophisticated displays of Art Deco styling.

The **Grand Lobby** (140 ft long, 45 ft wide, and 60 ft high) has walls of red marble above black marble wainscoting; the low ceiling is illuminated by dramatic circular light fixtures. The carpet of red, brown, gold, and black with abstract forms of musical instruments was designed by Ruth Reeves. The unity of the decorative features of the hall—carpets, wall coverings, statues, murals, and furniture—was coordinated by Donald Deskey, who reputedly spent his last $5,000 preparing his entry for the competition. Deskey had worked in Paris and attended (1925) the Exposition Internationale des Arts Decoratifs et Industriels Modernes, an exhibition generally credited with establishing the Art Deco style in the public taste.

Over the imposing staircase at the north end is a mural by Ezra Winter (1886–1949), *The Fountain of Youth*, its subject suggested by Professor Alexander and drawn from a legend of the Oregon Indians. It depicts an old man gazing at a gleaming inaccessible mountaintop on which bubbles the fountain of youth; across the sky marches a cloudy procession representing the vanities of life. Gold mirrored panels reflect the light from two 29 ft glass chandeliers (2 tons apiece).

Staircases at the ends of the Grand Lobby lead down to the **Main Lounge** and restrooms. The lounge is richly decorated in gray and black: Donald Deskey designed the plaid carpet; the nine piers are faced with black glass and edged with chrome trim; walls are covered with black Permatex, a novel material in 1932. Vignettes of famous theatrical figures decorate the walls.

William Zorach's (1887–1966) cast-aluminum nude *Spirit of the Dance* kneels in the center of the room. Along with Gwen Lux's statue of *Eve* (niche at top of south stairway leading to Grand Lobby) and Robert Laurent's *Girl with Goose* (south end of first mezzanine), this statue caused a scandal when installed, since Roxy declared the three nudes morally offensive. In view of his own racy reputation and the tameness of the statues, his outrage seems excessive. Nevertheless the nudes were removed; only later were they reinstated.

Even the **restrooms** (east side) are impressively decorated, though the original mural, *Men without Women* by Stuart Davis, was removed from the men's smoking lounge to the Museum of Modern Art. The women's lounge has a mural by Witold Gordon, *The History of Cosmetics.*

Return to the Grand Lobby. Separating it from the auditorium are 11 double stainless steel doors with bronze bas-reliefs representing theatrical scenes, designed by René Chambellan. The most impressive space in the Music Hall is the **auditorium,** which seats 6,200 people. The ceiling is egg-shaped, a form Roxy demanded for its supposed acoustic superiority. The great proscenium arch (60 ft high, 100 ft wide) dominates the room. Rising outward and forward from it are the successive overlapping bands of the ceiling, painted with perpendicular rays, whose effect has been compared to the aurora borealis, a sunburst, and the rays of dawn. Roxy liked to assert that a sunrise he had witnessed at sea inspired the design, but the model of the auditorium, complete with ceiling, had been photographed six days before he embarked on the inspirational voyage.

The stage machinery includes sections that can be raised or lowered on elevators, a revolving central turntable, and a movable orchestra pit. The stage can support twelve grand pianos, three Roman chariots with horses, or six elephants. While animals frequently appear in the Christmas pageant, the most famous performers of the Music Hall stage are the **Rockettes,** a troupe of precision dancers founded in 1925 by Russell Markert, who brought them from St. Louis to New York.

Leave the Music Hall and walk east on W. 50th St. Adjacent to the theater is the **Associated Press Building** (1938; DL). Above the main entrance (east side of building, facing Rockefeller Plaza) is Isamu Noguchi's stainless steel panel *News* (1940), depicting five men with the tools of the reporter's trade: pad and pencil, camera, telephone, teletype, and wirephoto.

International Building

Continue east along W. 50th St to the International Building (1935; DL).

Exterior

Over the entrance at 25 W. 50th St is a massive limestone screen by Lee Lawrie symbolizing the international purpose of the building. The four figures in the central rectangle on the bottom row represent the four races of mankind; above them are: a trading ship; three figures representing Art, Science, and Industry; and Mercury, messenger of trade. The upper-side panels represent regions of the Earth (whale's fluke, palm trees, mosque, and Aztec temple), while the lower ones symbolize the old order (Norman tower and lion, symbol of kings) and the new industrial, republican age (smokestacks and eagle). Panels at nos. 19 and 9 W. 50th St, also by Lawrie, represent *Swords into Ploughshares* and *St. Francis of Assisi with Birds.*

The main entrance of the building is on Fifth Ave, where a central doorway is flanked by two projecting wings. The south wing is known as the **Palazzo d'Italia** (1935; DL) and, like the British and French Buildings, it demonstrates the developers' desire to attract foreign tenants at a time when American ones were not readily available. Two bronze reliefs by Giacomo Manzu adorn the main entrance: a high relief of entwined grapevines and wheat stalks symbolizing fruitfulness, and a smaller low relief depicting an immigrant mother and child. These works, installed in 1965, replace earlier decorations by Attilio Piccirilli that were removed in 1940 when the U.S. was on the brink of war with Italy. In front of the central entrance of the International Building is a statue of *Atlas* (1937) supporting an armillary globe studded with signs of the zodiac. Designed by Lee Lawrie, this bronze, muscle-bound giant (height of figure, 15 ft; diameter of sphere, 21 ft; weight, 7 tons) impresses by his sheer size. The north wing of the building, known as the International Building North, retains its original decoration. Above the door is a glass panel by Piccirilli entitled *Youth Leading Industry* (c. 1936). Made of 3 tons of cast Pyrex, it depicts a charioteer reining in two plunging horses as a youth points out the road ahead.

Interior
The main lobby is tall and deep, with thin piers leading the eye to the **central escalators,** which dominate the room like the grand staircases of 18C–19C public buildings but suggest the fondness of Art Deco designers for machinery as a stylistic motif. The ceiling is covered with copper leaf and illuminated by indirect lighting. Ride up the escalator to the blank wall at the top, decorated with a bust of the aviator Charles A. Lindbergh. On the way down you have a great view through the rings of Atlas's sphere to the rose window and Gothic arches of St. Patrick's Cathedral across the street, an appealing juxtaposition of old and new.

52nd Street
Walk north to W. 52nd St and turn left. Between Fifth and Sixth Aves, 52nd St has been designated **"Swing Street"** to commemorate its place in the history of jazz.

History
Known simply as "The Street" among jazzmen, it attracted attention beginning in the late 1930s with its nightclubs, many of them former speakeasies. Most of the great innovators and performers of the period worked the row: Art Tatum, Dizzy Gillespie, Thelonius Monk, Lester Young, Kenny Clark, and, of course, Charlie Parker, for whom the club Birdland would later be named. In particular the street has been identified with bop, a style that emerged in Harlem in the early 1940s and came downtown when black musicians began working in the clubs of 52nd St. The best known were the Onyx, the Spotlight, the Three Deuces, the Famous Door, and, on nearby Broadway, the Royal Roost and Bop City. The period was a golden age for jazz and for 52nd St, but by 1948, when heroin abuse was widespread among jazz musicians, the street had become the territory of prostitutes, strippers, and drug pushers.

At 21 W. 52nd St is the **21 Club** (1872; Duggin & Crossman), with its lawn jockeys out front. It was the city's ritziest speakeasy during Prohibition, the place where café society came to eat, drink, and dance; the liquor is now legal but the atmosphere remains.

Museum of Television and Radio
25 W. 52nd St, New York, NY 10022. ☎ (212) 621-6800 for daily information on scheduled activities; ☎ 621-6600 for other information. Web site: www.mtr.org. Open Tues–Sun 12–6; until 8 on Thurs and 9 on Fri (theaters only). Closed Mon, Jan 1, July 4, Thanksgiving, and Dec 25. Admission charge. Daily screenings and radio programs; tours, children's programs; seminars. Gift shop. Accessible to wheelchairs; assisted listening devices available at the front desk; closed-caption programming.

Subway: Eighth Ave Local (E) to Fifth Ave–53rd St. Broadway Local (N, R) to 49th St–Broadway. Broadway–Seventh Ave (1, 9) to Broadway–50th St. Sixth Ave Express or Local (B, D, Q, F) to 47–50th St–Rockefeller Center. Bus: M1, M2, M3, M4, M6, M7.

Next door is the Museum of Television and Radio, called the Museum of Broadcasting when it was launched by CBS founder William Paley in 1975. The museum, which moved to this location in 1991, has a collection of more than 100,000 television and radio programs chosen for artistic, cultural, or historical importance. The radio shows date back to a speech in the 1920s by the labor leader Samuel Gompers; the TV shows begin in 1949. At the museum you can enjoy the scheduled performances in one of the theaters or listening rooms, or you can check out favorite programs and watch them on individual consoles.

Museum of Modern Art (MoMA)

11 W. 53rd St, New York, NY 10019. ☎ (212) 708-9400. Web site: www.moma.org. Open Sat, Sun, Mon, Tues, Thurs 10:30–5:45; Fri 10:30–8:15. Closed Wed, Thanksgiving, and Dec 25. Admission charge, except Fri 4:30–8:15, pay what you wish.

Exhibitions, screenings, gallery talks, and lectures. Restaurants, gift shops. For exhibition information, ☎ (212) 708-9480; for information about film screenings, ☎ (212) 708-9490. Accessible to wheelchairs.

Subway: Sixth Ave Local (F) or Eighth Ave Local (E) to 53rd St–Fifth Ave. Sixth Ave Express or Local (B, D, Q, F) to 47th–50th Sts–Rockefeller Center. Bus: M1, M2, M3, M4, M5, M6, M7, M27, M30, M31, M50, M57, Q32.

Not far north, on 53rd St west of Fifth Ave, is the Museum of Modern Art (MoMA) (1939; Edward Durell Stone & Philip L. Goodwin; East Wing, 1964, Philip Johnson; 1984 renovation and West Wing; Cesar Pelli & Assocs. with Gruen Assocs.). The museum has one of the world's greatest collections of European and American art from the end of the 19C to the present. It has stunning examples of painting and sculpture and also stellar collections of photography, film, and industrial design.

The museum is currently undertaking a massive expansion project, which will disrupt normal operations. Exhibitions will continue at the 53rd St building through spring 2002 and then be moved to MoMA QNS, a temporary facility at 45-20 33rd St, Long Island City (see Walk 50). The museum plans to reopen on 53rd St in late 2004–early 2005.

History

In 1929, when modern art was not considered art at all in many quarters, Abby Aldrich Rockefeller and two friends, Lillie P. Bliss and Mary Quinn Sullivan, founded a small museum in rented space in what is now the Crown Building on Fifth Ave. Their first exhibit was *Cézanne, Gauguin, Seurat, van Gogh,* a choice more daring than it seems today. The initial collection—donated by one of the trustees in 1929—was eight prints and one drawing. The collection got a major boost 1931, when Lillie Bliss left the museum masterworks by Cézanne, Gauguin, Matisse, Modigliani, Picasso, Seurat, and Degas.

The first director of the museum, Alfred H. Barr Jr., developed the concept of a museum that would include not just painting and sculpture but other visual arts—film, industrial design, prints, drawings, photography, and printed books—

and quickly shaped the museum into a major force. In 1932 the exhibit *Modern Architecture: International Exhibition* was influential in introducing the international style to the American public, and in 1935 an exhibition of van Gogh proved, in the words of the *WPA Guide to New York City*, that "art can attract as many people as a prize fight."

In 1932 MoMA moved to this site, leasing a brownstone from John D. Rockefeller Jr., who later donated the land. In 1939 the present building opened with an exhibition, *Art in Our Time*, with works from all the museum's departments. Throughout the 1940s and 1950s the museum continued to blaze new territory, dramatically increasing its photographic collection, mounting exhibitions on Matisse, Nolde, Rodin, Magritte, Turner, Pollock, de Kooning, and Oldenburg, and sending abroad the influential exhibition *The New American Painting*, which was devoted to abstract expressionism. As its astonishing collection increased, the museum gradually became more conservative: its strengths became those of conserving the past and offering a historical view of art from postimpressionism to relatively recent times. To counteract this trend, MoMA merged in 1999 with P.S. 1 in Long Island City, whose focus is avant-garde contemporary art.

The building too has evolved. It was renovated and enlarged in 1984, virtually doubling in size. Above the West Wing, constructed with the air rights above the rest of the museum, rises Museum Tower, a luxury apartment building whose rents help generate financial support for the museum. MoMA is expanding again, undertaking a $650-million fund-raising campaign—the largest ever by a museum—and purchasing three neighboring buildings on W. 53rd St to develop the sites and again double its space.

MoMA Highlights

The permanent collection contains a survey of modern European and American art from the late 19C to about 1960, with fine examples of European modernist movements beginning with cubism.

MoMA has an outstanding collection of works by **Picasso** and **Matisse,** as well as masterworks by van Gogh, Braque, and Mondrian.

The collection of postwar avant-garde **American abstract expressionists** is superb.

The **design collection** is unique in this country, as are holdings in **prints** and **photography,** which are shown in changing exhibitions.

Note: The works below are listed as they were shown in the museum before the renovation project began.

European Painting

Post-impressionism. In these galleries are many well-known paintings: Paul Cézanne, *The Bather;* Henri de Toulouse-Lautrec, *La Goulue at the Moulin Rouge;* Edgar Degas, *At the Milliner's;* Georges Seurat, *Evening, Honfleur;* Henri Rousseau, *The Dream* and *The Sleeping Gypsy;* Vincent van Gogh, *The Starry Night* and *Portrait of Joseph Roulin;* Paul Gauguin, *The Moon and the Earth.*

Fauvism, early Picasso, cubism. The collection features paintings by André

Drain, Georges Braque, and Henri Matisse, along with Pablo Picasso's *Les Demoiselles d'Avignon,* one of his most important works. There are examples of early "analytical" cubism by Picasso and Braque, as well as later "synthetic" works and cubist sculpture.

The museum has paintings by Gustav Klimt, Egon Schiele, Oskar Kokoshka, Wilhelm Lehmbruck, Otto Dix, and Ernst Ludwig Kirchner, and a fine collection of works by **Mondrian** that covers most of his career, culminating in *Broadway Boogie Woogie.* **Matisse** is represented by a whole gallery of wonderful paintings: *The Red Studio, The Moroccans, The Dance, Goldfish and Sculpture, Moroccan Garden, View of Notre Dame, Piano Lesson, Woman on a High Stool, Variation on a Still Life by De Heem.*

Sculpture includes many works by Constantin Brancusi and a few by Alberto Giacometti. Picasso of the late 1920s–30s is represented by *Seated Bather, Girl Before a Mirror,* and *Head of a Woman* (Marie Thérèse Walther). Museum favorites with visitors include Salvador Dalí, *The Persistence of Memory;* Frida Kahlo, *Self-Portrait with Cropped Hair;* and René Magritte, *The Empire of Light, II* and *The False Mirror.* There are large-scale works by David Alfaro Siqueiros, José Clemente Orozco, and Max Beckmann.

The museum owns three panels of **Claude Monet's *Water Lilies,*** as well as *The Japanese Footbridge. Charnel House,* a work of Picasso's from the 1940s, replaced *Guernica* when that painting was returned to Spain.

American Painting

The collection includes **figurative American painters,** including Andrew Wyeth *(Christina's World)* and Edward Hopper *(House by the Railroad).* There are also works by Georgia O'Keeffe and Stuart Davis. **Postwar painters** include **Jackson Pollock,** who is represented by a number of large, important canvases, notably the monumental *One (Number 31, 1950).* There are paintings by abstractionists Barnett Newman, Ad Reinhardt, Clyfford Still, Robert Motherwell, Mark Rothko, and Franz Kline. The museum owns works from Jasper Johns's Flag and Map series and many works by Andy Warhol, including *Gold Marilyn Monroe.* Artists in the collection from the pop and op movements of the 1960s include Claes Oldenburg, James Rosenquist, and Roy Lichtenstein.

Other Collections

The **architecture collection** includes models, drawings, and photographs of buildings, and owns the Ludwig Mies van der Rohe Archive. The **design collection,** more than 3,000 objects, ranges from household appliances and furniture to tools, textiles, sports cars—even a helicopter. The **graphic design collection** includes in excess of 4,000 examples of typography, posters, and other combinations of text and image. The museum owns 6,000 works on paper, with **drawings** in pencil, ink, and charcoal, as well as watercolors, gouaches, collages, and works in mixed mediums. The **photography collection** of more than 25,000 works dates from about 1840 to the present and includes work by artists, journalists, scientists, entrepreneurs, and amateurs. The **collection of prints** has historical and contemporary prints and books that reflect the history of modern art in both range and depth. There are prints made by the traditional techniques of lithography, etching, screenprinting, and woodcut as well as newer forms of printmaking.

American Folk Art Museum

45 W. 53rd St, New York, NY 10019. ☎ (212) 265-1040. Web site: www.folkart museum.org. Open Tues–Sun 10–6; Fri until 8. Closed Mon, national holidays. Admission charge. Changing exhibitions, workshops, lectures, educational events. Café; gift shop. Accessible to wheelchairs.

The museum, founded (1961) as the Museum of American Folk Art, is New York's only institution devoted solely to traditional and contemporary American folk art. Its new building (2001; Tod Williams Billie Tsien and Assocs.) is the city's first new art museum constructed from the ground up since the Whitney Museum opened its doors on Madison Ave in 1966. Surrounded by sites owned by the Museum of Modern Art, the building, according to the architects, was designed to make a quiet statement of independence, its form recalling an abstracted open hand.

The museum maintains a satellite branch across from Lincoln Center (see Walk 26).

The Collection

The collection includes 18C–19C traditional folk art as well as the work of modern self-taught artists. Among the traditional works are paintings, sculptures, trade signs, weather vanes, quilts, samplers, carvings, pottery, scrimshaw, and furniture. Some of these pieces are famous icons of American art: *Girl in a Red Dress with Cat and Dog* by Ammi Phillips; the *Darling Farm Flag Gate*, a wooden gate designed like an American flag, its red stripes "rippling" in an imaginary wind; and weather vanes depicting the Statue of Liberty and the archangel Gabriel. In addition to work by the self-taught 20C artists Eddie Arning, Harry Lieberman, Bill Traylor, and William Hawkins, the museum has the nation's largest holdings of paintings and manuscripts by Henry Darger. Darger, a Chicago recluse, devoted much of his life to a fantastic 19,000-page epic, *The Realms of the Unreal*, which he illustrated with several hundred watercolors.

Across the street from MoMA is the **Donnell Library Center** (20 W. 53rd St), a branch of the New York Public Library. Ezekiel J. Donnell, a cotton merchant, in 1896 bequeathed money for a library "in which young people can spend their evenings profitably away from demoralizing influences." It has the nation's best collection of children's literature, including English and American children's books from the 18C and 19C, as well as the original stuffed animals that inspired A. A. Milne's Winnie-the-Pooh stories. Milne, who had bought the animals for his son Christopher, loaned them to the president of E. P. Dutton in 1947 for a promotional tour of the United States. (Missing from the bunch is Roo, whom Christopher had lost in an apple orchard in Surrey.) Milne eventually gave the animals to Dutton, which donated them to the public library in 1987. In 1998 a member of the British Parliament unsuccessfully demanded that the creatures be returned to their rightful home in England.

American Craft Museum

40 W. 53rd St, New York, NY 10019. ☎ (212) 956-3535. Open Tues–Sun 10–6; Thurs open until 8. Closed Mon, national holidays. Admission charge; Thurs 6–8, pay what you wish. Changing exhibitions, lectures. Gift shop. Accessible to wheelchairs.

Adjacent to the library is the American Craft Museum (1986; Roche, Dinkeloo & Assocs), the city's foremost venue for 20C craft. Located in handsome quarters, which it owns as a condominium within the former E. F. Hutton Building, the museum has a 40 ft atrium fronting on 53rd St. Within are selections from the permanent collection and changing exhibitions of contemporary craft, including work in such traditional media as glass, ceramics, fiber, paper, wood, and metal. The beautifully mounted installations range from straightforward folk crafts to sophisticated modern works that stand between traditional craft and what is usually considered art.

In the plaza west of the former E. F. Hutton Building is *Lapstrake* (1987) by Texas sculptor Jesus Bautista Moroles, a pile of granite slabs, alternately rough hewn and polished, suggesting perhaps an ancient architectural ruin.

Just beyond the plaza (entrance at 51 W. 52nd St) is the **CBS Building** (1965; Eero Saarinen & Assocs; DL), "Black Rock," the home of the television network. Clad in dark gray granite, the 38-story tower is Saarinen's only skyscraper, notable for its reinforced concrete structure (as opposed to its steel-and-glass neighbors).

Equitable Center
One block south, facing Sixth Ave, is the **PaineWebber Building** (1961; Skidmore, Owings & Merrill).

PaineWebber Art Gallery
1285 Sixth Ave (between W. 51st and W. 52nd Sts), New York, NY 10019. ☎ (212) 713-2885. Web site: www.painewebber.com/about/comm/gallery. Open Mon–Fri 8–6. Closed weekends, holidays when the stock market is closed. Free. Accessible to wheelchairs.

Subway: Sixth Ave Express or Local (B, D, Q, F) to 47th–50th Sts–Rockefeller Center. Broadway Local (N, R) to 49th St. Broadway–Seventh Ave Local (1, 9) to 50th St. Bus: M5, M6, M7, M27, M50.

The ground-floor PaineWebber Gallery hosts changing exhibitions, most of them mounted by nonprofit institutions that could not otherwise afford Midtown exhibition space. Among the organizations who have had shows here are the Broadway Theater Institute, the Jacques Marchais Museum of Tibetan Art, the South Street Seaport Museum, the Bronx Museum, the Public Art Fund, and the Asia Society.

Galleria
Walk west through the PaineWebber Building, which along with the Equitable Tower to the west constitutes the Equitable Center. Between the two buildings is the Galleria, an open space with escalators to a concourse level. Here is Sol Le-Witt's *Wall Drawing: Bands of Lines in Four Colors and Four Directions Separated by Gray Bands* (1985). At the north and south ends respectively of the Galleria are Barry Flanagan's bronze *Young Elephant* (1985) and *Hare on Bell* (1983). In the center of the Galleria is the entrance to the bar of the Palio restaurant, which has a vibrantly colored mural by Sandro Chia (1985) depicting the Sienese horse race.

Equitable Tower

Walk west to the main entrance of the Equitable Tower (1986; Edward Larrabee Barnes Assocs.), 787 Seventh Ave (between W. 51st and W. 52nd Sts), formerly the headquarters of the Equitable Companies, involved in insurance and financial planning. Finished in smooth beige limestone framed with orange granite, the building rises 54 stories from a 723 ft arch facing Seventh Ave to a pair of 53 ft arched windows at the top. Inside, dominating the imposing 80 ft atrium is Roy Lichtenstein's *Mural with Blue Brushstroke*, a 68 ft painting whose images span the artist's career and include references to his early pop art period and his later paraphrases of art history. In the center of the atrium is Scott Burton's *Atrium Furnishment*, a 40 ft semicircular settee and circular table (19 ft in diameter) made of marble.

In the north corridor, **Thomas Hart Benton's murals** *America Today* (1930–31), painted for the New School of Social Research, reflect life in rural and urban America and the rise of technology. These muscular paintings are energized by an optimistic spirit that seems, with historical hindsight, at odds with Depression America, but as Benton pointed out, the Depression hit hard only when he had almost completed them. Bought by Equitable in 1984 for $3.4 million, the murals have been beautifully restored.

AXA Gallery

787 Seventh Ave (at W. 51st St), New York, NY 10019. ☎ (212) 554-4818. Web site: www.axa-financial.com/aboutus/gallery.html. Open Mon–Fri 11–6; Sat 12–5. Closed Sun, most public holidays. Free. Changing exhibitions; catalogs available at Hudson Newstand. Accessible to wheelchairs.

Also inside the lobby is the AXA Gallery. Formerly the Equitable Gallery (opened 1992; the name changed when the Equitable Companies became AXA Financial in 1999). The gallery hosts well-regarded shows (about four yearly) featuring work that would not otherwise be seen by New York audiences. Exhibition subjects have included narrative painting from the Pennsylvania Academy of Fine Arts, prints by African American artists from the 1930s and 1940s, and Thomas Jefferson's designs for Monticello.

From the Equitable Building walk west on 51st St to Broadway. Between W. 50th and W. 51st Sts at 1634 Broadway is the **Winter Garden Theatre** (1911; W. Albert Swasey; remodeling 1923; Herbert J. Krapp; interior DL), formerly the American Horse Exchange, a stable and auction market built in 1885 by William K. Vanderbilt, converted by the Shuberts to a theater. Through the years, the Winter Garden has hosted Fanny Brice in the *Ziegfeld Follies*, *West Side Story*, Barbra Streisand in *Funny Girl*, and *Cats*. The musical based on T. S. Eliot's poems opened Oct 7, 1982, and became Broadway's longest-running musical, reaching 7,485 performances before it closed on Sept 10, 2000.

West of Broadway on 52nd St are several other Broadway houses—the **Neil Simon Theatre,** originally the Alvin Theatre (1927; Herbert J. Krapp; DL), 250 W. 52nd St; and the **Virginia Theatre,** originally the home of the Theatre Guild (1925; Crane & Franzheim; DL), 245 W. 52nd St. The dance club **Roseland,** 239 W. 52nd St, opened at 1658 Broadway in 1919 and quickly became a popular jazz club, attracting big-name performers like Fletcher Henderson, Earl Hines, and

Ella Fitzgerald. When the building was demolished in 1956, the new Roseland Ballroom opened. Eight decades after its debut, it remains a popular nightspot.

Ed Sullivan Theater

Return to Broadway. On the west side between W. 53rd and W. 54th Sts is the Ed Sullivan Theater, originally Hammerstein's Theatre (1927; Herbert J. Krapp; interior DL), 1697 Broadway. Arthur Hammerstein (see Times Square History in Walk 15) named the theater for his father, producer Oscar Hammerstein I; architect Krapp fitted out the neo-Gothic interior with bronze grills, marble floors, and stained glass panels with scenes from operas produced by the great impressario. Hammerstein's failed as a legitimate theater and after a stint as a nightclub was converted in 1945 into a television studio. On June 20, 1948, the *Toast of the Town* made its debut with host Ed Sullivan, after whom the show was renamed in 1955. One of the longest-running prime-time shows in television history, the show closed in 1971.

The Ed Sullivan Show

Sullivan (1901–1974) began his career as a reporter, eventually replacing Walter Winchell as the *New York Evening Graphic's* Broadway columnist. His work as an emcee for vaudeville, radio shows, and benefits led CBS to offer him the TV job. Though the press ridiculed his stiff delivery, his journalist's instincts enabled him to sniff out talent and offer what viewers wanted—a mix that included the Bolshoi Ballet, the mechanical mouse Topo Gigio, and the ventriloquist Señor Wences. It was on Sullivan's show that Elvis Presley was broadcast live from the waist up, the Beatles performed to a record-breaking 73 million viewers, and Jim Morrison of the Doors disobeyed the producer and sang the taboo word *higher* in "Light My Fire." Sullivan also gave rare national exposure to black performers like Harry Belafonte and Richard Pryor. In 1967, the theater was renamed for Sullivan. In 1993, David Letterman's new program, *Late Show with David Letterman,* took over the theater.

Studio 54

Walk north to 54th St and turn left. Studio 54, 254 W. 54th St, now a theater, was a legendary disco in the late 1970s.

History

The building, which opened in 1927 as the Gallo Opera House, served time as a dinner theater, was taken over by CBS in 1943, and then converted to a sound studio. It was there that Jack Benny and later Johnny Carson held forth and the dubious *$64,000 Question* quiz show ran its course. In 1977, Ian Schrager and Steve Rubell opened Studio 54, which quickly became a celebrity haunt—Liza Minnelli, Truman Capote, and Andy Warhol regularly showed up—and a place for dancing and partying (cocaine became a staple) and intimate encounters in a basement lounge. Within 18 months the owners were arrested for tax evasion—

millions of dollars were reportedly hidden in false ceilings. Rubell and Schrager were sentenced to three years in jail. After they sold the club in 1980, things went downhill, the studio hosting a rock club and then a topless club in the early 1990s. In 1998, however, the Roundabout Theatre's successful revival of *Cabaret* moved to Studio 54, converting it once again to a legitimate theater.

Walk east on W. 54th St, back past Broadway and Seventh Ave. At 141 W. 54th St is the **Ziegfeld Theater,** the largest and only remaining traditional single-screen theater in Manhattan; the auditorium seats 1,200.

Return to Seventh Ave and turn right. At 854 Seventh Ave is the **Carnegie Deli,** which opened in 1934. Here you can sink your teeth into a double-digit (both price and weight) pastrami or corned beef sandwich, or opt for a bowl of their acclaimed matzoh ball soup. Regular customers have included Henny Youngman, Jackie Mason, and Woody Allen, who filmed much of *Broadway Danny Rose* here.

Walk north to W. 55th St and turn right. At 135 W. 55th St between Sixth and Seventh Aves is the domed and decorated **City Center for Music and Drama** (1924; H. P. Knowles, succeeded by Clinton & Russell; DL), built as the **Mecca Temple** of the Ancient Order of Nobles of the Mystic Shrine (Shriners). The city took over the building in 1943 and converted it into a theater (3,000 seats). The New York City Ballet and the New York City Opera called it home until their move to Lincoln Center. It is still a major dance venue and home to Off-Broadway's prestigious Manhattan Theater Club.

Carnegie Hall

Return to Seventh Ave and walk north. Carnegie Hall (1891; William B. Tuthill, architect with Dankmar Adler and William Morris Hunt, consultants; restored 1986; James Stewart Polshek; DL), 154 W. 57th St (southeast corner of the intersection at Seventh Ave), was built by Andrew Carnegie for the Oratorio Society, of which he was president. He also hoped to make money on his $2-million investment. Architecturally the building is not outstanding—a bulky, brownish, neo-Italian Renaissance hall with a high, square corner tower—but it is a musical landmark.

History

The acoustics of the original auditorium (2,760 seats) were legendary, delighting both audiences and performers, beginning with Tchaikovsky who appeared as guest conductor during opening week. Despite its popularity, the hall came close to demolition in the early 1960s when its owners began yearning for larger profits (Andrew Carnegie didn't make much money on it either), but preservationists headed by violinist Isaac Stern saved it. Although the New York Philharmonic, which first made Carnegie Hall its home and appeared here under the batons of Toscanini and Leopold Stokowski, now resides at Lincoln Center, major orchestras and soloists are still booked into the hall.

A major 1986 renovation left musicians and audiences complaining about the acoustics. In 1995, the stage floor was removed and the amount of "fill" beneath it was adjusted, restoring the acoustics. In 2000, Carnegie Hall decided to expand, choosing the only direction available—down—by digging out a new 688-seat auditorium underneath the main hall.

Weill Recital Hall

Carnegie Recital Hall, renamed Weill Recital Hall at Carnegie Hall, is a small (268 seats) but prestigious auditorium where less well-known artists display their talents.

Rose Museum at Carnegie Hall

154 W. 57th St (at Seventh Ave), 2nd floor, New York, NY 10019. ☎ (212) 903-9629. Web site: www.carnegiehall.org. Open to the public daily (except Wed) 11–4:30, and to concertgoers a half hour before the event through intermissions. Closed Wed, some holidays. Free. Permanent and changing exhibitions. Café in concert hall, open to concertgoers. Gift shop. Accessible to wheelchairs.

Subway: Broadway–Seventh Ave Local (1, 9), Sixth Ave Express (B, D), or Eighth Ave Express or Local (A, C, E) to 59th St–Columbus Circle. Bus: M5, M6, M7, M30, M57.

The Rose Museum at Carnegie Hall (1991) on the first-tier level has a permanent exhibition on the history of the hall as well as changing thematic shows drawn from the hall's extensive archives and those of other institutions.

In 1986, five years before its centennial, Carnegie Hall historians began a massive search to recover documents and memorabilia concerning the hall's past. Material arrived from all over the world, solicited by advertisements, stories in the media, and requests of former employees. More than 12,000 programs were recovered, and the museum now has an almost complete set from 1891 to the present. Past exhibitions include: *George and Ira Gershwin: Nice Work If You Can Get It*, which celebrated the 100th anniversary of their births; *The Piano Sonatas of Ludwig van Beethoven*, which displayed, for the first time in the U.S., over 200 pages in the composer's hand; and *Remembering the Art of Marian Anderson*, which ran on the occasion of her centennial.

The presence of Carnegie Hall has long made this neighborhood a center of musical activity, attracting instrument dealers and music stores. Still in evidence are the **Joseph Patelson Music House** behind Carnegie Hall (at 160 W. 56th St), whose bulletin board offers announcements of interest to musicians, and the **Steinway showroom** in the Manhattan Life Insurance Building (1925; Warren & Wetmore), 109 W. 57th St (between Sixth and Seventh Aves). Originally Steinway Hall, the building once had an upstairs concert hall.

Directly across from Carnegie Hall, 200 W. 57th St, in a brick building with terra-cotta ornament are the former **Rodin Studios** (1917; Cass Gilbert; DL). The former artists' studios with double-height windows facing north and two-story apartments have been converted to offices.

Diagonally across Seventh Ave from Carnegie Hall, 205 W. 57th St, are the **Osborne Apartments** (1885; James E. Ware; DL), a fine early building with a facade of reddish stone. The lobby maintains its former splendor but the rest of the ground floor has been converted into storefronts.

Next door, the **Art Students League** (1892; Henry J. Hardenbergh; DL) at 215 W. 57th St, an art school, enjoys a dignified French Renaissance building by the architect of the Plaza Hotel. Robert Henri and John Sloan were on the faculty; Edward Hopper, George Bellows, and Rockwell Kent were students.

Return to Seventh Ave and walk north to W. 58th St. On the southeast corner is **Alwyn Court** (1909; Harde & Short; DL), an apartment building lavishly encrusted with terra-cotta ornament: salamanders, crowns, portraits, urns. The original 14-room apartments (with five baths) were subdivided during the Depression.

Walk West on 58th St. At 213 W. 58th is a beautiful **carriage house** (1903; York & Saywer; DL), once owned by Helen Miller Gould, daughter of Jay Gould.

Continue west to Eighth Ave. At 959 Eighth Ave, on the southwest corner of 58th St, is the bizarre, theatrical **Hearst Magazine Building** (1928; Joseph Urban and George B. Post & Sons; DL), worthy of both its designer and original owner. Joseph Urban designed theaters and also theatrical sets for the stages of the Metropolitan Opera and the *Ziegfeld Follies.* This building, commissioned by the newspaper tycoon William Randolph Hearst, is adorned with oversize urns, fluted columns, and figures representing (left to right) Sport and Industry, Comedy and Tragedy, and Music and Art (Henry Kreis). The Hearst Corporation has hired architect Lord Norman Foster to design a tower above the building's existing six floors. William Randolph Hearst had originally planned such a tower but abandoned the idea during the Great Depression.

Walk south along Eighth Ave to W. 55th St and turn left to see one of New York's more unusual socioculinary institutions. At 259A W. 55th St. is **Soup Kitchen International,** whose owner, Al Yeganeh, became the model for the rule-obsessed "Soup Nazi" on the television sitcom *Seinfeld.*

18 · Midtown East: Murray Hill, 42nd Street, and Park Avenue

Murray Hill to 42nd Street

Subway: Lexington Ave Local (6) to 28th St. Sixth Ave Express or Local (B, D, Q, F) or Broadway Local (N, R) to 34th St.
Bus: M1, M2, M3, M4, M32.

History

Murray Hill, bounded roughly by E. 34th St, Third Ave, E. 42nd St, and Madison Ave, is named after Robert Murray, who had a country home here (at present-day E. 37th St and Park Ave) during the Revolutionary War. A myth later sprang up that after the British landing at Kips Bay, Mrs. Murray detained General Howe and his chief officers at tea, thereby allowing the American troops stationed in Lower Manhattan to escape up the West Side to Harlem Heights. In the mid-19C, real estate values soared as the upper crust built brownstone mansions along Fifth, Madison, and Park Aves.

Although most have been torn down, a few homes and carriage houses remain to suggest Murray Hill at its peak. The neighborhood remains a stable, upscale neighborhood. South of Murray Hill, from 34th to 23rd Sts, is a neighborhood sometimes called **Curry Hill** because of the many Indian and Bangladesh restaurants and shops along Lexington Ave. In recent years, this area has begun to gentrify.

Begin at Fifth Ave and 29th St. On the northwest corner is the **Marble Collegiate Church** (1854; Samuel A. Warner; DL), a Gothic revival contemporary of Trin-

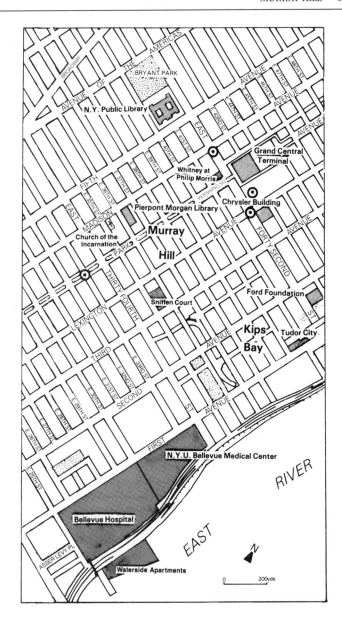

ity Church with roots dating back to the first Reformed congregation founded by the Dutch in 1628. Like West End Collegiate Church (see Walk 26), its ministers serve as equals to the members of the congregation and are called "colleagues." Norman Vincent Peale, prolific author and public speaker, made the church famous during his pastorate.

Church of the Transfiguration

Cross Fifth Ave and walk east on 29th St. The Church of the Transfiguration (Protestant Episcopal), 1 E. 29th St, is set in a quiet garden; it is better known as **the Little Church around the Corner.**

History
During the Civil War, the church was a station in the Underground Railroad. In 1870, actor Joseph Jefferson, trying to arrange the funeral of humble fellow actor George Holland, was rejected by the socially haughty minister of a nearby church; he was told to try "the little church around the corner." Jefferson replied, "God bless the little church around the corner." The church remains popular with actors.

Exterior
The main body of the church (architect unknown) dates from 1849; the Guild Hall and rectory by Frederick C. Withers were added in 1861, while the Lich Gate (from the Old English word for *corpse*) provided a covered resting place for a coffin before burial. Designed by Withers, the gate was donated (1896) by Mrs. Franklin Delano, aunt of President Franklin D. Roosevelt. The church, rectory, Guild Hall, Lich Gate, Lady Chapel, and Mortuary Chapel are designated landmarks.

Interior
The **nave** contains several memorials to actors. On the north aisle: Montague (Henry J. Mann), a handsome matinee idol (died 1878), is depicted in the first window wearing the robes of a pilgrim. The window depicting St. John the Beloved Disciple is dedicated to the American actor John Drew (died 1927). The **St. Faith Window** nearest the pulpit in the north aisle is said to be the oldest church window in America, made of 14C Belgian glass saved from a church destroyed during the Napoleonic Wars.

The **Joseph Jefferson Memorial Window** in the south aisle commemorates the incident that gave the church its nickname. Jefferson, in his role as Rip Van Winkle, is shown leading an enshrouded George Holland toward the Lich Gate. The bronze tablet next to the window honoring actor Otis Skinner is the work of Paul Manship.

On the west wall of the transept is the **Edwin Booth Memorial Window,** honoring the tragedian, who is depicted in the role of Hamlet. The Booth Window and its neighbor, the Drexel Window, are the work of John La Farge.

Walk east to Madison Ave and go north. Architect Stanford White modeled the Federal-style former **Colony Club** (1908; McKim, Mead & White; DL), 120 Madison Ave (between E. 30th and East 31st Sts), after 18C houses he had seen in Maryland. The club was the city's first private women's club, but since 1963 has housed the **American Academy of Dramatic Arts,** the oldest professional English-language acting school.

The former **Grolier Club** (1889; Charles Romeyn; DL), at 29 E. 32nd St, is a handsome brick-and-stone Romanesque revival building with an abundance of arches. America's oldest society for bibliophiles, the Grolier Club (founded 1884) moved uptown to 47 E. 60th Street in 1917.

Walk north on Madison Ave to E. 35th St. At 205 Madison Ave (northeast corner of the intersection at 35th St) is the Protestant Episcopal **Church of the Incarnation** (1864; Emlen T. Littel; rebuilt and enlarged after a fire in 1882). Founded as a mission of Grace Church, it is English Gothic in style. The interior is noteworthy for stained glass windows by Louis Comfort Tiffany, John La Farge, William Morris, and Edward Burne-Jones. The altar rail has carved oak angels by Daniel Chester French.

Turn right to 22 E. 35th St (between Madison and Park Aves), the Georgian revival **Collectors' Club** (1902; McKim, Mead & White; DL), was originally the residence of Thomas B. Clarke, an art dealer and decorator. The Collectors' Club (founded 1896) is devoted to philately.

Morgan Library

29 E. 36th St (between Madison and Park Aves), New York, NY 10016. ☎ (212) 685-0610. Web site: www.morganlibrary.org. Open Tues–Thurs 10:30–5; Fri 10:30–8; Sat 10:30–6; Sun 12–6. Closed Mon, holidays. Requested contribution. Exhibitions, lectures, concerts, films, tours. Café, gift shop. Accessible to wheelchairs, with the exception of several low steps leading into the original library building. Wheelchairs are available on request.

Subway: Lexington Ave Local (6) to 33rd St. Lexington Ave Express or Local (4, 5, 6) to 42nd St–Grand Central. Flushing Local (7) to 42nd St–Grand Central. 6th Ave Express or Local (B, D, Q, F) to 42nd St. Bus: M1, M2, M3, M4, M16, M34, Q32.

On 36th St, just east of Madison Ave, is the Morgan Library (1906; McKim, Mead & White; DL; extension to Madison Ave, 1928; Benjamin Wistar Morris), one of the great repositories of culture in the Western Hemisphere. The museum is known for its Renaissance manuscripts; Old Master drawings; early and rare printed books, including children's books; and ancient written records—Assyrian and Babylonian seals, cuneiform tablets, and Egyptian papyri. The legendary financier J. Pierpont Morgan (1837–1913) gathered most of the collection; his son J. P. Morgan Jr established the museum (1924). In 1988 the library bought the former home of Morgan's son (southeast corner of Madison Ave at E. 37th St) and renovated it (1991; Voorsanger & Assocs.), enclosing the former garden in a glass-walled court. The entire museum complex is elegant, civilized, and tranquil.

Exterior

Walk down E. 36th St toward Park Ave to see the original library (east of the annex containing the entrance), usually considered McKim's masterpiece. The simple classical building with a Palladian porch is faced with marble blocks fitted closely together without mortar, a procedure only possible where costs were no great object and labor was plentiful. Sculptured panels (Adolph A. Weinman) below the frieze represent (right to left) Truth with Literature, Philosophy, History, Oratory, Astronomy, and Music Inspiring the Arts. The marble lionesses guarding the doorway are by Edward Clark Potter, who later placed a more famous pair in front of the New York Public Library.

Interior

On view are three period rooms from Morgan's original library, plus changing exhibitions in several galleries, both in the old and new parts of the complex. The **Rotunda,** or vestibule, has richly colored marble decoration and a domed ceiling with murals by H. Siddons Mowbray. The **West Room,** Morgan's study, is preserved as it was during his lifetime. Displayed here are some of Morgan's favorite paintings and objects d'art, including bronzes, faience, and metalwork. Among the paintings are Hans Memling's *Portrait of a Man with a Pink* and Lucas Cranach's *Wedding Portraits of Martin Luther and His Wife.*

In the **East Room,** the actual library, are tiers of rare books and changing exhibitions of manuscripts, letters, and artifacts. Treasures on display here always include a Gutenberg Bible (Mainz, c. 1455), one of three in the Morgan collection. The 16C Brussels tapestry above the mantelpiece depicts *The Triumph of Avarice* and was designed by Pieter van Aelst, father-in-law of the elder Pieter Bruegel. The zodiacal signs in the ceiling decoration, also by H. Siddons Mowbray, refer to important dates in Morgan's life: his birth, the date of his first wife's death, the date of his second marriage.

On the northeast corner of Madison Ave and E. 37th St is the **Consulate General of the Polish People** (1905; C. P. H. Gilbert; DL), 233 Madison Ave, originally the Joseph Raphael De Lamar Mansion, built for a Dutch-born adventurer who made his money during the Gold Rush.

East 37th St, east of Madison Ave, is a quiet residential community with lovely, sometimes ornate, older homes. Two town houses dating from around 1900 remain at 19 and 21 E. 37th St (between Madison and Park Aves).

Continue east. At 57 Park Ave (between E. 37th and E. 38th Sts) is the **Guatemalan Mission to the United Nations** (1911; Horace Trumbauer; DL), built in Louis XVI style for the wealthy socialite Adelaide Douglas, ex-wife of William Douglas, the developer of Douglaston, Queens. The six-story granite-and-limestone building has a slate mansard roof and parapet. The finest detail is the grooved frieze with the bellflower motif at the fourth floor.

At 23 Park Ave (northeast corner of the intersection at E. 35th St) is the former **James Hampton Robb Mansion** (1898; McKim, Mead & White; DL), built of Roman brick, brownstone, and terra-cotta, with double-decker porticos. Robb was a cotton broker and Parks commissioner. In 1923, the Advertising Club of New York took over. The building was converted to co-ops in 1977.

East 35th St, between Park and Lexington Aves, is a fine brownstone block. At **123 E. 35th St** (1903; Hoppin & Koen) is an especially beautiful Beaux-Arts town house with a copper roof.

A block north on 36th St (between Lexington and Third Aves) is **Sniffen Court,** 150–158 E. 36th St. The Sniffen Court Historic District, named after builder John Sniffen, is a group of ten small Romanesque revival brick carriage houses (c. 1850–60) that have been attractively preserved.

Walk north on Third Ave; turn left on E. 38th St. The house set behind a walled garden at **152 E. 38th St** (1858; redesigned 1934–35; Robertson Ward; DL) seems to have been a gatehouse on an estate belonging one of Martin Van Buren's relatives.

Continue west to Lexington Ave and walk north to E. 42nd St. On the southeast corner is the former **Mobil Building**, 150 E. 42nd St (between Lexington and Third Aves), originally the Socony Mobil Building (1955; Harrison & Abramovitz). At the time of its completion it was the world's largest (1.6 million square ft) metal-clad office building; it had the city's largest office floor and the city's largest central air-conditioning system.

Chrysler Building

Across 42nd St is the city's most beautiful skyscraper, the **Chrysler Building** (1930; William Van Alen; DL), 405 Lexington Ave. It was built by the automobile magnate Walter P. Chrysler to express both the luxury and the mechanical precision of the automobile in its Jazz Age incarnation.

History

The building was undertaken by William H. Reynolds, a real estate speculator who also developed Dreamland, the turn-of-the-20C Coney Island amusement park. Like other ambitious men, reaching back through Frank Woolworth to the builders of the Tower of Babel, Reynolds aspired to erect the world's tallest tower, and hired the maverick architect William Van Alen to design it. Chrysler bought the lease and the plans in 1928, by which time the race for height had become a bitter rivalry between Van Alen and his former partner H. Craig Severance, then at work on the headquarters of the Bank of Manhattan (now 40 Wall St). Van Alen announced plans for a Chrysler Building of 925 ft. Severance in 1929 topped off triumphantly at 927 ft, having added a 50 ft flagpole and a lantern above the 60 stories and ten penthouses of his building. Meanwhile a team of steelworkers inside the fire shaft of the Chrysler Building constructed its 185 ft spire. When Severance declared himself the victor, they pushed the spire through a hole in the roof, bringing the building's height to 1,048 ft, 64 ft higher than the Eiffel Tower, previously the world's tallest structure. One year later, however, the Empire State Building soared above them all to 1,250 ft. (By 1999, the Chrysler Building was only the world's 18th tallest tower.)

Despite its stature in the cityscape, the Chrysler Building has never been very successful commercially and has had six owners since the Chrysler family sold it in 1953. The building's present owners are linking it to the undistinguished 666 Third Avenue, with an annex jazzed up by architect Philip Johnson.

Exterior

The Chrysler Building's slender tower rises to a shining stainless steel spire above concentric arches pierced by triangular windows. There is probably more stainless steel on the facade of the Chrysler Building than on any other building in New York, since stainless steel cost too much for all but the most lavish builders. Below the spire, winged gargoyles resembling hood ornaments stare off in four directions and a brickwork frieze of wheels studded with radiator caps, mudguards, and hubcaps encircles the building.

Interior

The lobby is one of the city's most beautiful interiors. The walls are veneered with sensuously veined Moroccan marble in warm tones of buff and red, while the floor is a yellow Siena marble. Overhead a mural by Edward Trumbull depicts two favorite Art Deco themes—transportation and human endeavor. Among its images are all sorts of modern innovations—ocean liners, airplanes, the Chrysler Corporation assembly line, and the Chrysler Building itself. The beautiful elevator doors and walls are inlaid with African woods in intricate floral designs, and the elevator cabs are marquetried, no two alike.

Cross Lexington Ave to the 1,400-room **Grand Hyatt Hotel** (1980; Gruzen & Partners with Der Scutt) on the north side of 42nd St. Built on the steel skeleton of the Commodore Hotel (1920; Warren & Wetmore), this chunky 30-story building is sheathed in gray mirrored glass that reflects its surroundings. Inside, the lobby exudes swank and glitter: Paradiso Italian marble pavement, bronze-covered columns, brass hardware.

Cross 42nd St to the **Chanin Building** (1929; Sloan & Robertson; DL), 122 E. 42nd St, decorated with geometric and floral bas-reliefs. The lobby is a treasure of Art Deco design in bronze and marble. René Chambellan, the architectural sculptor best known for his work at Rockefeller Center, collaborated on the design of the interior, including the lobby, whose theme is "City of Opportunity." The bas-reliefs and grillwork express, respectively, the active and intellectual life of the individual, with the geometric patterns, in Chambellan's conception, also symbolizing emotions and abstractions of thought. The whole design tells the story of a city where a man, through the exertion of his mind and hands, could rise from a humble state to wealth and power. The theme was especially applicable to Irwin Chanin, one of the city's first real estate developers. In 1919 Chanin borrowed $20,000 to build two houses in Bensonhurst, Brooklyn. Ten years later he had created 141 buildings in the city, including hotels and several Broadway theaters.

Just to the west is the former **Bowery Savings Bank** (1923; York & Sawyer), 110 E. 42nd St, a grand Romanesque palace with a dramatic deep-arched entrance, the work of one of the city's finest bank architects. Inside, the former banking room is suitably imposing with its beamed and coffered ceiling (65 ft high, 165 ft long, 80 ft wide), its varicolored marble columns, and its limestone floor inset with marble mosaics. Among the carvings in the frieze directly below the ceiling are motifs associated with money (the squirrel for thrift, the rooster for punctuality, the lion for power, the bull and bear representing Wall Street). Today, the bank houses Cipriani 42nd Street, a catering hall.

Just west of here is **Park Ave,** which began as Fourth Ave on the 1811 grid, but long remained undeveloped because a granite ridge ran its entire length. When the New York and Harlem Railroad requested a right of way for its tracks and permission to run its steam engines above 14th St (1832), the city granted it Fourth Ave. The railroad then blasted out the granite and laid the tracks in a cut from which coal smoke and noise polluted the neighborhood. In 1857 the city set 42nd St as the southern limit for steam engines; the trains were then pulled by horses downtown to their terminal. Fourth Ave was renamed in sections, with the final portion up to the Harlem River receiving the name Park Ave in 1888.

The intersection of Park Ave and E. 42nd St, though not properly a square, is named **Pershing Square** in honor of Gen. John Joseph Pershing, commander of the American forces in Europe during World War I. In 1999 the dark unused space under the Park Ave viaduct was filled by the handsome Pershing Square Café, whose ceiling replicates the underside of the viaduct.

Whitney Museum of American Art at Philip Morris

120 Park Ave, New York, NY 10017. ☎ (212) 663-2453. Web site: www.whitney.org. Open: gallery, Mon–Fri 11–6, Thurs until 7:30 P.M.; sculpture court, Mon–Sat 7:30 A.M.–9:30 P.M.; Sun and holidays 11–7. Free. Changing exhibitions, midday gallery talks, brochures. Coffee bar. Accessible to wheelchairs from 42nd St.

Subway: Lexington Ave Express or Local (4, 5, 6) to 42nd St–Grand Central. Flushing Local (7) to 42nd St–Grand Central. Bus: M1, M2, M3, M4, M5, M42, M98, M101, M102, M103, M104, Q32.

On the southwest corner of Park Ave and E. 42nd St (120 Park Ave) is the **Philip Morris Building** (1983; Ulrich Franzen & Assocs.), remarkable architecturally for having different facades on its different sides, the more elaborate of which faces Park Ave. In the lobby is the Whitney Museum of American Art at Philip Morris.

Exhibitions in the 900-square-ft gallery are mostly solo shows by living artists. Each year one or two exhibitions, usually of large-scale sculpture, are presented in the 5,200-square-ft sculpture court, a glass-enclosed atrium with public seating.

Further west, at 60 E. 42nd St (between Madison and Park Aves), is the **Lincoln Building** (1939; J. E. R. Carpenter), a 53-story skyscraper with a striking series of setbacks. The lobby's centerpiece is a bronze version of Daniel Chester French's seated Lincoln in the Lincoln Memorial in Washington, D.C., created by French from his original model.

Grand Central Terminal, Park Avenue, and Vicinity

Subway: Lexington Ave Express or Local (4, 5, 6), Flushing Local (7), or the Crosstown Shuttle from Times Square (S) to 42nd St–Grand Central Terminal.

Bus: M1, M2, M3, M4, M5, M42, M98, M101, M102, M103, M104, Q32.

Metro-North: Railroad from the Bronx, Westchester, Putnam, and Dutchess Counties and Connecticut stop at Grand Central Terminal. For information, ☎ (212) 532-4900 (in New York City) or (800) METRO-INFO (from elsewhere).

Grand Central Terminal

Begin at 42nd St and Park Ave. Though rail travel has declined in scope and grandeur since it was built, Grand Central Terminal (1903–13; Reed & Stem and Warren & Wetmore; DL) remains one of the world's great railroad stations and an enduring symbol of the city. It is a marvel of engineering and urban planning, bringing the railroad into the heart of the city while enhancing the surrounding neighborhood. It is also a major crossroads: more than 500,000 people pass daily through its marble corridors.

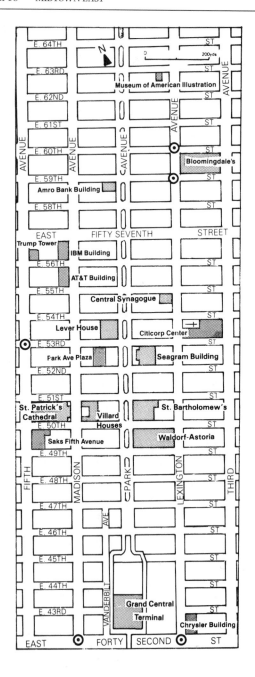

History

By 1869 Cornelius Vanderbilt, known as the Commodore because of his beginnings as a ferryboat entrepreneur, had seized control of all the railroads into New York by a series of bold financial maneuvers. He determined to consolidate the lines physically by erecting at Fourth Ave and 42nd St a Grand Central Depot, ambitiously named, since in 1869 42nd St was in the hinterlands. He then acquired sufficient land along Fourth Ave for storage and marshaling yards, land that constitutes practically all of the present Grand Central complex. A "head house," whose trains either backed in or backed out, designed by John B. Snook, rose between 1869 and 1871. Never really adequate, the station and its sheds and yards were enlarged and rearranged. An 1898 remodeling created a waiting room for immigrants in the basement so other passengers would not have to mix with them.

When the city demanded that the railroad electrify its lines or move the terminal to the outskirts, William J. Wilgus, brilliant chief engineer, submerged the tracks, introducing the two present levels of trackage and electrifying the lines as far as Mott Haven in the Bronx. He also suggested a new terminal that would use the air rights over the tracks (Madison–Lexington Aves, 42nd–50th Sts) for new, revenue-producing office and apartment buildings. A competition for the design of the station produced the innovative plan by architects Reed and Stem (Reed was Wilgus's brother-in-law) that wrapped Park Ave around the station on viaducts. Later the firm of Warren & Wetmore (Warren was a cousin of William K. Vanderbilt, then chairman of the board of the New York Central Railroad) was brought into the project. Warren & Wetmore won the power struggle between the two firms, but the basic design premises, including the elevated driveway around the station and the placement of piers for future office buildings along Park Ave, came from Reed & Stem.

At one time Grand Central was the terminus for two major railroads, the New York Central, which reached to the Mississippi River, and the New York, New Haven, and Hartford, which served New England. Today it is a commuter station.

The station covers three city blocks—E. 42nd–E. 45th Sts between Vanderbilt and Madison Aves—and beneath it are luggage tunnels, electric power facilities, steam, water, sewage, and electric mains, and loops of track where trains can turn around without backing out of the station.

It is not surprising that many assaults have been made on the architectural integrity of the terminal, sitting as it does on a prime Midtown site. A plan (1960) to slice the Main Waiting Room horizontally into four 15 ft stories (the upper three to contain bowling alleys) hastened designation of the terminal as a landmark in 1965. Thereafter the Penn Central Railroad, then operating the terminal and recognizing the value of surrounding real estate, proposed a 54-story tower over the Waiting Room, a design rejected by the Landmarks Commission. After several other plans to circumvent the designation failed, the railroad sued to have the landmark status withdrawn on the grounds of economic hardship, but in 1978 the Supreme Court upheld the city's right to protect architecturally or historically valuable buildings by this means.

In the late 1990s, the Metropolitan Transit Authority spent $200 million and four years restoring (architects, Beyer Blinder Belle) Grand Central to its original grandeur while simultaneously modernizing it.

<hr>

Grand Central Terminal Tours
Every Wed at 12:30 the Municipal Arts Society offers a free tour of the building; meet outside the information booth on the Grand Concourse. ☎ (212) 935-3960. Every Fri at 12:30, the Grand Central Partnership leads a free tour of the neighborhood, including Grand Central. Meet on 42nd St in front of the Whitney Museum at Philip Morris. ☎ (212) 883-2420.

<hr>

Exterior

The best view of the terminal is from Park Ave to the south. Whitney Warren, primarily responsible for the south facade, designed three great arched windows framed by pairs of columns to recall the triumphal arches of antiquity. Jules Felix Coutan created the 48 ft sculpture *Transportation* (1914) that crowns the facade. It depicts Mercury (Commerce) flanked by Hercules (Physical Energy) and Minerva (Intellectual Energy). Beneath the clock (13 ft in diameter) stands a heroic bronze statue of Cornelius Vanderbilt (1869; Albert De Groot), moved here from the former Hudson River freight station in 1929. Perched above a new entrance on Lexington Ave at 43rd St is a 3,000-pound cast-iron bald eagle, one of a dozen installed in 1898 but removed in 1910 when the present terminal was built.

Interior

Enter the terminal through the central doorway at Park Ave. Directly behind the Main Waiting Room is the **Main Concourse** (120 ft wide; 375 ft long), air-conditioned as part of the restoration. Sheathed in marble and simulated Caen stone, it rises to an elliptical vault (125 ft high) decorated with the constellations of the zodiac. Whitney Warren with Paul Helleu and Charles Basing designed the ceiling. (The constellations were mistakenly reversed north to south, because, some claim, Basing had held the blueprint in his hands below eye level rather than up against the ceiling.) Long darkened by grime, the ceiling is now restored to its cerulean color. (An unrestored patch has been left in the northwest corner to show the contrast.) Worked into the ornamentation throughout, even into the periphery of the heavens, are clusters of oak leaves, a Vanderbilt family emblem.

As part of the restoration, commercial intrusions like the former Kodak billboard on the east wall have been removed. The Tennessee quarry where the rose marble for the west staircase had been mined was reopened so that the new staircase on the Lexington Ave side would perfectly match the old one. (The eastern staircase was in the original plans but was never built.)

The restored station has attractive restaurants and shops, especially the new **Grand Central Market,** near the Lexington Ave/43rd St entrance. Here independent vendors offer delectable fresh fish, cheeses, spices, hams, breads, and pastries. In the market area is *Sirshasana* (1999; Donald Lipski), a work featuring 5,000 crystals suspended from a sculpted olive tree.

The renovation opened up the formerly dark and forbidding ramps down from the Main Concourse, creating a dramatic entry to the lower level. The **Lower Concourse** now has a food court as well as the famous **Oyster Bar** (accessible from the Grand Staircase at the west end of the concourse). This classic restaurant is architecturally interesting for its Guastavino tile ceiling (see Ellis Island Registry

Room in Walk 1) and gastronomically appealing for its 25 varieties of oysters, of which some 10,000 are opened and served daily.

Just north of the terminal is the **Metropolitan Life Building,** formerly the **Pan Am Building** (1963; Emery Roth & Sons, Pietro Belluschi, and Walter Gropius), 200 Park Ave. It is big (59 stories, with more than 2 million square ft of rentable space on a 3.5-acre site) and intrusive (spoiling the former vista down Park Ave).

Once this neighborhood was the focal point of the New York Central Railroad's vast real estate empire. Handsome hotels rose around the terminal: the Waldorf-Astoria and the Commodore Hotel (now the Grand Hyatt Hotel; originally named after the railroad's founder) on E. 42nd St at Lexington Ave. The Yale Club (1915; James Gamble Rogers) still stands at 50 Vanderbilt Ave, welcoming students and alumni of the university that was attended by several Vanderbilt offspring.

New York Central Building

Just north of the Met Life building is the New York Central Building (1929; Warren & Wetmore; DL), 230 Park Ave (between E. 45th and E. 46th Sts), former headquarters for the railroad and a visible reminder of its power. You can see it best from Park Ave, further north.

Interior

The central lobby has travertine, jaspé Oriental marble, and bronze fittings. (Burgundy and gold were the Vanderbilt colors.)

Exterior

The north facade is pierced by two vehicular portals that carry traffic on ramps around the railroad terminal. In the center is a large clock flanked by classical figures (Edward McCarten). The lower section of the 34-story tower was designed to match Grand Central's facade.

Park Avenue and the Railroad

The fortunes of Park Ave north of the New York Central Building have depended on the railroad. Before 1900, when the trains ran above ground, the street attracted modest dwellings and factories. The avenue began its upward swing when the Fourth Avenue Improvement Scheme (completed 1872–74) submerged the tracks below street level as far north as 56th St, although the neighborhood remained humble until the tracks were completely decked over during the construction of Grand Central Terminal (1903–13). By the 1920s, all the air rights over the tracks had been acquired by apartments and hotels, and luxury dwellings began appearing as far as 96th St, where the tracks emerge from the tunnel. Land values soared, increasing over 200 percent between 1914 and 1930.

After World War II, the drop in passenger revenues led the railroad to reexamine its real estate empire and to take advantage of the enormous inflation along Park Ave. Starting in the 1950s, Park Ave began changing from a fine residential neighborhood to a desirable commercial area, gradually becoming a stronghold of corporate America.

The building at **250 Park Ave** (1925; Cross & Cross), originally the Postum Building, is one of only a handful of buildings remaining above 46th St from the period before World War II. On the northwest corner of the intersection at E. 47th St is *Taxi!* (1983; J. Seward Johnson Jr.), a lifelike sculpture of a businessman hailing a cab.

Waldorf-Astoria Hotel

The Waldorf-Astoria Hotel (1931; Schultze & Weaver), 301 Park Ave (between E. 49th and E. 50th Sts), is still one of the city's finest hotels. It rises to two chrome-capped, 625 ft spires, the Waldorf Towers, whose private apartments, reached from a separate entrance on E. 50th St, once attracted the duke of Windsor, President Herbert Hoover, and Gen. Douglas MacArthur.

History

The first Waldorf-Astoria (1894) stood on the site of the Empire State Building (see The First Waldorf-Astoria in Walk 16). The names of several of the public rooms recall those fabled days: the Empire Room, the Palm Garden (its poshest restaurant), and Peacock Alley, where society's grand dames once flaunted their plumage. Oscar's, today a coffee shop, commemorates the legendary maître d'hôtel, Oscar Tschirky, whose command of the subtle points of social distinction raised him to the position of social arbiter. When the present hotel opened, the Starlight Roof had a ceiling that could be rolled back on balmy nights, making the room worthy of its name.

Interior

Inside, the lobby is a half-flight up, since like other Park Ave buildings the hotel stands over the railroad yards and needs space above ground for mechanical equipment. The tracks, though irksome for the architects, were a convenience for former guests arriving in private rail coaches, who could be shunted onto a special siding, bypassing the terminal altogether. When the hotel opened during the Depression, President Hoover lauded it as an "exhibition of . . . confidence to the whole nation," and surely its exquisite Art Deco interiors with marble, bronze, and matched woods suggested that the management foresaw better times.

The **lobby** is paneled in dark wood with beige friezes of classical figures above the wood and a ceiling decorated with mythological figures. The centerpiece of the room is a 9 ft, two-ton clock made for the Chicago Columbian Exposition in 1893.

Villard Houses

Walk north and west to Madison Ave and the **New York Palace Hotel** (1980; Emery Roth & Sons), 451 Madison Ave (between E. 50th and E. 51st Sts). The public rooms of this luxury hotel occupy part of the extraordinary Villard Houses (1886; McKim, Mead & White; DL), a U-shaped group of six sumptuous neo-Renaissance dwellings built for the railroad baron Henry Villard.

History

Villard came to America from Bavaria in 1853 with no money and no command of English. After a stint writing for German newspapers, he earned a small fortune reorganizing the Oregon and California Railroad, which had failed in 1873. At the peak of his power in early 1883, Villard began construction on a group of trophy houses, but by Christmas, he had lost his fortune (perhaps $5 million) and the presidency of the Northern Pacific Railroad (which he later recovered). The unfinished houses were transferred to trustees to be completed and sold. Their buyers included Villard's lawyer Artemas Holmes and Whitelaw Reid (editor of the *New York Tribune*), who with his wife, Elizabeth, bought Villard's own house for $350,000 in 1886 with wedding money from her father, the millionaire Darius Ogden Mills. The Reids hired Stanford White to do their interiors: White hired sculptors Augustus and Louis Saint-Gaudens, and painters John La Farge, Francis Lathrop, and Edwin Austin Abbey to make it a showplace.

After World War II, the publishing firm Random House, Capital Cities Communications, and the Archdiocese of New York all used the buildings as offices, fortunately leaving the interiors more or less intact. Thereafter exhaustive negotiations led to their conversion to a hotel, with the stipulation that the most important interiors be preserved. The current hotel is owned by the royal family of Brunei.

Exterior

Finished in warm Belleville (New Jersey) brownstone, the facade is modeled after the Roman Palazzo Cancelleria (1489–96), and was designed by Joseph Morrill Wells, first assistant in the office of McKim, Mead & White. Once when White boasted that one of his own drawings was as good "in its way . . . as the Parthenon," Wells, eating breakfast, replied, "Yes, and so too, in its way, is a boiled egg."

The courtyard in the center of the complex was once a carriage turnaround. On the left is the **Urban Center,** a group of organizations dedicated to historic preservation, architecture, and urban planning: among them are the Municipal Art Society, the Parks Council, and the Architectural League. Visitors may enjoy the reception rooms as they attend lectures, seminars, and exhibitions or browse in the superbly stocked Urban Bookstore, which specializes in architectural books.

On the right, in Villard's former home, is the famous **Le Cirque 2000** restaurant.

Interior

In the Grand Lobby of the hotel is a red fireplace mantel with marble figures above it representing Joy, Hospitality, and Moderation, designed by Augustus Saint-Gaudens, who, with Stanford White, also designed the zodiac clock near the top of the stairs.

Inside Le Cirque are rooms with some of the original details: a barrel-vaulted ceiling (30 ft high) gilded according to instructions by Stanford White, murals (completed 1888) by John La Farge representing Music and Drama, plaster casts of Luca della Robbia's marble *Cantoria* (1431–48) in Florence, and a ceiling supported by Corinthian columns, with gilt-bronze capitals.

St. Bartholomew's Church

Return to Park Ave. St. Bartholomew's Church (Protestant Episcopal) between E. 50th and E. 51st Sts (1919; Bertram G. Goodhue; DL) is one of the oldest buildings along the avenue. The congregation bought the site for $1.5 million in 1914 from the F. & M. Schaefer Brewing Co., which had been making beer by the railroad tracks since 1860.

Exterior

The ornate carved portico comes from the previous St. Bartholomew's Church (1902) on Madison Ave, designed by Stanford White, who styled it after a Romanesque church at St. Gilles in southern France and hired Daniel Chester French and Philip Martiny to execute the figures. The tympanum over the center doors contains a representation of the coronation of Christ.

Interior

The mosaics by Hildreth Meiere on the ceiling of the narthex tell the story of the Creation. The narthex opens into the three aisles of the nave, built facing east in the traditional cruciform shape with a barrel-vaulted ceiling. The structural elements are stone and marble veneered over concrete, and much of the wall surface has been covered with rough-textured Guastavino acoustic tiles. The west window is made of stained glass given as memorials for the earlier Madison Ave church. Along the north aisle (toward 51st St) are six stained glass windows by John Gordon Guthrie illustrating the Te Deum. Dominating the interior is a mosaic of glass and gold leaf (also by Hildreth Meiere) filling the ceiling of the apse. It represents the Transfiguration, with Christ in the center flanked by Elijah and Moses standing on the mountain and the disciples Peter (north side), James, and John (south side). The five tall windows in the apse below are filled with thin sheets of amber onyx and covered with grilles of the same material.

On the south side of the church is the **Community House** (1927; Bertram G. Goodhue Assocs. and Mayers, Murray & Philip; DL) added by Goodhue's successor firm after his death. The garden (1971) along with the Community House converts the church into an L-shaped complex whose pleasing proportions and open space provide a moment of grace along an avenue that is becoming increasingly an unrelieved wall of skyscrapers.

Providing a dramatic background to the church is the reddish orange brick and terra-cotta of the **General Electric Building** (1931; Cross & Cross; DL) at 570 Lexington Ave (southwest corner of the intersection at E. 51st St). Its spiked Art Deco crown suggests the fantasies of science fiction, as appropriate to the present tenant as to the original one, the RCA Victor Company. The lobby, with terrazzo floors, pale purple marble panels, aluminum light sconces, and silvery barrel-vaulted ceiling openings, is as coolly elegant as anything in the city. A corner clock at ground level on E. 51st St has projecting arms that grasp electric bolts. The building was donated to Columbia University in 1995.

Return to Park Ave along E. 51st St. On the south side of 51st St is a 12 × 20 ft bronze sculpture *Dinoceras* (1971; Robert Cook), suggestive of a struggling animal and named after a horned mammal of the Eocene period.

Seagram Building

On Park Ave (between E. 52nd and E. 53rd Sts) stands the Seagram Building (1958; Ludwig Mies van der Rohe and Philip Johnson; Kahn & Jacobs; DL), an elegant metal-and-glass curtain-wall building that occupies only 52 percent of its site. It rises on square columns to a height of about 500 ft (150 ft wide × 90 ft thick). All the materials—from the wall of custom-made amber glass and bronze, to the green Italian marble seating around the fountains, to the brushed aluminum and stainless steel hardware—were chosen for their quality. The building's excellence stems largely from the interest of Phyllis Lambert, daughter of the Seagram board chairman Samuel Bronfman, who persuaded her father to erect a monumental, not just serviceable, building, and who chose Mies van der Rohe as architect. (It is his only New York building.) The 38-story tower is thought to be the finest international style skyscraper in the last half century and is one of the most recently built of all landmark buildings.

Four Seasons Restaurant

Inside is the Four Seasons restaurant (1959; Philip Johnson & Assocs.), one of only three restaurants in the city to become interior landmarks. (Brooklyn's Gage & Tollner and the Oyster Bar are the other two, although the latter is landmarked as part of Grand Central Terminal.) Its decor—created at a cost of $4.5 million— caused an initial stir that has since subsided into enduring admiration. In the grill room is a sculpture of gold-dipped brass rods by Richard Lippold; a stage backdrop for *Le Tricorne* (1929) by Picasso occupies the corridor between the two dining rooms, each with ceilings 20 ft high.

Across the street from the Seagram Building, at 370 Park Ave (between E. 52nd and E. 53rd Sts), is the **Racquet and Tennis Club** (1918; McKim, Mead & White; DL), designed after White and McKim were dead and Mead had retired. Beneath the cornice of this brick-and-limestone club is a terra-cotta frieze with crossed racquets and netting.

The Racquet and Tennis Club now squats in front of a 575 ft office tower clad in aquamarine-tinted glass, the beneficiary of the club's air rights. In a complicated legal maneuver the developer, Fisher Bros., got permission to build the tower, called **Park Avenue Plaza** (1981; Skidmore, Owings & Merrill), with as much space as would be permitted on the site of the office building plus the site of the racquet club, thus "shoehorning" a big building onto a small site. In June 1981 the City Planning Commission proposed a new zoning law to discourage midblock "shoehorning" on the overbuilt East Side.

Lever House (1952; Skidmore, Owings & Merrill; DL), at 390 Park Ave (between E. 53rd and E. 54th Sts), was the first commercial structure in what was then a residential neighborhood, and the first steel-and-glass building in a file of stolid masonry apartment houses. The building takes its form from two slabs, one stretched out horizontally along the street, the other rising vertically. On the ground floor is an open interior courtyard. Lever House, once considered the ultimate corporate headquarters, is impressive today partly because it is smaller than it legally had to be, an act of restraint that later elicited proposals from developers to tear it down and build something bigger.

Walk east to Lexington Ave. Here, filling the block between E. 53rd and E. 54th Sts, is the mixed-use **Citicorp Center** (1978; Hugh Stubbins & Assocs.), a Midtown office tower as representative of 1970s architectural values as Lever House and the Seagram Building were of the values of the 1950s. The tower, sheathed in gleaming white aluminum, rises 915 ft from the street, resting on four 127 ft columns, which support it at the midpoints of the sides, not at the corners. The top of the building slants at a 45-degree angle; the large plane surface facing south, originally intended as a solar collector, is now conspicuous on the skyline among the domes, crowns, and spires of yesteryear and the flat tops of the previous generation. Inside is a skylit atrium with shops and restaurants.

On the northwest corner of the block is **St. Peter's Church** (Lutheran), founded in 1861, which has existed on this site since 1904. The church allowed Citicorp to buy its old building with the understanding that the corporation would erect a new one (1977; Hugh Stubbins & Assocs.). Inside are the sanctuary, which is acoustically isolated from the street and subway, a small theater, and the beautiful Erol Beker **Chapel of the Good Shepherd** (open for meditation during the day), enhanced by Louise Nevelson's wall sculptures: on the north wall, *Cross of the Good Shepherd* and *Trinity;* east wall, *Frieze of the Apostles;* west wall, *Sky Vestment—Trinity;* south wall, *Grapes & Wheat Lintel;* southwest wall, *Cross of the Resurrection.*

A block east and a little south, across Third Ave between E. 53rd and E. 54th Sts at 885 Third Ave, is the **"Lipstick Building"** (1986; John Burgee with Philip Johnson), an elliptical building on a rectangular site.

Central Synagogue

A block north on Lexington Ave is the Central Synagogue (1872; Henry Fernback; DL), 652 Lexington Ave (southwest corner of the intersection at E. 55th St). It is the oldest synagogue in continual use in the state and was designed by the first Jew to practice architecture in New York, Henry Fernback, known chiefly for his cast-iron work in SoHo. While Judaism has never had an architectural heritage similar to the Gothic tradition in Christianity, the Moorish style with its allusions to Judaic roots in the Middle East became the dominant style of synagogue architecture in the mid-19C, and the Central Synagogue is generally considered the finest example of Moorish revival architecture in the city. The onion-shaped green copper domes rise to 122 ft. The interior is colorfully stenciled in red, blue, and ocher.

History

The congregation was founded as Ahawath Chesed (Love of Mercy) on Ludlow St by 18 men, most of them immigrants from Bohemia. The congregation moved northward in several stages, acquiring the present site in 1870. A 1999 five-alarm fire started by a worker's blowtorch badly damaged the synagogue; Rabbi Peter Rubenstein raced into the blaze to rescue two antique Torahs. The temple reopened in 2001.

Walk west along E. 55th St, a block filled with row houses, many dating from the 1870s, some remodeled in the early 20C. Among the wonderful survivors are nos. 113–119 and 116–124 E. 55th St. The best, **116 E. 55th St,** has a gated entry and two black eagles on pillars flanking the doorway.

On the next block are the shiny and slick obelisklike **Park Avenue Tower** (1987; Murphy/Jahn) at 65 E. 55th St, with metal moldings and a decorative pyramid top (lit at night), and the neoclassical-inspired gray granite **Heron Tower** (1987; Kohn Pedersen Fox) at 70 E. 55th St, with nickel-plated grillwork and setbacks that minimize its bulk.

At 57 E. 55th St is the **Friars Club,** famous for its annual "roasts." It began in 1904 as a club for press agents and morphed into a club for entertainers (including composers and lyricists). Early members included Irving Berlin (who wrote "Alexander's Ragtime Band" for the first Friars Frolic in 1911), George M. Cohan (who wrote "Over There" at the clubhouse), Enrico Caruso, Oscar Hammerstein, and Will Rogers. Later members included Ed Sullivan, Frank Sinatra, Joe E. Lewis, Milton Berle, and Henny Youngman. The first female Friar, Liza Minelli, was allowed to join in 1988. The club is now trying to attract younger members, such as Jon Stewart and Drew Carey.

Sony Building

Continue west to Madison Ave. Occupying the block between E. 55th and E. 56th Sts is the 648 ft Sony Tower, originally built for AT&T (1984; Philip Johnson & John Burgee; altered 1994; Gwathmey Siegel & Assocs.). The building, which raised eyebrows when its design was announced in 1979, stands on a 131 ft masonry base of rose-gray granite and rises to a huge broken pediment, which prompted remarks about a "Chippendale" skyscraper. Eventually the building elicited critical praise for its monumental proportions, its beautiful materials, and its fine public spaces, including an atrium and covered colonnade. Now it is recognized as a trendsetter, rejecting the glass and steel of modernism in favor of the masonry and historical detail suggested by postmodern theory.

Sonywonder Technology Lab

550 Madison Ave, New York, NY 10022. ☎ (212) 833-8100. Web site: www.sonywondertechlab.com. Open Tues–Sat 10–6; Thurs until 8; Sun noon–6. Closed Mon, holidays. Reservations taken on Mon, Wed, and Fri 11–4; ☎ (212) 833-5414. Free. Exhibits, workshops, movies. Accessible to wheelchairs; services for hearing-impaired visitors; ☎ TTY (212) 833-6532 or voice (212) 833-8100.

Subway: Lexington Ave Express or Local (4, 5, 6) to 59th St. Eighth Ave Local (E) or Sixth Ave Local (F) to Fifth Ave–53rd St. Broadway Local (N, R) to Fifth Ave–60th St. Bus: M1, M2, M3, M4, M5, M57.

Located within the building is the Sonywonder Technology Lab, three floors of interactive exhibits on communications technology, not surprisingly promoting Sony products. The exhibits, many of them interactive and entertaining, include robotics, high-definition TV, and the Internet. The museum is popular with children and often very crowded.

IBM Building

At the corner of E. 56th St and Madison Ave is a sculptural fountain, *Levitated Mass* (1982; Michael Heizer), under which sluices a torrent of water. More conservative than the Sony Building, the 405 ft IBM Building (1983; Edward Larrabee Barnes, Assocs.), a block-long tower at 590 Madison Ave (between E. 56th and E. 57th Sts), is distinguished by its shape (a five-sided prism), its color (a dark gray-green), and its public spaces (an enormous, glass-enclosed garden atrium covered with a saw-toothed glass roof and an exhibition gallery). The 68 ft atrium, with its tall stands of bamboo, sculptures, seating, and kiosk for snacks (closed weekends), is a favorite Midtown rest stop.

On the lower level (reached from the 56th St entrance), the **First Amendment Center,** offers lectures and exhibitions. The center is sponsored by the nonpartisan Freedom Forum, a foundation concerned with issues of free speech and freedom of the press. For information, ☎ (212) 317-7596 or check the Web site at www.freedomforum.org.

On the corner of E. 57th St and Madison Ave is the bright orange *Saurien* by Alexander Calder (1975). At 45 E. 57th St (northeast corner of Madison Ave) is the **Fuller Building** (1929; Walker & Gillette; DL), a slender 40-story Art Deco building with white limestone set against black marble and terra-cotta. The clock and sculptural figures above the main doorway—laborers working in front of a futuristic cityscape—are by Elie Nadelman.

At E. 57th St and Park Ave (northeast corner) is the **Ritz Tower** (1925; Emery Roth and Carrère & Hastings), a vintage Park Ave masonry apartment building with all the trappings of its period—an elaborate top, swags, urns, cartouches, and balustrades marking the major setbacks.

Walk north to E. 59th St. At 500 Park Ave is the Amro Bank Building, originally the **Pepsico Building** (1960; Skidmore, Owings & Merrill; DL). This elegant aluminum-and-glass box was built for the Pepsi Cola Co., which fled to the suburbs around 1970. Its successor, the Olivetti Corporation, left in 1978, and the building was saved from demolition by selling its air rights to 500 Park Tower (1984; James Stewart Polshek), which is now "shoehorned" above it.

19 · United Nations, Turtle Bay, Beekman Hill, Sutton Place, and Roosevelt Island

Subway: Lexington Ave Express or Local (4, 5, 6) or Flushing Local (7) to 42nd St–Grand Central.
Bus: M15, M27, M42, M50, M104.

Turtle Bay

The neighborhood now dominated by the United Nations is known as Turtle Bay, after a cove in the East River that reached from about 45th to 48th Sts. Turtle Bay is one of the city's more genteel residential neighborhoods, its gracious brownstones and luxury high-rises attract diplomats, the affluent young, and a few celebrities.

History

The bay, filled in since 1868, got its name either from turtles in its waters or as a corruption of the Dutch word *deutal* (a bent blade), referring to its shape. The land of Deutal Bay Farm was granted in 1639 by Dutch Governor William Kieft to two Englishmen, George Holmes and Thomas Hall. In 1775, the Sons of Liberty, a group of belligerent, radical, mostly working-class patriots, sailed a sloop from Greenwich, Connecticut, through Hell Gate to Turtle Bay. They seized a military storehouse from its British guards and took its supplies back to Boston. Marinus Willett, after whom Willett St on the Lower East Side was named, led the foray. Later, Nathan Hale was captured near the former Dove Tavern (Third Ave at 66th St) and hanged as a spy and traitor to the king.

In the mid-19C, when Turtle Bay was still a rural suburb, publisher Horace Greeley brought his wife here to ease her grief at the death of several of her children. Margaret Fuller, writer and reformer, spent some years here, occasionally

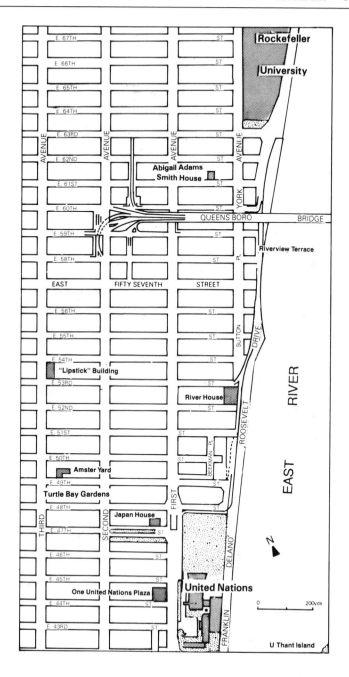

rowing across the river with a friend to visit the prison on Blackwell's (now Roosevelt) Island.

At Third Ave and 47th St, an enrollment office for the draft into the Union Army during the Civil War became the starting point of the **Draft Riots of 1863,** a three-day binge of rioting, looting, and burning. The riots began as a protest against a policy that allowed the affluent to buy their way out of the army for $300. The protesters, mostly Irish Catholics, first attacked members of the largely Protestant upper class, but within a day the rioters turned on blacks, also largely Protestant, who the rioters believed would flood the North and take Irish jobs if slavery ended. The protest became a race riot in which 18 blacks were lynched, the Colored Orphan Asylum on Fifth Ave was burned, more than 100 people (mostly blacks) were killed, and many were beaten and injured. Only when the military marched into the city was peace restored.

In the later 19C, modest brownstones replaced the country homes. The neighborhood to the north around the farm owned by James Beekman remained pleasant because of Beekman's careful development, but elsewhere the area deteriorated into slums, and the shores of Turtle Bay became a garbage dump. When the Third Ave elevated railway opened in 1878, followed by the Second Avenue El in 1880, the far East Side saw its brownstones converted to rooming houses or razed for tenements. In addition to immigrants who worked in local slaughterhouses, the area attracted the city's night people: actors, musicians, stagehands, and waiters who worked in the restaurants near Broadway.

The resurgence of Turtle Bay began around the end of World War I with the development of Turtle Bay Gardens, the renovation of individual brownstones, and the greening of Sutton Place and Beekman Hill, which began to attract literary and theatrical people such as Alfred Lunt and Lynn Fontanne, the Barrymores, Henry Luce, Irving Berlin, Billy Rose, and Humphrey Bogart. But only after the coming of the United Nations in 1947 were the cattle pens, slaughterhouses, breweries, and coal yards that had followed the opening of the Els dislodged from the shoreline.

Begin at 220 E. 42nd St (between Third and Second Aves) with the **News Building** (1930; Howells & Hood; DL), formerly the Daily News Building, an Art Deco skyscraper by Raymond Hood, considered the quintessential architect of the Age of Commerce. White vertical strips of brick alternate with dark strips of windows broken up by red-and-black brick spandrels. The water tower and other machinery atop the roof are concealed within a vertical extension of the building—a radical notion at a time when such fripperies as temples usually served as camouflage. Decorative brickwork and a bas-relief around the entrance form the only ornaments on this severe, cubistic building, which appeared in the Christopher Reeve *Superman* movies as the home of the mythical *Daily Planet.* Inside the lobby are meteorological displays, including a two-ton revolving globe that is 12 ft in diameter. The *Daily News* moved to 450 W. 33rd St in 1995.

Across the street, at 235 E. 42nd St, is the world headquarters of Pfizer, Inc., the pharmaceutical company. In the lobby is the *Pfizer Mural* (1961; Mikos Bel-Jon), a massive piece of burnished aluminum on thousands of handcut metal tesserae illuminated by colored lights. The mural explores the development of medical science and includes pictures of Emperor Shen-Nung, who discovered drugs and poisons in China in 2700 B.C.; Hippocrates; Rhazes, a 9C–10C Persian who was a pioneer in treating medicine as a science; William Harvey, who discovered the circulation of the blood, the bacteriologist Walter Reed; Alexander Fleming, who discovered penicillin; and Louis Pasteur. Overhead is British artist Brian Clarke's stained glass mosaic ceiling piece (1997), whose motifs include X-ray and microscopic images of joints, blood vessels, and viruses.

Continue east on 42nd St. Midway between Second and First Aves on the north side of E. 42nd St (main entrance, 320 E. 43rd St) is the **Ford Foundation Building** (1967; Roche, Dinkeloo & Assocs; DL.), justly admired for its beautiful interior garden, a quiet lush landscape filled with plants, trees, and a small pond. Surrounding the garden is the cube-shaped building, with piers of pinkish gray granite, a facade of weathering Cor-Ten steel, and large expanses of glass, all suitably elegant for a foundation that disburses millions of dollars to the arts, the humanities, and science. It was one of the few modern buildings in the city to become landmarked almost immediately after becoming eligible, 30 years after it was built.

Most of this immediate area is dominated by **Tudor City** (E. 40th–E. 43rd Sts between First and Second Aves), an ambitious and successful private effort at urban renewal (1928; Fred F. French Co. and H. Douglas Ives; DL). It included the Tudor Hotel (600 rooms, now the Crowne Plaza) and apartments (2,800 of them) rising on abutments over First Ave, all designed to create the feel of a suburb from which people could walk to work in the city. Developer Fred French bought more than 100 crumbling brownstones and tenements and erected 12 high-rise buildings in the American Tudor style popular in the 1920s—brick with an occasional stained glass window, Gothic doorway, and decorative lion or unicorn. Because the United Nations site was once occupied by slaughterhouses and breweries, the buildings face inward, with only occasional windows looking toward what is nowadays a splendid river view. The once-illuminated, now rusting, Tudor City sign remains on the first rental unit, Prospect Towers.

Continue east to First Ave. The East Side from about 27th to 40th Sts and Second Ave to the East River, is known as **Kips Bay.**

Kips Bay History

In 1655 Jacobus Kip owned a farm around Second Ave and E. 35th St reaching to the East River, which at the time curved inward, forming a bay. Kips Bay became a beachhead for invading British troops during the Revolutionary War, but thereafter remained pastoral until the mid-19C, when its country estates, subdivided around the time of the Civil War, gave way to rows of brownstone houses. The arrival of the Second and Third Avenue Els hastened its decline, bringing about a period of residential and industrial squalor from which it recovered only after the demolition of the Els. The bay itself has long since disappeared under tons of fill.

Turn left at First Ave and walk north to E. 43rd St. On the west side of the street is **Ralph J. Bunche Park,** named for the African American statesman (1904–1971) who received the Nobel Peace Prize in 1950 for his work as United Nations mediator in Palestine. The park's centerpiece is a steel sculpture, *Peace*

Form One (1972–80) by Daniel Larue Johnston; near it is inscribed a quotation from Bunche's acceptance of the prize.

United Nations (UN) Headquarters

First Ave at E. 46th St, New York, NY 10017. ☎ (212) 963-8687. Buildings open weekdays 9–5; Sat, Sun, and holidays 9:15–5. Visitors must pass through electronic metal detectors. Admission charge.

Tours in English and other languages leave from the Tour Desk in the General Assembly Building 9:30–4:45 daily (opening hour subject to change). Children under 12 must be accompanied by an adult; no children under 5 allowed. No guided tours on weekends in Jan, Feb. For tour information, ☎ (212) 963-8687 or check the Web site: www.un.org/tours. Delegates' dining room on second floor of the General Assembly Building open to the public 11:30–2:30; inquire at the Information Desk for a pass; reservations suggested; ☎ (212) 963-7625. Coffee shop (open 9–4:30). Gift shop. Accessible to wheelchairs.

The 18 acres of United Nations Headquarters at **United Nations Plaza** (First Ave between E. 42nd and E. 48th Sts) are not part of New York City, not even part of the United States; they are international territory belonging to the member nations of the United Nations.

History

Soon after the signing of the United Nations Charter (1945), the General Assembly voted to locate the UN's permanent headquarters in the United States. On December 11, 1946, John D. Rockefeller Jr. offered $8.5 million to buy a large parcel of land on the East River assembled by William Zeckendorf, a real estate operator who had obtained an option to buy it for private development. With unusual rapidity Congress accepted the gift and exempted it from the usual taxes, while the city agreed to contribute adjacent properties. A plan by Zeckendorf to condemn everything east of Third Ave between E. 46th and E. 49th Sts, including Turtle Bay Gardens and other areas just emerging from urban decay, was discarded in favor of a scheme sponsored by Robert Moses to widen 47th St between First and Second Aves and to tunnel First Ave beneath United Nations Plaza. The buildings were designed by an international committee of architects headed by Wallace K. Harrison, whose ties with the Rockefeller family went back to the building of Rockefeller Center. The UN is currently considering a $1-billion renovation and expansion plan.

Exterior

Across the avenue stand the UN buildings prefaced by a row of flags representing the member nations, arranged in alphabetical order in English from Afghanistan at 48th St to Zimbabwe at 42nd St. The number of member nations, and flags, has grown over the years from 51 to 189. The UN includes four buildings: the General Assembly Building, with a curving roof from which protrudes the dome covering the assembly hall; the Secretariat Building; the Dag Hammarskjöld Library; and the Conference Building, behind the General Assembly Building and not visible from First Ave.

In a circular pool in front of the Secretariat Building is a 21 ft high bronze sculptural abstraction, *Single Form* (1964) by Barbara Hepworth, placed there to honor Dag Hammarskjöld, the former secretary-general of the UN who was killed (1961) in a plane crash on a peace mission in the Congo.

Adjacent to the entrance to the Secretariat Building is a bronze *Reclining Figure* (1980) by Henry Moore, another memorial to Hammarskjöld, who had expressed hope to the sculptor that one of his works would someday join the UN collection.

Secretariat Building

When built, the Secretariat Building seemed a daring piece of architecture, a 544 ft slab (287 ft wide and only 72 ft thick) with white marble and walls and side walls of green glass set in an aluminum grid. Its long east-west exposure created air-conditioning problems that led critic Henry Russell-Hitchcock to predict, erroneously, the demise of glass-walled skyscrapers unless their western facades were shielded from the sun. Le Corbusier established the original design of the complex: a tall slab with offices for the bureaucracy, a low horizontal building for conferences, and a functionally shaped though imposing assembly building, all to be set on a landscaped site. When Le Corbusier withdrew, Wallace K. Harrison became responsible for implementing the details of the project.

General Assembly Building

The **Visitors' Entrance** is on the north side of the General Assembly Building. Near E. 46th St is the globe-shaped *Sphere within a Sphere* (1993; Arnaldo Pomodoro); to the right of the entrance is *Non-Violence*, a large sculptural pistol with its barrel tied in a knot (1988; Carl Fredrik Reutersward).

Interior

In the lobby of the General Assembly Building is a colorful tapestry of a jungle scene, *Mola Kuna*, executed by 50 Panamanian craftswomen. On the next wall is *Hope* (1994; Edite Pauls Vignere), a tapestry depicting a woman in white. At the left, or east end of the lobby, is a mural, *Brotherhood* (1968; Rufino Tamayo), a gift from Mexico. In front of it is a bronze cast of the famous 5C B.C. *Poseidon*, a gift (1952) from Greece (the original is in the National Museum of Athens). Hanging over the curve in the stairway is a **Foucault pendulum**, named after the French physicist Jean Bernard Léon Foucault, a gift (1955) from the Netherlands. A gold-plated sphere on 75 ft of stainless steel wire swings back and forth uniformly (thanks to an electromagnet underneath to counteract the friction of the air) as the earth rotates beneath it. It takes the sphere 36 hours and 45 minutes to complete its cycle. Nearby hangs a **replica of *Sputnik*,** the Soviet spaceship whose 1957 launching intensified the space race.

Near the lobby stairway arch is a case containing a gift of the U.S., a **moon rock,** collected in 1969 on the *Apollo 11* mission, man's first landing on the moon. Against the west wall is a 15 × 12 ft stained glass memorial window on themes of peace and human happiness designed by Marc Chagall. The **Meditation Room** (you may have to ask the guard for admission) has an abstract fresco by Swedish artist Bo Beskow.

On the left of the lobby is a **gallery** for changing exhibits, which can range from photographs of the earth taken from outer space to children's artwork from all over the world. Also on display are *Inukshuk*, a sculpture (donated 1989) derived from an Inuit path marker, given to help "discover paths to a peaceful future" and a *Dove of Peace* mosaic given in 1979 by Pope John Paul II.

UN Tours

You can see the meeting halls and nonpublic areas of the UN only on guided tours. Artwork on view includes a mosiac (1988) of Norman Rockwell's *Golden Rule* and an astonishingly detailed Chinese ivory sculpture (1974), the *Chengtu–Kunming Railway.*

UN Environs

The United Nations has one of the most impressive public **outdoor sculpture** displays in the city. On the paved **Visitors' Plaza** is a stainless steel sculpture by Eila Hiltunen (1983), a monument celebrating the composer Jean Sibelius, the gift of Finland.

Walk down the stairs past the flagpole; on the lawn to the left of the path near the river is Evgeny Vuchetich's bronze statue, *We Shall Beat Our Swords into Plowshares* (1958), a gift of the former USSR. The rose garden runs between the river promenade and the east wall of the General Assembly Building, on which there is an abstract relief sculpture (1961) by Ezio Martinelli.

From the promenade are good views of the East River, including the decaying Small Pox Hospital on the southern tip of Roosevelt Island, the Queensboro Bridge to the north, and the Williamsburg Bridge to the south. South of Roosevelt Island is a small island with a tree, a navigational marker, some shrubbery, and a metal peace arch; it is **U Thant Island,** named after the third secretary-general of the UN. It was formerly Belmont Island, named after August Belmont, a power behind the original IRT subway line. The island is man-made, built up of material excavated from the tunnel that now carries the Flushing Local (7) beneath the river. To the east is the industrial architecture of Queens.

Walk north along the promenade. The stainless steel sculpture on the north part of the lawn, *Roots and Ties for Peace* (1983) by Yolanda d'Augsburg Ulm, was presented by Brazil. To the west is *Solidarity among Sisters* (1996; Silvio Russo), a sculpture of a rising sun surrounded by people, presented by Arab women to the women of the world.

To the left is the 16 ft bronze equestrian *Monument to Peace* (1954; Antun Augustincic), given by Yugoslavia. Across the way is *Good Defeats Evil* (1990; Zurab Tsereteli), a 40 ft high sculpture in which St. George vanquishes a nuclear dragon made of actual Soviet and American ballistic missiles destroyed under a 1988 treaty. The work caused a stir because its Christian imagery seemed at odds with the usual notions of "godless" Communism, because artwork in the UN collection usually avoids religious imagery, and because the UN in the 1980s had declared a moratorium on art gifts to avoid clutter.

In the wooded area just north of the lawn are (east to west): a **memorial to Eleanor Roosevelt,** with a curved bench for quiet reflection; a bronze statue entitled *The Rising Man* (1975; Fritz Cremer), gift of the former German Democratic Republic; and a bronze bust of Francisco de Vitoria (1976; Francisco Toledo), a 16C Spanish Dominican theologian. In the northwest corner is a large bronze elephant (1998; Mihail) whose anatomy prompted protests and guffaws when it was unveiled. The gift from the governments of Kenya, Namibia, and Nepal was made from a cast of an actual African bull elephant, which had been tranquilized and captured for the sake of art. It is 11 ft high and weighs 7,000 pounds, but it was the creature's two-ft-long penis that prompted rumors of a UN-enforced reduction and ultimately resulted in carefully placed shrubbery to hide the potentially offensive organ.

On the northwest corner of the intersection at E. 44th St and First Ave is **One United Nations Plaza** (1976; Kevin Roche, John Dinkeloo & Assocs.), a 39-story, glass-walled tower with office space for the UN and a hotel. Because the UN Development Corporation has a charter forbidding the construction of any building taller than the Secretariat, this building stops at 505 ft. **Two United Nations Plaza** (1983; Kevin Roche, John Dinkeloo & Assocs.), a larger glass-and-metal tower, adjoins its predecessor to the west along 44th St, making an abstract formal composition that dominates the neighborhood skyline.

Three United Nations Plaza, the UNICEF Building (1987; Kevin Roche, John Dinkeloo & Assocs.), on the south side of E. 44th St completes the trio. Unlike the two earlier buildings, this one, only 18 stories high, slips unobtrusively into its surroundings. It is faced with light and dark granite that reflects the facade of the Beaux-Arts Apartments (1930; Murchison and Hood, Godley & Fouilhoux; DL) next door at 310 E. 44th St.

Just to the east, at 304 E. 44th St (1928; Dennison & Hirons), the **former Beaux-Arts Institute of Design**—with plaques on the facade depicting Rome, Athens, and Paris—is now the Permanent Mission of Egypt to the United Nations. The **United States Mission to the United Nations** (1961; Kelly & Gruzen and Kahn & Jacobs) faces UN Plaza on the southwest corner of 45th St (799 United Nations Plaza). Next door is **Uganda House** at 336 E. 45th St, built (1977) during the regime of Field Marshall Idi Amin. Its 14-story height was said at the time to be a deliberate attempt to overshadow the U.S. Mission to the east as an expression of Amin's outrage at American denunciations of his policies. The U.S. retaliated architecturally by installing a flagpole atop its mission. When Amin fell, the new team of Ugandan delegates discovered an elaborate system of electronic listening devices in the walls and hidden behind curtains.

Continue north on First Ave. The west side of the avenue from E. 42nd to E. 49th Sts was renamed (1985) **Raoul Wallenberg Walk** to honor the Swedish diplomat who saved thousands of Hungarian Jews during World War II. He disappeared and was presumably captured and killed. On the traffic island at 47th St is a sculpture called *Hope* (1998; Gustav Kraitz) that is dedicated to Wallenberg. Its five black granite posts symbolize a city destroyed, while the tallest post, at 21 feet, has a ceramic blue sphere on top to signify hope for the future. The work includes actual paving stones from a Budapest ghetto and a briefcase with the initials *RW*.

At First Ave and E. 47th St is **Dag Hammarskjöld Plaza,** expanded into a city park, which features the half-acre **Katharine Hepburn Garden** (1997), a tribute to the actress's love of gardens.

Rising at the northwest corner of First Ave and E. 47th St. is the **Trump World Tower** (2001; Costas Kondylis & Assocs.), another eponymous project of Donald Trump's. At a height of 856 ft, it is the city's tallest residential building and casts a huge shadow over the UN. It was built despite protests from noted public figures such as Walter Cronkite; Trump outmaneuvered them by transferring air rights from other properties, circumventing public hearings and environmental studies.

Japan House

Turn left (west) on E. 47th St to Japan House (1971; Junzo Yoshimura and Gruzen & Partners) between First and Second Aves. Designed by a Tokyo architect in a typically Japanese style but using primarily American building materials, Japan House is the headquarters of the **Japan Society,** which was founded in 1907 to promote understanding through cultural exchange.

Japan Society Gallery

333 E. 47th St, New York, NY 10017. ☎ (212) 832-1155. Web site: www.japansociety.org. Open during exhibitions Tues–Fri 11–6; Sat, Sun 11–5. Closed Mon, major holidays. Suggested donation. Changing exhibitions; lectures, films, language classes. Accessible to wheelchairs.

Subway: Lexington Ave Local (6) to 51st St. Eighth Ave Local (E) or Sixth Ave Local (F) to Lexington Ave–53rd St. Bus: M15, M27, M50, M101, M102.

On the second floor is the Japan Society gallery, which features exhibitions on Japanese life and culture.

On the block of E. 48th St block between Second and Third Aves is the former **William Lescaze residence,** 211 E. 48th St, which began as an ordinary 19C brownstone but was aggressively transformed (1934; DL) by architect Lescaze. Used as both a home and studio, the building makes dramatic use of glass block, a trademark of Lescaze's style. The facade, pushed forward to the building line, is covered with smooth gray stucco (originally white) and is brilliant when illuminated at night. In its day the house caused such a stir that for a while Lescaze and his wife set aside an hour on Mon for public visitation.

Turtle Bay Gardens Historic District

At 227–247 E. 48th St and 226–246 E. 49th St (between Second and Third Aves) is the Turtle Bay Gardens Historic District (remodeled 1920; William L. Bottomley and Edward C. Dean), two rows of 19C brownstones, back-to-back, with a common garden inside the block.

History

Inspired by houses with shared gardens in France and Italy, Charlotte Martin bought 20 deteriorating brownstones, filled in swampy areas, shaved six ft off each backyard to create a common garden, and redesigned the houses so that they faced inward to the garden, where she placed a replica of the fountain at the entrance of the Villa Medici in Rome. Famous residents include: Judge Learned Hand, Leopold Stokowski, Katharine Hepburn, Mary Martin, Tyrone Power, Stephen Sondheim, and E. B. White. To the essayist White, an old willow tree in the garden symbolized the city—life surviving difficulties, growth against all odds.

Walk around the block to E. 49th St (between Second and Third Aves). **Amster Yard** (1870; remodeled 1945; Harold Sterner), 211–215 E. 49th St, is another enclave, almost entirely secluded from the street. Originally the yard held workshops and small houses built on the site of what may have been the terminal stop of the Boston–New York stagecoach route along the Boston Post Rd. After the Second Avenue El was demolished in 1942, James Amster, a designer, bought the property and developed it into shops, apartments, and offices, around a central courtyard.

At 225–227 E. 49th St is the former **Efrem Zimbalist House** (1926), home of the violinist; his wife, diva Alma Gluck; their son, actor Efrem Zimbalist Jr.; and Gluck's daughter from a previous marriage, novelist Marcia Davenport. The cartouche over the door bears a violin, a staff with some unidentified musical theme, and an open-mouthed cherub. Later Henry Luce of Time-Life lived here, but between 1957 and 1960 the house became the 17th Precinct Police Station House.

Mitchell Place, 49th St on the east side of First Ave, is named for William Mitchell, a distinguished 19C jurist, who served as a member of the New York Court of Appeals and as presiding justice on the state supreme court. At the northeast corner of the intersection stands the former Panhellenic Tower (1928; John Mead Howells), once a residence and clubhouse for women college graduates, now converted to the **Beekman Tower Apartments.** The small park on the south side of Mitchell Place is called **General Douglas MacArthur Plaza,** after the controversial World War II hero who was relieved of his UN command post during the Korean War by President Harry S. Truman for disobeying Truman's orders.

Beekman Place

Walk along Mitchell Place, then turn left onto Beekman Place, at two blocks in length one of the smallest streets in the city. Named after the Beekman family, the street's location on a high bluff overlooking the river and its controlled development by the Beekmans made it as socially desirable early in its history as it is now. Among those who have lived here are John D. Rockefeller III, Irving Berlin, Gloria Vanderbilt, and Rex Harrison.

The Beekman Mansion

The Beekman mansion, Mount Pleasant (built 1765), stood near the river at about 51st St. During the Revolution it was confiscated and used as British headquarters. In 1783 James Beekman got his house back and entertained American officers returning to New York on Evacuation Day with punch made with lemons from trees in his greenhouse. In 1874 the house was demolished.

From 51st St a flight of steps leads to a footbridge across the Franklin D. Roosevelt (FDR) Drive. Walk north along the walkway next to the drive. One of the more imposing prominences overlooking the water is **River House** (1931; Bottomley, Wagner & White), at 433–437 E. 52nd St (east of First Ave). Completed the same year as the George Washington Bridge and the Waldorf-Astoria Hotel, River House quickly became synonymous with privilege and wealth. The apartments in the tower were built on two or three floors with as many as 17 rooms (one had nine bathrooms), while those in the body of the building were only slightly more modest. The serenity of the setting was disturbed by the arrival of the FDR Drive, begun downtown in 1936 and completed after World War II as a major artery linking the city with outlying highways.

Sutton Place

Cross back over the FDR Drive to Sutton Place, formerly and less glamorously known as Ave A. It was renamed after Effingham B. Sutton, a dry goods merchant who developed the area around 1875 with a fortune he had made in the California gold rush of 1849, not by striking the mother lode but by selling picks, shovels, and provisions to prospectors who hoped to do so. His venture with Sutton Place came about 50 years too soon, and the street remained modest until Anne Morgan, daughter of J. P. Morgan, and Mrs. William K. Vanderbilt (Anne Harriman) arrived in 1921.

The south part of the street was a later extension and is called Sutton Place South (E. 53rd to E. 57th Sts). The building at **1 Sutton Place South** (1927; Cross & Cross, with Rosario Candela) vies with River House as one of the city's premier apartments. **Sutton Square,** the block between E. 57th and E. 58th Sts, has a group of town houses sharing a common back garden, hence the name. At the foot of 57th St is a small park with a replica of Pietro Tacca's *Wild Boar* from the Straw Market in Florence, the model for which is in the Uffizi Gallery in Florence. On the north side of 57th St abutting the park (**1 Sutton Place**) is the neo-Georgian town house built (1921; Mott B. Schmidt) for Mrs. William K. Vanderbilt. At **3 Sutton Place** (1921; Mott B. Schmidt), originally the home of Anne Morgan, is the residence of the secretary-general of the UN.

At 58th St, east of Sutton Place, is another small park, and north of it, parallel to the river, is a small, cobbled, private street—**Riverview Terrace**—with five 19C houses looking out from the top of the ridge.

Queensboro Bridge

From the end of E. 58th St is a fine view of the Queensboro Bridge (1909; Gustav Lindenthal, engineer; Palmer & Hornbostel, architects; DL), which joins Long Island City in Queens with 59th St in Manhattan and was immortalized in Simon & Garfunkel's 1966 hit "59th Street Bridge Song."

History

As early as 1852 some of Long Island City's most powerful families—the Steinways and Pratts for example—began lobbying for a bridge, an enterprise furthered by the Long Island Railroad tycoon Austin Corbin and later by a Dr. Thomas Rainey, who foresaw the bridge as an aid to tourism, freight handling, and the funeral business (there were 15 cemeteries on Long Island at the time). Political and financial problems delayed its construction for some 40 years, and the collapse of another partially built cantilever bridge, the Quebec Bridge, called in doubt the safety of this one.

The span is 1,182 ft long and 135 ft above mean high water. About 50,000 tons of steel were used in construction at a cost of $20.8 million. Bicycle riders and pedestrians can still cross the bridge but can no longer descend to Roosevelt Island. Beneath the Manhattan approach to the bridge are handsome vaults with

Guastavino-tiled arches, which after years of delay have finally reopened in 1999 as **Bridgemarket,** featuring restaurants, food, and home furnishings.

Mount Vernon Hotel Museum and Garden

421 E. 61st St, New York, NY 10021. ☎ (212) 838-6878. Open Tues–Sun 11–4. Closed Mon, holidays. Call for summer hours. Admission charge. Tours, lectures, children's activities. Gift shop. Not accessible to wheelchairs.

Subway: Lexington Ave Express or Local (4, 5, 6) to 59th St. Broadway Local (N, R) to Lexington Ave. Bus: M15, M31, M57.

Walk north on First Ave and turn right on E. 61st St. Halfway down the block between First and York Aves is the Mount Vernon Hotel Museum and Garden, formerly the Abigail Adams Smith Museum (1799; DL), a survivor from the early years of the American republic.

History

In 1795 Col. William Stephens Smith and his wife, Abigail Adams Smith, daughter of President John Adams, bought 23 acres on which they planned a mansion. They would call their new home Mount Vernon in honor of George Washington, Smith's former commander. Unfortunately, Smith had financial difficulties and sold the property. In 1798 William T. Robinson bought it and completed what is now the museum building as a stable and coach house and the mansion as his residence. Later the mansion became the Mount Vernon Hotel, known for its turtle soup, and even later, a female academy, which was destroyed by fire in 1926. The stable, meanwhile, was converted to another hotel, also known as the Mount Vernon. From 1833 to 1905 it belonged to the Towle family, who sold it to the Standard Gas Light Co. In 1919 Jane Teller, an antiques dealer, rented and restored the site for displaying a collection of early American furniture. The Colonial Dames of America bought it five years later and opened it to the public.

Interior and Garden

Set on a half-acre of landscaped grounds, the house has been painstakingly restored and refurnished with period furniture (1800–1830) predominantly in the Federal style. Behind the house is a pleasant garden with herbs and plantings reminiscent of those popular around 1800.

Between E. 62nd and E. 68th Sts on the east side of York Ave is **Rockefeller University,** founded (1901) as Rockefeller Institute for Medical Research. The campus occupies the site of the former Schermerhorn family summer estate, which still had its original farmhouse when John D. Rockefeller Sr. bought the property. Today the university, small and prestigious—its scientists have earned 16 Nobel Prizes—is dedicated to advanced education and research in the biomedical sciences. (The grounds are not open to the public.)

New York Weill Cornell Medical Center

North of Rockefeller University between E. 68th and E. 70th Sts is the New York Weill Cornell Medical Center (1932; Coolidge, Shepley, Bulfinch & Abbott), a 6.4-acre complex for patient care, research, and teaching. The **main building** of glazed white brick constructed in Art Deco Gothic has been much admired for its skillful massing and spartan use of detail. At the time of completion it was also widely admired for its technical advances (air-conditioning, X-ray machines, and shadowless lights in the operating rooms) and for the humane quality of its interior design—the small wards subdivided by glass partitions into four-bed sections and lounges overlooking the East River.

History

New York Hospital was founded under a charter from King George III in 1771 as a hospital for the poor and, incidentally, as a medical school. During the Revolution it was used for British and Hessian soldiers but was not reopened to the public until 1791. In 1877 a new 200-bed hospital was built on W. 15th St near Fifth Ave with technological advances such as steam heat and artificial ventilation. The hospital formed an association with the Cornell University Medical School in 1912 and in 1927 decided to build this hospital, which opened for patients in 1932. In 1938 more than 100 anonymous donors gave $1,000 each to remove swastika designs, which had acquired sinister connotations with the rise of Hitler, from the 325 ft chimneys and to replace them with the present Greek crosses. Today the center is affiliated with the Hospital for Special Surgery (535 E. 70th St at York Ave) and the Memorial Sloan–Kettering Cancer Center (1275 York Ave at E. 68th St). In 1997 New York Hospital merged with Presbyterian Hospital (see Walk 29) to form New York–Presbyterian Hospital; in 1998 the Cornell University Medical School was renamed for its benefactors Stanford T. Weill, chairman of Citibank, and his wife, Joan.

Roosevelt Island

Roosevelt Island Tram: Station at 2nd Ave and E. 60th St open 6 A.M.–2 A.M.; weekends until 3:30 A.M. Tram leaves every 15 minutes on the quarter hour. Fare is $1.50 payable with a subway token or MetroCard.

Subway: Sixth Ave Express (B, Q marked 21st St–Queensbridge) to Roosevelt Island. Sixth Ave Local (F), Eighth Ave Local (E), or Broadway Local (R) to Queens Plaza; Broadway Local (N) or Flushing Local (7) to Queensboro Plaza; then transfer to Q102 bus to Roosevelt Island.

Roosevelt Island, a two-mile-long, 800 ft wide strip of land in the East River, long used as a place of exile for madmen, criminals, and incurables, emerged in the 1970s as "the New Town in Town," a planned community for people of all races and economic backgrounds. Only 300 yds off the shore of the East Side, the island is quiet and remote in feeling, untouched by the frantic energy of Manhattan to which it belongs politically. Traffic is minimal and there is plenty of open space. The island, however, benefits from its proximity to Manhattan, a five-minute tram (1976) or subway (1989) ride away.

In the island's midsection rise the towers of the new town whose housing, schools, transport, even rubbish removal were all planned by urban strategists, according to a master plan by Philip Johnson and John Burgee, a plan imperfectly implemented because of the city's fiscal problems in the 1970s. Down the island's midline runs a modern Main St, and girding the shoreline is a promenade, planned for its views and ornamented with occasional pieces of sculpture. At the ends of the island remain monuments of older, less orderly times—a decaying smallpox hospital on the south and a lighthouse built by inmates, and perhaps a lunatic, on the north end.

History

Dutch settlers referred to the island as Varckens, or Hog Island, and farmed it as early as 1639. After the English captured New Amsterdam, King Charles granted the island to Capt. John Manning, sheriff of New York in 1668. In 1675, Manning pleaded guilty to cowardice and treason for surrendering Fort James (at the Battery) to the Dutch and spent the rest of his years in exile on the island, which he then passed to his stepdaughter and her husband, Robert Blackwell. The Blackwell family owned and farmed the island until 1828 when the city bought it for penal uses, an objective for which, according to one 19C clergyman, J. F. Richmond, it was more than suitable: "Separated on either side from the great world by a deep crystal current, [it] appears to have been divinely arranged as a home for the unfortunate and suffering, a place of quiet reformatory meditation for the vicious." By the end of the 19C, its institutions included a workhouse, an almshouse, a madhouse, and the penitentiary where "Boss" Tweed served time and Mae West later (1927) lingered eight days after an obscenity conviction for performing her play *Sex*. In 1887, the journalist Nellie Bly went undercover in the island's lunatic asylum and wrote a series of scathing articles for the *New York World*, which led to reforms. But by 1921, when the island's name was changed from Blackwell's Island to Welfare Island, the place was still notorious—its workhouse overcrowded and obsolete, and its prison ruled by hard-core inmates who dealt in narcotics and lived well on the profits.

In 1934, a new commissioner of corrections, Austin H. McCormick, cleaned it up. The following year, when the Riker's Island Penitentiary opened, Welfare Island became a sanctuary for the aged and the ill, with a hospital for chronic diseases, the New York City Home for Dependents, a cancer hospital, and a charity hospital. Many of the older hospitals and asylums were left to decay.

In the boom years of the late 1960s, city planners—unwilling to leave so much valuable real estate lying fallow—began plans for redevelopment. The city leased the island to the state for 99 years, allowing a new quasi-public agency, the Urban Development Corporation (UDC), to take control of the project. The island was renamed Roosevelt Island to polish its image (1973), and the first apartments opened for rental in 1975. Originally the master plan called for two "towns," separated by a park, with a combined population of 20,000, a number deemed adequate for supporting restaurants, stores, and cultural activities. With construction delays, rampant inflation, and the fiscal collapse of the UDC, only one town, Northtown, has been built.

In 1984, the Roosevelt Island Operating Corporation (RIOC) was established, becoming the first independent agency charged with managing, developing, and operating the island, which today has about 8,500 residents. With development incomplete, the island has needed several million dollars each year in state subsidies.

Governor George Pataki, adamant about ending subsidies, has pressured RIOC to make the island more self-sufficient. There has been much tension in recent years, with many residents blaming the state and RIOC for bad day-to-day management and failure to develop the southern half of the island. Each merchant on the island has a monopoly (one pizza place, one liquor store, etc.), which gives them little reason to improve service or cut prices, especially with no new influx of customers as incentive. RIOC recently began developing Southtown, providing new apartments and ballfields, but it also has controversial plans for a hotel and convention center at Southpoint, which was intended for parkland.

The **Roosevelt Island Tramway** (1976; station by Prentice & Chan, Ohlhausen) crosses the river at 16 miles per hour, controlled automatically from the Roosevelt Island terminal, though the cabin attendant can override the automatic system. The tram has a rescue car with its own drive system and an emergency generator so that passengers won't dangle midriver during a power failure. Despite these precautions, however, the Swiss-made tram has suffered maintenance delays and breakdowns, as well as a hiatus in service when a film company leased the tram to make the thriller *Nighthawks*. Under optimal circumstances the ride takes 3½ minutes.

From the cable car station, walk south along the promenade. The low modern building near the terminal is a **Sports Park** (1977; Prentice & Chan, Ohlhausen), with a gymnasium and other facilities used by the island's schools. South of it is the **Goldwater Memorial Hospital** (1939; Isadore Rosenfield, senior architect of the New York Department of Hospitals; Butler & Kohn; York & Sawyer; addition, 1971), originally called the Welfare Hospital for Chronic Diseases. It has a central north–south corridor with short projecting wings to give patients, most of them chronically ill, maximal sunshine and river views.

Further south and east, beyond a fenced area, are the remains of the **Strecker Memorial Laboratory** (1892; Withers & Dickson; DL). Romanesque revival in style, the laboratory was the gift of a daughter of an otherwise unknown Mr. Strecker; it housed on the first floor an autopsy room and a mortuary as well as a laboratory for the examination of specimens and on the second floor had facilities for pathological and bacteriological research.

The other surviving 19C hospital at the south end of the island is the **Smallpox Hospital** (1856; James Renwick Jr.; south wing added 1904; York & Sawyer; north wing added 1905; Renwick, Aspinwall & Owen; DL), a Gothic ruin bathed in floodlights at night. The hospital replaced a group of wooden shacks on the riverbanks where smallpox sufferers were formerly quarantined. Although vaccination was common by the mid-19C, immigrants still brought the disease to New York, and as late as 1871 it reached epidemic proportions. In 1886 a new hospital for quarantining smallpox victims was built on North Brother Island, reducing the danger of spreading the disease to the Blackwell's Island population, which numbered some 7,000 by the end of the century; the hospital was converted to a nurses' home. Plans call for stabilizing the ruins and allowing public access to the south portion of the island.

Return along the promenade to the tram station and either continue walking north or take one of the electric minibuses (25 cents) along Main St. North of the station, just before the main residential area, is the **Blackwell Farmhouse** (1796–1804; DL), a simple, clapboard country house (not open to the public).

On the right side of Main St are the **Eastwood Apartments** (1976; Sert, Jackson & Assocs.), built for low- and middle-income tenants. The U-shaped buildings face industrial Long Island City in Queens and the smokestacks of a Consolidated Edison generator, Big Allis, named for its builder, the Allis Chalmers company. The richer tenants in the **Rivercross** co-ops (1975; Johansen & Bhavnani), across Main St to the west, look out on Manhattan's gilded East Side.

Nearby is the **Chapel of the Good Shepherd** (1889; Frederick Clarke Withers; restored 1976, Giorgio Cavaglieri; DL), the only refreshing piece of architecture in the town center. This stone-and-brick Victorian Gothic church once ministered to residents of the island's institutions and is now used as a community center. The church's bronze bell (1888) stands on the plaza.

Walk toward the East River through the apartment complex to the west prom-enade, whose loop around the island attracts joggers and strollers. Two more landmarks and a hospital stand at the north end of the island. The **Octagon Tower,** originally part of the New York City Lunatic Asylum (1839; Alexander Jackson Davis; DL), once stood as a central rotunda (dome added c. 1880; Joseph M. Dunn) at the intersection of two low granite wings demolished in 1970. (The building is fenced off from the public.) The tower was badly burned in 1982, and only the shell remains. There are plans to stabilize and preserve this ruin, perhaps even redevelop it into housing.

The New York Lunatic Asylum

The asylum was founded to fill a desperate need for accommodating the in-sane, who, up until then, were housed in overcrowded wards at Bellevue Hospital. Their early treatment could hardly have been enlightened since they were supervised by inmates from the penitentiary, but physical activity and labor were considered therapeutic, so patients were put to work in veg-etable gardens or conscripted to build seawalls that reclaimed land. Charles Dickens visited in 1842 and described it in his *American Notes* as "naked ug-liness and horror," and Nellie Bly exposed its horrific conditions in 1887.

Continue north past the **Bird S. Coler Hospital** (1952), a city hospital for the chronically ill. At the northernmost tip of the island in **Lighthouse Park** (1979) is a rock lighthouse (1872; James Renwick Jr., supervising architect; DL). Local legend states that the asylum warden allowed John McCarthy, a patient, to build a small fort on the point where the lighthouse stands because he feared a British invasion. When the lighthouse was planned, McCarthy was persuaded to demol-ish the fort and build the lighthouse in its place. A plaque to this effect disap-peared in the 1960s. It is more likely, however, that island inmates helped build the structure, which is 50 ft high and constructed of the gray Fordham gneiss quar-ried on the island, predominantly by convicts, and used for most of the older in-stitutional buildings of the period.

20 · Yorkville and the East River Islands

Subway: Lexington Ave Local (6) to 77th St.
Bus: M15, M18, M72.

Yorkville

In the late 18C Yorkville was a small hamlet between New York and the village of Harlem, its country estates attracting wealthy families of Germanic origin—

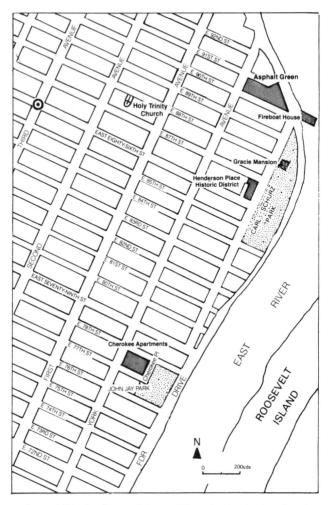

Schermerhorns, Rhinelanders, and Astors. When the New York and Harlem Railroad arrived in 1834, Yorkville quickly became a suburb drawing middle-class Germans, among them people like the Rupperts, who operated a brewery. Less-wealthy German immigrants usually settled first on the Lower East Side, notably around Tompkins Square in a neighborhood called "Kleindeutschland," but by 1900, as waves of eastern European and Italian immigrants poured in downtown, many Germans began moving to Yorkville. This migration was hastened in 1904, when the *General Slocum*, an excursion steamer jammed with Kleindeutschland women and children, burned and sank in the East River. More than a thousand people died, making it too painful for many surviving husbands to remain in the old neighborhood.

The opening of the elevated lines on Second and Third Aves in 1878–79 also opened up Yorkville. In the early 20C, its population included Irish, Germans, Hungarians, Jews, Czechs, Slovaks, and Italians, most clustered in separate ethnic enclaves.

Though Yorkville was never rich, it remained a solid neighborhood through the years of the Depression, a place where people worked close to home—either in small businesses or for the brewery—and enjoyed themselves at local restaurants, Bavarian beer gardens, or cafés modeled after those in Vienna. At some restaurants, presumably those for tourists, the doormen wore lederhosen and plumed Tyrolean hats. (Ironically, York Ave was called Ave A until 1928, when it was renamed after the World War I hero Alvin C. York, who single-handedly killed 25 Germans and took 132 prisoners on Oct 8, 1918, in the Meuse-Argonne campaign.)

In the years before World War II, Yorkville was a center of both Nazi and anti-Nazi activity. It was home to the Nazi-supported German-American Bund and its official paper, the *Deutscher Weckruf und Beobachter* (at 178 E. 85th St), and the German-American Business League, which published a list of Nazi-approved American business firms. On the other hand, the German Central Book Store (218 E. 84th St) carried books banned by Hitler, while the German Workers Club (1501 Third Ave) served as an anti-Nazi labor organization.

After World War II, the area saw a last wave of German immigration and later an influx of Hungarians following the uprising of 1956. After that, ethnic newcomers were largely Hispanics filtering down from Spanish Harlem on the northern edge of Yorkville. Nowadays high-rise buildings are rapidly changing the face of the neighborhood, attracting affluent young working couples and single people, so that Yorkville is not easily distinguishable from other middle-class neighborhoods. The eastern European population is largely gone and the luxury high-rises have priced out the remaining aging survivors.

Begin at E. 73rd St and First Ave. Here at the southern end of Yorkville lie the remnants of **Little Bohemia,** the Czech and Slovak quarter which centered around First Ave from the upper 60s to the mid-70s. Czechs moved here from the Lower East Side before World War I, and many Slovaks arrived after the war when Czechoslovakia became independent. Both Czechs and Slovaks continued coming here until the late 1940s, with another influx after the Russian invasion of Czechoslovakia in 1968. Like the rest of Yorkville, the area today has more tall apartment buildings than tenements and is more chic than Czech.

At 321 E. 73rd St (between First and Second Aves) stands an ornate, five-story, neo-Renaissance building, the former **Bohemian National Hall** (1896; William C. Frohne; DL), which was constructed to house Czech and Slovak social, athletic, and intellectual clubs. The building has been empty since 1988, and while interest in the hall was renewed after the Velvet Revolution of 1989 and Czechoslovakia's split into the Czech Republic and Slovakia in 1992, little has happened because New York's small Czech community is now based in Astoria. The Bohemian Benevolent and Literary Association, an umbrella group, owns the building and has been trying to persuade the Czech government to take over the building and restore it, allowing the association to keep one floor.

Sotheby's

Nearby, at 1334 York Ave (close to E. 72nd St), is Sotheby's, the American branch of the world's oldest firm of fine arts auctioneers.

History

Sotheby's was founded in 1744 by the London bookseller Samuel Baker, who established an auction room to find buyers for the private libraries he sold. When Baker died in 1778, his nephew John Sotheby took over. During the 19C, Sotheby's expanded into paintings, prints, coins, furniture, jewelry, porcelain, and antiquities, and by 1917 fine art had surpassed books in volume of sales.

In 1964 Sotheby's merged with an American company, Parke-Bernet, founded (1883) as the American Art Association. Its founders (1937) were Otto Bernet, who began working for the AAA at age 14, and Hiram Haney Parke, one of the country's great auctioneers.

Sotheby's is known for its high-profile auctions. The contents of Jacqueline Kennedy Onassis's home were sold in 1996, when the desk at which President John F. Kennedy signed the nuclear test ban treaty in 1963 fetched $1.43 million. "Sue," the largest, most complete and best-preserved Tyrannosaurus rex skeleton ever discovered, was sold to the Field Museum of Natural History in Chicago in 1997 for $7.6 million. And the Barry Halper baseball collection brought $21 million in 1999, setting a world auction record for a single-owner sale of sports memorabilia.

North of the Czech quarter is **Little Hungary,** which centered around Second Ave in the upper 70s and low 80s. The abortive Hungarian Revolution (1848) touched off the first wave of immigrants, who continued arriving until just before World War I and began moving uptown from the Lower East Side around 1905. A new wave arrived after the Soviet Union's invasion of Hungary in 1956.

Walk east of York Ave on E. 76th St, to **Cherokee Place,** named for the Cherokee Club, a branch of Tammany Hall (see Walk 13), which once stood on E. 79th St between First and Second Aves. Stretching across Cherokee Place from 507–523 E. 77th St to 508–522 E. 78th St are the **Cherokee Apartments** (1911; Henry Atterbury Smith; DL). Originally called the East River Houses, this six-story complex later became known as the Shively Sanitary Tenements because they followed Dr. Henry Shively's environmental notions for battling tuberculosis. The buildings have small balconies accessible from triple-hung windows and Guastavino-tiled tunnels leading to central courtyards. From the courtyard corner, stairways rise to upper floors, roofed against the rain with iron and glass. All these features—courtyards, balconies, passageways, triple-sash windows—were designed to enhance air circulation and sunlight. The exterior was extensively renovated in 1989–90.

John Jay Park, along the east side of Cherokee Place between E. 77th and E. 78th Sts, is a popular local gathering spot with a playground and a swimming pool. It is named after the first chief justice of the U.S. Supreme Court, drafter of the Constitution, and New York governor (1795–1801). Adjoining the park are two somewhat odd black steel sculptures, *Kryet-Aekyad #2* and *Eaphae-Aekyad #2* (1979; Douglas Abdell). The names are taken from the sculptor's private language in which the *Aekyads* are "letter sculptures" and can function as the basis of more complex structures, just as letters are the basis of words.

At E. 78th St, return to the York Ave side of the **City and Suburban Homes complex** (1901–13; Harde & Short, Percy Griffin, Philip Ohm; DL), which occupies the block bounded by E. 78th St, the FDR Drive, York Ave, and E. 79th St. This early attempt at working-class housing was the largest "model tenement" at the time, a block of six-story walk-ups, built by the City and Suburban Homes Co. to show that well-designed tenements could also produce profits. The **Junior League Hotel** (1910–12; Philip Ohm), 541–555 E. 78th St, later the East End Hotel for women and now apartments, was built for single women who paid $4–7 per week, including board.

Most of the Hungarian social clubs have vanished, but at 323 E. 79th St between First and Second Aves is the First Hungarian Literary Society, and at 213 E. 82nd St is the Hungarian House, with the Hungarian Library next door. Further east on 82nd St (between First and York Aves) is St. Stephen of Hungary Roman Catholic Church (1928; Emil Szendy). Nearby is St. Elizabeth of Hungary Roman Catholic Church at 211 E. 83rd.

Walk to E. 86th St, then east to East End Ave. Here is the well-preserved **Henderson Place Historic District,** named for the wealthy fur importer and developer John C. Henderson. It comprises 24 (originally 32) two-story, Queen Anne row houses (1882; Lamb & Rich) built of brick and rough stone. The buildings are set back with front yards, atypical for Manhattan.

Across East End Ave from Henderson Place is **Carl Schurz Park,** which extends from E. 90th St to E. 84th St on the East River, providing perhaps the most peaceful waterway views from the Manhattan side. This graceful, curving park is named for the most prominent German American of the 19C. Schurz (1829–1906), a hero of the German revolutionary movement of 1848, arrived in America in 1852 and became a brigadier general during the Civil War, a U.S. senator, secretary of the interior, editor of the *New York Evening Post* and *The Nation,* and, near the end of his life, a Yorkville resident. The upscale area around **Gracie Square** has been home to Gloria Vanderbilt and Robert Moses.

A promenade, **John Finley Walk,** honors John Huston Finley (1863–1940), president of the City College of New York, associate editor of the *New York Times,* state commissioner of education, and an unflagging pedestrian who was known to walk the 32 miles around Manhattan Island. Today, the park has a playground and dog run, but is best known as home of the city's mayor.

Gracie Mansion

Facing the river near the north end of the park is the chief official's official residence, Gracie Mansion (1799; additions, 1966; Mott B. Schmidt; restored 1984, Charles A. Platt; DL). Its high fences make it difficult to see from the park; there is a slightly better view from E. 88th St and East End Ave.

Exterior

With its 16 rooms and fine detailing—leaded glass sidelights and semicircular fanlight above the main doorway, railings around the roof and above the main floor—the mansion exemplifies Federal domestic architecture at the elegant end of the scale.

History

Loyalist Jacob Walton owned the first house on what was then called Horn's Hook, but during the Revolution the Colonial Army confiscated it and built a fort there. On Sept 15, 1776, the British demolished the house and the Americans retreated. The English used the site as an army camp until the war's end.

The present Gracie Mansion began as the country home of the merchant

Archibald Gracie, who had a downtown town house on State St across from Battery Park. Gracie's shipping business foundered in 1823 and he was forced to sell the house. In 1896, the city bought the property and it became part of the Parks Department; from 1924 to 1932, it housed the Museum of the City of New York. After a renovation, it became the mayor's residence in 1942 when Fiorello La Guardia rejected Charles M. Schwab's 75-room French château at Riverside Drive and W. 73rd St (now demolished). "What," exclaimed the fiery, 5´2˝ friend of the working class, "me in that?" In 1966, reception and conference rooms were added to the mansion.

Gracie Mansion Tours
The Gracie Mansion Conservancy offers house tours from mid-March to mid-Nov on Wed at 10, 11, 1, and 2. Admissions charge; reservations necessary. ☎ (212) 570-4751.

Along the river at this northern end is the **Fireboat House** (c. 1930), formerly one of 22 fireboat stations citywide. When peppier diesel boats replaced steam models in the 1950s, the stations were phased out, this one in 1976. Rebuilt in 1981 (Steven Robinson), the house served for nearly a decade as a community center for environmental studies. The Parks Department is demolishing the adjoining pier and building a new one that will provide local boaters with water access. (Part of the pier was already rebuilt for New York Waterway, which provides ferry service to Shea and Yankee Stadiums during the baseball season.) However, the Fireboat House was deemed too expensive to repair and the city has rejected community pleas for a new boathouse.

Visible to the West at E. 90th St is the former **Municipal Asphalt Plant** (1944; Kahn & Jacobs; DL), the first American parabolic arch built in reinforced concrete over a steel frame. Abandoned in 1968, when larger facilities were needed, the plant gained new life in 1972 when a citizens' group transformed it into Asphalt Green, a community center for arts and athletics.

East River Islands
To the north **Robert Wagner Walk** stretches up along the shoreline, idyllic except for the undeniable presence of the FDR Drive. A walk along here provides views of Mill Rock Island, owned by the Parks Department but not open to the public, and Randall's and Ward's Islands, which are of interest only to the extraordinarily thorough visitor. (Randall's and Ward's Islands were connected to one another by landfill in the 1950s; both are accessible by the Wards Island Pedestrian Footbridge at E. 103rd St, and by car or the M35 bus over the Triborough Bridge.)

Mill Rock Island
Mill Rock Island, the little 8.6 acre key-shaped island opposite E. 96th St, was, shockingly, the site of the largest intentional man-made explosion before the atomic bomb.

History

Mill Rock started as two islands, Great Mill Rock and Little Mill Rock, the name derived from a tidal mill (c. 1701–7) on the larger islet. During the War of 1812, a blockhouse there, along with fortifications on the shore, protected the northern entrance to the harbor. The isles were then home first to a squatter, who sold food and liquor to passing boats, and later to a farmer.

Great and Little Mill Rocks achieved international renown in 1885 as part of the U.S. government's efforts to clear the East River reefs and rocks that made the waters dangerous for ship traffic. From Great and Little Mill Rock Islands, the army's latest invention, "rack-a-rock," was produced and attached to Flood Rock, a partially submerged nine-acre navigational hazard. On Oct 10, 100,000 New Yorkers lined the shores and waterways to watch as 300,000 pounds of explosives were detonated, creating 50 geysers and sending sprays of water 200 ft high. Shocks were felt as far away as Princeton, New Jersey. Fragments of Flood Rock were used to fill in the space between Great and Little Mill. Since then, Mill Rock has essentially been unoccupied, a forgotten ward of the Parks Department since 1953.

Hell Gate

To the west of Mill Rock, the Harlem River runs along Manhattan's shore. The channel northeast of Mill Rock is Hell Gate, which has had a reputation for treachery since Dutch explorer Adraien Block sailed the *Tyger* through it in 1612. The name, however, is a corruption of the Dutch word *Hellegat*, which means "beautiful pass" and originally applied to the entire East River. Hell Gate is only 22.5 miles from the open sea via New York Bay but more than 100 miles in the other direction, via Long Island Sound, which accounts for three hours' difference in the tides at the two ends of the East River. These conflicting tides, along with reefs and rocks in the water, once made Hell Gate so tortuous that hundreds of ships were wrecked there. The most famous, the Revolutionary frigate *Hussar*, went down in 1780 and—according to legend—was carrying gold and silver coins worth $500 million as payroll for British troops. Neither the boat nor the coins have ever been found. Beginning in 1851, the Army Corps of Engineers blasted away such colorfully named rocks as Hen and Chickens, Hog's Back, Frying Pan, and Bald-Headed Billy, along with larger ones like Flood Rock.

Ward's Island

The large island to the north of Mill Rock is Ward's Island, now joined by landfill to Randall's Island as a single 486-acre mass.

History

Like its sibling, Randall's Island, Ward's Island has spent much of this century with an identity crisis, occupied by recreation areas, city institutions, and two major bridges that chop the open spaces into odd chunks. In the early 19C, Jaspar and Bartholomew Ward attempted to establish a farming community and cotton mill here. Later, the city began using its East River Islands as dumping grounds for society's undesirables. In 1847, the State Emigrant Refuge for "sick and destitute aliens" opened on Ward's Island after Ellis Island (before its immigrant-station days) was rejected; the facility also processed newcomers when Castle Garden, the state immigration depot, was overwhelmed. In fact, it was the deplorable conditions on Ward's Island that inspired Emma Lazarus to write the poem ("Give me your tired, your poor . . .") that adorns the Statue of Liberty. Later Ward's Island additions included the Inebriate Asylum, a rest home for Civil War veterans, and beginning in the 1890s, the Manhattan State Hospital, the world's largest insane asylum.

Today, the hospital, now known as the Manhattan Psychiatric Center, remains, albeit largely unoccupied because of deinstitutionalization. Other institutions on the island include a homeless shelter, a sewage treatment plant, and the Fire-fighters Training Center. Ballfields and barbecue areas are tucked in among the shadows of these institutions.

Randall's Island

Prior to the American Revolution, Randall's Island was known as Montresor's Island, owned by Capt. John Montresor, who secretly surveyed New York and the harbor for the British military. By 1776, he had fled, however, and Gen. George Washington established a smallpox quarantine on the island. But the British, viewing the islands as pivotal to control of the city during wartime, drove the Colonial troops from what are now Roosevelt, Randall's, and Ward's Islands, establishing army bases and hospitals there. On Sept 22, 1776, the Americans sent 240 men to recapture Montresor's Island, but the maneuver failed when many soldiers refused to attack.

A farmer named Jonathan Randel bought the island in 1784 and worked the land until his death in 1830. Five years later, Randel's heirs sold the island to the city, which built, among other things, a potter's field, an almshouse, the Idiot Asylum, and the notorious House of Refuge, where juvenile delinquents were often badly beaten and forced into sweatshop labor, caning chairs and making shoes for outside contractors.

In this century, both Randall's and Ward's Islands were transformed by Robert Moses, the city's master builder. On Randall's Island, Moses built Downing Stadium, where Jesse Owens broke several records while trying out for the 1936 Berlin Olympics and where Jimi Hendrix played his final concert in the continental United States. Moses also filled in the water between the two islands (and a third, small, unused island called Sunken Meadow) and created tennis courts and dozens of ball fields.

The future of Randall's and Ward's Islands began changing in 1992 when Karen Cohen founded the Randall's Island Sports Foundation, a public-private partnership working with the Parks Department to recast the island as the center of the city's sports and entertainment scene. After years of performing small tasks, like cleaning out overgrown areas where drug users hid, the foundation has hit its stride. It has repaired and reorganized the ball fields and begun restoring the shoreline and wetlands. In 2001, it demolished uncomfortable, old Downing Stadium and began work on a 19,500-seat amphitheater. An Olympic-quality track-and-field center is projected for 2002. Plans also call for a family-themed water park and improved access to the island.

Triborough Bridge

Randall's Island also supports the junction of the three arms of the heavily-used Triborough Bridge. The bridge was built by Moses, who then ran his empire from the Triborough Bridge and Tunnel Authority headquarters built in its shadows.

The Triborough's Y-shaped structure links the islands to Manhattan, Queens, and the Bronx. (All the roadways have footwalks allowing ambitious pedestrians to reach Randall's Island via the bridge.) The Bronx arm crosses the Bronx River and the Harlem Kills and can be converted into a lift bridge if the Kills is ever made navigable. The Manhattan arm starts at E. 125th St and crosses the Harlem River. Each of the twin 215 ft towers has a 1,000-ton cement counterweight and a 200-horsepower motor, which can lift the six-lane roadway and the span from about 55 ft above water to 135 ft above. The Queens arm, which runs from Astoria above Hell Gate, is a 1,380 ft suspension bridge with 315 ft towers and a roadway 143 ft above water.

History

Construction had begun on the Triborough Bridge (1936; Othmar Ammann, chief engineer), but the first $5.4-million allocation had been largely wasted on Tammany graft when the stock market crashed on Oct 29, 1929. After the crash, funds dried up, and in 1932 the only thing that existed of the future bridge was a lump of cement on Ward's Island that would ultimately become an anchorage. But soon after, Robert Moses gained control of the Authority and got a $37-million construction loan from President Roosevelt's Public Works Administration. By 1936 Moses had, astonishingly, completed the bridge. It has been suggested that Moses got the job done thanks to a sweetheart land deal with William Randolph Hearst, a deal that forced Moses to build the bridge across Randall's Island even though Ward's Island provided a more direct route to Queens.

Hell Gate Arch

The second bridge crossing these islands is Hell Gate Arch (1917; Gustav Lindenthal, engineer, and Henry Hornbostel, architect), a 1,017 ft span carrying four railroad tracks across the East River over Ward's Island. Lindenthal designed the Queensboro Bridge and was involved with the Williamsburg Bridge and the Brooklyn Bridge, but the structurally beautiful and imaginatively engineered Hell Gate Arch is considered his crowning achievement. The bridge is also the most prominent monument to Alexander Cassatt, the turn-of-the-20C president of the Pennsylvania Railroad, who planned a direct rail link between New England and the northeast corridor cities Philadelphia, Baltimore, and Washington.

The arch's design is unusual in that the upper arc curves upward at the ends, a pleasing visual note that also allows overhead clearance for locomotives and aids the bridge's rigidity by allowing deeper stiffening trusses. The handsome granite-faced towers with their arched openings reminded early observers of the portico to a mammoth temple. Among Lindenthal's engineering feats were the bridging of an underwater fissure in the bedrock beneath the Ward's Island foundation and his construction of the arch without scaffolding supporting the unfinished span, since that would have closed Hell Gate to navigation. When the final steel section was hoisted in place at the center, an adjustment of only $\frac{5}{16}$ of an inch was needed to close the arch.

21 · The Silk Stocking District, the Whitney Museum, and Environs

Subway: Lexington Ave Express or Local (4, 5, 6) to 59th St. Broadway Local (N, R) to Lexington Ave.
Bus: M101, M102, M103, Q32, M57, M31.

Silk Stocking District

The Silk Stocking District on the Upper East Side was once the nation's wealthiest congressional district, and while original district boundaries have been redrawn, the name still applies to the Upper East Side from about 61st St to 80th St. Its postal code, 10021, is the wealthiest zip code in the nation. Much of the neighborhood is included in the Upper East Side Historic District.

The neighborhood has beautiful houses and apartments, several interesting museums, and numerous consulates housed in former town houses. Madison Ave and its side streets from about E. 57th to E. 86th Sts have one of the city's denser concentrations of art galleries (the others are in SoHo, Chelsea, and on 57th St). It also has one of the city's ritzier shopping strips, including such shops as Versace, Armani, Ralph Lauren, D. Cenci, Baccarat, and Barney's. The population is mostly white.

Bloomingdale's

Begin at Bloomingdale's (between E. 59th and E. 60th Sts) on the east side of Lexington Ave, which in the past decades has been associated with whatever is "hot" in women's fashion. Known to its habitués as "Bloomies," it is one of the nation's most successful stores.

History

Lyman Bloomingdale, who with his brother Joseph founded the store in 1872, learned the retail business as a clerk in Bettlebeck & Co. Dry Goods in Newark, New Jersey, a firm with an all-star sales staff that also included Benjamin Altman (later of B. Altman & Co.) and Abraham Abraham (later of Abraham and Straus). Unlike the other 19C department stores, which began downtown and migrated uptown, Bloomingdale's started at 938 Third Ave, only a few blocks from its present location. In both its arrival and its demise, the Third Ave elevated railway was a blessing to Bloomingdale's, first bringing so many shoppers from downtown when it opened (1879) that within seven years the store had to move to larger quarters on the northwest corner of Third Ave and E. 59th St, a block it now completely occupies. Then, when the El was torn down (1954), the Upper East Side, its real estate formerly depressed by the dark and dirty El, began a swift climb to respectability and affluence. Fortunately, Bloomingdale's management had already begun upgrading the inventory from its former good-quality-but-sensible merchandise to the present stuff of fashion and fantasy.

Museum of American Illustration

128 E. 63rd St, New York NY 10021. ☎ (212) 838-2560. Web site: www.society illustrators.org. Open Tues 10–8; Wed–Fri 10–5; Sat noon–4. Closed Sun, Mon,

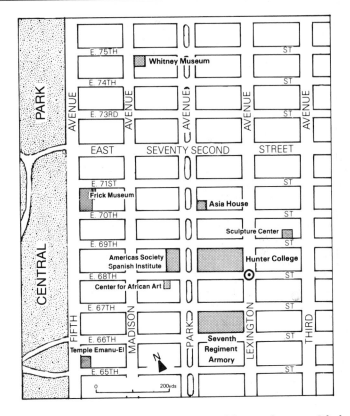

month of Aug, legal holidays. Free. Changing exhibitions, lectures. Gift shop. Ground-floor exhibition space accessible to wheelchairs.

A little further uptown is the Museum of American Illustration, located in an 1875 carriage house on E. 63rd St (between Park and Lexington Aves). It is the exhibition space for the Society of Illustrators and offers changing exhibitions designed to encourage interest in the art of illustration.

The Society of Illustrators dates back to 1901, when its monthly dinners attracted famous artists such as Maxfield Parrish, Frederic Remington, and N. C. Wyeth. The museum, however, dates from 1981 and now has a collection of about 1,500 works. Exhibitions include solo and group shows, historical and thematic exhibitions (air force art, stamps, sports' collectibles) and the Illustrators' Annual Exhibition, which showcases the best book, editorial, advertising, and institutional illustrations of the year.

East 64th St between Park and Lexington Aves features an eclectic mix of architecture, including the handsome Gothic-style **Central Presbyterian Church** (1922; Henry C. Pelton and Allen & Collens) with its soaring tower and several brownstones built in the 1870s, including nos. 116 and 118 E. 64th St. Some brownstones from the same period have been altered—for example no. 117 E.

64th St, which has a British neoclassical look (altered 1907; Theodore Visscher), and 121 E. 64th St, which has a stucco Tudor facade (altered 1919; James Casale). Here also are several conspicuous buildings by prominent modern architects. At 112 E. 64th St is the former Asia House, now the **Russell Sage Foundation** (1959; Philip Johnson & Assoc); its facade of glass and white-painted steel stands out on this street of stone. At 130 E. 64th is the former **Edward Durrell Stone residence** (original brownstone 1878; James E. Ware; makeover 1956; Edward Durrell Stone). Stone installed a massive concrete grille on the facade, which suggested a radiator cover to some observers. When his widow removed it in 1987, the Landmarks Commission issued a violation—ironic, since the building has long been out of character with its neighbors in the historic district. To avoid complicated negotiations, the family reinstalled the facade in 1999 when the building was on the market.

The Gothic-Moorish **Barbizon Hotel** (1927; Murgatroyd & Ogden), 140 E. 63rd St (southeast corner of the intersection at Lexington Ave), was founded as a women's residence in 1927. Young women needed three references to be considered for admission, and then they had to pass muster in terms of family, looks, dress, and demeanor. Afternoon tea was part of the package, as were regular drama, music, and discussion nights. Men were not allowed beyond the first floor lounges and had to leave by 10 P.M. Upstairs were pink-and-green, 9 × 12 ft dormitory-style rooms. Among the soon-to-be famous clientele were Joan Crawford, Lauren Bacall, Gene Tierney, Grace Kelly, Candice Bergen, Liza Minnelli, Ali MacGraw, and Cloris Leachman, as well as Eileen Ford models and employees of the Katharine Gibbs secretarial school. In *The Bell Jar,* Sylvia Plath renamed the Barbizon the Amazon and described its tenants as "mostly girls my age with wealthy parents who wanted to be sure their daughters would be living where men couldn't get at them and deceive them." The hotel's post-1960s decline was halted on Valentine's Day, 1981, when it began admitting men and underwent the first of several renovations. Today it operates as a traditional hotel.

Continue east on E. 63rd St. At 153 E. 63rd St is the Spanish-style **Hatch House** (1919; Frederick J. Sterner; DL), which features stucco walls, a red tile roof, a handsome iron gate, and an interior courtyard. It was built for William K. Vanderbilt's daughter Barbara Rutherford Hatch and her husband. The theatrical producer Charles Dillingham, the burlesque star Gypsy Rose Lee, and the artist Jasper Johns all subsequently lived in the building.

The building at **142 E. 65th St** (1871; Frederick S. Barus), between Third and Lexington Aves, was once home (1906–61) to federal judge Learned Hand; it later belonged to ex-president Richard Nixon, who paid $750,000 for it in 1979 after being rejected by co-op boards in the neighborhood. Two years later, Nixon sold the town house for nearly $3 million and moved to New Jersey.

On the north side of E. 65th St toward Lexington Ave begins the **Church of St. Vincent Ferrer complex.** The St. Vincent Ferrer School (1948; Elliot L. Chisling, Ferrenz & Taylor; DL), 151 E. 65th St, is the most modern and least interesting building. Next door, at 141 E. 65th St, is the Holy Name Society Building (1930; Wilfrid Anthony; DL), which echoes the church's architectural elements. On the northeast corner of E. 65th St at 869 Lexington Ave is the Priory (1881; William Schickel; DL), an English-Gothic building with pointed arches and a central pavilion. At the southeast corner of E. 66th St and Lexington Ave is the **Church of St. Vincent Ferrer** (1918; Bertram G. Goodhue; DL), faced with Plymouth granite and white limestone trim, with carvings (Lee Lawrie) that sprout from the octagonal turrets.

China Institute in America

Return to E. 65th St and walk east to the China Institute in America (between Lexington and Park Aves), a nonpolitical, nonprofit organization (founded 1926) that promotes the understanding of traditional and contemporary Chinese culture. The institute offers language courses, workshops for travelers and business people, and children's programs. It also sponsors the China House Gallery.

China House Gallery

125 E. 65th St, New York, NY 10021. ☎ (212) 744-8181. Website: www.china institute.org. Open Mon–Sat 10–5; Tues and Thurs until 8; Sun 1–5. Closed holidays and between exhibitions. Admission charge. Exhibitions, lectures, scholarly catalogs, gallery tours, performances. Not accessible to wheelchairs.

Subway: Lexington Ave Local (6) to 68th St–Hunter College. Sixth Ave Exp (B, Q marked 21st St–Queensbridge) to Lexington Ave. Bus: M101, M102, M103, M66.

The gallery mounts highly regarded exhibitions of Chinese painting, calligraphy, architecture, decorative art, folk art, photography, and textiles, which are curated by internationally recognized scholars.

Continue east to the **Sara Delano Roosevelt Memorial House** (1908; Charles A. Platt; DL) at 47–49 E. 65th St (between Park and Madison Aves). The domineering Sara, mother of FDR, built this double house—with a single entrance but connecting doors on several floors—as a wedding present for her son and his bride, Eleanor. Sarah lived in no. 47 and the young couple in no. 49. FDR recovered from polio in the fourth-floor bedroom (1921–22) and received congratulatory telegrams in the parlor when he was elected president in 1932. Roosevelt House became part of Hunter College of CUNY in 1943, two years after Sara's death; the college plans to restore the buildings and convert them into a conference center.

The eye-catching brick apartment building at **45 E. 66th St** (1908; Harde & Short; DL) drips with Gothic terra-cotta detail. From 1974 until his death in 1987, Andy Warhol, symbol of the radical downtown art scene, lived at 57 E. 66th St, a very posh uptown address.

Occupying the square block of Park to Lexington Aves and E. 66th to E. 67th Sts is the former **Seventh Regiment Armory** (1880; Charles W. Clinton), whose huge drill hall (187 × 290 ft) is one of the largest unobstructed indoor spaces in the city. Its private rooms, as befit an outfit known as the "Silk Stocking Regiment" for its socially prominent members, were designed by Louis C. Tiffany and Stanford White, among others, and remain superb examples of late-19C American interior design. The regiment now hosts antiques shows and other large-scale events.

In the 19C, carriage houses and stables were usually hidden away on the side streets, while the houses of the wealthy occupied the avenues. Several carriage houses survive on E. 66th St (between Park and Lexington Aves), the best of which is **no. 126 E. 66th St** (1895; W. J. Wallace and S. E. Gage), with its third-floor balcony and powerful brick archivolt surrounding the carriage doors. H. O. Havemeyer and Oliver H. Payne stabled their horses here before John Hay Whitney took it over for his cars.

A block north, at 149–151 E. 67th St, is the **Kennedy Child Study Center,** formerly the Mount Sinai Dispensary (1890; Buchman & Deisler and Brunner & Tryon; DL), brownstone below, with arched windows and upper-level terra-cotta trim. Next door is the **19th Precinct Station House** (1887; Nathaniel D. Bush), a limestone building with blue cast-iron trim, red brick, and multihued terra-cotta. Adjoining the precinct house is the station for **Engine Company 39, Ladder Company 15** (1886; Napoleon Le Brun & Sons), a brownstone-and-brick building, which once served as headquarters for the Fire Department.

The pièce de résistance, however, is the **Park East Synagogue** (1890; Schneider & Herter; DL) at 163 E. 67th St, a flamboyant, tan brick, Moorish-style building with asymmetrical towers, a central rose window, terrific terra-cotta detailing, and more than a dozen cutout arches of varying sizes.

Hunter College

On the west side of Lexington Ave, between E. 68th and E. 69th Sts, is the castle-like former main building of Hunter College (1913; C. B. J. Snyder). Hunter opened a more modern building at Park Ave and E. 68th St in 1940. The college added two new buildings in 1986.

History

One of the largest colleges in the City University system, Hunter College was founded in 1870 as a teacher's college for women. Men were admitted in 1964. Today the undergraduate student body, more than 18,000 and still 75 percent female, includes students from 80 nations. More than half are the first in their families to attend college and more than half are 23 or older. Hunter's programs in liberal arts, education, and social work are all highly regarded.

Continue west past Hunter's Sylvia and Danny Kaye Playhouse, which opened in 1993. At the southwest corner of Park Ave and E. 68th St is the former **Harold Pratt residence** (1919; Delano & Aldrich), 58 E. 68th St, a limestone mansion with rectangular, rounded-arch, and octagonal windows and a seashell motif. Pratt was the youngest son of the Brooklyn industrialist Charles Pratt (see Walk 48) and the only one to venture beyond the family's Brooklyn stronghold.

Occupying the block of Park Ave (between E. 68th and E. 69th Sts) is a group of houses built in the years after the turn of the 20C. In 1965 a developer wanted to demolish them for an apartment building, but the Marquesa de Cuevas, a granddaughter of John D. Rockefeller, bought them all and turned them over to their present owners.

The Americas Society

The first is the former **Percy R. Pyne residence** (1911; McKim, Mead & White; DL), 680 Park Ave, which houses the Americas Society, whose mission is to educate the people of the United States about the cultures, societies, and art of its Western Hemisphere neighbors.

Americas Society Art Gallery

680 Park Ave, New York, NY 10021. ☎ (212) 249-8950. Website: www. americas-society.org. Open Tues–Sun 12–6. Closed Mon, holidays. Free. Lectures,

concerts, group visits, and guided tours by appointment. Book shop. Entrance up two steps from street level; gallery on ground floor.

Subway: Lexington Ave (6) to 68th St–Hunter College. Bus: M1, M2, M3, M4, M101, M102.

Since 1967, the Americas Society Art Gallery has presented exhibitions documenting the achievements of the countries neighboring the U.S. to the north and south. The gallery presents exhibitions of the art of Latin America, Canada, and the Caribbean, from pre-Columbian times to the present. Some shows are devoted to emerging talents, some to prominent artists; others focus on indigenous Indian cultures and their pre-Columbian heritage.

Spanish Institute

684 Park Ave, New York, NY 10021. ☎ (212) 628-0420. Website: www.spanish institute.org. Open during exhibitions Mon–Fri 11–6; Sat 11–5. Closed Sun, holidays. Free. Changing exhibitions, lectures, symposia, language instruction, films, concerts. Entrance up three stairs from street. Main gallery on first floor.

The Spanish Institute (1926; McKim, Mead & White; DL), founded in 1954 to promote the understanding of Spanish culture and its influence in the Americas, features an exhibition program that offers some of the finest in contemporary Spanish art as well as historical shows.

Also on the block are the **Italian Cultural Institute** (1919; Delano and Aldrich; DL) at 686 Park Ave and the Consulate General of Italy (1917; Walker & Gillette; DL) at 690 Park Ave. Further north, on the corner of E. 69th St, is the stately limestone-and-granite home of the **Union Club** (1932; Delano & Aldrich), the city's oldest social club, dating back to 1836.

Asia Society and Museum

On the next block is the Asia Society and Museum (northeast corner of Park Ave and E. 70th St). The society, founded in 1956 by John D. Rockefeller III to foster understanding between Americans and Asians, offers programs that focus on political, commercial, cultural, and social issues in countries throughout Asia and the Pacific. Its home, **Asia House** (1981; Edward Larrabee Barnes Assocs.; renovated 2001; Voorsanger & Assocs.) bears the society's logo—a lion adapted from an 18C bronze Nepalese guardian figure. Inside are the society's headquarters and exhibition space.

Asia Society Museum

725 Park Ave (70th St), New York, NY 10021. ☎ (212) 288-6400. Web site: www.asiasociety.org. Open Tues–Sun 11–6. Closed Mon, major holidays. Admission charge. Changing exhibitions, lectures, gallery tours, concerts, films, arts programs, special events. Café; book shop; gift shop. Accessible to wheelchairs.

Subway: Lexington Ave local (6) to 68th St–Hunter College. Bus: M1, M2, M3, M4, M66.

In addition to mounting changing exhibitions, the society has a permanent collection, whose core holdings were gathered and donated (1979) by Mr. and Mrs. John D. Rockefeller III. The works date from 2000 B.C. to the present and include prehistoric Chinese bronze ritual vessels; Ming dynasty ceramics; Indian sculpture from the Kushan period; manuscript pages from the Rajput school in northern India; Buddhist sculptures from Thailand, Indonesia, and Burma; and Japanese woodcuts and ceramics.

The recent renovation, which doubled public and gallery space, allows masterpieces from the Rockefeller Collection to be on display at all times. At the reopening of the refurbished galleries, the society unveiled major works by contemporary Asian and Asian American artists, which were commissioned for long-term installation in the building.

The **Explorers' Club** at 46 E. 70th St, founded in 1904, includes on its roster some 3,500 members from 58 countries. Among the famous explorers, past and present: Sir Edmund Hillary, Tenzing Norgay, Buzz Aldrin, Neil Armstrong, Sally K. Ride, and Reinhold Messsner. The club (not open to the public except for occasional lectures) owns rare books, manuscripts, and paintings of historical value as well as memorabilia of famous explorers. The building (1912; Frederick J. Sterner) was originally the home of Stephen C. Clark, younger son of the Singer Sewing Machine magnate Edward Clark, who built the Dakota Apartments.

The Visiting Nurse Service of New York, at 107 E. 70th St (between Park and Lexington Aves), occupies the former Thomas W. Lamont residence (1921; Walker & Gillette), a Gothic-style home built for a parson's son who rose to chair the board of J. P. Morgan & Company. The **Paul Mellon House,** (1965; Mazza & Seccia) at 125 E. 70th St, is one of the few town houses built after World War II.

Turn right on Lexington and left on E. 69th St. Among the stables and carriage houses here, perhaps the most appealing is **no. 159 E. 69th St** (1882; Charles W. Romeyn), with its impressive entryway.

Sculpture Center

The carriage house at 167 E. 69th St (1909; Charles E. Birge) was built for George Gustav Heye, the founder of the Museum of the American Indian. It now houses the Sculpture Center, a nonprofit organization devoted exclusively to sculpture, which maintains both a school and a gallery.

Sculpture Center Gallery

167 E. 69th St, New York, NY 10021. ☎ (212) 879-3500. Open Tues–Sat 11–5. Closed Sun, Mon, and summer. Admission free. Changing exhibitions, catalogs. Accessible to wheelchairs.

Subway: Lexington Ave Local (6) to 68th St–Hunter College. Bus: M1, M2, M3, M4, M15, M66, M101, M102.

Exhibitions include emerging and midcareer artists, site-specific installations, and video installations.

Continue east to Third Ave and turn left, walking north to E. 73rd St. Turn left. Here is a wonderful row of carriage houses, including nos. 168–182 on the south side of the street and nos. 161–167 on the north side (built c. 1884–1902; various architects; DL). The house at **177 E. 73rd St** (1906; Charles F. Hoppe; DL), a harbinger of the future, was built as a garage for automobiles and is the fanciest garage in city. At one time Joseph Pulitzer owned the house at 166 E. 73rd St (1884; Richard M. Hunt; DL).

Continue west to the slender five-story neo-Federal townhouse at 127 E. 73rd St, originally the **Charles Gibson House** (1904; McKim, Mead & White), with a columned portico, second-story balcony beneath a large rounded-arch window, and a roof with a balustrade and three dormer windows. The house was designed by Stanford White for his friend Gibson, one of the leading illustrators and cartoonists of the late 19C; he was most famous for his Gibson Girls, pen-and-ink portraits of young society women.

Next door, at 129 E. 73rd, is a beautiful neo-Italian Renaissance mansion (1908; Harry Allen Jacobs), built originally for an attorney named Charles Guggenheimer and later home to the Leo Baeck Institute, devoted to the study of German Jewry (see the Center for Jewish History in Walk 12).

Return to Lexington Ave and walk north to E. 76th. **St. Jean Baptiste Church** (1913; Nicholas Serracino; DL), at 1067–1071 Lexington Ave (southeast corner of intersection at E. 76th St), was built to serve a Yorkville parish of French Canadian Catholics founded in 1882. The building, funded by the financier Thomas Fortune Ryan, its towered and domed silhouette anchoring the intersection, harks back to Renaissance Italian precedents. On the Lexington Ave side two bell towers, decorated with cherubs, pediments, scrolls, and swags, flank a globe supported by angels. On the corner of E. 76th St and Lexington Ave is an angel blowing his trumpet.

Whitney Museum of American Art

945 Madison Ave (at E. 75th St), New York, NY 10021. ☎ (212) 570-3676. Web site: www.whitney.org. Open Tues–Thurs 11–6; Fri 1–9; Sat–Sun 11–6. Closed Mon, national holidays. Admission charge. Thurs 6–9, pay what you wish. Changing exhibitions, lectures, gallery talks, symposia, performances, film, video. Restaurant. Gift shop. Accessible to wheelchairs.

Subway: Lexington Ave Local (6) to 77th St. Bus: M1, M2, M3, M4, M30, M79.

Walk west to Madison Ave and a block south to the Whitney Museum of American Art, founded (1930) by Gertrude Vanderbilt Whitney. The museum houses a superb collection of 20C American art and offers an active and sometimes controversial exhibition program.

History

In 1907 Gertrude Vanderbilt Whitney opened a studio in Greenwich Village. Linked by birth and marriage to two of the city's wealthiest and most eminent families, the Whitneys (oil and streetcars) and the Vanderbilts (shipping and railroads), she was nonetheless drawn to bohemianism and used her considerable means to support and exhibit young American artists. The Whitney Studio Club showed Stuart Davis, Edward Hopper, Charles Sheeler, Reginald Marsh, and John Sloan, among others, and Mrs. Whitney further supported the artists by buying many of the works she exhibited. In 1929 she offered her collection to the Metropolitan Museum of Art, which spurned it.

Understandably irritated with the establishment, she opened the first Whitney Museum on W. 8th St in 1931. In 1954 the museum moved uptown to W. 54th St, nearly quadrupling its attendance, and today the Whitney is the most important showcase of contemporary American art in the city.

Exterior

The building (1966; Marcel Breuer) has made the museum an architectural presence on Madison Ave. Breuer spoke of wanting the museum to have the vitality of the streets, the latitude of a bridge, and the weight of a skyscraper. What resulted is a building of three tiers of reinforced concrete clad in gray granite and cantilevered out like the steps of an inverted pyramid. The seven windows are randomly sized and placed; the entrance is reached by a concrete bridge over a sunken sculpture garden. In the early 1990s an annex was built for the staff, allowing the museum to add gallery space on the fifth floor of the main building.

Permanent Collection

In the spring of 1998, the Whitney opened redesigned galleries on the fifth floor that contain works from the first half of the 20C: painting, sculpture, prints, photographs, and drawings. The galleries are anchored by rooms dedicated to three artists whose work the museum has collected in depth: Edward Hopper, Georgia O'Keeffe, and Alexander Calder. Calder's *Circus* (1926–31) a work of performance art with whimsical figures of wire and other materials, is now installed upstairs next to a monitor that shows Calder himself "performing" the circus. In the fall of 2000, works created since World War II were reinstalled on the second floor. Mrs. Whitney bought many paintings by Charles Demuth, Charles Sheeler, Reginald Marsh, Joseph Stella, George Bellows, and The Eight, an influential group of early-20C painters led by Robert Henri, known for their unglamorized views of urban life; their work led to the creation of the Ashcan School. The museum has strong holdings in the works of Donald Judd, Willem de Kooning, Ad Reinhardt, Mark Rothko, and David Smith.

Across the street, at 940 Madison Ave, is the former **U.S. Mortgage and Trust Company,** once a handsome bank building and now an upscale home furnishings boutique with a restaurant in one of the old bank vaults.

Walk north to E. 79th St and turn right. The apartment building at **39 E. 79th St** (1926; Kenneth Murchison) was built by the etiquette expert Emily Post so she could live near her son and grandchild. Post, who lived here until her death in 1960, rounded up other buyers, including Murchison, the building's architect, Stanford White's widow, Bessie, and other members of the New York Social Register.

The rest of the block of E. 79th St between Fifth and Madison Aves has a series of landmark town houses: no. 53 (1917; Trowbridge & Livingston; DL), now the New York Society Library; no. 59 (1909; Foster, Gade & Graham; DL); no. 63 (1903; Adams & Warren; DL) and nos. 67–69 (1908; Carrère & Hastings; DL), now home to the Greek Consulate General.

On Park Avenue, just to the south, is the eye-catching Spanish-style **898 Park Ave** (1927), a 14-story apartment building wonderfully decorated with elaborate gold spiked lanterns, a gold leaf grill on the door, and unusual terra-cotta detailing. Above the doorway is a corbeled arcade, and above that, a five-bay arcade: each of the five bays features a terra-cotta old man in a different activity (sleeping in one, studying in another) on a blue terra-cotta background.

On the northwest corner, in the entryway to 900 Park Ave, is a huge, whimsical bronze *Cat* (1984) by Fernando Botero. In the early 1990s, Botero became the first artist to have his work displayed on the Park Ave malls, in what became an ongoing project sponsored by the Public Art Fund.

Walk north to E. 80th St, then turn right and walk east to another group of landmarked mansions. The home at **120 E. 80th St** (1930; Cross & Cross; DL) was built for George Whitney, head of J. P. Morgan & Co; it is the most elaborate of the group, with a columned portico with pedimented central window above and a slate roof with dormer windows above a balustrade. The building at **130 E. 80th St** (1928; Mott B. Schmidt; DL) belonged first to real estate mogul Vincent Astor but since 1947 has been home to the Junior League of the City of New York.

22 · Fifth Avenue: 59th Street to 79th Street

Subway: Lexington Ave Express or Local (4, 5, 6) to 59th St: Sixth Ave Local (F) or Eighth Ave Local (E) to Fifth Ave–53rd St. Broadway Local (N, R) to Fifth Ave. Bus: M1, M2, M3, M4, M5, M6, M7, M57.

Fifth Ave north of 59th St runs along the eastern edge of Central Park. Many of this area's mansions have been converted to other uses, yet it remains home to some of the city's most fabulously wealthy residents and is part of the Silk Stocking District. At 834 Fifth Ave, one must be worth over $50 million and pay $10 million cash and $12,000 a month maintenance for a duplex. Most residents at 960 Fifth Ave are worth over $100 million; their building features an in-house chef and maid and laundry service.

History
Fifth Ave between E. 59th and E. 79th Sts, one of the city's most attractive boulevards, remained undeveloped until the city purchased land for Central Park in 1856. Before then 59th St formed the frontier between the city's most exclusive residential section and a social and geographical wasteland called "Squatter's Sovereignty," which stretched almost to 120th St and contained poor people living in wooden shacks sometimes patched together with flattened tin cans. After the park was begun, the area was purged of its humble human and animal populations (pigs and goats) and began to receive many of the city's wealthiest and most powerful families. From the closing decades of the 19C to the years of World War I, the area displayed an imposing collection of monumental residences.

Eclecticism on Fifth Avenue
The period during which the great mansions rose coincided roughly with the eclectic period in American architecture. As the new millionaires, many of whom had made their fortunes during the post–Civil War boom, arrived on the social scene desirous of building suitably impressive homes, they turned for advice to the city's influential architects, who controlled the canons of taste. What the established architects—notably Richard Morris Hunt, Charles Follen McKim, and Stanford White—offered was eclecticism, a self-conscious selection of styles from the classical orders of the past. The new classical architecture depended on the availability of cheap, skilled

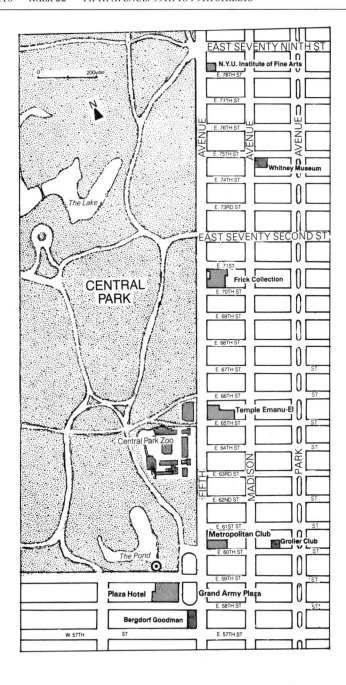

labor, supplied by the influx of immigrants, many of whom were experienced in masonry, ironwork, stone carving, painting and gilding, and ornamental plaster work. Eclecticism died after the end of World War I, when changing economic patterns and new building technology dictated the end of sumptuous masonry building and ushered in the era of the skyscraper and the high-rise apartment.

Although eclecticism made itself felt in other parts of the city, the greatest concentration of such buildings in residential uses is here in the vicinity of Fifth Ave—so much so that novelist Edith Wharton, whose privileged background and judicious eye made her a keen commentator on social developments of the period, once described this wide-ranging selection of detail as a "complete architectural meal."

Begin at **Grand Army Plaza** (between 58th and 60th Sts on the west side of Fifth Ave), usually called simply **the plaza.** The open square, one of the few deviations from the city's gridiron plan, provides a site for the **Pulitzer Memorial Fountain,** built in 1916 (Carrère & Hastings) with a $50,000 donation provided by the will of Joseph Pulitzer (1847–1911), publisher of the *New York World.* It is surmounted by Karl Bitter's statue of Pomona, goddess of abundance, a graceful young woman who is surely at home in this posh neighborhood. Bitter, a protégé of Richard Morris Hunt, was killed by a car in 1915 as he was leaving the Metropolitan Opera; his assistants completed the statue.

Plaza Hotel

Facing the plaza between 58th and 59th Sts on the west side is the opulent **Plaza Hotel** (1907; Henry J. Hardenbergh; DL), ideally situated with views of Fifth Ave and Central Park.

History

Built on the site of a previous, more restrained Plaza Hotel (1890; demolished 1905), the building has played host to such luminaries as Mark Twain, Eleanor Roosevelt, Groucho Marx, F. Scott Fitzgerald (who set short stories and a scene from the *Great Gatsby* here), and Frank Lloyd Wright, who had a permanent suite beginning in 1953 while he designed the Guggenheim Museum. (Solomon Guggenheim also had a suite at the Plaza.) The very first guests to sign the register were "Mr. & Mrs. Alfred G. Vanderbilt and servant."

Exterior

Architectural critics admire Hardenbergh's skill in manipulating the details of its French Renaissance design, using dormers, balustrades, high roofs, and rounded corner turnings to create a harmonious whole. On any given day, limousines are lined up around the block, making the entrance chaotic.

Interior

If you can't afford to stay at the Plaza, you can at least explore the lobby with its attractive mosaics and impressive marble columns and chandeliers. The lobby restrooms are a popular pit stop for tourists and New Yorkers alike.

On the east side of Fifth Ave (between 58th and 59th Sts) is the immense **F.A.O. Schwarz** toy store, where a fuzzy-hatted Beefeater doorman uncharacteristically waves to passersby. The store, founded in 1863 in Baltimore, moved to Lower Manhattan in 1870 and soon became successful. It has appeared in the movies *Miracle on 34th Street* and *Big.*

F.A.O. Schwarz occupies three floors in the **General Motors Building** (1968; Edward Durell Stone and Emery Roth & Sons), a 50-story, white, marble-clad skyscraper that replaced the Savoy Plaza Hotel, destroying the former gracious, traditional design of the square. Artificial turf carpets the sunken plaza. Developer Donald Trump recently bought the building and, as elsewhere, slapped his name on it, renaming it the General Motors Building at Trump International Plaza. On 59th St is the latest addition to the city's recent proliferation of street-level studios, used for CBS's *Early Show.*

On the west side of Fifth Ave, north of Central Park South, is one of the nation's finest equestrian statues, *General William Tecumseh Sherman* (1892–1903; Augustus Saint-Gaudens), the Civil War Union general best remembered for his destructive sweep through Georgia. Walking before the conqueror and waving an olive branch is a figure of Victory; the pine branch on the granite pedestal (Charles Follen McKim) signifies Georgia.

The city's horse-drawn carriage trade is appropriately situated here. Carriage drivers range from neatly attired men and women in black overcoats and top hats to grungy-looking stable boys. They provide tours of the park with various degrees of enthusiasm.

Cross Fifth Ave. On the northeast corner of 59th St and Fifth Ave is the **Sherry-Netherland Hotel** (1927; Schultze & Weaver), once part of a trio that included the Plaza and the Savoy Plaza. Its high-peaked roof adorns the skyline; gargoyles with huge lamps in their mouths decorate the doorway. The sculptured paneled doors originally decorated the porch of the extravagant mansion of Cornelius Vanderbilt II at Fifth Ave and 57th St. By 1893, the house had been extended west and north and had swollen to 137 rooms. When it was demolished to make space for Bergdorf Goodman in 1927, two of the six sculpture groups were snapped up by the hotel; both panels announce the arrival of guests.

Shops on the ground floor advertise the old and the new: **À La Vielle Russie,** established in 1851, sells czarist jewelry; **Geoffrey Beene**'s latest designs are displayed in a space (783 Fifth Ave) designed by architect Michael Graves (1984).

Begin walking north on Fifth Ave. On the northeast corner of 60th St and Fifth Ave stands the **Metropolitan Club,** an imposing Italian Renaissance palazzo (1892–94; McKim, Mead & White; DL). The club was founded by J. P. Morgan and other discontented members of the Union Club after the board of governors had blackballed a candidate whom Morgan had proposed for membership. One of the participants in the rejection remarked that Morgan's protégé had been voted down because, figuratively at least, he ate with his knife. An impressive wrought-iron fence and a colonnaded gateway guard the carriage entrance.

The **Hotel Pierre** (1928; Schultze & Weaver), 2 E. 61st St, is another of the city's older, prestigious hotels, its towered top a skyline landmark.

Although the majority of buildings in the eclectic style, like the Plaza Hotel and the Metropolitan Club, reflect French, Italian, or Roman originals, the **Knickerbocker Club** (1915; Delano & Aldrich; DL) at 2 E. 62nd St recalls a town house of the Federal period with its fine brickwork, marble lintels, and wrought-iron window gratings.

Diagonally across the intersection is the **Fifth Avenue Synagogue** (1959; Percival Goodman), at 5 E. 62nd St. Unlike many of New York's houses of worship—built as freestanding buildings and often located on the avenues—this one stands on a cross street and is attached to its neighbors on either side. The limestone facade has pointed oval windows filled with abstract patterns of stained glass; the shape of the windows is reiterated in the design of the sanctuary.

The intersection of Fifth Ave with 63rd St is graced with **820 Fifth Ave** (1916; Starrett & Van Vleck), one of the great apartment houses of the period. The original plans show each apartment occupying a full floor and including five fireplaces, a kitchen-pantry with four sinks, 6½ bathrooms, servants' rooms, and a conservatory. The exterior details—the copper cornice with a frieze beneath, pedimented windows, and balconies—were also features of the great private town houses of the period. Now a 12-story co-op with floor-through 18-room apartments, it remains one of the premier residences in the city. (Potential buyers' fortunes must be at least ten times the value of the apartment, which is usually in the mid-teen millions; maintenance is reportedly $14,000 a month.)

The **New York Academy of Sciences,** 2 E. 63rd St, is the third-oldest scientific organization in the United States, founded as the Lyceum of Natural History in 1817. It occupies the former William Ziegler Jr. residence (1920; Sterner & Wolfe). Ziegler, president of the Royal Baking Powder Company, was eventually followed by Norman B. Woolworth, of the five-and-dime family, who donated the building to the academy. The academy's gallery has exhibitions that explore the relationship between science and art; for information ☎ (212) 838-0230.

A block north, at 2 E. 64th St, is the former **Edward Berwind Mansion** (1896; N.C. Mellen), now converted to apartments. At one time reputedly the largest owner of coal mines in the nation, Berwind was also for many years the chief executive officer of the IRT (Interborough Rapid Transit). Described as Prussian in appearance, and as dour, close-mouthed, and acquisitive in business dealings, he was apparently socially charming and belonged to about 40 clubs and societies. This brick-and-limestone house in the style of an Italian palazzo was his town house; his country residence was "The Elms" at Newport, Rhode Island.

New India House (1903; Warren & Wetmore), home of the Indian Consulate and headquarters for the Indian delegation to the United Nations, 3 E. 64th St, is one of the few remaining buildings of modest scale designed by Warren & Wetmore, most famous for Grand Central Station. It originally belonged to Mrs. Marshall Orme Wilson, daughter of the dowager Mrs. Astor. The mansion of molded limestone with a slate-and-copper roof, arched drawing room windows, and small oval dormers, exemplifies the Beaux-Arts style.

The Arsenal

Across Fifth Ave inside the park, nestled among the trees near 64th St, is the Arsenal (1848; Martin E. Thompson; DL), an ivy-covered, eccentrically charming brick building surmounted by eight crenellated octagonal towers. The newel posts of the central staircase represent cannons, while the balusters supporting the railing resemble rifles.

History

Although it was constructed to replace an older ammunition depot downtown on Centre St, whose decrepitude made it an easy mark for thieves, the remoteness of the present building (in 1848) rendered it only dubiously effective as a place for stockpiling arms and ammunition. One critic complained that the cannons in the Arsenal, 4½ miles from the previous depot, would be utterly useless, since a mob could riot before the troops could drag the artillery into action. The building later housed the 11th Police Precinct, the Municipal Weather Bureau, the American Museum of Natural History, and a menagerie that predated the Central Park Zoo, before finally becoming home to the city's Parks and Recreation Department in 1934.

Parks Library

Within the building is the newly opened Parks Library, a public archive with 1,500 volumes on nature, recreation, architecture, sports, urban ecology, and New York City planning and politics. Located in room 240, the library is open Mon–Fri 9–6; ☎ (212) 360-8240.

Arsenal Gallery

Central Park at 64th St (Fifth Ave), New York, NY 10019. ☎ (212) 360-8163. Open Mon–Fri 9–5. Closed Sat, Sun, national holidays. Free. Art exhibits, occasional lectures and special events. Accessible to wheelchairs by prior arrangements.

Subway: Lexington Ave Local (6) to 68th St. Broadway Local (N, R) to Fifth Ave. Bus: M1, M2, M3, M4, M30, M66, M72.

The building also houses the Arsenal Gallery, whose changing exhibitions focus primarily on New York City parks, park history, recreation, and fine art depicting nature.

Temple Emanu-El

At 1 E. 65th St stands the largest synagogue in the world, Temple Emanu-El, with a seating capacity greater than St. Patrick's Cathedral. It is also the oldest Reform Jewish congregation in the city and the nation's third oldest, formed in 1845 as a German Jewish cultural society on the Lower East Side. After the congregation merged with Temple Beth El, another influential congregation, it moved from Fifth Ave and 43rd St, where it had been 60 years, to this massive limestone building (1929; Robert D. Kohn, Charles Butler, and Clarence Stein), an adaptation of Moorish and Romanesque styles symbolizing the mingling of Eastern and Western cultures. The three sets of bronze entrance doors bear symbols of the 12 tribes of Israel, as does the arch, which wraps around a magnificent wheel-shaped window (designed by Oliver Smith) with the traditional six-pointed Star of David embedded in the center.

Interior

Inside the 2,500-seat sanctuary, on the east wall (symbolically directing worshippers toward Jerusalem), is the Ark containing the Torah, the scrolls of Mosaic Law. In accordance with the Jewish restriction on visual images, sanctuary decorations are limited to a few traditional designs: the six-pointed Star of David seen in the mosaics and stained glass windows, the Lion of Judah, and the crown, a traditional Torah ornament. The mosaics are by Hildreth Meiere.

Beth-El Chapel

The synagogue's 350-seat Beth-El Chapel, set back from the avenue north of the main building, is Byzantine in flavor. The stained glass window over the ark is by Louis Comfort Tiffany; it adorned Temple Emanu-El's former temple at 43rd St and Fifth Ave, and when reinstalled here it was divided into three sections separated by marble frames. The synagogue sponsors lectures and musical programs, maintains a library and museum of Judaica, and offers tours. For information, ☎ (212) 744-1400 or check the Web site: www.emanuelnyc.org.

Mrs. Astor's Mansion

The temple replaced the mansion of Mrs. Caroline Schermerhorn Astor (wife of William Astor), also known as *the* Mrs. Astor, who dominated New York society in the closing years of the 19C. Her mansion, designed by Richard Morris Hunt, resembled a French Renaissance château. It featured a two-ton bathtub cut from a single block of marble and a ballroom, the capacity of which was said to correspond to the number of acceptable people in New York society, the "Four Hundred."

Since 1946, the **Lotos Club**, 5 E. 66th St, has occupied the former Margaret Vanderbilt Shepard residence (1900; Richard Howland Hunt), which is built in the French Renaissance style. The house passed on to their daughter, Maria, who married William Jay Schieffelin, great-great-grandson of John Jay, political reformer and pharmaceutical heir. The club, founded in 1870, is one of the oldest literary clubs in the country.

Next door, at 3 E. 66th St, a modest placard marks the site of a house where Ulysses S. Grant spent his final years (1881–85) and wrote his memoirs.

At 854 Fifth Ave, between 66th and 67th Sts, stands the town house formerly belonging to R. Livingston Beeckman, now the home of the **Permanent Mission of the Federal Republic of Yugoslavia to the United Nations** (1905; Warren & Wetmore; DL). Designed as a reflection of 18C classic French architecture of the Louis XV period, the house, crowned by a steep copper-covered mansard roof with two stories of dormers, maintains an air of dignity and monumentality, despite being hemmed in by two large apartment buildings.

Across Fifth Ave, at the intersection of 67th St and Central Park, is the **Seventh Regiment Monument** (1926–27; Karl Illava), a memorial to the men of the 107th Infantry who died in World War I. The sculptor was a sergeant in the 107th Infantry.

At the edge of the park, between 70th and 71st Sts, is a **memorial to Richard Morris Hunt** (1898; Daniel Chester French). It stands opposite the site of the former Lenox Library (1870), one of Hunt's finest achievements. The library was torn down and replaced by the Frick Mansion in 1914. Architect Bruce Price, a student of Hunt's, planned the granite monument on which rests a bust of his mentor flanked by two classically draped women: Sculpture and Painting (left) with a mallet and palette, and Architecture (right) with a replica of Hunt's Administration Building at the World's Columbian Exposition. The figures, six ft tall and 600 pounds each, were stolen in 1962 and almost melted down in a belt buckle factory before they were recognized and returned. The monument was restored and rededicated in 1998.

Frick Collection

1 E. 70th St, New York, NY 10021. ☎ (212) 288-0700. Web site:www.frick.org. Open Tues–Sat 10–6; Sun, Lincoln's Birthday, Election Day, and Veterans Day, 1–6. Closed Mon, Jan 1, July 4, Thanksgiving, Dec 24 and 25. Admission charge includes Artphone audio guide. Children under 10 not admitted; an adult must accompany children under 16. Accessible to wheelchairs. Exhibitions, concerts, lectures, special events; call for information. Gift shop.

Across the street is the Frick Collection, housed in one of the avenue's most elegant mansions (1914; Carrère & Hastings; enlarged as a museum, 1935, John Russell Pope; DL. Addition to the east, 1977; Harry Van Dyke and John Barrington Bayley). The house, designed in an 18C French style as a dwelling and gallery, contains Frick's magnificent art collection, including some of the best-known European paintings from the Renaissance to the end of the 19C. Magnificent French 18C furniture, sculpture, enamels, prints and drawings, and porcelains round out the collection.

History

Henry Clay Frick (1849–1919), a pioneer in the coke and steel industries, began collecting art seriously around 1895, indulging his taste for Daubigny, Bouguereau, and the Barbizon School. As his taste matured, he sold earlier acquisitions and began buying Flemish, Dutch, Italian, and Spanish paintings, aided by the English art dealer Joseph Duveen, whose taste he admired. In 1905 he abandoned plans for a new house and gallery in Pittsburgh (pollution from the steel mills would be hazardous to his collection) and commissioned Thomas Hastings of Carrère and Hastings to build a New York residence that could suitably display his artworks. After Frick's death the house and art collection were left in trust to establish a museum and art study center. After the death of Frick's wife in 1931, the building was enlarged and renovated as a museum (opened 1935) by John Russell Pope, who later designed the National Gallery of Art. The Frick Art Reference Library is open to researchers by appointment.

Highlights

The interplay between the superb paintings, the opulent house, and the fine collection of decorative arts, provides an experience unique in New York. Frick was drawn to the aristocratic art of 18C France. In bright, frivolously decorative rooms devoted to Fragonard and Boucher, ornate furniture, sculpture, and decorative arts complement the painted panels on the walls. There are examples of furniture by the master cabinetmakers of the period: Jean-Henri Riesener, Martin Carlin, and Louis Gilbert, as well as Sèvres porcelains and sculpture by Jean-Antoine Houdon.

Frick also enjoyed 18C English portraits. Examples by William Hogarth, Sir Joshua Reynolds, and George Romney are on view in the Dining Room and the Library, along with paintings by Joseph Mallord William Turner and Thomas Gains-borough, who is represented by *The Mall in St. James Park.*

The Living Hall contains some of the finest paintings in the collection. There are two portraits by Titian, *Man in a Red Cap* and *Pietro Aretino.* There are two portraits by Hans Holbein the Younger, *Sir Thomas More* and *Thomas Cromwell,* both beheaded but only one sainted. Giovanni Bellini's *St. Francis in Ecstacy* was one of Frick's favorites, a portrait of the saint in a luminous yet wild landscape. El Greco painted several versions of the ascetic scholar, visionary *St. Jerome;* another is in the Lehman Collection at the Metropolitan.

The Frick is fortunate to own three paintings by Johannes Vermeer: *Girl Interrupted at Her Music, Mistress and Maid,* and *Officer and Laughing Girl.* Jean-Auguste-Dominique Ingres's famous portrait of the *Comtesse d'Haussonville,* Rembrandt's *Self-Portrait* and the enigmatic *The Polish Rider* (even the attribution is disputed), and *King Philip IV of Spain* by Diego Velázquez are all gems of a brilliant collection. There are also portraits by Anthony Van Dyck, Frans Hals, Francisco de Goya, and James Abbott McNeill Whistler; landscapes by Jean-Baptiste-Camille Corot, Albert Cuyp, and Jacob van Ruisdael; religious paintings by Duccio di Buoninsegna, Piero della Francesca, Jan van Eyck, Gerard David, and Claude Lorrain.

Continue north on Fifth Ave. The **Lycée Français,** just off Fifth Ave at 72nd St, occupies two glorious French-style town houses. The house at **7 E. 72nd St** (1899; Flagg & Chambers; DL) features vermiculated stonework and a bulbous mansard roof, while **9 E. 72nd St** (1896; Carrère & Hastings; DL) was in its day praised as a compelling example of the modern French style. The porte cochère led to an interior court from which an imposing staircase arched upward to a grand salon that spanned the whole front of the house.

A block further north and a little off Fifth Ave, at 11 E. 73rd St, is the former **Joseph Pulitzer residence** (1903; McKim, Mead & White). Modeled on two Venetian palazzos, the publisher's house has a wide facade, arched windows, and colonnades. It stood empty much of the time Pulitzer owned it: his illness and near-blindness heightened his sensitivity to sound, and even the double walls of the house could not sufficiently mute the noise of the city.

Continue up Fifth Ave. At 1 E. 75th St is the home of the Commonwealth Fund, the former **Edward S. Harkness House** (1909; Hale & Rogers; DL), a remarkable example of the superb craftsmanship available at the turn of the 20C to those who could pay for it. Protected by a spiked iron fence and a "moat," the house, with its beautifully carved marble, resembles an Italian palazzo and is elegantly detailed from the elaborate cornice to the iron ground-floor gates. Harkness, a noted philanthropist, was the son of Stephen Harkness, one of the original partners of Standard Oil.

Further north, at 1 E. 78th St, is the former **James B. Duke Mansion** (1912; Horace Trumbauer; DL; interior remodeled 1958; Robert Venturi, Cope & Lippincott), now preserved as the New York University Institute of Fine Arts. Built of white limestone so fine that it looks like marble, it was modeled after an 18C mansion in Bordeaux. James B. Duke rose from humble beginnings on a North Carolina farm to dominate the tobacco industry, becoming president of the American Tobacco Co. in 1890 and maintaining his position of power even after the Supreme Court found his company in violation of the antitrust laws. He lived in this mansion until his death in 1925; his daughter Doris Duke and his widow donated the property to NYU in 1957.

The Cultural Services of the French Embassy, on Fifth Ave between 78th and 79th Sts (972 Fifth Ave), are located in the former **Payne Whitney House** (1906; McKim, Mead & White; DL), one of the earliest Italian Renaissance mansions north of 72nd St. It is notable for its gracefully curved and elaborately carved facade of light gray granite, a material not generally favored because of its extreme hardness. The house belonged first to Payne Whitney, philanthropist, financier, and an aficionado of horse racing who kept stables in Kentucky and on Long Island. His estate was calculated at $250 million. His wife, Helen Hay Whitney, was a daughter of John Hay, secretary of state under Presidents McKinley and Theodore Roosevelt. Their daughter, Joan Whitney Payson, was the principal owner of the New York Mets baseball team from its beginnings in 1962 until her death in 1975, and their son, John Hay (Jock) Whitney, was publisher of the *New York Herald Tribune* and ambassador to Great Britain.

The **Cultural Services of the French Embassy** schedules programs in the visual and performing arts; for information, ☎ (212) 439-1400.

The former Cook Mansion next door, at 973 Fifth Ave, was built 1902–5 by McKim, Mead & White and is visually continuous with the Payne Whitney House.

Ukrainian Institute of America

Looming up on the southeast corner of Fifth Ave and 79th St is the home of the Ukrainian Institute of America. The house (1899; C. P. H. Gilbert; DL) is a picturesque French Gothic mansion, with high slate roofs, pinnacled dormers, gargoyles, and a "moat" protected by an iron fence.

History

It was originally built for Isaac Fletcher, railroad investor and banker, who gave his art collection (including a portrait of the mansion) to the Metropolitan across the avenue. Fletcher sold the mansion to Harry F. Sinclair of Sinclair Oil, who sold it to Augustus Van Horn Stuyvesant, the last direct male descendant of the irascible one-legged Dutch governor, Peter Stuyvesant. Augustus, a successful real estate dealer, spent his declining years here, eventually becoming a complete recluse, attended only by his butler and his footman.

The institute (1948) maintains a collection of contemporary Ukrainian paintings, religious works, and Ukrainian arts and crafts (ceramics, folk costumes, woodcuts). It mounts occasional exhibitions; for information, ☎ (212) 288-8660.

23 · Museum Mile (Fifth Avenue, 79th Street to 104th Street) and Vicinity

Subway: Lexington Ave Local (6) to 77th St.
Bus: M1, M2, M3, M4, M79.

The section of Fifth Ave between 79th and 106th Sts has more museums, libraries, and cultural centers than any comparable stretch in the city. Dominating

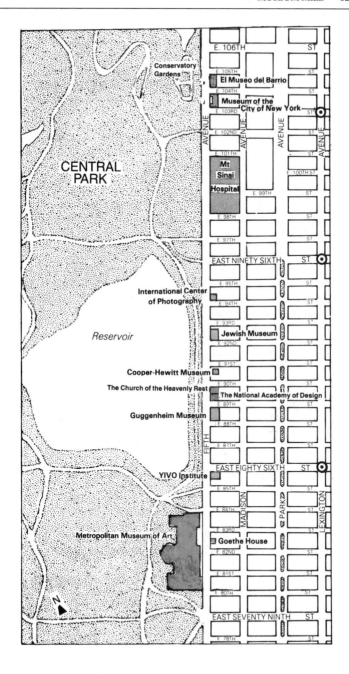

the group is the Metropolitan Museum of Art (Walk 24), but along the east side of the avenue are nine other institutions, most of them ensconced in the former homes of millionaires: the sector of Fifth Ave renamed Museum Mile in 1981 was once, before the debilitations of the income tax, known as Millionaire's Row. In 1979 the ten institutions formed a consortium to encourage joint ventures and shared resources.

Begin at Fifth Ave and 79th St. The palazzo-inspired house at 15 E. 79th St (1918; McKim, Mead & White), now occupied by the **Rudolf Steiner School,** was built for Thomas Newbold, a lawyer, state senator, and head of the New York State Department of Health. The uninspired brown-and-white brick, 27-story apartment house at 980 Fifth Ave (1968; Paul Resnick & Harry F. Green) replaced two town houses known as the Brokaw Mansions, built by Isaac Vail Brokaw, a real estate dealer and clothing manufacturer, for himself and his daughter. They were demolished in 1965 despite efforts of conservationists to save them, the first blows falling surreptitiously during the weekend.

Just north of 80th St, at 991 Fifth Ave, the **American Irish Historical Society** (1901; Turner & Killian) occupies a house once owned by William Ellis Corey, a president of U.S. Steel, who shocked society in 1907 by marrying Mabelle Gilman, a musical comedy star. The house with its swell front, ornamental cartouches, and slate mansard roof is a fine example of the Beaux-Arts style. The society has occasional events and exhibitions. For information, ☎ (212) 288-2263; Web site: www.aihs.org.

The 16-story apartment at 993 Fifth Ave (1930) exemplifies the work of Emery Roth père (see San Remo Apartments in Walk 26), who designed in the classical mode; now his firm is known for its blander, boxier towers (e.g., the General Motors Building, the tower of the Helmsley Palace Hotel).

On the southeast corner of 81st St and Fifth Ave is the **Stanhope Hotel** (1926; Rosario Candela). Its terrace is one of the more elegant places for people watching.

The building at **998 Fifth Ave** (1910; McKim, Mead & White; DL), on the northeast corner of 81st St, was the first apartment building to intrude upon territory previously occupied by a solid row of grandiose town houses. Its elegant good taste and spacious apartments (a typical simplex had 17 rooms) helped the wealthy succumb to the advantages of living under the same roof as their neighbors. Among the first tenants was Elihu Root, secretary of state and Nobel Peace Prize winner, to whom the rental agent reputedly offered a cut rate, hoping to lure his social peers into the building. Vanderbilts, Guggenheims, and Mortons followed.

Another Beaux-Arts town house, handsomely ornamented with wrought iron and limestone, stands at **1009 Fifth Ave** (1901; Welch, Smith & Provot; DL) (southeast corner of the intersection of 82nd St and Fifth Ave). Built speculatively, it was sold to Benjamin N. Duke, brother of the tobacco king James B. Duke, whose own house is at 78th St and Fifth Ave.

Most of the block facing Fifth Ave between 82nd and 83rd Sts remained unbuilt until the 1920s. Today, with its one early-20C town house squeezed in by newer, larger apartment buildings, it illustrates changing patterns of living in the second decade of this century, when expensive, impractical town houses gave way to more efficient apartments.

Goethe House New York

1014 Fifth Ave (at 82nd St), New York, NY 10028. ☎ (212) 439-8700. Web site: www.goethe.de/uk/ney/enindex.htm. Gallery hours: Mon, Wed, Fri 10–5; Tues and Thurs 10–7. Closed Sat, Sun, Aug. Free. Changing exhibitions, lectures, concerts, films, symposia, performances. Not accessible to wheelchairs.

Subway: Lexington Ave Express or Local (4, 5, 6) to 86th St. Bus: M1, M2, M3, M4, M79, M86.

The remaining town house on the block, at 1014 Fifth Ave (1907; Welch, Smith & Provot), first owned by the banker and broker James Francis Aloysius Clark, now houses **Goethe House New York,** a branch of the Munich-based Goethe Institute, funded by the German government and dedicated to promoting the understanding of German culture. Founded in 1957, Goethe House became part of the international Goethe-Institut in 1964.

Goethe House has an outstanding exhibition program that focuses on contemporary German artists, as well as a highly regarded film series. The library has more than 12,000 volumes on German culture and history as well as current issues of German newspapers and periodicals and an extensive collection of recordings and videos.

The **Marymount School,** on the southeast corner of Fifth Ave and 84th St, occupies a trio of town houses (nos. 1026, 1027, and 1028 Fifth Ave) previously owned by wealthy but otherwise unremarkable bankers, oil refiners, real estate dealers, leather manufacturers, and dairymen. The two southern houses (1903; Van Vleck & Goldsmith) were built as a pair; the corner house (1903; C. P. H. Gilbert) first belonged to Jonathan Thorne, an art lover who spent the last two decades of his life collecting beautiful objects for this Beaux-Arts house.

Only one early home survives on the block between 84th and 85th Sts; 1033 Fifth Ave (1878; Stephen D. Hatch) was designed as a brownstone but altered in 1912 to the then-fashionable Beaux-Arts style.

The 17-story apartment adorned with winged lions and human faces at 1040 Fifth Ave (between 85th and 86th Sts) is another work (1930) of Rosario Candela. Candela was born in Sicily, immigrated to the U.S. at the age of 19, and graduated from the Columbia School of Architecture (1915) three years later. In addition to building luxury apartments, he published two books on cryptography.

Neue Galerie New York

1048 Fifth Ave (at 86th St), New York, NY 10128. ☎ (212) 628-6200. Web site: www.neuegalerie.org. Open Fri–Mon 11–7. Admission charge. Changing exhibitions, lectures, films. Café. Accessible to wheelchairs.

The name of the Neue Galerie (New Gallery) harks back to the Neue Galerie Vienna, founded in 1923 to feature the work of Gustav Klimt, Egon Schiele, and other artists of the Secessionist movement. Like its European predecessor, the Neue Galerie New York (opened late 2001) focuses on early-20C Austrian and German art, including both fine and decorative works. In April 2001, the museum startled the New York art world by buying at auction for $22.5 million Max Beckmann's *Self-Portrait With Horn* (1938), described as a rare and haunting work.

The opening exhibition featured works by Beckmann, Klimt, Schiele, Vasily Kandinsky, Ernst Ludwig Kirchner, Paul Klee, and Oskar Kokoschka, as well as decorative arts from the Wiener Werkstätte and the Bauhaus.

The Building

The museum is housed in one of the finest mansions along the avenue, the former **William Starr Miller Mansion** (1914; Carrère & Hastings) on the southeast corner at 86th St. Miller, whose investments in railroads and banking totaled more than $3 million at the time of his death (1935), divided his time between this house and his Newport mansion, "High Tide." His daughter married an English baron. In 1944 Grace Wilson Vanderbilt, widow of Cornelius Vanderbilt III, bought the house; after her death (1953) the YIVO Institute for Jewish Research took it over. In 1993, YIVO moved downtown. The building was purchased in 1994 by Ronald S. Lauder, art collector, philanthropist, and chairman of the Estée Lauder Co., and Serge Sabarsky (d. 1996), an art dealer and gallery owner. Built of red brick and limestone, crowned with a slate mansard roof, the mansion is reminiscent of the 16C houses in the Place des Vosges in Paris, which is not surprising since both Carrère and Hastings studied at the École des Beaux Arts.

Solomon R. Guggenheim Museum

1071 Fifth Ave (at 88th St), New York, NY 10128. ☎ (212) 423-3500. Web site: www.guggenheim.org. Open Sun–Wed 9–6; Fri, Sat until 8. Closed Thurs, holidays. Admission charge; Fri 6–8, pay what you wish. Changing exhibitions, gallery talks, tours, lectures, films, concerts. Restaurant; gift shop. Accessible to wheelchairs.

Subway: Lexington Ave Express or Local (4, 5, 6) to 86th St. Bus: M1, M2, M3, M4, M86.

Facing Fifth Ave, between 88th and 89th Sts, is the Solomon R. Guggenheim Museum, Frank Lloyd Wright's masterpiece and the repository of some 4,000 paintings, sculptures, and works on paper from the impressionist period to the present.

More than any other New York museum, with perhaps the exception of the Whitney, the Guggenheim has a collection that reflects the tastes of a few individuals. Its exhibitions of modern and contemporary painting and sculpture are shown in one of the world's most remarkable modernist buildings, which itself is the jewel of the collection.

History of the Collection

Solomon R. Guggenheim (1861–1949), whose fortune was based on mining and smelting, started out collecting Old Masters, as did other millionaires of his vintage. This focus changed entirely in the late 1920s after he met Baroness Hilla Rebay von Ehrenwiesen, an intense, highly opinionated artist who introduced him to her artist friends (including Robert Delaunay, Fernand Léger, and Vasily Kandinsky) and to her taste for abstract art. In 1939 the Solomon R. Guggenheim Collection of Non-Objective Painting was shown in rented quarters at 24 E. 54th St with the baroness in charge.

James Johnson Sweeney followed Rebay as museum director in 1952 and under his guidance the Guggenheim Museum became less narrowly ideological, purchasing Picassos and Cézannes, for example, which Rebay would have outlawed on grounds that they were objective. A gift of impressionist and postimpressionist work from Justin K. Thannhauser, a noted dealer and collector, further enriched and broadened the collection. The bequest of Peggy Guggenheim put her entire collection of cubist, surrealist, and postwar painting and sculpture in the custody of the Guggenheim Foundation, though the collection remains in Venice and is shown in New York only on occasional exchanges.

The Building

The idea of building an architecturally remarkable museum and of hiring Frank Lloyd Wright to design it apparently came from Rebay, and since Guggenheim died long before plans came to fruition, the realization of the building was left to her and to Harry Guggenheim, Solomon's successor. One of the city's most controversial and distinctive buildings, the museum is a spiral with a ramp cantilevered out from its interior walls sitting above a horizontal slab. The ramp, 1,416 ft long (about a quarter-mile), rises 1.75 inches per 10 ft to a domed skylight 92 ft above the ground. The ramp diameter at ground level is 100 ft; at the top, 128 ft. Wright called the building "organic" architecture, imitating the forms and colors of nature, though his critics called it a bun, a snail, and an insult to art. Between the time of Wright's original design and the completion of the building, 16 years elapsed, many of them spent in arguments with the city's Department of Buildings, whose ideas on construction differed from Wright's, and in quarrels with former museum director Sweeney, who argued that Wright's design would create serious problems in storing and hanging the collection, reservations that proved accurate.

In 1992 the museum reopened after an expansion (Gwathmey Siegal & Assocs.) that allows more of its permanent collection and more of the Frank Lloyd Wright building to be seen.

Highlights of the Collection

The Justin K. Thannhauser Collection includes works by Camille Pissarro, Vincent van Gogh, Paul Cézanne, Paul Gauguin, Henri Rousseau, and other impressionist and postimpressionist painters. Pablo Picasso is represented by early paintings in the Thannhauser galleries and by later works elsewhere in the museum.

The Guggenheim has perhaps the world's largest collection of paintings by Vasily Kandinsky, as well as paintings by Paul Klee, Franz Marc, Piet Mondrian, Joan Miró, and other 20C European pioneers. Among the works by the postwar American painters are canvases by Willem de Kooning, Jackson Pollock, Mark Rothko, Franz Kline, Richard Diebenkorn, Andy Warhol, and Roy Lichtenstein.

Although Hilla Rebay collected only painting, the museum began to purchase sculpture after her departure. Alexander Archipenko, Constantin Brancusi, Alberto Giacometti, Henry Moore, Jacques Lipchitz, Isamu Noguchi, Louise Nevelson, and David Smith are all represented in the collection.

In 1990, the museum acquired the Panza di Biumo Collection of American minimalist art from the 1960s and 1970s. In 1993, the Robert Mapplethorpe Foundation gave the Guggenheim nearly 200 photographs and other works, introducing photography into the collection and inaugurating a photography gallery.

National Academy of Design

1083 Fifth Ave (between 89th and 90th Sts), New York, NY 10128. ☎ (212) 369-4880. Web site: www.nationalacademy.org. Open Wed–Thurs 12–5; Fri 10–6; Sat–Sun 10–5. Closed Mon, Tues, major holidays. Admission charge. Lectures, symposia, changing exhibitions. Book shop. Accessible to wheelchairs.

The National Academy of Design, a block north of the Guggenheim, is an artists' honorary association, with a museum and an art school. The town house at 1083 Fifth Ave (1914; Ogden Codman, Jr.), where the academy holds its exhibitions, was donated (1940) by Archer M. Huntington, whose wife, the sculptor Anna Hyatt Huntington, was an academy member. The academy, as the name implies, is a conservative institution, its members drawn from the ranks of the nation's established painters, sculptors, and graphic artists. Founded in 1825 as a school and exhibition center by the painters Samuel F. B. Morse and Rembrandt Peale, architect Ithiel Town, sculptor John Frazee, and engraver Peter Maverick, the academy has a collection of more than 2,000 paintings and 200 works of sculpture, in part the product of a ruling that members supply a representative sample of their work. The program includes loan exhibitions, works drawn from the collection, and an annual juried show.

Carnegie Hill

The area between Fifth and Park Aves, from E. 90th to E. 94th Sts., is known as Carnegie Hill.

North of the academy, on the corner of Fifth Ave at 90th St, is the Protestant Episcopal **Church of the Heavenly Rest** (1929; Hardie Philip of Mayers, Murray & Philip), a Gothic church with exterior sculpture by Ulrich Ellerhausen and a pulpit madonna by Malvina Hoffman. The rose window is by J. Gordon Guthrie.

Turn right and walk east along E. 90th St. Four landmark buildings of different eras survive here. The building at **11 E. 90th St** (1903; Barney & Chapman; 1929; alteration Wallace McCrea; DL) was once a more ornate Beaux-Art facade, but it was later altered to this staid limestone exterior. Next door is **15 E. 90th St** (1928; Mott B. Schmidt; DL), a small, charming, red brick Federal home with Flemish bond brickwork, a portico of Corinthian columns, and a second-floor balcony with a pediment over the window. The house at **17 E. 90th St** (1919; F. Burrall Hoffman Jr.; DL) is a Georgian revival home with a street-level arcade. At the corner is **1261 Madison Ave** (1901; Buchman & Fox; DL), a Beaux-Arts apartment house with an ornate entrance portico, a mansard roof, and iron balconies. Its arrival helped jump-start this neighborhood as an affluent residential area.

Walk north on Madison Ave to E. 91st St. The house at 11 E. 91st St (1911; Trowbridge & Livingston; DL) is a simple classical limestone residence that, like its neighbor to the west, is home to the **Consulate General of the Russian Federation**. At 9 E. 91st Street is the **John Henry Hammond House** (1909; Carrère & Hastings; DL).

John Henry Hammond, Legendary Talent Scout
Built for Emily Sloane, second daughter of W. D. Sloane and his wife, Emily Vanderbilt Sloane, the house has a star-studded history. Emily married John Henry Hammond, whose father had served as General Sherman's chief of staff in the Union Army; Emily's husband was of good enough family to have been educated at Yale and Columbia Law School but was not secure enough in social class to take a house of such proportions with equanimity:

"I'm going to be considered a kept man," he is said to have told his wife when shown the plans. Their son, also John Henry Hammond, spent a lifetime discovering, nurturing, and promoting musical talent, a career that shaped the direction of American music from the early years of the Depression until his death in 1987. He produced, among others, Billie Holiday, Teddy Wilson, and Count Basie. His support of Benny Goodman when the clarinetist hired Wilson and Lionel Hampton helped integrate the music world. During the 1960s and 1970s Hammond fostered the careers of Aretha Franklin, Bob Dylan, Paul Winter, George Benson, and Bruce Springsteen. His son, John Paul Hammond, became a respected blues musician. The house became the Soviet Consulate in 1942.

James A. Burden House

Nearby are the neo-Renaissance mansions of two more eminently successful capitalists. At 7 E. 91st is the James A. Burden House (1902; Warren & Wetmore; DL), now part of the Convent of the Sacred Heart at the corner. It was built by W. D. Sloane and his wife, Emily Vanderbilt Sloane, for their eldest daughter, Adele, who married James A. Burden, heir to the Burden ironworks in Troy, New York. The Burden ironworks produced most of the horseshoes for the Union Army during the Civil War (at a peak rate of 3,600 per hour) and eventually developed into the American Machine and Foundry Company, making James Jr. a brilliant match for Florence Adele Sloane, by reputation a beautiful and spirited woman.

Exterior and Interior

The architects of the house, Warren & Wetmore, who stood in the good graces of the Vanderbilts (they also built Grand Central Terminal), built a house that has been described as a modern French interpretation of an Italian palazzo: Italian in its massing and the simplicity of details, French in the inventive ornament and the presence of a service floor between the ground floor and what in a less imposing building would be called the parlor floor.

Cooper-Hewitt, National Design Museum

2 E. 91st St, New York, NY 10028. ☎ (212) 849-8400. Web site: www.si.edu/ ndm. Open Tues 10–9; Wed–Sat 10–5; Sun 12–5. Closed Mon and federal holidays. Admission charge; free Tues 5–9. Changing exhibitions, lectures, special events. Gift shop. For access to disabled visitors, ☎ (212) 849-8400.

Subway: Lexington Ave Express or Local (4, 5, 6) to 86th St. Bus: M1, M2, M3, M4, M86, M96.

Across the street at 2 E. 91st St (southeast corner of 91st St and Fifth Ave) is the Cooper-Hewitt, National Design Museum, part of the Smithsonian Institution, presiding over the neighborhood in a mansion built for the multimillionaire Andrew Carnegie (1901; Babb, Cook & Willard; DL).

The Carnegie Mansion

Carnegie (1835–1919), an immigrant from Scotland, amassed a fortune in iron, coal, steel, and steamship and railroad lines. In 1898 he announced his intention to build "the most modest, plainest, and roomiest house in New York." For this plain and roomy house, he chose a rocky, semirural plot far north of the trophy houses of his more fashionable financial peers. In 1891 he and his family moved into this 64-room mansion, a building remarkably comfortable and technically advanced for its time, and well-suited for his domestic needs and the philanthropic projects he administered from his first-floor office. The subbasement was filled with pumps and boilers, the most advanced and sophisticated available, with two of each major piece so that a spare was always available. If city water or electricity were interrupted, an artesian well and generator would relieve the family and servants of any inconvenience. Up in the attic, great fans pulled air through cheesecloth filters over tanks of cool water in a primitive system of air-conditioning. The house was the first private residence in the city with a structural steel frame, an Otis passenger elevator, and central heating.

Over the main door is an ornate copper-and-glass canopy. The marble vestibule leads to the Great Hall, which is paneled in Scottish oak, an indication of Carnegie's affection for his homeland, to which he returned yearly. At the east end of the hall stood the organ, its pipes in a shaft now used for the elevator. On the west end was Carnegie's study, now used as a gallery. Carnegie, like Fiorello La Guardia, was 5′ 2″ tall, and the doorways leading into the library and office are appropriate in scale. Along the south side of the first floor, facing the garden, were public rooms—the Music Room on the west, with a large crystal chandelier and musical motifs, including a Scottish bagpipe, in the ceiling moldings. Next to the Music Room is the garden vestibule, with leaded glass windows by Louis Comfort Tiffany. The formal dining room was east of the vestibule, and adjacent to it a breakfast room faced the garden and conservatory, which had an elevator to the potting shed below. All these rooms are currently used as exhibition space.

Upstairs were family bedrooms and a family library with elaborately carved teakwood trim designed by Lockwood de Forest, who used the same material on his own town house near Greenwich Village. Across the garden facing 90th St is a town house, formerly belonging to Carnegie's daughter, now used for museum administration.

The Museum

Sarah, Eleanor, and Amy Hewitt, granddaughters of industrialist Peter Cooper, impressed by the South Kensington Museum (now the Victoria and Albert) in London and the Musée des Arts Décoratifs in Paris, founded the Cooper Union Museum for the Arts of Decoration. Helped by such friends as J. P. Morgan, who donated European textiles, they began amassing decorative objects, prints and drawings, and things that appealed to them as good design—napkins, gloves, and cookie tins. Among their first acquisitions were Italian architectural and decorative drawings that had belonged to the curator of the Borghese Collection. Later came 1,500 drawings, sketches, and paintings by the American landscapist Frederick Edwin Church and the contents of Winslow Homer's studio. The Hewitt sisters admired both European culture and the kind of American industrial savvy represented by their grandfather (who along with his other accomplishments had designed the first American locomotive), and their acquisitions reflect these preferences.

The museum galleries at first were installed at Cooper Union. The collection continued to grow in size and quality over the years, broadening its focus after the last of the Hewitt sisters died in 1930, until by 1963 Cooper Union could no

The Cooper-Hewitt Museum. Built (1901) as the mansion of steel magnate Andrew Carnegie, the building now houses the design collections of the Smithsonian Institution. The granddaughters of another self-made millionaire, Peter Cooper, initiated the collections. (Courtesy of the Cooper-Hewitt Museum, the Smithsonian Institution's National Museum of Design. Photographer: Dave DeSilva)

longer maintain it financially, and supporters engineered its adoption by the Smithsonian Institution. In 1972 the Carnegie Foundation deeded the mansion to the museum, which reopened here in 1976.

Exhibitions

The museum was planned as a kind of visual reference library, so the collections include a little bit of everything, from architectural drawings to ceramics, glass, wallpaper, bandboxes, cutlery, jewelry, locks and keys, and a vast collection of fabrics and textiles. Exhibitions drawn from these encyclopedic holdings can range from 19C scenic wallpaper to photographs of the Latino landscape of Los Angeles.

In Central Park at Fifth Ave and 91st St is the **William T. Stead Memorial** (1913; George James Frampton), a bronze tablet commemorating this British journalist who died on the *Titanic* after helping other passengers into lifeboats. There is another tablet in London on the Thames embankment commemorating his heroism. The two figures beneath Stead's profile represent Fortitude (the knight) and Sympathy (the angel).

On the other side of the avenue, at 1 E. 91st St (northeast corner of Fifth Ave), is the **Convent of the Sacred Heart** (1918; C. P. H. Gilbert & J. Armstrong Stenhouse; DL), built as the mansion of Otto Kahn—financier, philanthropist, and patron of the arts. One of the largest and most restrained neo-Italian mansions in the city, the house has unusual arched carriage entrances. Kahn, a member of the

German Jewish elite known as "Our Crowd," was chairman of the board of the Metropolitan Opera, which he saved from artistic mediocrity by bringing in Giulio Gatti-Casazza as manager and Toscanini as conductor, and from financial bankruptcy by personally donating an estimated $2.5 million.

On the southeast corner of Fifth Ave and 92nd St is **1107 Fifth Ave** (1925; Rouse & Goldstone), a building remarkable for once having had the 54-room, three-story apartment of Marjorie Meriwether Post (the breakfast cereal heiress) and her husband, E. F. Hutton (the stock broker). The Palladian window facing the park two floors down from the cornice opened into the foyer; the porte cochère on 92nd St led to the vestibule of a private elevator.

Jewish Museum

1109 Fifth Ave (at 92nd St), New York, NY 10128. ☎ (212) 423-3200. Web site: www.jewishmuseum.org. Open Sun, Mon, Wed, Thurs 11–5:45; Tues 11–8. Closed Fri, Sat, major Jewish holidays, and certain legal holidays. Admission charge; Tues 5–8, pay what you wish. Changing exhibitions, lectures, family programs, panel discussions, films, concerts. Kosher café. Gift shops. Accessible to wheelchairs; to reserve wheelchairs, ☎ (212) 423-3213.

Subway: Lexington Ave Local (6) to 96th St. Bus: M1, M2, M3, M4.

In another recycled mansion across the street is the Jewish Museum (founded 1904), operated under the auspices of the Jewish Theological Seminary of America. The museum houses a collection of some 28,000 artifacts, works of art, ceremonial objects, and antiquities that is considered the most important collection of Judaica in the Western Hemisphere and one of the most important in the world. In addition to its permanent exhibition, the museum offers changing exhibitions.

The Collection

The permanent exhibition, **Culture and Continuity: The Jewish Journey,** occupies two floors and explores Jewish culture from its archaeological beginnings to the present. The first part, **Forging an Identity** (c. 1200 B.C.–A.D. 640), illuminates the early evolution of the Jews as a people with their own customs and rituals. On view are archaeological objects, vessels, implements, and a dazzling display from the museum's collection of Hanukkah lamps from places as unexpected as Morocco, Italy, and Australia. The second section, **Interpreting a Tradition** (640–1800), explores the cultures of Middle Eastern, Sephardic, and Ashkenazi Jews. Here are objects as diverse as a portion of a synagogue wall from 19C Persia showing the artistic influence of Islam, a metalwork Hannukah lamp from 18C Frankfurt, and a 20C Torah crown of silver and pearls designed by Moshe Zabari in 1959. The third section, **Confronting Modernity** (c. 1800–1948), deals with themes of the choices confronting Jews in modern times: assimilation or nationalism, religious orthodoxy or reform, capitalism or socialism. On view here is Moritz Daniel Oppenheim's painting *Return of the Jewish Volunteer from the Wars of Liberation to His Family Still Living in Accordance with Old Customs.* **Realizing a Future** contains contemporary art, painting, sculpture on themes such as the interaction between Jews and those around them, Jewish ritual, and spirituality. The plaster model of George Segal's *The Holocaust* (the bronze cast is in San Francisco) uses his familiar technique of casting living people.

The museum also mounts changing exhibitions, many exploring social history using interdisciplinary approaches, others offering in-depth explorations of individual artists. Artists whose works have been featured include Camille Pissarro, Marc Chagall, Chaim Soutine, Anni Albers, Ben Shahn, and George Segal.

The Building

The core of the museum was formerly the family mansion of Felix Warburg. Warburg admired the Isaac Fletcher House (see Ukrainian Institute of America in Walk 22) and hired its architect, C. P. H. Gilbert (son of Cass Gilbert), to design him something in the same French Gothic style. The mansion remained in the family until 1944, when the financier's widow, Frieda Schiff Warburg, donated it to the Jewish Theological Seminary for a museum. In 1990–93, the museum restored and expanded the building, doubling the exhibition space and replicating along Fifth Ave its intricately carved limestone facade, using stone from the original quarry.

Continue north on Fifth Ave. Walk east on 93rd St to Madison Ave. At **1321 Madison Ave,** on the northeast corner of 93rd St, is an attractive Queen Anne mansion (1891; James Ware; DL) that once stood in a row of five. It has a three-sided bay window, with a parapet over which are three round-arched windows with colonnettes. A cornice beneath the pyramidal roof and dormer window has a frieze with swags and scallops.

Cross Madison Ave. On the east side, between E. 94th and E. 95th Sts is the **facade of the Squadron A Armory** (1895; John Rochester Thomas; DL). At one time this facade, with its virtuoso brickwork and fanciful towers, machicolations, crenellations, and arched doorways, was part of a building that filled the block and housed Squadron A of the First New York Hussars, later the 105th Machine Gun Battalion. Until 1966, when it was threatened with demolition, the armory hosted horse shows and polo matches. Today it is the west wall of an open space belonging to the Hunter College Campus Schools (1971; Morris Ketchum Jr.), publicly funded schools for gifted students.

Continue east along E. 93rd St. At 56 E. 93rd St, the **Smithers Alcoholism Center of Roosevelt Hospital** (1932; Walker and Gillette; DL) occupies a house built for the stockbroker and sportsman William Goadby Loew. It is a fine example of the American Adam style with Palladian and bull's-eye windows and a white limestone facade curving around a small motor court. Later the house belonged to the theatrical producer Billy Rose.

The limestone Louis XV–style mansion (1930; John Russell Pope; DL) next door at **60 E. 93rd St** was designed for Virginia Graham Fair Vanderbilt, wife of William K. Vanderbilt II and daughter of Senator James Fair of Nevada, who hit paydirt with the Comstock Lode and the Big Bonanza mine. This and the Loew Mansion were among the last elegant town houses built in the city, because rising construction and maintenance costs as well as the vogue for palatial apartments made them obsolete. The building was long a home for the Lycée Français of New York, which put its six Upper East Side buildings up for sale in 2000.

Across the street and a bit further east is the **Russian Orthodox Church Outside Russia,** part of a complex of older buildings (67, 69, and 75 E. 93rd Sts) that centers on no. 75, the former home of financier Francis F. Palmer (1918; Delano & Aldrich; DL). In the late 1920s, this town house was sold to the banker George F. Baker Jr., who added the garden courtyard and the wing to the west with a ballroom. Beneath the house ran a spur from the New York Central line under Park Ave so that Baker could take his private railroad car all the way home.

At Park Ave, look across the street to **1185 Park Ave** (1929; Schwartz & Gross), a block-long apartment building with a beautiful triple ogee-arched entrance and plenty of decorative trim.

Walk south on Park Ave to the Louise Nevelson sculpture at E. 92nd St in the Park Ave mall. *Night Presence IV* (1972), a work of Cor-Ten steel (22 ft high, 13 ft wide, 9 ft deep) was given to the city by the artist, who felt New York represented "the whole of [her] conscious life." It is one of her earliest outdoor metal works, enlarged from a small wooden sculpture (1955), with turned doorknob forms and a cutout bird silhouette.

Return to Fifth Ave and walk north to 94th St. The house at **1130 Fifth Ave** (1914; Delano & Aldrich; DL) was built for Willard Straight, diplomat, financier, and founder of *New Republic* magazine. Straight, who spent much of his adult life in the Far East, volunteered for service in World War I and died of pneumonia contracted in the line of duty four years after the house was completed. For many years the building was the uptown home of the International Center of Photography.

Continue on Fifth Ave and walk north to 95th St. At 3 E. 95th St (1916; Horace Trumbauer; DL) is a French-style mansion with three tall arches on the ground level, a wrought-iron balcony above them, and a mansard roof on top. It also belonged to the Lycée Français of New York.

At **7 E. 95th St** (1916; Egisto Fabbri and Grosvenor Atterbury; DL) is an Italian Renaissance–inspired home built for a great-granddaughter of Cornelius Vanderbilt. It is now an Episcopal retreat center, the House of the Redeemer.

Return to Fifth Ave and walk north. At **7 E. 96th St** (1913; DL) and **15 E. 96th St** (1915; DL) are two houses designed by the influential architect Ogden Codman Jr. The one at no. 7, now the Manhattan Country School, was Codman's home. It features three dormer windows and a mansard roof and huge wooden shutters on the second- and third-story windows. Pierre Cartier, founder of the jewelry firm, lived in the companion house, no. 15, for many years.

Continue north up Fifth Ave and walk east again on 97th St. The **Russian Orthodox Cathedral of St. Nicholas** (1902; DL), just east of the avenue at 15 E. 97th St—with its five onion domes; gold crosses; red, blue, and yellow majolica tiles; and ornate terra-cotta—is an exotic form in a staid neighborhood.

Mount Sinai Hospital

Along Fifth Ave between 98th and 101st Sts is Mount Sinai Hospital, whose medical school is associated with the City University of New York.

History

Mount Sinai was founded in 1852 by a group of Jews that included Sampson Simson, one of the city's wealthiest citizens. Simson donated land for the original buildings on 28th St. The older buildings of the present complex date from 1904; the large, dark, rusty tower (436 ft, sheathed in Cor-Ten steel) is the **Annenberg Building** (1976; Skidmore, Owings & Merrill). In the central plaza, near 100th St, is a sculptural *Sphere* (1967) by Arnaldo Pomodoro.

Continue north. The **New York Academy of Medicine** (1926; York & Sawyer) at 2 E. 103rd St (southeast corner of Fifth Ave) is a picturesque, eclectic building

(Byzantine, Italian, Romanesque) with multihued bricks and top-floor columns. The library contains, in addition to the expected scientific tomes, a collection of cookbooks, the gift of Dr. Margaret Barclay Wilson, who in 1930 donated 4,000 volumes on food and nutrition to assist dietitians. The rarest item in the collection is a manuscript on roast boar that is duplicated only at the Vatican. Dr. Wilson also translated and edited one of history's earliest cookbooks, the *De re coquinaria* of Apicius Caelius.

Facing the Academy of Medicine from the other side of Fifth Ave at 103rd St is a **statue of Dr. James Marion Sims** (1892; Ferdinand von Miller II). Sims founded Woman's Hospital of New York and was a prominent surgeon, gynecologist, and philanthropist. With typical 19C emphasis on nationalism and progress, the inscription makes no mention of Sims's service to women but remarks only that he "carried the fame of American surgery throughout the entire world."

Museum of the City of New York

1220 Fifth Ave (between 103rd and 104th Sts), New York, NY 10029. ☎ (212) 534-1672. Web site: www.mcny.org. Open Wed–Sat 10–5; Sun 12–5; Tues 10–2 to preregistered groups. Closed Mon and all legal holidays. Suggested contribution. Gift shop. Accessible to wheelchairs: ramp entrance on 104th St.

Subway: IRT Lexington Ave Local (6) to 103rd St. Bus: M1, M2, M3, M4.

On the northeast corner of Fifth Ave at 103rd St is the Museum of the City of New York (1932; Joseph H. Freedlander; DL), whose exhibitions explore the city's complex history from its early days as a Dutch colony to its present eminence. Founded in 1923, the museum's collections contain more than 3 million artifacts—real and toy fire engines, maps and prints, ship models, portraits of prominent New Yorkers, and even the stripper Gypsy Rose Lee's hand-embroidered garter belt—which are shown in permanent and changing exhibitions.

Note: The museum expects to close at the present location in the spring of 2003 and reopen shortly thereafter at the Tweed Courthouse (52 Chambers St). At the courthouse a permanent exhibit organized chronologically will celebrate 400 years of New York City history, from the time when Native Americans were the only inhabitants to the new millennium. Temporary exhibitions on themes such as the city in art, the history of Broadway theater, and baseball—New York's indigenous sport—will supplement the permanent installation.

The Collections

The collections focus on six areas: **costumes, decorative arts, painting and sculpture, prints and photographs, theater,** and **toys.** Costumes range from Mrs. Cornelius Vanderbilt II's ball costume "The Spirit of Electricity" to Al Smith's derby hat, to shoes worn at George Washington's inaugural ball. The collection of American silver has elegant work by 18C New York silversmiths as well as florid 19C pieces from firms such as Tiffany and Co. The theater collection—set designs, costumes, caricatures of theater personalities, and manuscripts by luminaries such as Eugene O'Neill—documents the New York City stage from the mid-19C onward.

Period rooms re-create interiors from the homes of prominent New Yorkers, notably John D. Rockefeller Sr. The toy collection has more than 100,000 dolls, books, soldiers, trains, boats, and puppets from the colonial period to the present. The crowning glory of the dollhouse exhibition is the **Stettheimer Dollhouse,** whose meticulously executed interiors include miniature reproductions of works by Gaston Lachaise and Marcel Duchamp, as well as dolls representing Gertrude Stein, Virgil Thomson, and Edward Steichen.

El Museo del Barrio

1230 Fifth Ave (between 104th and 105th Sts), New York, NY 10029. ☎ (212) 831-7272. Web site: www.elmuseo.org. Open Wed–Sun 11–5. Closed Mon, Tues, legal holidays. Suggested contribution. Changing exhibitions, lectures, workshops, readings. Gift shop; café. Accessible to wheelchairs.

One block north, El Museo del Barrio is the city's only Latino museum devoted to Puerto Rican, Caribbean, and Latin American culture. Founded in an East Harlem School (1969) by Puerto Rican community activists and artists, the museum moved to its present location in 1977.

The Collection

The museum has an outstanding collection of **Santos de Palo,** wooden saints and religious figures, most made by self-taught Puerto Rican carvers. There is a permanent exhibition of Caribbean pre-Columbian artifacts, *The Taíno: Ancient Voyagers of the Caribbean.* Also in the permanent collection are traditional Latin American arts (musical instruments, miniature houses, dolls, nativity scenes, and masks), as well as paintings, 20C prints and posters, and sculpture.

The collections are shown in changing historical and contemporary exhibitions, some organized by the museum staff, others by outside curators. Exhibitions have included *Latin American Still Life,* with works by Frida Kahlo, Diego Rivera, and Fernando Botero; *Mexique,* an installation that re-created in miniature the Aztec capital of Tenochtitlan; and *Pressing the Point,* prints and posters by artists active in the artistic and social struggles of the 1960s and 1970s.

24 · The Metropolitan Museum of Art

1000 Fifth Ave (at 82nd St), New York, NY 10028. ☎ (212) 535-7710 for recorded information or (212) 879-5500 to reach a live person; (212) 570-3828 (TTY). Web site: www.metmuseum.org. Open Tues–Thurs 9:30–5:30; Fri–Sat 9:30–9:00; Sun 9:30–5:30. Closed Mon, Jan 1, Thanksgiving, Dec 25. Admission charge. On Sun certain galleries open at 11:00. Additional closings may also occur occasionally.

Exhibitions, lectures, concerts, tours, educational programs. Restaurant: reservations recommended. ☎ (212) 570-3964. Cafeteria, café. Great Hall Balcony Bar, Fri and Sat 4–8. Roof-garden beverage service in season. Book and gift shops. Accessible to wheelchairs; wheelchairs available; other services for disabled visitors, ☎ (212) 535-7710 or (212) 879-0421 (TTY).

Subway: Lexington Ave Express or Local (4, 5, 6) to 86th St.

Bus: M1, M2, M3, M4, M79, M86.

The Metropolitan Museum of Art (the "Met") is the largest art museum in the Western Hemisphere and perhaps the most comprehensive in the world. Its collections include more than 2 million artifacts spanning the course of human history.

Highlights of the Museum

Don't expect to see the entire museum in one, two, or even three visits. For your first visit, try a guided tour of museum highlights; check at the information desk for times.

European paintings: The Met's holdings are unrivaled on this continent. Especially popular are the galleries of **19C** European paintings, with impressionist and postimpressionist masterpieces. The galleries of European paintings from the **Renaissance through the 18C** contain dozens of world-famous paintings.

The **Egyptian Collection** is probably the best in the Western Hemisphere, a favorite with young and old. The reconstructed **Temple of Dendur** offers a unique opportunity to look at Egyptian architecture.

The galleries of **arms and armor** are fascinating both for the weapons themselves and for the pageantry of the installation.

The **French period rooms,** also unique in this country, offer treasures like Louis XIV's desk and Marie Antoinette's lacquered and gilded secretary in settings similar to those for which these beautiful objects were created.

The **American Wing** has a fine collection of American painting and decorative arts, including period rooms from the colonial period to Frank Lloyd Wright, and John Vanderlyn's marvelous panorama of Versailles.

History

The Metropolitan Museum of Art was founded (1870) just as the city was rising to eminence after the Civil War. Civic leaders and newly wealthy princes of industry foresaw that an art museum would indirectly be good for business, but they also believed in art's moral power to educate and improve the masses.

The Met's first president, John Taylor Johnston, oversaw negotiations with the state, which authorized the construction of a museum in Central Park, and with the city, which awarded the museum a handsome tax abatement. Eventually the city took title to the building while ceding its contents to the trustees, an arrangement that continues today.

The first acquisitions came from William T. Blodgett, a founder of *The Nation,* who donated paintings by Anthony van Dyck, Nicolas Poussin, and Francesco Guardi. Johnston was followed in office by the controversial Italian-born Luigi Palma di Cesnola, who had fought in the American Civil War and later became consul in Cyprus and an enthusiastic amateur archaeologist. Mistakenly convinced that Cyprus was the cradle of Greek civilization, Cesnola sold the Met hundreds of crates of antiquities, which form the nucleus of the museum's present collection of Cypriot art.

In the closing decades of the 19C the museum began capitalizing on the national wealth. In 1888, H. B. Marquand, a railroad financier, donated 37 paintings, including Vermeer's *Young Woman with a Water Jug.* Jacob S. Rogers, a locomotive manufacturer from Paterson, New Jersey, left $5 million to the Met, disappointing his relatives but propelling the museum into the ranks of wealthy institutions.

J. Pierpont Morgan, the financier, became president of the board in 1904 and continued to exercise his influence on the museum until his death in 1913. He brought the mighty collectors of his day—Henry Clay Frick and Stephen Harkness, for example—to serve on the board and engineered the appointment of art historian Roger Fry as curator of paintings. Fry made important purchases and recommended paintings by the French impressionists, who in 1907 had not yet achieved the popularity that would drive their prices skyward. Renoir's *Mme Charpentier and her Children,* for example, cost the museum a mere $20,000.

Despite Morgan's involvement with the museum, he did not leave the Met his $60-million collection, perhaps because the museum had not acted to house his treasures as he saw fit. His son J. Pierpont Morgan Jr., however, donated 40 percent of what remained after various sales and bequests: paintings, but also precious objects including jewels, gold work, and illuminated medieval manuscripts. That gift now comprises a significant part of the medieval collection.

Since the 1970s, the Met's collections have become truly encyclopedic rather than reflecting the spectacular holdings of a few great collectors. The Robert Lehman Wing (1975) with Old Masters and impressionist art; the Sackler Wing containing the Temple of Dendur (1978); the American Wing (1980) with paintings, decorative objects, and period rooms; the Michael C. Rockefeller Wing (1982) with arts of Africa, Oceania, and the Americas; and the Lila Acheson Wallace Wing (1987) for modern art have enlarged the building's footprint. The Henry R. Kravis Wing (1990), for European sculpture and decorative arts, and new galleries of Asian art and Greek and Cypriot art have expanded its exhibition space. The museum's holdings in Roman art are being reinstalled, with a new court for sculpture and galleries for Etruscan art. Proving its founders' financial instincts correct, the Met is today New York's single largest tourist attraction and a great financial and artistic power in its cultural life.

The Building

The museum building has grown from modest Ruskinian Gothic beginnings to 1.4 million square ft, its additions reflecting the reigning architectural styles of the past century.

The **original building** (1874–80; Calvert Vaux and Jacob Wrey Mould) faced Central Park; you can see parts of it from the Lehman Wing and the European Sculpture Court. Richard Morris Hunt designed the central **Fifth Ave facade** (1902); the north and south wings facing the avenue (1911 and 1913) are the work of McKim, Mead & White. The large uncarved blocks above the columns of Hunt's facade were to have allegorical groups representing major periods in the history of art, but funds never became available.

More recently, Roche, Dinkeloo & Assocs. redesigned the Fifth Ave stairs and added glass-walled wings on the other facades: the **Lehman Wing** (1975) to the rear, the **Sackler Wing** (1979) to the north and the **Rockefeller Wing** (1982) to the south. Conservationists have criticized the expansion, echoing sentiments of park designer Frederick Law Olmsted, who regretted allowing the museum a toehold in his territory.

Ground Floor

The Costume Institute

The Costume Institute contains a collection of more than 75,000 costumes and accessories from seven centuries and five continents. The clothing includes bull-fighters' capes, a bridal robe from Korea, and tribal headgear from central Africa. Among the urban garments are American and European dresses from the late 17C to the present time, lingerie, accessories, and notable examples of elegant couturier clothing. The collection is shown in special exhibitions, mounted with great style.

First Floor

Greek and Roman Art

South of the Great Hall are galleries with **prehistoric and early Greek art;** works from 4500–480 B.C. include ivories, terra-cottas, and bronze armor. A marble statuette of a *Seated Harp Player* (west gallery) is one of the earliest known representations of a musician.

The long barrel-vaulted central gallery contains **Greek art of the 6C–4C B.C.**, including *prize amphorae* (large vases that were filled with olive oil and presented to the victorious athletes) and **large-scale sculpture,** mostly marble copies of 5C–4C B.C. Greek bronze statues. The three galleries on the east (nearest Fifth Ave) are devoted primarily to **marble grave sculpture.** Early works include a *kouros,* or nude male figure, which shows Egyptian influences, and rectangular grave shafts with carved and painted reliefs of the deceased. In the second gallery are grave markers from the mid-5C B.C. to the early 4C B.C.; *Girl with Doves* is remarkable for its sweetness of expression.

The three galleries on the west contain **Greek art of the 6C–4C B.C.** Included here is the Met's remarkable collection of Greek vases. The vases, depicting scenes from everyday life and from mythology show the increasing skill of Greek artists in representing the human body.

Egyptian Art

The Egyptian galleries contain the finest collection of Egyptian art in the Western Hemisphere, with objects that date from prehistoric times to the Byzantine occupation during the reign of the emperor Justinian (A.D. 641). The galleries are organized chronologically in a U-shape, beginning with prehistoric and predynastic times just north of the Great Hall on the Fifth Ave side of the building.

Highlights

Highlights include wonderful tomb models illustrating everyday life; dazzling collections of royal jewelry; the Archeological Room, with mummies, coffins, and other funerary objects; the Temple of Dendur; Fayum portraits, used to cover the faces of mummies.

Galleries

Near the entrance is a reconstruction of the **tomb of Perneb** (c. 2440 B.C.), a high official of Dynasty 5. At the rear of the chapel is a false door through which

Perneb's spirit emerged from a subterranean burial chamber to enjoy the offerings arranged for it.

Gallery 4, Dynasty 11 (c. 2009–1998 B.C.), contains the finest collection of ancient Egyptian **tomb models** ever found, including models of boats, a brewery and bakery, a stable and garden. In **Gallery 8,** Dynasty 12–Early Dynasty 18 (c. 1929–1504 B.C.), are royal portrait statues and a display of **royal jewelry** including an exquisite pectoral with falcons and a scarab. **Gallery 9,** Middle Kingdom, Dynasty 12, Site of Meir, is the first of three rooms with objects that belonged to ordinary people. Among the smaller items is **"William,"** the museum's famous blue faience hippopotamus, originally an amulet for good luck.

The subject of **Gallery 12**—Queen Hatshepsut, Dynasty 18—was sister and wife of Tuthmosis II and became regent for Tuthmosis III. She declared herself Pharaoh and continued to rule, using the authority of powerful advisers. It is uncertain whether Tuthmosis III killed Hatshepsut or simply waited for her to die, but upon her death he saw to it that all her memorials were destroyed. There are 26 mutilated statues here, including the ***White Hatshepsut,*** a seated limestone figure showing her in masculine clothing but with a feminine body. **Gallery 14,** Hatshepsut–Tuthmosis IV (c. 1503–1417 B.C.), contains a magnificent collection of **gold jewelry,** some intended for the living, some for the dead.

In **Gallery 16,** The Amarna Reliefs, Dynasty 18: Amenhotpe IV changed the state religion, declaring Aton, the sun-disk, the only true god and himself, now renamed Akhenaton, Aton's only prophet. Running into resistance from the established priesthood, Akhenaton built a new capital downriver from Thebes near present-day Tel el Amarna. The **Amarna reliefs,** from his temple and palace, are carved in a mannered style that approaches caricature. Akhenaton, pictured as gaunt and long-jawed, was married to Nefertiti, pictured as beautiful. **Gallery 17,** The Amarna Room, Late Dynasty 18 (c. 1379–1320 B.C.) contains artifacts from the reigns of Akhenaton and Tutankhamun (Akhenaton's nephew). Tutankhamun restored Amun as state-supported god and renamed himself accordingly.

Gallery 21, The Archaeological Room, Dynasties 19–26 (c. 1320–525 B.C.), contains some of the best **tomb groups** in the world. Displayed in this claustrophobic room are coffins, canopic chests (for the organs not buried with the mummy), and servant figurines (to perform menial tasks for the dead).

In **Gallery 25:** The **Temple of Dendur** was built (c. 23–10 B.C.) by the Roman emperor Augustus, primarily as a public relations gesture to appease a conquered people. Centuries later it was given to the U.S. as a goodwill gesture for contributions to preserve ancient Nubian monuments upstream from the Aswan Dam. The Temple of Dendur honors Osiris, a god associated with the Nile and its fertility, as well as two brothers who drowned in the river during military campaigns.

Just beyond **Gallery 23** (with the massive **sarcophagus of Wennofer)** is **Gallery 26,** with facsimiles of **tomb and temple paintings,** which provide information on daily life in ancient Egypt.

Gallery 31, beyond the auditorium foyer, contains Roman art from the time of Augustus to A.D. 4C, notably a series of **Fayum portraits,** which sometimes were placed over the heads of mummies. Greco-Roman in style, these compelling portraits vividly bring ancient people to life.

Arms and Armor

The collection of arms and armor contains about 14,000 weapons, ranging from simple arrowheads to complex suits of armor. Many of the arms are ceremonial, chosen for their design rather than their military importance. The centerpiece of the galleries is the **Equestrian Court,** hung with colorful banners bearing the arms of King Arthur and the Knights of the Round Table. Several cases on the west side of the room contain English armor made at the royal workshops in Greenwich, which were established by Henry VIII. One masterpiece is a suit of field and tournament armor whose lavish decoration may have been designed by Hans Holbein the Younger.

In the galleries on the west (toward the American Wing) are displays of **European armor, 1400–1525.** Among the outstanding objects in the first gallery is a gilded Germanic *spangenhelm* from the Great Migrations period (early 6C), a style probably brought to the West during the invasion of Europe by the Huns; it is the only such helmet in the Western Hemisphere. Another important piece is a parade helmet (1543) signed by the Milanese master armorer Filippo Negrolo. Also on view are **European edged weapons** (rapiers, daggers, swords) and a collection of firearms from the 15C–19C.

On the other side of the Equestrian Court are the galleries of **Japanese armor.** On view are ferocious face masks from the Edo period (1615–1868), armor from the Kamakura period (early 14C), helmets in astonishing shapes ranging from an eggplant to a crouching rabbit, and a helmet from the Muromachi period (1392–1568) with antlerlike wings. A display of Samurai accessories (food boxes, drinking vessels) recalls both the physical needs of the warrior and the dignity of his role. The collection also includes **Islamic arms,** notably spectacular jeweled daggers and sabers, helmets, and firearms.

Medieval Art

The collection of medieval art contains Byzantine silver, enamels, glass, and ivories; medieval jewelry; Romanesque and Gothic metalwork, stained glass, sculpture, enamels, and ivories; and Gothic tapestries. The works were created from the 4C–16C, roughly from the time of the fall of Rome to the beginning of the Renaissance. In 1917 the financier and collector J. P. Morgan left the museum a gift that forms the nucleus of the more than 4,000 objects presently in the collection. Medieval art is also on display at The Cloisters.

Note: In 2000, the museum began a reinstallation of its collections of medieval art, with the galleries of secular and religious art of the Byzantine Empire, contemporaneous works from the Greco-Roman tradition, and examples of Judaica.

Works in the **Romanesque Chapel** (east wall of the Tapestry Hall) include *Virgin and Child in Majesty,* a masterfully carved wooden statue from the Auvergne on the front wall. On a side wall is a 12C stone *Head of King David* from the cathedral of Notre-Dame, Paris. Among the tapestries in the **Medieval Tapestry Hall** are a rare *Annunciation Tapestry* and the elegant *Rose Tapestries* depicting courtiers against a background of stripes and stylized rosebushes. In the center of the room is a monumental seated *Virgin and Child,* probably by Claus de Werve.

The **Medieval Sculpture Hall** is dominated by an impressive 17C choir screen from Valladolid, Spain. Among the many small and beautiful objects in this room are a reliquary *Crib of the Infant Jesus,* a popular devotional object during the early

16C; an alabaster *Mourner* from the Tomb of the Duc de Berry; and a carved representation of the Visitation, the visit of the Virgin Mary to St. Elizabeth—The crystal ovals probably covered tiny images of the Christ child and the infant John the Baptist. The **Medieval Treasury** contains beautiful and precious objects of gold, silver, ivory, and enamel, as well as utilitarian metalwork.

European Sculpture and Decorative Arts

The collection of European sculpture and decorative arts is one of the largest in the museum with furniture, silver, ceramics, metalwork, clocks and watches, and sculpture from the Renaissance to 1900.

Highlights

The featured English decorative arts include **stoneware, silver, porcelain,** and **furniture** from the 16C–17C. There are **English period rooms** from the 17C–18C, including a dining room decorated by Robert Adam in neoclassical style and a sitting room with remarkable Gobelins tapestries. Also on view are examples of English silver including work by the great **18C Huguenot silversmiths** (Simon Pantin, Paul Lamerie, Lewis Mettayer, Pierre Harache).

The **Studiolo for the Ducal Palace in Gubbio,** intended for meditation and study, was installed in the palace of Duke Federigo da Montefeltro. Its walls are carried out in a wood-inlay technique known as intarsia.

The **French 18C period rooms** are superb. The Paris shopfront is the only such facade remaining from the reign of Louis XVI. The room from the Hôtel de Crillon is a mirrored boudoir whose furnishings include a daybed and armchair that belonged to Marie Antoinette. The **Louis XV Room** has Hyacinthe Rigaud's portrait *Louis XV as a Boy.* Sèvres porcelains include an elaborate rose vase in the form of a ship.

The room from the Hôtel de Varengeville, the Paris town house of the wife of one of Louis XIV's great generals, contains Louis XV's own writing table from his study at Versailles. The centerpiece of the Louis XIV State Bedchamber is a bed with needlework hangings surrounded by four extraordinary needlework wall panels.

The **European Sculpture Court,** with its glassy roof and large windows, presents large French and Italian sculptures originally intended to be displayed out of doors. Among them is Jean Louis Lemoyne's *Fear of Cupid's Darts.* The north wall incorporates the original Italianate granite and red brick facade and carriage entrance to the museum (1888). Galleries adjacent to the sculpture court have decorative arts from the Renaissance through the early 20C.

The **16C patio from the castle of Los Vélez** in southeastern Spain serves as a sculpture garden containing a group of Renaissance works, notably Tullio Lombardo's *Adam* and *The Triumph of Fame,* an early-Renaissance Flemish tapestry believed to have been in the collection of Queen Isabella of Spain.

The Jack and Belle Linsky Galleries

This private collection was donated to the museum in 1982 with the stipulation that it be kept together. Here are European paintings, sculpture, and decorative arts. Among the Italian paintings are works by Carlo and Vittorio Crivelli, Giovanni di Paolo, and Andrea del Sarto. Two miniature panels by Cranach illustrate events from the New Testament, *Christ Blessing the Children* and *Christ and the*

Adulteress. Among the 17C Dutch paintings is Jan Steen's *The Dissolute House-hold.* Paintings from the 18C include three canvases by François Boucher and an elaborate still life by Luis Egigio Meléndez. In the Rotunda is Peter Paul Rubens's earliest known dated painting, *Portrait of a Man.*

The Robert Lehman Wing

This wing contains superb Italian, Flemish, and 19C French paintings, drawings, and decorative arts collected by Lehman, who gave them to the museum with the stipulations that they remain permanently together and that seven period rooms from the Lehman town house be re-created within the museum. The wing is set against the original Victorian Gothic west wall of the museum (1880; Calvert Vaux and Jacob Wrey Mould; DL). The lower galleries are used for changing exhibitions from the more than 1,600 drawings in the collection.

The **Grand Gallery,** nearest the central courtyard, contains **19C–20C French paintings** arranged chronologically: among them are Vincent Van Gogh's *Madame Roulin and Her Baby,* Balthus's *Figure in Front of a Mantle,* and works by Alfred Sisley, Camille Pissarro, Pierre-Auguste Renoir, and Pierre Bonnard.

In the first two period rooms (northwest side of the courtyard) are early **Sienese and Italian Renaissance paintings,** with works by Giovanni di Paolo, Lorenzo Veneziano, Carlo Crivelli, and Lorenzo Monaco.

The **Special Gallery** is illuminated by Jean-Auguste-Dominique Ingres's *Portrait of the Princesse de Broglie,* his last aristocratic portrait. The Red Velvet Room contains wonderful **15C Italian paintings** by masters from Siena, Florence, and Venice: Sassetta's *The Temptation of St. Anthony Abbot,* Giovanni di Paolo's *Expulsion from Paradise,* Giovanni Bellini's *Madonna and Child;* Sandro Botticelli's *Annunciation;* Jacometto Veneziano's *Portrait of Alvise Contarini* and *Nun of San Secondo;* and Lorenzo Costa's portraits *Alessandro di Bernardo Gozzadini* and *Donna Canonici.*

Beyond, the Sitting Room contains **16C–18C Spanish** and **17C Dutch paintings,** including El Greco's *Saint Jerome as a Cardinal* and Rembrandt's *Portrait of Gérard de Lairesse.* Velázquez, Hooch, Ter Borch, and Goya are also represented.

The final room, the **Flemish Room,** contains 15C northern European painting, including *The Annunciation* by Hans Memling; a pair of panels (painted on both sides), *Christ Bearing the Cross and the Crucifixion* and *The Resurrection with Pilgrims of Emmaus* by Gerard David; Petrus Christus's *St. Eligius;* Lucas Cranach's *Nymph of the Spring;* and *Venus and Cupid the Honey Thief* and *Portrait of Erasmus of Rotterdam* by Hans Holbein.

Arts of Africa, Oceania, and the Americas

Works in the architecturally dramatic Michael C. Rockefeller Wing (1982; Roche, Dinkeloo & Assocs.) span 3,000 years and three continents. Many of them were made to fill needs that were not purely aesthetic—appeasing the gods, declaring power, or adorning the body.

History

The wing, given by former New York governor Nelson A. Rockefeller, memorializes his son Michael, who died in a rafting accident (1961) while on a collecting expedition in Papua New Guinea. It houses the collection of the former Museum of Primitive Art, privately founded by Nelson Rockefeller, as well as his own personal collection, supplemented by gifts and other museum acquisitions.

Highlights

The first of two galleries devoted to **African art** focuses on the art of western Africa and has beautiful wooden sculptures from the Dogon, Bamana, and Senufo cultures. The second African gallery (to the left) is devoted to the arts of central Africa, the Guinea Coast, and Equatorial Africa. In the section devoted to the Guinea Coast is an extraordinary early-16C ivory pendant mask and a collection of bronze and brass objects from the court of Benin (Nigeria).

The galleries devoted to **art of the Americas** lie behind the African galleries. Here are Aztec and Toltec stone sculptures and ceramics from several cultures. Olmec artifacts include jade ornaments and a "baby" figure, possibly representing a god. The 6C *Seated Figure* is one of the few Maya wooden objects that have survived time, moisture, and infestation. From Veracruz comes a rare "smiling" figure. In the Treasury (to the south) are pre-Columbian and later objects of gold and silver, including nose and ear ornaments, vessels, and pendants.

The rest of the wing focuses on **arts of the Pacific Islands.** The large glass-walled gallery facing south contains an impressive group of objects from New Guinea. The **Michael C. Rockefeller Memorial Collection** includes Asmat art such as nine tall memorial poles, as well as reclining two-headed ancestor poles and remarkable costumes of straw and reed with woven masks. On a low platform near the window is a 25 ft long crocodile effigy.

The American Wing

The American Wing contains a superb collection of American art, furniture, and decorative arts from the late 18C to the early 20C. Floor plans on the walls of the galleries clarify the wing's labyrinthine design, which resulted when a new structure was wrapped around an older one. The 25 period rooms are organized chronologically, with the earliest exhibits on the top floor.

Highlights

The Garden Court has examples of 19C and early-20C American sculpture. The American paintings include important work by John Singleton Copley, Thomas Eakins, Winslow Homer, John Singer Sargent, and the Hudson River School of landscape painters. The panorama of *Versailles* by John Vanderlyn and the Frank Lloyd Wright room are historically and visually fascinating. The period rooms, with original woodwork and furnishings, provide a view of American domestic life during three centuries.

American Wing, First Floor

Behind the bank facade at the north end of the court are period rooms and furniture galleries from the **Federal period** (1790–1820), including work by Duncan Phyfe and Charles-Honoré Lannuier. Later furniture and decorative arts include painted furniture, Windsor chairs, and folk art. The **Shaker Retiring Room** is furnished in the simple utilitarian manner associated with this austere sect. John Vanderlyn's ***Panorama of the Palace and Gardens of Versailles*** occupies Gallery 119. In an age when travel was difficult, giant canvases depicting faraway places were a popular form of entertainment; they were rolled up and moved from city to city.

In the next galleries, groupings of furniture and period rooms reflect **19C revival styles** (Greek, Gothic, rococo, Renaissance, and Egyptian). Gallery 129 is the **Frank Lloyd Wright Room**, which re-creates a living room from the Francis W. Little House in Wayzata, Minnesota, with furniture and decoration by Wright.

The **Garden Court** is one of the best places in the museum to sit down; here you can admire 19C and early-20C sculpture, architectural elements, and stained glass by Louis Comfort Tiffany, John La Farge, and Frank Lloyd Wright. At the north end is the dignified marble facade of the United States Branch Bank once located on Wall St. Sculpture (changed occasionally) includes work by George Grey Barnard, Gutzon Borglum, Frederick MacMonnies, and Paul Manship. The gilded nude statue *Diana* is a reduced replica of the once-shocking original by Augustus Saint-Gaudens, which adorned Stanford White's Madison Square Garden.

Garden Court, Balcony

Galleries on the balcony survey **American decorative arts**, with examples of pewter, silver, glass, and ceramics, from simple utilitarian wares to opulent presentation pieces. A replica of Daniel Chester French's finest grave memorial, *Mourning Victory,* stands against the south wall.

American Wing, Second Floor

The Joan Whitney Payson Galleries contain a permanent display of **American paintings and sculpture** arranged chronologically. Among the 18C–early-19C paintings and sculpture are portraits by John Singleton Copley, Charles Willson Peale, John Trumbull, and Gilbert Stuart, whose early portrait of George Washington may have been done in part from life. George Caleb Bingham's *Fur Traders Descending the Missouri* is a masterpiece of genre painting. Among the **Hudson River School and 19C landscape painters** are Thomas Cole, Asher B. Durand, Albert Bierstadt, and Frederick Edwin Church. The museum owns several works by **Winslow Homer**, now rated as one of the nation's finest painters: among them are *Prisoners from the Front, Rainy Day in Camp, Snap the Whip,* and *Northeaster.* Emanuel Leutze's *Washington Crossing the Delaware* is a romantic reconstruction of history, inaccurate in its details but deeply imprinted on the American consciousness. Thomas Eakins, now also considered a major 19C painter, is represented by *The Champion Single Sculls (Max Schmitt in a Single Scull).* On the balcony are examples of trompe l'oeil painting, visionary painting, and Western art, including bronzes by Frederic Remington.

American Wing, Mezzanine

A stairway leads down to the mezzanine in the new wing. Featured here are late-19C–early-20C realists, featuring work such as Mary Cassatt's *Lady at the Tea Table,* James A. MacNeill Whistler's *Arrangement in Flesh Color and Black: Portrait of Theodore Duret,* and John Singer Sargent's *Madame X (Madame Pierre Gautreau),* a scandalous picture in its day.

Twentieth-Century Art

The Metropolitan came late to 20C art, but nevertheless has fine collections of the painters of the school of Paris—Braque, Picasso, and Modigliani; paintings and drawings by early American modernists nurtured by Alfred Stieglitz; large-scale paintings by the postwar abstract expressionists; and bronzes by Elie Nadelman and Gaston Lachaise.

First Floor: Paintings from 1900 to 1945

This collection includes French impressionists and their Belgian, British, Austrian, and American contemporaries. Among the paintings by Pablo Picasso are *The Blind Man's Meal* and *Gertrude Stein*, his most famous portrait. Also on display are works by Amedeo Modigliani and Giorgio de Chirico, and Henri Matisse's *Nasturtiums with the Painting "Dance,"* a painting in the Museum of Modern Art. Also on view are cubist works by Georges Braque and Picasso.

The museum owns works by American painters Childe Hassam, John Sloan, William Glackens, and Reginald Marsh. Paintings by Edward Hopper include *From Williamsburg Bridge, Tables for Ladies,* and *The Lighthouse at Two Lights.* American regional artists such as John Steuart Curry and Grant Wood are represented, as are Raphael Soyer, Paul Cadmus, Isabel Bishop, Stuart Davis, Thomas Hart Benton, and Charles Sheeler. The museum has a strong collection of the Stieglitz circle—Arthur G. Dove, Marsden Hartley, Charles Demuth, and Georgia O'Keeffe.

Mezzanine

On the mezzanine level are a sculpture gallery, with large-scale paintings and pieces of sculpture, and two galleries with reduced light for works by Paul Klee and drawings, prints, or other fragile works.

Second Floor: Paintings from 1945 to the Present

The museum owns early works by **Jackson Pollock** as well as important abstract expressionist paintings. Pollock's *Autumn Rhythm* and Willem de Kooning's *Easter Monday* are major works by the dominant figures of the movement; also represented are Clyfford Still, Mark Rothko, and Robert Motherwell. The collection includes abstract and color field paintings by Franz Kline, Ellsworth Kelly, Frank Stella, and Morris Louis. Other artists sometimes on view include R. B. Kitaj, Romare Bearden, James Rosenquist, Roy Lichtenstein, Red Grooms, Jim Dine, and Jasper Johns.

Second Floor

European Paintings

The museum holds one of the world's great collections of European paintings, spanning roughly the late 14C–18C, many familiar to every lover of art. The French, Italian, and Dutch schools are most strongly represented, but there are also wonderful works by British, Netherlandish, German, Spanish, and Flemish masters. Among the many masterpieces are exceptional examples of the work of Giovanni Battista Tiepolo and of Vermeer, whose five canvases at the Metropolitan surpass the number at any other museum in the world.

In a large gallery at the head of the Grand Staircase are large-scale works by Giovanni Battista Tiepolo. Beyond it are 18C English and Italian paintings, with aristocratic portraits by Sir Joshua Reynolds and Thomas Gainsborough.

Italian Paintings
The collection of Italian paintings is organized chronologically and geographically. Among the Florentine paintings are works by Giotto, Fra Filippo Lippi, Alessandro Botticelli, and Piero di Cosimo. Among the 15C–16C paintings are Andrea del Sarto's *The Holy Family with the Infant Saint John* and a beautiful Bronzino *Portrait of a Young Man*. Sienese paintings include works by Simone Martini, Giovanni di Paolo, and Sassetta's *The Journey of the Magi*. The works by Raphael include *The Agony in the Garden* and *Madonna and Child Enthroned with Saints*. Among the Venetian paintings are a *Madonna and Child* by Giovanni Bellini and two beautiful paintings by Titian, *Venus and the Lute Player*, and *Venus and Adonis*. Among the works by northern Italian painters are Andrea Mantegna's *The Adoration of the Shepherds* and *The Holy Family with Saint Mary Magdalen*.

Spanish Paintings
Works by El Greco include *Portrait of a Cardinal* and *Toledo*. Also on view is *Juan de Pareja*, one of Diego Velázquez's most famous portraits.

Flemish and Dutch Painting
The collection features works by Jan van Eyck, Rogier van der Weyden, Petrus Christus, Hans Memling, Gerard David, Pieter Bruegel, and Peter Paul Rubens. Dutch paintings include famous works by Rembrandt: *The Toilet of Bathsheba, Aristotle with a Bust of Homer, Self-Portrait,* and *Lady with a Pink.* There are portraits by Anthony van Dyck and Frans Hals as well as landscapes by major 17C–18C figures. **Johannes Vermeer** is richly represented by *Young Woman with a Water Jug, Portrait of a Young Woman, A Maid Asleep, Woman with a Lute,* and the atypical *Allegory of the Faith.*

French Painting
Here are works by Georges de la Tour, Claude Lorrain, Nicolas Poussin, as well as 18C paintings by Jean-Antoine Watteau, Jean-Baptiste Chardin, François Boucher, and Jean-Honoré Fragonard.

Photography
The collection of the Department of Photographs is shown in changing exhibitions. The museum has more than 15,000 works, mainly European and American photographs, dating from the 1830s to the present day. Especially important are the **Rubel Collection** (19C British photography); the **Alfred Stieglitz Collection** (masterpieces of the photo-secession movement (1902–17) and related pictorialist photography); the **Ford Motor Company Collection** (American and European photography between the world wars); and the personal archive of the American photographer **Walker Evans.**

Drawings and Prints
The Metropolitan Museum owns approximately 11,000 drawings and 1.5 million prints, most of them produced after the Middle Ages in western Europe and in North America. The collection of drawings is known particularly for its works by 15C–19C Italian and French artists. Several artists whose paintings are very rare—such as Michelangelo—are represented at the Metropolitan by drawings.

Other strong areas are northern Gothic, Renaissance, 18C Italian, and 19C French prints.

Nineteenth-Century European Paintings and Sculpture

The museum's collection of 19C European paintings and sculpture is one of New York's prime cultural attractions.

Note: Maps of the galleries are posted at the entrances. For part of each year paintings from the Annenberg Collection, promised to the museum, are also on view.

Highlights

There are outstanding works by the French impressionists and postimpressionists, including Degas and van Gogh. The central gallery has celebrated paintings by Manet; Courbet and Rodin also are richly represented. The museum owns 37 oil paintings by Monet and 21 by Cézanne.

The Galleries

The **corridor gallery** contains salon paintings, including Rosa Bonheur's *The Horse Fair.* There is sculpture by Rodin in bronze, marble, terra-cotta, and plaster, including a terra-cotta model of the head of Balzac and bronzes from *The Gates of Hell.*

The **first two galleries** (northeast corner, near Cypriot art) are devoted to precursors of impressionism. **Neoclassical** works include paintings by Jacques-Louis David, Jean-Auguste-Dominique Ingres, and Pierre-Paul Prud'hon. The galleries devoted to **romanticism** have works by John Constable, Joseph Mallord William Turner, Eugène Delacroix, and Théodore Gericault. The corner gallery, featuring the work of **Camille Corot,** includes figure paintings as well as the more familiar landscapes. Among the painters of the **Barbizon School** represented here are Charles-François Daubigny, Théodore Rousseau, Jean-François Millet, and Honoré Daumier. The museum has one of the world's largest holdings of the work of **Gustave Courbet,** displayed in two galleries at opposite ends of the Manet gallery.

The three galleries with **Degas sculpture, paintings, and pastels** contain many works collected by Mrs. H. O. Havemeyer, one of the museum's major benefactors. Through her friendship with Mary Cassatt, she knew the impressionist painters and was especially captivated by the work of Degas. On exhibit is his most famous sculpture, *Little Fourteen-Year Old Dancer,* the only piece exhibited during the artist's lifetime. Some of the Degas paintings in the collection include *The Dancing Class, Woman Seated Beside a Vase of Flowers,* and *The Collector of Prints.*

Adjacent to the Degas rooms is a large central gallery with paintings by **Édouard Manet,** including *Woman with a Parrot, Mademoiselle V . . . in the Costume of an Espada, The Spanish Singer, Young Man in the Costume of a Maja, Boy with a Sword, A Matador,* and *The Dead Christ with Angels.*

Impressionist and Postimpressionist Paintings

The remaining galleries exhibit the museum's stunning collection of impressionist and postimpressionist paintings.

The museum owns 37 works by **Claude Monet** that span his long career: among them are *Regatta at Sainte-Adresse, Garden at Sainte-Adresse, La Grenouillière, The Bodner Oak: Fontainebleau Forest, Cabin of the Customs Watch, Rouen Cathedral,*

Morning on the Seine near Giverny, The Houses of Parliament (Effect of Fog), Rouen Cathedral: The Portal, Bridge over a Pool of Water Lilies, Haystacks (Effect of Snow and Sun), and *Poplars* (1891).

Works by **Camille Pissarro** include *Barges at Pontoise; Poplars, Eragy; The Garden of the Tuileries on a Winter Afternoon; The Garden of the Tuileries on a Spring Morning;* and *The Boulevard Montmartre on a Winter Morning.*

Some of the paintings by **Paul Cézanne** in the collection are *The Gulf of Marseilles Seen from L'Estaque, Mont Sainte-Victoire and the Viaduct of the Arc River Valley, Dominique Aubert, Madame Cézanne in a Red Dress, The Card Players,* and *Still Life with a Ginger Jar and Eggplants.*

Pierre-Auguste Renoir's works include *Madame Charpentier and Her Children, A Waitress at Duval's Restaurant, Marguerite (Margot) Bérard,* and *Tilla Durieux.*

Other prominent works are **Paul Gauguin**'s *Ia Orana Maria, A Farm in Brittany,* and *Two Tahitian Women;* **Henri Rousseau**'s *The Repast of the Lion;* and **Vincent van Gogh**'s *Wheat Fields with Cypresses, Cypresses, Madame Ginoux (L'Arlésienne), Shoes, The Potato Peeler,* and *Self-Portrait with a Straw Hat.*

Georges Seurat is represented by *Circus Sideshow* and *Study for a Sunday Afternoon on the Island of La Grande Jatte.* Other highlights include **Paul Signac**'s *View of the Port of Marseilles* and **Odilon Redon**'s *Bouquet in Chinese Vase* and *Flowers in a Chinese Vase.*

Islamic Art

The collection, the most comprehensive in the world, is arranged chronologically and geographically to suggest the entire range of Islamic art, which developed over a span of 1,300 years in countries as far apart as Spain and western China. Outstanding holdings include glass and metalwork from Egypt, Syria, and Mesopotamia; 16C–17C carpets; and royal miniatures from the courts of Persia and Mughal India. Adjacent to the introductory gallery is the luxuriously paneled **Nur ad-Din Room** (1707) from Damascus, a traditional reception room of a well-to-do gentleman of the Ottoman period.

Ancient Near Eastern Art

These galleries contain pre-Islamic works from Mesopotamia and ancient Iran, along with selected objects from Anatolia, Syria, and southern Arabia—modern Iraq, Iran, Turkey, Syria, and Yemen. Chronologically the collection spans from 8,000 B.C. through the Arab conquest of Sasanian Iran in A.D. 651.

Lining the walls of the gallery for **Assyrian art** are large reliefs and imposing carvings from the palace of King Assurnasirpal II (883–859 B.C.) in Nimrud (now northern Iraq). Two enormous winged creatures, a bull and a lion, both with human heads, defend the door.

In a case near the entrance of the first gallery that features **Mesopotamian art** is a remarkable white gypsum figure of a bearded Sumerian worshiper wearing a long sheepskin skirt. Also on view are jewelry, metalwork, and sculpture. On the wall of the central gallery, devoted to **pre-Islamic Iranian antiquities,** are panels of glazed and molded brick depicting lions; the mosaic once was part of a wall marking a processional road in Babylon during the reign (c. 604–562 B.C.) of Nebuchadnessar II. In the last gallery are beautiful objects in gold and silver from the **Achaemenid dynasty** (550–331 B.C.) founded by Cyrus the Great and the later **Sasanian dynasty** (A.D. 224–651).

Ancient Cypriot Art

The museum has the most significant collection of ancient Cypriot art outside of Cyprus, with objects dating from about 2500 B.C. to A.D. 300.

History

The nucleus of the collection was gathered by Luigi Palma di Cesnola (1832–1904), an Italian military officer who fought in the American Civil War and later became consul on Cyprus. Cesnola sold his collection to the museum in 1872 and became its director in 1879.

Highlights

The long central gallery, **Geometric and Archaic Cyprus,** contains pottery with geometric motifs, metalwork, and terra-cotta and limestone figures. The most important work in the collection is the limestone **Amathus sarcophagus,** whose decoration, remarkable for preserving traces of color, shows Greek, Cypriot, and Near Eastern influences.

Asian Art

The collection of Asian art includes works from China, Japan, Korea, India, and Southeast Asia, dating from the second millennium B.C. to the 20C A.D.

Chinese Art

The collection of monumental Chinese Buddhist sculpture is perhaps the finest collection outside China. The Chinese Garden Court with its gallery of Ming dynasty furniture provides an exquisite view into the culture. The collection includes vessels from the Bronze Age, tomb models of human figures and architectural models, gold and silver vessels and ornaments, and T'ang tomb figures.

In galleries of **Chinese paintings,** works from the Sung, Yüan, Ming, and Ch'ing dynasties are shown on a rotating basis. The **Chinese Garden Court** between the two galleries is modeled on a scholar's garden in Suzhou, west of Shanghai, first built in the 12C by a public official as a place of retreat from the rigors of his administrative job. Like other Chinese gardens, this one is carefully designed so that contrasting principles—light and dark, hard and soft, high and low, crooked and straight, dynamic and static—balance and complement one another.

Japanese Art

Nine galleries contain Japanese painting, sculpture, ceramics, lacquer, textiles, metalwork, and woodblock prints, spanning more than 4,000 years, from the second millennium B.C. up to the present. Some of the most famous works are paintings from the Edo period: *Eight Plant Bridge* (also called *The Irises*) and *Rough Waves,* both by Ogata Korin. There are prints by artists such as Kitagawa Utamaro, Katsushika Hokusai, and Hishikawa Moronobu.

Arts of South and Southeast Asia

There are 18 galleries that contain objects from South Asia (India, Tibet, and Nepal) and from Southeast Asia (Thailand, Vietnam, Indonesia, Cambodia, Vietnam, and Burma). Objects date from the second millennium B.C. to the 18C. (To see the galleries chronologically, enter from the northeast corner of Early Chinese Sculpture off the Great Hall Balcony.)

In Gallery 3 are works from the **Gupta period** (early 4C–7C), which is often called India's Golden Age. Included is a sandstone *Standing Buddha,* whose flowing lines and posture of repose suggest the spirituality achieved by the god. In Gallery 5, **Kingdoms of Northeast India** (7C–12C), is a beautifully carved stone representation of *Durga as the Slayer of the Demon Buffalo.* Artists of the Chola period (880–1279) in **South India** were known for producing large-scale, cast-metal sculptures of Hindu gods—for example, the beautiful *Standing Parvati* in Gallery 7. The famous image of *Shiva as Lord of the Dance,* also in Gallery 7, shows the god in his three roles as creator, preserver, and destroyer of the universe.

In Gallery 12 are works from Nepal, including a *Standing Maitreya* and a *Chakrasamvara Mandala* from about 1100, the earliest known Nepalese painting on cloth.

A staircase leads down to the galleries of **Southeast Asian Art.** A seated image of *Avalokiteshvara, the Bodhisattva of Infinite Compassion* in Gallery 17, the **Khmer Courtyard, Angkor Period** (9C–13C), is one of the finest surviving large Khmer bronzes.

Musical Instruments

The collection of musical instruments is outstanding for its scope and for the beauty of the individual instruments. The galleries are arranged in a rectangle with instruments from Europe and the U.S. on the west (left) side, those from the Americas and the Pacific on the north, and from the Near East, Africa, and Asia on the east.

History

In the 1870s Mrs. Mary Crosby Brown, wife of a New York banker, began collecting instruments from all over the world, enlisting the help of missionaries, foreign officers in her husband's bank, scholars, and diplomats. By 1914 she had gathered some 3,000 instruments, the nucleus of the present collection.

Highlights

Among the European instruments are a group of rare baroque violins, the oldest extant piano, and courtly instruments from the Middle Ages and the Renaissance. Instruments from the Americas include pottery whistles, whistling jars, and rattles in human and animal forms. Among the African instruments are whistles, rattles, thumb pianos, and a marimba with gourd resonators. From the Far East come Japanese, Chinese, and Korean instruments, including a beautiful sonorous stone and a mouth organ of bamboo pipes in a lacquered bowl.

25 · Central Park

Subway: Lexington Ave Express or Local (4, 5, 6) to 59th St. Broadway Local (N, R) to Fifth Ave.
Bus: M1, M2, M3, M4, M30, M57.

Hours

Central Park is open from dawn to 1 A.M.; park drives are closed to traffic weekends from Fri at 7 P.M. until Mon at 6 A.M.; major holidays from 7 the night be-

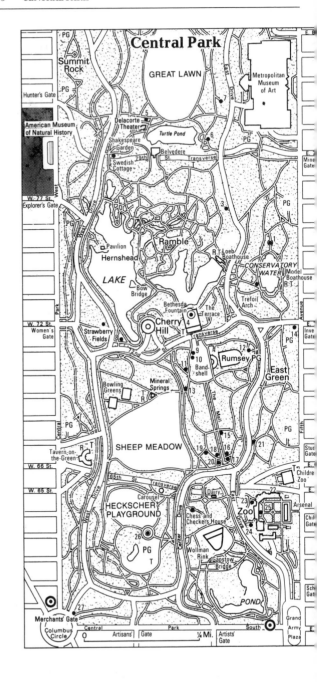

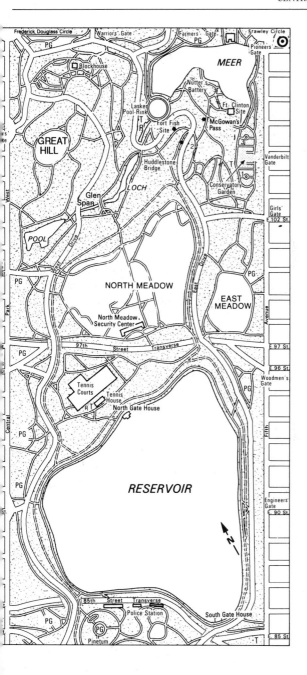

fore until 6 the morning after; and weekdays during nonrush hours, 10 A.M.–3 P.M. and 7–10 P.M.

Information and Maps
The **Central Park Conservancy** (a nonprofit organization founded in 1980) operates visitor centers at the Dairy, Belvedere Castle, and the Charles A. Dana Discovery Center. Maps and calendars of park events are available at the centers, which are open April–Oct 10–5; Nov–March 10–4. Information hotline for tours and activities, ☎ (212) 360-3456 or (800) 281-5722 (TTY) for the hearing impaired. For information about events, park history, and a virtual tour of the park, check the Central Park Conservancy Web site: www.centralparknyc.org.

Crime
Despite rumors to the contrary, Central Park is quite safe; the 22nd Precinct (i.e., Central Park) has one of the lowest crime rates in the city. Nevertheless it is unwise to wander around in remote areas of the park or to visit the park at night alone except to attend scheduled events. Don't leave bicycles unlocked. Precinct policemen, Urban Rangers, and park enforcement personnel patrol the park. Direct-line emergency call boxes are located throughout; they require no dialing and are connected directly with the police. The call boxes are identified with a brightly colored telephone logo. The first two digits on the metal plate attached to most park lampposts (some have been ripped off) tell the approximate cross street: thus 06413 means 106th St and 70235 means 70th St. For the **Central Park Police Precinct,** ☎ (212) 570-4820.

Toilets
Public restrooms are located at the Loeb Boathouse, Mineral Springs Pavilion, Model Boathouse, Delacorte Theater, the Arsenal, Tennis House, Zoo, Heckscher Playground, Conservatory Garden, Bethesda Terrace, Dana Discovery Center, and the North Meadow Recreation Center. Availability of restrooms may vary by season.

Dining
Refreshments are available at the Loeb Boathouse, Ice Cream Café, Mineral Springs Pavilion, Ballplayers' House (at Heckscher Ballfields), and the Zoo Café. **Snacks** are also available from carts and at additional seasonal locations. **Lunch** and **dinner** are served at Park View at the Boathouse (see Restaurants in Practical Information: Food and Drink) and the Tavern on the Green (see Tavern on the Green in Southern Central Park).

Tours
Walking tours are offered every weekend, free. Call the Central Park Conservancy, ☎ (212) 360-2727, or the Urban Park Rangers, ☎ (212) 628-2345.

Sports and Recreation

Ball Fields
Season opens in April. Permits required for organized athletic activities; ☎ (212) 408-0209 or (212) 408-0234. The **North Meadow Recreation Center** lo-

cated in midpark at 97th St provides recreational activities for young people and adults, including adventure programs involving new indoor and outdoor climbing walls, tai chi, and yoga. Public basketball and handball courts are also available; ☎ (212) 348-4867.

Bicycling
Best on roadways when park is closed to traffic, though there are bike lanes available. Cyclists must ride with traffic. Bicycles may be rented at the **Loeb Boathouse** (northeast corner of the lake, at 74th St) every day beginning in late March, weather permitting, 10–6. You must leave a credit card, driver's license, or passport for deposit. For information, ☎ (212) 517-3623.

Carriage Rides
Available from **Grand Army Plaza,** Fifth Ave or Sixth Ave at 59th St. Rate is $34 for a carriage with up to four passengers. Check with the driver on the length of the ride. For information, ☎ (212) 246-0520.

Gondola Rides
Available from **Loeb Boathouse** (northeast corner of the lake, at 74th St), spring through fall 5 P.M.–9 P.M. weekdays and weekends; up to six people, charge; ☎ (212) 517-3623; reservations required.

Horseback Riding
Rentals at **Claremont Stables,** 175 W. 89th St; reservations required. Open daily 6:30 A.M. to dusk. For riders experienced in English saddle, ☎ (212) 724-5100.

Ice Skating
Wollman Rink open mid-Oct until end of March, ☎ (212) 396-1010. **Lasker Rink** at 106th St, midpark, ☎ (212) 534-7639. Both rinks have admission charges and skate rental. Skating permitted on other bodies of water when signs indicate ice is sufficiently thick.

Lawn Sports
Lawn bowling and **croquet greens** just north of Sheep Meadow. Permits required; ☎ (212) 360-8133

Model Yachts
Conservatory Water at 72nd St and Fifth Ave. Races begin Sat at 10 A.M.

Picnicking
Sheep Meadow, the Great Lawn, the Great Hill and the Pinetum are great places for picnicking; no fires or cooking.

In-line Skating and Roller Skating
Use the closed road northeast of Sheep Meadow, weather permitting beginning in April, 10–5 weekdays; 10–6:30 weekends. In-line skating is also popular along the park drives. You can rent skates at **Wollman Rink,** ☎ (212) 396-1010; significant deposit required.

Rowboats

May be rented at the **Loeb Boathouse** (northeast corner of the lake, at 74th St), open seven days a week beginning in April, 11–5; deposit required; no reservations; ☎ (212) 517-3623.

Running

Soft track around the reservoir, 1.58 miles. Running on park drives is also very popular. Group runs organized by the **New York Road Runners Club;** ☎ (212) 860-4455.

Swimming

Lasker Pool, at 106th St at midpark. Open daily from July 4–Labor Day weekends; two sessions, 11–2:45 and 4–6:45; ☎ (212) 397-3106. Expect crowds.

Tennis

Located on the west side of the park, between 94th and 96th Sts; open March–Nov. Seasonal permits or single-play ticket required for admission; ☎ (212) 280-0205.

Cultural Activities

Get a seasonal schedule of events at any of the Central Park Conservancy's visitor centers. Check the Conservancy Web site at www.centralparknyc.org or ☎ the events hotline at 1-888-NYPARKS.

Concerts, Opera, and Dance

The **Metropolitan Opera** and the **New York Philharmonic** appear in the park during the summer. For the opera, ☎ (212) 362-3600; for the Philharmonic, ☎ (212) 875-5656. Multiethnic, multicultural **Summerstage** events, which include opera, dance, spoken word, and jazz, are held at **Rumsey Playfield.** Many events are free; ☎ (212) 360-2777 for schedule.

Delacorte Theater

There are productions of the Public Theater's New York Shakespeare Festival during the summer. George G. Scott, Kevin Kline, Denzel Washington, Gregory Hines, Raul Julia, and Michelle Pfeiffer are a few of the many stars who have appeared. Free tickets are distributed from 1 P.M. on the day of the performance; the line starts forming well before 10 A.M. Only two tickets per line member. For information, ☎ (212) 539-8750; Web site: www.publictheater.org. Tickets also available at the Public Theater (425 Lafayette St) and other locations in the five boroughs.

Children's Activities

Puppet Shows

Puppets perform "Jack and the Beanstalk," "Cinderella," and other classic tales at the **Swedish Cottage Marionette Theater** (79th St, enter at Central Park West and 81st St). Reservations necessary; admission charge. For information, ☎ (212) 988-9093.

Workshops for Children and Families
Free education, nature, art, and holiday workshops are provided at all three of the park's visitor centers. Call for times and reservations: Belvedere Castle, ☎ (212) 772-0210; the Dairy, ☎ (212) 794-6564; Charles A. Dana Discovery Center, ☎ (212) 860-1370.

Zoo
The **Central Park Wildlife Center and Zoo** is at 64th St and 5th Ave. The Children's Zoo, with domestic animals for petting and feeding, is open 10–5 weekdays; 10:30–5:30 weekends. Small admission charge. For information, ☎ (212) 861-6030.

Carousel
The **Carousel** is in midpark at 64th St. Open every day (weather permitting) April–Nov 10–6; Nov–April 10–4:30. Small fee. For information, ☎ (212) 879-0244.

Central Park, bounded by 59th St (Central Park South), 110th St (Central Park North), Fifth Ave, and Eighth Ave (Central Park West), is the heartland of Manhattan—843 acres set aside for the recreation of all its citizens. Although the park seems "natural," the largest surviving piece of Manhattan unencrusted with asphalt and masonry, its landscape and scenery are completely man-made, based on designs by Frederick Law Olmsted and Calvert Vaux.

History
In 1844, the poet William Cullen Bryant and other New York residents began calling for a public park, observing that commerce was devouring great chunks of Manhattan and the population sweeping over the rest. Andrew Jackson Downing, an architect and the preeminent landscape designer of the period, added his voice as did several politicians, and in 1856 the city bought most of what is now the park for $5 million. The land was desolate, covered with scrubby trees, rocky outcroppings, and occasional fields where squatters grazed their pigs and goats; a garbage dump, a bone-boiling works, and a rope walk added their own atmosphere. Egbert Viele was hired to survey the land and to supervise its clearing; he was aided by the police, who forcibly ejected the squatters and their livestock.

The Board of Park Commissioners (established 1857) arranged a design competition for the park in part because Andrew Jackson Downing, who probably would have been chosen, had recently drowned in a steamboat accident while trying to rescue his mother-in-law. Among 33 entries the Greensward Plan (1858) by Olmsted and Vaux was chosen, a plan based on enhancing existing land contours to heighten the picturesque, dramatic qualities of the landscape.

During the initial 20 years of construction, 10 million cartloads of dirt were shifted; 4–5 million trees of 632 species and 815 varieties of vines, alpine plants, and hardy perennials were planted; and a half-million cubic yds of topsoil were spread over the existing poor soil (some of it recovered from the organic refuse of the garbage dump). Sixty-two miles of ceramic pipe were laid to drain marshy areas and to supply water to lawns where hydrants were installed.

The Greensward Plan also incorporated the existing Arsenal and the Croton reservoirs, rectangular receiving pools for the aqueduct system that brought water from the Catskills. Curving drives, designed to keep would-be horseracers in check, carried traffic around these obstacles while straight transverse roads recessed below ground level took crosstown traffic unobtrusively through the park. North of the reservoir site (later filled in to become the Great Lawn as the present reservoir was created) the land was high and rocky, with good views, and the designers chose to leave this area as wild as possible. South of the reservoir were long, rocky, glacial ridges running north–south, which would be changed into open meadows, shady glens, and gently sloping hills. The formal element was to consist of a mall, an avenue of trees with a fountain at one end and statuary along its length.

Socially the park was intended as a democratic experiment, for the relief of the working classes whose daily lives were often confined to tenements and sweatshops as well as for the amusement of the wealthy, who could display their clothing, carriages, and horses along the tree-lined drives. It was also a public works project employing a staff of several thousand laborers, though it unfortunately attracted politicians who saw in its labor-intensive landscape a golden opportunity for patronage (controlling immigrant votes) and for letting out lucrative contracts to cronies in the building trades.

Even before its completion the park was a target for unwanted encroachments, beginning with a racing track for horses, which Olmsted blocked. While an airplane field (1919), trenches (1918) to memorialize World War I, an underground garage for 30,000 cars (1921 and frequently thereafter), and a statue of Buddha (1925) have not materialized, paved playgrounds, skating rinks, swimming and wading pools, a theater, and a zoo have taken park land. Robert Moses, zealous Parks Commissioner from the La Guardia era to 1960, advocated organized sports, accepted various buildings donated by philanthropists, and tore down structures of Olmsted's vintage, replacing them with boxy brick buildings. The present park environment represents therefore a compromise between the Olmsted vision of pastoral serenity and modern interests in active sports and recreation.

Restoring and Maintaining the Park
In 1980, the **Central Park Conservancy** was formed to restore Central Park to its former glory after many years of neglect. Working in conjunction with the City of New York Parks and Recreation Department, the conservancy has restored most of the park's major landscapes—including the Great Lawn, Sheep Meadow, Bethesda Terrace, and Harlem Meer—for the park's 20 million annual visitors. In 1998, the conservancy was officially named "Keeper of the Park" when the city awarded it a management contract. In addition to capital restorations and park maintenance, the conservancy also provides quality public programming at its visitor and recreation centers.

Southern Central Park
Subway: Lexington Ave Local (6) to 68th St.
Bus: M1, M2, M3, M4, M30.

Inventor's Gate
Just inside the entrance at 72nd St and Fifth Ave is Byron M. Pickett's bronze statue of **Samuel Finley Breese Morse** (1870), whose skill as a historical

painter and miniaturist was eclipsed by his fame as the inventor of the telegraph and Morse code. The statue depicts Morse as an inventor, one hand on the telegraph, the other holding a dispatch.

The entrance itself, inscribed with the words "Inventor's Gate," is one of three park entrances inscribed during the last century.

The Park Entrances

In 1862, the Central Park Board of Commissioners issued a report, which outlined a program for naming the park's 18 entrances after the industrial and intellectual pursuits of the day, giving the gates meaning and identity. This one, as well as Mariners' Gate at 85th St and Central Park West, Engineers' Gate at 90th St and Fifth Ave, and one additional gate not planned in the original draft, 76th St Gate at 76th St and Fifth Ave, were the only ones inscribed until recently. During the fall and winter of 1999–2000, the conservancy and city inscribed the remaining 14 blank entrances with the names originally proposed in 1862, including Merchants Gate (59th St and Eighth Ave), Miners' Gate (79th St and Fifth Ave), Pioneers' Gate (110th St and Fifth Ave), Farmers' Gate (110th St and Lenox Ave), and others.

On the left side of the road is a playground (1970; Richard Dattner & Assocs.), one of 21 playgrounds in Central Park.

Take the first right turn in the path on the north side of the roadway, and walk to the **Conservatory Water,** named after a conservatory planned here but eventually erected at 104th St. On the east shore of the pond is the **Model Boathouse** (1954; Aymar Embury II), where enthusiasts sail radio-controlled model yachts, some luxurious enough for model moguls. Regattas usually take place on Sat beginning at 10 A.M. during warm weather.

Walk around to the north end of the pond to José de Creeft's 11-ft bronze **statue of Alice in Wonderland** (1959) sitting on a mushroom and surrounded by the Mad Hatter, the Dormouse, the Cheshire Cat, and the March Hare. Children scramble all over it, but park purists would prefer all sculpture restricted to the Mall as Vaux and Olmsted originally desired. George T. Delacorte commissioned the statue of Alice to honor his wife, who read the classic story to all their children.

Continue around the pond to the west shore (good view of the East Side skyline from here) to the eight-ft seated bronze **statue of Hans Christian Andersen** (1956; Georg Lober) with a two-ft, 60-pound Ugly Duckling waddling in front. In 1973 a thief sawed the duckling off its base and stole it, but it was recovered undamaged several weeks later in a paper bag near a Queens junkyard.

Take the path that leads under the **Trefoil Arch** to the lake. The brownstone arch with its wooden ceiling, designed by Vaux, who planned the original park architecture, is part of a scheme that revolutionized traffic planning by separating different modes of transportation within the park, an innovative notion in the 19C, as were the sunken transverse roads across the park carrying city traffic.

Beyond the arch and to the right is the **Loeb Boathouse** (1954), donated by the banking family. In front of it is a small bronze statue of a rowboat (1967; Irwin Glusker).

North of the boathouse up the hill along East Drive is Edward Kemeys's ***Still Hunt*** (1881–83), a bronze panther crouched on a natural rock as if to pounce on the runners who jog obliviously along the road.

Return to the boathouse. Continue southwest around the lake to the formal **Terrace.** At the center is the **Bethesda Fountain** and its statue, ***Angel of the Waters*** (1868) by Emma Stebbins, one of the few works especially commissioned for the park. It depicts the biblical angel who stirred the waters of the Bethesda pool in Jerusalem and conferred healing powers on it. On the column beneath the angel are four plump cherubs representing the particularly 19C virtues of Temperance, Purity, Health, and Peace.

Long Side Trip for Energetic Walkers

Follow the shore of the lake to the beautiful cast-iron **Bow Bridge** (1859; Calvert Vaux), which crosses the lake to the **Ramble,** a heavily planted glen with intricately winding paths and carefully organized cascades in a meandering brook, the gill. Vaux and Olmsted included an artificial cave near the brook, but it has been walled up.

North of the Ramble, a favorite haunt of bird watchers, is Vista Rock (elevation 135 ft), site of **Belvedere Castle** (1869), since 1919 used as a weather station, now one of the park's three visitor centers and home to the Henry Luce Nature Observatory. North of the castle is Turtle Pond and the Delacorte Theater on the pond's west shore, with appropriate sculpture near the entrance, notably the bronze ***Tempest*** (1966; Milton Hebald) and ***Romeo and Juliet*** (1977; Milton Hebald), which is dedicated to Joseph Papp, the theatrical producer who brought Shakespeare to the park.

The **Shakespeare Garden** (east of West Drive, between the theater and the Swedish Cottage at the latitude of 80th St) contains plants mentioned in Shakespeare's plays and poetry. The **Swedish Cottage,** a replica of a Swedish schoolhouse made for the Philadelphia Centennial Exposition, houses the Swedish Cottage Marionette Theater.

Turtle Pond is the last trace of the old Croton Receiving Reservoir (drained 1931), which once filled the site now occupied by the **Great Lawn.** During the Depression squatters built shanties on the dry reservoir bed. Termed the "Great Dustbowl" in the 1970s, this expansive landscape was totally renovated by the conservancy between 1996 and 1998. Today ball games are played here and every summer both the Metropolitan Opera and New York Philharmonic give two free performances. Other summer megaevents staged here have included the debut of Disney's *Pocahontas* and a reunion of the singing duo Simon and Garfunkel.

To the southeast of the lawn near Turtle Pond is a bronze **statue of King Jagiello** (1939; Stanislaw Kazimierz Ostrowski), a heroic warrior under whom Poland became a major power. Jagiello, the first Christian grand duke of Lithuania, married the queen of Poland, uniting their lands. He is shown holding above his head the crossed swords of his adversaries. Ostrowski originally made the statue for a Polish competition; later it was used in the Polish Pavilion at the 1939 World's Fair.

North of this statue behind the Metropolitan Museum of Art is New York's oldest piece of outdoor sculpture, the 71 ft, 224-ton **Obelisk,** erected (c. 16C B.C.) by Thutmose (Tuthmosis) III at Heliopolis. It stood there a thousand years until toppled by some irate Persians and thereafter lay on the ground until the Romans set it up near the water in Alexandria (16 B.C.) not far from a temple built by Cleopatra, thus giving it its nickname, **Cleopatra's Needle.** The khedive of Egypt gave it to New York a few years after the Suez Canal opened (1869), but it didn't arrive in the city (1881) until William H. Vanderbilt paid the $100,000 shipping bill, which included constructing a railroad track to drag the pink granite statue up from the Hudson. Cecil B. de Mille, the film director and producer, presented the plaques translating the hieroglyphs.

Head back toward the Bethesda Fountain via the Delacorte Theater, the Swedish Cottage, and the west shore of the lake. On the shore south of 76th St is a promontory known as Hernshead with the **Ladies' Pavilion** (1871; Jacob Wrey Mould). Originally a shelter for ladies awaiting streetcars at Columbus Circle, it was moved here when the *Maine* Monument displaced it.

If you haven't taken the sidetrip, head west from the terrace along the 72nd St transverse.

At the intersection of West Drive and the 72nd St transverse is a 24 ft pedestal bearing a 14 ft **statue of Daniel Webster** (1876; Thomas Ball). In 1863 Ball modeled for mass production a two-ft statuette of the famous statesman and orator; the present work is a rather ungainly enlargement of that original.

Strawberry Fields

The 2.5-acre area near Central Park West and the 72nd St entrance is called **Strawberry Fields** in honor of former Beatle John Lennon, who wrote the song "Strawberry Fields Forever" and who was assassinated in the courtyard of the nearby Dakota Apartments in 1980. Lennon also wrote a song titled "Imagine," the word inscribed in the black-and-white pavement mosaic—a reproduction of a mosaic from Pompeii and a gift of Naples, Italy. The site is one of the most popular destinations for visitors, a shrine where fans leave flowers and other mementos. The garden, landscaped and set aside as a Garden of Peace, was donated by his widow, Yoko Ono.

History

The garden opened in 1985 after its planners overcame some unusual obstacles beginning with the wish of conservative City Council members to name the area for Bing Crosby instead of the politically controversial John Lennon. When Yoko Ono ran an advertisement in the *New York Times* requesting rocks and plants from nations around the world, many countries sent plants suitable to other climates or offered gifts inappropriate to the park—a totem pole, a tile bench, a large amethyst. Eventually the landscape architect Bruce Kelly decided on 161 varieties of plants for the 161 nations of the world.

Tavern on the Green

From here either go back to the Bethesda Fountain or continue south to the Tavern on the Green, a restaurant at 67th St and Central Park West, with a parking lot so conspicuous that critics once called the place the "Tavern On The Parking Lot." A sheepfold (1870; Jacob Wrey Mould) stood here and until 1934 sheltered a flock of white Southdowns who grazed in the Sheep Meadow. When the sheep were exiled to Prospect Park, Parks Commissioner Robert Moses converted the sheepfold to a restaurant, whose personnel included doormen in top hats, riding boots, and hunting coats, cigarette girls in court costumes, and a 12-piece orchestra dressed in forest green.

A Victory for Conservationists

In 1956 Moses wanted to enlarge the parking lot, a process which would have involved tearing down trees and paving over a play area. A brigade of parents and conservationists fought in the courts and in the park for the playground, wheeling baby carriages in front of Moses's bulldozers, which were stealthily brought in after midnight. Eventually the publicity made Moses relent and drop plans for enlarging the lot.

Skirt the northern edge of the Sheep Meadow and cut back to the Bethesda Fountain area. On the way is the **Mineral Springs Pavilion** (restrooms, and refreshments; closed in winter).

From the Bethesda Fountain, walk through the **Bethesda Terrace Arcade,** decorated with ornamental stonework and fine handcrafted Minton tiles designed by Jacob Wrey Mould. Nearly 16,000 ceiling tiles, weighing 50 tons, removed in 1983 after roof leakage threatened their stability, are now being restored. Installed in 1867, the decorative tiles were handmade at the Minton Tile Company of Stoke-on-Trent by embedding bits of colored clay into the tile body before firing. It is believed to be the only such Victorian encaustic tile ceiling ever created.

South of the arcade is the **Mall** (1,212 ft long) with its formal avenue of trees, the area Olmsted and Vaux considered an appropriate location for the park's statuary. Memorials elsewhere in the park result mainly from a passion for commemorative objects that gripped the city during the last half of the 19C. Near the beginning of the Mall is a statue of **Johann Christoph Friedrich von Schiller** (c. 1859; C. L. Richter), the first portrait statue erected in the park. Nearby are busts of **Beethoven** (1884; Henry Baerer) and **Victor Herbert** (1927; Edmond T. Quinn). On the east side of the Mall is the **Naumburg Bandshell,** sometimes used by the Parks Department for nonamplified concerts.

Behind the bandstand is the **Wisteria Pergola,** covered by Chinese wisteria, with the **Mary Harriman Rumsey Playfield** behind it, given (1936; rebuilt 1987) by the sister of former governor Averell Harriman. It replaced the Casino, an expensive play spot for adults, including former mayor James J. Walker, who entertained lavishly without always paying his bills. The statue of **Mother Goose** (1938) at the eastern edge of the playfield is by Frederick George Richard Roth.

Return to the Mall through the oak grove and cross over to the west side. The roadway between the Mall and the Sheep Meadow has been set aside for roller skating. When the weather is pleasant, skaters seemingly blessed with rubber joints dance to music from their own headsets or from the occasional blaring portable radio. Nearby is Christophe Fratin's *Eagles and Prey* (c. 1850), a bronze group of two ferocious eagles sinking their claws into a dead goat. Fratin belonged to a group of 19C French sculptors whose renderings of wild animals expressed a fascination with violence and terror.

Further down the Mall are (east side) statues of **Fitz-Greene Halleck** (1876; James Wilson Alexander MacDonald), a minor 19C poet who also served as John Jacob Astor's private secretary, **Sir Walter Scott** (1871; John Steell), and **William Shakespeare** (1870; John Quincy Adams Ward). In 1864, the tricentennial of Shakespeare's birth, the nation was preoccupied with proving its cultural sophistication and civic leaders felt that a statue in Shakespeare's honor would enhance the city's reputation as well as the poet's.

On the west side are **Robert Burns** (c. 1880; John Steell) and, opposite Shakespeare, a bronze statue of **Christopher Columbus** (1892; Jeronimo Suñol). To the west is *The Indian Hunter* (1866; John Quincy Adams Ward), a realistic bronze portrait of an Indian brave grasping his bow and arrow and leaning forward to hold his dog; Ward spent months in the Dakotas sketching Native Americans to prepare for this work, one of the best in the park.

Walk back north by *Shakespeare* and *Sir Walter Scott* to the Willowdell Bridge; beyond it is a statue of the canine **Balto** (1925; Frederick George Richard Roth), leader of a team of heroic huskies that carried diphtheria serum across 600 miles of stormy Alaskan wasteland to Nome in 1925.

Central Park Wildlife Center

830 Fifth Ave (at 64th St). ☎ (212) 861-6030. Web site: http://wcs.org/home/zoos. Open weekdays 10–5; weekends and holidays 10–5:30; earlier closing in winter. Admission charge. Children under 12 must be accompanied by an adult. No pets, no radios. Art gallery, special events. Café, gift shop. Accessible to wheelchairs.

From here a path leads south to the 5.5-acre Central Park Wildlife Center and **Children's Zoo** (redesigned 1988; Kevin Roche, John Dinkeloo & Assocs.).

Although park designers Olmsted and Vaux disapproved of caging animals in urban parks, the park commissioners were deluged with gifts of animals, including white mice, cattle, and deer, and to provide shelter for them established a menagerie in the Arsenal that remained there until 1934. The Central Park Zoo, which opened in 1935, originally had both large and small animals, most confined to barred cages; a renovation in 1988 has made the exhibits more suitable to the small scale of the zoo, retaining the popular sea lions and polar bears but concentrating on smaller animals. The name was also changed to the Central Park Wildlife Center, operated by the Wildlife Conservation Society (formerly the New York Zoological Society).

The zoo is divided into three zones—**temperate, tropic,** and **polar**—with animal exhibits and environments to match: real and artificial vegetation; an elaborate sprinkler system that exhales a humid jungle atmosphere; a man-made, pseudo-Antarctic icepack. Animals include red pandas, river otters, colobus monkeys, penguins, flying geckos, poison-arrow frogs, and Indian fruit bats, all chosen for their interest to visitors and their ability to adapt to zoo conditions.

Near the penguin exhibit and the Visitors Service Building, respectively, are

Honey Bear and *Dancing Goat* (c. 1935; Frederick George Richard Roth), fanciful fountain statues of great charm. In the Intelligence Garden is *Tigress and Cubs* (1866) by Auguste Cain, a prominent French sculptor whose commissions included works for the Jardins des Tuileries.

Delacorte Clock

At the south entrance to the Children's Zoo is the Delacorte Clock (1964–65; Andrea Spadini), commissioned by publisher George T. Delacorte, who admired the animated clocks of Europe. Every hour a parade of bronze animals about the size of the children watching them circles the clock while playing nursery tunes on musical instruments. A shorter performance takes place on the half hour.

Children's Zoo

Beyond the Delacorte Clock is the Children's Zoo, where young animal lovers can pet and feed goats, sheep, and a pot-bellied pig. In the Enchanted Forest is an aviary with birds, turtles, and frogs.

Nearby is the Arsenal (see Walk 22), home to the city's Parks and Recreation Department.

The Dairy

Central Park, New York, NY 10021. ☎ (212) 794-6564. Open Tues–Sun 10-5; closes at 4 Nov–March. Maps, calendars of events, gift shop. Short film and exhibit on the history of the park, family workshops, tours, and activities related to the history and design of the park.

Continue west of the zoo to the Dairy (1870; Calvert Vaux; restored 1979), built as a refreshment stand and resting place for mothers and children, the Dairy now serves as one of three information centers for the park.

When Olmsted and Vaux designed the park, they set the southern portion aside for children and their parents, the part most accessible to the city, which was then sparsely developed this far north. Here were the Dairy, the Children's Cottage, the carousel, and two rustic shelters—one on the Kinderberg, and the Cop Cot. At a time when milk was often contaminated, the Dairy was more than just a romantic pastoral feature. The park's herd of cows grazed in a field between the Dairy and what is now Wollman Rink.

The **Kinderberg,** the little hill near the Dairy, once held a summerhouse where the **Chess and Checkers House** (1952) now stands.

The Carousel

Cross under Center Drive via the Playmates' Arch just north of the Chess and Checkers House to the **carousel.**

History

According to park lore, the original carousel was turned by two animals in the basement, a blind mule and a horse, trained to respond to one or two knocks on the floor over their heads. The present carousel (1908; Stein and Goldstein), brought here in the 1950s from Coney Island after its predecessor was destroyed by fire, has 58 beautifully handcarved horses. It was restored completely (along with the machinery and the organ) in 1983, and again, in the 1990s.

From the carousel walk west toward the ball fields, on the site of one of the three playgrounds planned by Vaux and Olmsted. Unlike modern playgrounds equipped with swings, slides, and other mechanical aids to juvenile enjoyment, the original ones were simply meadows designated for field sports. Adults were not allowed, there were no permanent facilities (like backstops), and even the children had to have permits for all sports except sledding, a measure designed to protect the landscape. By 1927, compelled by overwhelming pressure for adult sports, the park managers installed five permanent fields with backstops.

Cross back under both Center Drive and South Drive. At the first sharp left intersection climb the hill to the **Cop Cot,** a rustic shelter crowning another rocky outcrop. The name means "little house on the crest of a hill," and the structure is a close replica (1984) of the original rustic summerhouse placed there when the park opened; it is built of tree limbs and trunks constructed where possible with such traditional joinery techniques as mortise and tenon instead of nails and bolts. The park once had dozens of such structures.

Follow the path northward back to **Wollman Rink** (1950), restored in 1987 by real estate mogul Donald Trump, to the embarrassment of the city government. Trump renovated the skating surface and rebuilt the rink building in five months for less than $3 million after the city had spent six years and $12.9 million without completing the job.

Walk up the hill past the chain-link fence enclosing the **Hallet Nature Sanctuary** (open only for special tours) and cross the Gapstow Bridge spanning the pond, where once both swan boats and real swans plied the waters. The latter have been replaced by pigeons and seagulls; the boats disappeared in 1924. During 1999–2001, the Central Park Conservancy restored the pond, which was partially filled in during the 1940s, and the surrounding landscape.

From here the path leads south to Grand Army Plaza at 59th St and Fifth Ave. Lined up along the sidewalk are horse-drawn carriages for hire.

On the southern edge of the park (Central Park South at Sixth Ave) stand three equestrian statues of South American liberators. Nearest Fifth Ave is a statue of **Simón Bolívar** (1919; Sally Jane Farnham), who fought against Spanish domination in South America. Facing straight down Sixth Ave is a statue of **José Julian Martí** (1959; Anna Hyatt Huntington), completed when the sculptor was 83 years old. Martí, a Cuban intellectual, organized Cuba's liberation from Spain while exiled in New York and returned to his homeland in 1895, where he was mortally wounded in a skirmish that marked the opening of Cuba's war for independence. He is shown dressed in a business suit, clutching his wound, about to topple from his horse. To its west is a statue of **José de San Martín** (c. 1950; Louis J. Daunas), who led the revolt of Argentina, Chile, and Peru against Spain. The intersection of Central Park South and Sixth Ave (officially renamed Ave of the Americas in 1945) is known (also officially) as Bolívar Plaza.

Northern Central Park

Subway: Lexington Ave Local (6) to 103rd St. Sixth Ave Express (B) or Eighth Ave Local (C) to 103rd St.
Bus: M1, M2, M3, M4.

The Reservoir

If you walk or take the bus uptown to the starting point of this route, you will pass the reservoir. Occupying 106 acres of Central Park, it reaches from about 86th St to 96th St and is a favorite spot for bird-watching and running, its soft track probably the most heavily run 1.58 miles in the city. Named the **Jacqueline Kennedy Onassis Reservoir** after her death in 1994, the 106-acre body of water used to be part of the city's water supply; now it supplies water for the loch, the pool, and the cascade. Calvert Vaux designed the gatehouses on the southern and northern shores, which contain equipment for controlling the water flow. The gate at E. 90th St, formerly Engineers' Gate, has been renamed Runners' Gate. Near the entrance is a gilded bust of one-term mayor **John Purroy Mitchel** (1926; Adolf A. Weinman). Mitchel was a reformer who got the reputation of being too friendly with the wealthy once he was in office. Shortly after he lost the 1917 election, Mitchel joined the air corps; he died in a plane crash while training as a pilot for World War I.

Conservatory Garden

Begin at Fifth Ave and 105th St. The **Vanderbilt Gate** formerly guarded the Cornelius Vanderbilt II Mansion where Bergdorf Goodman now stands (58th St at Fifth Ave). Made in Paris (1894), the wrought-iron gates were donated to the city (1939) by Gertrude Vanderbilt Whitney. Inside is the Conservatory Garden, which once had greenhouses and later a fine conservatory (1899; torn down, 1934) with impressive seasonal displays. The present garden (opened 1937) began as a Works Progress Administration project during the Depression to provide employment, with Gilmore D. Clarke as consulting landscape architect. In the 1960s and early 1970s it fell into disrepair, its broken fountains running dry, its hedges and trees growing unpruned. In 1983 the Central Park Conservancy began replanting the perennial gardens and, with the help of volunteers the following year, planted some 1,500 wildflowers on the slope to the southwest of the South Garden. Today the Conservatory Garden, with its magnificent displays of blooms and fine collections of perennials, has become a popular place to stroll, contemplate nature, and even get married.

The Gardens

The garden is divided into three sections. The **Center Garden** is Italian in style with borders of flowering quince, yew hedges, and symmetrical rows of crabapples. On the hillside is a beautiful mature Chinese wisteria on a wrought-iron arbor.

The **South Garden** contains the **Burnett Memorial Fountain** (1936; Bessie Potter Vonnoh) whose statues represents Mary and Dickon, the children in Frances Hodgson Burnett's classic *The Secret Garden*. The beds were redesigned by Lynden B. Miller (1983) as English-style herbaceous borders, with some 175 varieties of perennials. Along the garden's perimeter is a shade garden that combines native plants with other European and American species; the woodland slope is particularly lovely in the spring.

The **North Garden,** formal and French in style, centers around the **Untermeyer Fountain,** which features the bronze *Three Maidens Dancing* (1947; Walter Schott). The fountain was donated by Samuel Untermeyer. Its pedestal contains granite from the Yonkers home of the donor, a successful trial lawyer.

Circular beds surround the fountain, the outer ones planted with spectacular seasonal displays of tulips and chrysanthemums.

Continue past the Untermeyer Fountain and take the left fork of the path, which leads up the hill toward McGown's Pass. On the right are **Harlem Meer** (completed 1866) and the **Charles A. Dana Discovery Center** (1993; Buttrick, White & Burtis), one of the park's three visitor centers. The construction of the center and restoration of the meer and surrounding landscapes have attracted many visitors to the upper park. The center offers seasonal exhibits, family programs, and ecological education. For information, ☎ (212) 860-1370.

At McGowan's Pass take the right fork to the remains of **Fort Clinton,** built as part of a line of fortifications around the pass.

Central Park in Time of War

The Albany Post Rd, built over an old Indian trail, once ran northward approximately along the course of East Drive from 103rd St to 106th St, threading its way between two jutting hills where the remains of Fort Clinton and Fort Fish now stand. During the Revolutionary War the pass became an escape route for Col. William Smallwood's Marylanders, who were covering the retreat of the Colonial troops after the British invasion at Kip's Bay (Sept 15, 1776), and for the rest of the war British troops and German mercenaries were garrisoned there to protect the city from a northerly invasion. About 30 years later, during the War of 1812, the pass again gained strategic importance as New Yorkers realized, following the bombardment of Stonington, Connecticut, that their city was vulnerable to a land attack from the north. A volunteer force that included gentlemanly Columbia College students as well as butchers, lawyers, Freemasons, and tallow chandlers worked day and night to strengthen the old line of Revolutionary forts from Third Ave to the Hudson. In the McGowan's Pass area were Fort Clinton, named after Mayor De Witt Clinton; Fort Fish, named after Nicholas Fish, chairman of the defense committee; and Nutter's Battery.

Descend the hill and follow the path to the **mount** where McGowan's Tavern once stood, now a composting area. The early stone tavern bought from the Dyckman family was replaced in 1790 by a frame house that members of the McGowan family ran as an inn until 1845. Two years later the Sisters of Charity of St. Vincent de Paul bought it and added other buildings for use as a convent, Mt. Saint Vincent's. When the land was incorporated into the park, park commissioners used the convent buildings for administrative offices; Olmsted lived in one with his family for a while. Later it became a Civil War hospital, a restaurant with a sculpture gallery, and after burning down in 1881, a restaurant again; it was finally torn down in 1917. The nearby **bench** (1928) is a memorial to Andrew Haswell Green, park commissioner, lawyer, preservationist (he helped save Niagara Falls from exploitation), and moving force behind the consolidation of the five boroughs into one city. Green himself was murdered at the age of 81 by a madman who mistook him for someone else.

Take the path under the East Drive past the site of Fort Fish and continue to the Huddlestone Bridge. Through the arch you can see the **Lasker Pool-Rink,** aesthetically one of the park's less attractive structures but much appreciated by local children.

Near the bridge is a beautiful **cascade,** one of several along a watercourse that begins at the pool near Central Park West and leads to the Harlem Meer. All the bodies of water in the park are artificially created and filled with water from the city system. The **loch,** as this beautiful stream is called, flows through a wooded area of great natural beauty. Both the cascade and loch were recently restored by the conservancy. Follow the loch to the west.

At the west end of the loch the rocky Glen Span Arch leads through the ravine to the **pool,** formed by damming an old stream, Montayne's Rivulet (named after a Walloon family who farmed the area), which rose in high ground at Columbus Ave and 95th St and flowed into Harlem Creek at Fifth Ave and 107th St. Around the pond are tulip trees, weeping willows, and a handsome bald cypress with small leaves and fuzzy orange bark.

From here either leave the park by taking the left fork on the south side of the lake or take the right fork and walk up the **Great Hill** (134 ft), third-highest elevation in the park after Summit Rock (137½ ft) at 83rd St and Central Park West and Vista Rock (135 ft) at Belvedere Castle. Workmen here in 1864 found evidence of a Revolutionary War encampment—bayonets, shot, and pothooks.

From the summit take a path on the northwest side of the hill under the drive to **Block House No. 1,** built as part of the chain of fortifications for the War of 1812. At one time a cannon was mounted in a revolving turret on the platform roof of the fort so that it could fire over the parapet in any direction. From here descend the Great Hill along its west side to the Boys' Gate at Central Park West and 100th St.

26 · Upper West Side

The Upper West Side has long prided itself on being more middle class, more diverse, and definitely more liberal than the tony Upper East Side. While those distinctions have blurred in recent years as Upper West Side real estate prices have soared, the neighborhood still retains its singular flavor. While the Upper West Side is often said to run from Central Park to the Hudson River and from 59th to 110th St, the heart of the community lies between 72nd and 96th Sts.

History

In the early 19C, the Upper West Side was a series of small villages including Harsenville (in today's lower 70s), Seneca Village (a black community, in the 80s in present-day Central Park) and Bloomingdale Village (near 100th St). The opening of Central Park (1859), the widening of Bloomingdale Rd as a major boulevard (1867), and the arrival of the Ninth Ave elevated line (1879) all helped spur development. By the end of the 19C, elegant mansions and row houses were rising on Central Park West and around West End Ave and Riverside Drive, while tenements and businesses occupied Columbus and Amsterdam Aves. In the early 20C huge, luxurious apartment houses began to arrive.

The neighborhood flourished in the early 20C, attracting people involved in the arts, business, and politics, but after the Depression the community fell on hard times, especially the areas away from the park and the river, and increasingly became plagued by crime and drug use; Amsterdam and Columbus Aves became seedy. Urban renewal—mixed-income housing complexes in the upper half of the neighborhood—the construction of Lincoln Center, and the revitalization of 19C row houses helped revive the area. Through all these ups and downs, Upper Westsiders retained their sense of community and political activism, taking part in major political movements and causes, from Vietnam War protests to civil rights to historic preservation.

Today Columbus Ave has become a chic shopping district with boutiques selling designer children's clothing, bed linens, and tableware, while Amsterdam Ave, which lagged behind in the recovery, has become the community's hangout for Sunday brunch. Broadway is the principal local shopping strip and also the premier place in the city for food-lovers, who flock to Fairway (2127 Broadway, near W. 74th St) for produce, Citarella (2135 Broadway, near W. 74th St) for fish, Zabar's (2245 Broadway near W. 80th St) for every imaginable gourmet item, and H&H Bagels (2239 Broadway at W. 80th St) for fresh bagels. Climbing commercial rents, however, have forced many small local stores out of business. In their place chain stores have arrived and dominate the streetscape, particularly around Lincoln Center.

In 1992 the ubiquitous Donald Trump won a lengthy legal battle with neighborhood residents and is currently building Trump Place, known as Riverside South. In order to win approval, he had to cut back on projected population density and drop plans for the world's tallest building, but the sprawling project rising along the Hudson River from 59th to 72nd Sts will eventually have 16 commercial and residential towers (with 5,700 apartments). Trump has promised a 21-acre waterfront park to offset the vast increases in auto, pedestrian, and subway congestion.

Columbus Circle, Lincoln Center, Verdi Square
Subway: Broadway–Seventh Ave Local (1, 9), Eighth Ave Express or Local (A, C) or Sixth Ave Express (B, D) to 59th St–Columbus Circle.
Bus: M5, M7, M10, M57, M104.

Columbus Circle
Begin at Columbus Circle, the intersection of Central Park South (59th St), Central Park West (the extension of Eighth Ave), and Broadway. Atop a 77 ft granite column decorated with ships' prows stands a statue of **Christopher Columbus** (1892; Gaetano Russo), given by the Italian American community to commemorate the quadricentennial of Columbus's discovery. At the base of the column, a winged boy peruses a globe, while two bronze tablets depict the explorer's departure from Spain and his arrival in the New World.

After years of debate and delay, Columbus Circle is being redeveloped. The unloved New York Coliseum (1965; Leon & Lionel Levy) and a nearby office tower have been demolished allowing the developer, the Related Companies along with AOL Time Warner, to construct a 2.1 million-square-ft complex. The new **Columbus Center** (projected completion 2003; David Childs of Skidmore, Owings & Merrill) will include AOL Time Warner's headquarters, a hotel, apartments, a

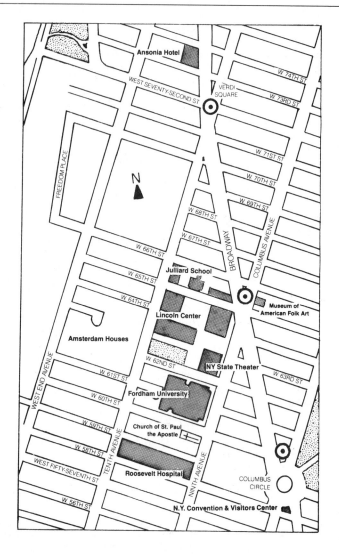

1,100-seat concert hall, a 600-seat performance atrium with a dance floor and 50 ft window, and a 140-seat jazz club as well as a jazz hall of fame. Also in the complex will be television studios for CNN and NY1 (owned by AOL Time Warner). The towers in the current plan are set back to avoid casting shadows over Central Park, a problem with earlier proposals.

The building at **2 Columbus Circle** (1965; Edward Durell Stone), at the south side of the circle, is a white marble box pierced with rows of round holes and raised above tall open arches. It was erected by A&P supermarkets heir Huntington Hartford to house his art collection. For a while it was the New York Cultural

Center (with galleries and exhibits) and later the headquarters for the city's Department of Cultural Affairs. Today it stands empty, its future uncertain.

Walk west along W. 58th St to Ninth Ave. On a slight rise near Ninth Ave in the upper W. 50s was an African American neighborhood known around the turn of the 20C as **San Juan Hill,** perhaps because of black Spanish-American War veterans who lived there or perhaps because of local racial battles. Many of its residents eventually moved uptown to Harlem.

Roosevelt Hospital, along Ninth Ave between W. 57th and W. 59th Sts, was founded in 1871 and is now part of the St. Luke's–Roosevelt Hospital Center. The oldest building on the site is the **William J. Syms Operating Theater** (1892; W. Wheeler Smith; DL) on the southwest corner of W. 59th St, named for its donor, a retired gun merchant. It is remarkable architecturally for the high semiconical skylight that illuminated the operating theater where observers, mostly medical students, could sit in its steeply raked gallery and watch the surgeons at work.

Walk north along Ninth Ave, which changes into **Columbus Ave** above W. 59th St, renamed in 1890 (as were West End Ave, Amsterdam Ave, Central Park West, and Central Park South at various times) to enhance its prestige. Those who petitioned the city for the name change regarded it as second in importance only to increased rapid transit in enhancing property values.

On the west side of Columbus Ave at W. 60th St is the Roman Catholic **Church of St. Paul the Apostle** (1885; Jeremiah O'Rourke), the home of the Paulist Fathers or Missionary Society of St. Paul, founded (1858) by Father Isaac Thomas Hecker to spread Catholicism in the largely Protestant U.S. and Canada. The bas-relief (Lumen Martin Winter) on the Gothic facade depicting the conversion of St. Paul contains 50 tons of travertine fixed against a mosaic background of Venetian glass tiles in 15 shades of blue. Stanford White designed the high altar and the altars at the ends of the north and south aisles. The mural *Angel of the Moon* (high on the south wall of the sanctuary), the Connemara marble altar of St. Patrick in the north aisle (second bay from the main entrance), the east window, and the two blue windows at the west end of the church were all designed by John La Farge.

Continue north. At 47 Columbus Ave (between W. 61st and West 62nd Sts) is the former **Kent Automatic Parking Garage** (1930; Jardine, Hill & Murdock; DL), a much admired Art Deco building, constructed as one of the city's first high-rise "automatic" (i.e., elevator-equipped) parking garages; later the Sofia Brothers Warehouse, it was recycled (1985) as the luxury **Sofia Apartments.**

Pressed up against it at 44 W. 62nd St is Lincoln Plaza Tower (1973; Horace Ginsbern & Assocs.), a 30-story apartment building with curved balconies and cylindrical columns—one of many residential buildings to rise after the construction of Lincoln Center set the neighborhood on its present upward course.

The **Lincoln Center Campus of Fordham University,** a Jesuit institution founded in 1841 with its main campus in the west Bronx, occupies the blocks bounded by Columbus and Amsterdam Aves, W. 60th and W. 62nd Sts. Built as part of the Lincoln Center urban renewal project, the campus has two main buildings: the Fordham Law School (1962; Voorhees, Walker, Smith, Smith & Haines) on the south and the Leon Lowenstein Center (1969; Slingerland & Booss) on the north.

Facing Columbus Ave at W. 61st St in front of the law school is Lila Katzen's *City Spirit* (1968), whose curved forms signify, according to the sculptor, the interlocking elements of the city. Closer to W. 62nd St is *Circle World #2*, (1969; Masami Kodama), a cube of black granite inserted in a broken circle of pink granite. In the plaza of the Lowenstein Center is the 28 ft bronze statue *Peter, Fisher of Men* (Frederick Shrady), casting a 14 ft bronze net across the plaza's reflecting pool.

Gallery at the American Bible Society

1865 Broadway, New York, NY 10023. ☎ (212) 408-1500; Web site: www.americanbible.org. Open Mon–Wed and Fri 10–6; Thurs 10–7; Sat 10–5. Closed Sun, holidays. Free. Exhibitions, special events, tours (call in advance). Gift shop. Accessible to wheelchairs.

Walk east along W. 61st St to Broadway. At 1865 Broadway (northwest corner at W. 61st St) is **Bible House** (1966; Skidmore, Owings & Merrill; glass entrance and stairs, 1998, Fox & Fowle), headquarters of the American Bible Society, which was founded in 1916 to make the Scriptures available to every literate person in a language each can understand.

The society maintains a library with some 50,000 volumes written in 1,900 languages and offers a permanent exhibition of rare and unusual Bibles, along with changing exhibitions. On view have been Helen Keller's Braille bibles, a Chinese Torah scroll made for a community of Chinese Jews who lived in Honan in the 13C–15C, and a full-scale reproduction of the Gutenberg printing press.

Walk north on Broadway to W. 63rd St. At 48 W. 63rd St is the **Iridium Jazz Club,** where octogenarian guitar legend Les Paul has been appearing on Mon nights (he is credited with inventing the electric guitar).

Dante Park, the southern triangle created by the intersection of Broadway and Columbus Ave at W. 63rd St, contains a bronze statue of **Dante Alighieri** (1921; Ettore Ximenes), erected to commemorate the 600th anniversary of the poet's death. The *Time Sculpture* (1999; Philip Johnson), a 28 ft bronze pylon with four clock faces, each bearing the name Movado, was installed over objections by some Lincoln Center officials and community activists who disliked its commercialism.

The family of tenor **Richard Tucker** erected the bronze portrait bust (1979; Milton Hebald) of the singer in the northern triangle near W. 66th St after his untimely death in 1975. Tucker, a native New Yorker, appeared in 499 performances in 21 seasons with the Metropolitan Opera and was one of the company's most popular performers.

Lincoln Center for the Performing Arts

140 W. 65th St (at Broadway), New York, NY 10023. ☎ (212) 875-1800. Web site: www.lincolncenter.org. Concerts, opera, music, dance, drama, film. Tours and Visitors' services include the "classic tour" (seven days a week) to the Metropolitan Opera House, Avery Fisher Hall, and the New York State Theater, with glimpses of rehearsals. Reservations recommended. Other group tours available by reservation. Admission charge. ☎ (212) 875-5350.

Restaurants: Fountain Café on the plaza, weather permitting, mid-May–Oct. Panevino Ristorante in Avery Fisher Hall, daily 11:30–4 (lunch), 4–curtain time (dinner), curtain time–one hour postperformance (supper); ☎ (212) 874-7000. The Grand Tier Restaurant in the Metropolitan Opera open two hours before performances for Metropolitan Opera ticket holders only (for reservations, ☎ (212)

799-3400). Gift shops. For information for the physically handicapped, ☎ (212) 875-5380.

Subway: Broadway–Seventh Ave Local (1, 9) to 66th St. Underground concourse to all buildings. Bus: M5, M7, M11, M20, M66, M104.

Bounded by Columbus and Amsterdam Aves, and W. 62nd and W. 66th Sts, Lincoln Center for the Performing Arts is a 15-acre complex of seven buildings devoted to drama, music, and dance. It is the nation's—and probably the world's—premier performing arts center.

History

Three events in the 1950s paved the way for Lincoln Center: the designation of Lincoln Square (the neighborhood around Broadway and Amsterdam Ave at W. 65th St) as a target for urban renewal, the desperate need of the Metropolitan Opera for new opera house, and the impending homelessness of the New York Philharmonic (Carnegie Hall at the time was scheduled for demolition). John D. Rockefeller III directed the fund-raising efforts while Wallace K. Harrison (of Rockefeller Center and the United Nations headquarters), who had worked with the Metropolitan Opera for a quarter of a century, headed the board of architects. In 1959 President Dwight D. Eisenhower dug up the first shovelful of earth, beginning a period of construction that ended with the opening of the Juilliard School in 1969. By 1987 most of the companies had outgrown their facilities and the trustees got out the shovel again to break ground for new buildings.

Today, Lincoln Center is home to the Metropolitan Opera, the New York Philharmonic, the New York City Ballet, the New York City Opera, Jazz at Lincoln Center, the Chamber Music Society of Lincoln Center, the Film Society of Lincoln Center, the Lincoln Center Theater, the School of American Ballet, the Juilliard School, and New York Public Library for the Performing Arts. Audiences can find opera, classical music, classical ballet, theater, rock and jazz concerts, and smaller, less conventional offerings. In the summer, the Lincoln Center Festival mounts innovative productions that might not otherwise reach the Lincoln Center audience; during the holiday season the Big Apple Circus camps out in Damrosch Park. The center attracts about 5 million people annually. Its payroll of over $100 million supports over 6,000 employees—musicians, actors, and dancers; stagehands, ushers, and ticket takers; costume makers, set builders, office personnel, and other staff.

Despite its obvious successes, or perhaps because of them, Lincoln Center has not escaped controversy. Social critics initially decried the destruction of a lower-income neighborhood rebuilt for the affluent: 1,647 families had to find new homes when their buildings were demolished to make way for the center. Acoustics in several buildings have been below par. Though time and familiarity have mellowed its big, glossy marble buildings, architectural critics never liked Lincoln Center, at worst citing it for mediocre and slick classicism, at best faintly praising the scale and relationship of its plazas and open spaces. Artists have sometimes found it too institutional, too rich, too powerful. The undeniable fact remains, however, that Lincoln Center, despite its initial cost overruns and ongoing budgetary struggles, is a vital cultural institution for both the city and the country and one that has helped revitalize a neighborhood.

In recent years Lincoln Center has begun planning yet another overhaul, which will cost anywhere from $875 million to $1.5 billion. In addition to major physical repairs and acoustical improvements, the proposals have included new buildings, a central ticket office, an opera museum, rooftop additions and sky boxes for Avery Fisher Hall, and the expansion of the Metropolitan Opera House lobby out into the plaza.

The Buildings

Architecturally Lincoln Center usually evokes the image of its three largest halls—the Metropolitan Opera House, Avery Fisher Hall, and the New York State Theater—which surround a plaza with a fountain and a pavement design of concentric circles and spokes. The fountain was designed by Philip Johnson, but the plaza, influenced by St. Mark's Square in Venice, was most likely a collaboration of all the architects working on the various buildings. The three halls, classical in inspiration, all have large expanses of glass looking out onto the plaza; they all have colonnades of one sort or another; and they all are finished with travertine, a creamy white marble from ancient quarries near Rome.

Metropolitan Opera House

The ten-story Metropolitan Opera House, the centerpiece of Lincoln Center (1966; Wallace K. Harrison), faces Broadway from the west side of the plaza. The **Metropolitan Opera** is known for the grandeur of its productions, most chosen from the traditional repertoire, and for its star-studded casts.

History

The Metropolitan Opera was founded by a group of "new" capitalists—i.e., Goulds, Whitneys, J. P. Morgan, and the occasional Vanderbilt—who were denied boxes at the Academy of Music on 14th St because the "old" nobility held title to them all. The first house (1883; J. C. Cady and Louis de Coppet Bergh), on Broadway at W. 39th St, had an auditorium whose deep "diamond horseshoe" gave box holders an unrivaled opportunity to look at one another, but it had disastrous sightlines, with some 700 seats having partial or obstructed view of the stage. The present house opened Sept 16, 1966, with the premiere performance of Samuel Barber's *Antony and Cleopatra,* whose title roles were sung by Leontyne Price and Justino Diaz.

Exterior

The main facade has five marble arches separated by columns, while the long side walls reach back the equivalent of 45 stories. At night, when the house is illuminated, two murals by Marc Chagall gleam through the windows.

Interior

Finished in red plush, gold leaf, and marble, the space recalls the color scheme of the old Met and attempts to reconcile the splendor of traditional opera houses with a contemporary approach, an attempt that some critics feel failed on the side of overdecoration and timidity. The crystal sunburst chandeliers were donated by the Austrian government. The concrete forms for the sweeping curves of the Grand Staircase were executed by boat builders.

The predominantly red **Chagall mural** on the south side, *Le Triomphe de la Musique,* contains references to opera, folk music, and jazz, as well as images of the New York skyline. Legendary Metropolitan general manager (1935–72) Sir Rudolph Bing appears in gypsy costume (central figure in the group of three on

Lincoln Center for the Performing Arts, the exterior of the Metropolitan Opera House. Visible through the windows are murals by Marc Chagall and the Austrian crystal sunburst chandeliers. The central fountain has become a popular meeting place and symbol for the city at large. (Winnie Klotz, Metropolitan Opera Association, Inc.)

the left). The yellow mural, *Les Sources de la Musique,* with a King David–Orpheus figure holding a lyre and a Tree of Life afloat in the Hudson River, has visual references to Wagner, Verdi, Bach, *Fidelio,* and *The Magic Flute.*

Backstage the building is equipped with a 110 ft fly loft above the main stage; three auxiliary stages as large as the main playing area; 20 rehearsal rooms, three of which are large enough to duplicate the main stage; and an orchestra pit that accommodates 110 musicians. The stage equipment, including six 60-ft hydraulic lifts and a revolving stage, was a gift from the government of West Germany.

The auditorium, also decorated in red, has 3,788 seats arranged in the traditional manner, though with a widened horseshoe to improve sightlines. Immense by European standards (Covent Garden has 2,158 seats), it offers a single row of boxes with otherwise "democratic" seating, in contrast to the old Met, which provided segregated elevators and less comfortable seats for patrons of the cheaper levels of the house. The free-form sculpture for the proscenium arch (1966) is by Mary Callery.

New York State Theater

On the south side of the plaza stands the New York State Theater (1964; Philip Johnson & Richard Foster), home to the New York City Opera and the New York City Ballet.

History

The resident New York City Ballet, founded in 1948 by general manager Lincoln Kirstein and artistic director George Balanchine, became famous for its performances of Balanchine's abstract, neoclassical ballets. The New York City Opera is a company of predominantly young American singers who perform an adventurous repertoire as well as standard operatic favorites in bold productions.

Exterior

Over the glass front wall rises a colonnade of paired square columns, interrupted by an outdoor balcony used as a promenade during intermissions.

Interior

On the front wall of the ground-level foyer are an *Untitled Relief* (1964; Lee Bontecou) and a painting entitled *Numbers* (1964) by Jasper Johns. On the stairway landings are two abstract sculptures of gold leaf on fiberglass by Kobashi entitled *Song* and *Dance*. One floor up is the Grand Promenade, with a marble floor, gold-leafed ceiling, beaded metallic curtains, and tiers of balconies for strolling. Since the state owns the building, the mayor and governor may use the foyer for receptions, as can private individuals—though for a fee. Two large, curvaceous statues at either end, one pair representing *Two Nudes*, the other, *Two Circus Women* (originals 1930 and 1931 by Elie Nadelman), were duplicated in Carrara marble at twice the original size by Italian artisans. Perhaps the most controversial objects in the theater, they have been called "absolutely pneumatic" by detractors, who also likened their polished whiteness to yogurt, while admirers have found them to combine "high style, sly levity, and swelling monumentality."

The auditorium (seats 2,792) was designed without a center aisle for better sightlines. It is decorated in a garnet color, with big jewel-like lights studding the tiers of balconies and a central chandelier that resembles a colossal, multifaceted diamond. The stage, engineered specifically to meet the demands of dancers, features a "sprung" floor with air spaces between its layers and is covered with dark gray linoleum. The theater's acoustics, despite two attempts to upgrade them, have remained inadequate to the demands of opera. In 1999 a sound enhancement system was installed, arousing consternation among opera patrons.

Avery Fisher Hall

Facing the New York State Theater is Avery Fisher Hall, originally Philharmonic Hall (1962; Max Abramovitz), a glass box surrounded by a colonnade of 44 tapered travertine columns. Renamed (1973) after Avery Fisher, manufacturer of high-fidelity components and donor of $10 million to Lincoln Center, the hall is the professional home of the New York Philharmonic.

History

From its opening (Sept 23, 1962), the hall's acoustics proved a nightmare to musicians, audiences, and its designers. Musicians complained of being unable to hear one another, while trained listeners in the auditorium were troubled by a lack of low-frequency sounds, a strident quality in the upper registers, and an echo. When adjustment of the original 106 sound-reflecting "clouds" hung over both the stage and the auditorium area failed to improve the acoustics, engineers resorted to increasingly radical measures, changing wall contours, replacing heavily upholstered seats with thinly padded, wooden-backed chairs, and filling in the space between the "clouds" with plywood. Even so, in 1974 the Boston and Philadelphia Orchestras, still dissatisfied, went back to Carnegie Hall for their

New York appearances. Finally, in 1976, using half of Avery Fisher's gift, architects Philip Johnson and John Burgee with acoustical guidance from Cyril Harris, consultant for the Metropolitan Opera House, had the hall completely gutted and rebuilt. However, even after the rebuilding and subsequent tinkering, many listeners still find the acoustics unsatisfactory.

Interior
In the entrance foyer at ground level are (east end) Seymour Lipton's *Archangel* (1964), an abstract sculptural work of bronze and Monel metal, and (west end) Dimitri Hadzi's dark bronze *K458—The Hunt* (1964), whose title recalls a Mozart string quartet. In the main foyer (up the escalator) is a two-part hanging work by Richard Lippold entitled *Orpheus and Apollo,* constructed of 190 strips of polished Muntz metal, a copper alloy, suspended from the ceiling by steel wires. At the south end (Broadway side) of the Grand Promenade (one level higher) is a bronze *Tragic Mask of Beethoven,* by Antoine Bourdelle, and (on the west side) a bronze head of Gustav Mahler, made by Auguste Rodin in 1901. The auditorium (seats 2,742) is used by the Philharmonic and other orchestras, by soloists, and by jazz and pop groups.

Vivian Beaumont Theater
The Vivian Beaumont Theater (1965; Eero Saarinen), named after a generous donor, has been praised as the center's visually most successful building; it has also suffered financial and artistic difficulties that long resisted changes in leadership and artistic direction. Since 1986, however, under the direction of Gregory Mosher and Bernard Gersten, the theater has attracted favorable attention from both audiences and critics, launching several shows that moved successfully to Broadway.

Situated west of the reflecting pool, the main facade appears as a horizontal slab of travertine projecting over a glass wall. Inside the entrance is a sculptural work, *Zig IV* (1961) by David Smith. The stage, designed when thrust stages were in vogue, was conceived as a compromise between a traditional proscenium arch and a thrust stage, with complex machinery for converting it from one to the other. The stage area is much larger than that of any other legitimate theater in the city and the auditorium is arranged as an amphitheater (seats 1,089). Also in the building is the **Mitzi E. Newhouse Theater,** a small house (seats 280) for more intimate and experimental drama.

New York Public Library for the Performing Arts
40 Lincoln Center Plaza, New York, NY 10023. ☎ (212) 870-1630. Web site: www.nypl.org. Open Mon 10–8; Tues–Thurs 12–8; Fri–Sat 10–6. Closed Sun, holidays. Free. Exhibitions, programs. Accessible to wheelchairs.

To the left of the theater and wrapped around it is the New York Public Library for the Performing Arts (1965; Skidmore, Owings & Merrill), which features circulating collections of some 250,000 items, including books, periodicals, music, and audio and video recordings.

The library has superb research collections. Highlights include manuscripts of Mozart and Bach, diaries of the ballet legend Vaslav Nijinsky, correspondence from stellar figures such as John Barrymore and Tennessee Williams, and rare cylinders of Metropolitan Opera performances dating to the turn of the 20C.

In Oct 2001, the library reopened after a two-year, $32-million renovation with a blockbuster exhibition, *Transformations*, that featured treasures from the collection as disparate as Lon Chaney's designs for *Phantom of the Opera*, a clip of Anna Pavlova dancing, examples of recorded sound on Amberol cylinders like those Thomas Edison used, and rare magic instruction manuals from the 18–19C.

Juilliard School

The Juilliard School lies on the north side of W. 65th St. It was founded in 1905 as the Institute of Musical Arts by Frank Damrosch and James Loeb and endowed in 1920 through a bequest from merchant and philanthropist Augustus D. Juilliard. Of all the buildings in the center the Juilliard School (1969; Pietro Belluschi) is the most complex, housing **Alice Tully Hall** (home of the Chamber Music Society of Lincoln Center) and the school itself, which offers professional training for performance in music, dance, and drama. Also on site are the Juilliard Theater (seats 1,026), a small recital hall (seats 278), a drama workshop theater (seats 206), 82 soundproof practice rooms, three organ studios, some 200 pianos, 35 teaching studios, and 16 two-story studios for dance, drama, or orchestral rehearsals.

Outside the building, on the terrace facing Broadway, stands a work of three tall, zig-zag columns of polished stainless steel entitled *Three by Three Interplay* (1971; Yaacov Agam). In the foyer of Alice Tully Hall is Antoine Bourdelle's bronze *Beethoven* (1901). Louise Nevelson's wood construction, *Nightsphere-Light* (1969), covers the west wall of the Juilliard Theater lobby; an untitled abstraction of black Swedish granite by Masayuki Nagare stands on the landing of the main staircase in the 65th St lobby.

Samuel and David Rose Building

The newest addition to Lincoln Center is the Samuel and David Rose Building with the **Meredith Willson Residence Hall** (1992; Davis Brody & Assoc. and Abramovitz Kingsland Schiff), which is home to several Lincoln Center constituents—the Film Society, the Chamber Music Society, the School of American Ballet—and also has living quarters for Juilliard and American Ballet School students, rehearsal studios, and the 300-seat Walter Reade Theater for the Film Society of Lincoln Center.

Between Avery Fisher Hall and Vivian Beaumont Theater is a reflecting pool containing Henry Moore's two-piece bronze *Lincoln Center Reclining Figure* (1965). Moore himself described the piece as "a leg part and a head and arms part." Near the library entrance is Alexander Calder's *Le Guichet* (1965), a stabile of blackened steel (22 ft long, 14 ft high). The name means "the ticket window."

On the southwest corner of the Lincoln Center site is **Damrosch Park** (1969; Eggers & Higgins), named for Walter Damrosch, director of the New York Symphony Orchestra (1903–27), composer, and pioneer of orchestral radio concerts.

Just west of Lincoln Center, between W. 64th and W. 65th Sts on Amsterdam Ave, is the **Fiorello H. La Guardia High School for Music and the Arts** (1984), a public high school open to city students by examination and audition. Among its graduates are Susan Strasberg and Al Pacino.

A block north, at 122 Amsterdam Ave (between W. 65th and W. 66th Sts), is **Martin Luther King Jr. High School** (1975; Frost Assocs). The memorial sculpture by William Tarr, constructed of self-weathering steel, resembles a huge printer's block, with letters and numbers suggesting milestones in the career of the slain civil rights leader.

Return to Broadway. While much of the area around Lincoln Center is given over to chain-store shopping and entertainment (Tower Records, a Loews multiplex, a Reebok health club), there are several survivors from the past.

American Folk Art Museum: Eva and Morris Feld Gallery

Two Lincoln Square (Columbus Ave at W. 66th St), New York, NY 10023. ☎ (212) 977-7298.

Open Tues–Sun 11:30–7:30. Free. Changing exhibitions, lectures, educational programs. Gift shop. Accessible to wheelchairs.

Subway: Broadway–Seventh Ave Local (1, 9) to 66th St. Eighth Ave Express or Local (A, C) to 59th St–Columbus Circle. Sixth Ave Express (B, D) to 59th St–Columbus Circle. Bus: M5, M7, M10, M66, M104.

Note: The main facility of the museum is on W. 53rd St (see Walk 17).

On the east side of Columbus Ave is the American Folk Art Museum, located in an attractive glassy atrium with benches for sitting. On display are changing exhibits and works from the permanent collection.

The museum's collections, which span the mid-18C to the present, contain portraiture, needlework, decoys, trade signs, and cigar-store Indians. Among the textiles are beautiful quilts, samplers, braided rugs, and Navajo blankets. Many of the works—Shaker rocking chairs, animal carvings from the southwest—have regional and ethnic connotations. Others, made by self-taught artists, express a deeply personal vision—for example, the work of the Reverend Howard Finster, who uses "other people's junk" to make artistic and devotional objects.

Walk north on Broadway to W. 70th St. Turn right and walk east to the **Pythian Apartments,** formerly the Knights of Pythias Temple (1927; Thomas W. Lamb), at 135 W. 70th St between Broadway and Columbus Ave. Thomas Lamb, designer of exotic movie palaces, created for this fraternal organization a fantastic mix of Assyrian, Sumerian, and Egyptian elements, including ten-feet-tall pharaohs who seem to have been abducted from King Tut's tomb and set down on the facade. Smaller terra-cotta pharaohs removed during a recent renovation now decorate the lobby. Once a recording studio, the building made its most significant contribution to music history when Bill Haley and His Comets recorded "Rock Around the Clock" here in 1954.

The ornate **Dorilton** (1902; Janes & Leo; DL) on the northeast corner of Broadway and W. 71st St was the first of several luxury apartment buildings built in this neighborhood. Its high stone arch, swelling mansard roof, and copious decoration—called importune by some, incendiary and voluptuous by others—all announced the building as a major social presence.

On the southeast corner of W. 72nd St and Broadway is **Gray's Papaya,** an Upper West Side institution, purveyor of the city's least-expensive hot dog. Gray's made headlines in 1999 by upping the price (from 50 cents to a whopping 75 cents) for the first time in 18 years.

Sherman Square, the triangle created by the intersection of Broadway and Amsterdam Ave at W. 72nd St is named after Gen. William Tecumseh Sherman (see Sherman statue in Walk 22), who lived nearby from 1886 until he died of pneumonia in 1891. The **subway kiosk** (1904; Heins & La Farge; DL), a little neo-Dutch colonial structure with limestone quoins and a Dutch gable, is no doubt intended to recall the founding of the city by the Dutch. Once three such "control houses," so called because riders entering them passed into territory "controlled" by the IRT, stood along Broadway, but the other two—at W. 103rd and W. 116th Sts—have not survived.

The triangle north of W. 72nd St is **Verdi Square** (DL), appropriately named in a neighborhood that attracted musicians long before Lincoln Center arrived. The **Verdi Monument** (1906; Pasquale Civiletti) depicts the composer in Carrara marble on a granite pedestal against which stand life-size figures of Aida, Otello, Falstaff, and Leonora (heroine of *La Forza del Destino*). During the 1960s and 1970s, Verdi Square was known as Needle Park because of its high concentration of drug dealers and users.

Facing Verdi Square, at 2100 Broadway (northeast corner of the intersection at W. 73rd St), is the **Apple Bank for Savings** (1926–28; York & Sawyer; DL). It was founded as the German Savings Bank in 1859 but renamed the Central Savings Bank in a period of anti-German feeling during World War I. York & Sawyer along with Samuel Yellin, responsible for the decorative ironwork, also designed the Federal Reserve Bank in the Financial District, after which this building is modeled.

Ansonia Hotel

Walk north on Broadway to the Ansonia Hotel (1904; Graves & Duboy; DL) at 2107 Broadway (between W. 73rd and W. 74th Sts), a grand old dowager among West Side apartment houses, not a hotel in the usual sense.

History

Although apartments had been built in the city toward the close of the 19C, people of means regarded multiple dwellings as the natural preserve of the working class and shunned close proximity to their neighbors and to their live-in servants, who could no longer be relegated to the attic or basement. Apartment hotels, like the Ansonia, however, offered suites and single rooms either furnished or not; their services included restaurants and full domestic staffs so that live-in servants were less necessary. Of the new apartments being built at the turn of the 20C, the 17-story Ansonia set the standard for luxury, featuring an English Grill, a large main dining room, a grand ballroom, tearooms, a lobby fountain with live seals, a Turkish bath, and the world's largest indoor swimming pool. The developer, William Earl Dodge Stokes, named the hotel for his grandfather, Anson G. Phelps, founder of the Ansonia Brass & Copper Co. in Ansonia, Connecticut. In nice weather, Stokes held orchestra concerts on the roof; he also raised goats, ducks, and chickens in a rooftop minifarm, selling the cheese and eggs at half-price to tenants.

At one time the New York home of Caruso, Toscanini, Ziegfeld, Stravinsky, Pinza, and Pons, the Ansonia still draws a musical clientele. Its most famous resident was Babe Ruth, who lived there from 1920 to 1929 at the height of his career with the New York Yankees.

Exterior
Imperiously facing down Broadway from its commanding site at a bend in the avenue, the Ansonia delights the eye with its copious Beaux-Arts decoration, rounded corner towers, and high mansard roof.

The Ansonia's Rivals
Similar in scale, though less exuberant than the Ansonia, is the **Hotel Belleclaire** (1903; Stein, Cohen & Roth; DL) at Broadway and W. 77th St. The Belleclaire provided a telegraph office as well as cafés and dining rooms in Moorish and Louis XV styles. The **Apthorp** (1906–8; Clinton & Russell; DL) at Broadway and W. 79th St, proclaimed the largest apartment house in the world upon completion, was developed by the Astor family. The **Belnord** (1908–9; H. Hobart Weekes; DL), at Broadway and W. 86th St, also advertised itself as the world's largest. Like the Apthorp, it is built around a central courtyard.

Riverside Drive and West End Avenue from 72nd Street to 107th Street and Vicinity
Subway: Broadway–Seventh Ave Express or Local (1, 2, 3, 9) to 72nd St.
Bus: M10, M30, M104.

Level Club
Begin at W. 72nd St and Broadway. Walk north to W. 73rd St. The condominium building at 253 W. 73rd St was erected as the Level Club (1926; Clinton & Russell), an ambitious business venture by the New York Masons. Art Deco terra-cotta friezes adorn the setbacks; the two large central columns above the third floor are topped by filigreed globes and supported by the crouching figures of King Solomon and Hiram Abif, the legendary builder of Solomon's Temple.

History
Much of the ornamentation, including the six-pointed stars and rams' heads, paid homage to King Solomon's Temple. Inside was an Olympic-size pool, a gym, and a 1,500 seat auditorium. The Masons, however, lacked Solomon's wisdom and ran up huge debts as they piled on the luxurious details. Eventually, the local group had to apologize to the national Freemasons and the public, explaining that the project was not sponsored by the Masons and was merely local entrepreneurship gone awry.

Continue west to West End Ave, then walk south to W. 72nd St. Turn right. At 309 W. 72nd St (1901; Gilbert Schellenger; DL) is the former **William Diller House,** a brick and limestone town house with an Ionic portico, two-story bowed bay windows, and sculpted flora along the trim. Next door, at the corner of Riverside Drive, is its stylistic companion, 311 W. 72nd St (1902; C. P. H. Gilbert; DL), with a similar portico and two-story bay. Known as the **John and Mary Sutphen House,** its distinctive feature is the steep mansard roof with

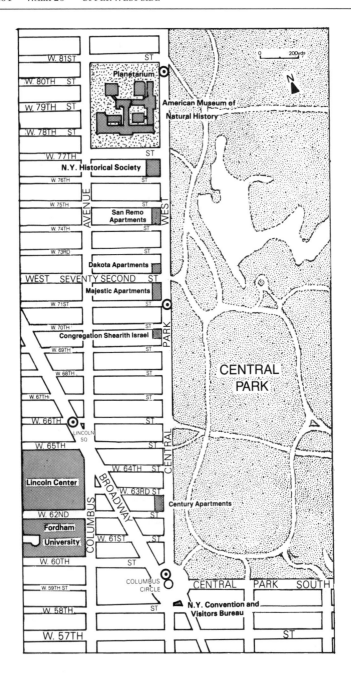

dormer windows. Sutphen's father, also named John, developed the area using restrictive covenants to ensure high-quality residences. The rules banned slaughterhouses and breweries, and also stipulated that Gilbert build this home and two others.

For the **Frederick and Lydia Prentiss House** (1901; C. P. H. Gilbert; DL), at 1 Riverside Drive on the northeast corner of W. 72nd St, Gilbert designed a companion building, with a turret topping off a conical roof in one section and a copper-trimmed slate mansard roof in another. Gilbert was more expressive with 3 Riverside Drive, the **Philip and Maria Kleeberg House** (1898; C. P. H. Gilbert; DL), a mix of French Renaissance and Gothic styles. Above a curved, four-sided bay with faceted pilasters on the first three stories are a balustrade and a steeply pitched roof with a wild assemblage of putti, gargoyles, shields, shells, wreaths, and foliage.

On the south side of W. 72nd St are the **Chatsworth Apartments and Annex** (1906; John Scharsmith; DL), 340–344 W. 72nd St, handsome Beaux-Arts luxury apartments with russet-colored bricks and limestone trim topped off by a three-story slate mansard roof.

Riverside Park

The buildings look out onto the southern edge of Riverside Park (1880; Frederick Law Olmsted and Calvert Vaux, with others; additions, 1941; Gilmore D. Clarke and Clifton Lloyd; DL), which stretches more than two miles from W. 72nd St to about W. 125th St. (A nonlandmarked green stretch, also called Riverside Park, runs from W. 135th to W. 158th Sts.)

History

The concept for a park and scenic drive to enhance the Upper West Side was born in the 1860s. In 1873, Frederick Law Olmsted was hired to design both the park and Riverside Drive, which he brilliantly combined in his landscaping plans. When Olmsted, whose career was repeatedly frustrated by city politicians, was fired from the Department of Public Parks in 1878, Calvert Vaux and other architects took over the plans for Riverside Park. Their early version was not completed for 25 years and, because the New York Central Railroad tracks ran through the site, much of the rustic pastoral design was not implemented.

Some of the ideas, however, were incorporated into a major renovation undertaken from 1937 to 1941 by Parks Commissioner Robert Moses, who added 132 acres, 140,000 feet of pathway, and eight playgrounds, much of it along shoreline extended by landfill.

The final result is a lovely terraced, sloping park, some of it, alas, in unfortunate proximity to the West Side Hwy. Moses also built a rotunda and marina at 79th St; the rotunda is now home to the **Boat Basin Café** (a good spot for summer outdoor dining), and the 110-slip public marina where the city's houseboats are docked.

At the southern entrance to Riverside Park, W. 72nd St at West End Ave, is an eight-ft bronze-and-stone **statue of Eleanor Roosevelt** (1996; Penelope Jencks). The former first lady is surrounded by three oak trees, a low granite wall, and benches.

The Former Schwab Mansion

One of the city's most majestic mansions once stood at Riverside Drive between W. 73rd and W. 74th Sts. Built in 1901 for Bethlehem Steel founder Charles Schwab, the house had 75 rooms, 40 baths, several eat-in kitchens, a gym, a private chapel, a bowling alley, a marble swimming pool, and a $65,000 pipe organ. After Schwab died in 1939, the Chase National Bank tried leasing or selling the property, but in 1947 the mansion was demolished for construction of an apartment building.

The **West End–Collegiate Historic District** runs from W. 74th St to W. 78th St between Riverside Drive and West End Ave. Most of the row houses here were built by speculators between about 1885 and 1900. To make the houses appealing, the developers hired well-known architects—C. P. H. Gilbert, Lamb & Rich, and Clarence True—who built in various styles with an eclectic mix of decorative touches. True designed 270 buildings in the area, and beginning in 1894 he bought up land on Riverside Drive below W. 84th St, becoming an astute developer himself.

Highlights of the West End–Collegiate Historic District

To see some of these residences, walk around the block bounded by W. 76th and W. 77th Sts, West End Ave, and Riverside Drive. Highlights include 337 W. 76th St (Clarence True), 301–305 W. 76th St (Lamb & Rich), 341–357 West End Ave (between W. 76th and W. 77th Sts) (Lamb & Rich), 302–306 W. 77th St (Lamb & Rich), and 334–338 W. 77th St (Clarence True).

Also at West End Ave and W. 77th St is the **West End Collegiate Church** and **Collegiate School** (1893; Robert Gibson; DL), whose congregation is descended from New Amsterdam's first church. The present building is Dutch in style, built of yellow-brown brick with an 18-step striped brick central gable and several smaller but equally exuberant gables on the sides. The school, founded in 1638 as part of the church, is now a separate institution, the nation's oldest private secondary school.

Walk north along Riverside Drive to W. 80th St. Clarence True also built houses in what is now the small **Riverside Drive–W. 80th–81st St Historic District**—for example, 307–323 W. 80th St. These houses have stained glass above the entrances, second-floor bay windows, and an elegant collection of gables, cornices, and terra-cotta tiles.

Return to Riverside Drive and walk north to W. 82nd St and a stretch of landmarked houses built by True in 1898–99. Avoiding the tedious repetition of brownstone, True built nos. 103, 104, 105 and 107–109 W. 82nd St in brick ranging in color from tan to orange to red. All of the bow fronts, stoops, and three-sided bays had to be removed after True lost a 1903 lawsuit in which a neighbor claimed the fronts blocked her view, light, and air. The house True designed at **332 W. 83rd St,** unaffected by the lawsuit, retains its steep tile roof, two-story rounded bay, and other decorative elements.

Return to Riverside Drive. Babe Ruth's third and final Upper West Side home was an 11-room apartment at **110 Riverside Drive** (83rd St). He lived here from 1942 until his death in 1948.

Continue north on Riverside Drive. Edgar Allan Poe spent two summers in 1843–44 in a farmhouse on W. 84th St east of Riverside Drive, about the time he began working on "The Raven." Turn right on W. 85th St. At 350 W. 85th is the **Red House** (1904; Harde & Short; DL), an attractive apartment building in a combination of French Gothic and Renaissance styles with a regal entrance. Faced with red brick and light terra-cotta trim, its ornamentation includes salamanders, leaf forms, crown motifs, and sculpted canopies above some windows.

Across the street, at **329–337 W. 85th St** (1891; Ralph Townsend; DL), is a row of five houses faced in textures of red brick and brownstone, adorned with first-story arches, rounded windows, stained glass, and carvings of foliage, faces, and masks. (Journalist Heywood Broun lived at 333 W. 85th St from 1921 until 1928.) Clarence True's effort on this block, at 316–326 W. 85th St (1892; DL), is an uninspired collection of squat red brick and brownstone row houses.

Continue to West End Ave, where True stars yet again with **520 West End Ave** (1892; DL), a five-story mansion built for cotton broker John Leech. This corner house of rusticated red sandstone with carved stone details is nicknamed the Castle. It had long been converted to apartments when it was landmarked in 1987 over the protest of the owner, who wanted to build a new apartment building on a platform above the house. The landmark designation was temporarily overturned on a technicality but was ultimately reinstated, defeating the apartment project.

Continue north to W. 86th St and the **Church of St. Paul and St. Andrew and Parish House** (1897; Robert H. Robertson; DL). Its dominant features are a towering octagonal campanile, huge terra-cotta Corinthian pilasters that split the entrance into three bays, flying buttresses, and a second, square tower.

Walk west to Riverside Drive. The **Riverside Drive–West End Historic District** stretches from W. 85th to W. 95th Sts and in most places from Riverside Drive to West End Ave. The district includes neo-Renaissance and Queen Anne row houses designed by architects C. P. H. Gilbert, Ralph Townsend, and Clarence True, as well as outstanding apartment houses, some of which follow the curve of Riverside Drive.

At 140 Riverside Drive (W. 86th St) is the block-long, 19-story **Normandy** (1939; Emery Roth & Sons, DL), one of the elder Roth's last works. Above the gracefully curved entrance is a gorgeous blue-and-gold mosaic.

Turn right on W. 88th St. Babe Ruth lived at **345 W. 88th St** from 1929 until 1942. Continue east along W. 88th St to **Congregation B'nai Jeshurun** (1918; Henry Herts and Walter Scneider), a flamboyant Moorish-style temple. This is the city's oldest Ashkenazic congregation, founded in 1825 by a group that split off from a Sephardic temple.

Return to West End Ave, turn right, and walk north to W. 89th St. Walk west to the southeast corner of Riverside Drive and the former **Isaac Rice Mansion** (1901; Herts & Tallant; DL) at 346 W. 89th St. Designed by architects better known for their theaters, this is one of only two freestanding homes surviving along Riverside Drive. It was built for lawyer and chess expert Isaac Rice and later sold to tobacco importer Solomon Schinasi, whose brother Morris owned his own mansion on Riverside Drive at W. 107th St.

Soldiers' and Sailors' Monument (1902; Stoughton & Stoughton with Paul DuBoy; DL), in Riverside Park at 89th St, memorializes the New York Regiments who fought in the Civil War. The monument is 100 ft high; its dozen 36-ft columns rise from a marble base decorated with laurel and oak leaves to a conical roof and marble finial. Above the door is a cornice with an eagle.

At W. 91st St, Riverside Drive splits into two roadways that wrap around an island of green guarded by an equestrian **statue of Joan of Arc** (1915; Anna Vaughn Hyatt) defiantly brandishing a sword.

Continue north to W. 94th St; turn right and walk east across West End Ave to **Pomander Walk** (1921; King & Campbell; DL). This small street, between West End Ave and Broadway from W. 94th St to W. 95th St, looks like a quaint old English village dropped into Manhattan. Developed by restauranteur Thomas Healy to re-create the sets of *Pomander Walk*, a popular Broadway play, the enclave has 16 two-story buildings facing a private walkway and 11 more facing the cross streets. Gloria Swanson, Rosalind Russell, Humphrey Bogart, and Lillian and Dorothy Gish are among those who have lived here.

Symphony Space

Continue east to Broadway. The towering new 22-story apartment complex at **2257 Broadway** (between W. 94th and W. 95th Sts) rising on top of an older building was constructed (2001; Costas Kondylis) as part of a real estate deal that provided funds for **Symphony Space,** the cultural institution at its base. This nonprofit performing arts center has endeared itself to its audiences since 1978 with offerings such as short story readings by Broadway and Hollywood actors, "Wall-to-Wall" celebrations of composers from Bach to Miles Davis, and an annual Bloomsday commemoration of James Joyce.

History

In 1979 **Symphony Space** moved into this building, originally constructed (1915) as a market and later used for an ice skating rink and a restaurant. The arts center sold the air rights, raising ten million dollars to fund an endowment and repair its auditorium. As part of the deal, a quarter of the 285 apartments have been set aside for lower-income tenants. Symphony Space's much-loved existing auditorium has been joined to the space of the empty Thalia movie theater, which once more shows art films and also serves as a venue for live performances. (The refurbished theaters [James Stewart Polshek] are expected to open in the spring of 2002.)

Continue north to W. 96th St and walk west to Riverside Drive. At the northeast corner of the intersection is the **Cliff Dwellers' Apartments** (1914; Herman Lee Meader), 243 Riverside Drive, a handsome tan brick building with Mayan-inspired trim and a frieze decorated with buffalo heads, masks, rattlesnakes, and mountain lions.

Continue north to W. 100th St and the **Firemen's Memorial** (1913; Attilio Piccirilli), whose bronze tablet commemorates even the "horses that shared in valor and devotion and with mighty speed bore on the rescue." The pink marble monument has a bronze bas-relief depicting the galloping horses of Engine Company 83. The sculpted figure of Sacrifice (or Courage) to the north depicts a woman supporting the body of a fallen firefighter; Duty to the south portrays the widow of a firefighter, holding a child and the firefighter's helmet.

Continue north to **294 Riverside Drive** (1901; Schickel & Ditmars; DL), a fine Beaux-Arts limestone mansion built for William Baumgarten, who worked for and later headed Herter Brothers, interior designers to the robber barons.

On the next block, at 310 Riverside Drive, is the **Master Building** (1929; Helmle, Corbett & Harrison and Sugarman & Berger; DL), an Art Deco high-rise with patterned brickwork that lightens in color as the building rises.

Continue north to the **Riverside Drive–W. 105th St Historic District.** At 330 Riverside Drive is another flowery Beaux-Arts mansion (1902; Janes & Leo), now home to the Riverside Study Center, a residence for young Catholic men. Next door, the **New York Buddhist Church** (1902; Janes & Leo) at 331 Riverside Drive occupies the former home of 1930s actress Marion Davies, paramour of William Randolph Hearst. (Hearst lived at Riverside Drive and W. 86th St.) In front is a bronze statue of **Shinran Shonin** (1173–1262), founder of the Jodo-Shinshu sect of Buddhism. The statue originally stood in Hiroshima less than two miles from ground zero when the atomic bomb was dropped. Astonishingly, it survived and was brought here in 1955 as a symbol of lasting hope for world peace.

On the northeast corner at W. 107th St is Riverside Drive's other remaining freestanding mansion, the former **Morris Schinasi House** (1909; William Tuthill; DL). Faced with Vermont white marble, it has 11 steps leading majestically to the entrance, and a green terra-cotta tile mansard roof with a copper spire.

Nicholas Roerich Museum

319 W. 107th St (near Riverside Drive) New York, NY 10025. ☎ (212) 864-7752. Web site: www.roerich.org. Open Tues–Sun 2–5. Closed Mon, holidays. Requested donation. Poetry readings, changing exhibitions, musical programs. Gift shop. Not accessible to wheelchairs.

Subway: Broadway–Seventh Ave Local (1, 9) to 110th St. Bus: M4, M5, M104.

At 319 W. 107th St is the Nicholas Roerich Museum (1923), a small, quiet site commemorating the life and work of Roerich (1874–1947), a Russian-born painter, mystic, archeologist, writer, and humanitarian. His artistic works included stage settings for Russian ballets—he established an international reputation working with Sergei Diaghilev. His humanitarian efforts led to the Roerich Pact, a treaty designed to protect cultural, scientific, and religious institutions and works of art during times of war. For this he was nominated for the Nobel Peace Prize in 1929.

Despite his achievements, Roerich is virtually unknown today. A major aim of the museum is to promote awareness of his ideas about art and culture, which are embodied in the museum's symbol, three red circles enclosed in a red ring, and its motto, *Pax Cultura* ("Peace through Culture").

The permanent exhibit contains about 200 of his paintings, many of them celebrating the beauty of the Himalayas and the spiritual quality of the people of the Tibetan highlands; a display of his writings; and a small collection of Indian and Asian artifacts and memorabilia.

Return south to W. 103rd St, then turn left and walk east. From 1925 to 1931, Ira and George Gershwin lived at 316 W. 103rd St with their parents and siblings. Humphrey Bogart grew up at 245 W. 103rd St.

At West End Ave, look south: **nos. 854, 856,** and **858 West End Ave** (1893; Schneider & Herter; DL) are among the best row houses in the area; they feature gables, pediment parapets, and ornamentation including lion's heads and carved capitals.

Walk north along West End Ave to W. 106th St where it intersects with Broadway. **Straus Triangle** is named for department store magnate Isidor Straus and his wife Ida, both of whom died on the *Titanic*. In the park is a memorial fountain whose bronze figure, Memory (1915; Augustus Lukeman and Evarts Tracy), reclines on a rock, her sandal dangling as she gazes into the water.

Central Park West and Vicinity

Subway: Broadway–Seventh Ave Local (1, 9) to 59th St–Columbus Circle. Eighth Ave Express or Local (A, C) to 59th St–Columbus Circle. Sixth Ave Express (B, D) to 59th St–Columbus Circle.
Bus: M5, M7, M10, M20, M104.

At 59th St, Eighth Ave becomes Central Park West, renamed after the opening of the park in 1876 to boost land values. The street is now an elegant boulevard whose venerable institutions and stately apartment buildings serve the cultural and spiritual needs of many New Yorkers as well as the domestic needs of a select few. The older buildings date back to the last decade of the 19C, when the arrival of the Ninth Ave elevated railroad in 1879 made the Upper West Side accessible to the middle class. The newer ones, with a few exceptions, date from before 1931, remarkable considering the city's penchant for tearing down and building up. Among the newer buildings facing the park are several splendid examples of Art Deco apartment architecture; among the older ones are fine masonry buildings. Along the side streets are long blocks of brownstone row houses dating to the late 19C, many with imposing stone stoops and exuberant ornamentation.

Begin at the north side of Columbus Circle in front of the **Trump International Hotel and Tower** (1997; Philip Johnson) a reconfiguration of the former Gulf & Western Building (1970; Thomas E. Stanley). The original office building was a white rectangular slab set down on a triangular site. When the wind blew hard, pieces of the stone facing sometimes fell off. Trump stripped it down and glitzed it up in golden bronze-tinted glass, adding a six-ton stainless steel globe (1997; Kim Brandell) out front.

Visible just at the edge of Central Park is the ***Maine* Memorial,** which commemorates the sinking of the U.S. battleship *Maine* (Feb 15, 1898), an incident that helped trigger the Spanish-American War. The memorial (1913; statuary by Attilio Piccirilli) consists of a granite stele (43.5 ft) with bronze and marble sculptures. On the top, the 15 ft Columbia Triumphant stands in a shell pulled by three hippocampi. At the base facing Broadway a boatload of marble figures includes Victory (a youth kneeling in the prow), accompanied by Courage (a male nude), and Fortitude (a mother comforting a weeping child). Behind them stands a robed figure representing Peace. Another group, facing the park, includes Justice, History, and a Warrior whose upraised hand once clenched a bronze sword.

The reclining youth looking downtown represents the Atlantic, while the Pacific, facing uptown, appears as an aged man.

Begin walking north up Central Park West. The Art Deco **Century Apartments** (1931; Jacques Delamarre and the Irwin S. Chanin Construction Co.; DL) at 25 Central Park West (between W. 62nd and W. 63rd Sts), has machinelike trim at the top and cantilevered terraces at the base of its twin towers. The building is named after the Century Theatre, a grandiose neoclassical fiasco (1909; Carrère & Hastings), too large and too far uptown to make a profit, even when Florenz Ziegfeld staged spectaculars there.

Behind the somber brick walls of the massive **West Side YMCA** (1930; Dwight James Baum), 5 W. 63rd St, are swimming pools, handball and squash courts, and an indoor track. (The Frederick Henry Cossett Dormitory, at 10 W. 64th St, offers rooms by the day and week.) A 1966 plan to create a landscaped mall between Central Park and Lincoln Center would have destroyed the "Y" and all its neighbors.

Filling Central Park West between W. 63rd and W. 64th Sts are two buildings of the **Ethical Culture Society,** founded in 1876 by Felix Adler to further morality independently of organized religion. The Ethical Culture school system began with the city's first free kindergarten (1878), establishing itself early as a force in experimental education. Today the society operates the Fieldston Schools in the Bronx as well as the Ethical Culture School here, all known for their progressive outlook. The northern building at 2 W. 64th St (1910; Robert D. Kohn with Estelle Rumbold Kohn, sculptor; DL) is a formal limestone Art Nouveau structure.

Standing boldly atop the **Liberty Warehouse** (c. 1891), at 43 W. 64th St between Central Park West and Broadway, is a 55 ft replica of the larger, more famous, more dramatically sited Statue of Liberty. Based on a scale model by sculptor Frédéric-Auguste Bartholdi, the figure was commissioned by the warehouse owner William H. Flattau and cast in a foundry in Akron, Ohio. It was shipped to New York by rail on a flatbed car, sliced in half lengthwise because it was too large to fit through the railroad tunnels, and then welded together again. Inside is a circular staircase, sealed by Flattau in 1912 because visitors were distracting his workers. The green color is paint, not verdigris.

The **Prasada** at 50 Central Park West, on the southwest corner of W. 65th St (1907; Charles W. Romeyn & Henry R. Wynne), started out with a grand mansard roof. The roof was removed in 1919, but the monumental entrance with its two-story striped columns remains.

The apartment house at **55 Central Park West** (1940; Schwartz & Gross), another Art Deco–inspired building, has a splendid ironwork canopy over the entrance and brickwork that shades from red at the bottom to tan at the top, giving the impression, observers have said, of a ray of sunshine perpetually shining on the facade.

Walk down W. 66th St as far as no. 56, once the **First Battery Armory of the New York National Guard** (1901; Horgan & Slattery), altered (1978) into television studios for the **American Broadcasting Company** (ABC). Across the street at 71 W. 66th St is another fanciful facade, originally the street side of the St. Nicholas Skating Rink (1896; Ernest Flagg and Walter B. Chambers). Nowadays ABC uses it for broadcast engineering operations. ABC, which is headquartered at 77 W. 66th St, occupies most of the block as well as 149 Columbus Ave and 7 Lincoln Square.

Return to Central Park West and continue north. West 67th St is a charming anomaly, with several studio buildings constructed expressly for working artists. Most famous of these is the **Hotel des Artistes** (1915; George Mort Pollard), 1 W. 67th St, just off the park, with large two-story windows opening into the studios and fanciful neo-Gothic statuary above the second story. Among its famous tenants have been Noel Coward, Isadora Duncan, Norman Rockwell, Rudolph Valentino, Alexander Woolcott, former mayor John V. Lindsay, and Howard Chandler Christy, whose elegant murals still adorn the posh ground-floor restaurant, Café des Artistes.

Just down the block at 15 W. 67th St (1906; Pollard & Steinam) is the **Central Park Studios,** featuring a beautiful wrought-iron and glass lamp above the doorway. The earliest studio building here is the **Cooperative Studio Building,** also known as the 67th Street Studios, at 27 W. 67th St (1905), erected by ten artists who occupied half and rented out the rest, realizing a 23 percent profit on their investment.

Free Synagogue

Return to Central Park West and keep walking uptown. On the southwest corner of W. 68th St is the **Second Church of Christ, Scientist** (1900; Frederick Comstock), topped off with green domes. At 68th St turn left and continue to 40 W. 68th St, originally the Free Synagogue (1923; S. B. Eisendrath and B. Horowitz), later the Hebrew Union College–Jewish Institute of Religion, a rabbinical training school, now York Preparatory School.

History

Under the leadership of its founder, Stephen Wise, a civic reformer and ardent Zionist, the Free Synagogue became a forum for public and religious issues. In addition to founding the synagogue (1907), Rabbi Wise organized the first section of the Federation of American Zionists and headed the delegation of the American Jewish Congress at the Paris Peace Conference following World War I. The present Stephen Wise Free Synagogue at 30 W. 68th St, just east of the original building, was added in 1941 (Bloch & Hesse) and remains in use.

Congregation Shearith Israel

Return to Central Park West and walk north to the southwest corner of W. 70th St. At 99 Central Park West is the newest home (1897; Brunner & Tryon; DL) of **Congregation Shearith Israel,** the nation's oldest Jewish congregation, which dates back to 1654 when the first Jewish refugees arrived in New Amsterdam fleeing the Inquisition (see Peter Minuit Plaza and Mill Lane in Walk 2).

New York's Oldest Jewish Congregation

Under Dutch rule Jews had to worship in secret, but in 1682, under a more tolerant British governor, they founded Congregation Shearith Israel (Remnant of Israel) and held organized services, first in a rented room on Beaver St, then in the upper story of a flour mill on Mill Lane and South William St. The first synagogue building (1730), at what is presently 26 South William St, is gone, but some of its artifacts and two large millstones from the Dutch mill are preserved in the Little

Synagogue here, which reconstructs the original sanctuary. (Open during services, Fri evening and Sat morning; ☎ (212) 873-0300 for times.)

Turn west onto 71st St for a look at some classic brownstone row houses.

"Brownstones"

Brownstone is a Triassic sandstone; its characteristic chocolate color comes from iron ore. A "brownstone" in the local dialect is a one-family row house faced with this material, usually dating from the late 19C, four or five stories high, two or three windows wide, featuring a tall stoop and a cornice at the top. Most brownstones were built by masons or builders, but the one at **20 W. 71st St** enjoyed the talents of an architect (1889; Gilbert A. Schellenger) who designed a row of four houses here. Most brownstones were constructed in small groups, and their widths became fractions of the standard city building lot (25 × 100 ft). The most spacious are 25 ft wide, while smaller varieties are 20 ft (a fifth of four lots), 18¾ ft (a quarter of three lots), or 16⅔ ft (a third of two lots). Because these houses were built for prosperous middle-class families, the interiors were executed in fine materials and the facades often elaborately decorated. Note, for example, the Cupids at the cornice of no. 24; the cartouches on nos. 26, 28, and 30; and the lions' heads on nos. 33–39.

Return to Central Park West and continue north past the **Majestic Apartments,** 115 Central Park West (between W. 71st and W. 72nd Sts), the second of four double-towered buildings that give the skyline along the park its distinction. Stylistically related to the Century nine blocks downtown, the Majestic was also built (1931; Jacques Delamarre; DL) by the Irwin S. Chanin Co. René Chambellan, better known for the fountains at Radio City, designed the brickwork patterns. Corner windows were frequently used in Art Deco buildings, their steel-cage construction allowed corners to be opened up (unlike masonry construction, where corners were load bearing).

Dakota Apartments

Across the street, at 1 W. 72nd St, are the **Dakota Apartments** (1884; Henry J. Hardenbergh; DL), architecturally one of the city's finest apartment buildings and socially the preeminent West Side address.

History

In 1884 apartments were just beginning to find favor with the well-to-do, so when Singer Sewing Machine heir Edward S. Clark undertook a magnificent apartment house on W. 72nd St, he was not acting without precedent. His choice of location, however, was daring—uptown, surrounded by shanties and vacant land, so far north and west of civilization that detractors called it "Clark's Folly," one of them remarking that the building might as well be in the Dakota territory. Clark liked the notion and told his architect to garnish the building with ears of corn, arrowheads, and a bas-relief of an Indian's head above the main gateway.

Exterior

Built around an open central courtyard, the Dakota is finished in buff-colored brick with terra-cotta and stone trim and embellished with balconies, oriel windows, ledges, turrets, towers, gables, chimneys, finials, and flagpoles. The railings on W. 72nd St and Central Park West feature griffins and Zeus-heads. The building is generally acknowledged to be the masterpiece of an architect outstanding for his sense of composition.

Interior

From the beginning, the Dakota has been a luxury building, its apartments originally fitted out with carved marble mantles, oak and mahogany paneling, inlaid marble floors, and hardware of solid brass. On the eighth and ninth floors, undesirable in the days before elevators, were rooms for servants, while the basement held boilers and generators to light the building, since the Edison Company's lines reached only as far as Spruce St.

Famous Dakotans

Not surprisingly, the building has attracted a striking clientele, notably people involved in the arts. Among them have been Boris Karloff, Zachary Scott, Leonard Bernstein, Lauren Bacall, Roberta Flack, Rosemary Clooney, Rudolf Nureyev, and scientist Michael Idvorsky Pupin. John Lennon, who lived here, was shot and killed in the courtyard by a deranged admirer on Dec 8, 1980, as Lennon was returning home from the recording studios. As fans heard the news, thousands flocked to the site, spending the night (and longer) singing Beatles songs by candlelight.

Continue north on Central Park West. At 135 Central Park West is another early luxury apartment, the **Langham** (1905; Clinton & Russell). When the Clark family sold the land for development, they initially restricted any new building from being taller than the Dakota, but that condition fell by the wayside and the Langham surpassed the Dakota. Early residents included prominent businessmen—Irving Bloomingdale, son of Lyman who founded the store; the theater promoter Martin Beck; and theater owner Edward Albee (grandfather of the playwright with the same name). A more recent resident, Mia Farrow, became famous for her role in *Rosemary's Baby*, filmed next door at the Dakota. Her Langham apartment was the backdrop for Woody Allen's *Hannah and her Sisters*.

The intersection of Central Park West and W. 74th St is infamous as the site of the first fatality from an auto accident. On Sept 13, 1899, 68-year-old Henry Hale Bliss exited a trolley car and turned back to help a young woman off. As he did, Bliss was hit by a car. He died within hours.

At 145–146 Central Park West (between W. 74th and W. 75th Sts) is the third of the boulevard's twin towers, the **San Remo Apartments** (1930; Emery Roth;

DL), finished in neoclassical garb with cartouches over the entrances and finialed temples on top.

Emery Roth

The firm of Emery Roth & Sons has built more than 100 glass-and-steel skyscrapers since World War II (few of them with much distinction), but Emery Roth père produced masonry apartment buildings and hotels ornamented with neoclassical detail between 1903 and the late 1930s. He came to the U.S. in 1886 at the age of 13 and four years later began working as a draftsman on the Chicago World's Columbian Exposition. Like other conservative architects, he was deeply impressed by the dignity of the Beaux-Arts buildings that dominated the exhibition, a style later reflected in his own work.

The San Remo is named after a hotel of that name which stood here before the turn of the 20C. It has been home to Rita Hayworth, Jack Dempsey, Dustin Hoffman, Diane Keaton, Elaine May, Mary Tyler Moore, and Steve Martin.

Continue to W. 76th St and turn left. The block between Central Park West and Columbus Ave has been designated the **Central Park West–76th St Historic District** because of its impressive row housing, built between 1889 and 1900. The earliest, nos. 31–37 W. 76th St (George M. Walgrove), have neo-Grec trim and then–newly fashionable rockface finishes; nos. 8–10 were built by John H. Duncan (better known for Grant's Tomb) in a neobaroque style. Elsewhere on the block are neo-Italian Renaissance, Romanesque revival, and neo-Gothic facades.

Return to Central Park West. Facing the park on the southwest corner of W. 76th St is the **Universalist Church of New York** (1898; William A. Potter), formerly the Church of the Divine Paternity, and originally the Fourth Universalist Society. Handsome inside and out, with a large Gothic tower, it was the church of Andrew Carnegie and others of the ruling class.

New-York Historical Society

170 Central Park West (between W. 76th and W. 77th Sts), New York, NY 10024. ☎ (212) 873-3400. Web site: www.nyhistory.org. Open Tues–Sun 11–5. Closed Mon, national holidays. Call for summer hours. Admission charge. Exhibitions, lectures, concerts. Gift shop. Accessible to wheelchairs; video displays hearing captioned.

Subway: Eighth Ave Local (C) or Sixth Ave Express (B, weekdays only) to 81st St. Broadway–Seventh Ave Local (1, 9) to 79th St. Bus: M7, M10, M11, M79.

A block further uptown is the New-York Historical Society (1908; York & Sawyer; north and south wings, 1938; Walker & Gillette; DL), the oldest museum in the city. Founded in 1804 by Mayor De Witt Clinton and others, the New-York Historical Society, which retains the old hyphenated spelling of the city's name, has collections and changing exhibitions that document the American experience as well as the history of the city. The building is a paragon of neoclassical severity, faced in hard gray granite and barely ornamented.

The society's collections include paintings, decorative arts, sculpture, drawings, watercolors, and trade artifacts. The research library, open to scholars, has a half-million books and 10,000 newspapers, including the city's first newspaper, the *New-York Gazette,* and John Peter Zenger's controversial *New-York Weekly Journal.* The collection of letters, manuscripts, and other documents pertaining to the founding of the Republic is second only to the holdings of the Library of Congress.

History
Plagued by fiscal and organizational woes almost from the beginning, the society was so deeply in debt by 1825 that the board contemplated selling the library. Nor was the institution settled geographically, bouncing from home to home for more than a century before finally settling here in 1908.

In the 1980s, the society became mired in controversy when it tried to ease mounting financial difficulties by selling the air rights over its building for an apartment tower. In the early 1990s, the galleries were closed and the research library's hours cut. The collections were poorly cataloged and critics charged that art works and artifacts were improperly stored. In 1994 former parks commissioner Elizabeth Gotbaum took over and gradually returned the society to respectability.

In a controversial move, the society auctioned off paintings and other objects, realizing almost $18 million, most of which was used to create an endowment. While it is extremely unusual for museums to sell works from the collection, Gotbaum argued that the society's survival was at stake and that some works, for example, ones by the European Old Masters, were rarely shown and had nothing to do with New York. The New York Supreme Court ruled that the society could sell some 200 Old Masters and other works by allowing public institutions to launch preemptive bids at modestly discounted prices, so that the art would still be available to the public: the Metropolitan Museum of Art bought a rare 15C painted tray celebrating a Medici prince's birth for $2.2 million.

After the sale, the society received grants, mostly from the government, for repairing the building, and from the Henry Luce and Andrew Mellon Foundations for restoring art and artifacts and cataloging the collections. It has teamed up with New York University, affiliating its library with the university's to catalog the collection and make it accessible online.

Highlights
The permanent collection includes landscapes by Asher B. Durand and John Frederick Kensett, painters of the Hudson River School; and Thomas Cole's five-part allegory *The Course of Empire,* which chronicles the ups and downs of a mythical civilization.

There are numerous portraits of distinguished New Yorkers by colonial artists, including one of Governor Edward Hyde (see Governors Island in Walk 1) dressed as a woman and another of Peter Williams (see John Street Methodist Church in Walk 3). Later works include portraits by Gilbert Stuart, John Trumbull, Thomas Sully, Charles Willson Peale, and Rembrandt Peale.

Among featured watercolors and drawings are John James Audubon's 431 watercolors for *The Birds of America* and George Catlin's *Outline Drawings of North American Indians.*

American silver on display includes pieces that belonged to Roosevelts,

Schuylers, and De Peysters, and ones that were made by outstanding silversmiths such as Cornelius Kierstede and Myer Myers. There are examples of practically every type of lamp created by **Louis Comfort Tiffany.**

Also featured are sculptures by Hiram Powers, John Quincy Adams Ward, Augustus Saint-Gaudens, and Frederick MacMonnies, and a large collection of work by the American Victorian sculptor John Rogers.

Exhibitions

Kid City is a permanent installation that features a child-size mock-up of Broadway between 82nd and 83rd Sts as it looked in 1901. Children can peer into the ovens of a German bakery, try on clothes in a turn-of-the-century apartment, and play store in a neighborhood market.

Changing exhibitions explore such topics as the historical development of "Uncle Sam," New York's political refugees, and the history of the Stork Club. A harrowing exhibit (2000) of photographs documenting lynchings in the American South from the 1870s though the 1950s received wide critical attention.

The American Museum of Natural History and the Rose Center for Earth and Space

On the next block is one of New York's, and indeed the world's, largest and most important museums, the American Museum of Natural History and its Rose Center for Earth and Space, the new home of the **Hayden Planetarium.**

American Museum of Natural History

Central Park West at W. 79th St, New York, NY 10024. ☎ (212) 769-5600. For recorded information, ☎ (212) 769-5100. Web site: www.amnh.org. Open Sun–Thurs 10–5:45; Fri and Sat until 8:45. Closed Thanksgiving and Dec 25. Suggested admission charge (entrance to museum and planetarium). For planetarium information, see Rose Center for Earth and Space.

Special exhibitions, guided tours, lectures, films, concerts, educational programs, symposia. Food court (no bag lunches) and restaurant. Gift shops.

Subway: Broadway–Seventh Ave Local (1, 9) to 79th St. Sixth Ave Express (B, weekdays only) or Eighth Ave Local (C) to 81st St. Bus: M7 and M11 uptown via Amsterdam Ave, downtown via Columbus Ave. M10 via Central Park West. M104 via Broadway. M17 crosstown on 79th St.

The American Museum of Natural History, along with the new Rose Center, should delight anyone interested in natural sciences ranging from astronomy to zoology. The collection contains some 36 million specimens (not all, fortunately, on display) ranging from the world-famous dioramas of animal habitat groups and the dinosaur exhibits to the world's largest cut gem.

History

Founded in the 1868 by scientist Albert Bickmore, the museum opened in the Arsenal (1869) and moved to its present building in 1877. The remote uptown location attracted few visitors, and the museum fell into debt. Morris K. Jesup, the museum's third president and a successful securities broker, boosted attendance by keeping the museum open on Sun (more radical than this seems now) and encouraged programs in paleontology, anthropology, and zoology. His successor, the wealthy and aristocratic Henry Fairfield Osborn, a paleontologist originally hired to bring the fossil collection up to speed, captured attention by sponsoring trips to Mongolia and Africa to search for human ancestors. In 1935, the Hayden Planetarium opened.

Throughout the years, the museum has evolved to keep up with changes in scientific theory and in public perception. In the 1940s and 1950s exhibits on ecology and cultural anthropology opened (Margaret Mead headed the anthropology department). Exhibits that reflected Osborn's racist views were replaced. New halls—for example, the Hall of Biodiversity—reflect present-day ecological thinking, and the reinstallation in the 1990s of the beloved dinosaur halls incorporates contemporary scientific insights.

The Building

The museum occupies the equivalent of four city blocks (W. 77th–W. 81st Sts between Central Park West and Columbus Ave), an area formerly called Manhattan Square and intended by the designers of Central Park as a park annex. The first museum building (1877) is now almost walled in by the wings and additions that have made the present museum an architectural hodgepodge of some 22 buildings.

The oldest visible part of the facade (1892; J. Cleveland Cady & Co.; DL) facing W. 77th St is also the most attractive. This wing (60 × 110 ft), Romanesque in style, faced with pink granite, has two round towers, a seven-arched arcade, and a central granite stairway that once swept up over the carriage entrance. The facade fronting onto Central Park West (1922; Trowbridge & Livingston) is faced with smooth blocks of the same granite. The central portion is the **Theodore Roosevelt Memorial**, its heroic arch framing a 16 ft statue of Theodore Roosevelt (1940; James Earle Fraser) that depicts him as an explorer; the flanking guides symbolize Africa and America.

Highlights

There is much too much to see in one, two, or even three visits. If time is limited, try a guided tour of the most popular exhibits; check with the Information Desk.

The **Fossil Halls** (i.e., the **Dinosaur Halls**) contain the world's best dinosaur exhibition. More than 85 percent of the specimens are real fossils as opposed to the look-alike reproductions. The halls were renovated over a seven-year period in the 1990s and are enhanced with state-of-the-art, multimedia, high-tech interactive displays. The exhibit is organized as an evolutionary "tree-of-life," beginning with primitive vertebrates and ending millions of years later with prehistoric mammals—mastodons and mammoths. The Tyrannosaurus rex (mounted in a scientifically accurate low-slung posture) and the Apatosaurus (formerly known as Brontosaurus), remounted with a longer tail and a new head, are all-time favorites. Other highlights include Stegosaurus and Triceratops, dinosaur eggs, a partial skull of a Velociraptor, and several dinosaur "mummies" with fossilized skin and soft tissues.

The **Hall of Biodiversity** on the first floor is the newest exhibit hall, part of the museum's efforts to alert the public to this important ecological issue. The walk-through Dzanga-Sangha diorama is a reconstruction of a rain forest in the central African Republic. On one wall is "The Spectrum of Life," a stunning display of some 2,500 models and specimens: bacteria, fungi, plants, and animals. Overhead hangs a museum favorite, a model of a giant squid, now complemented by a specimen of the real thing, a 250-pound, 25 ft-long male squid that came to the museum in 1998.

The **Animal Habitat Dioramas** date back to the first decades of the 20C and are world-famous for their beauty, workmanship, and accuracy. Most of the mounted specimens have been placed in habitat groups in environments carefully simulated down to the last leaf. In the African exhibit are elephants, giraffes, lions, and zebras. In the North American exhibit are big horn sheep, grizzly bears, Alaska brown bears, mountain lions, and wolves (many shown in national park settings).

The **Hall of Human Biology and Evolution** (opened 1993) celebrates the human body, and explores the beginnings of human culture. There is a hologram of a woman, viewed from the inside out, and a plastic model of the double-helical structure of DNA. Four startling dioramas show our hominid ancestors in their prehistoric habitats.

The centerpiece of the **Hall of Meteorites** is Ahnighito (the Eskimo name means "the tent"), the largest piece of the Cape York meteorite discovered in 1897. Near a photo montage of the back side of the moon are three moon rocks representing the three major lunar types.

The **Hall of Minerals** displays some 6,000 of the museum's 120,000 specimens. Some are spectacularly large: a half-ton copper block with malachite and azurite crystals, a giant topaz crystal (597 pounds, or 1,330,040 carats). Others are merely beautiful. In the **Hall of Gems** are diamonds; star sapphires, including the Star of India (563 carats, mined 300 years ago in Sri Lanka); the Brazilian Princess Topaz (21,005 carats), the world's largest cut gem; the Newmont Azurite from Namibia; and the uncut Patricia Emerald (632 carats).

Anthropological exhibits include extensive halls on African, South and Central American, and Asian peoples. The **Hall of Mollusks and Our World** has beautiful specimens from the museum's collection of more than 2 million shells. Outside the **Hall of Northwest Coast Indians** is a 63 ft long seaworthy Haida canoe built in 1878.

Rose Center for Earth and Space

Direct entrance on W. 81st St (at Central Park West and Columbus Ave); also accessible from the American Museum of Natural History. ☎ (212) 769-5200. Web site: www.amnh.org/rose. Open Sun–Thurs 10–5:45; Fri and Sat until 8:45. Closed Thanksgiving and Dec 25. Space Shows: Sun–Thurs 10:30–5; Fri and Sat 10:30–8. Entrance charge to Rose Center is included with entrance to the museum, but tickets (at the museum or by advance purchase) are required for the Space Show. Tickets can be purchased by telephone or at the planetarium.

Sky show, exhibitions, gift shops. Accessible to wheelchairs; video displays captioned for the hearing impaired; infrared hearing aids are available in the auditoriums and theaters.

The $210-million Rose Center for Earth and Space (2000; Polshek Partnership) replaced the former Hayden Planetarium (opened 1935); it provides a new architectural setting with sophisticated, up-to-the-minute exhibits. Visually stunning, this aluminum-clad sphere (87 ft in diameter) within a cube of water-white glass (more transparent than ordinary glass) on a gray granite base was designed by the firm of James Stewart Polshek and took less than six years from conception to completion.

Space Theater

Inside the top part of the sphere, still called the Hayden Planetarium, is the Space Theater. Its custom-built **Zeiss Mark IX Star Projector** can virtually re-create the night sky on the inner surface of the dome. The lower part of the dome holds **The Big Bang,** an exhibit with laser effects and big pulsing speakers that simulates the beginning of the universe. Other exhibit areas include the **Scales of the Universe** walkway, which attempts to convey the relative sizes of objects in the cosmos, from astronomically large to subatomically small. The **Cosmic Pathway,** a descending circular ramp, shows how the universe has changed over the last 13 billion years. All of recorded human history appears as the thickness of a hair at the very end of the ramp.

On display on the ground floor is the 15.5-ton Willamette Meteorite, found in Oregon and acquired by the museum in 1906.

The Willamette Meteorite

Known as "Tomanowos" to the Clackamas, Native Americans who lived in the Willamette Valley, the meteorite is revered by the Clackamas and their descendants. In June 2000, the museum signed an agreement with the tribe that ensures members an annual ceremonial visit to the meteorite. As part of the pact, the tribe dropped its claim for return of the meteorite and the museum agreed to place a description of the meteorite's spiritual significance to the Clackamas alongside the description of the meteorite's scientific importance.

From the front of the museum, walk west to Columbus Ave and north to W. 78th St. Between Columbus and Amsterdam Aves is a magnificent block, with more than a half-dozen buildings (121–131 and 118–134 W. 78th St) designed between 1885 and 1890 by Rafael Guastavino, best known for the tilework in the Registry Room at Ellis Island and in Grand Central Terminal. The brownstone and red brick buildings have elaborate cornices, wrought-iron railings, and elegant pillars.

Return to Columbus Ave and walk north to W. 81st St and east to Central Park West. At 211 Central Park West is the **Beresford** (1929; Emery Roth; DL), a triple-towered luxury apartment, with two of the towers visible from the east. Less impressive at street level than its twin-towered counterparts to the south, the building has attracted celebrity residents—Rock Hudson, Margaret Mead, John McEnroe, Peter Jennings, Diane Sawyer, Mike Nichols, Isaac Stern, Beverly Sills, and Tony Randall—and at least one notorious one, Meyer Lansky.

Continue north to W. 89th St. At 285 Central Park West is the **St. Urban** (1905; Robert Lyons), whose single tower has a dome and cupola (best seen from the north). It also features an arched entry and 16 broken-pediment dormers.

The twin-tower motif returns at 300 Central Park West with the **Eldorado** (1931; Margon & Holder with Emery Roth; DL), with a Southwestern-style base and bronze frames by the portals near the entrance decorated with Art Deco motifs. (The futuristic towers are best seen from the north or south.) Among those who have lived in the Eldorado are Groucho Marx, Marilyn Monroe, Faye Dunaway, and Richard Dreyfuss.

A block further is the **Ardsley** at 320 Central Park West (1931; Emery Roth), a Mayan-inspired Art Deco building that includes multihued brick-and-terrazzo reliefs. At 333 Central Park West is the **Turin** (1910; Albert Bodker), a beige building with medallions resembling Roman coins. Lorenz Hart (of Rodgers & Hart fame) lived here with his parents during the last decade of his life.

As recently as 1988, there were five row houses between W. 95th and W. 96th Sts, but today only **354** and **355 Central Park West** (1893; Gilbert Schellenger, DL) remain, a reminder of the transition from the wooden shacks that preceded them to the large apartments that now dominate the avenue. At 1 W. 96th St is the **First Church of Christ, Scientist** (1903; Carrere & Hastings; DL), a white granite building with an obelisk-capped spire and a stained glass window by John La Farge.

From Château to Condo

A half-mile north, at W. 106th St, are the ruins of the former **New York Cancer Hospital** (1886; Charles Haight; additions 1890; DL), one of the Upper West Side's most dramatic buildings. Funded by John Jacob Astor, it was America's first institution devoted entirely to cancer. The massive French château-style building of red brick with sandstone trim is dominated by five corner towers with conical roofs and gabled dormer windows. From 1956 until 1974, a nursing home occupied the premises but was closed amidst allegations of patient abuse. After slowly disintegrating for 25 years, the building is now being redeveloped as luxury condominiums (RKT&B Architects and Perkins Eastman Architects). The old hospital—its cellar cleansed of traces of radium, its facade restored—will be joined to a new 25-story apartment tower.

---

27 · Morningside Heights

Subway: Broadway–Seventh Ave (1, 9) to Cathedral Pkwy (110th St).
Bus: M4, M5, M11, M104 to Cathedral Pkwy (110th St).

Bounded by Cathedral Pkwy (110th St) on the south and the deep valley of W. 125th St on the north, Morningside Heights sits on the rocky ridge that runs the length of Manhattan. Harlem lies on low ground to the east, and on the west the terrain slopes down to the Hudson.

History

In one of the few success stories of the early part of the Revolution, the Continental Army defeated the British at Harlem Heights near present-day Broadway and W. 117th St on Sept 16, 1776. It was Washington's only significant victory in the campaign for Manhattan, where his efforts resulted in a series of lost battles followed by spectacularly successful retreats.

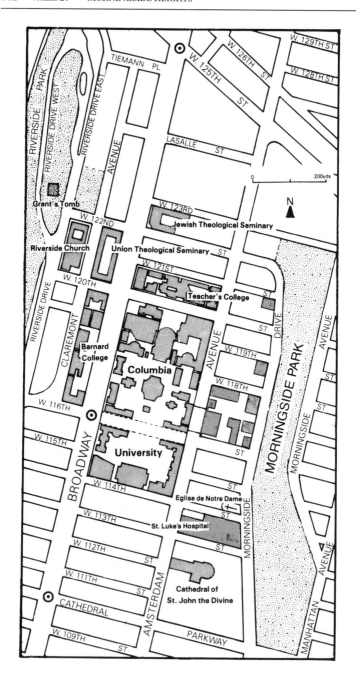

On Sept 15, the British Army had landed at Kip's Bay (on the East Side around 35th St), routing the defenders, and nearly trapping the main body of American forces in Lower Manhattan. The following day a force of American troops, encamped on Harlem Heights, moved south to encounter a British force in a buckwheat field where the Barnard College campus is presently located. The Americans hoped to lure some of the British down into the valley where 125th St lies, to outflank them, and eventually to cut them off, but the plan failed because the flanking party fired prematurely, revealing their whereabouts. Nevertheless, the Americans did hold off the British for several hours and forced them to retreat. While the battle had no great significance in the course of the war, it bolstered sagging American morale and demonstrated to Washington that his soldiers, despite several disastrous recent performances, were capable of standing up to the British.

Morningside Heights remained isolated, lacking adequate public transportation until the Ninth Avenue El opened in 1880. In its pastoral serenity dwelt the owners of small farms and houses and the squires of country estates, as well as the orphans of the Leake & Watts Asylum and the inmates of the Bloomingdale Insane Asylum. Riverside Drive also opened in 1880, touted as a new Fifth Ave, a prophecy that never quite materialized, and Morningside Park was completed in 1895. By century's end it seemed that the Heights would become a cultural, intellectual, and spiritual center of the city, as Columbia University, the Cathedral of St. John the Divine, Grant's Tomb, and St. Luke's Hospital were established there.

That promise has been partially fulfilled. Major institutions—not only Columbia but also Barnard College, Teachers College, St. John the Divine, St. Luke's, the Riverside Church, Union Theological Seminary, and the Jewish Theological Seminary—dominate the social and economic tone of the area. They boast beautiful and impressive buildings and own an estimated three-quarters of the real estate. During the Depression, however, many apartments and townhouses were turned into single-room-occupancy hotels, and shabby neighborhoods still impinge on the Heights from three sides.

The disparity between the wealth and power of the institutions and the struggles of the surrounding communities has sometimes engendered antagonism, especially apparent during the 1960s, when the institutions, seeking to secure their frontiers and to expand, tried to encroach on nearby park areas and residential space; the nadir came in 1968 when students closed down Columbia in protests that were spurred by the university's efforts to build a gym in Morningside Park. In recent years Columbia has been credited with trying to fit in better with the community, but tensions still exist.

Cathedral Church of St. John the Divine

Amsterdam Ave at W. 112th St, New York, NY 10025. ☎ (212)316-7540. Web site: www.stjohndivine.org. Open Mon–Sat 7 A.M.–6 P.M.; Sun 7 A.M.–8 P.M.; you can wander at will except during services. Grounds and gardens open during daylight hours.

Public tours: Tues–Sat 11 A.M., Sun 1 P.M. Admission charge. Vertical tours: climb 124 ft up stone spiral staircases to the top of the cathedral, first and third Sat of the month at noon and 2 P.M. Reservations required; admission charge. ☎ (212) 932-7347. Concerts, readings, lectures, and art exhibits. Gift shop, Mon–Sun 9–5. Restrooms on ground level behind the gift shop. Accessible to wheelchairs, except for restrooms.

Begin at Amsterdam Ave and W. 112th St, where the Cathedral Church of St. John the Divine (1892–1911; Heins & La Farge; continued 1911–42; Cram & Ferguson), rises in uncompleted splendor. The enormous stone arches erected to support the unbuilt dome and tower of the crossing stand exposed to the sky and to the eyes of passersby, who in all probability will never have the chance to see another masonry cathedral in construction. Even in its unfinished state, however, St. John the Divine, cathedral of the Episcopal Diocese of New York, is the largest Gothic church in the world.

Building the Cathedral

Although the idea of an American Episcopal cathedral in New York had been suggested as early as 1828, only after Bishop Horatio Potter proposed it to the diocesan convention in 1872 did it become a viable notion. Although the convention voted unanimously for the project, the financial panic of 1873 made fund raising impossible. Eventually (1887) a wooded plot of some 13 acres belonging to the Leake & Watts Orphan Asylum was purchased for a momentous $885,000, and the next year 60 entrants submitted designs in an architectural contest, from which the firm of Heins & La Farge emerged victorious. Like many of the other entries, the Heins & La Farge design, a Romanesque plan incorporating Byzantine elements, placed the long axis of the building along the spine of Morningside Heights, which would have given the church a spectacular flight of entrance stairs down to 110th St, but the tradition of building cathedrals with the nave running east–west was so strong that it eventually prevailed. In 1892, under Potter's nephew, Bishop Henry Codman Potter, the cornerstone was laid. Since then, the church has had to cope with engineering problems, financial woes, evolving trends in architecture, and the changing social fabric of the neighborhood.

Excavations for such a heavy building proved difficult, and J. P. Morgan poured a half-million dollars into an ever deeper hole before workers struck bedrock some 70 ft down. In 1911, almost 20 years after the digging had begun, only the choir and the four stone arches to support the dome were in place. Five years later, in the wake of personal disputes and changing canons of taste, the Heins & La Farge Romanesque plan was discarded, and Ralph Adams Cram (of the firm of Cram & Ferguson) redesigned the church on Gothic principles, solving the problems of the original plan, notably the width of the nave and the size of the crossing.

Cram added about 80 ft to the length of the nave, divided it into five aisles instead of the usual three, and proposed the use of alternate thick and slender piers to help in vaulting over its great width (146 ft; Westminster Abbey is 70 ft). He also made several proposals for covering the crossing, whose size presented aesthetic problems as well as difficulties in engineering. His ultimate solution involved reducing the 100 ft square to a 60 ft square by using intersecting arches and covering this smaller opening with a stepped-back 400 ft tower.

Ground was broken for the nave foundations in 1916; the nave itself was begun in 1925 and completed about ten years later, but excavations for the north transept went slowly and the money raised for its construction ran out when the walls had reached a height of about 40 ft. In 1939 the Romanesque choir was bricked up and remodeled to conform to Cram's Gothic interiors. Seven new clerestory windows were installed, but since the original Heins & La Farge roof still overhangs them, they are artificially lighted.

During World War II major construction was halted. In the 1960s a plan for completing the crossing in a contemporary style with an unattached 800 ft campanile (i.e., 250 ft higher than the Washington Monument, 184 ft shorter than the Eiffel Tower) was submitted but not approved. Then in 1967, during an era of intense national social awareness, the bishop announced that the building might never be completed; instead the church would devote its energies to the poverty in the community surrounding it. After more than a decade of social involvement, the trustees in 1978 announced a fund-raising campaign for completion of the crossing and the west facade, including the two towers.

A program for apprentice stonecutters, many from nearby neighborhoods, under the tutelage of master masons began in a shed adjacent to the cathedral. The apprentices cut the 21,000 pieces of Indiana limestone needed for the southwest tower, whose first stone was mortared into place in Sept 1982. High-wire artist Philippe Petit, who had attracted attention in 1974 walking the gap between the towers of the World Trade Center, opened the ceremonies walking across Amsterdam Ave, 15 stories above the road, with a ceremonial trowel for the bishop of New York, who awaited him on the cathedral roof.

Construction ground to a halt again in 1992, with 50 ft added to the tower above the nave roof. The stoneyard fell silent. Soon after, officials started talking of a $100-million building fund. The present dean, Harry Pritchett Jr., has shifted the focus to preserving the current structure (for $40 million) rather than trying to build more. The only stone work that continued was the carving of the Portal of Paradise, the central entrance to the cathedral. The statuary, comprised of 8 ft and 3 ft tall figures from the Old and New Testaments, was completed in 1997.

Cathedral Statistics	
Area of cathedral	121,000 square ft
Length of nave	248 ft
Length of choir	145 ft
Total length	601 ft
Width of west front	207 ft
Width of nave and aisles	146 ft
Width of crossing	100 ft
Height of nave roof	177 ft
Height nave vault	124 ft
Height of west towers (if completed)	291 ft

Exterior

The general appearance of the west front suggests medieval French cathedral architecture, though no single direct antecedent exists. The doors of four of the five portals are Burmese teak, while those of the central portal are bronze. The bronze lights on the front steps, salvaged when Penn Station was demolished (1963–66), were installed in 1967. The pierced window in the arch above the door contains a Crucifixion; on the gable is a statue of the archangel Michael.

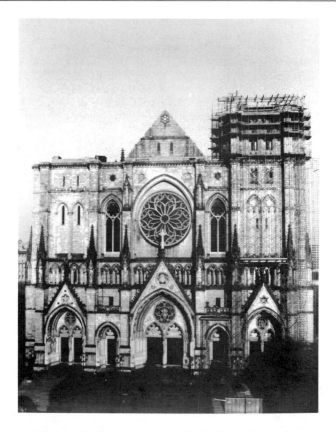

The Cathedral of St. John the Divine in 1988. The building, including the southwest tower, enveloped here by scaffolding, was erected using the traditional methods of masonry construction available to the builders of Europe's medieval cathedrals. The new addition to the tower began in 1982. (Robert F. Rodriguez)

Central Portal

The great bronze doors (sculptor, Henry Wilson) were cast in Paris by Barbedienne, the firm that cast the Statue of Liberty. Their 60 panels depict scenes from the Old Testament (north doors) and the New Testament (south doors). The frieze above the doors shows the peoples of all nations standing before the Lamb. The figure on the central post, his eyes raised heavenward, is St. John the Divine. Directly above him in the tympanum is a *Majestas,* showing Christ in Glory surrounded by the seven lamps and the seven stars of St. John's revelation. The spandrels contain symbols of the four Evangelists. The central coat of arms in the gable belongs to the See of New York.

Interior

Just inside the narthex are icons of Greek, Russian, and Byzantine origin, dating from the 15C–18C. Nearby is the **Peace Altar** (1986; George Nakashima), cut of walnut boards from a tree 300 years old.

The piers of the nave are alternately massive (16 ft) and slender (6 ft), an arrangement reflected both in the cathedral's exterior buttressing and in the design of the nave vaulting. The thick piers have an inner core of granite and are faced with limestone. The slender piers, made of solid granite, are constructed of 53 courses of single blocks, each weighing about four tons—a method of construction necessitated by the city building engineer, who would grant a permit only if each course was monolithic. The outer aisle on each side of the nave is divided by an arcade into seven bays, illuminated by stained glass windows—chapel windows 25.5 ft high and clerestory windows 44 ft high. The general theme of the windows is that of the religious spirit in human activity, and the iconography of the windows and other furnishings within each bay contributes to its individual theme. A general theme of the cathedral's iconography is internationalism, the cathedral as a house of prayer for all nations. This theme is reflected especially in the windows, in the decoration of the apsidal chapels, and in the Pilgrim's Pavement.

Medallions in the **pavement of the nave** (32,400 square ft) commemorate important people and sites in Christian history: those in the central aisle represent places identified with Christ's earthly life; those in the side aisles recall places and people venerated by pilgrims through the ages.

The bays in the **north aisle** (from west to east) are the Sports' Bay; Arts' Bay with the Poets' Corner (1984), whose tablets commemorate major American writers; Crusaders' Bay; Education Bay; Lawyers' Bay; Ecclesiastical Origins' Bay (tracing the growth of the Church of England and its translation to the New World); Historical and Patriotic Societies' Bay; and Fatherhood Window (this bay has only a clerestory window). Also displayed in the bays in the north and south aisles, are contemporary works of religious art and the Mortlake Tapestries, woven in England from a series of cartoons by Raphael and entitled *The Acts of the Apostles.*

The Mortlake Tapestries

Commissioned by Pope Leo X in about 1513, the cartoons, from which numerous sets of tapestries were woven, were dispersed throughout Europe and eventually lost. Sir Francis Crane, manager of the Mortlake tapestry works, rediscovered them in Genoa in 1623 and had them sent to England to be woven for Prince Charles (later Charles I).

In the **crossing** you can see the "bones" of the cathedral, the great granite piers, the uncompleted arches, and the remarkable temporary dome of red-brown Guastavino tile hastily installed in the summer of 1909 as a cheap alternative to covering the crossing with a conventional flat wooden roof supported by steel beams. Displayed in the crossing are the cathedral's other important set of tapestries, the

Barberini Tapestries, woven in the first half of the 17C on the papal looms founded by Cardinal Barberini. They depict scenes from the life of Christ and a map of the Holy Land; the cartoons by Jean François Romanelli are now in the Vatican.

The **choir** shows both the work of Heins & La Farge and Ralph Adams Cram. The lower part up to the balustrade below the clerestory windows remains from the original Romanesque plan (completed 1911); the work above (altered 1939–41) is Cram's Gothic remodeling. Dominating the choir are eight **granite columns** from Vinalhaven, Maine, originally quarried as monoliths but cut in two after the first two columns cracked while being turned and polished on a special lathe (lower sections, 38 ft high, 90 tons; upper sections, 17 ft high, 40 tons). Because the land slopes sharply downhill at this end of the church, the foundations for the columns go down 135 ft. Although the choir is relatively short (145 ft), a kind of false perspective makes it seem longer: the arcades at the east end are closer together and the floor slopes upward in that direction. The choir stalls were designed by Heins & La Farge after those in the Cathedral of San Domenico in Taormina, Sicily.

Among the interesting objects in the choir are the two menorahs near the altar. Designed after those in the Temple of Jerusalem as pictured on the Arch of Titus, they are the gift (1930) of the former *New York Times* publisher Adolph Ochs. The Magna Carta pedestal (south side of the main altar) was once part of the altar of the Abbey of Bury St. Edmunds on which (Nov 20, 1214), according to the inscription, "the barons swore fealty to each other in wresting the Great Charter from King John."

The original **organ** (Ernest M. Skinner, 1910) was remodeled and rebuilt in 1954 and a new stop, the State Trumpet, was added; its 61 silver pipes are directly under the Rose Window in the west front. The **Rose Window** itself, best seen from the east end of the nave, was designed by Charles Connick. It is 40 ft in diameter and contains more than 10,000 pieces of glass. From the central figure of Christ radiate symbols representing the gifts of the Holy Spirit, the Beatitudes, and the heavenly choir. The lesser Rose Window below it, also by Connick, develops the symbolism of the number seven: from a central monogram of Christ radiate seven fountains, seven growing vine forms, seven pairs of doves, and seven stars.

You can enter the **north ambulatory** from the archway in the crossing. The first structure in the ambulatory is the **baptistery** (1928; Frank Cleveland of Cram & Ferguson) donated by members of the Stuyvesant family, whose Dutch origins are symbolized in the decoration of the room. The coat of arms of the Stuyvesant family is in the spandrel of the ground-level arcade in the northeast wall. The baptismal font, octagonal in form and about 15 ft high, is built of Champville marble and modeled on the font in the baptistery of the cathedral of Siena, Italy.

An opening on the right of the ambulatory leads into the **presbytery.** The parapet at the ascent to the presbytery (in two sections at the south and north sides) is carved with figures representing notable men of the first 20 centuries of the Christian era.

Chapels

The chapels opening from the ambulatory are called the Chapels of Tongues, since each represents a different national or ethnic group, in keeping with the international ideal of the cathedral.

Note: The chapels are frequently locked, but are still visible through the gates.

The first chapel in the north ambulatory is **St. Ansgar's Chapel** (1918), named after the 9C Frankish missionary to Denmark, Sweden, and Germany. It is stylistically reminiscent of 14C English Gothic. The **Chapel of St. Boniface** (1916), next along the ambulatory, is named after the Apostle of Germany (c. 680–755), who was martyred by a heathen mob while preaching in West Friesland. The 11 ft bronze statue of the archangel Michael was made and donated in 1963 by Eleanor M. Mellon. **St. Columba's Chapel** (1911) next door is named after the Irish saint (521–597) who founded the monastery of Iona and worked to convert the Celts. The statues flanking the entrance are by Gutzon Borglum, of Mt. Rushmore fame, and represent influential figures in English church history. Architects Heins & La Farge designed this chapel in the Romanesque style they chose for the cathedral as a whole.

St. Savior's Chapel, the central chapel and the first one built (1904; Heins & La Farge), is dedicated to the Eastern Church, though its style is Gothic. The 20 figures flanking the entrance represent the heavenly choir and were also designed by Gutzon Borglum, as were the figures of scholars, bishops, and saints of the Eastern Church on either side of the window. The heavenly choir stirred up controversy when installed, since the figures are all female. The altarpiece showing scenes from the life of Christ was completed by Keith Haring in 1990, six months before his death from AIDS.

In the ambulatory directly opposite the entrance to the chapel is the tomb of Bishop Horatio Potter (1802–1887), designed after the tomb of Edward the Confessor in Westminster Abbey and occupying the spot behind the high altar traditionally reserved for a cathedral's founder.

The next chapel (open only for prayer and meditation) is the **Chapel of St. Martin of Tours,** the 4C Gallic bishop. Designed by Ralph Cram (1918) in a style reminiscent of 13C French Gothic, it is noteworthy for its beautiful windows (Charles Connick) depicting scenes from the lives of three French saints (left to right): St. Louis, St. Martin, and St. Joan of Arc. The **statue of Joan of Arc** (donated 1922) on the right wall is by Anna Hyatt Huntington and stands above a stone taken from the saint's cell in Rouen. A small chip of Reims Cathedral blasted away during World War I is embedded in the trefoil above the altar cross.

St. Ambrose's Chapel is named after the 4C bishop of Milan and is designed (1914; Carrere & Hastings) in a style Cram called "purely Renaissance." The **statue of St. Anthony** is by Luca della Robbia.

The **Chapel of St. James** (1916), the last in the south ambulatory, is dedicated to the people of Spain. The sacristy window (Henry W. Young) depicts figures in Spanish history, particularly those associated with the discovery of the New World, including Christopher Columbus. In the central bay of the south aisle is the tomb of Bishop Henry Codman Potter (1834–1908).

Continue along the south ambulatory and return to the crossing. The **bays in the south aisle,** like those on the north side of the nave, are devoted to religious aspects of various human activities. They are (east to west): Motherhood Window; Armed Forces' Bay with a 13C recumbent effigy of a knight in chain mail; Religious Life Bay, with the Earth Shrine (1986) and a memorial to St. Francis of Assisi, whose respect for the earth and its creatures is symbolized by a figure of the *Wolf of Gubbio* (1986; Kappy Wells); Medical Bay (with the AIDS memorial, 1985, commemorating those who have died of AIDS); Press or Communications Bay (with a marble statue of the *Return of the Prodigal* by William O. Partridge); Labor Bay, with a memorial to N.Y. firemen by Ralph Feldman, dedicated 1976; Missionary Bay, with the Holocaust Memorial (1978; Elliott Offner), the figure of a victim of Auschwitz; and finally the All Souls' Bay.

Auxiliary Buildings

Leave the cathedral by the west doors and walk south on Amsterdam Ave to W. 110th St to see the auxiliary buildings within the cathedral close. **Synod House,** a Gothic structure (1913; Cram & Ferguson) at the corner of Amsterdam Ave and Cathedral Pkwy, houses the offices of the bishops of the diocese. Near the sidewalk is the *Peace Fountain* (1985; Greg Wyatt), a bronze sculpture depicting the battle between good and evil as represented in the figures of Satan and the archangel Michael. The pedestal, in the form of a double helix, represents DNA, carrier of the genetic code. Around the rail are small bronze animal sculptures, cast from originals made by children and chosen in a juried contest. In the center of the lawn is the **Outdoor Pulpit** (dedicated 1916), an open-work Gothic spire 40 ft high, designed by architects Howells & Stokes. Outdoor services were formerly held on the lawn with a small choir and brass band.

Continue along the close road to **Diocesan House** (1909–12; Heins & La Farge), once a training school for deaconesses. The building now contains the cathedral library and archives. **Cathedral House,** across the road and east of Diocesan House, was originally the Bishop's House (1914; Cram & Ferguson); it was built like a Gothic château with money donated by J. P. Morgan. Morgan defended its elegance by opining that bishops should live "like everyone else," though he must have had a rarefied view of how "everyone else" lived.

Directly east is the **Deanery** (1914; Cram & Ferguson), and beyond it to the left is the **Cathedral School** (1913; Walter Cook and Winthrop A. Welch), formerly a day school for choirboys, now a coeducational elementary and middle school from whose enrollment the choir still draws its treble voices. The left fork of the road continues past the school to the **Biblical Garden,** planted with flora mentioned in the Bible. The road now leads back to Amsterdam Ave.

Walk north on Amsterdam Ave to the corner of W. 113th St. The small square building on the southwest corner of the intersection is a **gatehouse** (c. 1890) marking the end of a section of masonry aqueduct beneath Amsterdam Ave. Most of the water supplied from the city's reservoirs is carried by pipes, but during the later years of the 19C, when labor was cheap and pipe was expensive, the city built several masonry aqueducts. A second gatehouse stands at W. 119th St, where the pipes end and the masonry begins.

St. Luke's Hospital

Turn right at W. 113th St and walk east. Much of **St. Luke's–Roosevelt Hospital Center** (St. Luke's Division) on the north side of 113th St is new, but you can still see part of the original central pavilion, overshadowed by the modern wings.

History

The original hospital on this site, Saint Luke's, consisted of a central pavilion for administration and nine semidetached outbuildings, designed in the Beaux-Arts style by Ernest Flagg and built between 1893 and 1896. The hospital was founded in 1846 by the Episcopal Church; in the 1980s, the 780-bed facility merged with Roosevelt Hospital (founded 1871) in an effort to streamline the city's patchwork system of private, voluntary, and municipal hospitals. The hospital's Roosevelt Division is on Tenth Ave (between W. 58th and W. 59th Sts).

Morningside Park

Walk east on W. 113th St to Morningside Drive. Just across the drive is Morningside Park, 29.88 acres including a rocky cliff of Manhattan schist, which plunges down to the Harlem Plain.

History

In the mid-19C these precipitous slopes proved too steep for even the most ardent real estate developer, and so the area was handed over to Frederick Law Olmsted and Calvert Vaux to be developed as a park. Realizing that the most attractive feature of the area was the view to the east, the designers planned a walkway on top of the cliff studded with balconies facing the Harlem Plain below. But their original design was rejected and Jacob Wrey Mould, who designed the railings surrounding the terrace in Central Park, planned the massive, buttressed masonry wall that supports the overlooks. When Mould died, the original duo returned, with Vaux doing most of the design work. Down the hillside they laid out curving walks conforming to the topography of the land and placed small open meadows along the southern and eastern edges of the park.

Their plan has been altered through the years: P.S. 36 usurped an alpine rock garden at 123rd St, while concrete playgrounds were built in the south portion. Though Columbia's attempt to build a gym in the park was thwarted after the foundation was laid, the park's future really began to look brighter when Columbia student Thomas Kiel formed the Friends of Morningside Park in 1981. Beginning in 1989, a $5-million restoration cleared the park of both undergrowth and drug dealers, and the excavation for the gym foundation was converted into an ornamental pond. In 1996, Kiel, then 36, was killed in a trailbike accident and to fulfill his family's request for a memorial in the park, the Parks Department implemented part of the uncompleted Olmsted-Vaux plan, an arboretum with winding paths that would contain 112 species of trees and 169 kinds of shrubs. The Thomas Kiel Arboretum at W. 116th St and Morningside Ave was begun in 1998, with land set aside for expansion to 121st St; the planting program is based on the original Olmsted-Vaux description.

The Park

Inside the park, at the foot of the stairs at W. 114th St and Morningside Ave, the pond sits beneath a particularly dramatic cliff. Just to the north is the small **Bear and Faun Fountain,** also known as the Seligman Fountain (c. 1910; Edgar Walter). It features a bronze faun sequestered in the hollow of a bronze boulder on top of which stretches a bronze bear, its paw dangling over the edge. The rocks of the park form the pedestal on which the group rests. The work was given by the National Highways Protective Society to honor its vice president, Alfred L. Seligman, who died in an auto accident.

Just outside the park, along its eastern edge (Morningside Ave and Manhattan Ave at W. 114th St), is the statue *Washington and Lafayette* (1890; Frédéric-

Auguste Bartholdi), with the two figures shaking hands, a less successful evocation of Franco-American friendship than the Statue of Liberty. Charles "Broadway" Rouss (see Rouss Building in Walk 8) gave the statue to the city in 1900.

Continue north on Morningside Drive. At the northwest corner of W. 114th St is the Roman Catholic **Église de Notre Dame** (apse, 1909–10; Dans & Otto; remainder, 1914–28; Cross & Cross; DL). Originally built as a mission church of the Church of St. Vincent de Paul (on W. 24th St), it ministered to a congregation of French-speaking immigrants. The building, with its portico of Corinthian columns, recalls churches of Napoleonic France, for example, the Church of the Madeleine in Paris. The interior (open for services) is remarkable for its replica of the grotto at Lourdes. Since plans for a large drum and dome over the crossing, which would have brought natural light into the building, never materialized, the interior is artificially lighted.

Two blocks north, at the intersection of W. 116th St and Morningside Drive, is the **Carl Schurz Memorial** (sculptor, Karl Bitter; architect, Henry Bacon; 1913). Forced to flee Germany because of his revolutionary political sentiments, Schurz (1829–1906) emigrated to the U.S., where he became a leader of the Republican Party, a friend of Abraham Lincoln, a major general in the Union Army during the Civil War, a senator, and an editor. Bitter's bronze statue depicts Schurz as a strong, idealistic man; the low-relief panels on the monument portray the liberation of oppressed peoples: Native Americans, Asians, and blacks.

Columbia University

Directly across Morningside Drive are the outposts of Columbia University, whose main campus lies between Amsterdam Ave and Broadway, from W. 114th to W. 120th Sts. The university, one of the oldest, wealthiest, and most famous in the U.S., was founded as a gentlemen's college to "instruct youth in the learned languages and in the liberal arts and sciences." It is known for its professional schools—medicine, law, business, education, journalism, and architecture—and for the School of General Studies, where adults of any age can work toward degrees. Coeducational (formerly for men) Columbia College, Barnard (for women), and the School of Engineering and Applied Science are the undergraduate colleges. The university has a student body of about 22,000, including about 8,000 graduate students, and a faculty of 7,200.

For free campus tours, call the Visitors Center: ☎ (212) 854-4900.

History

By the mid-18C it became apparent to contemporary observers that while New York outstripped its American rivals commercially, it lagged behind culturally, its populace (according to observers from Boston or Philadelphia) afflicted by ignorance, their lives dominated by a sordid thirst for money. Consequently, a group of citizens set out to establish a center of learning that would lighten the intellectual gloom, in the process outshining Harvard, Yale, and the College of New Jersey (later Princeton). Among them were several vestrymen of Trinity Church who arranged a transfer of five acres of church property to the proposed college—a plot not far from the World Trade Center site, bounded by Church, Murray, and Barclay Sts and the Hudson River. It was Columbia's first piece of valuable real estate.

The college was chartered by King George II in 1754 and named King's College, the fifth such institution in the colonies. The first president was Dr. Samuel Johnson, an Anglican pastor from Stratford, Connecticut, and the first class of eight men, who bore such resounding old New York names as Verplanck, Van Cortlandt, and Bayard, met in the schoolhouse of Trinity Church.

Among the early students were Alexander Hamilton, who enrolled in 1775 and stayed about a year, later becoming the first secretary of the U.S. Treasury; John Jay, first chief justice of the U.S. Supreme Court; Gouverneur Morris, statesman and diplomat, minister to France; and Robert R. Livingston, first U.S. secretary of foreign affairs.

After the Revolution, the college, renamed Columbia, entered a period of intellectual dormancy that lasted well into the 19C. In 1814 the trustees appealed to the state for financial aid and received, instead of the share in the proceeds of a state lottery for which they had hoped, a plot of land west of Fifth Ave between 47th and 51st Sts, formerly the Elgin Botanic Garden. Appraised by the state at $75,000, it seemed worth much less to the trustees since it was rocky, remote from the city, and overgrown with weeds. In the long run it turned out to be worth much more: today Rockefeller Center stands on that 11.5-acre parcel, which in 1985 the university sold to the Rockefeller Group for $400 million.

In 1857 the college moved uptown, not to the Rockefeller Center site but to buildings formerly owned by an asylum for the deaf and dumb between Madison and Fourth (now Park) Aves, bounded by 49th and 50th Sts. The school remained there until its relocation to the Morningside Heights campus in 1897.

In 1902 Nicholas Murray Butler became president, and under his energetic guidance Columbia achieved its present high reputation. Its faculty has been illustrious, including such luminaries as John Dewey, Michael Pupin, Harold C. Urey, Isidor I. Rabi, Edward McDowell, and Franz Boas. Dwight D. Eisenhower was president of the university (1948–53) before resigning to run for president of the United States. Alumni include Paul Robeson, Allen Ginsburg, Jack Kerouac, and seven Supreme Court justices. The university has also had 60 faculty members, former faculty members, and alumni win the Nobel Prize.

On the northwest corner of Morningside Drive and W. 116th St is the house (1912; McKim, Mead & White) of the university president.

Walk east and cross Amsterdam Ave to the main campus. The university purchased the land from the Bloomingdale Insane Asylum in two parcels (1892 and 1903) for a total of $3.9 million. The original campus, built on the first parcel north of 116th St, contains the college's finest buildings, Low Library and St. Paul's Chapel. The **Morningside Heights Campus** of Columbia was designed (1893) by McKim, Mead & White, but is principally the work of Charles Follen McKim, who envisioned a densely developed area with small side courtyards and a narrow central quadrangle. McKim's original intentions can be seen in the brick-and-limestone classroom buildings with green copper roofs on the periphery of the main quadrangles, and in the placement of St. Paul's Chapel, Low Library, Earl Hall, and University Hall. The only side courtyard actually built is the one bounded by Schermerhorn, Avery, and Fayerweather Halls, and St. Paul's Chapel (and it has been altered by the Avery Library extension), since after McKim's death (1909) the university elected to retain the central open space and expand instead into surrounding city streets, a policy that has not been without social repercussions.

Continue along **College Walk,** the pedestrian extension of W. 116th St, to the center of the campus. The principal building in the Lower (or South) Quadrangle is **Butler Hall** (formerly South Hall), the main university library (1934; James Gamble Rogers). Named after President Nicholas Murray Butler, the library can accommodate 4 million volumes. The present Columbia collection, housed in several smaller libraries as well as Butler Hall, numbers more than 5 million volumes and is one of the largest in the nation. Weekdays during the academic year, there are free exhibitions in the sixth-floor **Rare Book and Manuscript Library; ☎** (212) 854-5153; Web site: www.columbia.edu/cu/libraries/indiv/rare/exhibits.html.

Dominating the Upper Quadrangle (north of College Walk) is Low Library, on whose broad steps sits Columbia's most famous piece of sculpture, ***Alma Mater*** (1903; Daniel Chester French). The statue, originally covered with gold leaf, was regilded in 1962 to the dismay of students and faculty members who demanded the removal of the gaudy gold in favor of the familiar gray-green patina. In 1970, the figure was slightly damaged by a bomb set off during student uprisings. *Alma Mater* sits on a throne flanked by torches implying enlightenment; her right hand holds a scepter topped with a crown, an emblem referring to Columbia's beginnings as King's College. An owl, symbolic of Athena and therefore wisdom, peers from the folds of her robe near her left knee; a laurel garland wreathes her head; a book, signifying knowledge, lies open on her lap.

Low Memorial Library

Low Memorial Library (1895–97; McKim, Mead & White; DL) dominates the quadrangle by virtue of its scale (dome, 136 ft above the terrace), its site atop three flights of stairs, and its imposing classicism. Seth Low, president of Columbia from 1890 to 1901, donated the building to honor his father, Abiel Abbot Low (1811–1893), the wealthy tea merchant and China trade pioneer whose warehouses still grace the South Street Seaport area. The younger Low resigned his office to become mayor of New York (1901–3), a position he won not because of special political acuity but because his opponents were flagrantly corrupt. Low Library remained the main university library until 1934 when Butler Hall superseded it. Today, it houses the university's central administration offices and **Visitors Center.**

Exterior

Low Library has its stylistic origins in the Roman Pantheon; its general plan is that of a Greek cross with an octagonal transition to a saucer dome. The outer dome of solid masonry covers an inner dome (diameter, 70 ft) of plaster on a steel frame, which forms the ceiling of the main reading room.

Interior

The former reading room, with its 16 polished granite columns capped by gilt bronze Ionic capitals, its galleries and heroic marble statuary, and its domed ceiling rising above semicircular clerestory windows, exemplifies the most elegant work of McKim, Mead & White. At one time the subbasement contained a large canvas tank and a stationary rowing rack for the Columbia crew.

Low Library (built 1895–97) at Columbia University is the focal point of McKim, Mead & White's Morningside Heights campus. On the steps sits Daniel Chester French's statue Alma Mater, *originally covered with glittering gold leaf. (Office of Public Information, Columbia University)*

Room 210 on the first floor houses the **Columbiana Collection,** which contains books, portraits, and memorabilia relating to the history of the university. To visit the collection, ☎ (212) 854-3786.

The picturesque three-story gabled brick building just east of Low Library is **Buell Hall,** the only building remaining from the days of the Bloomingdale Asylum. In front of **Philosophy Hall** is a cast of Rodin's most famous work, ***The Thinker*** (modeled 1880, cast 1930), originally a small figure intended to represent the poet Dante contemplating the tragic human condition.

St. Paul's Chapel

Just to the left (north) of Buell Hall is St. Paul's Chapel (1904–7; Howells & Stokes; DL), one of the campus's most beautiful buildings, originally affiliated with the Episcopal Church but now used for diverse religious services, weddings, and concerts. To view the chapel, ☎ (212) 854-1487.

Exterior

Constructed of brick and limestone, the building is shaped like a short Latin cross (140 ft long, 80 ft wide, 112 ft high) with a vaulted portico on the west and a semicircular apse on the east. A dome (interior diameter, 48 ft; height, 91 ft) covers the crossing. The capitals of the columns flanking the entrance are decorated with heads of cherubim by Gutzon Borglum.

Interior

The walls of the chapel are of tan brick and the fine Guastavino tile vaulting is in warm tones of salmon and buff. In accordance with the educational aspirations of Columbia, the three apse windows (John La Farge) show St. Paul preaching to the Athenians on the Areopagus (a hill west of the Acropolis); the windows in the transepts show teachers of the Old Testament (north transept) and the New Testament (south transept).

Just beyond the chapel is an overpass crossing Amsterdam Ave toward the east at W. 117th Street. On its plaza are several sculptures: *Three-Way Piece: Points* (1967; Henry Moore), a swelling, volumetric bronze abstraction resting on three points; *Tightrope Walker* (1979; Kees Verkade), an elongated aerialist with a second figure balanced on his shoulders, donated as a monument to Columbia alumnus and World War I leader William "Wild Bill" Donovan; and *Flight* (1981) by Gertrude Schweitzer. Also visible is Jacques Lipchitz's *Bellerophon Taming Pegasus* (cast 1973, installed 1977), which adorns the Law School (1961; Harrison & Abramovitz), a massive, white, high-rise building on the northeast corner of W. 116th St and Amsterdam Ave. According to the sculptor, the monumental statue (30 ft high, 28 ft wide, 23 tons) symbolizes the control by law over the forces of disorder.

Return to the main campus. Continue north along the sidewalk from the chapel to **Avery Hall** (1912; McKim, Mead & White), one of the early classroom buildings in the style designated by McKim. It houses the School of Architecture and the nation's largest architectural library (not open to the public).

Wallach Art Gallery
Open Wed–Sat 1–5. Free. ☎ (212) 854-7288; Web site: www.columbia.edu/cu/wallach.

Next door, in Schermerhorn Hall, is the Wallach Art Gallery, founded in 1986 under the Department of Art History and Archaeology. The gallery shows an eclectic mix of exhibits curated by graduate students, faculty, and others, with works drawn from public and private collections as well as from university collections.

Turn left in front of Avery Hall and walk west. In front of **Uris Hall** stands a 3-ton, hollow, black-painted steel sculpture (24 ft long, 11 ft wide, 12 ft high) by Clement Meadmore, installed in 1968 and entitled *Curl.* Meadmore, an Australian sculptor now living in New York, has left a similar work at the corner of Riverside Drive and W. 156th St.

Turn left again and walk south along the side of Low Library toward College Walk. Between the library and Lewisohn Hall to the southwest reclines the statue *The Great God Pan* by George Grey Barnard. Cast of bronze and weighing more than 3 tons, it was completed around 1898, intended for a fountain in the courtyard of the Dakota Apartments.

Turn right at College Walk and continue toward Broadway. On the left is the **School of Journalism** (1912–13; McKim, Mead & White), founded by the publisher Joseph Pulitzer in 1912. Considered the most prestigious journalism school in the nation, it comes into the public eye each spring when it announces the Pulitzer Prizes.

On the south side of the building is a **statue of Thomas Jefferson** (1914) by William Ordway Partridge, an alumnus of Columbia. Partridge's **statue of**

Alexander Hamilton (1908) stands in front of Hamilton Hall on the east side of the quadrangle.

Walk around the School of Journalism to College Walk, which leads out to Broadway through a gate guarded by two classically draped figures, *Science* (1925) and *Letters* (1916), both by Charles Keck. On the wall of the Mathematics Building on the east side of Broadway at about W. 117th St is a large plaque depicting the Battle of Harlem Heights.

Barnard College
Turn right (north) on Broadway. The campus of Barnard College lies on the west side of the street between W. 116th and W. 120th Sts.

History
Frederick A. P. Barnard became president of Columbia in 1864, following a string of men distinguished more for their piety than their administrative abilities. Among his liberal innovations was the institution of a women's course, which the trustees grudgingly accepted in 1883. Since women were not allowed to enter the classrooms and faculty members were not allowed to counsel or advise women outside class, the course was not notably successful. Nevertheless it was due to Barnard's efforts that the women's college was founded in 1889. The older buildings reflect the predominant style at Columbia.

Continue north along Broadway, which now begins to slope downhill. Near the corner of W. 120th St is the side of the **Marcellus Hartley Dodge Physical Fitness Center** (1974; Eggers Partnership), a gymnasium built after student and community hostility doomed the one proposed for Morningside Park.

Just north of the gymnasium are the **Pupin Physics Laboratories** (W. 120th St and Broadway), built in 1925 but named ten years later after Michael Idvorsky Pupin (1858–1935), a Serbian immigrant who became one of America's foremost inventors in the field of electricity and a revered professor of electrical engineering. In this building in the late 1930s and early 1940s, Harold C. Urey, Enrico Fermi, and I. I. Rabi did the work in nuclear fission that won them the Nobel Prize.

The row of red brick buildings on the east side of Broadway between W. 120th and W. 121st Sts houses **Teachers College,** an affiliate of Columbia University. Founded in 1889 by Nicholas Murray Butler, the college grew from humble beginnings as the Kitchen Garden Club of the Church of St. Mark's-in-the-Bowery, an organization for introducing manual training into the public school system and teaching working-class girls the elements of housekeeping and gardening. Since the days when John Dewey belonged to the faculty, Teachers College has earned a reputation for spearheading progressive causes in education.

Most of the red brick buildings date from around the turn of the 20C. On the northeast corner of the intersection is **Horace Mann Hall** (1901; Howells & Stokes and Edgar H. Josselyn), formerly the Horace Mann School, founded in 1887 and taken over by the college as an experimental school. Halfway down the block to the east, on W. 120th St, is **Main Hall** (1892; William A. Potter), the campus's earliest building, an elaborate composition of dormers, gables, pointed-arch windows, porches, and turrets.

Union Theological Seminary

Cross Broadway to the west side. Union Theological Seminary (1910; Allen & Collens, altered 1952 by Collens, Willis & Beckonert; DL) occupies the blocks between W. 120th and W. 122nd Sts. Founded in 1836 as a graduate school for Protestant ministers, the seminary has long enjoyed a reputation for liberal religious thought and involvement in social action. Its library (open to enrolled students and qualified scholars) is outstanding, containing the van Ess Collection, rich in manuscripts and incunabula, and the McAlpin Collection of British History and Theology. Among its faculty and graduates have been such luminaries as Reinhold Niebuhr, Norman Thomas, and Henry Sloane Coffin.

The Buildings

The classroom and residential buildings are organized in a quadrangle around a central courtyard dominated by the **Brown Memorial Tower** on Broadway and the **James Memorial Tower** on Claremont Ave. Constructed of rockface granite with limestone trim, the buildings belong to an era when American universities imitated the Gothicism of Oxford and Cambridge. The **interior quadrangle** and the **James Chapel** are especially attractive. For admission, inquire weekdays 9–5 at the Security Desk in the rotunda near the Broadway–W. 120th St entrance.

On the northeast corner of W. 122nd St and Broadway is the **Jewish Theological Seminary** (1930; Gehron, Ross, Alley), a large prosaic example of neo-Georgian architecture. Founded in 1886 to provide the Jewish population with American-trained rabbis and scholars, it has become a major center of Jewish education. Its library has the most comprehensive collection of Judaica and Hebraica in the Western Hemisphere and contains more than 300,000 volumes, including a fine collection of manuscripts from the repository of the Old Cairo Synagogue.

Walk west on 122nd St. The building housing the **Manhattan School of Music** (north side of W. 122nd St, between Broadway and Claremont Ave) was built in 1910 (Donn Barber) for the Institute of Musical Art; later with substantial additions (1931; Shreve, Lamb & Harmon) it was the home of the Juilliard School of Music. Distinguished alumni include the jazz pianist Herbie Hancock and soprano Catherine Malfitano.

Continue west on 122nd to Claremont Ave. Up a flight of stairs in Sakura Park is a **statue of Daniel Butterfield,** designed by Gutzon Borglum and erected in 1918. Butterfield (1831–1901) was a Union general in the Civil War but achieved his greatest fame off the battlefield as the composer of "Taps," the bugle call played as the flag is lowered at nightfall and at funerals.

Visible across the park is **International House** (1924; Lindsay & Warren), a residence for Columbia graduate students from almost 100 countries, built with funds provided by John D. Rockefeller Jr., who was chairman of the building committee. It was constructed during the years after World War I to foster international understanding across the chasms of cultural difference. Mrs. Rockefeller, later a founder of the Museum of Modern Art, had the assembly hall modeled after the Beneficent Street Church in Providence, Rhode Island, which she had attended as a child, and insisted that the rooms be furnished in an American colonial style—her way of introducing foreigners to the American experience.

Riverside Church

490 Riverside Drive (at W. 120th St), New York, NY 10027. ☎ (212) 870-6700.
Web site: www.theriversidechurchny.org. Open Tues–Sun 9–4:30. Sun services in
the nave begin at 10:45. A guided tour is given on Sun at 12:30 after the worship
service. The Visitors Center on the main level has a small book shop. Visitors are
welcome to have lunch in the cafeteria Tues–Thurs and after the Sun service. Restrooms located downstairs on the cloister level. Tours of the carillon, 9–4:30;
tickets at Visitors Center.

Subway: Broadway–Seventh Ave (1, 9) to 116th St. Walk north on Broadway
to W. 120th Street (Reinhold Niebuhr Place). Turn left and walk one block to
Claremont Ave. The entrance is a half-block north of W. 120th St on the left side
of the street. Bus: M104, M4, M5.

Walk south on Riverside Drive to the main entrance of Riverside Church (1930;
Allen & Collens and Henry C. Pelton; south wing, 1960; Collens, Willis &
Beckonert), which occupies a commanding site overlooking the Hudson River.
Originally affiliated with the Baptist Church, its membership is now interdenom-
inational, interracial, and international; the church has long been known for its
liberal appeal and community service.

History

The church began as a small Baptist congregation meeting on Stanton St on the
Lower East Side. About 1850 the group moved to Norfolk St and occupied the
landmarked building now owned by a Russian Jewish congregation, Beth Hame-
drash Hagodol. As the immigrant population overwhelmed the Lower East Side,
the Baptists moved uptown, first to 46th St just west of Fifth Ave, later to Park Ave,
and finally to the present location. The church was built largely with money from
John D. Rockefeller Jr., who though originally a Baptist was a leader in the interfaith church movement.

The Building

Despite its Gothic inspiration and particular indebtedness to the Cathedral of
Chartres, the Riverside Church is a modern, steel-framed building, its Gothicism
relegated to surface details. Although criticized when completed for its dispro-
portionately tall tower (392 ft), for its cultural servitude to Europe, and for its
eclecticism, the church is nonetheless distinguished for its fine stained glass, stone
carving, and woodwork, which represent the finest materials and craftsmanship
available.

Church Statistics	
Length (excluding south wing)	265 ft
Width	100 ft
Height of tower	392 ft
Length of nave	215 ft
Width of nave	89 ft
Height of nave	100 ft
Seating capacity of nave	2,500 people

Exterior

The building, faced with Indiana limestone, has its long axis parallel to Riverside Drive. The 22-story tower at the south end contains classrooms and offices as well as the carillon. The principal entrance on the west is elaborately carved and is clearly intended to recall the portals at Chartres. The tympanum depicts a seated Christ surrounded by emblems of the four Evangelists. Above the tympanum are five archivolts (moldings around the arch), the first and fifth depicting angels, the middle ones portraying scientists, philosophers, and religious leaders drawn from the whole sweep of human history—classical, Christian, and modern. The chapel door, just south of the west portal, is thematically devoted to the Nativity. You may also enter the church through the cloister entrance on Claremont Ave (east side), near which is a bronze *Madonna and Child* (1927) by Jacob Epstein, a work that emphasizes the humanity and humility of Christ.

Interior

Inside the revolving door is the **narthex.** In the east wall are two windows of 16C Flemish glass, the only windows not made specifically for the church. A small chapel in the northeast corner of the narthex contains Heinrich Hofmann's (1824–1902) painting *Christ in Gethsemane.* A door in the south wall of the narthex leads into **Christ Chapel,** inspired by the 11C Romanesque nave of the Church of St. Nazaire at Carcassone, France.

To the north of the narthex is the **nave,** finished in Indiana limestone and divided into three aisles by an arcade, above which is a triforium gallery and a clerestory. The clerestory windows are copies of the famous 12C–13C windows at Chartres, while those on the aisle level present modern motifs as well as historical ones. The 51 colored stained glass windows in the church were made by firms in Boston, Chartres, and Reims.

Continue along the nave to the **chancel.** The pulpit (weight, 9 tons) at the west side of the chancel is carved from three blocks of limestone; its niches (both upper and lower levels) contain figures of prophets; ten of the figures on the upper level stand beneath canopies representing the major cathedrals of France. In the center of the chancel floor a marble maze has been adapted from the labyrinth at Chartres, whose route medieval penitents traced out on their knees. The chancel screen portrays seven aspects of the life of Christ, shown in each panel, surrounded by people who have fulfilled the divine ideal, including Pasteur, Savonarola, Florence Nightingale, and J. S. Bach. The panels represent (left to right): Physicians, Teachers, Prophets, Humanitarians, Missionaries, Reformers, and Lovers of Beauty.

On the south wall of the nave at the gallery level, best seen from the chancel, is a work by Jacob Epstein, *Christ in Majesty;* finished in gold leaf, it measures 19.5 × 6 ft.

Return to the narthex to ascend the **carillon tower.** An elevator ascends 20 stories; stairs (147 steps) lead to the bell chamber and an open observation platform with spectacular views of Upper Manhattan and the rivers. The Laura Spelman Rockefeller Memorial Carillon, gift of John D. Rockefeller Jr., in memory of his mother, contains 74 bells, ranging from the 20-ton Bourdon (the largest tuned bell ever cast) to a ten-pound treble bell. Cast in three stages (1925, 1930, and 1956; Gillet & Johnston Foundry, England, and Van Bergen Foundry, Holland), it is the first carillon to exceed a range of five octaves.

Leave the church by the west portal and walk south. At 475 Riverside Drive (at W. 120th St), just south of the church, is the **Interchurch Center** (1958; Voorhees, Walker, Smith, Smith & Haines), originally built to house the offices of Protestant organizations. Its tenants now also include Catholic, Jewish, and Muslim religious organizations as well as other nonprofit organizations. The center hosts musical and cultural programs as well as art exhibitions. Open weekdays 9–5; ☎ (212) 870-2933.

Walk north on Riverside Drive past Riverside Church toward Grant's Tomb. On the northwest corner of the church is the Women's Porch, with sculptured figures of four women typifying the biblical ideal of womanhood. Facing north are Mary and Martha, the sisters of Lazarus; facing west are Eunice and Lois, mother and grandmother of Timothy. On the ridgepole of the roof is an Angel of the Resurrection.

General Grant National Memorial

Riverside Drive and W. 122nd St, New York, NY 10027. ☎ (212) 666-1640. Web site: www.nps.gov/gegr. Open daily 9–5. Closed Jan 1, Thanksgiving, and Dec 25. Free. Tours, exhibits. Annual celebration on April 27, Grant's birthday. Gift shop. Not accessible to wheelchairs.

On the west side of Riverside Drive, at about W. 122nd St, is the General Grant National Memorial (1891–97; John H. Duncan; DL), better known as Grant's Tomb, the largest mausoleum in North America.

One of the city's most imposing formal monuments, the massive granite sepulchre contains the remains of Ulysses S. Grant (1822–1885) and his wife, Julia Dent Grant. Intended to be unmistakably tomblike, despite objections that it would give a funereal tone to the neighborhood, it was once a popular site of pilgrimage but is now rather sparsely visited (only about 111,000 people in 1999).

History

After an illustrious career as commander in chief of the Union Armies in the Civil War and a scandal-ridden period as president (1868–76), Ulysses S. Grant died in 1885. He had requested burial in New York, at the U.S. Military Academy at West Point, or in Galena, Illinois. Because Galena seemed too remote and Mrs. Grant, a civilian, could not be buried at West Point, New York was chosen. In 1885, Grant's body was temporarily interred in a brick structure at 123rd St, and five years later John H. Duncan won the architectural competition for a tomb to cost about a half-million dollars (eventually 90,000 subscribers contributed about $600,000). Duncan's design was based largely on the tombs of Masolus at Halicarnassus (now in Turkey), Hadrian, and Napoleon.

Ground was broken in 1891, and the general's remains were quietly brought to the finished tomb in 1897. Despite the scandals that marred his administration, Grant himself remained a revered figure, and even while the tomb was under construction two attempts were made to claim his remains for other locales.

The site deteriorated in the 1980s, but in 1993 Frank Scaturro, a Columbia undergraduate who volunteered as a tour guide at the tomb, wrote a 325-page report describing the deplorable conditions and sent it to elected officials in Washington, D.C. The Grant family went to court threatening to exhume the bodies and bury them elsewhere, but Congress authorized $1.8 million to clean up the site, and the Grants withdrew the suit. The restored tomb was reopened in 1997 on the 175th anniversary of Grant's birth.

Exterior

The largest mausoleum in North America, Grant's Tomb has a cubelike base topped by a drum supporting a stepped conical dome. A broad flight of steps flanked by two large eagles leads to the Doric portico and entrance. (The eagles were moved here in 1939 from their roost on a former General Post Office in City Hall Park.) Above the cornice a tablet contains Grant's words, "Let us have peace," spoken upon accepting the presidential nomination of 1868; figures of two lamenting women recline against the tablet. The stepped cone is derived from reconstructions of the tomb of Mausolus (died c. 532).

Interior

The austere interior, inspired by Napoleon's tomb at the Hôtel des Invalides in Paris, is shaped like a cross and dominated by the sunken crypt directly below the dome. Above the windows, mosaics (1966; Allyn Cox) depict Grant's victories at Vicksburg (east) and Chattanooga (west) and the surrender of Robert E. Lee at Appomattox (north). Beneath the dome, sculptured women (by J. Massey Rhind) symbolize phases of Grant's life: birth and childhood (southeast), military career (northeast), civil career (northwest), and death (southwest). The two exhibition rooms on the north wall are devoted to Grant's civil and military career. A double staircase (public allowed only with Park Ranger escort) leads down into the crypt containing the imposing polished red granite sarcophaghi of General and Mrs. Grant. Niches in the wall at the crypt level contain bronze busts of Grant's generals Sherman and Sheridan (1938; William Mues), along with Thomas, Ord, and McPherson (done by Jens Juszko). Originally the windowpanes were clear glass over which were drawn dark purple curtains symbolizing mourning, but the curtains deteriorated and the windows were redesigned by the Tiffany studios and glazed with purple glass, which in its turn was found to be too somber and dark. The present yellow color seems to be some sort of compromise.

Grant Centennial Plaza

The park surrounding the monument, now known as Grant Centennial Plaza, was conceived to commemorate Grant's establishment (1872) of Yellowstone, the first national park. The free-form, free-spirited mosaic benches (1972–74; Phillip Danzig and Pedro Silva) were created as part of a community participation project. Directly behind the tomb, a fence encloses the Commemoration Tree, a ginkgo given (1897) as a gift by China to honor Grant.

Across Riverside Drive to the west (about opposite the public restrooms in the park), a fence near the footpath encloses a small stone urn inscribed "Erected to the Memory of an Amiable Child." The child was St. Clair Pollock, who at age five died in a fall from the rocks on July 15, 1797. His uncle, George Pollock, a wealthy linen merchant, had bought the land from Nicholas de Peyster and built his home at what is now Riverside Park and W. 123rd St, on a high piece of land commanding a view of the river. The house (c. 1783), called Strawberry Hill, stood at the north end of the landscaped oval behind Grant's Tomb. After the child's death, Pollock sold the house to Joseph Alston, husband of Aaron Burr's daughter Theodosia, and returned to Ireland, requesting that the child's grave remain untouched. In the mid-19C the house became the Claremont Inn, popular with travelers, and numbering among its illustrious guests the Morgans and Whitneys. It burned down and was demolished by the city in 1952.

Walk south along Riverside Drive to W. 116th St. The Paterno brothers, Charles and Joseph, built the two sumptuous corner apartments here, The **Paterno** and the **Colosseum** (1910; Schwartz and Gross). The Colosseum is particularly noteworthy for its curved facade that follows the flow of the street. (Inside it had mahogany dining rooms, wall safes, and a chauffeur's lounge on the ground floor.)

28 · Harlem

Like Coney Island, Greenwich Village, and the Lower East Side, Harlem is a neighborhood whose very name conjures up many images.

Geographically, Harlem is defined by the East and Harlem Rivers, the cliffs of Morningside Heights and St. Nicholas Terrace, and by 110th and 168th Sts. Its black residents are almost entirely African American, unlike Brooklyn's black population, which includes many middle-class Caribbean immigrants. East Harlem, east of Park Ave and north of 96th St, is largely Puerto Rican and is known as El Barrio or Spanish Harlem. A dwindling Italian community still remains around Pleasant Ave and E. 116th St, and other Latinos have joined the Puerto Ricans.

Early Harlem

Harlem's first settlement was a Native American village on the banks of the Harlem River between about the present-day location of 110th and 125th Sts. The fertile soil and the strategic advantages of the terrain attracted Dutch farmers, and in 1658 the Dutch founded Nieuw Haarlem, hiring a contingent of soldiers to build and defend their settlement. In 1672 black slaves, originally brought to this country by the Dutch, built a wagon road from Nieuw Haarlem to New Amsterdam, about ten miles south at the tip of Manhattan. Increasingly, this beautiful outlying land attracted gentlemen farmers or wealthy merchants who developed estates and built country mansions. By 1790 Harlem had a population of 203.

By 1837 the tracks of the New York and Harlem Railroad had been laid from City Hall to the Harlem River, opening the area for development, but simultaneously raising a barrier between the east and west sides of Harlem and creating a strip of blight where factories, squatters' shacks, and tenements quickly sprang up. By the 1840s, as the quality of the farmland deteriorated and many homesteads were abandoned, Irish squatters began to move in.

East Harlem, further depressed by the arrival of the Third and Second Ave elevated railroads in 1879 and 1880, was soon established as a working-class neighborhood. Speculators erected rows of tenements along the avenues, which became home to immigrants from Russia, Germany, Italy, Ireland, Hungary, Scandinavia, England, and Spain. Later it became a neighborhood largely of eastern European Jews and Italians.

The rest of Harlem, on the other hand, attracted middle-class German Americans. Speculators, anticipating the full-blown arrival of the middle class from

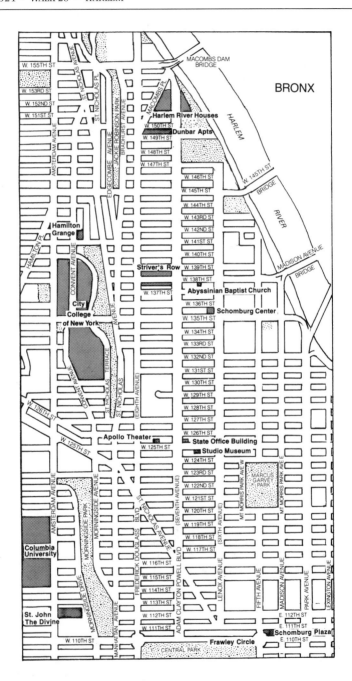

downtown, put up substantial apartment buildings and handsome row houses, particularly after the opening of the IRT subway along Lenox Ave in 1901. Oscar Hammerstein had opened the Harlem Opera House at 205 W. 125th St in 1889, expecting the same thing. Instead of a genteel middle class, however, more eastern European Jews from the Lower East Side showed up—and by 1917, Harlem was home to 80,000 Jews, not including the 90,000 in East Harlem. (The Jewish population, however, soon moved to the West Side and the outer boroughs. By 1930 only 5,000 remained, and many synagogues were converted to churches.) Without a new influx of more prosperous residents, the real estate market collapsed, leaving landlords with unrentable buildings.

In 1904 the black realtor Philip A. Payton stepped into the gap, taking over building management and guaranteeing high rents to landlords who would accept black tenants, making decent housing available to blacks for the first time in New York.

In 1827 the state had prohibited slavery, but its black population remained in a kind of civil limbo until the Emancipation Proclamation (1863) gave citizenship to all former slaves. At the close of the Civil War, New York's black population, estimated at 15,000, had been concentrated in ghettos in Lower Manhattan, notably around Thompson St in Greenwich Village. By the end of the century the black population was centered around the Tenderloin (west of Broadway between 32nd and 42nd Sts) and Hell's Kitchen districts (the 40s and 50s west of Seventh Ave). As demolition for the construction of the old Penn Station displaced them, blacks moved up into the San Juan Hill neighborhood (north and west of Columbus Circle). The next move was to Harlem.

Blacks began pouring into Harlem from other parts of the city, from the rural South, and from the West Indies. During the 1920s the black population of Harlem increased from 83,248 to 203,894, with a density of 236 people per acre, twice that of the rest of the city.

White business and property owners fought bitterly to keep Harlem white, but failed simply because it was too profitable to rent to blacks, although the arriving blacks were effectively barred from holding jobs in white-owned businesses. Later, landlords began subdividing apartments, increasing their own profits but beginning a policy of overcrowding and poor building maintenance that continues today.

The Harlem Renaissance

The 1920s were years of optimism and great artistic activity as writers, artists, and intellectuals made the pilgrimage to Harlem, by then the capital of black America. The era, particularly the years 1925–30, was considered the "Harlem Renaissance." A stream of hit Broadway plays, many of them written by and starring Harlem residents, began in 1921 with *Shuffle Along* by Noble Sissle and Eubie Blake. Black authors were published with greater frequency than ever before (Langston Hughes's *The Weary Blues* and *Not Without Laughter*, Walter White's *Fire in the Flint*, Wallace Thurman's *The Blacker the Berry*, Zora Neal Hurston's *Isis*). Painters Aaron Douglas, Romare Bearden, William H. Johnson, and Richmond Barthe broke new ground in terms of style and subject. Black newspapers like *Amsterdam News* and the *New York Age* flourished. Marcus Garvey awoke black self-respect and militancy with his back-to-Africa movement, while black and white intellectuals still enjoyed cordial relations.

To the outside world, Harlem was famous for its music. Whites flocked uptown to enjoy Harlem's ballrooms and cabarets, and the jazz at its famous nightclubs—the Cotton Club, Connie's, and Smalls' Paradise—many of which were white-owned and had white-only audiences. During the Roaring Twenties, entrepreneurs taking advantage of white curiosity billed W. 133rd St between Lenox and Seventh Aves as "Jungle Alley," a place where whites could see "the primitive essence" of Harlem.

The Cotton Club

Harlem's most famous nightclub during the 1920s was the Cotton Club, at 646 Lenox Ave (W. 143rd St). In 1923 mobster Owney Madden took over the Club Deluxe and renamed it the Cotton Club. Madden enforced a strict color line: permitting only whites to enjoy the club's entertainment. On any given night, Cadillacs, Studebakers, and Nashes would discharge their passengers, who then waited in line for entry. The patrons were a swanky mix of young college types, the Hollywood-Broadway bunch, and the Park Ave crowd. Among the regulars were Mayor Jimmy Walker, Jimmy Durante, George Raft, Tallulah Bankhead, and Babe Ruth. Blacks, preferably light-skinned ones, worked onstage, backstage, and out front as waiters and bouncers. The chorus line of light-skinned black women (including Lena Horne for a while) was so famous that white women tried to pass as black to join. Cab Calloway performed here, as did Louis Armstrong, Stepin Fetchit, trumpeter Doc Cheatham, and dancers Bill "Bojangles" Robinson and the Nicholas Brothers. Duke Ellington, whose band played here from 1927 to 1931, achieved his first brilliant success both musically and commercially through his association with the club.

In 1936, as business shrank during the Depression, the managers decided that Harlem had become unfashionable and moved the club downtown, to Broadway and W. 48th St. It remained open until 1940, when black stage revues lost their popularity. Today, a housing development occupies the original site on Lenox Ave.

The Depression and Beyond

The Depression devastated Harlem economically, revealing the poverty behind the glittering exterior. Throughout the city, the marginally employed were the hardest hit, and blacks, excluded from virtually all but menial jobs, were among the first to suffer. The 1930s were the years of "rent parties," where guests paid an entrance fee to hear the music, drink the bathtub gin, and help pay off the month's rent. Literary output dried up, housing deteriorated, racial tensions heightened, and Harlem became the ground for several unpleasant incidents and disturbances; a 1935 riot that followed false rumors of a black youth being beaten to death for shoplifting is generally considered the end of the Harlem Renaissance.

Music, however, continued to flourish with innovators like Dizzy Gillespie and Charlie Parker bringing life to the area's clubs. But by the late 1950s, black artists, actors, musicians, and dancers were permitted into the commercially more successful cultural scene in Midtown or Greenwich Village.

During the civil rights era of the 1950s and 1960s, Harlem again became the focus of both political and social activity. The Black Muslims founded the Temple of Islam at W. 116th St and Lenox Ave, and black civil rights leader Malcolm X worked there until he broke with the Muslims to found his own Organization of Afro-American Unity in 1964, also in Harlem. After riots in 1964 and 1968, federal, state, and local money was channeled into Harlem to improve housing and education, and to solve social problems.

In the 1970s, however, things grew worse. Empty, derelict buildings and rubble-strewn vacant lots accumulated. The combination of long-standing building-code violations, landlord neglect, tenant abuse, and tax delinquency resulted in the abandonment of many buildings by landlords who found it cheaper to walk away from their property than to pay the taxes on it. Some preferred arson with its insurance payoff. As a result of tax default and abandonment, the city became the *in rem* owner of 65 percent of Harlem's real estate.

Harlem, like other poor, minority neighborhoods, also suffered unduly during the crack epidemic of the late 1980s and early 1990s. In 1990, men in Harlem had a lower life expectancy than those in Bangladesh, many dying from TB and AIDS as well as violence. The rates of unemployment, crime, and drug addiction remain high, and school rankings are low relative to wealthier areas. Unemployment in 1996 was 9.8 percent compared to 5.5 percent for the entire city, while the median income was $10,000 lower than the city average. Asthma has risen dramatically in the past 15 years, particularly among children, and in 1997 the death rate in Harlem was five times the overall New York City rate, itself the highest in the country.

Harlem Today

Life is definitely on the upswing in Harlem. After years of population decline following World War II, middle-class families are again buying homes in Harlem's premier neighborhoods, including Striver's Row, Sugar Hill, Hamilton Terrace, and Mount Morris Park. Artistic institutions are flourishing once again. The year 1999 witnessed the birth of the Classical Theater of Harlem, which seeks to bring theater back to Harlem and has created nearly 60 professional theater jobs. The National Black Theater, which has survived in Harlem for 30 years, continues to prosper. In 2001, former president Bill Clinton shined the media spotlight on Harlem's renaissance when he leased office space on W. 125th St.

From river to river, hundreds of millions of dollars are being invested in the community, creating perhaps 10,000 jobs. The Upper Manhattan Empowerment Zone, initiated by the federal government, received $250 million in 1994 to lend out over ten years. From 1996 through 1999, Chase Manhattan Bank invested $150 million in Harlem. In a ten-year span ending around 2004, 15,000 new housing units will have been built here.

In East Harlem, at E. 125th St and Lexington Ave, a 50,000-square-ft Pathmark supermarket opened in 1999, anchoring a minimall. The City Council has approved the East River Plaza on the site of the long-abandoned Washburn Wire Company factory on the FDR Drive from E. 116th to E. 119th Sts. In Central Harlem, Renaissance Plaza, Harlem Center, and Harlem USA are adding retail space and new housing. And on the western edge, the celebrated New York supermarket Fairway opened a 35,000-square-ft store at W. 133rd St and Twelfth Ave in 1995.

Further north, between W. 137th and W. 145th Sts on the Hudson River, is the 28-acre, $129-million **Riverbank State Park** (proposed, 1969; opened 1993; Richard Dattner & Assocs.), a state park sited on a platform above a sewage treatment plant. Built to placate the Harlem community, who were understandably angry at having the plant foisted on them, the park features a regulation track and soccer field; skating rink; gym; community garden; playgrounds; tennis, handball, and basketball courts; and the city's only public Olympic-size indoor pool. While the sewage smells are not generally troublesome in the park, they are still annoying in the surrounding neighborhood.

Harlem Street Names

When touring Harlem, keep in mind that the major avenues take on different names as they pass through Central Harlem. Eighth Ave is Frederick Douglass Blvd. Seventh Ave was named Adam Clayton Powell Jr. Blvd shortly after the black Congressman's death in 1972 (see Abyssinian Baptist Church). Sixth Ave north of Central Park has been renamed twice—first it was Lenox Ave, after James Lenox who established the Lenox Library, now part of the New York Public Library, and later, Malcolm X Blvd, although most street signs and locals still refer to it as Lenox. While 125th St is officially Martin Luther King Jr. Blvd, New Yorkers still call it 125th St.

Harlem from 110th to 135th Street

Subway: Lexington Ave Local (6) to 110th St.
Bus: M1, M2, M3, M4

Begin at **Duke Ellington Circle** (formerly Frawley Circle), located at Fifth Ave and 110th St on Central Park's northeast corner. Its centerpiece is a 25 ft tall sculpture (1995; Robert Graham), featuring an eight-ft-tall **statue of Duke Ellington** standing next to his piano (facing east). The piano rests on three pillars; on top of each is a trio of nude female figures, sophisticated ladies, whom the sculptor cast as Ellington's muses. The bronze statue finished in black prompted protests from some women, including then–borough president Ruth Messinger, who demanded the nude women be removed, saying their location beneath Ellington was sexist. Most of the money for the statue was raised by the singer Bobby Short.

Towering above the circle is **Schomburg Plaza** (1975; Gruzen & Partners and Castro-Blanco, Piscioneri & Feder), its two 35-story octagonal towers a project of the state Urban Development Corporation.

Walk west along Central Park North. The playwright Arthur Miller *(Death of a Salesman)* was born at 45 Central Park North. Facing the park are handsome brownstones and elevator buildings, such as the **Semiramis Apartments** (c. 1905) at 137 Central Park North, built at the turn of the 20C for middle- and upper-class families. Like hundreds of other Harlem buildings, it was seized for taxes by the city (1974). The building was rehabilitated as condominiums in 1987.

At Lenox Ave (Malcolm X Blvd) is **Malcolm X Plaza,** which features Islamic patterns in its paving stones and flowers and trees that once flourished in Persia.

Turn right on Adam Clayton Powell Jr. Blvd. At 215 W. 114th St is the **Wadleigh School** (1902; C.B.J. Snyder; DL), a French Renaissance building with a majestic copper tower. It received a $47-million facelift in the 1990s.

Continue north to W. 116th St. At 1910 Adam Clayton Powell Jr. Blvd is the **First Corinthian Baptist Church,** built as the Regent Theater (1913; Thomas W. Lamb). Beset almost immediately by financial troubles, this neo-Venetian picture palace was saved by Samuel Lionel Rothafel, later famous as the movie theater mogul "Roxy."

At 1923 Adam Clayton Powell Jr. Blvd, on the northeast corner of the same intersection, are the once-elegant **Graham Court Apartments** (1901; Clinton & Russell; DL), the first in a series of three palatial court-centered apartments financed by the Astor family (the other two are the Apthorp and the Astor Court on Broadway and W. 90th St).

Continue north to W. 118th St and turn left, walking a half-block west to the corner of St. Nicholas Ave. In the Cecil Hotel is the former jazz club **Minton's Playhouse,** opened by sax player Henry Minton in 1938. Minton's, where Dizzy Gillespie, Charlie Parker, Thelonious Monk, and others used to riff into the wee hours, is usually considered the birthplace of bebop. While the lights out front have long been dark, there has been talk of reopening the club.

Across the street is **St. Thomas the Apostle Church,** (1907; T. H. Poole), 260 W. 118th St, an eclectic Gothic building with an arcaded porch and grand-entrance stairway.

Walk east to Lenox Ave, then walk south to W. 116th. At 102 W. 116th St is the **Malcolm Shabazz Mosque No. 7,** originally the Lenox Casino, converted to a temple (1965) by the addition of an aluminum onion-shaped dome. Elijah Muhammad established it as his Temple of Islam, and Malcolm X preached there before his break with Muhammad and the Black Muslims.

Diagonally across the street is one of Harlem's latest signs of revival, the $61-million **Renaissance Plaza,** with 241 moderate-income co-op apartments and 60,000 square ft of retail space (2001; Greenberg Farrow Architecture).

Walk north along Lenox Ave; from W. 119 to W. 123 Sts is the western border of the **Mount Morris Historic District.** At 201 Lenox Ave, on the northwest corner of 120th St, is one of the district's handsome churches, the **Mount Olivet Baptist Church,** which has the stately manner of a bank. Originally Temple Israel (1907; Arnold W. Brunner), it was built when the neighborhood's population consisted largely of well-to-do Protestant and German Jewish residents.

Marcus Garvey Park

Turn right on W. 120th St and walk a half-block east to Marcus Garvey Park, which straddles Fifth Ave between 120th and 124th Sts. Originally called Mount Morris Park, it was renamed (1973) to honor Garvey, a charismatic and flamboyant black leader fond of titles and prerogatives, who arrived in Harlem from the West Indies in 1914 and dedicated himself to the improvement of his race. He encouraged blacks to be proud of their color and to work toward their own social and political institutions, but his major interest was in leading his people back to Africa, of which he dubbed himself emperor and provisional president. To this end he formed two steamship companies whose vessels, along with many others of the period, attempted to subvert Prohibition by carrying some $3 million worth of liquor from New York to Cuba, a voyage that ended with government confiscation of the cargo. Later Garvey, convicted of mail fraud and imprisoned, was deported to Jamaica; he died an exile in London in 1940.

In 1839 the city established the park, mainly because its steep, rocky terrain was unsuitable for building. When the surrounding land was leveled, the central hill in the park (called Snake Hill by the Dutch) achieved a prominence that made the park visually dramatic. Its dominant man-made feature is a **cast-iron watch-tower** (c. 1855; Julius B. Kroehl, engineer; DL), the sole survivor of many that once served as fire lookout and warning stations (even the 10,000-pound bell remains). Today the park is home to a city swimming pool and recreation center.

Walk north along Mount Morris Park West to W. 122nd St. **Mount Morris Ascension Presbyterian Church** (1905; Thomas H. Poole), 15 Mount Morris Park West, is an atypical eclectic mix of styles with pale yellow brick and a neoclassical dome.

Turn left and walk west to **St. Martin's Episcopal Church** (1888; William A. Potter; DL) on the southeast corner of Lenox Ave and W. 122nd St, considered the finest Romanesque church complex in New York. The tower houses a carillon of 40 bells, second only to the 74 bells at Riverside Church.

Look one block to the north for two more churches: the **Ephesus Seventh Day Adventist Church** (1887; J. R. Thomas), originally the Reformed Low Dutch Church of Harlem at 267 Lenox Ave, and across the street, the picturesque Queen Anne revival **Bethel Gospel Pentacostal Assembly,** built as the Harlem Club (1889; Lamb & Rich) for businessmen and civic leaders.

Continue west along W. 122nd St, once known as **Doctor's Row.** The north side is lined with handsome row houses, especially the Queen Anne designs of nos. 133–141 W. 122nd St.

On the south side of the street is the renowned **Hale House,** 152–154 W. 122nd St, which has provided help for drug-addicted infants, children, and their families since 1969. It was founded by Clara Hale, better known as Mother Hale, and her daughter Lorraine, a physician. Mother Hale, who died in 1992 at age 87, is memorialized out front in a sculpture (1996; Robert Berks) that depicts her holding a small child. Surrounding the piece are bronze reliefs of children. The funding for this tribute came from a quintessentially odd New York assemblage including Donald Trump, Yoko Ono, Patti Labelle, Patrick Ewing, comedian Martin Lawrence, and Rupert Murdoch.

Continue to the corner. Across the street, at 2034–40 Adam Clayton Powell Jr. Blvd, is the **Washington Apartments** (1884; Mortimer Merritt; DL), one of the city's earliest apartment buildings and Harlem's first for middle-class families. It was built after elevated rail lines reached the neighborhood in the 1870s and brought an influx of newcomers.

Walk north. Look to the right, at 123rd St. Harlem is one of the few areas with so many churches that some are situated on side streets, where their presence is even more impressive, as is the case with the massive marble facade of the **Greater Metropolitan Baptist Church** (1898; Schneider & Herter; DL).

Just before reaching W. 125th St, at 2090 Adam Clayton Powell Jr. Blvd is

Theresa Towers, formerly the **Hotel Theresa** (1913; George and Edward Blum; DL). The tallest building in Harlem when it opened, this 13-story white brick and terra-cotta hotel excluded blacks until a black businessman, Love B. Woods, purchased it in 1937. When Joe Louis won the world heavyweight title that year, he celebrated at the Hotel Theresa, which soon became known as the "Waldorf of Harlem." Fidel Castro stayed here while visiting the United Nations in 1960, meeting with Soviet leader Nikita Khrushchev at the hotel.

Studio Museum in Harlem

144 W. 125th Street (between Lenox Ave [Malcolm X Blvd] and Adam Clayton Powell Jr. Blvd), New York, NY 10035. ☎ (212) 864-4500. Web site: www. studiomuseuminharlem.org. Open Wed–Thurs 12–6; Fri 12–8; Sat–Sun 10–6. Admission charge. Exhibitions, guided tours (by appointment), lectures, concerts. Gift shop. Café (to open). Accessible to wheelchairs.

Subway: Seventh Ave Express (2, 3), Eighth Ave Express or Local (A, C), Sixth Ave Express (B, D), or Lexington Ave Express or Local (4, 5, 6) to 125th St. Bus: M2, M7, M10, M100, M101, M102, BX15.

Turn right at W. 125th St and walk east to the Studio Museum in Harlem. Founded in 1968 to collect and exhibit the work of black artists, the museum has exhibits that feature emerging and established artists as well as traditional African art. The permanent collection of 19C–20C African American art, 20C Caribbean and African art, and traditional African art, includes works by Romare Bearden and historic photographs of Harlem by James VanDerZee.

Note: The museum is currently being renovated and expanded; expected completion date is 2002.

Next door, at 136 W. 125th St is the attractive tan brick former **Koch & Co. Building** (1893; William Hume & Son), which, with its five upper-tier arches, looks like it belongs downtown. Koch & Co. was a dry goods merchant that took a chance and moved uptown, all the way uptown. Today it's home to a medical center.

Cross to the north side of the street. Stretching toward Lenox Ave is the **site of the proposed Harlem Center,** an $85-million, 310,000-square-ft hotel, retail, and office complex to rise on state-owned land. It is being developed by Forest City Ratner, one of the city's leading real estate firms, and the Abyssinian Development Corporation, a community-oriented offshoot of the Abyssinan Baptist Church, one of Harlem's premier churches.

Return west. At the corner of Adam Clayton Powell Jr. Blvd and W. 125th St, in a large plaza, is the former Harlem State Office Building (1973; Ifill Johnson Hanchard), renamed (1983) the Adam Clayton Powell Jr. State Office Building.

Cross the boulevard, continuing west along W. 125th St. The first storefronts on the west side stand on the site of the Harlem Opera House built by Oscar Hammerstein in 1889 when the neighborhood population was beginning to change from German and Irish to Jewish and Italian. The theater was razed in 1959.

Apollo Theater

At 253 W. 125th St is the world-famous **Apollo Theater** (1913; George Keister; DL), which opened as a burlesque house for whites only.

History

In 1934, Leo Brecher and Frank Schiffman took over the theater, invited blacks, and turned the Apollo into Harlem's top spot. Brecher and Schiffman had previously opened the Lafayette Theater—now the Williams Christian Methodist Church at 2225 Adam Clayton Powell Jr. Blvd (between W. 131st and W. 132nd Sts)—to black performers in the 1920s, making it one of Harlem's premier performance palaces. During the Depression the Lafayette housed the WPA Federal Negro Theater, among whose productions was an all-black *Macbeth* directed by Orson Welles in 1937.

Louis Armstrong, Bessie Smith, Bill Robinson, Billie Holiday, Count Basie, Charlie Parker, Dizzy Gillespie, and Nat "King" Cole all graced the Apollo stage. Wednesday's Amateur Night drew a tough crowd, but not everyone got "the hook"—Sarah Vaughn, Ella Fitzgerald, and later the Jackson 5 got their big break here. Unlike many of its compatriots, the Apollo survived, even as the neighborhood declined and black artists were welcomed downtown. In later decades, the Apollo featured Marvin Gaye, Stevie Wonder, Bo Diddley, Gladys Knight, Aretha Franklin, and Smokey Robinson, who wrote "My Girl" backstage. B. B. King and James Brown recorded now-legendary live albums here.

But even the Apollo eventually hit hard times, and in 1976 it was converted to a movie theater. In 1983, former borough president Percy Sutton revived the Apollo for live performances, including Amateur Night. Since then, it has struggled financially and become ensnared in fiscal and political battles that led to AOL Time Warner taking over the theater's board of directors in an effort to turn it around.

The Tree of Hope

Inside the theater is the stump from the Tree of Hope, which once grew on the traffic triangle across from the Lafayette Theater (opened by the same producers who took over the Apollo). According to legend, struggling black actors and actresses kissed the tree for good luck. This stump is from the second Tree of Hope, donated by dancer Bill "Bojangles" Robinson when the original died. (A plaque still stands on the traffic triangle.)

Continue west on W. 125th St to Frederick Douglass Blvd and the brand new **Harlem USA** complex. It is the grandest of the new additions to Harlem, a 285,000-square-ft retail and entertainment center featuring stores and a Magic Johnson multiplex theater, which opened in July 2000, developed in part by the basketball legend who has opened movie theaters in inner city neighborhoods of Los Angeles, Houston, Atlanta, and Cleveland.

Return to Adam Clayton Powell Jr. Blvd and turn left, walking north to W. 128th St. At 151 W. 128th St is the **Metropolitan Baptist Church** (1884; John R. Thomas; DL), a low, massive Romanesque church with a heavy half-conical roof. It was built as the New York Presbyterian Church when Harlem was well-to-do and bourgeois.

Walk east to Lenox Ave and turn right. One block south on the east side of the street is **Sylvia's,** a premier soul food restaurant. Opened by Sylvia Woods in

1962—she had been working as a waitress when the owner decided to sell and offered it to his favorite employee—it is a major tourist attraction.

Head east on W. 127th St to Fifth Ave. At the corner is **St. Andrew's Church** (1873; Henry Congdon; DL), one of the city's prettiest Victorian Gothic churches. While many of the neighborhood's churches and temples have changed hands and even denominations, this is still occupied by its original Episcopal congregation.

Continue east to the former **Langston Hughes residence** (1869; Alexander Wilson; DL), 20 E. 127th St, an unremarkable Italianate brownstone. The great poet and playwright lived and worked on the top floor from 1947 until his death in 1967.

Return to Fifth Ave and walk one block north to 128th St. On the northwest corner is an empty lot at 2078 Fifth Ave, once the site of the notorious Collyer brothers' residence.

The Collyer Brothers

Homer (1883–1947) and Langley (1886–1947) Collyer are remembered for having the filthiest apartment in city history, a domestic disaster area discovered only after their deaths. Langley had been an aspiring concert pianist and Homer an attorney. By the 1930s Homer had suffered a stroke, which left him blind and paralyzed, and the brothers had become virtual recluses. No one could enter their home, and they lived without gas, water, electricity, or even a sewer connection—their sole link to society was an old radio. The Collyers collected everything and threw out nothing. They had numerous pianos and chandeliers plus thousands of empty bottles and cans and fading newspapers, which Langley had saved for the time when Homer regained his sight.

On March 21, 1947, the police received an anonymous tip that there was a dead body inside the house. In fact, there were two. When the police fought their way past the refuse into the house, they encountered cats, rats, and Homer's gaunt dead body. It took several weeks for the police to clear out the rest of the house, as onlookers gathered each day, curious about what would be found (dressmaker's dummies and the body of a Model T Ford) and what had happened to Langley. Eventually, the police found Langley's body, buried beneath debris that had been rigged to crush any intruders. Apparently, he had accidentally triggered the booby trap. After he had suffocated, Homer starved to death.

Other Points of Interest

The **Harlem Courthouse,** at 170 E. 121st St (corner of Sylvan Place), was built (1893; Thom & Wilson; DL) in the then-popular eclectic Victorian Gothic and Romanesque style. Once known as the Fifth District Prison (it had holding cells), it remained a magistrate's courthouse until 1961; since then it has served the city Parole Board and other agencies, including small claims court, an irony for such a majestic building.

Nearby, at 174 E. 110th St, is the **Aguilar Branch of the New York Public Library** (1899, expanded 1905; Herts & Tallant; DL), established in 1886 as a private library to satisfy the intellectual hunger of the predominantly Jewish immigrants who lived nearby. Named after Grace Aguilar, an English novelist of Spanish Jewish parentage, the building now serves as part of the public system.

Harlem, 135th Street and North

Subway: Sixth Ave Express (B) or Eighth Ave Local (C) to 135th St.
Bus: M3, M10.

St. Nicholas Historic District

Begin at W. 139th St and Frederick Douglass Blvd and walk east along W. 139th St. This two-square-block area of W. 139th and W. 138th Sts, between Frederick Douglass and Adam Clayton Powell Jr. Blvds, has had three names over time: the King Model Houses, Striver's Row, and the St. Nicholas Historic District.

History

The first name derives from the developer, David H. King Jr., who also built Stanford White's original Madison Square Garden. In 1891, hoping to create his own distinctive neighborhood, King put up four sets of row houses (146 in all) designed by three different prominent architects. White designed the Italian Renaissance, dark brick with brownstone and terra-cotta trim buildings on the north side of W. 139th St. On the south side of W. 139th St and on the north side of W. 138th St are Bruce Price's colonial revival rowhouses in yellow brick with terra-cotta and limestone trim. James Brown Lord's row, on the south side of W. 138th St, has neo-Georgian, red brick houses with brownstone trim.

King's project was a disaster, as the real estate boom shriveled during the 1895 depression and nearly all the properties were foreclosed. In 1919, they were sold to newly arriving blacks. Many were broken up into rooming houses, but the area became popularly known as **Striver's Row** because it attracted upper-middle-class, and presumably ambitious, black families. Among the strivers on this block were the "father of the blues," W.C. Handy (232 W. 139th St); bandleader Fletcher Henderson (228 W. 139th St); and Vertner Tandy, the first black architect allowed to register in New York State (221 W. 139th St). Around the block lived the surgeon Louis T. Wright (218 W. 138th St), composer Will Marion Cook (221 W. 138th St), and pianist Eubie Blake (236 W. 138th St).

Abyssinian Baptist Church

Walk east on W. 138th St to the Abyssinian Baptist Church (1923; Charles W. Bolton & Son; DL), 132 W. 138th St, built of New York bluestone.

History

The church was founded downtown on Worth St in 1808 and moved uptown in stages, following the black centers of population, stopping along the way on

Thompson St, Spring St, and on W. 40th St between Seventh and Eighth Aves. The church came into its own during the pastorate of Adam Clayton Powell Sr. Powell took over in 1908 and raised money to build a church in the new black mecca of Harlem. A charismatic and popular speaker, he stepped aside in 1938 for his son Adam Clayton Powell Jr., who brought even greater fame to the church and the family name.

After taking over the leadership of the church, Adam Jr. led boycotts of Harlem companies that refused to employ black workers. In 1941 he became the first black city councilman; four years later he was elected to Congress. He sponsored legislation focusing on civil rights and education, the minimum wage, and segregation in the armed forces, and became a powerful figure both in Congress, where he was the first black chairman of a major committee (Education and Labor), and in Harlem. Always controversial, Powell was censured by the House for financial irregularities in 1967 and stripped of his office; although the Supreme Court reinstated him in 1969, he was defeated in the Democratic primary the following year by Charles Rangel. (The church maintains a memorial room with memorabilia and photos spanning his career.)

Since 1989, the church pastor has been the outspoken and controversial Rev. Calvin O. Butts III, one of the city's most influential black leaders. Butts has spoken out against police brutality and negative advertising in Harlem (for example, cigarette ads that target poor neighborhoods); he has turned over his pulpit to Fidel Castro and attacked the white establishment for racism. He was a founder of the Abyssinian Development Corp., a community-based organization responsible for more than $100 million in housing (including 33 brownstones) and commercial development.

Continue east. At 120 W. 138th St (between Lenox Ave and Adam Clayton Powell Jr. Blvd) is the site of Liberty Hall, headquarters for Marcus Garvey's Universal Negro Improvement Association.

Walk south one block on Lenox Ave and turn right to 140 W. 137th St. Designed by George Foster, one of America's first black architects, **Mother African Methodist Episcopal Zion Church** (1925; George W. Foster; DL) is the "mother" church of A.M.E. Zion, the city's oldest black congregation. (The Zion group first held separate services from the John Street Methodist Church in 1796; they broke away completely in 1821.)

Harlem Hospital
Return to Lenox Ave and walk south to Harlem Hospital on Lenox Ave between W. 137th and W. 135th Sts. Founded as a municipal hospital in 1887, Harlem Hospital is now the main facility serving the local populace. Over the main doorway is a sculptural group of a black family by John W. Rhoden.

History
Here in 1920 Louis T. Wright became the first black physician to join a New York City hospital staff; he later became director of surgery. Martin Luther King Jr.'s life was saved at Harlem Hospital in 1958 after he was stabbed while making an appearance at a local department store.

Schomburg Center for Research in Black Culture

515 Malcolm X Blvd (Lenox Ave) (at W. 135th St), New York, NY 10037. ☎ (212) 491-2200. Web site: www.nypl.org/research/sc/sc.html. Open (exhibitions) Mon–Sat 10–6; Sun 1–5. Call for research and summer hours. Free. Changing exhibitions, lectures, group tours, musical programs. Gift shop. Accessible to wheelchairs.

Subway: Seventh Ave Express (2, 3) to 135th St. Bus: M5, M102.

Diagonally across the street is the Schomburg Center for Research in Black Culture (1978; Bond Ryder Assocs., renovated 1991), a branch of the New York Public Library and one of the finest facilities in the world for the study of the experience and history of peoples of African descent throughout the world.

History

The nucleus of the collection was gathered by Arturo Alfonso Schomburg, a Puerto Rican black bibliophile and scholar. It was purchased by the Carnegie Corporation in 1926 and merged with the New York Public Library's own collection of black history and literature. Schomburg, inspired to begin his archives by the remark of one of his schoolteachers that blacks had no history, was curator from 1932 until his death in 1938; the center was named for him in 1940. Today the collections have more than 5 million items—books, magazines, newspapers, pamphlets, photographs, paintings, recordings, sheet music, and art objects. Exhibitions drawn from this rich trove can range from Jacob Lawrence's paintings on the triumph over slavery to *Black New Yorkers/Black New York: 400 Years of African American History.*

On the north side of this building is the **Countee Cullen Branch of the New York Public Library** (1941; Louis Allen Abramson), 104 W. 136th St (southwest corner of Lenox Ave). Cullen, a poet, editor, and social critic, was an important figure of the Harlem Renaissance. The Countee Cullen Branch stands on the site of a mansion built in 1913 by Mme. C. J. Walker, a St. Louis laundress who discovered a hair-straightening process and reaped a fortune. Her daughter, A'Lelia Walker Robinson, was Harlem's outstanding hostess during the 1920s and for a time established one floor of the mansion as a café and gathering place for black poets and intellectuals.

At 103 W. 135th St is the original **135th Street Branch of the New York Public Library** (1905; McKim, Mead & White; DL), now part of the Schomburg Center. Next door, at 107 W. 135th St, was the first photo studio of James Van-DerZee, who depicted Harlem life from the 1920s through the 1960s.

Continue west. Another nearby literary landmark is the **Harlem Branch of the YMCA** (1932; James C. Mackenzie; DL) at 180 W. 135th St. In 1945 the Harlem Writers' Workshop was founded here and served as the temporary home of many aspiring blacks drawn to Harlem, including Langston Hughes and Ralph Ellison.

Across the street, at 187 W. 135th St, was the childhood home of pianist Fats Waller, later home to James Weldon Johnson, author of the poem "Lift Every Voice and Sing," *The Autobiography of an Ex-Colored Man,* and the history *Black Manhattan.*

On the southeast corner of W. 135th St and Adam Clayton Powell Jr. Blvd was once **Smalls' Paradise** (opened 1925), which ranked alongside the Cotton Club during the 1920s and featured roller-skating waiters. After years as a boarded-up wreck, it is being transformed into a public school, the **Thurgood Marshall Academy,** and three stories are being added. The local nonprofit group that owns the property hopes to attract a family restaurant for the ground floor.

Cross Adam Clayton Powell Jr. Blvd. The derelict row house at 220 W. 135th St was the home of Florence Mills, Harlem's most beloved celebrity during the 1920s, for most of her short life. The house is a National Historic Landmark.

Florence Mills

Mills got her first break in *Shuffle Along,* where as a member of the chorus line she stole the show from the featured performers. Her star reached its zenith in *Blackbirds,* which ran on Broadway, in Harlem, and then in London and Paris. Florenz Ziegfeld offered her a major role in the *Ziegfeld Follies,* but Mills, conscious of racial inequality despite her own stardom, turned it down. Following an illness, she died in New York City on Nov 1, 1927, at the age of 32. Over 3,000 mourners attended her funeral at the Mother Zion A.M.E. Church on W. 137th St, and more than 150,000 people crowded the streets to see the funeral procession. When it reached 142nd St and Seventh Ave, a low-flying airplane released a flock of blackbirds, which according to a contemporary account, "fluttered and flashed in the afternoon sun." Mills is buried in Woodlawn Cemetery in the Bronx.

Return to the corner of Adam Clayton Powell Jr. Blvd and walk north to W. 136th St. The blocks of W. 136th and W. 137th Sts between Powell and Frederick Douglass Blvds feature an eclectic but attractive mix of row houses, some in superb condition, some in disrepair. Gone completely is 267 W. 136th, where Iolanthe Sydney ran a rooming house whose residents included Langston Hughes and Zora Neale Hurston.

Continue west to Edgecombe Ave, then turn south to W. 135th St. At St. Nicholas Park, turn right and head west through the park to St. Nicholas Terrace. On the corner is the **A. Philip Randolph Campus High School at City College** (1924; DL), one of Harlem's most successful public schools.

Continue west to Convent Ave and turn left. Convent Ave is named after the Convent of the Sacred Heart (established 1841), which stood between St. Nicholas and Amsterdam Aves (then called Tenth Ave) until it burned down in 1888.

City University of New York

Along Convent Ave between W. 130th and W. 135th Sts is the south campus of the City University of New York (CCNY), originally the City College of New York.

History

CCNY was founded in 1849 after the state legislature authorized the Board of Education to establish a free academy for qualified city students. Its policy of free admissions for city residents long made City College a stepping stone out of the ghetto. In 1903 more than 75 percent of the students were Jewish, and in 1910 almost 90 percent, most coming from eastern European families. Nowadays, though tuition is no longer free and the student body is more black and Hispanic than Jewish, CCNY still provides an educational outlet for the city's aspiring young. Today the college is part of the city university system (CUNY), but this campus is still known as CCNY.

South Campus
The grounds are divided into a north and south campus. The south campus originally belonged to the Academy and Convent of the Sacred Heart, which moved to Westchester County as the Manhattanville College of the Sacred Heart in 1952. The medieval-looking day-care center (1912) on the northeast corner of Convent Ave and W. 133rd St originally served as the gatehouse of Manhattanville College. **Aaron Davis Hall** (1978; Abraham W. Geller & Assocs. and Ezra D. Ehrenkrantz & Assocs.), at the southeast corner of Convent Ave and W. 135th St, has three theaters and an outdoor amphitheater. At the southwest corner of W. 135th St and Convent Ave, between the two campuses, is a brownstone-and-granite **gatehouse** (1890; DL) for the Croton Aqueduct, marking the end of the masonry aqueduct that leads into Manhattan from High Bridge. From here the water is piped underground to the next gatehouse, at W. 119th St and Amsterdam Ave.

North Campus
Continue north along Convent Ave to the north campus, between W. 138th and W. 140th Sts. Designed in 1905 by George B. Post, the original buildings and the gates that frame the central walkway were built of dark Manhattan schist excavated from this site and from nearby subway construction. The buildings were then trimmed with white terra-cotta and adorned with more than 600 gargoyles completing the quintessential Gothic feel that makes the buildings seem ideal either for a medieval town or an American university. Massive **Shepard Hall,** which curves around the northeastern end of the campus, is the main building.

North of the campus, along Convent Ave between W. 141st and W. 145th Sts is the **Hamilton Heights Historic District,** an enclave of fine row houses built between 1886 and 1906. On the northeast corner of W. 141st St is **St. Luke's Church** (1892; R. H. Robertson), the brownstone Romanesque revival home of an Episcopalian congregation founded on Hudson St in Greenwich Village. The tower was never finished.

Hamilton Grange National Memorial
287 Convent Ave (between W. 141st and W. 142nd Sts), New York, NY 10031. ☎ (212) 283-5154. Web site: www.nps.gov/hagr. Open Fri–Sun 9–5. Closed national holidays. Free. Not accessible to wheelchairs. Exhibitions, programs, group tours (call ahead).

Subway: Broadway–Seventh Ave Local (1, 9) to 137th St. Walk east to Convent Ave, then north to W. 141st St. Eighth Ave Express or Local (A, C) or Sixth Ave Express (B, D) to 145th St. Walk west to Convent Ave and south to W. 141st St. Bus: M4, M5, M100, M101.

The district's centerpiece is Hamilton Grange (1802; John McComb Jr.; DL), the country home of founding father Alexander Hamilton. In front is a heroic bronze **statue of Alexander Hamilton** (1889; William O. Partridge). The grange, one of the finest Federal houses of its day, was the only home Hamilton ever owned.

Alexander Hamilton

Hamilton was born in 1755 in the West Indies, the illegitimate child of Scottish and French Huguenot parents. He arrived in America in 1772 and enrolled in King's College (now Columbia University), where he soon began making speeches and writing articles urging unity against interference from Britain. He was one of the earliest American leaders to argue that whites were not inherently superior to blacks, and though he was an abolitionist he did own slaves himself. After the Revolution, Hamilton helped found the Bank of New York, wrote many of the *Federalist* papers that argued for the ratification of the United States Constitution. He was later secretary of the Treasury and a key adviser to President George Washington. A flamboyant and controversial figure, Hamilton was killed in a duel with Aaron Burr in 1804.

The Grange

Hamilton built the grange on a 32-acre farm, then eight miles from the city, as a respite from politics. After his death, the grange had various owners until 1889, when it was donated to St. Luke's. The church moved it two blocks southeast, removed the front and side porches, and turned the house around so it could be squeezed into its current site. The American Scenic and Historic Preservation Society took over the house in 1924 and in 1933 opened it to the public. Since 1962, it has been run by the National Park Service, which hopes to move the house to a more spacious setting at the northern edge of St. Nicholas Park at W. 141st St. After being closed for seven years in the 1990s, the house has been stabilized and reopened.

Inside are three rooms with some of Hamilton's belongings (the chairs and dining room centerpiece, for instance), period furniture (the pianoforte), and reproductions of Hamilton's belongings (the painting of George Washington).

Across the street, at **280–298 Convent Ave** (1902; Henri Foucheaux), is a row of limestone-faced Beaux-Arts houses. Further up the street are **nos. 311–339** (1890; Adolph Hoak), a picturesque Romanesque row, and **nos. 320–328** (1890; Horace B. Hartwell) and **330–336** (1892; Robert Dry), all constructed at about the same time.

Just west of Convent Ave, at 467 W. 142nd St, is **Our Lady of Lourdes Church** (1904; O'Reilly Brothers; DL), an astonishing exercise in architectural recycling, incorporating parts of three unrelated buildings. The National Academy of Design (1865; Peter B. Wright), which once stood at Park Ave South and E. 23rd St, contributed its gray-and-white marble Ruskinian-Gothic facade. The apse and parts of the east wall came from the Cathedral of St. John the Divine when the east wall there was altered to make way for the Lady Chapel. The pedestals flanking the main entrance were salvaged from the department store millionaire A. T. Stewart's mansion (1867; John Kellum) on the northwest corner of 34th St and Fifth Ave.

Continue north to W. 145th St, turn right and then left onto St. Nicholas Ave. This section of Harlem—the heights between St. Nicholas and Edgecombe Aves, from about W. 143rd to W. 155th Sts—is known as **Sugar Hill,** where the black bourgeoisie lived the "sweet life." Among the prominent figures who lived here were musicians Duke Ellington, Count Basie, and Cab Calloway, and boxing champion Sugar Ray Robinson.

Walk north to W. 150th St, then east to St. Nicholas Place bordering Colonial Park. On the south corner are two former residences, a row house, and a handsome shingle-style structure, now part of the Dawn Hotel, a family shelter (6 St. Nicholas Place, 1888; 8 St. Nicholas Place, 1885).

At 10 St. Nicholas Place, on the northeast corner of W. 150th St, is the former **James A. Bailey House** (1888; Samuel B. Reed; DL). This rockface limestone mansion with Flemish gables and a tower was built by the circus entrepreneur James Anthony Bailey, partner of P. T. Barnum and cofounder of the Barnum & Bailey Circus, "the greatest show on earth." Today it is a funeral home. Next door is an attractive shingle-style home at 14 St. Nicholas Place (c. 1890).

At the north tip of Sugar Hill (and Harlem), turn right onto W. 155th St, then right again onto Edgecombe Ave to the **409 Edgecombe Avenue Apartments** (1917; Schwartz & Gross; DL). This 12-story building looking down on Central Harlem from its ridge was the crème de la crème of Harlem living from the 1930s to the 1950s. The writer, editor, and activist W. E. B. Dubois lived here (1944–51), as did the NAACP leader Walter White and his successor, Roy Wilkins, painter Aaron Douglas, singer and actor Julius Bledsoe (the original Joe in *Show Boat*), and civil rights lawyer and future Supreme Court justice Thurgood Marshall.

Polo Grounds Towers

Return to W. 155 St and turn right, heading east along the rocky spine of Harlem, known as **Coogan's Bluff.** The Polo Grounds Towers apartment buildings stand on the site of one of New York's most famous ball fields, the **Polo Grounds,** which stretched from W. 157th to W. 159th Sts between Eighth Ave and what is now the Harlem River Drive.

History

In 1876, the New York Giants began playing at what was called the Polo Grounds, in a field at 110th St and Fifth Ave where polo had once been played. When the city decided to build a traffic circle there in 1889, team owner John Day moved the team uptown and built a wooden ballpark under Coogan's Bluff. When the park burned down in 1911, it was replaced by a massive concrete-and-steel structure. Like the wooden park, its successor was bathtub-shaped with short fences in left and right fields and a "death valley" in center field (stretching 483 ft away at its longest part). In deepest centerfield (in fair territory) was a five-ft-high memorial to Eddie Grant, the first big leaguer to die in World War I.

Under its fiery manager John McGraw, the Giants were baseball's best team—playing in nine World Series from 1905 to 1924 and winning four championships. After 1912, the Yankees shared the Polo Grounds with the Giants for a decade, until McGraw forced the Yankees to leave when he became jealous of Babe Ruth's popularity; McGraw preferred singles and stolen bases to home runs.

In 1920 at the Polo Grounds, Yankee pitcher Carl Mays caused baseball's sole fatality when his pitch hit Cleveland shortstop Ray Chapman in the head, killing him. In 1951, in the final game of a National League playoff with the archrival Brooklyn Dodgers, Giants outfielder Bobby Thomson hit the "Shot Heard 'round the World," a ninth-inning, three-run homer into the left field stands to win the pennant. In the 1954 World Series, Willie Mays, the greatest Giant ever, made "The Catch," chasing down a seemingly unreachable ball in deep center field, then whirling and firing it back to the infield to stop two base runners from advancing.

Three years later, however, Mays and the Giants were gone, moving to San Francisco. Baseball returned briefly to the Polo Grounds when the New York Mets played the 1962–63 seasons there before moving to their permanent home in Queens. The football Giants had moved from the Polo Grounds to Yankee Stadium in 1955 after 30 years, and the ballpark was destroyed in 1964 to make way for the housing project.

Turn right (south) on **Macombs Place,** which takes its name from Alexander Macomb, a hero of the War of 1812, who had his home nearby. His son John built a toll bridge and dam in 1813, harnessing the river's power to run a mill. The dam obstructed shipping and turned much of the river upstream into a large millpond, and so in 1838 irate citizens bashed a hole in Macomb's dam with picks and shovels, restoring the river's navigability, an action later upheld by the courts. The **Macombs Dam Bridge** across the Harlem River at W. 155th St (opened 1895; Alfred Pancoast Boller; DL) is the modern descendant of that bridge, and the oldest metal truss swing bridge in the city.

Between W. 151st and W. 153rd Sts, Macombs Place, and the Harlem River Drive, is one of Harlem's oldest redevelopment projects, the **Harlem River Houses** (1937; Archibald M. Brown, Horace Ginsbern, Charles F. Fuller, Richard W. Buckley, John L. Wilson, Frank J. Forster, and Will R. Amon; DL). These four-story red brick walk-ups, grouped either around central open spaces or facing the river, represent a period of high hopes for public housing and redevelopment that were not later fulfilled. At a time when black families living in filthy Old and New Law tenements often paid half their incomes for rent, the fortunate 574 black families in these houses paid less than $32 monthly for rent and enjoyed such amenities as playgrounds, steam heat, cross ventilation, and tiled bathrooms.

The **Dunbar Apartments** (1928; Andrew J. Thomas; DL), six well-designed low-rise buildings bounded by W. 149th and W. 150th Sts, and Adam Clayton Powell Jr. and Frederick Douglass Blvds, represent a private attempt to solve ghetto housing problems. John D. Rockefeller Jr. constructed them as a housing cooperative for which tenants had to pay $150 down plus $50 a room and a monthly fee. All the apartments sold quickly and the project succeeded until the Depression, when most tenants lost their jobs and defaulted on their mortgages. Rockefeller foreclosed in 1936, returned the tenants' equity and thereafter offered the apartments as rentals. Named for the black poet Paul Laurence Dunbar, the buildings, grouped around a central courtyard, attracted an illustrious clientele: poet Countee Cullen, labor and civil rights activist A. Philip Randolph, dancer Bill "Bojangles" Robinson, and Arctic explorer Matt Henson.

29 · Upper Manhattan: Washington Heights and Inwood

Note: Since the distances on this route are long and the traffic not too heavy, the route lends itself to car travel.

Upper Manhattan, with a population of about a quarter-million, is largely unknown to visitors except for The Cloisters. It has some of the city's best scenery, several museums, some of the city's oldest homes, and many of its newest immigrants. The area from W. 155th St to Dyckman St is known as Washington Heights; north of that it is called Inwood.

At the northern tip of Manhattan, where the island narrows to a slender peninsula, the leveling effects of the city's developers are less evident than elsewhere in the city. Elevations rise to more than 200 ft, hardly alpine but high enough to affect the street plan, whose pleasant deviations from the downtown grid follow early roads built over Indian trails, which in turn followed the contours of the land.

Manhattan Bedrock

Two ridges of Manhattan schist—the bedrock upon which the city's first skyscrapers depended–run from north to south: the Fort Washington Ridge on the west and the Fort George Ridge on the east, which ends on Dyckman St. Between them is a basin known as the Inwood Lowlands, beneath whose soil and architectural accretions lies a base of Inwood marble, a stone more easily eroded than the schist. In Washington Heights, the valley between the ridges forms the natural roadbed for Broadway, formerly the Boulevard in this part of town until, in 1899, its full 15½–mile length from Bowling Green to Spuyten Duyvil was given one name.

History

As the names of the ridges suggest, the high ground had strategic importance during the Revolutionary War, when they were fortified with three outposts. Overlooking the Hudson River was Fort Washington, whose outlines are still recognizable in Bennett Park just west of Fort Washington Ave at W. 183rd Street. Fort Tryon was just to the north in the park now bearing the same name. Fort George was on the east ridge near the current intersection of Fort George Ave and Fort George Hill (formerly an extension of St. Nicholas Ave, renamed in 1962).

The area remained rural well into the 19C, attracting gentlemen farmers and others who located their country homes here, among them the newspaper publisher James Gordon Bennett and the naturalist John James Audubon.

Dinners on Horseback

The extravagant **C. K. G. Billings,** heir to a Chicago gas fortune, owned the land where Fort Tryon Park is today. He built a stable near the former Speedway, a road for fast trotters that opened in 1898 along the Harlem River. The 25,000-square-ft stable was designed by architect Guy Lowell and included quarters for entertaining guests and a lodge with views south to the Statue of Liberty. To celebrate the completion of the $200,000 stable in 1903, Billings invited 36 friends to an affair catered by Sherry's Restaurant; guests were to sit on oversize rocking horses. When huge crowds gathered to witness the party, Billings moved the gala to Sherry's at 44th St and Fifth Ave, where waiters were dressed as grooms, the floor was covered with grass and hay, and the food was served on little tables attached to the saddles of real horses, who had been brought upstairs in the freight elevator.

Soon after, Billings built a full-time residence on his property, with room for nearly two dozen servants and more than a dozen cars, autos having replaced horses in Billings's heart. There was also a swimming pool, bowling alley, squash court, and formal gardens.

The turning point for the region was the completion of the IRT subway in 1906, which hastened the end of aristocratic exclusivity at the northern end of the island. The process of urbanization was essentially completed by the arrival of the IND line in 1932.

Upper Manhattan then developed as a working-class residential community and has remained one. At first it was largely Irish, with Armenian and Greek communities; during the 1930s an influx of Jews fleeing Nazi Germany moved into the western half, while blacks from Harlem moved north to the east of Broadway. (Count Basie and Paul Robeson moved to a luxury building at 555 Edgecombe Ave.) Many of the Irish and Jews left in the 1960s and the neighborhood became increasingly Puerto Rican, black, and Cuban. In the 1980s, Washington Heights attracted more immigrants than any other neighborhood, most of them Dominicans. In neighboring Inwood, 80 percent of the arrivals were also from the Dominican Republic. By 1990, two-thirds of the 200,000 residents living in Washington Heights and Inwood were Latinos, a percentage that continues to grow. Some blacks and a dwindling number of German Jews and Irish remain, while Koreans, Soviet Jews, and white professionals seeking affordable rents with quick subway access to Midtown move in.

In the late 1980s and early 1990s, the region was devastated by the crack epidemic—not just because of use by poverty-stricken minorities, but because of Washington Heights's accessibility to drug-buying suburbanites from Westchester and northern New Jersey. The problem was compounded by the worst police corruption in a generation, which prompted the creation of the Mollen Commission. Ultimately 30 officers from the 34th Precinct were convicted of or pleaded guilty to crimes ranging from perjury to heroin dealing. Distrust of the police sparked several near riots. By the late 1990s, however, crime had dropped precipitously, and tensions have eased.

Washington Heights

Begin at Broadway and W. 155th St. Washington Heights runs north from W. 155th St to Dyckman St. The area around Audubon Terrace has its own distinctive identity.

Audubon Terrace
Subway: Broadway–Seventh Ave Local (1) to 157th St.
Bus: M4, M5

Between W. 155th and W. 156th Sts along the west side of Broadway, on the former estate of the ornithologist and painter John James Audubon, is the **Wash-**

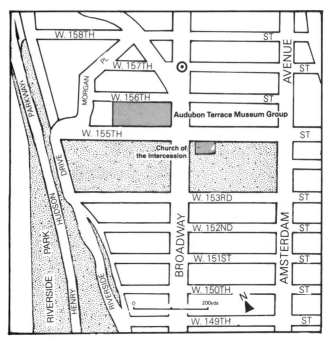

ington Heights Museum Group in Audubon Terrace. Formerly also the home of the Museum of the American Indian, which moved downtown in 1994, the site still hosts the Hispanic Society of America, the American Numismatic Society, and the American Academy of Arts and Letters. The buildings were financed largely by Archer Milton Huntington, son of Collis P. Huntington, the transcontinental railroad builder and steamship magnate. The younger Huntington's interests, however, ran to poetry, archaeology, and scholarship, not railroads, and he is remembered more for the money he gave away to libraries and museums than for the money that he made. In 1904 he started buying up parcels of the former Audubon estate for a kind of American acropolis, a concentration of cultural and intellectual institutions that would serve scholars and also be available to the public.

Originally the buildings looked north to W. 156th St. But around 1911, as apartment buildings began rising around Audubon Terrace, the architects changed their plan and faced the buildings inward across a paved courtyard. Nowadays the museum buildings, grand and classical in manner, seem incongruous in a modest neighborhood remote from the intellectual life of the city.

On the south side of Audubon Terrace are the former home of the Museum of the American Indian (1916); the Hispanic Society of America (1908), founded by Archer M. Huntington; and the American Numismatic Society (1908)—all designed by Charles Pratt Huntington, nephew of the donor; and the Administration Building (1923; William M. Kendall) of the American Academy of Arts and Letters. On the north side of the courtyard are (east to west) the former headquarters of the American Geographical Society (1916; Charles Pratt Huntington), now occupied by Boricua College; the courtyard of the Hispanic Society; and the auditorium and gallery of the American Academy of Arts and Letters (1930; Cass Gilbert).

The Plaza

Dominating the plaza is a group of statues by Anna Hyatt Huntington, already well known as a sculptor at the time of her marriage to Archer M. Huntington. The largest is a bronze equestrian **statue of El Cid Campeador** (1927) surrounded by four seated warriors, a piece that celebrates the legendary medieval hero who defended Spain against the Moors. Known for her animal sculptures, Anna Huntington also contributed the two limestone lions flanking the Hispanic Society entrance (1930) and the north building's limestone groups of bears, jaguars, boars, and vultures (1936), as well as the limestone equestrian **reliefs of Don Quixote,** Cervantes's legendary knight of La Mancha, and **Boabdil,** the last Moslem king of Granada (1942 and 1944); the inscriptions beneath them are taken from the poetry of her husband.

Hispanic Society of America

Broadway and W. 155th St, New York, NY 10032. ☎ (212) 926-2234. Web site: www.hispanicsociety.org. Open Tues–Sat 10–4:30; Sun 1–4. Closed Mon, major holidays, and for two weeks at Christmas (call for times). Free. Exhibitions, library. Gift shop. Not accessible to wheelchairs.

The Hispanic Society of America (founded 1904) houses a collection gathered mainly by Archer M. Huntington, whose fascination with Spanish and Portuguese culture dated from his first visit to Spain.

Today the collection ranges from prehistoric times through the periods of Roman and Moorish domination, to the present. The library contains over 100,000 volumes and manuscripts, mainly on Spanish and Portuguese history, literature, and art. The society recently acquired the empty building that formerly housed the American Indian Museum and plans to expand into that space.

Interior

The Main Court, two stories high and illuminated in part by skylights, with its archways of deep red terra-cotta ornately worked in Spanish Renaissance style, is one of the city's more remarkable interiors. On view are examples of Spanish painting from the Middle Ages to the present, with works from the Spanish Golden Age (1550–1700), the 19C, and the early 20C. There are paintings by El Greco, Diego Velázquez, Francisco de Zurbarán, Jusepe de Ribera, Alonso Cano, Bartolomé Esteban Murillo, and Juan Carreño de Miranda. The society is especially rich in works by Francisco Goya. In the **Sorolla Room,** murals by Joaquin Sorolla y Bastida, Spain's most celebrated artist at the turn of the 20C, depict street scenes and regional Spanish festivals. Also on display are decorative arts: ceramics, including Hispano-Moresque lusterware; gold and silver work; archaeological artifacts; sculpture; and textiles.

American Numismatic Society

Broadway and W. 155th St, New York, NY 10032. ☎ (212) 234-3130. Web site: www.amnumsoc.org. Open Tues–Fri 9–4:30. Closed Sat–Mon and holidays. Free. Exhibitions, lectures, library. Not accessible to wheelchairs.

The American Numismatic Society (founded 1858) contains an extraordinary collection of more than a million coins, bills, and medals, as well as the world's finest numismatic library. Although the society is scholarly in nature, the permanent exhibition on coinage, from prehistory to the present, should both profit (intellectually) and delight anyone interested in either history or money.

Note: The society is relocating in 2003 to new headquarters at 140 William St (corner of Fulton St).

Galleries

The museum has two galleries. In the **east gallery** are changing displays of coins and medals. In the **west gallery** a permanent exhibition, **The World of Coins,** surveys the history of coinage from about 1000 B.C., when coins were invented more or less contemporaneously in China, India, and Asia Minor, to the present day. Examples of ancient, medieval, and modern coins are displayed in settings that make their historical and artistic significance intelligible to the numismatically innocent.

American Academy of Arts and Letters

Broadway and W. 155th St, New York, NY 10032. ☎ (212) 368-5900. Call for dates of exhibitions. Open during exhibitions, Thurs–Sun 1–4. Not accessible to wheelchairs.

The American Academy of Arts and letters is an honorary organization dedicated to furthering interest in literature, the visual arts, and music.

The academy has two annual exhibitions: in March, an invitational exhibition of painting and sculpture by candidates for art awards; and in May, a show of works, including literary and musical manuscripts as well as fine art, by newly elected members and the winners of honors and awards. The permanent collection contains works by members.

History

In 1898 the National Institute of Arts and Letters was founded, its 250 members selected to represent the highest achievements of the era. Among the favored few were Henry Adams, William and Henry James, and two future presidents—Woodrow Wilson and Theodore Roosevelt, who were chosen for their literary output. In 1904 the American Academy, limited to 50 members, was founded as the inner circle of this august group. In 1976 the two organizations merged; in 1992 the members voted to have a single category of membership (limited to 250 members) and to take the present name. The roster also includes 75 foreign members and 10 special American members—for example, the choreographer Twyla Tharpe and the drummer Max Roach—whose work falls outside the established categories.

The Building

The Administration Building (1923; McKim, Mead & White) stands on the south side of the courtyard. The other building, on the north side, contains the north gallery and auditorium (1930; Cass Gilbert). The bronze doors at the entrance of the Administration Building were designed by Adolph A. Weinman and those leading to the galleries by Herbert Adams.

Boricua College

The building on the northeast corner of the complex, now occupied by Boricua College, was constructed as the home of the **American Geographical Society**, which moved in 1978 to the University of Wisconsin at Milwaukee, taking with it the largest map collection (some 325,000 maps) in the Western Hemisphere. Boricua College, a private four-year liberal arts school, offers courses designed to meet the educational needs of Spanish-speaking students.

Church of the Intercession

Directly across Broadway, on the southeast corner of W. 155th St, is the Church of the Intercession (1914; Cram, Goodhue & Ferguson; DL), formerly a chapel of Trinity Parish, built by the preeminent ecclesiastical architect Bertram G. Goodhue. The church complex, which includes a bell tower, cloister, parish house, and vicarage, has been praised for its site design, which recalls the time when the neighborhood was still rural and evokes the Gothic revival ideal of the country church. Noteworthy in the interior are the wooden ceiling supported by stone piers, the wood carving, the high altar inlaid with some 1,500 stones collected from the Holy Land and other shrines of early Christianity, and the wall tomb of its architect, Goodhue, decorated with reliefs of some of his buildings. Behind the church is part of the original graveyard, including the burial plot of John James Audubon.

Trinity Cemetery

Trinity Cemetery occupies a plot of land from Riverside Drive to Amsterdam Ave, W. 153rd to W. 155th Sts. Open 9–4:30 daily, entrance on W. 155th St near Riverside Drive.

History

In 1842 Trinity Parish, realizing the scarcity of land in Lower Manhattan, bought a 23-acre parcel from Richard F. Carman (the area was then known as Carmanville) and set aside part of it for a cemetery. Its hilly, broken topography sloping toward the Hudson River suggests the 19C landscape before developers exercised their leveling powers. When Broadway was extended northward, the parcel was cut in two and Trinity Corporation built a suspension bridge (1871; Vaux & Withers) joining the two halves, so that visitors could wander between them without having to descend to the street. Although the bridge was demolished in 1911, the high granite wall supporting its ornamental iron fence with gateways (1876), the gatehouse, and keeper's lodge (1883; Vaux & Radford) still remain.

In the eastern sector of the cemetery, near the Church of the Intercession, is the grave of **John James Audubon** (1785–1851), who after long struggles achieved fame and financial security with his *Birds of North America*. The gravestone, a tall brown Celtic cross decorated with reliefs of animals and birds, rests on a pedestal with sculpted rifles and a powder horn, a palette, and paintbrushes. Also in the eastern parcel is the grave of **Fernando Wood** (1812–1881), whose tall marker is surmounted with a shrouded urn. Wood was mayor of New York during the "Boss" Tweed years; he made his fortune selling questionable liquor to sailors and investing the returns in ships and real estate.

Enter the western parcel from Riverside Drive near W. 153rd St. **Clement Clarke Moore,** who is popularly thought to have written the verses beginning "'Twas the night before Christmas . . . ," is buried in the northwest part of the cemetery (lower slope near the Riverside Drive retaining wall and W. 155th St). Further up the hill is the Astor plot containing the remains of **John Jacob Astor** (1822–1890), philanthropist and grandson of the patriarch, and his wife, Charlotte Gibbes Astor. Astor, who administered the family estate during the later years of his life, funded the Astor Library, the Children's Aid Society, and the New York Cancer Hospital. Higher up the slope lies **Eliza Bowen Jumel** (see Morris-Jumel Mansion). **Alfred Tennyson Dickens,** son of the novelist, godson of the poet, lies on the hillside near Broadway and the W. 155th St gate. He died of a heart attack at the Hotel Astor while on a lecture tour and was buried here with great ceremony; Andrew Carnegie was one of the honorary pallbearers.

In a small park near W. 160th St and Edgecombe Ave is the Morris-Jumel Mansion and the Jumel Terrace Historic District, with a group of modest 19C row houses.

Morris-Jumel Mansion

W. 160th St and Edgecombe Ave, New York, NY 10032. ☎ (212) 923-8008. Information available at the Web sites of the Historic House Trust, www.preserve. org, and the New York City Parks and Recreation Department, http://nycparks. completeinet.net. Open Wed–Sun 10–4; Mon–Tues group tours by reservation. Admission charge. Tours, exhibitions, special events. Not accessible to wheelchairs.

Subway: Eighth Ave Local (C) to 163rd St–Amsterdam Ave. Bus: M2, M3, M18, M100, M101.

Five blocks north and a block-and-a-half east is one of the city's few remaining pre-Revolutionary buildings and Manhattan's oldest house, the Morris-Jumel Mansion (1765; remodeled with portico added, 1810; DL). Situated in small, peaceful Roger Morris Park at Jumel Terrace and W. 160th St, just east of St. Nicholas Ave, the home, now a museum, has a commanding view, nowadays of Yankee Stadium and the South Bronx.

Built as the summer home of Lt. Col. Roger Morris and his wife, Mary Philipse, the house still has its original Georgian hipped roof, wooden corner quoins, and wide-board facade.

History

Morris served under General Edward Braddock during the French and Indian War and was a friend of George Washington, who may have been romantically linked to Mary Philipse before her marriage. But when the war broke out, Morris remained loyal to the king and returned to England, as did other wealthy loyalists. Attracted by its view of the surrounding countryside, Washington used the house as his headquarters from Sept 14 to Oct 21, 1776, and was quartered here on Sept 16 when the successful Battle of Harlem Heights took place (see Morningside Heights History in Walk 27). When the Colonial Army left Manhattan, British and Hessian officers took over the house.

After the war, the land was farmed and the house became a tavern called Calumet Hall. As president, Washington returned for a celebratory dinner in

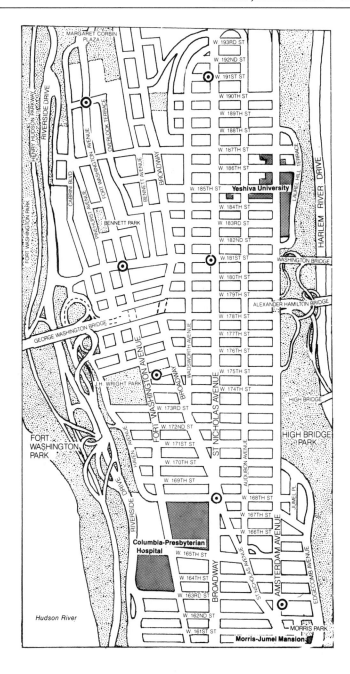

1790 with John, Abigail, and John Quincy Adams; Thomas Jefferson; and Alexander Hamilton.

Eliza Jumel

Eliza Bowen Jumel was born in Providence, Rhode Island, probably in 1775. Forced into prostitution by poverty, Eliza's fortunes turned in 1804 when she married Stephen Jumel, a wealthy French wine merchant. Wagging tongues said that the brilliant and beautiful Eliza, already Jumel's mistress, feigned a deathbed crisis to lure him into wedlock. In 1810, the Jumels bought the house and restored it, adding the portico and enlarging the doorway in the Federal style.

Mme. Jumel had an imperious tongue and boundless social ambition, which remained unfulfilled in New York. In 1815, the Jumels went to Paris, where they did find acceptance; she became an outspoken Bonapartiste, unwise in the first years after Napoleon's exile, and was asked to leave France. She brought back Empire furniture, an extensive wardrobe, and Francophilic tastes.

In 1832, Jumel was injured in a carriage accident and died. In 1833, Eliza, then about 58 and one of the city's richest women, married 77-year-old Aaron Burr. He was apparently fortune hunting and the marriage was stormy and brief; Burr only lived in the house about a month before they separated. Eliza sued for divorce, which was granted in 1836, ironically on the day of Burr's death.

Mme. Jumel lived on in the mansion, becoming eccentric and reclusive. She died there in 1865 at the age of 90. After 20 years of litigation, the house was leased in 1887 to Augustin Le Prince, who wanted to use it to demonstrate his invention, the motion picture camera. Le Prince never actually lived in the house and disappeared in Europe in 1890. In 1897, the patent for a motion picture camera was granted to Thomas Edison, again after years of litigation.

Interior

On view are 12 period rooms with furnishings that include many Jumel family pieces, notably a mahogany sleigh bed in which Napoleon is said to have slept. George Washington may have used the office on the second floor, which is furnished with 18C English and American furniture.

Environs

Across Jumel Terrace, between W. 160th and W. 162nd Sts, is **Sylvan Terrace,** once the carriage drive of the Morris-Jumel Mansion. Two rows of modest wooden houses, built (c. 1882) for workers, face one another across this quiet street.

East of the mansion lies Edgecombe Ave, whose name (from the Saxon *combe,* for "hill") implies its situation on the side of a ridge or bluff. **Highbridge Park** (1888; Calvert Vaux & Samuel Parsons Jr.), which runs from W. 155th St to Dyckman St along the east side of the escarpment, gets its name from **High Bridge** near W. 174th St, the oldest remaining bridge joining Manhattan to the mainland, i.e., the Bronx. High Bridge was originally called Aqueduct Bridge (1839–48; John B. Jervis; DL) and was part of the Croton system bringing water into the city from tributaries of the Hudson River in Westchester County. Built of closely spaced granite piers supporting 15 arches, resembling the aqueducts of the Roman campagna, the bridge once attracted tourists who enjoyed views from the promenade across the top (closed many years ago because of vandalism and crime). In 1923, during construction of the Harlem Ship Canal, the navy replaced several of the center spans with a steel arch to provide a wider ship channel. The campanile, **Highbridge Tower** (1872; attrib. John B. Jervis; DL), at W. 173rd St in the park, was once a water tower with a 47,000-gallon tank providing pressure to keep the water flowing in its regular 13 ft-per-mile downhill course to the reservoirs in Central Park.

Return east to the heart of Washington Heights. At W. 165th St and Broadway stands the former **Audubon Ballroom** (1913; Thomas W. Lamb), where black activist and civil rights leader Malcolm X was assassinated in 1965. The ballroom and the adjoining San Juan Theater, originally the Audubon Theater, an impressive movie palace in its prime, were acquired by the city in the mid-1970s. In the early 1990s Columbia University bought the property and incorporated it into a biotechnology research center with additional space for retail and a community mental health clinic. The destruction of the theater incited howls of protest from preservationists; the university preserved some of the polychrome terra-cotta facade (adorned with motifs that included fox heads, for theater owner William Fox) but razed the interior.

New York–Presbyterian Hospital, Columbia-Presbyterian Center

The New York–Presbyterian Hospital, Columbia-Presbyterian Center (1928–47; James Gamble Rogers, Inc.; additions, 1947–64; Rogers & Butler; 1964–74; Rogers, Butler & Burgun) fills the blocks from W. 165th to W. 168th Sts, between Broadway and Riverside Drive, on high ground along the hillside overlooking the Hudson River.

History

The site is fitting for one of the largest and most prestigious medical centers in the nation, founded in 1868 as the Presbyterian Hospital by James Lenox at Park Ave and E. 70th Street. Since 1911 it has embraced both the teaching and research facilities of Columbia University's College of Physicians and Surgeons and the patient care facilities of the Presbyterian Hospital. In the 1990s, the hospital spent $1.3 billion on new construction and renovations and also opened seven outpatient clinics in the community, which historically has felt estranged from this elite institution.

In 1997, the hospital merged with New York Hospital, uniting these two world-class academic medical centers. Together they are today known as New York–Presbyterian Hospital, the University Hospitals of Columbia and Cornell. The West Side campus (here) is the Columbia Presbyterian Center, while the East Side campus (around York Ave between E. 68th and E. 71st Sts) is affiliated with the Weill Medical College of Cornell University. New York–Presbyterian Hospital has about 2,268 beds and a staff of 13,658, with 6,217 physicians.

The Columbia Presbyterian Center also includes Babies' and Children's Hospital, whose old-fashioned name harks back to its founding in 1887. The world's first successful pediatric heart transplant surgery took place here. The hospital has the nation's largest heart transplant program and the nation's largest burn unit. The Sloane Hospital for Women was the first to perform amniocentesis and the first to perform surgery on a fetus in utero. The new Complementary Care Center is one of the first academic-based centers to investigate alternative methods of healing.

On Broadway and W. 175th St stands the former **Loew's 175th Street Theater** (1930; Thomas W. Lamb), whose facade mixes Oriental, Indian, Mayan, Islamic, and classical motifs. Lamb, a famous theater architect, said he chose this exotic mélange to create an atmosphere in which the mind was "free to frolic." In the theater's heyday, the lobby was a modern, gilded version of a Moorish seraglio and the auditorium was redolent with Byzantine and Romanesque elements. In the 1970s the theater became the pulpit of the Reverend Ike, a charismatic preacher.

George Washington Bridge

The approaches to the George Washington Bridge (1931; Othmar H. Ammann, engineer, and Cass Gilbert), cut across town between W. 179th and W. 180th Sts. Like the Brooklyn Bridge, the George Washington Bridge, which crosses the Hudson River to Fort Lee, New Jersey, and forms part of the interstate highway I-95, represented a step forward in technology, while also becoming an object of beauty and imaginative inspiration. Its 3,500 ft span doubled the record for suspension bridges and its soaring steel towers and curving cables inspired Charles Edouard Jenneret (better known as Le Corbusier) to call it "the only seat of grace in the disordered city."

History

A trans-Hudson Bridge had been contemplated as early as 1868, when the state of New Jersey authorized one at the southern boundary of Union Township, a move the state of New York ignored. Conflicting interests and difficulties in financing and engineering kept the involved agencies squabbling until the Port of New York Authority was formed in 1921 and brought the project to fruition. Chief engineer Othmar H. Ammann, who had emigrated from Switzerland in 1904 expressly to participate in American bridge projects, studied the political, financial, and structural problems surrounding previous attempts at a Hudson River crossing. It was he who proposed an automobile crossing, not a railroad bridge, thus cutting costs and anticipating America's romance with the internal combustion engine. The Port Authority funded the bridge ($59 million) by selling bonds, a difficult task in the years before 1929, when stock prices were booming. Groundbreaking ceremonies took place in 1927, and four years later 5,000 people came to listen to speeches marking the completion of the project. When the bridge was opened to the public, the first to cross were two boys from the Bronx on roller skates.

Between 1958 and 1962, a lower deck was constructed without disturbing traffic on the existing bridge, a feat accomplished by raising 76 steel sections from below, either from the shores or from barges. The lower deck, snidely nicknamed the Martha Washington Bridge, brought the total cost to $215.8 million and took longer to build than the original structure but increased its capacity 75 percent, making it the world's only 14-lane suspension bridge. Today, it remains one of the world's busiest, with about 54 million cars using it annually in the eastbound direction (where the tolls are taken; if the traffic is equal in both directions, then the bridge carries more than 108 million cars each year).

On the New York side the huge U-shaped anchorage in Fort Washington Park also serves as a roadway arch. To avoid placing such a bulky object on the New Jersey Palisades, Ammann had workers tunnel into the rock of the cliffs, place eyebar chains in the tunnels (which were large enough to accommodate four trolley tracks), attach the cables to the chains, and fill the tunnels with cement. The 604-ft New Jersey tower stands 76 ft out in the river, but the 604-ft New York tower is on land—Ammann needed the bridge to connect the two sides at about the same elevation (300 ft) and placed the towers where they could best carry the cables' weight. The original plans called for sheathing the towers in masonry, for which Cass Gilbert produced appropriate designs, but by 1931 the Port Authority, having just bought the Holland Tunnel, was unwilling to spend money for cosmetic purposes.

Bridge Statistics	
Length of span between anchorages	4,760 ft
Width of bridge	119 ft
Height of roadways above mean high water	115 ft and 212 ft
Number of strands in each cable	26,474 wires
Total length of steel wire in cables	105,000 miles
Height of towers above water	604 ft
Tons of steel	113,000
Tons of cable wire	28,000
Cubic yds of masonry	200,000

At the east end of the George Washington Bridge, between Fort Washington and Wadsworth Aves, is the **George Washington Bridge Bus Station** (1963; Pier Luigi Nervi and the Port of New York Authority). The concrete wings of its butterfly-shaped roof rise to allow the fumes from the buses to escape from beneath. The station, which connects with the Eighth Ave Express (A) subway, serves some 11 million commuters yearly.

The **Bridge Apartments** (1964; Brown & Guenther), between W. 178th and W. 179th Sts, Wadsworth and Audubon Aves, represent an early attempt to use the air rights over a highway for residential purposes. Unfortunately the roadway is not completely decked over and the noise, smell, and dirt from this major artery rise to assault the senses of those living above.

Little Red Lighthouse

At W. 181st St and Pinehurst Ave, a set of steps descends via a footbridge at Riverside Drive and an underpass at the Henry Hudson Pkwy to Fort Washington Park along the river. Just under the tower of the bridge stands the Little Red Lighthouse

(1921), whose light and foghorn warned ships of the shoals off Jeffrey's Hook until 1947. The lighthouse, a conical iron tower, stands 40 ft high and has an observation deck reached by a spiral staircase. The Northern Park Rangers give occasional tours: ☎ (212) 304-2365.

History

Moved here from Sandy Hook, New Jersey, the lighthouse was commissioned in 1921. When the navigational lights on the George Washington Bridge took over its function, the lighthouse went up for auction (1951) but was saved by the pleas of admirers, many of whom had read Hildegarde Hoyt Swift's children's tale *The Little Red Lighthouse and the Great Gray Bridge* (1942), in which the lighthouse symbolized the importance of small things in a big world. Today the Parks Department maintains the lighthouse.

Bennett Park

Return to Pinehurst Ave. Bennett Park, between W. 183rd and W. 185th Sts, Fort Washington and Pinehurst Aves, stands on the site of **Fort Washington,** a Revolutionary War fortification. The park contains the **highest natural elevation in Manhattan,** a rocky outcropping that reaches 265.05 ft above sea level.

History

After defeats on Long Island and in Manhattan, Washington led his troops north, leaving behind a garrison at Fort Washington, a crudely fortified earthwork with five bastions under the command of Col. Robert Magaw. On Nov 16, 1776, Hessians scaled the outworks on Long Hill (the ridge in what is now Fort Tryon Park) from the north and east and attacked the Americans. General Cornwallis invaded Manhattan across the Harlem River at the present site of 201st St; the 42nd Highlanders crossed the Harlem more or less where High Bridge now stands, and British troops led by Lord Percy marched up from downtown, while warships bombarded the fort from the Hudson. The defenders of the outworks were killed or pushed back into the fort, which quickly surrendered after it became clear that the American troops were outnumbered. The loss of 54 lives and the capture of 2,634 of Washington's best-equipped troops were severe blows to the ragged, inexperienced Colonial army.

In 1871, the land where the fort stood was bought by James Gordon Bennett, founder of the *New York Herald.* In 1901, the Sons of the American Revolution, with the permission of James Gordon Bennett Jr., built a monument (Charles R. Lamb) to commemorate the Battle of Fort Washington. The younger Bennett was said to have intended to give the city the land for a park, but he died in 1918 without mentioning it in his will. Although the property was divided and sold, the part where Fort Washington stood was kept intact at the request of the American Scenic and Historical Preservation Society. In 1928, the city bought the site of the fort and additional land to create a park. Paving stones in the 1.8-acre park mark the outlines of the fort.

Pinehurst Ave, which runs along the west side of the park, is named after the country estate of C. P. Bucking. Facing the park, from W. 183rd to W. 185th Sts, are the **Hudson View Gardens,** built by Morningside Heights developer Charles Paterno (1924; George F. Pelham) in the Tudor style with peaked roofs and landscaped indentations. The apartment complex features small private streets between the buildings, creating a peaceful enclave. Like many of the other co-ops of the day, it was "restricted," i.e., no minority or Jewish tenants were allowed.

Fort Tryon Park

About five blocks north is 66-acre Fort Tryon Park, which contains The Cloisters, the branch of the Metropolitan Museum of Art devoted to medieval art. It has landscaped terraces, lawns, and gardens, along with wonderful views of the Hudson River.

Park History

In 1909, and later in 1916, John D. Rockefeller Jr. bought property (some of it from C. K. G. Billings's estate) but was initially stymied in his effort to raze the estate and give the land to the city for Fort Tryon Park. Architectural admirers of Billings's lodge and stable persuaded Rockefeller to rent out the buildings while he negotiated with the city about the park. In 1925, a fire consumed the mansion. At an elevation of 250 ft above the waterline, Billings's much-heralded private pumping system failed, as did the city's water pressure. Hundreds of thousands of gawkers watched the mansion burn.

Eventually, Rockefeller's gift was accepted by the city, and Fort Tryon Park was completed in 1935. The landscape architect was Frederick Law Olmsted Jr., son of Central Park's designer. Visible from Riverside Drive near the car entrance are the gateposts and part of the arcaded drive of the former Billings estate.

Margaret Corbin Drive

From the plaza at Fort Washington Ave and Mother Cabrini Blvd, a roadway and a footpath enter the park. The roadway is named after **Margaret Cochran Corbin,** a 26-year-old Revolutionary War heroine who fought beside her husband John in the Battle of Fort Washington. When he was killed, she took over his gun and continued firing until she herself was severely wounded. After the war, Corbin, known familiarly as "Captain Molly," became a domestic servant and was known to have an unbridled tongue and an indifference to the niceties of dress. She died in 1800 and was buried in modest circumstances until the Daughters of the American Revolution had her body exhumed and reinterred in the Post Cemetery at West Point.

The Footpath

The footpath leads past flower gardens and the café (open all year 10–5 with slight variations according to the weather) to the site of the old fort. Built in the summer of 1776 as an outwork to Fort Washington to the south, it fell (Nov 16, 1776) to Hessian mercenaries. After the American defeat, the British renamed it Fort Tryon in honor of William Tryon, last British governor of New York (1771–78). From the site of the fort, a path leads north along the side of the hill to The Cloisters, offering beautiful views of the river and the New Jersey Palisades.

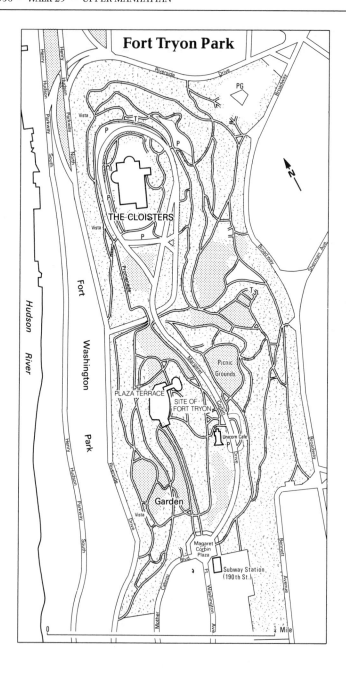

Fort Tryon Park

Riverside Drive

PG

Henry
Hudson
Parkway
South

Henry
Hudson
Parkway
North

Vista

P

T

P

THE CLOISTERS

P

Vista

P

Promenade

Fort

Washington

Park

Hudson

River

Henry
Hudson
Parkway
South

Riverside
Drive

T

Margaret Corbin Drive

Picnic
Grounds

PLAZA TERRACE

SITE OF
FORT TRYON

Unicorn Cafe
P

Garden

Vista

Magaret
Corbin
Plaza

Blvd

Fr. Washington Ave

Mother Cabrini Blvd

Bennett Avenue

Broadway

Sherman Ave

Overlook

Subway Station
(190th St.)

0   ¼ Mile

The Cloisters

Fort Tryon Park, New York, NY 10040. ☎ (212) 923-3700. Web site: www.met museum.org (then click on "The Collection"). Open March through Oct, Tues–Sun 9:30–5:15; Nov through Feb, Tues–Sun 9:30–4:45. Closed Mon, Thanksgiving, Dec 25, Jan 1. Admission by voluntary contribution; you must pay something, but the amount is discretionary. Limited free car parking around museum.

Exhibitions; gallery talks for adults, Sat at 12 and 2. Museum café in covered walkway near Trie Cloister, open May–Oct during museum hours. New Lease Café in park south of museum, open every day except Mon; ☎ (212) 568-5323. Picnicking in park. Programs of recorded music, concerts, special events, and exhibitions. Limited wheelchair accessibility. Restrooms accessible to wheelchairs.

Subway: Eighth Ave Express (A) to 190th St. Exit by elevator, take M4 bus or walk through park to museum. Bus: M4. Car: Henry Hudson Pkwy north to first exit after the George Washington Bridge.

The Cloisters, the only branch museum of the Metropolitan Museum of Art, is located at the north end of Fort Tryon Park. Named after the medieval cloisters incorporated within the building, it has outstanding collections of medieval art and architecture, lovely gardens, and beautiful natural surroundings.

The Building

The museum building, large parts of the collection, and Fort Tryon Park were donated by John D. Rockefeller Jr., who also bought land across the Hudson River and donated it as a park to New Jersey, ensuring an unspoiled view from the museum. The building (1934–38; Charles Collens of Allen, Collens & Willis) was not copied from a single model, but was developed around pieces of medieval architecture recovered from five ruined French monasteries and other sites, with an effort to make the modern additions as unobtrusive as possible. Cloisters—quadrangles surrounded by a walkway or arcade—often had gardens in the center, and the three courtyard gardens at the museum are based on information from medieval documents and works of art. While the medieval collections at the Metropolitan Museum itself have a broad geographical and chronological focus, those at The Cloisters emphasize the Romanesque and Gothic periods in Europe.

Highlights
The Unicorn Tapestries
The *Altarpiece of the Annunciation* triptych in the Spanish (Campin) Room
The medieval gardens

Interior

The museum is organized more or less chronologically, beginning with the Romanesque Hall and ending with the Late Gothic Hall and the Froville Arcade. The **Romanesque Hall** incorporates three doorways suggesting the evolution of the sculptured church portal in the 12C–13C: a 12C French Romanesque doorway, the late-12C Reugny doorway (transitional between the Romanesque and Gothic styles), and a magnificent 13C Burgundian Gothic doorway. The **Fuentidueña Chapel** is decorated with limestone sculpture, including large pier figures of St. Martin (left) and an Annunciation group (right). The frescoes date from the 12C and depict the Virgin and Child with the three magi and the archangels Michael and Gabriel, the Temptation of Christ, and the Healing of the Blind Man and Raising of Lazarus.

The **Saint-Guilhem Cloister** is built around a series of capitals, shafts, and columns (before 1206) from a Benedictine abbey near Montpellier. The capitals are carved with motifs including historical themes, stylized acanthus leaves, naturalistic vine leaves, and animals; several of the column shafts are handsomely carved.

Incorporated in the walls of the **Langon Chapel** is stonework from a 12C church near Bordeaux. The wooden Romanesque *Enthroned Virgin and Child* is one of the few surviving wood sculptures from an artistically important area of Burgundy.

With the exception of the plaster vaults and the floor, the **Chapter House from Pontaut** is a reconstruction, stone by stone and brick by brick, of a room from a 12C abbey in Gascony. The chapter house served as a meeting room where the monks gathered to discuss monastery business. The pink-and-white marble elements of the **Cuxa Cloister** come from a 12C Benedictine monastery in the eastern Pyrenees. The reconstruction, about half the size of the original, was made according to evidence of fragments, on-site excavations, and notes and drawings from the 18C–19C. The simplest and perhaps the earliest capitals are undecorated; more elaborate ones include a capital with rearing lions at the corners and a group with leaf forms and primitively designed heads. In the center is a garden with fragrant plants.

The **Nine Heroes Tapestry Room** features about two-thirds of a 14C set of French tapestries, one of only two known existing sets from that period. The Nine Heroes—Hector, Alexander, and Julius Caesar (pagan), David, Joshua, and Judas Maccabeus (Hebrew), and Arthur, Charlemagne, and Godfrey of Bouillon (Christian)—were a popular theme of medieval legend. The set of tapestries, cut up and dispersed over the centuries, has been reassembled from 95 fragments.

In the **Early Gothic Hall** are examples of 13C–14C sculpture, painting, and architectural elements (ceiling beams and stained glass windows). From this room a short stairway leads down to the **Gothic Chapel** with tomb sculpture and stained glass. The tomb effigy of Jean d'Alluye shows the young man fully armed, with his hands joined in prayer and his feet resting against a crouching lion.

Next in chronological order is the **Bonnefont Cloister,** whose gray-white marble columns and capitals come from a Cistercian abbey near Toulouse. The capitals (first half of the 14C) are carved to represent natural and imaginary plants. The garden is planted with herbaceous plants cultivated during the Middle Ages.

Next to the Bonnefont Cloister is the **Trie Cloister** from a former Carmelite convent southwest of Toulouse, destroyed except for the church in 1571 by the Huguenots. The capitals, probably carved between 1484 and 1490, show scenes from the Bible, saints' legends, and coats of arms of local families. The plants of this garden were selected from those shown in the Unicorn Tapestries.

In the **Glass Gallery** windows are 75 panels and roundels of stained glass (15C–early 16C), usually found in secular buildings but with sacred subjects. Be-

The Cloisters, which houses part of the Metropolitan Museum's medieval collection, incorporates architectural elements from churches, monasteries, and other medieval European buildings. Pictured here is the Bonnefont Cloister from late-13C or early-14C France. (Marilynn K. Yee, New York Times pictures)

yond the doorway to the Trie Cloister is elaborately carved woodwork from a house at Abbeville that once opened onto a spiral staircase.

In the **Treasury** are smaller objects of exceptional quality and value used for religious and state ceremonies; there are examples of Limoges enamels, illuminated manuscripts, including the *Belles Heures of the Duke of Berry;* carved ivories; reliquaries; a flabellum used for keeping flies off the eucharistic vessels; and chalices. The walrus tusk ivory cross, a 12C English Romanesque cross with more than 100 carved figures, attributed to the abbey of Bury Saint Edmunds, is one of the outstanding objects in the collection.

Return to the main floor and the **Boppard Room** with six late-Gothic stained glass panels (15C), originally made for the church of a Carmelite convent at Boppard on the Rhine. Beyond the Tapestry Hall is the **Hall of Unicorn Tapestries** with a famous series of six late-medieval tapestries along with fragments of another that depict *The Hunt of the Unicorn,* a legendary creature rich in both religious and secular symbolism during the Middle Ages. The Unicorn Tapestries, donated by John D. Rockefeller Jr., are remarkable for their naturalistically rendered animals and flowers: over 100 different species of plants appear, of which 85 are recognizable. The most famous panel, *The Unicorn in Captivity,* may have been woven as a separate work, not part of the series. The seed-laden pomegranates shown in the tapestry were medieval symbols for fertility, and the tapestries may have been woven to celebrate a wedding.

The **Spanish Room,** sometimes known as the **Campin Room,** with its 15C painted Spanish ceiling, has been decorated like a room in a house whose furnishings serve as a backdrop to the *Altarpiece of the Annunciation* by Robert Campin (c. 1425), an early Flemish masterpiece. The *Altarpiece* has three panels: two kneeling donors on the left, the central Annunciation, and St. Joseph in his workshop on the right. The **Late Gothic Hall** contains late-15C works, including sculpture and painting. The **Froville Arcade,** just outside the Late Gothic Hall, is built around nine pointed arches from the 15C Benedictine priory of Froville in eastern France. The arches, grouped in threes and separated by buttresses as they were in their original setting, are typical of 14C–15C cloisters, which depended for effect on their proportions rather than on great skill in decoration or stonecutting, as did earlier Gothic and Romanesque arcades.

Other Points of Interest: Two Bridges over the Harlem River

In the eastern section of Washington Heights are two bridges that cross the Harlem River: the **Washington Bridge** (1888), at W. 181st St, and the **Alexander Hamilton Bridge** (1964), between W. 178th and W. 179th Sts, which carries the Cross Bronx Expressway into Manhattan.

The Washington Bridge (best seen from a boat tour around the island, the Major Deegan Expwy across the Harlem River, or Laurel Hill Terrace, located a block east of Amsterdam Ave between W. 183rd and W. 188th Sts) is one of the city's most handsome bridges. A double steel arch (each arch 510 ft across) spans the river and the railroad tracks on its east bank. The present design is a simplified version of a prize-winning plan submitted to the city by C. C. Schneider. Granite viaducts with masonry arches lead from high bluffs on both the Manhattan and Bronx sides, 151.6 ft above mean high water, making the bridge 16 ft higher than the Brooklyn Bridge and 6 inches higher than the Statue of Liberty.

Yeshiva University

North of the bridges sits Yeshiva University, between W. 183rd and W. 187th Sts along Amsterdam Ave (seven blocks east of Fort Washington Ave). The Yeshiva evolved from the first Jewish parochial school (1886) in the nation and a theological seminary founded ten years later. The Main Building (1928; Charles B. Meyers Assocs.), on the southwest corner of W. 186th St and Amsterdam Ave, is an exotic Near Eastern conglomeration of minarets, towers, arches, domes, and buttresses executed in orange stone, ceramic tile, copper, and brass. The school provides undergraduate and graduate education in the arts, sciences, and Jewish studies, while the associated **Rabbi Isaac Elchanan Theological Seminary** trains rabbis and cantors. The main exhibition space of the Yeshiva University Museum has moved downtown to the Center for Jewish History (see Walk 12), but exhibitions are still held here in the Leiferman Galleries.

Yeshiva University Campus Galleries

2520 Amsterdam Ave (at W. 185th St), New York, NY 10033. ☎ (212) 960-5390. Web site: www.yu.edu/museum/yum_at_cjh.htm. Open Mon–Thurs 10–5. Closed Jewish holidays. Free. Limited wheelchair accessibility.

Subway: Broadway–Seventh Ave Local (1, 9) to 181st St. Eighth Ave Express (A) to 181st St. Walk east to Amsterdam Ave. Bus: M101.

In addition to changing exhibitions from the permanent collection, there is a long-term installation, **From Aleph to Tav: Collecting at the Turn of the Century,** which focuses on recent acquisitions of artworks, silver, textiles, and photographs.

Inwood

North of Dyckman St is the Inwood section of Manhattan, which is two-fifths greenbelt. Inwood Hill Park, the city's only primeval park, and Isham Park take up its entire northwest corner. The neighborhood was developed largely in the 1930s and still has many buildings from that period. In the northeast corner is a transport hub with subway yards and a brick bus barn. Nearby are a Con Ed generating station and a number of garages, car washes, and other service industries.

Dyckman House

4881 Broadway (at W. 204th St), New York, NY 10034. ☎ (212) 304-9422. Open Tues–Sun 11–4. Closed Mon, holidays. Admission free. Not accessible to wheelchairs.

Subway: Eighth Ave Express (A) to 207th St. Broadway–Seventh Ave Local (1) to Dyckman St; walk north three blocks. Bus: M104 to 125th St, transfer to the M5 to 168th St, transfer to the M100 to Dyckman House; takes up to an hour from Midtown depending on traffic and bus connections.

At the corner of W. 204th St and Broadway is Dyckman House (1783; DL), the only Dutch colonial farmhouse remaining on Manhattan. Situated across from a gas station, the house is a surprising survivor from the 18C. It remains only through the determination of two Dyckman descendants who bought it in 1915, restored it, furnished it with family furniture, and donated it to the city, thereby rescuing it from the ambitions of an apartment developer.

History

The Dyckmans were one of early Manhattan's most prominent families. Jan Dyckman arrived in 1661 from Westphalia in Germany via Holland. A bookkeeper and woodcutter, Dyckman went into partnership with Jan Nagel (after whom nearby Nagle Ave is named) and began buying farmland. Nagel and Dyckman first acquired 74 acres, which they leased in 1677 to tenant farmers for two hens a year for seven years provided that the tenants planted 50 fruit trees a year, a policy which resulted in extensive peach, apple, and cherry orchards. Eventually the Dyckman farm became the largest in Manhattan and remained active for 200 years, until 1868. The builder of the present house was William Dyckman, a grandson of Jan Dyckman.

Exterior

Once the center of the 300-acre Dyckman farm, whose meadows reached to the Harlem River, the present house was built to replace an earlier Dyckman homestead destroyed by the British during the Revolutionary War. It is believed to incorporate materials from the original house, which was probably not on this site. Constructed of brick and wood on a fieldstone foundation, it has the overhanging eaves and gambrel roof of the Dutch colonial style.

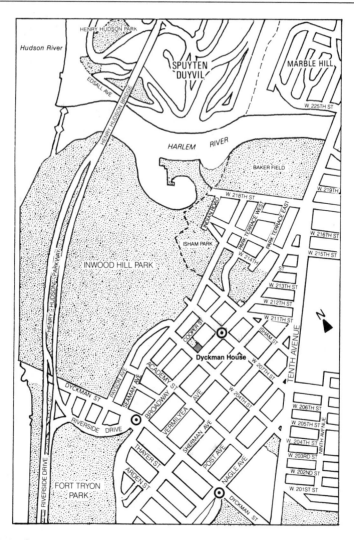

Interior

Inside are six period rooms decorated with early American furnishings. On the ground floor is a winter kitchen, its staircase built around a slab of Inwood marble too large to dig out. A small room behind the dining room contains relics, many of them from the Revolutionary War, excavated in the neighborhood during the first decades of the 20C.

Behind the house are a reconstructed smokehouse and a well. In another corner of the garden is the reconstruction of a small military shed, similar to those used by the British during the Revolutionary War, when both British and Hessian soldiers camped on the Dyckman farm.

Inwood Street Names

Like Dyckman St and Nagle Ave, other street names in this part of Inwood commemorate early landowners. **Vermilyea Ave** is a corruption of the name of Isaac Vermeille, who settled nearby in 1663. **Post Ave** is named after a family whose early settlers called themselves Postmael. John Seaman, a captain who arrived in 1630 and 20 years later owned 12,000 acres on Long Island, gave his name to **Seaman Ave,** near which his descendants lived. **Sherman Ave** is named after a humble family who lived along a little waterway called Shermans Creek, which flowed into the Harlem River; the Shermans seem to have settled along the creek in about 1807 and in 1815 occupied a fisherman's shack at the bottom of Fort George Hill. **Sickles St** brings to mind the family of that name whose American progenitor, Zacharias Sickels, followed Peter Stuyvesant here from Curaçao in 1655. **Arden St** recalls Jacob Arden, a butcher, whose land lay between 170th and 177th Sts. **Ellwood St** was named in 1911, but no one knows the honoree. When the street was being cut and graded, however, workers found the remains of crude military huts, presumably from Hessian soldiers during the Revolutionary War, a belief based on the fact that the British and their allies occupied this part of New York for most of the war. As the dates of these street names suggest, the Inwood section of Manhattan was developed relatively late. Many of its apartment buildings show the brickwork patterns, typical setbacks, construction materials, and window forms of the Art Deco architecture of the 1930s.

Two blocks north of Dyckman House, Isham St crosses Broadway. The street is named after a prominent family who owned the surrounding land and in 1912 gave 20 acres to the city for Isham Park. The main part of the park adjoins Inwood Hill Park and is indistinguishable from it, while the smaller sections to the east lie south of 214th St.

To the north lie the Columbia University athletic grounds. **Baker Field,** including Lawrence A. Wein Stadium (1905–30; rebuilt 1986), named for a generous alumnus, is the stadium where the Columbia University football team has pursued its recently melancholy fortunes. Also on the grounds at 5145 Broadway (opposite W. 220th St) is the **Allen Pavilion, New York–Presbyterian Hospital,** (1988; Skidmore, Owings & Merrill), a community hospital and acute care facility.

Indian Rd, formerly Isham Ave, is a small street intersecting W. 218th St at its western end along the border of Inwood Hill Park. It was renamed in 1911, when evidence of an Indian settlement was uncovered in the park lowlands. The Indians belonged to the Weequaesgeek tribe, who also inhabited much of what is now Westchester County, and the settlement was called *Shorakapkock* (generally translated "between the hills"), a name reflected in modern Kappock St in the nearby Bronx.

At the west end of the ball fields near the beginning of the woods is a boulder in the pathway bearing a plaque that marks the site as the place where Peter Minuit "bought" Manhattan Island from Native Americans. Historians, however, generally believe that the famous transaction transpired in the vicinity of the Dutch settlements around the Battery.

Inwood Hill Park

The 196 acres of Inwood Hill Park stretch west to the Hudson River, north to the Harlem River, and south to Dyckman St. It is Manhattan at its most primitive, with a wide variety of trees and wildflowers and steep rocky slopes (which saved the park from development). On the lagoon at its northern edge remains the sole surviving patch of salt marsh in Manhattan. Like the rest of Washington Heights–Inwood, it consists of two ridges with a valley between. Geologically, the park is a microcosm of the city at large: there are outcroppings of Manhattan schist, exposures of Inwood marble, and boulders of Fordham gneiss, as well as glacial striations and potholes, scoured out of the bedrock by the gravel-bearing water of the melting glacier.

History

The park became the last refuge for Manhattan's Native Americans as the white settlers pushed them back. There are still caves where the Indians either stored food or retreated for emergency shelter; pottery shards, arrowheads, and other artifacts have been found there. A number of Native Americans remained in the area into the 19C, some of them intermingling with the black slave laborers who worked the Dyckman and Nagel farms.

During the Revolution a five-sided earthen fort occupied the high ground sometimes known as Cock Hill (perhaps a corruption of the Indian *Shorakapkock*), part of a chain of fortifications commanding the river. British and Hessian troops occupied the area. Pewter buttons bearing Hessian regimental insignias, as well as blue-patterned earthenware and musket shot, have been found in the park.

Until the 1930s the park remained in its pristine state. When the Henry Hudson Pkwy was developed and pushed through the park, some of the park was landscaped, and during the WPA era of the Depression, the paths were laid out. Nowadays the park is overgrown and wild again, but the ten miles of walking paths remain.

Beyond the grassy fields of the park flows the Harlem River, which was not navigable to the Hudson River until 1895, when a channel was cut through a bulbous promontory that formerly extended north of where Baker Field and Ninth Ave are presently located. Before then a narrow stream, Spuyten Duyvil Creek, flowed in a looping curve marked by the present boundary of Manhattan.

Spuyten Duyvil

Some historians believe that Henry Hudson first anchored in Spuyten Duyvil Creek and was there received by a party of friendly Native Americans. The origin of the creek's strange name is unknown. One explanation was offered by Washington Irving in his *Knickerbocker's History of New York:*

Anthony Van Corlaer, sent by Peter Stuyvesant to warn the settlers north of the creek of an imminent British attack, reached the waterway in the midst of such a storm that he could find no one to ferry him across. Emboldened by a few swigs from his flask, Van Corlaer swore he would swim across *"en spijt den Duyvil"* (in spite of the devil), threw himself into the wild waters, and drowned. Others suggest that *spuyten* could refer to a cold spring that once spouted in the area presently covered by the ballfields and *duyvil* could be a corruption of *duyvel*, a Dutch word for meadow.

Henry Hudson Bridge

To the west can be seen the curve of the Henry Hudson Bridge (1936; Emil F. Praeger), which spans the Harlem River with a fixed steel arch 2,000 ft long, and at its highest point is 142.5 ft above the river. The bridge (span 800 ft) was part of the West Side Improvement project, conceived and brought to fruition by Robert Moses during the 1930s; it joins two sections of the Henry Hudson Pkwy, which links the West Side Hwy with the Saw Mill Pkwy to the north. It opened on Dec 12, 1936. The bridge was built originally as a single-deck, four-lane structure because the bankers underwriting the project would only authorize $3.1 million in bonds, unable to believe that commuters would choose a toll bridge over the nearby free bridge on Broadway. When the bridge quickly proved itself financially viable, the second deck was added.

Marble Hill

When the ship channel (400 ft wide and 15 ft deep) was finished, Spuyten Duyvil Creek was filled, making the area now known as Marble Hill physically a part of the Bronx. Over the years the residents of Marble Hill (currently about 7,000) have been embroiled in a debate over the political affiliation of their 52 acres. The battle reached a climax in 1939 when Bronx Borough President James J. Lyons climbed to high ground in Marble Hill, planted the Bronx flag, and claimed the territory for his borough. In 1984 the State Supreme Court ruled that Marble Hill belonged politically to the borough of Manhattan, but is part of Bronx County, constituting the single exception to the coincidence of the five counties and the five city boroughs. Today Marble Hill is a quiet neighborhood whose apartment houses are relieved by occasional old frame buildings. This 52-acre piece of Manhattan now geographically indistinguishable from the Bronx was given its name at the end of the 19C because of its terrain and its former quarries.

Borough of the Bronx/Bronx County

Home of the Bronx cheer (or raspberry), the Bronx Zoo (or Wildlife Conservation Park), the Bronx Bombers (or New York Yankees), the Bronx has suffered in reality and reputation in recent decades but is now recovering from its social and financial woes.

The Bronx is the only borough of New York City attached to the mainland of North America, and even so it is surrounded on three sides by water: the Hudson River on the west, the Harlem and East Rivers on the south, and Long Island Sound on the east. Its area of 43.1 square miles and population of approximately 1.2 million make it the second smallest borough in both categories. The population began to rise in the mid-1990s after several decades of decline.

The eastern Bronx is largely flatland, some of it originally salt marsh, sliced into long peninsulas by inlets and tidal rivers. Tons of garbage, euphemistically known as landfill, have been dumped onto the marshes since World War II and the areas along Eastchester Bay including Throgs Neck, parts of Baychester, and Co-op City are now densely populated residential areas. West of the flatlands are three north–south ridges which give the middle and western sections of the borough their hilly terrain. The westernmost ridge runs through Riverdale near the Hudson and west of Broadway, with Broadway following the lowland valley. The second ridge crosses Van Cortlandt Park and runs south to the Macombs Dam Bridge area with the Grand Concourse laid out along its spine. The third and lowest proceeds through the Bronx River Park and Crotona Park, falling away to the flatlands along the East River.

Most of the Bronx is residential, developed with apartment houses that range from the onetime luxury Art Deco buildings along the Grand Concourse and the well-kept high-rises overlooking the Hudson River to the institutional towers of Co-op City and the intimidating housing projects throughout the South Bronx. The strip along the East River that includes Mott Haven, Port Morris, and Hunts Point has long been industrial.

The Bronx is fortunate in having beautiful parks, nearly 6,000 acres of them or about 23 percent of its total area, most acquired by the city fathers in the years between 1880 and 1900. A plan to link them by wide, tree-lined boulevards resulted in two attractive parkways, the Mosholu Pkwy and the Bronx-Pelham Pkwy. Unfortunately, the city's straitened finances in the 1960s and 1970s, along with changing government priorities, brought hardship to the parks and many other facilities in the outer boroughs. A Greenways Plan, for bike and walkways throughout the borough going east-to-west, was approved in 1993, but its implementation has been slow.

History

In 1639 the Dutch West India Co. purchased from Native Americans the land that now constitutes the Bronx, and in 1641 Jonas Bronck, a Dane who arrived in the New World by way of Amsterdam, purchased 500 acres along the river,

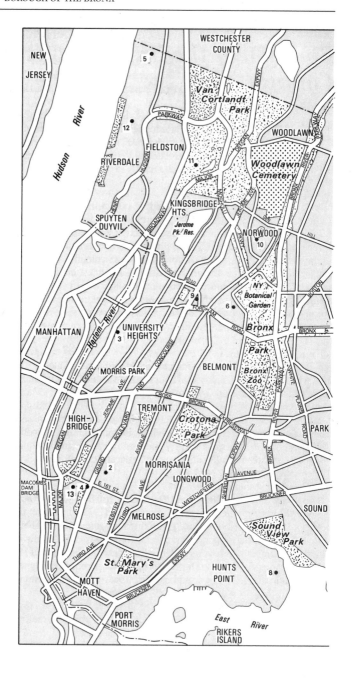

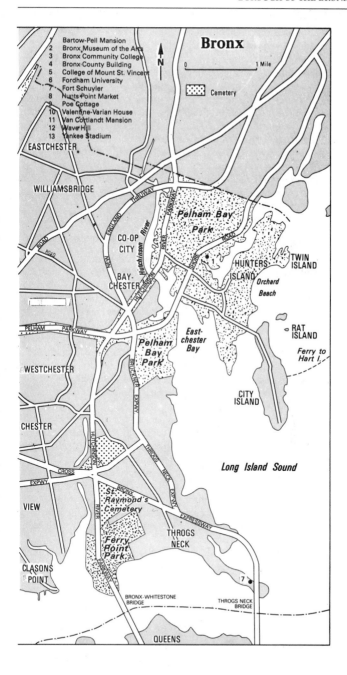

Bronx

1 Bartow-Pell Mansion
2 Bronx Museum of the Arts
3 Bronx Community College
4 Bronx County Building
5 College of Mount St. Vincent
6 Fordham University
7 Fort Schuyler
8 Hunts Point Market
9 Poe Cottage
10 Valentine-Varian House
11 Van Cortlandt Mansion
12 Wave Hill
13 Yankee Stadium

N

0   1 Mile

Cemetery

EASTCHESTER

WILLIAMSBRIDGE

THRUWAY

Pelham Bay Park

PARKWAY

CO-OP CITY

NEW ENGLAND

Hutchinson River

ROAD

SHORE

ROAD

1

HUNTERS ISLAND

TWIN ISLAND

Orchard Beach

BAY-CHESTER

HUTCHINSON

ROAD

PELHAM   PARKWAY

Pelham Bay Park

East-chester Bay

RAT ISLAND

Ferry to Hart I.

WESTCHESTER

BRUCKNER EXPWY

CITY ISLAND

CHESTER

Long Island Sound

HUTCHINSON

THROGS NECK EXPWY

CROSS

EXPWY

VIEW

BRONX RIVER

St. Raymond's Cemetery

EXPRESSWAY

THROGS NECK

Ferry Point Park

CLASONS POINT

PARKWAY

7

BRONX-WHITESTONE BRIDGE

THROGS NECK BRIDGE

QUEENS

which soon was known as Bronck's River. The borough today takes its name from this original settler. A few years later other settlers arrived in the area, including religious dissenter Anne Hutchinson who, in 1637, was expelled as unfit for society by theocrats of the Massachusetts Bay Colony, who could not tolerate her liberal religious views or her quick tongue. With her husband, children, and followers, she moved to Rhode Island; her husband's death and continued controversy again sent her packing, this time to the shores of what is now Pelham Bay, where she settled in the early 1640s. Around the same time, John Throgmorton, an Anabaptist, arrived in the area with 35 families who shared his religious views. Soon after, Native Americans attacked both colonies and though some of Throgmorton's followers were able to escape, Anne Hutchinson's colony was annihilated except for one of her daughters, Susannah, who was taken hostage. After a two-year stay with her captors, Susannah was returned, unwillingly, when the Dutch and Native Americans made a treaty to settle their differences. The place names Throgs Neck and Hutchinson River remain as evidence of these early sojourners.

Other British settlers arrived including Thomas Pell, via Connecticut in 1654, and Richard Morris in 1662, but both the Dutch and the Native Americans were (understandably) so entrenched that it was not until 1664, when the British took over, that settlement of the Bronx began in earnest. Still, the Bronx remained quietly rural, its land divided between modest farmers and large landowners whose style of life imitated that of the English landed gentry. Part of Westchester County, the Bronx had a population of only 3,023 as late as 1830.

Villages evolved along the post roads to Albany and Boston—Mott Haven, Kingsbridge, Morrisania, East Chester, Pelham—later to become the commercial centers of borough neighborhoods. Railroads followed the general course of the roads and also fostered development in both the east and west sectors of the borough. Riverdale became a fashionable country retreat for the wealthy, accessible not only by rail but also by steamboat.

After 1840, however, advances in transportation and technology and the crush of immigrants resulted in the influx of a population that ended with the Depression in the early 1930s. The first newcomers to the territory were the Irish, who started to arrive in the 1840s to labor on the railroads and the Croton Aqueduct. After 1848 Germans followed, most remaining farmers as they had been in their native land. The two decades from 1840 to 1860 saw the population quadruple (from 5,346 to 23,593). In 1888 the Third Ave elevated railway reached the hinterland of 169th St and a flood of newcomers began settling near it—more Irish and Germans, Jews, Italians, Poles, and Greeks—attracted to the Bronx because it seemed almost rural.

Politically, the Bronx joined New York in two sections: first (1874) the western towns of Kingsbridge, West Farms, and Morrisania; then (1894) the eastern towns of Eastchester, Westchester, and part of Pelham voted to become part of the city. According to the provisions of the Greater New York charter in 1898, these two separately annexed areas officially became the borough of the Bronx, with a population of 200,507.

Long considered the stronghold of working-class families—Jews, Italians, Irish, and others who had improved their lot sufficiently to escape the Lower East Side—the Bronx of the first half of the 20C conjures almost as much nostalgia among its former children as Brooklyn does. During the "golden age" of the Bronx, which lasted from about 1920 to the early 1950s, the borough was divided into tightly knit neighborhoods, usually dominated by one ethnic group, which became centers of social life. City services—education, transportation, parks—made life comfortable and attractive.

The arrival of the automobile, however, and the construction of superhighways, enabled the population, or at least the upwardly mobile part of it, a greater choice of where to live; Westchester County and Long Island attracted many borough residents. Public transportation began to deteriorate; the last trolley ceased running in 1948. Jobs became less plentiful.

As middle-class whites left after World War II, poor minorities—mainly blacks and Latinos—increasingly dominated the population, though some neighborhoods, particularly in the northeast and northwest, remained largely middle class and white. In the 1970s, parts of the South Bronx, riddled with burned, abandoned buildings and rubble-filled lots, evoked comparisons with Dresden at the end of World War II. In the last two decades, however, the Bronx has been slowly recuperating, and now, like Harlem, it is polishing its public image.

From 1990 to 1996, 107,567 immigrants (about 14 percent of the city's total) settled in the Bronx, which has about 14 percent of the city's total population. More than 40 percent of the immigrants came from the Dominican Republic, with another 13 percent from Jamaica and 11 percent from Ecuador, Honduras, and Guyana. Nearly 3,500 Irish—a quarter of those arriving in the city—settled in the Bronx, mainly in the Williamsbridge-Norwood area, which attracted more immigrants than any other Bronx neighborhood. University Heights, Morris Heights, and Highbridge—neighborhoods just east of Upper Manhattan (the city's largest immigrant destination)—also saw a large influx of immigrants.

While life in the borough is improving, the Bronx still struggles with unemployment, crime, and unusually high asthma rates. This health issue, activists argue, is the result of environmental racism; indeed, many of the city's garbage facilities, bus depots, highways, and other polluters are concentrated in poor neighborhoods in the Bronx.

Touring the Bronx

Many sights in the Bronx are easily accessible. Historic houses stand in Van Cortlandt Park and Pelham Park, the latter near City Island, a unique island community. The Bronx Zoo and nearby New York Botanical Garden are among the finer attractions in the city and can be reached by express bus, commuter train, or subway from Midtown. Riverdale offers fine views of the Hudson River, an assortment of educational institutions, and examples of upper-class domestic architecture including Wave Hill.

For other areas a car is desirable mainly because distances are great; while some neighborhoods still have crime problems, most blocks with notable sights are relatively safe during the day. Get a map, because the streets are not laid out regularly.

30 · The South Bronx: Mott Haven, Port Morris, Hunts Point, Melrose, Morrisania, and Highbridge

The name South Bronx once designated only Mott Haven and Melrose, but when much of the borough deteriorated in the 1960s and '70s, the term came to include crime-ridden neighborhoods as far north as University Heights at Fordham Rd. The appellation inaccurately evokes the image of a single sprawling, burned-out ghetto, but as the communities of the Bronx slowly rebound, they are struggling to reclaim their individual identities.

Although much of the damage done to these neighborhoods in the 1960s, '70s, and '80s was wrought by individuals, the decimation of the region began with a series of bad governmental policies, some driven by institutional racism, others merely by pure stubbornness. Population shifts beyond anyone's control also affected the borough adversely: after World War II, while many industrial jobs were moving to the South, thousands of uneducated workers arrived from the rural South and the Caribbean looking for blue-collar jobs.

After World War II, Robert Moses, then in charge of "slum clearance," demolished housing for the poor in northern Manhattan without providing adequate replacement housing. Some 170,000 people, mainly Puerto Ricans, headed to the South Bronx. In addition, the city Welfare Department "dumped" the city's poorest newcomers into the housing projects Moses built in the South Bronx and offered the landlords of older tenements and buildings above-market rents for taking welfare clients. In the long run, this proved disastrous. The housing projects warehoused and isolated poor people. Because rent control (implemented during World War II) prohibited landlords from raising rents to cover their costs, they subdivided their apartments into tiny units and cut back on maintenance. The tenements and apartments, most erected before 1915, rapidly deteriorated.

Two final blows finished off the area. In the 1950s, Moses rammed the Cross Bronx Expressway through several thriving neighborhoods, refusing to compromise on its placement. The expressway displaced tens of thousands of working- and middle-class Jewish, Irish, and Italian residents, many of whom looked around at the other changes and decided to leave. Their departure drained the borough's powerful Democratic machine of much of its influence, leaving the new, poorer residents with no political voice.

Then in 1968, the state sponsored Co-op City, a $413-million, 15,000-unit apartment complex in an isolated corner of the north Bronx. Bronx activists argued that if such high-quality housing had been built in South Bronx neighborhoods, the region might have stabilized. Instead, Co-op City lured away what remained of the South Bronx's middle class. Although the federal government poured money into the South Bronx, most of these funds went for massive housing projects; in some cases the government even razed tenements without fully funding new projects, leaving empty lots and homeless residents in its wake.

Then, around 1970, the fires started. Some were genuine accidents caused by aging electrical systems, but more were attributed to arson. Some were set by landlords seeking to collect insurance money, others by tenants knowing that people who were burned out got priority for public housing. By the mid-1970s, the South Bronx averaged an astonishing 12,000 fires a year; 40 percent of its housing stock vanished; 300,000 people moved away.

The city, immobilized by a fiscal crisis, did little. President Jimmy Carter visited in 1977 and promised help but accomplished nothing. His successor, Ronald Reagan, came and then slashed federal government contributions to related programs, cutting the affordable housing budget by two-thirds. The 1981 movie *Fort Apache, The Bronx* and Tom Wolfe's 1987 novel *Bonfire of the Vanities* sealed the area's reputation as a disaster area beyond salvation.

By this time, however, the region had begun inching out of the depths. The dedicated work of community organizers, who bought back buildings and lots from the city and rehabilitated them, played a large role, but the key was broad-based, intelligently targeted intervention by the government. After his reelection in 1985, Mayor Edward I. Koch pushed through a ten-year plan for affordable housing. Of the $5.1 billion allocated for citywide reconstruction, more than a quarter went into the South Bronx. (The total was more than the combined affordable housing outlay of the next 50 largest U.S. cities.) Most of the money went not to high-rise housing projects but to low-density housing geared to individual ownership. The city also rebuilt parks and branch libraries and subsidized retailers who moved in and lived above their stores. Federal government assistance brought banks and private companies back to the South Bronx.

Despite these improvements, the South Bronx is still beset by problems including high unemployment and pollution (perhaps caused by a disproportionate number of bus terminals and waste transfer stations). Drugs and crime are still serious issues, although the number of shootings and robberies in the South Bronx has plummeted.

Mott Haven

Mott Haven, along the Harlem River in the southwest corner of the borough, was the home of Swedish immigrant Jonas Bronck, who established a farm in 1639 around present-day E. 132nd St and Lincoln Ave. However, Mott Haven became industrial when Jordan Mott, inventor of a cast-iron, coal-burning stove, built an iron works (1828) along the river around E. 134th St. Mott purchased the land from Gouverneur Morris, scion of the aristocratic Morris family (see Morrisania History). When asked whether he minded that this section of Morrisania were renamed Mott Haven, Morris allegedly snapped, "I don't care what [Mott] calls it; while he is about it, he might as well change the name of the Harlem [River] and call it the Jordan." The Mott Iron Works flourished until 1906, attracting successive waves of immigrants, first Irish and German, later Jewish and Italians. Some of the factory buildings are still visible from the western side of the Third Ave Bridge.

Mott Haven became a suburb with the arrival of the Third Ave elevated line, attracting middle-class residents and also piano manufacturers in the later decades of the 19C. As the subway was extended into the Bronx, upscale row houses were built, complementing the tenements constructed for the earlier immigrants.

By the 1940s the piano companies had left; during the 1950s Mott Haven's population became largely African American and Latino and began to suffer the problems of other communities in the southern part of the borough.

Today, however, the area has a new lease on life. Both Alexander Ave and Bruckner Blvd bustle with stores selling and restoring antiques and furniture. Kelly's Furniture, 20 Bruckner Blvd, housed in a former Ruppert's Brewery warehouse for 24 years, has been joined by a dozen smaller newcomers. Many are owned by Caribbean and African immigrants who used to work for the city's big auction houses and are now taking advantage of the South Bronx's combination of easy accessibility (the Major Deegan and Bruckner Expwys have exits nearby), improved image, and affordable rents. The commercial strip has new "antique" lighting, benches, and planters.

Points of Interest

There are still traces of **"Pianotown."** At the corner of Bruckner Blvd and Lincoln Ave is the former **Estey Piano Factory** (1885; A. B. Ogden & Son), a brick building with a corner clock tower, now used for storage by Touro University. The former **Krakauer Brothers Piano Company** and **Kroeger Piano Company** buildings remain on E. 132nd St between Alexander and Lincoln Aves.

The **Alexander Ave Historic District** runs along the avenue between E. 137th and E. 141st Sts. Its main attractions are handsome row houses (1860s–80s), particularly those between E. 139th and E. 140th Sts, and two churches. **St. Jerome's Roman Catholic Church** (1898; Dehli & Howard) on Alexander Ave between E. 137th and E. 138th Sts and the **Tercera Iglesia Bautista** (Third Baptist Church), originally the Alexander Avenue Baptist Church (1902; Ward & Davis), on the corner of E. 141th St and Alexander Ave, today look out onto housing projects. Also in the district is the **Mott Haven Branch of the New York Public Library** (1905; Babb, Cook & Willard), between E. 140th and E. 141st Sts, resembling a humbler version of Andrew Carnegie's mansion, which was designed by the same architects.

To the east, at 414–432 E. 136th St (between Willis Ave and Brown Place), are the yellow brick **Bertine Block row houses** (1891; George Keister; DL), built for developer Edward D. Bertine. These Queen Anne homes with gables, mansards, cornices, and other details exemplify the substantial and often stylish housing constructed for the then-middle-class population of the Bronx. Bertine himself chose to live at 416 E. 136th St.

Indicative of relatively recent philosophies in renewal housing are the **Plaza Borinquen town houses** (1974; Ciardullo-Ehmann) on several sites in the area, including E. 137th St (between Willis Ave and Brown Place). While they lack charm and character, the three-story houses made of reddish brown masonry blocks keep residents close to the streets, instead of isolating them in high towers.

The two- and three-story town houses (1888–97) of the **Mott Haven East Historic District** on E. 140th St (between Willis and Brook Aves) are typical of the finest late-19C housing in the Bronx. Some have picturesque Dutch and Flemish details.

Nearby is modest fieldstone **St. Ann's Church** (Protestant Episcopal) **and graveyard,** 295 St. Ann's Ave (between E. 139th and E. 141st Sts). The borough's oldest church (1841; DL), it is set back from and facing away from the street (which did not exist when the church was built). The cemetery holds the graves of Morris family members including railroad pioneer Gouverneur Morris II (1813–1888), a genius in the eyes of his acquaintances and something of a rake. Morris built the little church to honor his mother, Anne Carey Randolph Morris, said to be a descendant of the Indian princess Pocahontas. Also buried here is the first Gouverneur Morris (1752–1816), who helped draft the U.S. Constitution, and Lewis Morris (1726–1798), a signer of the Declaration of Independence.

The Piccirilli Brothers, Monumental Sculptors

A block and a half west of St. Ann's Ave (between Willis and Brook Aves) is an empty lot where 467 E. 142 St once stood. Here, beginning in 1893, the Piccirilli Brothers produced some of the city's most important public sculptures, including the lions at the New York Public Library and the Firemen's Memorial (W. 100th St and Riverside Drive). The six brothers—Ferruccio, Attilio, Furio, Orazio, Masanielo, and Getulio—who arrived with their father from Tuscany in 1887, got their big break in 1901 when Attilio was chosen to create the sculpture for the *Maine* Monument at the Columbus Circle entrance to Central Park. Soon the brothers' handiwork (often made from designs by other sculptors) could be seen all over the city: in the pediment group at the New York Stock Exchange (1904); in Daniel Chester French's *Four Continents* at the U.S. Custom House (1907); in *Civic Virtue* (1922), which was banished from City Hall and sent to Queens (see Kew Gardens in Walk 51); and in French's facade sculpture for the Brooklyn Museum. Eventually, the Piccirillis extended their range, carving likenesses of Thomas Jefferson for the Virginia State Capitol and of James Monroe for his Ashland Plantation. The brothers reached their peak when French hired them to carve Abraham Lincoln (1922) for the Lincoln Memorial. As fewer public monuments were built the brothers were largely forgotten; Attilio died at the studio in 1945 and the building was demolished around 1960.

Hilly **St. Mary's Park,** bounded by St. Ann's and Jackson Aves, St. Mary's and E. 149th Sts, takes its name from a modest Gothic-style wooden Episcopal church that stood on Alexander Ave near E. 142nd St until 1959. Once the hill was called Janes's Hill after Adrian Janes, whose iron works stood nearby. The amalgamated Janes, Kirtland & Co. Iron Works (1863), on Westchester Ave between Brook and St. Ann's Aves, produced architectural ironwork, most notably the 8.9 million-pound dome of the U.S. Capitol Building in Washington, D.C.

Across from the park, at 519 St. Ann's Ave (between E. 148th and E. 149th Sts), is the limestone, brick, and terra-cotta **P.S. 27** (1897; C. B. J. Snyder; DL), one of the earliest works of New York's most famous school architect. The main features of P.S. 27 are the scrolled gables, carved escutcheon over the main entrance, and octagonal bell tower.

Around the block, at 454–464 E. 148th St (southeast corner of Brook Ave), the South Bronx Overall Economic Development Corporation has converted a former factory (1887) into **Brook Avenue Gardens** (2000; Urban Architectural Initiatives), a low-income housing complex. One of the first garment buildings in the city, the factory was used for the manufacture of silk trimmings; its last use, before closing around 1970, was as a casket factory. Tenants of the 79 apartments enjoy high ceilings, parquet floors, and exposed brick walls.

Port Morris

East of Mott Haven is tiny Port Morris, first developed by the Morris family in the 19C as a deep-water port. For many years its main industry was Richard Hoe & Co., Printing Machinery and Saws, a firm whose founder invented the rotary printing press. The Hoe factory was demolished in 1977.

In the last few years, Port Morris has been revived, with an 88-acre industrial complex built at the defunct Harlem River Yards just north of the Bronx Kill. Businesses include a *New York Post* printing plant, a paper recycling plant, and a waste-transfer station. A small rail line, the Oak Point Link, is designed to reduce truck traffic to and from the Hunts Point Markets and the Port Morris waste-transfer site.

Hunts Point

In the southeast corner of the Bronx, bounded by Westchester Ave to the north and Prospect Ave to the west, is Hunts Point, named for 17C settler Thomas Hunt. Like much of the South Bronx, this area boasted large estates until the subway arrived, bringing with it row houses and apartment buildings for the working class. German and Irish immigrants were followed by Italians and Jews, and then in the mid-20C, Puerto Ricans and blacks.

Bronx Verse

The Hunt estate was subsequently owned by the poet Joseph Rodman Drake, who died in 1820 and is buried in Drake Park (at Hunts Point and Oak Point Aves) along with members of the Hunt family and other elite early Bronxites. Drake wrote of his borough in the early 19C, "Yet I will look upon thy face again / My own romantic Bronx, and it will be / A face more pleasant than the face of men." The street names around the park recall other 19C American poets: Whittier, Bryant, Longfellow, and Fitz-Greene Halleck.

The former home of the **American Bank Note Company** (1911; Kirby, Petit & Green), once the world's largest printer of paper currency and stock certificates (mostly for South and Central American countries), is at 1241 Lafayette Ave and Tiffany St. Like many other businesses, the company fled the South Bronx (1984), taking hundreds of jobs to the suburbs. The community, however, has brought new life to the building complex, first using it for various small textile businesses and later for community-oriented groups, including a social services organization and second-opportunity high school. **The Point,** a community-development corporation, has undertaken the construction of artists' studio space and a 125-seat dance theater. Occupying the old machine shop and currency warehouse at 940 Garrison Ave (corner of Manida St), now redecorated with vibrant murals, The Point also operates a 225-seat theater and a photo gallery. For information, ☎ (718) 542-4139.

Across the street, at Lafayette Ave and Baretto St, is the **Corpus Christi Monastery** (1890; William Schickel), a convent of cloistered Dominican nuns. The main building occupies 2.5 acres of the 7.5-acre tract of land.

Nearby, at 812 Faile St (northeast corner of Lafayette St), is **Sunnyslope** (c. 1860; DL), the former home of businessman Peter Hoe. The Gothic revival mansion, with its pointed chimney pots, was once part of a 14.6-acre estate; it became Temple Beth Elohim in 1919 and is now the Bright Temple African Methodist Episcopal Church.

Hunts Point today is best known as the site of the **New York City Terminal Market** (1965; Skidmore, Owings & Merrill), on Halleck St (between Lafayette and East Bay Aves), the city's primary fruit and vegetable wholesale market, and the **Hunts Point Cooperative Meat Market** (Hunts Point Ave, south of East Bay Ave), which dates from 1976 (Brand & Moore). The market, which moved here from Lower Manhattan in the 1960s, is the largest food distribution center in the northeast, with 650 businesses and 19,000 employees. The historic Fulton Fish Market (see Walk 2) may be moved here.

The market sits along the southern reaches of the 23-mile Bronx River, which is idyllic near its source in Westchester County and near the New York Botanical Garden, but becomes increasingly foul as it wends through the South Bronx to the East River. A long-range plan is being developed to rescue the Bronx River; The Point recently provided the first real access to the water with a 1.5-acre park in Hunts Point. The wetlands at water's edge are being restored, and work has begun north of Hunts Point on Starlight Park near E. 174th St and on Soundview Park near the East River.

Longwood

A subsection of Hunts Point, on the other side of the Bruckner Expwy, is Longwood, which got its name from a large estate in its western portion. This area boasts several clusters of new housing created by community groups. They are purposefully far more modest than the government's behemoth housing projects and have therefore been enthusiastically greeted by urban planners, who see such small-scale buildings as a way to reverse urban blight.

On Kelly St, between Intervale Ave and E. 163rd St, is the **Banana Kelly Project.** When the city sent demolition crews in 1977 to raze three tenements on Kelly St, the 30 families living there formed a human chain around their buildings; in the glare of publicity, the city backed down. The victors incorporated as the Banana Kelly Community Improvement Association (named for the bend or "banana" in Kelly St) and capitalized on the publicity to attract government and bank loans to repair their buildings. Adopting the slogan "Don't Move, Improve," they completed renovations at an astonishingly low $26,000 per apartment, far less than the then-usual gut rehabilitation estimates of $85,000 per apartment. The association now manages 1,000 units and has built 1,500 more new, cooperatively owned units. In recent years, however, the group has been criticized for shoddy management and upkeep, and its leader has also taken fire for living in Riverdale and owning a house in Connecticut. In 2001, the group was forced to turn over management of its buildings to other nonprofit groups, including the Southeast Bronx Community Organization.

A block east, at 878 Tiffany St, is **St. Athanasius Church,** the home of Father Louis Gigante, a charismatic community and parish leader. In front of the church is **Tiffany Plaza.** If one site might be taken to symbolize the potential resurrection of the South Bronx, it is this plaza, created through community and city effort, its fountains and trees untouched by vandalism. Gigante, who arrived at St.

Athanasius in 1962, founded the Southeast Bronx Community Organization (SEBCO) in 1968 and over the following decades successfully organized his Hunts Point constituents to rebuild dozens of abandoned buildings and thousands of units for low-income local people. In the 1980s, Gigante was also one of the first developers in the city to embrace modular construction, a system in which building sections are constructed in a factory, transported to the site, and erected on the foundation.

Several blocks south of the church at Fox and Prospect Aves are the **Villa Maria Homes** (1990; DeLuxe Homes), another group of modular homes and one of the most visually charming developments in the Bronx. The houses have pitched roofs with dormer windows and stone stoops leading to covered front porches.

To the north is the seven-block **Longwood Historic District** (1897–1901), bounded roughly by Longwood and Leggett Aves, Hewitt Place and Fox St, which survived the neighborhood's rough years intact. The district's bay-fronted double houses represent some of the best domestic architecture built at a time when the Bronx was becoming an urban extension of Manhattan.

Melrose

West of Longwood and north of Mott Haven is the small neighborhood of Melrose. From the 1850s until the 1940s, its largely German population enjoyed local beer gardens and worshiped in German churches. The Third Ave elevated line reached the area in the 1890s, as did the subway in 1904. Italians and other groups moved in during the early 20C.

Through the 1950s, the **Hub**—the intersection of E. 149th St and Westchester, Third, Willis, and Melrose Aves, where trolley and subway lines converged—was the main shopping and entertainment district for the entire borough. Around the turn of the 20C, theaters arrived, offering vaudeville, drama, amateur nights, and, eventually, movies. Alexander's first department store opened at 2952 Third Ave in 1928. Although the Hub is no longer the centerpiece of the Bronx, it is still a busy commercial area.

Morrisania

North of Melrose is Morrisania, bounded to the north by the Cross Bronx Expwy, to the south by E. 161st St, to the east by Crotona Park and Prospect Ave, to the west by Webster Ave. It is the remnant of the original town of Morrisania, incorporated in 1785.

History

The first members of the Morris family to come to the colonies were Welshmen Richard and Lewis Morris, who arrived in the Bronx after successful careers as merchants and privateers in Barbados. Their original holdings, purchased from Jonas Bronck's lands in about 1670, were increased by a royal grant from William of Orange. The Morrises became one of the leading families of New York, their descendants achieving national prominence. The first Gouverneur Morris, great-grandson of the first Richard Morris (Richards, Lewises, and Gouverneurs abound in the family) and a framer of the U.S. Constitution, delivered the eulogy at George Washington's funeral.

The Lewis Morris who first owned Morrisania died in 1691. His grandson, the fourth Lewis Morris, also signed the Declaration of Independence and after the

Revolution attempted to sell his estate as a site for the nation's capital. The original town of Morrisania began to develop with the arrival of a railroad in the 1840s, evolving into the borough's social and civic center, a role it retained until the 1920s, when new housing developments in the northern Bronx drained the population.

One symbol of the neighborhood's lost power is the former **Bronx Borough Courthouse** (1915; Oscar Bluemner and Michael J. Garvin; DL), 513 E. 161st St (at Third Ave), a handsome granite-and-marble Beaux Arts building with vaulted ceilings, a spectacular rotunda, and a sculpture of Justice (J. E. Roine) above the entrance. The building took more than a decade to complete and ran far over budget. Garvin, who was politically connected, often received sole credit for the design, but he subcontracted out to Bluemner, who actually designed the building. In 1998, after having been closed for almost two decades, the building was auctioned off for $300,000 to developers who hope to resell it for five times that amount, rather than undertake a massive restoration. A community group, Nos Quedamos, hopes to raise the money and buy it.

North and east of the courthouse is **St. Augustine's Church** (1894; Louis Giele), 1183 Franklin Ave (at E. 167th St), a Renaissance and baroque church with two cupola-topped towers. The church replaced an original wooden structure (one of the borough's first Catholic churches) built by German and Irish immigrants in 1850 and a later brick church destroyed by fire. The size of the present church, whose sanctuary seats 1,500, reflects the large Roman Catholic population of the Bronx at the end of the 19C. Many of St. Augustine's parishioners were Italians who helped build and landscape such institutions as the Bronx Zoo and New York Botanical Garden. The congregation dwindled in the 1940s as blacks, largely Protestant, began moving to the neighborhood; attendance fell 70 percent before rebounding in the last decade with the influx of Catholic Latinos.

About five blocks north of the church is 127.5-acre **Crotona Park,** the only large swath of green in the South Bronx. The Bathgate family, who owned the land in the 19C, allowed picnicking on the shores of its Indian Lake. In 1883 the city bought the land, from which the new Brooklyn Bridge could be seen in the distance, and named the park for a Greek city famed for its athletes. Fittingly, a local kid named Hank Greenberg hit his first home run here before going on to a Hall of Fame baseball career. The park was not landscaped as was Central Park, but it was altered when concrete walls replaced Indian Lake's shoreline in 1914. Robert Moses, using Works Progress Administration (WPA) money, added a swimming pool, the Crotona Play Center (1936), and other sports facilities. As the area deteriorated in the 1960s and '70s, the park became a war zone, and in one area of the park regular dog fights were held. Today most of the playgrounds have been renovated and the dog pit is now a community garden. In 1998, Friends of Crotona Park was formed to rehabilitate the park.

On the eastern border of the park is **Charlotte St,** a short street whose houses with green lawns and picket fences exemplify the rebirth of the neighborhood. (These blocks are sometimes considered part of Morrisania, West Farms, or Crotona Park East.) Charlotte St became a national symbol of urban despair after President Jimmy Carter's 1977 visit exposed its derelict buildings and rubble-strewn lots to nationwide publicity. Carter proposed a 732-unit high-rise housing project, an idea rejected by the city because of its size. In the 1980s, the Mid-Bronx Desperadoes, officially the MBD Community Housing Corporation, built

89 single-family, prefabricated suburban-style ranch houses called **Charlotte Gardens**, financed with federal, city, and state assistance. The nearby commercial area is also slowly rebounding. In 1999, European American Bank opened the neighborhood's first bank in more than a decade on Southern Blvd at Jennings St, a block from Charlotte Gardens.

East of Charlotte St, Russian revolutionary **Leon Trotsky** lived briefly at 1522 Vyse Ave (between E. 172nd and E. 173rd Sts), after being expelled from France and Spain, biding his time until returning for the Bolshevik Revolution in 1917.

Highbridge

Along the Harlem River, north of E. 161st St and south of the Cross Bronx Expwy, lies **Highbridge**, which takes its name from the aqueduct crossing the Harlem River in the northern part of the district. As with neighboring communities, nearly two-thirds of the immigrants who arrived during the early-to-mid-1990s were Dominican.

Its most famous landmark is Yankee Stadium, "the house that Ruth built," at E. 161st St, southwest corner of River Ave.

Yankee Stadium

Between 1913 and 1923 the New York Yankees shared the Polo Grounds (see Walk 28) with the New York Giants. In 1923, Babe Ruth's popularity led Yankee owner Jacob Ruppert (of brewery fame) to build Yankee Stadium on a corner of the William Waldorf Astor estate, tailoring the park to the left-handed slugger's skills by building a short right field fence. The nation's first three-tiered major league ballpark, and the first to be called a stadium, was completed in only 284 days. The right and left field fences were 295 and 281 ft from home plate, but left-center field became known as Death Valley because the fence was (originally) a remote 500 ft away.

Opening Day at Yankee Stadium drew 74,200 customers (25,000 more were turned away), breaking baseball's attendance record by nearly 30,000. John Philip Sousa led the Seventh Regiment band and Governor Al Smith threw out the first ball. Fittingly, Ruth scored the first run with a home run to right field. Powered by Ruth and first baseman Lou Gehrig, the Yankees began winning the World Series seemingly at will; their lineup was known as Murderers' Row.

By the time the 20C ended, the franchise would capture a record 25 championships, led by successive generations of heroes: Ruth and Gehrig, followed by Joe DiMaggio, Bill Dickey, Yogi Berra, Whitey Ford, and Mickey Mantle. Yankee Stadium saw Don Larsen pitch the only perfect World Series game (1956) and Roger Maris break Ruth's single-season home run record (1961). Equally memorable but sadder were Lou Gehrig's farewell (1939), when the dying star told cheering fans, "Today I consider myself the luckiest man on the face of the earth," and the cancer-stricken Babe Ruth's farewell nine years later.

In the 1970s, when CBS, which owned the club, threatened to move the Yankees to New Jersey, the city bought the stadium and embarked on a renovation originally estimated at $21 million, promising to pour money also into the surrounding community. The project altered the ballpark in numerous ways. While sight lines were improved and new concession areas were built, plastic seats replaced wooden ones; the scalloped copper frieze was removed from the upper deck and replaced with a plastic replica atop the new giant scoreboard in right-center field; decorative tiles were painted over; and the entrance facades were lost to escalator towers. The dimensions were also made more modest—310 ft in right field, 312 ft in left field, and 417 in centerfield (altered again in 1988; the dimensions are now 314, 318, and 408 ft respectively). The final bill footed by taxpayers has been estimated as more than $160 million (including debt service); no money went to the community.

In the late 1970s, Reggie Jackson, Catfish Hunter, Thurman Munson, Ron Guidry, and Sparky Lyle created a new dynasty nicknamed the Bronx Zoo after the club's rambunctious, often fractious personnel. Principal owner George Steinbrenner, who bought the club in 1973, captured as many headlines as the players with his bombastic and tyrannical ways. Toward century's end, Steinbrenner, who had long denigrated the South Bronx, began hinting that he might move the team to New Jersey. Most New Yorkers were appalled, but were equally unhappy with a plan for a new Yankee Stadium in Manhattan's far W. 30s. However, when the Yankees won four World Series between 1996 and 2000, Steinbrenner appeared to mellow both in his leadership of the club and in his belief that the Yankees had no future in the Bronx. In 2002, when the team's lease expires, the stadium will be baseball's third oldest, after Boston's Fenway Park and Chicago's Wrigley Field. (The Boston Red Sox are currently considering plans to move out of Fenway Park.)

Yankee Stadium also formerly hosted the football Giants, who arrived in 1956 and soon dominated the league. With stars like Frank Gifford, Y. A. Tittle, Sam Huff, and Andy Robustelli, the Giants played in five championship games over a seven-year span, including the 1958 championship game that they lost to Baltimore, one of football's most exciting games and the first to be nationally televised. The Giants left in 1973 when the stadium renovations began, ultimately moving to New Jersey.

Thirty championship boxing matches were also staged at Yankee Stadium. The most famous were Joe Louis's 1936 defeat of German Max Schmeling and Ingemar Johansson's 1959 upset of heavyweight champ and New York native Floyd Patterson. After a 17-year hiatus, boxing returned to Yankee Stadium in 1976 for one final title fight, when Muhammed Ali won a controversial decision over Ken Norton.

As the premier stadium in the city, Yankee Stadium has also hosted other memorable events. In 1957, 125,000 followers turned out for the Billy Graham Crusade. Pope Paul VI held the first papal mass in America here in 1965, and Pope John Paul II visited the stadium in 1979. Nelson Mandela's capped his triumphant trip to America in 1990 with a speech at the Stadium.

Yankee Stadium Tours

The Yankees offer daily tours of the stadium, taking visitors into the dugout, clubhouse, press box, and to Monument Park (monuments and plaques honoring legendary Yankee figures), which was created after the 1976 renovation. For information, ☎ (718) 293-4300.

Other Points of Interest

At 936 Woodycrest Ave, just west of the stadium, is the former **American Female Guardian Society and Home for the Friendless** (1901; William B. Tuthill). Built as a mansion and converted to Muhammad's Mosque of Islam, this imposing building overlooks Macombs Dam Park.

At 1005 Jerome Ave, near E. 165th St, is the **Park Plaza Apartments** building (1928; Horace Ginsbern; DL), one of the finest Art Deco apartments in the borough. Its facade, designed by Marvin Fine, is garnished with Mayan motifs and terra-cotta ornaments including squirrels, wolves, frogs, and winged creatures. Terra-cotta tiles depict fountains, the city skyline, the rising sun, and even an architect humbly presenting a model of his building to the Parthenon.

At 1257 Ogden Ave, near W. 168th St, is one of the borough's oldest school buildings, P.S. 11, originally **P.S. 91** (1889; George W. Debevoise; additions 1905, C. B. J. Snyder and 1930, Walter Martin; DL). Made of brick and Harlem River stone, it features a central tower with a ground-level arch, narrow round-arched windows on the second floor, a bull's-eye window on the third floor and, finally, a corbeled cornice topped off by a peaked dormer window and pyramidal roof.

Across the street, at 1272 Ogden Ave, is the charming stone **Presbyterian Church of Ghana,** formerly the Union Reformed Church of High Bridge (1889; Alfred E. Barlow). The congregation was founded in 1860.

The Birth of Hip-Hop?

According to legend, hip-hop music was born in northern Highbridge. At 1520 Sedgewick Ave during a 1973 birthday party for his younger sister, Jamaican-born Kool Herc (Clive Campbell) became the first hip-hop DJ, using two turntables to extend the drum breaks by hip-hopping from one turntable to the other, thus giving the dancers more time to perform their moves. Break dancing was subsequently born from this music. Other influential early hip-hop stars—for example, Grandmaster Flash (whose 1982 hit "The Message" was considered the first serious rap song)—also hailed from the Bronx.

---

31 · The Grand Concourse

Subway: Sixth Ave Express (D) or Lexington Ave Exp (4) to 161st St–Yankee Stadium.
Bus: Bx1, Bx2 to E. 161st St–Grand Concourse. Bx6 to E. 161st St–Grand Concourse. Number 4 Liberty Express to E. 165th St and Grand Concourse.
Car: From Manhattan, take FDR Drive to Major Deegan Expwy; exit at Grand Concourse; Continue to E. 161st St. Or take West Side Hwy onto Cross Bronx Expwy; exit at Jerome Ave; right on Jerome to E. 165th St; left to Grand Concourse.

East of Highbridge is the borough's most famous address, a street that transcends neighborhood distinction, creating its own linear identity: the Grand Concourse. (In general, Bronx residents define the borough by its streets rather than its neighborhoods, saying, "I live just off the Concourse" or "I live on Gun Hill Road," as opposed to "I live in Melrose." In other boroughs, people live in Park Slope or on the Upper West Side, not "on Seventh Avenue" or "just off Broadway.")

History

Formally named the Grand Boulevard and Concourse, the roadway was laid out by Louis Risse, who called it the "Speedway Concourse." It was constructed between 1892 and 1909. Risse purposely placed the Concourse on a natural ridge so that the side streets would slope down away from it, providing a sense of grandeur, a view, and a breeze on even the hottest days. Risse's road, which runs from E. 161st St to Mosholu Pkwy, is 182 ft wide and has eleven lanes that were originally designated separately for carriages, cyclists, and pedestrians who used the thoroughfare as a route to Van Cortlandt Park. In 1917, the Concourse was extended south to E. 138th St, swallowing up newly widened Mott Ave, but the newer section is neither as wide nor as grand as the older part and is lined with fast-food restaurants and auto-parts shops.

The opening of the IRT subway nearby in 1918 led to the construction of large apartment buildings, and during the Depression, while most construction in Manhattan was halted, the arrival of the IND subway encouraged the building of many of the Concourse's finest apartments. Thus, the avenue became one of the city's finest residential areas, the Park Ave of the Bronx, its residents (including Milton Berle and E. L. Doctorow) mostly well-to-do Jewish families drawn from the managerial and professional classes.

As the population aged and moved out in the 1960s (with many going to Co-op City), many blacks and Latinos moved in and synagogues were converted to churches. Asian immigrants began arriving in the 1990s.

Although the neighborhoods east and west of the Grand Concourse began deteriorating rapidly, the Grand Concourse was better able to withstand the stresses of these years and was still considered a posh address relative to its surroundings. The grand facades of its Depression-era buildings make the street even now a showcase of Art Deco and Art Moderne architecture. There are plans for a $30-million redesign of the Concourse and a movement afoot to have the strip declared a historic district.

While there is a historic landmark at E. 149th St, the **Bronx Post Office** (1937; Thomas Harlan Ellett; DL), which features noteworthy WPA-era murals by Ben Shahn, the Concourse's most impressive stretch starts at E. 161st St.

Begin at the **Bronx County Courthouse** (1934; Joseph H. Freedlander & Max Hausle; DL), 851 Grand Concourse, officially the Mario Merola Courthouse, named for the borough's lead district attorney for 14 years before his death in 1988. Decorating the massive limestone facade is a wraparound frieze whose heroic figures (by Charles Keck) portray the working man. The eight freestanding sculptures of pink Georgia marble were carved or supervised by Adolph A. Weinman and represent such themes as achievement and progress.

The housing complex for the elderly on the northeast corner of the same intersection (900 Grand Concourse) is the former **Concourse Plaza Hotel,** which opened in 1923 with Governor Al Smith speaking at the dedication dinner. With its three levels of banquet rooms, the hotel was *the* place to be seen in the Bronx. In its heyday, the hotel was a temporary home for Yankee players including Roger

Maris and Mickey Mantle, as well as members of visiting baseball and football teams. Franklin Roosevelt, Harry Truman, and John Kennedy campaigned for the presidency here.

On the northwest side of the Concourse, from E. 161st to E. 164th Sts, is **Joyce Kilmer Park,** named for a 31-year-old soldier who was killed during World War I but is best remembered for his poem "Trees" (1914). In 1999 the Heinrich Heine Fountain, also called the **Lorelei Fountain** (1899; Ernst Herter), was renovated after years of vandalism and moved from the park's northern end to Lou Gehrig Plaza (originally Grand Concourse Plaza) at the south end of the park, across from the Bronx County Courthouse.

Heinrich Heine in the Bronx

The fountain's principal figure, made famous in Heine's lyric *Die Lorelei,* is the Teutonic siren whose beauty and song led incautious sailors to a watery death. The statue was commissioned in 1887 for Dusseldorf, Heine's birthplace, but was rejected there and later in Mainz for political reasons: Heine was Jewish. The German American Arion Verein, a New York choral society, offered to sponsor the work, hoping to install it on Fifth Ave near the southeast corner of Central Park where the Sherman statue now stands. The Municipal Arts Commission demurred, and the fountain eventually found its way to the Bronx—no safe haven as it turned out. The Christian Temperance Union condemned the work as pornographic, and in 1900 a vandal decapitated the Personification of Poetry, one of the figures at the statue's base. For a while the statue was guarded around the clock by police. Through the years the statue continued to be defaced, until in 1975 it was considered the most deteriorated monument in the city. During summers of the 1990s, a dentist from Dusseldorf who vacationed on Long Island voluntarily removed graffiti from the figure, for which he was dubbed the "Heine-schrubber" in the German press. Beginning in 1998, with money from public and private sources, the statue was completely dismantled, cleaned of its graffiti (the paint had penetrated deeply into the stone), replumbed, and reinstalled.

Bronx Museum of the Arts

1040 Grand Concourse (at E. 165th St), Bronx, NY 10456. ☎ (718) 681-6000. Open Wed 3–9; Thurs and Fri 10–5; Sat and Sun 1–6. Suggested donation; free admission to galleries every Wed. Gift shop. Accessible to wheelchairs. Changing exhibitions, children's programs, educational programs; concerts, lectures, seminars.

Just past the park, on the east side of the street, is one of the borough's major cultural institutions, the **Bronx Museum of the Arts.** Founded in 1971 as part of a community effort to revitalize the Bronx, the institution is the borough's flagship visual arts museum. It has grown from modest beginnings at the Bronx Borough Courthouse, moving into a former synagogue at its present location in 1982, and expanding through the years to its present form, with its most recent addition in 1998. It is currently planning yet another expansion, which will include a new building next door.

The museum is known for its contemporary and historical exhibitions, which showcase local and ethnic art and explore issues that affect the borough; other shows examine issues and trends in the art world at large. The permanent collection has some 800 works, mainly by contemporary artists from Africa, Asia, and Latin America, which are shown in changing exhibitions.

Andrew Freedman Home

On the next block, at 1125 Grand Concourse, is the former Andrew Freedman Home (1924; Joseph Freedlander and Harry Allan Jacobs; wings 1931, David Levy; DL), an Italian Renaissance–style building of soft gray-and-yellow limestone set back from a lush lawn hidden behind a frontage of trees.

History

Freedman was a Tammany Hall insider, who invested in building the IRT subway and owned the New York Giants baseball team from 1894 to 1902. The 1907 stock market collapse impressed upon him the transitory nature of wealth, and when he died in 1915, he created a charitable trust to build and maintain a refuge "for aged and indigent folk" of "culture and refinement"—i.e., well-to-do people who had lost their money.

Residents could enjoy the library and billiard room, the Oriental rugs on the floors and the fine art on the walls. Each "guest" room had a shower stall of white marble. Formal dinner dress was required. But by the 1960s, operating costs outstripped income. Plastic plates replaced the bone china, guests were asked to pay some rent, and the building itself deteriorated. In 1983 the once-elegant mansion was sold to the Mid-Bronx Senior Citizens Council, which turned it into a residence for the elderly poor and a community center.

North of McClellan St, on the east side of the street, is **1150 Grand Concourse** (1937; Horace Ginsbern), a tan-and-black building with a colorful mosaic of sea life flanking the main doors. Like lobbies of many Art Deco buildings, this one is worth poking into for its floor mosaics and murals of nature scenes. Nearby **1188 Grand Concourse** (1937; Jacob Felson) features a stylish sawtooth design, although the gold bands need cleaning. Other handsome buildings with nice detail along this stretch include 1227 and 1235 Grand Concourse, between E. 167th and E. 168th Sts.

At 1275 Grand Concourse is the former **Temple Adath Israel,** now a Seventh Day Adventist Church, one of many such buildings along the Concourse to be converted. At 1455–1499 Grand Concourse (between E. 171st and E. 172nd Sts) is the former **Roosevelt Gardens** (1924), once one of the Concourse's most impressive structures. It suffered years of abuse and was abandoned before being rehabilitated in the 1980s (though most of its mission-style detail has been stripped away).

Across the street is **1500 Grand Concourse** (1935), designed by Jacob Felson, who along with Horace Ginsbern created many of the Concourse's finest buildings. This limestone building has orange-and-brown brick in vertical and horizontal bands. Felson also designed the chic **1675 Grand Concourse** (1936), at

E. 174th St, another Art Deco classic with vertical inlaid bricks of contrasting colors. The **Lewis Morris Apartments** (1923; Edward Raldiris), at 1749 Grand Concourse, a massive Greek-style tower, was once one of the Bronx's most desirable addresses.

Two blocks east of the Concourse, in the neighborhood of Tremont, is the **Shuttleworth House** (1896; Neville & Bagge; DL), on the corner of Mt. Hope Place. Built for Edwin Shuttleworth, an affluent stone dealer, this decorative private residence has two corner towers, a gracious veranda with wooden columns, and details that include human figures, portrait busts flanking the door, griffins, fleurs-de-lis, and nautical elements. A survivor from earlier times when the Bronx boasted fine suburban-style houses, it is now surrounded by inelegant apartment buildings. The neighborhood of **Tremont,** north of Crotona Park and east of the Grand Concourse, long a neighborhood of Jewish, Italian, and Irish families who had moved up from Manhattan's immigrant neighborhoods, was one of the areas most devastated by the intrusion of the Cross Bronx Expwy. Houses in the path of the road were demolished and a stable population was displaced, leaving a neighborhood bisected by an excavated roadway choked with traffic. In the years after completion of the road in 1955, the population became largely Latino and black.

At 1882 Grand Concourse, near East Tremont and Monroe Aves, is **Mt. Hope Court** (1914; Otto Schwarzler), also known as the Flatiron of the Bronx. This ten-story apartment was the borough's tallest building for many years. The building at **1947 Grand Concourse** (H. Herbert Lilien; 1939), at E. 178th St, features horizontal colored bands and vertical brick piers; **2121 Grand Concourse** (1936; Horace Ginsbern), at E. 181 St, is a zigzag-style Art Moderne building with cantilevered corners; **2327–2331 Grand Concourse** is the Art Deco Concourse Hotel.

At 2417 Grand Concourse is the former **Loew's Paradise Theater** (1929; John Eberson; DL), a symbol of the borough's faded glory and the fits and starts associated with restoring it. The theater closed in 1994 and deteriorated badly, but it was landmarked in 1997. New investors took over, hoping to open a hall for concerts, wrestling, and boxing. After $5 million in renovation, however, the project stalled. The building remains empty. Its exterior is cream-toned terra-cotta and red levanto marble.

Just north of Fordham Rd is a branch of the **Emigrant Savings Bank,** originally the Dollar Savings Bank (1932; Halsey, McCormack & Helmer; DL), designed by the creators of Brooklyn's towering Williamsburgh Savings Bank. The original building was a modest granite bank, but as Dollar Bank prospered it added a ten-story tower with a four-faced clock (1938). The decoration includes quotations encouraging thrift: "Without Economy No One Can Be Rich. With It, Few Can Be Poor." Inside are marble, limestone, terra-cotta, bronze, and gold- and silver-leafed plaster details as well as five murals depicting the borough's early history.

Edgar Allan Poe Cottage

Poe Park, East Kingsbridge Rd and Grand Concourse, Bronx, NY 10458. ☎ (718) 881-8900. Open Sun 1—5; Sat 10—4. Closed mid-Dec–mid-Jan. Admission charge; children under 12 free.

Subway: Lexington Ave Express (4) to Kingsbridge Rd; Walk three blocks east to Grand Concourse. Sixth Ave Express (D) to Kingsbridge Rd.

Car: Take Major Deegan Expwy to Fordham Rd. Go east to Grand Concourse and turn left (north) to Kingsbridge Rd.

Poe Cottage (c. 1812; DL), in Poe Park at E. 193rd St, a humble white frame farmhouse, was moved here from Valentine St and Kingsbridge Rd in 1913. Edgar Allan Poe, already author of "The Tell-Tale Heart" and "The Raven" but still stalked by poverty and his own bleak disposition, came to this little house in 1846 hoping the country air would cure his wife Virginia's tuberculosis. She died during the first winter, but the poet stayed on to write "Ulalume" and "The Bells" and perhaps part of "Annabel Lee," a eulogy to his bride, whom he had married when she was just 13 years old. Poe rented the cottage out in 1849 and headed south, dying in Baltimore in Oct of that year.

The house has been converted to a simple museum, with a few period furnishings, memorabilia, and an audiovisual exhibit that evokes Poe's tragic life and literary achievement.

North of Poe Park the population shifts from being largely Latino to a mix of established German and Irish families and newer Albanian, Indian, Pakistani, and Korean arrivals. **Town Towers** (1931), 2830 Grand Concourse (at E. 197th St), is another of Horace Ginsbern's fine works. The facade includes striped brick piers, palm fronds, and a crenellated parapet; inside is another attractive Art Deco lobby. The arched doorway of **2888 Grand Concourse** is supported by sculptures of two weary hooded gnomes. Above them, the building has an unusual array of multicolored bricks.

32 · Central Bronx: Bronx Zoo, New York Botanical Garden, Fordham University, Belmont, West Farms, and University Heights

The main geographical and cultural feature of the Central Bronx is Bronx Park, which includes the Bronx Zoo and the New York Botanical Garden. Nearby are the campus of Fordham University and the neighborhoods of Belmont and University Heights. While these neighborhoods are sometimes considered part of the South Bronx, they never suffered the same destructive destabilization.

Bronx Zoo

Fordham Rd at Bronx River Pkwy, Bronx, NY 10469. Recorded information hotline, ☎ (718) 367-1010; to reach a live person, ☎ (718) 220-5100. Web site: www.wcs.org. Open every day of the year (rides and some exhibits closed in winter): April–Oct, Mon–Fri 10–5; weekends and holidays 10–5:30; earlier winter closings except during Nov–Jan holiday period. Admission charge; general admission free on Wed. Additional fees for Congo Gorilla Forest, Children's Zoo (seasonal), Butterfly Zone (seasonal), and rides.

Special events, exhibits, educational programs. Terrace Café and Flamingo Pub open year-round; African Market and Asia Plaza open seasonally. Zoo map included with entrance fee. Baby strollers for rent at entrances. All buildings except Monkey House and Astor Court restroom accessible to wheelchairs. To reserve an adult stroller, ☎ (718) 220-5188 a week in advance.

Subway: Seventh Ave Express (2) to Pelham Pkwy. Lexington Ave Express (5) to E. 180th St, transfer to Seventh Ave Express (2) to Pelham Pkwy. Walk west to the Bronxdale entrance.

Bus: Bx9, Bx19 to Southern Blvd entrance. Bx12, Bx22 to Fordham Rd and Southern Blvd. Walk east on Fordham Rd to entrance. Q44 to E. 180th St and Boston Rd. Walk north to entrance. Express Bus: Liberty Lines express service on BxM11 from Manhattan (various stops on Madison Ave) to the zoo's Bronx Pkwy entrance. For information about fares, schedule, and stops in Manhattan, ☎ (718) 652-8400.

Car: From the East Side, take Triborough Bridge to Bruckner Expwy east to Bronx River Pkwy north. Take exit 6 and turn left to Bronxdale parking lot. From the West Side, take West Side Hwy to the Cross Bronx Expwy east to Bronx River Pkwy north. Take exit 6; turn left to Bronxdale parking lot. Parking: Large lots (parking charge) along the Bronx River Pkwy near exit 6; additional parking available.

The Bronx Zoo is the largest urban zoo in the U.S. It covers 265 acres and is home to more than 6,000 animals of 612 species. One of the city's major tourist sites (2 million visitors annually), it also serves as an international center for environmental education and a facility for perpetuating rare and endangered species.

History

In the years since its opening (1899), the zoo, established and operated by the Wildlife Conservation Society (formerly the New York Zoological Society), has changed both physically and in its philosophy. During earlier decades administrators emphasized rarity and quantity—in 1910 there were 5,163 animals of 1,160 species. Today there are more than 6,000 animals but only 612 species, with herds and flocks replacing single animals where possible, a policy that has increased breeding potential. In 1998 there were 292 births and hatchings. The zoo has also replaced most of its older cages with more natural habitats, an approach extended indoors with such exhibits as Wild Asia, World of Darkness, and World of Birds. The Wildlife Conservation Society has helped establish more than 100 wildlife sanctuaries around the world.

Highlights

The zoo's main entrance and parking area is off exit 6 of the Bronx River Pkwy. Just beyond the entrance is **World of Birds** (1972; building by Morris Ketchum Jr. & Assocs.) a two-tiered naturalistic indoor habitat with more than 100 species, including birds of paradise, hornbills, and curassows. An artificial waterfall plummets 40 ft from a 50 ft fiberglass cliff, and periodically a shower drenches the rain forest exhibit (but not the visitors).

Just northwest of World of Birds, near the bison exhibit, is **Fountain Circle,** marked by the 36 ft bronze Rainey Memorial Gate (1934; Paul Manship, sculptor), whose stylized tree-of-life motif has 22 full-size animals. In the center of the Fountain Circle parking lot stands a white limestone fountain (17C–early 18C) from

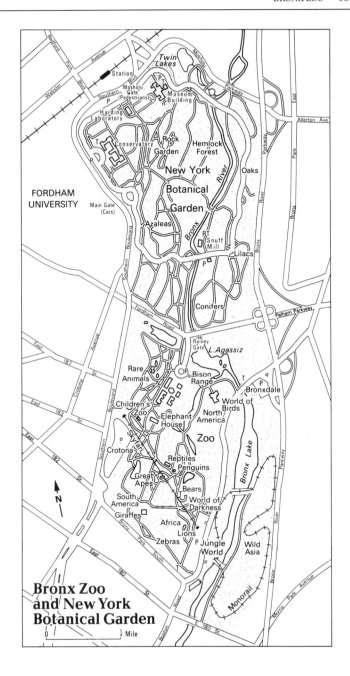

Bronx Zoo
and New York
Botanical Garden

0   ¼ Mile

Como, Italy, with sporting dolphins, sea horses, mermaids, and mermen, a gift (1902) from William Rockefeller. The stone jaguars near the stairs are the work of Anna Hyatt Huntington (1937) and were modeled after Señor Lopez, the first big cat in the Carnivore House (opened 1903).

West of Fountain Circle is one of the zoo's continental exhibits, the **Sea Bird Colony,** which re-creates the rugged Patagonian coast of South America with Magellanic penguins, Inca terns, guanay cormorants, and other indigenous species.

South of the sea birds is **Astor Court,** formerly Baird Court, named after 19C naturalist Spencer Fullerton Baird and renamed in the 1980s for philanthropist Brooke Astor, who helped fund restoration of the area and its historic buildings, once the zoo's main exhibit area. This formally designed area, which includes the Lion House (1903), the Administration Building (1910), the Main Bird House (1905), and the Heads and Horns Building (1922), is now used largely for administrative offices. The Primate House (1901, later renamed the Monkey House) still houses monkeys, while the Elephant House (1908; Heins & La Farge), with its green-tinted dome and sculpted pachyderms as well as real elephants, tapirs, and rhinos, is a visitors reception center.

Also inside Astor Court is one of the zoo's newest and most popular exhibits, the **Butterfly Zone** (open late May–early Oct, weather permitting). Inside this walk-through, caterpillar-shaped structure—21 ft high, 42 ft wide, and 170 ft long—are nearly 1,000 North American butterflies and moths of 35 species who fly freely around visitors. Visitors can also view the metamorphosis of pupae as they develop and eventually emerge as damp, wrinkled butterflies or moths, fluff their wings, and join the other Butterfly Zone inhabitants.

In the southern part of the park is **World of Darkness** (1969; building by Morris Ketchum Jr. and Assocs.), an indoor exhibit with more than 40 nocturnal species. Low levels of light turn day into night so visitors may see these animals, including bats, owl monkeys, porcupines, and bush babies at their liveliest.

The southern section of the zoo is also home to some of the zoo's continental exhibits. The **African Plains** features lions, slender-horned gazelles, zebras, and others. The new **Congo Gorilla Forest,** a 6.5-acre African rain forest habitat, is the new home of the zoo's lowland gorillas (one of the largest breeding populations in North America) as well as Wolf's monkeys, gray-cheeked hornbills, African rock pythons, assassin bugs, and other native neighbors. Visitors walk through a lush landscape, made up of more than 15,000 plants representing 400 species, which is home to 400 animals of 55 species. Hidden in the trees are electronic feeders that release food at intervals, encouraging the gorillas to forage and explore their environment.

Elephants, gaur (largest of the world's cattle), antelope, Siberian tigers, rhinoceroses, and many species of deer of which the Formosan sika deer is the rarest, inhabit the 40 acres of **Wild Asia** (open May–Oct, weather permitting). The **Bengali Express,** a monorail (20-minute narrated tour), is the only way to see the exhibit; this monorail leaves from the Asian Plaza beginning 10:30 A.M.

New York Botanical Garden

E. 200th St at Kazimiroff (Southern) Blvd, Bronx, NY 10458. ☎ (718) 817-8700. Web site: www.nybg.org. Open April–Oct, Tues–Sun and Mon holidays 10–6; Nov–March, same days 10–4. Closed Mon except holidays. Extended holiday hours late Nov–early Jan. Admission charge for grounds, with additional fees for conservatory and some specialized gardens. Admission to grounds is free Wed all day and Sat 10–noon. Garden passport combination ticket available.

Lectures, seasonal events, guided tours, tram and golf-cart tours (fee), plant information, programs for children and adults; for information about educational programs, ☎ (718) 817-8747 or inquire at the Watson Building reception desk. Lunch and snacks in Garden Café year-round. Picnic tables. Garden shop and plant shop (seasonal). Accessible to wheelchairs; tram tours.

Subway: Involves a one-mile walk to the garden. Lexington Ave Express (4) to Bedford Park Blvd (Jerome Ave). Cross Jerome Ave and walk southeast on Bedford Park Blvd, which ends at the garden; turn left and proceed to the garden's entrance (next to the bus stop). Depending on connections, the subway will take 30–45 minutes from Grand Central Station; the walk from the subway to the garden takes about 20–25 minutes. If you cross Paul Ave, you are going the wrong way.

Train from Grand Central: More convenient than the subway. Take Metro North Harlem Line Local from Grand Central Station to Botanical Garden Station. **Note:** Be sure to take a local train as express trains do not stop at the garden. Schedules (different on weekends and holidays) available at the Grand Central Station information booth.

Shuttle Bus: The garden operates a shuttle to and from Manhattan on weekends, April–Oct. ☎ (718) 817-8700 for reservations.

Car: Take Pelham, Bronx River, or Mosholu Pkwys to Kazimiroff (Southern) Blvd exit. Follow signs to vehicular entrance. Ample car parking (charge).

The New York Botanical Garden, a national historic landmark, is one of the city's great open spaces, with 250 acres of specialty gardens and plant collections, a glorious conservatory, an arboretum, and a 40-acre tract of original forest with the Bronx River running through it. It is also a major educational institution sponsoring biological and environmental research, expeditions, and scientific publications; the plant science library is one of the world's largest, and the herbarium, a collection of preserved plants, has more than 6.5 million specimens.

History

In 1884 the city bought 661 acres from the Lorillard family, tobacco dynasts, of which 250 became the site of the Botanical Garden. Urged by Nathaniel Lord Britton, a Columbia University botanist, the state legislature founded the garden (1891) and was happy to see such eminences as Andrew Carnegie, J. P. Morgan, and Cornelius Vanderbilt sit on its board of directors. The 34-room Lorillard Mansion burned down in 1923, but in 1938 the city transferred other buildings from the estate to the garden, including the Snuff Mill, the carriage house (now a maintenance center), and a stone cottage (private residence to the vice president of horticulture).

Garden Tour

Free maps and tour information are available at the **information booth** next to the **Great Garden Clock,** not far from the main entrance.

Highlights

Follow signs to the conservatory, walking along Perennial Garden Way, first passing the **Herb Garden,** designed by English landscape designer Penelope Hobhouse, with 160 species of herbs and ornamental plants in a traditional knot design. The nearby **Perennial Garden,** designed by the city's public garden designer Lynden B. Miller, features "mixed borders," displays combining perennials, annuals, biennials, and bulbs that re-create English borders but tolerate New York's harsher climate.

The **Enid A. Haupt Conservatory** (1902; William R. Cobb for Lord & Burnham, greenhouse manufacturers; altered in 1938 and 1953; restored 1978; Edward Larrabee Barnes & Assocs.; restored 1997; Beyer Blinder Belle; DL) is the best Victorian glasshouse in the United States. During a four-year, $25-million restoration 17,000 panes of glass were replaced by hand and state-of-the-art technical systems were installed.

The central building is a commanding presence with a 90 ft high dome and a rotunda 100 ft in diameter. Flanking it are ten interconnecting greenhouse galleries, which together recall London's former Crystal Palace and the greenhouses of the Royal Botanical Gardens in Kew outside London. The permanent exhibition, **A World of Plants,** has flora from lowland and upland tropical rain forests, desert plants from the Americas and Africa, aquatic plants, and subtropical plants. **Palms of the Americas,** in the dome, offers more than 100 species of palms as well as cycads (the world's most ancient plants) and ferns. Two galleries are dedicated to seasonal flower shows.

Not far from the conservatory is the **Seasonal Walk.** In autumn chrysanthemums bloom here in colors like the tones of Persian carpets. In the spring 13,000 tulip bulbs flower in a rainbow of color. The **Demonstration Gardens** nextdoor include fragrance, vegetable, cutting, wildlife, native, autumn, and shade gardens.

Beyond the café and the Mosholu Gate is the magnificent **Main Building,** a 99-year-old Beaux-Arts masterpiece housing the library and herbarium, the largest collection of preserved plant specimens in the Western Hemisphere. (After 2001 these facilities will move to the Plant Studies Center, a five-story, 70,000-square-ft facility now being constructed as an addition to the Main Building; the Main Building will revert to its original function as a museum.) In front of the building stands the bronze ***Fountain of Life*** (1905; Carl Tefft), vitality in this case symbolized by plunging horses, nude figures, a mermaid, and a merman.

The **Rock and Native Plant Gardens** are especially beautiful in April and May, when wildflowers are in spectacular bloom. The rock garden features a heath bed and an alpine meadow, with delicate mountain and rock-loving flowers from around the world.

East of the Rock and Native Plant Gardens lies a 40-acre **forest,** one of the city's few remaining tracts of natural uncut woodland, home to migratory and resident birds, mammals, reptiles, and amphibians. On the hills are hemlock, oak, and hickory trees, while beeches, tulip trees, red maples, and sweet gums grow at lower elevations.

Running through the forest is a stretch of the 23-mile **Bronx River,** which originates near the Kensico Dam in Westchester County and spills into the East River at Hunts Point. East of the forest is an arboretum with collections of oaks, maples, conifers, and flowering trees and shrubs—lilacs, magnolias, crabapples, and cherry trees.

The **Rose Garden,** with 260 varieties of antique and modern roses, was designed in 1916 by famous landscape designer Beatrix Jones Farrand but not actually constructed according to her plans until 1971, when David and Peggy Rockefeller financed the project. In 1999 the garden won the President's Award for the most outstanding All-America Rose Selections in a public rose garden.

The **Snuff Mill** (1840; restored 1954; DL) was built by the Lorillard brothers, Peter and George, who harnessed the waterpower of the Bronx River to grind their tobacco with millstones instead of rubbing it over graters as other firms did. This innovation, devised by their father, Pierre, in part accounted for the success of the family business. Diarist Philip Hone remarked on Pierre Lorillard's death (1843): "He led people by the nose for the best part of a century and made his enormous fortune giving them to chew that which they could not swallow."

In April on **Daffodil Hill** thousands of naturalized daffodils burst into bloom. The **Wild Wetland Trail** provides a walk through a lush environment of grasses, greens, and wildlife that teaches the importance of wetlands. At the end of the trail is the **Children's Adventure Garden,** a 12-acre indoor-outdoor hands-on botany and horticulture museum that opened in 1998. Whimsically designed with hedge mazes, climbing boulders, and giant topiaries as well as an activity center with laboratories and microscopes, it makes the botanical garden and, on a larger scale the planet, relevant to children.

Fordham University
The third major institution in the Central Bronx is Fordham University, east of Webster Ave between E. Fordham Rd and Southern Blvd.

History
Founded on Rose Hill in 1841 as St. John's College by the Right Reverend John Hughes, later the city's first Roman Catholic archbishop, it was led in its early years by John McCloskey, later the nation's first cardinal. In 1846 it became a Jesuit institution (as it remains today). Fordham University also has a residential campus at Lincoln Center in Manhattan, as well as academic centers in Tarrytown and Armonk, New York. Today Fordham enrolls more than 14,600 undergraduate and graduate students overall.

The Campus
Located on 85 acres, the campus features traditional collegiate Gothic architecture and cobblestone streets. The fieldstone Greek revival **Rose Hill Manor House** (1838; additions 1907; DL), with its dentiled cornice and cupola, was originally a country house and is now the main administration building. **Alumni House** (1840; William Rodrigue; DL), a smaller, fieldstone building, now serves as the housing office. William Rodrigue, who built Alumni House along with **St. John's Church** (1845; DL) and **St. John's Residence Hall** (1845; DL), was Hughes's brother-in-law and a teacher at the college. The Gothic revival church, with its pinnacled tower, and the fieldstone residence hall form the **Queen's Court** or Old Quad. The church's transept, chancel, crossing, and latern were added in 1929.

Belmont

Belmont, bounded by E. Fordham Rd, the Bronx Zoo, E. 187th St, and Arthur Ave, is named for Jacob Lorillard's estate, which included much of the surrounding land. At the end of the 19C, Belmont became an Italian enclave peopled by immigrants from Sicily and southern Italy who flocked here to construct and landscape the Bronx Zoo. Most of the older Italians have moved on, and the neighborhood today is filled with Albanians, blacks, and Latinos. Yet Arthur Ave remains a vibrant Italian commercial district, far more coherent than Manhattan's Little Italy. The Italians who moved to Westchester County or more-affluent sections of the Bronx still return to shop and dine; the strip also attracts hordes of other New Yorkers.

Many of the neighborhood establishments measure time in terms of generations. For example, **Biancardi's Italian Market,** 2350 Arthur Ave, has been selling meats (including goat, rabbit, and suckling pig) since 1932. **Borgatti's Pasta Store,** 632 E. 187th St, has also been around for more than 60 years, while **Addeo's Bakers,** 2352 Arthur Ave, dates back to 1929, and **Mario's** restaurant at 2342 Arthur Ave opened in 1919. Oddly, the oldest store (dating to 1915), which sells cheese, cold cuts, and olive oil, is **Teitel Brothers** (at 2349 Arthur Ave), which was founded by Austrian Jewish immigrants and has been run by their descendants.

The merchants work hard at preserving Arthur Ave's flavor, particularly with the **Ferragosto di Belmont,** founded in 1997, one of New York's most distinctive street fairs. Unlike most street fairs, which have become increasingly generic, this festival (on or around Aug 15) is limited to neighborhood merchants and resembles a country fair in old Italy. Costumed performers roam the streets, musicians perform Italian songs, and local merchants prepare authentic Italian food including spit-roasted pigs.

Also keeping the Italian spirit alive are the **Belmont Italian American Playhouse,** 2385 Arthur Ave, founded in 1981, and the **Enrico Fermi Cultural Center,** 610 E. 186th St, in the local library branch, which since 1981 has housed books, records, films, and other documents about Italian immigrants and Italian Americans. The center's Italian Heritage Collection features reference books in both English and Italian.

West Farms

Immediately south of the zoo and reaching east to the Bronx River is the neighborhood of West Farms. The river attracted industry, and glass, pottery, paint, and bleaching factories, along with flour mills and coal yards were built after 1812. From the 1860s through the 1930s, the area was a thriving port. Today, it is home to several forgotten historic sites.

The **Old West Farms Soldiers' Cemetery**—the borough's oldest public burial ground for veterans, containing the graves of soldiers from the War of 1812, the Civil War, the Spanish-American War, and World War I—lies at 2103 Bryant Ave and E. 180th St, next to the modern Lambert Houses (1973; Davis, Brody & Assoc.). In 2000, Bronx borough president Fernando Ferrer rededicated the deteriorated site and allocated money for restoring the fence.

The main attraction of **River Park,** just to the east along E. 180th St, is a 19C man-made waterfall once used to power nearby mills. Locals also enjoy fishing and wading in the river. Further east, at 1129 E. 180th St (between Devoe and Bronx Park Aves), is the **Fire Alarm and Telegraph Bureau,** an attractive buff brick building with three archways and a terra-cotta roof. When built by the Fire Department in 1923, it was at the cutting edge of technology and is still used for fire-alarm dispatches.

One of the city's grandest subway stations is the former **New York, Westchester & Boston Railway Company Administration Building** (1912; Fellheimer & Long, and Allen H. Stem; DL), at E. 180th St and Morris Park Ave. Now the **entrance to the E. 180th St subway station** for the Seventh Ave Express (2) and Lexington Ave Express (5), it was created in the style of a Florentine villa, with two square towers, arched windows, and a red tile roof. The building was more successful than the original railroad line, which folded in 1937.

University Heights

On the western edge of the Central Bronx, lying on a ridge that descends to the Harlem River on the west, is the neighborhood of University Heights, dominated by the former campus of New York University. The community is now largely Dominican, Jamaican, and Guyanese, and of the more than 9,000 immigrants who arrived here between 1990 and 1996, more than half were Dominican. During the same period, 407 refugees moved here from Vietnam, more than any other neighborhood in the city.

Bronx Community College

Bronx Community College, part of the City University of New York, occupies the former **University Heights campus of New York University,** on University Ave between W. 180th St and Sedgwick Ave. NYU officials, seeking a traditional collegiate setting, created the campus at the end of the 19C when the Washington Square area seemed too urban and commercial. Because of fiscal problems, the university sold the campus back to the city in 1973, and it was taken over by Bronx Community College.

The Bronx Cheer

According to legend, the Bronx cheer was invented in the 1950s at Bronx Community College (then located at nearby E. 184th St and Creston Ave). When students were suspended for spitting at visiting basketball teams, sophomore Allen Van Wersh hit upon the idea of sticking out his tongue and vibrating his lips to razz opponents. The rest is history.

The Campus

The classical and Renaissance buildings of tawny Roman brick with terra-cotta and limestone trim were designed by McKim, Mead & White and are considered one of Stanford White's crowning achievements. The true masterpiece here is **Gould Memorial Library** (1912; DL), completed eight years after White's death and influenced by Rome's Pantheon. Inside is a beautiful three-story rotunda with sculptures of classical figures and 16 columns of green Connemara marble, perhaps the largest display of this marble in the nation. White further embellished the interior with wood, bronze, mosaic, and Tiffany glass details. In 1919, when the city's leading architects wanted to create a memorial for White, who had been murdered (see The First Two Madison Square Gardens in Walk 13), they chose this site, designing a set of bronze doors in their colleague's honor.

Hall of Fame for Great Americans

Campus of Bronx Community College of CUNY, University Ave and W. 181st St, Bronx, NY 10453. ☎ (718) 289-5161. Open daily 10–5. The rotunda in Gould Memorial Library is open during the school year weekdays 9:30–2:30. Free. Permanent exhibition of sculpture; guided and self-guided tours. Restrooms in Gould Memorial Library. The colonnade is accessible to wheelchairs; the library rotunda is not.

Subway: Lexington Ave Express (4) to Burnside Ave. Bus: From George Washington Bridge Bus Station in Manhattan, Bx3 via University Ave.

Nearby is the Hall of Fame for Great Americans (1901, 1914; McKim, Mead & White; DL), with 98 bronze busts of famous Americans mounted between the columns of a majestic open-air, semicircular colonnade. The colonnade, with Guastavino vaulting and a tile roof, sits on the brow of a hill that offers sweeping views across the Harlem River to the Harlem plains and the distant hills with the towers of The Cloisters rising above the trees.

History

The Great Americans were chosen by a college of electors appointed by the trustees of the Hall of Fame. Those honored include such obvious candidates as George Washington, Benjamin Franklin, and Abraham Lincoln, as well as dark horses such as John Lothrop Motley (a historian whose definitive works were *The Rise of the Dutch Republic* and *The History of the United Netherlands*). Sculptors of the busts also range from the well-known, including Jean-Antoine Houdon (*George Washington* and *Robert Fulton*, both replicas) and Frederick J. MacMonnies (*Simon Newcomb* and *James Abbott McNeill Whistler*), to less-renowned figures—for example, Rudulph Evans (*Grover Cleveland* and *Henry Wadsworth Longfellow*). In 1992 the newest bust, *Franklin Delano Roosevelt*, was installed, but there are four honorees whose statues have not yet been cast: Louis Brandeis, first Jewish Supreme Court justice; Clara Barton, founder of the American Red Cross; Luther Burbank, horticulturist; and Andrew Carnegie, industrialist and philanthropist. The once-popular site is now largely forgotten. Elections have not been held since 1976, and the elector panel has been disbanded. Still, the hall received a much-praised restoration recently. There have been talks of completing the missing busts and renewing the electoral process.

Other Buildings

Complementing the Hall of Fame and the Gould Memorial Library are the **Hall of Philosophy** (1912; DL) and the **Hall of Languages** (1895; DL), also designed by White. Symmetrical, classical buildings with Ionic porticos and cornices set on low roofs, they complete White's grand architectural composition.

Across Hall of Fame Terrace from the main campus is **MacCracken Hall** (c. 1880), the one time residence of Henry Mitchell MacCracken, the NYU chancellor who founded the campus.

Other Points of Interest

South of the campus, on W. Burnside Ave at the southeast corner of Phelan Place, stands a battered **gatehouse** (1890) built for the New Croton Aqueduct (1885–93), a system of tunnels that delivers water to the city. The course of the aqueduct is visible in a strip of parkland paralleling University Ave.

At W. Fordham Rd and the Harlem River is the **University Heights Bridge** (1895; William Burr; relocation 1908; Othniel Nichols; reconstructed 1987–92; DL), a steel-truss bridge with a central revolving swing span, stone pavilions, and ornate iron railings. It was originally the Harlem Ship Canal Bridge but was floated south to this site after serving for about a decade at the northern end of the Harlem River.

33 · Eastern Bronx: Throgs Neck, Parkchester, Westchester, Morris Park, Pelham Bay Park, City Island, and Co-op City

Throgs Neck

Throgs Neck is a peninsula stretching from the southeast extremity of the Bronx into Long Island Sound. The neighborhood's 30,000 residents are mostly of Italian, Irish, and German descent. The name recalls John Throgmorton (or Throckmorton), who arrived here with a band of followers in 1643 and was driven out by Native Americans. In the 19C wealthy industrialists Collis P. Huntington (railroads) and H. O. Havemeyer (sugar) had summer homes here. Nowadays it is a modest residential neighborhood, through the center of which cut the approaches to the **Throgs Neck Bridge** (1961; Othmar H. Ammann).

Fort Schuyler

Subway: Lexington Ave Local (6) to Westchester Square–E. Tremont Ave. Transfer to Bx40 bus marked "Fort Schuyler" and take it directly to the gate of Maritime College, the last stop.

Bus: New York Bus Service offers express bus service between Manhattan and Throgs Neck; ☎ (718) 994-5500 for information. The stop for Fort Schuyler is at the intersection of Pennyfield and Harding Aves, approximately a half-mile from the Maritime College campus.

Car: From Manhattan, take Triborough Bridge and follow "New England" signs to Throgs Neck Bridge; take Fort Schuyler exit just before the Throgs Neck Bridge. At stop sign turn right, go to traffic light, turn left onto Pennyfield Ave, proceed approximately one mile to Maritime College entrance.

At the end of Pennyfield Ave beneath Throgs Neck Bridge is the former Fort Schuyler, now the **Maritime College of the State University of New York.**

History

Fort Schuyler (1834–38; I. L. Smith; DL), built of granite and shaped like an irregular pentagon, dates from a period between the War of 1812 and the Civil War when the city, in no immediate danger, was completing the system of coastal fortifications begun around 1812. Before this period the waters of Hell Gate were considered sufficient protection, but with the development of steam propulsion, the military establishment closed this "back door" into the city. Fort Schuyler, paired with Fort Totten on Willets Point in Queens, was designed to rake the lower part of Long Island Sound with crossfire.

Although garrisoned during the Civil War, Fort Schuyler never saw action and was abandoned in 1870, remaining empty until restored (1934) by public funds and converted to the Maritime College, founded in 1874 to train officers for the U.S. Merchant Marine. The college became part of the State University of New York in 1948. In 1967, architect William A. Hall converted the gun galleries into a library.

Maritime Industry Museum

6 Pennyfield Ave, Fort Schuyler, Bronx, NY 10465. ☎ (718) 409-7218. Web site: www.maritimeindustrymuseum.org. Open Mon–Sat 9–4. Closed Sun, Jan 1, Thanksgiving, Dec 25. Free; free parking. Changing exhibits. Gift shop. Only the ground floor is accessible to wheelchairs.

Since 1986, Fort Schuyler has been home to the Maritime Industry Museum, which documents the history of the merchant marine, ports, and related industries. On the second floor is the main exhibit, **The Evolution of Seafaring,** a chronological survey that begins with the Phoenicians and includes paintings, ship models, tools, and navigational instruments. Other exhibits focus on the history of the school, the tragedy of the *Morro Castle* (which burned off New Jersey in 1934), clipper ships, and modern passenger liners. The museum also has an intricate and detailed model of the Brooklyn Naval Yard during World War II.

Parkchester

Parkchester, bounded to the north by E. Tremont Ave, to the east by Purdy Ave, to the south by McGraw Ave, and to the west by White Plains Rd, is the site of one of the nation's first large-scale housing projects (1938–42; Board of Design, Richmond H. Shreve, chairman). Before the arrival of Parkchester, the eastern Bronx was sparsely developed, with small residential neighborhoods, occasional business centers, and large expanses of marshland. Less famous than nearby Co-op City, this 129-acre complex is virtually self-sustaining; it has 100 stores, 35 offices, and its own security force, maintenance staff, and recreation department.

History

The 171-building, 12,271-unit complex was created during the Depression by the Metropolitan Life Insurance Company, which administered it for some 30 years. While its curving roads and expanses of lawns earned the praise of city planners, the apartments were originally available to whites only. Accusations of racism led Metropolitan Life to sell the complex to the Helmsley-Spear real estate firm, which turned it into condominiums. Today, Parkchester—indeed, the entire eastern section of the borough—still attracts fewer minorities than the Bronx at large: between 1990 and 1996, more immigrants from the former Soviet Union than from the Dominican Republic moved into this area.

By the early 1990s the development was aging and the neighborhood deteriorating. In 1998, Helmsley-Spear sold the complex to the Community Preservation Corporation, the city's largest private financer of multifamily housing. Plans for renovation have been announced, but the complex continues to struggle with a high vacancy rate and unhappy tenants.

Nearby, at the intersection of E. Tremont Ave, Poplar St, and Castle Hill Ave, is the **Church of St. Raymond's** (1898), one of the borough's oldest Roman Catholic parishes, established in 1842. This striking Byzantine building has two main towers, each with a dome atop a colonnade and surrounded by four miniature colonnaded domes. Above the church entrance is a large rose window, which dominates the front of the church.

Westchester
Westchester Square, at the intersection of Westchester Ave and E. Tremont Ave, was the village green of the colonial town of Westchester, called *Oostorp* by the Dutch who founded it in 1653. Today it is an undistinguished commercial center. The area to the north, Westchester Heights, has in recent decades become home to several large state mental institutions and to the Albert Einstein College of Medicine of Yeshiva University (Morris Park Ave, southwest corner of Eastchester Blvd). The Bronx State Hospital Rehabilitation Center (1971; Gruzen & Partners), the Bronx Children's Psychiatric Hospital (1969; office of Max O. Urbahn), and the Bronx Developmental Center (1976; Richard Meier & Assocs.) all occupy a tract of land bounded by the Hutchinson River Pkwy and Eastchester Rd.

Near Westchester Square is **St. Peter's Church** (Episcopal) complex and cemetery, 2500 Westchester Ave (church 1855; Sunday School and chapel building 1868; Leopold Eidlitz; DL). The third church of a congregation that dates back to 1693, Gothic revival St. Peter's has a steeply pitched roof and towering spire. It was built by Leopold Eidlitz, a Czech, who became one of the most influential 19C American architects; his son, Cyrus, restored and somewhat altered the church after an 1877 fire. Today, the elevated train line runs overhead, depriving the church and cemetery of their quiet dignity. The cemetery includes the graves of Revolutionary War soldiers.

Morris Park
To the northwest lies Morris Park, one of the borough's most stable neighborhoods, its population mostly middle-class Italian Americans. Morris Park has been untouched by the extremes of urban decay or gentrification.

History
The community dates back to 1889, when John Albert Morris built a 307-acre thoroughbred racetrack, which attracted hotels and restaurants frequented by Manhattan society. The Belmont Stakes were run there until 1905. When racing was moved to Belmont Park, the Aeronautic Society of New York held meets at the

racecourse; inventor Alexander Graham Bell partnered with aviation pioneer Glenn Curtiss in a failed attempt to launch a plane there in 1908.

After Morris's death, the city took over Morris Park from a bankrupt real estate syndicate and began constructing streets. In 1913, it auctioned plots of land to buyers, including Astors and other notable families. Morris Park remained sparsely populated until after World War II, when Italians from Manhattan moved here. Morris Park Ave, the main shopping street, has genuine Italian butchers, bakers, and cheese makers.

St. Lucy's Church

To the northeast of Morris Park, at the corner of Bronxwood and Mace Aves, is St. Lucy's Roman Catholic Church (1939). On its grounds is the **Lourdes of America,** an outdoor stone replica of the French grotto where the Virgin Mary appeared to Bernadette Soubirous in 1858. The grounds also contain a replica of the Holy Steps in Rome, which, like the grotto, was built in the early 1940s by founding pastor Pasquale Lombardo. A steady stream of visitors—older Italians, younger Albanians, blacks, and Latinos—comes to the grotto to pray or touch the trickle of holy water. The water once supposedly flowed from a natural spring beneath the shrine but today is regular New York City tap water blessed once a year. The Holy Rome replica attracts less attention but is more elaborate. Statues of saints, angels, and sheep adorn the steps leading to a large scene of the Crucifixion. The church gift shop sells books, candles, and figurines.

Pelham Bay Park

In the 1880s, the city bought land to create Pelham Bay Park—now 2,764 acres of salt marsh, lagoon, forest and upland, meadow and seashore. In addition to Orchard Beach, its most famous recreational facility, the park contains the Split Rock Golf Course and the Pelham Bay Golf Course, bridle paths, and facilities for hiking, bicycling, tennis, boating, and running. There is also a police shooting range (not open to the public).

History

Religious pioneer Anne Hutchinson (1591–1643) and her followers are believed to have settled somewhere near the site of Pelham Bay Park in the early 1640s. In 1654 Englishman Thomas Pell bought more than 9,000 acres from the Siwanoy Indians, including the present parkland, but had to swear allegiance to the Dutch to keep his land. Presumably he felt relieved when the British took over the colony and he was granted (1666) a royal patent for the land.

The Park

Today, the park is divided into two sections by the mouth of the Hutchinson River opening into Eastchester Bay. **Garbage Mountain,** the dominant topographical feature of the southwest sector of the park, began as an imposing mound of trash; it was closed to dumping in 1979 and seeded with grass. Nearby, the **Pelham Bay War Memorial,** a tall column (c. 1925; Belle Kinney, sculptor) crowned by a winged figure, stands south of the road.

Isaac L. Rice

In the southern end of the park once stood Isaac L. Rice Stadium, built in 1916 with a $1-million gift from Rice's widow, Julia. Rice was an editor, lawyer, inventor (electric storage batteries for cars and submarines), and chess master (creator of the opening known as Rice's Gambit). The stadium deteriorated over time and was knocked down in the 1980s. However, Rice is remembered in the street names just south of the stadium site—Watt, Ampere, and Ohm Aves. The Parks Department hopes to raise money to restore *The American Boy* (1916; Louis St. Lannes), the statue that once crowned Rice Stadium, and to place it once again in the park.

In the park's northern section are golf courses, Orchard Beach, and the Bartow-Pell Mansion Museum, which lies just east of Shore Rd near the golf greens.

Bartow-Pell Mansion Museum

895 Shore Rd, Pelham Bay Park, Bronx, NY 10464. ☎ (718) 885-1461. Open Wed, Sat, Sun 12–4. Mansion closed Aug. Carriage house open April–Oct during museum hours. Gardens open Tues–Sun 8:30–4:30. Call to confirm. Admission charge; children under 12 free when accompanied by an adult. Grounds and carriage house accessible to wheelchairs; mansion not accessible.

Subway: Lexington Ave Local (6) to Pelham Bay Park. Take Westchester Bee Line bus into the park itself.

Car: From Manhattan, take Triborough Bridge to Bruckner Expwy and New England Thruway; take Orchard Beach exit.

The present mansion is the third on the site of Thomas Pell's original estate. Robert Bartow, a descendant of the Pell family, built this unusually fine Greek revival stone manor sometime between 1836 and 1842 (DL). In 1888 the city bought the house and grounds from Westchester County as part of a program for developing parks but let the building stand vacant until 1914, when the International Garden Club restored it and planted its now-lovely gardens. Behind the house, past the flower beds, herb garden, and lawn, a walkway leads to the family graveyard, where descendants of Thomas Pell are buried. Mayor La Guardia spent two summers in the house.

Interior

The interior of the house has been furnished with period pieces from private collections and city museums, including examples of American Empire furniture (c. 1810–40). The elliptical stairway and elegant carved woodwork exemplify Greek revival domestic architecture at its best. The newly restored three-story carriage house, with a hay loft and tack room, serves as an exhibit facility.

Orchard Beach

From the mansion, follow Shore Rd to Orchard Beach. Its sweeping crescent was created in the 1930s by Parks Commissioner Robert Moses by filling the space between Hunter and Twin Islands on the north and Rodman's Neck on the south with white sand dredged from the Rockaways. Its colonnaded bathhouses (1936;

Aymar Embury II) are reminiscent of another Moses project, Jones Beach. Orchard Beach was restored in the mid-1990s and regularly draws tens of thousands of sun-worshipers, mainly Latinos from the rest of the Bronx. There are plans to build a privately owned water amusement complex on an acre of city-owned parkland near the main pavilion at Pelham Bay Park, just off the beach. For information on Orchard Beach, ☎ (718) 885-3273.

Hunter Island

Nearby Hunter Island has 166 acres of forest, wetlands, and rocky shoreline. Around 1811 John Hunter, an auctioneer and art collector, built a Georgian mansion that became famous for its lavish hospitality. Hunter's art collection included paintings by Leonardo da Vinci, Rembrandt, and Rubens; his guests included Governor De Witt Clinton and President Martin Van Buren. Robert Moses razed the residence in the 1930s, though traces of Hunter's gardens remain, including a grove of white pine trees and flowers that now grow wild.

This section of the park almost became a garbage dump, but local naturalist and historian Theodore Kazimiroff led a grass-roots fight to protect the former island. In 1986 the **Kazimiroff Nature Trail** was named in his honor. Depending on the season, you can see wild geraniums, periwinkles, dogwood, honeysuckle, and black locust trees. Birds in the park include pheasants, red-winged blackbirds, great horned owls, and an occasional wild turkey.

Twin Island

West of Hunter Island is Twin Island—formerly two cigar-shaped islands called East and West Twin Islands—a 19-acre point of land at the northeast end of Orchard Beach, joined to the park by landfill. It has several glacial boulders, including the Lion (or Sphinx) Rock (northeast end of the point), which was revered by the Siwanoy Indians.

City Island

City Island Ave in the midsection of the park leads across a bridge to City Island, a small community with a long maritime history.

History

In 1761, local inhabitants conceived a plan to develop a port rivaling that of New York (hence the name "City" Island), a scheme that never got off the ground. In the middle of the 19C, the island became known for oystering and, more important, as a center of shipbuilding. Yachts such as Vincent Astor's *Nourmahal,* Jules Bache's *Colmena,* J. P. Morgan's *Corsair,* and other pleasure boats slid down the ways at City Island. In 1902 Ratsey & Lapthorn Inc., the American branch of the famous English sailmaker, opened a sail loft on Scholfield St. Several America's Cup defenders were also built on City Island: the famous Minneford Yacht Yard, founded in 1926, built four of them. During World War II, minesweepers, PT boats, tugs, and landing craft were also built here. The end of the war, the introduction of fiberglass for boat-building, and cheaper operating costs elsewhere helped kill off City Island's boat-building industry. Minneford's remained in business until 1983, the island's last boatyard.

Many of the natives—who refer to themselves as clam diggers and outsiders as mussel suckers—have ties to City Island's nautical past; from the 1860s until 1950 many of the islanders worked in the industry.

Today the 230-acre island is still synonymous with boating, but the boats are mostly the recreational variety—party boats, sightseeing and excursion vessels, and jet skis. While the island is still insular, it has in recent years seen an influx of newcomers attracted to new condominiums, the first of which arrived in the 1980s when some 70 of them began rising on land formerly owned by the United Shipyard. In the 1970s, a small group of artists also moved to City Island; in recent years CIAO (the City Island Arts Organization), has operated a cooperative and gallery, organized local events, and lent support to local artists.

City Island Avenue

City Island Ave, the island's main street, runs from the mainland bridge to Belden Point at the southern tip. Along it are many of the island's restaurants, most of them seafood places that range from fairly elegant dining spots to open-air shacks. Also along the avenue are several art galleries, including Focal Point (321 City Island Ave) and the Starving Artist (269 City Island Ave). There are also unusual shops such as **Mooncurser Antiques** (229 City Island Ave), a vinyl-lover's paradise where 75,000 albums of every genre are for sale. Further along the avenue is Le Refuge Inn, at 620 City Island Ave, a bed-and-breakfast serving superior French cuisine and owned by a renowned Manhattan chef, Pierre St. Denis.

Other Points of Interest

At the island's northern tip, a small bridge leads to private **High Island.** It was a bungalow community from around 1913 until the 1960s, when a local radio station bought the island and relocated their transmission towers there.

At the foot of Fordham St, facing Long Island Sound, is a slip from which departs a ferry bound for **Hart Island,** where the city's potter's field (not open to the public) has been since 1869. Louisa Van Slyke, who died in the city's Charity Hospital, was the first of about 800,000 unclaimed or unknown men and women and stillborn babies buried there. Prisoners from the Rikers Island Penitentiary bury the dead four days a week.

North of the ferry slip is the **Pelham Cemetery,** with some Pell family gravestones dating back to the mid-18C. **Rat Island,** a two-acre rocky islet visible offshore, has at various times sheltered yellow fever victims from Pelham, convicts escaping from the Hart's Island Reformatory, and an artists' colony.

The house at **175 Belden St** (c. 1880; DL) is one of the few remaining clapboarded Victorian cottages in the city. On the other side of City Island, at **21 Tier St,** which overlooks Eastchester Bay, is a huge, three-story, brown-shingled home (1894) with conical roofs, protruding oriels, and intersecting gables. It was featured in the 1962 film *A Long Day's Journey into Night.*

The **City Island Museum,** a former school building (1898; C. B. J. Snyder) at 190 Fordham St, has paintings, photographs, and documents that emphasize City Island's place in the yachting industry. Staffed by volunteers, it is open Sun 1–5; for information, ☎ (718) 885-0008.

Co-op City

Rising from the marshland near the Hutchinson River Pkwy are the towers of Co-op City (1968–70; Herman J. Jessor), the nation's largest housing development. Co-op City consists of 35 bulky apartment towers, 236 clustered town houses, eight parking garages, a firehouse, a heating plant, three shopping centers totaling 150 stores and 40 offices, and an educational park with five schools.

Freedomland

The complex was built on the site of Freedomland U.S.A, a $65-million theme park, shaped like a map of the United States, which offered exhibits on the Civil War, the Chicago Fire, San Francisco's Barbary Coast, Little Old New York, and the Old West. Unfortunately the park, which opened in 1960, drew fewer than a third of its anticipated 5 million annual visitors and shut down after four years.

History

Co-op City's more than 15,000 apartments were built to house more than 57,000 mostly working-class and middle-class people. Initially, many residents were Jewish and Italian, fleeing decaying neighborhoods elsewhere in the Bronx, ironically pushing the old neighborhoods downward even faster. Today Co-op City is more diverse, reflecting more accurately the make-up of the city.

Co-op City has been criticized for being overwhelming in size and lacking any intimate neighborhood feel, but its problems have generally been unrelated to its size. It garnered a reputation for corruption well before the first spadeful of marsh muck was turned. The marshy land under Co-op City caused ongoing construction problems: more than 50,000 pilings had to be driven to support the buildings. While the roads and buildings are now stable, the ground around them continues to sink so that all the gas lines have had to be replaced. By the late 1990s, much of the complex was aging and in need of repair.

34 · Northwest Bronx: Riverdale and Fieldston

Riverdale

Riverdale, a beautiful neighborhood of winding streets and hilltop vantage points overlooking the Hudson River and the Palisades on its western bank, stretches along the east side of the river from Spuyten Duyvil to the Westchester County line west of Van Cortlandt Park. It was largely undeveloped until 1852, when wealthy businessmen, attracted by the new Hudson River Railroad (1849), which made downtown Manhattan an easy commute, bought 100 acres to build summer retreats. Industrialist William Earl Dodge hired James Renwick Jr., architect of St. Patrick's Cathedral, to design his mansion, Greyston, while Percy Pyne, president of the National City Bank of New York, built Alderbrook, a Gothic revival mansion. Not surprisingly, the area became known as the Gold Coast of the Bronx.

In the 1930s, the Henry Hudson Pkwy sliced lengthwise through Riverdale, and after World War II most of the estates were sold to institutions or developers. High-rise apartment buildings (many of them now cooperatives) were built along the parkway, diminishing Riverdale's exclusivity. Nonetheless, Riverdale is still mostly upper-middle-class, and while there is a large elderly population in the high-rises, an increasing number of young couples with children, priced out of Manhattan, are buying Riverdale apartments.

While Riverdale has had a large Jewish population for decades, there has been a growing Orthodox Jewish community in the neighborhood. Nearly 40 percent of Riverdale's residents are Jewish and more than 20 percent of those are Orthodox. In fact, the last census found that after English and Spanish, the most common language was Yiddish. Although there are few Hasidim (the ultra-Orthodox sect), many of the Orthodox Jews in Riverdale (as elsewhere) are becoming increasingly fundamentalist and insular, creating strained relations with non-Jews and non-Orthodox Jews.

Along the river, in the northwest section of the community, is the **Riverdale Historic District,** bounded by Palisade Ave, W. 254th St, Independence Ave, and W. 252nd St. Its 15 acres include seven of the original estates linked by a carriage alley, now Sycamore Ave. The district's 34 structures—ranging from 19C villas and carriage houses to 20C colonial revival homes—are set regally on steeply sloping land overlooking the river and the Palisades.

Touring Riverdale

A car is recommended for visiting the winding streets and hilly terrain of Riverdale, where homes sit often hidden from sight on narrow, winding roads. Potholes and bumps scar the roads, suggesting that residents prefer to discourage casual sightseers. Wave Hill may be reached using public transportation followed by a reasonable hike.

To access Riverdale by car, take the Henry Hudson Pkwy across the bridge to the Kappock St exit. Follow Kappock St past Knolls Crescent to Johnson St, which then becomes Palisade Ave.

Palisade Ave skirts the river and offers a good view of the undeveloped New Jersey Palisades, whose remarkable beauty T. H. Huxley found equal to that of some of the finest Himalayan landscapes. Expensive houses built during the decades following World War I line the road along the river, and further inland stand tall apartment houses, most dating from a later period.

Begin at Independence Ave and Kappock St, near Riverdale's southern edge. At 2570 Independence Ave is the former **Riverdale Presbyterian Chapel** (1889; Francis H. Kimball; DL), now the Edgehill Church at Spuyten Duyvil, whose eclectic, asymmetrical design combines elements of the shingle style with those of the neo-Tudor and Romanesque revival traditions.

At Independence and Palisade Aves are the homey and charming **Villa Charlotte Bronte apartments** (1926; Robert Gardner), which look out onto the river. Across the street is Henry Hudson Park, bounded by Kappock St, Independence Ave, and Palisade Ave, with a 100 ft column on which rests a statue of **Henry Hudson** (1938; Karl Bitter and Karl Gruppe), keeping an eye on the river he discovered. Gruppe, Bitter's student, made the statue from a plaster model Bitter had executed some years before his death in 1915, when he was hit by a car and killed as he was leaving the opera.

Greyston

Head north on Palisade Ave and turn inland at W. 247th St. At the southwest corner of Independence Ave (690 W. 247th St) sits one of Riverdale's earliest estates, Greyston, the former William E. Dodge residence (1864; James Renwick Jr.; DL), a gray granite mansion adorned with teal-blue "gingerbread." Dodge cofounded the mining company Phelps Dodge & Co. and supported the YMCA. His daughter, Grace, a social worker, helped found Teachers College. She bequeathed both her interest in education and the mansion to her nephew Cleveland, who eventually willed the estate to the college. After serving as a conference center for the college, it became a Zen Buddhist retreat, and today is again a private residence.

Return to Palisade Ave, where joggers exercise along the path of Riverside Park, and continue north. On the north side of Spaulding Lane, between Palisade and Independence Aves, is part of the campus of the **Riverdale Country School,** formerly the property of George W. Perkins, benefactor of Wave Hill.

Alderbrook

At 4715 Independence Ave, just south of W. 248th St (which intersects Spaulding Lane), is **Alderbrook** (c. 1880; DL), a brooding Gothic revival mansion built for the banker Percy Pyne, whose Park Ave town house is now a landmark (see The Americas Society in Walk 21). From 1920 until 1946, **Alderbrook** belonged to sculptor Elie Nadelman (1882–1946). Nadelman, already successful when he came to America in 1914, married a wealthy widow and a year later bought Alderbrook as well as a town house on E. 93rd St. The couple lived in Manhattan and turned one of the buildings on the Alderbrook estate into a folk art museum, ultimately spending a half-million dollars on their collection. After the stock market crash of 1929, the Nadelmans sold their Manhattan home and moved to Alderbrook, where he established his studio. During this period Nadelman continued to work, but withdrew from the art world; he never exhibited after 1930 and rarely sold anything. In 1935 workers repairing his studio damaged much of his work, and Nadelman never recovered from this blow, consigning the damaged works as they were to the attic and cellar, where they remained until after his death in 1946. Though Nadelman spent the later years of his life isolated from the art scene, he did enroll in the Riverdale Air Warden Service and later volunteered for two years teaching ceramics and modeling to wounded soldiers at Bronx Veterans' Hospital. Eventually Alderbrook was subdivided, and today there are several other small homes on the former estate.

Head north on Independence Ave and turn left. The former **Count Anthony Campagna residence** (1930; Dwight James Baum; DL), at 640 W. 249th St (southeast corner of Independence Ave), is now the ultra-Orthodox Jewish Yeshiva of Telshe Alumni School. On warm days the students can be seen playing on the grounds of the Italian Renaissance–inspired estate with its grand cobblestone drive and Tuscan-style villa. The Italian-born Campagna, with his brother-in-law Charles Paterno, made his fortune developing apartment buildings, especially on Morningside Heights.

Across the street, at 4970 Independence Ave, is the **Coachman's House** (1880; Charles W. Clinton; DL) of **Parkside,** businessman Henry Foster Spaulding's estate. The lovely stick-style cottage with a slate roof and jigsaw ornamentation was moved here from the west side of the avenue. Today Yeshiva of Telshe Alumni School owns the property.

Wave Hill

675 W. 252nd St (entrance on Independence Ave at W. 249th St), Bronx, NY 10471. ☎ (718) 549-3200. Web site: www.wavehill.org. April 15–Oct 14: Open Tues–Sun 9–5:30; Wed until sunset. Oct 15–April 14: open Tues–Sun 9–4:30. Closed Jan 1, Thanksgiving, Dec 25. Greenhouses open Tues–Sun 10–noon and 2–4 P.M. Glyndor Gallery is open Tues–Sun 10–4:30. Admission charge to Wave Hill March 15–Nov 14 Wed–Sun; free Tues all day and Sat mornings. Also free Nov 15–March 14.

Art exhibitions, outdoor sculpture shows, concerts, horticultural exhibitions, workshops, lectures. Gift shop. Café. Wave Hill House, the Great Lawn, and flower gardens are accessible to wheelchairs. Wheelchair on request at the front gate and at the reception desk.

Subway and Bus: Broadway–Seventh Ave Local (1, 9) to 231st St. Change to Bx7 or Bx10 bus at the northwest corner of W. 231st St and Broadway. Leave bus at W. 252nd St and walk across parkway bridge; continue two long blocks on W. 252nd St to Independence Ave. Turn left to Wave Hill gate at W. 249th St.

Express Bus: Liberty Lines runs Mid-Manhattan Riverdale Express via East Side and West Side routes to W. 252nd Street; ☎ (212 or 718) 652-8400 for information and schedule. Follow walking directions above. Liberty Lines bus returns from W. 252nd St rather than W. 249th St stop. Van: The Mosholu Van Service also offers van service between Wave Hill and points in Manhattan. For information, ☎ (718) 543-6900

Train: Take Metro North Railroad from Grand Central Station to the Riverdale Station. Wave Hill is a five-block, uphill walk from the station. For train schedule, ☎ (212) 532-4900.

Car: From Manhattan, take Henry Hudson Pkwy to 246th St exit. Continue on service road to W. 252nd St. At W. 252nd St, turn left over the parkway and turn left again. Turn right at W. 249th St and continue straight to Wave Hill gate.

On the west side of Independence Ave lie the grounds of Wave Hill, a nonprofit cultural institution that offers 28 acres of lawns, beautiful gardens, and woodlands overlooking the Hudson River, as well as historic buildings and greenhouses.

History

Wave Hill began as the country estate of the jurist William Lewis Morris. The oldest building on the site is his fieldstone mansion (central wing 1844, with later additions; DL), built of locally quarried Fordham gneiss. After Morris died, the house was sold in 1866 to publisher William Henry Appleton, who built gardens and greenhouses. His guests included the naturalists Thomas Henry Huxley and Charles Darwin. Theodore Roosevelt's family rented Wave Hill during the summers of 1870–71, which perhaps inspired the future naturalist in Teddy, then about 12 or 13 years old. Mark Twain leased the estate from 1901 to 1903 and is said to have built a tree house in one of the chestnut trees. In 1903, the estate was sold to the financier George F. Perkins, whose interests in conservation led him to purchase two additional nearby estates, which are now part of the campus of the Riverdale Country Day School.

Perkins added greenhouses, gardens, stables, an underground recreation building with a bowling alley, and a neo-Georgian mansion called Glyndor. He worked personally with Albert Millard, previously a royal landscape gardener in Vienna, to lay out gardens emphasizing the beauties of the site. Orchards and vegetable gardens planted on the lower slopes of the estate (now wooded) and greenhouses used for cultivation of both flowers and vegetables made the estate relatively self-sufficient. Perkins was also pivotal in preserving the beauty of the Palisades across the river. The Perkins family lived in **Glyndor House,** which had been purchased along with adjacent property from Oliver Harriman, and often leased out the Wave Hill mansion. In 1928, Bashford Dean, curator of arms and armor at the Metropolitan Museum (and also of reptiles and fishes at the Museum of Natural History), who had a long-term tenancy, asked eminent Riverdale architect Dwight James Baum to design the **Armor Hall,** now used for lectures and chamber music. Arturo Toscanini lived at Wave Hill (1942–45), followed by the British ambassadors to the U.S. (1950–56).

In 1960, Perkins's daughter deeded the estate to the city for an environmental-nature center. It is operated by an independent nonprofit organization; the city owns the buildings and grounds. Since 1967, Marco Polo Stufano has been the director of horticulture. When he arrived only traces of the formerly beautiful gardens remained visible beneath acres of tangled vegetation. Today the gardens are among the most beautiful in the country.

Gardens

The **Great Lawn** and **Pergola Overlook** offer solitude and glorious views of the Hudson River and the 500-ft Palisades across the river. The **Flower Garden** is planted with old-fashioned and modern annuals, perennials, shrubs, and bulbs. Next to it the **conservatory** and **greenhouses** offer tropical and arid plants, palms, and seasonal displays (especially welcome in winter). The **Herb Garden** features plants used for culinary, medicinal, and religious purposes, while the **Dry Garden** showcases plants that thrive in warm, dry climates. The **T. H. Everett Alpine House** has high-altitude and rock-garden plants, many with small, delicate, confettilike blooms. Especially beautiful is the **Aquatic Garden,** with ornamental grasses and plants—among them lilies and lotuses—sprouting from formal garden pools (best viewed late summer through autumn). There is also a **Wild Garden,** with plants from around the world, and a **Monocot Garden,** displaying the diversity and beauty of a class of plants that includes grasses, bamboo, asparagus, and such flamboyantly flowering types as irises, cannas, and daylilies. Around the outer verges of Wave Hill is a ten-acre **woodland** with a walking path.

Return to Independence Ave, turning left onto W. 252nd St, where the Riverdale Historic District begins; the street becomes Sycamore Ave as it bends to the right. **Stonehurst** (1858; DL), 5225 Sycamore Ave, which takes its name from the gray building stone, is an Italian-style villa sited below street level. It belonged first to importer William Cromwell, one of the original Riverdale investors. In 1859, after Cromwell died, it was sold to Robert Colgate, a paint and lead manufacturer; later Nicholas de B. Katzenbach, U.S. attorney general under President Lyndon Johnson, lived there.

Continue up Sycamore Ave. The **Salanter Akiba Riverdale Academy** (1974;

Caudill Rowlett Scott Assocs.), cut into the hillside at 655 W. 254th St (between Independence and Palisade Aves), is an Orthodox Jewish school that is architecturally at odds with the rest of community. Turn left to Palisade Ave and follow it around the campus. The neo-Tudor Administration Building (1905), originally the mansion of Henry W. Boettger, was Toscanini's last Riverdale home. Recent additions have altered the original house almost beyond recognition.

Follow Palisade Ave past Ladd Rd with its modern houses, past the Monastery and Retreat of the Passionist Fathers and Brothers to W. 261st St. Near the intersection is the **Hebrew Home for the Aged** (5901 Palisade Ave) with handsome additions (1968; Kelly and Gruzen; additions 1975).

Judaica Museum

Hebrew Home for the Aged at Riverdale, 5961 Palisade Ave (at W. 261st St), Bronx, NY 10471. ☎ (718) 581-1787. Web site: www.hebrewhome.org/museum. Open Sun 1–5; Mon–Thurs 1–4:30. Closed Fri–Sat, federal and Jewish holidays. Free. Changing exhibitions, lectures, educational programs, workshops. Accessible to wheelchairs.

Subway and Bus: Broadway–Seventh Ave Local (1, 9) to 231st St, then take Bx7 or Bx10 bus to Riverdale Ave and W. 261st St.

Car: Take Major Deegan Expwy north to Van Cortlandt Park South exit. From exit turn right; at Broadway turn right (under the El) and continue to W. 261st St. Turn left onto 261st and continue straight past Riverdale Ave. At end of 261st, turn left and right into Hebrew Home for the Aged.

On the sixth floor of one of the buildings at the Hebrew Home For the Aged is the small Judaica Museum. The museum (1982) began with a gift from Ralph and Leuba Baum of about 1,000 pieces of Judaica from Europe, Israel, and the United States. The collection now includes manuscripts, contemporary paintings, and sculpture, as well as embroidered textiles and other decorative arts. The museum mounts displays from its permanent collection as well as changing exhibitions.

College of Mount St. Vincent

At W. 261st St turn right. On the left is the campus of the College of Mount St. Vincent. The main gate is on Riverdale Ave at W. 263rd St. The college, founded as the Convent and Academy of Mount St. Vincent by the Sisters of Charity, moved here from its former quarters in Central Park when the park was developed. The centerpiece of the property was previously 19C-actor Edwin Forrest's picturesque Gothic revival residence **Fonthill** (1852; DL), which was modeled after its English predecessor, Fonthill Abbey. The house, now used for the admissions department, is dominated by six octagonal towers upon which the eccentric Forrest bestowed individual names. Forrest never really got to live in Fonthill Castle, and it never served his desired goal of becoming a home for indigent actors after his death.

Across from Fonthill (to the east) is the **Original College Building** (1857–59; Henry Engelbert; additions 1865, 1883, 1906–8; DL), now the Administration Building, a handsome brick building with Victorian charm and a 180 ft bell tower overlooking the river. The best view of these buildings is from the most westerly campus road, closest to the river.

The **Lourdes Grotto,** just before the gatehouse (1859), was built in 1873 as the goldfish pond, part of the original Forrest estate. It is reputed to be the oldest outdoor grotto in the country. The area was described in *Long Day's Journey into*

Night by playwright Eugene O'Neill, who received his First Communion in the chapel in 1900.

The campus has beautiful trees, including the largest **Japanese lace maple** in New York State. It stands in front of Marillac Hall (1860; additions), a residence hall.

Although the college is officially open only to those connected with it, and parking is controlled, benign-looking visitors are usually allowed to view the campus. Check with the gatekeepers.

To return to the parkway, take W. 261st St inland (east) to Riverdale Ave and turn right; follow Riverdale Ave to exit 16 of the parkway.

Fieldston

Between the Henry Hudson Pkwy and Broadway is the privately owned neighborhood of Fieldston, an enclave of Riverdale, known for its educational institutions and fine houses. Among the former are Horace Mann High School (231 W. 246th St, corner of Tibbett Ave); the Fieldston Schools (Manhattan College Pkwy at Fieldston Rd), run by the Ethical Culture Society; and Manhattan College (Manhattan College Pkwy, Tibbett Ave, and W. 242nd St), a Catholic college founded as an academy in 1849.

History

In 1829 Maj. James Delafield bought about 250 acres and named his estate Fieldston after the family home in England. Around 1913 his descendant Edward Delafield, along with other landowners, began developing Fieldston and Riverdale as an area with winding streets (which would not conform to the rectilinear grid imposed elsewhere) and attractive houses.

The main street, **Fieldston Rd,** shaded by an umbrella of venerable trees, is lined with handsome, rather formal suburban houses from the 1920s and 1930s in a variety of then-popular styles—Spanish colonial, Georgian, and English country. Many were built by Dwight James Baum (who lived in Fieldston himself) and Julius Gregory. The former **C. E. Chambers House** (c. 1923), at 4670 Waldo Ave (between College Rd and Livingston Ave), is an example of Gregory's work.

35 · Northern Bronx: Van Cortlandt Park, Woodlawn Cemetery, Kingsbridge and Kingsbridge Heights, and Norwood

Van Cortlandt Park

Subway: Broadway–Seventh Ave Local (1, 9) to 242nd St–Van Cortlandt Park. Bus: M100 via Broadway to Isham St in the Inwood section of Manhattan; change to Bx20 and take to Van Cortlandt Park.

Car: From the West Side, take the Henry Hudson Pkwy to 246th St exit; go right to Broadway to park entrance. From the East Side, take the FDR Drive north to the Willis Ave Bridge; follow the Major Deegan Expwy north to Van Cortlandt Park South; follow that west to Broadway and go north to the park entrance at W. 246th St. Parking on street along Broadway.

Van Cortlandt Park is less celebrated than either Manhattan's Central Park or Brooklyn's Prospect Park, but at 1,146 acres, it is far larger. The park offers both recreational facilities and natural beauty. In its center, crisscrossed by walking trails, is a natural forest, with pin oak, sweet gum, red maple, hickory, tulip, black walnut, sugar maple, and American sycamore trees. Tibbetts Brook flows through the park from north to south and toward its southern end widens into man-made Van Cortlandt Lake, the largest body of fresh water in the borough.

Intrusions began in the 19C. The Croton Aqueduct (1837–42) runs north–south through the eastern part, punctuated with red brick service towers, as do the remains of the city's first rail line to Boston. The Henry Hudson Pkwy and the Major Deegan Expwy, modern encroachments masterminded by Robert Moses, also slice through the park, obliterating wetlands and isolating one section of the park from another.

Recreation areas include ball fields and playgrounds on the perimeter. Local athletes play baseball, football, and cricket on the Parade Ground. The Van Cortlandt Golf Course was the nation's first public course (1895). The Mosholu Golf Learning Center (a nine-hole short course with a driving range), the Van Cortlandt Park swimming pool, and the Riverdale Equestrian Centre in the park at Broadway and W. 254th St offer other athletic opportunities.

History

The first settlers in what is now Van Cortlandt Park were Native Americans who farmed, hunted, and fished in its meadows, forests, and streams. In 1646 the Dutch West India Company, who had "bought" most of the Bronx from the Native Americans, sold the land to lawyer Adraien Van der Donck. After his death, the property passed through various hands until Frederick Philipse bought it in 1693. Philipse's daughter Eva married Jacobus Van Cortlandt, who was given some 50 acres at the time of the marriage. Jacobus kept adding to this land until he owned all of what is now the park. Here he farmed and milled grain, damming Tibbetts Brook (and thus creating Van Cortlandt Lake) in about 1690 to power his gristmills. The Van Cortlandts continued to farm the land until the 1880s.

During the 1840s the Croton Aqueduct was laid through the park, bringing water from upstate to a reservoir that stood where Bryant Park (42nd St near Fifth Ave in Manhattan) is today. Later, around 1881, the Putnam Division of the New York Central Railroad laid rails across the land. The city took over in 1888, opened the Parade Ground, improved a few parts of the park, but left much of it wild.

During the fiscal crises of the 1970s, the park suffered as maintenance budgets were cut back. In 1992 local activists responded by forming the Friends of Van Cortlandt Park, a volunteer organization that preserves and protects the park's natural beauty and develops programs for its public use.

Hiking Trails in Van Cortlandt Park

Three nature trails cross the park: the **Cass Gallagher Nature Trail** in the Northwest Forest off Broadway and Mosholu Ave; the **John Kieran Nature Trail,** through the lake and freshwater wetlands; and the **John Muir Nature Trail,** the park's only east–west path, which crosses the steepest section at the park's center. Other trails are the **Old Croton Aqueduct Trail,** on the National Register of Historic Places, and the **Putnam Trail,** which follows the route of the former Putnam Division of the New York Central Railroad. Along it are remains of trestles, bridges, and even a station.

Stones for Grand Central Terminal

On the west side of the Putnam Trail, near a path leading to the Parade Ground, are 13 slabs of stone, placed there before 1903 under the aegis of Cornelius Vanderbilt to test their durability. Ultimately, Vanderbilt, who controlled all the railroads into New York City as early as 1869, chose the stone for Grand Central (Indiana limestone—the second southernmost stone on the trail) not because it best withstood the ravages of weather but because it was the cheapest to transport on his railways.

Van Cortlandt House Museum

In Van Cortlandt Park near W. 246th St and Broadway, Bronx, NY 10471. ☎ (718) 543-3344. Open Tues–Fri 10–3; Sat–Sun 11–4 (call to confirm). Admission charge. Exhibits. Occasional concerts, lectures, events. Gift shop. Not accessible to wheelchairs.

Bus: Bx9 to W. 244th St. Liberty Lines BxM3 to W. 244th St.

In the southern part of the park, not far from Broadway, is the oldest building in the Bronx, the Van Cortlandt Mansion (c. 1748; DL).

History

The first American Van Cortlandt, Oloff Stevensen Van Cortlandt, came here in 1638 as a soldier for the Dutch West Indies Company and stayed on to amass one of the four biggest fortunes in the colony by the time he died (1684). His descendants—merchants, shipbuilders, and frequent holders of city office—married well (into the Jay, Philipse, Van Rensselaer, Schuyler, and Livingston families), increasing their wealth and influence. Jacobus Van Cortlandt (1658–1739), was the first Van Cortlandt associated with this part of the Bronx. Frederick Van Cortlandt, who built the mansion, was the grandson of Oloff Stevensen Van Cortlandt; the house was occupied by Van Cortlandts until deeded to the city in 1889.

The House

The house is built of rubble stone masonry with brick around the windows, above which are keystones with grotesque carved faces, unique in colonial architecture but not uncommon in Holland. It is furnished with English, Dutch, and colonial furniture, including pieces that belonged to the Van Cortlandt family. On view are an 18C kitchen with the appropriate tools and utensils, two parlors, a dining room where George Washington and Rochambeau dined, and bedrooms, including one where Washington slept during his peripatetic conduct of the Revolution.

Environs

In front of the manor a formal garden once grew in the area below the terrace. Today some of that land has been taken over by the swimming pool. In the rear is the **Sugar House Window,** taken from the old warehouse on Duane St built by the Rhinelanders to store sugar from the West Indies. In 1776 the British used the warehouse as a prison for American soldiers, and when it was torn down a section of its wall and window, with iron bars, was rebuilt here. Also in the rear of the house is a statue of lawyer and soldier **Josiah Porter** (1902; William Clark Noble). A remnant of an early burial ground, the Kingsbridge Burying Ground (1732), a small fenced area, lies east of the mansion near the **Urban Forest Ecology Center**. For information, ☎ (718) 548-0912.

In the **Memorial Grove,** near Broadway and W. 246th St, 30 pin oaks and Norway maples were planted in 1949 to honor Bronx citizens killed in World War II; some of the plaques bearing the names of fallen soldiers survive at the base of the trees.

The **Parade Ground,** east of Broadway and north of the grove, was first an army staging area. Fifteen bison spent the summer of 1907 grazing on its grasses, before being sent west and reintroduced to the Oklahoma plains.

North and east of the Parade Ground (about a half-mile from the mansion) is **Vault Hill,** site of the original Van Cortlandt family burial ground. Here Augustus Van Cortlandt, city clerk during the Revolution, secreted the municipal records in a strongbox. They are now on display within the mansion along with several of the vault markers. The family remains have been removed to Woodlawn Cemetery, and the vault has been sealed. Vault Hill has one of New York's few meadows with switchgrass, little bluestem, and wildflowers like birdsfoot trefoil, ironweed, and sweet white clover.

In the eastern sector of the park, at E. 238th St, a cairn of stones and a plaque in **Indian Field** memorialize the Stockbridge Indians who were ambushed by British troops in 1778 while the Indians were scouting for the colonists.

Woodlawn Cemetery

329 E. 233rd St (at Webster Ave), Bronx, NY 10470. ☎ (718) 920-0500. Open daily 9–4:30. A free map with grave locations is available at the cemetery office. Occasional walking tours; concerts and events celebrating those buried here; annual birthday salute on the Fourth of July to "Yankee Doodle Dandy" George M. Cohan; annual tree lighting ceremony.

Subway: Lexington Ave Express (4) to Woodlawn. Walk to main gate of the cemetery on Jerome Ave. Train: Harlem Division train from Grand Central Terminal to Woodlawn. The Webster Ave entrance to the cemetery is just west of the tracks at E. 233rd St and Webster Ave.

Car: Take Bronx River Pkwy to E. 233rd St exit, or Major Deegan Expwy to E. 233rd St or Jerome Ave to intersection of Bainbridge Ave. Car parking inside gates.

Woodlawn Cemetery, first called Wood-Lawn, lies on a high ridge of land east of Van Cortlandt Park near the northern border of the borough. Regarded by many aficionados as America's most beautiful cemetery, Woodlawn is renowned for its setting, its statuary, the architecture of its mausoleums—designed by Stanford White, Louis Comfort Tiffany, and James Renwick among others—and the fame of those buried here.

History

In 1863 the Reverend Absalom Peters and the cemetery trustees bought 400 acres of farmland for a rural cemetery that mourners from New York could reach by a special Harlem River Railroad train in 35 minutes. The park saw its first burial in 1865 and since then has become the final resting place of more than 300,000 people. While not as beautifully landscaped as Green-Wood in Brooklyn, Woodlawn boasts a more impressive roster.

Who's Who in Woodlawn Cemetery

Mayor Fiorello La Guardia has a simple tombstone, while Robert Moses, who built on a grand scale, has only a small plaque in a community mausoleum. Composers W. C. Handy, Victor Herbert, Irving Berlin, and George M. Cohan are buried here. Jazz greats Duke Ellington and Miles Davis lie across from one another—Davis's headstone is elaborately carved with a trumpet and the opening bars of his song "Solar," while Ellington's small slab simply says "DUKE" EDWARD KENNEDY ELLINGTON. Novelist Herman Melville; painter Joseph Stella; actress, director, and producer Antoinette (Tony) Perry Freauff, for whom the Tony Awards are named; and ballroom dancers Vernon and Irene Castle are buried here. The most famous athlete is Hall of Fame second baseman Frankie "The Fordham Flash" Frisch.

The worlds of politics and journalism are also well represented: suffragist Elizabeth Cady Stanton; newspaper publisher Joseph Pulitzer; pioneering journalist Elizabeth Cochran, better known as Nellie Bly; William "Bat" Masterson, sheriff and U.S. marshal, gambler, Indian scout, and sportswriter. Others include Adm. David Glasgow Farragut, the Civil War hero for whom the navy created the rank of admiral; Ralph Bunche, undersecretary-general to the United Nations and the first African American to win the Nobel Peace Prize; political cartoonist Thomas Nast, who gave us the Democratic donkey, Republican elephant, and white-haired, potbellied image of Santa Claus; and Charles Evans Hughes, New York governor, U.S. secretary of state, and chief justice of the Supreme Court.

There are familiar names from the world of business as well: Rowland H. Macy, James Cash Penny (J.C. Penny), Charles C. Loehmann, and Jay Gould, all moneymakers with impressive memorials. Two sphinxes guard dime-store millionaire F. W. Woolworth's mausoleum, while brokerage head Jules S. Bache is buried in a mausoleum recalling the Temple of Isis at Phylae. Railroad builder Collis Huntington's monument suggests a miniature Greek-style temple. John Harbeck, who inherited a Brooklyn real estate fortune then earned millions more in Boulder, Colorado, has a massive and ornate mausoleum (1910; Theodore Blake) with a tower emerging from a turret. It is reportedly Woodlawn's most expensive monument.

Financier Oliver Hazard Perry Belmont and his wife, Alva Vanderbilt Belmont (formerly married to William Kissam Vanderbilt), hired architect Richard Morris Hunt (who designed the Statue of Liberty pedestal as well as several Vanderbilt mansions) to create a mausoleum modeled after the Chapel of St. Hubert at the Château d'Amboise in France.

The pinkish mausoleum for meatpacker Herman Armour was designed by

James Renwick, architect of St. Patrick's Cathedral. Department store magnate and *Titanic* victim Isidor Straus (see Macy's in Walk 14) is buried in a tomb decorated with a ship at sea. It lies in front of a large mausoleum where Isidor and Ida Straus's children are buried. Ida also died on the *Titanic* in 1912, but her body was never recovered.

The most recent prominent burial occurred in 1997, when real estate magnate Harry Helmsley, then owner of the Empire State Building, was buried in a $350,000, 20 × 30 ft granite mausoleum, decorated with stained glass windows depicting the New York skyline.

Perhaps the strangest epitaph in the cemetery belongs to one George Spenser (1894–1909): "Lost life by stab in falling on ink eraser, evading six young women trying to give him birthday kisses in office of Metropolitan Life Building."

Woodlawn also has six "Great Trees" designated by the Parks Department in 1985, more than any other location. These include a weeping pendant silver linden with a limb more than two ft wide, a weeping beech, and an ancient white oak. An American elm infected with Dutch Elm disease was cut down in 1995, but the stump remains in tribute. Interestingly, the formaldehyde used in embalming kills most flowers but not the trees.

Kingsbridge and Kingsbridge Heights

Kingsbridge, in a valley between the ridges of Riverdale to the west and Kingsbridge Heights to the east, dates back to the 1660s and is one of the borough's oldest neighborhoods. The King's Bridge was a toll bridge at Spuyten Duyvil Creek at what is today Kingsbridge Ave, just south of W. 230th St. Built by wealthy landholder Frederick Philipse in 1693, it was the first link between Manhattan and the mainland. (The creek was filled in after the digging of the Harlem River Ship Canal in 1895.) Once largely Irish, Kingsbridge is today also home to Dominicans and other Central American immigrants.

Step Streets

Kingsbridge has some slopes so steep that stairs were built into the hillsides to allow people to get around; the steps, often 100 or more, are known as "step streets." Uphill roads generally angle across slopes, while step streets decrease the distances that pedestrians must travel if walking along the streets.

In the middle-class neighborhood of Kingsbridge Heights, on the hills and ridges south of Van Cortlandt Park, is the **Jerome Park Reservoir,** occupying part of the site of a racetrack built by Leonard W. Jerome. Known best as the father of Jennie Jerome (Winston Churchill's mother), he was equally fond of horses and women, a founder of the American Jockey Club, and the moving force behind the racetrack, where he and his well-to-do colleagues raced their thoroughbreds from 1876 to 1890. In 1905 the reservoir was built as part of the Croton system, covering 94 acres and holding 773 million gallons of water bound for the city. A second basin to the east (which extended to Jerome Ave) was filled in, its land given over to the De Witt Clinton High School, Herbert H. Lehman College (until 1968 the uptown campus of Hunter College and now part of the city university system), and the **Bronx High School of Science** (which moved uptown from 184th St in 1959). The latter is one of the nation's most prestigious public schools, the alma mater of several Nobel Prize winners, including Leon N. Cooper (1972, physics) and Sheldon L. Glashow and Steven Weinberg (1979, physics).

Filling the rest of the site are subway yards and the imposing **Kingsbridge Armory** (1912; Pilcher & Tachau; DL), at 29 W. Kingsbridge Rd (between Jerome and Reservoir Aves), a two-towered, square-block monolith on five acres, reputedly the largest armory in the world. The National Guard pulled out in 1994; since then it has been used as a homeless shelter and training ground for a local cadet corps. The city has proposed transforming the now-empty building into a sports, entertainment, and retail complex; local activists favor community-oriented projects instead.

Norwood

The neighborhood of Norwood, east of Kingsbridge and south of Woodlawn Cemetery, was traditionally an Irish neighborhood but is today a diverse community. Puerto Ricans arrived in the 1970s, followed in the 1980s by new Irish immigrants as well as Albanians, Koreans, Pakistanis, Bangldeshis, Russians, and Latin American immigrants. In the 1990s, it welcomed a mix of Dominicans, Russians, Jamaicans, Filipinos, Irish, and others.

Museum of Bronx History

3266 Bainbridge Ave (between Van Cortlandt Ave and E. 208th St), Bronx, NY 10467. ☎ (718) 881-8900. Web site: www.bronxhistoricalsociety.org. Administrative headquarters and research library of Bronx County Historical Society, 3309 Bainbridge Ave, Bronx, NY 10467. Museum open Sat 10–4; Sun 1–5. Tours by appointment during the week. Closed mid-Dec–mid-Jan and major holidays. Admission charge. Exhibitions. Research library, by appointment. Gift shop. The Bronx Historical Society offers tours, lectures, special events (not all at Valentine-Varian House). Limited wheelchair access.

Subway: Sixth Ave Express (D) to 205th St–Norwood. Lexington Ave Express (4) to Mosholu Pkwy, then walk east on E. 208th St. Bus: Bx10, Bx16, Bx28, Bx30, Bx34 to Bainbridge Ave and E. 208th St.

Car: Take Major Deegan Expwy to Van Cortlandt Park exit. Follow Van Cortlandt Park South and Gun Hill Rd to Bainbridge Ave; turn right and follow Bainbridge Ave to the museum. Street parking.

Just south of Gun Hill Rd is the second-oldest house in the Bronx, the **Valentine-Varian House,** today the Museum of Bronx History, owned and operated by the Bronx County Historical Society.

Isaac Valentine, a well-to-do farmer, built this sturdy two-story fieldstone farmhouse (1758; DL) on land purchased from the Dutch Reformed Church. During the Revolution the family fled, endangered by skirmishes nearby, and for a while the house was occupied by British and Hessian soldiers. In 1791 Isaac Varian bought the house along with some 260 acres of land. It remained in the Varian family until 1905, when the building was sold at auction to William F. Beller. Caretaker tenants occupied the house until the 1960s. In 1965 Beller's son donated the house to the Bronx County Historical Society and it was moved across the street to its present site in Williamsbridge Oval Park, where it serves as a museum.

Exhibitions

The permanent exhibition offers an overview of the history of the Bronx from the Native American period through the beginning of the 19C. Two other galleries contain special exhibitions, which change about twice yearly and focus on some aspect of Bronx history. There are gardens outdoors, including an herb garden, and also the **Bronx River Soldier Monument.**

Rescued from the River

The Civil War monument, a granite figure of a Union soldier, once stood on a pedestal in the middle of the Bronx River below the bridge at Gun Hill Rd. Sculpted by John Grignoloa, the statue was intended for a plot in Woodlawn Cemetery that belonged to a Civil War veterans' post, but the figure was damaged in an accident and never made it to Woodlawn. Grignoloa gave it as a gift to John Lazzari, who lived along the west bank of the river at Williamsbridge. In 1898 Lazzari installed the statue on an unused granite pier that had formerly supported a wooden bridge to his property. After construction of the Bronx River Pkwy, the statue came under the jurisdiction of the Parks Department but remained on its pedestal in the middle of the river until 1959, when strong winds and floodwaters swept it into the river. At the request of early members of the Bronx County Historical Society, the Parks Department rescued and stored it until it was installed here.

Behind the Valentine-Varian House an earthen embankment curves around a large playground on the site of the former (1888–1923) **Williamsbridge Reservoir,** part of the city water system. The reservoir held water from the Bronx River that flowed into it from behind the Kensico Dam through the Bronx River pipeline. When the reservoir was abandoned, tunnels were cut through the dam and playground equipment was installed. The former **Keeper's House** (c. 1890; DL) still remains on Reservoir Oval East at the intersection of Putnam Place. After being occupied by one family from 1946 until 1998, the house has been converted into headquarters for the Mosholu Preservation Corporation, the *Norwood News,* and the local business improvement district.

The startling upswept roof of **St. Brendan's Roman Catholic Church** (1966; Belfatto & Pavarini), Perry Ave between E. 206th and E. 207th Sts, resembles the prow of a ship, understandable since St. Brendan is the patron saint of navigators and, according to legend, voyaged to America. The church (open during services) also has fine stained glass windows.

Montefiore Hospital and Medical Center, E. Gun Hill Rd between Kossuth and Tryon Aves, was founded in 1884 on the centenary of the birth of Sir Moses Montefiore, Anglo-Jewish leader and philanthropist. It was the first hospital in the country to use insulin therapy for diabetes and radioisotopes in cancer therapy. The first heart pacemaker was developed here, as were pioneering techniques in microsurgery and organ transplant. Begun as a home on the East Side (at Ave A and E. 84th St) for Jewish invalids and chronically ill patients, the hospital moved first to W. 138th St and Broadway (1889) and then to the Bronx (1912), searching for open space and fresh country air for its many tubercular patients. It is affiliated with Yeshiva University's Albert Einstein College of Medicine and has earned a reputation as one of the city's more socially active hospitals, assuming responsibilities for the care of neighborhood patients long before federal policy encouraged large academic institutions to do so. It is the largest employer in the Bronx, with some 8,000 employees. During the turbulent 1970s, Montefiore worked with neighborhood activists to preserve residential buildings; in 1981 it helped found the Mosholu Preservation Corporation, a nonprofit organization that provides local economic development and community support.

Borough of Brooklyn / Kings County

Once a separate city, Brooklyn today still preserves a distinctive identity and an almost mystical hold on the hearts and imaginations of its admirers. Some of its aura derives from a brighter past, illuminated by the radiance of memory and nostalgia for which the departed Brooklyn Dodgers are the most powerful symbol. It evokes fierce pride, even chauvinism, in some of its residents (past, present, and spiritual) who defend its populace as the most stalwart, its nurturing qualities as the most conducive to worldly success, its neighborhoods as the most halcyon. People write books, songs, and poems about Brooklyn as they do not, for example, about Queens, the Bronx, or Staten Island.

The very name Brooklyn conjures up clichéd, often inaccurate images of endless blocks of row houses and apartments, some handsome and gracious, others gutted, barricaded, or in the final throes of urban decay. (Much of the borough is filled with detached or semidetached one- and two-family homes.) Its stereotypical inhabitant is an aggressive, humorous, streetwise, and ambitious character, not precisely like any of the many famous people who were born or raised there but something like all of them: Walt Whitman, Mickey Rooney, Mae West, Jackie Gleason, Woody Allen, S. J. Perelman, George Gershwin, Spike Lee, Barbra Streisand, Joe Papp, Joseph Heller, Al Capone, Mel Brooks, Vince Lombardi, Jimmy Smits, Zero Mostel, Danny Kaye, Jerry Lewis, and Mike Tyson.

Geographically, Brooklyn occupies the western tip of Long Island and is bounded by the East River, the Narrows, and Upper New York Bay on the west and north, by the Atlantic Ocean on the south and the borough of Queens on the east. Rocky ridges created by the Wisconsin glacier run east and west through its central and western portions, while the south and east parts of the borough are largely coastal plain, created by glacial outwash. Many neighborhood names describe local geography: Brooklyn Heights, Park Slope, Crown Heights, Bay Ridge, Flatbush, Flatlands, and Midwood. Even the name Brooklyn, first applied to the 17C village near the present intersection of Fulton and Smith Sts, refers to a topographically similar Dutch town, *Breuckelen* ("Broken Land").

Much of Brooklyn is residential, but the waterfront has long attracted industry and shipping. The downtown area is focused around Fulton St. The pattern of settlement was influenced by transit lines—first horsecars, then elevated railways, and eventually subways—fanning outward through the borough. Its area of 78.5 square miles makes it the second-largest borough geographically, while its 2.5 million inhabitants make it the largest in population.

Brooklyn History

The Dutch first settled Brooklyn in the 17C, buying land from the Canarsee Indians and chartering five of its six original villages: Breuckelen (1657); 't Vlacke Bos, now Flatbush (1652); Nieuw Utrecht (1662); Nieuw Amersfoort, now Flatlands (1666); and Boswijck, now Bushwick (1660). The sixth charter, for Gravensande, now Gravesend, went in 1645 to Lady Deborah Moody, an Englishwoman.

Dutch culture, agrarian and conservative, endured in Brooklyn long after the Revolution, especially inland, although New Yorkers, many of them of British origin, were attracted to the waterfront and northern districts. Steam ferry service to Manhattan began in 1814, accomplishing on a small scale what the Brooklyn Bridge would do more grandly in 1883—linking this rural area to the big city, making it a desirable place to live and do business. From 1820 to 1860, Brooklyn's population nearly doubled every decade.

Brooklyn rejected overtures to join New York politically in 1833, accepting Gen. Jeremiah Johnson's opinion that the two cities had "nothing in common, either in object, interest, or feeling—nothing that even apparently tends to their connection unless it be the waters that flow between them," and in the following year (1834) became an independent city, covering 12 square miles and boasting a population of some 30,000 inhabitants. As the century progressed, Brooklyn gradually absorbed outlying towns: New Lots, Flatbush, Gravesend, New Utrecht, and Flatlands, and became known as the City of Churches for its many houses of worship. In 1898, its destiny dictated by short-term fiscal needs and geography, Brooklyn voted by a slim majority to join Greater New York.

The late years of the 19C and the early ones of the 20C were a golden period for Brooklyn, its cultural institutions (the Brooklyn Museum, now the Brooklyn Museum of Art; the Brooklyn Academy of Music; the Brooklyn Botanic Garden; the Long Island Historical Society, now the Brooklyn Historical Society) finding fertile soil in which to flourish, its major industries (oil and sugar refining, brewing and distilling, publishing, glass and ceramics, cast iron) providing jobs for its large population. Major public works projects (Prospect Park, the Brooklyn Bridge, the development of the Atlantic Basin in Red Hook) as well as the construction of sound housing along the rapid transit lines testified to its economic health. Most of the city and America visited Brooklyn for a different reason—from the 1890s until the 1940s, Coney Island's beaches and fantastical amusement parks were the nation's playground.

After the turn of the last century, however, Brooklyn's demography began to change as immigrants poured in from Europe and, after the 1930s, from the American South, seeking jobs in the great manufacturing and port center that Brooklyn had become. It also became a hotbed for the Mafia. By 1930 half of Brooklyn's adults were foreign-born, most gravitating to ethnic neighborhoods: Bushwick, Brownsville, Bensonhurst, and Greenpoint.

The Depression hit the new immigrants hard and by the mid-1930s some of these areas had become slums. Established middle-class families moved further out to suburban neighborhoods in Flatbush, Flatlands, or Canarsie. The borough's population kept growing—between 1890 and 1940, it soared from 1.2 million people to 2.7 million. Despite the setbacks of the Depression, Brooklyn remained economically sound through the end of World War II, when the exodus to the suburbs of much of the remaining middle class, governmental policies favoring other regions of the country, and changes in the structure of capitalism eroded Brooklyn's economic base. The port lost thousands of jobs, the breweries of Bushwick shut down, the Navy Yard was abandoned by the Defense Department, and large neighborhoods became derelict, bombed-out slums, most poignantly Brownsville, long a working-class Jewish area noted for its social and intellectual vitality. The end of the era was symbolized by the folding of the borough's daily newspaper, *The*

Eagle, in 1955, and the departure of the Brooklyn Dodgers for Los Angeles after the 1957 season. The decline continued and grew worse in many neighborhoods through the 1960s, '70s, and '80s.

More recently, Brooklyn has slowly rebounded, though at greatly different rates in different neighborhoods, thanks to the efforts of neighborhood associations, cultural groups, families undertaking the renovation of brownstones, civic organizations like the Bedford-Stuyvesant Restoration Corporation, and government programs like the city takeover of the Brooklyn Army Terminal and the downtown development of Metrotech. A new flood of immigrants has helped reinvigorate the borough, with 283,000 settling in Brooklyn from 1990 to 1996, more than 35 percent of the city's total and far more than in any other borough. Nearly three-quarters of the city's 107,000 immigrants from the former Soviet Union settled in Brooklyn, as did one-quarter of the 80,000 Chinese, nearly half the 45,000 Jamaicans, and two-thirds of the 25,000 Poles and the 21,000 Haitians.

As the cost of residential real estate in Manhattan skyrocketed during the 1990s, Brooklyn became the first alternative for many artists and entrepreneurs (in DUMBO, Williamsburg, Red Hook) and families (Park Slope, Fort Greene, Carroll Gardens, Cobble Hill). This new energy resulted in a groundswell of popularity—with developers deciding to invest in the borough and with tourists traversing the bridges in search of the "real" New York.

Today the borough grapples with the number-one land-use issue vital to shaping Brooklyn's future—how to redevelop its waterfront. It is a particularly momentous problem as only 8.6 percent of Brooklyn's land is devoted to parks, less than in any other borough. On the table are waterfront redevelopment plans that will affect neighborhoods from working-class Sunset Park and Red Hook, to affluent Cobble Hill and Brooklyn Heights, to artsy DUMBO, to the Farragut housing projects west of the Navy Yard. The affected communities and their political representatives have differing, often conflicting, visions for their waterfronts. The state legislature, in 1998, financed the nonprofit Brooklyn Bridge Park Development Corporation, which includes politicians and residents working together to develop a master plan for the waterfront.

Touring Brooklyn

Where distances are short, walking tours have been suggested and subway stops indicated. For outlying areas a car is necessary. Various companies and groups also offer guided tours of the borough.

Note: Until 2004, the rehabilitation of the Manhattan Bridge will cause major service changes on the Sixth Ave Express lines (B, D, and Q). For further information, see Subways in Practical Information.

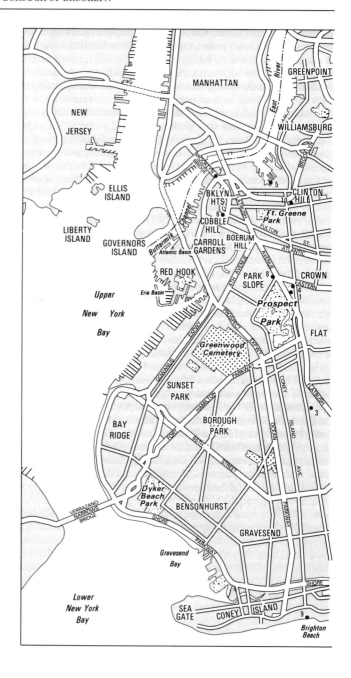

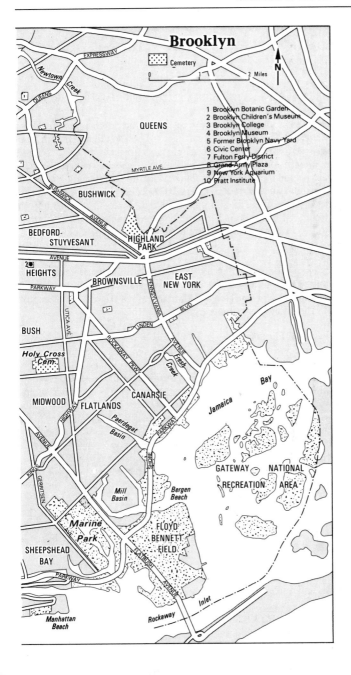

Brooklyn

Cemetery

0   2 Miles

N

1 Brooklyn Botanic Garden
2 Brooklyn Children's Museum
3 Brooklyn College
4 Brooklyn Museum
5 Former Brooklyn Navy Yard
6 Civic Center
7 Fulton Ferry District
8 Grand Army Plaza
9 New York Aquarium
10 Pratt Institute

QUEENS

Newtown Creek

EXPRESSWAY

MYRTLE AVE.

BUSHWICK

BEDFORD-
STUYVESANT

HIGHLAND
PARK

AVENUE

HEIGHTS

PARKWAY

BROWNSVILLE

EAST
NEW YORK

PENNSYLVANIA

BLVD.

LINDEN

BUSH

UTICA AVE.

Holy Cross
Cem.

Fresh Creek

ROCKAWAY PKWY.

AVENUE

Bay

MIDWOOD

CANARSIE

Jamaica

FLATLANDS

Paerdegat
Basin

PARKWAY

KINGS

AVENUE

GERRITSEN

Mill
Basin

Bergen
Beach

GATEWAY   NATIONAL
RECREATION   AREA

Marine
Park

FLOYD
BENNETT
FIELD

SHEEPSHEAD
BAY

PARKWAY

FLATBUSH AVE.

Inlet

Manhattan
Beach

Rockaway

36 · Fulton Ferry, DUMBO, and Vinegar Hill

Subway: Eighth Ave Express (A) to High St–Brooklyn Bridge. Follow Cadman Plaza West toward the bridge.

To Walk across the Brooklyn Bridge: Take Lexington Ave Express (4, 5) to Brooklyn Bridge–City Hall or Nassau St Express or Local (J, M) to Chambers St in Manhattan. To walk across from Manhattan, climb the stairs under the bridge opposite the William St extension to the bridge promenade. The stairs are also accessible from the plaza behind the Municipal Building; walk through the building via the south arch (past the subway station) and take the pedestrian underpass beneath the bridge approaches; there are signs pointing to the stairs up to the bridge. To walk to Manhattan from the Brooklyn end, follow Cadman Plaza East beneath the Brooklyn-Queens Expwy to Front St and the stairs to the promenade.

Fulton Ferry

The **Fulton Ferry Historic District** lies north of Brooklyn Heights on low ground fronting the East River. Before the advent of bridges and tunnels, the Fulton ferry—the first linking Brooklyn and Manhattan—offered easy access across river and was the catalyst for economic growth.

Crossing Brooklyn Ferry

As early as 1642, one Cornelis Dircksen operated a regular rowboat service to what was then New Amsterdam. During the pre-Revolutionary period, The Ferry—as the district was known—became the focus of industry and business, with slaughterhouses, taverns, a brewery, and a distillery. After the disastrous Battle of Long Island in Aug 1776, Washington's forces, barely escaping annihilation, were ferried across the East River from here in rowboats manned by Massachusetts fishermen serving in the army. When a new ferry was established nearby at the foot of Main St in 1796, the district became known as Old Ferry, until it was renamed after Robert Fulton, who introduced steam service in 1814 to supplement his other ferries, which included boats powered by horses on treadmills. Steamboats made the trip across the river in just a few minutes, compared to the typical 90-minute trip powered by sails or oars.

Fulton Ferry evolved into a vibrant mercantile and commercial center that prospered until the Brooklyn Bridge destroyed its economy. By the time the last ferry crossed in 1924 the district had degenerated into a skid row with the requisite flophouses and greasy spoons.

Today Fulton Ferry is enjoying new life with a beautiful waterfront park, thriving restaurants, and the conversion of former warehouses and commercial buildings to offices and residences.

Begin at the **Fulton Ferry Pier** (1976), at the foot of Old Fulton St, a small park offering spectacular, panoramic views of Manhattan and the Brooklyn Bridge. A tablet marks the "Brookland Ferry Landing" from which the Revolutionary Army embarked during the night of Aug 29, 1776, under the direction of George Washington. The pier has been redesigned with wooden decking, bronze historic plaques, cleat-shaped benches, and a fence etched with excerpts from Walt Whitman's poem "Crossing Brooklyn Ferry." It was unveiled in 1995.

Bargemusic

Fulton Ferry Landing, Brooklyn, NY 11201. ☎ (718) 624-2083. Web site: www.bargemusic.org. Concerts Thurs–Sun. Snack bar. Accessible to wheelchairs.

Subway: Seventh Ave Express (2, 3) to Clark St; Eighth Ave Express or Local (A, C) to High St–Brooklyn Bridge.

Moored to the pier at the foot of Furman St is Bargemusic, a 102 ft solid-steel barge formerly used by the Erie Lackawanna Railroad to haul coffee. Today it is the venue for perhaps the most prolific chamber music series in the world—concerts four times a week, 52 weeks a year. Bargemusic was founded (1977) by violinist Olga Bloom, who lived on the barge, which she had towed from Staten Island to Brooklyn, until the city prohibited living on the river. As befits chamber music, the barge offers an intimate if somewhat spare setting, seating 130 people. Musicians play against a wall of glass, with the starry lights of Manhattan as backdrop.

To the right of the pier is another neighborhood pioneer, the **River Café,** 1 Water St, which opened in 1977. It is an elegant barge-turned-restaurant with a sumptuous view and fine dining.

Brooklyn Bridge

Overhead is the Brooklyn Bridge (1883; John A. Roebling and Washington Roebling; reconstruction 1955; David B. Steinman, consulting engineer; DL), still thought by many to be the world's most beautiful bridge. The world's first steel suspension bridge, it was an engineering triumph (in 1883 only Trinity Church was higher) and a product largely of immigrant labor. The view from the pedestrian promenade is wonderful, both down to the river and up to the cables and granite arches.

History

John A. Roebling, an immigrant from Prussia in 1831, started his American career as a farmer but soon began working on canal systems, where he developed the wire rope that later would make the bridge possible. His plans (1869) for an East River bridge included the towers with their pointed openings, the iron trusses that stiffen the roadway, and the system of inclined stays that run diagonally from the towers, giving the bridge its particular beauty and, he contended, making it so stable that even if all the cables snapped, the bridge would sag but not fall.

Only a week after the plans gained final approval, a boat docking at Fulton Ferry crushed Roebling's right foot and he died of tetanus three weeks later. His son Washington Roebling took over actual supervision of the work, which went slowly, hampered by blowouts of the compressed air in the caissons, fire, the dangers of "caisson disease" (the bends, whose cause was not yet understood), fraud, a taxpayers' suit against the bridge, and lack of funds. During the last decade of construction (it took 14 years), Washington Roebling was rendered an invalid by the bends and Emily Roebling became the liaison between the bridge workers and her husband, who watched the project from his window with a telescope.

The bridge opened May 24, 1883, amidst triumphal celebrations. Since then it has inspired artists (John Marin, Joseph Stella) and writers (Walt Whitman, Hart

Crane, Thomas Wolfe). Folklore surrounds it, beginning with the tragedies in the Roebling family and the death of 20 workers during its construction. The week after it opened, 12 pedestrians died, crushed by a panic-stricken mob that believed the bridge was collapsing. In 1884 P. T. Barnum took 21 elephants across, declaring himself satisfied thereafter as to its stability. In 1885 one Robert Odlum, a swimming instructor, jumped to his death wearing a bright red swimming shirt and trunks. Steve Brodie, a personable unemployed Irishman, claimed to have survived a jump in 1886; to prove it he opened a tavern featuring an oil painting of the event and an affidavit from the barge captain who allegedly fished him out of the river.

The Brooklyn Bridge Anchorages

Both the Brooklyn and Manhattan bridge anchorages have imposing vaulted spaces within them. For many years the Manhattan vaults—cool, dark, and partly underground—were used as storage by a commercial wine merchant, though they were sealed during Prohibition. Today, the city's Department of Transportation uses both anchorages for storage. (They are scheduled to be rehabilitated; projected completion date is 2010.)

Creative Time, an alternative arts organization known for its use of public spaces, has an annual Art in the Anchorage exhibition on the Brooklyn side. For information, ☎ (212) 206-6674 ext. 201; web site: www.creativetime.org. The anchorage can be reached from the foot of Cadman Plaza West, which becomes Old Fulton St close to the river.

Bridge Statistics	
Length of river span	1,595.5 ft
Total length of bridge	5,989 ft
Width of bridge floor	85 ft
Number of cables	4
Diameter of cables	15.75 inches
Length of each cable	3,578.5 ft
Number of wires in each cable	5,434
Total wire length	3,515 miles per cable
Depth of Brooklyn foundations	44 ft 6 inches below high water
Depth of Manhattan foundations	78 ft 6 inches
Height of towers	276 ft 6 inches above high water
Height of roadway	119 ft above high water at the towers
Total weight of bridge exclusive of masonry	14,680 tons

Walk away from the water and into the Fulton Ferry Historic District proper. At the corner of Furman St and Old Fulton St (Cadman Plaza West), which was known as "The Road to the Ferry," is the former headquarters of the **Brooklyn City Railroad** (1861; David Morton; DL), now loft apartments. The company was established in 1853, replacing a former stagecoach line that brought people to and from the Fulton Ferry Terminal.

Continue walking away from the water. **Grimaldi's Pizzeria** (opened 1990; the building dates back to c. 1748), 19 Old Fulton St, has one of the city's few coal-fired brick ovens and some of its best pizza. Prepare for a wait on weekends and in the evenings. Grimaldi's, which is closed Tues, does not take reservations and accepts cash only.

A Short History of New York Pizza

Modern pizza was "invented" in 1889 in Naples. Asked to cook up something special for visiting Queen Margherita, Raffaele Esposito, a local restaurateur, reproduced the red, white, and green of the Italian flag with tomatoes, basil, and mozzarella cheese on top of a round of dough, producing the first Pizza Margherita. It was a smash hit with the queen and also with Esposito's other customers. By the turn of the 20C, pizza had traveled to New York with immigrants.

In 1905 Gennaro Lombardi opened Lombardi's, a legendary pizzeria on Spring St in Little Italy. One of his employees was Patsy Lancieri, who subsequently opened Patsy's on First Ave in East Harlem, when that neighborhood was still an uptown Little Italy. Patsy Grimaldi worked there for Patsy Lancieri before opening the present store in Brooklyn. Two of the city's other leading pizza men, John Sasso of John's in Greenwich Village and Anthony (Totonno) Pero of Totonno's, in Coney Island, also started at Lombardi's, which was reopened in 1994 by Gennaro Lombardi's grandson, also named Gennaro. Grimaldi's was originally called Patsy's but changed its name after a feud with the new owners of the East Harlem store.

Across the street is the former **Eagle Warehouse and Storage Co.** (1893; additions 1910; Frank Freeman), 28 Cadman Plaza West (southeast corner of Elizabeth Place). This monumental brick building with a machicolated top stands on the site of the original offices of the *Brooklyn Eagle* newspaper. Freeman so loved the *Eagle* that he incorporated its three-story pressroom into the warehouse. The outline of the old building—with its first floor green grilles—can be seen from cobblestoned Elizabeth Place at the corner of Doughty St. The warehouse addition begins just above the third floor of the *Eagle* structure. The building, whose beautiful glass clockface has become a penthouse window, was converted to condominiums in 1980.

The Brooklyn Eagle

The *Eagle* was founded (1841) as an organ of the Brooklyn Democratic Party. Its first editor was Henry C. Murphy, elected mayor of Brooklyn in 1842. Walt Whitman edited the paper from 1846 to 1848 but was relieved of his job either because of his strong antislavery views or because he was "slow, indolent, heavy, discourteous, and without steady principles," as his publisher stated. The paper was directed at a stable, business-oriented,

---

Protestant readership, and thrived as long as this population dominated Brooklyn, reaching its peak between 1890 and 1930. In 1950 the *Eagle* won a Pulitzer Prize for a series of articles uncovering crime, gambling, and police corruption; five years later (March 16, 1955), during a labor strike, the paper folded.

Cross the street to the corner of Front and Old Fulton Sts (Cadman Plaza West) and the former **Long Island Safe Deposit Company** (1869; William Mundell), 1 Front St. This cast-iron palazzo was built as a bank during the high tide of prosperity following the Civil War. Next door, at 5–7 Front St, is perhaps the city's earliest surviving office building, originally home to the **Long Island Insurance Company** (1835).

Follow Front St under the bridge approach; turn left at Dock St and right at Water St. The brick **Empire Stores,** at 53–58 Water St (between Dock and Main Sts), date from the years after the Civil War (west group 1870; east group 1885) when they were used to warehouse goods brought to the waterfront on railroad cars, which were then loaded onto barges. Later the Arbuckle Brothers, prominent Brooklyn coffee merchants, filled the warehouses with coffee.

Next door, at 25–39 Water St (between Dock and New Dock Sts), is the former **Tobacco Inspection Warehouse** (c. 1860–70), neglected and deteriorated, its foundation crumbling. In 1999 the state planned to raze the building to provide more parkland, but preservationists halted the demolition at least temporarily, seeking to stabilize the shell of the historic structure.

The nine acres between the warehouses and the water are **Empire–Fulton Ferry State Park.** Virtually undiscovered by outsiders and relished by locals, the park is a wonderful place for the solitary contemplation of New York Harbor, the Manhattan skyline, and the mighty Brooklyn and Manhattan Bridges. As a first step toward expansion of the park, the state has recently added restrooms and a permanent office for the Park Rangers.

DUMBO

Just east of the Fulton Ferry Historic District is the newly-named DUMBO neighborhood, an acronym for Down Under the Manhattan Bridge Overpass. Sometimes considered part of Fulton Ferry, the 72-acre area is also called Between the Bridges because of its location between the Brooklyn and Manhattan Bridges.

This forgotten piece of real estate—long a bleak landscape of factories and warehouses with gorgeous skyline views—became quietly hip in the 1970s, when artists, attracted to the huge, cheap spaces, converted the warehouses (often illegally) into studios and residences. The 1990s brought the rush of a new artsy crowd and higher rents, although the neighborhood still lacks basic amenities like banks and grocery stores.

Development in DUMBO

Developer David Walentas, who owns real estate in DUMBO and has already exercised residential conversions of warehouses, proposed a $300-million redevelopment for Empire–Fulton Ferry State Park and its environs, including the state-owned Civil War–era warehouses on Water St, part of the Fulton Ferry Historic District, and portions of the waterfront site owned by the city. The controversial plan, which called for a large hotel, parking garage, and retail outlets, would have dramatically changed the tranquil character of the area. The Brooklyn Bridge Park Coalition fought privatization of the waterfront and called for an expanded park that would encompass all the publicly owned properties between the Brooklyn and Manhattan Bridges. In 1999, the City Planning Commission rejected Walentas's plan. In the meantime the city and state await an overall master plan for the borough's waterfront from park advocates. The park proposal will probably include cultural institutions for the Empire Stores (including a historical museum) and athletic facilities. In 2001, Walentas offered a scaled-down plan focusing on the Empire Stores.

Other Points of Interest

David Walentas's first residential conversion was the former Gair Building (c. 1888; conversion 1999; Beyer Blinder Belle), a 16-story concrete warehouse, now the **Clock Tower Building**, at 1 Main St, a 124-unit, luxury condominium loft building with water views.

Art galleries—including the **Smack Mellon Studios** (1995), at 56 Water St, which is housed in an old spice mill factory, and the **d.u.m.b.o. arts center,** 69 Washington St—line the side streets. **Excalibur,** an iron foundry established on Bleecker St in Manhattan in 1967, and in DUMBO at 85 Adams St around 1980, specializes in bronze sculpture and historical restoration.

Vinegar Hill

East of DUMBO, centered around Hudson Ave, Plymouth St, and Front St, is the tiny **Vinegar Hill Historic District,** one of Brooklyn's oldest residential communities, known for its Greek revival and Italianate row houses (1830s–early 1850s). The neighborhood's name is derived from the 1798 Battle of Vinegar Hill in Ireland. The area once boasted a large Irish community, many of whose members worked in the nearby Brooklyn Navy Yard. The brothels and bars of Sands St, which borders the yard, so irritated officials at the Navy Yard that they locked the Sands St entrance. The old warehouses and row houses of Vinegar Hill have attracted a small population of artists.

37 · Brooklyn Heights

Subway: The nearest stops are the Seventh Ave Express (2, 3) at Clark St (access to street via an elevator) and the Eighth Ave Express (A) at High St–Brooklyn Bridge. A little further away are stops for the Seventh Ave Express (2, 3) and Lexington Ave Express (4, 5) at Borough Hall.

Brooklyn Heights, bounded by the East River, Old Fulton St, Atlantic Ave, and Court St, is an old residential neighborhood distinguished by its tree-shaded streets, superlative riverfront views, and its many well-preserved 19C houses of brick, brownstone, and even wood. New York's first suburb, it also became its first designated historic district (1965), a classification that preserves the facades of its buildings from wanton change.

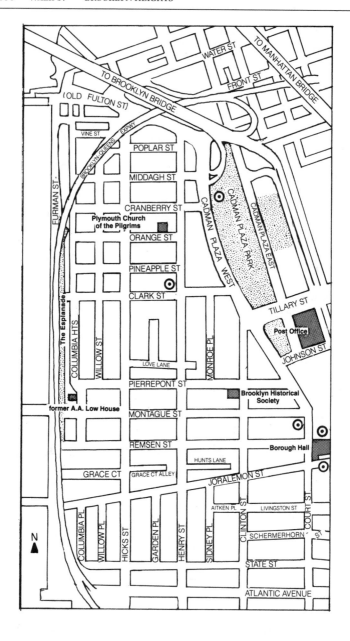

History

The Heights played a crucial role in the Revolutionary War. After a crushing defeat in the Battle of Brooklyn in 1776, the Americans, under Gen. Israel Putnam, retreated to Brooklyn Heights, where George Washington was headquartered. With nowhere to run and forced to confront the possibility of surrender, Washington instead engineered a stunning escape for his army, silently crossing the East River in small boats under the cover of a nighttime fog that enabled the troops to slip past the unsuspecting British Navy.

Part of the village of Brooklyn, Brooklyn Heights started thriving after 1814 when Robert Fulton's steam ferry began scheduled crossings to and from New York, the big city across the river. Not long thereafter prominent landowners (whose names, including Hicks, Pierrepont, Middagh, Remsen, and Joralemon are commemorated in local streets) divided their farms into standard 25 × 100 ft building lots. Development flourished from the 1820s onward, with houses growing larger and more ambitious in style. While many Brooklyn Heights streets are named after prominent 19C families, five of them—Pineapple, Orange, Cranberry, Poplar, and Willow—have botanical names. Legend attributes this to the ire of one Miss Middagh, who allegedly tore down street markers bearing the names of neighbors she disliked and substituted the present ones.

Victorian Brooklyn Heights was known for its fine families, churches, and clergymen. But the Brooklyn Bridge (1883), the merger with New York City (1898), the arrival of the subway (1908), and the Manhattan Bridge (1909) all contributed to the exodus of patricians from the Heights. Several large hotels—for example, the St. George—were built, but by the Depression even the middle class was gone and many of the private homes had been converted to rooming houses; a few had even become brothels, seamen's clubs, or missions.

Beginning in the 1940s, many writers—including W. H. Auden, Truman Capote, Norman Mailer, Arthur Miller, Tennessee Williams, and Carson McCullers—moved in. In the 1950s, development including construction of the Brooklyn-Queens Expwy led to the demolition of many old brownstones. The Heights remained in social limbo until the late 1950s and early 1960s, when young couples willing to put labor and money into redeeming the faded brownstones and brick row houses galvanized the borough's first preservationists' movement. In the 1980s, co-op conversions in the old hotels and apartment buildings also helped stabilize the neighborhood.

Today, the Heights is one of the city's most beautiful and expensive neighborhoods, with "handyman's specials" priced as high as $1 million and two- and three-family houses being reconverted into one-family dwellings. Homes seem to be in a perpetual state of restoration as evidenced by the many work permits taped to windows and doors. And, after years of disputes and delay, in 1998 the state legislature financed the nonprofit Brooklyn Bridge Park Development Corporation to create a plan to develop the piers below Brooklyn Heights as parkland.

Brooklyn Heights's largest landowner is the Jehovah's Witnesses, a proselytizing religious group that believes in the second coming of Christ. Founded in Pennsylvania in 1872, the sect established their headquarters here in 1909 and gradually began buying property, today owning more than $190 million of real estate, much of it residences for young Witnesses.

Plymouth Church of the Pilgrims

Begin in front of the Plymouth Church of the Pilgrims, on Orange St between Henry and Hicks Sts. This plain, red brick Italianate church (1849; Joseph C. Wells; DL), often described as barnlike, is best known for its minister, Henry Ward Beecher, who used its pulpit for 40 years (1847–87) to address the great issues of the day: temperance, woman suffrage, and, most notably, slavery. (Beecher's sister was Harriet Beecher Stowe, author of the renowned antislavery novel *Uncle Tom's Cabin*.)

Henry Ward Beecher, Preacher and Abolitionist

Beecher began his Brooklyn pastorate in a more modest church building on nearby Cranberry St. When that building was damaged by fire, the founders decided that given his growing appeal they would build a new church on Orange St. Beecher was apparently responsible for much of the design of the present church, whose sanctuary accommodates 2,800 people. The theater-style interior, virtually unaltered from Beecher's day, influenced the design of subsequent churches.

At the height of the preacher's popularity, "Beecher boats" ferried throngs of New Yorkers across the river to hear him, while policemen patrolled the crowds who had gathered hours before services. Always theatrical, Beecher once brought a nine-year-old slave girl, Pinky, to the church with the avowed intention of selling her to the highest bidder. Roused to indignation by Beecher's imitation of a slave auctioneer, the congregation purchased her freedom; one congregant, poet Rose Terry, threw her ring into the plate; Beecher placed it on Pinky's finger, saying, "Remember, with this ring, I do wed thee to freedom." Because of the antislavery activities of Beecher and members of the congregation, the church became known as Grand Central Depot of the Underground Railroad.

The charismatic preacher was nearly brought down in 1874 by a civil suit alleging an adulterous affair with a newspaper editor's wife. Though Beecher was acquitted and continued preaching at his church until his death, the media circus that surrounded the trial irreparably damaged his reputation.

The Church

The opalescent stained glass windows (c. 1915) of the sanctuary were designed by the Lamb Studios—the oldest-known American stained glass studio (founded 1857). They depict the history and influence of Puritanism. In the garden to the left of the sanctuary, a dramatic statue by Gutzon Borglum, sculptor of Mt. Rushmore, depicts Beecher auctioning off Pinky. Borglum also executed the nearby bas-relief of Lincoln, who, as a presidential aspirant in 1860, trekked to Brooklyn to hear Beecher. Hillis Hall, given by coffee merchant John Arbuckle, has stained glass windows from the Tiffany Studios, originally in the Church of the Pilgrims on Remsen St, which merged with Plymouth Church in 1934.

The arcade between the church house and sanctuary contains a historical exhibit, which includes a fragment of Plymouth Rock and the freedom ring Beecher gave to Pinky. In 1927, on the church's 80th anniversary, Rose Ward Hunt, by then a mature married woman, returned the ring.

Walk east to Henry St and turn left. The towering structure on the right side of the street belongs to one of Brooklyn's more successful public housing efforts, **Cadman Towers** (1973; Glass & Glass and Conklin & Rossant). Although visually unremarkable, the urban renewal project combines high- and low-rise buildings, shopping, and parking.

Continue north on Henry St. As you pass Cranberry St, look right toward the housing project. Until 1964 the Rome Brothers' Printshop stood a block to the east. In 1855 the Rome Brothers set type for Walt Whitman's *Leaves of Grass.*

At 70 Henry St is a squat, unprepossessing movie theater, the **Brooklyn Heights Cinema.** Unremarkable when it was built, it is one of the city's last surviving independent movie theaters, a monument to a bygone era.

Continue on Henry St to Middagh St, where the former **Mason Au & Magenheimer Candy Company Building** (1885; Theobald Engelhardt; reconstructed 1975) still stands. An advertisement (repainted) for Peaks and Mason mints is visible at the top of the south wall. The building has been revamped as residences, many with loft spaces, and renamed the Henry Street Studios.

Turn left at Middagh St and walk west to Willow St. The house on the southeast corner of Willow and Middagh Sts, **24 Middagh St,** is a well-preserved clapboarded house (1824) with fine carved Federal detailing around the door, dormer windows, and quarter-round attic windows visible from Willow St. The cottage behind it, now joined to it by a wall, was originally the carriage house. In 1848 Henry Ward Beecher lived at 22 Willow St, across the intersection.

Walk south on Willow St to **57 Willow St** (c. 1824), on the northeast corner of Orange St, a house exemplifying the Federal style: dormers, pitched roofs, Flemish bond brickwork, tooled stone lintels, and a parapet between the chimneys concealing the roof gable.

Turn right on Orange St and walk a block to **Columbia Heights,** which runs parallel to the spectacular Brooklyn Heights Promenade. For almost 100 years, the Hotel Margaret (1889; Frank Freeman) occupied the northeast corner of the intersection; it burned down in 1980 when it was being converted to apartments. The Margaret Apartments (1988; Ehrenkrantz Group) is one of the many Jehovah's Witnesses residences in the area. Other residential facilities line the streets, including 124 Columbia Heights, which was built on the site of the house (110 Columbia Heights) from which Washington Roebling oversaw construction of the Brooklyn Bridge after he suffered the bends in 1872 and became housebound.

Turn left on Clark St. The former **Leverich Towers Hotel** (1928; Starrett & Van Vleck), at 25 Clark St, once glittered as one of Brooklyn's brighter social spots, its four corner towers spotlighted at night. Today it is yet another Jehovah's Witnesses residence hall.

On the next block, between Hicks and Henry Sts, is the **St. George Hotel,** an eight-building complex named after a nearby 18C tavern and now well past its prime. Built in various stages (1885; Augustus Hatfield; additions 1890–1923; tower 1930; Emery Roth), it was for a while the city's largest hotel (2,632 rooms), famous during the 1920s for its Art Deco ballroom and pool—the world's largest indoor saltwater swimming pool. In 1995, a fire destroyed the hotel buildings on Clark St; today the remaining sections are cooperative apartments and student housing. A proposal for an 11-floor "boutique hotel" on the vacant lot left by the fire is pending.

For a peek at some of Brooklyn's best Gothic revival row houses, slip briefly down Hicks St (to the right) to **nos. 131 and 135 Hicks St** (c. 1848). Note the dark brownstone facades, the Tudor arches above the doors, the small-paneled casement windows with horizontal hoods and molds.

Return to Willow St and walk south. The houses at **108–112 Willow St** (c. 1880) best exemplify in Brooklyn the offbeat architectural style known as Queen Anne, which flourished from 1880 to 1900 after its introduction to this country from England at the Philadelphia Centennial Exposition (1876). The style combines medieval and Renaissance elements in a freehanded, nonacademic manner. The houses form one visual unit, displaying a variety of forms (gables, bay windows, chimneys, dormers; round, square, and elliptical openings) and materials (brick, stone, terra-cotta, ironwork, shingles).

Continue south to 151 Willow St, a handsome red brick carriage house set back from the street. At **155–159 Willow St** are a trio of pristine small Federal row houses (c. 1829) with sidelights, leaded transoms, and paneled front doors flanked by colonnettes. Between 151 and 155 Willow St is a towering dawn redwood tree *(Metasequoia glyptostroboides)*, planted here in the 1950s. Until 1941, when a Chinese forester came upon an ancient tree he could not identify, the dawn redwood was known only from fossil records. Botanists were astounded to discover that the tree was a dawn redwood, thought to have died out eons ago. The Brooklyn Botanic Garden was one of the first to receive seed specimens, one of which ended up here.

Turn right at Pierrepont St and walk toward the water. Pierrepont St takes its name from Hezekiah Beers Pierpont, landowner and gin distiller, one of the first to recognize the advantages of opening Brooklyn Heights for suburban development. He backed the Fulton Ferry (1814) and by 1823 was offering 25×100 ft lots to "gentlemen whose duties require their daily attendance in the city." His estate faced the harbor, running north and south from Remsen St to Love Lane and westward to a point beyond Clinton St. Hezekiah's children reverted to an earlier, fancier spelling of Pierrepont.

At **6 Pierrepont St** (c. 1890) is an unusual Romanesque revival town house with a rockface entrance stairway and posts carved with flourishing stone plant forms.

Continue west to Columbia Heights; turn right. Outstanding among the many fine Italianate town houses in the area are **210–220 Columbia Heights** (1852–60), amply proportioned with wide doorways; the elaborate door hoods are carved with acanthus leaves.

Turn around and walk back to Pierrepont St. Continue east, crossing Willow and Hicks Sts to 82 Pierrepont St, the former **Herman Behr Mansion** (1890; Frank Freeman), on the southwest corner of Henry St. With an addition in 1919, this handsome Romanesque revival mansion became the Palm Hotel. It later lost its luster, was reduced to a brothel, but then was redeemed by the Franciscans of nearby St. Francis College, who took it over as a residence for novitiates. It has now been converted to apartments.

Continue east on Pierrepont St. Between Henry and Clinton Sts—the latter named after De Witt Clinton, governor of New York State, mayor of New York City, and builder of the Erie Canal—are several fine town houses. The house at **104**

Pierrepont St (c. 1857) is a four-story brownstone with elaborately carved console brackets on the first and second stories. The building at **108–114 Pierrepont St** (1840) was once a Greek revival double house with a central cupola, but drastic remodeling has made it a strange hybrid, half Greek revival and half Romanesque revival. The doorway pediment and corner quoins on one half remain from the original facade. The other half was given its present Romanesque revival form for the publisher Alfred Barnes with the addition of brownstone facing, terra-cotta ornament, a turret, and a rounded bay.

Walk east to Monroe Place, named after James Monroe, the nation's fifth president, who finished his life in straitened circumstances in New York. On the northwest corner of Monroe Place and Pierrepont St is the **Appellate Division of the New York State Supreme Court** (1938; Slee & Bryson). Stately, but somewhat incongruous in this residential neighborhood, the courthouse has Doric columns and gold filigree. On the northeast corner stands Minard Lafever's (1844) **Church of the Saviour,** also called the First Unitarian Church. Some windows (the Low, Woodward, Farley, Frothingham memorials and possibly the other opalescent windows) are by the Tiffany Studios. The building at **46 Monroe Place** has Brooklyn Heights's only remaining ironwork basket urn, topped with the traditional pineapple for hospitality.

Brooklyn Historical Society

128 Pierrepont St (at Clinton St), Brooklyn, NY 11201. ☎ (718) 624-0890. Web site: www.brooklynhistory.org.

Subway: Seventh Ave Express (2, 3) or Lexington Ave Express (4, 5) to Borough Hall. Eighth Ave Express or Local (A, C) or Sixth Ave Local (F) to Jay St–Borough Hall. Nassau St Local (M) or Broadway Local (R) to Court St.

Return to Pierrepont St and turn left. At 128 Pierrepont St (the southwest corner of Clinton St) is the Brooklyn Historical Society (1878; George B. Post; DL), founded in 1863 as the Long Island Historical Society. The society, which maintains a library, museum, and educational center dedicated to Brooklyn history and culture, changed its name in 1985. The grand, historic building is currently closed for renovations and is expected to reopen in fall 2002. The society's offices are temporarily housed at 2 MetroTech Center, Suite 4200, Brooklyn, NY 11201; ☎ (718) 254-9830.

Interior and Exterior

While the landmarked interior, with its Minton tile floors, ash and oak woodwork, Corinthian columns, and stained glass is presently closed, the glorious exterior remains a feast for the eyes. On the facade are terra-cotta heads of a Norseman and a Native American (over the main entrance) and busts of Johann Gutenberg, Benjamin Franklin, Michelangelo, Christopher Columbus, William Shakespeare, and Ludwig van Beethoven. All are by Olin Levi Warner, who studied at the École des Beaux Arts in Paris and returned to New York in 1872. His work here is an early example of architectural sculpture by a successful artist. Warner later went on to sculpt the bronze doors of the Library of Congress, where he reused the Norseman and Native American motifs. He died after a bicycle accident in Central Park in 1896. The stylized American plant forms on the column capitals and friezes are by Truman H. Bartlett.

When the museum reopens, it will have a new educational center and a major new exhibition, **Brooklyn Works: 300 Years of Making a Living in Brooklyn.**

Across the street, at 129 Pierrepont St, is the prestigious and private **St. Ann's School** (1906; Frank Freeman), the former home of the Crescent Athletic Club. The school is known for its arts programs.

Turn right on Clinton St and walk one block to **Montague St,** the community's commercial thoroughfare. It is named after the English writer Lady Mary Wortley Montagu, neé Pierrepont. The final *e* in Montague is a misspelling that, needless to say, has stuck. Long the neighborhood's main commercial street, many of the boulevard's ethnic restaurants and shops are housed in old brownstones. One unfortunate change in recent years, however, has been the increasing presence of chain stores.

On the northwest corner of Clinton and Montague Sts is the brownstone Gothic revival church last known as **St. Ann and the Holy Trinity Episcopal Church** (1847; Minard Lafever). The Holy Trinity parish (founded 1847) was dissolved in the 1950s and the church closed. It remained empty until the 1970s, when St. Ann's (founded 1784) moved in, giving way to the secular **St. Ann Center for Restoration and the Arts,** formed in 1980. After 21 years of providing avant-garde performances and programs, as well as greatly restoring the building, that organization left in 2000, citing issues of control with the church. It is hoping to reopen in DUMBO. Shortly after, the church, with its cast-terra-cotta ornaments, stained glass windows by William Jay Bolton, and a reredos by Frank Freeman, closed to the public, citing structural problems.

Walk west on Montague St. At Henry St turn left and walk south to the northeast corner of Remsen St. Originally the **Church of the Pilgrims** (1846; Richard Upjohn; DL), the first congregational church erected in Brooklyn, this historic church has served Middle Eastern Catholics of the Maronite rite as **Our Lady of Lebanon Church** since 1944. The first round-arched, early–Romanesque revival ecclesiastical building built in the United States, it is faced with ashlar stonework instead of the usual brownstone and represents a brief departure from Upjohn's more familiar Gothic revival style. The church doors in the west and south portals come from the luxury liner *Normandie,* which burned (1942) and sank at its Hudson River berth. They depict Norman scenes, including famous castles and cathedrals. The 3,200-pound church bell dates from 1864 and sounds the note *D* when tolled. The Church of the Pilgrims merged with Plymouth Church in 1934.

Return to Montague St and make a left. The **Hotel Bossert** (1909; addition on the south 1912; Helmle and Huberty), 98 Montague St (on the southeast corner of Hicks St), gets its name from founder Louis Bossert, a Bushwick millwork manufacturer. In the 1920s and 1930s the Marine Roof, decorated by theatrical designer Joseph Urban, afforded visitors a vista of the Manhattan skyline while they dined and danced. It is now residential space for Jehovah's Witnesses.

Continue until you reach the foot of Montague St and the waterfront. The **esplanade,** known locally as the **promenade** (1951; Andrews and Clark, engineers; Clarke & Rapuano, landscape architects), is a five-block walkway from Remsen St to Orange St, providing spectacular views of the Manhattan skyline—from the Chrysler Building to the Battery—as well as the Statue of Liberty and Ellis Island. It is cantilevered over the Brooklyn-Queens Expwy, which accounts for the constant whooshing sound of cars and trucks below. A plaque at the entrance recalls the former site of Four Chimneys, the original Hezekiah Pierpont Mansion, where George Washington made the decision to retreat with his army across the East River during the ill-fated Battle of Brooklyn.

Exit the promenade and look left to **2–3 Pierrepont Place,** two superb Renaissance revival brownstones (1857; Frederick A. Peterson) by the architect of Cooper Union. An 1858 city directory lists the owners as Abiel Abbot Low (teas) and Alexander M. White (furs). Low, a Yankee from Salem, Massachusetts, got into the China trade early, made a fortune, and settled here with his family including son Seth, later mayor of Brooklyn and of New York City. From his opulent home— four stories elaborated with quoins, a heavy cornice, Corinthian pilasters at the entrance, and a conservatory added on the south end—Low could watch his ships setting out to sea. Housing reformer Alfred Tredway White lived at no. 2 from 1868 to 1880. A playground now stands on the site of no. 1, which once had a mansion belonging to Henry E. Pierrepont—Hezekiah's son, an important city planner and a founder of Greenwood Cemetery.

To the right of the promenade entrance is Montague Terrace. Follow it and turn left onto Remsen St—named after landowner Henry Remsen—and then right onto Hicks St. Walk a short block to **Grace Court Alley** (on the left), once a mews for the horses and carriages of the Remsen and Joralemon St gentry; the stables converted to apartments now house the gentry itself.

Across the street, on the southwest corner of Grace Court, is **Grace Church** (1847; Richard Upjohn), whose architect returned to his usual Gothic revival manner a year after his experiment with the Church of the Pilgrims. A glorious old elm tree shades the courtyard south of the church; three Tiffany windows adorn the sanctuary.

Turn right on Joralemon St—named after Teunis Joralemon, a 19C landowner—and follow it downhill toward the harbor. On the west side of the street, between Hicks and Furman Sts, are 24 modest Greek revival houses, **29–75 Joralemon St,** many with their original iron railings and doorway trim. The steel-shuttered **58 Joralemon St** (c. 1847; converted 1908), once someone's home, is, strangely enough, a ventilator and emergency exit for the Lexington Ave subway, whose Battery–Joralemon St tunnel runs deep beneath the street.

Continue to the corner of Joralemon St and Columbia Place. On the southwest corner are the **Riverside Buildings** (1890; William Field & Son), aptly named until the Brooklyn-Queens Expwy usurped the shoreline. These model tenements at 4–30 Columbia Place were built by Alfred Tredway White, whose good works also enhance Cobble Hill.

Turn around and walk back up sloping Joralemon St to Willow Place. Then turn right and walk south. In New York, Gothic revival town houses were never as common as other styles, so **2–8 Willow Place** (c. 1847) are unusual survivals. Their Gothicism is expressed mainly in the coupled porches with clustered colonnettes, diamond-paned sidelights and transoms, and recessed chevron patterns. The buildings at **43–49 Willow Place** (1847) make up Brooklyn's sole remaining colonnade row, four Greek revival houses joined by a wooden colonnade. Unlike the city's other such rows, which were intended for the wealthy, this one housed more humble folk, accountants and merchants.

Turn left on State St and walk five short blocks to Clinton St. Make another left and walk to the northeast corner of Livingston St and the former Protestant Episcopal **St. Ann's Church** (1869; James Renwick Jr.), now the Auditorium of Packer Collegiate Institute. An exuberant Ruskinian Gothic building, its brownstone facade is banded with white limestone and topped with spires and traceried openings. The church is smaller but more flamboyant than Renwick's famous Manhattan churches—for example, Grace Church on Broadway and St. Patrick's Cathedral on Fifth Ave. Next door, at 170 Joralemon St, is the Gothic revival campus of the **Packer Collegiate Institute** (1854; Minard Lafever), which started out as a girls' school but is now a private secondary school.

38 · The Civic Center and Downtown Brooklyn

Subway: Seventh Ave Express (2, 3) or Lexington Ave Express (4, 5) to Borough Hall. Eighth Ave Express or Local (A, C) or Sixth Ave Local (F) to Jay St–Borough Hall.

The Civic Center, today devoted to borough affairs, was formerly the seat of government of the independent city of Brooklyn established in 1834, the descendant of the town of Breuckelen, chartered by the Dutch in 1658. Downtown Brooklyn, which includes the Civic Center, lies east of Brooklyn Heights and south of the Fulton Ferry District.

Long the focal point of Brooklyn's far-flung system of elevated railways, the Civic Center got a facelift in the 1950s when the trestles were torn down and the streets widened during the construction of Cadman Plaza and the Brooklyn-Queens Expwy. Critics of Robert Moses, who spearheaded the project, assert that this "improvement" destroyed more than it enhanced, cutting off the downtown from Brooklyn Heights. The main shopping street, once the commercial hub for all of Brooklyn, is Fulton St, now home to a pedestrian mall. In recent years, the success of Metrotech, an ambitious commercial development, has brought new life to downtown Brooklyn.

Borough Hall

Begin at Borough Hall (1848; Gamaliel King; cupola 1898; Stoughton & Stoughton; DL), at 209 Joralemon St (between Fulton and Court Sts).

History

The city hall of the independent city of Brooklyn was begun in 1836 after a design by New York architect Calvin Pollard, but construction was halted during the 1837 financial panic. Building resumed eight years later, with the new hall opening in 1848. Like certain other things in Brooklyn, the city hall began as a copy of its counterpart in New York across the river, but financial crises and political realities resulted in several changes of design. The present building, faced in Tuckahoe marble, was designed by Gamaliel King, a former grocer and carpenter. It is Greek revival in style but smaller and less elaborate than the building Pollard had originally planned.

Exterior

The building is best viewed from the plaza side, where the steep steps climb toward six fluted Ionic columns. Its original wooden cupola was destroyed in an 1895 fire. The current cast-iron cupola with copper shingles made its debut in 1898, the same year the building was downgraded to the role of Borough Hall when Brooklyn joined Greater New York. The entire building was restored in 1989.

To the right of Borough Hall is a set of verdigris lamp standards saved from the former (1905) Kings County Hall of Records, which was razed during the 1950's redevelopment.

Cadman Plaza

Borough Hall looks out onto Cadman Plaza, officially S. Parkes Cadman Plaza, named after a noted Brooklyn Congregationalist minister and radio preacher. The plaza is bounded by Cadman Plaza West, Joralemon, Adams, and Court Sts, and the viaducts to the Brooklyn Bridge.

Walk through the plaza. On the right, just before the entrance to the **New York State Supreme Court** (1957; Shreve, Lamb & Harmon), is a bust (1972; Anneta Duveen) of **Robert F. Kennedy,** who was a U.S. senator from New York State from 1964 until he was assassinated in 1968 during his run for the presidency. The tribute features quotations from the presidential hopeful. Behind the bust is a plaque honoring Washington A. Roebling, engineer and supervisor of the Brooklyn Bridge. Directly in front of the courthouse is a statue of **Christopher Columbus** designed in 1867 by Emma Stebbins and moved here from Central Park in 1971.

Continue north past the courthouse. The plaza's finest sculpture is John Quincy Adams Ward's eight-ft bronze statue of **Henry Ward Beecher** (1891), standing on a granite pedestal by Richard Morris Hunt with the Manhattan Bridge as backdrop.

Beyond the statue on the right, at 271 Cadman Plaza East (northeast corner of Johnson St), is the **General Post Office** (1885–91; Mifflin E. Bell, first designer; William A. Freret, successor; addition to the north 1933; James Wetmore, supervising architect; DL). The building is a grand example of Romanesque revival architecture, with a facade of polished and rough granite, steep slate-covered roof, dormers, half-round turrets, and massive arcaded windows at ground level. In 2000, a $130-million renovation began on the largely unused building to add courtrooms for the Federal Bankruptcy Court and offices for the U.S. Attorney and other agencies. When it is finished in 2002, the building will be renamed the U.S. Post Office and Courthouse.

Continue through the plaza, crossing Tillary St. Directly ahead, at the plaza's north end, is the **Brooklyn War Memorial** (1951; Eggers & Higgins, architects; Charles Keck, sculptor), with two larger-than-life classical figures in front of a wall commemorating heroes of World War II.

Return to Tillary St and turn left (east) and walk several blocks to Jay St. Turn left to **St. James Cathedral** (1903; George H. Streeton), between Father James F. Hinchey Place and Chapel St, a Georgian-style brick church with a verdigris copper steeple. Before the first Roman Catholic church on Long Island was erected here in 1822, Brooklyn Catholics had to take the ferry to Manhattan to attend mass. In 1853, when the Diocese of Brooklyn was created, St. James became its cathedral—i.e., the seat of the bishop. In 1868 the first bishop, John Loughlin, began building a much larger and grander church in the Fort Greene section of Brooklyn that was slated to become the new cathedral. Work continued there for ten years before the funds ran out. In 1896 Loughlin's successor designated St. James a procathedral (a parish church used as a cathedral). St. James was not re-designated a cathedral until 1972, when it was clear that the larger church would never be completed.

Metrotech

Turn around and walk south on Jay St. At Myrtle Ave turn left into the commons of Metrotech, Brooklyn's most ambitious development project of recent years. Begun in 1986 in the hopes of luring Manhattan businesses seeking cheaper rents for back-office space, Metrotech includes 12 buildings (mostly shiny new glass-and-brick structures) on 16 acres bounded by Tillary St, Flatbush Ave Extension, and Willoughby and Jay Sts.

History

Metrotech was financed largely by the city, which spent more than $166 million in capital improvements in the neighborhood and gave Metrotech incentives and tax breaks worth over $300 million. The project was also financed in part by Polytechnic University, which at first had promoted the idea of a Brooklyn Silicon Valley that would improve the neighborhood and attract students. Although the Metrotech concept was altered (back-office operations instead of high-tech jobs) for pragmatic reasons, it has been quite successful. Unlike the Citicorp Tower built in an isolated section of Long Island City, Metrotech was developed in an existing neighborhood, which has gained 25,000 new jobs, many through the rental of Metrotech space to major corporations.

Metrotech Commons

Metrotech Commons, the four-acre pedestrian plaza, hosts rotating sculpture exhibitions sponsored by the Public Art Fund, a nonprofit organization dedicated to showing contemporary art in public places. In front of 2 Metrotech Plaza is the one permanent piece—Tom Otterness's ***Alligator*** (1996), a whimsical rendering of New York's mythological sewer dweller. This bronze predator has slithered out from a manhole to nab a banker, who has a moneybag for a head.

Polytechnic University, founded in 1854 as a college preparatory school in Brooklyn Heights, occupies several buildings here, including the former **First Free Congregational Church** (1846–47; DL), at 311 Bridge St. Now incongruous among its modern neighbors, this sturdy Greek revival church was home to the Bridge Street African Wesleyan Methodist Episcopal Church between 1854 and 1938. Escaping slaves hid in the basement when the church was a stop on the Underground Railroad. Later a factory, it is now Wunsch Hall, a student center.

Renaissance Plaza

Return to Jay St. Directly across the way, at Renaissance Plaza (1998; William B. Tabler), is the new, 384-room **Marriott Hotel,** part of a 32-story tower that contains the Brooklyn offices of the city's corporation counsel and district attorney. The hotel boasts Brooklyn's largest ballroom and, as the first new hotel in Brooklyn built in several generations, indicates that both Metrotech's success and Brooklyn's comeback are for real.

Turn left onto Jay St. Between Myrtle Ave and Willoughby St is the former **City of Brooklyn Fire Headquarters** (1892; Frank Freeman; DL), 365–367 Jay St. Now overshadowed by Metrotech, this building, best viewed from across the street, was once a Romanesque revival masterpiece, rated the finest work of Brooklyn's best architect. Built of rock-face granite, dark brown brick, and red sandstone with terra-cotta ornament, the firehouse has a large archway for fire engines (pulled by horses in the old days) and a tall tower for spotting fires. Today, it is a run-down apartment house.

Continue along Jay St to the **Fulton Mall** at Jay and Smith Sts. In the 1930s–40s, this part of Fulton St was the center of downtown Brooklyn, with large department stores—Frederick Loeser & Company, Abraham & Straus (A & S), and Namm's—drawing shoppers from all over Brooklyn. But as middle-class Brooklynites fled to the suburbs in the 1950s, Fulton St lost its attraction as a retail hub; Namm's and Loeser's closed, and the area deteriorated until the 1970s when a group of merchants banded together to work for renewal. The sidewalks along Fulton St between Boerum Place and Flatbush Ave Extension were widened and vehicular traffic restricted. Today, the Fulton Mall is once again bustling, especially popular with African American shoppers from nearby neighborhoods. Sadly, most of the shops are chain and discount stores, lacking local color.

At 374 Fulton St (between Smith St and Red Hook Lane) is **Gage & Tollner's** (1875; redesigned as a restaurant 1892; interior restored 1995; DL), a highly regarded steak-and-seafood restaurant. A Brooklyn gustatory landmark for more than a century, it opened nearby in 1879 and moved to this wooden storefront in 1892. The landmarked interior features cherry-wood trim and the original gaslight fixtures; the walls are covered by golden brown Lincrusta, an embossed linoleumlike product invented in 1877 as a cheaper alternative to plasterwork.

At 420 Fulton St (between Gallatin Place and Hoyt St), a branch of Macy's now occupies the Art Deco building (c. 1929; Starrett & Van Vleck) that was originally the flagship store of **Abraham & Straus,** long the neighborhood's commercial anchor. A & S eventually occupied eight buildings along Fulton St. Earlier, this site was home to Brooklyn's first free public school, which opened July 4, 1661.

Abraham & Straus

A & S was founded as a small dry goods business in 1865 by Joseph Wechsler and Abraham Abraham, who had clerked in Newark with his future rivals Benjamin Altman and Lyman Bloomingdale. Called Wechsler and Abraham, the store moved to Fulton St in 1883, the year the Brooklyn Bridge opened. While others scoffed at the store's remote location, the owners had confidence that the new bridge would help trade, and Abraham continued to lobby for a subway that would connect Brooklyn with Manhattan and further enhance the business. After Wechsler sold his interest in 1893 to three Macy's partners, including Isidor and Nathan Straus, the store became known as Abraham & Straus, but was not part of Macy's. In the 1920s Abraham & Straus went public and in 1949 became part of Federated Department Stores (to which Macy's also belongs); in 1995 Federated dropped the A & S name completely.

Continue east on Fulton to Albee Square. On the left, on DeKalb Ave at Albee Square West, is the **Gallery at Metrotech**, 1 DeKalb Ave, formerly the Albee Square Mall (1978; Gruen Assoc). Such stores as Black Family Books, Gifts, and Cards and ABC Contemporary Art give the gallery the local ambience missing from the Fulton Mall. Until 1977 the RKO Albee Movie Theater, named for Edward F. Albee, a vaudeville impresario and grandfather of the playwright, stood here; when it was demolished it had outlasted the Brooklyn Strand, the Brooklyn Paramount, the Loew's Metropolitan, the Fox, the Orpheum, and a number of burlesque houses.

Just past the mall, at the corner of DeKalb, Fulton, and Fleet Sts, is the **Dime Savings Bank** (1907; Mowbray and Uffinger; DL), a monumental building in the classic mode with an Ionic colonnade and classical figures flanking a clock above the entrance. Inside is a low leaded-glass dome and a decor that features impressive gilded dimes. While the city's commercial banks in the high-rent financial district were usually ensconced at street level in tall buildings, savings banks, especially those in outlying areas, could afford to build exclusively for their own use. They also felt it necessary to communicate architecturally their fiscal stability, especially during times of economic upheaval.

Junior's

Walk along DeKalb Ave on the right side of the bank to the corner of Flatbush Ave and one of Brooklyn's most beloved culinary institutions, Junior's. This family-owned restaurant-bakery, at 386 Flatbush Ave Extension, features a memorable orange-and-white color scheme, wooden blinds, Art Deco light fixtures, and a solid, basic diner menu. All those factors, along with friendly service, helped it weather the neighborhood's tough times. But Junior's lasting fame—it has become a stop for tour buses, campaigning politicians from Robert Kennedy to Bill Clinton, and local officeholders including Abe Beame and Ed Koch—can be attributed to one menu item: cheesecake. Junior's rich, creamy cheesecake with its atypical sponge cake bottom was, in 1973, voted the city's greatest cheesecake by both the *Village Voice* and *New York* magazine, cementing its longstanding word-of-mouth reputation.

Junior's Cheesecake

Founder Harry Rosen began his career with a restaurant-nightclub called Enduro on this spot in 1929. Twenty years later, when Enduro fell on hard times, Rosen closed it down and hit upon the idea of Junior's, a family-style eatery that opened a year later in 1950. He named it for his sons, although their names are Marvin and Walter, not Harry Jr. Shortly after, he and Danish baker Eigel Peterson conspired to create the perfect cheesecake. The recipe was long a tightly held secret, known only to Peterson, the subsequent two bakers, and Harry Rosen's sons and grandsons, who currently run Junior's. However, a memoir-cookbook by Harry's sons offered the recipe, as did Harry's obituary when he died at 92 in 1996. In 1999 the corner of Flatbush Ave Extension and DeKalb Ave was officially renamed Harry Rosen Way–Cheesecake Corner.

Return west along De Kalb Ave one block; cross Fulton St at Bond St where it intersects with De Kalb and follow Bond St two blocks south to Schermerhorn St. Turn right and follow Schermerhorn St three blocks (west) to Boerum Place.

New York City Transit Museum

Corner of Boerum Place and Schermerhorn St, Brooklyn, NY 11201. ☎ (718) 243-8601. Web site: www.mta.nyc.ny.us/museum.

Subway: Seventh Ave Express (2, 3) or Lexington Ave Express (4, 5) to Borough Hall. Broadway Local (N, R) to Court St. Eighth Ave Express or Local (A, C) to Hoyt St–Schermerhorn St or to Jay St–Borough Hall.

Located down a flight of stairs in the restored former Court St subway station (which closed as an actual subway stop in 1946) is a wonderful tribute to the city's enormous mass transit system. It opened as a temporary exhibition in 1976 but was so popular that it evolved into a permanent museum.

Note: The museum is closed for renovations until 2003. The gallery annex and store at Grand Central Terminal remain open.

Exhibitions included classic subway cars with wicker seats, leather straps, and Miss Subway ads; turnstiles; early maps from the days when the IRT and BMT were rival, privately held lines; and station mosaics, like one from Chambers St that depicts New York Harbor from the Brooklyn Bridge to the Statue of Liberty. (These mosaics were partly decoration, partly visual aids for immigrants who could not read English.) The museum plans to renovate and open to the public two historic sites: the former City Hall Station (in downtown Manhattan) and the Willow Place Electrical Substation in Brooklyn.

Diagonally across the street is the **Brooklyn Friend's Meeting House** (1857; attrib. Charles T. Bunting, builder; DL), 110 Schermerhorn St (southeast corner of Boerum Place), which reflects the simple, even stark character of Quaker architecture.

39 · Cobble Hill, Boerum Hill, Carroll Gardens, Red Hook, and Gowanus

Subway: Seventh Ave Express (2, 3) to Borough Hall. Sixth Ave local (F) to Bergen St.

South of Brooklyn Heights, in the northwest part of the borough, are the historic neighborhoods Cobble Hill, Boerum Hill, and Carroll Gardens. Formerly considered part of South Brooklyn (i.e., the southern portion of the original city of Brooklyn), they were renamed in the late 1950s and early 1960s to polish their images and boost their real estate values.

Atlantic Avenue, West to East

Stretching along the border between Brooklyn Heights and Cobble Hill and Boerum Hill to the east is Atlantic Ave, one of the borough's main thoroughfares and one of its most interesting commercial strips. It is also a center for the city's Arab population. Between Fourth and Third Aves, Arabic food shops and Islamic bookstores offer sustenance for body and mind. In the two blocks from Third Ave to Bond St are clothing stores, upholstery and lace shops, and antique galleries.

On a building at the northwest corner of Nevins St and Atlantic Ave is one of the city's most entertaining examples of public art. Every year since 1982, Jerry Johnson, a local sign painter and artist, has painted brightly colored satirical billboards with faux advertisements; one sign mocked the "greed is good" ethic of the Reagan-era 1980s, showing a dapper trio with a shiny new car. The ad, supposedly "Courtesy of the President's Council on Appearances," reminded passersby to "Dress right . . . and get a better shake out of life."

Between Bond and Court Sts are an **Antiques Row,** a jail, bail bondsmen's and lawyers' offices, and an occasional Arab market.

Arab Brooklyn

The center of Brooklyn's Arab population is between Court and Henry Sts. The population includes Syrians, Palestinians, Yemenis, Iraqis, Jordanians, and Egyptians, most of them Christian, except for the Yemenis who are Muslim. The Brooklyn colony began after Little Syria (north of Battery Park around Washington St in Manhattan) was displaced by excavations for the Brooklyn-Battery Tunnel. Many of the present residents are descendants of these former Manhattanites. Shops here sell fruits, nuts, coffee, dates, and olives, as well as brass water pipes, belly dancing costumes, backgammon sets, and CDs of Middle Eastern music. There are Arab bakeries and pastry shops, falafel stands, and more formal restaurants, many of them Lebanese.

Cobble Hill

Residential Cobble Hill, running south from Atlantic Ave and west to the Brooklyn-Queens Expwy, dates back to the 17C, when it was settled by Dutch farmers. Once there was an actual Cobble Hill, which the Dutch called *Ponkiesbergh*, rising at the present-day intersection of Court St, Atlantic Ave, and Pacific St. Here stood a fort used during the Revolutionary War. The name Cobble Hill was revived in the late 1950s with the area's brownstone resurgence. Most of Cobble Hill is a New York City historic district, except for the northwest corner occupied by Long Island College Hospital.

The "Poor Man's Brooklyn Heights"

Cobble Hill remained sparsely populated until ferry service in 1836 between Whitehall St in Manhattan and Atlantic Ave spurred development. Attractive town houses were built in the 1840s and 1850s for the upper-middle-class families who settled here just south of fashionable Brooklyn Heights. By the early years of the 20C, however, Cobble Hill had become "the poor man's Brooklyn Heights," attracting Irish, Italian, and Middle Eastern immigrants. Today the neighborhood retains much of its Italian and Middle Eastern flavor, despite decades of gentrification (and housing prices that almost rival those in Brooklyn Heights).

Begin at Atlantic Ave and Henry St. Walk south down Henry St for 3½ blocks, just past Congress St. On the left side of the street, facing Cobble Hill Park, is **Verandah Place,** a short block lined with small town houses and former stables (some converted into garages). It was less pleasant in 1931 when Thomas Wolfe lived at no. 40. In *You Can't Go Home Again,* he described his basement abode as more like a dungeon than a room, its windows barred "to keep the South Brooklyn thugs from breaking in."

Return to Henry St and walk to the next corner, turning right onto Warren St. Halfway down the block on the south side is Warren Place, which you can enter through the gate. This little hideaway is lined with red brick **Workingmen's Cottages,** each only 11½ ft wide. They were constructed in 1879 by housing reformer and philanthropist Alfred Tredway White. At the time of construction, the wrought-iron flower box holders, arched doorways, shared gardens, and even the indoor toilets were remarkable amenities in lower-income housing.

The cottages were part of a larger social experiment spearheaded by White and designed by William Field & Son. The complex includes the neighboring **Tower Buildings** (1879), which fill the western half of the block between Warren and Baltic Sts, and the **Home Buildings** (1877) along Hicks and Baltic Sts (439–445 Hicks St and 134–140 Baltic St). The apartments provided stairwells entered from outdoor balconies (for fire safety), good light and ventilation, and bathing facilities in the basement. Though the project was philanthropic in nature, White sought a modest 5 percent return to show that low-income housing could be built for profit. Today Hicks St overlooks the noisy, fume-laden Brooklyn-Queens Expwy.

Return to Henry St and turn right. The houses at **412–420 Henry St** (1888; George B. Chappell) once belonged to F.A.O. Schwarz, the toy seller.

Continue to DeGraw St and turn left. On the northwest corner of Degraw St and Strong Place is the **St. Frances Cabrini Chapel,** originally the Strong Place Baptist Church (1852; Minard Lafever), a stone church with a buttressed square tower designed by one of the city's eminent architects. The earlier Strong Place Baptist Church Chapel (1849; Minard Lafever), 56 Strong Place, is now a day-care center.

Return to DeGraw St and turn left. At Clinton St turn left again. On a block dominated by traditional row houses, **334 Clinton St** (1850; James Naughton) stands out with its mansard roof, corner tower, and wrought-iron fringes. Naughton was the primary architect for Brooklyn's school system in the 19C.

Christ Church (Protestant Episcopal), at 320 Clinton St (northwest corner of Kane St), was designed (1842) by Richard Upjohn, architect of Trinity Church in Lower Manhattan, and has furnishings designed by Louis Comfort Tiffany, including an altar and altar railings, the reredos, pulpit, lectern, and chairs. The Upjohns lived a block away, at 296 Clinton St (northwest corner of Baltic St), in a house that was built in 1843 but has been so altered since then there is little left worth seeing. This section of Clinton St, along with Kane St and Tompkins Place, contains some of the neighborhood's nicest Italianate row houses.

Turn right onto Kane St. At 236 Kane St, on the corner of Tompkins Place, is the **Kane Street Synagogue** (1856). Originally the Middle Dutch Reformed

Church, it is now home to Congregation Baith Anshei Emes, Brooklyn's oldest continuously functioning Jewish congregation, whose first sanctuary stood on Boerum Place and State St near Borough Hall before the congregation bought this building in 1905.

Return to Clinton St, turn right, and continue to **219 Clinton St** (on the corner of Amity St), one of the area's oldest surviving mansions. When it was built (1845) for Abraham J. S. DeGraw, a Manhattan commission merchant, it had a view of the harbor. Ralph L. Cutter, a seller of dry goods, added the tower in 1891 because neighboring buildings by then were blocking his view. To reach his tower, Cutter installed Brooklyn's first residential elevator.

Turn right on Amity St. The building at **197 Amity St** (between Clinton and Court Sts), now looking a bit ragged, was the birthplace in 1854 of Jennie Jerome, who became mother of Winston Churchill. A few years later her father, Leonard Jerome, moved the family to a new mansion on Madison Square.

Continue east to Court St and turn right at the corner of Congress St, where **St. Paul's, St. Peter's, Our Lady of Pilar Church** stands on what was once farmland owned by Cornelius Heeney (1754–1848). A penniless Irish immigrant who succeeded financially as a furrier, Heeney was the second Roman Catholic elected to the state legislature. He also served as guardian of a fatherless boy, John McCloskey, who grew up to be the United States's first cardinal. Heeney donated this land to **St. Paul's Church** (1838; Gamaliel King), the second Catholic church built in Brooklyn. His other charitable donations included land on Fifth Ave in Manhattan for St. Patrick's Cathedral and a bequest of $2 million to Brooklyn's poor and homeless. Heeney is buried in the churchyard. The church, originally Greek revival in style, has been altered and expanded, veneered with brownstone, and topped off with a steeple (c. 1860). Frank McCourt, author of *Angela's Ashes*, was baptized here as an infant before his family moved back to Limerick. The present name reflects a merging of congregations.

On **Court St,** the local shopping strip, neighborhood butcher shops and bakeries alternate with trendy cafés, Moroccan gift shops, Japanese restaurants, and antique stores. Technicolor murals on the **Cobble Hill Cinema,** 265 Court St, depict film classics and screen stars such as Jimmy Durante and Clark Gable.

Boerum Hill

Boerum Hill begins on the east side of Court St and is bounded roughly by Fourth Ave and State, Wyckoff, and Warren Sts. Long considered part of South Brooklyn, it was renamed Boerum Hill (in the 1970s when it was undergoing gentrification) after a Dutch family who had farmed the land during colonial times. Today a neighborhood with middle-class professionals and historic brownstones, Boerum Hill also has two large public housing projects. Young people from outside the neighborhood have moved here, imbuing the area with vitality, particularly on the main drag, Smith St, where boutiques and well-reviewed restaurants have opened in recent years.

History

Boerum Hill was first developed between 1840 and 1870, when middle-class business people built the Greek revival and Italianate row houses that still give the area much of its appeal. In the 1920s Irish moved in; Puerto Ricans followed in the 1940s and 1950s. By the 1960s, many row houses had become rooming houses as the neighborhood took a downward course. In 1973 a six-block area, irregularly shaped and bounded by Pacific, Nevins, Wyckoff, and Hoyt Sts, was designated a historic district, a portent of forthcoming gentrification. Today the population is a polyglot mix of whites, blacks, Latinos, Asians, Arabs.

Points of Interest

The east side of Hoyt St between Bergen and Wyckoff Sts (nos. 157–165 Hoyt St) in the historic district has row houses built between 1854 and 1871. Twenty-three row houses (1847–74) on State St between Smith and Hoyt Sts outside the historic district are also landmarked.

During Prohibition, the **Boerum Hill Café** (1851), 148 Hoyt St (at Bergen St), was one of several neighborhood speakeasies. Today it is the Brooklyn Inn.

The **Atlantic Ave Tunnel,** underneath Atlantic Ave from Boerum Place to the waterfront, is the oldest railway tunnel in Brooklyn and had long been forgotten until railroad buff Bob Diamond rediscovered it in the 1980s. Part of the Long Island leg of the Boston–New York railroad, the tunnel, which is 17 ft high and 21 ft wide, was built in 1844 by the Brooklyn and Jamaica Railroad (later part of the Long Island Rail Road), closed for political reasons in 1859, and sealed in 1861. Diamond conducts periodic tours of the 2,500 ft former byway; for information, call the Brooklyn Historic Railway Association, ☎ (718) 941-3160.

Carroll Gardens

Carroll Gardens begins where Cobble Hill ends, at DeGraw St, and extends south to the Gowanus Expwy; it runs east to west from Hoyt St to the Brooklyn-Queens Expwy. The name was adopted in the 1960s to help distinguish the neighborhood from deteriorating Red Hook next door. Charles Carroll, for whom the district is probably named, was the only Roman Catholic signer of the Declaration of Independence.

History

In 1864, the neighborhood was developed by a land surveyor, who set his brownstone back from the streets behind large front gardens. In 1973, several of the most attractive blocks, President and Carroll Sts between Smith and Hoyt Sts as well as Hoyt St between President and First Sts, became a historic district.

The Irish settled here in the early 19C, but from the end of the century onward, the neighborhood became more and more Italian, with many of its residents working at the Brooklyn Navy Yard or the Red Hook docks. In 1918, Al Capone was married at St. Mary's Star of the Sea Church on Court St between Nelson and Luquer Sts.

Despite the influx of middle-class professionals that began in the 1960s, the neighborhood retains an Italian ambience: regional dialects are still spoken, social clubs remain, and many front gardens are decorated with religious shrines and statues. Christmas is particularly colorful with neighbors outdoing one another with extravagant lighting and other holiday effects.

Points of Interest

The F. G. Guido Funeral Home at 440 Clinton St (southwest corner of Carroll St), originally the **John Rankin residence** (1840; DL), is a freestanding masonry

Greek revival town house sometimes touted as the finest in the city. Its brickwork and gray granite trim are handsomely preserved.

The **South Congregational Church complex** (chapel 1851; DL; church 1857; DL; ladies' parlor 1889; Frederick Carles Merry; DL; rectory 1893; Woodruff Leeming; DL), 253–269 President St and 358–366 Court St, is no longer exclusively a religious destination. The congregation now worships in the ladies' parlor, while the Romanesque revival church and chapel have been converted into apartments, as have two other nearby churches at 423 and 450 Clinton St.

Red Hook

Red Hook, named Roode Hoek by the Dutch (hoek meaning a point of land and roode describing either the soil color or the onetime cranberry bogs), originally referred to all the land below Atlantic Ave from the Gowanus Canal to Buttermilk Channel. Today, however, as Cobble Hill and Carroll Gardens have been renamed to divorce them from disagreeable associations with Red Hook, the name refers only to the section south of the Gowanus Expwy. It has long been a commercial area dependent on its piers and waterfront industry, having received its initial impetus from the opening of the Erie Canal in 1825.

The Brooklyn Docks

The Atlantic Dock Co. developed the pier and terminal facilities in the Atlantic Basin area in the early 1840s. William Beard, a railroad contractor, developed the Erie Basin with its rocky breakwater in 1864. During the Civil War the warehouses served as a supply base for the Union Army and also as military prisons and hospitals. After the turn of the last century, the Brooklyn docks became one of the world's great grain ports. In the 1920s the Tebo Yacht Basin, now gone, oversaw the dry-docking of the yachts of the wealthy, including J. P. Morgan's *Corsair*. During World War II, the Todd Shipyards, facing the Erie Basin, turned out landing craft for the Allied invasion; just after the war the rusted hull of the *Normandie*, destroyed by a fire (1942) at Pier 88 in the Hudson, was towed here to be readied for scrapping.

Red Hook's Decline

Since World War II, with the rise of containerized cargoes, the Brooklyn piers, lacking sufficient upland space for the handling of containers, have diminished in importance. Although there is a containerport in Red Hook operated by the Port Authority, most port activity takes place across the Hudson River in New Jersey.

For years the residential communities of Red Hook rivaled Hell's Kitchen in density and bleakness. In the opening years of the 20C Red Hook was mostly Italian and Irish. A few survivors from these days still remain, especially near the waterfront, in "the back," as it is called. Al Capone's family moved here to 38 Garfield Place from the area around the old Navy Yard, and it was on Red Hook's mean streets that Capone is said to have received the gash that earned him the nickname Scarface. Longshoremen, rope makers, ship chandlers, and others tied to the port lived here, sometimes without ever leaving the neighborhood, for it was and still is isolated, beyond the reach of the subway, accessible only by long bus rides. This was the setting for Arthur Miller's *A View from the Bridge*, Budd Schulberg's *On the Waterfront*, and Hubert Selby Jr.'s *Last Exit to Brooklyn*.

Red Hook has never been affluent, but the area was severely debilitated by the arrival of the Brooklyn-Queens Expwy (1958), a Robert Moses inspiration, and the Gowanus Expwy (1941), which isolated the shopping neighborhood around Columbia St, overshadowed blocks of housing on Hicks St, and polluted the air. More recently the loss of jobs on the docks has further depressed the area. Early slum-clearance projects like the Red Hook Houses (1939), stretching from Clinton St to Dwight St, may have been heralded when completed, but today these blockbusters (2,881 apartments) reflect rather than relieve the surrounding squalor; about 8,000 people live in the projects, nearly three-quarters of the neighborhood's population. Newer housing attempts on Visitation Place between Van Brunt and Richards Sts and between Verona and Dwight Sts (1972; John Ciardullo Assocs.) are more humane in scale.

In 1936 the **Red Hook Play Center,** at Bay and Henry Sts, with its outdoor, Olympic-size swimming pool, replaced a Hooverville that had sprung up as the Depression deepened. It still offers one of the few recreational facilities in an isolated neighborhood.

Red Hook's Recovery

Optimists have staked their dreams of improvement in recent years on spillover from the brownstone revival to the north and on industrial ventures like the Port Authority shipping terminal, which opened in 1981, today Brooklyn's only operating containerport. Now run by American Stevedoring Inc. and supported financially by the city, state, and Port Authority, the 80-acre site handles 55,000 containers annually and more than half the cocoa arriving on the East Coast.

While there have been blockbuster plans to dig a rail freight tunnel under the Hudson River and dredge the harbor to accommodate deep-draft ships, the neighborhood's tentative economic recovery has been nurtured by realistic small-scale ventures. In the late 1980s, retired police detective Greg O'Connell bought Piers 49 and 41 and 28 acres of waterfront land from the Port Authority, as well as several old warehouses. He has renovated the warehouses, including **499 Van Brunt St** (ca. 1865), leasing space to small businesses including film production companies, a glass engraver, and a brewery.

Artists and artisans discovered Red Hook in the 1970s and 1980s when a city program encouraged them to buy homes in low-income areas; some were fortunate enough to purchase four-story houses for as little as $2,500. Today there are more than a dozen glasswork businesses in Red Hook. While the lack of public transportation will likely prevent the area from flourishing as Williamsburg and DUMBO have, it may be possible for Red Hook to improve its lot without losing its character.

Touring Red Hook

Red Hook is not easily reached by public transportation. A car is recommended.

Points of Interest

Several old Red Hook warehouses remain, including the **Brooklyn Clay Retort & Firebrick Works** (c. 1860) at 76–86 Van Brunt St, 99–113 Van Dyke St, and 106–116 Beard St. These granite factory buildings and warehouses produced and stored brick fired from New Jersey clay, which was ferried from Perth Amboy to the Erie Basin. Also near the basin are the **Beard & Robinson Stores** (1869), at 260 Beard St, and the **Van Brunt's Stores** (c. 1869), at 480 Van Brunt St.

As part of Greg O'Connell's deal with the Port Authority, he has opened a **public promenade** next to the Beard St Pier and 499 Van Brunt St. The pier, open dawn to dusk, offers straight-on views of the Statue of Liberty and the Bayonne Bridge. The Brooklyn Waterfront Artists Coalition holds a festival there each spring; for information, ☎ (718) 596-2507.

The 1,500 ft of track in front of 499 Van Brunt St may someday carry a trolley line to downtown Brooklyn. (The last trolley line closed in 1956.) Bob Diamond, who founded the Brooklyn Historic Railway Association, is awaiting final approval to lay another half-mile of track into Red Hook, which would connect with abandoned trolley tracks that run to downtown. The trolleys make short runs on Sun from April through Nov; ☎ (718) 941-3160.

Pier 45, at the edge of Conover St, is home to the small **Hudson Waterfront Museum.** Founded in 1986, the museum settled here in 1994 on **Lehigh Valley Railroad Barge No. 79** (built in 1914). It offers programs for school groups year-round and special events for the public May through Sept. The small permanent collection of artifacts related to dock work (hooks, barge shovels, foghorns) overlooks the pier's community garden. For information, ☎ (718) 624-4719; Web site: www.waterfrontmuseum.org.

Just beyond Pier 45 is **Pier 41,** at the foot of Van Dyke St, which offers occasional art shows in the summer.

At the foot of Coffey St, looking out onto Buttermilk Channel and Governors Island beyond, is **Louis Valentino Jr. Park and Pier,** a well-tended 300,000 square ft park (1997). The shore area is landscaped with native grasses, but the highlight is a 357 ft pier jutting out into New York Harbor, providing a stunning vista that includes the Statue of Liberty, the Verrazano-Narrows Bridge, and Lower Manhattan. The park was named after firefighter Louis Valentino Jr., who died battling a blaze in Flatlands in 1996.

Gowanus

South of Carroll Gardens and Boerum Hill and west of Park Slope is the neighborhood of Gowanus, allegedly named for Gouwane, a chief of the Canarsee Indians. The Dutch settled the area in the 1640s, and it remained rural until the 1840s, when the Gowanus Canal was built.

The Infamous Gowanus

The 2½-mile Gowanus Canal, 5,700 ft long and 100 ft wide, begins at Gowanus Bay in New York Harbor, narrows through the neighborhood of Gowanus, and ends at Douglass St. Before there was a canal, there was Gowanus Creek, a winding tidal creek surrounded by marshy land, known for its delicious oysters. In 1840 the creek was drained, straightened, and bulkheaded to give barges access to New York Harbor. The arrival of the canal turned the neighborhood into a rough industrial area: coal, lumber, brick, and stone yards, as well as ink factories and paper mills lined its banks. The area's cheap housing and bars attracted transient sailors.

With tides unable to cleanse its northern end, the Gowanus became a foul byway by the late 19C. In 1911, with great fanfare, the city opened a much-needed flushing tunnel that drew stagnant water from the canal and pumped in fresh water from Buttermilk Channel. After World War I, 6 million annual tons of cargo made the canal the nation's busiest and dirtiest. Pollution worsened severely in the 1960s when the flushing mechanism stopped working and was not repaired. Untreated sewage poured into the water. Large-scale containerized shipping forced many of the surrounding industries to close or relocate to bigger, deeper ports, usually in New Jersey, and the opening of the Verrazano-Narrows Bridge drew business away from the canal. Currently only about ten firms still operate along its banks.

Gowanus Reborn
In 1999, the flushing tunnel was repaired, and within two months its effects became apparent. Not only has the stench lessened, but fish have returned to the canal, although the health department still cautions against eating them. The oxygen level of the water is almost as high as that in New York Harbor itself. There have been several proposals to redevelop land along the canal that rely heavily on large commercial retailers. The developers have become ensnared in lawsuits, and each proposal has promoted community protests.

Some smaller companies are moving back near the canal, and warehouses and factories are being converted to cooperatives and studio spaces for artists. Some art galleries have popped up along its shores, but the area remains gritty. The population is primarily black and Hispanic. Housing consists of a few row houses and some co-ops where white-collar workers live.

There is a small southern Italian enclave, with its own social club, just east of the canal around Carroll St, near Our Lady of Peace Roman Catholic Church. **Monte's Italian restaurant** on Carroll St has been owned by the same family since opening in 1906 (the date of its mahogany-and-oak bar). The Venetian murals were painted in 1938 and restored in the 1990s. Customers have included Al Capone, Frank Sinatra, and Sammy Davis Jr.

The Gowanus by Boat
The Brooklyn Center for the Urban Environment occasionally sponsors boat tours of the Gowanus Canal, which sell out quickly. For information, ☎ (718) 788-8500.

Points of Interest

Old Stone House Historic Interpretive Center
On 3rd St (between Fourth and Fifth Aves), Brooklyn, NY 11217. ☎ (718) 768-3195. Web site: www.oldstonehouse.org. Open Sat 12–3 and for special events. Changing exhibits, permanent exhibit on the Battle of Brooklyn, school programs.

The Old Stone House, in the center of James J. Byrne Memorial Park, is a replica of a Dutch stone farmhouse that witnessed one of the bloodiest battles of the Revolutionary War.

The original Stone House (1699), also known as the Vechte-Cortelyou House, once stood beside Gowanus Creek. British troops occupied it in 1776, forcing the Americans to retreat. But 400 soldiers of the William Smallwood's Marylanders counterattacked the British in six consecutive valiant encounters, recapturing the house twice but losing 250 American lives. The determination of these men not only restored morale, but bought the disorganized Colonial Army time to regroup.

The two-story building remained a residence until about 1852. The area around it later became Washington Park and a ball field, with the stone house becoming the clubhouse for a team that eventually became the Brooklyn Dodgers. Later, street grading left only the second story of the house above grade level, and this remnant was demolished and buried in 1897. The city eventually bought the property, built the current park, and rebuilt the house some 20–30 ft from its original spot, using fieldstones excavated from the original foundation. By the 1970s, the building was shuttered and forgotten. Local historians restored the building, and it reopened to the public in 1997. The site is operated by the First Battle Revival Center, which is dedicated to preserving the history of the Battle of Brooklyn.

Public Bath No. 7 (1906–10; Raymond F. Almirall; DL), at 227 Fourth Ave (corner of President St), predates indoor plumbing. Faced in brick and polychromatic terra-cotta with a glazed white surface to connote cleanliness, and ornamented with fish, tridents, and shells, the building has been restored as the **Brooklyn Lyceum,** a performing arts center. For information, ☎ (718) 857-4816.

A nondescript, largely unnoticed piece of wall on Third Ave (between 1st and 3rd Sts) is the oldest section of any major league ballpark standing in America. It was formerly the outfield wall of Washington Park, home of the Brooklyn Dodgers (then known as the Superbas and the Trolley Dodgers) from 1898 until the club moved to Ebbets Field in 1913. The rest of the stadium was razed in 1926, and the site was taken over by Con Edison, which preserved the wall.

The **Carroll St Bridge** (1889; Robert Van Buren, chief engineer; DL; restored 1989), on Carroll St at Second Ave, one of three bridges spanning the Gowanus Canal, is one of only four retractile bridges in the country. Instead of raising, the bridge slides back onto the shore to allow boats to pass.

The **tallest subway viaduct** in the city is at Smith and 9th Sts (on the F line), with a clearance above the canal of 87.5 ft.

40 · Park Slope

Subway: Seventh Ave Express (2, 3) to Grand Army Plaza. Sixth Ave Express (D, Q) to Seventh Ave.

Park Slope, which reaches from the lowlands around the Gowanus Canal to the hilltops of Prospect Park, is often seen as two distinct neighborhoods. The **North Slope,** which runs from Prospect Park West as far west as Fourth Ave and as far south as 9th St, has a high concentration of Victorian architecture, particularly brownstones, and draws well-to-do professionals. **South Slope,** also on the western flank of the park and bounded by 9th St, 17th St, and Fourth Ave, has long been a working-class district, developed in the 19C for dockworkers on the Brooklyn waterfront as well as Irish and Italian laborers working for the gentry or in factories. In recent years, the value of its real estate has been steadily on the rise. The neighborhood today has a mix of professionals, including writers, and longtime residents, many of them Irish American. (The local Irish American Day parade is the largest in Brooklyn.)

The mansions, brownstone and brick row houses, and churches of Park Slope's impressive historic district, the borough's largest, are located mostly in the North Slope and along the park. These impressive buildings date from the years surrounding the turn of the 20C.

History

During the 1850s, the rural land that later became Park Slope belonged almost exclusively to lawyer and railroad developer Edwin C. Litchfield, whose Italianate mansion survives on high ground in Prospect Park. The development of Park Slope gained momentum after the opening of Prospect Park in the 1870s and the Brooklyn Bridge in 1883, making the neighborhood convenient for prosperous professionals who worked in Lower Manhattan. Large Victorian mansions were built, including some monumental ones on Prospect Park West, which overlooks the park.

After World War II, Park Slope lost its appeal and many single-family homes were converted to rooming houses. But beginning in the 1960s, young professionals bought and restored these late-19C and early-20C residences, sparking a revival that has made Park Slope one of Brooklyn's most desirable neighborhoods, an area that attracts many Manhattanites to its brownstone blocks and row houses. Rising prices for residential real estate have driven many native Brooklynites out of the North Slope, while rising commercial rents have driven small stores and neighborhood restaurants from Seventh Ave. Quirky shops have recently been opening on Fifth Ave to the west, once considered the hinterland. In the last decade, restaurants and small shops have also opened above 9th St (in an area formerly considered part of the lower-rent South Slope) and row house prices there now sometimes reach $500,000.

Montauk Club

Begin at the Montauk Club (1891; Francis H. Kimball), 25 Eighth Ave (northeast corner of Lincoln Place), one of the few remaining private clubs in the borough. During its heyday before World War I, this five-story brownstone, brick, and terra-cotta structure served Brooklyn's social, business, and political elite. The decoration, an eclectic composition of Venetian Gothic and Native American motifs, pays tribute to the Ca d'Oro in Venice and also to the Montauk tribe of eastern Long Island, whose history appears in the terra-cotta frieze. Above the main entrance on Eighth Ave a terra-cotta panel depicts the club founders and builders laying the cornerstone; the wrought-iron fence and building's capitals are decorated with Indian faces. The building's three facades are all different: on the Eighth Ave side is wonderful terra-cotta; on Plaza St the Venetian style dominates; and Lincoln Place has a broad balcony with an arcade. The building's north side was left unadorned.

Interior

The interior is finished in oak and mosaic tile, with occasional Venetian arches in the woodwork. The first, second, and third floors were originally used for dining and entertaining, while the basement had a bowling alley (long gone); the top two floors contained residential rooms for members. Faced with an aging membership and high maintenance costs, the club's board recently sold the upper three stories (which have been converted into luxury condominiums) and basement, while continuing to operate on the first two floors.

Walk east to Plaza St West; turn right. Proceed one block to Berkeley Place; turn right again, stopping at **276 Berkeley Place** (1891; Lamb & Rich), a sturdy Romanesque revival house with cupid and scallop-shell ornamentation. The house originally belonged to George P. Tangeman, who made his fortune from the Royal and Cleveland Baking Powder Companies. Unlike the millionaires of New York's Fifth Ave, who dealt in railroads, real estate, and oil, Park Slope's industrialists generally owed their wealth to more homely commodities, such as chewing gum, hot dogs, and cleansing powder.

Walk west (away from the park) to Eighth Ave; turn left and go south to President St; turn right. Among the attractive 19C homes along President St between Eighth and Seventh Aves is **869 President St** (1865; Henry Ogden Avery), a robust brick structure built for a former U.S. ambassador to Spain, Stuart L. Woodford. It features two bracketed oriel windows and radial decorations over the ground-floor windows and door. The orange-colored, Roman brick residences at **878** and **876 President St** (1889; Albert E. White) are late Romanesque revival in style with round and elliptical-arched openings and random ashlar stone walls. The building at **874 President St** (c. 1888) is a real curiosity with its massive anchor sculpture and gate flanked by sea serpents. It was remodeled in the first half of the 20C, inspired by Tudor architecture with its random brickwork, stone, and stucco.

Cross Eighth Ave to the other side of President St for a look at **944–946 President St** (1886–90; Charles T. Mott), a brownstone and brick house with wrought-iron balconies, terra-cotta, stained glass, and a whimsical "1886" in a triangular adornment.

Walk toward the park and turn right on Prospect Park West. On the southwest corner of Prospect Park West and Carroll St are two limestone Renaissance revival apartments, formerly private houses, at **18** and **19 Prospect Park West** (1898; Montrose W. Morris); the former retains its glass-and-bronze canopy.

Turn right on **Carroll St.** The block between Eighth Ave and Prospect Park West, developed by several eminent 19C architects, is architecturally one of Park Slope's most eclectic. Noteworthy are **nos. 861–855** (1892; Stanley M. Holden), four Romanesque revival houses built in an alternating *ABAB* pattern with differing carved leaf forms, stained glass, terra-cotta window roofs, and faces ornamenting the windows; **nos. 872–864** (1887; William B. Tubby) are picturesque brick and shingled Queen Anne houses, with an "eyebrow" window at **no. 870;** those at **846–838** (1887; C. P. H. Gilbert) are each 40 ft wide, with no. 838 standing out because of its bronze-tipped conical tower.

Continue to Eighth Ave. On the northeast corner of Eighth Ave and Carroll St stands the former **Thomas Adams Jr. residence** (1888; C. P. H. Gilbert), now apartments. While the corner of this outstanding Romanesque revival mansion is engraved "117 Eighth Ave," the structure is a double house: 119 Eighth Ave (the Adams house) and 115 Eighth Ave (which served another Adams family member). The latter has an elaborately carved entrance arch on Carroll St. Adams invented Chiclets chewing gum.

On the southwest corner of the same intersection stood (until 1950) the equally spectacular mansion of Charles Feltman, inventor of the hot dog, whose Coney Island restaurant Feltman's earned him fame and fortune.

Turn left on Eighth Ave. At the northeast corner of Eighth Ave and Garfield Place is the imposing **Congregation Beth Elohim,** also known as Garfield Temple (1910; Simon Eisendrath and B. Horwitz), with a large dome, huge stained glass window, and a main entrance flanked by Ionic columns and set diagonally from the corner. It serves a Reform Jewish congregation.

Return to Eighth Ave and walk north, turning right onto **Montgomery Place,** which is named after Gen. Richard Montgomery, the hero of the Battle of Quebec (1775). It is one of the Slope's loveliest blocks. In the 1880s and 1890s, developer Harvey Murdock commissioned architect C. P. H. Gilbert to design many of the buildings, including nos. 11, 17, 19, 21, 25, 14–18, 36–46, 48–50, and 54–60. Murdock lived at no. 11, with its striking Dutch stepped gable, red tile roof, and third-floor windows with small-paned upper sash typical of the period. Unlike its neighbors, no. 46 Montgomery Place, smaller in scale, has a parapet instead of an attic story.

Walk toward the park and turn right onto Prospect Park West. At the corner of Carroll Street and Prospect Park West is the former **Horace Pratt residence** (1901; Charles Brigham), notable for its detail. The Indiana limestone walls have a hammered surface and sculptures of animals, human masks, and stone relief panels.

For a long time **49 Prospect Park West** (1892; Montrose W. Morris), between 1st and 2nd Sts, was the biggest building in the neighborhood. It belonged first to Henry J. Hulbert, whose financial interests included paper, Pullman cars, and life insurance. The mansion's towers allowed Hulbert a fine view of the harbor. Its whitish gray limestone is unusual for the Romanesque revival style. Today it is the Poly Prepatory Lower School.

Hulbert's next-door neighbor, at **53 Prospect Park West,** was William H. Childs, inventor of Bon Ami, precursor of the modern battery of cleansing powders. His former house is one of the city's best examples of the rare neo-Jacobean style. Today the red brick and limestone mansion (1901; William B. Tubby) serves the Brooklyn Ethical Culture Society.

Other Points of Interest

The **Brooklyn Conservatory of Music,** founded in 1897, occupies a brick-and-brownstone Victorian Gothic mansion at 58 Seventh Ave (1881; S. F. Evelette), northwest corner of Lincoln Place. It was built for William M. Brasher, owner of a Brooklyn oil cloth factory and, in 1924, was sold to the Park Slope Masonic Club, which occupied it for 20 years. In 1944, the conservatory moved in. Today the conservatory is one of the oldest and largest community schools of the arts in the nation, providing vocal and instrumental instruction and offering recitals and concerts. It recently completed a $2.5-million renovation, retaining as much original architectural detail as possible, and has built a lovely garden area on Lincoln Place with benches, fountains, and famous musical themes etched on clay bricks in the pathway walls.

Next door is the Romanesque revival former **home of Frank L. Babbott** (1887; Lamb and Rich), son-in-law of Charles Pratt, the founder of a major oil refinery in Brooklyn. It stands at 153 Lincoln Place, next to the conservatory. This brick building with brownstone trim and elaborate stone ornamentation was substantially enlarged in 1896. It became a rooming house in 1936, a residence of the Presbyterian Home for the Aged in 1945, and, in 1957, the Lincoln Plaza Hotel, a transient hotel where rooms are available by the hour, an unlikely neighbor on this block of brownstones.

At 116 Sixth Ave, between Sterling and Park Places, is the magnificent high-Victorian **St. Augustine Roman Catholic Church** (1892; Parfitt Brothers), with an unusual double apse. On top of the tower is a figure of the angel Gabriel, sculpted by a German company in Park Slope. The interior stained glass door windows and transoms were created by Tiffany Studios. The original pulpit, though no longer in use, features a life-size bronze angel, which won first prize at the 1893 Chicago Exposition. Since the 1960s, the church has had an active social outreach program and offers masses in English, Spanish, and Haitian Creole. However, the church's minority membership has been dwindling slowly as Park Slope real estate prices soar.

A Plane Crashes in Brooklyn

The empty lot on the corner of Seventh Ave and Sterling Place is an unusual sight in this highly sought-after neighborhood. On the morning of Dec 16, 1960, two commercial airplanes collided over New York Harbor. One, a TWA Constellation, crashed onto a military airfield in Staten Island. The second, a United Airlines DC-8, after an abortive attempt to land in Prospect Park, reached its final resting place at this corner. The resulting fire consumed more than ten nearby buildings, including a church (the former occupant or this lot) and a funeral home; 84 passengers and six people on the ground were killed. In 1999, nearly 40 years after this devastating accident, a Manhattan developer proposed a five-story, 19-unit condominium for the site.

The four Romanesque revival mansions at 21–27 Seventh Ave, across the street from the crash site, on the southeast corner of Sterling Place and Seventh Ave, were built in 1887 by Laurence B. Valk, an architect perhaps best known for his churches. The one at **21 Seventh Ave,** on the corner, with its elegant turret with curvilinear peaked roof, belonged to singer Lillian Ward.

The former **Ansonia Clock Company Factory** (1881), at Seventh Ave and 12th St in the South Slope, was once the world's largest clock factory, employing 1,500 workers, many of them Polish and Irish immigrants. In 1982 it was converted to co-ops and renamed Ansonia Court, for its landscaped interior courtyard.

The mammoth, imposing, and solid **14th Regiment Armory, N.Y. National**

Guard (1895; William A. Mundell; DL), at 1402 Eighth Ave (between 14th and 15th Sts), is another of the city's great fortresses. The patinated **_Doughboy_** (1923; Anton Scaaf) out front was a gift from Gold Star Mothers, women whose sons or husbands died in World War I. The 14th Regiment, also known as the Brooklyn Chasseurs and the "Red-Legged Devils," for their bright Zouave-style uniforms, was organized in 1847. The unit saw its glory days in the Civil War at Bull Run, Antietam, Gettysburg, and the Battle of the Wilderness, and also fought in the Spanish-American War and World War I. The National Guard unit was relocated in 1993. Today the armory shelters homeless women, though plans are under consideration for conversion to community uses.

Cut off from the neighborhood by the Prospect Expwy and somewhat incongruous with its surroundings is the opulent **Grand Prospect Hall,** 263 Prospect Ave (between Fifth and Sixth Aves). Built in 1903 by developer John Kolle to replace the original Prospect Hall (1892), which was destroyed by fire in 1900, it was a public concert hall and community meeting place with bowling alleys, a billiard room, a German-style oak-paneled beer hall, an open-air roof garden, dining rooms, and a ballroom 40 ft high, 70 ft wide, and 125 ft long. The ballroom hosted a political rally by William Randolph Hearst (1906), addresses by former governor Al Smith and Mayor James J. Walker (1929), and Works Progress Administration theater presentations (1930s). Ten years later, the Kolle family sold the hall to a Polish group, who used it for union and fraternal organization meetings. Over the years, the building deteriorated, until in 1981, Michael and Alice Halkias purchased it, added "Grand" to its name, and brought it back to its former glory—even finding and restoring the Bavarian-style murals long gone from the beer hall. Today, the revamped Grand Prospect Hall hosts parties and events.

41 · Prospect Park

Subway: Seventh Ave Express (2, 3) to Grand Army Plaza. Sixth Ave Express (D, Q) to Prospect Park or Parkside Ave. Sixth Ave Local (F) to Seventh Ave or 15th St–Prospect Park.
Car: From Manhattan take Manhattan Bridge to Flatbush Ave; follow it south to Grand Army Plaza. From points east, take Brooklyn-Queens Expwy to Tillary St exit; turn left onto Flatbush Ave Extension; follow it to Grand Army Plaza. Parking on park perimeter and, during business hours, at Wollman Rink or at Litchfield Villa.

Prospect Park, 526 acres of meadows, woods, and lakes designed by Frederick Law Olmsted and Calvert Vaux, is one of the chief and most cherished ornaments of Brooklyn. Laid out by its designers (1866–67) after they had cut their teeth on Central Park, the park is thought by many to be their masterpiece. Today, in addition to Olmsted's beautifully enhanced landscape, there are picnic grounds, baseball diamonds, a zoo, a carousel, playgrounds, a historic house museum, and a skating rink.

Crime
Prospect Park has in the past had an unpleasant reputation, but in recent years the crime rate has dropped significantly and police statistics indicate that the park

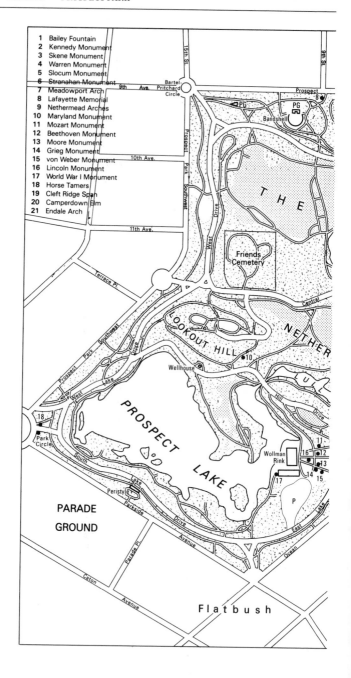

1 Bailey Fountain
2 Kennedy Monument
3 Skene Monument
4 Warren Monument
5 Slocum Monument
6 Stranahan Monument
7 Meadowport Arch
8 Lafayette Memorial
9 Nethermead Arches
10 Maryland Monument
11 Mozart Monument
12 Beethoven Monument
13 Moore Monument
14 Grieg Monument
15 von Weber Monument
16 Lincoln Monument
17 World War I Monument
18 Horse Tamers
19 Cleft Ridge Span
20 Camperdown Elm
21 Endale Arch

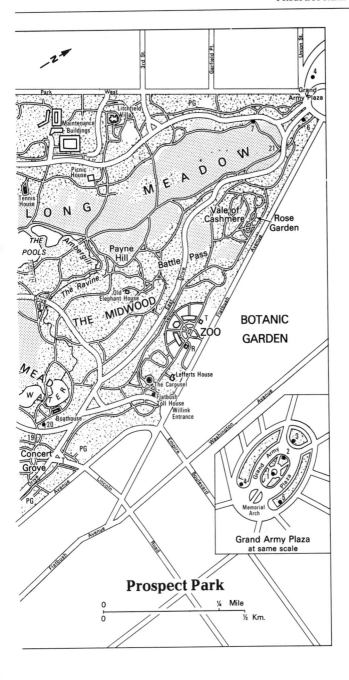

Prospect Park

is safer than even the "better" neighborhoods surrounding it. It is still an urban park. Use common sense. Do not wander in its more isolated areas alone and don't go there at night. As elsewhere, company is the best security.

Recreational Facilities

Ice skating at Wollman Rink, begins mid-Nov and continues through mid-March; skate rental is available. For rink information, ☎ (718) 287-6431. Horses to ride on the bridle path can be rented at Kensington Stables, 51 Caton Place at E. 8th St; ☎ (718) 972-4588. Pedal boating: mid-May–Sept at Wollman Center and Rink; ☎ (718) 282-7789. The carousel, near Empire Blvd and Flatbush Ave, features 51 wooden horses and other animals. Open April–Oct; for information, ☎ (718) 965-6512.

Maps and Guides

Maps of Prospect Park and *A Guide to Nature in Prospect Park* can be purchased Mon-Fri 9–5 at the Prospect Park Alliance office in Litchfield Villa (95 Prospect Park West, near 5th St), and weekends at Wollman Rink and the carousel. For information about the guide, ☎ (718) 965-8985.

Nature Tours

For guided tours of the ravine on Sat and Sun at 3 P.M., ☎ (718) 965-6988. The Brooklyn Bird Watchers Club organizes walks; ☎ (718) 875-1151. Nature tours will also be offered at the Prospect Park Audubon Center beginning in late spring 2002. The Urban Park Rangers offer periodic historical and environmental walking tours; for information; ☎ (718) 421-2021 or (866) NYC-HAWK.

Trolley

The free Heart of Brooklyn Trolley runs Sat, Sun, and holidays, noon–5, year-round. It leaves from Wollman Center and Rink on the hour and stops throughout the park, as well as near the Brooklyn Public Library, Brooklyn Museum of Art, Prospect Park Wildlife Center, and Brooklyn Botanic Garden. There is a connection to the Brooklyn Children's Museum Trolley at the Brooklyn Museum of Art and Grand Army Plaza.

Weekly Information about Park Events

Call the events hotline at ☎ (718) 965-8999 or visit the Web site at www.prospect park.org.

History

In 1859, sparked by the success of Central Park across the river, Brooklyn civic leaders, headed by James S. T. Stranahan, moved to purchase a $4-million parcel of land for a "pleasure ground." Egbert Viele, formerly the chief engineer of Central Park, developed a plan that included much of the present parkland as well as the area now occupied by the Brooklyn Museum of Art and the Botanic Garden. Fortunately, the Civil War halted construction, giving the commissioners time to reconsider Viele's plan. Unhappy with it, they hired Calvert Vaux, who convinced them to give the site its present form, eliminating Flatbush Ave, which would have cut a swath down the middle, and adding enough land for a large lake. Vaux brought in Frederick Law Olmsted and the two worked on Prospect Park from

1866 to 1873, authorizing some $5 million in improvements, enhancing the natural contours of the land, providing rustic park shelters, building archways and roads, planting and replanting trees and shrubs. Work continued into the 1890s, though the exact date of completion is unknown.

At the end of the century the firm of McKim, Mead & White designed the peristyle and a number of park entrances, and oversaw the formal placement of statuary in the Concert Grove. Later intrusions have included fenced ball fields on the Long Meadow, the zoo, and the skating rink, greatly enjoyed by their users but unloved by those who cherish the original design.

After a period of neglect and serious vandalism, Prospect Park today is enjoying a resurgence. The Prospect Park Administrator's Office (created 1980) oversees a master plan to restore and preserve landscaping and park structures. Increased security, including antigraffiti stakeouts, are making the park safer.

Begin at Brooklyn's answer to the Place de l'Étoile, **Grand Army Plaza** (1870; Frederick Law Olmsted and Calvert Vaux)—on Flatbush Ave at the intersection of Prospect Park West, Eastern Pkwy, and Vanderbilt Ave—a monumental oval plaza with a triumphal arch honoring the Union forces in the Civil War. John H. Duncan designed the 80 ft arch (1892), on top of which rides a bronze **Columbia** (1898; Frederick W. MacMonnies) in a four-horse chariot (quadriga) accompanied by trumpeters. The figure is commonly believed to represent Victory, but according to park archives she represents Columbia, the Union. On the pedestals, two monumental groups also by MacMonnies (both 1901) represent the **Army** (west) and the **Navy** (east), while above the inner doorway to the arch are bas-reliefs of **Lincoln** and **Ulysses S. Grant** (1894; Thomas Eakins and William R. O'Donovan).

Art in the Arch
The Grand Army Plaza Arch is open for art exhibitions in the autumn and spring on weekends only. Free. For information, ☎ (718) 965-8999.

North of the arch is an ellipse surrounded by formally planted London plane and Callery pear trees. In the center is the **Mary Louise Bailey Fountain** (1932; Eugene F. Savage, sculptor; Edgerton Swartwout, architect), with a grotesque openmouthed Neptune and sportive Tritons. North of it stands the city's sole official **monument to John F. Kennedy,** a modest marble tablet with a small bronze bust (1965; Neil Estern); still further north across the road is a bust of **Alexander Skene** (1905; J. Massey Rhind), onetime dean and president of Long Island College Hospital.

Walk back toward the park. On the west, across the road, is Henry Baerer's bronze statue of **Gouverneur Kemble Warren** (1896), Civil War engineer and soldier, defender of Little Round Top in the Battle of Gettysburg, some of whose boulders have been incorporated in the statue's base. In the same position on the other side of the arch is a bronze statue of **Henry Warner Slocum** (1905; Frederick W. MacMonnies), a Civil War general who hailed from Brooklyn and served under Sherman on his infamous march to the sea. In New York, Slocum is best remembered perhaps for the ill-fated steamboat named after him (see Tompkins Square Park in Walk 10).

Enter the park through its most formal approach, whose eagle-topped Doric columns and 12-sided classic temples (1894; Stanford White) express the reigning classicism of the period. Just inside the park entrance stands a statue of **James S. T. Stranahan** (1891; Frederick W. MacMonnies), Parks commissioner, public servant, and originator of Brooklyn's boulevard systems.

Take the right pathway (nearest Prospect Park West). The berm, or earth mound, that girds the entire park was designed by Olmsted and Vaux as a visual and acoustic barrier, distancing the park from its urban surroundings. Take the left fork of the path and cross under the roadway (here, as in Central Park, Vaux and Olmsted have separated vehicular and pedestrian traffic); walk through the **Meadowport Arch** (1872; Calvert Vaux) and into the Long Meadow.

Over a mile in length, the **Long Meadow** provides 90 acres of gently rolling grassland whose pastoral serenity Olmsted felt to be essential to an urban park, so essential that he had workers remove a narrow glacial ridge to enlarge the sweep of the land, creating what is the longest unbroken park vista in North America. He planted trees either singly (and some have grown to wonderful proportions) or in selected groups, sometimes using a tree-moving machine he and Vaux invented in 1867. Workmen with picks and shovels scooped out and packed into place the dips and rises that today seem to have been put there by nature itself.

Follow the path past the **Picnic House** (1927; J. Sarsfield Kennedy; restored 1984), used for various park programs (restrooms in basement) and as a rental facility for weddings, meetings, and other events. Keep walking west to the **Tennis House** (1910; Helmle & Huberty; restored 1997) of brick and limestone with open Palladian arches. It was built in the days when lawn tennis was a portable sport played on lawns; today it houses the Brooklyn Center for the Urban Environment (BCUE), which offers courses, exhibitions, programs for children and adults, and walking tours of Brooklyn and other city neighborhoods. For information, ☎ (718) 788-8549.

Side Trip

Take the path along the road and cross under it to the newly rebuilt **Harmony Playground** (2002). Behind it is the bandshell (1939), which stages the park's **Celebrate Brooklyn!** performing arts festival, June–Aug. At the 9th St entrance to the park is Daniel Chester French's (1917) **Lafayette Memorial,** a ten-ft bronze tablet with a high relief of Lafayette in the uniform of an American Revolutionary soldier. The park maintenance buildings between 8th and 7th Sts (inside the park) used to be the stables of the early park.

Since 1890, **Litchfield Villa** just to the north (inside the park opposite about 4th St), has been the headquarters of the Parks Department for Brooklyn. The villa (1857; Alexander Jackson Davis; DL) was built as a home for Edwin C. Litchfield, a lawyer who made a fortune developing midwestern railroads. In 1853 he hired Davis to design this Italianate mansion, which is romantic, asymmetrical, towered, turreted, and balconied.

Davis called it Ridgewood; the Litchfields called it Grace Hill (Mrs. Litchfield's maiden name was Grace Hill Hubbard).

After the Civil War, Litchfield donated 24 acres of his land to Prospect Park, but, according to the *Brooklyn Eagle*, the park commissioners "lusted" after Litchfield's castle and appropriated his estate and home, allowing the family to rent it back for $2,500 a year. The bunches of corn and wheat on the porch column capitals (instead of the classic acanthus leaves) perhaps reminded Litchfield of the Midwest, where he first achieved financial success. Return to the Long Meadow.

Cross the Long Meadow to the **pools**—modified glacial kettles that are natural bodies of water unlike, for example, Prospect Lake.

Take the path along the shore to the rustic bridge, cross it, and continue on via **Rocky Pass.** On either side is a wooded area—the **ravine** (restored 1996–99). The steep hills, waterfalls, rustic shelter, and plantings here were designed to satisfy the 19C taste for wild, romantic scenery and to complement the gentler landscape of the Long Meadow. Inside the ravine is the **Ambergill,** a 15 ft gorge with lush vegetation and a waterfall.

The ravine is currently (2001) behind fences to allow the new plantings to take root. However, special **Behind the Fences** free tours are offered April–Nov at 3 P.M. on Sat and Sun; ☎ (718) 965-6988.

Continue along Rocky Pass, past the stone staircase, to the **Nethermead Arches** (1870; Calvert Vaux), whose three spans accommodate walkers, horseback riders, and the brook. Inside the arches are vaults with fine brickwork. Beyond is the **Nethermead,** or lower meadow, surrounded by woods and seemingly isolated from the city.

Continue upstairs and along the path to the right, following it along Central Drive to an unused paved road leading up Lookout Hill. On the west side of the drive is the fenced **Friends' Cemetery** (generally locked; apply to the keeper if he is available; Urban Park Rangers sometimes lead tours of the cemetery), a 15-acre Quaker burial ground established (1846) before the park was built and still in immaculate condition. The actor Montgomery Clift is buried here about halfway up the hill near the right (north) fence.

Take the unused carriage drive up **Lookout Hill,** the highest elevation (170 ft) in the park, planned as a gathering place with separate concourses for carriages and pedestrians. Before the vegetation became so dense, the hilltop, rather abandoned nowadays, offered views of the city and harbor. Today it's a great place for birding. Its restoration will complete the restoration of the woodlands and waterways in the park.

Walk down the east stairway. Near the bottom of the hill, not far from the bridge, is the **Maryland Monument** (1895; Stanford White; restored 1993), a memorial to the heroism of a Maryland regiment whose holding action allowed the main body of Washington's troops to escape encirclement by the British during the Revolutionary War.

Continue downhill to the lake. Off to the right (as you face the water), hugging the hillside, is the **Well House** (1869), whose pumps once raised water to a reservoir on top of Lookout Hill. From here it flowed down into the pools and thence through the ravine into the Lullwater and Prospect Lake. City water came into the park at the turn of the 20C and the well was covered over.

From the foot of the hill, cross the Terrace Bridge and continue straight on to the **Concert Grove** (1872–74; Calvert Vaux and Thomas Wisedell), laid out as a formal garden with avenues of trees and statues of musicians (not original to the design); it has some of the most ornate sandstone carvings in the country. At the edge of the lake stands the **Wollman Center and Rink** (1960; Hopf & Adler). It replaced a small cove and an offshore island that once served as a natural bandstand and obliterated the beautiful formal vistas from the Concert Grove. In the grove today are busts of composers: **Mozart** (1897; Augustus Mueller), **Beethoven** (1894; Henry Baerer), **Thomas Moore** (1879; John G. Draddy), **Grieg** (1914; Sigvald Absjornsen), and **von Weber** (1909; Chester Beach). Directly behind the rink is Henry Kirke Brown's **Abraham Lincoln** (1869), formerly in Grand Army Plaza.

Walk around the rink past the parking lot to the **World War I Memorial** (1921; Augustus Lukeman, sculptor; Daniel Chester French, architect), a shrouded bronze angel sheltering a soldier.

From here either follow the lakeshore south to the Park Circle exit or return to Grand Army Plaza past the zoo, carousel, the Lefferts Homestead, and the Vale of Cashmere.

To Continue to Park Circle

Continue along the shoreline to a re-created rustic shelter (restored 2000) jutting out into the lake opposite the classical-style Parkside-Ocean Ave entrance to the park. Cross left over the drive, following the path to the **peristyle** (1906; McKim, Mead & White; DL), its limestone columns finished off with terra-cotta Corinthian capitals. Further along is the Park Circle entrance (1897; McKim, Mead & White), adorned with Frederick W. MacMonnies's wonderful, athletic **Horse Tamers** (1897), two bronze groups flanking the roadway.

To Return to Grand Army Plaza

Walk back to the Concert Grove. Along its main axis furthest from the rink is the **Oriental Pavilion** (1874; Calvert Vaux; restored 1988), a fine example of Victorian exotic tastes in architecture, its hipped roof and posts modeled on a medieval Hindu temple.

At the pavilion turn left and walk under the **Cleft Ridge Span** (1872; Calvert Vaux; restored 1989). Its vaulted interior is finished with polychrome blocks of molded concrete, a process called Beton-Coignet that was developed in France; the Cleft Ridge Span was the first structure in the United States to utilize this process. Beyond, on the left, is a Himalayan pine, and on the right, the park's most famous tree, a gnarled and twisted Camperdown elm, given to the park in 1872.

The Camperdown Elm

The poet Marianne Moore wrote about it; its devotees raised money to fill its hollows and truss its branches. Created by grafting a prostrate Scotch elm onto an upright elm trunk, the tree is descended from a crawling elm that grew (c. 1850) near Camperdown House in Dundee, Scotland.

Continue straight ahead to the **boathouse** (1905; Helmle, Huberty, and Hudswell; DL; restored 2001), faced with white terra-cotta. Serenely set along the Lullwater, this Beaux-Arts building was inspired by Sansovino's Library of St. Mark built in 16C Venice.

The Boathouse is currently closed for renovation. It is scheduled to reopen in spring 2002 as the Prospect Park Audubon Center. The new center will offer educational programs, exhibits, visitor information, a gift shop, and a café. Leading from it will be a network of interpretive paths focusing on Prospect Park's environment, design, and history.

The **Lullwater Bridge** (1869; McKim, Mead & White; restored 1986), a single steel arch, crosses the pond.

Past the boathouse, take the right fork of the path under the East Wood Arch toward the **Willink entrance** to the park (1888–90; McKim, Mead & White; restored 1994) and nearby comfort station (1887; Helmle & Huberty; restored 1995) with its beautiful Guastavino ceiling. On the left is the **carousel** (1921; Charles Carmel; restored 1990), whose wooden horses and other animals were salvaged from two merry-go-rounds at Coney Island and moved here in 1952. Nearby is the octagonal **Flatbush Toll House** (c. 1855), which originally stood on the boundary between the independent towns of Brooklyn and Flatbush, perhaps at the intersection of Flatbush and Lefferts Aves, not far from where it stands today.

Lefferts Homestead Children's Historic House Museum

Prospect Park (at Flatbush Ave and Empire Blvd), Brooklyn, NY 11215. ☎ (718) 965-6505. Web site: www.prospectpark.org. Open to the public Apr–Nov (call for hours) and to school groups year-round. Wheelchair ramp to first floor. Free. Permanent and changing exhibits, seasonal festivals, and workshops. Gift shop.

Subway: 6th Ave Express (D, Q) to Prospect Park.

On the right is the Lefferts Homestead (1783; DL), a clapboard Dutch farmhouse burned by the American troops under George Washington during the Revolution and rebuilt afterward.

The house is one of the few surviving Dutch colonial farmhouses in Brooklyn. Built by an 18C Flatbush landowner, Peter Lefferts, the house (threatened by demolition) was donated to the city in 1918 and moved from its original location on Flatbush Ave between Maple and Midwood Sts to Prospect Park. It is now a children's historic house museum, with programs that explore Brooklyn's rural past and its urban present.

Prospect Park Wildlife Center

450 Flatbush Ave, Brooklyn, NY 11225. ☎ (718) 399-7339. Web site: www.wcs.org. Open 365 days a year 10–5 (earlier closing in winter). Admission charge. Exhibitions and special events. Gift shop. Cafeteria. Accessible to wheelchairs.

Subway: 6th Ave Express (D, Q) to Prospect Park. Walk north on Flatbush Ave.

The Prospect Park Wildlife Center (formerly the Prospect Park Zoo) is a 14-acre state-of-the-art urban zoo with engaging exhibits directed to teaching children about animals in their natural habitats. Operated by the Wildlife Conservation Society, which also manages the Bronx Zoo, the center displays 400 animals of about 80 species in authentic environmental replicas.

Sculptor Mags Harries's aluminum-frame animals (1993)—including an octopus and a snake that is swallowing a frog—surround the walkway leading to the zoo from the subway station. Boxwood growing through the frames will eventually create a topiary zoo.

Inside is the ever-popular **Sea Lion Pool,** whose rockwork suggests the coast of California. The **World of Animals,** one of three main exhibits, explores the relationship between animals and their environments: young visitors can meet prairie dogs almost face-to-face or climb into kid-size birds' nests. **Animal Lifestyles** demonstrates how animals adapt to their environments; the intelligent and sociable hamadryas baboons in their rocky "African" habitat draw crowds of visitors. **Animals in Our Lives** includes an outdoor barnyard exhibit, with cows, sheep, and goats.

Evolution of the Zoo

By the end of the 19C, Prospect Park had a menagerie, many of them animals who had been donated. In 1902, zoo records mention an alligator, ring-tailed monkeys, and porcupines. Around 1915, the zoo bought 90 animals from European collections.

During the Depression, under the aegis of Robert Moses, the powerful Parks commissioner, the zoo was rebuilt and modernized. Moated enclosures and rocky dens replaced the old metal-barred cages, and a large central rotunda was built for elephants and hippos. The zoo opened to great fanfare in 1935. By the 1980s the zoo had once again become obsolete. It closed in 1989 for a four-year, $36-million renovation and opened, once again to great fanfare, in 1993.

Continue north toward Grand Army Plaza. East Drive follows the course of a colonial road that passed through a narrow rocky defile in the hills left by the glacial moraine. **Battle Pass,** along the road, is named after a Battle of Long Island skirmish fought here in which an outnumbered American force led by Gen. John Sullivan tried to hold off Hessian mercenaries attacking from the south. The Colonials got off only one volley before they were overrun and captured or killed.

Beyond Battle Pass, on the right of the road, is a meadow with a path leading to the **Vale of Cashmere** (c. 1894), a secluded hollow planted with azaleas and rhododendrons, once ornamented with rustic arbors and pedestals bearing Grecian urns. At its northern end, a flight of stairs leads up to the rose garden (1894), now a stretch of lawn with empty lily pools. From the garden, continue north past the Endale Arch (1867) to the park exit at Grand Army Plaza.

42 · The Brooklyn Public Library, Brooklyn Museum of Art, and Brooklyn Botanic Garden

Subway: Seventh Ave Express (2, 3) to Grand Army Plaza. Sixth Ave Express (D, Q) to Seventh Ave, within four blocks of the library.
Car: From the Manhattan Bridge, at bridge exit go straight on Flatbush Ave; continue to Grand Army Plaza; follow Eastern Pkwy signs around the traffic circle; library is two-thirds around the circle. From the Brooklyn Bridge, continue straight ahead to Atlantic Ave and turn right; continue one mile to Flatbush Ave and turn right to Grand Army Plaza; continue as above.

Near the end of the 19C, when Brooklyn was experiencing a great cultural awakening, the triangle bounded by Flatbush Ave, Eastern Pkwy, and Washington Ave, originally named **Institute Park,** was set aside for museums and educational buildings. Today it contains three of Brooklyn's major institutions: the Brooklyn Museum, the Brooklyn Botanic Garden, and the Central Library of the Brooklyn Public Library.

Central Library of the Brooklyn Public Library

Grand Army Plaza, Brooklyn, NY 11238. ☎ (718) 230-2100. Web site: www.brooklynpubliclibrary.org. Open Mon–Thurs 9–8; Fri–Sat 9–6; Sun 1–5. Closed holidays and Sun in summer. Accessible to wheelchairs. Exhibits; special events; educational programs.

The Central Library of the Brooklyn Public Library (1941; Githens & Keally; DL) is the flagship of Brooklyn's public library system and the largest of its 60 branches (the central library itself, the business library at Cadman Plaza, and 58 branches throughout the borough).

History

Brooklyn's first library, a subscription library for apprentices, was proposed in 1823, but it was not until 1892 that the mayor of Brooklyn suggested a public library system. The public library was voted into existence in 1897, the year the first branch was established in the former School No. 3, a wooden schoolhouse in a cornfield on Bedford Ave. Within four years, eight more branches had opened, and by 1923, thanks to a grant from Andrew Carnegie, the library had 30 branches.

Although planning for a main building began in 1907 and the cornerstone was laid in 1912, the proposed building—a classic, ornate marble edifice to complement the ambitious Brooklyn Museum—was delayed. Funds for Brooklyn projects vanished in the aftermath of the city's consolidation (1898) and subsequent fiscal crises. Finally, in 1941, after the uncompleted Beaux-Arts building had been partially torn down, a stripped-down, more modern version was completed, faced with Indiana limestone instead of marble. To one early observer the building suggested an open book, its spine on Grand Army Plaza and its two wings opening like pages along Eastern Pkwy and Flatbush Ave.

The library has continued to grow. The second floor opened in 1956, and further expansions were completed in 1972 and 1989. Beneath the library are four subterranean floors of stacks (not open to the public). The building has free Internet access throughout. The library has 13 divisions and 3 million books, magazines, videocassettes, CDs, and other multimedia materials.

Highlights of its holdings include the Brooklyn Collection, with the morgue of the *Brooklyn Daily Eagle* newspaper, which ceased publication in 1955, and the Brooklyn Photography Collection, with more than 25,000 photos of Brooklyn people and places dating back to 1870. The Multilingual Center (opened in 1997), with a staff of bilingual librararians, offers almost 80,000 books and newspapers in Chinese, Haitian Creole, Spanish, Hebrew, and Russian—the major languages spoken in Brooklyn—as well as materials in Arabic, Bengali, French, Hindi, Italian, Polish, and Yiddish.

Exterior

The 15 panels of the decorative bronze screen above the entrance depict characters from American literature: Hester Prynne from Nathaniel Hawthorne's *The Scarlet Letter;* the eponymous raven from Edgar Allan Poe's poem; Moby-Dick, from Herman Melville's novel; and Rip van Winkle, from Washington Irving's story. They were sculpted by Thomas Hudson Jones, sculptor of the Tomb of the Unknown Soldier in Arlington National Cemetery in Virginia. Inscriptions near the entrance were written by Roscoe C. E. Brown, a trustee and later president of the Brooklyn Public Library. One reads: "While men have wit to read and will to know, the door to learning is the open book." More quotations from Brown, as well as from Shakespeare and Goethe appear elsewhere on the facade. Flanking the doors are gold-leafed figures by C. Paul Jennewein, known for his work at Rockefeller Center; they depict the evolution of art and science.

Interior

The entrance foyer, designed as an "outer temple," leads between tall columns into the "great hall," paneled with Appalachian white oak. Above the doorway is a 300-pound zinc eagle (1892; Neils Poulson and Charles Eger) with a wingspan of ten ft. It is one of four that adorned the headquarters (see Eagle Warehouse and Storage Co. in Walk 36) of the *Brooklyn Daily Eagle* from 1892 to 1955. The eagle belongs to the Brooklyn Historical Society and is temporarily on loan.

Brooklyn Museum of Art

200 Eastern Pkwy (at Washington Ave), Brooklyn, NY 11238. ☎ (718) 638-5000. Web site: www.brooklynart.org. Open Wed–Fri 10–5; Sat–Sun 11–6; first Sat of each month open 11–11. Closed Mon, Tues, Jan 1, Thanksgiving, and Dec 25. Suggested contribution.

Changing exhibitions, gallery talks, lectures, films, children's programs. First Sat programs include lectures, dance, films, other entertainment. Café. Gift shop. Accessible to wheelchairs. Parking lot.

Subway: Seventh Ave Express (2, 3) to Eastern Pkwy–Brooklyn Museum.

Car: For museum and botanic gardens, follow directions to the library, then follow Eastern Pkwy to Washington Ave and turn right. Metered street parking. Large enclosed pay parking lot behind the museum adjacent to the gardens.

The Brooklyn Museum of Art (1897; McKim, Mead & White; 1978; additions and alterations; DL) is to Brooklyn what the Metropolitan Museum is to Manhattan. Its wide-ranging collections (1.5 million objects) and imaginative exhibitions make it one of the nation's largest and most prestigious institutions.

Highlights

The Egyptian Collection
Period Rooms from historic Brooklyn
18–19C American paintings
Arts of Africa, the Pacific, and the Americas

History

The Brooklyn Museum began humbly in 1823 as the Brooklyn Apprentices' Library, which accumulated not only books but also models of machinery, tools, and "specimens of the arts and natural productions," in order to teach "the mechanic arts" to its youthful members. In 1831, it added its first painting, a commissioned portrait of one of the founders. Later the library joined with the Brooklyn Lyceum to form the Brooklyn Institute, whose emphases included natural history and fine art. By 1878, however, the institute owned only 15 paintings (seven of them portraits of museum officers), but the natural history collections included stuffed birds, reptiles preserved in jars of alcohol, and large numbers of shells.

Then in 1883 the Brooklyn Bridge opened, and the independent city of Brooklyn, its population swelling, saw for itself a brilliant future. In 1893, the institute was reconfigured as the Brooklyn Institute of Arts and Sciences, embracing organizations that eventually would become the Brooklyn Botanic Garden, the Brooklyn Academy of Music, and the Brooklyn Children's Museum, as well as the Brooklyn Museum of Art.

The institute hired McKim, Mead & White to design a grand new home. The architects came up with a blockbuster plan for four buildings grouped around a central quadrant: it would be the world's largest museum—bigger than the Metropolitan Museum of Art, bigger than the Louvre. In 1897, the West Wing was finished and the building opened to the public.

The following year, however, Brooklyn joined the city of New York and its loss of independence ultimately shattered the museum's grand dreams. Plans for the museum building were scaled back. When the structure that houses the museum today was completed in 1927, the institute announced that the other three buildings to complete the quadrant would not be built.

While the Brooklyn Museum remained a popular and important institution, it was long overshadowed by museums in Manhattan and considered in some quarters a "local" Brooklyn museum. In the 1990s, however, following the lead of the Brooklyn Academy of Music, the Brooklyn Museum of Art began creative programming that brought it back onto the radar screen of New Yorkers beyond the boundaries of Brooklyn.

The museum is in the midst of a major expansion, which is based on a master plan developed by a partnership between Arata Isozaki Inc. and James Stewart Polshek Associates. It will include the redesign of the Eastern Pkwy entrance, whose grand staircase was demolished in 1934 in the interests of making the museum less elitist and more "modern." The revamped entrance, which will be surrounded by an outdoor plaza with fountains and seating, will open into a new glass-and-steel lobby.

Exterior

The Brooklyn Museum of Art, in the neoclassical style at which its architects excelled, grandly faces Eastern Pkwy with a six-column Ionic portico, an imposing pediment, and a huge dome. On the frieze above the cornice heroic sculptures of great thinkers and artists include four Chinese figures (sculptor, Karl Bitter) representing (beginning at the far left of the facade) Law, Art, Religion, and Philosophy; Mohammed (Charles Keck), left of the pediment; and, right of the pediment, Homer, Pindar, and Minerva (Daniel Chester French); followed by Plato, Phidias, Praxiteles, and Demosthenes (Herbert Adams). On the pediment itself, eight heroic figures by Adolph A. Weinman and Daniel Chester French represent (left to right) Sculpture, Painting, Architecture, Art and Science, Geography, Astronomy, and Biology.

Manhattan and Brooklyn

The statues of *Manhattan* and *Brooklyn* (1916; Daniel Chester French) flanking the main entrance on Eastern Pkwy formerly stood near the Manhattan Bridge on the Brooklyn side but were placed here (1963) when the bridge ramps were widened. In the 1960s Robert Moses, head of the Triborough Bridge and Tunnel Authority, whose obsession with ever larger and wider highways led to some of New York's finer arteries and some of its more blighted neighborhoods, proposed an expressway through Lower Manhattan. He asked the city Art Commission for permission to demolish the bridge approaches, claiming that removal of the sculpture was necessary for bridge connections to the proposed roadway. Since it appeared that the road was inevitable and that the bridge approaches were doomed, the commission sadly gave permission, under the condition that some of the sculpture be moved to other sites. The Brooklyn Museum volunteered to take these two sculptures, and in 1963 they were moved here. Unlike many urban preservation stories, this one had a happy outcome, since the roadway project was defeated in 1969.

The Collections

First Floor

The main exhibition area on the first floor is devoted to the **Arts of Africa, the Pacific, and the Americas.** The Brooklyn Museum, the first in this country to show African art as art, has an important collection, especially strong in works from Central Africa. There are masks, wooden and brass statues, and household objects. A carved ivory gong from the Edo people of Benin is the only example of its kind in the United States. Also unique in this country is a figure of the king Mishe MiShyaang maMbul of the Kuba people of Zaire, an 18C figure representing the king's spirit double.

Included in **Arts of the Americas** are beautiful woven and painted fabrics, including the **Paracas textile** (300 B.C.?), said to be the most exquisitely executed fabric produced in the Western Hemisphere, and stone sculpture from the Mayan, Aztec, and Huastec cultures. The museum recently acquired an important set of portraits of **Kings of the Inca Empire,** painted by anonymous Peruvian artists from the 14C–18C.

Also on view is an imposing display of wood sculpture representing the **Cultures of Oceania:** New Zealand, Polynesia, New Guinea, Indonesia, and Melanesia. Here are masks, wicker shields decorated with fine shellwork, and ceremonial figures. **Native American Art** includes totem poles and other works by the Northwest Coast Indians; a remarkable hide shirt from the Blackfeet tribe, decorated with porcupine quills and glass beads; and fine examples of basketry, beadwork, masks, and pottery.

Second Floor

The second floor houses the museum's collection of **Islamic and Asian art.** In the galleries of Islamic art are displays of ceramics, textiles, rugs, illustrated manuscripts, and calligraphy. The galleries of Asian Art include Chinese, Japanese, and Korean sculpture, ceramics, prints, paintings, Indian stone and bronze sculpture, and terra-cottas.

Third Floor

Third floor galleries are devoted to ancient civilizations. In the **Gallery of the Ancient Middle East** are 12 Assyrian reliefs from the palace of Ashurnasirpal II (9C B.C.) in Kalhu (Nimrud).

The **Egyptian Collection,** reinstalled (1993) in the West Wing and arranged chronologically, is one of the finest in the nation. The collection covers four millennia, from the predynastic period (4000–3000 B.C.) to the Muslim conquest in the 7C A.D. (The earliest material is installed in the square of galleries opening from the Assyrian reliefs and will be reinstalled.)

The chronological installation (up a few steps) in the West Wing ranges from about 1350 B.C. during the reign of Akhenaton and his wife, Nefertiti, to the rule of Cleopatra VII (died 30 B.C.). Works on view include tombstone reliefs, sarcophagi, carved wooden tomb statues, idealized granite figures of pharaohs, decorated coffins, and small elegant objects such as cosmetic jars and gold jewelry. Famous pieces include the cartonnage (i.e., a decorated container for a body) of Nespanetjerenpere and the **"Brooklyn black head"** (47–44 B.C.), a diorite head of a man remarkable for being rendered in a style that owes nothing to Greek or Roman traditions. The bird-shaped coffin for a sacred ibis once contained a mummified ibis, a bird believed to be a manifestation of the god Thoth. Highlights of the final section of the exhibition, **Temples, Tombs, and the Egyptian Universe,** are a 2,600-year-old coffin and its intricately wrapped mummy, as well as reliefs from the tomb of the 8C B.C. vizier Nespeqashuty.

Fourth Floor

The fourth floor is devoted to decorative arts including **period rooms,** two of them from early Brooklyn. The two-room **Jan Martense Schenck House** (c. 1675), which originally stood in the Flatlands section of Brooklyn, has been reconstructed and filled with period furniture. The **Nicholas Schenck House** (c.

1775), from the Canarsie section of Brooklyn, is a small farmhouse with a gambrel roof. Much of its furniture belonged to old Brooklyn families. Other American period rooms are organized chronologically and geographically. Of particular interest is the **Moorish Room from the John D. Rockefeller town house** on W. 54th St in Manhattan, with the dark tiles, brocaded walls, and wood paneling that pleased the exotic tastes of the period. Also on this floor are galleries with excellent examples of metalware, glass, and ceramics—including objects designed and produced in Brooklyn.

Fifth Floor

The fifth floor is devoted to painting and sculpture. The Brooklyn Museum has a fine collection of **American paintings,** known for its 18C–19C portraits and landscapes. Here are works by Ammi Phillips, John Singleton Copley, Charles Willson Peale, and Gilbert Stuart (the last two represented by portraits of George Washington). Among the early landscapes is one of Edward Hicks's many treatments of *The Peaceable Kingdom.* Francis Guy's *Winter Scene in Brooklyn* depicts (1817–20) life on Front St when it was the center of the village of Brooklyn.

Paintings from the 19C include works by members of the Hudson River School and other romantic landscape painters, as well as history paintings, portraits, and genre scenes. Frederick Church, Albert Bierstadt, Asher B. Durand, Thomas Cole, George Inness, Winslow Homer, Thomas Eakins, John H. Twachtman, and John Singer Sargent are among the artists represented. Works by early-20C painters usually associated with the urban scene are also featured, including Childe Hassam, John Sloan, and William Glackens.

The galleries of **European art** contain works ranging from the early Italian Renaissance to the impressionist and postimpressionist periods. Highlights are altarpieces for the 14C–15C, especially Nardo di Cione's *Madonna and Child Enthroned with Saints.* The **Rodin Sculpture Gallery** displays groups from the sculptor's best-known commissions—*The Gates of Hell, The Burghers of Calais,* and the *Monument to Balzac*—as well as portraits, mythological subjects, and erotic groups that suggest the scope of Rodin's long career.

Brooklyn Botanic Garden

1000 Washington Ave (at Eastern Pkwy), Brooklyn, NY 11225. ☎ (718) 623-7200. Web site: www.bbg.org. Grounds open April–Sept: Tues–Fri 8–6; weekends and holidays 10–6. Oct–March: Tues–Fri 8–4:30; weekends and holidays 10–4:30. Closed Mon (except public holidays), Jan 1, Thanksgiving, and Dec 25. Native Flora Garden and Rose Garden closed Nov–March. Conservatory, gift shop, and Visitor Center: open April–Sept, Tues–Sun and holidays 10–5:30; Oct–March, Tues–Sun and holidays 10–4. Admission charge; children 16-and-under free. Free every Tues (except holidays) and Sat until noon.

Concerts, seminars, workshops, exhibits, festivals, seasonal events, educational programs, research library. Public tours weekends at 1 (except major holiday weekends); meet in front of the Visitor Center. Café. Gift shop. Most of the garden is accessible to wheelchairs.

Subway: Sixth Ave Express (D, Q) to Prospect Park. Seventh Ave Express (2, 3) to Eastern Pkwy–Brooklyn Museum. Car: See directions to Brooklyn Museum of Art.

The Brooklyn Botanic Garden, a carefully tended and intensively planted 52-

acre oasis hedged around by asphalt and apartment houses, is an unexpected Eden enjoyed by neighborhood visitors and revered by horticulturists and plant lovers the world over. Its grounds include formal and informal areas, a world-renowned Japanese garden, an herb garden, a rose garden, a world-famous collection of flowering cherries, stands of conifers and monocots, a native plant garden, a rock garden, a Shakespeare garden, a fragrance garden, mixed perennial borders, ponds with water lilies, and an outstanding conservatory.

History
The Botanic Garden was founded (1910) as a department of the Brooklyn Institute of Arts and Sciences for the education and enjoyment of the public, a remarkable goal at a time when botanic gardens were still primarily attached to universities. Initially funded with a donation from the Brooklyn philanthropist Alfred Tredway White on land made available by the city of New York, the garden—a wasteland at first—was enriched in its early years with the by-products of nearby breweries and stables. Its collections now include more than 12,000 species of plants.

Highlights
The **Visitor Center** is housed in the Beaux-Arts-style Administration Building (1918; McKim, Mead & White). Here you can find out what is currently in bloom and pick up a garden map and calendar with upcoming events and programs. Outside the main entrance is **Magnolia Plaza,** spectacular in early April when more than 20 varieties are in full bloom. The figures on the armillary sphere representing the signs of the zodiac are by Rhys Caparn, daughter of Harold Caparn, landscape architect for much of the garden.

The **Japanese Hill-and-Pond Garden** (1914–15; restored 1999–2000) is the masterpiece of Takeo Shiota, who came to America in 1907. Architectural elements include a Viewing Pavilion and a vermilion *torii,* or gateway, to a Shinto shrine, in this case dedicated to a harvest god, on the hillside beyond. Here and there are stone lanterns and wooden bridges. Five small waterfalls with echo caverns beneath them splash onto a landscape of miniature trees and shrubs. The pond contains turtles and koi fish. Outside the entrance is a three-ton **Komatsu stone lantern** (1652) given by the city of Tokyo in 1980. A **Celebrity Path,** with names of famous people who were born or achieved their success in Brooklyn, rims the south shore of the pond.

The **Cherry Walk** and the **Cherry Esplanade** offer one of the most famous collections of Oriental flowering cherries outside Japan, with more than 200 trees of 40 varieties; they flower in early May against a backdrop of red foliage provided by Schwedler maples planted on Armistice Day, 1918. The Cherry Esplanade has trees of one spectacular variety—the deep pink double-flowered *Prunus serrulata* "Kwanzan."

The **Cranford Rose Garden** has more than 5,000 roses, including many All-America Selections. At their peak in May and early June, they fill the garden with color and scent.

The **Lily Pool Terrace,** two large pools, is gorgeous in summer, with 100 varieties of water lilies and lotus flowers.

The **Steinhardt Conservatory** (1988), a complex of greenhouses, holds the garden's indoor plant collections, including the **Bonsai Museum**—the country's oldest and perhaps finest collection of bonsai (dwarfed, ornamentally shaped trees and shrubs grown in shallow pots). The central exhibit, the **Trail of Evolution,** traces the development of plant life from the Precambrian era (some 3.5 billion years ago) to the present, from simple single-celled organisms to "modern" flowering plants. The **Aquatic House** has shallow and deep pools as well as displays on bogs, insectivorous plants, and orchids. On the lower level three environmental pavilions—**Tropical, Desert,** and **Temperate**—offer giant banana trees, cactii, a fern grotto, and a limestone cave with a display of mushrooms.

The **Children's Garden** (1914) is a cherished local institution where each year hundreds of children learn to grow vegetables and flowers, absorbing the human virtues associated with gardening. The **Discovery Garden** is a horticultural hands-on site for kids.

43 · Southwestern Brooklyn: Sunset Park, Bay Ridge, Bensonhurst, Bath Beach, and Borough Park

Sunset Park

The neighborhood of Sunset Park, along Upper New York Bay south of Gowanus Bay, is named after a high, sloping park that stretches from Fifth to Seventh Aves and from 41st to 44th Sts, offering sunset views of the harbor to the west. Although the park was built in the 1890s, the area was not formally named Sunset Park until 1969, before which it was considered part of Gowanus (to the north) and Bay Ridge (to the south).

History

Sunset Park's first European settlers were Dutch farmers, who worked land that had previously belonged to the Canarsee Indians, raising grain and tobacco for cash crops. The local village was Gowanus, between present-day 24th and 28th Sts along the bay. Agriculture dominated the area until the mid-19C, when Green-Wood cemetery was developed and the Gowanus Canal to the north was widened to encourage commerce.

In the 1840s Irish immigrants came, fleeing the potato famine, and often found work as laborers in the construction trades. They were followed by Poles and then in the 1880s by Norwegians, who continued to work as shipbuilders, dockworkers, and maritime bankers or insurers. They were followed in turn by Finns, many of them skilled craftsmen, who became known for their communal organizations. The Italians who arrived at the turn of the 20C worked as longshoremen, as laborers digging the subways, and in construction, especially as masons and bricklayers.

In the 1930s Sunset Park began to fall on hard times. The Depression hit hard, and the arrival of the elevated Gowanus Expwy in the next decade (completed 1941) further blighted the area, bringing noise and pollution and destroying much of the commercial strip along Third Ave. With the rise of the automobile after World War II and the opening of the Verrazano-Narrows Bridge in 1964, the middle class defected to the suburbs or Staten Island.

By the late 1960s things looked bleak. Containerization drew shipping jobs to other ports. Fraud and corruption in financing federal housing led to the abandonment of hundreds of houses in Sunset Park. Unemployment soared. In 1972, Lutheran Medical Center, the major local institution, began a $67-million expansion and increased its hiring of local residents, helping to spur investment from the public and private economy.

Sunset Park Today

The last traces of the Scandinavian community have been obliterated, and Sunset Park is now largely Hispanic (initially Puerto Rican, increasingly Dominican and Mexican) with a burgeoning Asian population that includes the city's fastest growing Chinatown. Between 1990 and 1996, more than 3,000 of Sunset Park's 15,000 immigrants came from the Dominican Republic while 4,400 came from China—making it the third-most-popular destination after the Chinatowns in Manhattan and Flushing (Queens) for Chinese immigrants. Many of the newcomers are Fujianese and a large number arrived illegally. More than 200 Asian businesses line Eighth Ave between 40th and 60th Sts, including numerous restaurants between 55th and 59th Sts. Attracted by low rents, the Chinese garment industry has set up factories in old warehouses and tenements that churn out low-quality clothing. Unfortunately, many operate as sweatshops and are among the city's worst offenders against humane labor practices. Crime is down in Sunset Park compared to the early 1990s, but gangs, particularly Mexican gangs, remain a problem.

Sunset Park's turn-of-the-20C brownstone and limestone homes along the side streets to the east are now attracting professionals priced out of nearby Park Slope. The section from 38th to 64th Sts between Fourth and Seventh Aves is listed on the National Register of Historic Places.

In the late 1990s, spurred by a strong national economy, Sunset Park began to return to its historic position as a vital industrial zone. Three proposed development projects, if implemented, may significantly change its future: the reconstruction of the Gowanus Expwy (an expensive but preferable alternative proposal recommends tearing it down and routing the roadway underground and at street level), the rebuilding of the port, and the construction of a rail freight tunnel to Staten Island or New Jersey.

Green-Wood Cemetery

500 25th St, Brooklyn, NY 11232. ☎ (718) 768-7300. Web site: www.green -wood.com. Only the main gate is open for visiting hours, daily 8–4. The guard at the gatehouse will direct you to the office for permission to view the cemetery. On weekdays a map is available at the office inside the main gate. Privately sponsored tours on weekends during spring and autumn. For information, call the cemetery or check their Web site.

Subway: Broadway Local (N, R) to 25th St. Bus: B63 runs east across Atlantic Ave and then south along Fifth Ave past the main gate.

Green-Wood Cemetery, Fifth to McDonald Aves, 20th to 37th Sts, is Brooklyn's Père Lachaise, renowned for the famous people buried there and its Victorian tombstone architecture. Green-Wood's 20 miles of paths wind through 478 acres, past four lakes, thousands of trees, and the highest elevation in Brooklyn (216.5 ft).

In 1838, when Green-Wood was established, most burials took place in family plots or churchyards, so New Yorkers were reluctant to be buried here. In 1845, however, the widow of De Witt Clinton (died 1828), former New York mayor and governor, allowed his remains to be moved from their grave in Albany, New York, to Green-Wood. After that the cemetery became *the* fashionable place to be buried—even for people who lived as far away as Michigan or Ohio. The cemetery was also a popular spot for outings, its landscaped hills and winding roads offering Victorian visitors both fresh air and fine views of New York Harbor. Several glacial lakes have been filled in to increase available land for burials.

Who's Who in Green-Wood Cemetery

Buried among the nearly 600,000 at Green-Wood are 38 Union and two Confederate generals, the Reverend Henry Ward Beecher, Samuel F. B. Morse, Nathaniel Currier, James Merritt Ives, William M. "Boss" Tweed, Samuel Chester Reid (who devised the notion of adding stars to the American flag for new states), Peter Cooper, Horace Greeley, Charles Ebbets (owner of the Brooklyn Dodgers), Louis Moreau Gottschalk (the most successful 19C American composer), James Kirke Paulding (who wrote "Peter Piper picked a peck of pickled peppers"), Margaret Sanger, and Leonard Bernstein. There is still space available for contemporary plots.

Green-Wood's **Victorian statuary** has attracted art historians and scholars. To memorialize particular lives and deaths, monuments depict sinking steamboats, mangled railroad cars, fire hydrants, empty children's beds, empty chairs, and flights of angels kneeling, standing, or stooped with grief.

Main Gate

The majestic **main gate** (1861; Richard Upjohn & Son; DL), on Fifth Ave at 25th St, represents the full flowering of the Gothic revival style and was probably designed by R. M. Upjohn, son of the famous architect of Trinity Church. Built of brownstone, with multicolored slate roofs on the flanking gatekeeper's lodge and office, the gate bristles with spires, turrets, finials, and crockets, its portals covered by tall traceried gables. The decorative features, depicting religious themes relating to death and resurrection, are carved from Nova Scotia sandstone. Other gates and gatehouses are at 20th St opposite Prospect Park West (1920; Warren & Wetmore) at 37th St and Fort Hamilton Pkwy (1875; Richard M. Upjohn).

Points of Interest

Across from Green-Wood's main gate is McGovern Florists, formerly the **Weir & Company Greenhouse** (1895; G. Curtis Gillespie, DL), the only remaining Victorian greenhouse in the city, a wood-and-glass building with an octagonal dome supported by corner pavilions.

The Fifth Ave Bus Depot at 36th St is nothing much to look at, but will warm the hearts of fans of the classic TV sitcom *The Honeymooners.* Ralph Kramden, Jackie Gleason's beloved character, worked nearby and the depot was renamed the **Jackie Gleason Bus Depot** in 1988.

The Romanesque revival former **68th Precinct House** (1892; George Ingram and Emile Gruwe; DL) towers over Fourth Ave at 43rd St like a fortress. Most impressive is the massive corner tower with decorative stone faces and foliate motifs. The precinct closed in the early 1970s, and the building today is in dismal shape.

In the early decades of the 20C, **Finntown,** one of two major Finnish settlements in New York (the other was in Harlem), lay north and east of Sunset Park. (**Little Norway** lay to the south.) Finntown had a half-dozen public saunas and many small restaurants and mom-and-pop stores. Few traces remain today. The most noticeable, the **Alku Toinen Finnish Cooperative Apartments,** 816–826 43rd St (between Eighth and Ninth Aves), date from 1916 and are among the city's first cooperative apartments. *Alku* means "beginning" in Finnish; other Finnish apartment houses were given names translatable as "Poorhouse," "Old Maids' Home," and "Drop of Sweat."

Beginning in about 1920, the **Bush Terminal District,** along the waterfront from about 28th to 50th Sts, was one of Brooklyn's major port facilities—manufacturing, warehousing, and distributing goods, and employing some 30,000 workers at its peak. The terminal complex was founded in 1890 by Irving T. Bush on land his father used for an oil business. By about 1960 container shipping had rendered much of it obsolete. In the late 1980s, prostitutes and drug addicts populated the neighborhood from 41st to 50th Sts, but in recent years the area has been revitalized, largely by the Southwest Brooklyn Industrial Development Corporation, and is now home to 150 small companies. As part of the deal with city, Dominick Massa, a member of the development corporation, opened Massa's Café Harborside, at 1 43rd St, right off the water in an old longshoreman's cafeteria. Across from it is a statue of Irving T. Bush, holding his hat in his hand.

South of Bush Terminal, on Second Ave between 58th and 65th Sts, is the former **Brooklyn Army Terminal,** or **New York Port of Embarkation and Army Supply Base,** built at the end of World War I to relieve the strain on the city's port facilities. During World War II, about 80 percent of the goods and personnel for the war effort passed through the terminal. After the war the waterfront declined, and in the 1970s the terminal closed. In 1984 the city bought and redeveloped it as manufacturing space; it reopened in 1987 and today generates about 25,000 jobs. Aficionados of industrial architecture find much to admire in the **Beaux-Arts warehouses** (1918; Cass Gilbert), with their eight-story skylit central atriums.

Bay Ridge
Subway: Broadway Local (R) to Bay Ridge Ave.
Bus: Express bus B27 from 57th St and Madison Ave in Manhattan runs along Shore Rd in Bay Ridge to Fourth Ave. Brooklyn local bus B37 runs from the Borough Hall area to Bay Ridge.
Car: Take the Brooklyn Battery Tunnel to the Gowanus Expwy. The Gowanus Expwy merges with the Brooklyn-Queens Expwy (I-278 west); follow the Brooklyn-Queens Expwy westbound and exit onto the Belt Pkwy; take exit 1 from the Belt Pkwy to 65th–67th Sts in Bay Ridge.

Bay Ridge, south of Sunset Park, is a quiet residential community with fine waterfront property. It is named for the terminal moraine of the Wisconsin glacier, which ran southwest from Prospect Park to the bay before crossing the Narrows to Staten Island; Ridge Blvd more or less follows its course in Bay Ridge. The neighborhood formerly had a large Scandinavian and Italian population, and while many Italian Americans and some Scandinavians remain, new immigrants have arrived. (The annual Norwegian Parade attracts mostly people of Norwegian heritage who live elsewhere.) Most of the new arrivals are Chinese, spilling over from Sunset Park to the north, and Russian, but there are also Latinos and Arabs.

History

The Dutch settled the area and called it *Nieuw Utrecht* (1662), which also included Borough Park, Bath Beach, and part of Bensonhurst. Bay Ridge remained rural until after the Civil War, when industrialists built mansions there as summer retreats. (Today, houses and apartments have replaced nearly all these mansions.) In the later 19C Scandinavians, mostly Norwegian sailors and shipbuilders, settled in its more modest inland areas. The Scandinavian community remained essentially stable until after World War II, when it was augmented by Irish and Italians. The most dramatic (some say disruptive) new arrival was the Verrazano-Narrows Bridge, which opened in 1964 after displacing 8,000 residents for its construction.

Saturday Night Fever

The neighborhood and bridge supplied the setting for the 1978 movie *Saturday Night Fever.* Its dance scenes were filmed in **2001 Odyssey,** a discotheque at Eighth Ave and 64th St. While the dance floor remains intact, the club, renamed Spectrum, now caters primarily to a gay and lesbian clientele.

Points of Interest

Owl's Head Park, Colonial Rd and Wakeman Place, with its handsome old beech trees, offers panoramic hilltop views of the Verrazano-Narrows Bridge and Manhattan skyline. The property was once the estate of Democratic politician Henry C. Murphy, first editor of the *Brooklyn Eagle.*

The west side of Bay Ridge also features some elegant homes, including **131 76th St** and **122 76th St,** both on a bluff overlooking the Narrows. Most memorable is the **Howard E. and Jessie Jones House** (1916–17; J. Sarsfield Kennedy; DL), at 8200 Narrows Ave. Known locally as the Gingerbread House, this rare example of arts-and-crafts design is built of boulders, with a faux-thatch (real asphalt) roof and an extravagant fieldstone chimney.

Another house, remarkable for its survival, is the **James F. Farrell House** (c. 1847; DL), 119 95th St (between Marine Ave and Shore Rd), a wooden Greek revival dwelling with wooden clapboards and Italianate paneled front doors with central medallions; its columns, shutters, trim, and cornice remain intact. The house, which once had views of the harbor, was moved 100 ft back from Shore Rd in 1913 to save it from demolition and is now surrounded by apartments.

A few tastes of Scandinavia remain on the commercial streets. At **Nordic Delicacies,** 6909 Third Ave (between Bay Ridge and Ovington Aves), you can buy herrings, cardamom, troll dolls, and, should you desire, cod liver oil. Try **Mejlander and Mulgannon,** at 7615 Fifth Ave (between 76th and 77th Sts), if you are looking for flatbread and lingonberry jam to spread on it. Nearby **Leske's Bakery,** at 7612 Fifth Ave, turns out Danish pastry and authentic *lempe*, Swedish rye with molasses.

Bay Ridge's most famous store is **Kleinfeld,** at 8202 Fifth Ave, once the country's busiest bridal shop, which sells wedding dresses to prospective brides from as far away as Japan and Ethiopia. Isadore Kleinfeld founded the business as a fur emporium in 1941; the company went bridal in 1968 and garnered a reputation for personal attention and its huge selection of designer gowns. In 1999, it was purchased by a group of investors that includes actor Wayne Rogers.

At 9818 Fort Hamilton Pkwy (near 99th St) is **St. John's Church** (1834), a modest Protestant Episcopal church known as the "church of the generals" because of its proximity to neighboring Fort Hamilton. Robert E. Lee served as vestryman and Stonewall Jackson was baptized here at the age of 30.

Verrazano-Narrows Bridge

Overhead soars what was once the world's longest suspension bridge, the Verrazano-Narrows Bridge (1964; Othmar H. Ammann, engineer), a 4,260 ft span linking Staten Island and Brooklyn. It is also a major link in the interstate highway system, providing the shortest route between the middle-Atlantic states and Long Island.

History

Proposed as early as 1926, the bridge became mired in politics, and Bridge Commissioner Robert Moses spent almost 20 years subverting and crushing opposition to the project. Ground was broken in 1959. As a consolation to those in the Italian community of Bay Ridge whose homes were destroyed for the approaches, the bridge was named after Giovanni da Verrazano, the Florentine explorer who discovered New York Bay in 1524. The bridge's massive eastern tower occupies what was Hendrick's Reef, a tiny ledge of land in the Narrows and once home to Fort Lafayette, a Civil War garrison. Today, the Staten Island side of the bridge is the starting point for the New York City Marathon.

Bridge Statistics	
Length of bridge including approaches	13,700 ft
Height of roadway above mean high water	228 ft
Height of towers	693 ft
Weight of each tower	27,000 tons

Fort Hamilton

Fort Hamilton, named after Secretary of the Treasury Alexander Hamilton, was built (1825–31) after the War of 1812 had demonstrated the importance of coastal forts in the defense of the city. The first fortification on the site was an early

Dutch blockhouse built to protect the town of Nieuw Utrecht. During the Revolution a battery stood here. It was followed by Fort Lewis, an earth-and-timber work that served during the War of 1812. Fort Hamilton was built facing Fort Wadsworth on Staten Island across the Narrows, protecting the entrance to New York Harbor.

The 155-acre government reservation includes the Fort Hamilton Officers' Club, originally **Casemate Fort** (1825–31; DL), one of the city's earliest granite fortifications (not open to the public).

Harbor Defense Museum at Fort Hamilton

Fort Hamilton, Brooklyn, NY 11252. ☎ (718) 630-4349. Open Mon–Fri 10–4 (call ahead). Closed ten days during the Christmas holidays. Free. Permanent exhibition. Accessible to wheelchairs.

Subway: Broadway Local (R) to Bay Ridge–95th St. Bus: B8, B16, B37, B63, B70.

Car: Take Brooklyn Bridge to Brooklyn-Queens Expwy; continue east to Belt Pkwy; exit at Fort Hamilton–Fourth Ave. Take Fourth Ave right onto Marine Ave; turn right again onto Fort Hamilton Pkwy; follow to end. Once within the fort, follow signs past Officers' Club to the museum.

Also on the grounds is the Harbor Defense Museum (enter through the 101st St gate), whose exhibits chronicle the contribution of coastal fortifications in the city and New York Army units in national defense.

The permanent collection includes guns, uniforms, banners, and other military equipment and memorabilia. There are a Civil War mine and a flank howitzer dating from 1841, part of the original armament of the fort. Outside is an experimental Rodman gun, the largest artillery piece of the Civil War, named for its designer, Thomas J. Rodman. The exhibits are housed in a building known as a *caponier* (literally, "chicken coop"), designed as a flank battery to protect the fort from attack by land.

Bensonhurst
Subway: Sixth Ave Express (B) to Bay Pkwy.

East of Bay Ridge and south of Borough Park is Bensonhurst, long a largely Italian middle-class residential neighborhood. In Sept the community celebrates the weeklong Feast of Santa Rosalia (patron saint of Sicily), which brings many visitors to the heart of the Italian community. Along Eighteenth Ave, between 68th and 77th Sts, are cafés selling espresso and elaborate pastries, shops selling Italian shoes and clothing, and grocery stores with Italian cheeses and cold cuts.

History

Bensonhurst dates back to 1652, when Cornelis Van Werckhoven, a member of the Dutch West India Company, bartered the land from the Canarsee Indians for an assortment of knives, shoes, shirts, and combs, and established a homestead. The town, which grew up around the present intersection of New York and Eighteenth Aves, was chartered in 1657 and named Nieuw Utrecht after Van Werckhoven's home town.

It remained rural for a long time, and in 1887 one square mile of the community consisted of nine farms, four owned by members of the Benson family. When the Benson holdings were broken up in 1889, Bensonhurst was opened to development. In the early years of the 20C, it became a resort area. For several generations thereafter, Bensonhurst was predominantly a community of Italians and Jews, with Sicilians arriving in the 1950s.

Bensonhurst has often been the neighborhood that, for better or for worse, defined Brooklyn to much of America. First, in the 1950s, it was home to Ralph and Alice Kramden of television's *The Honeymooners*. In the 1970s, the "sweathogs" of the TV sitcom *Welcome Back, Kotter* attended a fictionalized New Utrecht High School. John Travolta moved on from the show to *Saturday Night Fever*, which took place in Bensonhurst and Bay Ridge. In 1989, the racist killing of black teenager Yusef Hawkins by a gang of whites presented a far uglier picture of the neighborhood, while highlighting its homogeneity.

In 1980, nearly 80 percent of Bensonhurst's residents were of Italian descent, but in recent years the neighborhood has become one of the prime settlement spots for immigrants from the former Soviet Union; between 1990 and 1996, 12,363 arrived here, third-most of any community in the city. During the same period, 2,000 Chinese immigrants moved in. Of the few Italians who emigrate to New York nowadays, more settle in Bensonhurst than anywhere else in the city.

Points of Interest

On a spacious lot on Eighteenth Ave between 83rd and 84th Sts stands the handsome brick **New Utrecht Reformed Church** (1828; DL), with its stone tower and Federal-style roundel window. The masonry of this early-Gothic-style church includes fieldstones from its predecessor, the Protestant Dutch Reformed Church erected here in 1699, which was used by the British as a hospital and training ground during the Revolution. On the grounds is the historic **New Utrecht Dutch Reformed Cemetery** (c. 1653; DL), with graves of early New Utrecht families—Cortelyous, Bennetts, Van Brunts—and a communal unmarked grave for Revolutionary War soldiers. Also on the site is one of the last remaining Revolutionary War–era **Liberty Poles,** where in 1783, the first American flag in New Utrecht was flown celebrating the nation's triumph over the British. Most Liberty Poles in the metropolitan region are long gone, but community members have replaced this one five times through the years (most recently in 1946), and the pole still flies the Stars and Stripes.

Bath Beach

Southwest of Bensonhurst, along the shore east of the Verrazano-Narrows Bridge, is Bath Beach, a fashionable seaside resort at the turn of the 20C. (The Belt Pkwy and housing built on landfill have effectively obliterated the resort.) The population, long predominately Italian, as in neighboring Bensonhurst, now has increasing numbers of Russian Jews and Asian immigrants. Bath Beach was home to one of the earliest African American settlements in Brooklyn, a four-block area off Bath Ave where a small community of freed slaves settled during the Underground Railroad days of the Civil War.

Borough Park

Borough Park, like Bensonhurst to its south, was once a part of the Dutch settlement of Nieuw Utrecht and began developing following the extension of the subway system from Manhattan. In 1930, the neighborhood was about half Jewish with many Italian residents. During the Depression, Hasidic Jews arrived from Poland and more Italians came from the Lower East Side. Later, many of the Italians moved on to Bensonhurst, and the neighborhood became increasingly Hasidic as Hasidim arrived from Hungary after the 1956 uprising and from nearby Crown Heights and Williamsburg, displaced by the construction in 1957 of the Brooklyn-Queens Expwy. Nearly half the 11,000 immigrants settling here from 1990 to 1996 came from the former Soviet Union and Poland, and most were Hasidic or Orthodox Jews. In contrast to earlier immigrants who adopted American culture, the new residents resolutely maintain their Old World customs, including their style of dress.

Borough Park has perhaps 300 synagogues, many in private homes, and dozens of yeshivas. The neighborhood is primarily residential and lower middle class, divided by the street grid into monotonously regular blocks of small one- and two-family houses and apartments. Thirteenth and Sixteenth Aves are the main commercial streets, with discounted clothing shoes, dry goods, and electronics stores. As a result of the neighborhood's insularity, there are more wig salons and small bakeries than video stores or national retail chains. As in other predominantly Jewish areas, the shops close Fri afternoons around three and reopen on Sun.

44 · South Central Brooklyn: Flatbush, Including Prospect Park South and Midwood

Flatbush

Subway: Sixth Ave Local (D) to Church Ave or Beverly Rd, or Sixth Ave Express (Q) to Church Ave.
Car: Manhattan Bridge to Flatbush Ave. Follow Flatbush Ave south past Prospect Park to Church Ave.

Flatbush is a quiet residential neighborhood stretching south of Prospect Park to Kings Hwy. This large area includes the smaller enclaves of Prospect Park South, Ditmas Park, and Midwood.

The Dutch settled Flatbush in 1634, chartering the town in 1652 and calling it *'t Vlacke Bos*, or "wooded plain." The farmers of Flatbush were determined to remain apart from the burgeoning city of Brooklyn nearby and until 1893 even imposed a toll on visitors entering their community. (One of the old Flatbush Turnpike toll booths survives in Prospect Park.) Annexed to the city of Brooklyn in 1894, Flatbush remained rural and isolated until steam railways—the Brooklyn, Flatbush, and Coney Island Railroad, later electrified as the Brighton Line of the BMT and IND—made rapid transportation possible. Thereafter it evolved into a well-to-do suburb, much of which still maintains elements of gentility.

Beginning in 1920, Jews from the Lower East Side and other Brooklyn neighborhoods, including Brownsville and Williamsburg, moved here. During Brooklyn's heyday, from the 1920s until the late 1950s (marked in the common memory by the 1957 departure of the Dodgers), Flatbush was considered the heart of Brooklyn, a neighborhood that today inspires even more nostalgia than glamour spots like Brooklyn Heights or Park Slope. (This is in part because the Brooklyn Dodgers were commonly associated with Flatbush, even though Ebbets Field was just over the border in Crown Heights.)

In recent decades, however, especially in northeastern and eastern Flatbush, where apartment houses dominate, the Jewish population has moved away and immigrants from Asia, Pakistan, Afghanistan, the former Soviet Union, Central America, and the Caribbean have moved in. There is also a large Haitian population.

Points of Interest

The **Flatbush Dutch Reformed Church** (1798; Thomas Fardon; DL), 890 Flatbush Ave (southwest corner of Church Ave), was established by Peter Stuyvesant in 1654. Stained glass windows in the present fieldstone building, its third, depict the homes of old Flatbush families. Some of the windows, including the one depicting Samson, were made by the Tiffany Studios. The tower contains a Dutch bell, donated in 1796, which tolled the death of George Washington (1799) and every president since then. The nearby **parsonage,** on Kenmore Terrace at the northeast corner of E. 21st St, is a Greek revival house (1853) with a colonnaded veranda.

Kenmore Terrace is part of the tiny Albemarle–Kenmore Terraces Historic District, which also encompasses the small cul-de-sac around the block. Some of the houses of Kenmore Terrace (1918), built in the English garden city style, have ground-floor garages for those new fangled automobiles. On Albemarle Terrace (1917) are colonial revival brick row houses designed, like those on Kenmore Terrace, by the firm of Slee & Bryson.

Erasmus Hall Academy, founded in 1786, once occupied the white clapboard Federal-style building (1787; DL) at Flatbush Ave on the southeast corner of Church Ave. It now contains offices and a small museum of education; ☎ (718) 856-3571. The building is surrounded by a Gothic quadrangle dating from 1905 to 1925; a statue of Dutch philosopher **Desiderius Erasmus** (copied from a 1622 Dutch original) stands in the courtyard. Funded by Alexander Hamilton, Aaron Burr, and John Jay among others, the academy opened with a student body of 26 boys. It cost one guinea to enter, and tuition was a sizable six pounds sterling. Students came from as far as the West Indies, Brazil, Spain, and Sweden. The academy eventually evolved into Erasmus Hall High School, joining the city public school system in 1896. Its alumni include Barbara Stanwyck, Neil Diamond, Barry Manilow, Barbra Streisand, quarterback Sid Luckman, pitcher Waite Hoyt, and chess champion Bobby Fischer, who dropped out to work on his game.

Flatbush Town Hall (1876; John Y. Cuyler; DL), at 35 Snyder Ave (near Flatbush Ave), was built by the citizens of Flatbush two years after they voted down a proposal to join the city of Brooklyn. The red brick and stone Victorian Gothic building now serves the Flatbush Historical Society and other community groups.

Prospect Park South

Prospect Park South, a designated historic district, is Flatbush's most elegant neighborhood, a tree-lined community bounded by Church Ave, E. 16th St, Beverley Rd, and Coney Island Ave. In 1899, developer Dean Alvord bought this land to create a rural environment insofar as possible within the limitations of regular city blocks. Before he built the houses, Alvord planted the now-stately maples, put in utilities, paved the roads, and established building restrictions that defined the community. He instructed his architect, John J. Petit, to build large, commodious homes in different styles that ranged from shingle style, to Queen Anne, to Swiss chalet, and today there are noteworthy homes on every block in the district. Early residents included business executives from major corporations and the *Brooklyn Eagle*, and journalist Nellie Bly. Alvord himself lived at 1522 Albemarle Rd, which was destroyed by fire in 1958. The Prospect Park South Association founded in 1905 is one of the nation's longest continuously operating neighborhood groups.

A Walking Tour of Prospect Park South

Begin at the edge of Prospect Park South at Buckingham Rd and Church Ave. Walk south toward Albemarle Rd. The house at **100 Buckingham Rd** (1908; Arthur Loomis Harmon) is notable largely because it was designed by an architect who later became a principal of the firm that designed the Empire State Building. (Coincidentally, Chrysler Building designer William Van Alen was the architect of 1215 Albemarle Rd.)

Across the street and down the block, at **115 Buckingham Rd** (1900; John J. Petit), is a shingle-style home with a gambrel roof and a bell-capped corner tower.

One of the neighborhood's most striking homes is **131 Buckingham Rd** (1902; John Petit), known locally as the "Japanese house," because its corbels, brackets, cornices, and pediment suggest a Japanese temple. Created by Petit with the help of three Japanese artisans, it has three stained glass windows with dragon motifs and originally had Japanese tile on the roof. Next door, at **143 Buckingham Rd** (1906; Walter Cassin), is one of the area's few brick homes, an asymmetrical Italian villa-style house with a corner tower.

Turn right on Albemarle Rd. At **1510 Albemarle Rd** (1900; John Petit) is a huge temple-fronted mansion with four massive columns topped by a pedimented roof. Across Marlborough Rd, on the southwest corner, is **1440 Albemarle Rd** (1905; Robert Bryson & Carroll Pratt), a colonial revival mansion featuring a two-story front porch with fluted Ionic columns and a Palladian dormer window.

On the other side of the street, the Queen Anne–style home at **1423 Albemarle Rd** (1899; John Petit) has a two-story gable, a peaked roof porch, and a rounded corner tower.

Continue to the corner of Argyle Rd. The building at **1305 Albemarle Rd** (1905; H. B. Moore) is a large mansion with huge two-story Ionic columns flanking the entrance beneath an entablature with a central oval window. Above the entrance is a wrought-iron balcony; on either side are two-story porches. Inside is a full-fledged ballroom. Across the street, **1306 Albemarle Rd** (1905; John Petit) features a corner tower with conical roof and finial, a projecting gable on the Argyle Rd side, and, most notably, a long porch that curves gracefully around the corner.

Across Beverly Rd, to the south of the Prospect Park Historic District, is **Beverly Square West** (Theodore Benton Ackerson), another development begun in 1898, with a mix of large Victorian houses and smaller two-family homes. South of Dorchester and west of Ocean Ave is the **Ditmas Park Historic District,** begun in 1902 by developer Lewis Pounds. Inspired by Prospect Park South, Pounds developed this neighborhood primarily with colonial revival houses, but included neo-Tudor, Renaissance, and arts-and-crafts homes as well. The house at **415 E. 19th St** is an English cottage built for Arthur Ebinger, who founded Ebinger's Bakery, nostalgically remembered and locally famous for its all-chocolate black-out cake. (Ditmas Park West, which extends from E. 16th St to Coney Island Ave, has similarly impressive homes.)

Midwood

The neighborhood of Midwood, roughly bounded on the north by Ave H and Glenwood Rd, on the east by Nostrand Ave, on the south by Kings Hwy, and on the west by Ocean Pkwy, gets its name from the Dutch *Midwout,* meaning "Middle Wood." Midwood became a township in 1652 but began to flourish in the early 20C when the BMT Brighton subway line reached deep into Brooklyn.

The Vitagraph Studio

The pioneering Vitagraph film studio opened here in 1906 at Locust Ave and E. 15th St off Ave M. Cecil B. DeMille and Rudolph Valentino were among those who made silent films here. NBC began using the building in the 1950s, most famously for *The Cosby Show,* a 1980s hit sitcom. In the late 1990s, CBS took over, using the studio for its soap opera *As the World Turns.*

History

Throughout the 20C, Midwood's population was mostly Italian American and Reformed Jewish, although in the last two decades, Orthodox and Hasidic Jews have been moving in, sometimes demolishing older houses with small gardens to build massive, double-lot homes. In the 1980s, Pakistanis and Indians settled along commercial Coney Island Ave, while in the 1990s, immigrants from Haiti and the former Soviet Union arrived.

Among Midwood's famous sons is the filmmaker Woody Allen, who graduated from **Midwood High School**, at the corner of Bedford Ave and Glenwood Rd. It was once a neighborhood school but today draws students from all over the borough, attracted by its prestigious magnet programs and affiliation with neighboring Brooklyn College.

Points of Interest

Brooklyn College of the City University of New York, 2900 Bedford Ave (at Ave H), was founded (1930) as a coeducational liberal arts college and housed in rented facilities in downtown Brooklyn. The current 26-acre campus opened in 1937 on what had been a golf course that occasionally hosted the tent shows of the Barnum & Bailey Circus. Today, the college enrolls about 10,500 undergraduates and 4,500 graduate students. Its library, undergoing a $62-million renovation and expansion, is the largest in the City University system. The **Brooklyn Center for the Performing Arts at Brooklyn College** (BCBC) offers concerts, recitals, dance programs, and theatrical events in the George Gershwin Theater (500 seats) and the Walt Whitman Theater (2,450 seats).

The **Wyckoff-Bennett House** (c. 1766; DL), 1669 E. 22nd St (southeast corner of Ave P), is considered the finest Dutch colonial farmhouse still standing in Brooklyn. The house, built for Henry and Abraham Wyckoff, has the overhanging eaves and columned porch typical of the style. During the Revolutionary War, Hessian soldiers who were quartered here scratched their names on two panes of glass: "Toepfer Capt of Reg de Ditfurth" and "MBach Lieutenant v Hessen Hanau Artilerie." The date of construction, 1766, is carved into a beam of the old barn.

45 · Southern Brooklyn: Coney Island, Brighton Beach, Manhattan Beach, Sheepshead Bay, and Gravesend

Coney Island

Subway: Sixth Ave Express or Local (B, D, F) or Broadway Local (N) to Coney Island–Stillwell Ave.
Car: Take the Belt System around the shoreline to the Coney Island–Ocean Pkwy exit (no. 7) and go south. Or take the Brooklyn-Queens Expwy to the Prospect Expwy and follow Ocean Pkwy through Brooklyn to Coney Island. Large pay parking lot (includes one adult aquarium admission) at the New York Aquarium (Surf Ave at W. 8th St).

Coney Island, joined to the mainland early in the 20C by filling part of Coney Island Creek, is no longer the "world's largest playground," as it once billed itself, but still survives as an archetype of American honky-tonk.

Geographically, Coney Island encompasses the communities of Manhattan Beach, Brighton Beach, and Sea Gate, along with the famous amusement area (formerly known as West Brighton). Legend shrouds much of Coney Island's history, including the origin of its name, which most likely comes from the "coneys," or rabbits, who inhabited the island during the colonial period.

History

Its history as a resort began when the Coney Island House (1829) opened at Sea Gate, soon followed by other establishments whose restaurants and bathing pavilions attracted a genteel clientele. By 1870, however, Coney Island, particularly the western section called Norton's Point (ironically, today's gated community of Sea Gate), had declined; under the corrupt administration of Gravesend political boss John Y. McKane, gambling and prostitution flourished. Despite new hotels and other physical improvements to Coney Island, pickpockets and prostitutes continued to thrive under McKane's averted gaze until the 1890s.

In 1875 Andrew R. Culver, a lawyer and railroad entrepreneur with interests in Coney Island, had built a railroad from Prospect Park to Coney Island, and the following year an elegant boulevard, Ocean Pkwy (1876; Frederick Olmsted and Calvert Vaux; DL), was completed along the same stretch. When transportation made the island accessible, hotels followed. In 1877 Austin Corbin, a banker and railroad investor, opened the spectacular Manhattan Beach Hotel at the island's eastern end. While it quickly became the "in place" for Manhattan's elite, two other colossal hotels just to the west, the Brighton Beach and Oriental Hotels, soon followed. Tourists sipped draft champagne, listened to John Philip Sousa's band, and watched fireworks.

The Coney Island Hot Dog

Charles Feltman, an immigrant from Bavaria, is credited with "inventing" the hot dog—i.e., putting a sausage in a roll. He sold them first from a cart, perhaps around 1870, and later from an oceanside stand in Coney Island. In 1874 Feltman bought land on which he opened the Ocean Pavilion, which eventually he developed into a huge restaurant–beer garden. Feltman's remained a family business until 1946.

In 1884, a new era dawned when L. A. Thompson invented the roller coaster at Coney Island. His first model, whose cars were pushed by attendants back to the top of the track, peaked at six mph. By the turn of the 20C, the construction of three spectacular amusement areas ushered in the area's golden age: George C. Tilyou's Steeplechase Park (1897), Luna Park (1903), and Dreamland (1904). Steeplechase was named for a horserace of wheeled wooden horses on an 1,100 ft inclined and undulating track. Steeplechase Park also had funhouse-style attractions: distorting mirrors, rotating barrels that knocked people off their feet, a Human Roulette Wheel that caromed people into one another by centrifugal force, and, later, air jets that blew up women's skirts. Luna Park was hailed for its fantasy architecture created by Frederick Thompson and Skip Dundy, who embellished their "electric Eden" with a Venetian lagoon, a Chinese theater, an electric tower, and a multitude of candy-colored spires, onion-shaped domes, and minarets all illuminated with 250,000 light bulbs, in an era before most homes had electricity. Dreamland essentially copied Luna Park on a grander scale (taller towers, a million light bulbs) but was less popular; it burned down in a devastating fire in 1911.

After the Dreamland fire, Coney Island began changing again—a sideshow sprouted up on the Dreamland site, the big hotels were razed for residential housing, and with the arrival of the subway between 1915 and 1920 Coney Island became the playground of the common man, the "empire of the nickel." During the 1920s and 1930s huge crowds thronged the boardwalk (opened 1923) or lay thigh-to-thigh on the sand. In hot weather people slept on the beach rather than in their suffocating tenements.

By the 1940s, the amusement areas began deteriorating. Luna Park succumbed to a series of fires in the 1940s. Several factors brought about Coney Island's decline: the rise of the automobile and the introduction of air-conditioning after World War II; the flight to the suburbs; and the policies of Robert Moses, who promoted such spots as Long Island's Jones Beach (which he built, along with the roads to get there) at the expense of honky-tonk Coney Island. In fact, Moses saw Coney Island as a place to isolate blacks and poor people in housing projects. In 1964 Steeplechase Park closed; in the following two decades crime and drugs became prevalent in the amusement area.

While the density of its high-rise housing projects condemns much of the community to a role as home to the old and the poor, in the last fifteen years, Coney

Island has improved. Local nonprofit groups have built nearly 1,000 homes on empty lots and lured retailers to fill the stores, while the amusement area has expanded a bit and cleaned up a lot. A new minor league baseball park opened in 2001 to rave reviews and capacity crowds, sparking talk of more redevelopment. In addition, the community is seeking landmark status for several buildings. Coney Island may not be as crowded as it was in 1945, but in summertime, its beaches, boardwalk, and amusement area still pulsate with life.

New York Aquarium

Surf Ave at W. 8th St, Coney Island, Brooklyn, NY 11224. ☎ (718) 265-FISH. Web site: www.nyaquarium.com. Open 365 days a year, 10–4:30 in winter (last ticket sold at 3:45), with later closings the rest of the year. Changing exhibitions; educational programs; marine mammal demonstrations. Indoor ocean-view cafeteria and outdoor snack bar. Picnic tables. Gift shop. Accessible to wheelchairs.

Subway: Sixth Ave Express or Local (D, F) to W. 8th St–NY Aquarium. A pedestrian bridge leads from the subway station across Surf Ave to the aquarium entrance.

Car: Same directions as for Coney Island.

One of Coney Island's highlights is the New York Aquarium, the oldest public aquarium in the U.S. but somewhat underused because of its remoteness from the rest of the city. Situated on 14 acres off the Atlantic Ocean, the aquarium moved to its present building (1955; Harrison & Abramovitz) from its former home in Battery Park. On display are beluga whales and bottle-nosed dolphins, moray eels, penguins (viewable from underwater), and many exotic fish. Favorite exhibits include the **shark tank** and the **Sea Cliff exhibit.** The **Touch-It Tank** and **Tide Pool** allow children to get up close to rays, star fish, and other forms of marine life. Recent additions include exhibits of seahorses—giant, pot-bellied, and pygmy—and "Alien Stingers"—corals, jellyfish, and sea anemones.

Points of Interest

The **Coney Island amusement area** stretches from about W. 8th St, near the aquarium, to W. 16th St and consists of two main amusement parks—Astroland and Deno's—as well as several smaller amusement areas.

Astroland Amusement Park

1000 Surf Ave (at W. 10th St), Coney Island, Brooklyn, NY 11224. ☎ (718) 265-2100. Web site: www.astroland.com. Open, weather permitting, daily mid-June–Labor Day noon–midnight; weekends only in Sept.

Astroland has the world-famous **Cyclone roller coaster** (1927; Harry Baker, inventor; Vernon Keenan, engineer; DL). One of a dwindling number of wood-track roller coasters, it is considered by some classicists to be the country's best. Its first drop is 85 ft at a stomach-churning 60-degree angle; during the 110-second ride the coaster reaches 68 mph, hurtling through nine drops and six curves.

Deno's Wonder Wheel Amusement Park

Boardwalk at W. 12th St, Coney Island, Brooklyn, NY 11224. ☎ (718) 372-2592. Web site: www.wonderwheel.com. Open daily, weather permitting, May–Sept 11 A.M.–midnight; April and Oct, weekends 11 A.M.–midnight. Snack bar; kiddie rides.

Deno's has the **Wonder Wheel** (1920; Charles Herman, inventor; DL), a 150 ft tall, 200-ton steel wheel, which has taken more than 30 million customers in circles. During the power outage of 1977, the operators hand-cranked the wheel to bring the passengers down safely.

Coney Island USA

1208 Surf Ave (at W. 12th St), Coney Island, Brooklyn, NY 12244. ☎ (718) 372-5159. Web site: www.coneyislandusa.com.

Coney Island USA is a nonprofit group founded by Dick Zigun, a graduate of the Yale School of Drama. It runs the nation's only (nonprofit) freak show, **Sideshows by the Seashore,** and is dedicated to preserving this lowbrow form of Americana. It also oversees the small **Coney Island Museum,** whose permanent collection contains memorabilia from the heyday of the amusement area. Coney Island USA hosts the wonderfully garish **Mermaid Parade** on the first Sat after the summer solstice. Marchers dress as mermaids, mermen, mer-babies, mer–biker chicks, and King Neptune in every imaginable variation.

At 1310 Surf Ave (corner of Stillwell Ave) is **Nathan's Famous,** a beloved eatery founded in 1916 by Nathan Handwerker, a roll-slicer and delivery boy at Feltman's. Handwerker saw Coney Island's future as a workingman's resort and charged a nickel for his hot dogs, half the price of the stylish Feltman's. Every year, Nathan's hosts a wild and wacky Fourth of July hot dog eating contest, in which competitors wolf down as many franks (and buns) as possible in 12 minutes (the current record is 50, set by Japan's Takeru Kobayashi); ☎ (718) 946-2202.

At W. 16th St and the Boardwalk is the abandoned **Parachute Jump** (1939; James Strong, inventor, Elwyn Seelye & Co. engineers, 1939; DL), nicknamed the Eiffel Tower of Brooklyn. The ride first appeared at the 1939 World's Fair, its 11 colored parachutes with double seats giving riders "all the thrills of bailing out without any of the usual hazards or discomforts." After the fair it was moved here to Steeplechase Park.

The Demise of the Thunderbolt

In Nov 2000, the Thunderbolt roller coaster (1925; designer, John A. Miller) was demolished, despite local efforts to save it. Unused since 1983, the Thunderbolt is best remembered for a small wooden house under the first turnaround, which was featured in Woody Allen's movie *Annie Hall.*

KeySpan Park (2001; Jack L. Gordon Assocs.), at 1904 Surf Ave between W. 17th and W. 19th Sts, brings professional baseball back to Brooklyn for the first time since 1957, when the Dodgers abandoned the borough. The stadium stands on the site of Steeplechase Park, with views of the Parachute Jump beyond the right field wall, the Atlantic Ocean beyond the outfield, and the neon-lit amusement park beyond the left field wall. The home team, the Brooklyn Cyclones (named for the famous roller coaster a few blocks away), is a farm club of the New York Mets and belongs to the Class A New York–Penn League, to which the Staten Island Yankees also belong. KeySpan Park, which seats about 6,500, was the second minor league ballpark that opened in New York in 2001 and at $39 million the second-most expensive minor league stadium ever built, outdone by the $71-million new home of the Staten Island Yankees. In their inaugural season, however, the Cyclones stole the show, finishing in first place and beating their Staten Island rivals in the playoffs. Brooklyn's ardor for their new ball club produced sold-out crowds, astonishing merchandise sales, and increased coverage by the major newspapers.

While most of Coney Island today is black and Latino, there are some remnants of its old Italian population. **Gargiulo's Restaurant** has been serving traditional Italian fare at 2911 W. 15th St since 1907. At 1524 Neptune Ave is one of the city's oldest and finest pizza establishments, **Totonno's,** which has been making pies in its coal-fired brick ovens since 1924.

Coney Island's Future

Steeplechase Park closed in 1964, and there have been numerous plans to redevelop the site since then. In April 2000 the City Council passed a $91-million redevelopment plan for Coney Island, including funds for the stadium, neighborhood improvements, sports complex, and money to stabilize the Parachute Jump.

Brighton Beach

Brighton Beach, east of Coney Island, can be reached by walking along the Boardwalk past the aquarium. In the past two decades the neighborhood, nicknamed Little Odessa, has absorbed a huge influx of Russian immigrants, mostly Jews. In fact, from 1990 to 1996 Bay Ridge, Bensonhurst, Gravesend, Sheepshead Bay, and Brighton and Manhattan Beaches have together become home to 42,000 immigrants from the former Soviet Union, about 40 percent of the city's total. The shops along the main commercial strip, **Brighton Beach Ave,** are stocked with black bread, herring, kasha, and even delicacies such as sturgeon and caviar. Cafés attract a Russian-speaking clientele who can be seen taking tea or vodka to refresh themselves after a stroll. There are also Russian and Georgian restaurants and nightclubs.

Manhattan Beach

On the eastern edge of the former island is the upper-middle-class neighborhood of Manhattan Beach, between Ocean Ave and MacKenzie St. Many second-generation and successful Russian immigrants have started moving away from the cramped homes and apartments of Brighton Beach to larger homes in Manhattan Beach. Thanks to an extreme paucity of parking it has the area's mellowest, most pleasant beach. The neighborhood is also home to Kingsborough Community College, which occupies the site of a World War II naval training station.

Holocaust Memorial Park

Overlooking Sheepshead Bay, along West End Ave (between Shore Blvd and Emmons Ave), is the **Holocaust Memorial Park** (1997; architect, George Vellonakis), fittingly established in Brooklyn, which is home to more Holocaust survivors and their relatives than any other place in the country. The centerpiece is a flame rising out of a 14 ft steel chimneylike tower, broken away near the top to reveal barbed wire. It is inscribed with the word "Remember." The rest of the site consists of dozens of tomblike granite stones with inscriptions providing reminders of, explanations about, and quotes related to the Holocaust. They touch on everything from the Nuremberg Laws to Anne Frank to the *St. Louis* (the ship loaded with Jewish refugees that was turned away by the U.S.). Thirteen years in the making, the memorial ran into several controversies. Vellonakis, a Parks Department architect, wanted to include stones recounting the plight of gypsies, homosexuals, Jehovah's Witnesses, and the disabled slaughtered by Hitler. But community groups and funders rejected the last-minute addition, since those groups were included on the centerpiece and the memorial was a place for the area's Jewish population to mourn. After its completion, many residents complained about a sculpture resembling a graveyard in a city park. (Children do run and play around the stones.) Others defended the memorial as a fitting reminder of the 20C's greatest tragedy.

Sheepshead Bay

Sheepshead Bay is a modest residential community of about two square miles northeast of Coney Island. The bay, from which the neighborhood gets its name, juts inward from the east. It is said to be named because its shape resembles a sheep's head or because sheepsheads (described as black-banded fish with sheeplike teeth) once abounded in its waters. A quiet fishing village existed here until the land boom of 1877, followed by the opening of the Sheepshead Bay Race Track in the late 19C, which attracted wealthy horsemen, including August Belmont and William K. Vanderbilt, and high rollers such as Diamond Jim Brady and Lillian Russell. The area has long been home to Italian- and Irish-Americans, although there is a small but diverse mix of newer immigrants too.

Moored along the Emmons Ave waterfront (between Ocean Ave and 27th St) is a small fleet of fishing boats, many for hire, which depart early in the morning and return in the late afternoon with their catch, sometimes offered for sale along the pier. While the fishing business has suffered in recent decades, casino boats began departing in the late 1990s from Sheepshead Bay to the three-mile mark where New York's border ends and gambling laws do not apply.

Points of Interest

For nearly a half century, one of Brooklyn's most popular restaurants was F.W.I.L. Lundy Brothers Restaurant, known to everyone simply as **Lundy's** (1934; Bloch & Hesse; restoration 1996; Van J. Brody; DL). Located at 1901–29 Emmons Ave, in a massive Spanish-style building with sand-colored stucco walls and tile roofs, it was the nation's largest restaurant (seated 1,700) when it opened. Founded by the family that had been operating the local Lundy Brothers Fish Market since 1880, the restaurant became renowned for its seafood, biscuits, and its noisy, convivial atmosphere. At its peak in the 1950s, Lundy's fed 10,000 people on a Sun and 15,000 on a holiday. The restaurant closed two years after founder F. W. I. Lundy died in 1977 but reopened on a smaller scale in 1996.

Down the block, at 2005 Emmons Ave, is **Pips,** the country's first comedy club when it opened in 1962. Before then comedians played at venues like Manhattan's Village Gate and the Bottom Line, where comedy alternated with musical entertainment. The original owner, George Schultz (who sold it in 1994), helped launch the careers of David Brenner, Robert Klein, Andy Kaufman, Steve Landesberg, and Andrew Dice Clay. For information, ☎ (718) 646-9433.

Further inland, at 1926 E. 28th St (between Aves S and T), is the **Elias Hubbard Ryder House** (c. 1834; DL); its white shingles and shutters in the Dutch colonial style set it apart from the flat brick, attached houses on the block. The original family lived in the house until 1966.

Gravesend

Gravesend, south of Bensonhurst and west of Sheepshead Bay, was probably named after the English seacoast town at the mouth of the Thames River. The *graves* part of the name seems to come from an Anglo-Saxon word meaning "groves." Gravesend has been an Italian American community for much of the 20C, although immigration in the last two decades has made it more diverse. While most of its housing stock consists of well-kept private homes and some apartment buildings, the neighborhood is also home to the large Marlboro Houses public housing project (notorious for violent crime), which is near W. 8th St and Ave W.

History

Gravesend, the only one of Brooklyn's original six towns not settled by the Dutch, was established by Lady Deborah Moody, an English woman who in 1643 with her Anabaptist followers fled the religious intolerance of the Massachusetts Bay Colony and settled here by the water. In 1645 the town was granted a charter and enjoyed both religious freedom and a degree of self-government. Unlike the other early Brooklyn settlements, which grew up haphazardly, Gravesend was formally planned in the manner of the English colonial towns in Massachusetts or Connecticut with a central green centered around what is today McDonald Ave and Gravesend Neck Rd. Along with the original cemetery, the square remains the only trace of the original town plan.

Points of Interest

Gravesend Cemetery (1650; DL), the oldest city-owned cemetery, is on Village Rd South between Van Sicklen and Lake Sts. Lady Deborah Moody is buried here, though the precise location of her grave is unknown. Unfortunately, all of the pre-18C gravestones are gone and there is little of interest to see in the tiny 1.6-acre burial ground.

At 27 Gravesend Neck Rd is the **Hicks-Platt House,** which is said to date either from the mid-17C or the mid-18C, although it has been considerably altered. In the 1890s, it was passed off by real estate entrepreneur William Platt as Lady Moody's house.

L & B Spumoni Gardens, at 2725 86th St, has been making homemade spumoni and ice cream since 1939 and offers a taste of Italian Gravesend.

The clapboard **Hubbard-Lucchelli House** (c. 1830s), at 2138 McDonald Ave (between Aves S and T), was almost a goner, until John Antonides, a Brooklyn Museum editor, purchased it in 1998 and embarked on an extensive restoration of this rare Dutch colonial farmhouse. Antonides moved into the house in 2001 and is currently seeking landmark protection.

46 · Southeastern Brooklyn: Floyd Bennett Field, Marine Park, Flatlands, and Canarsie

Floyd Bennett Field

At the southern terminus of Flatbush Ave, along its east side, is Floyd Bennett Field, which occupies more than 800 acres on Jamaica Bay and is part of the National Park Service's Gateway National Recreation Area. It features the only campgrounds in the five boroughs (open April–Nov), nature trails, a large community garden, and old airport hangers with historic planes. It offers seasonal nature walks and programs, miles of open runways for cycling or in-line skating, and hosts several annual ethnic festivals and other special events. For information, ☎ (718) 338-3338.

History

The land was once Barren Island, off the shoreline, a garbage dump and rendering facility in the late 19C, home to a poor community whose residents worked in its glue factories and horse rendering plants. In the 1920s, the residents were evicted and the island was joined to Brooklyn by landfill, to create the city's first municipal airport (dedicated 1930), Floyd Bennett Field, named to honor the pilot who flew Admiral Byrd over the North Pole in 1926. The field failed as a commercial airport because it was too far from central New York, although during the days before World War II, when aviators competed for long-distance flight records, it served as the takeoff point for Wiley Post (1933), who flew solo around the world (7 days, 18 hours, 49 minutes, 30 seconds) and for Howard Hughes and companions, who halved that record five years later.

Flatbush Ave leads south across the **Marine Pkwy–Gil Hodges Bridge** (toll) built across Rockaway Inlet (1937) to Jacob Riis Park in Queens. The bridge has three spans totaling 4,022 ft and a 540 ft central lift span. Gil Hodges, whose name was added to the bridge in 1978, was the first baseman for the Dodgers during the team's final years in Brooklyn and later managed the New York Mets to their first World Series championship. He lived in nearby Midwood.

Marine Park

Marine Park is both a park and a neighborhood. The park, lying west of Flatbush Ave and south of Ave U along the shore, consists of some 2,000 acres donated mostly by the Whitney family during the 1920s. The park has a two-mile oval for running and cycling as well as baseball diamonds and basketball courts.

In the surrounding neighborhood of Marine Park, at 1940 E. 36th St (between Fillmore Ave and Ave S), is the **Hendrick I. Lott House** (small wing 1720; larger wing 1800; DL), a Dutch colonial with overhanging eaves supported with round pillars in the front and square ones in back. It is the only Dutch farmhouse in Brooklyn still on its original property. The house is situated on a large lot and faces south away from the street, since city streets had not yet been laid out in a grid. The smaller wing, the original house built in 1720 by Johannes Lott, has ceilings only six ft high and one tiny bedroom. In 1800, his grandson Hendrick built a larger house, with arched dormer windows, closets, and wide plank wood floors, incorporating the original house.

The Lotts of Southern Brooklyn

The Lotts, major landowners in southern Brooklyn, owned 35 slaves in the early 1800s, freeing them two decades before slavery was abolished. In the 1920s, their holdings much reduced, they sold off the surrounding acreage, keeping only this large yard and house. Although the Lott family occupied the farmhouse until the 1980s, it then sat vacant as the paint faded and chipped and the interior deteriorated. When the house was landmarked in 1989, the family sued because developers had offered $1 million for the lot if they could raze the house. The house fell apart as a legal battle ensued. Then in 1997, the Historic House Trust won control of the house. It will restore the house and make it a museum that examines one family in Brooklyn over a period of 300 years. The museum is currently slated to open in 2003.

Flatlands

Flatlands, southeast of Flatbush, was one of the original Dutch towns in Brooklyn, also called *Nieuw Amersfoort.* Chartered in 1666, it took its name from its terrain, low coastal plains adjoining the salt marshes to the south. During the 17C a small Dutch town centered on what is now the junction of Flatbush Ave and Kings Hwy. Today the area is primarily residential with some industrial development. The population remains primarily Jewish, Italian, and Irish, but immigrants from Jamaica, Guyana, and Haiti are starting to find their way here.

Points of Interest

The **Flatlands Dutch Reformed Church,** 3931 Kings Hwy (between Flatbush Ave and E. 40th St), is one of three churches in Brooklyn established (1654) by Peter Stuyvesant and is the third church building on this site (1848; DL), a simple white clapboard Greek revival building with a cemetery whose markers bear prominent old Brooklyn names: Lott, Kouwenhoven, Wyckoff. The earliest church on the site had stocks and a whipping post. Pieter Claesen Wyckoff (see Pieter Claesen Wyckoff House Museum), who arrived in America as an indentured servant (c. 1637) and rose to local prominence, is buried beneath the pulpit.

The three names of the **Stoothof-Baxter-Kouwenhoven House** (c. 1747; new wing 1811; DL), 1640 E. 48th St (between Aves M and N), belong to three prominent and related Brooklyn families who owned it for a century and a half. It is a simple shingled wood-frame farmhouse with projecting eaves.

Canarsie

Canarsie, east of Flatlands along Jamaica Bay, is named after its first inhabitants, the Canarsee Indians, a tribe of the Leni Lenape or Delawares of the Algonkian linguistic group. Both the Native Americans, and the Dutch after them, cultivated maize, squash, and beans on the fertile plains and fished the bay for shellfish; the Dutch cut the salt hay from the marshes for fodder. Canarsie remained rural well into the 20C, when it became a suburb reached primarily by automobile, built up with two-family row houses that were occupied for a long time by Italian Americans and Jews. When Puerto Ricans and blacks were bused into neighborhood schools in the 1970s, outbursts of racial violence occurred. The neighborhood became more thoroughly integrated in the 1980s as immigrants from the Caribbean began settling there.

Points of Interest

The **Canarsie Pier** (foot of Rockaway Pkwy) is part of the Gateway National Recreation Area, attracting fishermen and strollers and providing a rare and lovely water view.

The **log cabin** at the corner of 93rd St and Flatlands Ave was built around the turn of the 20C from huge logs (and without a single nail) on a fieldstone base, supposedly by a local eccentric known as Mr. Doubleday. It served as a luncheonette and ice cream parlor in the 1940s and 1950s and has been a realty office since 1970.

The **Brooklyn Terminal Market** at E. 87th and Foster Ave began as a farmers' market in 1942 and is now a major source of foods and plants for retailers and savvy Brooklynites seeking wholesale or discounted retail prices.

Pieter Claesen Wyckoff House Museum

5816 Clarendon Rd (at Ralph Ave), Brooklyn, NY 11203. ☎ (718) 629-5400. Open Tues–Sun 10–4. Not accessible to wheelchairs. Permanent exhibition, special events.

Subway and Bus: Seventh Ave Express (2) or Lexington Ave Express (5) to Newkirk Ave. Then take B8 bus to Beverly Rd and E. 59th St. Walk one block south to the museum.

Car: Take Belt Pkwy to Flatbush Ave; go north to Ave T; turn right to Ralph Ave; turn left to Clarendon Rd. Or take the Manhattan Bridge to Flatbush Ave; continue to Clarendon Rd; turn left to E. 59th St.

On the edge of Canarsie near the Brooklyn Terminal Market are two very different historic homes. The **Pieter Claesen Wyckoff House Museum** (c. 1652; DL), possibly the oldest building in the state is a low, wood-shingled farmhouse in the Dutch colonial style.

Surrounded by block-long Fidler Wyckoff Park, the house contains furniture and artifacts that reflect rural life in Nieuw Amersfoort (renamed Flatlands by the British after 1664) during the 17C–18C. Pieter Claesen arrived in the colonies in 1637 as an indentured servant to Killian Van Rennselaer, a merchant who had large landholdings around Albany. Wyckoff moved to Nieuw Amersfoort around 1649, where he became a prosperous farmer and eventually the town's wealthiest citizen. After the British took over in 1664, Pieter Claesen had to take an English name, as did every other Dutch resident, and chose Wyckoff.

Jackie Robinson Residence

At 5224 Tilden Ave, on the corner of 53rd St, is an unremarkable unattached house, which is nonetheless listed on the National Register of Historic Places.

Jackie Robinson lived there between 1947–1950, during his first three seasons with the Brooklyn Dodgers. The house is a reminder of a time when athletes did not command staggering salaries.

47 · East Central Brooklyn: Crown Heights, Bedford-Stuyvesant, Brownsville, East New York, and Cypress Hills

Subway: Seventh Ave Express (2) to Grand Army Plaza (on the western edge of Crown Heights) or to Eastern Pkwy–Brooklyn Museum.
Car: Take Manhattan Bridge to Flatbush Ave. Follow Flatbush Ave south to Eastern Pkwy at Grand Army Plaza. Eastern Pkwy cuts through the center of Crown Heights.

Crown Heights

Crown Heights, formerly considered part of Bedford, lies south of Bedford Stuyvesant and north of Flatbush, roughly between Ralph Ave on the east and Washington Ave on the west. Largely residential, its population includes African Americans, blacks of Caribbean descent, and Jews, many of them Lubavitch Hasidim from the former Soviet Union.

History
The first local blacks were slaves belonging to Dutch farmers, but in the 1830s and 1840s the free black communities of Weeksville and Carrville flourished here. The name Crown Heights seems to be a corruption of the 19C place name *Crow Hill*, which was either the name of a local hill or a racial slur.

Crown Heights's first moment in the spotlight came in 1870–74 when **Eastern Pkwy** (DL), the world's first six-lane parkway, opened between Grand Army Plaza and Ralph Ave. Frederick Law Olmsted and Calvert Vaux, masterminds of Central and Prospect Parks, intended this wide, tree-lined roadway bordered by access roads to become part of a system of residential arteries that would reach eastward to Manhattan, leading to Central Park and then to the Hudson River. Olmsted bestowed the name *parkways* on these roads because they brought greenery and open space to urban neighborhoods. Ocean Pkwy, which originally ran southward from Prospect Park to Coney Island, is the only other completed segment.

The wealthy soon began building homes along the resplendent new avenue, and after the Brooklyn Bridge opened in 1883, the whole neighborhood became fashionable. When the IRT subway was dug beneath the parkway in 1920, some of the mansions were replaced by apartment buildings, which attracted middle-class professional residents.

In the early 20C, a Caribbean contingent lived in Crown Heights, but from the 1920s through the 1950s the neighborhood was mostly Jewish. In the 1940s, the ultra-religious Lubavitch Hasidim from the Soviet Union began settling here, and today, Crown Heights is the city's largest Lubavitch Hasidim enclave. During the

Jewish holidays the Lubavitch Movement headquarters at 770 Eastern Pkwy near Kingston Ave draws thousands of the faithful.

White flight in the 1950s led to the neighborhood's decline, hastened by the departure of the Brooklyn Dodgers after the 1957 season. During the 1960s and '70s, a new wave of Caribbean immigrants arrived (Haitians, Jamaicans, Trinidadians, Barbadians, Grenadians, creating what is today New York's largest West Indian population). As the immigrants became more established, the neighborhood gradually stabilized. While the commercial strips like Nostrand and Utica Aves seem a bit weary and some blocks are blemished with graffiti and boarded-up buildings, there are many well-kept, attractive homes on the side streets.

Immigration to Crown Heights continues today. Between 1990 and 1996, 16,000 newcomers arrived, including the second-biggest Haitian settlement and large numbers from Trinidad and Tobago. About 63 percent of Crown Heights's immigrants come from these countries, along with Guyana and Jamaica.

Long-simmering racial tensions between Caribbeans and the insular Hasidim exploded in 1991 after a Lubavitcher driver accidentally killed a Guyanese child. Local blacks rioted, killing a Lubavitcher visitor from Australia; racial strife spilled beyond Crown Heights's borders. In the aftermath of the riots, community groups began working to ease the tensions, creating a local Unity Day to bring the various ethnic groups together.

During the West Indian–American Day Carnival over the Labor Day holiday (early Sept) millions of participants celebrate with steel bands, street dancing, colorful and elaborate costumes and floats, and a parade down Eastern Pkwy, which has been a tradition since 1969. For information, call the Caribbean American Center; ☎ (718) 625-1515.

Points of Interest
At **1700–1720 Bedford Ave** (between Montgomery St and Sullivan Place) stands a dull and architecturally undistinguished apartment building to which people—mostly middle-aged men—still make pilgrimages. Ebbets Field, the stadium of Brooklyn's beloved Dodgers, stood here until 1960.

Ebbets Field and the Brooklyn Dodgers
Club owner Charles Ebbets selected the location because the land was cheap (the area was called Pigtown, replete with shacks, garbage dumps, and pigpens), because it lay between suburban Bedford and bustling Flatbush, and because it was close to public transportation. The intimate ballpark, replete with quirky angles and dimensions, opened in 1913 and was soon packed with fans, including many colorful characters. According to local lore, the team owed its affectionate nickname, Dem Bums, to a loudmouthed, frustrated fan—a truck driver with a Brooklyn accent.

On Aug 26, 1939, Red Barber announced the first televised baseball game, a broadcast from Ebbets Field of the Dodgers playing the Cincinnati Reds. But it was the Dodgers of the 1940s and '50s who captured the hearts of Brooklynites. In the stands, Hilda Chester banged her cowbell, while the Dodgers Sym-Phony Band rooted and tooted for the club with great volume and limited musical skills. Clothier Abe Stark's 30 ft long ad on the outfield wall dared longball hitters to "Hit Sign Win Suit," providing Stark with the publicity that elected him Brooklyn borough president. Such stars as Dixie Walker, Pee Wee Reese, Duke Snider, Carl Furillo, and Gil Hodges led the club to seven National League pennants between 1941 and 1956. But "Wait 'til next year!" became the borough's rallying cry as Brooklyn lost each World Series to the hated Yankees, before finally winning it all in 1955.

On April 15, 1947, **Jackie Robinson** trotted onto Ebbets Field, breaking baseball's color barrier, an accomplishment that transcended baseball and eventually gave momentum to the civil rights movement. While Robinson's presence increased Dodger attendance and profits, the influx of blacks into the neighborhood around Ebbets Field helped prompt then-owner Walter O'Malley to look for a new home. In addition to his concern about white flight, O'Malley wanted a larger ballpark and parking lot. While O'Malley has long been cast as the sole villain, Robert Moses blocked O'Malley's efforts for a new stadium at Atlantic and Flatbush Aves, where the Atlantic Center shopping mall is today.

The 1957 season was the Dodgers' last. Three years later, with several ex-Dodgers on hand, Ebbets Field regular Lucy Monroe sang the National Anthem one last time and the ballpark was demolished. It was a loss that cut across social, racial, and economic lines.

Murals at **Jackie Robinson Intermediate School,** around the block at 46 McKeever Place, depict Robinson and other prominent and accomplished blacks, including Malcolm X, Booker T. Washington, and Aretha Franklin. Another mural honoring George Washington Carver, Jesse Owens, and Bob Marley, among others, dominates Bedford Ave from Crown to Carroll Sts.

About a half-mile north, at the intersection of Bedford Ave and Dean St, is **Grant Square,** occupied by a statue of Gen. Ulysses S. Grant astride his horse. Designed in 1896 by William Ordway Partridge, it was commissioned by the neighborhood's premier institution, the **Union League Club,** founded in 1888 as a social and political organization for Republicans of high standing. The club occupied the southeast corner of Dean St, a Victorian brownstone (1892; Lauritzen & Voss) adorned with medallions of Ulysses S. Grant and Abraham Lincoln and garnished with stone lions and American eagles. Today it is a senior citizens' center.

One block north, at 1322 Bedford Ave, is the **23rd Regiment Armory of the New York National Guard** (1892; Fowler & Hough; DL). This massive fortress is the most impressive of the eight 19C armories in Brooklyn, with an imposing 136 ft main tower and two 70 ft towers flanking the two-story arched main entrance. Inside is a 24 ft high fireplace. The armory is now a part of the city's homeless shelter system.

Across Bedford Ave, at 1198 Pacific St, stands the **Imperial Apartments** (1892; Montrose W. Morris; DL), dating back to Crown Heights's days as a prestigious neighborhood. Developer Louis F. Seitz followed up his successful Alhambra Apartments for the middle class in Bedford-Stuyvesant (see later this walk) with the Imperial, which is reminiscent of a 16C French château and executed in light-colored brick with terra-cotta trim.

At 1227 Pacific St is **St. Bartholomew's Church** (1886–90; George P. Chappell; DL), a quaint, small, red brick and granite Romanesque revival church with a semiconical roof.

Brownstones and Limestones in Crown Heights
Crown Heights has blocks of brownstone and limestone row houses that would do Park Slope or Cobble Hill proud: on St. Mark's Ave along Brower Park between Kingston and Brooklyn Aves, and at Park Place and Dean Sts between Franklin and Bedford Aves. Some of the houses on Dean St between Bedford and Nostrand Aves are run-down and defaced with graffiti, but there are ten wonderful 1890 Queen Anne houses (1164–1182 Dean St), with an array of stepped, peaked, and domed gables, terra-cotta, wooden shingles, and limestone facades. Like St. Bartholomew's Church, they were designed by noted Brooklyn architect George Chappell.

In addition to fine apartments and row houses, the community also had numerous mansions. At 839 St Mark's Ave, near Brower Park, the former **Dean Sage residence** (1869; Russell Sturgis), a handsome Romanesque revival brownstone, is now a community home for the mentally disabled.

Brooklyn Children's Museum
145 Brooklyn Ave (at St. Mark's Ave), Brooklyn, NY 11213. ☎ (718) 735-4400. Web site: www.bchildmus.org. Open Wed–Fri 2–5 when school is in session; weekends and school holidays 10–5. Closed Mon–Tues, Jan 1, Thanksgiving, Dec 25. Suggested contribution. Children's resource library, exhibits, workshops, films, special events. Gift shop. A café is planned.

Subway: Seventh Ave Express (3) to Kingston Ave. Walk one block west on Eastern Pkwy; turn right onto Brooklyn Ave and walk six blocks to St. Mark's Ave. Eighth Ave Express (A) to Kingston–Throop Aves. Walk west on Fulton St one block to Brooklyn Ave; turn left (south) and walk six blocks to the intersection of Brooklyn and St. Mark's Aves.

Trolley: The BCM Trolley Express (free) runs every hour from 10:15 to 4:15 on weekends from Grand Army Plaza, with a stop at the Brooklyn Museum of Art.

Bus: B43 or B44 to St. Mark's Ave or B45, B65, or B25 to Brooklyn Ave.

Car: Take Atlantic Ave to Brooklyn Ave; turn south on Brooklyn Ave and continue four blocks to St. Marks Ave. Street parking.

The world's first children's museum (1899), the Brooklyn Children's Museum has evolved from a collection of natural history specimens housed in the parlors of an old mansion to a truly modern museum and educational resource for children. Today the museum's 200,000 yearly visitors enter through a 1907 trolley kiosk and a sewer culvert with a stream whose waterpower children can harness with sluices, gates, and waterwheels.

Inside the museum are hands-on, push-and-pull, jump-and-climb exhibits. Children can play musical instruments from all over the world, crank the jaw of a "horse" to see how animals chew, and test their measuring skills in a greenhouse exhibit. **Together in the City** explores New York's cultural diversity by offering children the opportunity to make a virtual pizza or (virtually) visit Yankee Stadium. The collections—some 27,000 objects—include fossils of plants and animals, African and Asian masks, a mammoth's tooth, a pickled human brain, and 2,000 dolls from many countries. There is a performance area and an exhibit for small children.

The Building
The original museum occupied a Brower Park mansion built for historian James Truslow Adams. By 1929 the museum had expanded into the nearby L. C. Smith (of typewriter fame) Mansion. Those buildings gradually deteriorated, and in 1977 the present subterranean 35,000-square ft facility designed by Hardy, Holzman, Pfeiffer opened on the site of the Smith Mansion.

Weeksville
On the border of Crown Heights and Bedford-Stuyvesant are the remains of Weeksville, a 19C village that was Brooklyn's first black community. The survivors are four tiny frame homes at 1698–1708 Bergen St between Rochester and Buffalo Aves. Known as the **Hunterfly Rd Houses** (1840–83; DL), they stand in stark contrast to the towering Kingsborough Houses across the street.

History
The village was settled by free blacks shortly after the abolition of slavery in New York State in 1827 and is named for James Weeks, a Virginian who purchased land here from the Lefferts family estate in 1838. Weeksville grew during and after the Civil War, its 40 families occupying an area bounded by what is today Fulton St, and Ralph, East New York, and Troy Aves. Susan McKinney Steward, the state's first black female physician (and the third in the nation), was born in Weeksville in 1847; Moses Cobb, the first black policeman in the city of Brooklyn, also owned a house in Weeksville. Important neighborhood institutions included the Howard Colored Orphanage Asylum, the Zion Home for the Aged Relief, and the African Civilization Society.

With the opening of the Brooklyn Bridge in 1883 and the building of new streets, burgeoning white communities swallowed up Weeksville. A few local institutions have survived from the days when Weeksville thrived. The **Bethel Tabernacle African Methodist Episcopal Church** was founded in 1847 on the corner of Schenectady Ave and Dean St; since 1978 it has occupied a former school building at 1630 Dean St across from its original location. The **Berean Missionary Baptist Church** (1894) on Bergen St (between Utica and Rochester Aves) was founded about 1854 and originally served a mixed-race congregation. **Colored School No. 2** (1847) became P. S. 243 (the Weeksville School) at 1580 Dean St.

The historic homes, set back from Bergen St, face the remnants of Hunterfly Rd, a colonial highway that joined Bedford and Canarsie. They were rediscovered in 1968 at a time when nearby buildings were being leveled for housing projects. Long forgotten and unoccupied since the 1950s, the homes were standing derelict among weeds when an aerial photographer and historian, who had studied old maps, decided to fly over the neighborhood and noticed four small buildings set along a lane deviating from the street grid.

Society for the Preservation of Weeksville and Bedford-Stuyvesant History

1698 Bergen St, Brooklyn, NY 11213. ☎ (718) 756-5250. Web site: www.weeks villesociety.org. Exhibits, programs, tours by appointment only. One of four houses is accessible to wheelchairs.

Subway: Eighth Ave Express (A) or Seventh Ave Express (3) to Utica Ave.

Present exhibits include articles found during an archeological dig on the site as well as a donated pair of slave shackles. There are plans to further restore the buildings and construct a museum and cultural center on an adjacent empty lot.

Bedford-Stuyvesant

Bedford-Stuyvesant, the largest black community in the country, used to be two neighborhoods: Bedford on the west, settled by the Dutch in the 17C, and the Stuyvesant Heights district to the east, settled later. The playground of P.S. 26, at Malcolm X Blvd and Lafayette, Greene, and Stuyvesant Aves, is the **geographic center of New York City.**

History

Like other outlying Brooklyn areas, Bedford-Stuyvesant went through several stages of development: first as farmland, later as a suburb with freestanding frame houses, then as an urban neighborhood with brick and brownstone row houses for a prosperous middle class, and finally as a black ghetto.

Unlike other neighborhoods, however, Bedford (the origin of the name is obscure) had a significant black population long ago, with slave laborers on Dutch farms making up 25 percent of the population in 1790, and later, the 19C black communities of Weeksville and Carrville. Meanwhile, Stuyvesant Ave in the Bedford Corners section attracted retail magnates like F. W. Woolworth and Abraham Abraham (of Abraham & Straus), who built mansions. Between the two world wars, Jews, Italians, Irish, and blacks from the West Indies and the American South began settling in the aging-yet-still-attractive neighborhood. By 1940, 65,000 blacks lived in Bedford-Stuyvesant; the dramatic increase of black arrivals after World War II made Bedford-Stuyvesant the nation's second largest black community after Chicago's South Side. Whites began moving out, and some of the housing stock and commercial strips deteriorated, creating the lasting image of Bedford-Stuyvesant as a slum. In the 1980s, black immigrants from the Caribbean began arriving, although the neighborhood attracts far fewer immigrants than nearby Crown Heights, Williamsburg, and Bushwick.

Today, much of the neighborhood is stable, home to working- and middle-class blacks. Nearly 85 percent of the community is black and most of the other residents are Latino. The southern, or Stuyvesant, end of the neighborhood is safer, cleaner, and has fewer housing projects and more noteworthy sites. Home buyers priced out of places such as Fort Greene, Clinton Hill, and Park Slope are increasingly looking to Bedford-Stuyvesant's more reasonably priced brownstones. Development of the neighborhood's commercial real estate, however, is lagging behind. The northern, or Bedford, side is battling encroachment from Williamsburg as Hasidic Jews have begun buying up properties on the Williamsburg—Bedford-Stuyvesant border and lobbying the city to convert commercial and manufacturing zoning to residential, allowing them to redevelop these blocks as housing.

Points of Interest

The **Antioch Baptist Church and Church House** (church 1892; Lansing Holden and Paul Higgs; church house 1893; Langston & Dahlander; DL) was built to fit in with its row house neighbors. The church has towers (of differing heights), round-arch stained glass windows, and a rounded projecting center featuring three rounded stained glass windows, light brick, and russet slate shingles. When the present African American congregation bought the building from the largely white Greene Avenue Baptist Church in 1950, the church became a pivotal Brooklyn institution, visited during the civil rights era by Martin Luther King Jr., Ralph Abernathy, and Rosa Parks.

On the north side of Tompkins Park (designed by Vaux and Olmstead), between Marcy and Tompkins Aves, is one of two trees in New York that have been designated landmarks. The ***Magnolia grandiflora*** (c. 1885; DL) qualifies as Brooklyn's second-most-famous botanical specimen after the Camperdown elm in Prospect Park.

A Tree Grows in Bedford-Stuyvesant

In 1965 Hattie Carthan, the 64-year-old "tree lady" of Brooklyn, began working to preserve and plant trees in Bedford-Stuyvesant. When the giant magnolia was marked for destruction in 1968 (an apartment complex would have risen in its stead), Carthan persuaded the Landmarks Preservation Commission to designate it a living landmark. Eventually, she engineered the purchase of three city-owned brownstones, 677–679 Lafayette Ave, and oversaw their conversion to the Magnolia Tree Earth Center. By the time she died in 1984, her efforts had also brought some 1,500 thriving trees to the streets of Bedford-Stuyvesant. Alongside the tree is a mural in Carthan's honor, and nearby, at the southwest corner of Marcy and Lafayette Aves, is a lush community garden named for her.

About eight blocks south, at 832 Marcy Ave (between Putnam Ave and Madison St), is the former **Boys' High School** (1891; James W. Naughton; additions 1910; C. B. J. Snyder; DL), built by the longtime superintendent for Buildings of the Brooklyn Public School system. The three street facades of this grand Romanesque revival building, with their gables, dormer windows, round-arch windows, and terra-cotta detail, give the impression of several adjoining buildings. At the intersection of Marcy and Putnam Aves, the school has a soaring campanile with a steep pyramid roof. Distinguished graduates of its distinguished past include Aaron Copland, Isaac Asimov, and Norman Mailer. It was joined with Girls' High in the 1970s and then moved to Fulton St. The building now houses Street Academy, an alternative high school.

Concord Baptist Church of Christ

Across the street, at 833 Marcy Ave, is the Concord Baptist Church of Christ (1956), noted more for its history than its architecture. (The original building was destroyed by fire in 1952.)

History

The church was founded in 1847 for Brooklyn members of Manhattan's Abyssinian Baptist Church, who were tired of commuting to services; it moved here from Concord St in 1872. Among its early pastors were abolitionist Samson White and Leonard Black, a fugitive slave. From 1863 until 1990, the Concord Baptist Church of Christ had only four pastors; the most celebrated and influential, Louisiana-born Gardner C. Taylor, led the congregation from 1942 to 1990. A national leader among Baptist ministers, active in the civil rights movement, Taylor brought Martin Luther King Jr. to speak at the church, served as one of King's advisers, and led protests against job discrimination in the city's building trades. He also served on the Board of Education and was the first black president of the New York City Council of Churches. Among his many community projects, Taylor helped establish a credit union, a nursing home, a senior citizens' residence, an elementary school, and a clothing exchange.

A little further south is a section of Bedford-Stuyvesant with blocks of brownstones that could rival any in Park Slope or Brooklyn Heights. Outstanding blocks include Hancock St between Marcy and Tompkins Ave and the two blocks of Halsey St from Marcy to Bedford Aves and Macon St in the same vicinity. Among the standouts is the stately Renaissance-style home at **247 Hancock St** (1880s; Montrose W. Morris), a freestanding mansion built across three lots. Another beauty is the elaborate **74 Halsey St** (c. 1880s), with two stories of three-sided projecting bay windows topped by a wrought-iron balcony and a triangular pediment.

Nearby, along Nostrand Ave (between Hancock and Macon Sts), are three impressive landmarked buildings. The entrance of the former **Girls' High School** (1886; James Naughton; addition, 1912; C. B. J. Snyder; DL), at 475 Nostrand Ave, has a stone portico with a second-story balustrade. Above is a pyramid-topped tower with a square belfry. Graduates included the singer Lena Horne and Shirley Chisholm, the first black woman elected to Congress (1968). The building is now the Brooklyn Adult Training Center.

Down the block, at 488 and 500–518 Nostrand Ave, are the **Renaissance Apartments** (1892; DL) and the **Alhambra Apartments** (1890; DL), designed by Montrose Morris for prominent local developer Louis Seitz. Stylistically similar to the Imperial, which Seitz and Morris built in Crown Heights that same year, the Renaissance is faced with pale yellow brick, banded with terra-cotta, and topped off with a slate mansard roof. At the corners are round towers with conical roofs. It was recently renovated after sitting empty for years—completely gutted and so derelict that trees grew inside. The architect built the Alhambra two years earlier than the Renaissance, using the same materials but placing more emphasis on the mansard roof with pedimented dormer windows and open loggias and arcades.

Several blocks to the east is the **Stuyvesant Heights Historic District,** an L-shaped area bounded partially by Chauncey and Macon Sts, Stuyvesant and Tompkins Aves, which was built up largely between 1880 and 1910. Local street names bestowed during a period of patriotic fervor recall historic naval figures: Thomas MacDonough, Stephen Decatur, William Bainbridge, and Isaac Chauncey. The avenues commemorate New York governors: Morgan Lewis, Enos T. Throop, Daniel D. Tompkins, and Peter Stuyvesant. Sumner Ave used to be called Yates Ave after Governor Joseph C. Yates, but the name was changed to avoid confusion with Gates Ave.

Mansions (including 87 and 97 MacDonough St), handsome brownstones, and other row houses with elaborate and eclectic architectural flourishes line these streets. Noteworthy blocks include Bainbridge St (between Lewis and Stuyvesant Aves) and the west side of Stuyvesant Ave (between Bainbridge and Decatur Sts).

There are three fine churches in the district—**Our Lady of Victory Roman Catholic Church** (1895; Thomas Houghton), on the corner of Throop Ave and MacDonough St; **St. Philip's Episcopal Church** (1899; Arni Delhi), on Mac-Dounough St between Lewis and Stuyvesant Aves; and **Mount Lebanon Baptist Church** (1894; Parfitt Brothers), on Decatur St at Lewis Ave. The **First A.M.E. Zion Church** (1889; George Chappell) on the southwest corner of MacDonough St and Tompkins Ave, with its huge campanile, sits just across the street from the district.

A new museum in the making is aptly called the **Planning Headquarters of the Museum of Contemporary African Diasporian Arts (MoCADA),** at 281 Stuyvesant Ave (between Jefferson Ave and Hancock St). It was founded by Laurie Cumbo, who will devote the next several years to fund-raising so she can make her dream a reality. For information and exhibit schedule, call ☎ (718) 602-4041 or access their Web site at www.mocada.org.

The **Bedford-Stuyvesant Restoration Center,** (1976; Arthur Cotton Moore) 1368 Fulton St (southeast corner of New York Ave), is a complex that includes stores, offices, and a theater named after Billie Holiday, the great jazz singer. The project, on the former site of the Sheffield Dairy, is a major achievement of the Bedford-Stuyvesant Restoration Corporation, founded (1967) after a widely publicized visit by Senator Robert F. Kennedy focused attention on the area. Although the Restoration Corporation had to reduce its staff and agenda because of federal funding cuts during the years of Ronald Reagan's presidency, it has continued providing jobs and low-interest loans, financing low-income housing, and encouraging supermarkets and other local businesses to settle in the area.

Brownsville

Southeast of Bedford-Stuyvesant is Brownsville, long synonymous with urban squalor but experiencing some revitalization through new housing.

History

The neighborhood is named after Charles S. Brown, who subdivided what had been farmland for housing in 1865. Two decades later, a group of realtors erected cheap housing and encouraged Jews from the Lower East Side to relocate here, an influx hastened by construction of the Fulton St elevated line in 1889. By 1900, 15,000 sweatshop workers worked in Brownsville, which had become a slum with unpaved streets, no sidewalks or sewers, and only one public bathhouse.

Between the 1920s and World War II, however, things improved as the population prospered. A pushcart market sprang up on Belmont Ave between Christopher St and Rockaway Ave, selling leftovers from the nearby produce market at Junius St.

From the Brownsville ghetto came a generation of eminent actors, artists, businessmen, and politicians, including Danny Kaye, Aaron Copland, and Sol Hurok, who launched his career as an impresario by persuading violinist Efrem Zimbalist to play for a local cultural society.

After World War II, the Jews, drawn by the suburbs or pleasanter parts of the city, began leaving, replaced by a poorer, mostly nonwhite population. During the 1960s and 1970s efforts at slum clearance eradicated some of the worst housing, but it was replaced by public housing projects. A lack of local jobs and social services further depressed the area, which was soon plagued by crime, arson, and rioting. Heavyweight champions Mike Tyson and Riddock Bowe both grew up in the Brownsville slums.

Point of Interest
The once majestic **Loew's Pitkin Theater** (1930; Thomas W. Lamb), at the corner of East New York and Pitkin Aves, harks back to an era when elaborate movie palaces filled the borough. Today the ground level of this light brick building with ornate terra-cotta details is occupied by retail shops.

East New York
East New York, bounded on the north by Atlantic Ave, on the east by Conduit Ave and the Queens County line, on the south by Linden Blvd, and on the west by Pennsylvania Ave, was founded as a commercial venture by Connecticut businessman John R. Pitkin, whose schemes for a town rivaling New York were dashed by the 1837 fiscal panic. It was developed later as a working-class neighborhood and attracted Russians, Germans, Italians, and Jews, many arriving from Brownsville. During the 1960s and early 1970s many longtime residents, some pressured by block-busting real estate dealers, sold their property and moved away; today the population is mostly black. Corruption in the U.S. Department of Housing and Urban Development caused federally owned urban renewal housing to go into foreclosure. Those buildings were destroyed by arson as poverty and crime spread.

Gradual revitalization of East New York and neighboring Brownsville was spearheaded in the 1980s by the East Brooklyn Congregations, which used a concept developed by commercial builder I. D. Robbins and began building the **Nehemiah Houses,** small, affordable two-story, one-family houses to encourage home ownership. Led by Rev. Johnny Ray Youngblood of the St. Paul Community Baptist Church, the group has built more than 2,000 homes.

Point of Interest
The **New Lots Dutch Reformed Church** (1823; DL), 630 New Lots Ave (southeast corner of Schenck Ave), was built of local oak by local farmers tired of trekking to the Flatbush Reformed Church. This simple, dignified church with pointed arch stained glass windows sits in an old graveyard.

South of East New York, but often thought of as part of that neighborhood, is the nation's largest federally subsidized housing project, Starrett at Spring Creek, originally known as **Starrett City** (1975; Herman Jessor). The city within a city has 20,000 residents living in 46 apartment buildings, with its own power plant, security force, and even a local cable station. When it first opened, Starrett City's managers, hoping for middle-class residents, imposed a quota, reserving 65 percent of the units for whites. The applicants however were generally lower income, and the system was taken to court in 1979; management claimed it was maintaining the quota to preserve integration, even though blacks were left waiting while apartments sat empty. Even after losing in court in 1988, Starrett again tried attracting only middle-class residents who could pay more, leaving poorer blacks and Latinos waiting while apartments sat empty. Today, however, the project is considered a model of integration; 50 percent of the residents are white (many of them immigrants from Russia and eastern Europe) and 50 percent belong to minorities.

Cypress Hills

Cypress Hills, bordered by Jamaica Ave, the Queens County line, and Atlantic Ave, is often considered part of East New York, with which it shared similar patterns of development until the 1960s and 1970s, when Cypress Hills remained more stable. From 1990 to 1996, more than 17,000 immigrants settled in the East New York–Cypress Hills area, more than one-third of them from the Dominican Republic; significant numbers of Jamaicans and Guyanese also moved here.

Points of Interest

P.S. 65K, at 158 Richmond St (between Ridgewood Ave and Fulton St), is also known as the **Little Red Schoolhouse** (1870; Samuel Leonard; facade 1889; James Naughton; DL). The Romanesque revival facade was added nearly 20 years after the school opened and features round-arched windows, a roof and tower entablature with a frieze of terra-cotta plaques, and a balustrade capping the tower.

Several cemeteries line Jamaica Ave, including **Cypress Hills National Cemetery** (636 Jamaica Ave), the city's only national cemetery, established in 1870 when land was purchased from nearby Cypress Hills Cemetery. More than 21,000 people are interred here, including 3,100 Union and 461 Confederate prisoners of war as well as the last survivor of the War of 1812, Pvt. Hiram Cronk, buried here in 1903 at the age of 114. The remains of 14 British sailors, buried in a vault shortly after the end of the Revolution and unearthed in 1908 at the Brooklyn Navy Yard, were reinterred here a year later, after the British government showed little interest. The national cemetery was closed for burials in the 1950s.

48 · Fort Greene and Clinton Hill

Fort Greene

Fort Greene, east of downtown Brooklyn and south of the Brooklyn Navy Yard, is a residential and commercial neighborhood whose diverse population reflects that of the city at large. On its southern edge are its two most famous landmarks—the legendary Brooklyn Academy of Music, focus of a small historic district, and the towering Williamsburgh Savings Bank. The main commercial strips run along Flatbush Ave and Fulton St. Beautifully kept 19C row houses line the streets of the

Fort Greene Historic District near the park of the same name, but the neighborhood also has several public housing projects.

History

The first European settler was Italian pioneer Peter Caesar Alberti, who bought land from the Dutch and started a tobacco plantation in 1639. The neighborhood's name honors Revolutionary War hero Nathanael Greene, who oversaw the construction of a fort in what is now Fort Greene Park. Housing for the upper middle class was developed in the late 19C and the street names reflect the propriety of the first residents: the north–south streets bear the names of fashionable London streets (Adelphi, Carlton, Portland, Oxford, Cumberland, and Waverly); the east–west avenues bear the names of American Revolutionary War heroes (Gates, DeKalb, Greene, Willoughby, Lafayette). The neighborhood has long had a black population; in the 1870s Dr. Susan McKinney Steward, the state's first black woman doctor, lived here.

Fort Greene deteriorated in the mid-20C, especially after the closing in 1966 of the Brooklyn Navy Yard on its northern border. Since the 1980s, however, it has been rejuvenated by middle-class blacks (about two-thirds of the population is black), though the neighborhood is still grittier than nearby Park Slope, Cobble Hill, and Brooklyn Heights. Fort Greene has become popular with people in the performing arts: residents have included the actor Wesley Snipes, jazz musicians Wynton and Branford Marsalis, writer Doris Lessing, and the late jazz singer Betty Carter. Former resident Spike Lee still maintains his film production company, 40 Acres and a Mule, here. Bordered by major thoroughfares but not mutilated by them, Fort Greene has a small-town feel.

Large-scale development at the neighborhood's periphery may threaten its present character. Just beyond the intersection of Atlantic and Flatbush Aves is the ugly, boxy **Atlantic Center Mall,** whose suburban-style chain stores opened in the mid-1990s.

The developer, Forest City Ratner, also responsible for Metrotech Center in downtown Brooklyn, is planning a 400,000-square-ft mall, Atlantic Center Plaza, adjacent to the first one in the area above the Long Island Rail Road Flatbush Terminal and the Atlantic Ave subway station. Here Brooklyn Dodger owner Walter O' Malley hoped to build a new stadium; in early plans the mall's exterior resembled Ebbets Field's facade.

Brooklyn Academy of Music (BAM)

Main Building (BAM Opera House, BAMcafé, and BAM Rose Cinemas): 30 Lafayette Ave (between Ashland Place and St. Felix St), Brooklyn, NY 11217. BAM Harvey Theater: 651 Fulton St (between Ashland Place and Rockwell Place). ☎ (718) 636-4100; BAM Rose Cinemas, ☎ (718) 623-2770. Web site: www.bam.org. Box office open Mon–Sat 10–6; Sun (performance days only) 12–4.

Operas, concerts, films, plays, jazz, dance, performance art. Bamcafé: open Thur–Sat 5–10:30 and Sun noon–8 (brunch until 4, concession service thereafter); also open Mon–Wed 5–7:30 when there are performances in the Opera House or Harvey Theater. Accessible to wheelchairs.

Subway: To Main Building, Seventh Ave Express (2, 3), Lexington Ave Express (4, 5), or Sixth Ave Express (D, Q) to Atlantic Ave. To BAM Harvey Theater, Seventh Ave Express (2, 3) or Lexington Ave Express (4, 5) to Nevins St. Bus: The

BAMbus departs from the Whitney at Philip Morris, 120 Park Ave (at E. 42nd St), one hour before most BAM performances. For information, ☎ (718) 636-4100.

Car: From the Manhattan Bridge, continue straight off the bridge to Flatbush Ave; follow it to Fulton St. Turn left onto Fulton St; the BAM Harvey Theater is one block ahead on the left (parking on your right). For the BAM Opera House, continue two blocks to Ashland Place; turn right; parking is immediately to your right.

Begin at the Brooklyn Academy of Music (1908; Herts & Tallant). BAM, as it is known locally, is the nation's oldest performing arts center, founded in 1859. After its original Montague St building burned down in 1903, the academy moved into this Italian Renaissance–style theater.

A Pioneer in Terra-Cotta

The building was a pioneer in the use of colored terra-cotta glazes. Earlier attempts failed either because the darker color selections blended into the buildings, or because the areas of terra-cotta were too small to be visible from a distance. The designers resolved those problems by using broad fields of terra-cotta, primarily in bright colors.

Performers as famous as Charles Dickens and Paul Robeson have appeared at BAM; Enrico Caruso suffered a throat hemorrhage onstage on Dec 11, 1920, and gave his final performance in New York 13 days later. By the 1960s, the Brooklyn Academy of Music was virtually moribund. It was revived almost singlehandedly by Harvey Lichtenstein, a former dancer, who served as executive director from 1967 to 1999. Lichtenstein instituted adventurous programming that ranged from the Royal Shakespeare Company to blues legend Albert King. The **Next Wave Festival,** begun under his aegis in 1983, put BAM on the map as a home for avant-garde music and theater, attracting talent and audiences from Manhattan and abroad. In 1998 BAM opened **BAM Rose Cinemas,** the borough's premier art-house movie theater.

The Majestic Theater: Renovation without Renewal

Nearby, at 651 Fulton St (between Rockwell and Ashland Places), is BAM's **Majestic Theater** (1904; renovated 1987; Hardy Holzman Pfeiffer), renamed (1999) the Harvey Lichtenstein Theater and locally known as "the Harvey." During the renovation the former vaudeville theater was structurally stabilized, but the years of water damage and neglect were allowed to remain, making this "ruin" beautiful in its own way. BAM uses it for theater, dance, and music.

Williamsburgh Savings Bank

Around the block from BAM's main facility is Brooklyn's tallest building, the 512 ft **Williamsburgh Savings Bank** (1929; Halsey, McCormack & Helmer; DL), at

1 Hanson Place. The bank (chartered in 1851) was taken over by the Republic National Bank of New York in 1987, but the building is still called the Williamsburgh Savings Bank.

Exterior

The base is polished rainbow granite; the first floor is limestone. Ornamentation on the lower facade includes relief carvings of industrious and thrifty animals (bees, squirrels, pelicans) and metal grilles showing four continents. The upper levels are clad in buff-colored brick and terra-cotta; some of the setbacks are highlighted by rounded arches and terra-cotta bands. The four-faced clock on the tower was the world's largest when the building opened. (Each face is 27 ft in diameter.) The gilded copper dome above it intentionally resembles the dome of the bank's former headquarters at 175 Broadway in the Williamsburg section of Brooklyn.

Interior

The interior has suggested to some observers "a cathedral of thrift." The ceiling vaults in the lobby are covered with blue, red, and gold mosaics. René Chambellan's sculpted metal figures of working men ornament the doors leading to the main banking room, resplendent with 22 varieties of marble. A mosaic ceiling features the signs of the zodiac (Angelo Magnenti) and a mosaic mural depicts an aerial view of Brooklyn (executed by Ravenna Mosaics of Berlin).

From the bank, walk east down Hanson Place to the Hanson Place Seventh Day Adventist Church, originally the **Hanson Place Baptist Church** (1860), at 88 Hanson Place (southeast corner of S. Portland Ave). The facade of this handsome wood-trimmed brick church is reminiscent of an ancient temple: four tall Corinthian columns lead to a Greek revival entry with triangular frames above each doorway.

Continue east on Hanson Place to Fulton St. The strip of Fulton St from Flatbush Ave to S. Oxford St is a vibrant center of African culture. The **Brooklyn Moon Café,** 747 Fulton St, has become one of several hot spots for spoken-word events; **Keur N'Deye,** 737 Fulton St, serves Sengalese food; **Moshood Creations,** 698 Fulton St, has a colorful African-style mural on its sidewalk; **Nigerian Fabrics & Fashions,** 701 Fulton St, sells traditional African garb; and the **4W-Circle of Art,** 704 Fulton St, is a cooperative of local artists.

The Bogolan Strip

The local merchants association has dubbed the strip Bogolan, short for *bogolafini*, the West African (Bambara) word for a traditional cloth dyed with fermented mud and leaves. The use of the name is meant to suggest African reemergence and the influence of African American culture in the community.

At Fulton and S. Oxford Sts, turn left (north) onto S. Oxford St and walk to the corner of Lafayette Ave. The large brownstone **Lafayette Avenue Presbyter-**

ian Church (1862; Grimshaw & Morrill) at 85 S. Oxford St, its nave flanked by towers, has an impressive history. Theodore L. Cuyler, its 19C leader, was a leading abolitionist and teacher, and the church became a stopover on the Underground Railroad. Among Cuyler's pupils was Robert Gould Shaw, who led the black troops of the 54th Regiment, celebrated in the movie *Glory*. President Abraham Lincoln sent his son Robert Todd Lincoln to represent him at the church's groundbreaking. In 1862, Cuyler held meetings in the Parlor Room (now the Theodore Cuyler Library) with a committee that included Frederick Douglass, Horace Greeley, and Henry Ward Beecher. The group sketched an early draft of the Emancipation Proclamation and sent representatives to Washington to pressure Lincoln. In the church library are the shovel Robert Todd Lincoln used during the groundbreaking, its handle made from a fence rail split by his father, and a copy of Cuyler's sermon "Father Abraham," delivered two days after the president's assassination.

Tiffany in Brooklyn

The church has 13 Tiffany stained glass windows, including *The Creation* (a copy is at the Metropolitan Museum of Art) in the Lecture Room. It also owns the largest Tiffany stained glass work outside a museum, *The Apostle Paul Preaching at Mars Hill*, on the north wall of the sanctuary.

Cuyler originally deemed "art glass" to be "frivolous," but Louis Comfort Tiffany eventually changed the reverend's mind by asking him to be the model for St. Paul. The Greeks were modeled on church board members, while the girl at Paul's feet is nine-year-old parishioner Elise Woodward Stutzer. Decades later, as an elderly woman, Stutzer donated money for the *Mighty Cloud of Witnesses* (1973; Hal Prussing), said to be the largest mural inside any church anywhere. Created by a 23-year-old Pratt Institute student, it stretches from the balcony to the roof and around the entire circumference of the sanctuary. (The "witnesses" are based on photos of actual people from 1973.)

Continue on S. Oxford St to DeKalb Ave. This street and S. Portland Ave to the west are among Fort Greene's finest blocks. Their superb Italianate row houses suggest Fort Greene's prominence in the 1860s, when it was the next suburb beyond Brooklyn Heights.

Turn right on DeKalb Ave and walk one block to **Washington Park,** the name of Cumberland St as it runs along the eastern border of Fort Greene Park. (Fort Greene Park was originally called Washington Park.) This street was once one of Brooklyn's finest addresses, its houses, elaborated with mansard roofs and dormer windows, attracting notable figures such as the publisher Alfred C. Barnes (no. 182). William C. Kingsley, the political power behind the Brooklyn Bridge, lived at no. 176, and Abner Keeney, his partner in a contracting business, lived next door at no. 175. Together, Kingsley and Keeney spearheaded the paving of Brooklyn's streets, the laying of its sewers, and major construction work in Prospect Park. Kingsley expanded into building materials and real estate, became publisher of the *Brooklyn Eagle*, and was a major force in Brooklyn politics.

Fort Greene Park

Enter Fort Greene Park from Washington Park and Willoughby Ave. During the Revolution, Fort Putnam occupied the high ground of this hilly 30-acre park.

During the War of 1812, the fort was rebuilt and renamed after Nathanael Greene, who had supervised its original construction. The city of Brooklyn set aside the site for a park in 1845 and hired Frederick Law Olmsted and Calvert Vaux (1860) to lay out the grounds, which would contain a memorial to the Prison Ship Martyrs.

The **Prison Ship Martyr's Monument** at the summit of the hill was designed by Stanford White (1908), with a granite column (148 ft 8 inches) whose crowning bronze brazier (Adolph A. Weinman) was intended to support an eternal flame. A crypt below (not open to the public) contains the remains of some of the 11,500 American soldiers who died on British prison ships in Wallabout Bay between 1780 and 1783. The dead, who had succumbed to starvation, disease, flogging, and exposure, were first buried in shallow graves along the water by their companions, but the bodies kept washing up on the shores of Brooklyn and Manhattan, and in 1808 the bones were moved to a private estate in Brooklyn. In 1873 they were moved to the present crypt. The monument is currently in sorry shape—the bronze door has been replaced with plywood, two plaques are missing, and the eternal flame has not been lit for years. Four bronze eagles that once stood atop the monument's corner pillars were removed for their safety in 1962 by the Parks Department. One local effort hopes to have the federal government assume responsibility for the monument, which was built with government money. (In the early 1990s, drug dealers overran the park, but since then the park, like the brownstones surrounding it, has been reclaimed.)

The novelist Richard Wright, who lived nearby at 175 Carlton Ave, supposedly wrote much of his masterpiece *Native Son* while sitting in the park.

Leave the park via Willoughby Ave and walk three blocks east to Clermont Ave. Turn right and walk two blocks to Lafayette Ave. Here, along the Fort Greene–Clinton Hill border, are three unusual buildings. The **Brooklyn Masonic Temple** (1909, Lord & Hewlett and Pell & Corbett), 317 Clermont Ave (corner of Lafayette Ave), is an imposing Classical revival brick temple with stellar polychromatic terra-cotta detail. The building is now owned by the African American Masons, a group unaffiliated with the white Brooklyn Masons who built it.

On the northwest corner of the intersection at Lafayette and Vanderbilt Aves is the massive French Gothic **Our Lady Queen of All Saints Church** (1913; Gustave Steinack), executed in cast stone. Gargoyles representing women and animals and relief sculptures of two dozen saints adorn the facade.

Diagonally across the intersection, at 200 Lafayette Ave, is the former **Joseph Steele House** (1812; with 1850 additions; DL), a yellow clapboard Greek revival dwelling with an octagonal cupola and a dentiled cornice.

Clinton Hill

Subway: Sixth Ave Local (F) or Eighth Ave Local (E) to Queens Plaza. Change to the Brooklyn-Queens Crosstown local (G) to Clinton–Washington Aves. Or take the Eighth Ave Express (A) to Hoyt–Schermerhorn Sts in Brooklyn and change there to the G train to Clinton-Washington Aves.

History

Clinton Hill, east of Fort Greene, named for De Witt Clinton, mayor and governor, was first built up with grand homes (and carriage houses) in the 1840s. It evolved from rural retreat to suburban neighborhood after the Civil War, when developers began building row houses, many of them in the Clinton Hill Historic District, which is south and west of Pratt Institute. When the oil millionaire Charles Pratt moved to Clinton Ave in 1875, he transformed the neighborhood, first building palatial homes for his family and then establishing the Pratt Institute. Soon the Pfizers (of the pharmaceutical firm), the Bristols (of the Bristol-Myers pharmaceutical company), and the Underwoods (whose money came from typewriters) followed Pratt to Clinton Hill.

The neighborhood, like many others, declined after World War II. Many homes were converted to rooming houses; Robert Moses cleared areas and built housing projects. Today, however, Clinton Hill is on the upswing as the brownstone revival reaches east from Fort Greene.

In addition to Pratt Institute, the neighborhood is home to St. Joseph's College, a commuter school that offers courses in business, law, education, and health care management. The Roman Catholic bishop of Brooklyn has his residence here. The population is generally middle class. The housing is a mix of exquisite row houses, mansions (some of them run-down), apartment buildings, and housing projects.

Begin at the **Church of St. Luke and St. Matthew,** originally **St. Luke's Episcopal Church** (1889; John Welch; DL), 520 Clinton Ave (near Fulton St). Considered the masterpiece of a Brooklyn architect known mostly for Greek and Gothic revival churches, St. Luke and St. Matthew is eclectically Romanesque revival. Above the large rose window is a corbeled cornice flanked by small octagonal towers. To the left is the main tower, resembling a campanile from 12C northern Italy. The mixture of rough and smooth stone and terra-cotta adds beauty to the facade. Inside are windows by the Tiffany Studios.

Walk north on Clinton Ave to the corner of Gates Ave and the brick-and-limestone **Royal Castle Apartments** (1912; Wortmann & Braun; DL), 20–30 Gates Ave. Look up to see the fanciful corbels and arched gables on the roofline.

Along Clinton Ave, between Gates and DeKalb Aves, stand the former residences of the wealthy and the merely well-to-do. While most have been broken up into apartments and some are in major need of repair, the strip still offers an architectural feast. Among its offerings: a Renaissance revival limestone house at **463 Clinton Ave** (1902; Mercein Thomas); a Queen Anne mansion with bay window, pointed roof, dentils, and swags at **410 Clinton Ave** (1882; Parfitt Bros.); the neo-Flemish Romanesque porch and pediment of **405 Clinton Ave** (1889; William Tubby); the minibalcony and tiered, green-tiled roof of **356 Clinton Ave** (1905; Theodore Visscher); and the brick, brownstone, and terra-cotta of **315 Clinton Ave** (1888; Montrose Morris).

At DeKalb Ave turn right and walk one block to the corner of Waverly Ave. Here are two more massive structures from Clinton Hill's heyday: **282–290 DeKalb Ave** (1890; Montrose Morris) and **285–289 DeKalb Ave** (1889; Montrose Morris), with an array of cylindrical turrets, conical roofs, and other details.

Return to Clinton Ave and turn right (north). The **former Pratt family houses,** by and large better preserved than other nearby mansions, stand on Clinton Ave between DeKalb and Willoughby Aves. On the west side of the street (232 Clinton Ave) stands the **Charles Pratt Mansion** (c. 1875), home of the founder of the Greenpoint's Pratt Astral Oil Works, which he merged secretly and advantageously with John D. Rockefeller's Standard Oil Company in 1874. On the other side of the street are homes Pratt built for three of his five sons. The **George DuPont Pratt House** (1901; Babb, Cook & Willard; later extensions to the south), 245 Clinton Ave, built by the architects of the Andrew Carnegie Mansion, now belongs to **St. Joseph's College**. The **Charles Millard Pratt Mansion** (1893; William B. Tubby), next door at 241 Clinton Ave, is now the residence of the Roman Catholic bishop of Brooklyn. This Romanesque revival brick house has a great arched porte cochère on one side, balanced by a semicircular conservatory on the other; an eyebrow dormer window peers through the tile roof. The **Caroline Ladd Pratt House** (1898; Babb, Cook, & Willard), 229 Clinton Ave, first belonged to Frederick B. Pratt and is now a residence of the Pratt Institute. The columned arbor on its north serves as an entranceway to the gray-and-white Georgian revival house.

Pratt Institute
Continue on Clinton Ave to the corner of Willoughby Ave; turn right and walk three blocks east to Pratt Institute, which fills the blocks between Willoughby and DeKalb Aves, Hall St and Classon Ave.

History
Charles Pratt, a self-made man, founded Pratt Institute as a trade school for young people situated as he had been in his youth. It opened with a drawing class in 1887 and soon expanded to include courses in engineering and science, a school for librarians, and courses in home economics. The school's buildings originally faced the city streets but were enclosed as a campus in the 1950s. Today, the school is known for its programs in architecture, art, and design. Graduates include the actor Robert Redford, artist Peter Max, photographer Robert Mapplethorpe, and cartoonist Jules Feiffer.

The Campus
The Pratt campus is a mishmash of landmarks dating back to Pratt's day and uninspired modern buildings. Rotating exhibits in the outdoor **Sculpture Garden** have included works by well-regarded sculptors such as Tom Otterness and Louise Bourgeoise. The university has in recent years undertaken a multimillion dollar rehabilitation of its landmarked buildings.

Ryerson Walk, once Ryerson St, bisects the campus. On its eastern side is the sturdy Romanesque revival **Main Building** (1887; Lamb & Rich; DL), along with the adjoining three-story brick **South Hall** (1891; William Tubby) and **Memorial Hall** (1927; John Mead Howells; DL). The portico with brownstone arches was added by William Tubby in 1894.

Also on the east side is the **East Building** (1887; William Windrim), originally called the Mechanical Arts Building, which contains the engine room and boiler for the original power plant. It was designed so that Pratt could convert his educational experiment to a shoe factory if the school failed. Today it is the oldest continuously operating, privately owned, steam-powered electrical generating plant in the country. There is a viewing area from which the **working steam turbines** are visible, along with a collection of Brooklyn memorabilia. On New Year's Eve and during graduation ceremonies, visitors can try out the collection of steam whistles, pulling the levers on whistles from locomotives, riverboats, and the U.S.S. *Normandy*.

Across the lawn, on the west side of Ryerson Walk, is the **Library** (1896; William B. Tubby; DL), another of Pratt's philanthropies, founded as Brooklyn's first free public library and annexed to the college only in 1940.

Thrift Hall (1916; Shampan & Shampan), on the east side of Ryerson Walk at DeKalb Ave, now contains offices. It opened as a savings and loan company (in a building where Memorial Hall now stands), organized by the philanthropic Pratt to make low-cost mortgages available to workers and to teach the virtue of thrift.

Schafler Gallery

Pratt Institute, 200 Willoughby Ave (between Hall St and Classon Ave), Chemistry Building, Brooklyn, NY 11205. ☎ (718) 636-3517. Open during the academic year, Mon–Fri 9–5. Call for summer hours. Free. Occasional lectures, tours, performances. Limited wheelchair accessibility.

Subway: Brooklyn-Queens Crosstown Local (G) to Clinton–Washington Aves.

Inside the Chemistry Building, near the Willoughby Ave entrance, is the Schafler Gallery (1985), which mounts shows on sculpture, graphics, painting, architecture, and photography. Some show the work of faculty members or students; others draw on outside sources.

On three separate blocks around the campus are the remaining **Pratt Row Houses** (1907; Hobart Walker; DL). The Pratt family built a complex of 38 workers' houses, which he connected to Pratt's central heating plant. Twenty-seven survive: 220–234 Willoughby Ave, 171–185 Steuben St, and 172–186 Emerson Place. During the 1920s, one was used to teach "household science" to Pratt students. The houses are now faculty housing.

Return to Willoughby Ave and walk west to Washington Ave; turn left (south). At 320 Washington Ave (between DeKalb and Lafayette Aves) is the former **Graham Home for Old Ladies** (1851), once a shelter for elderly females indigent but too genteel for the public poorhouse. It was founded as the Brooklyn Society for the Relief of Respectable, Aged, Indigent Females, but the name was changed in 1899 to honor paint manufacturer John B. Graham, who donated the land and also helped finance the building. The home lasted well into the 20C, but by the 1980s the neo-Georgian building had become a cheap hotel for prostitutes and then a welfare hotel, before being closed.

Continue to Lafayette Ave and turn left, walking one block east to the corner of St. James Place. Another of Charles Pratt's projects was the **Emmanuel Baptist Church** (1887; Francis H. Kimball; DL), 279 Lafayette Ave. Pratt belonged to the Washington Avenue Baptist Church, but when the minister, Emory Haynes, published a novel that included satire aimed at monopolies, Pratt took offense. While 180 others joined Pratt in defecting, it was largely his money that financed the Emmanuel Baptist Church. Contemporary newspaper articles called it the Astral Church or the Standard Oil Church.

The square twin towers, the trio of arched and pedimented doorways, and the large pointed-arched window above the doors give the church a French Gothic feel. Inside is a 900-seat sanctuary with a vaulted roof. In 1999, the church was restored. The stenciled pattern on the lower walls is based on a Coptic cross, a style associated with Ethiopia, which reflects the black congregation's heritage.

Other Points of Interest

St. James Place has some of the neighborhood's better mid-19C row houses, as do nearby Clifton and Cambridge Places and Grand Ave. Other interesting blocks include Washington Ave between Gates and Greene Aves, which offers a mixture of detached homes and row houses, and Waverly Place, which has carriage houses.

Outside the Clinton Hill Historic District, at the edge of Bedford-Stuyvesant, is the **Lincoln Club** (1889; Rudolph Daus; DL), at 65 Putnam Ave (between Irving Place and Classon Ave). This extravagant Queen Anne brick, stone, and terra-cotta building with an intensely decorated roof gable was built for a men's social and political club (founded 1878), whose members hoped to further the interests of the Republican Party. It disbanded in 1931, and since the 1940s the building has belonged to the Mechanics Temple, Independent Order of Mechanics of the Western Hemisphere.

49 · Northern Brooklyn: Greenpoint, Williamsburg, and Bushwick

Greenpoint

Subway: Eighth Ave Local (E) or Sixth Ave Local (F) to Queens Plaza. Change to Brooklyn-Queens Crosstown Local (G) in direction of Smith–9th Sts, Brooklyn, to Greenpoint Ave.

Greenpoint, the neck of land north of the Brooklyn-Queens Expwy between Newtown Creek and McCarren Park, whose proximity to the water long made it an industrial area, is today a quiet residential district, with significant enclaves of Poles, Italians, Puerto Ricans, and other ethnic groups. Greenpoint has long been a modest working-class neighborhood, but in recent years artists have been attracted by its affordable rents, turning old warehouses and factories into studios. Despite the bleak condition of the East River piers, residents sunbathe and fish among the ruins, enjoying the water and Manhattan views.

History

Greenpoint was undoubtedly verdant in 1638 when the Dutch bought it from the Indians. After 1832, however, when Eliphalet Nott and Neziah Bliss surveyed the land and laid out streets and lots for development, Greenpoint gradually became industrial. Shipbuilders worked on its shoreline by 1840. During the Civil War period the Continental Ironworks stood on West St between Oak and Calyer Sts. In 1861 the works began production of the hull of the *Monitor*, and on Jan 30, 1862, the ironclad ship slid down the ways into the East River.

The shipbuilding industry declined during the maritime depression after the Civil War, replaced by the "black arts" (printing, porcelain making, glassworking, iron casting, and oil refining), which attracted Polish, Russian, Irish, and Italian immigrant workers. These industries used Newtown Creek both for transportation and for dumping waste. By the early 20C, Newtown Creek, the second busiest waterway in the country after the Mississippi River, was so polluted that the water corroded the paint on ships and bridges.

After World War II the factories closed, leaving Greenpoint an industrial ghost town. As the neighborhood declined, its low rents attracted immigrants, some Puerto Ricans but mostly Poles. Gradually Greenpoint became the city's Polish capital, a claim it maintains today. While many other immigrant neighborhoods are now filled with largely assimilated second- and third-generation descendants of the original settlers, Greenpoint continues to experience an influx of Poles: 7,600 of them between 1990 and 1996, nearly one-third of all Polish newcomers to the city. These new immigrants keep alive the mother tongue and the customs of the old country. The commercial strips, Manhattan and Nassau Aves, are filled with Polish bakeries, bookstores, restaurants, and candy shops. This group also maintains active ties with Poland: in Poland's first free elections in 1990, the neighborhood contributed 5,000 absentee ballots.

Greenpoint, the Cradle of "Brooklynese"

Greenpoint (or sometimes Flatbush) is allegedly the birthplace of Brooklyn-ese, a dialect of American English that substitutes *d* for *th*, as in "dem Bums," and interchanges *oi* and *er*, as in "Greenpernt." However, linguists do not believe that there is an actual "Brooklyn" dialect or accent, although there is one that pervades the greater New York region.

The following short walking tour of Greenpoint includes remnants of the old industrial era, several blocks of attractive and well-kept 19C homes, and the commercial institutions of the middle-class Polish American community along Manhattan Ave.

Begin at the Greenpoint Ave subway station (Manhattan Ave at Greenpoint Ave). The local historic district encompasses the area between Java, Calyer, and Franklin Sts and Manhattan Ave. One of Greenpoint's finest blocks architecturally is the section of **Kent St between Manhattan Ave and Franklin St.** To reach it, walk a block north of the subway station and turn left.

St. Elias Greek Rite Church (1870), at 149 Kent St, a brown-and-white striped brick, Ruskinian Gothic building, began as the Greenpoint Reformed Church. Along the other side of the street are handsome 19C houses, built for working-class and middle-class families. The architectural mix includes neo-Grec houses (148–152 Kent St, dating from 1889) and Italianate houses (144 and 146 Kent St, dating from 1874). The houses at **134–136 Kent St** (1885), also neo-Grec in style, have fine ironwork, which may have been cast in Greenpoint's foundries. The one at **130 Kent St** (1859; Neziah Bliss) has a high stoop with a portico.

Continue west to Franklin St. Turn right and go one block north. Just outside the historic district, at 184 Franklin St (between Java and India Sts), are the **Astral Apartments** (1886; Lamb & Rich; DL), built by Charles Pratt for the workers in his oil refinery. Designed after the Peabody Apartments in London, the Astral Apartments were a milestone in the tenement reform movement, providing every room with daylight and fresh air. Pratt's Astral Oil was located on the East River at Bushwick Creek from Kent Ave to N. 12th St. In 1870 the refinery daily processed 1,500 barrels of petroleum into 1,100 barrels of Astral Oil, a high-quality kerosene that replaced whale oil and other fuels as an illuminating oil. The street names here—Java, India—recall the 19C spice trade that flourished along the waterfront.

Return along Franklin St; continue past Kent St and Greenpoint Ave to Milton St. Turn left. Another architecturally attractive block is **Milton St between Franklin and Manhattan Aves,** with more late-19C row houses and several churches. Noteworthy among the houses are 122–124 Milton St, a brick-and-brownstone Queen Anne pair with attractive ironwork (1889; Theobold Englehardt), and 141–149 Milton (1894; Thomas Smith), which are set back off the street and have wrought-iron balconies.

The **Greenpoint Reformed Church** (c. 1867; Thomas C. Smith), 138 Milton St, moved to this Italianate-Greek revival building from its former site on Kent St. **St. John's Evangelical Lutheran Church** (1892; Theobald Engelhardt), 155 Milton St, served an immigrant congregation whose German name is still inscribed on the building. Closing off the end of Milton St is the red brick **St. Anthony of Padua–St. Alphonsus Church** (1874; P. C. Keely), 862 Manhattan Ave, whose towering 240 ft tall spire makes it a neighborhood landmark.

Turn right and continue down Manhattan Ave to Calyer St. On the corner is the limestone-and-granite **Greenpoint Savings Bank** (1908; Helmle & Huberty), with a pantheon dome, Doric columns, and a fish-scaled slate pattern.

Turn right onto Calyer St and right again onto Lorimer St, which has another attractive row of small town houses.

Points of Interest

The imposing, ornate Roman Catholic **St. Stanislaus Kostka** (c. 1878), 607 Humboldt St (corner of Driggs Ave), serves the largest Polish congregation in the city. St. Stanislaus Kostka, the pious but physically frail second son of a Polish noble family, was the first Jesuit to be beatified (1605). Determined to become a Jesuit but prevented for political reasons from joining the order in Vienna where he attended school, he walked hundreds of miles to Rome, where he was accepted. After ten months as a novice, he died on Aug 15, 1568. He was canonized in 1726.

In **Monsignor McGolrick Park** (between Driggs and Nassau Aves, Russell and Monitor Sts) the ***Monitor* Monument** (1938; Antonio de Filippo) depicts a bronze sailor straining at a bronze hawser. The park also contains a **shelter** (1910; Helmle & Huberty; DL) inspired by the Trianon at Versailles. The park is named for Monsignor Edward J. McGolrick, an Irish immigrant who served for 50 years as the pastor of the local parish.

On the Greenpoint-Williamsburg border stands the Byzantine-style **Russian Orthodox Cathedral of the Transfiguration** (1921; Louis Allmendinger; DL), 228 N. 12th St (at Driggs Ave). Its five copper verdigris onion domes mounted on octagonal belfries hover above the low industrial and residential buildings. The yellow brick exterior is otherwise modest but inside (entrance on Driggs Ave, services Sun at 11 A.M.) the church is richly decorated in bright colors with wall paintings of saints, stained glass windows, and columns painted to simulate marble supporting a high, sky-blue dome. During services the lighted crystal chandeliers, ornately vested priests, incense, and music, seem doubly exotic in this humble neighborhood.

At 227 India St is the **Bedi-Makky Art Foundry,** where the famous Iwo Jima Memorial statue was cast.

Williamsburg

Subway: Nassau St Local (J, M) to Marcy Ave.
Car: Take Williamsburg Bridge to Hooper St. Go left to Lee Ave, the center of Hasidic commercial activity. A car is recommended for points of interest beyond this area.

South of Greenpoint and along the East River is Williamsburg, which runs south to Flushing Ave and east to the Queens border.

History

Once part of the town of Bushwick, Williamsburg became independent about 1810 and took its name from Col. Jonathan Williams, who surveyed the area. A ferry to Corlear's Hook in Manhattan gave inland farmers a market for produce, but Williamsburgh (spelled with an *h* until it became part of the city of Brooklyn in 1855) remained isolated. In the mid-19C, Williamsburg still attracted industrialists and sportsmen—Commodore Cornelius Vanderbilt, William C. Whitney, and Jim Fisk—to its resort hotels, while affluent businessmen built mansions along its avenues.

A distillery (c. 1819), later superseded by a brewery, was its first industrial plant, and after Williamsburgh was incorporated as a village, industry began to arrive. Shipyards, mills, foundries, small sugar refineries, and some of the world's largest industrial firms began along the Williamsburg waterfront, employing the neighborhood's Irish, Germans, and Austrians. The Pfizer Pharmaceutical Company was established here in 1849 by German-trained chemist Charles Pfizer; Charles Pratt's Astral Oil Works opened in 1867 on Bushwick Creek, and later became part of Standard Oil Company. William and Frederick Havemeyer, in 1857, established a large, technologically advanced sugar plant with its own docks and warehouses, which today survives as Domino Sugar. Later the F & M Schaefer Brewing Company (founded by German immigrants Maximilian and Frederick Schaefer in 1842) set up shop at S. 10th St and Kent Ave in 1915.

The **Williamsburg Bridge** (1903; Leffert L. Buck), built to ease traffic on the Brooklyn Bridge, was the longest and heaviest suspension span in the world and the first with towers made entirely of steel. Its opening transformed the neighborhood. Dubbed "the Jews' Highway" by the press, the bridge brought a flood of poor and working-class immigrants (mostly Polish and Russian Jews and Italians) from the Lower East Side, eventually turning parts of Williamsburg into a slum. During the 1930s these immigrants were joined by Jewish refugees from Europe.

Beginning in 1946, Williamsburg became the first American home of the Satmar Hasidic Community, an ultra-Orthodox Jewish sect (*hasidim* means "pious ones") founded in 18C Poland but now including groups from Hungary and elsewhere as well. Today, almost all the Jews in Williamsburg are ultra-Orthodox Hasidim. Sect members are highly visible because of their clothing: men wear black garments with wide-brimmed or sable hats, full beards and sidelocks, while the women, modestly garbed in dark, long-sleeved dresses, have shaven heads covered with wigs and scarves if they're married. The boys wear sidelocks and yarmulkes.

Manufacturing continued to attract immigrants, including Puerto Ricans, in the 1950s; many moved into public housing projects built to alleviate overcrowding. The Williamsburg Houses, built in 1937, were the country's first public housing project; later projects were less humane in scale and design.

As manufacturing jobs decreased—Schaefer closed in 1976, eliminating 2,500 jobs—the neighborhood fell on even harder times; it was overpopulated, had poor housing and high crime.

In recent years, parts of Williamsburg have made a comeback, particularly the Northside, which began attracting artists and young hipsters who opened trendy restaurants, cafés, shops, and galleries among the old Polish stores on and around Bedford Ave on the Greenpoint border. East Williamsburg, near the Bushwick border, retains some of its former Italian flavor. The Southside is Hasidic and Hispanic, with the largest group of newcomers hailing from the Dominican Republic; Lee Ave is the Hasidic commercial strip, while Broadway caters to the Hispanic population.

Points of Interest

Crowded **Lee Ave** feels like the Lower East Side 100 years ago, with its Hebrew and Yiddish signs advertising kosher butchers and bakeries, clothing stores selling Hasidic garments and wigs, and other shops geared to the Hasidic clientele.

Along Bedford Ave, south of the Brooklyn-Queens Expwy, Jewish institutions and schools have taken over several former mansions and clubs that remain from pre-bridge days. A lack of concern for historic preservation has left many of the buildings run-down. The building at 571 Bedford Ave on the corner of Rodney St, now occupied by Young Israel of Brooklyn and Bais Yaakov of Adas Yereim, was formerly the **Oscar F. Hawley Mansion** (c. 1875; Lauritzen & Voss; remodeled 1891) and later the Hanover Club. Hawley was president of a nearby box manufacturing factory and his mansion was considered one of the architectural landmarks of the neighborhood. The yeshiva at 505 Bedford Ave, northeast corner of Taylor St, once belonged to Frederick Mollenhauer (1896), a sugar refiner. Rebbe Joel Teitelbaum, who established the Hasidic community here in the 1940s, lived in the building (500 Bedford Ave, at the northwest corner of Clymer St) now used by the Ravtov International Jewish Rescue Organization.

Near the foot of the Williamsburg Bridge is the former **Williamsburgh Savings Bank** (1875; George B. Post; additions 1905; Helmle, Huberty & Hudswell; 1926; Helmle & Huberty; DL) at 175 Broadway (northwest corner of Driggs Ave). Its grand dome and monumental entrance recalls the era when Mollenhauers and Havemeyers lived nearby. One of the nation's first Italian Renaissance revival buildings, the bank anticipated the surge of interest in Renaissance architecture that made the careers of such firms as McKim, Mead & White. In 1995, plywood panels that had covered 20 oval etched-glass windows since World War II were removed, allowing light once again to enter.

Williamsburg Art and Historical Center

135 Broadway, Brooklyn, NY 11211. ☎ (718) 486-7372. Web site: wahcenter. org. Open weekends 12–6 and Mon by appointment. Galleries, lectures, films, performances.

Up the street is the former **Kings County Savings Bank** (1868; King & Wilcox; DL), 135 Broadway (northeast corner of Bedford Ave), a four-story Second Empire masterpiece with its ornate Victorian interior still intact. Today it houses the Williamsburg Art and Historical Center, a multifaceted cultural center, which opened in 1996.

Directly across from the bank, at 178 Broadway, is the **Peter Luger Steak House,** believed by many to serve up the best aged porterhouse steak in the city. Founded in 1887, this German beer hall–style restaurant attracts a large and loyal clientele, including politicians, city power brokers and gadflys, and civil servants. The interior is casual—floors are sprinkled with sawdust, ceilings are pressed tin, and its dark wood-paneled walls suggest its beginnings as a café and billiard parlor.

Near the formal Brooklyn entrance to the Williamsburg Bridge is **Continental Army Plaza**—bounded by Roebling, S. 4th, and S. 5th Sts—which gets its name from its centerpiece, an equestrian statue of *George Washington at Valley Forge* by Henry M. Shrady (1906), his first public work. The tiny, three-quarters of an acre park was built by the Department of Public Works in conjunction with construction of the bridge, which opened in 1903. The statue, cast at Roman Bronze Works in Brooklyn and anchored to a granite base, was dedicated three years later.

The impressive domed building with terra-cotta detail across the street is the former home of the **Williamsburgh Trust Company** (1906; Helmle & Huberty), now the Ukrainian Autocephalic Orthodox Church in Exile.

The first public housing built in this country, the **Williamsburg Houses** (1937; Board of Design with Richmond H. Shreve, chief architect), still stands between Maujer, Scholes, and Leonard Sts and Bushwick Ave. Lauded in their day for their small scale, private entries, outdoor courtyards for recreation, and floor plans admitting generous amounts of air and light, today they are weathered and run-down.

Brooklyn Brewery

79 N. 11th St, Brooklyn, NY 11211. ☎ (718) 486-7422. Free tours of its 25-barrel brewery, tasting room, beer-related events.

When it opened in 1996 in a 1860s-era former steel foundry, the Brooklyn Brewery, at 79 N. 11th St (corner of Wythe Ave), became Brooklyn's first commercial brewery in 20 years and one of the largest in the East. (The microbrewery started making beer upstate in 1987.) A century ago, there were about 48 breweries in Brooklyn; the last two, the F & M Schaefer Brewing Company and Rheingold, closed in 1976, done in by mass-market competition and by huge commercial breweries.

At 270 Union Ave is the former **Colored School No. 3** (1879; DL), a reminder of former segregation policies. The school began as the African Free School (founded before 1841). It was taken over by the city of Brooklyn in 1887, and after the consolidation of Greater New York in 1898 became part of the New York Public School system. In recent years, it has been restored as a residence and artist's studio.

Brooklyn Navy Yard

The former Brooklyn Navy Yard, once the nation's premier shipbuilding and ship repair facility, is today largely a city-run industrial park (closed to the public). It stretches from the East River inland to Flushing Ave, from Kent Ave to Navy and Hudson Sts.

History

In 1781 John Jackson and William Sheffield started on the shores of Wallabout Bay a small shipyard whose facilities included a sawmill and a pond for seasoning ship timbers. The yard was sold in 1801 to the federal government for $40,000. During the War of 1812, it became an important base for servicing ships, though the first warship built there, the 74-gun ship-of-the-line *Ohio*, was not launched until 1820. Robert Fulton's famous steam frigate, the *Fulton*, was built there and launched in 1815. Among the long line of distinguished ships produced in the yard are the battleship *Maine*, blown up in Havana harbor in 1898; the *Arizona*, sunk at Pearl Harbor in 1941; and the battleship *Missouri*, on whose decks Japan signed the surrender ending World War II. Activity peaked in the Navy Yard during World War II, when 70,000 workers on continuous shifts turned out battleships and destroyers and overhauled some 5,000 vessels. The yard was decommissioned in 1966 with the loss of thousands of jobs. The federal government sold most of it (264 acres) to the city, which in 1993 leased the yard to the Brooklyn Navy Yard Development Corporation, a nonprofit city agency formed to oversee the yard's renaissance as an industrial park. In 1996, the city committed $101 million to this project.

The Navy Yard Today

The park currently has 200 tenants, mostly manufacturing and distribution companies but also two shipbuilders, and employs 3,000 people. There are plans afloat to build a major television and movie production studio on 15 acres at the northern edge of the yard.

The remainder of the yard was owned by the federal government until 2001, when it gave the city most of the property. Sadly, **Admiral's Row,** a series of ten Victorian houses, the last one built in 1910, has badly deteriorated. The property is owned by the Army Corps of Engineers. There are four landmarks on site. Visible from Flushing Ave, between Ryerson St and Williamsburg Place, is the former U.S. Naval Hospital, originally the **U.S. Marine Hospital** (1838; Martin E. Thompson; DL), austerely constructed of Sing Sing marble, now closed and boarded up. Nearby stands the brick Second Empire–style home of the hospital's chief of surgery, officially known as the **Surgeon's House, Quarters R-1, Third Naval District** (1863; True W. Rollins and Charles Hastings, builders; DL). These 28 acres are owned by the federal government.

The oldest structure in the yard is the former **Commandant's House,** also known as Quarters A (1806; attrib. Charles Bulfinch associated with John McComb Jr.; DL), south of Evans and Little Sts in the western part of the yard, barely visible through the gates. The three-story white clapboarded house with handsome porches and elegant details—hewn oak floor beams 32 ft long, interior wood trim of carved mahogany—is one of the city's finest Federal structures. It is privately owned.

On Dock St, at the foot of 3rd St, is **Dry Dock No. 1** (1851; William J. McAlpine, engineer, and Thornton MacNess Niven, architect and master of masonry; DL), the oldest granite-walled dry dock in the nation and a great structural tour de force in 19C American engineering.

Bushwick

Bushwick was one of Brooklyn's original six towns, chartered in 1660 as *Boswijck*, "town of the woods." The neighborhood, which stretches northeast of Broadway to the Queens border and the Brooklyn-Queens Expwy, is industrial in its northern reaches and residential further south.

History

Bushwick's German population dates back to the end of the Revolutionary War, when some of the Hessian mercenaries who had billeted here chose to remain, mostly as farmers. German immigration picked up after abortive 1848–49 uprisings in Germany, and Bushwick simultaneously became known as a center of the beer industry. Otto Huber, Caspar Illig, Joseph Fallert, Ernest Ochs, and Samuel Liebermann (founder of the Rheingold Breweries) all established factories within a 14-block area known as Brewers' Row (bounded by Scholes and Meserole Sts, and Bushwick Place and Lorimer St). Many of these men lived in Bushwick, giving it its staid Germanic atmosphere. In the 1840s, Peter Cooper (see Cooper Union in Walk 10) had a glue factory on the site of the housing project now named after him, and other industries thrived along Maspeth Creek.

In the 20C the demography of Bushwick changed. After the Depression, Italians, many of them Sicilians, replaced the Germans. Beginning in the 1950s, as the Italians moved out to Queens, blacks, Puerto Ricans, and, later, Dominicans moved to Bushwick. Today the population is mostly Latino and black, with a small number of whites (mainly Italians) and Asians.

Bushwick is one of the poorest communities in the city. The neighborhood lost its economic base after World War II, as factories closed and prosperous residents moved elsewhere. It was particularly hard hit by looting, arson, and rioting during the citywide blackout in 1977. In the early 1980s, there were more than 1,000 empty lots in Bushwick, and as recently as the early 1990s, drug dealers openly sold their wares on street corners. Today, unemployment is still high and drug dealing remains prevalent, though the dealers have mostly been chased from the streets and violent crime has dropped sharply. Additionally, thanks to such local groups as the Bushwick Local Development Corporation and the Ridgewood Bushwick Senior Citizens Council, as well as the New York City Housing Partnership, hundreds of new homes (mostly two-family) have been built and fewer than 50 empty lots remain. Still, housing projects are mixed with the neighborhood's old homes, many of which are physically depressed.

Touring Bushwick

A car is recommended. Take the Williamsburg Bridge to Broadway; follow Broadway south to Myrtle Ave. Turn left on Myrtle Ave and right on Bushwick Ave.

Points of Interest

On Bushwick Ave, south of Myrtle Ave, occasional mansions remain—most falling into decay, left behind by departing brewers, manufacturers, and other prosperous families. Some have been taken over by Black Muslim and Rastafarian groups. At 670 Bushwick Ave (on the southwest corner of Willoughby Ave) is the former **William Ulmer Mansion,** built by the brewer and later owned by Arctic explorer Frederick A. Cook. The former **Catherine Lipsius residence** (c. 1886; Theobald Engelhardt), 680 Bushwick Ave (on the southeast corner of the same intersection), built by a brewer's widow, was once an elegant Italianate home. Both mansions are boarded up.

The **South Bushwick Reformed Church** (1853; DL) stands on the northwest corner of Bushwick Ave and Himrod St, a white frame Greek revival survivor of the days when Dutch influence was still strong in Brooklyn. The scale of the building, its grand Ionic columns and high tower, suggest the affluence of the mid-19C congregation, but today it is in dire need of a paint job. Himrod St is named after its first minister.

Further south are former mansions of other affluent men: the former **Gustav Doerschuck residence** (c. 1890), with a corner tower topped by a pyramid roof, at 999 Bushwick Ave (northwest corner of Grove St); the former **Charles Lindemann home** (c. 1890), on the northeast corner at 1001 Bushwick Ave, with turrets and dormer windows; and the former **Louis Bossert residence** (1890), 1002 Bushwick Ave (southeast corner of Grove St), which has a mansard roof. Bossert, a millwork manufacturer, built the once-elegant Bossert Hotel in Brooklyn Heights; his former home has been converted to a church.

Perhaps the most imposing building is the Roman Catholic **St. Barbara's Church** (1910; Helmle & Huberty), on Central Ave at the northeast corner of Bleecker St, a Spanish baroque church of buff brick with wedding cake terracotta ornamentation, which rises like an apparition in this otherwise depressed area. Inside are statuary, carvings, frescoes, bas-reliefs, and stained glass by turn-of-the-20C German craftsmen. The church's earliest parishioners were Germans, then Italians, followed by today's largely Hispanic congregation, who have donated many dollars to the upkeep of this magnificent church.

Borough of Queens/Queens County

The borough of Queens, the largest in the city, covers 112.2 square miles (37 percent of the city's total area) and is located geographically in the western portion of Long Island. It is nearly as large as Manhattan, the Bronx, and Staten Island combined and is bounded by Brooklyn on the west, with Newtown Creek forming part of the border, by the East River on the north, by the Atlantic Ocean on the south, and by Nassau County on the east.

Topographically, it resembles the rest of Long Island, with a chain of hills created by glacial deposits running across the north and a low outwash plain in the south. The northern shore is indented by Flushing and Little Neck Bays, while the Rockaway peninsula juts westward across the mouth of Jamaica Bay in the south to form a ten-mile oceanfront.

Home to 1,998,853 people, Queens is the second-most populous borough, surpassed only by Brooklyn. More than a third of Queens residents are foreign born, a percentage unmatched in any other borough. It is also second only to Brooklyn in the number of immigrants it attracts—between 1990 and 1996, 240,000 foreigners settled here. The largest number, more than 27,500, came from China, many of them from Taiwan. Also settling in Queens were two-thirds of the 20,800 arrivals from India, three-quarters of the 15,800 Colombian newcomers, more than half of the 16,900 new Bangladeshis, nearly three-quarters of the 11,800 new Koreans, almost two-thirds of the 8,500 new Peruvians, half of the city's 5,200 new Salvadorans, nearly three-quarters of the 4,500 new Romanians, three-fifths of the 3,330 Iranians, and more than 85% of all arrivals from Afghanistan.

In other words, while Brooklyn welcomed the most immigrants altogether and Manhattan the most Chinese and Dominicans, Queens became home to a more diverse group of heavily concentrated ethnic communities than any other borough, and most likely, any other place on earth. The Flushing Local (7) subway train, which runs through many immigrant neighborhoods from Long Island City to Flushing, has been called the International Express (although it's often a painfully slow local), and in 1999, it was named a "National Millennium Trail" by the White House.

Queens is largely residential, with more than 253,000 one- and two-family homes, comprising 75 percent of the borough's housing stock. It has apartment towers of various heights, but lacks the concentration of 19C brownstones and tenements that characterize Brooklyn and the Bronx. Queens is also distinguished by strong neighborhood identities. Some of its neighborhoods—Kew Gardens, Forest Hills, Douglaston—are almost suburban in character with detached houses, attractive gardens, and garages. Queens also has the highest median income of any borough. Among its suburban amenities are more than 6,400 acres of parkland, more than any other borough.

At the other end of the economic scale are slums in South Jamaica, the Rockaways, and in some older industrial areas. While Queens has earned a reputation

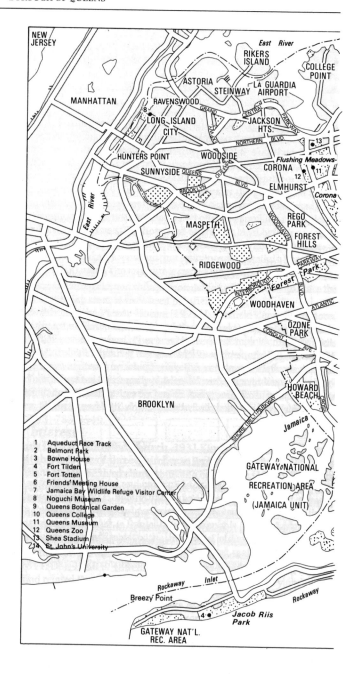

1 Aqueduct Race Track
2 Belmont Park
3 Bowne House
4 Fort Tilden
5 Fort Totten
6 Friends' Meeting House
7 Jamaica Bay Wildlife Refuge Visitor Center
8 Noguchi Museum
9 Queens Botanical Garden
10 Queens College
11 Queens Museum
12 Queens Zoo
13 Shea Stadium
14 St. John's University

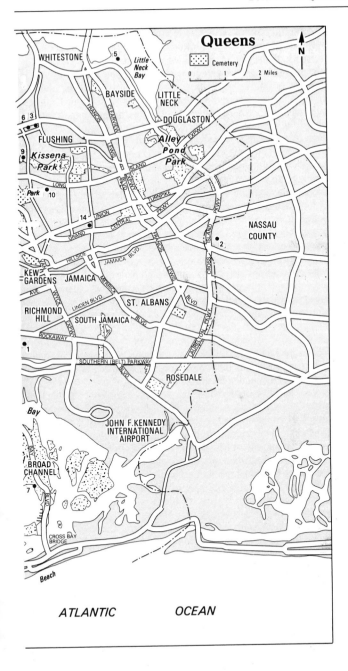

Queens

Cemetery

0 1 2 Miles

N

WHITESTONE

Little Neck Bay

5

BAYSIDE

LITTLE NECK

DOUGLASTON

Alley Pond Park

6 3

FLUSHING

9

Kissena Park

Park 10

NASSAU COUNTY

14

2

KEW GARDENS

JAMAICA

ST. ALBANS

RICHMOND HILL

SOUTH JAMAICA

1

SOUTHERN (BELT) PARKWAY

ROSEDALE

Bay

JOHN F.KENNEDY INTERNATIONAL AIRPORT

BROAD CHANNEL

7

CROSS BAY BRIDGE

Beach

ATLANTIC   OCEAN

FRANCIS

CLEARVIEW

LEWIS

ISLAND

CROSS

UTOPIA

TURNPIKE

PKWY

ISLAND

PKWY

EXPWY

LONG

UNION

GRAND

CENTRAL

HILLSIDE

JAMAICA BLVD

FRANCIS

LEWIS

CROSS ISLAND PKWY

MERRICK

AVE

WYCK

LINDEN BLVD

BLVD

BLVD

LAURELTON PKWY

ROCKAWAY

BLVD

as a bedroom community in the past half century, those areas that developed earlier became industrial, with concentrations of factories in the vicinity of Long Island City, Maspeth, College Point, and along the right-of-way of the Long Island Rail Road, although most heavy industry has moved out of Queens (and indeed the entire Northeast). Commercial centers are scattered throughout the borough, usually located at the crossroads of earlier towns, established independently before the creation of Greater New York in 1898: the most important ones are Jamaica, Flushing, and Elmhurst.

Because of its former spaciousness, Queens became the resting place of uncounted souls whose remains lie buried in a belt of cemeteries that begins on the Brooklyn-Queens border and stretches eastward along Jackie Robinson (formerly Interborough) Pkwy, an area known by the waggish as the "terminal moraine." This includes Union Field, Bethel, Mt. Carmel, Mt. Neboh, Cypress Hills, Mt. Lebanon, and Mt. Judah cemeteries. Other large graveyards in the borough, which also owe their impetus to an 1851 law prohibiting further burials in Manhattan, are St. John's, Mt. Olivet, Lutheran, Mt. Zion, and Calvary.

More than any other borough, Queens bears the stamp of Robert Moses, who as Parks commissioner preserved acres and acres of land—forests, meadow, beaches, marshes—while as master roadbuilder (and head of various public authorities) he blighted equally large areas by lacing the borough with highways: the Grand Central Pkwy, Interborough Pkwy, Clearview Expwy, Cross Island Pkwy, Laurelton Pkwy, Long Island Expwy, Brooklyn-Queens Expwy, and the Whitestone Expwy.

Queens is also the city's aviation center—home to both LaGuardia and Kennedy Airports as well as the College of Aeronautics and many aviation-related industries. It is the city's television and motion picture production center, with most of the grip, lighting, costume, and scene-building companies on the East Coast located within its borders. Queens also hosts Shea Stadium and the USTA National Tennis Center.

As Queens embraces its future, it is also trying to preserve its past. Frustrated by its comparative lack of official city landmarks (it has fewer designations than any other borough, including Staten Island), the Queens Historical Society took it upon itself in 1996 to create "Queensmark." The program honors Queens structures and sites worthy of special recognition for their architectural, cultural, or historical significance. (Queensmarked sites are identified by bronze plaques.)

History

The first inhabitants of Queens were Native Americans, the Rockaway tribe, whose name lives on in the peninsula stretching across Jamaica Bay. The first European settlers were Dutch and arrived around 1635. Most of the earliest settlements were short-lived, in part because of losing battles with Native Americans. Governor Willem Kieft purchased title to the land from Native Americans in 1639, and shortly thereafter the first towns were chartered: Mespat (now Maspeth) in 1642, and Vlissingen (Flushing) in 1643. Middleburgh, which became Newtown in 1655, was founded in 1652 between the two earlier settlements, its first residents immigrants from France and England as well as Holland. Indeed, as settlement continued, the Dutch staked out their claims in the western part of Long Island while the English colonized the eastern portion, including the towns of Hempstead and Jamaica (1650).

In 1683, 19 years after the British took title to the former Dutch colony of New Amsterdam, Newtown, Flushing, and Jamaica were organized as Queens County, one of 12 making up the British province of New York. The name honors Catherine of Braganza, queen of Charles II. During the Revolution most residents of Queens were British sympathizers, and after the war many loyalists emigrated to Newfoundland.

Although a few industries established plants in Queens during the 19C, notably the Steinway piano factory and the Edward Smith & Co. paint factory, the borough remained rural and agricultural until almost the turn of the 20C. (The Queens County Farm Museum, a historical restoration, recalls this era.) As the railroads pushed eastward across Long Island, the beaches of both the northern and southern shores began attracting summer residents. At the turn of the last century, the land LaGuardia Airport now occupies held an amusement park, and the Rockaways, whose remoteness is enshrined in the place name of its easternmost settlement, Far Rockaway, attracted the well-to-do, who enjoyed its grand hotels or the privacy of their own mansions. The major roads were used by farmers taking their produce to New York markets or by residents in outlying communities seeking the amenities of the commercial districts closer to the city.

In 1898 Queens joined Greater New York, although several of the eastern towns chose to remain independent—Hempstead, North Hempstead, and Oyster Bay—and were then absorbed into Nassau County. At the time (1900), the population of the borough was only 152,999, a figure that tripled in the next 20 years and doubled again between 1920 and 1930, as bridges, tunnels, and rapid transit opened Queens to development. In 1910 the Queensboro Bridge and the East River tunnel of the Pennsylvania Railroad allowed direct access to Manhattan, while the subways came during the next decades with the BMT and IRT both reaching the outer areas of the borough and the IND going all the way to Jamaica in 1937. The Triborough Bridge (1936), the Bronx-Whitestone Bridge (1939), the Queens-Midtown Tunnel (1939), and, most recently, the Throgs Neck Bridge (1961) made Queens readily accessible by car.

In 1939–40 the first of two world fairs was held in Flushing Meadows, and several of these public works projects, along with the development of LaGuardia Airport, were undertaken to coincide with its opening. After World War II, Queens experienced its second great boom, one that took the form of suburban development as builders grabbed whatever open space remained and erected acre after acre of tract housing, small homes on small lots, monotonously repeated row upon row, block upon block. Despite the blandness of much of Queens's suburban development, its very newness has saved the borough from some of the problems of urban blight that afflict Manhattan, Brooklyn, and the Bronx.

Touring Queens

Several large sections of Queens are inaccessible by subway and more easily seen by car. A casual glance at a road map may make it appear that Queens is laid out in a recognizable rectilinear pattern, but it is deceptively difficult to find your way around. Numbered avenues generally run east and west, but they are sometimes interspersed with roads, drives, and even an occasional court bearing the same number; streets run generally north and south and seem to be more regular than avenues in their numbering. The pattern is further complicated by the vestiges of old roads, dating from the colonial period and themselves often following Native American paths, wandering across the modern grid according to topographical variations long erased by landfill or leveling. New highways running through old neighborhoods have disrupted the continuity of street layouts as well as the social fabric of the neighborhoods themselves. Finally, developers have created special patterns—arcs or crescents, for example—in communities such as Forest Hills Gardens, Rego Park, or Kew Gardens that were developed all at once as planned communities or for real estate speculation.

50 · Northwestern Queens: Hunter's Point, Long Island City, Ravenswood, Astoria, Steinway, Sunnyside, and Woodside

Long Island City

Long Island City is an industrial and residential neighborhood on the east bank of the East River opposite Roosevelt Island. The name can refer both to the smaller community of Long Island City proper and to a larger geographical area that includes Hunter's Point, Ravenswood, Dutch Kills (a long-obsolete name now being revived), Sunnyside, and Astoria.

History

Long Island City's low-lying flood-prone terrain remained largely undeveloped before the Civil War, when the area around Hunter's Point was industrialized. When the swamps were drained (1870–74), industry began to arrive as oil refineries, lumberyards, asphalt factories, gas plants, and chemical factories were built. Proximity to the waterfront, which made Long Island City attractive as a manufacturing center, also made it a focal point for transportation. Railroad terminals had been built before and during the Civil War and a ferry ran to Manhattan as early as 1859. In 1892 piano maker William Steinway backed a tunnel for a trolley car connection to Manhattan. Franchise disputes, an explosion, and the Panic of 1893 halted the project, and though the Steinway Tunnels were eventually completed in 1907, they sat empty until 1913, when they were converted for subway use as part of the IRT Flushing line, which opened in 1915. By the opening years of the 20C, Long Island City boasted the IRT and BMT subway lines, the Long Island Rail Road, the Penn Central Railroad, and the Queensboro Bridge.

As Long Island City became congested, heavy industry began leaving, replaced by other kinds of manufacturing. In the 1930s, the neighborhood's 1,400 factories turned out 5 million loaves of bread, 10 million gallons of paint and varnish, and undisclosed quantities of spaghetti, candy, and shoes. Gradually, much of this lighter industry moved on as well, although today a "new Long Island City" is emerging. The huge neon sign that once heralded the Silvercup commercial bakery (Queens Plaza to Forty-third Ave, between 21st and 22nd Sts) has since 1983 publicized the Silvercup Studios, the city's largest film and television production facility.

Neon in Queens

A neon sign with a giant blue-gray stapler and the slogan "SWINGLINE STAPLERS—Easy Loading" once adorned the factory building at 32-00 Skillman Ave. It was dismantled and sold in 1999, despite public opposition. Swingline, one of the city's oldest and largest manufacturers, was founded in 1925 by Russian immigrant Jacob (Jack) Linsky, who sold it in 1970. Linsky and his wife, Belle, donated their significant art collection to the Metropolitan Museum, where it is displayed in special galleries bearing their names.

As industry departed, some observers projected that Long Island City, including Hunter's Point, would become the next artists' colony. However, despite the departure of some companies, the commercial area remained relatively stable, unlike Williamsburg, which was largely abandoned and offered artists plenty of cheap loft space. While Long Island City does have several important art institutions and numerous artists do work here, it never became an art mecca.

Rising above old factories in Hunter's Point is the 48-story Citicorp Tower, the intended anchor for a new business community that has not yet materialized. Waterfront development is belatedly arriving in the form of Queens West, an ambitious, 74-acre residential and commercial development sure to change the area.

Hunter's Point

Hunter's Point, the southern part of Long Island City, takes its name from the British sea captain George Hunter, who owned land here during the colonial period. Its development dates from after 1860, when the first steam ferry made regular crossings to Manhattan. Around the landing at 34th St, a prosperous community arose, with inns and hotels for travelers and comfortable homes for commuters. Hunter's Point was gradually urbanized during the Civil War, a process that accelerated dramatically with the opening of the Queensboro Bridge.

Points of Interest

At 48 stories and 663 ft, the **Citicorp Tower** (1989; Skidmore, Owings & Merrill), 44th Drive to Forty-fifth Ave near Jackson Ave, is the tallest building in the outer boroughs.

Near the Citicorp Tower is the ornate **N.Y. State Supreme Court, Long Island City Branch** (1876; George Hathorne; rebuilt 1908; Peter M. Coco; DL), reconstructed in its present Beaux-Arts style after a fire.

Memorable Words and Pictures

Ruth Snyder, a Long Island housewife, was tried here in 1927 for murdering her husband and found guilty. She was one of the first women electrocuted (at Sing Sing in 1928). A photograph of Snyder taken at the moment of her death by a reporter who had sneaked a camera into the death chamber was published on the front page of the *Daily News;* it became one of journalism's most controversial pictures. Willie "the Actor" Sutton allegedly uttered his celebrated defense of his profession here: he robbed banks, he said, because "That's where the money is."

The block of Forty-fifth Ave between 21st and 23rd Sts has been declared the **Hunter's Point Historic District.** Its Italianate row houses (early 1870s) owe their good condition to their building material, Westchester stone, which is harder and less friable than the usual brownstone.

P.S. 1 Contemporary Art Center

22-25 Jackson Ave (at Forty-sixth Ave), Long Island City, NY 11101. ☎ (718) 784-2084. Web site: www.ps1.org. Open Wed–Sun 12–6. Suggested donation. Changing exhibitions, music, video and film, studio program for artists, performances, public programs. Gift shop. Café. Accessible to wheelchairs.

Subway: Eighth Ave Local (E) or Sixth Ave Local (F) to 23rd St–Ely Ave. Exit onto 44th Rd to Jackson Ave; walk two blocks south on Jackson Ave to Forty-sixth Ave. Or take Flushing Local (7) to 45th Rd–Courthouse Square. Exit onto Jackson Ave; walk one block south to Forty-sixth Ave. Or take Brooklyn-Queens Crosstown Local (G) to 21st–Van Alst Sts. Exit onto 21st St. Walk one block north to 46th Rd. Turn right. Walk one block east to Jackson Ave. Bus: Q67 to Jackson and Forty-sixth Aves; B61 to Forty-sixth Ave.

Car: Via the Queens-Midtown Tunnel, exit at Van Alst St. Follow 21st St three blocks. P.S.1 is on the right. Via the Queensboro-59th St Bridge, from the lower level, turn right onto Jackson Ave, go five blocks to Forty-sixth Ave; from the upper level, exit at 21st St, turn right, and follow to Forty-sixth Ave.

Queens Artlink Shuttle

Queens Artlink offers a courtesy weekend shuttle service that runs from Manhattan to cultural attractions in Queens. There are two buses. The first leaves the Museum of Modern Art on W. 53rd St (between Fifth and Sixth Aves) in Manhattan every hour on the half hour from 11:30 A.M. to 4:30 P.M. This bus travels to P.S. 1 Contemporary Art Center. The second bus, which leaves P.S. 1 on the hour, makes a loop continuing on to the Isamu Noguchi Garden Museum, Socrates Sculpture Park, and the American Museum of the Moving Image. For information, ☎ (212) 708-9750.

P.S.1 Contemporary Art Center is one of the best places in the city to see new and adventurous art. In the galleries, stairwells, corridors, basement, and courtyard of what was once a public school, are exhibitions of sculpture, painting, and video art. P.S.1 has long focused on emerging artists but also has shown impressive retrospectives of now-mainstream figures. In 1999, P.S.1 merged with the Museum of Modern Art (MoMA), a partnership that keeps MoMA on the cutting edge and gives it more exhibition space in a less formal environment, while P.S.1 gains financial support and exponentially increased visibility.

The Building

The center occupies the former Ward 1 School (1892), which was refurbished (1976; Shael Shapiro) by the Institute for Art and Urban Resources as an experimental art center with studios and exhibition space. In 1997, P.S.1 undertook an imaginative renovation (1997; Frederick Fisher), creating 36 galleries and making it one of the world's largest contemporary art museums.

The biggest development in Long Island City in the last decade has been the start of the **Queens West project,** which, when completed, will have 19 buildings with 6,300 apartments and 2.5 million square ft of commercial and retail space along the waterfront. The project will be built in stages over years, if not decades. The first building, the 522-unit **Citylights,** at 5th St and Forty-eighth Ave (across the river from the United Nations), opened in 1997. Two-acre **Gantry Plaza State Park** (1998) is named for the two historic gantry float bridges, huge black iron structures that once loaded railroad freight cars onto barges. The park has two piers (one will eventually accommodate ferry traffic), spectacular views of Manhattan, a "mist" fountain, a plaza for musical performances, and quirky carved wooden benches.

Old Calvary Cemetery

South of Long Island City is Old Calvary Cemetery (bounded to the north by the Long Island Expwy, to the east by Laurel Hill Blvd, to the south by Review Ave, and to the west by Greenpoint Ave). The Roman Catholic Archdiocese of New York purchased 115 acres of former farmland in 1845 from the Alsop family, whose burying ground with monuments dating back to 1743 survives inside the cemetery. The first Calvary interment was in 1848; burials were originally reserved for poor Irish immigrants from Manhattan.

Who's Who in Old Calvary Cemetery

Among the famous interred here are baseball Hall of Famer "Wee Willie" Keeler (1872–1923), remembered for his strategy "Hit 'em where they ain't"; Governor Alfred E. Smith (1873–1944); Tess Gardella, who portrayed "Aunt Jemima" in television commercials; and Joseph Petrosino, an Italian immigrant who became the New York Police Department's first Italian American detective. Petrosino tirelessly fought the Italian crime organization, the Black Hand. But in 1909, on an investigative trip to Palermo, Italy, the detective was gunned down, making him the only NYPD officer killed in the line of duty outside the United States. More than 200,000 people attended his funeral.

Also noteworthy in the cemetery are a **chapel** (1895) off Review Ave, whose dome imitates that of Sacre Coeur in Paris, and the Queen Anne–style **gatehouse** (1892) at the Greenpoint Ave entrance, opposite Gale St, decorated with inlaid leaves and flowers. Old Calvary Cemetery sits atop a hill, straddles the busy Brooklyn-Queens Expwy, and is as densely packed as Manhattan, which looms in the near distance. Together with what is sometimes called New Calvary Cemetery, an additional 250 acres in nearby Woodside, the graveyard contains more than 3 million people, exceeding any other cemetery in the United States.

Long Island City Proper and Dutch Kills

North of Hunter's Point, around the bridge approaches, is Long Island City proper and Dutch Kills, an area of railroad yards and factories (old and recycled) and a hub of transportation. The **Queensboro Bridge** (1909; Gustav Lindenthal, engineer; DL) sweeps overhead at 41st Rd, linking Queens to 59th-60th Sts in Manhattan. Just north of the bridge, (Vernon Blvd to 21st St, Fortieth Ave to Bridge Plaza) are the **Queensbridge Houses** (1939; William F. R. Ballard, chief architect), once the largest public housing project in the nation (3,161 apartments in 26 buildings on 62.5 acres).

Much of the area is zoned industrial, including the Silvercup Studios, which with Kaufman-Astoria Studios in Astoria and two other smaller studios, has two-thirds of the city's film and television space. The latest addition is Silvercup Studios East, on Starr Ave between Greenpoint and Borden Aves, about a mile from their present studios near the Queensboro Bridge. It includes five new drive-on studios, each with approximately 16,000 square ft of space.

Points of Interest

Embedded in the ground on a concrete triangle on **Queens Plaza North** are two **mill stones** that were brought over from Holland in 1650, the oldest European artifacts in the borough. They were used in a mill in Queens that dated back to the 17C and was powered by a sluice paralleling Northern Blvd. The Long Island Rail Road razed the mill in 1861; the stones were installed here near the bridge entrance and across from a bank in 1920. The stones, 4½ ft high and 6 inches thick, will soon be lifted out of the ground and incorporated into the centerpiece of a new garden here.

Not far from the foot of the bridge is a group of rehabilitated industrial buildings, intended as part of an 1980s rejuvenation. The project, the **International Design Center** (1985; I. M. Pei & Partners, master plan), was intended to create a complex of showrooms for the design and furniture industries in such former factories as the **Adams Gum Building** (1919; Ballinger and Perot), at 30-30 Thomson Ave (between 30th Place and 31st St), home of Chiclets and Dentyne; the **American Eveready Battery factory** (1914); and the **Loose-Wiles Sunshine Bakery** (1914; William Higginson). After the market for corporate furniture collapsed following the 1987 stock market crash, the soaring atriums and low-rent showrooms sat empty. Today the 400,000-square-ft space is leased as offices and to the DeVry Institute of Technology, a local trade school.

MoMA QNS (The Museum of Modern Art, in Queens)

45-20 33rd St (at Queens Blvd), Long Island City, NY 11101. ☎ (212) 708-9400 for information and hours. Web site: www.moma.org.

Subway: Flushing Local (7) to 33rd St.

Car: Take lower level of Queensboro Bridge to Queens; follow signs to Queens Blvd (Rte 25). Turn right on Van Dam St and left on Forty-seventh Ave. Turn left again on 33rd St. The entrance is on the left between Queens Blvd and Forty-seventh Ave. Parking lot (fee) at the Factory Building (Forty-seventh Ave at 31st St), also metered street parking.

In 1999 the Museum of Modern Art bought a former Swingline staple factory, the Leemar Building (c. 1950), and beginning in 2002 the factory, renovated and redesigned, will take on new life as MoMA QNS, an exhibition and storage space for the museum. Masterpieces from MoMA's permanent collection, including Vincent Van Gogh's *The Starry Night,* Pablo Picasso's *Les Demoiselles d'Avignon,* and Andy Warhol's *Gold Marilyn Monroe,* will be shipped across the river for installation at MoMA QNS, which will also mount traveling exhibitions.

The former factory will remain the main exhibition space of the Museum of Modern Art until late 2004, while the museum's 53rd St home undergoes a major expansion. When the expansion is finished, MoMA QNS will house the museum's archives, some of its library collections, and its collection of film stills.

Michael Maltzan Architecture of Los Angeles is designing the entrance and galleries, while Cooper, Robertson and Partners of New York will oversee the whole project, creating state-of-the-art offices, study centers, and workshops where heavy machinery once turned out miles and miles of little wire staples.

Ravenswood

Ravenswood is the neighborhood of Long Island City lying along the East River north of the Queensboro Bridge. Big Allis (the Con Ed generator familiar from Manhattan's East Side), public housing including the Ravenswood Houses, and some new waterside enterprises mark the area.

Points of Interest

Isamu Noguchi Garden Museum

32-37 Vernon Blvd (at 10th St), Long Island City, NY 11106. Entrance on Thirty-third Rd near 11th St. ☎ (718) 721-1932. Web site: www.noguchi.org. Open April–Oct including holidays; Wed, Thurs, and Fri 10–5; Sat and Sun 11–6. Suggested contribution. Accessible to wheelchairs. Changing exhibitions, films, educational programs. Gift shop. Café. Free guided tours 2 P.M. daily.

Subway: Broadway Local (N) to Broadway (in Queens). Exit at Broadway and 31st St; walk west on Broadway (toward Manhattan). Broadway ends at Vernon Blvd; turn left on Vernon and continue for two blocks.

Bus: Take the Steinway Transit Q101 (not the bus labeled "Rikers Island") from E. 59th St and Second Ave on the south side of the Queensboro Bridge and ask for a transfer. At Broadway and Steinway St in Queens, transfer to the Q104. Get off at Thirty-second Ave and Vernon Blvd. For more information, call Steinway Transit: ☎ (718) 445-3100. For information about shuttle bus service from Manhattan, ☎ (718) 721-1932. For the weekend Queens Artlink shuttle, see P.S. 1 Contemporary Art Center.

Car: From Manhattan, take the lower level on the Queensboro Bridge and exit right at 25A (Jackson Ave). Make a right at the first light and turn onto 27th St.

Drive two blocks to Forty-third Ave and turn right. Forty-third Ave ends at Vernon Blvd. Turn right onto Vernon Blvd and continue for a mile and a half.

The Isamu Noguchi Garden Museum (1985; Shogi Sazao), created by Noguchi himself, exhibits more than 250 works by this Japanese American sculptor, who died in 1988.

Installed in a former photoengraving factory, this small museum, with its 13 galleries and outdoor sculpture garden, shows the span of Noguchi's work. Featured are examples of his basalt-and-granite stone sculpture, geometric steel works, and polished marble forms. There are also models of public sculpture, set designs, and a gallery of early work. A sense of tranquillity pervades the garden, with its stone sculpture, trickling fountain, and carefully placed trees.

Socrates Sculpture Park

31-29 Vernon Blvd (at Broadway), Long Island City, NY 11106. (Mailing address: P.O. Box 6259, Long Island City, NY 11106.) ☎ (718) 956-1819. Web site: www.socratessculpturepark.org. Open daily 10–dusk. Free. Sculptures are installed in an open field. Gift shop; catalogs. Accessible to wheelchairs.

Bus: Same as for Isamu Noguchi Garden Museum, but get off at Broadway and Vernon Blvd.

Nearby is Socrates Sculpture Park, located in a windswept field facing the East River. Dedicated to the philosopher who dedicated himself to the search for truth, it is one of the few places in New York to see large-scale outdoor sculptures, and probably the only place to see them actually being constructed. The 4.5-acre waterfront site is striking—remote, a little wild, and exposed.

Bordering and crisscrossing the park are walls and walkways. The rocks by the waterside near the remains of pilings surrounding the old slip have been brightly painted by Anthe Zacharias. Changing exhibitions by well-known and emerging sculptors are mounted in the spring and fall. Much of the work is created on-site, so visitors can watch art in process. Children are encouraged to touch, climb, and explore.

From Garbage Dump to Sculpture Park

Formerly a marine terminal, then an abandoned lot filled with garbage and rubble that took about a year to clear, the park was leased in 1986 from the city and developed by Mark di Suvero, whose studio was nearby, and other sculptors. Although a developer had hoped to build a marina and luxury apartments here, the city designated Socrates a permanent park in 1998.

Astoria

Subway: Broadway Local (N) to Astoria Blvd–Hoyt Ave.

Car: Take Queensboro Bridge to Northern Blvd; turn left (north) at 31st St in Queens and follow it north to Ditmars Blvd. Or take the Triborough Bridge to 31st St and turn left (north) to Ditmars Blvd.

Parking: Difficult, especially on weekends; there is a municipal lot on 33rd St, south of Ditmars Blvd.

North of Long Island City proper and just across the East River from Ward's and Randall's Islands is Astoria, a solid working- and middle-class community. First known for its association with the Steinway piano company and later for its Greek population, today Astoria is more diverse.

History

Formerly known as Hallett's Cove, after William Hallett, to whom Governor Peter Stuyvesant granted a patent for 1,500 acres in 1654, Astoria got its present name in 1839 when it was incorporated as a town. The name was accepted despite the bitter opposition of John Jacob Astor's local detractors. Local fur trader Stephen Halsey had hoped Astor would pour money into the community if it took his name, but the multimillionaire only dished out $500 to a local women's seminary.

The town grew as a suburb after a steam ferry began crossings to Manhattan, and during the 1840s it became the center of a thriving shipping business, some of whose entrepreneurs traded in exotic woods. Successful shippers built their mansions along the waterfront, though none has survived. German immigrants, many of them farmers, settled in the area.

In the 1870s, William Steinway, the son of a German immigrant piano maker, bought 400 acres of farmland in Long Island City and then built a piano factory and a factory village with a church, library, kindergarten, and trolley line, establishing the community of Steinway.

Active in community affairs, Steinway, along with brewer George Ehret, founded the North Beach Amusement Park. The beach resort lasted from 1886 until Prohibition in 1919. After World War I, Astoria played a pivotal role in the development of the film industry, with the pioneering Famous Players Film Co. opening here in 1919.

Beginning around that time, Italians became the largest presence in Astoria. But after immigration laws were relaxed in 1965, Greeks began pouring in. Although Italian Americans still maintain numerical superiority, Astoria became known as the city's largest Greek enclave as immigrants transformed empty storefronts into restaurants, bakeries, and nightclubs.

While the flavor of the shopping district is still distinctly Greek, the neighborhood demographics have been shifting again. Many second-generation Greek Americans are moving to Bayside, Flushing, Whitestone, and Long Island. Astoria's Greek population dropped 20 percent from 1980 to 1990 and continues downward, while Bangladeshis, Albanians, Indians, Irish, Egyptians, and others move in. Many of the remaining Greeks are elderly; many speak little English and maintain strong ties to their community and churches.

Points of Interest

To get a feeling for the neighborhood, walk along one of the commercial strips: Thirtieth Ave, 31st St, Ditmars Blvd, or Steinway St. Among the numerous Greek restaurants, pastry shops, and markets are **Greek House Foods** (32-22 Thirtieth Ave), **Kalamata Market** (38-01 Ditmars Blvd), and **Titan** (25-56 31th Street), perhaps the largest Greek supermarket in the country.

At Thirtieth Ave between 29th and 30th Sts is **Athens Square Park** (Stamatios P. Lykos), which since 1990 has been transformed from a playground into a neighborhood gathering place with artifacts honoring Greek culture. While the park still has a basketball court and playground, it also has an amphitheater and a bronze statue of the philosopher **Socrates** (1993; Anthony Frudakis), sitting on a granite base as if engaged in dialogue. In 1996 three granite fluted Doric columns were installed near the amphitheater in a manner that suggests the Tholos of Athena Pronaia in Delphi, a circular building that serves as the gateway to the Temple of Apollo. In 1998, the park received from Demetris Avramopoulos, the mayor of Athens, a bronze replica (Stavros Georgopoulos and Spiro Goggakis) of the **Piraeus Athena,** a 4C B.C. statue of the goddess discovered in 1959 and now in the Archaeological Museum of Piraeus.

Astoria Park, bounded by Shore Blvd, 19th St, Astoria Park South, and Ditmars Blvd, was developed as a WPA project in the 1930s during the construction of the Triborough Bridge. The facilities include playing fields, tennis courts, and an Olympic-size swimming pool. In summer, area residents wait in long lines stretching several blocks to get into the pool. The bridge is a huge presence, its abutments looming large and casting shadows; there are abutments from the Hell Gate Bridge in the park's northern section.

The **Remsen House** (1835), 9-26 Twenty-seventh Ave (southwest corner of 12th St), in a shabby neighborhood, survives from the period when Hallett's Point, a bulbous peninsula protruding into the East River just south of Astoria Park, was a fashionable summer colony with grand houses. Once handsome, this Greek revival house still has its pilastered doorway, tall parlor-floor windows, and iron fence.

Across the street is the former **Doctor Wayt House** (1845), 9-29 27th Ave (northwest corner of 12th St), an Italianate mansion once grander but now being restored. In poor condition is the two-story colonnaded former **Robert Benner House** (1852), at 25-37 14th St (between Astoria Park South and Twenty-sixth Ave).

The city's lone surviving old-time beer garden is **Bohemian Hall,** at 29-19 Twenty-fourth Ave (near 29th St), a reminder of the first half of the 20C when thousands of Czech and Slovak immigrants settled here. Today part of the Czech Republic, Bohemia belonged to the Austro-Hungarian Empire before World War I. The Bohemian Citizens Benevolent Society, which founded the hall in 1910 as a schoolhouse and added the 125 ft × 110 ft beer garden in 1919, still runs the hall and garden. Today ethnic groups rent it for weekend festivals: Czechs and Slovaks (of whom several thousand remain in Astoria), Cubans, Greeks, and even Bangladeshi local societies all take a turn. The season ends with an Oktoberfest.

The First Xerox

On Oct 22, 1938, in a small lab behind a beauty salon in an unremarkable building at **37-02 Broadway,** Chester Carlson, a physicist turned patent lawyer, duplicated a printed page that read "10-22-38 Astoria." It was the first image ever photocopied, the original Xerox. Carlson hawked his new product to 20 companies, including IBM, Kodak, RCA, and General Electric, all of whom declined. In 1944 he persuaded a nonprofit research institute in Ohio to develop his invention. The term *xerography* was coined by a professor of classical languages who put together the ancient Greek words for "dry" *(xeros)* and "writing" *(graphos).* In 1947 the Haloid Company, a maker of photographic paper, made a deal with Carlson for the commercial rights and in 1958 introduced the first office copier. In 1961 Haloid changed its name to Xerox, and Carlson ultimately reaped a fortune.

St. Irene Chrysovalantou Greek Orthodox Cathedral, 36-07 Twenty-third Ave, is home to the weeping icon of St. Irene, Greek Orthodox patron saint of peace and of the sick. The icon attracted international attention in 1991 when it reportedly shed tears. Thousands came to see the saint, who is said to have healing powers. Not long afterward, the small portrait of St. Irene, painted by a Greek monk in 1919 and encased in a bejeweled frame, was stolen by four armed intruders. Five days later, the image was returned to the church by mail, its frame removed.

In the days before Hollywood became the nexus of the American film industry, the **Famous Players–Lasky Corporation** on Thirty-fifth Ave (stretching from 34th to 38th Sts) was one of the nation's first major studios. More than 110 silent movies were made at the 13-building complex and stars such as Gloria Swanson, Maurice Chevalier, Paul Robeson, the Marx Brothers, and Rudolf Valentino worked here. The company later became a part of Paramount Pictures. When films moved west, the complex became the Eastern Service Studios, its facilities devoted to educational and comic shorts. During World War II, the U.S. Army took over the property, turning out training films and propaganda. After the government abandoned the property in 1971, the Astoria Motion Picture and Television Foundation was formed to restore the studios. Developmental rights went to George Kaufman, who renovated eight sound stages and renamed them the Kaufman Astoria Studios. Today, this is the biggest, most successful studio outside of Hollywood. In 1999, the studio began building its seventh sound stage, an 18,000-square-ft facility on 36th St, between Thirty-fourth and Thirty-fifth Aves.

American Museum of the Moving Image

Thirty-fifth Ave at 36th St, Astoria, Queens, NY 11106. ☎ (718) 784-0077. To reach a live person, ☎ (718) 784-4520. Web site: www.ammi.org. Open Tues–Fri 12–5; Sat and Sun 11–6. Screenings Sat–Sun 6:30. Admission charge. Lectures, screenings, changing exhibitions, tours. Gift shop. Café. Accessible to wheelchairs.

Subway: Broadway Local (N) train to Broadway (in Queens). Walk east to 36th St; turn right and walk two blocks to Thirty-fifth Ave. Or Broadway Local (R) to Steinway St. Use the Thirty-fourth Ave exit near end of train. Walk south on Steinway St; turn right on Thirty-fifth Ave. Continue 2½ blocks to museum entrance.

Bus: Steinway Transit Q101 (not the bus labeled "Rikers Island") departs from E. 59th St and Second Ave in Manhattan. Get off at Thirty-fifth Ave in Astoria and walk west on Thirty-fifth Ave. For the weekend Queens Artlink shuttle, see P.S. 1 Contemporary Art Center.

The Astoria Motion Picture and Television Foundation also operates the American Museum of the Moving Image, three floors of exhibition space devoted to the history and art of movies.

The collection of 80,000 film and video artifacts, the largest such private collection in the country, includes oddities such as the jowls Marlon Brando wore in *The Godfather,* a *Bride of Frankenstein* wig, and a *Get Smart* lunchbox. The museum also has cameras, props, fan magazines, reassembled movie sets, and commissioned works of art, including *Tut's Fever Movie Palace,* an installation by Red Grooms and Lysiane Luong. Film screenings and retrospectives take place in its 200-seat theater.

Steinway

East of Astoria lies Steinway, developed by piano manufacturer William Steinway, who moved his factory from Park Ave and 53rd St in Manhattan to a 400-
acre site along Bowery Bay in 1872, surrounding it with a company town that
included a park, library, ball fields, a kindergarten, and some row houses that still
stand. Steinway was attracted by the availability of land and lumber in Queens,
but he also chose this then-isolated spot to remove his workers from the influence of union organizers.

Points of Interest

The **Steinway & Sons factory** is still at the northwest corner of Nineteenth Ave
and Steinway Place. A master cabinetmaker, Henry Engelhard Steinway made
his first piano in his Seesen, Germany, home. After immigrating to the United
States, he opened his first piano factory in 1853. The first piano produced there
belongs to the collection of the Metropolitan Museum of Art. Today, this factory,
as well as one in Hamburg, Germany, crafts thousands of pianos. In 1995 the
piano company merged with Selmer, a maker of band instruments, and is now
known as Steinway Musical Instruments. For information about public tours, ☎
(718) 721-2600.

The former **Steinway Company Housing** (c. 1880), a stretch of Victorian
brick row houses, remains on Twentieth Ave (between Steinway and 42nd Sts)
and 41st St (between Twentieth Ave and 20th Rd). Stone nameplates bearing the
names Albert, Theodore, and Winthrop are embedded in corner houses, remaining from the days when the streets were named for Steinway family members.

The **Lent Homestead** (c. 1729; DL), 78-03 19th Rd (at 78th St), is the second-
oldest dwelling in Queens, a Dutch-style farmhouse of fieldstone with hewn timbers and shingles, built by Abraham Lent, grandson of Abraham Riker, whose
family once owned Rikers Island. Hidden behind trees and vines, the house has
been handsomely modernized, though the shingles and original timbers at one
end and the shape of the large, dormered, overhanging Dutch roof remain to tes-
tify to its antiquity.

At 20th Rd and 35th St is the **Lawrence Cemetery** (DL), where the remains
of 89 Lawrence family members reside, including 12 high-ranking military officers and seven members who held government posts. The earliest grave is that of
Maj. Thomas Lawrence (died 1703); the last belongs to Oliver Lawrence, buried
in 1975.

The **Steinway Mansion** (c. 1858; DL) survives at 18-33 41st St (between
Berrian Blvd and Nineteenth Ave), on a hill overlooking the East River. Benjamin
Pike, an optician, built the Italianate villa for himself, with rough stonework, romantically asymmetric bays, arcades, and towers. William Steinway bought it in
1870. Once graced by lawns, tennis courts, orchards, and stables, it now stands
obscured by trees in a rather sinister neighborhood whose tone is established by
a sewage treatment plant, some junkyards, and ferocious guard dogs. It is privately owned.

Nearby, at the intersection of Nineteenth Ave and Hazen St, is the bridge (1966)
to **Rikers Island,** politically part of the Bronx but joined to Queens by this bridge
(not accessible to the public). On the island are ten city penal institutions with a
total population of more than 16,000. Built in 1935 to replace the old Welfare
(now Roosevelt) Island prison, it was heralded as a model penitentiary, but today

it is obsolete and the subject of controversy. The island at low tide lies only about 100 ft from the runways of LaGuardia Airport and historically had relied for security on the currents and tides of the river. Today, armed guards and barbed wire fences provided needed security. The island is named after Abraham Rycken (later spelled Riker) and his descendants, who owned it for generations after 1664.

Near Rikers Island is **North Brother Island,** site of the former Riverside Hospital for communicable diseases, whose most famous resident was "Typhoid Mary" Mallon, a cook who unknowingly communicated the disease, probably starting several epidemics. The burning excursion steamer, the *General Slocum,* beached here in 1904, but not before more than a thousand passengers had lost their lives, most of them women and children on an outing from the Tompkins Square neighborhood of the Lower East Side. **South Brother Island,** also part of the Bronx, is about seven uninhabited acres.

Sunnyside

Sunnyside, a modest residential community centered around the intersection of Roosevelt Ave and Queens Blvd, is hemmed in by cemeteries, industrial zones, and the former Sunnyside Yards of the Pennsylvania Railroad. The community has a large population of Colombian, Ecuadorian, Korean, Chinese, Indian, Romanian, and Irish immigrants, many of the latter spilling over from Woodside. The fringes of the neighborhood, near the railyards and cemeteries, are plagued by drug-dealing and crime, while tidy Sunnyside Gardens boasts a members-only park.

Sunnyside Gardens (1924; Henry Wright, Clarence Stein, and Frederick Ackerman), bounded by Skillman and Thirty-ninth Aves, from 43rd to 50th Sts, is a community of detached homes and small apartment buildings, an early and successful experiment in urban planning undertaken by a limited-profit agency that developed these 70 acres of unpromising land during the boom years of the 1920s. It was one of America's first planned garden communities, with jointly owned and maintained homes for working-class residents. During the Depression, First Lady Eleanor Roosevelt led a protest march to help save homes from foreclosure. Although some women barricaded themselves in or chained themselves to the porches, more than half the residents lost their homes during the 1930s. Later, during the white flight of the 1960s, many established families left and poorer newcomers replaced them. The sense of unity suffered when the original deed restrictions expired in the 1960s and some residents fenced in their yards while others cut through the original curbs to build driveways.

The social centerpiece of Sunnyside Gardens is a 3.5-acre park, one of two members-only parks in the city. (The other is Gramercy Park in Manhattan.) The park was established in 1926 and is run by the Sunnyside Gardens Community Association, a private trust that collects yearly membership dues from residents. Unlike quiet and refined Gramercy Park, this park is geared toward family fun, with tennis courts, basketball courts, a wading pool, and a picnic area.

The **Sunnyside railyards** (between Skillman and Jackson Aves) opened in 1910, along with a tunnel beneath the East River to Pennsylvania Station that allowed direct train travel from New England to New York for the first time. Today lines leading into the yards accommodate the trains of Metro-North, a commuter and freight line to points north and east, the Long Island Rail Road, and Amtrak, the long-distance national railroad. The yards may eventually accommodate a

Long Island Rail Road station that will enable Queens residents to commute to the East Side of Manhattan.

Woodside

Woodside, northeast of Sunnyside, is a lower-middle-class residential community developed after 1917, when the Flushing line of the IRT put it within minutes of Manhattan. Long called Irishtown, the neighborhood began welcoming middle-class Korean, Chinese, and other immigrants in the 1980s. However, in the 1990s, changes in the visa lottery system encouraged immigration from European countries, including Ireland and Poland, and from 1990 through 1996 more Irish settled in Woodside than in any other neighborhood in the city.

51 · Central Queens: Jackson Heights, East Elmhurst, Maspeth, Ridgewood, Corona, Elmhurst, Forest Hills, Kew Gardens, and Rego Park

The first settlement in central Queens was Middleburgh (1652), between Maspeth and Flushing, established by English settlers with the permission of Peter Stuyvesant, then the Dutch governor of the colony. Many of the English referred to their town as "the new town," New Town, or NewTown, to distinguish it from an earlier settlement to the west that had been abandoned in 1644 after attacks by Native Americans. In 1683, the English, who had taken the colony from the Dutch in 1664, established Queens County and divided it into three large governing districts: the towns of Newtown, Flushing, and Jamaica. Newtown's original boundaries encompassed the modern communities of Jackson Heights, Corona, Elmhurst, Forest Hills, Maspeth, Ridgewood, and Rego Park, which range economically from the exclusivity of Forest Hills Gardens to the industrial blight and economic depression of parts of Ridgewood and Maspeth.

Jackson Heights

Subway: Flushing Local (7) train to 82nd St–Jackson Heights. From the subway stop, walk west along Roosevelt Ave to 80th St; turn right and walk north past Thirty-seventh Ave to the Greystone Apartments.

Car: Take the Queensboro Bridge; the ramp off the bridge becomes Queens Blvd (exit 25); exit left onto Northern Blvd (exit 25A) and follow it east to 80th St. Turn right (south) and continue to 35th Ave.

Jackson Heights lies east of Long Island City and between Astoria Blvd and Roosevelt Ave. Some of the nation's first garden apartments and first middle-class cooperatives were built here, most of them within the Jackson Heights Historic District, which runs about from 76th to 88th Sts and from Roosevelt Ave to Northern Blvd. Today the neighborhood remains a quiet, well-kept community with neat gardens, courtyards, and other green space. It is named after John C. Jackson, president of the Hunters Point and Flushing Turnpike Company, which built Jackson Ave (now Northern Blvd).

History

Once rural, the region was known as Train Meadows and nicknamed "the corn-fields of Queens," when 350 acres of it were bought by a consortium of investors, eventually headed by Edward A. MacDougall and called the Queensboro Corporation. MacDougall's planned community would capitalize on its proximity to Manhattan, particularly after the opening of the Queensboro Bridge in 1909 and an elevated subway eight years later. The buildings were designed largely by two architects, George H. Wells and, more notably, self-taught Andrew J. Thomas, who grew up in a tenement and started his architectural career building tenements. One of Thomas's innovations was to use the full city block as his design unit, constructing low-rise buildings set back from the lot line and occupying only 30 to 50 percent of the lot, allowing for front gardens and spacious interior courtyards that provide light, air, and a suburban feel.

The neighborhood was marketed as a "restricted" community for people of modest means, so long as they were not Jewish, black, or Catholic. The Queensboro Corporation built a community clubhouse, playgrounds, tennis courts, and a golf course; it published the *Jackson Heights News* and donated land for churches.

After World War I, with housing in short supply and rents high, the Queensboro Corporation introduced tenant-ownership (i.e., cooperative apartments). The concept, usually reserved for the wealthy, made the development attractive to home buyers and provided the capital to continue building. (In the 1920s, the company also built private homes.) Beginning with the construction of Linden Court (1919), designed by Thomas, buildings became more elegant, until the mid-1920s, when their cost made them prohibitive.

Soon some of the apartments were converted to rentals and divided; the corporation started selling property to outside developers, and buildings from this era feature minimal ornamentation and less regard for open space. Queensboro itself even built on the golf course it had previously provided. After World War II, Robert Moses attempted to build public housing in Jackson Heights without holding public hearings. The community, furious at the thought of institutional housing intruding upon their planned community, banded together to hand Moses one of his rare defeats.

Without MacDougall, who died in 1944, Queensboro lost sight of its original vision. In response to the city's housing shortage, the corporation constructed 38 apartment houses in 1950 alone, which displaced gardens, trees, and tennis courts. These new buildings changed the neighborhood's character—the increased density drove many old-timers to the suburbs, and a Supreme Court decision of 1947 against advertising for "restricted" neighborhoods forced Queensboro to accept those it had formerly rejected to fill vacancies. Many Jewish and Catholic families moved in. In recent decades, they have been gradually replaced by Peruvians, Colombians, Mexicans, Argentinians, Chinese, and, especially, Indians. Indian restaurants, jewelry stores, and sari shops began blossoming on 74th St—Little India—in the 1980s. The most renowned restaurant is the **Jackson Diner,** formerly in a converted diner, now in a funky, postmodern venue at 37-74 74th St (between Roosevelt and Thirty-seventh Aves).

More recently, Ecuadorians, Dominicans, and more Colombians joined the mix, arriving in numbers equal to those from Bangladesh and India. From 1990 to 1996, 12 percent of the city's 15,859 new Colombians settled here. Manhattanites seeking more space for less money have also discovered the neighborhood. In 1988, local citizens founded the Jackson Heights Beautification Group and lobbied for the historic district designation. It continues fighting to preserve the neighborhood's historical and aesthetic integrity, which has been particularly challenging on the commercial streets.

Begin at 35-15 80th St (between Thirty-fifth and Thirty-seventh Aves), the site of Jackson Heights's first major project, the **Greystone Apartments** (1917; George Wells). Built in English Gothic style, these 14 five-story limestone and gray brick buildings were originally named the Garden Apartments, but by 1925 the term *garden apartments* had become generic and the complex was renamed. Ironically, Greystone is not truly a garden-apartment complex because although each individual building has a garden, there is no central interior garden.

Continue south to Thirty-seventh Ave and turn left, walking east to 82nd St. Turn right. At 37-06 82nd St is a Jamaica Savings Bank in the original **Queensboro Corporation headquarters** (1929; Morrell Smith), a stylish three-story, neo-Tudor building that was outfitted with fireplaces, exposed beam ceilings, and a squash court in the basement. (Much of the rest of the block's commercial space was designed in a similarly charming Anglo style and called English Gables.) Queensboro moved during the Depression, leasing the space to a drugstore in 1934. The signs on the present bank are out-of-character with the original architecture.

Return to Thirty-seventh Ave and turn right, then right again on 85th St. **Linden Court** (1919; Andrew Thomas) occupies the west side of the block as well as the east side of 84th St. It was Jackson Heights's first co-op, its first genuine garden apartments (a central garden runs the length of the block between the buildings), the first garden-apartment group on an urban block designed as a single unit, and one of the city's first apartments to include driveways and garages.

Across the street is the block-long **Cambridge Court** (early 1920s; Andrew Wells), built after Linden Court with a more stylish mansard roof and dormer windows. The building covers only 35 percent of the lot; the rest was green space, until 1990, when much of it was paved for a parking lot. During the Depression the Queensboro Corporation realized that people could not afford seven-room apartments and divided many of the units into two- and three-room suites, which were then converted to rentals.

Walk north on 85th St, crossing Thirty-seventh Ave. **Roosevelt Terrace** (1954; Philip Birnbaum), 35-11 85th St, 35-31 85th St, and 35-50 85th St, symbolizes the destruction of MacDougall's original vision. The Queensboro Corporation sold the site, originally a playground, to a private developer, who built this plain, nine-story building, Jackson Heights's tallest.

Return to Thirty-seventh Ave and walk east to 87th St. Turn left. By the 1920s, the increasingly ambitious building designs were pushing prices to levels where the only people who could afford the apartments would prefer living in private houses. While these slate-roofed, English garden–style homes with dormer windows (C. F. and D. E. McAvoy) are unified in groups of two to five houses, they also boast individuality in their varying roof lines and entryways. The Queensboro

Corporation, using various architects, eventually filled more than 15 blocks with these houses (most between 70th and 90th Sts, Thirty-fourth Ave and Northern Blvd). The houses cost from $20,000 to $38,500 in an era when a typical Queens home went for under $15,000. By 1929, the value of Jackson Heights land had soared so high that single-family homes ceased being feasible and Queensboro focused on apartments again.

Continue north to Thirty-fifth Ave, then turn left. Walk west to 82nd St. The **Community Church** (1923; F. P. Platt Brothers), at 35th Ave and 82nd St, is notable mainly for being the site where architect Alfred Mosher Butts, unemployed during the Depression, developed a board game he called Criss-Crosswords (hand-drawn with his architectural drafting equipment) that later (1940) evolved into **Scrabble.**

Turn right and walk north to 82nd St. The **Colonial Apartments** (1915; George Wells), 34-31 to 34-51 82nd St, were built as rental space. In 1920 the building became one of the nation's first to convert to co-op apartments.

Continue north, crossing Thirty-fourth Ave. Just before Northern Blvd, at 33-05 to 33-21 82nd St, is **Laurel Court** (1914), Queensboro's first apartment building. It was built near Northern Blvd because it was then the only transportation artery. Surrounding the four five-story tan brick buildings were dirt roads and empty lots.

Return to Thirty-fourth Ave and turn right. On the north side of the street, between 82nd and 83rd Sts, is **Hayes Court** (1923; Andrew Thomas), a handsome building that may have been influenced by the Dakota apartment building in Manhattan. This was one of three smaller buildings erected as rentals when Queensboro realized many families could not afford their increasingly expensive co-ops.

Continue west to 81st St. On the south side of the street is **The Chateau** (1923; Andrew Thomas), an elaborate garden-apartment complex built like a French château, with slate mansard roofs and carved limestone entries. It was architect Thomas's warm-up for **The Towers** (1924; Andrew Thomas), easily the neighborhood's most ambitious and opulent complex. The eight six-story buildings (33-16 to 33-52 81st St and 33-15 to 33-51 80th St) have orange tile roofs with boldly projecting eaves and stone and terra-cotta trim. Griffins guard the gates, which lead into side gardens decorated with classical columns. Inside are marble hallways, oak parquet floors, and fireplaces. MacDougall himself moved from Flushing into a top-floor, 14-room duplex, which had views of Manhattan from the Battery to Hell Gate. A seventh-story penthouse served as rooftop apartments for family servants. Apartments in The Towers cost $18,000–25,000, more than most private homes, and even at those exorbitant prices the developers would have lost money. Although Queensboro hired architect Ernest Flagg (famous for the Singer Tower, mansions for the wealthy, and housing for the poor), to design a Georgian-style building even more luxurious than The Towers, the corporation was forced to drop the idea when it could not find buyers for The Towers. The financial failure of The Towers also prompted Queensboro to build more private homes and sell lots to outside developers.

Walk south down 80th St toward Thirty-fifth Ave. On the west side is **Elm Court** (1922; George Wells), the first apartment building in New York to use self-operated push-button elevators.

Continue one block west to **Dunnolly Gardens** (1939; Andrew Thomas), on the north side of Thirty-fifth Ave (between 78th and 79th Sts). Thomas's last

Jackson Heights apartment complex and the first one in a Moderne style, Dunnolly Gardens marked Queensboro's first block-long complex in 13 years. Mayor Fiorello La Guardia attended the dedication. It also signaled the beginning of the end of Queensboro's purist devotion to open space, since it was developed on the former golf course.

East Elmhurst

Across Astoria Blvd from Jackson Heights, in the shadow of LaGuardia Airport, is tiny East Elmhurst. Considered by some as simply an extension of Jackson Heights or Corona, it is dominated by hotel chains, car rental agencies, and other airport-related businesses along Ditmars Blvd.

East Elmhurst's side streets are lined mainly with single-family homes, most of which are owned by middle-class and upper-middle-class black families who have been in the neighborhood for many years. Past residents have included Ella Fitzgerald and Malcolm X, whose home was firebombed.

The **College of Aeronautics** is located on a six-acre site bounded by Ditmars Blvd, 90th St, and Twenty-third Ave. It moved here from Newark, New Jersey, in 1945 and offers degrees in aeronautics and aerospace-related fields: airplane maintenance, air traffic control, and airport management. Half the students come from Queens. (East Elmhurst also is home to P.S. 127, which offers programs related to aerospace. Nearby, in Long Island City, is Aviation High School, providing an educational continuum for students, many of whom find internships and ultimately jobs at LaGuardia.)

LaGuardia Airport

LaGuardia Airport, on Grand Central Pkwy bordering Flushing Bay and Bowery Bay, was the city's second municipal airfield after the economically unsuccessful Floyd Bennett Field in Brooklyn.

From Resort to Airport

In the 1880s William Steinway (pianos), George Ehret (beer), and Henry Cassebeer (patent medicines) developed the area between Bowery Bay and Flushing Bay as a resort called Bowery Bay Beach; the name was changed (1891) to North Beach when the Bowery in Manhattan picked up tawdry connotations. The amusement park (picnic tables, rides, dance halls) occupied the site until Prohibition took its toll. In 1929 it was converted to a private flying field, the Glenn H. Curtiss Airport. In 1934, Mayor Fiorello La Guardia was flying from Chicago to New York and refused to land at Newark Airport, then the biggest local airport, saying he had paid to be flown to New York. The mayor was taken to Floyd Bennett Field.

In 1937, using Works Progress Administration and city funds, La Guardia took over Curtiss Airport, renaming it North Beach Airport. It was enlarged by landfill and the purchase of additional property, and opened to commercial traffic in 1939. In 1947 the airport was leased to the Port Authority and renamed LaGuardia Airport, and in the 1960s it was modernized and expanded.

LaGuardia Terminal Buildings

Today the facility occupies more than 680 acres. The **Central Terminal Building** (1965; Harrison & Abramovitz) handles most scheduled airlines. The central section was revamped in the 1990s, while the east and west wings were totally rebuilt, a multimillion dollar project undertaken by the Port Authority to make the terminal resemble a consumer-friendly shopping mall filled with name-brand retailers.

The round Art Deco **Marine Air Terminal** (1939; Delano & Aldrich; DL), the original terminal, was built close to the water, where the "flying boats" landed. It is now used by commuter shuttles and other flights. In 1980, an indoor aviation mural, **Flight** (1942; James Brook), which had been painted over, was restored. In the 1990s, the terminal, decorated with a frieze of winged fish representing the Pan Am Clipper flying boats for which it was built, received a major overhaul.

Other terminals include the **Delta Air Lines Terminal** (1983), the **US Airways Shuttle Terminal** (formerly the Eastern Airlines Shuttle Terminal) (1981), and the newest one, the **US Airways Terminal,** opened in 1992.

Maspeth

Maspeth, a blue-collar neighborhood with small-town charms, owes much of its industrial development to Newtown Creek, an oily tidal arm of the East River. It lies east of the Brooklyn border and is bounded by the Brooklyn-Queens Expwy on the north and Metropolitan Ave on the south. Today, the western section remains largely industrial, but the northern part, cut off from the rest by the Brooklyn-Queens Expwy, has remained residential. Maspeth has two major cemeteries—Mt. Olivet and Mt. Zion, where there is a monument to the victims of the Triangle Shirtwaist factory fire.

History

The area was first settled in 1642 by the Reverend Francis Doughty, a New England minister, and his followers, who received a land grant from the Dutch. They were violently forced out by the indigenous Mespat people, who had long occupied the headwaters of Newtown Creek. De Witt Clinton (who later served as governor of New York State from 1817 to 1828) had a summer home at the headwaters of the creek, and here he planned the Erie Canal. The rural area turned industrial in the 19C, with smelly oil refineries, copper smelters, and rendering and carbon plants built near the creek, and rope factories further inland.

In the 1950s, Maspeth was bisected by the Long Island Expwy, which makes it inconvenient to drive from one side of town to the other.

Points of Interest

Maspeth Town Hall, 53-37 72nd St, was built in 1898 as the Binkerhoff School, named for one of the area's original settlers. The 1½-story wooden structure remained a school until 1932. During the Depression, it housed a girls' club and federal Works Progress Administration offices. From 1936 to 1971, it was the 112th Police Precinct. Twice abandoned, it was later saved by a coalition of local citizens, businesses, and government interests. Today it is a nonprofit community center offering cultural and recreational programs.

The former Episcopal **St. Saviour's Church, Parish Hall, and Rectory** (1848; Richard Upjohn), on Rust St (between 57th Rd and 57th Drive), occupies a beautifully wooded square block, a site incongruous with this primarily industrialized area of Maspeth. The church was damaged by fire in the 1970s. It closed in the early 1990s and was sold to San Sung Fortress, the Korean Methodist Church of New York (founded 1992). Today, the 19C rectory is boarded up.

Ridgewood

Named for its once-forested terrain, Ridgewood lies south of Maspeth and east of the Brooklyn border. In the 19C, Ridgewood attracted German homesteaders who grew tobacco, fruit, and grains. Later breweries, beer gardens, and knitting mills sprang up in the area, employing mostly German immigrants. To accommodate these workers, thousands of row houses were built between 1895 and 1920, many of them constructed with yellow brick from what was then Kreischerville (now Charleston) on Staten Island. The popular Mathews Model Flats, built by Gustave X. Mathews, were featured at the 1915 Panama-Pacific Exposition in San Francisco. Paul Stier built a similar development from 1908 to 1914. Competition from large national firms and rising land values eventually killed off the local beer business. In the 1930s, Germans were joined by Romanians, Italians, and Slovenes. More recently, eastern Europeans, particularly Romanians, Poles, and immigrants from the former Yugoslavia, have gradually replaced the dwindling population of Germans. The Welcome Inn, once a favorite German restaurant, is today a private Serbian club. Nearly 13 percent of New York's immigrants from the former Yugoslavia settled here between 1990 and 1996.

In the 1960s and 1970s the crime, drugs, and arson that plagued adjoining Bushwick in Brooklyn threatened to spread to Ridgewood. In 1979 Ridgewood voters changed the area's zip code from a Brooklyn to a Queens number, hoping to dissociate themselves from Bushwick, at least in the eyes of the post office. In 1983, about 3,000 row houses were named to the National Register of Historic Places, bringing a sense of pride to the community, which had been losing oldtime residents to Long Island. The neighborhood's commercial strip, Myrtle Ave, was hit hard by competition from large shopping malls in the late 1980s, leading to the closing of many mom-and-pop shops. In 1988, a business improvement district was formed to help fund security, sanitation, and storefront improvements.

Points of Interest

A particularly nice stretch of **historic row houses** (c. 1905; Louis Berger & Co.) is on Stockholm St between Onderdonk and Woodward Aves; even the street is paved with Kreischerville brick.

St. Aloysius Roman Catholic Church and Rectory (1907, 1917; Francis J. Berlenbach), 382 Onderdonk Ave, sits on a hill some 60 ft above sea level, with towers rising 165 ft. Founded in 1892, the neo-Renaissance church is the tallest structure in Ridgewood.

Vander Ende–Onderdonk House

18-20 Flushing Ave (between Cypress and Onderdonk Aves), Ridgewood, NY 11385. ☎ (718) 456-1776. Open Wed and Sat 2–4:30. Admission charge. Not accessible to wheelchairs. Gift shop. Guided house tours, lectures, videotape history programs, genealogy workshops, craft classes, special events.

Subway: 14th St–Canarsie Local (L) to Jefferson St. Walk five blocks north (right) along Flushing Ave to the museum.

Car: From north and east take Long Island Expwy to Woodhaven Blvd exit.

Turn right on Metropolitan Ave and bear left onto Flushing Ave (two blocks). From south and west, take Belt Pkwy to Cross Bay Blvd exit; go north along Cross Bay–Woodhaven Blvd to Metropolitan Ave and bear left onto Flushing Ave (two blocks). Parking lot available.

The area's only remaining Dutch farmhouse built of stone is the Vander Ende–Onderdonk House (1709; DL), at 1820 Flushing Ave, now a museum and home to the Greater Ridgewood Historical Society.

The house is named for two Dutch farming families who lived there—the Vander Endes beginning in the early 18C, the Onderdonks beginning about 1821. During the 20C, the house was used as a speakeasy and later as a factory for spare parts for the Apollo space program. It was abandoned in the 1970s and nearly destroyed by arson in 1975. That year the historical society was formed to save the house, whose stone walls and chimney had remained intact. In 1982, the gambrel-roofed home, now reconstructed, reopened to the public.

The museum features a room furnished in Victorian style as well as archaeological artifacts dug from the site, rotating exhibits, and an extensive reference library focusing on genealogy and local history.

Arbitration Rock, a car-sized chunk now on the grounds of the house, served as the starting point for an 18C survey that resolved property disputes by establishing the Brooklyn-Queens border.

Cemeteries of Queens (and nearby Brooklyn)

In Ridgewood, Glendale, Middle Village, and spilling over into Cypress Hills (Brooklyn) is a greenbelt of cemeteries, many of them small Jewish graveyards.

Machpelah Cemetery (1870s), 82-30 Cypress Hills St (in Glendale on the west side of the street, north of the Jackie Robinson Pkwy), is known for the grave site of the master magician **Harry Houdini** (Ehrich Weiss). Weiss, who died on Halloween (1926), spent much of his life exposing psychic and spiritual frauds. His wife, Wilhelmina Beatrice "Bess" Houdini (née Rahner), held seances for ten years after his death to prove Houdini's belief that it was impossible to return from the dead. Her name is also on Houdini's tomb, but the cemetery refused to bury her because she was Catholic. Bess is buried in Gate of Heaven Cemetery, in Hawthorne, New York. For decades, the Society of American Magicians paid tribute to the magician at his grave site, a highly publicized annual Halloween event that attracted large crowds. The grave site was eventually vandalized and a bust of Houdini smashed. Starting in the 1990s, the cemetery has prohibited the general public from visiting the site, but it still allows the magician's society to continue its "Broken Wand" ceremony once a year on an undisclosed date. With financial help provided by magician David Copperfield, the magicians have replaced Houdini's bust, which they bring to and from the grave site for their ceremony.

The actor Edward G. Robinson (Emmanuel Goldenberg) is buried in **Beth El Cemetery** (1864), just north of Machpelah, while Borscht Belt comic Henny Youngman and Yiddish writer Sholem Aleichem are buried in **Mount Carmel Cemetery** (1904), on the east side of Cypress Hills St. Poet Emma Lazarus, who wrote the "New Colossus" of Statue of Liberty fame, and Supreme Court Justice Benjamin Cardozo are both in **Beth Olom Cemetery** (1866), south of the Jackie Robinson Pkwy and west of Cypress Hills St.

The westernmost cemetery in this stretch is **Cemetery of the Evergreens**

(1849), beginning along Bushwick Ave in Brooklyn and extending to Cypress Ave in Queens. Buried here are the tap-dancing legend Bill "Bojangles" Robinson and jazz great Lester Young. Evergreens, as well as other nearby Jewish cemeteries, pays tribute to the victims of the 1911 Triangle Shirtwaist factory fire. Additional memorials here recall 5,000 indigent seamen from 28 nations (a marble monument topped by a globe; 1853) and forgotten actors designated by the Actors Fund Memorial (with its tall spire; 1887).

East of the Jewish cemeteries is **Cypress Hills Cemetery** (1848), 833 Jamaica Ave, the first nonsectarian cemetery corporation organized in Queens (actually it is two-thirds in Queens and one-third in Brooklyn). This is the final resting place of Jackie Robinson, whose simple stone reads, "A life is not important except in the impact it has on other lives." Here also are Mae West, boxer Jim Corbett, and Jewish engineer Leo Frank, who was wrongfully convicted of rape and murder in Georgia and then taken from jail and lynched in 1915 by anti-Semites.

Northeast of Cypress Hills Cemetery is Roman Catholic **St. John's Cemetery** (1880), 80-01 Metropolitan Ave, Middle Village. The bodybuilder Charles Atlas is buried amid a crowd of Mafia figures, including Salvatore "Lucky Luciano" Lucania and Salvatore Maranzano, who was murdered in his office in 1931 on orders of Lucky Luciano. Also interred here are Carmine Galante, Vito Genovese, Joseph Profaci, and Joe Colombo, head of the Colombo family from 1963 until 1978. He was shot in the head in 1971—supposedly on orders of Carlo Gambino, head of the Gambino family—and remained in a coma until his death. Gambino is also buried in St. John's, as is Wilfred "Willie Boy" Johnson, a Gambino associate and informer who refused to enter the witness protection program and was shot to death in front of his Brooklyn home.

West of St. John's Cemetery is the **Lutheran Cemetery,** founded in 1852 when St. Paul's German Lutheran Church in Manhattan bought 225 acres for a cemetery to serve Lower East Side immigrants of all faiths. Buried here are 1,021 victims of the excursion boat *General Slocum*, which burned and sank in the East River during an outing in 1904.

Corona

Settled in the 17C by Dutch and English farmers, Corona is now a densely populated residential community on the west side of Flushing Meadows–Corona Park and south of Flushing Bay.

History

Originally known as West Flushing, the area's rural landscape began to change with the building of the National Race Course (later named Fashion Race Course after a well-known horse), which operated from 1854 to 1866. Property for the racetrack had been bought from Samuel Willets, a devout Quaker and one of New York City's richest men. When he discovered the land would be used for racing and gambling, he tried to buy it back but failed.

In 1870, developer Benjamin W. Hitchcock bought a farm and subdivided land for development, advertising what he called Corona, or "crown of the hill," a workingman's paradise. The development included long-gone Shady Lake at 108th St and Corona Ave, which was enjoyed by the many Lower East Side immigrants—particularly Italians—who moved across the river for better conditions.

The former **Tiffany Studios factory,** at 96-13 Forty-third Ave, produced Tiffany lamps from 1893 to 1938. Here Louis Comfort Tiffany experimented with glass colors and pottery glazing and perfected techniques of assembling stained glass windows.

Corona's most famous resident, however, was Louis Armstrong, who despite his fame chose to live among small, one- and two-family homes from 1943 until his death in 1971.

Corona is the fictional home of *All in the Family,* a 1970s sitcom whose main character, Archie Bunker, was famous for his narrow-mindedness. At the time the area was absorbing an influx of Dominicans, Puerto Ricans, and Colombians as well as Asians, South Americans, East Indians, and Guyanese. Today the neighborhood, which has struggled with crime and drug-dealing, continues as a magnet for immigrants: from 1990 to 1996, Corona, along with neighboring Elmhurst and Flushing, became home to 54,000 new arrivals, most of them Dominican, Chinese, emigrés from the former Soviet Union, and Ecuadorians, but also Jamaicans, Indians, Colombians, and Peruvians. In 1999, the *Daily News* hailed the block bounded by 97th Place, Corona Ave, Forty-fifth Ave, and 97th St as the world's most ethnically diverse block, with immigrants or descendants of immigrants from Greece, Puerto Rico, India, China, Italy, Germany, England, the Dominican Republic, and elsewhere residing there. There is also a remnant of the earlier Italian American population, some of whom pass the time playing bocce at William Moore Park (108th St, Fifty-second and Corona Aves).

Also in Corona is **Lefrak City,** a 5,000-unit apartment complex at Junction Blvd and the Long Island Expwy. Proclaimed a "city within the city" and named for its innovative developer, Samuel J. Lefrak, it has 20 18-story towers and such amenities as security and a swimming pool. When it was built (1960–68), Lefrak City was a model of modern middle-income housing.

Points of Interest

The modest brick **Louis Armstrong House** (1910; Robert W. Johnson; DL), at 34-56 107th St, was the home of the famous jazz trumpeter from 1942 until his death in 1971. Born in New Orleans, Louis "Satchmo" Armstrong moved to New York in 1930. The house was clapboarded until Armstrong covered it in brick in 1970. Upon her death in 1983, Armstrong's wife, Lucille, willed the house to the city for a museum. The collection of hundreds of reel-to-reel tapes, scrapbooks, photographs, sheet music, and, of course, trumpets is administered by Queens College as part of its Louis Armstrong Archive. The college is working to open the house as a museum and educational center. For information, ☎ (718) 478-8274 or (718) 478-8299.

Louis Armstrong's Grave

Armstrong is buried nearby in Flushing Cemetery, 163-06 Forty-sixth Ave, his black marble stone (section 9, division A) decorated with a white trumpet.

The former **Edward E. Sanford** residence (1871; DL), at 102-45 Forty-seventh Ave (between 102nd and 104th Sts), is a rare survivor from the village of Newtown. This freestanding two-story frame house, surrounded by a detailed, white picket fence, is designed in a vernacular Italianate style with decorative porch.

When **Benfaremo,** "The Lemon Ice King of Corona," at 52-02 108th St, opened in 1944, it served only lemon ice. Today, the neighborhood institution churns out about 25 flavors and is considered by many aficionados to have the city's best ices. Open during warm months until midnight; ☎ (718) 699-5133.

Flushing Meadows–Corona Park

Subway: Flushing Local (7) to Willets Point–Shea Stadium, except for the Queens Wildlife Center and the Hall of Science, accessible via the same train to 111th St. Some organizations run shuttle buses from the subway.

Car: From the Long Island Expwy, take exit 22. From the Grand Central Pkwy, take exit 9-E to the park.

Flushing Meadows–Corona Park, girded by the Grand Central Pkwy and the Van Wyck Expwy, occupies 1,255 acres running north–south along what was once the Flushing River, a navigable waterway to the old town of Flushing. It is the borough's largest park, with acreage in both Corona and Flushing. Within its boundaries are the Queens Theatre in the Park, the Queens Museum of Art, the Queens Wildlife Center, the New York Hall of Science, the Queens Botanical Garden, the USTA National Tennis Center, Shea Stadium, an indoor ice skating rink, and a marina on Flushing Bay. The park also offers ballfields and picnic areas, as well as 124 acres of natural areas, including Meadow Lake, an 84-acre man-made, freshwater lake—the city's largest. For park information, ☎ (718) 760-6565.

From Dump to Park

Originally the land of Flushing Meadows was salt meadow, marshland inundated by tides, and therefore useless for housing. Saved thus from development, the marsh became the Corona Dump and the river an open sewer. By the 1920s train-loads of trash and garbage that arrived daily from Brooklyn smoldered nightly, giving the place a Dantesque aura and inspiring novelist F. Scott Fitzgerald to name it the Valley of Ashes in his novel *The Great Gatsby.* The swamp disappeared beneath tons of filth, one mound rising high enough to earn the name Mt. Corona.

In the 1930s Robert Moses, at the time commissioner of the city's parks, undertook a massive reclamation effort to convert the marsh into the grounds for the 1939–40 World's Fair. (The 1964–65 World's Fair also took place here.) The park, built on the site of the 1,200-acre fairgrounds, took about 30 years to create, a project that involved channeling part of the Flushing River into a conduit as large as a tube of the Holland Tunnel, building sewage plants to decontaminate Flushing Bay, and removing hundreds of thousands of tons of garbage.

Begin near the park's eastern edge, where the fair mall began, not far from the Van Wyck Expwy. While little remains from the 1939–40 World's Fair, there are notable survivors from the 1964–65 World's Fair, including Donald De Lue's 45 ft statue *The Rocket Thrower,* a modestly draped, heavily muscular bronze athlete hurling a missile through a circle of stars. On the lawn to the right is a statue of **George Washington** (1959) by the same sculptor. Straight down the mall is the **Unisphere** (1963–64; DL), 700,000 pounds of stainless steel, 12 stories high and 120 ft in diameter. As the centerpiece of the 1964–65 World's Fair, it was said to symbolize peace through understanding; today it is a symbol of the park and also of Queens.

Off to the left is the former **New York State Pavilion** (1964; Philip Johnson & Richard Foster), hailed for structural innovations when built for the fair; its concrete tubular columns originally supported two roofs, one above the other, sheathed in colored transparent plastic.

Queens Theatre in the Park

Flushing Meadows–Corona Park, Queens, NY 11368. ☎ (718) 760-0064. Web site: www.queenstheatre.org.

Subway: Flushing Local (7) to Willets Point–Shea Stadium. A free trolley from the subway station runs continuously for one hour before and after all Main Stage performances.

Car: Take Grand Central Pkwy to Shea Stadium exit (9-E); follow the signs to the theater. Park in parking lot (free).

Today, the pavilion—renovated in the late 1990s—houses the Queens Theatre in the Park, with a 476-seat main theater and a 99-seat experimental theater. The theater presents programs for adults and children, with local, national, and international artists.

Queens Museum of Art

New York City Building, Flushing Meadows–Corona Park, Queens, NY 11368. ☎ (718) 592-9700. Web site: www.queensmuse.org. Open Tues–Fri 10–5; Sat–Sun 12–5. Suggested contribution. Lectures, films, programs for children. Gift shop. Accessible to wheelchairs.

Subway: Flushing Local (7) to 111th St. Walk south on 111th Street to park entrance at Forty-ninth Ave and follow yellow signs to museum; it's a fifteen-minute walk.

Car: Take Grand Central Pkwy to Shea Stadium exit (9-E); follow the signs to museum. Park in parking lot.

At the head of the mall stands the Queens Museum of Art, housed in the former **New York City Building** (1939; renovated 1994; Rafael Vinoly), which once held the city's exhibition for the 1939–40 World's Fair.

The schedule of changing exhibitions includes work by contemporary artists, traveling shows, and exhibitions with themes related to New York. Permanently on view is **Tiffany in Queens,** with finished works of art glass and industrial artifacts from the former Tiffany factory in Queens, and the famous **Panorama of the City of New York** (1964; Robert Lester & Associates).

The Panorama of the City of New York

Created at the request of Robert Moses for the 1964–65 World's Fair to show the development of the city and to help with urban planning, the

9,335-square-ft panorama contains models of some 835,000 buildings, as well as parks, rivers, bridges, roads, and even an airplane taking off from La-Guardia Airport—all executed at a scale of 1 inch to 100 ft. The panorama was updated in 1994 by designers who flew over the city, checked maps, and made field trips. Perhaps the most noticeable change from the original version is the suburban sprawl on Staten Island.

The museum will expand in 2003, when the ice rink with which it currently shares space departs for a new home near the tennis center.

Queens Wildlife Center

Flushing Meadows–Corona Park, 53-51 111th St, Flushing, NY 11368. ☎ (718) 271-1500. Web site: www.wcs.org. Open daily April–Oct 10–5 and until 5:30 on weekends and holidays; earlier closing in winter. Admission charge; children under 3 are free. Children's zoo, educational programs, special events. Gift shop. Vending machines with food. Accessible to wheelchairs.

Subway: Flushing Local (7) to 111th St. Walk south to park; bear right through Hall of Science parking lot to Queens Wildlife Center.

Car: Take Midtown Tunnel to Long Island Expwy; go east to 108th St exit. Turn left onto 108th St, right on Fifty-second Ave, and right on 111th St. Parking lot is between Fifty-fourth and Fifty-fifth Aves.

Two overpasses lead to the western section of the park beyond the Grand Central Pkwy. Near the road is the Queens Wildlife Center, the best place in Queens to see bison, elk, mountain lions, bald eagles, and other North American species in replicas of their natural habitats.

The center focuses on North American wildlife, but there are also exhibits on South American spectacled bears and a petting zoo. The aviary is housed in a geodesic dome designed by Buckminster Fuller for the 1964 Fair. "Otis," the coyote retrieved from Central Park in 1999 (he had probably traveled down from the Bronx), has been joined by other coyotes found wandering in New Orleans.

History

The zoo, which opened in 1968 as the Flushing Meadows Zoo, was renovated in 1992 by the Wildlife Conservation Society according to contemporary standards of animal management. The society also runs the Bronx Zoo, the New York Aquarium, and the wildlife centers in Central and Prospect Parks.

New York Hall of Science

47-01 111th St, Flushing Meadows–Corona Park, Queens, NY 11368. ☎ (718) 699-0675. Web site: www.nyhallsci.org. Open July 1–Aug 31: Mon 9:30–2, Tues–Sun 9:30–5; Sept 1–June 30: Mon–Wed 9:30–2, Thurs–Sun 9:30–5. Closed Jan 1, Labor Day, Thanksgiving, Dec 25. Admission charge, but free Sept 1–June 30, Thurs–Fri 2-5. Additional fee for Science Playground. Lectures, workshops, films, special events, science library. Gift shop, automated cafeteria. Accessible to wheelchairs.

Subway: Flushing Local (7) to 111th St. Walk south to entrance at Forty-eighth Ave and 111th St.

Car: From Manhattan via Midtown Tunnel, take Long Island Expwy eastbound to 108th St exit; left on 108th St to Fiftieth Ave, right at Fiftieth Ave to 111th St. Enter driveway across 111th St at Forty-ninth Ave. Parking is available in the hall's private lot, with a fee on weekends, holidays, and weekdays in the summer. No parking during the U.S. Open tennis tournament.

Beyond the Terrace on the Park, a catering service, is the New York Hall of Science (1964; Harrison & Abramovitz), one of the finest science museums in the country. The building, with its seven-story wavy wall of cobalt-blue stained glass, was designed for the 1964–65 World's Fair to house exhibits on the space program. Ranked as one of the best science museums in the country, it features over 225 hands-on science and technology exhibits. A $68-million renovation now under way will include a 55,000-square-ft new wing.

Long-term exhibits include **Marvelous Molecules: The Secret of Life,** which explores the shared chemical structure of living things (compare your molecular makeup to that of a cockroach or a piece of broccoli). Other exhibits tune in to audio technology and look at microbes, light, and cyberspace. The 30,000-square-ft **Science Playground** (open spring–fall) offers children the chance to crawl, climb, hang upside down, make noise, and get wet—all in the interests of science.

The Building

Over the years this dramatic building has been expanded and updated to fit its new role. It started as a modest science museum in 1966, then it closed in 1981 and was expanded in 1986 with 25,000 square ft of exhibition space and updated hands-on exhibitions. In 1996 the building was again expanded (Polshek Partnership), doubling its public space and introducing the Science Playground. A second phase of expansions will add more space and new exhibits.

USTA National Tennis Center

The United States Tennis Association (USTA) National Tennis Center, which lies just south of the Long Island Rail Road tracks, is the site of the U.S. Open championships. The facility has three stadiums, as well as 33 outdoor courts and 9 indoor courts, which are available to the public when the U.S. Open is not in session.

History

The tournament moved here in 1978 from Forest Hills, where the matches were played on grass (and briefly clay) in the elite, private West Side Tennis Club. The first stadium, the Singer Bowl (built by the Singer Sewing Machine Company for the 1964–65 World's Fair), was remodeled by the USTA and renamed **Louis Armstrong Stadium.**

In the 1990s, the USTA spent $254 million to redesign the center, building **Arthur Ashe Stadium** (1997; Rossetti Associates Architects), a four-tier, 22,547-seat facility, the largest tennis stadium in the world. Ashe, who won the U.S. Open in 1968 as well as titles at Wimbledon and the Australian Open, was the first black male to win a Grand Slam singles title. Louis Armstrong Stadium (its top tier removed) serves as a second stadium; the more intimate **Grandstand** serves as a third.

The U.S. Open

The U.S. Open is considered by many to be the most challenging of the tennis Grand Slam events, in part because the wind and the planes flying to and from La-Guardia Airport can be disruptive, but also because New York fans are vocal and even rambunctious. Jimmy Connors and John McEnroe—both outsized person-alities and local favorites, won the first seven men's championships at the new site. Connors particularly captivated the public's imagination in 1991, when at the age of 39 he reached the semifinals by winning two five-set comeback marathons. The dominant women have been Steffi Graf (five titles), Martina Navratilova (four), Chris Evert (three), and, most recently, Venus Williams (two).

Shea Stadium

North of the Long Island Rail Road tracks is Shea Stadium (1964; Praeger-Kavanagh-Waterbury), home turf of the New York Mets, one of the city's two major league baseball teams. The Mets were created in 1962 to ease the pain of National League fans still mourning the departure of the Brooklyn Dodgers (see Ebbets Field and the Brooklyn Dodgers in Walk 47) and the New York Giants (see Polo Grounds Towers in Walk 28). After playing for two years at the Polo Grounds, the club moved here in 1964 to a new ballpark named for lawyer William Shea, who helped broker the deal that brought the club into existence. The Yankees played at Shea for two years while their stadium was being renovated, and the football Jets called it home before they moved to New Jersey in 1984. The Beatles concerts here in 1965 and 1966 symbolized the peak of Beatlemania.

Memorable Moments at Shea Stadium

Lovable losers for their first seven years, the Miracle Mets shocked the world in 1969, defeating the Baltimore Orioles to win the World Series at Shea. In 1973, the Mets came from last place in Aug to win the pennant before los-ing in the World Series. Pitcher Tug McGraw's rallying cry—"You gotta be-lieve!"—has since become part of the nation's sports lexicon. Shea's most magical moment, however, came on Oct 25, 1986, when the Mets staged an improbable comeback in Game Six of the World Series when Mookie Wil-son's slow ground ball rolled through Red Sox first baseman Bill Buckner's legs, allowing the Mets to win the game and eventually the Series.

While the stadium lacks Ebbets Field's charm or Yankee Stadium's sense of his-tory, it is now baseball's sixth-oldest stadium. The Mets are planning a new ball-park nearby that will resemble Ebbets Field in style but have a retractable dome, luxury suites, and other modern touches.

Elmhurst

West of Corona and Flushing Meadows–Corona Park, south of Roosevelt Ave and north of the Long Island Expwy, is Elmhurst, near the center of the old town of

Newtown. Densely populated today, Elmhurst is touted as New York's most ethnically diverse neighborhood, with a mix of Indian, Chinese, Korean, Filipino, Ecuadorian, Peruvian, and Colombian immigrant residents. Earlier arrivals—of German, Italian, and Irish descent—today mostly live south of Queens Blvd.

History

One of the oldest English settlements on Long Island, Elmhurst began as Middleburgh (the old Dutch name) in 1652 and was later known as NewTowne, or Newtown. The area had streams, salt marshes, and meadowlands, and Newtown boasted fine apple orchards, from which Newtown Pippins were exported to England for cider. During the American Revolution, western and central Queens together had only 99 residents, most of them Loyalists.

In the late 1890s, Cord Meyer, a wealthy politician, began developing land for a residential community in western Newtown. He used his political clout to change the town's name in 1896 to Elmhurst, a name whose idyllic, suburban overtones avoided any association with Newtown Creek, by then foul with sewage and industrial waste. To further enhance his community, Meyer helped finance the New York and Queens trolley and started a water company.

Points of Interest

The **First Presbyterian Church of Newtown,** at Fifty-fourth Ave and Queens Blvd, is the city's oldest church, founded in 1652. The first building served as a village church and town hall, and stood at Dongan St and Broadway. In 1715 the church received a charter from the Presbytery of Philadelphia, becoming the First Presbyterian Church of Newtown, and the old building was replaced by a new church with a small spire and bell. British sympathizers (who made up much of the local populace) sawed off the steeple during the Revolution; the British used the church as prison and guardhouse. A white wooden church with a Dutch-style steeple was built in 1787 and used until 1928, when it was destroyed by fire. Today, the bell (1788) of the old church hangs in the 85 ft tower of the present granite Gothic structure (1893; Frank A. Collins). In the 1930s, the bodies in the churchyard were reinterred in Evergreen Cemetery to make way for the subway. The church has supported diversity since the 18C, when it accepted African Americans as full communicants; today, its congregation includes members from about 40 countries.

The **Reformed Dutch Church of Newtown** (1831; DL), 85-15 Broadway (at Corona Ave), is a white clapboard Georgian structure with Victorian stained glass, now serving a large Asian population. Its cupola is a neighborhood landmark. **Fellowship Hall** (1860; DL), Greek revival in style, was built as a chapel and moved to its present site in 1906.

Newtown High School (1897; C. B. J. Snyder; additions 1930s and 1960s), 48-01 90th St (between Forty-eighth and Fiftieth Aves), recalls a time when education was synonymous with architectural excellence. Construction began just before Newtown was incorporated into Greater New York, but the building wasn't dedicated until May 4, 1900, delayed by scandal and poor workmanship caused by Tammany Hall politics. Originally Newtown Union School, which included kindergarten through 12th grade, the school became Newtown High School in 1910 and lays claim to being the first agricultural school in the state.

Elks Lodge No. 878 (1923), at Queens Blvd and Grand Ave, was once one of the borough's premier social and political clubs with a swimming pool, banquet hall, gym, 700-seat theater, and a large bronze elk outside. At its peak, the club had 5,000 members; admission was considered a prerequisite for rising in politics. In recent decades, membership has dropped and the tax bill has risen; in 2000, the building, once known as the "powerhouse," was sold to the New Life Church.

Forest Hills

Subway: Eighth Ave Local (E), Sixth Ave Local (F), Brooklyn-Queens Crosstown Local (G), or Broadway Local (R) to Seventy-First Ave–Forest Hills.
Train: Long Island Rail Road to Forest Hills (Austin St and Seventy-First Ave).
Car: Take Queens Midtown Tunnel to Long Island Expwy (I-495); Long Island Expwy east to exit 20, Queens Blvd eastbound; turn right onto Continental Ave—Seventy-First Ave.

Forest Hills, west of Flushing Meadows–Corona Park and south of Corona, is famous for tennis and city planning. In addition to the Tudor and Georgian homes of the Forest Hills Gardens, a historic planned community, Forest Hills has many apartment buildings, most of them along and north of Queens Blvd. The area has a large Jewish population and in the 1990s was the top destination outside Brooklyn for immigrants from the former Soviet Union. It has also attracted concentrations of Chinese, Indian, Israeli, and Iranian newcomers. Specialty stores, national chains, and movie theaters occupy Austin St, Continental Ave, and Queens Blvd, while small antique shops are found on Metropolitan Ave. A section of 70th Rd between Austin St and Queens Blvd is known as Restaurant Row.

History

In 1906 wealthy politician Cord Meyer, who had already developed Elmhurst, bought 600 acres in an area called *Whitepot* (from a Dutch word meaning "pit") and named his venture Forest Hills after nearby Forest Park (and possibly after its high ground or simply because the name sounded good). Three years later, he sold 142 acres to Margaret Olivia Slocum Sage, widow of the financier and industrialist Russell Sage. She organized the charitable Russell Sage Foundation, which undertook Forest Hills Gardens, one of the country's oldest planned communities. In 1910 the Long Island Rail Road built a link through Forest Hills, bringing Manhattan within a 14-minute train ride.

Points of Interest

The 12-acre **West Side Tennis Club,** bounded by Sixty-ninth Ave, Burns St, Dartmouth St, and Tennis Place, long hosted American Davis Cup matches as well as the U.S. championships (after 1968, the U.S. Open). The club was started in 1892 in Manhattan with three dirt courts on Central Park West. After moving several times in Manhattan, it bought the Forest Hills property in 1913 and built a Tudor clubhouse in keeping with the surrounding architecture. In 1978, when heightened interest in tennis made the stadium (capacity 13,500) less than optimally profitable, the United States Tennis Association moved the championships to the present National Tennis Center in Flushing Meadows. Today the club, which maintains 43 tennis courts and hosts small tournaments, is one of a few in the country to provide four types of court surfaces: grass, Har-Tru, red clay, and Deco-Turf.

Forest Hills Gardens

Forest Hills Gardens, bounded on the north by the Long Island Rail Road tracks, to the east by Union Turnpike, to the south by Greenway South, and to the west by Seventy-first Ave, looks like an English village with Station Square, a brick-paved public plaza and an elegant railroad station; winding tree-lined streets; half-timbered Tudor-style homes and apartments; and neo–Old English streetlights.

History

Sponsored by the philanthropic Russell Sage Foundation, the development (began 1913) was intended as a model community for middle-income families, but the costs of development according to plans by architect Grosvenor Atterbury and landscape architect Frederick Law Olmsted Jr ultimately pushed prices upward. Atterbury, who had designed houses for the wealthy and also model tenements, set the architectural standards, designing some arts-and-crafts-style houses and the Church-in-the-Gardens, a nondenominational church (1915) at 50 Ascan Ave, donated by Mrs. Sage.

In 1922, the Forest Hills Gardens Corporation, which still oversees the community, took over and instituted strict design covenants, paving the way for today's exclusivity. Public parking is prohibited on its streets, but pedestrians are free to roam this lovely neighborhood.

A brilliant mosaic tile mural on the facade of the otherwise bland-looking **Greenpoint Savings Bank** at 71st Rd and Queens Blvd depicts Forest Hills in the foreground, with the towers of Manhattan in the distance.

Eddie's Sweet Shop, 105-29 Metropolitan Ave (near 72nd Rd), considered by some the best ice cream parlor in New York, is at least 85 years old and has been operated since 1968 by the same family. The decor remains from a simpler time: tile floors, tin ceilings, dark wood walls, a marble counter, and a vintage wooden phone booth. The homemade ice cream is served in old-fashioned metal bowls and plates.

Statues of two doughboys and a World War I memorial form the centerpiece of the **Remsen Family Cemetery** (DL), between Alderton St and Trotting Course Lane, just off Metropolitan Ave. Early Queens settlers, the Remsens established the graveyard in the mid-18C, although the oldest stone dates to 1790. It belongs to Col. Jeromus Remsen, who led the Kings and Queens County Militia during the American Revolution's Battle of Long Island. The cemetery is beautifully maintained by American Legion Post 1424, which has owned the plot since 1964.

Kew Gardens

South and east of Forest Hills is Kew Gardens, a residential and commercial neighborhood with concentrations of upper-class Asians, Indians, and Jews from Iran, the Soviet Union, and Israel as well as Colombians, Afghans, and others.

History

When the area was purchased in 1868 by Manhattan lawyer Albon Platt Man, it was considered the hilly, northern part of Richmond Hill, which Man also developed. It was Man's heirs, however, who renamed the area Kew Gardens, after the botanical gardens in England, and developed it with English and neo-Tudor styles.

High-rises were built once the subway opened in 1936. Before World War II, Kew Gardens attracted refugees from Nazi Germany, who arrived early enough to be financially secure.

Point of Interest

In front of the **Queens Borough Hall** (1941; William Gehron & Andrew J. Thomas), on Queens Blvd between Union Turnpike and Eighty-second Ave, stands Frederick MacMonnies's enormous (57 tons), extremely controversial marble statue *Civic Virtue* (1922). When originally placed in front of City Hall in Manhattan, the statue disturbed onlookers—in part for the near-nudity of its central figure, a muscular male whose modesty is protected by wisps of seaweed and bubbles of foam, and in part because of the symbolism of the two writhing female forms on whom the hero appears to be trampling. Women had achieved suffrage only two years earlier and many booed the unveiling. MacMonnies defended his work by pointing out that Virtue's foot does not actually tread upon the women, but since feminist groups, the Women's Christian Temperance Union, and the president of Harvard all objected, the statue was moved in 1940 to this less-conspicuous site in Queens.

Rego Park

West of Forest Hills is Rego Park, a residential neighborhood of apartment houses and private homes, with bustling commercial strips along Queens Blvd and 63rd Drive. Many residents are Jewish and Asian; the 1990s saw Rego Park become a mecca for those fleeing the former Soviet Union.

History

While the land was still rural, Chinese farmers grew produce for sale in Chinatown. Many were bought out in the 1920s by the Real Good Construction Co., who put up row houses and multifamily dwellings, boasting that their new homes were "*Real Good*" places to live. Although a trolley reached Rego Park from the Queensboro Bridge beginning around 1913, the area remained somewhat isolated until 1928, when the Long Island Rail Road opened its station at 63rd Drive and Austin St, spurring development. The 1939 World's Fair had a similar effect; that year Howard Johnson's, a restaurant chain that began in Massachusetts, built its first New York City restaurant in Rego Park, at Junction Blvd and 62nd Drive. It lasted until 1969, when it was razed to make way for the 11-story Queens Tower.

Lost Battalion Hall

Also in 1939, Lost Battalion Hall, nearby at 93-29 Queens Blvd, was built as a monument to the U.S. Army's heroic "Lost Battalion." The 679-man unit, composed almost entirely of troops from New York City, was cut off and surrounded by Germans in the Argonne Forest in 1918; without food for five days, subjected to machine gun and rifle fire and bombarded by grenades, the unit refused to surrender. When the fighting was over, only 252 had survived. The two-story brick building is now a city-run recreation center.

52 · Northeastern Queens: College Point, Whitestone, Bayside, Little Neck and Douglaston, Flushing, and Floral Park

Unlike the central and western parts of the borough, northeastern Queens has a suburban feel, due largely to its lack of subway access. The neighborhoods here attract perhaps one-tenth as many immigrants as such locales as Flushing, Astoria, or Woodside.

College Point

College Point lies along the shore of Long Island Sound north of Flushing. Known earlier as Tew's Neck, Lawrence's Neck, and Strattonport, it owes its present name to St. Paul's College, founded (1836) as a seminary by Episcopalian minister William A. Muhlenberg. The college, which opened in 1839, lasted only about ten years, but the name endures. College Point's rural complexion began to change in the mid-19C with the arrival of hard-rubber industry pioneer Conrad Poppenhusen.

Conrad Poppenhusen, Entrepreneur and Philanthropist

An immigrant from Germany, Poppenhusen got a license in 1852 to manufacture and sell Charles Goodyear's vulcanized rubber, which did not get sticky in hot weather. Poppenhusen purchased land in the west-central part of what is now College Point and created a model town for his workers, draining marshes, paving roads, and building houses and schools. He went on to found the Flushing and North Side Rail Road, which connected College Point to New York City, and eventually he became a majority stockholder in the Long Island Rail Road. When his sons mismanaged the railroad business, Poppenhusen went bankrupt; he died in 1883 and is buried in Hamburg, Germany.

Throughout the 19C and early 20C, College Point prospered, its factories, mills, and breweries employing Swiss and German immigrants. Its picnic grounds and beer gardens attracted Manhattanites of Germanic descent, who arrived via excursion steamers that plied Long Island Sound. The last rubber factory closed in the 1970s. Today College Point remains largely residential, but its small-town atmosphere has been compromised by huge retail developments built nearby.

Points of Interest

Poppenhusen Institute

114-04 14th Rd, College Point, NY 11356. ☎ (718) 358-0067. Museum open Mon–Wed 10–4; Fri and Sat by appointment. Admission charge. Partially accessible to wheelchairs.

Subway and Bus: Flushing Local (7) to Flushing–Main St; then take bus Q65 to 14th Rd.

Car: Take Triborough Bridge toward Long Island (I-278 west) to Grand Central Pkwy. Continue past LaGuardia Airport to exit 9, Whitestone Expwy (I-678) and Northern Blvd (NY25A). Take the Whitestone Expwy north toward the Whitestone Bridge to exit 15, Twentieth Ave westbound; follow Twentieth Ave west to College Point Blvd; turn right and follow College Point Blvd north to 14th Rd; turn left to Poppenhusen Institute.

The Poppenhusen Institute (1868; Mundell & Teckritz; DL), at the southeast corner of 14th Rd and 114th St, is Conrad Poppenhusen's greatest legacy. Built primarily as an adult evening school offering English language instruction, art, literature, and history classes, it also contained the nation's first free kindergarten for the children of working mothers. The five-story structure, built in the French Second Empire style, once had a library, a savings bank, and a jail whose cells, according to local tradition, occasionally held those visiting Manhattanites who had drunk too deeply in the nearby beer gardens. In 1980, the institute could no longer fund the school; three years later, Citizens for Poppenhusen Institute took over, making the building a community cultural center.

Inside, a small museum offers ongoing exhibits on the Matinecock Indians, College Point's first inhabitants, and its former summer resorts and beer gardens. You can also visit the jail cells and the original kindergarten room.

The **Poppenhusen Memorial** (1884), on College Point Blvd at College Place and Eleventh Ave, marks the approximate site of Conrad Poppenhusen's home. Several unimpressive buildings from his India Rubber Co. (1889, 1921) still stand at 127th St and Twentieth Ave. The India Rubber Co. later became the Hard Rubber Comb Co. and then the I. B. Kleinert Rubber Co., a maker of dress shields.

Frilled with gingerbread, the **First Reformed Church of College Point** and **Parish House** (1872), Fourteenth Ave at the northwest corner of 119th St, are fine examples of the carpenter-Gothic tradition.

Hermon A. MacNeil Park, 28.87 acres, occupies the site of the former St. Paul's College. On the grounds stood a mansion built with stone originally intended for the college building; when stonework became too expensive for Muhlenberg's straitened finances after the Panic of 1837, he sold whatever was not already in the foundation to his sister. Later (c. 1848) Mary Rogers, Muhlenberg's niece, and her husband, William A. Chisolm, lived in the mansion. Even later (1937) Fiorello La Guardia used it as a summer city hall. In about 1941 Parks Commissioner Robert Moses leveled the mansion and created the park, formerly known as Chisholm Park.

Hermon A. MacNeil, Queens Sculptor

Hermon Atkins MacNeil, who lived in College Point, was a sculptor of national reputation. He sculpted the figure of *Washington in War* on the memorial arch in Washington Square Park, as well as four of the busts in the Hall of Fame for Great Americans in the Bronx. MacNeil also designed the Standing Liberty quarter, minted between 1916 and 1929, modeling the figure of Liberty on a College Point neighbor.

Whitestone

Whitestone lies east of College Point, along the North Shore of Long Island between the footings of the Bronx-Whitestone and Throgs Neck Bridges. It is mostly
an upper-middle-class community with a suburban feel and pleasant waterfront
neighborhoods (the subway is a 15-minute bus ride away in Flushing). The
Beechhurst section in the north, along Powell's Cove Blvd between the Bronx-
Whitestone and Throgs Neck Bridges, is home to the **Le Havre Houses,** formerly
known as the Levitt Houses, along 166th St and Utopia Pkwy, a 32-building
apartment complex built along the shoreline by Alfred Levitt (1958; George G.
Miller), brother of the founder of Levittown, Long Island.

Whitestone's most exclusive neighborhood is **Malba** (on the western side), with
winding streets, million-dollar-plus houses, and gorgeous views of the Bronx-
Whitestone Bridge and a bit of Manhattan. Malba is an acronym of the last names
of the five men who developed the community in 1908. A private community
until the 1980s, the old guardhouse stands empty on a grassy triangle called R.
L. von Bernuth Park, at Malba Drive and Parsons Blvd.

History

Settled in 1645 by Dutch farmers who paid Native Americans an axe for every 50
acres of land, Whitestone took its name from a large, white boulder that once
stood at the landing place and served as a navigational aid for passing ships. In
1735 the discovery of a large clay deposit made the area a manufacturing site for
pottery and clay pipes. During the governorship of De Witt Clinton, Whitestone
called itself Clintonville, reverting to its old name in 1854 when a post office was
established. In the mid-19C some called the area Iron Springs, after a spring discovered on a farm at 14th St and Old Whitestone Ave was touted as healthful for
anemic patients.

Points of Interest

Directly on the waterfront near the footings of the Whitestone Bridge is 16.8-
acre **Francis Lewis Park.** It is named for a signer of the Declaration of Independence, whose house near present-day 152nd St and Seventh Ave was burned
by the British during the American Revolution. The park's designers had the fore-
thought to put the handball courts under the bridge, leaving the grassy expanse
open to breezes coming off the water.

Beechhurst lays claim to the **Hammerstein House** (1924; Dwight James
Baum; DL) at 168-11 Powells Cove Blvd, built by the theatrical producer Arthur
Hammerstein, uncle of lyricist Oscar Hammerstein II. Hammerstein named the
15-room house Wildflower for a hit Broadway musical he produced (1923); the
show's profits enabled him to build the neo-Tudor mansion, which once sported
gardens and a breakwater for docking yachts and seaplanes. Hammerstein sold
Wildflower in 1930 to support his theatrical enterprises. It later became a yacht
club and a restaurant and is now slated to be the centerpiece of a waterfront condominium community.

Grace Episcopal Church (1859; Gervase Wheeler; additions 1904, 1939,
1957), 140-15 Clintonville St, is known for the bronze bell in its belfry, which is
tolled the old-fashioned way—by pulling a rope.

On the next block, in sharp contrast to the surrounding community, is the fantastical **St. Nicholas Russian Orthodox Church** (1969; Sergei Padukow), 14-65 Clintonville St, with its shiny, turquoise bulbous top.

Bayside

East of Whitestone is Bayside, bounded on the north and east by Little Bay and Little Neck Bay. Bayside's first settler was Englishman William Lawrence, who arrived via a Dutch land grant in 1664. Once part of the town of Flushing, Bayside became a rural resort for wealthy Manhattanites in the late 1800s. The opening of the North Shore Rail Road (later part of the Long Island Rail Road) in 1866 encouraged well-to-do New Yorkers to build large estates. By the 1920s, Bayside was a prosperous suburban community. Filmmaking in nearby Astoria attracted celebrities including John Barrymore, Buster Keaton, Marie Dressler, Irving Berlin, Norma Talmadge, and Rudolph Valentino. W. C. Fields lived here between 1919 and 1921 and starred in *Sally of the Sawdust*, which was made in Bayside.

Development intensified after World War II, with improved public transportation and major highways making Bayside more accessible. Bay Terrace, a massive apartment complex on 200 acres, was built in 1952. Today, Bayside is a mainly white, middle- and upper-middle-class, suburban-style community dominated by one-family detached houses. The main commercial streets are Northern and Bell Blvds, the latter named for a lane that ran across the large farm of shipping merchant Abraham Bell. His country manor built in 1849 stood at Thirty-ninth Ave and Bell Blvd until 1971, when it was demolished by developers.

Points of Interest

World heavyweight boxing champion (1892–97) **"Gentleman" Jim Corbett** lived with his wife, Vera, in a modest Queen Anne–style house at 221-04 Corbett Rd (corner of 221st St) from 1902 until he died in 1933. He is buried in Cypress Hills Cemetery.

Crocheron Park, at Thirty-fifth Ave and Little Neck Bay, occupies the site of the 19C Crocheron Hotel, whose restaurant was famous for its clambakes. During the latter half of the 19C, proprietor James C. Crocheron's hospitality attracted a celebrity crowd that included New York politicians and socialites. William Marcy "Boss" Tweed, the notorious Tammany Hall chief, allegedly used the hotel as a hideout when he was under investigation for graft. The hotel burned down in 1878, was rebuilt, and burned to the ground again in 1907, having never regained its earlier glory. The city acquired the property in 1924 and, in 1935, developed it into a 45-acre park with grassy slopes and beautiful John Golden Pond.

John Golden, Theater Impressario

Golden, a theatrical producer and founder of ASCAP (American Society of Composers, Authors, and Publishers), lived here on a 20-acre estate that he purchased from Pearl White, star of the silent movie melodrama *The Perils of Pauline.* He left the property to the city for a park, which was dedicated in 1965. A Broadway theater is named for him.

The 12-room **Cornell-Appleton House,** 33-23 214th St (corner of 33rd Rd), is thought to be Bayside's oldest (c. 1852) residence. Mrs. Archibald Cornell, who inherited the house and its 100-acre grounds in the early 19C, was aboard the *Titanic* when it hit an iceberg and sank. She and her sister were rescued by the ship *Carpathia.*

The **Lawrence Family Cemetery** (DL), at Forty-second Ave and 216th St, is a remnant of Bayside's colonial past. This land, and a lot more, came into the Lawrence family in 1645, granted by Dutch governor Willem Kieft. Formerly a family picnic ground, it became a graveyard in 1832; 48 family members are interred here including Cornelius Van Wyck Lawrence, mayor of the city of New York (1834–37), as well as a Native American named Moccasin, a Lawrence family servant. The Bayside Historical Society sometimes offers guided tours; ☎ (718) 352-1548.

Fort Totten

In the northeast corner of Bayside, on a peninsula that juts out into Long Island Sound at Little Neck Bay, stands Fort Totten, formerly called the Fort at Willets Point. In 1898 it was named for Brig. Gen. Joseph G. Totten, a military engineer who planned the nation's 19C coastline defense. Together with Fort Schuyler across the East River in the Bronx, Fort Totten was built to protect New York Harbor during the Civil War. It saw no action but was used as a training ground.

After the Civil War, the fort became a center for the Army Corps of Engineers as they developed torpedoes, underwater mines, and mercury-fed searchlights. Today, it houses the nation's largest Army Reserve Center, the 77th Army Reserve Command. In 1983 the federal government gave the city 11.4 acres of the Fort's grounds, including its battery. In 1995, the U.S. government announced the 163-acre fort's closing; except for the reserve base and small Coast Guard facility, everything will eventually be turned over to the city. Certain sections of the military complex are open to the public (be prepared to show identification at the guard post on Totten Ave before entering the campus).

The former **Officers' Club** (c. 1870, enlarged 1887; DL), a picturesque wooden crenellated building, is used today by the **Bayside Historical Society** and other community organizations. It is one of the few surviving examples of the Gothic revival castellated style, characteristic of 19C American architecture. Located at the periphery of the parade grounds, the building has a dignified symmetrical facade and roof-level parapets. The Bayside Historical Society mounts long- and short-term exhibitions on the history of Bayside and the fort. Exhibits open Mon–Fri 11–3; summer hours Mon, Tues, Thurs, and Sat, 11–3. For more information, ☎ (718) 352-1548. Web site: www.baysidehistorical.org.

The **Old Fort Museum** was started by the Army Corps of Engineers in 1904 and since 1967 has been run on a volunteer basis by unofficial Fort Totten historian Jack Fein, a veteran of World War II. The museum contains newspaper clippings, snapshots, and other military memorabilia, including an old uniform from the Spanish-American War. After seeing the museum, visitors can walk through the cool, dark tunnel leading to the **Fort Totten Battery** (1862–64; William Petit Trowbridge, engineer; DL). The huge gunports in the unfinished two-story granite fort (it was originally intended to be five stories) look out onto Little Neck Bay. In 2000 the city's Parks Department secured 60 acres of Fort Totten and is expected to take over the museum in the near future. For now, the museum is open seven days a week from morning until evening; ☎ (718) 352-0180.

Little Neck and Douglaston

Train: Long Island Rail Road's Port Washington line to Douglaston station.
Car: Take Long Island Expwy (east) to the Cross Island Pkwy (north) to exit 31. Turn right onto Northern Blvd, left onto 235th St, then make a slight right onto Douglaston Pkwy.

Little Neck, south of Little Neck Bay and east of Bayside, is today a neighborhood of quiet streets and moderately priced houses. It is often linked with Douglaston, its wealthier neighbor to the north.

History

The Douglaston Peninsula was first inhabited by the Matinecock Indians, who found the waters of Long Island Sound a rich source for shellfish, whose shells were used for making wampum—beads of polished shells strung in belts or sashes—a Matinecock specialty. Later the Dutch settled the area and farmed. During the 19C the area boasted delicious oysters and "Little Neck" clams, as sloops and schooners operated from the foot of Old House Landing Rd, now Little Neck Pkwy. Pollution forced the beds to close in 1909.

In 1835, Douglaston was carved out of Little Neck when wealthy Scotsman George Douglas purchased the land and mansion of Wynant Van Zandt, a successful merchant and alderman of New York City. Douglas began remaking the peninsula into a gentleman's estate, with guest houses, stables, and a pier. Douglas's son William inherited the property in 1862 and continued to improve it. Exotic specimen trees remain from this period, possibly planted by Samuel Parsons (1819–1906), the famous nursery man, who lived nearby. The younger Douglas was devoted to sailing, and his yacht, the *Sappho*, won the America's Cup in 1871; the mast stood for years at the Douglaston Dock. With the introduction of rail connections to Manhattan (the railroad reached Douglaston in 1866), the North Shore of Long Island soon became a playground to the rich. Douglaston's planned garden suburb was largely developed from 1906 to 1940, after the Douglases sold the estate to the Rickert-Finlay Realty Company, which touted the area as a private park more beautiful even than Central Park, because it was surrounded by water. The neighborhood, particularly Douglaston Manor, which makes up the bulk of the peninsula, is laid out with a slightly curving grid of streets that conform to the hilly topography and capitalize on vistas of Little Neck Bay, the body of water that forms the mouth of Long Island Sound. The Douglaston Historic District includes 615 beautiful single-family homes in Tudor, Mediterranean, and colonial revival styles, but, mostly, the arts-and-crafts style (of which there are more here than in any other neighborhood in New York City).

Start at the northern side of the Long Island Rail Road station on 235th St at the **weeping beech tree.** William Douglas convinced local officials to name the town Douglaston (instead of Marathon, also under consideration) in 1866, by donating a farm building to the LIRR for a station house. The original station house is gone, but the weeping beech survives, a legacy of nurseryman Samuel Parsons, who planted the first one in the United States at nearby Flushing. That tree died in 1998 and this one was grown from a cutting of the original.

Walk north past the stores and shops of what locals refer to as **"The Village."** Pass the Colonial revival–style **Community Church** (1922). On the west side of the street (Douglaston Pkwy) are farmhouses built in the 1850s through 1870s by Irish immigrants who worked on the Douglas estate.

At 38th Rd, turn right (east). At the crest of the hill is **140 Prospect Ave** (corner of 38th Rd), a square stucco house designed by arts-and-crafts master Gustav Stickley. One of three Stickley houses in the Douglaston Historic District, this one was built from plans ordered from Stickley's magazine, *The Craftsman.*

Continue down the hill. The medieval Spanish baroque revival mansion at **309 38th Rd** (1916; Elbert McGran Jackson) was built by Jackson, an architect by training who made his living as a magazine illustrator, designing many covers for the *Saturday Evening Post* through the 1930s. He expanded the copper-roofed house over the years, adding a second story with Moroccan-inspired stained glass windows and a two-story studio for painting.

Udalls Cove Wildlife Preserve

Train: Long Island Rail Road's Port Washington line to Little Neck Station, then walk two blocks to the water.

Car: Take Long Island Expwy south to Little Neck Pkwy exit. Follow parkway for about two miles to the end (Virginia Point), where there is a parking lot.

At the end of the street is Udalls Cove Wildlife Preserve, a 100-acre tidal wetland that attracts thousands of shore birds during fall migrations and through parts of the winter and is home to other wildlife. It is a protected New York City park, although limited public access is allowed.

Turn left (north) on Douglas Rd, then left on Forest Rd. The house at **329 Forest Rd** (1916) was built by Trygve Hammer, a Norwegian sculptor who designed the bas-reliefs of the now-demolished Bonwit Teller Building (site of Trump Tower) in Manhattan. The house, with weathered boards and a carved peak, evokes Hammer's homeland.

Follow Forest Rd west to where it intersects with Center Drive. The **Allen-Beville House** (1848; DL), at 29 Center Drive, is a Greek revival–Italianate mansion complete with third-story cupola for scanning the bay. The house has wide porches front and back; grand entryways with transoms; tall, shuttered windows; and a beautiful garden.

Follow Center Drive north to Ridge Rd, turn left and head west to 1 Alston Place. Behind the evergreen hedge is the **Cornelius Van Wyck Farmhouse** (1735, with 18C additions; DL), which is perfectly preserved. The main two-story facade faces the bay, acknowledging the dominance of water transportation when the house was built.

Return east to West Drive, turn left and head north to 600 West Drive, the former **Wynant Van Zandt Mansion** (1819), now the **Douglaston Club.** The sweeping lawn contains some old trees planted by Parsons and Douglas in the mid-19C. This boxy Greek revival house with a servants' wing attached to the back was originally the summer house of New York merchant and alderman Wyant Van Zandt and his 15 children. The third-story ballroom replaced a cupola destroyed by a fire in 1921. Today the private clubhouse has tennis courts (John McEnroe learned to play here), a restaurant, bowling alley, and swimming pool.

Continue up West Drive to Knollwood Ave. At 303 Knollwood Ave is a Mediterranean revival house with a beautiful medieval-style front door surmounted by elegant wrought-iron work by architect William F. McCulloch. The front facade is accented by small turquoise tiles and leaded glass windows, designed for the original owner, Miss Edythe L. DePalezieux-Falconnet.

Continue north on West Drive to Bayview Ave. Here a circle of hedges marks the original carriage turnabout for the pleasure road of the Douglas estate, which culminated at "The Point," with views of Little Neck Bay at the west end of Long Island Sound. Directly across the bay is Great Neck, where F. Scott Fitzgerald wrote *The Great Gatsby.* The Douglaston Peninsula and Great Neck were the inspiration for the fictional "East Egg" and "West Egg" of this famous novel. To the east, beyond Great Neck, is Kings Point and the Merchant Marine Academy, and in the very far distance, Stepping Stone Lighthouse.

Continue south on Shore Rd, past Douglaston Manor's biggest homes, including **1114 Shore Rd** (1907; John Sarsfield Kennedy), built for stage star William Collier in 1907. The house has an unusual cedar shingle roof: the shingles were steamed and bent to imitate thatch, emulating the informal English houses they were based on. This particularly beautiful arts-and-crafts-style house has two huge, ogee-shaped stained glass windows (morning glories decorate the eastern window) that orient the house to the views of the bay.

The large stucco house at **1915 Shore Rd** (1917; Buchman & Fox) was designed for Norbert Bachman, the owner of a New York department store. Buchman & Fox designed many large department stores in Manhattan's Ladies' Mile Historic District.

Continue south to the corner of Manor Rd. At **204 Shore Rd** (1922; Frank Forester) is a handsome brick Georgian house with twin beech trees brought to the site as full-grown specimens when the house was built and now well over 100 years old. Two blocks south, at the corner of Arleigh Rd, is a throwback to the more typically "Victorian"-era homes that preceded the styles that typify Douglaston Manor: **28 Arleigh Rd** has an open porch, corner tower, and wonderful carriage house in back, all taking advantage of the location of this house on the bay. Just to the west, at the base of the Douglaston Peninsula, is all that remains of Cozy Point, the Parsons estate—a shingled barn with a red roof.

Points of Interest

The **Zion Episcopal Church** (1925; additions 1960), at 243-01 Northern Blvd (between Douglaston Pkwy and 244th St), is a lovely, colonial-style church built on a hill set back from Northern Blvd and Douglaston Pkwy. The original church, which gets its name from the biblical hill in Jerusalem, was built in 1830 on land donated by Wynant Van Zandt, who is buried along with family members in a vault beneath the church. The church and its outbuildings were destroyed by fire on Christmas Eve, 1924, though the **Parish Hall** (1896–97) survived. The church has a beautiful cemetery, which contains an Indian burial ground. The remains of Matinecock Indians were moved here when Northern Blvd was widened in the 1930s. A split boulder with a maple tree growing between its halves marks the spot. According to the pastor, anyone with Matinecock blood may enjoy the privilege of burial here.

Alley Pond Park

Alley Pond Environmental Center. 228-06 Northern Blvd, Douglaston, NY 11163-1890. ☎ (718) 229-4000. Open Mon-Sat 9–4; Sun 9:30–3:30. Trails open daily, dawn to dusk. Programs, lectures, tours. Nature shop, picnic tables.

Subway and bus: Flushing Local (7) to Main St–Flushing. Change to Q12 bus to the Northern Blvd stop in front of the park.

Car: Take Long Island Expwy (I-495) east to Springfield Blvd; north on Springfield Blvd to Northern Blvd; go east on Northern Blvd. The park is just past Cross Island Pkwy.

Note: While this is a good place to start, some trails are accessible from other parts of the park.

Alley Pond Park is the second largest park in Queens and is divided between Bayside and Douglaston. Although transected by four highways—Northern Blvd, Grand Central Pkwy, Cross Island Pkwy, and Long Island Expwy—its 655 acres offer protected woodlands, fresh and salt water marshes, kettle ponds, and meadows, much of it accessible by trails.

The park began in the 1920s, when the city bought 330 acres of what was once the "Alley," a bustling 19C hamlet with a blacksmith, gristmill, general store, and homes clustered around Alley Pond. The Alley was named for the long, narrow ravine created by Alley Creek. All that remains of the pond is a patch of phragmites; the pond was filled in to accommodate construction of the Long Island Expwy in the 1950s. Despite the obliteration of pond and creek, the park remains a paradise with old tulip trees, including one 250-year-old giant, and a red oak forest on its northwest edge. The 132-acre southern forest, with its stands of sweet gum, American beech, oaks, white ash, and other native trees, is impressive.

Flushing

Subway: Flushing Local (7) to Main St–Flushing.
Train: Long Island Rail Road on Port Washington line to Flushing–Main St.
Car: Take either the Long Island Expwy to exit 23 and go north on Main St, or follow Northern Blvd to Main St.

Flushing, first settled in 1642 and chartered in 1645, lies east of the Flushing River. The name is a corruption of the Dutch *Vlissingen,* the name of a town in Holland from which some of its early settlers emigrated. It has been associated with the development of religious freedom in the U.S. ever since the 17C struggles between Peter Stuyvesant and the Quakers, whom he wished to suppress. During the 18C, the western end of Flushing hosted the country's first commercial nursery, 113 acres planted by Robert Prince. It was so impressive that George Washington visited it and Lewis and Clark supplied it with specimens from their expeditions. The offspring of Prince's industry account for many of the 140 genera and 2,000 species of trees and shrubs that enhance Flushing.

Eventually, other nurseries that gathered trees and plants from around the world for resale were started here, including Linnaean Gardens (owned by Prince's grandson Robert and later combined with Prince's Nursery) and Parsons Nursery, located on the site of Flushing High School and founded by Quaker Samuel Parsons in 1838. During the 19C Flushing was a summer colony and remained a quiet residential town until the highways constructed for the first New York World's Fair led to its rapid development.

Today it is still residential though not particularly quiet as it is intersected by major avenues and girded by expressways. The population is a mix of old-timers, many of them Jewish, and more-recent Asian residents, mostly Chinese (particularly Mandarin-speaking and middle-class Taiwanese) and Koreans as well as Vietnamese, Japanese, and East Indians. Asians first arrived in the 1970s, revitalizing the downtown's empty storefronts and investing in the neighborhood. Of the nearly 20,000 immigrants who settled in Flushing between 1990 and 1996, 5,800 were from China, 2,500 from Korea, and 2,000 from India. Additionally, it became home to one-third of the city's 2,550 Afghan newcomers, making it the city's center for this new group. Today Flushing has the city's second largest Chinatown; more than 43 percent of its residents are of Asian descent. The neighborhood's bustling commercial strip, Main St, bursts with Asian food markets and restaurants, sari shops, and Indian and Pakistani restaurants. Off the busy thoroughfare several historic sites reflect the neighborhood's diversity and commitment to religious freedom: from a Quaker meetinghouse to Hindu temples and Korean churches.

Begin at Main St and Roosevelt Ave and walk north. (Street numbers will decrease.) **St. George's Episcopal Church** (1854; Wills & Dudley; DL), on Main St between Thirty-eighth and Thirty-ninth Aves, is built of brownstone and Manhattan schist with a wooden steeple that was added later. It replaces an earlier church (1761), where Francis Lewis, signer of the Declaration of Independence, served as vestryman.

Continue on Main St to Northern Blvd. William Prince's Linnanean Gardens once flourished on the site of the now-vacant **RKO Keith Theater,** which screened its last film in 1986. Despite its landmarked interior, the once-regal theater has been neglected and allowed to deteriorate.

Friends Meeting House
137-16 Northern Blvd (between Linden Place and Main St), Flushing, NY 11354. Open during worship, Sun 11–12. ☎ (718) 358-9636.

Turn right and walk to Linden Place. The Friends Meeting House (1694; enlarged 1716–19; DL), a simple wooden building with a steep hipped roof and very small windows, which offers a moment of serenity in a hectic and fast-paced neighborhood. The back of the house faces busy Northern Blvd while the front opens onto a garden and small graveyard, whose stones were unmarked until 1848 in accordance with the Quaker belief that death equalizes everyone. Except for a period during the British occupation (1776–83) when it served as a prison, hay barn, and hospital, the Friends Meeting House has been used continuously for religious services since its construction. Worshiping must have been uncomfortable, however, during its first 50 winters, as iron stoves were not installed until 1760; central heating followed two centuries later (1965).

Across Northern Blvd is the most imposing 19C structure in town, the former **Flushing Town Hall** (1862; Cornelius Howard, builder; DL), 137-35 Northern Blvd (northeast corner of Linden Place). This tan brick building with chocolate-brown trim, usually described as Romanesque revival, is overlaid with Victorian detail—a heavy cornice, gables, turrets, and a porch. Once it held a courtroom, bank offices, a library, a meeting hall, and a jail. During its prime it hosted Flushing's most important events—town meetings, opera performances, balls—and its most illustrious visitors—Theodore Roosevelt, Ulysses S. Grant, Tom Thumb, P. T. Barnum, and Jenny Lind. After years of abandonment, the Flushing Council on Culture and the Arts (founded 1979) began restoring the building in 1990 and three years later began offering programs in the performing and visual arts. Its Fri night jazz concerts are particularly popular.

Turn left at Leavitt St for the **Lewis H. Latimer House** (c. 1887–89; DL), 34-41 137th St. The son of former slaves, Latimer (1848–1928) had the distinction of being the only African American member of the Edison Pioneers, the engineering division of the Edison Electric Light Company. He joined Thomas Edison's company in 1884, where he improved on Edison's electric light bulb with a carbon filament. He also made the original drawings for Alexander Graham Bell's telephone. To save it from demolition, the small, butterscotch-colored house—where Latimer spent the last 20 years of his life—was moved from nearby Holly Ave in 1988 to its present site across the street from the Latimer Gardens housing project. It is scheduled to open as a historic house museum, showcasing Latimer's life and work; ☎ (718) 961-8585.

Return to Northern Blvd past the **Flushing Armory** (1905), 137-58 Northern Blvd, and Flushing High School to Bowne St. Turn right. About 100 yds down the street on the right is a boulder called the **Fox Oaks Rock**. It gets its name from George Fox, English founder of the Religious Society of Friends (i.e., Quakers), who came to North America in 1672 and preached here under a stand of oaks.

Bowne House

37-01 Bowne St (at Thirty-seventh Ave), Flushing, NY 11354. **Note:** The house is currently (2001) closed to the public during restoration. For information, ☎ (718) 359-0528.

On the southeast corner of Bowne St and Thirty-seventh Ave is the oldest dwelling in Queens, the Bowne House (1661, with later additions; DL), built by John Bowne and inhabited by nine generations of his family until 1945, when it was opened as a museum. It is important not only for its antiquity but for its association with religious freedom in this country. The museum contains 17C–18C furnishings, including pieces that belonged to the Bowne family.

A Landmark of Religious Freedom

The Quakers' heretical beliefs, fanaticism, and ecstatic form of worship (hence the name *Quakers*) drew the wrath of conforming Christians, notably Governor Peter Stuyvesant, who particularly abhorred the sect. Stuyvesant could not prevent members of the sect from meeting secretly to practice their religion, but he did arrest those who allowed Quakers to meet in their homes. John Bowne, a Quaker convert, nonetheless let the group meet in his kitchen. In 1657 Stuyvesant issued an edict declaring the Dutch Reformed Church the only permitted religion in the colony. The townspeople responded with the **Flushing Remonstrance,** which rebuked Stuyvesant for curbing religious freedoms that had been promised them by the original charter of the town. (A plaque in the garden recounts the re-

> monstrance.) Stuyvesant then arrested and fined some of those who signed the statement, and, in 1662, fined Bowne and banished him to Holland. Bowne pleaded his cause with the Dutch West India Company and the business-minded company directors advised Stuyvesant to moderate his antagonism, stressing that increased immigration to the underpopulated colony was more important than religious conformity.

Kingsland Homestead

143-35 Thirty-seventh Ave (actually on 37th St, west of Parsons Blvd), Flushing, NY 11354. ☎ (718) 939-0647. Open Tues, Sat, Sun 2:30–4:30. Admission charge. Not accessible to wheelchairs. Exhibitions, lectures, programs.

Walk out through the Bowne House garden to Thirty-seventh Ave and past the playground to the Kingsland Homestead (1774; DL), a Dutch-style house with gambrel roof and a columned porch built by Charles Doughty, a Quaker farmer. Doughty's son-in-law, Joseph King, inherited the house and settled there after an adventurous career as a British sea captain. King's daughter Mary married Lindley Murray, of the family for whom Manhattan's Murray Hill was named. The house was moved twice from other locations in Flushing, and since 1968, has been headquarters for the Queens Historical Society.

Inside are a small collection of memorabilia from Joseph King, historical photographs, maps of Queens and neighboring Nassau County, a Victorian period room, and special exhibitions on local history and decorative arts.

Next door to the Kingsland Homestead once stood Queens's most famous tree, a **weeping beech** (1847; DL) towering 60 ft tall with a spread of about 85 ft and a trunk circumference of 14 ft. It was born in Belgium and planted as a four-inch sprig in 1847 by renowned horticulturist Samuel Parsons, who supplied trees and shrubs for Central and Prospect Parks. The tree, one of the city's two living landmarks and the first weeping beech in North America, died in 1998 and was cut down the following spring, leaving a 12 ft stump. It is surrounded by eight of its healthy descendants, which retain landmark status.

Return to Bowne St. Along this street and the side streets just off it are several of Flushing's many religious institutions. Flushing hosts more than 100 Korean churches, the largest of which is the 3,500-member **Korean American Presbyterian Church of Queens** (143-17 Franklin Ave, just off Bowne St).

On the northeast corner of Bowne St and Roosevelt Ave is the **Bowne Street Community Church** (1892), a red brick building with a large bell tower, which was built for the Protestant Reformed Church, a descendant of the oldest denomination in the city, the Dutch Reformed Church of 1628.

Continue on Bowne St for about a half-mile to the **Hindu Temple Society of North America** (1977; Baryn Basu Assocs.), at 45-57 Bowne St. Although built in the Dravidian style of some 2,000 years ago and enhanced with ancient deities, the temple—the fancy neighbor in this working-class area—boasts electronic sliding doors and interior television monitors that show what is happening inside. Within the temple barefoot pilgrims pray to Vishnu, Lakshmi, Shiva, and other Indian deities, as spiritual leaders chant mantras.

Other Asian temples serving Flushing's immigrant population include the Japanese **Nichiren Shoshu Temple** (1984; Ashihara Assocs.), at 42-32 Parsons Blvd (at Ash Ave), and the Korean **Won Buddhist Temple,** in the Song Eun Building (1986; Bo Yoon & Assocs.) at 43-02 Burling St. On one crowded stretch of Bowne St between Cherry and Forty-Fifth Aves are the Swaminarayan Temple, Boon Church of the Overseas Chinese Mission, and Gurdwara Singh Sabha, as well as the Kissena Jewish Center, which suffers from dwindling attendance and rents the building to a Korean congregation on Sun.

Other Points of Interest

Queens College

Queens College, its 76-acre campus bounded by Reeves and Melbourne Aves, Main St, and Kissena Blvd, opened in 1937 and is part of the City University of New York. The college offers degrees in science and liberal arts, attracting some 15,000 students—40 percent of them first-generation college students, 44 percent of them foreign-born.

Frances Godwin and Joseph Ternbach Museum

Mattis Room, Paul Klapper Library, Queens College, Flushing, NY 11367. For information and exhibition schedule, ☎ (718) 997-4747.

In Klapper Hall is the Frances Godwin and Joseph Ternbach Museum at Queens College, with a permanent collection of European art, ancient and antique glass, prints by American artists commissioned by the WPA, and examples of Asian and Egyptian art. The museum offers changing exhibitions of painting, sculpture, and drawing. It is named for Frances Godwin, a professor at the college, and Joseph Ternbach, an art restorer and collector.

Benjamin Rosenthal Library

Queens College. 65-30 Kissena Blvd, Flushing, NY 11367. ☎ (718) 997-3770. Web site: www.satchmo.net. Open Mon–Fri 9–5; Sat 10–5 (appointments recommended); hours may vary with college schedule.

The **Louis Armstrong Archives** are housed in the Benjamin Rosenthal Library on campus. There are two exhibitions each year; topics have ranged from *Breaking the Barriers,* which followed Armstrong's career as he became a mainstream figure in popular music and film, to *Red Beans and Ricely Yours, Louis Armstong,* which explored his relationship to food, drink, and dieting.

Queens Botanical Garden

43-50 Main St (at Dahlia Ave), Flushing, NY 11355. ☎ (718) 886-3800. Web site: www.queensbotanical.org. Open 8–dusk; earlier closing in winter. Closed Mon except legal holidays. Free. Group tours, educational programs, lectures. Plant shop (seasonal). Accessible to wheelchairs. Free on-site parking.

Subway and bus: Flushing Local (7) to Main St–Flushing; transfer to bus Q44 to Elder Ave.

Car: Take Long Island Expwy to exit 23 (Main St); follow Main St north for seven traffic lights. Left onto Dahlia Ave.

The Queens Botanical Garden may not be as spectacular as its Bronx or Brooklyn brethren—22 of its 39 acres are an arboretum—but it is beautiful in its own right. More than 13,000 tulips and a stand of Kwanzan cherry trees steal the show in late April and early May, while June blooms with the brilliance of thousands of roses in the Charles H. Perkins Memorial Rose Garden. Among the gardens are those designed to attract bees and birds, a Victorian-style Wedding Garden, and an herb garden. The Oak Allée flanks a formally planted area with seasonal beds of bulbs and annuals.

The garden is an offshoot of a 1939–40 New York World's Fair horticultural exhibit, which went to seed after the fair closed. In 1946, horticulturally concerned citizens formed the Queens Botanical Garden Society and brought the exhibit to life again, expanding its original five acres to 20, and opening the Queens Botanical Garden on June 5, 1948. The garden was moved across the street to its current address to make way for the 1964–65 New York World's Fair. Two Mount Atlas blue cedars from the 1939–40 fair flank the garden's main entrance.

Kissena Park (bounded by Kissena Blvd, Booth Memorial Ave, Rose and Oak Aves, and Fresh Meadow Lane) is a 219-acre park with a small spring-fed lake on the site of Samuel Parsons's nurseries, founded in 1838. A group of horticulture students discovered within the park a grove of rare Oriental trees, planted a century ago, presumably during Parsons's tenure.

Floral Park

South and east of the Douglaston Peninsula is the residential neighborhood of Floral Park, named (as are some of its streets) for a 19C commercial nursery.

Queens County Farm Museum

75-50 Little Neck Pkwy, Floral Park, NY 11104. ☎ (718) 347-3276. Web site: www.queensfarm.org. Grounds open Mon–Fri 9–5 all year. House open Sat–Sun 10–5. Free; charges for some events. Limited wheelchair accessibility. Workshops and events; farmstand, greenhouses, festivals and fairs; self-guided tours of grounds, guided tours of house.

Subway: Eighth Ave Local (E) or Sixth Ave Local (F) to Union Turnpike–Kew Gardens. Transfer to Q46 bus to Little Neck Pkwy. Walk north three blocks to entrance.

Car: Via Triborough Bridge, take Grand Central Pkway to Little Neck Pkwy (exit 24). Go south on Little Neck Pkwy three blocks to entrance.

The Queens County Farm Museum is the only historic working farm within the borders of New York City. The centerpiece of this museum (opened 1975) is the Adriance Farmhouse (earliest section c. 1722; DL). The building has the typical overhanging eaves and long front of the Dutch colonial style. Inside, the farmhouse has been appointed with period furniture and artifacts. Outside are barns and sheds, as well as gardens producing fruits, vegetables, and herbs, and a three-acre orchard. Dedicated to preserving the agricultural history of New York, the museum offers events that have included experiments in candle making and quilting, corn-husking and pie-eating contests, a Civil War encampment, an annual Indian Powwow, the annual Queens County Agricultural Fair, and shows of antique autos and motorcycles.

History
The first farm here dated back to the closing years of the 17C, when the rich soil of the glacial outwash plain attracted settlers. The present house was built in the 18C by Jacob Adriance and enlarged (c. 1830) by subsequent owners. At the end of the 19C the land was a truck farm. In 1926 the Creedmore branch of the Brooklyn State Hospital, for psychiatric patients, acquired the property and used it to cultivate vegetables, with some patients working in the gardens as therapy. The patients left in 1973, and two years later the farmhouse and gardens opened as a museum.

53 · Southern Queens: Jamaica, Jamaica Estates, St. Albans and Hollis, Richmond Hill, Woodhaven, and Ozone Park

Most of what is now southern Queens was contained within the original boundaries of the town of Jamaica settled in 1656 by the English, who had secured a patent from the Dutch (who referred to the area as *Rustdorp*, which means "restful" or "peaceful" village). The English took over in 1683, renamed the area Jamaica and established the first Queens County seat here. The origin of the name is uncertain, though the accepted source is an Algonquin word for "beaver" (which gives the name a different etymology from that of the island in the West Indies, whose origin is a Carib word meaning "land of wood and water").

Jamaica
Early in the 18C, Jamaica, then (as now) located at the intersection of major roads, became a trading center for Long Island farmers taking their produce to Brooklyn and Manhattan. Large-scale development did not take place until the Long Island Rail Road was electrified in 1910 and the elevated line and subway along Jamaica Ave arrived in 1918. During the 1930s and 1940s Jamaica—nestled between Jamaica Estates, Queens Village, Hollis, and Richmond Hill—was one of the major urban centers in Queens and in the late 1950s was the fourth-largest retail center in the city. From then on, with shopping malls rising elsewhere in Queens and the white middle class moving further out to Long Island, Jamaica began to deteriorate. A branch of Macy's located at 165th St and Eighty-ninth Ave closed in 1978. The Gertz Department Store at Guy R. Brewer Blvd and Jamaica Ave closed in 1980 after 69 years in business.

In 1979 the elevated train along Jamaica Ave from Sutphin Blvd to 168th St was torn down in the hope that Jamaica Ave would be transformed, just as Third Ave in Manhattan bloomed commercially once the "el" there was removed (1955). While the commercial strip is less robust than it was in its heyday, many independent and chain stores, primarily discount shops, now do a steady business. Streets and parks in northern Jamaica are cleaner. The main switching point and headquarters of the Long Island Rail Road, the flagship branch of the Queens

Public Library, and an influx of government offices are also here, while the Greater Jamaica Development Corporation is working to again make Jamaica—home mainly to Hispanics and blacks (most immigrants are from Guyana)—a destination.

South Jamaica, with its sizable housing projects and gangs, has not fared as well. However, the neighborhood's Allen AME Church under Senior Pastor and longtime Congressman Floyd Flake has bought land, built housing, and invested in local businesses in an effort to revitalize the community.

King Manor Museum

150-03 Jamaica Ave, Jamaica, NY 11432. ☎ (718) 206-0545. Open Mar–Dec, Sat and Sun noon–4; Tues, one tour offered at noon. Closed Jan and Feb. Admission fee. Partially accessible to wheelchairs; call for information. Tours (some bilingual, Spanish and English) available during weekend hours. Changing exhibits devoted to local history; special events. Gift shop.

Subway: Eighth Ave Local (E) or Nassau St Express (J, Z) to Jamaica Center–Parsons/Archer. Sixth Ave Local (F) to Parsons Blvd.

Begin at the King Manor Museum, 150-03 Jamaica Ave (north section, 1730; west section, 1755; east section 1806; DL), in 11-acre Rufus King Park between 150th and 153rd Sts. This large, white-shingled house reflects three stages of construction in three styles, Georgian, Federal, and Greek revival. Originally a small farmhouse, it was bought and expanded by Rufus King (1755–1827), Federalist statesman, member of the Continental Congress, signer of the Constitution, U.S. senator, presidential candidate, abolitionist, and father of John Alsop King, who became governor of New York in 1857. It remained a family residence until 1897, when the then-village of Jamaica purchased it. It is owned by the city and since 1900 has been managed by the King Manor Association of L.I., Inc. The house has been restored to reflect the King family's tenancy in the early 1800s.

On the southeast corner of 153rd St and Jamaica Ave is the **First Reformed Church of Jamaica** (1859; Sidney J. Young; renovated 1902; Tuthill & Higgins; DL), one of the best early Romanesque revival churches in the city, its two towers flanking a broad, gabled facade. Between 153rd St and Parsons Blvd is the Gothic revival brownstone **Grace Episcopal Church and Graveyard** (1862; Dudley Fields; additions 1901–2; Cady, Berg & See; graveyard c. 1734; DL), 155-03 Jamaica Ave, where Rufus King and his son John King are buried. Founded in 1702, the church was the official church of the British Colonial government.

Continue east on Jamaica Ave; turn left on 160th St to what was a Depression-era jazz club, **La Casina** (c. 1933; DL), 90-33 160th St, built in the streamlined Moderne style. Today it is the Jamaica Business Resource Center.

Cross Jamaica Ave, walking south to what is left of **St. Monica's Church** (1857; Anders Peterson, builder; DL), 94-20 160th St, on the campus of **York College.** One of the few Roman Catholic churches in the city built in the early Romanesque revival style, it once boasted an unusual freestanding bell tower. In the 1960s, much of the land around the church was condemned to make way for the college. The church's last service was held June 24, 1973. Thereafter negligence led to the tower's collapse during a 1998 storm.

Behind the church, at 159th St and the southwest corner of Beaver Rd (and difficult to see from the street), is the **Prospect Cemetery** (1668; DL), the oldest public burial ground in Queens. Overgrown and locked to the public, it contains Revolutionary War veterans and members of the Van Wyck and Sutphin families, who gave their names to an expressway and a local boulevard. A small Romanesque revival chapel, which has been vandalized over the years, was built in 1857 by a successful New York hardware store owner, Nicholas Ludlum, in memory of his three daughters—Mary Cecelia, one year old (d. 1828); Cornelia, 13 (d. 1837), and Mary, 21 (d. 1855). There have been periodic efforts to restore both the memorial chapel and cemetery.

Jamaica Center for Arts and Learning

161-04 Jamaica Ave, Jamaica, NY 11432. ☎ (718) 658-7400. Web site: www.jcal.org. Open Tues–Sat 10–5.

Return to Jamaica Ave and walk east to the former **Register Building** (1898; A. S. Macgregor; DL), 161-04 Jamaica Ave, a neo-Italianate Renaissance structure built as the city office for registering titles and deeds. It is home to the Jamaica Center for Arts and Learning (formerly the Jamaica Arts Center), a multidisciplinary arts organization offering workshops in art, drama, computer skills, music, dance, and more, for toddlers through seniors. A Community Gallery features the work of local artists or students enrolled in the center's classes and workshops.

Continue east to 162-24 Jamaica Ave and the former **J. Kurtz and Sons furniture store** (1931; Allmendinger & Schlendorf; DL), a huge, colorful, six-story Art Deco building attesting to Jamaica's former commercial eminence. The building features polychromatic terra-cotta panels and black-and-white glazed tile pylons, its style reflecting the furniture that was once sold inside. The store closed in 1978.

A few blocks east, on the north side of the street, is the elaborate **Loews Valencia Theater** (1929; John Eberson; DL), 165-11 Jamaica Ave, built in 1929 as a Spanish-style movie palace seating 3,500. Since 1976, it has been the **Tabernacle of Prayer For All People Pentecostal Church.** The facade has ornate polychromatic terra-cotta work and a diamond brick pattern, while the ceiling inside is sprinkled with lights to look like stars. Although the church has kept the exterior facade virtually intact, some figures of nude women on an arch over the pulpit have been given wings and clothes, converting them to angels. The old ticket booth remains outside.

Jamaica Estates

North of Jamaica is the enclave of Jamaica Estates, its steep hills created by the Wisconsin glacier, whose terminal moraine rested at Hillside Ave. In 1907, a consortium of wealthy New Yorkers, including Timothy Woodruff, lieutenant governor of the state of New York under Theodore Roosevelt, purchased 503 acres of hardwood forest from the city. The partners, presumably Anglophiles, developed the land as an exclusive community, giving the streets names like Kent, Wareham, Cambridge, Hovenden, and Edgerton. The winding streets were laid out to fit the contours of the land; many neo-Tudor style, one-family homes were built, most with large lawns and trees. When the Jamaica Estates Company went bankrupt in the 1920s, the 275 property owners formed the Jamaica Estates Association, determined to preserve the original building restrictions: only detached, two-story houses with attics; no flat roofs; and no house costing less than $6,000, quite a sum at the time. Apartment buildings were permitted only along the periphery of the development. Today, the development includes more than 1,700 homes—in various styles including Tudors, colonials, Georgian-style mansions, and ranch houses. Its stone gatehouse entrance is preserved on Hillside Ave.

Points of Interest

St. John's University

In the northwest corner of the neighborhood is the campus of St. John's University, a Roman Catholic college founded in 1870 by the Vincentian Fathers, now enrolling some 18,300 students, most of them from families in the city and on Long Island. Approximately 85 percent of St. John's alumni live and work in the greater New York metropolitan area. The school's graduates have a tradition of performing public service; perhaps best known are former governor Mario M. Cuomo and his predecessor Hugh L. Carey. The school's popular Big East basketball team recently changed its name from the Red Men to the Red Storm, in deference to protests from Native Americans. The college also has a campus in Grymes Hill, Staten Island.

Chung-Cheng Art Gallery

Sun Yat Sen Hall, St. John's University, Jamaica, NY 11439. ☎ (718) 990-1526. Open Mon–Thur 9–4; Fri–Sat noon–4. Closed holidays. Free. Accessible to wheelchairs.

Subway and bus: Eighth Ave Local (E) or Sixth Ave Local (F) to Union Turnpike–Kew Gardens; change to Q46 bus to 173rd St and Union Turnpike.

Car: Take Grand Central Pkwy east to Utopia Pkwy exit.

Dedicated in 1973, **Sun Yat Sen Hall,** the pagoda-style building that houses the university's Department of Asian Studies, also contains the Chung-Cheng Art Gallery, with a collection of Chinese and Japanese art.

The collection began with a donation of artifacts from the 1964 World's Fair and includes samurai swords, porcelain and cloisonné ware, ivory carvings, and lacquerware. Changing exhibitions show the work of contemporary Asian artists.

Cunningham Park

Six blocks east of the neighborhood is 358-acre Cunningham Park, named for W. Arthur Cunningham (1894–1934), a decorated World War I veteran and city comptroller under Mayor Fiorello La Guardia. The city bought land for the park, originally known as Hillside Park, between 1928 and 1944.

Long Island's Appian Way

After about 1908, a strip of the Long Island Motor Pkwy ran through what is now the park's midsection. William K. Vanderbilt, who loved fast cars and had the wherewithal to buy them, built this private toll road, which became the nation's first highway intended solely for automobiles. It was paved with concrete and had bridges and overpasses to avoid intersections. The press dubbed it "Long Island's Appian Way." In the 1920s, more than 150,000 cars traveled the parkway (and paid its tolls), but competition from the public highways that Robert Moses was developing in the 1930s brought its glory days to an end. In 1938 the property was given to the city. Today it is a path for runners and cyclists.

Also in the park are tennis courts, a bocce court that attracts a steady following, playgrounds, stables, bridle paths, playing fields, and picnic areas. For nature lovers, there are swamp-encircled kettle ponds and stands of old oak in the park's 60-acre Southern Forest. For information, ☎ (718) 217-6452.

Southeast of Jamaica Estates are the middle-class black communities of Hollis, Springfield Gardens, Laurelton, Cambria Heights, and St. Albans. (While many of the immigrants moving here are from the island of Jamaica, there is an increasing Asian presence as well.)

St. Albans and Hollis
In the 1940s and 1950s, Jackie Robinson, Count Basie, Lena Horne, Roy Campanella, and other prominent blacks lived in **St. Albans.** This well-maintained, suburban-style neighborhood continued to be racially integrated in the 1950s and 1960s but became mainly black by the 1970s. A Veterans Administration hospital and the 30-year-old Black Spectrum Theatre occupy part of a 125-acre site that once belonged to the St. Albans Golf Course, built in 1915 and once visited by celebrities.

Hollis gained fame more recently as the hometown of rappers Run-DMC, the group—Joseph Simmons (Run), Darryl McDaniels (DMC), and Jason Mizell (Jam Master Jay)—that catapulted rap music into the mainstream. They were the first rappers to have gold (1984) and platinum (1985) albums, to go multiplatinum (1986), to have their videos on MTV, and to appear on *American Bandstand* and the cover of *Rolling Stone.*

Richmond Hill
Subway: Nassau Street Express or Local (J, Z) to 121st St (and Jamaica Ave).

West of Jamaica is Richmond Hill, long a working-class community with residents of Irish, Italian, and German descent, now more diverse. Between 1990 and 1996, more Guyanese immigrants (4,716, or 11 percent of the city's total) moved to Richmond Hill, particularly the southern half, than to any other community in the city. Dominicans, Indians, and Caribbeans have also moved here. North Richmond Hill, on the other hand, which has Queen Anne Victorian houses, many designed by Henry E. Haugaard, is still home to many old-time residents. It was the first community to receive the "Queensmark" designation—for architectural or historical significance—from the Queens Historical Society.

History

Richmond Hill's farmland was developed after the Civil War (1867) when attorney Albon P. Man bought the Lefferts and Welling family farms and subdivided the land. From 1952 to 1963, Beat Generation writer Jack Kerouac lived on and off at his mother's house at 94-21 134th St.

The community center, the **Triangle,** formed by the intersection of Lefferts Blvd with Myrtle and Jamaica Aves, is in decline. The former Triangle Hofbrau (1864), a stagecoach stop and later a favorite eating spot of Mae West and Babe Ruth, is now a medical clinic, while the RKO Keith's marquee (1920s) sadly is covered with bingo signs. **Jahn's Ice Cream Parlor,** in Richmond Hill since 1923, survives with its 25-cent nickelodeon piano and famous Kitchen Sink sundae, enough for eight people. There is growing community interest in revitalizing the Triangle.

To view some Queensmarked structures, walk from the Triangle to the corner of Hillside Ave and 118 St, continuing down 118th St to **85-19 118 St.** More colonial revival than Queen Anne, this house has a grand circular porch and stairs and a unique balustrade above the porch and Palladian window. Next door, at 85-09 118th St, is the Tudor-and-Gothic-style Episcopal **Church of the Resurrection** (1874), with leaded stained glass windows and copper-clad conical-roofed parish house. Make a left on Eighty-fifth Ave to **117-03 85th Ave,** a classic Queen Anne with a small balcony shaded by a conical roof, a lone eyebrow dormer window, and paired columns supporting a wraparound porch. Continue on Eighty-fifth Ave to **85-14 111th St,** with its beautiful staggered shingle work.

Turn right onto Eighty-sixth Ave and left on 109th St. The exquisite Queen Anne with colonial revival elements at **86-22 109th St** features Ionic columns on the porch and symmetrically placed dormers on a hipped roof. Turn around and walk up 109th St to Park Lane South, stopping at its intersection with Myrtle Ave and the site of a memorial to the the World War I doughboy, known in the neighborhood as the **"Buddy Monument"** (1925; J. P. Pollia).

Woodhaven

West of Richmond Hill is Woodhaven, which reaches to the Brooklyn border. Woodhaven maintains a mix of Italian and Irish as well as Asian, Hispanic, and some black residents.

History

Woodhaven was founded in the 1830s by the same John R. Pitkin who tried to build a rival to Manhattan in East New York, today a battered Brooklyn neighborhood. Pitkin called his town Woodville and it began to prosper after two Frenchmen opened the Lalance & Grosjean tinware factory on Atlantic Ave in 1863, eventually employing 2,100 people. (This section is today considered Ozone Park.) The factory closed in 1955.

Baseball history was made at the 15,500-seat Dexter Park baseball field, east of Franklin K. Lane High School and behind the C-Town Supermarket, when in 1930 the first engineered lighting system for night games was installed. The field, home turf of the semiprofessional Bushwicks, closed in 1951 and was replaced by brick row houses.

Points of Interest

In 1821, the popular **Union Race Course** was built between 78th and 82nd Sts. A competition in 1823 between the best horses of the North and the South drew more than 50,000 people to the then-rural area. All that remains of the racecourse is the Old Pump House, today the Union Course Tavern at 87-48 78th St (northwest corner of Eighty-eighth Ave). The oldest bar in Queens, it is reportedly the place where ten-year-old Brooklynite Mae West (1893–1980) got started when it was Neir's Hotel, a combination tavern/inn/vaudeville house. Today, the tiny, dark bar with tin ceilings and walls caters to the neighborhood's old-timers, who bemoan the community's transformation. Scenes in Martin Scorsese's 1990 movie *Good Fellas* were filmed here.

Surprisingly, perhaps, Betty Smith's novel *A Tree Grows in Brooklyn* was written in Queens in 1943 in the basement of a house at 85-34 Forest Pkwy.

Forest Park

Richmond Hill and Woodhaven share Forest Park, located near the Brooklyn-Queens border. The 538-acre park also borders nearby Kew Gardens, Forest Hills, and Glendale. In 1895, Brooklyn officials bought 124 separate tracts of land in Queens to create what was then called Brooklyn Forest Park. Like Central and Prospect Parks, Forest Park was designed by landscape architect Frederick Law Olmsted's firm. Park Lane South and Forest Park Drive offer scenic vantage points.

The eastern section features 411 acres of oak forest with many trees more than 150 years old. The woodlands can be traversed by three trails. There are also seven miles of bridle paths. The western portion offers ball fields, tennis courts, a track, an 1890s **Daniel Muller carousel** (at Park Drive and Woodhaven Blvd), and a golf course. Its Dutch colonial revival–style clubhouse, known as **Oak Ridge** (c. 1914), houses Parks administration offices and the Queens Council on the Arts.

Seuffert Band Shell

About a half-mile from the park's Woodhaven Blvd entrance is the renovated Seuffert Band Shell (at Forest Park Drive and Woodhaven Blvd), on the site of an earlier bandstand and concert grove built in 1920. The bandshell is named for George Seuffert Sr., friend of march-king John Philip Sousa and founder of the 54-member Concordia Military Band (1898), later called the Seuffert Band. Seuffert led free outdoor concerts at the bandshell until 1932, when his son, George Seuffert Jr., a native of Ridgewood, took up the baton. The elder Seuffert died in 1964 at the age of 89. When Seuffert Jr. died in 1995, it was feared that the music would die with him. Instead, the Queens Symphony Orchestra continues the tradition of providing free, Sun afternoon concerts each summer at the bandshell. For information, ☎ (718) 235-4100.

Ozone Park

Ozone Park, south of Woodhaven and north of the Belt Pkwy, is a modest residential community that traditionally attracted Italians and some German, Irish, and Polish families. In the last decade Caribbeans and Hispanics have moved here, though there is still an Italian flavor on 101st Ave, one of the neighborhood's commercial strips. (Liberty Ave, the other commercial strip, has a more West Indian flavor.)

History

Railroad service in 1880 spurred the area's development by Benjamin Hitchcock, a music publisher, and Charles C. Denton, who called this former part of Woodhaven "Ozone Park," boasting of the healthy air from nearby Jamaica Bay and the ocean beyond. (Development in nearby Howard Beach has long blocked the breezes.)

Points of Interest

In 1984, the site of Lalance & Grosjean's tinware factory (Atlantic Ave between 89th and 92nd Sts) became a shopping mall. A few brick buildings remain, but more impressive is the beautiful **clock tower** (1876) at the corner of 92nd St. Some faded workers' houses (1884), badly covered in vinyl siding, remain at 85-02 to 85-20 Ninety-fifth Ave and 85-01 to 85-21 Ninety-seventh Ave.

Aqueduct Racetrack, bounded by Rockaway Blvd, Southern Pkwy, the Eighth Ave Express (A) line right-of-way, and 114th St, is the only raceway remaining within the city limits. It dates back to 1894 (reconstructed 1959; Arthur Froehlich & Assocs.) and is named for an aqueduct that runs along Conduit Ave, the service road south of the Southern Pkwy, which once brought water from sources further east on Long Island to the Ridgewood Reservoir near the Brooklyn-Queens border. In 1955, the New York Racing Association came into existence as a nondividend, tax-paying organization and purchased the assets of several racetracks, including Aqueduct. A year later, the old Aqueduct was torn down and the new "Big A" reopened in 1959. In 1975, a track was constructed to allow for winter racing. The season at Aqueduct runs from Oct to May. From May through Dec, there is a large weekend flea market. For information, ☎ (718) 641-4700.

John F. Kennedy International Airport

John F. Kennedy International Airport, at the south end of the Van Wyck Expwy along Jamaica Bay, is New York's largest airport, covering 4,930 acres, an area equivalent to all of Manhattan from the Battery to 42nd St. Construction began in 1942, when the first landfill was dumped onto the salt marshes bordering the bay in preparation for a planned 100-acre New York International Airport on the site of the Idlewild Golf Course. Commercial flights began in 1948—the same year the Port Authority began operating the airport—and since then the facility has become the city's most important airport, serving primarily long-distance domestic and international flights. After the assassination of John F. Kennedy in 1963, the airport was renamed.

The airport has two pairs of parallel runways aligned at right angles and a fifth general aviation runway for private, business, and commuter planes, a total of nine miles of runways served by 25 miles of taxiways. The airport is currently undergoing a major expansion, which includes new airline passenger terminals, an air traffic control tower, roadways, parking garages, and a light rail transit system.

JFK Terminals

The airport's 880-acre **Central Terminal** is home to nine airline passenger terminals, many of them built in the 1950s and 1960s. Virtually the entire complex, however, is being rebuilt. There will be more ticketing and baggage-handling space, along with expanded and improved retail and restaurant facilities. A new **Terminal 1**, shared by Air France, Japan Airlines, Korean Air, and Lufthansa, opened in 1998 on the site of the former Eastern Airlines Terminal. The former International Arrivals Building, now **Terminal 4**, underwent a major renovation that began in 1997. In 1999, plans to replace two American Airlines Terminals—**Terminals 8** (1960; Kahn & Jacobs) and **9** (1961; Skidmore, Owings & Merrill)—with a new 2.2-million-square-ft complex began. Noteworthy in Terminal 8 was the world's largest stained glass wall (Robert Sowers, designer). When completed, the new terminal will be the airport's largest.

The most significant and controversial terminal has been the **Trans World Airlines International Building** (1962; Eero Saarinen & Assocs.; DL). Its innovations included enclosed "jetway" passages from the gates to the aircraft, baggage carousels, and "satellite" clustering of gates away from the main terminal. While the airline welcomed the landmarking of its exterior, whose swooping concrete form expresses the notion of flight, TWA objected to landmarking much of the interior, saying it was functionally obsolete. The landmark status will likely prevent the terminal's demolition.

Getting to Kennedy

The biggest issue for people flying out of Kennedy Airport has always been simply getting there. For three decades, proposals for a rail line linking the airport directly to Manhattan have been defeated because of cost, environmental issues, and protests from adjacent communities. The Port Authority is presently building a partial version, eight miles of track for what it calls AirTrain. This rail line will link passengers from the Jamaica subway and Long Island Rail Road stations and the Howard Beach (A train) subway station to Kennedy. The Port Authority estimates that AirTrain will attract 34,000 users daily, reducing traffic on the roads to Kennedy and pollution in Queens. The $1.9-billion project should be completed in 2003.

54 · Howard Beach, Broad Channel, Jamaica Bay, and the Rockaways

The southern portion of Queens, once the haunt of the Canarsee and Rockaway Indians and later noted for its fine fishing, clamming, oystering, and resort areas, has long been defined by Jamaica Bay, a shallow bay of about 20 square miles spotted with thousands of acres of marshy islands, some of them in danger of eroding, thereby diminishing resting and feeding areas vital to area wildlife. Jamaica Bay, lying southwest of Kennedy Airport, is part of the Gateway National Recreation Area, which maintains a wildlife refuge on the bay's largest land mass, an island known in its various parts as Black Bank Marsh, Ruler's Bar Hassock, Big Egg Marsh, and Broad Channel.

Howard Beach

North of Jamaica Bay is Howard Beach, once called Ramblersville, where squatters, attracted to Hawtree Creek and the bay, lived in shacks on stilts in the water. The area between Hawtree Creek and the airport is referred to as Hamilton Beach, accessible to the rest of Queens by a small, wooden bridge on 102nd St.

History

Howard Beach's current name comes from the leather manufacturer William J. Howard, who arrived in the 1890s and set up a goat farm. His ambitions later drove him to fill in the marshy land, build cottages and a hotel, and eventually develop homes and streets. Howard's first model home opened in 1913, the same year that the Long Island Rail Road opened a station here along its Rockaway line. In 1950, fire destroyed the railroad trestle in the bay and the Long Island Rail Road stopped service to the community. The following year, subway service to the area was initiated. Today the old resort community is mainly middle-class Italians and Jews with a mix of old and new private homes, condominiums, and apartment complexes.

The main street, Cross Bay Blvd, is lined with hotels, restaurants, chain stores, and a huge catering hall. The neighborhood is divided into "Old Howard Beach," east of Cross Bay Blvd, and "New Howard Beach," to the west. Howard Beach was thrust into the spotlight in 1986 when a group of bat-wielding white men chased three black men—without provocation—onto the busy Belt Pkwy. A passing car killed one of the blacks, Michael Griffith. One of the city's uglier racial incidents in recent years, it captured national attention. In 1999, the street where Griffith had lived—Pacific St, between Albany and Ralph Aves in Brooklyn—was renamed in his honor.

Broad Channel

Smack in the middle of Jamaica Bay is the 1,200-acre island of Broad Channel, the only settlement in the bay, which dates back to the 1860s when it began as a fishing village. The area remained sparsely populated until 1880, when the New York, Woodhaven, and Rockaway Railroad built a trestle across Jamaica Bay to the Rockaways. The line made four stops, including one at Broad Channel. In 1915, real estate developer Pierre Noel leased a 500-acre parcel from the city and created a summer bungalow community in this isolated area.

During Prohibition, Broad Channel's isolation was used to advantage and it became known as Little Cuba, with visitors enjoying bootleg liquor in its yacht clubs and speakeasies. In 1925, Cross Bay Blvd made Broad Channel accessible to motorists, enhancing its popularity. But when Noel's Broad Channel Corporation went bankrupt during the Depression, the property reverted to the city, which became landlord to thousands of tenants who now lived year-round in the winterized bungalows. For nearly 50 years, residents owned their homes but paid rent to the city for the land beneath them. After much protest, the city began selling residents their properties in 1982. Today the insular island community has about 2,400 people, many of them blue-collar, Irish Americans whose families have lived on the island for generations. Most houses are small former bungalows and there are a handful of shacks on pilings, which gives the community a pleasingly archaic appearance. New land titles, however, have spurred development;

some cottages have been enlarged or knocked down to make room for double-lot homes.

Jamaica Bay Wildlife Refuge

North of Broad Channel is the Jamaica Bay Wildlife Refuge, whose ponds and marshlands form a full-time or seasonal habitat for 325 bird species. The city opened the 9,155-acre refuge in 1953 but never really had the money to fund it. In 1972, the refuge was turned over to the U.S. Department of the Interior and the newly created Gateway National Recreation Area. Since then, the refuge has become one of the country's most important urban wildlife refuges. Located on the Atlantic flyway, it is most interesting during the autumn and spring migrations, when thousands of ducks and geese stop over in its wetlands. It is also home to white-rumped sandpipers, black-bellied plovers, egrets, black-crowned night herons, and an array of butterflies, turtles, and amphibians.

Most visitors walk the 1.75-mile **West Pond Trail,** which begins at the Visitors Center, or the more challenging 3-mile **East Pond Trail,** a mucky but rewarding trek, that begins across the street from the Visitors Center. Park Rangers offer free nature walks.

The Visitors Center is about a mile northwest of the Broad Channel subway station of the Eighth Ave Express (A) on the west side of Cross Bay Blvd. Self-guided trail maps available. For schedule of events, ☎ (718) 318-4340. Web site: www.nps.gov/gate.

The Rockaways

The southernmost portion of Queens is the 11-mile-long Rockaway Peninsula reaching westward from the mainland of Long Island across the mouth of Jamaica Bay. After Native Americans sold the neck of land to a colonist in the late 17C, it remained part of the town of Hempstead until the city of New York was incorporated in 1898. While some towns chose not to become part of the city, the Rockaways opted otherwise, despite its only land connection to Nassau County. Like Howard Beach and Broad Channel, the Rockaway Peninsula first attracted fishermen. Its remoteness and inaccessibility eventually turned it into an exclusive summer resort until railroads put it within reach of the common man, thereby driving the more aristocratic visitors eastward to the Hamptons and other areas further out on Long Island. The Rockaways enjoyed a period as a middle-class summer resort with seaside hotels and bathhouses. Playland, a popular amusement park between Beach 97th and 98th Sts opened in 1901, with a roller coaster and fun house arriving in 1925. The park, which had entertained some 180 million visitors by its 70th anniversary, was demolished in 1987.

The land lay fallow for more than a decade; in 1999, a private developer began building 90 homes on the site. Other redevelopment is slowly coming to the Rockaways too, including 40 new homes on part of a 308-acre urban renewal site in the Arverne section, vacant since the 1960s, when thousands of summer bungalows were razed.

Points of Interest

Gateway National Recreation Area, Breezy Point

Breezy Point Unit, Rockaway Point Blvd, Queens, NY 11697. ☎ (718) 318-4300. Visitors Center open daily 9–5. Offers an overview of Fort Tilden's military history as well as nature exhibits. It also dispenses free parking permits necessary to visit the tip of Breezy Point from April 15 to Sept 15; at other times permits are not required. Restrooms.

Much of the western portion of the Rockaways is public land, maintained by the National Park Service as part of the Gateway National Recreation Area. Its communities—Belle Harbor and Neponsit (which doesn't allow renters)—are affluent. At the tip is **Breezy Point,** a private, gated community often called the Irish Riviera, which started as a tent colony at the turn-of-the-20C. The tents were gradually replaced by cottages, and in 1961 the Breezy Point summer colony became a cooperative and bought the land (about 500 acres) under the houses. Today the co-op still owns the land while members own their homes; its 2,800 one-family houses have a year-round population of 5,000 and a summer population of 12,000. The Breezy Point Cooperative also owns the nearby gated communities of Roxbury and Rockaway Point.

Although Breezy Point's residential streets are closed to outsiders, the **Breezy Point Tip,** at the very end of the point, is federal property open to the public. Here the National Park Service oversees colonies of rare birds; the area with its beautiful sand dunes is closed only when the birds are breeding. About a dozen pairs of piping plovers—a species of tiny, shy coastal bird on the federal endangered and threatened list—lay their eggs here during late April and May. Together with Fort Tilden and Jacob Riis Park, Breezy Point is part of Gateway's Breezy Point Unit.

Just east of the Breezy Point community is the site of **Fort Tilden,** built in 1917 as part of the city's outer coastal defenses and paired with Fort Hancock at Sandy Hook, New Jersey. It is named for Samuel J. Tilden, New York State governor and unsuccessful presidential candidate (1876), who left much of his money to the New York Public Library. The 317-acre former U.S. Army base was decommissioned in 1974. Visitors can hike the property and explore the beach, coastal uplands, and vestiges of the military era. The beaches along Fort Tilden contain one of the last natural dune systems in New York City. Battery Harris East and Battery Harris West, two World War II bunkers, are used as platforms by birdwatchers during the Northeast's annual hawk migration and provide magnificent vistas year-round. There are also ball fields, summer concerts, and nature exhibits scattered throughout the site. The Rockaway Theater Company recently took over an old army base moviehouse, transforming it into a local theater, while the Rockaway Artists Alliance is renovating two equipment warehouses into an arts and cultural center.

Jacob Riis Park

Bus: Green Bus Lines operates from southern and central Queens, and an express bus from Manhattan, to Jacob Riis Park. For information, ☎ (718) 995-4700.

Car: Take Belt Pkwy (eastbound) to exit 11-S. Cross the Marine Pkwy Bridge (toll) to the Rockaway Peninsula and turn left.

Next to Fort Tilden is Jacob Riis Park, named after the 19C journalist who crusaded for better housing and parks for the poor. Developed by Robert Moses, the one-mile-long boardwalk and beach—one of the finest beaches in the metropolitan area—opened in 1937 but, in quintessential Robert Moses fashion, was left largely inaccessible to public transportation. Its 7,000-car parking lot is one of the largest parking areas in the city. The park became part of the Gateway National Recreation Area in 1974. Each July, Gateway sponsors its All-Women Lifeguard Tournament at Riis Park. The exterior of the park's historic bathhouse, a WPA-sponsored project, was recently restored as part of an overall rehabilitation. The interior has yet to be renovated and is closed to the public.

Rockaway Beach

Subway: Eighth Ave Express (A) to Rockaway Park–Beach 116th St. **Note:** The A train schedule is divided into several routes: from Manhattan to Lefferts Blvd, Far Rockaway, or Rockaway Park. Make sure you take the train to Rockaway Park. The Rockaway Park branch stops at Beach 90th St, Beach 98th St, Beach 105th St, and Beach 116th St. The Far Rockaway branch stops at Beach 67th St, Beach 60th St, Beach 44th St, Beach 36th St, Beach 25th, and Mott Ave.

Bus: Green Bus Lines also operates from southern and central Queens, with an express bus from Manhattan, to the Rockaway Peninsula. For information, ☎ (718) 995-4700. A city bus, Q35, operates from Brooklyn and Queens to the Rockaways.

Car: Take Belt Pkwy (eastbound) to exit 17 (Cross Bay Blvd). Turn right, drive all the way down Cross Bay Blvd, crossing two bridges. The second is the Veterans Memorial Bridge (toll), which leads to the Rockaway Peninsula and Rockaway Beach.

East of the Cross Bay Veterans Memorial Bridge is Rockaway Beach, the former home of Playland and still the heart of Irish Rockaway. Arverne and Edgemere are economically depressed with empty lots, a handful of bungalows, and a few large-scale housing projects that seem foreign to this low, windswept land. Far Rockaway is racially mixed with blacks, Russian immigrants, and Orthodox Jews living in houses ranging from old 1900s mansions and colonials to Tudors and new, modest, suburban-style homes.

Curiously out of place amid three run-down hotels in Rockaway Beach—the Hotel Lawrence, Baxter's Hotel, and the Rockaway Park Hotel—is an odd cultural attraction, located in the lobby of Baxter's Hotel. The **Rockaway Park Playhouse,** 160 Beach 116th St, was opened in 1994 by hotel owner John Baxter, who emigrated from Ireland in 1952. It stages primarily Irish plays, often with Baxter as the star performer. For information, ☎ (718) 474-3030.

The **Rockaway Museum,** 88-08 Rockaway Beach Blvd, is a tiny, fledgling community museum housed in the Wave Building; the *Wave* is the Rockaway's 106-year-old weekly newspaper. The museum is open Mon–Fri 11–4 and is free. It features changing exhibits on local history. For information, ☎ (718) 474-6760.

In the 1960s, all the **bungalows** south of Rockaway Beach Blvd and between Beach 32nd and Beach 84th Sts were bulldozed, but four blocks with about 150 bungalows built (1921) during Rockaway's heyday surprisingly survive on Beach 24th to Beach 27th Sts (between Seagirt Blvd and the boardwalk) in Far Rockaway. Today, the Beachside Bungalow Preservation Association, founded by resident Richard George, is trying to get them named city landmarks. Some of the tiny, 20 × 40 ft cottages have fallen into disrepair or are boarded up, but others are glorious year-round homes. Built by Richard Bainbridge, these 1½-story homes have front porches and pitched roofs in a variety of styles; common lanes lead directly to the beach.

Bayswater Point State Park

Subway: Eighth Ave Express (A) to Far Rockaway–Mott Ave. Walk 13 blocks north on Mott Ave to the park.

Car: Take Marine Pkwy Bridge or Cross Bay Bridge to Beach Channel Drive all the way to Far Rockaway. Turn left onto Mott Ave for one mile to the park's entrance.

Bayswater Point State Park, at the north end of Mott Ave in Far Rockaway, is a 12-acre state park with a woodchip trail leading to gorgeous views of Jamaica Bay. It occupies the grounds of a former waterfront mansion built in 1903 by a Wall Street magnate, A. M. Heinsheiner, who commuted to Manhattan by private boat. The park was created in 1991 as one of a series of Jamaica Bay ecopreserves managed by the New York City Audubon Society, under a formal agreement with the state. For schedule of guided tours, call the New York City Audubon Society at ☎ (212) 691-7483.

Borough of Staten Island / Richmond County

To the world at large, Staten Island is famous as the end point of one of the greatest free rides in the domain of tourism, the Staten Island Ferry. From 1948 until 2001, it was also infamous as the dumping ground for New York's garbage, the Fresh Kills Landfill. But to Staten Islanders and those in the know, there is much more to this borough.

The island is separated from Manhattan by Upper New York Bay, from Brooklyn by Lower New York Bay and the Narrows, and from New Jersey by the Kill Van Kull and the Arthur Kill (the word *kill* is a Dutch term for "channel"). It is 13.9 miles long and 7.3 miles wide in its largest dimensions, making it the third-largest borough (60.9 square miles). While far and away the smallest in population (443,728 in 2000), it is growing faster than any other borough, increasing by 15 percent in the 1990–2000 decade.

Down the center of the island, from St. George to La Tourette Park, runs a spine of rocky hills whose highest point, Todt Hill (409.2 ft), is the highest natural point in the city and the highest point on the Atlantic seaboard south of Maine. During the years before and after the turn of the last century, the wealthy built mansions along the crest of these hills. Many of these residences survive along Howard Ave in Grymes Hill and in the neighborhoods of Emerson Hills and Dongan Hills, though some have been adapted to use as educational or charitable institutions. Others have surrendered land to subdivisions or ostentatious homes as new money moves to the island. East of the central ridge lie low coastal plains, now densely developed with back-to-back rows of tract housing and continuous commercial strips. Areas that once were separate towns have been built up with small, single-family houses, town houses, and condominiums, which threaten to merge into one giant tract of suburban sprawl.

Southern Staten Island, one of the island's fastest growing sections, was once dominated by the sea, and though the fishing villages and oystering communities no longer exist, some of its former charm remains. Unfortunately, developments of cookie-cutter town houses and condos threaten this area too. The west, fronting the Arthur Kill, is lowland, much of it salt meadow. Some has been filled and built up with more housing or turned to commercial and industrial uses. Three thousand acres were befouled by the nation's largest garbage dump, the Fresh Kills Landfill (1948–2001), which received 13,000 tons of residential garbage daily.

The far north, facing New Jersey across the Kill Van Kull, has several of the island's oldest industrial and residential settlements, some of which have declined in recent decades. Across the Kill stand the unsightly oil tanks of New Jersey refineries.

In the Kills are three islands that flourish as bird sanctuaries in spite of the pollution around them. Since the Clean Air and Clean Water Acts of the 1970s, fish have returned to these heavily trafficked waters, and now herons, egrets, and other birds nest on Shooter's Island in the Kill Van Kull and on Prall's Island and Isle of Meadow in the Arthur Kill. The islands are part of the Harbor Herons Project and are overseen by the city's Parks Department, the New York City Audubon Society, and other agencies.

Despite the onslaught of suburbia, Staten Island retains many historic buildings, with more structures from the 17C through the early 19C than any other borough. It also has wonderful parks, including the city's largest stretch of green, the 2,500-acre Greenbelt in central Staten Island, made up of 12 contiguous parks. The National Park Service controls some of the oceanfront through the Gateway National Recreation Area, which (on Staten Island) includes Great Kills Park, built largely on landfill, and Miller Field, a former army base. Both parks have fine recreational facilities. Recent laws have been enacted to preserve wetlands from indiscriminate use.

Joining the island to its neighbors are four major bridges whose construction spans 36 years. Three of them connect Staten Island with New Jersey, and their long-standing presence explains why much of the island is culturally and economically linked more to New Jersey than to the rest of New York City. The Outerbridge Crossing (1928) and the Goethals Bridge (1928) were the first facilities built by the Port Authority of New York (changed in 1972 to the Port Authority of New York and New Jersey). The Outerbridge Crossing, a 750 ft span, joins the Charleston section of Staten Island with Perth Amboy, New Jersey, and is named after Eugenius H. Outerbridge, the first chairman of the New York Port Authority. About 15 million eastbound (the direction in which the tolls are taken) vehicles cross it yearly. The Goethals Bridge, a cantilever structure (span 672 ft), reaches from Howlands Hook to the Bayway section of Elizabeth, New Jersey, and carries an estimated 13 million eastbound vehicles yearly. The Bayonne Bridge (1931) is a graceful steel arch (span 1,675 ft) linking Port Richmond with Bayonne, New Jersey; it carries 3 million eastbound vehicles yearly.

The most recent arrival, the elegant Verrazano-Narrows Bridge (1964), crosses the Lower Bay (span 4,260 ft) from Fort Wadsworth to Bay Ridge, Brooklyn, carrying more than 69 million vehicles yearly. Its arrival triggered a land boom that changed the face of the island forever and still has not slowed. In much the same way, the Staten Island Expwy (1964) and the West Shore Expwy (1976) encouraged uncontrolled development, particularly on the island's south and west coasts.

Staten Island History

In the 16C–17C, Staten Island was home to Lenape (or Delaware) Indians, a tribe related to the Algonquin people. Both Giovanni da Verrazano (1524) and Henry Hudson (1609) made note of Staten Island during their explorations of the New World. The former stopped off at a spring to refill his water casks and the latter gave the borough its name, *Staaten Eylandt*, after the States General, governing body of the Netherlands. In the years that followed, the Dutch attempted to colonize the island at least three times, but hostile Native Americans, roused to anger by the provocative actions of the colonists, attacked the settlements. It wasn't until 1661 that a group of farmers—French Huguenots and Dutch Walloons—established the first permanent settlement, *Oude Dorp* ("Old Town"), near present-day Fort Wadsworth. When the British took over New Amsterdam, Staten Island

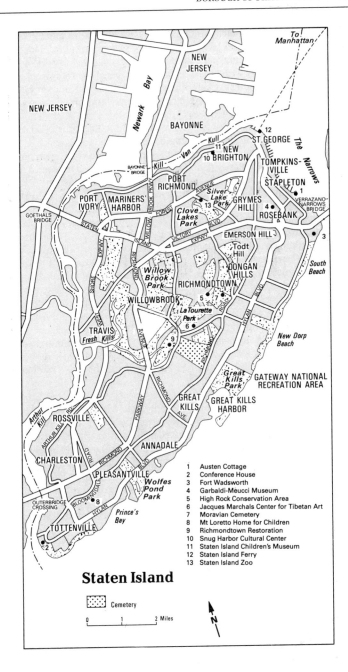

1 Austen Cottage
2 Conference House
3 Fort Wadsworth
4 Garbaldi-Meucci Museum
5 High Rock Conservation Area
6 Jacques Marchals Center for Tibetan Art
7 Moravian Cemetery
8 Mt Loretto Home for Children
9 Richmondtown Restoration
10 Snug Harbor Cultural Center
11 Staten Island Children's Museum
12 Staten Island Ferry
13 Staten Island Zoo

Staten Island

Cemetery

0   1   2 Miles

N

took the name of Richmond after the Duke of Richmond, illegitimate son of Charles II.

During the British colonial period, Staten Island continued to develop as an agricultural community with its less-fertile areas devoted to raising stock, while its long coastline and protected waters made fishing, oystering, and shipbuilding important factors in the economy. Along the Kills several tidal mills were built for grinding grist and sawing lumber.

In the early summer of 1776 the arrival of some 30,000 British soldiers and Hessian mercenaries disrupted the agrarian quiet of the island, which soon became a vast military camp from which the British would stage operations on Long Island. Although the population was largely loyalist and welcomed the arrival of the British forces, the billeting of so many soldiers strained the resources of the 3,000 islanders and tensions developed. At the end of Aug the British attacked and took the west end of Long Island (present-day Brooklyn), using barges built on Staten Island. That Sept the Billopp House in present-day Tottenville became the site of abortive negotiations to end the war. Throughout the rest of the fighting, the British maintained fortifications at Fort Hill in St. George. Staten Island is said to have been the site of the last shot of the war: an unknown soldier departing down the bay fired at the jeering crowds lining the shore.

After the war, Staten Islanders continued farming, oystering, and fishing, largely unaffected by the heady changes across the bay, although the federal government did see the strategic importance of the island and fortified it during the War of 1812. In 1829, teenaged Cornelius Vanderbilt, who was born near Stapleton, started a regular ferry service to Manhattan, the first step in a business empire that would eventually make him the borough's wealthiest and most famous son.

Soon Staten Island burgeoned as a seaside resort, especially New Brighton, where such hotels as the Pavilion attracted prominent New Yorkers and a large clientele from the South. A literary circle formed around eye surgeon Samuel MacKenzie Elliott, whose practice was located in Manhattan. Dr. Elliott treated historian Francis Parkman (who later claimed that Elliott had nearly blinded him), James Russell Lowell, Henry Wadsworth Longfellow, and Richard Henry Dana. Elliott's residence still stands in West New Brighton. Judge William Emerson had a summer house called the Snuggery on what is now Emerson Hill, where he entertained his brother Ralph Waldo Emerson and hired Henry David Thoreau for a short time in 1843 to tutor his son. Enthusiasts of sport also were attracted to the island, which was home to the first American canoe club and the site of the first lawn tennis court (1880).

Other notable visitors were Giuseppe Garibaldi, who remained for three years during his exile from Italy; Herman Melville, who frequently visited his brother Tom, governor of Sailors' Snug Harbor from 1867 to 1884; and Frederick Law Olmsted, who tried his hand at farming before finding his life's work as a landscape architect.

During the Civil War the island again became a training ground and assembly point for troops, who set up camps in the fields and orchards and whose presence provoked hostility in a population with strong Confederate sympathies. Many Southerners sent their families to the safety of the hotels they had formerly visited for pleasure. During the Draft Riots (July 1863) abolitionist Horace Greeley came here and was hidden from angry mobs by his friend George W. Curtis, whose house still stands, also in West New Brighton. In Stapleton, Factoryville (now West New Brighton), and New Brighton, mobs burned and pillaged buildings and attacked those blacks who had not escaped into the woods or across the Kill to New Jersey.

Toward the end of the 19C, Staten Island became less rural, but again changed more slowly than the other boroughs. Industries began to dot the northern and western parts of the shoreline—brick and linoleum factories, breweries, dye works, chemical plants—but the Atlantic seacoast still attracted summer visitors. South Beach on the Lower Bay and Midland Beach, just south of it, became popular resort areas. The first railroad (1860) was extended along both sides of the island, linking formerly isolated communities, and charitable institutions aware of the growing shortages of land in Manhattan began buying sites for hospitals, orphanages, and schools.

In 1898, when Staten Island became part of Greater New York (voters favored consolidation four to one), it had only about 67,000 inhabitants, a population slightly larger than that of Manhattan in 1800.

Staten Island Today

Today Staten Island is struggling to maintain its heritage and preserve what natural beauty remains, while growing in some orderly fashion. Since the opening of the Verrazano-Narrows Bridge, the borough has seen not just a population explosion, but a concurrent rise in crime and in the number of people on welfare. Staten Island has eight housing projects, mostly in the northern section. Pollution is also a problem, some of it coming from the industrial plants of New Jersey. When the wind is from the west, the residents of Tottenville can inhale the fumes of Perth Amboy. Rural and small-town Staten Island are virtually gone, and the island has become another outpost of suburbia.

Some neighborhoods have seen the arrival of new immigrants. Port Richmond—its main street long pockmarked with empty storefronts—is being reinvented by Mexican newcomers. Hasidic and Orthodox Jews, Chinese, Indians, Russians, and Albanians, many with more money than earlier immigrants, have also staked out lives on Staten Island. The borough is home to the second-largest mosque in the city (the Albanian Cultural Center on Victory Blvd) and the largest Liberian community outside Africa.

The island, however, remains predominantly white (80 percent), is the only Republican-leaning borough, and has the highest per capita income—$29,159— of any borough. Interestingly, about 40 percent of the white residents are Italian Americans, mostly former Brooklynites. (While the Mafia's presence on Staten Island is often exaggerated, it undeniably exists, as the number of Mafia-related arrests and killings attests.) As an island, the borough remains more insular in personality than any other borough—it has its own daily newspaper, the *Staten Island Advance* (founded 1886)—and every few years some residents rally around the idea of seceding from the city entirely.

> **Touring Staten Island**
> While you can easily reach some parts of Staten Island using public trans-
> portation, it is better to visit outlying areas by car. Staten Island Rapid Tran-
> sit runs from the ferry terminal at St. George to Tottenville. Buses also leave
> from the ferry terminal.
>
> Except for the Greenbelt, Richmondtown, and the Snug Harbor Cultural
> Center, most of the island's sights are small in scale, yet they are intriguing
> to anyone who is interested in history, architecture, or community devel-
> opment, or who simply wants to see the city as a whole.

55 · Northern Staten Island: St. George and New Brighton, Snug Harbor, West New Brighton, Port Richmond, and Westerleigh

St. George and New Brighton

St. George, where the ferry docks, is the gateway to Staten Island and the seat of
borough government. It is also the island's primary transportation hub and its
most densely developed section.

History

During the American Revolution, the British built earthen redoubts on what became known as Fort Hill. After the war, the area remained rural until the 1830s,
when the section facing the Kill Van Kull became a fashionable resort with luxury
hotels. The neighborhood was considered part of the village of New Brighton
until St. George developed its own identity as home to the ferry.

New Brighton was one of the region's earliest planned suburban communities, begun (1835) by English immigrant Thomas E. Davis and named for the English seaside resort. The project ended in foreclosure after the financial panic of
1837, and development did not begin in earnest until the ferry terminal and rail
lines were opened in St. George.

Erastus Wiman, a Toronto-born entrepreneur who understood the importance
of proximity to New York City, moved the ferry station from Tompkinsville to St.
George, shaving a few minutes off the trip to the Battery. He also gave St. George
its name, allegedly persuading railroad investor George Law to sell him land for the
terminal by offering to name the town after Law, canonizing him in the process.

St. George Terminal

Begin at the St. George Terminal for the **Staten Island Ferry,** which marks the
end of a 6.2-mile, half-hour trip from the Battery in Manhattan, with a view
guaranteed to lift your spirits. The panorama includes the Lower Manhattan sky-

line, Governors Island, Ellis and Liberty Islands, the Verrazano-Narrows Bridge, and, finally, the steep hills of Staten Island with the spires and towers of St. George.

For ferry information, ☎ (718) 815-2628. An exhibit on ferry history from the collection of the Staten Island Institute of Arts and Sciences is displayed in the waiting room.

Ferry Fares

Astonishingly, this breathtaking experience is free, though it has never been expensive. As recently as 1976, a round-trip journey cost ten cents; then the fare climbed to a quarter, and in 1989 doubled to 50 cents. In 1997, it was eliminated altogether by Republican mayor Rudolph Giuliani, who owed a large political debt to Staten Island's Republican voters.

Ferry History

The city began to operate the ferry in 1905, taking over the service from the Baltimore and Ohio Railroad. The boats were steam powered from 1857 until 1981, when large diesel ferries came into service. Today the ferry carries 70,000 riders daily as well as cars.

Next to the original terminal, its developer, Erastus Wiman, built the Staten Island Amusement Company, with a casino where visitors were entertained by an electrically illuminated fountain, a 60-piece band, showgirls, and stage shows. The 1888 spectacle *The Fall of Rome* included elephants, which were stabled in New Brighton and driven daily past the home of political cartoonist William A. Rogers, who lived on St. Mark's Place. Soon the pachyderms began appearing in Rogers's cartoons, eventually becoming the symbol of the Republican Party. Wiman also converted the St. George Cricket Ground into a pro baseball stadium as another attraction for his ferry customers, and sometimes the stage productions literally spilled over into deep right field.

The St. George Revitalization Project

An ambitious renewal plan for the area around the terminal is now under way. The terminal itself is getting an $81-million facelift (completion date 2003), which will include a bigger and brighter waiting room, a concourse for restaurants and shops, and a rooftop promenade. An esplanade will wrap around the borough's northwest corner, the first section extending from Jersey St in New Brighton to the ferry terminal.

Also planned are a National Lighthouse Center and Museum on a ten-acre site once used by the U.S. Light-House Service and later as a Coast Guard station. The now-crumbling U.S. Light-House Service, Third District, Staten Island Depot Office Building (1871; Afred B. Mullett; DL), was built to store records. In addition, the Staten Island Institute of Arts and Sciences hopes eventually to build a Waterfront Museum, dedicated to the history of New York Harbor.

North of the terminal is the **Richmond County Bank Ballpark at St. George,** 75 Richmond Terrace. On June 24, 2001, it opened to a sellout crowd of 6,854 enthusiastic fans, who watched the Staten Island Yankees, a Class-A minor league franchise of the New York Yankees, defeat the Hudson Valley Renegades, 3–1. The $71-million stadium, built on land once used for railyards, has a view from home plate of New York Harbor, including the Statue of Liberty and the downtown skyline. The ballpark was designed by the firm of Helmuth, Obata & Kassabaum (HOK), architects of the much-admired Oriole Park at Camden Yards in Baltimore, Maryland.

Across from the terminal, facing the harbor at 2–10 Richmond Terrace, is **Staten Island Borough Hall** (1906; Carrère & Hastings; DL), an impressive monument to municipal government. Built in the style of a 17C French château, Borough Hall features a central pavilion highlighted by a limestone Doric colonnade and flanked by projecting wings that include Flemish bond brickwork and an elaborate cornice. A two-story mansard roof tops off the building. John Carrère, whose prestigious firm also designed the New York Public Library on Fifth Ave, was a Staten Island resident.

Adjacent, at 12–24 Richmond Terrace, is the **Richmond County Courthouse** (1919; Carrère & Hastings; DL). The Corinthian details on this solemn building reflect the influence of the Pantheon. Borough Hall and the Richmond County Courthouse were the only two buildings actually constructed in a civic center planned after Staten Island joined Greater New York in 1898. The **Richmond County Family Court House** (1930; Sibley & Fetherston; DL), 100 Richmond Terrace, has a terra-cotta facade and detailed Ionic columns.

Staten Island Institute of Arts and Sciences

75 Stuyvesant Place, Staten Island, NY 10301. ☎ (718) 727-1135. Open Mon–Sat 9–5; Sun 1–5. Suggested admission charge. Gift shop. Accessible to wheelchairs.

Up the hill to the north is the Staten Island Institute of Arts and Sciences. Founded in 1881, it is the island's oldest cultural institution. The institute houses a museum, which opened to the public (1907) in Borough Hall before getting its own home (1917). It offers changing exhibitions of fine and decorative arts, photography, and Staten Island history.

In addition to documents and artifacts from Staten Island's past (including the Staten Island Ferry Collection), painting, sculpture, and decorative arts, the institute has a remarkable natural science collection: a half-million insect specimens, including the world's largest cicada collection; 25,000 plant specimens; thousands of shells; and more than 2,000 bird eggs.

Continue up Wall St to St. Mark's Place. One block to the left is the new **Brighton Heights Reformed Church.** The original white wooden Gothic revival church (1863) was known for its octagonal spire, which rose above the treetops and provided a visual landmark from afar. In 1996, when a careless worker left his heat gun on, the church burned to the ground. Parishioners raised $2.8 million, and in 1999 a new brick church arose (the fire code prohibits new wooden churches). Its 70 ft steel-and-fiberglass tower now graces the skyline.

Return on St. Mark's Place past Wall St to Hamilton Ave. At the corner is **Curtis High School** (1904; C. B. J. Snyder; DL), the borough's first secondary school. Set on a landscaped lawn, the brick-and-limestone building with a central medieval tower and gabled pavilions has a collegiate feel.

St. George–New Brighton Historic District

Walk west along St. Mark's Place (with the school on your left). The St. George–New Brighton Historic District contains 78 houses, most on Carroll Place, St. Mark's Place, and Westervelt Ave.

Historic District Revival

During the real estate boom of the 1880s and 1890s, Queen Anne, shingle-style, and colonial revival houses were built in what is now the island's only residential historic district. While many of these homes became apartments or boarding houses when the neighborhood declined after World War II, the area has recently experienced a revival, led by preservationists who have long lived here and newcomers—some of them artists, playwrights, and musicians—eager to buy spacious, affordable homes near Manhattan.

At 125 St. Mark's Place is the Queen Anne–style **Camman House** (1895; Edward A. Sargent), with "eyebrow" windows in its conical roof. Sargent, Staten Island's leading late-19C architect, also designed three neighboring houses: 119, 115, and 103 St. Mark's Place. The single institution in the historic district is the neo-Romanesque **St. Peter's Roman Catholic Church** (1903; Harding & Gooch) at 49 St. Mark's Place. The interior has a vaulted ceiling constructed without pillars to provide unobstructed sightlines. The bell tower was added in 1919. Next door is the handsome Renaissance **rectory** (1912; George H. Streeton), whose tan brick and terra-cotta mosaics depict religious symbols.

Also of architectural interest are the three similar houses (1886–87) at 48–56, St. Mark's Place, 17–19 St. Mark's Place (c. 1875), and 1–5 St. Mark's Place (c. 1860), a funky house with a "witch's hat" roof. Unfortunately, some of these houses have been broken into apartments.

Walk left on Westervelt Ave; bear left onto Hamilton Ave and follow it to Phelps Place. The handsome shingle-style double houses at 7–8 and 9–10 Phelps Place and the freestanding 11 Phelps Place (all c. 1890; Douglas Symth) sit on this quiet cul-de-sac, once the estate of Anson Phelps Stokes.

Return to Hamilton Ave; turn right and walk back along Westervelt Ave. The double brick house at 30–32 Westervelt Ave was built (1878–82) by saloon keeper Joseph Wilks when ferry transportation improved.

Continue down the hill to Richmond Terrace. Just to the right of the intersection is the oldest house in the district, **404 Richmond Terrace** (c. 1835), originally the residence of Henry P. Robertson, now a catering firm. In the 19C nine other Greek revival mansions were ranged along this then-fashionable street, overlooking the waters of the Kill Van Kull. Today the view across the Kill includes the oil tanks of Bayonne, New Jersey.

Just outside the historic district are several other buildings of note. Richmond Terrace leads west to Franklin Ave. At 105 Franklin Ave is the **Hamilton Park Cottage** (c. 1864; Carl Pfeiffer; DL). When built, this Italianate brick house stood in one of the nation's first limited-access suburban developments, Hamilton Park (laid out 1851–52), named for its founder, Charles Hamilton. The 12 Hamilton

Park "cottages" were among German architect Pfeiffer's first American commissions.

Continue along Franklin Ave. Turn left onto Park Place and left again onto Harvard Ave. At 66 Harvard Ave is the **Pritchard House** (c. 1853), a yellow stucco Italianate residence with stone trim and a wooden porch, balcony, and window hood. It is the only survivor from the original Hamilton Park development, about a decade earlier than Pfeiffer's cottages.

Return to Park Place; turn right onto Franklin Ave and left onto **Pendleton Place,** developed in the 1850s and 1860s by William S. Pendleton, a successful Boston lithographer who moved to Manhattan. He built several houses on this block, renting some to New Yorkers looking for suburban retreats and others to his relatives. One of the few remaining is the 2½-story Gothic revival **W. S. Pendleton House** (c. 1855; attrib. Charles Duggin, DL), at 22 Pendleton Place, which sits high on the hill with views of the Kill Van Kull. It has steeply pitched gable roofs, a square, spire-topped tower, and beautiful scalloped scrollwork. Even higher on the hill is **1 Pendleton Place** (c. 1862; Charles Duggin), Pendleton's second house, a large, asymmetrical stick-style residence, whose fourth-floor, eight-sided lookout provides a great vantage point.

Return to Franklin Ave and turn left onto W. Buchanan St. The dilapidated **New Brighton Village Hall** (1871; James Whitford; DL) at the corner of Lafayette Ave, a once-stately French Second Empire brick building, has been empty since 1968.

Walk two blocks toward the water to Richmond Terrace. Turn left to 806 Richmond Terrace (between Clinton Ave and Tysen St), the **Tysen-Neville House** (c. 1800; DL), one of the city's last remaining colonial houses. Owned by retired British naval officer Capt. John Neville, the stone house has an unusual two-story veranda, probably added in the late 19C. During the early 1900s it became the Old Stone Jug, where sailors from Snug Harbor enjoyed hospitality and libations. Snug Harbor eventually bought the place and closed it down. It is again a residence.

Snug Harbor Cultural Center

1000 Richmond Terrace, Staten Island, NY 10301. ☎ (718) 448-2500. Web site: www.snug-harbor.org. Grounds open daily dawn to dusk; extended hours for special events. Free admission to grounds. See individual museums for hours and fees. Free guided tours Sat and Sun at 2; tours depart from Visitors Center near parking lot by West Lawn. Café (open Mon–Fri 11–2); gift shop (open Wed–Sun 1–4:30). Wheelchair access limited to grounds and Veterans Memorial Hall, Newhouse Center for Contemporary Art, Visitors Center, and Music Hall.

Bus: From St. George Terminal, S1 to Snug Harbor Gate.

Car: From Verrazano Bridge, take Bay St exit (five miles from bridge), continue on Bay St to Richmond Terrace. Free parking; enter via the west gate on Kissel Ave off Delafield Place.

Just to the west of the Tysen-Neville House is Snug Harbor Cultural Center, once a sailors' retirement home, now a fast-growing center for the visual and performing arts. The Newhouse Center for Contemporary Art, the Staten Island Children's Museum, the Staten Island Botanical Garden, and the John A. Noble Collection are located on its 83-acre grounds. Mature trees, fountains, gardens, and magnificent Greek revival architecture grace the area.

History

Sailors' Snug Harbor, the nation's first retirement home and hospital for elderly and disabled sailors, was established by the will of merchant Robert Richard Randall. His father, Thomas, had made a fortune at sea in activities that could charitably be described as "profitable commerce" or "privateering" but with equal accuracy could be called piracy. Robert died in 1801 directing that his assets be used to construct on his Manhattan farm a home for "aged, decrepit and worn-out sailors." During two decades of litigation with relatives who wanted Robert's money for themselves, the city expanded to encroach on the farm. Therefore Snug Harbor's trustees leased out the Randall property (near present-day Washington Square) and bought a Staten Island farm (1831). The first building was completed in 1833.

After more than a century as a retirement home, Sailors' Snug Harbor was sold in the 1970s to a developer and the remaining sailors—fewer than 100—were moved to more modern facilities in North Carolina. The new owner proposed high-rise buildings on the site, but in 1973 concerned citizens convinced the city to buy the land and its 28 buildings. Snug Harbor Cultural Center opened in 1976, undertaking a program of restoration and renovation that continues today.

The **iron fence** surrounding the property (1841–45; Frederick Diaper; DL) was put up not so much to bar intruders as to keep the old salts from wandering off to neighboring watering holes. The **North Gatehouse** (1873; Richard P. Smyth; DL), which provides access from Richmond Terrace, was one of four built in hopes of preventing the sailors from smuggling liquor onto the premises.

Begin at the **west gate.** Inside stands the **Governor's House** (late 1880s), built as the Chief Steward's House; the original Governor's House stood across the road, but was demolished in 1955.

Staten Island Botanical Garden

The nearby **Rose Garden,** like all of the center's plantings, is maintained by the Staten Island Botanical Garden. Across the way is the **Pond Garden,** where sailors once sailed model boats. On the right is **Cottage Row,** a group of mansard-roofed Victorian cottages (1885) constructed for employees; some are now used for artists-in-residence.

New York Chinese Scholar's Garden

Staten Island Botanical Garden, 1000 Richmond Terrace, Staten Island, NY 10301. ☎ (718) 273-8200. Web site: www.sibg.org. Open April–Oct, Tues–Sun 10–5; for hours in late fall and winter, call ahead. Guided tours Wed, Sat, and Sun. Admission charge. Café open for lunch daily during spring, summer, and fall; open weekends in early winter. Gift shop. A few pavilions have steps; otherwise, wheelchair accessible.

Just beyond the cottages is the New York Chinese Scholar's Garden (opened 1999), part of the Staten Island Botanical Garden. It is not so much a formal garden as a series of courtyards and pavilions enhanced by nature.

Modeled after Ming dynasty (1368–1644) scholars' gardens—private retreats for reflection and the contemplation of nature—the garden is unique in the United States. It was built by Chinese artisans using Chinese materials and incorporating Chinese plants: lotus, bamboo, banana, and jasmine. Traditional materials include light and dark goose-egg pebbles embedded in the paving and limestone quarried from the floor of Taihu Lake near Suzhou used as sculpture or to suggest hills. A mosaic floor mural depicting cranes contains objects found on site—among them slices of glass from beer and soda bottles.

Within the garden are three ponds and a waterfall, whose recirculating water represents the rejuvenation of life. Trees, shrubs, and flowers have been selected for their shape, seasonal character, and symbolic meaning, with pine, bamboo, and plum used extensively. Walkways, some covered, bend and twist, offering new perspectives of viewing. One of the two main pavilions serves as a scholar's study and the other as a viewing pavilion. The study is closed to keep out distraction, while the viewing room is open, overlooking 20 acres of wetlands, which support egrets and herons.

Connie Gretz's Secret Garden

Children should be delighted by Connie Gretz's Secret Garden (opened 2000), a maze whose intricate pathways are enclosed by three-ft evergreens. The maze leads to a walled secret garden inspired by Frances Hodgson Burnett's classic children's novel. Overlooking it is a 38 ft castle with a drawbridge and moat.

The **Carl Grillo Glass House** (open 9–5), on Chapel Rd, is a 3,000-square-ft conservatory housing plants and flowers from temperate, tropical, and desert environments. Just beyond the conservatory are perennial gardens and a gazebo (1905), the lone survivor of four such structures built to mask air shafts.

Across the way is the Snug Harbor **Visitors Center** (Building H), housing a historical exhibit. Along Melville Rd are a **Butterfly Garden** and a **Sensory Garden,** containing tactile and scented plants.

Staten Island Children's Museum

1000 Richmond Terrace, Staten Island, NY 10301. ☎ (718) 273-2060. Open during the school year Tues–Sun, 12–5; during the summer, Tues–Sun 11–5. Open most school holidays. Closed Mon, Jan 1, Easter, July 4, Thanksgiving, Dec 25. Admission charge. Changing exhibits. Café; gift shop. Wheelchair accessible.

Behind the gardens is the **Staten Island Children's Museum,** whose delightful hands-on exhibits exploring science, history, and the arts are geared to children ages 2–13. Permanent exhibits include **Block Harbor,** a harbor-waterfront environment with a walk-in wooden frigate; **Bugs and Other Insects,** with more than 200 mounted specimens, and **Portia's Playhouse,** an interactive theater space with costumes, props, and sound effects.

Founded (1974) in a Stapleton storefront, the museum moved to Snug Harbor in 1986, expanding from a single exhibit to four floors of exhibition space. The main building (1911), formerly a maintenance building, is now connected by a glass-enclosed walk-through to the barn (renovated 2000), which once was used for storing vegetables. The "silo" now holds the elevator.

Snug Harbor's Beaux-Arts **Great Hall** (1918), now a banquet hall and catering service, was once the Recreation Building. Inside was a reading room graced by tall Palladian windows and a vaulted ceiling. Across the street is **Veterans Memorial Hall** (1855–56; James Solomon; DL), formerly the chapel, where daily attendance was once mandatory; the bell tower was added in 1883. It is now used for concerts and weddings.

Next to the Great Hall is the **Music Hall** (Building T), the second-oldest (1892) theater in New York City (Carnegie Hall is one year older), where the sailors once enjoyed vaudeville and films. Though larger in scale, the Music Hall echoes the Greek revival style of the center's original buildings. Continued renovation will increase the auditorium's capacity from 400 to its original 850 seats.

On the lawn in front of the Music Hall is a bronze replica (1987) of J. W. Fiske's zinc **King Neptune Fountain** (1898) showing a determined Neptune brandishing a harpoon. (The original is on display in the John A. Noble Collection.)

The magnificent **row of five Greek revival buildings** (Buildings E–A, east to west) facing the Kill is the architectural centerpiece of Snug Harbor. The end buildings (Buildings E and A) were designed by Richard Smyth (1879–1881). The three central ones (Buildings D, C, and B) are the work of the famous architect Minard Lafever. Except for Building C, all were dormitories.

John A. Noble Collection

1000 Richmond Terrace, Staten Island, NY 10301. ☎ (718) 447-6490. Web site: www.johnanoble.com. Open Tues, Wed, and Fri 10–5; Thurs 1–7; Sat and Sun 1–5. Restricted hours during winter months (call ahead). Closed Jan 1, Thanksgiving, Dec 25. Admission charge. Educational programs, changing exhibitions, printmaking classes, lectures. Gift shop. Accessible to wheelchairs.

Building D (1840–41; Minard Lafever; DL) houses the John A. Noble Collection of maritime art (opened 2000), which includes oil paintings, lithographs, photographs, and drawings. Other resources at the museum include a maritime library and printmaking studio. Noble (1913–1983) was a well-known artist who had worked as a seaman and in the marine salvage industry. He painted the ships of New York harbor and the sailors of Snug Harbor.

In 1928, while working on a schooner in the Kill Van Kull, Noble discovered the former Port Johnston coal docks, which had become a graveyard of wooden ships. The sight changed Noble's life. In the following decades he committed himself to documenting the history of the harbor, working from a floating studio on a houseboat that he had salvaged and built in 1941, as he said, "out of the small bones of larger vessels." Later Noble became one of the passionately committed activists whose work saved the grounds and buildings of Snug Harbor from development. Exhibitions focus on Noble's work and on the history of New York Harbor.

Newhouse Center for Contemporary Art

1000 Richmond Terrace, Staten Island, NY 10301. ☎ (718) 448-2500. Open Wed–Sun noon–5. Admission charge. Gift shop. Wheelchair accessible.

Building C, with its majestic Ionic portico, was formerly **Main Hall** (1831–33; Minard Lafever; DL), the administration building. The oldest and architecturally most important structure of Snug Harbor, it is Lafever's earliest known work. It is constructed of brick and sheathed in Westchester marble quarried by Sing Sing prisoners. Inside is the Newhouse Center for Contemporary Art.

The Newhouse Center was founded in 1977 as a community gallery, and its exhibitions often feature Staten Island artists or focus on issues of local interest. On the second floor is a 20 × 100 ft ceiling mural of a billowy haired Neptune (1884;

restored 1993). The upstairs passageway between Main Hall and the adjacent building (once the dining hall), with its two rows of windows and benches, which suggests the seating on a ferry boat, was once a predinner gathering place for the sailors.

The **obelisk** on the front lawn facing Main Hall marks the tomb of founder Robert Richard Randall. When he died in 1801, Randall was buried in the graveyard at Manhattan's St. Mark's-in-the-Bowery Church. In 1834, he was reinterred here. Further along the path is a statue (1884) of Randall.

West New Brighton

West of Snug Harbor is the neighborhood of West New Brighton, sometimes called West Brighton. In the 19C its industrialized western sector was called Factoryville. This racially mixed neighborhood, mainly built up with modest one- and two-family homes, also has public housing projects, mansions, renovated 19C houses, and several colonial-era landmarks.

Points of Interest

The house at **69 Delafield Place** (c. 1850) is a dark stone Gothic revival residence, one of 22 houses built as an investment by the noted eye surgeon, oculist, and abolitionist Dr. Samuel MacKenzie Elliott. Legend has it the house was a stop on the Underground Railroad.

The **Cornelius Cruser House** (DL), also known as the **Kreuzer-Pelton House,** at 1262 Richmond Terrace, is best seen from Pelton Place. Its three sections reflect Staten Island history. Cornelius Van Santvoord, minister of the Dutch Reformed Church in nearby Port Richmond, built the simple one-room Dutch colonial cottage in 1722; Cornelius Cruser enlarged it with the steep-roofed central section in 1770; and Daniel Pelton added the two-story brick extension in the Federal style (1836).

The **Scott-Edwards House** (c. 1730; addition 1840; DL), at 752 Delafield Ave, began as a modest one-story sandstone dwelling; the Greek revival portico was added about 1840, perhaps when it belonged to Judge Ogden Edwards, a cousin of Aaron Burr and the first New York supreme court justice from Staten Island.

The impeccably restored **Julia Gardiner Tyler House** (c. 1835; DL), at 27 Tyler St, is an elegant, white Greek revival mansion with an imposing four-columned portico. Julia Gardiner Tyler, widow of President John Tyler and a rabid Confederate sympathizer, lived here after 1868. Once part of a large estate, the house, which today looks out on the headstones of St. Peter's Cemetery Annex, is a dignified anomaly in a neighborhood of ranch houses.

Staten Island Zoo

614 Broadway (Colonial Court; rear entrance on Clove Rd at Martling Ave), Staten Island, NY 10310. ☎ (718) 442-3100. Web site: www.statenisland zoo.org. Open daily 10–4:45. Closed Thanksgiving, Dec 25, Jan 1. Admission charge; voluntary donation on Wed after 2. Food concession; gift shop. Accessible to wheelchairs.

Bus: From St. George Terminal, S48 to Forest Ave and Broadway. From Bay Ridge, Brooklyn, S53 to the zoo entrance.

Car: Take Staten Island Expwy to Slosson Ave exit; continue north to Martling Ave; turn right onto Martling Ave.

Several blocks north of the Gardiner House is the eight-acre Staten Island Zoo, founded in 1936 on the former Barrett family estate; it is the only zoo in the five boroughs not administered by the Wildlife Conservation Society.

The Staten Island Zoo may not have lions and tigers, but it does have a spectacular reptile collection featuring boa constrictors, cobras, and some 30 varieties of rattlesnakes. The new **African Savannah at Twilight** offers leopards, baboons, and antelopes. There is a tropical forest habitat, a state-of-the-art aquarium, a colony of vampire bats, and, for children, a petting zoo and pony rides.

Mandolin Brothers Ltd., 629 Forest Ave, has been called "a toy shop for guitar players"; it counts George Harrison, Bob Dylan, George Benson, and Paul Simon among its clientele. On the ferry home from a visit to the store, Joni Mitchell penned "Song for Sharon," which begins, "I went to Staten Island, Sharon, to buy myself a mandolin." Paul McCartney turned to Mandolin Brothers when his original Hofner Violin Bass needed repairs. The store sells new and vintage acoustic and electric guitars, as well as mandolins, banjos, bass guitars, and ukeleles. Prices in the "High-End Room" soar to $50,000 for a Gibson 1960 Les Paul Standard with a graduated sunburst finish. For information, ☎ (718) 981-8585.

Port Richmond

West of West New Brighton and south of the Kill Van Kull is Port Richmond, an ethnically diverse community with a significant black and Hispanic population as well as longtime white residents. Port Richmond is currently recovering from decades of decline.

History

In the early 19C the area became a transfer point for freight and passenger travel on the Kill. Vice President Aaron Burr, infamous for fatally wounding his political rival Alexander Hamilton in a duel (1804), spent the last weeks of his life at the Winants Hotel (2040 Richmond Terrace; demolished long ago), where he died in 1836.

In the mid-19C Irish and German immigrants worked in the whale-oil processing plant or the lumber and coal yards near the waterfront. By the end of the century there was a black community. During World War I, Italians, Poles, and Scandinavians labored at the shipyards, which closed after the armistice and reopened during World War II.

Until the advent of the Verrazano-Narrows Bridge and the Staten Island Mall, Port Richmond Ave was the main commercial street of the North Shore. Thereafter the population shifted southward, and the commercial area declined. Today it is enjoying a renaissance, as new immigrants, particularly Mexicans, have established businesses.

Points of Interest

Built as the **Northfield Township District School 6** (1891; addition James Warriner Moulton; 1898; DL) and later the P.S. 20 Annex, this beautiful Romanesque revival building at 160 Heberton Ave has striking textured brickwork and a four-story pyramidal bell tower. Converted into housing for the elderly (1993–94), it is a fine example of the adaptive reuse of a historic structure. Next door in Veterans Memorial Park is a fountain dedicated to the memory of Eugene G. Putnam (1865–1913), principal of P.S. 20 for 17 years.

Temple Emanu-El (1907; Harry W. Pelcher), at 984 Post Ave (between Decker and Heberton Aves), a classical revival synagogue modeled after the Great Synagogue of Warsaw, is Staten Island's oldest synagogue and its second largest. It dates back to the turn-of-the-20C, when Port Richmond was a small town and many of the temple's congregants owned stores in the thriving commercial district. While there is no longer a sizable Jewish community in Port Richmond, the socially liberal Conservative congregation numbers about 200 families, many from surrounding neighborhoods.

Faber Park and Pool, 2175 Richmond Terrace (between Ferry and North Sts), is located on what was once the North Shore home of the Faber family, of lead-pencil fame. Caspar Faber started the business in Stein, Germany (1761). A century later Eberhard Faber came to New York, building the first lead-pencil factory in the United States. The property became parkland in 1928; in 1932 a municipal pool was built as an alternative to the polluted Kill Van Kull.

The **Staten Island Reformed Church,** formerly the Old Dutch Reformed Church, 54 Port Richmond Ave, occupies the site of the first religious congregation (1663) on Staten Island. Standing on a forlorn commercial strip, the church, now sadly weathered, replaced two earlier ones. The first (1715) was destroyed by fire during the Revolutionary War and rebuilt in 1787. The current structure was built in 1844. Its burial ground is the resting place of some of the North Shore's earliest settlers.

Ralph's Ices, 501 Port Richmond Ave, still a family business, has been a local landmark since 1949; it was founded in 1928 in a garage by Italian immigrant Ralph Silvestro. The store boasts 60 flavors of Italian ice and long lines of customers in the summer. Ralph's is closed from mid-Oct to early April; ☎ (718) 273-3675.

Westerleigh

Westerleigh, just south of Port Richmond, is an attractive residential neighborhood with an intriguing history: it was settled by Prohibitionists.

Prohibition Park

In 1887, in what is roughly the center of today's Westerleigh, the National Prohibition Party bought 25 rural acres as a summer haven and called it Prohibition Park. Three-acre Westerleigh Park, some homes, and many street names survive from the temperance community. Some streets honor the party's presidential candidates, including Clinton B. Fiske, Neal Dow, and John G. Woolley, while Willard Ave is named for Frances E. Willard, leader of the Woman's Christian Temperance Union. Other streets pay homage to formerly "dry" states—Ohio, Virginia, and the Dakotas—while the "wet" state of New York is named simply in deference to being the community's home. Well-organized and influential, the Prohibitionists had a 4,000-seat meeting hall on The Boulevard for lectures and rallies. When Westerleigh Collegiate Institute was built in 1895, the name Prohibition Park was abandoned.

Among the houses remaining from the early days of Prohibition Park is **42 The Boulevard** (c. 1893), a beautifully shingled house with a stone first story and a Palladian window. Others include 6–8 The Boulevard (1893) and 682 Jewett Ave (1890), originally the home of Rev. William H. Boole, a cofounder of Prohibition Park.

The **Peter Housman House** (c. 1730; addition c. 1760; DL), at 308 St. John Ave (named for the Prohibitionist governor of Kansas), predates the temperance movement. To the original one-room stone wing, Housman, a successful mill-wright, added a large clapboard addition with dormer windows.

56 · Eastern Staten Island: Tompkinsville and Ward Hill, Stapleton and Stapleton Heights, Grymes Hill, and Rosebank

Tompkinsville and Ward Hill

South of the St. George Terminal is Tompkinsville, the oldest village (1814) in eastern Staten Island, named for Daniel D. Tompkins (1774–1825)—abolitionist, governor of New York, and vice president of the United States. In colonial times it was known as the **Watering Place,** where ships refilled their casks as they left the harbor. Today it is a working-class neighborhood, home to the city's only secular commune, Ganas (founded 1979), which owns several homes along Scribner and Corson Aves and has helped stabilize the area.

Southwest of Tompkinsville is Ward Hill, a well-to-do area named for Caleb T. Ward, who bought the hill in 1826. The monumental Greek revival **Caleb T. Ward Mansion** (c. 1835; Seth Geer; DL) on its summit, at 141 Nixon Ave, was once surrounded by the 250 acres of Ward's estate. Now hemmed in by elegant 20C homes, it has stupendous views of the harbor.

Stapleton and Stapleton Heights

Stapleton, along Upper New York Bay and south of Ward Hill, is racially, ethnically, and economically mixed. Housing ranges from the 693-unit Stapleton Houses, a New York State housing project, to large 19C homes in Stapleton Heights, especially around St. Paul's Ave.

History

The area was rural when future steamship and railroad magnate Cornelius Vanderbilt (1794–1877) was born on the nearby family farm. The village of Edgewater preceded modern Stapleton, which took shape in 1832 when William J. Staples, a Manhattan merchant and entrepreneur, and Minthorne Tompkins, son of Daniel D. Tompkins, bought land from the Vanderbilts, laid out streets, and established ferry service to Manhattan.

Staten Island Beer

In the mid-19C, German immigrants arrived, attracted by the terrain, which reminded them of their homeland. Natural springs provided the fresh water necessary for producing beer; the hillsides provided sites for caves, useful for fermentation vaults and cool storage. The most successful firm, the **Rubsam & Horrmann Atlantic Brewery,** lasted well into the 20C, surviving Prohibition and the Depression; in 1953 Piels Brothers, Inc., bought the brewery but closed it a decade later.

At one time the deepwater piers extending into the bay at Tompkinsville and Stapleton were municipal piers built (1921–23) by Mayor John Hylan to bring trade to the waterfront. This plan failed, and in 1937 the piers were designated a free port where foreign cargoes could be unloaded and stored for transshipment without paying duty. This plan also failed. In the mid-1970s some of the piers were converted to a facility for container shipping, but later they were demolished. The **Stapleton piers** were rebuilt as a U.S. Navy base, the Staten Island Homeport, which operated only from 1990 to 1994. The city, which inherited the $226-million facility, has considered and rejected an array of plans—a pier for casino boats, an auto raceway, a sports complex, a film studio—leaving its future in doubt.

Points of Interest

St. Paul's Ave, a one-way winding and hilly street in Stapleton Heights, is built up with Italianate, Queen Anne, and Tudor houses, some of them originally the homes of well-to-do brewers. Before the advent of storm sewers and pavement, mud from the hillsides regularly washed down the street, then known as Mud Lane.

A tall butterscotch-colored clock tower defines the former **P. S. 15** (1897–98; DL) at 98 Grant St (corner of St. Paul's Ave). Built by Edward A. Sargent, a leading Staten Island architect who also did houses in the St. George–New Brighton Historic District, the school now houses offices for the Department of Education.

The Episcopal **St. Paul's Memorial Church and Rectory** (1866–70; Edward T. Potter; DL), at 217–225 St. Paul's Ave, has been described as one of the finest high-Victorian Gothic religious complexes in the city. The church is faced in dark stone and trimmed with Connecticut brownstone. The 2½-story rectory, which complements the church in style and materials, suggests an English country parish house.

Among the avenue's well-kept homes is **387 St. Paul's Ave** (c. 1885), a salmon-colored Victorian beauty festooned with "gingerbread."

Serpentine Art and Nature Commons

Box 040252, Stapleton Station, Staten Island, NY 10304-005.

On St. Paul's Ave (between Van Duzer St and Broad St) is a 35-acre wooded hillside. Open to the public for hiking and picnicking, the Serpentine Art and Nature Commons has good views of the harbor. In the 1970s a group of committed neighbors saved the hillside from developers who wished to regrade the slope for housing. Its rare ecological environment, a "serpentine barrens," includes plants such as green milkweed and slender knotweed. For special events, see the Web site: preserve.org/serpentine/serpentine.htm.

Unlike Stapleton Heights, much of Stapleton is run-down. One exception is the former **Edgewater Village Hall** (1889; Paul Kühne; DL) in Tappen Park, the only vestige of the 19C village (incorporated 1866) that preceded modern Stapleton. The Romanesque revival brick building houses a children's health center and offices for Staten Island district attorneys.

Uphill from the park, the house at **390 Van Duzer St** (18C?; DL), between Wright and Beach Sts, is an architectural hybrid moved here from elsewhere, its Greek revival portico perhaps recycled from some other building. The house at **364 Van Duzer St** (c. 1855; DL), between Beach and Prospect Sts, was built by Capt. Robert M. Hazard, who bought the land from Minthorne Tompkins and William J. Staples. The Greek revival house, with a double portico, two-story columns, and tall parlor windows, also has the traditional overhanging eaves of the Dutch colonial style.

Farther south is the **Dr. James R. Boardman House** (1848; DL), at 710 Bay St, a wood-frame Italianate house on a hill overlooking the Narrows. Boardman was the resident physician at the Seamen's Retreat. The former **Seamen's Retreat** (1834–53; Abraham Maybie, builder; DL), at 732–38 Bay St (northwest corner of Vanderbilt Ave), is now the **Bayley-Seton Campus of St. Vincent's Catholic Medical Centers.** The earliest building, the **Main Building,** dates from 1834 to 1837, when the New York State legislature operated a seamen's hospital here. Nearby is the former **Physician-in-Chief's Residence** (1842; Staten Island Granite Company, builder; DL), similar in style to the Main Building. Non-landmarked 1930s buildings dominate the site.

A Historic Hospital

The federal government took over this site from the state in 1883, moving the U.S. Marine Hospital here from Bedloe's (now Liberty) Island to make room for the Statue of Liberty. The Marine Hospital then became a U.S. Public Health Service Hospital, which continued serving seamen. The National Institutes of Health, now in Bethesda, Maryland, began as a one-room Laboratory of Hygiene for Bacteriological Investigation in the attic of the hospital. After the government left in 1981, the Sisters of Charity reopened the hospital, naming it for Dr. Richard Bayley, physician of the old quarantine station, and his daughter, who was canonized as St. Elizabeth Ann Seton, the first native-born American saint and founder of the American Sisters of Charity.

Behind the Seaman's Retreat, at 119 Tompkins Ave (between Vanderbilt Ave and Tompkins St), is the former **Mariners' Family Asylum of the Port of New York** (1855; J. Graham Glauber), built as a refuge for female relatives of seamen being treated next door. Both the Bayley-Seton complex and the former Mariner's Family Asylum are in **Clifton,** a neighborhood south of Stapleton and north of

Rosebank. Historically associated with the Vanderbilts, Clifton is now home to a large number of Liberian and West African immigrants.

Grymes Hill

Southwest of Stapleton is fashionable **Grymes Hill.** Like other Staten Island hills, Grymes Hill (elevation 354 ft) has long attracted the wealthy, leaving the flatlands below to the less affluent.

During the 19C, grand estates arose on Grymes Hill, some of them the homes of beer barons—for example, August Horrmann, who built the 40-room Horrmann Castle in 1891. The castle was sold in 1945, used as a convent until 1965, and razed in 1968 to make way for the Enclave, a gated community of very big, very expensive homes, many owned by Italian Americans whose families lived in Bensonhurst or other heavily Italian Brooklyn neighborhoods. At the top of the hill are older and more tasteful Tudor, Victorian, and colonial houses. Garden apartments and ranch houses dominate the hill's lower reaches.

Queen of the Hill

Grymes Hill is named for **Susana Grymes,** widow of Louisiana's first governor, William Charles Cole Claiborne. After Claiborne died in 1817, Susana moved to Paris, returning two years later to Louisiana, where in 1822 she married a distinguished lawyer, John R. Grymes, a union that lasted about 13 years. In 1836, the strong-willed Susana left her husband to move to New York. Grymes provided money to buy a house on Staten Island, where she lived in seclusion on the hill that bears her name. In 1843, she moved to Europe. She died in 1881.

Points of Interest

Wagner College, bounded by Howard Ave, Campus Rd, Pleasant Valley Ave, and a network of small streets on the east, sits atop Grymes Hill enjoying a fine view of the harbor. Founded in 1883 in Rochester, New York, as Wagner Memorial Lutheran College, Wagner is now a nonsectarian, private, largely undergraduate institution. In 1918 it moved to Staten Island, purchasing 38 acres from the estate of Sir Edward Cunard, of the English shipping family, and 16 acres from Jacob H. Vanderbilt. The present 108-acre campus offers a mix of modern academic architecture, older collegiate-style structures, and assorted buildings dating back to the Cunard days.

Bellevue (c. 1851), the former Cunard residence in the East Campus on Howard Ave, is now Cunard Hall, with offices and classrooms. The red brick mansion once commanded spectacular views of the harbor, which are now blocked by newer buildings, but the view is still breathtaking from the upper tier of the nearby main parking area. Howard Ave was originally called Serpentine Rd, either after serpentinite, the local greenish, striated stone, or after the winding course of the road itself.

Also on the East Campus are the ivy-covered brick neo-Tudor **Main Hall** (1930; Smith, Conable & Powley), now used for the theater and visual arts departments, and several **Victorian houses,** which were guest houses and servants quarters during the Cunard days.

Around the corner, at 144 Campus Rd, set back from the street, is the abandoned and sadly deteriorating **Augustinian Academy** (1927; Wilson Eyre & McIlvaine), formerly a Roman Catholic school. Security gates barricade the broken asphalt road leading to the school. The building, with its gabled, red-tiled roofs, stands on the site of Jacob H. Vanderbilt's home. In 1993, when the school was threatened with demolition, Wagner College purchased it, a move that thwarted a proposed town house development but left uncertain the future of the 29-acre property.

Further along Howard Ave is the **Staten Island Campus of St. John's University,** situated on the former estate of shipping tycoon John H. Gans and the grounds of Notre Dame Academy (opened 1903). The academy had purchased 13 acres from several former estates, including that of Dr. Louis A. Dreyfus, said to have invented a chewing gum base and a permanent water-based house paint.

Rosebank

East of Grymes Hill is working-class Rosebank. First farmed by the Dutch, Rosebank became a summer retreat for wealthy Manhattanites in the 1830s. It was initially considered part of Clifton to the north but is said to have taken its name from a bed of roses on St. Mary's Ave. In the late 1840s the Irish arrived, driven from their homeland by the potato famine, their presence reflected in street names like Shaunessy Lane and Donley Ave. Since the 1880s, Rosebank has been largely blue-collar Italian.

Points of Interest

Garibaldi-Meucci Museum

420 Tompkins Ave (near Chestnut Ave), Staten Island, NY 10301. ☎ (718) 442-1608. Open Tues–Sun 1–5. Closed Mon and major holidays. Free. Accessible to wheelchairs.

Bus: From St. George Terminal, S52 or S78 to the corner of Chestnut and Tompkins Aves.

This small house-museum memorializes the Italian freedom fighter, Giuseppe Garibaldi, who lived here with his friend Antonio Meucci between 1850 and 1853. Exiled from Italy after the fall of the Roman Republic in 1849, the impoverished Garibaldi sought refuge in the United States, awaiting the opportunity to return home. He was taken in by Antonio Meucci, the inventor of a prototype telephone. The two barely supported themselves hunting and making candles. Garibaldi left New York permanently in the autumn of 1853 and returned to Italy to continue the struggle for Italian unification and independence.

By the late 19C, especially after Garibaldi's death in 1882, the house had become a shrine to which hundreds made pilgrimages. Meucci died in 1889 and, in 1906, the Garibaldi Society of Staten Island raised money to move the house two blocks to its present location and erected a Pantheon-like structure (demolished in 1952) to protect it. Since 1919 the building has been overseen by the National Order Sons of Italy, which opened it as a museum in 1956.

The museum contains letters, photos, military artifacts, and other memorabilia documenting Garibaldi's life. There is also a small exhibit on Meucci, who was declared the first inventor of the telephone by the U.S. Supreme Court in 1886, though by then it was too late for him to benefit from his invention.

Alice Austen House Museum and Garden

2 Hylan Blvd (at Bay St), Staten Island, NY 10301. ☎ (718) 816-4506. Web site: www.aliceausten.8m.com. Open Thurs–Sun 12–5. Closed Jan, Feb, and major holidays. Suggested donation. Gift shop. Gallery talks, lectures, family events. Accessible to wheelchairs by prior arrangement (museum accessible, gravel pathways difficult to navigate, but arrangements can be made for different entrance route).

Bus: From St. George Terminal, S51 to Bay St and Hylan Blvd; then walk to waterfront.

This charming Victorian cottage is the former home of photographer Alice Austen (1866–1952), whose pioneering work depicts New York life at the turn of the last century. Austen came to live here when she was quite young (in the 1860s) and stayed until she was forced to leave by illness and poverty at age 70. The house, furnished with Victorian period pieces, has a magnificent view of New York Harbor and a pretty garden replanted, following Austen's photographs, with weeping mulberry, flowering quince, and other shrubs.

History

When the cottage (1691–1710; altered c. 1846 and later; DL) was bought in 1844 by Austen's grandfather, John Austen, a wealthy businessman, the original Dutch colonial house had already been enlarged. His wife named it **Clear Comfort**, and he remodeled it in the Gothic revival style. When Alice Austen's father deserted Alice Cornell Austen, her mother, during pregnancy, the mother (who thereafter never used her married name) moved back with her financially comfortable parents, bringing the baby Alice with her.

Alice Austen, Victorian Photographer

Alice Austen was given a camera at age ten. She became one of the first female photographers in the nation to work outside the studio, her photos documenting the social customs of her generation, the influx of immigrants to New York City, and the workings of the former Staten Island Quarantine Stations.

Though her early life was comfortable, her finances became straitened as she grew older, and the 1929 stock market crash dealt her a blow from which she never recovered. Eventually she lost her home and moved to the Staten Island Farm Colony, the poorhouse. Not long before her death, Austen's contributions to photography were finally recognized, and she was able to spend the final six months of her life in a nursing home. The Staten Island Historical Society owns more than 4,000 of her negatives, which form the basis of exhibitions at the museum.

Down the block from the Austen cottage and set back from the street, at 30 Hylan Blvd, is the former **Henry McFarlane House** (c. 1841–45, with additions; DL). Originally the residence of the merchant McFarlane, the building served the **New York Yacht Club** between 1868 and 1871. Now run-down, it is owned by the

City Department of Parks, which has been leasing it to residential tenants until it can be restored.

St. John's Episcopal Church (1869–71; Arthur D. Gilman; DL), the granite, Victorian Gothic edifice at 1331 Bay St (southeast corner of New Lane), replaces an earlier frame church in which Cornelius Vanderbilt (born 1794) was the first baby baptized.

South of the church (Bay St at the northeast corner of Nautilus St) is the former **Rosebank U.S. Government Quarantine Station** (opened 1938), where passengers from abroad suspected of carrying communicable diseases were kept under observation; the station has been converted to housing for the U.S. Coast Guard.

New York Quarantine Stations

The city's first official quarantine was established at Bedloe's (now Liberty) Island in 1758, but after a cholera epidemic spread to Manhattan, detainees were shuffled off to Governors Island, and later, in 1801, to Tompkinsville in northeastern Staten Island. This quarantine station angered the local population because workers went in and out freely, spreading disease. After a yellow fever epidemic in 1848, politicians began building a new station at Seguine's Point on the southern part of the island, but protesters there burned it to the ground. When the state returned the quarantine station to Tompkinsville, outraged residents dragged patients out and set the buildings ablaze.

Panicked, health officials turned their sights offshore, constructing two artificial islands about a quarter-mile from land. Hoffman and Swinburne Islands began operating as quarantine stations in the 1870s but were abandoned in the 1920s when restrictive laws decreased immigration. Now deserted and undeveloped, they are part of the Gateway National Recreation Area.

The estate of Arthur Von Briesen (1843–1920), a German American attorney who in 1876 helped found an organization offering free legal services to German immigrants (and which 20 years later became the Legal Aid Society), once stood at the top of the hill where **Von Briesen Park** (Bay St at School Rd) is now located. The park offers superb views of the harbor, the Verrazano-Narrows Bridge, and the fortifications to its south.

Fort Wadsworth

Fort Wadsworth, Staten Island, NY ☎ (718) 354-4500. Open Wed–Sun 10–5. Free. Ranger tours Sat and Sun 10:30 and 2:30; Wed–Fri 2:30. Gift shop. Accessible to wheelchairs.

Bus: From St. George Terminal, S51 to park entrance on Bay St.

Car: From Brooklyn and the Verrazano-Narrows Bridge, take Bay Street exit to park entrance.

Fort Wadsworth, commanding the entrance to New York Harbor, occupies the site of one of the city's oldest military fortifications. Jutting out into the bay beneath the Verrazano-Narrows Bridge are the stern granite walls of **Battery Weed** (1845–61; DL), built before the Civil War and later named for Stephen H. Weed, who was killed in the Battle of Gettysburg. Since 1995, it and **Fort Tompkins** (1858–76; DL), which is farther up the hill, have been part of Gateway National Recreation Area. Until the navy departed in the early 1990s, the forts were part of the Fort Wadsworth Military Reservation, the oldest continually staffed military facility in the country.

History

As early as 1663, the Dutch built a blockhouse here to defend themselves from Indian attacks; the British, who controlled the area during the Revolution, elaborated the fortifications. In 1812 the U.S. government erected Fort Richmond, which faced Fort Lafayette (across the Narrows on a man-made island where the eastern tower of the Verrazano-Narrows Bridge now stands).

Before the Civil War, two new forts were built—Fort Tompkins at the top of the hill and, on the site of Fort Richmond, Battery Weed, with 102 mounted cannons. In the 1890s, when pointed projectiles capable of piercing the walls rendered the forts obsolete, the army erected 12 small gun batteries.

After World War II, the fort accommodated antiaircraft guns and later a radar control center for the Nike missile system, which protected New York until the 1970s. The army withdrew in 1983 and the navy took over. In 1995 the National Park Service assumed control, as had been mandated in 1972 when the Gateway National Recreation Area was created.

Inside are a central courtyard and three tiers of arched galleries. A 1.5-mile trail walk with spectacular panoramic views encompasses both forts and the remains of the gun batteries. Exhibits on site detail the evolution of the city's coastal defense system.

57 · Central Staten Island: Dongan Hills, Todt Hill, New Dorp, Lighthouse Hill, Willowbrook, Bull's Head, New Springville, and Richmondtown

Central Staten Island is largely defined by a range of hills that begins at St. George and runs southwest to La Tourette Park. The name Dongan Hills formerly referred to the whole range of hills but today is used to specify a single neighborhood. The communities built on the hills—Ward Hill and Grymes Hill (in northern Staten Island), Fox Hills, Emerson Hill, Todt Hill, Dongan Hills, and Lighthouse Hill—contain some of the island's most expensive real estate.

Dongan Hills

Dongan Hills is an affluent community, between Todt Hill and South Beach, with the Richmond County Country Club on one border and the South Beach Psychiatric Center on another. During the 17C a mining town was built to exploit nearby lodes of hematite; it was named for Thomas Dongan (1634–1715), an Irish aristocrat who became governor of the province of New York in 1682.

Points of Interest
The **Billiou-Stillwell-Perrine House** (1662–1830; DL), at 1476 Richmond Rd (between Delaware and Cromwell Aves), began as a one-room stone farmhouse, with a Dutch-style fireplace large enough to roast an ox. Pierre Billiou, leader of the Oude Dorp settlement (1661), built the oldest part with its medievally steep roof; the Stillwells and Perrines added on to it. Still a private residence, it is the third-oldest house in the city.

Todt Hill
The community of Todt Hill, sometimes considered part of Dongan Hills, boasts its own identity as Staten Island's wealthiest residential neighborhood. Flamboyant new mansions, some walled to protect privacy, have supplanted older estates. The most expensive houses, whose prices soar into the millions, stand on the grounds of the 135-acre Richmond County Country Club, the city's only privately owned golf course.

At 410 ft above sea level, **Todt Hill** is the highest natural point in New York City and on the Atlantic Coast south of Acadia National Park in Maine.

History
During the 17C, when the Dutch worked the local iron deposits, Todt Hill was known as *Yserberg* ("Iron Hill"). The origin of its present name ("Death Hill") is uncertain. Some believe it refers to the burial ground (now the Moravian Cemetery) at the foot of the hill, while others trace it to the dangerous work of Dutch ice vendors who harvested ice from ponds on the heights and hauled it downhill to sell in New Amsterdam.

Points of Interest
Stone Court (1898–c. 1917; Ernest Flagg; DL), at 209 Flagg Place (between W. Entry Rd and Iron Mine Drive), was the country home of architect Ernest Flagg. The original 71-acre estate included a main house, a gate, and gatehouse as well as a stable, palm house, water tower, and gardener's cottage, all faced in serpentine rock, a striated stone quarried locally. Flagg (1857–1947) designed several famous Manhattan buildings, including the Singer Tower (demolished 1968), St. Luke's Hospital, and the Scribner Building, as well as the U.S. Naval Academy in Annapolis, Maryland. He was also deeply interested in tenement reform and low-cost housing.

The design of the mansion—with its gambrel roof, colonnaded veranda, twin chimneys, clapboarded upper stories, and whitewashed fieldstone walls—is both unusual and original. To some observers it suggests the Dutch colonial style of early Staten Island homes, to others the mansions of wealthy Dutch colonists in the Caribbean. The estate was sold after Flagg's death in 1947; today the mansion and some of the grounds belong to Scalabrini Fathers of St. Charles.

Copperflagg Estates, 23 homes built on eight acres formerly belonging to the Scalabrini Fathers, were intended to be affordable yet well-designed middle-class housing. Architect Robert A. M. Stern, hired by the developer, studied Flagg's designs, but the houses turned out to be large (3,800–7,000 square ft) and very expensive. The development is divided into two sections. One area is landmarked; here Stern designed six French Norman houses of fieldstone and stucco (all 1987–88; Robert A. M. Stern) at 15–71 Flagg Court, and converted the former **stable** (79 Flagg Court), **gatehouse** (79½ Flagg Court), and **palm house** (61 Flagg Court) into residences; the Landmarks Preservation Commission oversaw the design of these structures. Houses outside the landmarked site (on Copperflagg Lane and Copperleaf Terrace) are built in styles that reflect Greek revival, Regency, Georgian, federal, and Dutch colonial traditions.

Flagg's own efforts to build middle-class housing were more appropriate in scale. The experimental **Todt Hill Cottages** (1918–24; DL) on the grounds of his estate reflect his conviction that good design need not be costly. Among them are **Bowcot** (1918; DL), at 95 W. Entry Rd (accessible from Flagg Place), and **Wallcot** (1919–21; Ernest Flagg; DL), also known as the **House-on-the-Wall**, at 285 Flagg Place. Both are small, picturesque stone houses that feature Flagg's signature "mosaic rubble" construction, a technique of embedding broken stone in a concrete wall.

The **McCall's Demonstration House** (1925; Ernest Flagg; DL), at 1929 Richmond Rd (across from Hunter Ave), was designed at the request of *McCall's* magazine to exemplify economy, modern technology, and convenience for the housewife. Flagg incorporated his ideas about building technology (the roof was a slate-rubberoid combination) and rented the cottage to his secretary. It is shrouded by trees and difficult to see from the road.

New Dorp

History

The neighborhood of New Dorp is centered around New Dorp Lane, which runs between Richmond Rd and Hylan Blvd. The town was settled by the Dutch in 1671, ten years after Dutch and Huguenot families had established Staten Island's first permanent European settlement, Old Dorp (now Old Town, south of present Fort Wadsworth). Farming and fishing were its main economic resources during the 17C and 18C.

In the 19C William Henry Vanderbilt (1821–1885), the eldest son of Cornelius Vanderbilt, established a racetrack on the southern part of his farm, which included land that is now part of the Gateway National Recreation Area. Cornelius, known as the Commodore, thought William dull and unambitious and kept him down on the farm, which yielded an annual income of about $12,000, pennies by Vanderbilt standards. The dullard turned out to be a brilliant manager of railroads, beginning with the lowly Staten Island Railroad, whose stock rose from almost nothing to $175 a share under his administration. He also succeeded as a farmer, increasing his original 80 acres fourfold. When the Commodore's favored son, George Washington Vanderbilt, died in 1864, the old tyrant redirected his attention to William, making him vice president of the New York and Harlem Railroad. William continued to prove himself worthy, and when the Commodore died in 1877, William inherited more than $90 million, the bulk of his father's estate, and the presidency of the New York Central Railroad. In the eight years that remained to him before his death, William doubled the family fortune to an estimated $200 million. He enjoyed fine horses and owned the famous trotter Maude S.

Vanderbilt's Staten Island Railroad spurred development in New Dorp with shops and businesses built near the station, then located on New Dorp Lane. Hotels were constructed for visitors coming from New York by rail to see the horse races and for tourists coming to enjoy the beach. New Dorp long remained a quiet outpost, especially after World War II when pollution made the beaches less attractive. The opening of the Verrazano-Narrows Bridge brought new residents to the area as well as to the rest of central and southern Staten Island. Today the population is mostly white and includes many Italian Americans.

The **Moravian Cemetery,** at Todt Hill Rd and Richmond Rd, contains the **Vanderbilt Family Mausoleum** (1886; Richard Morris Hunt), an ornate granite tomb holding the remains of the first Cornelius Vanderbilt and other family members. (The Vanderbilt burial ground is not open to the public.) Within the cemetery is the **Old New Dorp Moravian Church** (1763), with overhanging Dutch eaves; it now serves as the cemetery office. Also buried here is **Eberhard Faber** (1822–1879), manufacturer of lead pencils.

The **New Dorp Moravian Church,** at 1265 Todt Hill Rd (north of Richmond Rd), a classical revival church (1844) that replaced the one in the cemetery, was given by William H. Vanderbilt, son of Cornelius. The Vanderbilt family association with the Moravian sect dates back to the conversion of Jacob Van Der Bilt in the 18C.

Just south of the cemetery, at the north end of Altamont St, stands the small, wooden **New Dorp Lighthouse** (c. 1854; DL), a clapboard house topped by a short square tower. The tower rises 40 ft above the ground and 192 ft above sea level. The beacon remained operational until the U.S. Coast Guard retired it in 1964. The lighthouse, privately owned since 1974, is best seen in winter, when leaves have dropped from surrounding trees.

Lighthouse Hill

The more imposing Staten Island Lighthouse on Edinboro Rd gives its name to the surrounding community, Lighthouse Hill, an attractive neighborhood with winding roads and hilltop vantage points.

Points of Interest

Jacques Marchais Museum of Tibetan Art

338 Lighthouse Ave (near Windsor Ave), Staten Island, NY 10306. ☎ (718) 987-3500. Web site: www.tibetanmuseum.com. Open April–Nov: Wed–Sun 1–5; restricted winter hours (call ahead). Closed holidays. Admission charge. Permanent

and changing exhibitions; films, special events. Gift shop. Not accessible to wheelchairs. Resources for visually impaired visitors; call ahead.

Bus: From St. George Terminal, S74 to Lighthouse Ave (30 minutes). Walk up the hill (15 minutes).

One of the island's more unexpected sights is the Jacques Marchais Museum of Tibetan Art, a remarkable private collection displayed in an idyllic, meditative setting. The collection was gathered over more than two decades by Jacques Marchais, the professional name of Mrs. Jacqueline Klauber, a dealer in Asian art.

Jacques Marchais

Jacques Marchais, née Edna Coblentz, born (1890) in Illinois, was captivated as a child by a collection of bronze Tibetan figures she found in the attic, apparently souvenirs her seafaring great-grandfather had brought back from Asia. She changed her name to Jacqueline and then, eventually, masculinized that to Jacques in order to be taken more seriously in her business. Though she grew up to become absorbed in Asian culture and religion, she never visited the Far East but bought pieces from other collections, at private sales and through dealers. Marchais died in the 1950s; a board of directors now operates the museum.

On display are sculpture, scroll paintings, and ceremonial pieces that range from jewel-encrusted images to humble devotional objects of bone. The two museum buildings suggest Tibetan mountain monasteries: sturdy structures with thick stone walls pierced by small windows. They are set in a small garden with stone and metal sculpture.

At the top of the hill, Lighthouse Ave veers sharply left into Edinboro Rd and the **Staten Island Lighthouse** (1912; DL), a tall, octagonal, yellow brick tower sandwiched between two homes. Despite its landlocked location, the light stands on such high ground that its 350,000 candlepower beacon is easily seen by ships in New York Harbor. Before the lighthouse was electrified, draft horses climbed the hill bringing oil to light the beacon. The lighthouse, operated by the Coast Guard, is not open to the public.

Go down Edinboro Rd; turn left onto Rigby Ave and left again onto Manor Court. **Crimson Beech,** at 48 Manor Court, is the only residence in New York City designed by Frank Lloyd Wright. Originally the **William and Catherine Cass House** (1958–59; Frank Lloyd Wright; DL), this prefabricated dwelling represents Wright's last try at designing moderately priced housing. In 1999 Catherine Cass, who had lived there for 40 years, sold it for $800,000, along with the original drapes, furniture, built-in intercom system, and stereo.

Return to the intersection of Edinboro Rd and Rigby Ave. Edinboro Rd runs west to Richmond Hill Rd, which crosses 540-acre La Tourette Park, part of Staten Island's Greenbelt. **La Tourette Park** is named for the La Tourette family, who farmed this land from the early 1800s until 1928, when the city bought the property. The **David La Tourette House** (1836; DL), a brick Greek revival mansion, survives as the clubhouse of what is now a public golf course.

High Rock Park and Conservation Center

200 Nevada Ave, Staten Island, NY 10301. ☎ (718) 667-2165. Open daily 9–5. Free. Ranger hikes weekends and most holidays. Maps to the entire Greenbelt available.

Bus: From St. George Terminal, S74 to Rockland Ave. Walk up Nevada Ave to park gates.

Car: Take Richmond Rd to Rockland Ave; turn right to Nevada Ave; turn right on Nevada Ave to park entrance. Parking lot on Summit Ave.

Just northeast of La Tourette Park is High Rock Park, the gateway to the Greenbelt and the first of its natural areas saved (1964) from development.

A former Girl Scout camp, the 90-acre park is primarily a forest preserve with five ponds and several hiking trails. Its woods and waters are home to owls, wood ducks, great blue heron, warblers, and woodpeckers. One of the trails leads to man-made "Moses" Mountain, whose name derisively recalls Robert Moses, autocratic head of the city's Parks Department, head of the Triborough Bridge and Tunnel Authority, and relentless roadbuilder.

"Moses" Mountain

In the 1960s Moses supported a highway project that would have destroyed the Greenbelt. Tons of rock blasted during construction of the proposed parkway were piled up to be used later for filling valleys, smoothing the path of the new highway. During the 20 years residents fought the highway, nature covered the huge rock pile with green. Eventually, the highway plan was defeated.

From the summit of "Moses" Mountain, there's a 360-degree panoramic view that takes in Lighthouse Hill to the south, Heyerdahl Hill to the west, Seaview Hill to the north, High Rock to the east, and Todt Hill to the northeast. (A ramp from the unfinished parkway can be seen from the park's Blue Trail.)

The Staten Island Greenbelt

Designated parkland in 1983, the Greenbelt encompasses more than 2,500 acres, linking 12 individual parks. Natural areas include tidal and freshwater wetlands, oak and beech forests, open meadows, rolling hills, swamp, marsh, and bogs. A stop on the Atlantic flyway, the Greenbelt is a birder's paradise. Its 35 miles of trails provide ample opportunities for hiking and, in season, viewing the autumn foliage.

Other facilities include the **Greenbelt Native Plant Center,** at Victory Blvd and Travis Ave, devoted to propagation of common, rare, and endangered plants native to Staten Island and the northeast, and the nearby 803-acre **William T. Davis Wildlife Refuge** (established 1928), the first such refuge in the city.

To the east of High Rock Park is the **New York City Farm Colony–Seaview Hospital Historic District,** bounded roughly by Walcott and Colonial Aves, Manor Rd, and Rockland Ave. (The buildings are severely deteriorating and the site is surrounded by fences and difficult to access.) The two institutions, lying on about 320 acres on both sides of Brielle Ave, were founded separately by the city as a tuberculosis hospital and a poor farm.

Farm Colony

East of Brielle Ave, the Farm Colony (1903–14) was built by the city on the site of the former Richmond County Poor Farm. Here the able-bodied poor were sent to learn "self-discipline and independence" through farming—growing vegetables for the colony and other public institutions. Work was not mandatory.

The original colonial revival **dormitories** and other structures were made of local rubble stone and designed by Renwick, Aspinwall, & Owen. Additional buildings, designed by Charles B. Meyers, were added between 1930 and 1934. The Farm Colony closed in 1975. The site continues to be the focus of an ongoing struggle between environmentalists (who would like to see the land incorporated in the Greenbelt) and preservationists (who hope for adaptive reuse of the historic buildings) and those who see different uses for the land. In 1999, in a controversial move, some of the landmarked ruins were demolished in favor of a Little League ball field.

Seaview Hospital

On the west side of Brielle Ave is the **Seaview Hospital** complex (1905–38), once the country's largest and most expensive municipal facility for treating tuberculosis. (While the old buildings are empty, the site is accessible, and the buildings can be viewed from outside.)

Architect Raymond F. Almirall planned the early buildings to have maximum therapeutic value: patients enjoyed fresh air, light, and landscaped views. Inside, the buildings were decorated with colorful ceramic friezes and murals, manufactured in Delft, Holland. In 1951 the first clinical trials of a nontoxic cure for tuberculosis were undertaken at Seaview. When antibiotic therapy drastically reduced the incidence of TB in the late 1950s, Seaview was turned over to other uses. Today the Seaview Hospital Rehabilitation Center and Home operates on the site.

Willowbrook

West of the historic district is the neighborhood of Willowbrook, named for a stream that flows into the Arthur Kill.

Points of Interest

The Central Campus of the **College of Staten Island** (opened 1994), part of the City University of New York, occupies the grounds of the former Willowbrook State School. The 204-acre site is the city's largest college campus, serving some 12,000 students. Fourteen renovated neo-Georgian buildings from earlier institutions serve as offices, classrooms, and laboratories.

The Willowbrook Scandal
The former Willowbrook State School, a state institution for the mentally disabled, is remembered for its failures. In 1938, the state bought 375 acres for use by the Department of Mental Hygiene, but in 1942 the federal government commandeered the site and built the nation's largest facility for wounded soldiers, Halloran General Hospital. The state took over again in 1952. By 1963 more than 6,000 mentally handicapped children were crowded into a facility intended for 4,200. Public protest, spurred by local television reporter Geraldo Rivera's exposé of the horrendous conditions at the school, led to government investigation, court intervention, and ultimately the closing of the institution, which had become indelibly stained in the public mind.

West of the campus at the northern end of the Greenbelt is idyllic **Willowbrook State Park,** with ball fields and facilities for fishing and picnicking. The handcarved wooden figures on the **carousel** (1999) represent wild and endangered animals (open warm-weather months).

Bull's Head
West of the park is Bull's Head, a residential and commercial neighborhood with the congested intersection of Victory Blvd and Richmond Ave at its center. Until the coming of the Verrazano-Narrows Bridge and the Staten Island Expwy (which cut off part of the area), Bull's Head was rural, its population dominated by immigrants from Naples. Today the neighborhood has more Asian Americans than any other section of the island.

New Springville
South of Bull's Head is New Springville, a suburban neighborhood whose oldest residential subdivisions date back to the 1950s. The population surged after the nearby Staten Island Mall opened in 1973. Along with neighboring Castleton Corners, New Springville is home to nearly 30 percent of Staten Island's immigrants, attracting Chinese, Russian, Indian, and even Egyptian and Israeli immigrants.

Points of Interest
The former **Asbury Methodist Church** (1849; remodeled, with tower added, 1878; DL), at 2000 Richmond Ave, is named for Francis Asbury, who became the first bishop of the American Methodist Episcopal Church in 1784. Sent to America by John Wesley, founder of Methodism, Asbury remained at this church for 45 years. Col. Ichabod B. Crane, said to have lent his name to Washington Irving for "The Legend of Sleepy Hollow," is buried in the church graveyard. (The obelisk was broken by vandals and removed for safekeeping.) It is now the Son-Rise Interfaith Charismatic Church.

South of the church and just north of La Tourette Park, at 435 Richmond Hill Rd (between Forest Hill Rd and Bridgetown St), is the **Silvanus Decker Farm-**

house (c. 1880; DL), a gray-and-white clapboarded farmhouse, now a private residence. Richard Decker, a descendant of the original owner, donated it to the Staten Island Historical Society in 1955.

Richmondtown

Richmond Hill Rd continues east through La Tourette Park into Richmondtown, a middle-class residential neighborhood, known mainly as the site of Historic Richmond Town.

History

Richmondtown dates back to around 1690, when the village was called Cocclestown, probably because of the island's abundant oysters and clams. The name degenerated to Cuckoldstown but had been prudently changed to Richmondtown by the end of the Revolution. Located at a crossroads in the middle of the island, Richmondtown grew and prospered until in 1728 it became the seat of Richmond County (i.e., Staten Island). During the Revolution, some of its buildings were destroyed, including the original Dutch Church and the courthouse.

In the 1830s, as New York City across the bay was feeling the pressures of rapid growth, Staten Island became a suburban retreat. A new civic center was built in Richmondtown, including the Third County Courthouse (1837) and, later, the County Clerk's and Surrogate's Office (1848) and the jail (1860; demolished 1953). By the late-19C the population of the island had shifted to the coastal areas, leaving Richmondtown a rural backwater. When Staten Island joined Greater New York as the borough of Richmond in 1898, St. George superseded Richmondtown as the seat of government.

Historic Richmond Town

441 Clarke Ave (near Arthur Kill Rd and Richmond Road), Staten Island, NY 10306. ☎ (718) 351-1611. Web site: www.historicrichmondtown.org. Open July–Aug, Wed–Fri 10–5; Sat and Sun 1–5. Sept–June, Wed–Sun 1–5. Closed major holidays. Admission charge. Snack bar. Picnic grounds. Gift shop. Maps and schedules available at the Visitors Center.

Bus: From the St. George Terminal, S74 to Richmond Rd and St. Patrick's Place.

Car: Take Verrazano-Narrows Bridge to Richmond Rd–Clove Rd exit. Turn left onto Richmond Ave; follow Richmond Rd approximately five miles. The restoration is on the left. Or take West Shore Expwy to Richmond Ave; turn left onto Arthur Kill Rd; continue to Clarke Ave.

Historic Richmond Town, an undertaking of the Staten Island Historical Society, was established in 1958, 23 years after the society purchased its first building. The historic village's 28 restored buildings and museum exhibits illuminate four centuries of Staten Island history.

The Visitors Center is in the Greek revival **Third County Court House** (1837; DL). To its left, near Tysen Court, is the Reseau–Van Pelt Cemetery, a small private graveyard dating back to the 18C. Across Center St from the Third Court House is the **Second County Clerk's and Surrogate's Office** (1848; DL), now the **Staten Island Historical Museum,** containing exhibitions on local history.

The restored buildings, about half of them on their original sites, include houses, stores, a carpenter shop, a sawmill, and a parsonage. In July and Aug, costumed craftsmen demonstrate carpentry, spinning and weaving, quilting, fire-place cooking, tinsmithing, and printing. Among special events offered annually are a Civil War encampment and the Richmond County Fair.

One of the most important structures in Richmondtown is the **Voorlezer's House** (c. 1695; DL), the first building purchased by the society. This small frame house was built by the Dutch Reformed congregation for its *voorlezer*, or lay reader, who lived and also taught school there; it is believed to be the nation's oldest elementary school building.

Other Points of Interest

At the marshy edge of La Tourette Park, picturesque Episcopal **St. Andrew's Church** (1872; William H. Mersereau; DL), 4 Arthur Kill Rd (southeast corner of Old Mill Rd), looks as if it had been transplanted from rural England, with its fieldstone walls, bull's-eye windows, and steep gables, all intact. The original church (1712) was destroyed by fire, and the present structure stands on its foundations. Dr. Richard Bayley, father of St. Elizabeth Ann Seton and officer of the quarantine station (see A Historic Hospital in Walk 56), in Stapleton, is buried in the churchyard.

At the other end of Historic Richmond Town is **St. Patrick's Church** (1860–62; DL), 45 St. Patrick's Place (between Center St and Clarke Ave), a brick Romanesque revival church with narrow, roundheaded windows, built just before the Civil War, when the Roman Catholic population of Staten Island was increasing rapidly.

58 · Southern Staten Island: Tottenville, Pleasant Plains, Prince's Bay, Annadale, and Eltingville

At the southern tip of the island are Tottenville, Pleasant Plains, and Prince's Bay, all founded as fishing villages. The towns are accessible by Staten Island Rapid Transit.

Tottenville

Tottenville is one of the oldest communities on the South Shore, containing the most southerly point of New York City and New York State. Historically, its waterfront facing the Arthur Kill and Raritan Bay has turned the local economy toward shipping, shipbuilding, and fishing. The flavor of the past remains in Tottenville's older single-family homes, from tiny bungalows to more elaborate Victorian houses.

History

Ferries linked Tottenville economically to New Jersey as early as the 18C; later, from 1867 until 1964, a ferry to Perth Amboy's Smith St commercial district made it easy for Tottenville residents to spend their money across the bay. In 1898 the Atlantic Terra Cotta Company, whose architectural ornaments still grace New York's subway stations and the Flatiron Building, established a factory in Tottenville. Several boatyards and a smelting and refining company also flourished around the turn of the 20C.

Although the arrival of the Verrazano-Narrows Bridge did not affect southern Staten Island as quickly as its more northerly neighborhoods, Tottenville's population surged 41 percent, from 6,486 in 1980 to about 11,000 today. Big, ostentatious houses, rows of town houses, and semidetached houses now awkwardly stand alongside older homes. Rapid development has brought such problems as school overcrowding, but zoning laws of the late 1990s now restrict most of Tottenville to detached one-family homes.

Points of Interest

Main St, Tottenville's commercial center, is quiet and unremarkable. The former **Masonic Temple** (c. 1900), at 236 Main St, decorated with polychromed terracotta, today houses a tavern. The gabled and dormered Victorian frame house at **127 Main St** is a relic of a more prosperous past.

Conference House

7445 Hylan Blvd, Staten Island, NY 10307. Mailing Address: P.O. Box 171, Staten Island, NY 10307. ☎ (718) 984-6046. Open April 15–Nov 15, Fri–Sun 1–4. Call to confirm. Closed major holidays. Admission charge.

Bus: From the St. George Terminal, S103 to the last stop on Craig Ave near the park.

Train: From St. George Terminal, to Staten Island Rapid Transit Tottenville Station. Follow Bentley St to Craig Ave; turn right and continue to Hylan Ave; follow Hylan Ave a block to the park (about 1 mile altogether).

At Hylan Blvd and Satterlee St stands the historic Conference House (c. 1680; DL), also known as the Billopp House. Surrounded by idyllic 226-acre **Conference House Park,** it commands views of Raritan Bay and Perth Amboy.

History

The manor house was built by British sea captain Christopher Billopp and remained in the family until the Revolution. Billopp's great-grandson, also named Christopher, sympathized with the British cause, for which he would later lose his property. On Sept 11, 1776, when American prospects for victory looked bleak, the Continental Congress sent Benjamin Franklin, Edward Rutledge, and John Adams to a conference at the Billopp House with Gen. William Howe, commander in chief of the British Army in North America. Howe offered to pardon those who had taken up arms against the Crown if the colonies would rescind the Declaration of Independence signed just two months earlier, but the American delegates replied that independence was not negotiable.

After the war, New York State confiscated the property, which at its most extensive totaled some 1,600 acres, and the house fell into disrepair; in the early years of the 20C it became a factory for making rat poison. The house was deeded to the city of New York in 1926, and three years later the newly formed Conference House Association began to rehabilitate the building. Today the City Parks Department, which oversees the grounds, is constructing a waterfront pavilion.

The house is built of local rubblestone with ground seashells mixed into the mortar. Inside are an impressive basement kitchen and a vaulted root cellar. Most of the furnishings are from the 18C, though a 17C sea chest remains as the sole Billopp family possession.

There is a short trail in the park at **Ward's Point,** the southernmost tip of the island, once the site of a Delaware Indian village. Ward's Point is named for the same Caleb T. Ward who gave his name to a hill in northern Staten Island.

Another historic house (not open to the public) overseen by the Conference House Association is the **Henry Hogg Biddle House** (c. 1840s; DL), nearby at 70 Satterlee St. It is remarkable for its unusual combination of Dutch colonial overhanging eaves and Greek revival two-story porticoes front and back.

Pleasant Plains

Mount Loretto Mission of the Immaculate Virgin

The neighborhood of Pleasant Plains, north of Tottenville, contains one of Staten Island's most scenic spots, the Mount Loretto Mission of the Immaculate Virgin.

History
Owned by the New York Archdiocese, the mission was founded in 1870 in Manhattan by Father John C. Drumgoole as a refuge for homeless newsboys. Ten years later the orphanage moved to Staten Island, where it continued to serve homeless and disabled children until the 1990s. When the 650-acre property, with its sweeping views of Raritan Bay and the Atlantic Ocean, came under pressures from developers, the Trust for Public Land and the state of New York interceded. In 1998 the state bought a 194-acre waterfront parcel, which will be developed as a park.

The site includes the only natural red clay bluffs in the city, as well as grasslands, coastal woodlands, freshwater and tidal wetlands, and shoreline. Remaining on the property are the **Church of St. Joachim and St. Anne** (1891; Bejamin E. Lowe; new nave 1976) and the former mission residence (off Hylan Blvd, west of Sharrott Ave), originally the **Prince's Bay Lighthouse and Keeper's House** (c. 1845). **St. Elizabeth's Home for Girls** (1897; Shickel & Ditmars), an institution for orphaned and abandoned girls, was destroyed by fire in 2000.

Prince's Bay
The neighborhood of Prince's Bay, founded as a fishing village, was once known for oysters so delicious that the menus of upscale New York restaurants designated them by name. By the 1830s the industry supported every family from Prince's Bay to Tottenville. Oystering continued to flourish throughout the 19C as oystermen developed underwater cultivation techniques, seeding the beds and transplanting young oysters into deeper waters. By 1916, however, the waters were dangerously polluted and the industry died.

Points of Interest
Both the **John H. Ellsworth House** (1879), at 90 Bayview Ave overlooking the Lemon Creek salt meadow, and the **Abraham Wood House** (1840; DL), at 5910

Amboy Rd, were built for oystermen. The area around the Prince's Bay rapid transit station also has charming old homes from the oystering days. **Amboy Rd,** one of Staten Island's oldest streets, was laid out in 1709.

The **Joseph Seguine House** (1837; DL), at 440 Seguine Ave (between Wilbur St and Hank Place), sits on high ground overlooking Prince's Bay. Seguine inherited land and a thriving oyster business from his French Huguenot family, which had settled on Staten Island in 1706. Sometimes known as the Burke-Seguine House, the 2½-story Greek revival mansion has a classical pediment and an impressive portico supported by six squared piers. In 1981, architectural designer George Burke bought the 18-room house at auction and subsequently restored and donated it to the city, while keeping a lifetime interest. The Urban Park Rangers offer occasional house tours. For information and reservations, ☎ (718) 667-6042.

Further down Seguine Ave, toward the water, is another landmark that has not fared as well. The privately owned **Manee-Seguine Homestead** (late 17C–early 19C; DL), 509 Seguine Ave, is empty and derelict. Joseph Seguine was born in this house, which the Seguines had bought from Abraham Manee, also an oysterman, in the 1780s.

At the end of Seguine Ave is 84-acre **Lemon Creek Park,** one of the city's newest parks and the last undisturbed tidal creek and salt-marsh ecosystem on the South Shore. The Native Americans who inhabited the area harvested the oyster beds in the creek and surrounding waters. Today, birders may spot piping plovers, egrets, herons, and cormorants on the beach; flocks of purple martin swallows return here each April from their winter retreats in Brazil.

The **Memorial Church of the Huguenots** (1923–24; Ernest Flagg; 1955 addition; James Whitford Jr.; DL), now the Reformed Church of Huguenot Park, 5475 Amboy Rd, testifies to the impact of Huguenot immigrants (French Protestants of the 16C and 17C) on Staten Island history. The church, built to commemorate the 300th anniversary of Huguenot religious freedom, is a late work of Ernest Flagg and incorporates his interests in medieval architecture and moderately priced construction techniques. Reminiscent of the vernacular Norman architecture of northwest France and England, the church has concrete walls inset with serpentine rubble stone quarried from Flagg's Todt Hill estate.

Annadale

North of Prince's Bay is Annadale, named for Anna Seguine, member of the Huguenot family who settled here in the 17C. In the mid-19C German and Irish immigrants moved into Annadale, but the area remained rural as late as the 1970s when suburban town houses arrived in force. In the last decade this middle-class neighborhood has also seen the construction of 6,000-square-ft neomansions and the sectioning off of "mini-communities" (for example, Arden Heights).

Blue Heron Park

267 Poillon Ave, Staten Island, NY 10312. Friends of Blue Heron Park: ☎ (718) 317-1732. Web site: www.preserve2.org/blueheron/blueheron.htm. Urban Park Rangers: ☎ (718) 967-3542. Nature Center open 11–4. Nature walks, environmental education, workshops, events. Handicapped-accessible trail.

Bus: From St. George Terminal, S78 to Poillon Ave. Walk north a half-mile.

Train: From St. George Terminal, Staten Island Rapid Transit to Annadale Station. Walk uphill on Annadale Rd to Poillon Ave. Follow Poillon a half-mile to park.

Car: Take West Shore Expwy or the Korean War Veterans Memorial (Richmond) Pkwy to Arden Ave exit. Follow Arden Ave south to Hylan Blvd; turn right and travel a half-mile to Poillon Ave. Turn right and follow Poillon Ave a half-mile to park entrance. Via Hylan Blvd, Poillon Ave is about a mile past Richmond Ave when traveling toward Tottenville.

Offsetting some of this development is Blue Heron Park, which began (1972) with 26 acres but now encompasses 222 acres of meadows, ponds, streams, and woodlands. Hiking trails wind past glacial kettle holes (pond basins). The Great Old Oak, now a quarter century old, stands on the bank of Blue Heron Brook.

Eltingville

Just north of Annadale is Eltingville, named for a local 19C family. In the 20C the area remained sparsely populated, mainly by Scandinavians, until the Verrazano-Narrows Bridge brought accelerated development and an influx of Italian American arrivals from Brooklyn.

Points of Interest

St. Alban's Episcopal Church and Rectory (1865; R. M. Upjohn; enlarged 1872; DL), at 76 St. Alban's Place (between Winchester and Pacific Aves), is a charming carpenter-Gothic wood-frame building, one of the few examples of board-and-batten construction in New York City. The paint colors, beige and maroon, are historically accurate.

The **Frederick Law Olmsted House,** formerly the Poillon House (early 18C; additions 1830s; DL), at 4515 Hylan Blvd, is set back from the road, visible from what appears to be a driveway but is actually Orchard Lane. In 1848, the 26-year-old Olmsted bought the house and an adjoining 125 acres (with his father's help). The property had been owned by agricultural reformer Samuel Akerly; Olmsted named it Tosomock Farm and lived there, farming and experimenting with landscape gardening, until 1853. The property was farmed until the 1880s; later it became a summer resort called Woods of Arden, with the farmhouse serving as an inn.

59 · Western Staten Island: Charleston, Rossville, and Travis

Western Staten Island, mostly lowland, encompasses the communities of Charleston, Rossville, and Travis. In the early 20C, ferries linked these isolated villages and factory towns to New Jersey across the Arthur Kill, and though the ferries are long gone, residents are still more likely to venture west than to travel to Manhattan. Before the West Shore Expwy was completed in 1976, the area was difficult to reach by road—Travis, for example, was accessible only by Victory Blvd—but the completion of the expressway transformed these sleepy hamlets into outposts of suburbia.

Charleston and Rossville had hometown industries that survived into the 20C, but when the local factories closed, the sparsely populated region was used for facilities unwanted anywhere else—gas and oil storage tanks, marine salvage companies, railroad yards, and a city sewage disposal plant—many of them built on city land. Most notorious was the Fresh Kills Landfill just outside Travis, which closed in 2001.

Charleston

In the 19C Charleston, rich in deposits of clay and kaolin, was called Kreischerville. Bavarian immigrant Balthasar Kreischer opened a brick-making factory in 1854; by 1860 its Irish and German workers were producing a million firebricks annually. The factory closed in 1927, but Kreischer bricks survive in buildings here and elsewhere in the city—for example, in the Mathews Model Flats in Ridgewood, Queens.

Points of Interest

The only **Kreischer House** remaining was built for Balthasar's son Charles. The stick-style Victorian house (c. 1888; attrib. Palliser & Balliser; DL) stands at 4500 Arthur Kill Rd near Englewood Ave. Formerly a restaurant, it is currently empty.

Kreischerville, the company town surrounding the brickworks, included housing, a church, and a school. The **Kreischerville Workers' Houses** (c. 1890; DL), four identical pairs of houses, still stand on Kreischer St (near Androvette St), facing sidewalks paved in Kreischer brick. **St. Peter's German Evangelical Reformed Church of Kresicherville** (1883; Hugo Kafka; DL) survives as the Free Hungarian Reformed Church in America, at 25 Winant Place (near Arthur Kill Rd). Built of Kreischer brick, the **Westfield Township School No. 7**, later, **P. S. 4** (1896; enlarged 1906–7; C. B. J. Snyder; DL), 4210–4212 Arthur Kill Rd, remains from the days when the Kreischer Brick Works operated at full capacity. Today it is a public school for special education.

Clay Pit Ponds State Park Preserve

83 Nielsen Ave (at Carlin St off Sharrotts Rd), Staten Island, NY 10309. ☎ (718) 967-1976. Open all year sunrise to sunset. Self-guided hiking trails, equestrian trails (no horse rental), nature programs.

Bus: From St. George Terminal, S74 to Sharrotts Rd. Walk along Sharrotts Rd a quarter-mile; turn left onto Carlin St and continue to the end.

Car: Take I-287 (Staten Island Expwy) west to Rte 440 (West Shore Expwy) south. Continue about six miles to Bloomingdale Rd (exit 3). Turn left onto Bloomingdale Rd. Go about one mile to Sharrotts Rd and turn right. Go about one mile, turn right onto Carlin Rd, and continue to the end.

The site of a former clay mine is preserved at Clay Pit Ponds State Park Preserve, a 260-acre natural area just north of the historic buildings and east of Arthur Kill Rd. With its wetlands and woodlands, fields and spring-fed streams, and sandy pine-oak barrens—a habitat more typical of the South than of the Big Apple—this park is New York City's only state preserve. Established in 1977, the park gets its name from the white kaolin clay deposits that provided raw material for bricks and architectural terra-cotta in the late 19C and early 20C. Once the pits were abandoned, natural springs, rain, and vegetation filled in the depressions.

In the park grow rare wildflowers such as cranberry, lizard-tail, possum-haw, and bog twayblade; northern black racer snakes, box turtles, Fowler's toads, green frogs, and spring peepers also live here. Two state-designated protected areas—90 acres of freshwater wetlands and a 70-acre area with rare and endangered plants and wildlife—remain off-limits to the public.

Rossville

Rossville was originally called Blazing Star after the Blazing Star Tavern, which stood here during the American Revolution. In 1836 the town was renamed for wealthy landowner William E. Ross. Its rural character changed radically when the Woodbrooke development (1979–91) added 1,200 town houses and semidetached homes to the landscape.

Points of Interest

Just north of the intersection of Arthur Kill Rd and Rossville Ave is the **Sleight Family Graveyard** (DL), also known as the Blazing Star Burial Ground, one of Staten Island's oldest cemeteries. Graves date to 1751, and those who lie there include Winants, Seguines, Poillons, and Sleights—families also enshrined in local place names. The small cemetery is overgrown and difficult to see from the road.

To the west, at 2543 Arthur Kill Rd, is the city's last commercial marine-salvage yard, the **Witte Marine Equipment Company,** whose oldest derelict vessels predate World War I. Formerly ships were left intact until a buyer was found, but increasingly they are dismantled and sold for parts. (The company does not welcome visitors.)

Sandy Ground

Sandy Ground, one of the oldest black settlements in the nation, is a community within Rossville, founded in the 1830s primarily by oystermen from Snow Hill, Maryland, who fled laws restricting the rights of freed slaves. These men farmed the rich oyster beds of Raritan Bay, and by the mid-19C Sandy Ground had grown into a self-sufficient community of about 150 families. In 1916, the city prohibited fishing and oystering in waters that had become polluted, and Sandy Ground's residents turned to other ways of making their living. Only a handful of families remain, centered around Bloomingdale, Woodrow, and Clay Pit Rds. Today the community is surrounded by the town houses and "estates" of newer arrivals, most of them whites.

Sandy Ground Historical Society
The Sandy Ground Historical Society was founded in 1979 to preserve the heritage of this site and to educate the public. 1538 Woodrow Rd, Staten Island, NY 10309. ☎ (718) 317-5796. Call for hours. Features local history exhibits.

Sandy Ground's spiritual and social center is the **Rossville African Methodist Episcopal Zion Church,** at Bloomingdale and Woodrow Rds. Its **cemetery** (1852; DL) contains the graves of at least 34 African American families, including that of George H. Hunter, described in journalist Joseph Mitchell's 1956 essay, "Mr. Hunter's Grave." The cemetery was badly vandalized in 1997 but has been restored.

Travis

The area now known as Travis, first called Jersey Wharf and later New Blazing Star, has undergone several identity crises. It was named Travisville for the first time in the 19C after a property owner, Col. Jacob Travis; later it became Deckertown, for a prominent local family, some of whose descendants still live nearby. After 1873, when the American Linoleum Company was established here, it became Linoleumville. Travis boasts the city's longest-running Fourth of July parade, launched in 1911.

History

Much of the company's early workforce came from England, where linoleum was invented, although Poles and Germans also lived nearby. At the beginning of the 20C, the factory employed 700 people, half of Linoleumville's population. The innovative company developed machinery for making linoleum and pioneered inlaid and decorative styles, but it closed in 1931 during the Depression. A few years later the town revived the name Travis. Today an immense Con Edison power plant at the foot of Victory Blvd occupies the factory site.

Index